Maven in Blue Jeans

Maven in Blue Jeans

A Festschrift in Honor of Zev Garber

Steven Leonard Jacobs, editor

Purdue University Press
West Lafayette, Indiana

Printed in the United States of America.

Library of Congress Cataloging-in-Publication Data

Maven in blue jeans : a festschrift in honor of Zev Garber / Steven Leonard Jacobs, Editor.
p. cm. — (Shofar supplements in Jewish studies)
Includes bibliographical references.
ISBN 978-1-55753-521-4
1. Holocaust, Jewish (1939–1945) 2. Judaism—Relations—Christianity. 3. Christianity and other religions—Judaism. 4. Bible—Criticism, interpretation, etc. 5. Rabbinical literature—History and criticism. I. Jacobs, Steven L., 1947- II. Garber, Zev, 1941-
D804.3.M385 2008
296—dc22 2008042887

Contents

A Scholar's Creation

Susan Garber

(*Inspired by memories of French vanilla coffee and my husband's pipe*)

Autumn's light casts a warm glow upon the bookcases.
He leans back into the big chair at his study desk.
Comfortable and secure, he puffs upon his pipe.
The scent of cherry-blend tobacco permeates the air.
One hour pleasantly passes as he begins his work.
He hopes it will be good.

He contemplates the volume opened before him
And his mind interacts with its printed pages.
He jots down words on a notepad,
Slowly, purposefully as the second hour goes by.
A new creation has begun.

His thoughts separate from those of the volume
And he saw this was good.
His effort begins to bear fruit in the third hour
As words become sentences, paragraphs, and then pages.
It is good.

Day has now become night,
The setting sun replaced by the moon and the stars.
Enthusiastically he continues his endeavor
With all his energy, his soul and might.
The fourth hour, amazingly good.

His ideas have multiplied greatly;
The writing pad almost full.
He is tiring now
But his dog, sitting at his feet, nudges him awake.
And during the fifth hour,
He is reminded all is good.

In the sixth hour,
From what was once emptiness,

Has come a notepad full.
Contained within it is his mind's work
And it is very good.

His wife steps into the room,
Bringing warm coffee to her beloved sage.

"Six hours you have worked, my husband, And now, the seventh, you must rest." And he knows his life is good.

17 Kislev 5767 December 8, 2006

Maven in Blue Jeans

A Brief Introduction

Steven Leonard Jacobs

It was, perhaps, most propitious that I called Zev Garber on the occasion of his sixty-fifth birthday with a proposition: Would he honor those of us who respect him and his scholarship, and to and for whom he has been both a mentor and a friend to so many of us, by allowing me to edit a *Festschrift* in his honor? Taken somewhat aback by my proposal, he humbly and honestly demurred, but promised to share this request with his wife, Susan, and get back to me within the week. Which of course he did with a positive reply, and this collection of essays is the result. (Susan's poem, which graces and introduces this entire volume, is an especially meaningful and therefore most appropriate way to begin.)

Step 2 in the process involved the following questions: First, would he furnish me with a list of those colleagues with whom he has interacted over his long and productive career that I might personally invite them to contribute? (All but very, very few responded to my invitation most enthusiastically!) Second, would he also suggest before the invitational letter was sent out those academic intellectual scholarly categories in which he himself has invested himself and which, in turn, would provide something of a guideline for our colleagues? And, finally, as we neared submission of the manuscript, would he also contribute a bibliography of his own writings which those of us who know him can peruse and continue to marvel at his productivity; and those who do not know him personally but acquire this volume nonetheless can behold a true scholar of diverse interests hard at work over many, many years? Needless to say, Zev was more than happy to honor all three requests.

On a personal note, I first met Zev (and Hank Knight and Jim Moore) at the seventeenth annual Scholars Conference on the Holocaust and the Churches (founded by Franklin Littell of Temple University and Hubert Locke of the University of Washington in 1970) in Nashville in 1987—the first time that particular conference had journeyed outside its normal venue of Philadelphia. Together, the three warmly welcomed me into their fellowship with a genuine sincerity that has resulted in numerous academic collaborations over the years, as Zev and I (the Judaic scholars) and Hank and Jim (the Christian scholars) have interacted in a post-Shoah dialogue that enlarged not only our own understandings of both the Hebrew Bible and the New Testament but that of the many, many friends we four have acquired over the years through our public midrashic interpretative readings of different passages of these two sacred texts at that annual gathering. Spearheaded by Zev's own commitments and initiatives, we have also been privileged to publish our work in three separate and distinct venues: *SIDIC*; *Shofar*, published by Purdue University Press (and to whom we are collectively grateful for the publication of this *Festschrift*, especially Tom Bacher and Rebecca Corbin); and the University Press of America.[1] I continue to treasure both the relationship with my three colleagues and, especially, the leadership Zev has provided trying to balance the two elements.

More important, however, and central to this volume of collegial essays, is the man and his work. First the man: Zev, with his long hair, beard, customary blue jeans, turtleneck-style shirts, casual jackets, and ever-present pipe, remains the quintessential "child of the '60s" long after the sixties have passed. Yet, even for those among us who have conservatized our own wearing apparel and tonsorial concerns, we too must admit that Zev is Zev, and his whole persona is uniquely his and him—and we would not have it any other way! Master of the teachable moment, as soon as he opens his mouth to speak and teach, we are spellbound by his words, his ways of interweaving the diverse strands of his vast knowledge, the profundity of his insights, and the passionate moral commitments that undergird and overgird his intellect.[2]

Then, too, that commitment manifests itself in his welcoming presence to other and younger scholars with whom he does not always necessarily agree. Passionate as noted, Zev is equally encouraging of those new to the discipline of academics as well as those of us of longer standing. He continues to mentor and nourish younger scholars. Those of us no longer young still draw intellectual sustenance from his writings and public addresses.

Then, too, there are his many and varied contributions to the academy. Zev Garber remains a major figure in post-Holocaust Jewish and Christian thought, most especially in the area of Jewish-Christian relations and biblical exegesis and eisegesis of both the Hebrew Bible and New Testament. While scholars, including those who have contributed to this volume, may disagree regarding its organization and whether or not one or more essays should have been placed elsewhere, the six categories that comprise this work are Zev's categories and clearly reflect the far-reaching nature of his intellect.[3]

Significantly, part 5, "Shoah Theology and Other Shoah Matters, Including Antisemitism," has the largest number of contributors and reflects well in its own way both Zev as scholar and Zev as committed Jew. The world that created the Shoah and brought with it the murders of nearly six million Jewish men, women, and children continues to shatter the worlds of the Jews, raising questions of enormous complexity even now, questions that continue to defy easy resolution. That tragic reality, coupled with the rise and virulence of Middle Eastern antisemitism throughout the Arab world, has had its impact on Zev's writings as well as his thinking and his public presentations and pronouncements. Issues of the physical and religious survival of the Jewish people in our post-Shoah world occupy a central place in Zev's work. At the same time, we see in Zev Garber the religiously committed human being, one equally comfortable in the worlds of the academy and the Jewish people, true to his rearing as a product of both a classical yeshiva education and that of secular Western humanity.

All those of us who have contributed to this volume are delighted to do so; the quality of our contributions speaks for itself as does the incredible diversity of contributions and scholars in the different disciplines. That all of us collectively embraced this project is also a fitting tribute to a unique human being whom we count as mentor, colleague, and friend. This *Festschrift* is intended to be an honoring, a well-deserved and too-long-overdue tribute, and a celebration of the life, work, and teaching of one passionately committed to making sense of our world. And, as the Jewish Religious Tradition itself records in the tradition of *Moshe Rabbeinu* (Moses our Rabbi), to Zev Garber: *Ad meah esrim shana,* "May you, too (like Moses of old) live to 120 years—with full vigor of mind, body, and spirit!"

Steven Leonard Jacobs
Tuscaloosa, Alabama
January 8, 2009

Notes

Note: Special thanks to Professor Lawrence Baron of San Diego State University, who suggested the title of this *Festschrift*. It could not be a more fitting tribute and description of Zev himself.

1. *SIDIC* 35, no. 1 (2002); *Shofar* 15, no. 1 (1996); and *Post-Shoah Dialogues: Re-Thinking Our Texts Together* (Lanham, Md.: University Press of America, 2006).

2. For a look-see into what makes Zev Garber "tick," see his own academically autobiographical essay, "Teaching Shoah Matters: A Personal Memoir," in *Teaching about the Holocaust: Essays by College and University Teachers*, ed. Samuel Totten, Paul R. Bartrop, and Steven Leonard Jacobs (Westport, Conn.: Greenwood Press, 2004), 65–79.
3. Zev also suggested a seventh category, that of "Language and Memory," as a possible avenue for contributors. Yet when the essays themselves were finally organized, they fell quite easily and naturally into the sections indicated.

Part 1

Exegesis and Eisegesis:
Hebrew Bible, New Testament, and Rabbinic Literature

The Domestication of a Radical Jew

Paul of Tarsus

S. Scott Bartchy

I

The eminent Harvard sociologist Orlando Patterson observes in his 1991 prize-winning book titled *Freedom in the Making of Western Culture*: "Paul [of Tarsus] is the greatest figure in the history of Western religious and social thought, not only because he was the first to pose" the most profound questions about freedom, "but because the answers he gave have determined all subsequent reflections on them."[1] This strong claim is open to discussion, of course. But even if regarded as only partially correct, such an evaluation has created serious perplexity among many historians and culture analysts, who in their research have repeatedly found sentences taken from Paul's letters used not at all to encourage freedom but, on the contrary, to reinforce an oppressive status quo.

For example, did not Paul insist on returning a runaway slave to his owner, thus setting the example followed many centuries later by American Christians who opposed the Underground Railroad and who captured all the runaway slaves they could find and returned them to their owners? Did not Paul urge all followers of Jesus as the Christ to "remain in the social condition" in which they were converted (1 Cor. 7:17–24), thus severing the nerve of social change in his own time and laying the foundation for the sanctification of rigid social stratification in many subsequent cultures? Are not sentences from Paul's letters routinely cited by various contemporary ecclesiastical authorities who oppose the ordination of women to positions of Christian leadership?[2]

If Patterson is only half right in his judgment about Paul's importance as a strong advocate of freedom, we are faced with serious questions: Why and how did Paul's legacy become so radically distorted? And what can our awareness of how Paul's words have been used and misused tell us about ancient texts and those readers who have received these documents as inspired and holy?

II

One intriguing confirmation of Patterson's primary contention has been offered by Daniel Boyarin in his profound and provocative book *A Radical Jew: Paul and the Politics of Identity*. Here this leading scholar of Talmud and Midrash explores the positive and negative ramifications of Paul's radical baptismal teaching that "there is neither Jew nor Greek, there is neither slave nor free, there is no male and female, for you are all one in Christ Jesus" (Gal. 3:28). Together with the earlier book by Alan Segal, *Paul the Convert: The Apostolate and Apostasy of Saul the Pharisee*, Boyarin's study signals a greatly to be welcomed stage in Pauline scholarship, in the field of the history of religions, and in American intellectual life. For in these books, two important Jewish intellectuals have taken major steps in reclaiming Paul as an important example of the wide range of Judaism(s) in the first century of our era.[3]

Boyarin presents Paul of Tarsus "as a Jewish cultural critic" and then asks "what it was in Jewish culture that led him to produce a discourse of radical reform of that culture?"[4] This is a very productive question, and I welcome the fact that Boyarin assumes that Paul was not motivated "by an abnormal psychological state but by a set of problems and ideas generated by his cultural, religious situation." It is in this context of a growing critical emphasis on the fact that the historical Saul/Paul[5] never stopped regarding himself as a resident in the House of Israel, even after becoming a follower and apostle of Jesus of Nazareth as Messiah, that I am especially pleased to be able to dedicate this essay to my esteemed colleague, Zev Garber.

III

In my own forthcoming book, *"Call No Man Father": The Apostle Paul's Vision of a Society of Siblings*, I seek to understand Paul not only as a Jewish cultural critic but also and especially as a critic of the dominant cultural values and social codes that largely defined who was regarded as a good and honorable person among all societies in the ancient Mediterranean world. I argue there that it was Paul's astonishing personal behavior, using his powers for the sake of others rather than himself, that made credible his "discourse of radical reform." And in that discourse Paul reached beyond specifically Jewish issues to challenge some of the characteristic features of the broader Mediterranean world in which he was raised. He expressed the radicality of his vision by:

- undermining patriarchal authority in general and the constraints of consanguineal family ties and loyalties;
- seeking to resocialize all his converts as "brothers and sisters" of each other, now based on their baptismal initiation into a new kind of "family" created by a gracious invitation from a nondiscriminatory God;
- rejecting traditional patterns of male socialization in an agonistic culture that was becoming increasingly addicted to interpersonal violence;
- turning upside down the conventional and enormously important conceptions of honor and shame by redefining how honor is to be won: not in self-aggrandizement but by using one's powers for the sake of others;
- and by redefining power not as the ability to dominate, control, and effectively have one's own way with others but rather as the ability to lift up the fallen, to reconcile the alienated, to forgive the sinner, to empower the weak, and radically and inclusively to restructure community boundaries.

IV

Yet to designate Paul of Tarsus a radical of any sort would seem to contradict conventional wisdom in light of how dictators and oppressors, within and without the established Church, have widely and frequently cited various sentences from the writings bearing Paul's name to justify hierarchical policies and practices of both State and Church, and to resist any lessening of male privilege and of traditional male domination of females in both the domestic and ecclesiastical spheres. Are not the phrases "women should be silent in the churches" and "I permit no woman to teach or to have authority over a man" among the best-known exhortations in the Pauline legacy?

There can be no question that both men and women have used selected parts of the Pauline tradition through the centuries to sanctify systems of domination in various cultures. What can be and must be questioned, however, is whether Paul's basic teachings with respect to male dominance and privilege have been appropriately understood in the context of the cultural values and social codes taken for granted by virtually everyone living in the Mediterranean basin during the first century of our era.

V

Indeed, in the discussions known to me of Paul's teaching regarding the roles of "Christian" women,[6] what has been missing is an analysis of his exhortations to male Christ-followers to modify sharply their concept of "manhood," including their anticipation that however low their social status, simply because they were males they would be served by women and by at least some men whom they could dominate. That is, any treatment of Paul's teaching regarding the behavior and roles of Christian women is inevitably incomplete and distorted without a thorough examination of his views regarding the status, roles, and privileges of Christian men.[7] A close reading of Paul's letters shows that in his specific instructions regarding male and female gender roles, Paul's primary relational framework for all men and women in his house-based congregations and his most frequent form of speaking to them had become that of "sisters and brothers," even when addressing married couples (see 1 Corinthians 7).[8] And this emphasis on a kind of family relations not based on blood-ties points to the strong influence Paul felt of the radical social codes and antipatriarchal traditions associated with the historical Jesus of Nazareth.[9]

Within this frame of thinking, Paul praised such female Christian leaders as Phoebe and Priscilla (Rom. 16:1–5) and Euodia and Syntyche (Phil. 4:2), and he described Junia with the title and role that he most highly prized for himself: apostle. Indeed, Paul states that this Junia and her companion Andronicus were not only apostles before him but highly esteemed as such by him and other Christ-followers (Rom. 16:7).

Thus in distinct contrast to much that has been written on the subject, I argue that Paul's vision included neither a hierarchical nor an egalitarian structure for his house-based communities. Rather, according to my cultural context–based analysis, Paul sought to create well-functioning surrogate families of people, without anyone in patriarchal authority.[10] These people had answered Paul's challenge to reject the loyalties of blood-kinship and ethnic identity in favor of embracing the radically inclusive Rule of Israel's Compassionate God, as proclaimed by Jesus of Nazareth. As in any family, there were the relative strong and weak, measured in a variety of ways. And as in any well-functioning Mediterranean family, the honor and solidarity of the kin-group, sharing what they had without keeping score and eschewing internal competition, took precedence over individual "rights" or religious experiences.

VI

Furthermore, since patriarchal systems arrange human relationships so that not only may men dominate women but also some men may dominate most other men, an analysis of Paul's relation to patriarchy and male dominance must include his instructions about how "Christian" men were to treat each other in light of the hierarchical structures in which they had been socialized as males into manhood. Among these structures, the most extreme form of domination in principle had long been institutionalized as chattel slavery. Thus the letter written by Paul to the slave owner Philemon about his slave Onesimus can serve as a critical test case of Paul's intentions.

During the eighteenth and nineteenth centuries in the United States, a vast number of readers found in this brief letter "the Pauline Mandate" to justify Christian support both of slavery and of the dreaded Fugitive Slave Law. In the context of the early Roman empire, however, it is highly unlikely that the slave Onesimus would have been regarded by anyone as a fugitive or runaway, as recent research has demonstrated.[11] And it is highly probable that Paul was encouraging Philemon to set Onesimus free, as the first step in returning him as a freedman back to the circle of Christ-followers who were caring for the imprisoned Paul. In any case, Paul confronted Philemon with the choice of continuing to regard himself as Onesimus's owner or of beginning to see himself as Onesimus's brother, and to act radically as his new "beloved brother . . . in the Lord" (v. 16) because of the message that had made personal, and thus social, transformation possible for all three of them.

Paul set a personal example of "holy self-humiliation" for his converts by giving honor to all persons without respect to their social status and by using his influence on behalf of the least honorable persons. See, for example, Paul's employing in an upside-down way the familiar image of the human body to represent positive social relations among his house-congregations:

> God has so arranged the body, giving the greater honor to the inferior member, that there may be no dissension within the body, but the members may have the same care for one another. (1 Cor. 12:24–25 NRSV)

Paul's teaching further clarified and reinforced his attempt to undermine among the early Christ-followers the traditional anticipation and toleration of elite privilege that characterized conventional socialization in the first century—and now. The radical Paul had begun to measure the strength of the strong not by their ability to control those whom they sought to dominate but by their capacity and readiness to empower those whom they knew to be weak.

VII

Much more could be said to clarify the historical Saul/Paul's challenge to the dominant cultural values and social codes of his world. Yet I hope I have written enough here to make plausible my claim that this practical theologian and community organizer has been used and abused by many if not most of his post-third-century readers—especially following the Emperor Constantine's co-opting and undermining of the Christian tradition and its institutions by declaring himself the patron of the Christians, whom he anticipated would become his dutiful clients.

Quite often overlooked is the fact that Constantine chose to become Christianity's patron without embracing any of the revolutionary cultural values and social codes of the early Christians. He never renounced violence; rather he even had members of his own family killed whom he suspected of having become his enemies. He never rejected the dominant Roman values of male or elite privilege. He never sought to follow Paul's admonition to excel in giving honor to others rather than demanding honor for himself. In short, Constantine opened wide the door to the thorough domestication of Pauline radicalism.

VIII

Before focusing on specific cases of the domestication of this first-century radical Jew, it is important that the reader keep in mind that Paul wrote his letters in a so-called high-context culture, that is, a culture identified by anthropologists as one in which the speakers and writers rely on a rich and extensive repertoire of social knowledge shared with their hearers and readers.[12] In a "high-context" culture, speakers and writers simply assume that their audiences can and will use the appropriate cultural scripts, their sense and experience of how "life works," to "fill in the gaps" and "read between their lines." And here is where much interpretative trouble starts. Most later readers of Paul have also lived in their own "high-context" cultures in which they have taken for granted a large amount of unspoken social knowledge, including cultural values and social codes that have often been different from, and even seriously at odds with, the critical social knowledge shared by Paul and his first readers. This fact alone has further opened the door to various expressions of domestication of this radical Jew.

Yet, even some of Paul's contemporaries who shared his cultural context found the radical Paul too extreme. An early second-century Christian writer put the matter delicately:

> Our beloved brother Paul wrote to you according to the wisdom given him. . . . There are some things in them hard to understand, which the ignorant and unstable twist to their own destruction, as they do the other scriptures. (2 Pet. 3:15–16 NRSV)

To be sure, already some first-century documents in the Pauline tradition contain the so-called domestic codes, Martin Luther's "Haustafeln," found in the letters to the Colossians, to the Ephesians, and to Timothy and Titus. These codes seek to modify the patriarchal behavior of husbands, fathers, and slave owners without rejecting hierarchical relations in principle. These hortatory passages, apparently written by students and admirers of the historical Saul/Paul, provide evidence for the fact that Paul's initial radicality was difficult to sustain as the Christian movement attracted an increasing number of patriarchs and persons used to holding controlling power over others.

IX

From the beginning, this movement existed in a strong tension created by its radical inclusivity and aggressive outreach on the one hand—tending toward lowering what could be called "the repentance threshold"—and its mission to transform both individuals and their social relationships on the other, which in order to accomplish called for keeping the repentance threshold high. In classical Christian terminology, this is the tension between evangelism and sanctification.

For example, my close analysis of the exhortations to husbands and wives in chapter 5 of the Letter to the Ephesians has convinced me that these words were indeed intended radically to modify traditional patterns of male domination and to do so in this case by challenging husbands to serve their wives as Christ did and does the church—even unto death. The passage reads:

> Husbands, love your wives, just as Christ loved the church and gave himself up for her in order to make her holy by cleansing her with the washing of water by the word. (Eph. 5:25 NRSV)

That is, in Paul's name the rhetorical strategy has been shifted from emphasizing "brother-sister" relationships to a Christological critique of male power that seems even more radical. Yet the fact that the text leaves open the possibility of retaining patriarchy, albeit in a beneficially and sharply modified form, seems to point both to its immediate pastoral practicality in the first century and to its potential for use in the future to justify patriarchal privileges, as the history of the interpretation of this passage makes overwhelmingly clear.[13]

My own critical thinking about the possibility that attempts to domesticate Paul were made part of the New Testament canon was jump-started by James Robinson of Claremont Graduate School in a lecture he gave at Harvard Divinity School about forty years ago. Robinson argued that the letters addressed to Timothy and Titus in the name of Paul, the so-called Pastoral Letters, were composed at least in part to show that Paul, "if rightly understood," was less threatening to the pervasive cultural values than many were claiming. Some who had read Paul's radical ideas expressed in his letters to the Corinthians, the Galatians, and the Romans had apparently concluded that he was too bold, too dangerous, and therefore had to be brought back to mainstream values, that is, "domesticated."

In the years since hearing that lecture, I have concluded that Paul was even more dangerous than Robinson had discerned. For in those early letters Paul not only emphasized freedom from the Torah, freedom in the Spirit, and the resulting egalitarian access to charismatic leadership. He also challenged the authority of all patriarchs, including that of the emperor as the *pater patriae*, he showed no respect for blood-kin solidarity, and he rejected the fundamental values by which all honorable males were socialized and all leaders were judged.[14] Paul's calling Jesus, whom the world had profoundly humiliated, the Lord of life (e.g., 2 Cor. 4:5), functioned as antilanguage, the co-opting use of words to undermine the status quo.[15] Paul used such antilanguage frequently (e.g., "Lord" forty-four times in Romans and sixty-four times in 1 Corinthians) implicitly to call into question the authority of all conventional rulers: emperors, governors, elders, fathers, and husbands, in the name of one who had refused to dominate anyone.

X

Now I turn to what I regard as the most far-reaching case of domestication of the radical Paul by later interpreters, at least one of whom was well intentioned but who got it all wrong while getting part of it right—namely, Martin Luther. The passage in question is 1 Cor. 7:20–21, which I translate:

> Each person should continue in the calling into which one was called. Were you a slave when you were called? Do not be concerned about it. But if, indeed, you become manumitted, by all means [as a freed person] live according to [God's calling].[16]

For centuries, interpreters have puzzled over the appropriate completion of the elliptical Greek phrase at the end of verse 21: μαλλον χρησαι ("rather use . . ." "freedom"? or "slavery"? or something else?).[17] Should a slave confronted with legal release from slavery, manumission, grasp freedom or seek to remain a slave—or grasp something else altogether? While there are many factors that must be evaluated together to answer this critical question, in this essay I discuss my solution to this vexing puzzle only in relation to the meaning of the Greek word κλησις in verse 20.

In the New Revised Standard Version the term κλησις is rendered with "condition"—"Let each of you remain in the condition in which you were called." The translators reflect here a view that has become common wisdom about Paul, which Leander Keck states succinctly in a widely used handbook, *Paul and His Letters*: "Paul's ethic appears to be so thoroughly influenced by his expectation of the imminent parousia that it produces a 'conservative' stance, for he actually urges his readers not to change their roles in society (1 Cor. 7:17–24)."[18] But this common view of Paul is based on an egregious mistranslation of the key term κλησις.

While in English we can use the word "calling" to refer to a person's occupation, the term κλησις never carried that extended meaning in ancient Greek. Within the New Testament and in every Pauline usage of this term and the cognate verb καλειν, the calling in question is God's call to belong to Christ, except in Rom. 11:29 when the analogous calling of Israel is his subject.[19]

How then did the Greek term for "calling" or "invitation" or "summons," translated correctly with "vocatione" in the Latin Vulgate, come to be translated into English as "condition" or "station in life" or "social status," with the result that Paul is read as one who has firmly shut the door on all possible changes in the status quo and given such social conservatism a divine sanction?

XI

The story begins not in the first or second century but in the sixteenth, for prior to that time *vocatio* in this context was understood specifically as the call from God into a covenant relationship with God. But when Martin Luther translated the New Testament from Greek into German, he decided to enrich—or shall we say, distort—Paul's intended meaning by substituting the term *Beruf* ("occupation/status") for the correct German word *Ruf*: "Ein jeglicher bleibe in den Beruf darin er berufen ist" (1545).[20] His apparent motivation was to assure his readers that they need not torture themselves with such existential doubts as he had suffered, that had motivated him to seek to become pleasing to God by changing from a raucous student of the law to becoming a celibate priest and then on to becoming an Augustinian monk. As part of his emphasis on the importance of the laity in the Church, Luther hoped to encourage each person to believe that there was no need to change one's status from lay to clergy, or priest to monk, to please God. Likewise, there was no need for a German peasant to aspire to a higher social position, for God had called him to be a good Christian precisely as a peasant.[21] Not only monks had a vocation from God; every Christian in secular employment had such a vocation as well. Thus to seek to change one's status, however lowly, would be to go against God's will.[22]

Despite Luther's intent to comfort and empower the laity by translating κλησις with the word *Beruf*, it was a daring move fraught with disastrous potential—and a radical domestication and distortion of the historical Paul's apparent intent. Thus the late-nineteenth-century German critic of culture Karl Holl commented in his famous essay "Die Geschichte des Wort Beruf" that when Martin Luther translated κλησις with *Beruf*, he executed "eine kühne Wortumprägung [a bold restamping of the word's meaning]."[23] And Max Weber's judgment expressed in his essay "Die protestantische Ethik und der Geist des Kapitalismus" there is no Greek word that bears Luther's meaning that still stands: "Im Griechischen fehlt eine dem deutschen Wort [*sic* 'Beruf'] in der ethischen Färbung entsprechende Bezeichnung überhaupt [In Greek there is no word at all with the ethical coloring of the German term 'Beruf']."[24]

Thus despite the opinion of the great German lexicographer Walter Bauer, who lists "Beruf" (station in life, position, occupation) as a secondary meaning of κλησις, there simply is no evidence to support such a rendering.[25] What then might have influenced the esteemed Walter Bauer, who should have known better, to insist on such an insupportable translation? I suggest that it was the enormous influence of the German *Standesethik*, the code of ethics that came to define the relations among the classes as a result of the German Reformation in the sixteenth century.

XII

A personal story will reinforce my assertion of the enormous and continuing influence of this *Standesethik* in contemporary German culture. In 1977, while teaching in the Protestant faculty of the University of Tübingen, I was one of the local committee hosting the annual meeting of the international Society for New Testament Studies. As a host I was more assertive than I would have been otherwise in opening up conversations with members of the Society who were arriving from all over the world. Among them was a colleague from northern Germany with whom I had had some casual correspondence on issues in Pauline studies. He seemed to me to be a progressive and analytical thinker. So I mentioned to him that I had been invited by a prominent German publisher to make more accessible my work on slavery in a book to be titled simply *Paulus und die Sklaverei.* Many experiences in Tübingen classrooms had taught me well that it would be pointless for me to present my evidence and conclusions regarding Paul's words in 1 Cor. 7:21 to enslaved Christians without first dealing with his admonition in the previous sentence to remain in Christ's calling. For all the German translators' understanding of 7:20 continued to be strongly colored by Luther's mistranslation of κλησις with the term *Berufung*. Especially as an American I sensed that I needed help here from the inside of German culture. So I asked my German colleague if he could direct me to some up-to-date analyses of the *Standesethik* tradition by German scholars, since it was clear that I needed their authoritative support in writing my first chapter.

My colleague's response rocked me back on my heels. Instead of recommending any books or articles to me, he wagged his warning finger under my nose and whispered urgently, "Passen Sie auf, Herr Bartchy, Auch der Hitler war gegen die Standesethik." That is: "Be careful, Mr. Bartchy, Hitler was also opposed to the Standesethik." Wow! He was not smiling. This was no joke. To be sure, Hitler had opposed this class-based ethic because of the traditional authority it gave to those in the German aristocracy, especially men holding high rank in the military. But how could a scholar's attempt to clean up a longstanding and widely influential mistranslation of Paul be compared to Hitler's envy and criticism of the *Stand* of the German military aristocracy? Until then I had not realized how very, very deep and pervasive this way of justifying the ordering of life in social classes had become in German culture. It can be no wonder that Walter Bauer felt that he had to find such a meaning as *Stand*, if only as a secondary one, for Paul's use of κλησις in 1 Cor. 7:20.[26]

XIII

Not only the meaning of κλησις in verse 20 but also Paul's use of the term in the immediate context should have alerted translators of Paul's letters since Luther to Luther's intentional mistranslation. For two sentences earlier, verse 18, Paul wrote, "Was anyone at the time of his call [κλησις] circumcised?" As Neil Elliott, in his excellent book *Liberating Paul: The Justice of God and the Politics of the Apostle*, puts it, "Surely no one would argue that the 'calling' here was a matter of God calling a man *to be circumcised.* Why, then, should anyone suppose that in 7:21 Paul speaks of God calling a person *to be a slave*?"[27]

And in sharp contrast to the conventional wisdom expressed by Leander Keck and noted above about Paul's general opposition to social change in view of the impending end, throughout chapter 7 of 1 Corinthians, Paul repeatedly suggests that under the proper circumstances his Christian readers may very well change their social status without sinning or rejecting God's "call to peace" (7:15). Indeed, as Elliott correctly stresses (following my emphasis of two decades earlier),[28] the structure of this chapter is based on Paul's offering alternatives to his personal preferences for conduct or marital status. For example, in 7:2–6 Paul strongly encourages sexual relations in marriage although his preferred missionary ideal is celibacy (7:7)—but this is only for those who are comfortable in their single state (7:9). He recommends unmarried and widowed persons to marry, although it is not his first choice (7:8, 39).

He approves of a woman remaining separated from her husband (7:11), although Paul not only prefers that Christ-followers not divorce, he even quotes a command from Jesus against divorce (7:10). And at the end of this chapter Paul states that a widowed woman may indeed remarry, and he urges her to marry "in the Lord," that is, another Christ-follower, even though Paul states that he feels that she would be happier if she remained single (7:39–40).

Rather than writing as a social conservative who reinforced the status quo with divine sanctions, in 1 Corinthians 7 Saul/Paul of Tarsus redefined sexual politics in marriage as a partnership of equals—the man's body belongs to his wife in the very same way (ὁμοιως) as everyone took for granted that the woman's body belonged to her husband (7:4–5). Further, a woman did not have to be married or become pregnant to be regarded as a full person in Paul's communities. Nor did a man have to prove his virility or gain honor for his blood-family by siring children, preferably boys.

The image of Paul as social conservative is the result of undermining his social vision while claiming his authority. Ignorance of the cultural values and social codes in his "high context" has kept even serious scholars enthralled to the domestication of this radical Jew. Paul's domestication has been thorough and long lasting. Many of his translators profoundly betrayed him—with serious and detrimental theological and social consequences.

XIV

Now to conclude with some hermeneutical observations. As all historians are aware, the reading of any sentence, paragraph, and document outside of its original context is prone to anachronistic and ethnocentric distortions. This problem becomes especially acute with far-reaching results when the text in question is regarded as a sacred text, when—as in the case of the writings of Paul of Tarsus—the words of a human being become regarded as the Word of God. For as revelation from God, the words are assumed to be eternally true, severed from the limitations of time and space—and thus of culture. As divine words, their vulnerability to being read in accord with the changing cultural values and social scripts of various readers through the centuries has had enormously wide-ranging social and psychological effects.

An irony: The more that words are believed to have an unchangeable meaning, the greater is their vulnerability to distortion of their original intent. In the case in question here, the radical Paul who undermined patriarchy by redefining the family and gender roles, who rejected the use of power to dominate others, and who was finally executed as a disturber of the peace of the Roman empire, has been tamed and domesticated by a large number of those who claim to hold his words in the highest regard. The result: those in positions of power often feel quite at home with their greatly distorted readings of his words. Historians have inherited the task of joining social critics and theologians in making such folks much less comfortable in the presence of the radical Paul of Tarsus.

Notes

1. Orlando Patterson, *Freedom in the Making of Western Culture* (New York: Basic Books, 1991), 326.
2. For example, the authority of Paul is called on by the Southern Baptist Church, the Lutheran Church–Missouri Synod, the Lutheran Church–Wisconsin Synod, congregations in the noninstrumental Church of Christ and the independent Christian Churches, the Church of Jesus Christ of the Latter Day Saints, and in part by the Roman Catholic Church and the Eastern Orthodox Church, as a primary basis for rejecting the ordination of women to leadership ministry. The passages cited most frequently are 1 Cor. 14:33–35 ("women should be silent in the churches") and 1 Tim. 2:11–15 ("I permit no woman to teach or to have authority over a man"). Based on the evidence of ancient manuscripts, many scholars regard the first passage as a later gloss by a misogynist copyist, that is, not written by Paul. And the majority of university-based church historians and New Testament exegetes have concluded that 1 Timothy was written by a later follower of Paul who sought to extend Paul's authority by making him appear to be less radical than in his earlier letters. Without exception, when these two admonitions are cited to restrict leadership roles and ordination to ministry solely to men, the function of the passages in their respective documents and the particular historical contexts that provoked these exhortations have simply been ignored. See my discussion below.

3. Daniel Boyarin, *A Radical Jew: Paul and the Politics of Identity* (Berkeley: University of California Press, 1994); Alan Segal, *Paul the Convert: The Apostolate and Apostasy of Saul the Pharisee* (New Haven: Yale University Press, 1990).
4. Boyarin, *A Radical Jew*, 2.
5. In distinct contrast to the convention of referring to "Saul of Tarsus" as "Paul of Tarsus" to mark his "conversion" to the Jesus-movement, there is strong evidence that he was still called Saul even when he was preaching about Jesus as the Christ among diaspora Judeans (see Acts 9:19b–28; 11:25–30; 12:25–13:2). When describing Saul's evangelistic activities with Barnabus on Cyprus, the author of Acts observes: "Saul, who was also called Paul, [was] filled with the Holy Spirit" (13:9). It seems highly likely then that whether he was called "Saul" or "Paul" was a consequence of his immediate cultural context and that as a resident of Tarsus he may well have been known as Saul or Paul from his childhood and throughout his life, depending on who was speaking to him.
6. In his letters Paul never uses the term "Christian" to refer to those who have been baptized into Christ. Rather his most frequently used terms by far are "brother" and "sister" and also when referring to them as groups he addresses them with such terms as "God's beloved," "holy ones in Christ Jesus," and "God's assembly." In only two New Testament documents are these converts called "Christians": Acts 11:26 (in Antioch apparently at the point of the group's no longer being regarded there as a faction within the House of Israel) and 1 Pet. 4:16 (in the context of being reviled and persecuted because of "the name of Christ"). See John H. Elliott, "Jesus the Israelite Was Neither a Jew nor a Christian. On Correcting the Nomenclature," *Journal for the Study of the Historical Jesus* 5, no. 2 (2007): 119–54.
7. See my "Undermining Ancient Patriarchy: Paul's Vision of a Society of Siblings," *Biblical Theology Bulletin* 29 (1999): 68–78.
8. See the chart on p. 70 of my "Undermining Ancient Patriarchy" and also the subtle analysis of Paul's use of sibling terms in all of his uncontested letters by Reidar Aasgaard, *"My Brothers and Sisters!" Christian Siblingship in Paul*, JSNTS 265 (New York: T&T Clark, 2004).
9. See my "Who Should Be Called Father? Paul of Tarsus between the Jesus Tradition and *Patria Potestas*," *Biblical Theology Bulletin* 33 (2003): 135–47.
10. See my "Undermining Ancient Patriarchy," 77, and "Who Should Be Called Father?" 145–46.
11. See Peter Lampe, "Keine 'Sklavenflucht' des Onesimus," *Zeitschrift für die neutestamentliche Wissenschaft* 76 (1985): 135–37, and my "Philemon, Epistle To," *Anchor Bible Dictionary* 5:305b–310a.
12. See Bruce J. Malina, *Christian Origins and Cultural Anthropology: Practical Models for Biblical Interpretation* (Atlanta: John Knox Press, 1986), esp. 1–12, and his challenge to become "a considerate reader of the Bible."
13. While in this passage more than twice as many words are addressed to the husband (93) as are written to the wife (40), the behavior enjoined on the wife seems to echo traditional expectations for wives, except for the final, rather puzzling admonition that she "should respect her husband" (5:33). This exhortation suggests that the husband "in Christ" was making changes in his way of being a husband that went against traditional gender norms, creating psychological confusion and making such an apparently banal statement an important admonition to the wife as new, more egalitarian, ways of marital relating were being worked out according to the overarching challenge to traditional values stated in 5:21: "Subordinate yourselves to each other in awe of Christ."
14. See my "'When I'm Weak, I'm Strong': A Pauline Paradox in Cultural Context," in *Kontexte der Schrift: Kultur, Politik, Religion, Sprache–Text*, Band II, ed. Christian Strecker (Stuttgart: Kohlhammer, 2005), 49–60.
15. One of the main features of "antilanguage" is the *relexicalizing* of the received meaning of words for the purpose of strengthening the self-identity of a resistance movement or "antisociety" (see M.A.K. Halliday, "Anti-Languages," *American Anthropologist* 78 [1976]: 570–84).
16. S. S. Bartchy, *First Century Slavery and the Interpretation of 1 Corinthians 7:21* (Missoula, Mont.: Scholars Press, 1973), 183.
17. See the two-page chart displaying the history of the interpretation of this verse in *First Century Slavery*, 6–7.
18. Leander Keck, *Paul and His Letters* (Philadelphia: Fortress Press, 1979), 94–95.
19. Rom. 11:28–29: "On the one hand with regard to the gospel they [a part of Israel—see v. 25] are enemies for your sake; but on the other hand with regard to election they are beloved for the sake of their ancestors; for the gifts and calling of God are irrevocable" (my trans.).
20. Note that this mistranslation, now with the closely related word *Berufung*, has continued down to the most recent version of the Luther Bibel (1984): "Jeder bleibe in der Berufung in der er berufen wurde."
21. This meaning is still emphasized in the International Bible Society's German translation, *Hoffnung fuer Alle*: "Jeder soll an dem Platz dienen, an dem ihn Gottes Ruf erreichte" as well as in the *Gute Nachricht* translation: "Alle sollen Gott an den Platz dienen . . ."

22. Perhaps the best-known defender of this radically conservative position is Albert Schweitzer, who derived from 1 Cor. 7:17–24 Paul's "theory of the status quo," according to which the natural condition of the Christian's existence has "become of no importance, not in the general sense that it does not matter what is done to it, but in the special sense that henceforth nothing must be done to it." *Mysticism of Paul the Apostle* (New York: Black, 1968), 194–95.
23. Thus the ecumenical *Einheitsuebersetzung* (1980): "Jeder soll in dem Stand bleiben, in dem ihn der Ruf Gottes getroffen hat." And the widely used Elberfelder translation (1985) reads: "Jeder bleibe in dem Stand in dem er berufen worden ist." Karl Holl, "Die Geschichte des Worts Beruf" (1928), 190.
24. For an extensive discussion of this critical issue, see Bartchy, *First-Century Slavery*, 135–55. Max Weber, "Die protestantische Ethik und der Geist des Kapitalismus" (1920), 63.
25. Walter Bauer, *Griechisch-Deutsches Woerterbuch zu den Schriften des Neuen Testaments under der übrigen urchristlichen Literatur*, 5th ed. (Berlin: Töpelman, 1958), col. 862.
26. In the most recent edition (the third) of the English translation of Baur's magisterial word book, thoroughly revised and edited by Frederick Danker (University of Chicago Press, 2000), Danker continues to posit a secondary meaning as "the position one holds" or "condition," citing references that seem quite ambiguous and weak and then noting scholars who hold "another perspective" on this postulated secondary meaning in 1 Cor. 7:20, that is, they reject it.
27. Neil Elliott, *Liberating Paul: The Justice of God and the Politics of the Apostle* (New York: Orbis Books, 1994), 34.
28. See Bartchy, *First-Century Slavery*, 166–72.

A "Seminal" Study of the Jesus *Drasha* in the Gospel of Matthew

Herbert W. Basser

My association with the esteemed professor in blue jeans goes back to the early 1980s when he was the dynamic editor and manager of various scholarly writings connected with the National Association of Professors of Hebrew (NAPH) and I was a relative newcomer to academia. Zev, just "Zev" with no pretentious titles, encouraged me to publish and speak in his forums, to meet the accomplished scholars of that era, to write reviews for his journals. When I was unable to attend a conference at the last moment owing to a personal tragedy, Zev Garber, quite unknown to me at the time, got hold of my lecture notes and presented my paper for me (improvising while speaking). The editor of *Bible Review* heard the brilliant delivery and published the piece. The energetic ball of fire in blue jeans (so congenial in his affection for all junior scholars) helped and mentored, taught and encouraged, reviewed my most complex books with acumen and broad grasp. He brought me to wide notice by including me in one of his early edited books on methodologies in the teaching of Jewish Studies. By some stroke of good fortune, he caught a slew of egregious typing mistakes the secretary had created just as this book, which would bring me to public attention, was about to go to press. Perhaps the most embarrassing "typo" was a reference to a sublime passage in the Gospel of Matthew which was (as if meant to entertain my *Freudian* readers) rendered as the *Semen on the Mons*. I owe it to him, my savior, to include here my latest thinking on this very passage that will soon be published by Academic Studies Press, provisionally titled: *The Mind Behind The Gospels: A Commentary to Matthew: Chapters 1–14.*

* * *

Chapters 5–7 in the Gospel according to Matthew contain teachings for those who need to hear the moral fiber of the *hasid*—the pious and humble servant of God—and are commonly called the Sermon on the Mount. The trichapter sermon presents a list of exhortations in a form that seems to be that of a manifesto in which, along with the teachings, Jesus encourages his disciples to keep their spirits up while remaining both humble and willing to accept whatever persecutions might afflict them. Jesus assures his disciples that those who suffer persecution either for his sake or for the sake of righteousness shall share in the ultimate reward: *The Kingdom of Heaven.* I do not read these three chapters as a message directed at Matthew's own church. Rather Jesus' words, making no personal claim, are aimed at strengthening his disciples and the Jewish people of his time. Much later in the Gospel, the Kingdom of Heaven will be promised to a different group, the nations of the world who are the enemies of Israel (24:24; 28:19).

Jesus uses the Galilean preacher's style to teach his disciples. "As attendants of the elders, the scribes had no authority to offer decrees on their own. They could only give exhortations of faith and elucidate scriptures." In this chapter Jesus will overstep the boundary that defines the scribe in the manner in which he teaches but not in the content of his teaching. That is, while Jesus does not say anything in this chapter that would contravene any of the laws of the sages and Pharisees, nonetheless in six places in it (5:21–42) he teaches in the form of a teacher of law, not citing prior teachers. The scribes had no authority on their own to offer opinions on the law. There is no scriptural exegesis in his sermon beyond what was the common understanding of the verses. His teaching on divorce and oaths will require some attention as here it is not clear at all what he wants to do. His use of exaggeration is not surprising. What may be surprising are some cases where it seems he wants to be taken literally.

The sermon opens with a hymn of consolation and praise for the humble and the afflicted. Tightly structured, the hymn seems repetitive (there are eight beatitudes in it), but it is not boring as each phrase is developed from a biblical verse that has the word "*anav*" (meek).[1] It is written in a proto-*piyyut* style (a kind of liturgical poetry that blends scripture, *midrash*, and the poet's values).[2] The hymn locates scriptural constellations concerning the phrases alluding to "next world" and "face of God" together with "humble" and "afflicted" (in Hebrew *anav* and *ani*). In it there are allusions to biblical texts but none of these are directly cited.[3]

The ninth and final beatitude (5:11) begins a new unit. The *piyyut* style is abandoned and instead Jesus begins to address his hearers directly. Be worthy examples and shining lights, he says to them (5:13–16). Thereafter Jesus speaks of the importance of keeping every law, however minor (5:17–20); for as he says he has not come to abolish the law but rather to see to it that its every part is fulfilled, is practiced. The language recalls the teaching of the Mishna:

> Rabbi Yonatan says: All who fulfill the Torah in poverty will in the end fulfill it in wealth, while all who annul the Torah in wealth will in the end annul it in poverty. (Avot. 4:9)

Many have thought that once Jesus has declared that he has not come to abolish the law but rather to fulfill its every part, he then refers to six age-old laws of the Jews and states what, according to him, it really means to fulfill them. For him a desultory compliance of the law is not enough.[4] I do not agree. The sermon uses these verses to introduce sermonic exhortations on related matters but does not imply literal compliance is anything less than mandatory. The word "murder" introduces a sermon on anger, and adultery a sermon on lust. The material of these sermons is standard fare for Jewish teaching.

For the preacher, divine laws are designed to transform human behavior. Sermons tease out of scriptural passages old messages in new ways. The messages are based on a desire to transform one's character and ultimately the society in which one lives. That was the job of the preacher. As in the works of Philo, Josephus, Ben Sirah, and many others, the Jews are not only to refrain from bad behavior; they are also to refrain from any social activity and/or emotional involvement that might in some way lead toward bad behavior. That is the goal of the rabbinic laws of Mishna and Talmud. In laying out these moral laws in this way, what Jesus is doing here in form is very roughly akin to what the rabbis called "making a fence around the Torah" (M. Avot 1:1).[5] To "make a fence around the Torah" is to extend the law beyond what it minimally requires one to do. The rabbis extended the reach of certain laws in order to either prescribe or else prohibit matters that, if not prescribed or prohibited, might lead to the transgression of the laws around which the fence was built. Jesus appears to be doing more than the scribes did but in effect he is artistically rephrasing age-old messages. Matthew 23:23 tells us that the scribes and Pharisees added tithes on mint and other spices that are never eaten alone; by doing this they erected a fence, so to speak, around the ritual law concerning the tithing of staple vegetables. That is, if such things as mint and dill are tithed, then obviously the staple vegetables, as the law enjoins, are to be tithed, too. Yet, as Jesus points out, the Pharisees would not lift a finger to safeguard the moral law: "Woe to you, scribes and Pharisees, stage-actors! You tithe mint, dill, and cumin, and you leave aside the more serious things of the Torah, judgment, mercy, and faith." Yet, we must be wary of reading the later portrayals of Jesus into the pastoral sermonic setting.

To say that rabbinic authority was somewhat lenient in demanding higher standards of conscience is to make a valid critique. The rabbis did not often legislate on matters that were thought to be unenforceable. However they did at least encourage people concerning right behavior in these unenforceable matters. So, for instance, while prurient behavior was understood by all to be prohibited, still there were few legal safeguards against it. There were rules for keeping males and females from being alone together—but little beyond that was practical. However a text in Avot de Rabbi Natan, version A (chap. 2), shows the extent to which this matter was of concern. In the text of the biblical verse, the foundation upon which the fence was built is interpreted in a most creative way (the careful manipulation of a scriptural text to make a point was considered an art).

> "*Keep your way far from her*" (Pr 5:8): ["Her"] refers to a prostitute. A person tells you, "Do not go near a certain market or do not go in a certain lane-way because there is a certain prostitute of dazzling beauty who frequents these places"—Do not then think to yourself, "That warning is of little concern to me. I know my will power will withstand the temptations. Even if I do happen to meet her in these places, I trust in myself that nothing will happen." Even so, do not go there for perhaps you will stumble.

A rabbinic text from Midrash Tannaim (ed. Hoffman), Deut. 22:4, shows similar intent. The matter here is mercy toward an injured animal, and again the rabbis do not legislate. However they do make known that, in this case, it is their preference to show mercy, even if doing this is not strictly required by law. The text reads:

> *You shall not* [stand by] *and watch the donkey of your brother or his ox* [suffer]. This is a negative commandment. How do I know it is also a positive commandment?—Scripture says, "When you see the donkey of your enemy or ox going astray, etc." (Exod. 23:5).
>
> *And scripture says "And can you [can] ignore it."*—[Indecisive syntax] For some, this is meant to be read as an exclamatory question. Can you ignore the suffering? [Surely not!] But for others it is meant to be read as a declaration. You can ignore it. [Surely so!] . . . This latter reading applies to an elderly and dignified sage. [For it would be considered dishonorable for such a one to be seen to be coming to the aid of an animal.] Nevertheless, if he is a *hassid* he will always do more than what is permitted, or less than what is proscribed, by the minimalist reading of the law. And this is the preferred way for all.

A text in BT Baba Metsia 30b comments on supererogatory mechanisms and suggests that the Hebrew Scriptures have already advised that they are normative. In this text, Exod, 18:20 is read so that no part of it is seen to be free of meaning:

> "And thou shalt teach them the statutes and the laws, and shalt show them the way wherein they must walk, and the work that they must do." (Exod. 18:20)
>
> Rabbi Yosef interpreted the verse . . .
>
> "*and the work*," this word refers to the actual law,
>
> "*which should be done*" means: "go beyond the minimum requirements of the law."

Having said all this, I do not find Jesus legislated in the sermon at all. The two exceptions are his teachings on divorce and oaths, which I take as Matthean additions since they are absent in Luke's parallels. The teaching on divorce has been put into the sermon form here but it is taken from a later statement (chap. 19) where Jesus has already turned away from teaching and encouraging but instead argues and debates.

I had initially thought to take the approach that Matthew's scheme in the sermon was to add what later rabbis termed "duties of the heart." I do not think so now. In form it might seem to imply duties but in actuality it really does not demand much more than plucking out eyes and cutting of hands, hardly serious legislation. What we do have is a series of minisermons introduced by some scripture or allusion to scripture. The scripture then is really left alone. Jesus goes on to speak about other matters suggested by the scripture. It is not exegesis at all. There is a hint of wanting to extend prohibitions but the sheer shock of the rhetoric argues strongly against that. In sum, he did not say more than the scribes did, but his form is that of the religious authority promulgating law. In the language of the rabbis we could say he teaches *midrash aggada* but he sounds like he is teaching *midrash halacha.*

What can we as historians of religion learn from the sermon? There are very few fully preserved synagogue sermons, designated as such, in Jewish literature. Matthew has taken some sources and shaped them into a sermon. Even so, he shows us that much of what we find in Talmudic literature is closely related in style, structure, and content to much earlier preaching. In general, the value of the gospels for understanding the continuity of Jewish customs and word usage cannot be overemphasized. Time and again in his important work David Flusser makes this point. For instance, he points out that the custom of the father naming the male child at circumcision, about which we are told in Luke (1:59–64), is not attested in the Talmudic texts.[6] Nor is the practice of passing around the "kiddush cup of wine" for which those at the table are to drink, about which again Luke tells us (22:17), attested in these texts either.[7] Only because both of these customs are referred to in the gospels can it be said that they date from the Second Temple period.

Aside from confirming that certain practices mentioned in late Jewish sources (and also certain types of exegesis) were current in the days of the Second Temple period, the New Testament also shows us that certain phrases or words that appear in the late Jewish sources were also being used in this earlier period.[8] For instance, in Acts 21:21 the phrase "the Jews who are among the Gentiles," used by the author to refer to the Diaspora Jews whom Paul is said to be turning away from the Mosaic law, remains unattested in Jewish sources until its appearance in BT Talmud Shabbat 88b–89a.[9] There Moses is said to have replied to the angels who wanted to possess the Torah:

> Of what use is the Torah for you? I ask you moreover, what is written in it?
> "Thou shalt have no other gods . . ." Do you live among the Gentiles who worship idols?

And in *Shemot Rabba* (*Va'era*) 3:7 and BT Berakhot 9b there is a parallel to the phrase found in Matt. 6:34: "Each day has enough trouble of its own," which reads: "There is sufficient trouble for its time frame alone" (i.e., "Each time frame has enough trouble of its own").

Also, the word "*Hosanna*" is found in Matt. 21:9; Mark 11:9; John 12:13; and in each case it means "praised be you." The word is found with other meanings in BT Sukka (a "palm branch" in 31a, 33b, 37a, 46b) and in a *midrash* (The Great *Hoshanna*—the title of the last day of the Festival of Sukkot) (*Vayikra Rabba* 37:2). Only in medieval *piyyut* do we find that it means "praise to God." In the current liturgy there is a pertinent alphabetical "*hoshanna.*" Midrash Tehillim 17:5 relates that after the destruction of the Temple a synagogue official stood in the center of the synagogue on a platform while the congregants encircled him. This practice continues to this very day. Praises called "*Hoshanna*" are now sung and the phrases of the poems are generally begun by the word "*Hoshanna.*"

Finally, I need to say something about my methods in this work as a whole and in chapters 5, 6, and 7 in particular. I have read a large chunk of the various books and articles dealing with the interpretation of the Gospel of Matthew. Moreover, colleagues who have looked at my work, and in particular Prof. Dale Allison, who also sent me articles and unpublished papers, have wondered about my methods. I seem to use Jewish exegetical materials indiscriminately without care for date or provenance and reject the "blatantly" obvious suggestions offered by scholars that have been current for forty years or longer.

Any scholar faces the following question (since we do not have a tradition handed down from Bultmann from Matthew from Jesus from the Mount of Sermons): (a) Is it better to *invent* an exegesis that nowhere exists by using sources that might have been available to Matthew's sources or to Jesus using extant Jewish and Hellenistic writings; or (b) is it better to find an exegesis that *does exist* but comes from any time and any place within the interpretive culture of Judaism? To my mind the latter presents, at the very least, a real possibility of what a Jewish interpreter in the second century might have thought since someone did cite such a tradition at some point. It was not fabricated by a scholar with Matthew in mind. When the very language and images of Matthew's story are so visible in these "later" statements that come from deep within the conservative culture of rabbis who breathed the same civilization (to use Mordecai Kaplan's apt term) as did Jesus and the early Christians, it seems to me to be the better option. However, there is latitude for speculation as well and using the Hebrew Bible where the genre of writing indicates one was meant to do that. This is the case in the Beatitudes, which begin chapter 5. Hebrew poetic forms are riddles that require the listener or reader to scan scripture for the language the poet uses and the traditions attached to those scriptures. Of course, all rules of thumb have their exceptions and I have used my own judgments on where to draw lines. The question of method and viable approaches were discussed eighty-five years ago by Strack-Billebeck in their "After-Word to the Sermon on the Mount" (*Evangelium nach Mattaus*, 470–74). Around the same time Joseph Klausner noted, "So extraordinary is the similarity that it might almost seem as though the Gospels were composed simply and solely out of matter contained in the *Talmud* and *Midrash*."[10] If modern scholars need convincing and the battle is to be up hill, what better place to begin than with the "sermon on the mountain"?

The final verses, 43 to 48, of chapter 5 show us in bold strokes the richness of Matthew's exegetical skills. Here are the verses and my comments.

> 43–44. "You have heard that it was said, 'Love your neighbor' (Lev. 19:18) and [you might infer from this that it also means to] hate your enemy. But I say, Love your enemies and pray for those who persecute you."

We would do well to approach this unit (vv. 43–45) carefully, for it is of a different order than the other units in this section of the Sermon on the Mount. For unlike in the other units, here Jesus gives a full sermon on the biblical text that introduces the unit (Lev. 19:18), the commandment to love one's neighbor. In this sermon it is not the written law to love one's neighbor that Jesus objects to; rather it is the inference that one might draw from the verse, that loving one's neighbor means that one should hate one's enemy.

We begin our discussion with an explanation of how the rabbis went about transforming the meaning of certain laws that seemed to them no longer acceptable to their cultural sensitivities and worldview. The method used to transform the meaning of these laws might be characterized in this way: "literal unacceptable; stretch apt." For with this method the literal meaning of a biblical text was rejected for whatever reason, after which the text was then reinterpreted in such a way that a new meaning was found for it which was more in keeping with the current worldview of the rabbis. In the rabbinic literature this three-step exegetical method appears like this: (1) the text is given; then (2) the plain meaning of the text is stated, followed by objections to this meaning; then (3) the new meaning is established. To show how this method worked, and also to show that both the rabbis and Matthew's Jesus used this same method to interpret both biblical and oral law, we shall first present several examples from the rabbinic literature, before turning again to the gospel text. Our first example is from BT Zebahim 22b.

> 1. The prophet Ezekiel proclaimed: *Thus says the Lord: Any stranger, uncircumcised in heart, and uncircumcised in flesh, shall not enter into my sanctuary* (Ez. 44:9) . . . And also: *In that you have brought strangers, uncircumcised in heart, and uncircumcised in flesh, to be in my sanctuary, to profane it, my house* (44:7). . .
>
> The Rabbis taught: 2. Any stranger—might I think Ezekiel literally means a stranger [a non-Israelite, who could under no circumstances officiate in the Temple]? The Scripture state his disqualification, "uncircumcised in heart." [So it was not a non-Israelite the rabbis were speaking of here, but a Jewish priest who was "uncircumcised in heart," that is, whose intentions were impure.] 3. So why call him "stranger"? It means "one whose characteristic behaviors have estranged him to his Father Who Is in Heaven."

For the rabbis the "stranger" in this text from Ezekiel, who was not to enter the Temple, did not mean a non-Israelite, which is what it originally meant. Rather for them it meant an Israelite, who because of his being "uncircumcised in heart" was "estranged" from God. The rabbis used this text from Ezekiel to make known that a Jewish priest with an impure heart was as unfit for divine service as any non-Israelite would have been. Both circumcised flesh and a circumcised heart were required for a priest to officiate in the Temple.

As can be seen from this example, in reinterpreting the legal texts from the scriptures and the oral documents to fit the needs of their current worldview, the rabbis stretched the meaning of the words in the texts far beyond what the context would seem to allow. It was never the texts alone they were interpreting but rather the value system of their current worldview that provided the context for their interpretations. But this "stretching" of the meaning of the words in these texts was in no way seen to be a violation of the texts, since it was done using the standard hermeneutical methods universally accepted by the rabbis. That is, for reasons that were wholly intelligible to the community, the rabbis set aside the literal meaning of these biblical texts and replaced them with a new meaning that was, if not opposite to, at least far removed from the original meaning of it.[11] Let us look at another example of this three-step interpretive method from the rabbinic literature (there are hundreds to choose from), this one from BT Menahot 99b. The three steps—statement of the verse; objection to its literal meaning; then reinterpretation—are clearly apparent in it.

> 1. *And thou shall set upon the table show bread before me continually* (Ex. 25:30).
>
> It was taught: 2. Rabbi Yosi said [the literal is impractical], If the old show bread was removed after a part of the morning and the new set down during a part of the evening there would be no problem. 3. So what meaning do I establish for the words of Ex. 25:30, "before me continually"?—That the table not rest [for a whole night or day] without bread on it.
>
> Said Rabbi Ammi, From the words of Rabbi Yosi we can derive that even if one reads a mere chapter of Torah in the morning and a chapter at night he can fulfill Joshua 1:8: *"This book of the Torah shall not depart out of thy mouth; [but you shall meditate in it day and night].*

In interpreting Exod. 25:30, Rabbi Yosi determined that the show bread did not need to be on the table at all times, as the biblical text says literally that it should be. That is, new loaves did not have to be set on the table before the old ones were removed to fulfill the requirement that the bread be "before [God] continually." It is not made clear what Rabbi Yosi's objection to the word "continually" was. Nevertheless what he understood by "continually" is far removed from what is normally meant by the word. As a result of this interpretation, rabbis such as R. Ammi, as the text points out, found reason to shorten the times required for daily Torah study. It should be noted that Rabbi Yosi's interpretation of Exod. 25:30 was dismissed long ago but his intention, as usual, was to alleviate unnecessary strain and hardship in the community.[12] This was always the reason for uncovering a new meaning for these legal texts.

Let us now turn back to the gospel text in which, as I say, by applying the same exegetical method to Lev. 19:18, Jesus determines that the word "neighbor" also means "enemy." Here is the text with the steps (differing in a minor way from the examples we have seen from the rabbinic literature above in that in it they appear 1-3-2) marked in it.

> 1. (Mt. 5:43) "You have heard that it was said, *'Love your neighbor'* and [by implication] hate your enemy. (5:44) But I tell you: 3. Love your enemies and pray for those who persecute you. . . . 2. (5:46) If you love those who love you, what reward will you get? Are not even the tax collectors doing that? And if you greet only your brothers, what are you doing more than others? Do not even pagans do that?"

Since scripture has no need to talk about loving one's friend and/or one's neighbor, Jesus suggests that the real point here concerns hating one's enemy. The text from Leviticus does not say explicitly that loving one's neighbor means that one should then hate one's enemy, but this is accepted as if it were written. Since scripture commands one to love one's neighbor, which means God will reward one for fulfilling the commandment, why should He bother to reward what comes naturally between friends anyway? A friend is by definition someone one loves. That is, it is unnecessary for the scriptures to command one to love one's friend or neighbor, for people do this anyway. Thus Jesus must establish a different meaning for the text, namely, "love your enemies."[13]

> So that in this way you will be children of your heavenly father, because he causes his sun to shine upon the evil and upon the good, and he sends rain upon the righteous and the unrighteous both. (5:45)

The homiletic mechanisms Matthew uses (and further on we will look at them in some detail) to produce the argument Jesus makes in this unit—which is that you must love one's enemies because that is exactly what God does and you are to be just like him—are fairly complex. What Matthew wants to develop here is the sermonic materials that will confirm the argument Jesus makes and so we must now take a wider look at what Jesus says in his argument—that one must be like God.

I begin with what most would consider a very late written text from Exodus Rabba 46:4, which comments on Deut. 14:1: "You are children of the Lord your God." This text teaches that the Children of Israel must be like God because they are also his children. In its present form the *midrash* is somewhat corrupt but for our purposes we need look only at a short parable from it. The text reads:

> A parable: There was a *synkletos*-officer [i.e., a senator] who had children who associated with riffraff and turned to evil ways. . . . [T]he father claimed they were not really his children. . . . [B]ut he was told: Everyone knows they are your children for they are similar to you.
>
> The key to the parable: The "synkletos" symbolizes God; "his children" symbolize the Children of Israel, as it is said, You *are children of the Lord your God* (Deut 14:1).

The point of this parable seems to be that in the end Israel shall be redeemed because as God's children they innately share in his goodness. Though living among the nations has corrupted them, they will be welcomed back by God because he is their father and they are "similar" to him. The parable does not let us know in what way Israel is "similar" to him.[14] We are only told that the key to its meaning lies in Deut. 14:1. Israel is set apart from the nations because they are God's own children and therefore deserving of salvation.

Another midrash, from Tanhuma Deuteronomy Ekev 5:5, which also refers to Deut. 14:1, states that the Israelites are God's children only when they are obedient to his commands.

> "You are children of the Lord your God" (Deut 14:1). When are you my children? When you are of the Lord your God by obeying my commandments.

In still another midrash, from the Mekhilta of R. Ishmael to Exod. 15:2 (see also YT Peah 1:1 and BT Shabbat 33b), it is said that to be like God means to be generous in spirit as he is.

> This is my God, and I will glorify Him; [my father's God, and I will exalt Him] (Ex. 15:2). Abba Shaul says, "Be similar to him (*hidameh lo*). As he is kind and merciful so you also be kind and merciful."

Note here the joining of "kind" and "merciful."

Finally, in a text from Tanhuma Vayishlah 10:10 (abbreviated in what follows), which serves as a midrash on Deut. 13:5 and 8:6, the command to imitate God is confirmed by several citations from the scriptures.[15]

> When Moses told Israel "after the Lord your God you shall go" (Dt 13:5) and "to go in his ways" (Dt 8:6)? (They said: who can go in his ways . . . ?) Moses said to Israel: That is not what I said to you—rather [follow] his ways which are kindness and truth and charity as it is written, "All the paths of the Lord are mercy and truth" (Ps 25:10), and charity. . . . So you also, go after these traits of the Holy One.

In Luke 6:35 Jesus gives us a reworking of Deut. 14:1: "And you shall be a) *children of* b) *the Highest,* c) for he is kind to the thankless and the wicked" (blanket universal statement), which is followed by: "Be therefore merciful, as your Father also is merciful" (6:36).

For Luke, that God is kind to the thankless is visible and obvious. Although biblical texts were available as proof, Luke's Jesus does not make use of them. Using empirical data is sometimes preferred by midrashists even when biblical texts are readily available to them.[16] The midrashic themes concerning *imitatio dei*, which we saw in the examples from the rabbinic literature above, are simply stated by Jesus in Luke 6:35 as the conclusion of a somewhat intricate exegesis of Deut. 14:1. Matthew's approach is different and we will dwell on that shortly.

Finally, we should also consider Targum Pseudo-Jonathan to Lev. 22:28. This biblical text reads: "And whether it be cow or ewe, you shall not kill it and its young both in one day," concerning which the targum comments: "My people, the children of Israel, just as our [var. your] father is merciful in heaven [var. in heaven is merciful], so shall you be merciful on earth."[17]

The substance of Luke 6:35 was likely available as a midrash, not unlike the one attached to Lev. 22:28 in the Targum Pseudo-Jonathan. As I say, in Luke 6:35 Jesus does not cite any verse for his assertion that God is kind to the thankless and the wicked but instead relies on the well-known fact that God is kind, which he appends to his paraphrase of Deut. 14:1: "You shall be children of the Lord your God."

Likewise in our text from Matt. 5:45 Jesus does not cite any verse as a proof-text for his assertion that God too loves those who do not love him, but uses the well-known fact of God's beneficence toward all, including the wicked, as proof that he is indeed kind to his enemies. However, in the next sections of chapter 5 (46–48) Matthew goes beyond Luke to find scriptures and traditions that bolster the claim that God is perfect and kind and so are we to be. I cited Luke at length here because the sections that follow will show Matthew's stunning ability to simplify complex exegesis in going beyond Luke's version.

> For if you love those who love you, what reward do you have? Do not the tax collectors do the same? And if you greet only your siblings, what especially are you doing? Do not the Gentiles do the same? (5:46–47)

Jesus has made the case that the command to love one's neighbor does not also mean that one should hate one's enemy, but rather just the reverse. And now to confirm this claim, Jesus gives us several examples of what loving one's neighbor normally meant—loving those who love you in return, and greeting those whom you already know—and he explains why there is nothing special about doing either of these things. How can that be, he asks, if both the Gentiles and the despised Jewish tax collectors do the same? (It is of interest that Jesus groups together the Gentiles with the tax collectors here.) Initially in Matthew's gospel Jesus shows an anti-Gentile bias; but after a time he begins to show an anti-Jewish bias, which then remains. But here Matthew presents Jesus as a completely loyal Jew who has no sympathy for pagans. As we proceed into chapter 8 we will find the Gentiles are destined to dine with Abraham, Isaac, and Jacob at the great feast in the next world, while the Jews will be kept out gnashing their teeth. Progressively, Jesus turns away from the Jews until he orders that scribes be made of all the nations, all the Gentiles.

> "So you shall be perfect, as your Father in heaven is perfect." (5:48)

Here Jesus tells the members of his audience that it is in loving their enemies that they will become perfect, as their Father in heaven is perfect. They are not to be like the Gentiles and the tax collectors whose imperfection means that they love only those who love them (vv. 46–47).

Jesus' argument here is essentially that of Luke's Jesus (6:35–36): be like God; God loves his enemies (those who are "ungrateful and the selfish"); therefore to be like God means to love one's enemies. But unlike in Luke, here in Matthew Jesus also states that the proof of God's love for those who do not love him is found in the fact that he does not withhold the sun and rain from them, when certainly he could.[18] Moreover in Matthew Jesus ends his sermon not with a syllogism, as he does in Luke, but with a close paraphrase of Deut. 18:13.

Matthew's literary achievement in this brief unit is masterful, but especially here in this final verse in which he brings into play the various rabbinic *midrashim* which had come to be associated with Deut. 18:13. In Matthew's version of Deut. 18:13—"So you shall be perfect as your Father in heaven is perfect"—the text demands *imitatio dei*. Let us take a closer look at what lies behind Matthew's rendering of Deut. 18:13.

First, to see the way Deut. 18:13 was written in the various biblical texts from antiquity will be helpful here. The Masoretic version of the text reads: "You shall be perfect with the Lord your God." Now the Hebrew for "perfect," "*tamim*," is used in the Scriptures to mean either "without blemish," which gives the word a passive sense (e.g., "If his offering is a burnt offering from the herd, he shall offer a male without blemish ['*tamim*']" [Lev. 1:3]), or to act kindly or justly, which gives the word a more active sense (e.g., "The Rock, his work is perfect ['*tamim*'] for all his ways are justice" [Deut. 32:4]). The Septuagint and Peshitta (the Syriac version) give us: "You shall be perfect before the Lord your God." That is, before God be both without blemish and also act kindly and/or justly toward others. The Targum Onkelos gives us, "You shall be perfect in the fear of the Lord your God," which gives us an essentially submissive sense to the word; whereas Targum Neofiti has, "You shall be perfect in good deed with the Lord your God," which gives the word a somewhat more active sense.[19] The Vulgate brings together both the completely active and passive senses of "*tamim*" in its version of the text: "You shall be perfect and without defect with the Lord your God." As can be seen, none of these versions of Deut. 18:13 above is very close to Matthew's version of it.

Now let us return to the Masoretic version of Deut. 18:13: "You shall be perfect with the Lord your God." The word "with" in Hebrew is "*im*," but "*im*" can also mean "even as," in the sense of being "similar to." For example, a tradition found in Midrash Tanhuma Vayera 23 states that before Abraham went up the mountain with Isaac he said to his servants, who had just before responded to a question of his in such a way as to make their obtuseness obvious: "Stay here with ['*im*'] the donkey [Gen. 22:5], for you are even as ['*im*'] he is."[20] That "*im*" can mean "even as" explains why in Midrash Tehillim 119:10 Deut. 18:13 is rendered in this way: "You shall be perfect with the Lord your God— even as he is perfect."

In another tradition from Midrash Tehillim, but from 119:3 (some texts 119:10), it is said that the word "*im*" from Deut. 18:13 means "similar to," and not "before," as in the version of the text in either the LXX or Peshitta. The midrashist then reminds that one should be perfect and states that it is in being perfect that one is "similar to" God, for God too is perfect. (However, the proof-text he uses here to confirm his claim that God is perfect is not entirely apposite, for in it the word "perfect"—"*tamim*"—does not in its biblical context refer to God but to his work. The midrashist has purposely read the verse only partially to make his point.) The tradition reads:

> Blessed are the perfect ones of the way who go in the instruction (Torah) of the Lord (Ps. 119:1).
>
> King Solomon said: The righteous one who walks in His perfection, his children are blessed on account of him (Pr 20:7). Now if his children are blessed [only] on his account, he himself all the more so [is blessed].
>
> And likewise Moses said to Israel:
>
> You shall be perfect with the Lord your God (Deut. 18:13).
>
> *"Before"* the Lord your God is not written here but rather *"with/similar to"* the Lord your God. *If you would be perfect then you would be with/similar* to *the Lord your God.*—Why is this?—Because he is also perfect.—This is as it is said*: the Rock, his working is perfect* (Deut. 32:4).

The following variant from Midrash Tehillim 119:10 goes out of its way to try to harmonize the meanings for "*im*" that we have seen in several of the versions of Deut. 18:13 above—"before" (in the LXX and Peshitta), and "even as" (in Matthew and in Midrash Tehillim 119:3). The text reads:

> For perfection is congenial [*yafeh*] before God, as it is said: *You shall be perfect with the Lord your God—even as he is perfect.* This is as it is said: the Rock, his working is perfect (Deut. 32:4).

As is obvious, Matthew's rendering of Deut. 18:13 is similar to that which appears in Midrash Tehillim above: "So you shall be perfect even as (Greek "hos") your Father in heaven is perfect."

Both Matthew and the rabbis in Midrash Tehillim produced such a similar rendering of Deut. 18:13 because they both had in mind Lev. 19:2, whose opening injunction, "*You shall be* holy," is a close parallel to "*You shall be* perfect" of Deut. 18:13. Moreover the latter part of Lev. 19:2 reads: "for ['*ki*'] I the Lord your God am holy." Now the rabbis understood that like "*im*," "*ki*" could also mean "even as," which is why in a tradition found in both Midrash Tanhuma Leviticus, *Kedoshim*, 2 and Yalkut Shimoni Leviticus 604, we read:

> [God said,] "Tell Israel, 'And you shall be for me a kingdom of priests and a holy nation' (Ex 19:6). —Why? Even as ("*ki*") I the Lord [your God] am holy so you shall be holy . . . As it is said, 'You shall be holy, for ("*ki*," even as) I the Lord your God am holy' " (Lev 19:2).

The clearest proof that both Matthew and the rabbis understood that Deut. 18:13 was a close parallel to Lev. 19:2 is found in an antique source, Sifra (to Leviticus) Kedoshim, parashah 1. In discussing Lev. 19:2 in this text, Abba Shaul says: "[Israel is the family] of the King—and so how must she act? She imitates the King." This midrash is also very much like the midrashim we have seen in the rabbinic traditions above concerning Deut. 14:1, in which we are told that the children of Israel are to imitate God because they are also his children.

It now remains to show, finally, that Lev 19:18—"And you shall love your neighbor as yourself [I am the Lord]"—which was the starting point for this sermon, has also been made part of the network of traditions concerning Israel's call to imitate God. Lev. 19:18 concludes with the declaration from God that "I am the Lord," and this declaration connects with the phrase "the Lord your God" found in all the other biblical texts that lie behind this sermon on love of one's neighbor in Matthew—Deut. 14:1, 18:13, and Lev. 19:2. The traditional exegesis of these latter texts connects with the commandment to love one's neighbor by way of the declaration from God that "I am the Lord" (Lev. 19:18). In his sermon here Jesus has found the connection between these two latter parts of Lev. 19:18. "I am the Lord" is the pointer that explains that "your neighbor" refers to both the righteous and the wicked; for which reason Jesus can intimate that because God loves both and then everyone else should love both too.[21]

For Luke it was enough to incorporate the substance of Deut. 14:1—"You are children of the Lord your God"—to establish the principle that one should act as God does (Luke 6:35). By including in his version of the sermon a paraphrase of Deut. 18:13—"You shall be perfect *with/as* the Lord your God"—Matthew not only goes beyond Luke, he also greatly enhances the sermon.

In essence then, Matthew does give us here (v. 48) a *midrash* that incorporates the rabbinic understanding of Deut. 18:13, which he then combines with a paraphrase of Deut. 14:1—"You are sons of God"—to drive home the point that because God is Israel's father, it is necessary for Israel to imitate him. Thus Deut. 18:13 is to be rendered precisely as Matthew has it.

The appreciation of Matthew's literary skill here suffers when we avail ourselves only of the English translations of the verses. The richness of the midrashic traditions associated with these various texts allows us to see that Matt. 5:45–48 was part of a complex and ongoing homiletic performance. Indeed his text here is nothing short of sheer poetry constructed from various biblical texts and the midrashim associated with them, whose overall purpose is to show that the word "neighbor" must be stretched so that it can also mean "enemy."

I am honored to offer this endeavor to my friend, the word being meant in its most basic sense needing no stretch or metaphoric reworking. For Zev Garber is straightforward and direct, a man of many talents and limitless energy, a true friend to every human being whose love for all is in small measure returned by the writers in this volume.

Notes

1. In his collection *Ha-Esh Ve-Ha-Etzim* (The Fire and the Wood) (Jerusalem: Schocken, 1962), S. Y. Agnon has devoted his first story, "According to the Suffering Is the Reward," to this theme. A *paytan* (modeled after the geonic descriptions given of Yehudai Gaon, c. 800) writes such poetry until one day he meets an afflicted soul, a suffering servant figure. At the end the paytan learns in a revelation that the poet whose art is the expression of a meek life which is immersed in human suffering makes a mark in heaven. So much for Agnon's story. Jesus' sermon begins with a series of beatitudes celebrating the purity of the meek. In alternating usages of blessed we sometimes find the phrase, "Blessed are the nouns who are X," and other times, "Blessed are those who do X." In order to make contact with his hearers he ends by adding a blessing—"Blessed are those who are persecuted," "Blessed are you, the persecuted." This blessing sums up Jesus' liturgical "Ode to the Harassed."
2. A. Mirsky, *Yesodot Tzurot Hapiyyut* (Jerusalem: Magnes, 1985). See also by the same author, "From Midrash to Piyyut to Jewish Poetry," *Leshonenu* 32 (1967–68): 129–39 (Hebrew).
3. Scholars have studied these beatitude forms in Qumran scrolls and other literature of the Second Temple period. While the form and genre are fixed, the meaning of any piece is open to the listener or reader to decide. See Benedict T. Viviano, "Beatitudes Found among Dead Sea Scrolls," *Biblical Archaeology Review* 18, no. 6 (November/December 1992): 53–55, 64–66; John P. Meier, *A Marginal Jew* (New York: Doubleday, 1994), 2:323; Joseph A. Fitzmyer, *The Dead Sea Scrolls and Christian Origins* (Grand Rapids, Mich.: Wm B. Eerdmans, 2000), 116–18; and perhaps most important, Emile Puech, *Qumrân grotte 4, XVIII: Textes hébreux (4Q521–4Q528, 4Q576–4Q579)*, Discoveries in the Judaean Desert 25 (Oxford: Clarendon Press, 1998).
4. See E. P. Sanders, *The Historical Figure of Jesus* (London: Penguin Books, 1995), 210–12.

5. Chapter 6 continues his encouragement to go beyond the externals of religious observance and reach through to the inner core. We shall address these issues as we meet them in the commentary.
6. *Machzor Vitry*, dating from the twelfth and thirteen centuries, knows the custom, and Tirna (1380, *Sefer Ha-Minhagim*, "Laws of Milah circumcision," 94) claims to have seen a *baraita* which gives the source of the practice. Abraham received his full name after his circumcision. Thus, that day is the earliest opportunity for bestowing a name.
7. See D. Flusser, *Jewish Sources in Early Christianity* (Tel Aviv: Mod Books, 1989), 10. In chap. 10 of the same work he demonstrates that midrashim which surfaced in very late collections are attested as early as New Testament times.
8. L. Ginzberg and S. Kraus have noted that midrashic themes appear in the works of the Church Fathers some 700 times. All of these appearances are attributed to Jewish informants and they all appear in the works of the Fathers before they appeared in written Jewish texts. See L. Ginzberg's notes to vols. 5 and 6 of *Legends of the Jews* (1948), and in particular *Die Haggada bei den Kirchenvätern und in der Apokryphischen Litteratur*, in *Monatsschrift* (1898; repr., Berlin, 1900), xlii. *et seq*. See also S. Kraus, "Church Fathers," in *Jewish Encyclopedia* (1906), 4, 82. See also his "The Jews in the Works of the Church Fathers," *Jewish Quarterly Review* 6 (1894): 233–58.
9. There are other places in the Babylonian Talmud where the phrase occurs with this meaning, e.g., BT Berakhot 59a.
10. Joseph Klausner, *Jesus of Nazareth: His Life, Times, and Teachings* (New York: Macmillan, 1927; Boston: Beacon, 1964), 388–89.
11. Sometimes a similar principle is said to be "If it does not suit its immediate scriptural context find another where it will fit." BT Shabbat 70a, BT Pesahim 23b–24a, BT Yoma 32b, and a hundred more places in the Talmud and halachic midrashim.
12. H. Basser, "Uncovering the Plots: The Image of Rabbi Shimon bar Yohai," in *The Mathers' Lectures and Other Papers in the Study of Judaism at Queen's University*, ed. J. Neusner (Binghamton: Global, 2001), 53–56.
13. A text from Avot de Rabbi Natan, version A, chap. 16, wonders then who is excluded from the love commandment. "What constitutes [the grave sin of] misanthropy? We have been taught that one [who is a scholar] cannot [infer from 'And you shall love your neighbor'] that it means 'love scholars' and [by extension] 'hate disciples.' [Or for one who is a disciple] 'love disciples' and 'hate the untutored.' [This is misanthropy.] But 'love everyone' and [by exclusion] 'hate the apostates, renegades, and those who hand Jews over to the Romans.' "
14. The sermon of which this parable is but a small part is so inscrutable that R. Zeev Einhorn, one of the greatest commentators on Midrash Rabba, declared it to be far beyond his grasp.
15. BT Sotah 14a tells us that Rabbi Hama son of Rabbi Hanina knew another version of this idea: Why is it written "to go in his ways" (Deut. 13:5)? Can anyone really go after the Shekhina? Does Scripture not say, "For the Lord your God is a consuming fire" (Deut. 4:24)? But Deut. 15:5 means to follow after the attributes of the Holy One.
16. See, e.g., B Pesahim 21b.
17. "As I am merciful," is also reflected in Y. Berakhot 5:3. In this text R. Yosi, from the fourth century, complains about the midrashic addition to Lev. 22:28 in the targum: "R. Yosi, son of [R] Buna, said: 'They do not do well who make the injunctions of the Holy One, Blessed be He, into traits of mercy and render' " (Lev. 22:28): "My people, children of Israel, just as I am merciful in heaven, so shall you be merciful on earth." Yet Matthew's sermon's reference to "your father" has a sound basis. In the Maher edition of *Targum Pseudo-Jonathan*, he points out that the text in the London library reads: ". . . Children of Israel, just as our father is merciful in heaven . . ."
18. BT Taanit 7a records in the name of Rabbi Abbahu: "The day of rain is greater than the resurrection of the dead. The resurrection of the dead is reserved only for the righteous but rain falls both on the righteous and on the wicked."
19. Mishna Avot 3:9 puts fear of God and good works on the same level.
20. Gen. 30:8 seems to know this meaning for *im;* at least Onkelos and Rashi assume so: "Then Rachel said, 'God has heeded my requests in my pleadings, in my dearest prayers, that I might have a child even as (*im*) my sister, yea it was given to me'; so she called his name Naphtali." Numerous other examples of texts in which "*im*" means "even as" or "similar to" are found in *Bereschit Rabba*, ed. J. Theodor and Ch. Albeck (Jerusalem: Wahrmann, 1965), 893 (at the bottom).
21. I am grateful to the panel of the Society of Biblical Literature (annual meeting, Washington, D.C., November 2006) for mentioning the importance of this point while discussing my paper, "Imitatio Dei: A Note on the History of Exegesis based on Luke, Matthew and the Rabbis."

The Messy Realities of Life

A Rereading of Numbers 19 and 20

Joseph A. Edelheit

The "happenstance" of textual contiguity has always been a source of fascination to me. Does the writer intend for the reader to understand that the willful placement of words, sentences, paragraphs, and even chapters are themselves valuable insights to the meaning of the text as a whole? For example, does rereading Numbers 19 and 20 provide a "*remez*"—a hint—of a deeper meaning of these enigmatic chapters? In Numbers 19 we read of the *parah adumah*, the Red Heifer, a paradoxical ritual that need only be described as a *chok*, a biblical commandment that has no rationale except being commanded by God. In Numbers 20 the text offers a narrative regarding the deaths of Miriam and Aaron, the people once again whining and rebelling over water and Moses' sin of striking the rock for which he is denied entrance to the land. These two chapters are seemingly disconnected except for the happenstance of contiguity, yet the more I reread the texts, the more certain I am that the seeming "happenstance" of textual position is itself a significant resource of meaning.

I dedicate this contemporary interpretation of Numbers 19 and 20 to Zev Garber, whose life as a Jew, teacher, dialogue partner, and exemplar of Jewish survival is itself worthy of significant consideration. These two chapters illuminate important themes in Zev's passion for the Jewish people, Jewish learning, and the hope of dialogue. Unlike many academics whose writings are lofty, arcane, and entirely theoretical, Zev has created a significant corpus and discipline of "praxis," the practical and immediately applicable ideas and ideals of Jewish learning. He has not sought learning for the mere sake of learning, but has participated at every level he could find in venues in which learning and teaching led to action. This commitment to realistic application of learning and dialogue was the reason I always found time for any project in which Zev participated.

Numbers 19 is often characterized as a *kushiya*, an extremely difficult *halachic* (legal) question for which one must wait for Elijah to come and answer just prior to the Messianic times. The Red Heifer is a ritual required for the "cleansing" of those made impure/unclean by the physical contact or even close proximity to the dead. Yet, in the Torah's most dense paradoxical language, the priest and his helpers who prepare the ritual are themselves made impure/unclean by the very process of preparing the cleansing or purifying ashes and additional ingredients. The paradox is stated most unequivocally in the *Pesikta de Rav Kahana* 4:6: "They purify the defiled and defile the pure." How can the very act of preparing a purification ritual be an act which makes the priest impure? *Yalkut Me'am Lo'ez* explains this eternal intellectual quandary:

> This commandment is one of the very deep secrets of the Torah which cannot be investigated, nor can its observance be explained. It is to be fulfilled as a divine edict, in awe and love of God. The secret of the Red Cow was revealed to our teacher Moses alone, as indicated in the word "you" ("bring you a completely red cow"). That is, only to "you" was this explained, not to anyone else. Even King Solomon, whom the scripture calls the wisest of all men and expert in every realm of knowledge, did not penetrate the secret of the Red Cow. He says in Ecclesiastes (7:23), "I said, I will be wise; but it was far from me."[1]

The explanation in the *Pirke de Rav Kahana* in the name of Rabbi Yochanan ben Zakkai concludes: "That of which the Torah speaks here is a divine law, a commandment which encloses a great secret. Therefore, do not try to fathom it, for it is a law that God has mandated, a decree issued that you are not permitted to question."

There are many different attempts to clarify the ritual as a *hatta't*, a burnt offering that is usually the means of providing purification, but during such a sacrifice the use of the blood from the animal plays a key role in the ritual purification. In the case of the Red Heifer, the blood is not sprinkled on the person seeking purification. Further, the rabbinic tradition teaches that the actual Red Heifer was very rare. We learn that there were only nine, perhaps only seven actual such sacrifices:

> Moses prepared the first and Ezra the second and five [were prepared] after Ezra, [according to] the view of R. Meir; but the Sages say, Seven [were prepared] after Ezra. (*m. Parah* 3:5)

Joseph Blau in his review of the Red Heifer in rabbinic literature notes,

> [A] conservative interpretation has been proposed that ties the constantly recurring rabbinic references to the rite of the Red Heifer to the eschatological theme in Judaism. Central to Jewish eschatology is the belief that the coming of the Messiah will be prologue not only to the gathering of the scattered children of Israel from the four corners of the earth into the Promised Land, but also to the rebuilding of the Temple and the restoration of its sacrificial rites. . . . [W]e find [them] preoccupied with the priestly duties in connection with the slaughtering of the Red Heifer and the preparation of the water of purification.[2]

It is interesting that today if you Google the idiom "Red Heifer," there are many links to various Messianic Christian sites. Whatever the reality of the Red Heifer as a sacrifice required for purification during the ancient Israelite culture, it surely remains a source of textual and theological complexity for any reader of the Torah.

Numbers 20 begins and ends with the deaths of Miriam and Aaron respectively and yet there is not a single mention of the very ritual of purification required by the mere presence of the dead, which is commanded in Numbers 19. The theme of death is a central shared link between the two chapters, as is a shared use of "water." In chapter 19, the water is required to mix with the ashes of the sacrifice to create the "waters of lustration" which is the commanded ritual for purification, while in chapter 20 it is the recurring need for water which becomes the narrative focus of Moses' conflict with the people. Jacob Milgrom, in his essay/excursus "Magic, Monotheism, and the Sin of Moses," refers to Numbers 20 "as one of the Gordian knots of the Bible: The punishment is clear; but what is the crime?"[3] For Milgrom, both of these chapters from Numbers pose significant challenges for interpretation. He sets out to clarify the severity of Moses' sin for which he is denied entrance to the land. He reviews the many possibilities, arguing that, ultimately, it was not merely striking the rock twice instead of talking to it as God had commanded, but that he and Aaron refer to themselves as the source of the miracle, in verse 10b: "shall *we* get water for you out of this rock?" Whether Milgrom is correct in his review and conclusion is itself an act of interpretation and our current rereading does not require us to make such a final determination.

One can make a strong argument for several different readings about Moses' behavior and the reasoning or rationale of his ultimate punishment. For instance, one could argue that Moses once again loses his temper with the people's behavior at a time of personal grief and loss over his sister's death for which there is no mention of any burial or communal grieving as with Aaron. Moses has not taken any time for himself after his sister's unexpected death and immediately must respond to the people's recurring neediness. His inability to remember the difference between God's command in Exod. 17:1–7, when he was told to strike the rock, and here, when he is told to speak to the rock, seems to illuminate Moses' all-too-real humanity, his vulnerability as a leader and prophet. Miriam consistently links Moses to water from the moment she puts him into the Nile to save him through the song she leads after they cross the *Yam Suf* to the midrashic well which she provides the people during their time in the desert. It is more than mere irony that with Miriam's death Moses is thrust into a transformative struggle with the people over their insatiable thirst for water. Moses once again reacts striking the rock twice and is punished for not publicly sanctifying God in the communal presence of the people. Would a single strike have been understood as a mere outburst of rage without the severity of the punishment? Regardless of the depth of the question, only an interpretive answer is possible from within the text. Like the previous chapter, God's punishment of Moses seems to be a divine decree for which any rational explanation is hidden.

We are left with significant gaps in our understanding of each chapter and the deeper meaning, if any, of their connection to each other. I would venture that a reading of the two chapters as inherently united will also guide us to understanding the deeper levels of meaning in each of them. Since Numbers 19 is characterized as the paradigm of the *chukah*, the divine decree for which there is no human understanding, I will use it as an extreme example of how the Bible might have expressed a theory or ideology for which little or no meaningful application is possible. I argue that this is a possibility based on the immediate contiguity of the detailed procedures involved in the Red Heifer as the necessary purification of anyone/everyone who is defiled by contact with or the presence of the dead and the opening verse of Num. 20:1b, "Miriam died there and was buried there." There is no other detail offered about her burial, who attended to her or whether the elaborate and paradoxical ritual of the Red Heifer is used to purify whoever attended to Miriam's remains or buried her. With the rabbinic literature offering us that only Moses really understood the meaning of the commandment and that he prepared the first Red Heifer's ashes and waters of purification, it would also be reasonable to conclude through interpretation that Moses would have used the ritual after the deaths of his sister and brother. The absence of any mention in either the biblical text or any rabbinic passage suggests that regardless of the paradigmatic importance of the Red Heifer, it is a theory that is not applied. While the argument of silence is not in and of itself sufficient to prove my point, it is enough to suggest that the text is willfully ambiguous about the inherent applicability of the ritual. Perhaps in the ancient world it was enough to provide a divine decree/theory of how death and the dead could be ritually nullified without ever having to perform the act itself.

If Numbers 19 is the theory, then Numbers 20 offers the context/narrative for the application or praxis. The complex ritual required for sanctification from the impurity of death seems on the face of it to pale in comparison to an exhausted leader who is beset by the community's insensitivity about death when it demands water without offering even a nuance of condolences after Miriam's death. Numbers 20:1 ends with "Miriam died there and was buried there," and then verse 2 reads, "The community was without water, and they joined against Moses and Aaron." The absence of any textual buffer is starkly obvious to even the less-educated reader. Was Moses enraged at the people offering no concern for the great prophetess, his sister Miriam? Was a context of "death" necessary for Moses' most human fallibility as a leader to be challenged to its core, a tragic mix of rage and his self-destructive work ethic? Exodus 18:17–18 offered the reader a dark forecasting: "But Moses' father-in-law said to him, 'The thing you are doing is not right; you will surely wear yourself out, and these people as well. For the task is too heavy for you; you cannot do it alone.'" Moses never asks for help especially in the face of his own sister's death. Rabbinic tradition has it that he might well have been the only mortal to understand God's paradoxical commandment regarding death and purification, but even that degree of discernment fails to protect him from the people's insatiable neediness. Whether it is because he strikes the rock a second time as an act of public faithlessness or it is his arrogance in referring to "we," he and Aaron, as the source of the miracle that would provide the water, it is clear that Jethro's warning actually came true in Numbers 20: both Moses and the people were worn out. Beyond Moses' sin of hubris, the arrogant plight of most leaders, there is the obvious disconnect between the theory in Numbers 19 and its applied value in the next chapter.

Numbers 19:20 warns, "If anyone who has become unclean fails to cleanse himself, that person shall be cut off from the congregation, for he has defiled the Lord's sanctuary." Numbers 20:12 explains, "But the Lord said to Moses and Aaron, 'Because you did not trust Me enough to affirm My sanctity in the sight of the Israelite people, therefore you shall not lead this congregation into the land that I have given them.'" Is Moses unclean because of his contact with his dead sister, which then distorts his trust of God? The text hints that the sacrifice cleanses "the defiled sanctuary" while the sin defies the "public sanctity" of God. Both the ritual and the sin are linked to God's holiness, in place and public stature. Is it merely curious that Moses who is called to lead the people from slavery is unique in his knowledge of divine sanctity and then fails in a moment of complete humanness to publicly affirm the very sanctity that he alone uniquely understands? These two chapters of Torah offer us the lesson of disconnects between the complex details of theory and the messy ambiguous realities of life. Moses may be the only person to whom God provides secrets that explain the law, but Moses is also that same person who, in the face of life's unexpected tragedies, consistently fails to apply his intimate spiritual knowledge of God's presence in response to the rebellion of a community thirsty for its own immediate entitlements.

There are many examples of leaders who fail their communities when the messy realities of life challenge their pristine understandings of their theoretical visions. For the sake of our discussion, I offer one contemporary analogy for our consideration, the serious disconnect between the "oppression-model," the theory often used to describe the plight of the Palestinians, and the application of the theory in any attempt to offer a balanced explanation of the most current violence in the Middle East. The theory assumes a two-dimensional analysis of all victims (especially in this case, the Palestinians), yet fails to comprehend the ambiguous and complex realities of Israelis and Jewish survival in its application. Recently Christopher Caldwell in his review of "The Trouble with Diversity" notes, "More likely, the problem is that the ideological style of argument—of pitting an untainted abstraction such as 'equality' or 'progress' or 'democracy' against the messy realities of complex modern societies—has come to seem dangerous."[4]

The Uncivil University: Politics and Propaganda in American Education deals with the issue of the failed application of the "oppression-model" to the complex realities of the Middle East, which have now resulted in a crisis of both flawed education and rise of antisemitism on campuses all over America. Tobin, Weinberg, and Ferer argue:

> The unique set of issues that Israel, Palestinians, and other Middle Eastern nations face are framed on campus to fit within the politics of race and inequality. Palestinians are portrayed as poor and brown, while Israelis are rich and white. Israelis are colonists; Palestinians are indigenous. . . . The Palestinian cause is . . . [e]mbraced as representative of the struggle against colonialism, white supremacism, economic exploitation, and nearly all other forms of oppression. However for Palestinians to effectively play the part of the ultimate victim and inherit the legacy of black South Africans . . . there must also exist an ultimate white oppressor. . . . If Palestinian nationalism is righteous, then Jewish nationalism is sinful.[5]

This is the conclusion of several significant studies done at various campuses, where identity politics activists argue that the theory of "oppression" can and should be applied regardless of its flawed logic or provocative rejection of Jewish survival. "A Brown University alum, Sarah McDermott, wrote in the campus paper, 'If progressives have an anti-Israel bias, it is for good reason. Zionism, liberal Zionism included, is discriminatory by definition, and is used as a tool of colonialism and imperialism. It is, therefore, incompatible with progressive politics.' A professor from Yale who spoke at Duke argued, "Zionism is a 'diseased' ideology of ethnocentric nationalism and racism that we are familiar with from South African apartheid and European fascism." The "oppression-model" becomes so distorted in its twisted application to the Palestinians that some have argued that the Holocaust, the historical event that fostered the global sensitivity in 1948 which prompted the United Nations vote on Israel's statehood, is no longer linked to Israel but now the Palestinians. The following was written for the *Daily Bruin* at UCLA: "[T]he mass graves being built in the West Bank [. . .] eerily parallel a scene out of the genocide in Bosnia. Witnessing the Israeli army rounding up all the men in Palestinian villages [. . .] And then branding them with identification numbers brings back horrific images of a concentration camp somewhere in Auschwitz." This is obviously factually wrong, but, in the discourse of identity politics, the revision to/for whom one applies terms like "Auschwitz" is so symbolic that few if any will ask for proof of such assertion.[6]

The use of media coverage of the summer 2006 conflict between Lebanon and Israel is another easily distorted tool among those proving that these are the victims of white, powerful, Western-wealthy, military imperialists. Few people can or would want to defend the bombing of homes or the mistakes that kill eighteen children, and even the Israeli assertion that Hezbollah hid rocket launchers in homes and that they knew they were using their own citizens as "human shields" is difficult to prove. The visual power of the Israeli defense forces is all too often a confirmation of the charge/characterization that Palestinians or Lebanese are poor, innocent victims of overwhelming Western power. The contemporary circumstances in the Middle East are an ideal example of how ambiguous complex realities defy the analysis of a simple theory/ideology. Regardless of how much the discourse of identity studies/politics has advanced campus politics and activism for more than twenty-five years, its use as the template for analysis today is itself an indictment of a theory's failure to help us understand as much as we all need. The use of the "oppression-model" only exacerbates the polarization of all discourse, and the students who are exposed to such analysis are not guided in making a critical decision, but often intimidated into accepting the correct view for the sake of the victims being described. For Jewish students, faculty, and staff on campuses experiencing these conflicts, there is little if any margin that saves them from a community goaded with a discourse that offers little distinction between the Jew, the Zionist, the Israeli, and the oppressor. I have myself had such an experience when, even in my absence, one of the speakers in responding to a question about the Israeli position baited the audience: "Inviting the Israeli position would be like asking for the rapist's [*sic*] position!" Since I had argued for the right to present an Israeli position regarding the conflict in Lebanon, I felt that it was me, my office of Director of Jewish Studies, that was being compared with a rapist.

The most distorted element of the theory's application comes in the explanation of the oppressed victim's justified acts of terrorism. "Suicide bombers are a symptom of the problem. Resistance is a symptom of oppression." At the University of Georgia, a history professor "explained that suicide bombings are the 'result of hopelessness' . . . [and] anger at the current situation. . . . Palestinians are unique and deserve special consideration due to their hardships."[7] When the flawed application of the theory can even be used to justify acts of murder that are willfully intended to kill as many innocent civilians as possible, then we must all admit that the "oppression-model" fails at every level of honest education. If the best we can offer students is that helpless Palestinians cannot be held to basic human norms of behavior, then we have failed to understand and teach anything about the reality of the Middle East. *The Uncivil University* is a valuable tool for analyzing the polarized circumstances of discourse on our campuses, and, as such, illuminating at least one significant example of a theory that cannot be applied to the messy realities of life.

Numbers 19 and 20 teach us that the paradoxical demands of a theoretical purification ritual fail to provide Moses with the necessary insights that will ultimately sanctify God amidst the messy realities of grief and whining and insatiable communal thirst. If the theory cannot be applied within the messy realities of life, then we have not understood anything in our learning the theory. A return to Gadamer's foundational philosophical hermeneutics is necessary in order to recover the meaning from what seems to be a closed system of theory that fails in its immediate application to real life. The requirement that knowledge be applied is central to Gadamer's hermeneutics.

> [T]here is an inextricable connection of the theoretical and the practical in all understanding and interpretation—that hermeneutical understanding shapes our practical lives [and is not a purely disinterested, theoretical activity]. All understanding involves not only interpretation but also application. . . . It is here we discover the fusion of hermeneutics and *praxis and phronesis*.
>
> . . . *Phronesis* is a form of reasoning and knowledge that involves a distinctive mediation between the universal and the particular. . . . The "intellectual virtue" of *phronesis* is a form of reasoning, yielding a type of ethical know-how in which what is universal and what is particular are codetermined. . . . Understanding, for Gadamer, is a form of *phronesis*.[8]

Gadamer links praxis and *phronesis* to the centrality of dialogue and conversation as "fundamental for grasping what is distinctive about hermeneutical understanding. . . . For Gadamer's entire corpus can be read as showing us what we truly are, what is most characteristic of our humanity is that we are dialogical or conversational beings."[9]

David Tracy reframes Gadamer's work into a model of interpretation as conversation.

> A fundamental characteristic of good conversation is the ability to take seriously the existence of different interruptions. These interruptions include things like the radical plurality disclosed in postmodern studies of language and the "terror of history" which is so pervasive in the late twentieth century. Other interruptions come from voices protesting against the systemic "isms" surrounding this century: "sexism, racism, classism, elitism, cultural parochialism". . . . Tracy again insists that every act of interpretation involves a moment of practical application. . . . In this sense the contemporary hermeneutical concern with praxis is entirely correct. . . . Within the context of this emerging tension between hermeneutics and praxis he [Tracy] acknowledges his own preference for a theology of the interpretation of the religious classic.[10]

Tracy's model takes us full circle to where this project began, with a rereading of Torah and specifically two chapters that offer every reader texts that have permanent surplus meaning.

The original "happenstance" of the positioning of these two chapters can now be more fully developed. The contiguity of the chapters does permit us to view a textual reality of "between," a literal to-and-fro position between chapters 19 and 20 that contextually creates the very conversation from which interpretation itself takes place. Numbers 19 is the ultimate example of Israelite sacrificial ritual purification that requires a complete paradox—a *chok*—a law whose sole purpose is hidden within God's command of it. Numbers 20 is a narrative about death and the need for water, which can only be achieved through an act sanctifying God. The mediation of the two chapters comes with the discipline of interpretation, the conversation between the paradoxical requirement of the ritual theory and its obvious absence within the messy realities of actual death and thirst. If the theory does not satisfy the real but always ambiguous moment of human application, then there is no sanctifying *praxis*. Gadamer and Tracy are correct in offering us the dialogue—the serious conversation—as the only means for recovering understanding from the inherent disconnect between Numbers 19 and 20. It is also the dialogue that offers us our only hope from the failed application of an "oppression-model," which itself promised meaning and understanding as one of the "systemic 'isms' of the late twentieth century" as noted above. Yet it is the rejection of a public communal dialogue by anyone making a claim on behalf of the Palestinians as an oppressed community which illuminates that the theory is philosophically flawed and is now a grave disservice to the complex ambiguous issues that deserve serious reflection.

Those of us like Zev Garber whose lives and responsibilities as teachers link us to both the universal ideals of the academy and the parochial demands of Jewish survival must take the complexity of Numbers 19 and 20 very seriously. We cannot risk remaining statically committed to the discourse of theories that themselves become texts within textbooks which can no longer be applied within the real history that emerges with today's unexpected ambiguous challenges. Garber's career offers a model of such risks and his willingness to engage in the dialogues that mediate the universal and parochial, in particular the conversations of interfaith partners that continue to illuminate a continually emerging post-Shoah reality that requires a foundational commitment from all dialogue participants to the survival of the Jewish people. Any serious conversation about Israel and the Palestinians must take the survival of the Jewish people as its first-order assumption or the dialogue will merely become a stressful attempt to apply a theory that results in striking words as if they were rocks at least twice, even as all the actual suffering people die in an endless cycle of violence that denies everyone a chance to enter the land of their destiny, and fails to sanctify either God or humans.

Notes

1. Yitzchok Magriso, *MeAm Lo'ez—The Torah Anthology*, ed. Aryeh Kaplan (New York: Moznaim Publishing, 1991), 67–103.

2. Joseph L. Blau, "The Red Heifer: A Biblical Purification Rite in Rabbinic Literature," *Numen* 14 (March 1967): 70–78, www.jstor.org.
3. Jacob Milgrom, "Magic, Monotheism, and the Sin of Moses," in *The JPS Torah Commentary: NUMBERS* (Philadelphia: Jewish Publication Society, 1990), 448–56.
4. Christopher Caldwell, "Affirmative Distraction," *New York Times Book Review*, December 24, 2006, 7.
5. Gary A. Tobin, Aryeh K. Weinberg, and Jenna Ferer, *The Uncivil University: Politics and Propaganda in American Education* (San Francisco: Institute for Jewish and Community Research, 2005).
6. Ibid., 116, 120, 133.
7. Ibid., 139, 141.
8. Richard Bernstein, *Beyond Objectivism and Relativism: Science, Hermeneutics, and Praxis* (Philadelphia: University of Pennsylvania Press, 1983), 141, 146.
9. Ibid., 162.
10. Dermot A. Lane, "David Tracy and the Debate about *Praxis*," in *Radical Pluralism and Truth: David Tracy and the Hermeneutics of Religion*, ed. Werner G. Jeanrond and Jennifer L. Rike (New York: Crossroad, 1991), 18–37.

A Cosmopolitan "Student of the Sages"

Jacob of Kefar Nevoraia in Rabbinic Literature

Steven Fine

My first academic lecture was given at a regional conference of the National Association of Professors of Hebrew in Long Beach, California. My topic was "On the Use of Rabbinic Literature in Interpreting the Synoptic Gospels: The *Amidah* in Luke 18?" I remember fondly my excitement at my first paper, and my even greater enthusiasm at entering into what was for me foreign and somewhat subversive territory, New Testament studies. The chair of this session was our own Zev Garber, by then an old friend of mine. I will never forget Zev's gentleness and professionalism as I proceeded to overread the relationship between rabbinic sources and the Gospels in a way that might allow both to live comfortably within my own curious soul. For over two decades I have been honored to call Zev my friend and, on more than one occasion, my mentor. On the occasion of this *Festschrift,* I return to my early interest in Jewish-Christian relations. Truth said, my gaze is no less subversive here than it was in 1987, though here my eyes are set on the models of scholarly discourse on Jewish-Christian relations in antiquity, and their implications for contemporary scholarship and community. I hope that Zev is pleased.

It has become axiomatic that the writing of biography on the basis of rabbinic literature is deeply fraught, since the lives of the rabbis, like the lives of biblical characters, were the objects of literary construction that included deindividuation and often a deeply hagiographic impulse.[1] It is absolutely the case that we cannot know exactly what a particular rabbi actually said and did at any particular time. That said, by broadly contextualizing rabbinic traditions, we can get a sense of the "stage" upon which the rabbis functioned, and of the concepts that existed at the time that the story was formed. Through this kind of holistic reading, we can come as close as possible to the characters that the authors of our literature were quite certain had existed and once walked the earth. Archaeology and geography are important in this type of reconstruction, for they provide nonliterary evidence of Jewish life in antiquity. In the pages that follow, I will attempt to broadly contextualize the traditions of one member of the rabbinic community of late antique Palestine, Jacob of Kefar Nevoraia. I will draw upon rabbinic sources, Roman law, Karaite, Samaritan, and Patristic sources, archaeology, and geography in my attempt to read the traditions of Jacob of Kefar Nevoraia holistically. I will also refer to current scholarship on ethnic identity. For almost a century, scholars have identified Jacob as a "Jewish-Christian." Rather than being evidence for Jewish-Christianity in antiquity, however, I will argue based upon my holistic reading that Jacob served the rabbis as a point from which to reflect upon the ambiguities of

Jewish life in the cosmopolitan world of the Roman empire, particularly within "diaspora" communities on the borders of Eretz Israel.

The Jerusalem Talmud and classical Amoraic and post-Amoraic midrashim all preserve traditions of Jacob of Kefar Nevoraia.[2] The most complete classical Amoraic presentation of Jacob's exploits appears in *Genesis Rabba,* chapter 7:

1. "Let the waters bring forth [swarms of living creatures, and let birds fly above the earth across the firmament of the heavens]" (Gen. 1:20, RSV).
2. Jacob of Kefar Nevoraia ruled in Tyre:
3. Fish require ritual slaughter.
4. Rabbi Haggai heard of this and said to him: Come and be whipped.
5. He [Jacob] said to him: A man who said a word of Scripture should be whipped?
6. He [R. Haggai] said to him: How is it Scriptural?
7. He [Jacob] said to him: For it is written: "Let the waters bring forth swarms of living creatures, and let birds fly" etc.
8. Just as the bird must be ritually slaughtered, so must the fish be ritually slaughtered.
9. He [R. Haggai] said: You have not ruled well.
10. He [Jacob] asked: Whence can you prove this to me?
11. He [R. Haggai] responded: Lie down [to be lashed] and I will prove it to you.
12. He [R. Haggai] said to him: It is written: "If flocks and herds be slaughtered for them, will they suffice them? [or if all the fish of the sea be gathered together for them, will they suffice them?]" (Num. 11:22).
13. Shall be slaughtered is not written here but "will be gathered together."
14. He [Jacob] said: Whip me, for your explanation is good.
15. Jacob of Kefar Nevoraia ruled in Tyre:[3]
16. "It is permitted to circumcise the son of a gentile woman on the Sabbath."
17. Rabbi Haggai heard of this and said to him: Come and be whipped.
18. He [Jacob] said to him: A man who said a word of Scripture should be whipped?
19. He [R. Haggai] said to him: How is it Scriptural?
20. He [Jacob] said to him: For it is written: "And they declared their pedigrees after their families, by their fathers' houses" (Num. 1:18).
21. He [R. Haggai] said: You have not ruled well.
22. He [Jacob] asked: Whence can you prove this to me?
23. He [R. Haggai] responded: Lie down [to be lashed] and I will prove it to you.
24. He said: It is written: "Now therefore let us make a covenant with our God to put away all the wives, and such as are born of them" (Ezra 10:3).
25. He [Jacob] said: And on the basis of Tradition [that is, a non-Pentateuchal text from the Hagiographa] you will whip me?
26. [He (R. Haggai) said: And let it be done according to the Torah (ibid.).]
27. He [Jacob] said: Whip your whip, for it is well taught![4]

Jacob of Kefar Nevoraia is presented in Amoraic traditions as a younger contemporary of the Amora Rabbi Haggai. Rabbi Haggai flourished during the third and fourth Palestinian Amoraic generations, circa 280–340 CE.[5] Jacob, who did not acquire the title "Rabbi," appears in these traditions functioning in Tyre on the Phoenician coast.

Kefar Nevoraia, today called Nabratein, was located in the Upper Galilee near the ancient Tyrian backcountry. A late antique synagogue was discovered at this site,[6] and the tomb of Jacob has been venerated there since medieval times.[7] Jacob's presence in Tyre would not have been unusual for a Jew of Kefar Nevoraia. Rabbinic sources suggest close relations between Tyre and the Upper Galilee and considerable contact between the rabbinic community and the Jews of Tyre.[8] *Sifre Deuteronomy* reflects this relationship in its interpretation of Deut. 32:13, interpreting the word *zur,* "rock," to mean *Zur*, Tyre: " 'and oil from the flint of Tyre (*tsur,* Deut. 32:13):' These are the olives of Gush Ḥalav."[9] The preponderance of bronze Tyrian coins from Meiron, Khirbet Shema, and Gush Ḥalav is indicative of the fact that the Upper Galilee region was part of the agricultural backcountry of Tyre.[10]

We know little about the Jews of Tyre during the late third and fourth centuries. Three and possibly a fourth funerary inscription from Tyre have been published. All are in Greek. The Tyrian Jews commemorated in these inscriptions had both biblical and Greek names. One Greek/Latin name and three biblical names appear in these inscriptions: "Josephos son of Simonos" and "Saras daughter of Marcellus." Priests were apparently buried separately at Tyre. A Greek inscription reads: "Burial place of the most honored priests."[11] The markers of individual priests are not known. Inscriptions from the Galilee provide additional evidence for Tyrian Jews that corresponds closely with the evidence from Tyre itself. Inscriptions in Greek discovered in Beth She'arim, a Jewish necropolis in the lower Galilee, suggests that some Tyrian Jews, like other Jews from the nearby Diaspora, sent their bodies for burial in this necropolis. From the extant inscriptions, which we might assume reflect a more wealthy and perhaps more rabbinically connected or generally pious element of the Tyrian Jewish community,[12] we may suggest that knowledge of Greek and use of Greek names is pervasive.[13]

Hebrew appears on one inscription. Above the entrance to catacomb 19 at Beth She'arim, a tablet was discovered *in situ* that bears a Greek epitaph in which both the son and father bear biblical names; "Daniel, son of Iddo from Tyre," is followed by the Hebrew "Shalom." Nahman Avigad notes that the scribe of this inscription "was familiar with the Greek letters but not with the Hebrew." He postulates that this marker was carved in Tyre and brought to Beth She'arim "together with the deceased." In Diaspora and Palestinian communities, the simple and emblematic Hebrew word "shalom" is a common formula following Greek and Aramaic epitaphs.[14] One woman at Beth She'arim had a double Greek/Hebrew name. On an inscribed lintel at the western entrance of catacomb 21, we read: "The tomb of Theodosia, also [called] Sarah, from Tyre." Avigad considers this double naming to be "an accepted practice among Diaspora Jews,"[15] though this phenomenon may have been known in the Land of Israel as well.[16] The use of biblical names in the Tyre inscriptions and in the Tyrene inscriptions at Beth She'arim is also similar. Like Saras daughter of Marcellus, who was interned in Tyre, "Esther daughter of Anthos from Tyre," interned in catacomb 12 at Beth She'arim, had a biblical name, while her father had a Greek name.[17] One rabbi was from Tyre, "Rabbi Simeon son of Jacob from Tyre."[18] His name fits well among the biblical examples chosen by epigraphic Tyrian Jews. "Severianus the most illustrious synagogue leader (*archisynagogos*) from Tyre" appears together with a Sidonian synagogue leader in a Greek dedicatory inscription on a lintel from a Sepphoris synagogue.[19] Sidonian and Tyrian Jews, like Babylonians and Capadocians, seem to have settled in Sepphoris. Lea Roth-Gerson suggests that it "apparently dates to the fifth century [*Le-khol ha-nireh*]."[20] From the little that we can glean about the actual Jews of Tyre, they were not atypical of other Syrian communities, or of Greek-speaking communities in Palestine itself. Their names give us no sense that they were more or less Hellenized than other communities, or any more or less prone to tolerate behaviors that Rabbi Haggai would find difficult. The extant evidence suggests a community where Jewish identity construction was set firmly within the cosmopolitan context of Roman Syria, a region that both Palestinian and Syrian Jews considered the close-by Diaspora.[21]

Rabbinic sources present Jacob of Kefar Nevoraia as a "student of the Sages," as a junior member of the rabbinic community. In every place where Jacob appears acting in rabbinic literature, he is shown interpreting biblical texts. In y. Bikkurim 3:3, 65d Jacob is presented expounding (*tirgem*) biblical verses in an extended criticism of the deteriorating social position of the rabbis and the rising status of the urban aristocracy during the third and fourth centuries. Appointments to positions of communal prominence in exchange for payments and the appointment of the nonlearned (from the standpoint of the rabbis) were particularly disturbing to him. These inappropriate appointments are contrasted with "Rabbi Isaac b. Elazar [who adjudicates] in the synagogue of Madrata (or Marudata) of Caesarea." Jacob's mention of a specific rabbi and his location in a specific Caesarean synagogue assumes a relationship between Jacob and this city. Jacob's presence in Caesarea is taken for granted by the parallel to this tradition in *Midrash Samuel,* a late, perhaps Palestinian, collection.[22] *Midrash Samuel* 7:10 places Jacob's exposition in Caesarea.[23] There we read: "Jacob of Kefar Nevoraia expounded one verse in the Synagogue of Marudata of Caesarea and the Sages praised him [for it]." An unrelated tradition in *Ecclesiastes Rabba* 7:47, to be discussed below, has a Caesarean rabbi brand Jacob a "heretic."

A tradition preserved in a Byzantine-period collection, the *Midrash on Psalms,* also presents Jacob in Tyre, expounding (*tirgem*) a biblical text in a way that is completely within rabbinic norms.[24]

In the *Genesis Rabba* tradition that I have cited, Jacob adjudicates Jewish law on two parallel occasions. Jacob Neusner is undoubtedly correct that "[t]he two stories obviously have been joined together prior to their insertion here."[25] This midrashic collection contains both exempla, suggesting a basic tie between them. Jacob of Kefar Nevoraia pushed the bounds of rabbinic halakhah on two separate, though formulaically linked, occasions. Interpreting Gen. 1:20, Jacob required the ritual slaughter of fish. He legitimized this procedure through standard rabbinic exegetical method. Jacob's exegesis of Gen. 1:20 assumes relationship between the two parts of the verse. Just as birds require slaughter, he reasoned, so do fish. Louis Ginzberg notes that the *Damascus Document* (12:13–14) forbade the consumption of fish blood, though Ginzberg was not of the opinion that ritual slaughter was practiced. Samaritans were apparently strict regarding the consumption of fish blood, and later the Karaites "even insist that the killing of fish requires a certain procedure, corresponding to the procedure of ritual slaughter of kosher mammals and birds [*shehitah*], an opinion that stands in obvious conflict with the sectarian prescription in our [Damascus] document."[26] *Pirqe de-Rabbi Eliezer,* an eighth- or ninth-century document, explicitly rejects the ritual slaughter of fish (and of locusts) through an alternate exegesis of Gen. 1:20. It reads almost like a response to Jacob's interpretation:[27]

> . . . And these, that swarmed from the water—fish and locusts, and are eaten without ritual slaughter, but the bird is not eaten without ritual slaughter.
>
> These [the fish] that were created from water, their blood is to be poured out like water.
>
> And these [the birds] that were created from the earth, their blood is to be poured out in the dust.

The point is that fish slaughter was not beyond discussion by "law-abiding" Jews during late antiquity and the early medieval period, though it was soundly rejected by the Talmudic rabbis.

In the second example, Jacob determines that the son of a Jewish man and a non-Jewish woman may be circumcised on the Sabbath. In rabbinic law, circumcision of the son of a Jewish mother on the eight day overrides Sabbath prohibitions that would normally not allow such a procedure. Jacob suggests that Jewish paternity is sufficient to override Sabbath law, and thus established that the son of a Jewish man is a Jew (ancient "paterliniarity").[28] The parallel in *Pesikta de-Rav Kahana,* and versions of *Genesis Rabba,* add the following Halakhic excursus after line 22 of our *Genesis Rabba* text:[29]

> He [Jacob] said to him [Rabbi Haggai], In accord with which [passage of] the Torah?
>
> He [Rabbi Haggai] said to him [Jacob], From this which Rabbi Johanan in the name of Rabbi Simeon son of Yoḥai said:
>
> "Neither shall you make marriages with them, your daughter you shall not give to his son [and his daughter your son shall not take], For he will turn away your son from following me . . ." (Deut. 7:3–4).
>
> "Your son" born of a Israelite woman is called your son.
>
> "Your son" born of a gentile woman is not called your son.

In both the *Genesis Rabba* and *Pesikta de-Rav Kahana* versions, Jacob accepts the punishment meted out by Rabbi Haggai, but only after Rabbi Haggai proves to him through biblical exegesis the error of his position. Significantly, the earlier version of this episode, preserved in y. Yevamot 2:6, 4a and Qiddushin 1, 60a, adds considerable ambiguity to the story. There, it is the people of Tyre who "came and asked" for Jacob's opinion. He does not offer it with the kind of stature assumed by *Genesis Rabba* and *Pesikta de-Rav Kahana*. Further, the Yerushalmi traditions suggest that Jacob only "thought (or, intended) to permit them" (למישרי לון סבר), but apparently had not yet done the deed—as he has in the later versions. His stature and resolve are clearly greater in *Genesis Rabba* and *Pesikta de-Rav Kahana*! In all versions, Jacob is a loyal, if in the opinion of Rabbi Haggai, errant, student of the rabbis.[30]

In another case of personal status set in Tyre, we hear of Rabbi Ḥiyya bar Ba, a generation before Jacob,[31] coming to Tyre and finding a proselyte who was circumcised, but who had not been ritually immersed as the rabbis would require. He said nothing. Upon approaching his teacher, Rabbi Johanan, with this episode in Tiberias, Rabbi Johanan vindicated Rabbi Ḥiyya bar Ba's decision not to interfere,

"Well you did not disqualify him," said the elder scholar. From the episode of Jacob allowing the circumcision of the son of the non-Jewish child and from this text, we might assume that laws of Jewish status were, at least at times, followed less stringently by some in Tyre than the Amoraic rabbis might have preferred.

The cases of Jacob of Kefar Nevoraia and of Rabbi Ḥiyya bar Ba suggest a certain fluidity of Jewish identity among Tyrian Jews. Both exogamy and proselytism are evidenced in the relatively small corpus of rabbinic sources that deal with Tyre. Issues of personal status were significant in the other known locus of Jacob's activities, Caesarea Maritima. Lee I. Levine cites the *Vita of Saint Susanna,* a work included in the *Acta Sanctorum,* as referring to a marriage between a wealthy pagan priest in Caesarea and the Jewish mother of the child who became the Christian Saint Susanna! The complexity of religious identification in Roman Caesarea, and no doubt all cosmopolitan Roman contexts, is expressed in Susanna's mother's complex statement: "Her name [Susanna] will derive from the people of her ancestors, and not from the Greeks." The text goes on to describe that "[t]he mother educated her daughter according to the customs and the teachings of the Jews." Whatever the historicity of this document, it is significant for our discussion of Jacob of Kefar Nevoraia and his apparent willingness to circumcise the child of a non-Jewish mother and a Jewish father in third-century Tyre.[32] Intermarriage between Jews and non-Jews in the Roman empire during late antiquity is evidenced in a law of Valentinian II and Theodosius I in 388 that requires that "[n]o Jew take in marriage a Christian woman, nor a Christian engage in matrimony with a Jewess."[33]

It seems to me that Jacob's rulings, and Rabbi Haggai's strong response to them, reflect the complexities of cosmopolitan Greco-Roman life meeting the academic piety of the rabbis in the Land of Israel. The possible incruence of rabbinic standards with those of more cosmopolitan communities is known from within the rabbinic heartland itself, as the fourth-century synagogue mosaic with its nude, uncircumcised figure of Libra and well-developed image of Helios within the zodiac wheel at Hammath Tiberias B so well illustrates.[34]

The issue of fish slaughter, however, does not reflect the kind of religious laxity or "assimilation" usually ascribed to cosmopolitan life. This is a real stringency and impediment to social integration that extends the control already exerted by Jewish dietary laws. If actually carried out, the ritual slaughter of fish would be quite cumbersome. It would have meant that Jews could only procure live fish, which they would have had to ritually slaughter very soon after the fish was actually caught. What connects the two cases ascribed to Jacob of Kefar Nevoraia is the issue that in turn connects them to Jacob's appearance in the synagogue of Madrara in Caesarea. In each of these cases Jacob took positions counter to the established approach through his interpretation of scripture. The extant midrashim present us with a very complex character—though they do not present enough information to allow us to determine a clear ideological identity (if, in fact, Jacob had one). Far from the agricultural village of Nabratein in which he was apparently reared, and functioning in what the rabbis referred to as the culturally liminal "cities of the sea," Jacob seems to have lived a fascinatingly liminal existence that he legitimized through biblical exegesis. This is the sort of autonomous and self-constructed existence that cosmopolitan environments in fact encourage—in Roman times as in our own. As Sylvia Barack Fishman suggests, paraphrasing Frederik Barth's important work on ethnic identity, "ethnicity functions as a kind of boundaried vessel, within which the enclosed culture is continually adjusted, with some elements being emphasized and others de-emphasized according to a shifting spectrum of influencing factors."[35] Modern experience shows that negotiation and redefinition, which can include within it laxity and the identification of new stringencies at the very same time, are part and parcel of minority identities—particularly in cosmopolitan settings. Assuming that the two incidents in which Jacob's decisions were rebuked reflect the life experience of a single individual (as *Genesis Rabba* clearly does), then perhaps this approach to identify formation helps to explain this fascinating, and enigmatic character.

Jacob of Kefar Nevoraia's heresy is presented more stridently in *Ecclesiastes Rabba.* This Byzantine-period midrashic collection is dated by Marc Hirshman to the sixth or seventh century CE.[36] *Ecclesiastes Rabba* 7:47, comments on Eccles. 7:26, "I find more bitter than death the woman, whose heart is snares and nets and her hands are fetters: he who is good before God shall escape from her; but the sinner shall be ensnared by her":[37]

> Rabbi Nisi[38] of Caesarea explained this verse in terms of heretics (*minin)*:
> "Good before God": This is Rabbi Eleazar,
> "And the sinner will be ensnared by her": This is Jacob of Kefar Nevoraia.
> "Good before God": This is Rabbi Eliezer son of Dama,
> "and the sinner will be ensnared by her": This is Eliezer of Kefar Sama.
> "Good before God": This is Ḥanania son of the brother of Rabbi Joshua,
> "and the sinner will be ensnared by her": These are the people (*bene*) of Kefar Nahum.
> "Good before God": This is Judah son of Naqusa,
> "and the sinner will be ensnared by her": These are the *minin.*
> "Good before God": This is Rabbi Nathan,
> "and the sinner will be ensnared by her": This is his student.
> "Good before God": These are Rabbi Eliezer and Rabbi Joshua,
> "and the sinner will be ensnared by her": This is woman.

That Jacob's heresy is recounted in the name of a Caesarean rabbi is not surprising, owing to his association with Caesarea elsewhere. Jacob is categorized as a *min* in this composite list of culture heroes who avoided heresy, and of infamous "*minin*" who did not. The referent of the term "*min*" here is unclear. Basing itself primarily on this text, modern scholarship has long held that Jacob was a Judaeo-Christian.[39] We find this stated quite unproblematically by Samuel Safrai, who writes, and I translate, that Jacob "converted, or at least was suspected [of being a] Jewish-Christian."[40] Other scholars have taken a much more circumspect approach.[41] The identification of Jacob as a Judaeo-Christian is made tentatively by Oded Irshai, who recognized the significance of the cosmopolitan context for interpreting the traditions dealing with Jacob. In the end, however, Irshai admits that the identification of Jacob as a Judaeo-Christian is not unambiguously supported by the evidence.[42]

The identification of *minim* has perplexed scholars and clerics for the greater part of two millennia. Much of this discussion has its roots in the rabbinic "benediction against the *minim.*"[43] As Samuel Krauss aptly wrote, "how much blood has been spilt [as a result of it], and how much more ink."[44] Almost every major European or American scholar of rabbinic literature and history has voiced an opinion regarding the identification of the *minim,* in no small measure reacting to the significance of this question for early Christian studies. A consensus has developed among rabbinicists that is well stated by Shaye J. D. Cohen:

> The Rabbis lumped together all those who questioned Rabbinic Judaism. It made no difference to the Rabbis whether their opponents were Gentile Christians, Jewish Christians, Gnostics of any variety, pagans, or dissident Jews; all of them, to the exasperation of later scholars, were called *minim.* From the Rabbinic perspective they are all the same.[45]

Daniel Sperber writes in a similar vein that "Any attempt to identify *minim* with one single sectarian group is . . . doomed to failure."[46] Stuart S. Miller too suggests that *minut* (heresy) represents "a broad range of possibilities." He argues that at Sepphoris, and by extension throughout the rabbinic corpus, "all encounters [presented in rabbinic literature] are between individual *minim* and rabbis. To extrapolate from these few instances cohesive groups, movements, or distinct communities of like-minded *minim* is to go beyond the evidence."[47] Setting aside the historical question, Richard Kalmin notes that "overly careful attempts to determine the precise heresy described in the sources may be misguided. These sources give us rough stereotypes and sketches drawn in extremely broad strokes rather than finely nuanced portraits or scientifically precise descriptions."[48] The term *min,* applied to Jacob of Kefar Nevoraia, serves to categorize Jacob among the rabbinically liminal—those who are close enough to the rabbis to be part of them, yet whose behavior sets them apart negatively. This term is never used to describe Jacob in classical midrashim, sources that are closer to his own time, but rather reflects a later classification.

To conclude: the traditions of Jacob of Kefar Nevoraia, like so many others in rabbinic literature, leave us with more questions unanswered than with answered questions. The relationship of the sources on Jacob of Kefar Nevoraia with the village of Kefar Nevoraia in the Upper Galilee was well known during the Middle Ages. Jacob's specific ideology is difficult to pin down, though there is no evidence to brand him a Jewish-Christian. He was—or at least is—portrayed as a member of the rabbinic community attempting to deal with life in the complex culture mix of the eastern Mediterranean coast who, in the course of adapting to that environment, came into dispute with at least one Palestinian rabbi. In offering this interpretation, I use models of ethnic identity that have recently been developed. Jacob's connection to the rabbinic movement and the gravity of his "error" must have both been quite intense, for Jacob of Kefar Nevoraia's exploits were remembered by the rabbis and, ultimately, he was memorialized in a list of infamous "*minim*."

The case of Jacob of Kefar Nevoraia provides us with a window into the complexities of rabbinic story-telling. Archaeological sources from Tyre, Nabratein, and elsewhere, read together with other rabbinic and non-Jewish literary sources, help to set the contexts for the Jacob stories. While we ultimately cannot know whether Jacob of Kefar Nevoraia ever spoke in Tyre and Caesarea, lived in Nabratein, or came into conflict with Rabbi Haggai, for the storytellers all of this was quite real. By focusing upon the world that the Jacob of legend and the storytellers of our literature shared, I have offered this broadly holistic interpretation of the traditions of Jacob of Kefar Nevoraia in honor of another "student of the sages," my friend Zev Garber.

Notes

Note: Many thanks to Joseph M. Baumgarten, Richard Kalmin, and Eric M. Meyers for discussing the contents of this paper with me, and to Professor Stuart S. Miller for commenting on the manuscript.

1. On the complexities involved in rabbinic biography see J. Neusner, *The Development of a Legend: Studies on the Traditions Concerning Yohanan ben Zakkai* (Leiden: E. J. Brill, 1970); W. S. Green, "What's in a Name? The Problematic of Rabbinic Biography," in *Approaches to Ancient Judaism: Theory and Practice,* ed. Jacob Neusner (Missoula: Scholars Press, 1978), 1:77–96; J. Fraenkel, "Hermeneutical Problems in the Study of the Aggadic Narrative," *Tarbiz* 47 (1978):140–358 (in Hebrew). See also Fraenkel's *Studies in the Spiritual World of the Homiletical Story* (Israel: Hakibbutz Hameuchad, 1981, in Hebrew) and his *The Ways of Aggadah and Midrash* (Israel: Yad la-Talmud, 1991, in Hebrew). For recent discussions of the problem of rabbinic biography, see A. Goshen-Gottstein, "Rabbi Eleazar ben Arakh: Symbol and Reality," and M. Hirshman, "*Shmuel ha-Katan,*" both in *Jews and Judaism in the Second Temple, Mishna and Talmud Period: Studies in Honor of Shmuel Safrai,* ed. I. Gafni, A. Oppenheimer, and M. Stern (Jerusalem: Ben Zvi Institute, 1993), 173–97 and 165–72 respectively (both in Hebrew); Hirshman's brief comparisons of rabbinic biography with general Greco-Roman modes of biography are particularly enlightening.
2. The philological and historical contexts for these traditions have been discussed with great attention to detail by Oded Irshai. Though my conclusions differ from his, Irshai's study has been invaluable in the preparation of this essay. See O. Irshai, "Ya'akov of Kefar Niburaia—A Sage Turned Apostate," *Jerusalem Studies in Jewish Thought*, 2, no. 2 (1982/83): 153–68 (in Hebrew).
3. *y. Yev.* 2:6, 4a: "Jacob of Kefar Nevoraia went to Tyre. They came and asked him . . ."
4. J. Theodor and Ch. Albeck, eds., *Genesis Rabba* 7 (Jerusalem: Wahrmann, 1965), 51–52. Parallels are discussed and analyzed by Theodor. This translation follows the base text, British Museum Add. 27179 as cited by Theodor-Albeck and discussed by Irshai, "Ya'akov," 157–58, 163–64. See especially *y. Yev.* 2:6, 4a; Qid. 1, 60a. On the date of *Genesis Rabba,* see H. L. Strack and G. Stemberger, *Introduction to the Talmud and Midrash*, trans. M. Bockmuehl (Edinburgh: T&T Clark, 1992), 303–5.
5. Ch. Albeck, *Introduction to the Talmud, Babli and Yerushalmi* (Tel Aviv: Dvir, 1969), 323, 337 (in Hebrew).
6. E. M. Meyers, J. F. Strange, and C. L. Meyers, "Preliminary Report on the 1980 Excavations at en-Nabratein, Israel," *BASOR* 244 (1981), 1–25; Y. Tsafrir, L. di Segni, and J. Green, *Tabula Imperii Romani Iudaea-Palestina: Eretz Israel in the Hellenistic, Roman and Byzantine Periods; Maps and Gazetteer* (Jerusalem: Israel Academy of Sciences and Humanities, 1994), 164.
7. Irshai, "Ya'akov," 156 n. 17, collects the relevant data. See Meyers, Strange, and Meyers, "Preliminary Report on the 1980 Excavations," 3; A. Yaari, *Journeys to the Land of Israel: Jewish Pilgrims from the Middle Ages to the Beginning of the Return to Zion* (Ramat Gan: Massada, 1976), 91, 141, 434 (in Hebrew).
8. For sources, see S. Klein, *Sefer ha-Yishuv* (Tel Aviv: Dvir, 1939), 126–29 (in Hebrew); Irshai, "Ya'akov," 168 n. 72.
9. L. Finkelstein, ed., *Sifre on Deuteronomy* (New York: Jewish Theological Seminary, 1993), 316, p. 358. See b. Men. 85b, and Rashi to Deut. 32:13; Meir Loeb ben Jehiel Michael Malbim, *Sefer Torah ve-ha-Mitzvah* (Israel: Mefarshei ha-TaNaKH, n.d.), to *Sifre Deut.* 316, p. 815.

10. Meiron: J. Raynor and Y. Meshorer, *The Coins of Ancient Meiron* (Winona Lake, Ind.: Eisenbrauns, 1988); Khirbet Shema: R. S. Hanson and M. L. Bates in *Ancient Synagogue Excavations at Khirbet Shema', Upper Galilee, Israel, 1970–1972*, ed. E. M. Meyers, A. T. Kraabel, and J. Strange (Durham, N.C.: Duke University Press, 1976), 148–50; Gush Ḥalav: J. Raynor, "Numismatics," in *Excavations at the Ancient Synagogue of Gush Halav*, ed. E. M. Meyers, C. L. Meyers, and J. F. Strange (Winona Lake, Ind.: Eisenbrauns, 1990), 230–34; H. Hamburger, "A Hoard of Syrian Tetradrachms and Tyrian Bronze Coins from Gush Halav," *IEJ* 4 (1954): 201–26, 247. J. Raynor notes, "The major difference between the early numismatic evidence from Nabratein and the evidence from Meiron, Khirbet Shema, and Gush Halav can be seen in the lack of Phoenician autonomous and Tyrian city coins found at Nabratein" (Meyers, Strange, and Meyers, "Preliminary Report on the 1980 Excavations," 16). See also pp. 18–19. This paucity of excavated Tyrian coins clearly is not, in my opinion, enough to suggest that the relationship between Tyre and Nabratein was substantially different from that of the nearby sites. It simply reflects the fact that Tyrian coins in great numbers were not uncovered.
11. L. Roth-Gerson, *The Jews of Syria as Reflected in the Greek Inscriptions* (Jerusalem: Zalman Shazar Center for Jewish History, 2001), cat. nos. 34–37, pp. 174–76 (in Hebrew), and the bibliography cited there.
12. See Tessa Rajak's excellent reassessment of scholarly interpretation of Beth She'arim, "The Rabbinic Dead and the Diaspora Dead at Beth She'arim," in *The Talmud Yerushalmi and Graeco-Roman Culture I*, ed. P. Schäfer (Tubingen: Mohr Siebeck, 1998), 349–66, and the bibliography cited there.
13. Roth-Gerson, *The Jews of Syria*, 101, notes that "It is well known that one of the most prominent signs of the hellenisation of Jewish communities in the diaspora was the use of Greek names" (my translation).
14. N. Avigad, *Beth She'arim* (New Brunswick, N.J.: Rutgers University Press, 1976), 3:82, 118; Roth-Gerson, *The Jews of Syria*, no. 41, p. 178, 153 n. 24; D. Noy, "'Peace upon Israel': Hebrew Formulae and Names in Jewish Inscriptions from the Western Roman Empire," *Hebrew Study from Ezra to Ben-Yehuda*, ed. W. Horbury (Edinburgh: T&T Clark, 1999), 135–46.
15. Avigad, *Beth She'arim*, 3:86; M. Schwabe and B. Lifshitz, *Beth She'arim* (New Brunswick, N.J.: Rutgers University Press, 1974), 2:185; Roth-Gerson, *The Jews of Syria*, no. 40, p. 177.
16. See *Lev. Rabba* 32:5, ed. M. Margulies (Jerusalem: Jewish Theological Seminary of America, 1993), 747–48.
17. Avigad, *Beth She'arim*, 3:27; Schwabe and Lifshitz, *Beth She'arim*, 2, no. 147, p. 131; Roth-Gerson, *The Jews of Syria*, no. 39, p. 177.
18. See Albeck, *Introduction to the Talmud*, 190. On rabbinic connections with Tyre, see A. Oppenheimer, *The Galilee in the Mishnaic Period* (Jerusalem: Shazar Center, 1991), 154–56 (in Hebrew).
19. On this inscription, see Chiat, 85–86; L. Roth-Gerson, *Greek Inscriptions in the Synagogues in Eretz-Israel* (Jerusalem: Yad Ben Zvi, 1987), 105–10 (in Hebrew), and the bibliography cited there.
20. Roth-Gerson, *Greek Inscriptions*, 105, 107 n. 13.
21. Roth-Gerson, *The Jews of Syria*, 44.
22. Y. Elbaum, "Midrash Samuel," *Encyclopedia Judaica* (New York: Macmillan, 1970), 11:1517–18; Strack and Stemberger, *Introduction to the Talmud and Midrash*, 390–91.
23. *Midrash Samuel*, ed. S. Buber (Cracow, 1893), 34b. On the historical context of this statement, see L. I. Levine, *The Rabbinic Class of Roman Palestine in Late Antiquity* (New York: Jewish Theological Seminary of America), 173–75.
24. *Midrash on Psalms*, ed. S. Buber (Vilna: Romm, repr. New York: Om, 1947), 19, 2, p. 164, and n. 21. On the date of this collection, see Strack and Stemberger, *Introduction to the Talmud and Midrash*, 350–51.
25. J. Neusner, *Genesis Rabbah: The Judaic Commentary to the Book of Genesis: A New American Translation* (Atlanta: Scholars Press, 1985), vol. 1, chap. 7.
26. L. Ginzberg, *An Unknown Jewish Sect* (New York: Jewish Theological Seminary, 1976), 79–80, 148, 346–47. Cf. Irshai, "Ya'akov," 164–67.
27. *Pirke de-Rabbi Eliezer*, chap. 9, following Hebrew Union College, Klau Library, HUC MS.2043, folio 6a, a Yemenite manuscript thought to date to the fifteenth century. Mounted at http://www.usc.edu/dept/huc-la/pre-project/graphics/pre05/pre0506a.jpg. See Ginzberg, *An Unknown Jewish Sect*, 80. On the date of *Pirke de-Rabbi Eliezer*, see Strack and Stemberger, *Introduction to the Talmud and Midrash*, 356–59.
28. See *y. Shab.* 19, 17b, and Irshai, "Ya'akov," 160, for another context where Jacob and R. Haggai discuss the timing of ritual circumcision.
29. See *Pirque de Rav Kahana*, ed. B. Mandelbaum (New York: Jewish Theological Seminary, 1962), 65. On the date of this text, see Strack and Stemberger, *Introduction to the Talmud and Midrash*, 321. See Theodor and Albeck, eds., *Genesis Rabba*; E. Z. Melamed, *Halachic Midrashim of the Tannaim in Babylonian Talmud* (Jerusalem: Magnes, 1973), 400, n. 36a (in Hebrew).

30. Richard Kalmin suggests that "cases in which amoraim exhibit hostile or ambivalent attitudes toward one another . . . most likely date from the period roughly contemporary with the amoraim involved." If this is the case in Palestinian materials as well, as Kalmin suggests it may be, then the disputes between Jacob and Rabbi Haggai fall into the category of interactions that may at some level be accepted as historical. See R. Kalmin, "Christians and Heretics in Rabbinic Literature of Late Antiquity," *HTR* 87, no. 2 (1994): 2 n. 2, and personal communication.
31. Third-generation Palestinian Amora. See Albeck, *Introduction to the Talmud,* 236–37.
32. L. I. Levine, *Caesarea Under Roman Rule* (Leiden: E. J. Brill, 1975), 72–75. See now K. Holum, "Identity and the Late Antique City: The Case of Caesarea," *Religious and Ethnic Communities in Later Roman Palestine* (College Park: University Press of Maryland, 1998), esp. 166–69.
33. *Codex Theodosianus* 3.7.2; A. Linder, *The Jews in Roman Imperial Legislation* (Detroit: Wayne State University Press, 1987), no. 18. See S. W. Baron, *A Social and Economic History of the Jews,* 2nd ed. (New York: Columbia University Press, 1952), 2.2:229–35, 401–2. Cf. Feldman, *Jew and Gentile in the Ancient World* (Princeton, N.J.: Princeton University Press, 1993), 79.
34. M. Dothan, *Hammath Tiberias: Early Synagogues* (Jerusalem: Israel Exploration Society, 1983), 39–48; Joseph Baumgarten, "Art in the Synagogue: Some Talmudic Views," in *Jews, Christians and Polytheists in the Ancient Synagogue,* ed. S. Fine (London: Routledge, 1999), 71–86; Levine, *Rabbinic Class,* esp. 176–81; and my *Art and Judaism During the Greco-Roman Period: Towards a New Jewish Archaeology* (Cambridge: Cambridge University Press, 2005).
35. Sylvia Barack Fishman, *Negotiating Both Sides of the Hyphen: Coalescence, Compartmentalization and American-Jewish Values* (Cincinnati: University of Cincinnati Judaic Studies Program, 1995), 42; Frederik Barth, *Ethnic Groups and Boundaries* (Boston: Little, Brown, 1969), 38. See my discussion of identity theory in *Art and Judaism During the Greco-Roman Period.*
36. M. Hirshman, "Midrash Qohelet Rabbah (Ch. 1–4)," doctoral diss., Jewish Theological Seminary of America, 1983, 25, 106–7, and "The Greek Fathers and the Aggada on Ecclesiastes: Formats of Exegesis in Late Antiquity," *Hebrew Union College Annual* 59 (1988): 37.
37. Ms. Vatican 291, p. 260b, and the variants cited by Irshai, "Ya'akov," 153–55.
38. See Irshai, "Ya'akov," 154 n. 4. A Palestinian Amora of fourth generation. See Albeck, *Introduction to the Talmud,* 344–45.
39. W. Bacher, *Die Agada der Palastinensischen Amoraer* (Strassburg: K. J. Trubner, 1892–99): 3:776; M. Seligsohn, "Jacob of Kefer Neburaya," in *Jewish Encyclopedia,* ed. A. Singer (New York: Funk and Wagnalls, 1904), 7:35; Ginzberg, *An Unknown Jewish Sect,* 346, writes that Jacob was "known for his Judeo-Christian tendencies"; Z. Vilnay ("Ya'akov Ish Kefar Nevoraia," *Ariel: Entsiklopedyah li-Yediat Erets Yisrael* [Tel Aviv: Sifriyat ha-Sadeh, 1969–84], 4:3776 [in Hebrew]), who writes simply that Jacob "was apparently a *min,* and believed in Jesus of Nazareth" (my translation); Meyers, Strange, and Meyers, in "Preliminary Report on the 1980 Excavations," 1, write that Eccl. R. tradition "is usually understood to mean that Jacob embraced Christianity." See Irshai, "Ya'akov," and the additional bibliography cited there. The most significant recent volume that deals with "Jewish Christianity" is A. H. Becker and A. Y. Reed, eds., *The Ways That Never Parted: Jews and Christians in Late Antiquity and the Middle Ages* (Minneapolis: Fortress Press, 2007). See esp. A. S. Jacobs, "The Lion and the Lamb: Reconsidering Jewish-Christian Relations in Antiquity," 95–118.
40. . . . *asher hafakh, oh nehshad, ke-yehudi-nozri.* S. Safrai, *In Times of Temple and Mishnah: Studies in Jewish History* (Jerusalem: Magnes, 1996), 224 (in Hebrew).
41. See Albeck, *Introduction to the Talmud,* 337, who ignored the *minut* charge altogether, as did A. Hyman, *Toldoth Tannaim Ve'amoraim* (repr. Jerusalem: Machon Pri Ha'aretz, 1987), 2:772 (in Hebrew). Hyman was indeed sensitive to this issue. See the entry for Jacob of Kefar Sakhneh on the same page.
42. Irshai, "Ya'akov," 167–68, and more clearly in the English summary, s.v.
43. The bibliography on this subject is vast. The most recent discussion, with a very extensive bibliography, is by W. Horbury, *Jews and Christians in Contact and Controversy* (Edinburgh: T&T Clark, 1998), 8–11, 67–110.
44. S. Krauss, "Zur Literatur der Siddurim: christliche Polemik," *Festschrift fur Aron Freidmann* (Berlin, 1935), 137, translated by Horbury, *Jews and Christians,* 72.
45. S. J. D. Cohen, "A Virgin Defiled: Some Rabbinic and Christian Views on Heresy," *USQR* 36 (1980): 3.
46. D. Sperber, "Min," *Encyclopaedia Judaica,* 12:2.
47. S. S. Miller, "The Minim of Sepphoris Reconsidered," *HTR* 86, no. 4 (1994): 400, esp. Miller's encyclopedic notes 92 and 93.
48. Kalmin, "Christians and Heretics in Rabbinic Literature of Late Antiquity," 169.

Floating Letters

Mayer I. Gruber

The story is told in the Babylonian Talmud, Tractate Abodah Zarah 18a, that when Rabbi Hanina son of Teradyon was set afire by the Romans along with the Torah scroll held to his chest, his students asked him, "What do you see?" He responded, "Leaves of parchment are burning while letters are floating."[1]

The commentary of Tosafot ad loc concerning the question "What do you see?" implies that the phenomenon of "floating letters" was interpreted by the Tosafists as what we would call a "miracle," that is, "an event that appears unexplainable by the laws of nature and so is held to be supernatural in origin or an act of God as an unusual phenomenon outside of Nature," or "one [i.e., an event] that excites admiring awe."[2] Thus, the Tosafists:

> *What do you see.* It seemed to them [the students] that he [Rabbi Hanina son of Teradyon] should have seen something which would inspire wonder[3] or angels or something else,[4] or alternatively,[5] that [they asked the question] because they were hearing the sound of the floating letters, but they did not know what it [the process described by the four Hebrew words "parchments burning; letters floating"] was.

It was my personal experience with letters "floating off the page" in the summer of 1992 that suggested to me that the expression did not refer to a miraculous incident, but a natural phenomenon. Animal skin on which letters are written in ink is consumed by fire at a higher temperature than blank parchment burns up. How is this possible?

In the summer of 1992 I was visiting several libraries in northern Italy together with my son, now Rabbi Hillel Boaz Gruber, to peruse some manuscripts of Bible commentaries by Rashi (Rabbi Solomon Isaaki, 1040–1105). The goal was to research, collect, and catalog examples of the approximately twelve diagrams that Rashi had added to his commentary as an integral part of the attempt to illuminate both the Bible and previous interpretations thereof.[6]

During the course of our library journey, we arrived at the Turin Municipal Library one day to look at a very important collection of 274 medieval Hebrew manuscripts,[7] which had been catalogued in an exemplary manner.[8] Unfortunately, in 1904 a fire damaged most of the manuscripts. Many were burned up entirely, while others seemed to be more like huge pieces of phyllo dough. The Turin librarians who are custodians of the collection are making a yeoman effort to restore the Hebrew manuscripts that were damaged by the flames. These dedicated librarians gave me a free hand to study the Rashi manuscripts to clarify if they contained evidence of the maps and other diagrams that formed a part of Rashi's biblical commentaries. While studying the manuscripts, I came across letters that seemed to be nearly "suspended across an abyss" (cf. Job. 26:7) with the surrounding parchment almost entirely burnt. The letters seemed to be floating in air almost like the letters of Rabbi Hanina son of Teradyon's Torah scroll as described in the Babylonian Talmud.

The letters floating on air from the medieval Hebrew manuscripts housed in the Turin Public Library were not borne to Heaven by an angel or anything else (*dabar aher*). After floating through the air, those letters or parts of letters landed on the table or the floor. I asked the librarians to take those deteriorating manuscripts back and return them to their place so that they could treat them with the latest restoration techniques. I told them that I preferred to risk having people say I had not seen all of the existing evidence on all of the Rashi diagrams than to expose those manuscripts to the risk of further deterioration.

I was convinced by one aspect of my Turin experience: I saw, face to face, the terrible reality undergone by Rabbi Hanina son of Teradyon's holy scroll, the phenomenon that had been described in the Babylonian Talmud and which the Tosafists had not understood. Because they had not seemed to understand it, I concluded that this was a natural process and that the Tosafists quoted in the margin of our printed editions of the Talmud with specific reference to the passage under discussion here had not seen book burning or did not relate such experience to the case at hand.

My personal experience, that which I "would see with my own eyes" (Job 19:27), enabled me to explain the story in the Talmud not as a miracle but as a natural phenomenon. Based on studies of the type of ink on Hebrew manuscripts in Palestine in the days of Rabbi Hanina son of Teradyon, and the animal skin employed as a writing material at that time,[9] I concluded that the sections of his scroll that were blank burned completely at a temperature about 359 degrees Celsius,[10] while the letters burned only at a temperature above 450 degrees Celsius.[11]

According to studies of the ink used in Hebrew manuscripts in Europe during the thirteenth century CE,[12] such as the manuscripts I saw in Turin, we may conclude that letters are burned up entirely when temperatures rise above 450 degrees Celsius, while parchment without writing burns up at a temperature of 359 degrees Celsius (see above). What is most important here is the difference of 91 degrees between the temperature at which the inked parchment will burn and the temperature at which the surrounding uninked parchment will burn. This difference accounts both for the appearance of letters that are hanging over an abyss and for the floating of letters, which are no longer attached to surrounding parchment.

Of course, exact science cannot confirm that the incident reported concerning Rabbi Hanina son of Teradyon's scroll indeed happened. But I have no doubt that what was related in the Talmud shows that at an early stage of Talmudic legend, the narrator was aware of the material reality that I learned about in Turin. Luckily, the Tosafists quoted above were not familiar with this aspect of book-burning.[13]

Nevertheless, it has been suggested to me by a number of learned scholars that more likely "leaves of parchment are burning while letters are floating" may simply be a fixed expression. That is to say, "Why do I assume that the expression should be explained against the background of the burning of a Torah scroll and then related to the fact, which I observed, that letters inscribed in black ink on animal skin do indeed float?" To this brilliant question I must respond that the expression "letters are floating" occurs a total of two times in the entire Babylonian Talmud, once in the passage quoted above from Tractate Abodah Zarah, and once more in Babylonian Talmud Tractate Pesahim 87b.

The attestation of "letters are floating" in Babylonian Talmud Tractate Pesahim comes about in the following manner: R. Alexandri is quoted as saying, "Three returned to their original home: Israel, Egypt's wealth, and the writing on the Tablets [of the Decalogue that Moses smashed according to Exod. 32:19]." It is explained in the Talmud that when Israel was exiled to Babylonia, the nation was returning to the home of Abraham and Sarah, who originated in Babylonia (see Gen. 11:26–31). Consequently, the Babylonian exile was actually a return to Israel's original home. Likewise, when according to 1 Kings 14:25–26 Pharaoh Shishak took away to Egypt the temple treasuries and the royal treasuries, he was only restoring to Egypt the silver and gold that the Israelites had taken from Egypt according to Exod. 12:35. In the same vein, the Talmud explains, when Moses declared, "I broke them [the tablets of the Decalogue] before your eyes" (Deut. 9:17), this means that "the tablets are broken while the letters float [up to God who gave them]."

Indeed, the text quoted in Pesahim mentions not parchment but stone tablets and would, according to the logic of some contemporary Jewish scholars, call into question my attempt to relate "floating letters" to parchment by correlating my own experience in Turin with the narrative found in Abodah Zarah 18a. My defense is as follows: I deliberately compared the text in Abodah Zarah to my own experience because my own experience is genetically related to what is described in Abodah Zarah. Both are accounts concerning letters inscribed on animal skin. The text in Pesahim, on the other hand, speaks of stone tablets rather than animal skin. How do I account for this? Not by the unwarranted assumption that "floating letters" is simply a ubiquitous expression that does not mean anything in particular. On the contrary, I assume that the text in Abodah Zarah refers to a phenomenon closely related to what I saw in Turin while the text in Pesahim refers to something further removed from the reality of letters inscribed on animal skin. The fact is that while letters inscribed on burnt animal skin do indeed float, letters incised on stone do not float except in a Talmudic imagination, which has been influenced by the story of Hanina son of Teradyon, which, most likely, reflects familiarity with the physical reality I saw replicated in Turin. It should now be obvious, therefore, that since there are only two attestations of the expression "floating letters" in all of the Babylonian Talmud, one of which reflects an empirical reality and one of which must be a secondary, derived usage, there is no reason to assume that "floating letters" is "simply an expression" either in Abodah Zarah or in Pesahim or in my account of my visit to the municipal library of Turin.

Notes

Note: The author expresses his sincere thanks to Prof. Catherine Delano Smith, director of the Maps in Bibles Project at London, and to the Committee on Research and Publications of the Faculty of Humanities and Social Sciences at Ben-Gurion University of the Negev, who funded my research on line-drawings in medieval manuscripts of Rashi's Bible Commentaries. In the course of pursuing this research during the summer of 1992, I came across the answer I provide here to the question, "What is the origin of the expression 'floating letters'?" I am also abundantly grateful to many Israeli scholars, whose numerous insightful leading questions enabled me to expand this study beyond the simple facts of what, apparently, lies behind the expression "floating letters" in the Hanina son of Teradyon narrative.

1. This is the reading in the Vilna edition. However, in New York JTS Ms. 44830, which was written at Ubeda, Spain, in 1290 CE, we read as follows: "Letters are floating while leaves of parchment are burning." For the text of this highly regarded manuscript, see Shraga Abramson, ed., *Tractate Abodah Zarah of the Babylonian Talmud: Ms. Jewish Theological Seminary of America* (New York: Jewish Theological Seminary of America, 1957). Raphael Rabinowitz, *Diduke Sophereim,* pt. 10 (Munich: H. Roesel, 1879), 22b n. 50, notes that the reading "leaves of parchment" (Heb. *gewilin*) is found also in Ein Ya'akov and Menorat ha-Maor, while in the editio princeps of the Talmud (Venice: Bomberg, 1520–23) the reading is "Page [*sic*] (*gilayon*) are burning while letters are floating." The latter reading is problematic because in the first clause the subject of the nominal sentence, "page," and the predicate thereof, "are burning," do not match in number.
2. The source of this definition of "miracle" is *American Heritage Dictionary,* 2nd college ed. (Boston: Houghton Mifflin, 1976), 801. It is not claimed here that Tosafot employs the term "miracle." What is claimed here is that the string of three possible explanations for "floating letters/burning parchment" employed by Tosafot are functional equivalents of the definitions provided by the *American Heritage Dictionary* for the modern English term "miracle."
3. Heb. *debar temah*, which Eliezer Ben Yehuda, *A Complete Dictionary of Ancient and Modern Hebrew* (Ramat-Gan: International Publication Society, 1959), 16:7789, defines as "wonder or miracle." N. H. Tur-Sinai (the editor of vols. 15–16 of Ben Yehuda, *Thesaurus*) notes that the term *temah* is first attested in this meaning in the Geniza version of Ben Sira 16:11. Rashi in his commentary on 1 Sam. 10:12 defines *temah* as something new which is not generally found. As for *temah* in the sense "miracle, wonder" in Ben Sira, see now Haim Dihi, "The Morphological and Lexical Innovations in the Book of Ben Sira," Ph.D. diss., Ben-Gurion University of the Negev, 2004, 716–19 (in Hebrew).
4. The Hebrew term *dabar aher,* literally "something else," has a variety of meanings in rabbinic Hebrew. Possibly the most widely attested meaning is "an alternative interpretation." The term may also refer to something that one is forbidden to mention by name such as a) idolatrous worship; b) a pig; c) leprosy; or d) incest. For the nuances of *dabar aher* in ancient rabbinic Hebrew, see Jacob Levi, *Neuhebräisches und chaldäisches Wörter-*

buch, 2nd ed., rev. Heinrich Lebrecht Fleischer, ed. Lazarus Goldschmidt, 4 vols. (Berlin: Harz, 1924), 1:374; Marcus Jastrow, *A Dictionary of the Targumim etc.* (New York: Choreb, 1926), 278; and Yitzhak Frank, *The Practical Talmud Dictionary* (Jerusalem: Ariel, 1991), 56–66. One Judaic scholar who saw an earlier version of this paper was exceedingly angered that I dared to mention the latter dictionary. He said, "Why mention this dictionary? I never heard of it." It is worth mentioning this remark because, unfortunately, the attitude of "if I never heard of it, it cannot be right or even important" is ubiquitous in contemporary Judaic scholarship. Zev Garber, in whose honor I present this study has been in the forefront of scholars who have encouraged the expression of reasonable ideas without respect to the academic or other affiliation of the particular lexicographer, historian, theologian, or what-have-you. Another Judaic scholar reacted with frustration that I sought a nuance of *dabar aher* more precise than "something else." In fact, elementary philological method suggests that we seek a nuance of the term *dabar aher,* which would account for its juxtaposition in the Tosafistic context with the terms *temah* and angels, both of which suggest that Tosafot seek an explanation, which falls under the definition(s) of "miracle" as defined in the *American Heritage Dictionary.*

5. Aram. *'iy name,* lit., "or also," which is employed throughout the Babylonian Talmud to encode an alternative interpretation; see Frank, *Practical Talmud Dictionary,* 9–10; Michael Sokoloff, *A Dictionary of Jewish Babylonian Aramaic of the Talmudic and Geonic Periods* (Baltimore: Johns Hopkins University Press, 2002), 108b, s.v. *'iy*, p. 756a, s.v. *'iy name.*
6. Mayer I. Gruber, "What Happened to Rashi's Pictures?" *Bodleian Library Record* 14, no. 2 (April 1992): 111–24; Gruber, "Light on Rashi's Diagrams from the Asher Library of Spertus College of Judaica," in *The Solomon Goldman Lectures,* ed. Gruber, vol. 6 (Chicago: Spertus College of Judaica Press, 1993), 73–85; Gruber, "Notes on the Diagrams in Rashi's Commentary to the Book of Kings," *Studies in Bibliography and Booklore* 19 (1994): 29–41; Gruber, "The Sources of Rashi's Cartography," in *Letters and Texts of Jewish History,* new and expanded ed., ed. Norman Simms (Hamilton, New Zealand: Outrigger Publishers, 1999), 61–67; Gruber, "Rashi's Map Illustrating His Commentary on Judges 21:19," in *Proceedings of the Rabbinical Assembly 2004 Convention* (New York: Rabbinical Assembly, 2006), 135–41; Catherine Delano Smith and Mayer I. Gruber, "Rashi's Legacy: Maps of the Holy Land," *The Map Collector*, no. 59 (Summer 1992): 30–35; Gabrielle Sed-Rajna, "Some Further Data on Rashi's Diagrams to His Commentary on the Bible," *Jewish Studies Quarterly* 1 (1993/94): 149–57; Therese Metzger, "Exegese de Rashi et Iconographie biblique juive au Moyen Age," in *Rashi et la culture juive en France du Nord au moyen Age,* ed. Gilbert Dahan, Gerard Nahon, and Eli Nicolas (Paris: E. Peeters, 1997), 203–24; Avraham Grossman, *The Early Sages of France* (Jersualem: Magnes, 1997), 207–9 (in Hebrew); Avraham Grossman and Ben-Zion Kadar, "The Maps of the Land of Israel Drawn by Rashi: Their Historical Meaning," *Iggeret* 25 (2003): 26–29 (in Hebrew).
7. See Bernardinus Peyron, *Codices Hebraici Manu Exarati Bibliothecae quae in Taurinensi Athenaeo Asservatu* (Rome: Fratres Bocca, 1880); and see Binyamin Richler, *Guide to Hebrew Manuscript Collections* (Jerusalem: Israel Academy of Sciences and Humanities, 1994), 188–89. There (p. 188) Richler indicates that ninety manuscripts survived the fire. Moreover, he notes that six additional Hebrew manuscripts, which were not mentioned in Peyron's catalogue, were discovered in the Library of Turin in recent years.
8. See the previous note for data concerning the exemplary catalogue of this collection prepared by Bernard Peyron.
9. Yoram Nir-El and Magen Broshi, "The Black Ink of the Qumran Scrolls," *Dead Sea Discoveries* 3 (1986): 164: "Visual examination of the black ink on the Qumran scrolls shows that the black colour and the geometrical definition (sharpness) of the inscribed letters were maintained for a very long time (approximately 2000 years). On the other hand, old texts which were written with iron-based black ink show a tendency to turn brown-red. This phenomenon is explained as due to the formation of iron oxide (rust) and was observed even in 200-year old Torah scrolls. This serves as additional support for our claim that the black ink used in the Qumran scrolls was not iron-based, but of a carbonaceous nature."
10. S. H. Graf, "Ignition Temperatures of Various, Papers, Woods and Fabrics," *Engineering Experiment Station, Oregon State College, Bulletin* 26 (1949). I express my sincere gratitude to Prof. Ronald Hoffman, Department of Chemistry, Cornell University; Prof. Peter Kuniholm, Department of History of Art and Archaeology, Cornell University; John F. Dean, Director, Department of Preservation and Conservation, Olin Library, Cornell University; Marianne Hansen, researcher in the Olin Library; who expended considerable time and energy in search of the Graf article until finally Jill H. Powell, Reference/Instruction Coordinator, Engineering Library, Cornell University, found the article for me.
11. See Zvi Gopher, "The Composition of the Ink and Attempts to Strengthen the Script," in Yohanan Aharoni and Joseph Naveh, *Arad Inscriptions,* translated by Judith Ben-Or, ed. and rev. Anson F. Rainey (Jerusalem: Israel Exploration Society, 1981), 180.

12. I. Ta-Shma, *Law, Custom and Reality in Ashkenaz 1000–1350* (Jerusalem: Magnes, 1997), 287–96 and esp. 295 (in Hebrew). He explains that medieval Hebrew manuscripts include both texts that were written in ink of vegetable origin, which retain their blackness until now, and texts written in ink that included metallic materials, which through oxidation have turned brown, and he shows that variant traditions attributed to halakhic authorities justified both the continued use of ink of vegetable origin and the adoption of ink which included also metallic particles.
13. Cf. Robert Chazan, *European Jewry and the First Crusade* (Berkeley: University of California Press, 1987), 197–210. I do not deny that anti-Judaism expressed itself in the Middle Ages as in modern times by the systematic ceremonial burning of Jewish sacred texts. I simply suggest that the particular passage in Tosafot, which finds the description of "floating letters" totally mystifying, must stem from a person or persons who had never seen the phenomenon of "floating letters," which I observed in Turin in 1992. The unfamiliarity of Tosafot with the physical reality of "floating letters" is, of course, shared by contemporary scholars, who suggested to me that "floating letters" is "simply an expression." Obviously, no one with proper philological training would take anything written in a canonical literary or theological text as "simply an expression."

Dialogue as Praxis

A Midrashic Reading of Numbers 19–20 and Hebrews 9

James F. Moore

My relationship with Zev Garber now spans more than twenty years. He has helped me to develop a special approach to dialogue that not only shapes all of my work but also has led to the forming of a group that has now engaged in a dialogue on sacred texts for nearly fifteen years.[1] It is this aspect of my relationship with Zev that I illustrate in this essay and offer as a contribution to this *Festschrift* dedicated to him. I do so by engaging in a dialogue with another colleague whom I have now known for twenty-five years and with whom I have had an ongoing dialogue for those twenty-five years: Joseph Edelheit. Joe has also written his own contribution to this *Festschrift,* and his work forms a beginning point for me to offer my reflections in the following essay. The approach we have taken, all of us, has been dialogue on texts, which involves both the effort to fully respect the other as equal and to think about our texts together in a post-Shoah context. The theme is dialogue, but the focus is on a text that is full of ambiguity and questions. I offer my reflections on the "Red Heifer" text from Numbers 19 by turning to an equally puzzling text in Hebrews 9.[2] My hope is that what I present here will both show the process of dialogue on texts that Zev has been so instrumental in helping me to develop and will open up the possibilities for dialogue presented in the texts and for my friend Joe Edelheit.

The Task at Hand

I begin with the text from Hebrews 9 even though it stands as a secondary text, that is, as an interpretation of the text from Numbers 19. I believe, however, that I will be led back to Numbers 19 in ways quite revealing for dialogue by beginning with Hebrews 9. First of all, the relationship between Christian texts and the Hebrew Scriptures is not always so clear as it appears to be in Hebrews 9. It is obvious that the author of Hebrews 9 intends the words to be taken as a commentary on a text and on a practice. In both cases, however, the reader is left with puzzling questions, and those questions are where we must begin with this effort at dialogue.

First, while the writer of Hebrews apparently refers to a text, Numbers 19, in talking about the sacrificial offerings of the priests, the Hebrews text shows a curious lack of awareness of the details of the Numbers text. The tradition, whatever that may be, of the offering of the Red Heifer is confused in the Hebrews text with various other types of priestly acts that are partly connected with ideas of sin offering and with the role of establishing the covenant relationship of Yahweh with the people of Israel.

Thus, while the offering of the Red Heifer is clearly the task of the priest, Eleazar, the writer of Hebrews links this with actions by Moses. While the offering of the Red Heifer focuses attention on the ashes produced by a whole burning, the writer of Hebrews talks about the blood of the sacrifice. This mixing of forms of ritual may be a conscious effort to make a sweeping judgment about the whole role of the priests, but it confuses the link with the text from Numbers 19. In what sense can we say that Hebrews 9 is a commentary on Numbers 19? There are certainly problems for us here.

Second, the text in Hebrews includes reference to the Red Heifer as if it were a natural, normal, indeed, frequent activity of the priests. What we know of the ancient traditions leads us to conclude that, in fact, the rituals of the Red Heifer were very infrequent practices.[3] Despite the instructions of Numbers 19, the act may have actually been conducted as little as three times during the entire history of the ancient sacrifices. Because the writer of Hebrews confuses this ritual with other practices, indeed, of practices that may or may not have been priestly, we do not have a clear picture of how well the writer of Hebrews actually knew the sacrificial practices. We can assume that the writer understood his comments as based on actual reference to activities that were being done and meant something in particular to the Jewish people of his time. However, the references made lead us to question this and to wonder in just what way the text of Hebrews can actually be a commentary on such practices.

A third puzzle for us upon which to expand is just what are we to make of the practice of the Red Heifer? It is called an eternal command but is, in fact, almost nonexistent in the actual practice of the people. If this is the case, then we are puzzled about what to do with the claims of Hebrews 9, which are as close to what many have called a replacement theology as we find in the entirety of the Christian scriptures. If there is a replacement, we are puzzled about exactly what is being replaced. This replacement idea may also help us to link back to Numbers 20 in which there is another kind of replacement that is happening—the replacing of the first generation of leadership of the covenant people. But the ambiguity of Hebrews 9 is as troubling on this matter as the strangeness of the original text of Numbers 19 and its link to chapter 20.

Let me suggest a fourth puzzle, which lies hidden under the connections attempted by the writer of Hebrews. Numbers 19 and 20 are linked by the theme of death (particularly dead bodies), but that link is extremely vague even in the original text just as it is inviting for the reader of the text to explore. Hebrews 9 is also about death, but this comes across as something very different. The issue of Numbers is the question of clean and unclean. Hebrews 9 seems unaware of this dimension and misses a central point of the original text in the process. In addition, this matter of clean and unclean links it with the way that the community decides who is inside of and who is outside of the covenant people. That question becomes central to Hebrews 9, but I wonder if we can reverse the pattern of reading texts by seeing that Numbers 19–20 can help us rethink Hebrews 9 and its exclusivist claims around who is inside of and who is outside of the community.

These four puzzles are enough for one essay and, if left as openings for dialogue, will serve us well to offer a dialogue connection to what Joe Edelheit has to say about Numbers 19. In fact, his reading of that text may well provide the insight for which my listing of puzzles calls, and may show clearly how and why a dialogical reading of texts (what our group has called a "midrashic reading" over the years) is not only fruitful but vital for the ongoing dialogue between Christians and Jews. I will delight in the possibility that the Book of Numbers reread can become a pathway for rethinking Hebrews 9 and the whole history of Christian supercessionism.

Puzzles One and Two

The combination of textual references that we see in Hebrews 9 is not really so surprising. Such a practice may have been common in the ancient religious communities. If the author of Hebrews knew of the ambiguity of the Numbers 19 text, this linking may well be a way of resolving the problem as the early rabbis would also do. But the mixing of factual data leads to a real problem of understanding. We wonder who might have been the audience of Hebrews that could read or hear the text with some level of understanding, but at the same time recognize that it is full of inaccuracies. Who would care about this and why? The author seems completely oblivious to this as an issue. We must, therefore, presume that the linking is already a pattern that had become familiar to many in the early church so that the author is picking up an established tradition. If so, then the problem only pushes back the matter and does not resolve our puzzle. The reason for the linking is clear as the author wishes to use this connection of textual references in order to create an argument that the whole system of sacrifice is replaced by the perfect sacrifice of Jesus. That point is obvious, but the point has little relation to the actual text of Numbers 19. The Red Heifer is *not* the whole system of sacrifice, nor is it intended to represent that. In fact, the ritual of the Red Heifer seems very specialized and is linked specifically to the question of cleanness (particularly related to death and dead bodies). We have little reason for understanding the ritual itself except as linked to this very specific question. There is no mention at all that the sacrifice is intended as a sin offering.

The writer of Hebrews may have cared little about this problem since it does not prevent the effort to make the point of replacement. It does show, however, that the writer was not very conversant with the traditions of ancient Israel and may not have known much about the actual practices of the Temple priests (here the reference in fact is to the tent, which is a link to the scenario of the people in the desert and not to the Temple). If this is all true, then Hebrews 9 is not a commentary on Numbers 19—*despite* the fact that it is the only reference to the Red Heifer in all of Christian scriptures. We can, however, read Hebrews 9 as if it *were* a commentary and find surprising results in doing so.

If we do this, then we can say that the destruction of the Temple does indeed eliminate the entire sacrificial system attached to the Temple. The issue is not one of supercession, but rather what to do without the Temple. For the author of Hebrews, there is in the death of Jesus a response for those who look to that for meaning. I will follow this line shortly as I try to midrashicize this text. But the problem we are now facing is not resolved by this realization, even if we can push the replacement theology of the text and subsequent tradition to the side by rethinking this text in this way. The issue that faces us, though, is that the obligation of the sacrifice of the Red Heifer is not really linked with the Temple-system even if the task is given over to the priest. The Red Heifer stands outside of the normal practice and requires a separate treatment.

So what can be done? Two factors connected to the Red Heifer are of interest for us in thinking about Hebrews 9. First, the sacrifice is linked with ritual uncleanness both of the one sacrificing and of the people who are made clean by the water of the ashes. Second, the sacrifice is especially linked to our relation to the dead (especially interesting in that the next chapter in Numbers speaks of the deaths of central figures of the wilderness journey even as there is almost no mention of the Red Heifer or of uncleanness in these accounts). In addition, the sacrifice is clearly connected with the issue of who is to be regarded as inside of the community (who is accepted) and who is outside. The strangeness of the Numbers text presents us with this irony that the sacrifice itself is "outside of the camp." Thus, the priest becomes an outsider who must proceed through a ritual in order to again become an insider.

Is it possible that the question of insider/outsider is for both textual settings a key matter that must be resolved not so much for religious reasons but for the sake of the well-being of the community? It is likely the case for the audience of the writer of Hebrews. Is it the case, in some sense, for the audience of Numbers (not the people of the story but the people who have inherited the story)? If so, we may look in this direction for a possible rethinking of the text from Hebrews and maybe for a post-Shoah reading in dialogue.

Puzzles Three and Four

In fact, though, I have tried to indicate that there is no ground for presuming a supercessionist position for the community of Hebrews. But to push aside replacement theologies is not to set aside the whole matter of replacement. Indeed, the issue is clearly front and center for Numbers since the scene unfolds as the context for the "replacement" of the original generation of the leaders of the people of Israel. We are also clearly led to see that Miriam, Moses, and Aaron are not replaced simply because they grow old and must die. Instead, they are removed from the role of leading the people into the land of promise because of a fault (of their failing). But even the rabbis are a bit undecided about what this actually means. Who does not fail? Who is in and who is left out if this is the criterion for judgment?

This is the persistent question of the Numbers text and actually links us to the other odd theme of how we are to think about the dead.

I am convinced that this question is not merely the question of the text, that is, the question of the desert, but is in fact a key question for the continuing life of the people. Formulated as it is by the story in Numbers, we have a fascinating way of leading the reader to consider the issue of who is in and who is out, who is acceptable and who is not. The entire theme of uncleanness surely has to do with this question in the context of the Numbers story. And we wonder, what does this do to our rethinking of the Hebrews text? If we are now thinking along with the Numbers text, the issue in Hebrews becomes very different than it first seems. If the issue is not that one people replaces another but rather one of leadership and how to think about the question of those who fail, then we read Hebrews in a different way.

Creating a New Way

I have argued that the Hebrews text need not be read as a replacement theology in what has been the traditional sense but, rather, can be read as a replacement born of necessity like the issues found in Numbers. If there is no Temple, then there is no priesthood and no sacrificial system. The writer of Hebrews responds by arguing that, in Jesus, there is no need to reconstruct this system, since the Christ provides a new way forward. But this point does not suggest that the older system was false or inadequate. The system could have continued, but the catastrophe of the destruction of the Temple means that the system can no longer be continued. Thus, the way provided by the Christ is not a supercession but a new way forward.

This means that the Book of Hebrews must be read as an attempt to answer the question how this new way is to be understood, that is, how it impacts the life of those in the community. It is clear that for these "Christians" the path taken is very different from the path chosen by the rabbis who also must contend with the destruction of the Temple in order to find a new way forward. For the rabbis, this way forward becomes eventually the halakhah and unfolds in a life pattern that no longer depends on the sacrificial system of the Temple. For the writer of Hebrews, the way forward is not halakhah, at least not as it will be developed in Judaism. But the way forward is a life pattern that is shaped by the following of the Christ.

It is not clear to me that the writer of Hebrews fully knew or was in conversation with Jewish communities in the diaspora. The apparent lack of knowledge we have noted suggests that the writer was not aware of how Judaism was taking a new shape as well. That is speculation on our part and not really pertinent for us. What is more significant is that the writer of Hebrews links all this to the Red Heifer, and the reason is that this writer must or wants to connect this with the whole matter of dealing with death. The Christ provides a new way in that the Christ has passed into the "eternal temple" (tent) according to this writer. But this does not mean that, somehow, this gives the Christ a superior position, only an eternal position. That is, the sacrifice is transformed not merely in understanding how we deal with dead bodies but into a theology of how we face death. The Christian response is clearly to look to the resurrection, which is presented directly in this symbolism of the Christic sacrifice.

Different Paths, but Dialogue?

The issue becomes for us now: Can these two ways so strikingly different be brought into dialogue? Given our present reflection, is the story of the Red Heifer a possible route to such dialogue? Finally, I want to pose this discussion as a post-Shoah discussion that takes account of how either response to the catastrophe of the Temple destruction can be viable in a post-Shoah world.

If the view as presented by the writer of Hebrews does not presume a supercession of the priestly tradition, and if it represents a typical Christian perspective, we may ask why there is any need for dialogue other than pure curiosity. Indeed, we have suggested that the writer of Hebrews may not have been very familiar with either the Temple traditions or with contemporary Jewish communities and their developing practices. It is surely possible for communities to develop without significant contact or conflict. If there is no actual animosity or open aggression, then this isolated development might be sufficient. Dialogue becomes an option for the intellectually curious. We will see, though, that a benign isolation does not work to take account of the actual progress of Western religious development. Christians did gain imperial power with that additional reason to read their traditions not just as another way forward but as a replacement, even a superior one, that requires full replacement, supercession. The exclusivism that finally accompanies the wedding of Christianity with Roman power does give reason for dialogue. The ultimate expression of this triumphalism in ideologies like that of Nazism and the resultant devastation, genocide with a catastrophe even more cataclysmic than the destruction of the Temple, makes dialogue imperative. That post-Shoah consideration we will come to shortly.

But before we move in that direction, I want to pursue a question also pertinent. Is dialogue also a necessary option even if we begin by assuming a coexistent pluralism and not a replacing supercessionism? Maybe the strange text of the Red Heifer can help us toward a midrashic approach to this question. What we see in the Numbers text is that the ritual of the sacrifice of the Red Heifer is a prototype of worship that is designed to create boundaries. There is an outside and inside and, as we have said, even the sacrifice itself is done *outside* of the camp. But the ritual is designed to bring people in and not to push people out. Only those who refuse to accept the practice are left on the outside (presumably).

On the other hand, this is just the point. Rituals create a form of exclusivism that defines a community's identity and, with that, those individuals who are "inside" of the group. To refuse is to define oneself as outside of the group. All of this is okay, but the ritual is designed to specifically stigmatize those on the outside (they are perpetually unclean). The Red Heifer is a symbol, in this way, of much of religious practice and the dangers of ritual. If to be a Jew is to accept a ritual and also to define the outsider as "unclean," then we have not merely a problem with exclusivism but also xenophobia with the potential for aggressive violence. I speak here of Numbers, but in actuality, Christians often taking a position like that of the writer of Hebrews have been as likely to think this way and have often also possessed the power to put that thinking into destructive action.

On the other hand, we face an oddity with the story of the Red Heifer in that this ritual is commanded as an eternal commandment but is actually performed very rarely. There are, apparently, only some circumstances that require the dramatic form of exclusivism I have described (the historic moments of catastrophe perhaps). In other moments, the communities *can* act with greater openness to the other, which is in fact shown by the commands as we see in Leviticus 19. But to cultivate this kind of openness, to truly accept the stranger as one of us, we need dialogue. There is a necessity for such dialogue, which is challenged only in rare moments when the community itself is under threat of annihilation and, thus, extinction. Then we need the Red Heifer to determine who can be safely accepted as one of us.

Of course, this is the great danger of Hebrews 9, since the text can verge on making the sacrifice of the Christ a form of the Red Heifer and see history as one great cataclysm. Christians *must* avoid this tendency and can do so only by taking seriously that the Red Heifer is offered only rarely. Otherwise, we are also driven by the command of love even of the stranger. This command to make any sense at all has to mean dialogue (including a form of dialogical living, community). So I suggest a form of reverse midrash to allow Numbers 19 to become a way of reading Hebrews 9.

Post-Shoah Reading

All of this is made problematic in our post-Shoah world since the Nazi genocide and its ideological foundations put the Jewish community forever at the brink of catastrophe, annihilation. If there is no point at which the community can relax and accept openly the other but must always maintain some suspicion of the other, then dialogue is not only risky but perhaps a delusion. The temptation on the horizon is to live as if the ritual of the Red Heifer is the standard shape of Jewish identity. Indeed, this is the terrible pull of the Shoah that it might become the center of the community's identity. Much of post-Shoah Jewish reflection has been an effort *not* to do this, but it remains the dark cloud always present.

My aim, though, is to speak of a midrashic reading of Hebrews and of the Christian communal identity and I hope for a dialogical interchange on this and on Jewish identity from my friend Joe Edelheit. Christians do not live in such a moment of catastrophe, but they do live in a moment of disintegration, which is the aftermath of the Shoah for Christianity. To be an insider in the sense of the writer of Hebrews means for us now to be the ones who carry the identity, thus stigma, of the killers. We are the ones who have touched dead bodies, indeed, millions of them, many of them children. How do we make ourselves clean? Is the blood of the eternal lamb of the Hebrews text sufficient as a way forward now? There is a fundamental problem with saying this and even more of a problem if this is said in an exclusivist tone.

So we return to the strange story of Numbers for some possible insight since this story does have to do with touching the dead and with uncleanness. Perhaps there is need far more for a ritual like the Red Heifer, but, in this case, not so much as a sign of insider/outsider but rather to face squarely the issue of being unclean. I am reminded that the sacrifice takes place "outside" of the camp and, in addition, is performed not by Aaron but by Eleazar. Is it so surprising that in a post-Shoah world this text should lead us to see that our way forward must come from outside (truly dialogue is a necessity)? Not even the eternal possibility can promise that we are once again made clean. But I am talking here not about guilt but about uncleanness, for we have touched dead bodies without undergoing the ritual of washing.

I am inclined to think that this now becomes an eternal command in that we are not talking about an episode through which we can be changed and the past can go away. We are actually talking about moving through the catastrophe toward a new way, the way that now does bring Jews and Christians together. If the writer of Hebrews was trying to search through the confession of the crucified and risen Christ for a new way forward, we now must move past the disintegration of this hope to a new way forward which strikingly now brings us back to dialogue with the Jewish community and to the strange ritual of the Red Heifer. This is no conclusion or absolute finish to a problem but an ongoing effort to move forward to some new form of community.

Forward to Dialogue

Now we must reconsider the argument that has brought us to this point. Even if we now think of uncleanness—rather than guilt—as the point that initiates a new dialogue, we are confronted by the striking claim found in Joe Edelheit's essay in this volume. Edelheit has argued that the model of oppression, which has served some groups well in raising up real oppression and moving toward righting those wrongs, is now close to bankruptcy as a workable model. We must admit that, if this is true, our move to embrace uncleanness as a mode of understanding our present, taking up our past as Christians, runs the real risk of reinforcing this model of oppression. Those who would be quite ready to accept our guilt and responsibility for the Christian past may well be the same ones who now use this model for condemning not only Israelis but also the whole American Jewish community for complicity in oppression. Does one stage lead directly to the other?

I have argued before that there is a real possibility that the moral model for understanding Christian complicity in the Shoah can easily become an unworkable way of imposing a different moral standard on the current State of Israel.[4] Even more, this judgment leads to an impossible and unworthy association of all Jews, be they Israelis or Jews in the Diaspora, with failed policies of the Israeli government. But this is not all, since this high moral standard can lead to an assessment of the Israeli presence in the Palestinian Territories as equivalent to the Nazi policies in their occupation. If we see this actually happening, then the model is truly bankrupt, without any real moral cogency and certainly without potential for producing dialogue. But this means that even the conclusion I have drawn from this Midrash of Hebrews and Numbers cannot stand as it is.

Do we know a way forward and can the approach I have used so often lead to at least a glimmer of possibility? Joe has suggested that truth may lie in the recognition within the Numbers text itself that theory (I would suggest liturgy) does not play out in practice. What is needed is a new theory that can produce real praxis, a theory that Joe argues is embedded in our midrashic model of dialogue (the model kept alive and carried out annually by the Midrash group).[5] Thus, we must abandon the oppression model and fully embrace our midrashic approach, which forces a real encounter based on deeply held claims—taking the other seriously as other. Perhaps this does produce a praxis in itself that leaves us in a better place than we are left usually.

But this model must move beyond theory to liturgy as religious practice, since this is the true insight of Numbers 19–20. We cannot expect a dialogue to emerge if our liturgies continue to produce language that draws lines, excludes, and judges the other as less. Our religious praxis must match our theory if honest dialogue is to become a workable praxis. This is a challenge that we are still yet to understand and achieve. There is much work to be done to actually make this happen beyond mere talk among those of us doing Midrash.

Yet another challenge arises from Joe's invitation to a new theory that is truly risky for Jews. If the oppression model is to be abandoned, then this model is also not useful to apply to Israeli (and, more broadly, Jewish) views of Israel. But we cannot know what it means to stop thinking of Israel under siege, and, if this is simply chosen by one side, then we have a true dilemma that implies full vulnerability. Maybe this is an important step for Jews in America (I leave this as a dialogical question), but I cannot know nor do I wish to predict what this could mean or whether it could be accomplished in Israel. But if the risk is now made fully as an offer to dialogue, then we start with a new sort of beginning. We cannot fall back on models of oppression as that which sustains encounter. This must become fully a conversation that produces respect in reality. Perhaps this is what I have actually called for in trying to envision a dialogical community.[6] But, in this community, barriers are dismantled (figuratively and literally), even if we are left with difference because difference does not cause inequality but is the basis for a rich newness. The issue is, can we move to this beyond so that dialogue means praxis in the fullest sense? This is more than simply entering the promised land or waiting for a new generation of leaders but is before us as an urgency that we must take up now before it is again, yet again, too late.

Notes

1. This group, which includes Steven Jacobs and Henry Knight as well as Zev and myself, has come to be called the "Post-Shoah Midrash Reading Group," and our collective work of dialogue together (Jews and Christians) on sacred texts always joined together a text from Hebrew scripture and a text from Christian scripture, and has now appeared in many formats. Most especially, this can be seen in our book, *Post-Shoah Dialogues: Re-Thinking our Texts Together* (Lanham, Md.: University Press of America, 2004). Samples of our work have also appeared as special issues in *Shofar* (Fall 1996), *Sidic* 35, no. 1 (2002), and the *Bulletin of the Council of Societies for the Study of Religion* (September 2006).
2. All texts for this paper are taken from the NRSV version of the Christian scriptures.
3. For example, see W. Gunther Plaut, *The Torah: A Modern Commentary* (New York: Union of American Hebrew Congregations, 1981), 1144ff.
4. The argument is made much more fully in the essay that appears in my book: James F. Moore, "The Israel-Shoah Link," *Toward a Dialogical Community* (Lanham, Md.: University Press of America, 2004), 73ff.
5. Our dialogues have been conducted on a regular basis principally as part of the Annual Scholars' Conference on the Holocaust and the Churches since 1993.
6. James F. Moore, *Toward a Dialogical Community* (Lanham, Md.: University Press of America, 2004).

Testing the Results of Richard Kalmin

A Null Hypothesis Examined in the Setting of Mishnah and Bavli Tractate Moed Qatan

Jacob Neusner

I. Richard Kalmin's hypothesis

Dr. Richard Kalmin, professor of Talmud at the Jewish Theological Seminary of America, has undertaken a variety of studies, yielding these results, based on his accompanying studies:[1]

1. "Formal aspects of Amoraic discourse provide evidence of generational contrast indicative of the diversity of talmudic source material . . . statements by later Amoraim are formally distinguishable from statements by earlier Amoraim."[2]
2. We may adduce "differences between the introductory formulae introducing statements by early, later, and middle-generation Amoraim. These differences . . . support my claim regarding the presence of diverse sources in the Bavli, distinguishable along chronological lines."[3]
3. "Middle generation Babylonian Amoraim [are] transitional. . . . [T]hese transitional features may reveal the role of third- and fourth-generation Amoraim in the editing of earlier Amoraic statements."[4]

These statements of Kalmin aim at a historical outcome: "early Amoraic generations . . . played a role in the editorial process."[5] By implication he wishes to validate attributions of sayings to named sages and so confirm the historical value of attributions. Kalmin's studies open the way to the present project, which is systematically to find evidences of layers of knowledge that are preserved in the final, coherent statement of the Talmud at the end of its development.[6]

One need not follow every detail of Kalmin's inquiry into the interplay of forms and attributions to appreciate his basic proposition, which is that the Bavli embodies the culmination of generations of cumulative results, and that we may follow the historical formation of the document by these layers. That history of the formation of the text defines Kalmin's purpose.

II. Survey of data

I pursue three questions, the third of which brings us to the problem of attributions.

First, do the same types and forms of Mishnah-exegesis and of Halakhah-analysis persist throughout the Bavli-tractate Moed Qatan and in what proportions? The analysis shows that they do. The work of form-analysis renders moot any distinction between the rhetorical form and the analytical type. The rhetoric ("where in Scripture do we find . . .") and the type (the foundation, in scripture, of the law of the Mishnah) are identical, the one providing a label for the logic of the other. The form embodies what the analytical logic requires, for example, this/not that, and/or, this and—all the more so—that. The forms and types of Mishnah-exegesis are listed in Table 1.

How shall we characterize the types and forms of Mishnah-exegesis? In the main—over half of our sample—Mishnah-exegesis in the sample before us is comprised by the citation and gloss of the Mishnah, its language and its law. Nearly a quarter of the sample is made up of inquiries into the meaning of the language of the Mishnah, a subset of citation and gloss. Add to that the citation of the Mishnah and the question, "whence in Scripture do we find proof that . . . ," and we have 82 percent of the whole. More to the point, we are able to classify with other-than-generic indicators (concession of a simple case, challenge to a complex one, perfection of the Mishnah, authority behind an anonymous rule, and the like) only a scattering of items. It suffices to say that the types and forms of Mishnah-exegesis yield few indications of differentiation and many of homogenization (see Table 2).

The types and forms of Halakhah-analysis come down to a single item: citation of a law, set forth whether in the Mishnah or in the Tosefta or in a baraita, joined by a gloss. That generic type encompasses 86 percent of the sample. The glossing is miscellaneous and not readily classified by indicator traits. The other entries are episodic. They suggest the possibility of taxonomy of analytical initiatives but prove too random to sustain such an exercise. Some categories are identical to those of the Mishnah, for example, how the exegesis of a verse yields the rule at hand, concession of an obvious case yielding a question on a complex one. Others have no clear counterpart in Mishnah-exegesis

Table 1. Mishnah

Citation of a rule + gloss on the application of the rule	39	54%
Concession of a simple case, challenge to a complex one	2	3%
Consistency of versions of the law	3	4%
Identification of the Named Authority behind the Anonymous Rule	3	4%
Meanings of words and phrases	16	22%
Perfection of the Mishnah: No redundancy, perfect cogency	3	4%
Reason behind the Mishnah's law	2	3%
Whence in Scripture do we find an indication that . . .	5	6%
Total	73	100%

Table 2. Halakhah

Clarification of what is subject to dispute	2	2%
Classification or clarification of an interstitial case	2	2%
Concession of an obvious case yielding a question on a complex one	2	2%
Declaration of a law and analysis thereof	84	86%
Declaration of the decided law	1	1%
Derivation of an inference of law from a clarification of a rule	1	1%
Distinction between an action for a licit purpose and for an illicit one	1	1%
How the exegesis of a verse yields the rule at hand	2	2%
Limitation placed on the applicability of a general rule	1	1%
Reasoning behind the law	1	1%
Sorting out interstitial occasions	1	1%
Total	98	100%

and validate the distinction between Mishnah-exegesis and Halakhah-analysis, for example, reasoning behind the law, distinction between an action for a licit purpose and for an illicit one.

Second, how do the several types and forms of Mishnah-exegesis and Halakhah-analysis relate: is it in fixed sequences, or not in a clearly indicated order? The outline of the tractate proves that they do follow fixed sequences. We now classify by authority the forms and types surveyed just now and determine the distribution by named authorities of the compositions of Bavli-tractate Moed Qatan. We want to know whether a particular type of exegesis or analysis is favored by a particular authority or set of authorities. We further should like to find out whether authorities assumed to have flourished early in the process of making the Talmud exhibit a preference for the more elementary type of exegesis or analysis—meanings of words and phrases, wording of the Mishnah, scriptural foundations of the Mishnah-law—and whether authorities reckoned as coming later in that process asked a type of question that took for granted the completion of that elementary program.

The issue is, do particular authorities of the Bavli specialize in particular types and forms of Mishnah-exegesis and Halakhah-analysis? Or do we find a random distribution of types and forms scattered among named authorities? The answer is that I discern no clear preference of a given authority for a type of exegesis or analysis. The catalogues of types and forms and how they are distributed that follow yield a one-sided result, with some noteworthy, but undemonstrated, tendencies.

Specifically, authorities who are assumed to have come early in the unfolding of the Talmud, such as Rab, Samuel, and Judah, do not predominate in the elementary initiatives, for example, the search in scripture for a foundation of a law, the explanation of the meanings of words and phrases. And authorities who are assumed to have flourished later on in the same process, such as Abbayye and Raba, are not excluded. There is a tendency to attribute to earlier figures, such as Judah, inquiries into the meanings of words and phrases. The key-category of Mishnah-exegesis and Halakhah-analysis, the citation of a law and the glossing and analysis of that law, encompasses authorities early, middle, and late. There is a tendency to attribute to later figures analytical initiatives.

But these two tendencies do not validate the proposition that the earlier authorities focused their attention on Mishnah-exegesis, with special attention to the meanings of words and phrases, the correct reading of the Mishnah-rules, and the scriptural foundations of the Mishnah-law. And they do not support the proposition that the middle and later authorities concentrated on the analysis of problems of law and legal theory, deeming the exegetical work to have been completed.

The catalogues that follow yield a negative conclusion, that *there is no correlation between types and forms of Mishnah-exegesis and Halakhah-analysis in our probe.*

Authorities of Mishnah-Exegesis by Types

Whence in Scripture do we find an indication that . . .

1:1–2 VII.1–3+4	Simeon b. Pazzi/Rabina/Ashi; Abbahu; Abbayye; Pappa; Hinena; Joshua b. R. Idi; Mar Zutra; Ashi; Rabina; glossed by a free-standing composition that cites Joshua b. Levi
1:7–8 I.2	Anonymous
3:5–6 I.5	Anonymous
3:5–6 I.12	Hiyya bar Abba, Ammi, Isaac Nappaha
3:5–6 I.22	Mattenah/Ina

Perfection of the Mishnah: No redundancy, perfect cogency

1:1 I.1	Anonymous
2:1 I.1	Shisha b. R. Idi/Ashi
2:2 I.1	Anonymous

Meanings of Words and Phrases

1:1 I.2	Anonymous
1:1 III.1	Judah

1:1 V.1	Abba
1:4 I.1	Judah/Raba bar Ishmael
1:5C–G II.1	Rab
1:6 I.1	Judah
1:6 II.1	Judah
1:6 III.1	Judah
1:7–8 IV.1	Yannai
1:7–8 V.1	Yohanan/Rabbah bar Samuel
1:7–8 VI.1	Dimi
2:5 I.1	Hiyya bar Abba/Assi
2:5 II.1	Anonymous
3:5–6 I.2	Anonymous
3:5–6 I.13	Said Rabbah bar bar Hannah said R. Yohanan

Identification of the Named Authority behind the Anonymous Rule set forth in the Mishnah

1:1 I.3	Huna, Pappa (Abbayye)
2:2 I.2	Isaac bar Abdimi
3:1–2 II.1	Raba
3:5–6 I.3	Amram/Rab
3:5–6 I.4	Abbayye (glosses foregoing: the decided law . . .)

Citation of a rule + gloss on the application of the rule

1:1 II.3	Jeremiah, Abbayye
1:1 VI.1	Jacob/Yohanan. Ashi
1:1–2 VII.6–7+8	Anonymous. The passage is glossed by Judah/Samuel, Judah bar Ammi/Judah, Pappa
1:1–2 VIII.1	Eleazar/Yose bar Hanina
1:3 I.1–3	Judah; Huna
1:4 I.2	Simeon b. Gamaliel/Yemar bar Shalamayya/Abbayye
1:4 II.1	Anonymous
1:4 II.2	Simeon b. Eleazar
1:4 III.1	Joseph
1:5C–G III.1	Kahana/Judah/Rab
1:7–8 I.1	Judah/Samuel, Eleazar/Oshaia or Hanina; Rabbah bar R. Huna + Abbayye
1:7–8 II.1	Hisda
1:7–8 II.2	Hisda/Hina bar Hinnena
1:7–8 III.1	Judah
1:10 I.1	Joseph
1:10 III.1	Hisda
1:10 IV.1	Raba, Abbayye
2:2 I:5	Huna/Rabbah bar R. Huna
2:3 I.1	Anonymous
2:3 II.1	Jeremiah/Zira
2:4A I.1	Raba/Nahman
2:4B–E I.1	Abbayye
2:4B–E II.1	Pappa/Raba
2:5 II.5	Huna/Kahana
3:1–2 III.1	Jeremiah/Zira
3:1–2 III.2	Hisda/Rabina bar Shila
3:1–2 III.3	Hisda/Shila
3:1–2 III.4	Ulla
3:1–2 IV.1	Assi/Yohanan/Jeremiah

3:1–2 IV.2	Raba/Abbayye/Bar Hedayya
3:3 I.1	Samuel
3:4 I.1	Samuel glosses
3:4 II.1	Samuel glosses
3:5–6 I.1	Rab/Huna/Sheshet
3:5–6 I.9–11	Huna/Hiyya bar Abba/Yohanan; Raba/Rabina
3:5–6 I.21	Case involving Rabbah bar bar Hanna illustrates Tannaite teaching
3:5–6 I.23–27	Idi bar Abin (minor gloss)
3:5–6 I.28–29	Hiyya bar Abba/Yohanan
3:5–6 I.30–31	Hiyya bar Kameda/*colleague of R. Abba bar Hiyya/R. Abba/R. Zira*
3:5–6 I.32	Abbayye
3:5–6 I.33	Rabbah bar bar Hanna
3:5–6 I.34	Anonymous
3:5–6 I.35	Simeon b. Eleazar
3:5–6 I.36	Abbahu
3:5–6 I.37	Anonymous
3:5–6 I.38	Rabin–Yohanan/Hiyya bar Abba/Hisda
3:5–6 I.40	Joshua b. Qorhah
3:5–6 I.41	Anonymous
3:5–6 I.42	Pappa
3:5–6 I.43	Anonymous/gloss (3:5–6 I.44) Abbayye and Raba
3:5–6 II.1	Judeans, Galilaeans
3:5–6 II.2	Yohanan
3:5–6 II.3–4	Yohanan/Samuel
3:5–6 II.6	Samuel/Rab
3:5–6 III.1	Giddal bar Menassia/Samuel
3:5–6 IV.1	Annani bar Sasson/Ammi
3:5–6 IV.2	Sheshet
3:5–6 IV.3	Pappa
3:7A–B I.1	Anonymous (+3:7A–B I.2: Safira)
3:7C–E 3:8A–C II.1	Pappa
3:7C–E 3:8A–C III.1	The Nehardeans

Concession of a simple case, challenge to a complex one

1:1–2 IV.1	Zira, Abba b. Mamel
1:10 II.1	Anonymous

The reason behind the Mishnah's law

1:1–2 IV.2	Amemar
3:1–2 I.1	Anonymous; glossed by Rabbah bar bar Hana

The consistency of versions of the law of the Mishnah or Tosefta: Clarifying conflicting traditions

1:5A–B I.3	Anonymous
1:5C–G	Abbayye

Authorities of Halakhah-Analysis by Types

Classification or clarification of an interstitial case

1:1 I.4	Rabbah, Joseph (Abbayye)
3:5–6 I.7	Abbayye/Rabbah

Concession of an obvious case yielding a question concerning a complex one

1:1 II.1	Ilaa/Yohanan v. Ashi

1:1 V.1	Anonymous. But a set of case-reports follows, with Abbayye, Jeremiah, and Ashi.

Citation of a rule + gloss on the application of the rule: Only if . . . even if . . .

1:1 II.3	Pappa vs. Ashi

Derivation of an inference of law from a clarification of a rule: What is at stake is . . . that leads to the inference that . . .

1:1–2 VIII.2	Jacob/Yohanan, Zebid, Mesharshayya

Limitation placed on the applicability of a general rule

1:4 III.2	Hisda

Clarification of what is subject to dispute

1:5A–B I.2	Raba
1:5A–B I.3	Anonymous
1:5A–B I.4	Glossed by Abbayye and Raba

How the exegesis of a verse yields the rule at hand

1:5A–B I.5	Abbayye/Raba
3:5–6 I.20	Ammi bar Hama

Distinction between doing an action for a licit purpose and doing it for an illicit purpose

1:9 I.6	Raba

Sorting out interstitial occasions or situations: The comparison of the laws governing an interstitial category

2:2 I.4	Hama bar Guria said Rab

The reasoning behind the law and the conflicting rulings yielded by that reasoning

3:1–2 I.2	Abbayye

Declaration of a law and analysis thereof

3:1–2 II.2	Samuel/Phineas/Ashi
3:1–2 II.2	As above
3:1–2 II.4	Anonymous
3:1–2 II.5	Joseph/Abbayye
3:1–2 II.6	Abbayye
3:1–2 II.7	Anonymous
3:1–2 II.8	Joseph/Abbayye
3:1–2 II.9	Pappa
3:1–2 II.10	Joseph/Abbayye
3:1–2 II.11	Rab
3:1–2 II.12	Anonymous
3:1–2 II.13	Anonymous
3:1–2 II.14	Anonymous
3:1–2 II.15	Joseph
3:1–2 II.16	Joseph
3:1–2 II.17	Joseph
3:1–2 II.18	Joseph/Abbayye
3:1–2 II.19	Joseph/Abbayye
3:1–2 II.20	Raba
3:1–2 II.23	Anonymous

3:1–2 II.24	Hisda
3:1–2 II.39	R. Tanhum b. R. Hiyya of Kefar Akko said R. Jacob bar Aha said R. Simlai
3:1–2 II.40	Joseph
3:1–2 II.45	Giddal/Rab, Pappa
3:5–6 I.6	Huna b. R. Joshua
3:5–6 I.15	Said R. Yose bar Abin/Adda of Caesarea-Yohanan
3:5–6 I.16	Mani/Hanina
3:5–6 I.17	Tannaite citation, no attributed gloss
3:5–6 II.7	Samuel/Yohanan
3:5–6 II.8	Rabin bar Ada/Raba
3:5–6 II.9	Oshaia and Bar Qappara
3:5–6 II.10	Raba
3:7A–B I.16–20	No telling attribution
3:7A–B I.21	Anonymous
3:7A–B I.22	As above
3:7A–B I.23	As above
3:7A–B I.24	Helbo/Huna
3:7A–B I.26	Helbo/Ulla/Eleazar
3:7A–B I.27	Anonymous
3:7A–B I.28	Hisda
3:7A–B I.29	Hisda
3:7A–B I.30	Anonymous
3:7A–B I.31	Ulla
3:7A–B I.32	Anonymous
3:7A–B I.33	Nahman/Samuel
3:7A–B I.34	Anonymous
3:7A–B I.35	Mattenah and Mar Uqba
3:7A–B I.36	Anonymous
3:7A–B I.37	Pappa
3:7A–B II.1	Anonymous
3:7A–B II.3	Anonymous
3:7A–B II.4	Anonymous
3:7A–B II.5	Anonymous
3:7A–B II.6–7	Anonymous
3:7A–B II.8	Anonymous
3:7A–B II.9	Anonymous
3:7C–E 3:8A–C I.1	Anonymous
3:7C–E 3:8A–C I.2	Anonymous
3:7C–E 3:8A–C II.3	Anonymous
3:7C–E 3:8A–C II.4	Yohanan
3:7C–E 3:8A–C II.5	Judah/Rab
3:7C–E 3:8A–C II.6	Anonymous
3:7C–E 3:8A–C II.9	Levi
3:8D–E 3:9 I.6	Yohanan
3:8D–E 3:9 I.7	Abbahu
3:8D–E 3:9 I.10	Levi bar Haita

Declaration of the decided law

3:5–6 I.8	Rabin/Yohanan; Eleazar, Pedat

Third and concomitantly, do compositions attributed to sets of authorities generally assumed to have flourished early in the period in which the Talmud took shape—Rab and Samuel, for example—

pursue a logical inquiry that is primary in the unfolding of the Halakhic-analysis, while compositions attributed to sets of authorities generally supposed to have flourished later in that period—Rabbah, Raba, and Abbayye, for instance—pursue analytical problems that rest on a logic subordinate to that governing in the inquiry assigned to earlier figures?[7] They do not.

Clearly, I pursue a null hypothesis. For such a correlation of sequences of authorities and the logical order of what is attributed to those authorities would provide a test of falsification of attributions. For attribution to an early authority of an analysis subordinate in logic or premise to what is assigned to a late authority would call into question the validity of the attribution: how could Rabbi X, who flourished in the third century, have assumed as an established rule of law what is otherwise subject to debate among authorities who flourished 200 years later?

III. Does Bavli Moed Qatan yield indications of layers of Talmudic knowledge?

When we attempt to correlate the types and forms of exegesis and analysis with the names of authorities associated with them, we produce no pattern that sustains differentiating discourse by layers, however indicated. I see no patterns of attribution of a determinate type of composition to a particular authority or set of authorities. For the most part, we have come up with a single governing pattern: citation and gloss, whether in Mishnah-exegesis or Halakhah-analysis. The attributions appear random and scattered.

If successive layers of writing accumulated in the process of the agglutination of the Bavli on Moed Qatan, we are unable to find the detritus of that process: forms characteristic of one generation but not of another. The thesis of a cumulative process produced a null hypothesis: if we deal with layers of knowledge, we should find formal indications thereof. But we find no evidence to sustain that hypothesis.

IV. Richard Kalmin's main results compared with those yielded by Bavli Moed Qatan

Richard Kalmin states: "formal aspects of Amoraic discourse provide evidence of generational contrast indicative of the diversity of talmudic source material . . . statements by later Amoraim are formally distinguishable from statements by earlier Amoraim."[8]

My form-analysis briefly summarized here and in detail set forth in *Contours of Coherence in Rabbinic Judaism* does not replicate Kalmin's result.[9] His articles are richly documented, and this contradictory outcome requires an explanation.

I went in search of recurrent patterns of a gross order, repeatedly characteristic of large blocks of writing, and I came up with one principal pattern, the citation and gloss of a passage of the Mishnah, Tosefta, or external Halakhic source. I did not attempt to distinguish one citation + gloss exegesis or analysis from another; to me they conform to a single pattern.

Kalmin proceeds to another claim I could not replicate in my sample:

> We may adduce "differences between the introductory formulae introducing statements by early, later, and middle-generation Amoraim. These differences . . . support my claim regarding the presence of diverse sources in the Bavli, distinguishable along chronological lines."[10]

Here Kalmin focuses on "introductory formulae," which I took to mean, "Our rabbis have taught on Tannaite authority" and similar rhetorical cliches. He clearly has in mind a much more refined set of criteria.

> Middle generation Babylonian Amoraim [are] transitional. . . . [T]hese transitional features may reveal the role of third- and fourth-generation Amoraim in the editing of earlier Amoraic statements.[11]

Here Kalmin produces a correlation that I could not demonstrate. But the difference is in premise, not form-analysis. He seems to me to rely on attributions for his indicative data, working from the attribution to the classification of "early/middle/late." But I assume nothing about attributions, except that they represent data requiring verification. So Kalmin's path was closed to me by the question that precipitated the inquiry: do we find correlations of type or form and sequence of attributions? I could not assume at the outset what I set out to investigate.

Accordingly, I account for the contradictory results produced here in a simple way. First, in the first two of his three propositions Kalmin understands by form, and by form-analysis, much more refined data than the gross indicators that governed my classification. Second, Kalmin is less troubled than I am by the problem of testing the reliability and intent of attributions.

V. Does an exegetical program govern throughout? Do analytical initiatives of a particular type recur?

Let me now articulate the outcome of my probe into the layers of Talmudic knowledge in Bavli Moed Qatan.

First, do the same types and forms of Mishnah-exegesis and of Halakhah-analysis persist throughout the Bavli-tractate probed here and in what proportions? Yes, citation and gloss, subdivided into a few specific types of exegetical inquiry, account for nearly the whole of the exegesis of the Mishnah. The counterpart exercises of the Halakhic-analyses produce the same result. Nearly the whole of the Talmud's work of exegesis and analysis requires citation and gloss for its form, clarification of issues of consistency, and coherence for its content. That is without regard to the names or provenance of the authorities to whom sayings are attributed.

Second, how do the several types and forms of Mishnah-exegesis and Halakhah-analysis relate: is it in fixed sequences, or not in a clearly indicated order? Mishnah-exegesis invariably takes priority over Halakhah-analysis. The program is fixed: first clarify the Mishnah, then pursue analytical questions of law. My reference system, with its ordinal enumeration of compositions, signals that result throughout; a glance at the outline of the tractate confirms that impression.

Third, analytical initiatives of a particular type do recur and do predominate in all types of compositions and among all named authorities: citation of the received formulation of the law, whether in the Mishnah or in the Tosefta or in a collection external to both, then exposition or refinement of the law.

VI. Do determinate types of exegesis and analysis recur in particular names or sets of names?

The indicated types of exegesis and analysis are randomly scattered among particular names or sets of names. This result is particularly troubling in light of Kalmin's contrary result.

VII. Is it true that with adequately classified data in hand, we may describe the generative logic of Talmudic analysis as that exegetical and analytical process unfolded in sequences signified by the requirements of a pure, atemporal dialectics?

The Mishnah and the Tosefta are so composed as to permit the correlation of logic and attribution. What is assigned to an early authority is fundamental in logic; what is assigned to a later authority that intersects is subordinate in logic. With that result in hand, I asked, do we discern evidences of temporal sequence, signaled by successive generations of rabbinic authorities in the Bavli? I wanted to know whether sets of authorities generally assumed to have flourished early in the period in which the Talmud took shape—Rab and Samuel, for example—pursue a logical inquiry that is primary in the unfolding of the Halakhic-analysis, while sets of authorities generally supposed to have flourished later in that period—Rabbah, Raba, and Abbayye, for instance—pursue analytical problems that rest on a logic subordinate to that governing in the inquiry assigned to earlier figures.

Even if we were to follow Kalmin's lead in taking for granted that the rabbinic sages really said what is attributed to them, we could not reconstruct an unfolding logic corresponding in its development from simplicity to complexity as successive generations of sages joined in the exegetical and analytical work. What the Mishnah and the Tosefta exposed—a correspondence between the sequence of generations and the unfolding from fundamental to secondary, primary to subordinate—the Talmud simply does not make manifest. That is not because discussions do not unfold in ever more refined and complex sequences of thought. Protracted dialectical arguments do just that. But those dialectical arguments are constructed in response to applied logic that transcends attributions to named authorities of particular components of the composition.

In general, in the Bavli, questions of a primary character may surface in the names of authorities, early, middle, and late. A survey of sayings attributed to "middle" and "late" authorities will sustain that claim.

But we need not invoke the alleged sequence of named generations. Rather, the Talmud's sustained and systematic expositions simply are not constructed in accord with, and do not take account of, sequences of generations. They pursue their own logic, their own dialectics, without matching primary to early names, subordinate to later ones. The Bavli exhibits its own traits of composition and the agglutination of composites, and its interest in attributions is for considerations not comparable to those that govern in the Mishnah and the Tosefta.

It is solely by paraphrasing the Talmud itself that we may indeed describe the generative logic of Talmudic analysis as that exegetical and analytical process unfolded in sequences signified by the requirements of a pure, atemporal dialectics. Stating the matter simply: the attributions of sayings to named authorities within a dialectical analysis of the law do not bear upon the exposition of the analytical process.

VIII. Deciphering the architectonics of Talmudic knowledge: What, exactly, can we make of attributions?

Kalmin aims at a historical outcome: "early Amoraic generations . . . played a role in the editorial process."[12] Thinking in historical terms, he has interpreted the data of attributions to yield historical results: order, correlation of time and sequence of intellectual events. I have not found it possible to replicate his results. I could not establish the correlations required to validate his results.

Two reasons account for the difference. First, as I said, I think each of us invokes for "form-analysis" different criteria for defining what is meant by "forms." And second, what Kalmin takes as a datum I subject to doubt. He seems certain that attributions bear a fixed significance wherever they occur, in all documents meaning a given authority, at a given time and venue, really said what is stated in his name. I do not share his certainty, which is why where he concludes, I commence, the inquiry.

The experiment conducted here produced a negative result: the classification of types and forms of the Talmud yields no correlation with attributions. The distinct compositions are randomly distributed among diverse authorities, whose sayings exhibit no patterns—sequences of logic corresponding to attributions of statements to sequences of historical order for example. The outcome of the probe conducted here is to recast the issue of attributions as a medium for identifying the layers of Talmudic knowledge. Different documents use attributions—what they claim attributions represent as firm knowledge adumbrates the way forward. It is to ask how, in the Bavli in particular, do attributions function?

Notes

1. Collected in Richard Kalmin, *Sages, Stories, Authors and Editors in Rabbinic Babylonia* (Atlanta: Scholars Press for Brown Judaic Studies, 1995). I checked with him about this brief precis of his main results and he confirmed that it is an accurate account.
2. "Unique formal characteristics of later Amoraic discourse," in ibid., 111.
3. "Quotation forms in the Babylonian Talmud," in ibid., 127.
4. "Middle-Generation Amoraim as among the editors of the Talmud," in ibid., 169.
5. Kalmin, *Sages, Stories*, 172.
6. I know of no other systematic work on the problem, and his extensive notes in *Sages, Stories* do not suggest otherwise.

7. My *History of the Mishnaic Law*, 43 vols. (Leiden, 1974–86), pursued a comparable problem. It is, can we correlate the attributions of sayings to authorities of the Mishnah assumed to have flourished early in the sequence of generations with the standing of what is attributed to them in the larger unfolding of the law? That is, do we find that what is assigned to early authorities concerns primary and generative conceptions of the law, while what is attributed to later ones addresses secondary and derivative ones? If that is the case, then we have sequences of ideas matching sequences of sets of authorities, the order of authorities matching the logical standing of what is assigned to those same authorities. I found that that is the case where the inquiry is sustained by the evidence, that is, where we have sequences of authorities and sets of rules set forth in ordinal relationships of persons, bearing rulings that intersect and exhibit the traits of logical unfolding, there the process yields an affirmative result. It is most, most unusual for a saying assigned to an early authority to rest on premises attested only by sayings attributed to a later one. The great exception to that rule is the Houses of Shammai and Hillel, who are not uncommonly represented as disputing secondary and derivative issues otherwise first attested in disputes among mid-second-century figures, Judah, Meir, Simeon, and the like. I showed that that is the case for the entirety of tractate Makhshirin in *Form Analysis and Exegesis: A Fresh Approach to the Interpretation of Mishnah* (Minneapolis: University of Minnesota Press, 1980).
8. "Unique formal characteristics of later Amoraic discourse," 111.
9. Neusner, *Contours of Coherence in Rabbinic Judaism* (Leiden: E. J. Brill, 2005).
10. "Quotation forms in the Babylonian Talmud," 127.
11. "Middle-Generation Amoraim as among the editors of the Talmud," 169.
12. Kalmin, *Sages, Stories*, 172.

Creation and Mortalization

A Religio-Literary Perspective

Sara R. Mandell

It is an honor and privilege to write for a *Festschrift* paying tribute to Zev Garber. He is an exceptional scholar; but, more importantly, he is a kind and considerate man, who shows a depth of feeling for those with whom he interacts.

* * *

Although we generally approach Gen. 1:1–3:24, the first *major* pericope in the Hebrew Scriptures,[1] as a religious text, the narrative as many have noted contains a number of intertwined and powerful literary *topoi* that are frequently found in epic.[2] This is not surprising since this pericope, although not an epic unto itself, is the introduction to the remainder of Genesis as well as the prose epic work, Genesis through 2 Kings (Primary History).[3]

Gen. 1:1–3:24 does use some of the same myth types as non-Israelite works with which it is sometimes compared, but this does not primarily result from the presence of epic genre, "mix and match" precepts regarding a universality of folklore elements, and it is not an emanation from some "collective unconsciousness" that itself generates archetypes. Rather, even expecting there to be a number of identical myth types in the same or related genres, the similarity of development as well as the congruity of those found in non-Israelite works and Gen. 1:1–3:24 are quantitatively beyond what is plausible or probable.[4] More important than the quantity of individual, specific, thematic as well as architectonic parallels is that even complex pericopes are developed analogously despite the intricacy of their structure.[5]

The two redactors of Gen. 1:1–3:24, J and P, undoubtedly changed what they received to fit their theoliterary preconceptions while retaining a sufficient amount of its earlier integrity. Because they were not contemporaneous, they have among other things very disparate world and theological viewpoints that reflect the different centuries and locales in which they wrote and the different cultic environment in which they participated.[6] Gen. 1:1–2:4a is attributed to P, whose dating has been debated. The *communis opinio* but not *consensio opinionis* is that P completed it during the Babylonian Exile or the Restoration,[7] or the early Second Temple Era.[8] It is possible that the tradition or the school from whence P emanated was something relatively new, arising during the exile. There is, however, a *communis opinio*, but no *consensio opinionis*, that the Priestly School had been in existence long before this time.[9]

The Priestly Redactor seems primarily interested in the "Philosophy of Order" and, as many have noted, in the cultic, and this is both reflected and introduced in Gen. 1:1–2:4a.[10] His cultic-theo-philosophical narrative, which now forms the introduction to the entire Hebrew Scriptures, acts as one part of a frame that enhances J's storytelling of the Creation-Garden-Expulsion narrative. So, the interest in ordering in Gen. 1:1–2:4a sets the philosophical and concomitantly literary "tone" for P's redaction of the Tetrateuch.

Gen. 2:4b–3:24 is attributed to J, whom some believe early (tenth century BCE), and some later, or as late as the Second Temple Era.[11] Unlike P, J does not seem to be particularly interested in cultic matter or philosophic discourse. Sometimes J might act as an original author rather than a redactor. And at times being "storyteller" and others, a "remembrancer," he may, but does not always, hand down stories long in circulation. We cannot consistently categorize him as either one or the other since in antiquity both authors and redactors followed much the same procedures: editing, altering, and adapting traditional oral and/or written materials to serve their own ends, be they ideological, theological, or literary.[12]

Despite his cultic focus, P was clearly not a literary "hack," without consideration of and feel for literary context. Nor was he so blinded by his own theological or theopolitical beliefs that he could only understand what he read from his own faith perspective. So we must assume that when he set Gen. 1:1–2:4a before Gen. 2:4b–3:24, he was clearly aware of the differences between his view of creation and J's, both in its theological outlook and in its literary style. And he did not excise J's portion either because it served his own ends to retain it or because it was so commonly accepted that he could not get rid of it. Although it seems unlikely but not impossible that P made internal alterations in J's narrative save for having possibly lopped off its beginning, he significantly modified the text simply by prefacing J's account in such a way that his work subsumed J's pericope into what is now the composite Gen. 1:1–3:24 pericope.[13] This simple act definitively altered both the theology and literary format of J's pericope so that the reader reads J's pericope in context of P's introduction rather than as an independent entity or within the framework of the following Yahwistic episode (Genesis 4).[14]

Thematically, once P has prefaced J's work, the narrative describes the creation of everything, including the precursor of humankind, but not of the Lord-God himself. It is characteristic of the entirety of Primary History, to which Gen. 1:1–3:24 is the introduction, that the Deity's existence is taken for granted and not justified by the unidentified implied narrator of the pericope, who is "reporting" the events and telling the story.[15] The inversion of the order in which "Man" *adam* or "the Man" *ha'adam* is created in the now combined pericope merely stresses the focal nature of that specific act of creativity from a literary perspective.

The important status of the created being, which is called Man, includes what is "other," that is, its or his female component, be it included or derivative.[16] The female "other" is treated as an inclusive component of the creation of Man in P's portion of the combined pericope insofar as he (actually it), that is the Man, was defined as having been created as a male, who is explicitly and immediately redefined as both male and female.[17] In J's portion, the female "other" is treated as derivative insofar as she is created from the rib or side of the Man. Moreover, there is a temporal differentiation. The Priestly Redactor's other was created as a component of the singular, but, because of the immediacy of the redefinition, he seems to have been created simultaneously as a dual entity that is both male and female. The Yahwist's other was the result of a separate and later act of creation in which the Deity facilitates the birth of the Woman/other, who is clearly but not explicitly defined as female, from the Man, who is clearly but not explicitly defined as male. The Priestly Redactor's other was not created to serve a different end than that of the differentiated and explicitly designated male component of the entire created entity, itself designated as Man.

Although we learn that the purpose of the Man's creation is to keep and tend the Garden,[18] there is focus on his role as suzerain of all the created beings within the Garden both because he was appointed to that role (Gen. 1:26) and by virtue of the power to name. But the Man is not suzerain of the Garden itself since that belongs to the Lord-God. So the Man's violation of his suzerain's, that is, the Lord-God's, interdiction not to eat of the tree that is in the center of the Garden is conjoined with his own acquisition of "knowledge," which leads to the possibility that he may also obtain eternal life. This, however, is a conundrum since he is already in the Garden, in which there is no delimiting time of life. So, it is meaningful that Gen. 1:1–3:24 concludes with what had been J's depiction of the mortalization and expulsion of that being, now by virtue of naming become respectively a specific and individual man and woman, Adam and Eve, who are the forbears of all of humankind from the Garden and from the possibility of eternal life.

Part(s) of this composite pericope may have once circulated in the secular or folk tradition.[19] Although this may have occurred prior to their being taken up by those redactors to whom we attribute them, there is no basis for assuming that they ceased to exist as such once they had been incorporated into the religious perception of the two redactors or of their forebears. Moreover, we must not assume that some matter had been incorporated into a redactor's text because he was composing in a particular period or that it had been received by him solely in writing as a religious formulation. Various sagas or other forms of narrative presentation may have been part of the traditions of a school represented by the redactor. They would have been incorporated into those traditions either orally or in writing prior to the period in which the redactor worked.[20] If they had been transmitted orally, no matter how formulaically, the very act of presentation would have altered them, causing them to change and develop as time passed unless there were a written formulation within the tradition itself with which the oral rendering could be compared. But even if there were some written rendering in some other tradition, it is not likely that a redactor would "check" his received tradition against a foreign one, either oral or written, and it is not a requirement that he would check it against one that came from some other segment of his greater ethnic or "faith" group.[21] Although we must analyze and comprehend the completed theoliterary composite pericope as if it were a unified entity, we must not forget that parts of it may or more likely had to have been perceived differently when they were part of the secular tradition, and would continue to be perceived differently by those for whom they were still part of a folk or secular tradition, just as parts of it may or more likely had to have been perceived differently even within the religiohistorical tradition as it developed before P prefaced J's creation narrative with his own. Moreover, no matter how the composite major pericope appears in the received tradition, it was, is, and must be perceived, understood, and valued differently by different readers insofar as the reader interacts with the text. This is as true today as it was at the time of its redactors, whose dating is still in debate (above).

This variance in perception, and therefore in its resultant analysis of the pericope, is mainly due to the way in which the reader interacts with the text. But it is also due to what is *not* said or described, that is, to the gaps or *lacunae* in the narrative. Since each reader, generally albeit unconsciously, fills in the "legitimate" gaps in any narrative accordance with his own life-experiences and worldview, he will interpret and understand what he reads differently than do others.[22] This filling in of the gaps results in textual uncovering or deconstructing hypertexting (literary), which itself is defined as the layering(s) of the narrative. In practical terms this is one, but not the only, process of getting "under" the text as presented. Once done, it helps the reader give a fuller meaning to and thereby gain what seems to him to be a more complete understanding of the text, *albeit from his own perspective*, thereby representing his own "interaction" with the text. Therefore it is consequential for each reader that not all of the hypertext, (layering[s] of text), in Gen. 1:1–3:24 emanates from P, who is responsible for the partial framing of the narrative of that pericope as it stands within the received tradition and therefore even for the way in which the reader perceives what really had been J's. Because P framed the text by prefacing his own creation narrative to it, he is responsible for the entirety of the final form of the pericope.[23]

Precisely because someone, probably J, had reshaped traditional material "into a new and original literary myth of origins,"[24] or someone else, probably P, had reshaped traditional or even cultic material that may once have been a myth accompanying a ritual practiced when the Jerusalemite Temple (either First or Second Temple) still stood or what the redactor thought would have been practiced if the Temple had been standing, we look at at least four, and possibly more, levels of hypertext in a relatively reverse temporal order: (1) that intended by P in the entirety of Gen. 1:1–3:24, which he made his own by framing J's pericope; (2) that intended by P in his own minor pericope (Gen. 1:1–2:4a); (3) that intended by J in the minor (although major prior to its prefacing by P) pericope that we attribute to him (Gen. 2:4b–3:24); and (4) that intended by those tradents or keepers of the cult who were responsible for the various traditions prior to their assumption by the known redactors.[25]

We do not know whether the redactors to whom we assign the responsibility of reformulation were in fact the first to include specific gaps in the narrative or whether they existed in the traditions these redactors inherited. Granted that both J and P may but need not have yet other prior traditions, we can state that whoever was responsible for reformulating what ultimately became P's or J's portion respectively as a sacred myth of origins, be it for ritual usage, "historical respective"[26] or not, must have been responsible for making some type of hypertexting fit his narrative perception, whether he presented his narrative in such a way as to formulate these gaps or whether he allowed gaps that were in what he had received to remain. We cannot say how conscious he was of what he was doing. This would necessitate a "psychological profile" of the redactor or his predecessors, which we do not have any data to substantiate and which we cannot recreate. But, in any case, the better a craftsman he was, the more meaningful would his hypertexting have been whether its delimitation was a consciously crafted literary device or not.

Biblical scholars have attempted to get behind the present text insofar as determining the genre and "remembrancing" status, including the individual minor pericopes' former *Sitz im Leben* or even series of *Sitzen im Leben* by applying form criticism, and the "remembrancing" as well as the literary status by applying tradition history, and redaction or higher criticism. And they have also used various literary theory methodologies such as new criticism, structuralism, reader response criticism, deconstruction, and so on. In general, literary criticism demands that all these as well as other methodologies be applied. From a (modern) literary perspective, which is different from although included in what biblical scholars define as literary critical studies per se, we must work with the final form of the text, while remembering and taking into account the affect that redactoral activity has had on the narrative. Consequently, we work as if we can assume that what we have today is pretty much what P and J presented although P's prefacing as well as his framing of J's material makes J's intent dubious. So if we interpret the data properly, we can still only theorize about the way in which these two respective redactors wished the reader to understand their myth of origins. But although we can do so with a greater degree of certainty for P than for J, this too may be problematic. For who is to say what is the proper interpretation of that data which is even today so controversial.

Granting all of these uncertainties, J seems to have begun his work with what is now Gen. 2:4b.[27] Clearly the combined P and J work makes some matters problematic; however, it is precisely this that renders the narrative interesting from theoliterary and literary-politico perspectives. In P's narrative, creation is presented as a sequenced list of events that commences with "In the beginning, (when) God created the Heavens and the Earth" (Gen. 1:1), and seemingly ends with "These are the generations of the Heavens and the Earth" (Gen. 2:4a), a verse which, as Cross has observed, P uses to introduce J's version of the creation story.[28] As others have commented, this formulaic statement that is generally deemed to conclude P's creation narrative, but which Cross treats as introducing J's, can also properly be translated: " 'this is the origin of the heavens and the earth,' i.e., the story of their origin."[29] Although both accounts show Ancient Near Eastern influences, P's in particular may have been influenced by Babylonian mythology of very old provenience,[30] and J's account may be partially dependent on or related to Mesopotamian traditions and literature, some of which is also of very old provenience.[31] We know for example that the Garden (and tree) Myth is not (specifically) of Israelite origin.

While it is sometimes thought that P's account is more purely Judahite and less tainted by both the written and oral Near Eastern traditions than is J's, this is not the case.[32] Certainly, if P were exilic, his exile in Babylon would have exposed him to at least the SB *Gilgamesh*, and most likely other Sumero-Assyro-Babylonian traditions as well. Even if P did live in Judah and Jerusalem during the Second Temple Era, it is quite likely that he was familiar with these same traditions and literary works, or he may have known stories coming from them without knowing their provenience. And, in any case, the absence of the Man's mortalization in P's account reflects P's exilic or Second Temple Era theopolitical ideology, which demands that there be a type of human chain analogous to the "Great Chain of Being" directly linking them with "the Man," whom the Deity created. At the same time, by retaining J's delineation of mortalization, P does allow the concept of mortalization to be part of the narrative. The Priestly Redactor built his story on a model in which the hero or a "hero," who is both a singular male and at the same time a plurality, being male and female, is created in the image of the Deity, who himself is both a singular and plural entity.[33] In J's narrative, nothing is said about the hero's creation in the image of the Deity.[34] So it is significant that only J built the mortalization of the hero into his story in such a way that it becomes one of the pericope's two major motifs.[35] The hero's likeness to the Deity in J's account may reflect J's orientation to his surroundings, whatever they were, as well as his man centered mythological universe.[36]

What does matter is that P seems to have allowed J's creation account to stand.[37] Whether or not P actually textually modified J's account other than the framing type of modification resultant on his prefixing it has not been ascertained, and in any case is not pertinent to this discussion.[38] The Priestly Redactor retained J's account because it included a discussion of the created being's imperfection and consequent mortalization.[39] By retaining J's account, which he or one of his sources had already conjoined with an "older" stratum in which creation is represented by "a series of births," P could present his own philosophically oriented version of creation by the divine word.[40] Meaningfully, the combination allowed him to depict the Man, whom the Deity created without intervention, as virtually the creator's own hypostasis at the same time as he presented him as a male and female being.[41] So without saying that the Deity is himself in the form of a male-female entity, the combined text itself would lead the implied reader to that conclusion. At the same time, J's presentation would allow him to account for that hypostasis' disobedience without showing the allomorph of what is perfect to be imperfect. Notably, then, this matter must have presented P with an interesting conundrum if the expulsion from the Garden was part of the tradition P inherited, which is likely, and/or would or could not discard. Hence, when P edited the work, placing his own creation account before that of J, he let the interesting distinction between his representation of creation and that of the Yahwist remain in the narrative so as to suit his theological, not his cultic or literary, ends.[42]

Despite the elaborations in the verse, we cannot take the statement in Gen. 1:27 to refer to "humankind" as the created entity, as many scholars wish, precisely because the noun "Man" is articulated.[43] And we must not forget that unlike the generic term "man," in J's own verse in Gen. 1:26, which we must not read as a hypertext having reference to females camouflaged by a specifically male referent, the specification of the Man rather than simply Man in verse 1:27 of J's creation story must be deemed specific. So the term cannot represent humankind, but some paradigmatic male figure having the female implicit in it.[44] And when we see a lack of clear delineation of gender in Gen. 1:27 where gender is noted, despite the stress on the superior status of the maleness as the likeness of Elohim, it becomes clear that that creation is liminal despite the specification of it as Man or the Man.

Because he has the potential to remain in the Garden forever, the Man has an even greater potential to be liminoid, that is, permanently liminal. But J's narrative shows the inevitability of the limitation of his stay, thus defining him as liminal, when it depicts the Man as not even questioning the Woman when she gives him the fruit of the interdicted tree to eat. This is not to be hypertexted so as to understand what they may have or have not said to one another. Clearly, this was not meaningful to J or he would have included it. Rather, the "gaping" here has a functional significance. So when, according to the Yahwistic narrative, the Man simply takes and eats, he is thereby performing both the forbidden and yet symbolic action that in and of itself will and does bring about an alteration of state. Once he has eaten, both his own sense of physical exposure and whatever punishment is to be inflicted are each after the fact. It is not that he has "sinned," as later interpretations would have it, as others have noted. It is that he has become different from what he was. Therefore, it goes without saying that this alteration has itself altered his state to the extent that he is no longer the same as he was before having eaten. So, by definition, he cannot remain liminoid, as defined by being permanently in a liminal state, since this is his state prior to alteration. Only at this point in the narrative does he enter a true, transitional state of liminality.

But it is precisely Man's or the Man's prior liminoid rather than liminal status that suggests that he is to be thought of as the paradigmatic initiand,[45] and the text is the narrative for a creation/birth and humanization rite of passage.[46] So, the critical reader may and in fact must ask what role the Woman plays in this creation/birth and humanization initiation ritual. The narrative depicts her as a facilitator rather than an initiator, although she might have been the latter in earlier traditions. In Gen. 1:1–3:24 she is not the model anything. This is totally in accord with the traditions of male birthing that anthropologists have found in societies in various parts of the world.[47]

From an anthropological perspective, it is important that P in the received text defines "the Man" as created in the image of Elohim (Gen. 1:27) and as created both male and female (Gen. 1:27c).

That is, he is created as if he, in and of himself, were a complete set of doubles or nonidentical twins. The Priestly Redactor shows that the male part of this twin may have priority over the female by virtue of the "stair-like parallelism" he employs in Gen. 1:27b–c ("in the image of Elohim he created him/it; male and female he created them"), by virtue of which male and female both emanate from the male image, which itself is the likeness of Elohim. So Man is also created in the likeness/image ("in our likeness/image"), that is as an icon or a hypostasis of the Deity (Gen. 1:26–27).[48] In fact, the creation of man in Elohim's image, that is as a hypostasis of Elohim, is stressed by the parallelism inherent in the near repetition of the statement in Gen. 1:26a ("and Elohim said let us make Man in our image, according to our likeness") with chiastic parallelism in Gen. 1:27ab ("And Elohim created the Man in his image: in the image of Elohim, he created him"), to which is appended almost as an afterthought, by stair-like parallelism as I have already noted, the interesting conundrum in Gen. 1:27c ("he created them male and female").[49]

The basic *personae* are also doubles in J's story: but they were not created simultaneously as in P's account. The creation of the Woman from the rib or from the side of the Man is representative of a twofold creature, that is, a creature whose components are siblings and possibly nonidentical twins.[50] The Yahwist does not give us any indication of how long the Man was in existence prior to the Deity's creation of the Woman. From a New Critical perspective, this would mean that it is not important to J's narrative. But from a "deconstruction"-oriented perspective, this is meant to open the various possibilities to the reader's interpretation.[51] In either case, because of her creation from the Man's rib, the Woman is younger and therefore presumably lesser than the Man.[52] Significantly, in both P and J, *the Man and the Woman are created fully grown.*

Anthropologically, the role of twins and/or doubles is of great importance in understanding the relationship between the Man and the Woman. In primal societies, when there are twins, either death or the denial of the relationship between the two or sometimes of the existence or status of one of the two is almost always predicated. Hence, in looking at the way in which primal societies view twins, we see something about the monstrous nature and the ultimate mortality of this abnormal and thereby terrible birth. It is because this monstrous thing is intolerable that the Man and the Woman had to be categorized and distinguished from one another: he as a male and a farmer as his name indicates, and she as a female and a life-giver as her name indicates. This is accomplished by naming, which itself represents a transformation as well as a classification. So the Man and the Woman were changed, categorized, and most important distinguished from one another by becoming Adam and Eve respectively.

Only after they have been acknowledged as separate, named, and thereby classified entities, "catechized"—the real significance of the so-called curse—and reclothed in the skins that will now become their dress, could they be expelled from the Garden and sent out into sacred but nonliminal space. At this point, the ritual initiation into humanization, which is emphasized by the denotation of the name Eve—the mother of all life— is complete.[53] Meaningfully, Woman now becomes the "birther" of life, which is no longer from the earth, thus giving an etiologic explanation of why human males do not give birth to their offspring by creation or by fiat as both Elohim and various gods in other societies often do.[54] Gen. 1:1–3:24 is not an etiologic saga, and so this must be considered an offshoot of the far more basic ritual. As such, it defines humanization as being characterized by female birthing rather than explaining how female birthing came to be. But this is not the only ritual depicted in Gen. 1:1–3:24. So at the same time as the humanization ritual is being brought to completion, another ritual, that of mortalization, is brought to the point where the potential for but not actual experience of mortalization is also complete.

The problem of the mortalization of Man in this pericope has been much debated. But the basic relationship of the two trees in the Garden to that mortalization is viewed in varying ways. The fundamental conundrum is that according to J, the Man is threatened with immediate death should he eat of the Tree of Knowledge of Good and Evil (Gen. 2:17; 3:3), but he does not die on the day in which he has eaten. Meaningfully Northrop Frye, Kenneth Burke, and others before them, such as J. G. Frazer, either call the Tree of Knowledge of Good and Evil a "tree of death"[55] or sometimes simply treat the tree's spirit as related to death.[56] Frazer suggests that the tree was not even a tree of knowledge, but exclusively a death tree.[57] If he is correct, this Tree of Death can be viewed as standing opposed to the

Tree of Life.[58] But, clearly, J or his predecessors had modified this set of matched opposites to bring it in line with "Wisdom" precepts regarding both creation and destruction.[59]

The nature of the two central trees in the Garden is of great importance to the narrative. Meaningfully the lack of seeds in this fruit of the Tree of Knowledge shows it to be an unbroken entity, which like the egg is representative of the life cycle. So, P, from whose perspective the fruit of the Wisdom Tree in J's account is at once different from and yet must be the same as the fruit of the Tree of Life and the Tree of Death—although J himself only seems to recognize the disparity, not the identity—is actually reverting to an archetypal Tree of Life paradigm by granting Man permission to eat of any seed-bearing plant or fruit. Whereas the fruit of the Tree of Life may have been available to Man and Woman in the Garden in J's account, as Fewell and Gunn note, this is no longer to be seen as viable once P has prefaced J's pericope with his own account.[60]

If we include the full received title of the tree, including the term "Good and Evil," we can arrive at an important aspect or definition of the tree. Since "Good and Evil" may mean "everything" as others have noted,[61] and since there may well be a "tie-in" between Israelite and Egyptian saga, and since analogies between the Gen. 1:1–3:24 and Middle Egyptian sagas as well as morphology vis-à-vis the creation from clay and "Adam's" rib have been noted,[62] I suggest that there is a hidden meaning, implicit in the text, that is also dependent on Middle Egyptian morphology. The term "Good and Evil" may be a play on the Middle Egyptian, in which the same sign has two different meanings: 𓎟 = nb, without the determinative means "everything"; but with it 𓎟𓏤, it means "lord" or "master." Significantly, it is the Man who is the master of everything in the Garden, with only the Tree of Knowledge of Good and Evil not under his jurisdiction. So, by implication, that tree of which he is not the suzerain is the tree of the knowledge of himself as well as of the Deity. It is really the Tree of Death precisely because it is the tree of knowledge of man, and therefore of mortality. As such, it is opposed to the Tree of Life, which is also the tree of the Deity and, therefore, of immortality; this is why J may have envisioned the two trees (Tree of Life and Tree of Knowledge of Good and Evil) rather than the ubiquitous World Tree. That the Tree of Life had potentially been available to the Man and the Woman is not relevant since, had they eaten of it, they would indeed have become like Elohim and lived forever.

But if we delete from the tree's name "Good and Evil," a term that not only represents a figure of speech and means "everything," "lord," or "master" and which may make insinuations regarding the Man's and the Woman's knowledge or at least awareness of their sexuality, we may say that they eat of the "Wisdom Tree." This is both the Tree of Death and, in the cycle of things, of human Life, which comprehensively defines it as the tree of mortality. Its fruit, being seedless, unlike that of the explicitly named Tree of Life that gives eternal life, must have been able to give mortal life by an asexual type of creation. If this type of creation represents a form of divine creativity, then its fruit itself may be a product of nonsexually effected birth that is analogous to the other types of nonsexually effected birthing that had already occurred in both P's and J's narratives. But here it is the tree's fruit rather than the creator deity himself that can be classified as the parent. This presentation may reflect J's understanding that the Tree of Life was also the sacred *asherah*, which itself was a cultic symbol of the goddess Asherah. Notably, since J delineates Yahweh alone as creating without sexuality, Eve may here be a demythologized form of Asherah, which is why J would have his implied narrator depict what happened in such a way that more of the onus seems to be on her than on her man/husband.[63] The Yahwist may well have recognized the origins of the *persona* and her relationship to Asherah. However, even if he did not realize the broader religious inferences of his presentation, he may well have recognized the sexual intimations into which he was weaving his narrative, or had simply inherited from the *Vorlagen* of his narrative even though he excluded them from specific portions of it.[64]

Since "Wisdom" is directly related to knowledge of divine creativity, this eating of the fruit of the Wisdom Tree, then, is relevant to far more important matters than sexuality: it indicates that they had acquired Godlike knowledge about unisexual creativity as well as other things, but not necessarily omniscience.[65] And, like J's deity, P's creator deity himself is not omniscient since it is only after he has created any entity that he judges its outcome.[66] The Priestly Redactor's superimposed preface (Gen. 1:1–2:4a) shows the Deity creating by the divine word and additionally by another, albeit undefined, means. So P does not tell us how Elohim created the heavens and the earth (Gen. 1:1) or how he separated the light from the darkness (Gen. 1:4b), for example. He simply notes that the Deity created them, and it was good.

Since this very knowledge of creativity, basic to the "Wisdom" tradition which is a component genre of Gen. 1:1–3:24,[67] is inherent in the precept that the word of the Deity is creative, eating the fruit of that particular tree enabled the Man and the Woman to become informed of divine creativity.[68] For this reason the Deity *must* curse and expel them once he acknowledges that they have disobeyed him; otherwise, they truly would become not just like gods, but God(s), having the knowledge of creativity.[69]

Consequently, although the threat expressed in J's portion of the pericope states that the Man will die on the day in which he eats, the events depicted contradict this.[70] Accordingly, subtending the explicit threat of immediate death is the implicit and clearly differentiated delineation of that threat, which itself renders the statement regarding immediate death a puzzle. At the same time as it promises that the Man will die on the very day in which he eats its fruit, it insinuates otherwise: he will not die on the day in which he eats it.[71] It really means that he will become subject to death: that is, he will become (at least potentially) mortal on that day.[72] Moreover, since mortal man can achieve a kind of immortality via the continuation of his line, it is meaningful that once *he* has eaten and hence become potentially mortal, both the Woman, who had eaten first, and the Man become aware of their potential for sexuality[73] as well as their nakedness. This is indicated by the fact that they cover *only and specifically* their genitalia when, realizing that they are no longer alone, they hide, and then the Deity calls to them (Gen. 3:7).

Because both the Man and the Woman are depicted as flat characters, the reader does not know what either felt, thought, or even experienced after first she and then he had eaten. He only learns what both the Man and the Woman did in the presence of the Deity: namely, they acted like intruders in a garden that from their perspective was no longer theirs and they hid. But the implied narrator, who had informed the reader of the interdiction against the eating or even touching of the tree, knows it had never really been theirs so the reader understands why they hide. That the implied narrator does not indicate how long a time intervened between the eating of the fruit and the Deity's stroll in the Garden is of no importance. What matters is that the stroll took place in *what is now* clearly established as a Garden that the Deity had created for his own pleasure.[74]

Because we are not told how long a time intervened between the Woman's eating and her giving the fruit to her man/husband, whom we are specifically told was "with her" (Gen. 3:6), we cannot ascertain if the Woman had become aware of her sexuality as soon as she had eaten or after the Man had eaten. However, the narration in Gen. 3:7, which begins with a waw conversive, continuing the sequence of waw conversives in verse 6, suggests that the awareness and the covering of the loins were immediately consequent on their sequenced act of eating. Obviously, none of this matters to the plot development or the redactor would have had the implied narrator say something to make the reader aware of it—presuming of course that we have a well-wrought work of literature. The absence of a discussion of the immediate effect the eating has on the Woman allows and possibly invites the reader to ask what happened.

By juxtaposing authorial silence, the redactor then provides a source of literary tension that not only raises the reader's expectations of what will happen, but also allows for all sorts of mutually exclusive interpretations to be proffered by the real reader. The implied reader on the other hand is expected to know what happened. So when the implied narrator hints at the Man's and the Woman's awareness of their sexuality when the Deity is walking in his Garden, but juxtaposes that walk with their awareness that they are naked, both of which lead to a covering of their genitalia (Gen. 3:7–8), he does so because his plot development demands that some explanation or statement be made at precisely this point and not earlier.[75] Therefore it is notable that again he introduces the couple's awareness of the Deity (Gen. 3:8) by a waw conversive, thus keeping it in tandem with the couple's awareness of their nakedness (Gen. 3:7). The chain of events leads them from blindness to vision to hearing; and, this is analogous to their innocence—which is neither noted nor acknowledged— their knowledge of their own nakedness, and their awareness of the Deity.

Accordingly, I believe that the lack of thematic importance renders the presence or absence of sexual intercourse irrelevant simply because it does not matter to the *omniscient* implied narrator and his narrative's development. What matters is the alteration of states from blind and presumably mute innocence to observable, sensory knowledge and awareness, which includes sexuality. The text is not really cryptic. Rather, the gaping inherent in the text stresses what is important to both the implied narrator and possibly the redactor as well. Consequently, in contrast to Hauser, who suggests that the depiction of the Man and the Woman in Gen. 2:24 as being of one flesh must not be viewed as referring solely to or excluding sexual relations, I believe that the sexual aspects of this are not explicitly presented because their awareness is what really matters *at this point* in the implied narrator's narrative.[76] The redactor, however, as well as the implied narrator clearly wished there to be sexual *overtones*, as that is important to the *topos* itself.[77] Hence the Man is "seduced" when he is given the fruit of the Tree of Knowledge of Good and Evil. However, the *omniscient* implied narrator's ambiguity, which I believe J treated as an intentional narrative device so as to hint strongly at, but still leave the issue in abeyance for literary ends, has led scholars to differ about whether this was sexual. Although this awareness of sexuality may seem to be out of accord with what the implied narrator is reporting, it is just what the redactor wants the critical reader to infer.

No matter what we see as having happened, within a literary context we can only say that the Man is seduced by the Woman, who herself was seduced by the Creeping Thing, who offered her the food, traditionally but not realistically or religio-historically an apple or a fig.[78] By the time P superimposed his own schema on the Tetrateuch, many people may well have accepted J's narrative as representing a particular fruit that was known to and consumed by humans in their own day. But this must have been unacceptable to P himself, who by his own classification excluded what was not seeded.

We must remember that P, whose deity had given Man permission to eat of any seeded food be it plant or fruit of the tree, allowed J's narrative, *which does not have this restriction*, to stand. But, as I have noted (above), P unconditionally altered J's account by virtue of the fact that he prefaced it with his own.[79] This alteration sets the literary tone and mood as well as the sense that the reader perceives in the narration.[80] For that reason, the reader perceives J's account in a different way than he would if it had stood alone or even if it had stood with a different preface than what it now has by virtue of J's efforts. So the Priestly Redactor need not have made internal textual modifications in J's narrative so as to accomplish his own ends: he has done it by external modification.

One notable and very important aspect of this alteration imposed by P's "preface" to J's creation story is the limitation on the nature of the fruit of the Tree of Knowledge. It is *now defined* as seedless precisely because, according to P, the Deity has permitted Man to eat of every plant and tree yielding seed (Gen. 1:29). That is, he allowed man to eat from any *life-giving plant or fruit* which, once created by the Deity, derived from pre-existent life.[81] But, on the other hand, he forbade him to eat from the fruit of the Tree of Knowledge of Good and Evil, which by exclusionary definition then must have been different or "wholly other." Moreover, the fact that the Deity did not forbid the Man to eat of the Tree of Life is also significant.[82] Although this tree must have been viewed as "wholly other" by J as well as by some of those from whom he received his traditions, it need not have been viewed as such by all who preceded him or even by all who were subsequent to him. In fact, since the Deity did not interdict the Man from eating the fruit of the Tree of Life, this must have been a tree that yielded seed. Consequently, despite its cosmic importance, it was a tree that belonged to the realm given over to the domain of the Man, who is after all an iconic figure, and before his humanization was a hypostasis or at least an alter ego and, as I have already noted, even an icon of the Deity. Moreover, it seems as if the delineation of the creativity, by propagation of seed in accordance with its species, of what had been created according to P leads me to believe that P did not consider the Tree of Life in J's account to be "wholly other" no matter how J interpreted it. Only the Tree of Knowledge of Good and Evil then is wholly other for P, by implication at least.

Since nothing is in Genesis 1 by chance and the statements are to be held as completely and bindingly valid in their literal sense,[83] we must assume that P specified seeded plants and fruit for some reason,[84] and this is related to the story J is telling as well as to P's conception of "order." Despite modern genetic engineering's having given us the boon of nonseeded fruits, "natural" fruits are seeded. Consequently, when P limited what is edible in the vegetable/fruit world to seeded plants and fruits, he must have been eliminating something that was not part of the "natural" world, but only part of what was considered divine.[85] He would have done this so as to conform to his sense of order by species, presenting what is included in those mechanisms of mundane propagation about which he knew.

Then, J's fruit of the Tree of Knowledge was defined as something unto itself because of the limitations imposed by P.[86] It was unique and not part of what had been portrayed as "*an emergence of the species*" when P represented "*the creation of plants and animals*."[87] And for the implied narrator as well as for his implied reader, it is the seduction by the unique type of "food" that not only looks good but is good to eat, not the classification within a species or the sexuality that is consequent upon eating, that is of significance.[88] So even without the snake, the seduction would not have been accomplished by the fruit of the Tree of Life, only by that of the Tree of Knowledge.

The "seduction" by eating pericope is well arranged and highly structured insofar as the Woman is tempted and she eats. Only after she eats does she give the fruit to her man/husband, who eats it. There is no question of Eve, however called, tempting the Man, defined as her man/husband, who is merely obedient to her or at least does not question her motivation or the correctness of eating. In fact the narrative does not tell us why the Man eats: only that he does so.[89]

It is most likely that prior to J's account, the tree from which the Woman ate was most likely that of Knowledge and of Life combined, the fruit of which defied human classification. And the separation into two trees as well as the restrictive definition of the Tree of Knowledge of Good and Evil was a later addition, possibly made by J, that had been appended to explain why its fruit was forbidden.[90] Conceivably in an earlier tradition, there was no need to incorporate another tree into the story.[91] So eating of that tree may well have given both knowledge and sexuality even though J presents the event in such a way that his implied narrator is not yet explicitly concerned with sexuality. The redactor understood that the Man and the Woman did not become subject to death until they became expressly aware of their potential sexuality (Gen. 3:16) and hence their potential for the only type of immortality permissible to mortals (Gen. 3:15), and, this occurred after the Lord God had ascertained from them that they had eaten of the Tree of Knowledge of Good and Evil, which itself must have been equated with the endless cycle of death and renewal, be it of the world or of man.

Before they ate, both the Man and the Woman were in what seemed to be a permanently liminal state, being and having the potential to remain liminoid: two states that are not identical. Although the period between their eating and their acknowledgment of what they had done, when they had not yet been deprived of their protected status in the Garden and they had not yet become subject to death, is itself liminal since the two are no longer what they were, and they had effectually started the process whereby they would ultimately become mortal, they were neither deities nor were they mortalized. Hence for this unspecified time, in which they had the knowledge of creativity, knowledge although possibly not experience of their own and what may be termed "human" sexuality—as is indicated by their ultimately covering their genitalia in the presence of the Deity—and the potential of eternal life since they had not yet been subject to death, they were in no specific status. It is precisely because they are neither immortal nor mortal—since they have not yet been either excluded from the Garden paradise or made subject to death[92]—they are not yet given names *on a permanent basis*.[93]

In the received text, the treatment of the Man and the Woman while in the Garden suggests that they must have been "gatherers." So the plucking of the fruit of any tree, even one from which they were interdicted to eat, would have been a natural act, be they mortal, immortal, or, as they were for almost the entirety of their stay in the Garden, liminoid, or for the timeless moment between the eating and the Deity's walk in the Garden, liminal. And it was only the interdiction against that one specific object of their gathering, not the nature of the tree or its fruit, that had made it unlawful albeit not unnatural to pluck and eat. In any case, both the Man and the Woman are shown as belonging to the precivilized "hunting-gathering" primal world. And this suggests that they had not yet attained to civilization although they had the potential to become civilized.

But in the Man's showing dominion over the animals by virtue of naming them, he and the Woman show themselves to be acting as at least potentially a nonsolitary couple even before they experience shame in the Deity's presence.[94] Their companions, however, are nonhuman. And since the implied narrator does not tell us anything about the relationship between the Man, the Woman, and their nonhuman companions, who nevertheless are not gods, we do not know what either's relationship to the latter is. But clearly, neither the Man nor the Woman experiences a sense of shame about nakedness in their presence, as J indicated (Gen. 2:25).[95]

It is no accident that when J clearly stated that they did not experience shame about their nakedness (Gen. 2:25) prior to this act of disobedience, he did so immediately after he insinuated that or possibly even presented a metaphor for the actualization whereby a man and a woman were to have sex (Gen. 2: 24), in what may be an etiologic set of verses.[96] The implied narrator specifies that they realized they were naked and they were ashamed.[97] Knowledge of nakedness itself would of course lead to the observation of sexual difference,[98] which may be the basis of their shame. Perhaps nakedness shows difference from other animate beings, who after all are clothed with "skins,"[99] but whose genitalia are not hidden possibly in order that and clearly with the result that the sexual difference could be observed.[100] But in any case the implied narrator either does not explain because it is unimportant to his narrative or because he wants the reader to understand the implicit ramifications of the ambiguous presentation and the gaping stresses what is unstated. This allows the narrative to allude to what may well be unspeakable.

There is no change in their psychological makeup whereby their shame or guilt (Gen. 2:25) is itself the differential that distinguishes them from their former selves after the Man has eaten (Gen. 3:7).[101] The implied narrator does not tie this altered state and potential aggregation to the world that awaits them into the account as viewed from the Man's or the Woman's perspective of what the Deity will think about them. In fact the implied narrator basically ignores the Man's and the Woman's thought processes because they are not pertinent to his own account. What does matter to the implied narrator is that together with the Man's and the Woman's potential to be civilized, they have acquired the potential for mortal creativity by sexuality that may have been hinted at, or merely etiologically described, in Gen. 2:24. Farming and childbirth, with both of which they will soon be respectively cursed, is an extension of this type of creativity.[102] Hence, we have a pericope in which the Woman suffers in childbirth (Gen. 3:16), the Man suffers in getting food (Gen. 3:17–18), and both by implication suffer by becoming subject to death (Gen. 3:19). This suffering is related to their acquisition of names although their future names are not etymologically related to that concept. But the woman has to undergo an additional form of suffering: namely, a determined, not an implied—as in P—diminution of status by virtue of being named by the Man. Because of this (Gen. 3:20), the Man not only subjects her to his dominion to which the Deity had just condemned her (Gen. 3:16b), but he incorporates her into the greater community of plants and beasts over which he already has dominion. So even in Eden, then, some type of society exists.

Before they suffer what is the life of (civilized) humankind and can be condemned to farming and birthing, they must become at least potentially mortalized, and this requires that they must become subject to the potential of death.[103] Either J or some earlier, albeit unknown, remembrancer may have separated the Tree of Life—which is by virtue of its effective but not stated exclusion of non-deities from eating, must also be deemed the Tree of Death—from the Tree of Knowledge traditions to make it seem that in Eden mortality and knowledge are separate entities. Since it is no accident that in most traditions, there is only one World Tree as I have noted (above), this may well be what has led various anthropologists to see the Tree of Knowledge as the Tree of Death as depicted in this pericope as I have already noted.[104] If so, it also explains why the received text represents the Creeping Thing as enticing the Woman to eat of the Tree of Knowledge of Good and Evil rather than the Tree of Life.

The Creeping Thing is in effect enticing the Woman to her death, be it immediate or ultimate. But the implied narrator does not tell the reader what the Creeping Thing actually intends, just as he does not tell him what the Woman intends when she offers the fruit to the Man. The implied reader would be expected to know the implications. It is also no accident, then, that J only depicts the Man as being threatened with death should he eat of the Tree of Knowledge of Good and Evil ("And do not eat from the Tree of Knowledge of Good and Evil. For on the day in which you eat of it, you will surely die"), but nothing is said about the Tree of Life (Gen. 2:17). Since, in reality, this threat only and specifically means that he will become mortal,[105] as the statement, "And Elohim said: do not eat from the fruit of the tree that is in the midst of the Garden. Do not even touch it lest you die" (Gen. 3:3), indicates by not giving a date certain for that death.

Contact with the sacred and/or totem is dangerous because it liminalizes and sacralizes.[106] That is, by its contagion, it transmits manna that can empower or kill those who come into contact with it. This is irony at its best. Because of what could have meant divine empowerment and sacralization, man will become empowered over the birds and beasts alone, and he will be subject to mortalization. The reader understands the full implications of this: expulsion from the world of the sacred; obviation of creation by the divine word—creation is to be a work of labor for both man and woman alike[107]—and ultimately, death. Thus, J treats the liminoid creature, the Man, as liminalized together with the other liminoid creature, the Woman, after having eaten and precisely because they both had eaten of the *totem, therefore, taboo and thereby death prefiguring fruit of the Tree of Knowledge of Good and Evil.* In fact it is only its status as both totem and taboo that renders the Tree of Knowledge, the Tree of Death, thus making it the mirror image of the Tree of Life, which is by definition also a tree of death.[108]

But the narrative does not present this matter explicitly. Rather, it reflects what may have been known only in very early stages of the tradition in which the ritual of initiation into mortality had been tied into its mythic narration. From a literary perspective, however, the only ostensible result of the Woman's eating is that she offers the fruit to her man/husband to eat (Gen. 3:6), and he does so without question. Once *he* has eaten, the eyes of both were opened.[109] Before this then they or at least the Woman saw without the benefit of having had their eyes opened (e.g., Gen. 3:6); thus, they may have seen as do "blind" seers in many traditions.[110] This demands that we properly presume they were physically blind.[111] That is, they had knowledge, which implies that they already had some type of wisdom, but not divine Wisdom.

Although we may and in fact must treat this blindness metaphysically and as related to Wisdom, from a literary-critical perspective we must take the text at its "base" level as well unless there is some indication to the contrary. In the latter case, we must presume that the opening of their eyes means that they had been closed prior to the event. Therefore they were at least blind insofar as they lacked physical sight via the eyes. But other than the fact that their eyes had been opened, there is no indication that they had been physically blind previously. In fact, the implied narrator says that Eve saw that the forbidden tree was in fact a food tree and it also looked pleasing (Gen. 3:6). From a ritualistic perspective, this is the truth.

Eve must eat and she must somehow or other cause the Man to eat for the rites of humanization and mortalization to take place. So she saw what she saw; and it does not matter whether she saw as human beings do or not. Because human vision is not really important to the narrative, or at this point to the ritual either, there is no indication that they "saw" by the means of human vision, the eyes. So we must either presume that their closed eyes are a symbolic representation of their exclusion from divine Wisdom prior to their eating or they had a different type of vision that was changed as they began the process of mortalization and humanization.

This clearly indicates that for J as well as his sources, the Man and the other animate beings including the Woman were not created as human beings, and they did not represent a generic "mankind" as is generally thought.[112] It even hints that the creation of Man in the image of the Deity was not necessarily anthropomorphic as we conceive of it. If so, Man may originally have been created for the Deity's amusement, and placed in the Garden just as our children might place their dolls in a dollhouse. He was not to function as humankind but as a miniature deity, whose eyes at least were not the vehicles of sight. But this "miniature deity" is to "cultivate and maintain" Yahweh's garden, which is more than a "park of trees" as Ezek. 31:8 seems to think.[113] So he is a toiler in Yahweh's park. He is a caretaker, whose relationship to the Deity may well resemble what P construes as his own relationship to that same deity.[114]

Notes

1. Like many others, I treat this first pericope as ending at Gen. 3:24. The Yahwist's narrative (Gen. 4:1–26), in which Adam and Eve have been expelled from the Garden and procreate, may be treated as an independent pericope that is linked with the genealogical report (Gen. 5:1–32) P appended so as to bring the narrative to the flood pericope. But, for an extended narrative, see George W. Coats, who does *ultimately* treat the end of

Genesis 3 as the end of the story itself, in accordance with the demands of the plot. Coats, *Genesis: With an Introduction to Narrative Literature,* vol. 1 (Grand Rapids: Eerdmans, 1983), 28–35, 57.

2. Some of these are clearly related to the text's relationship to its literary *Weltanschauung*. Sarna's assumption of the superficiality of parallels outside of "cultural moorings" would set the biblical text apart from its surrounding world: something we now know to be invalid. Nahum M. Sarna, *Understanding Genesis (*New York: Schocken, 1970), 4. The argument against its classification as epic because it is not in verse is not justified. Our modern presupposition that in antiquity all epic was always formatted in verse or that it remained in verse as long as it was classified as epic, may well be based on Aristotle, whose opinions are not always to be trusted or correct.

3. There is a great body of work dealing with Primary History (PH). In particular, for naming PH and treating it as a nine-book epic, see, David Noel Freedman, *The Unity of the Hebrew Bible* (Ann Arbor: University of Michigan Press, 1991), passim; Freedman, "The Earliest Bible," in *Backgrounds for the Bible,* ed. Michael Patrick O'Connor and David Noel Freedman (Winona Lake, Ind.: Eisenbrauns, 1987), 29–37. See also Sara Mandell and David Noel Freedman, *The Relationship between Herodotus' History and Primary History* (Atlanta: Scholars Press, 1993), passim. For P's narrative in Gen. 1:1–2:3 (*sic:* we generally conclude P's part of the narrative at 2:4a) as "a prelude to the rest of the Genesis narrative," see J. Richard Middleton, "Creation Founded in Love: Breaking Rhetorical Expectations in Genesis 1:1–2:3," in *Sacred Text, Secular Times: The Hebrew Bible in the Modern World,* ed. Leonard J. Greenspoon and Bryan F. Lebeau (Omaha: Creighton University, 2000), 64–65.

4. N. Wyatt suggests that it is possible that "in using other people's myths (if that is the way it was) the people of ancient Israel felt that these were meaningful and powerful forms; perhaps in adapting them they were using them in the time-honoured way, by actually shaping and articulating their own experience by means of mythic expression, for this is an important quality of myth; and perhaps they did not feel, as do many of their modern interpreters, a compulsion to deny the long-standing intellectual perception of this traditional past in favour of post-Enlightenment categories." Wyatt, "The Mythic Mind," *SJOT* 15 (2001): 16.

5. So it is meaningful that in general, material in Primordial History that is compared with that of the Ancient Near East is mainly concerned with "episodes and motifs." See J. W. Rogerson "Genesis 1–11," *Currents in Research* 5 (1997): 76.

6. For the "claims for the authority" of texts in antiquity on the basis of ritual, see James W. Watts, "Ritual Legitimacy and Scriptural Authority," *JBL* 124 (2005): 404. For historicity, see, e.g., Philip R. Davies, who states: "texts cannot verify their own historical value." Davies, "Biblical Histories, Ancient and Modern," in *Can a "History of Israel" Be Written?* ed. Lester L. Grabbe (Sheffield: Sheffield Academic, 1997), 105.

   The ideological bases of PH have been noted by many. See, e.g., Robert P. Carroll, "Madonna of Silences" (in *Can a "History of Israel" Be Written?,* ed. Grabbe, 89 et passim), who also notes that some scholars do not wish to use the term ideology in reference to biblical writings (89 n. 15). In the case of P, David M. Carr notes P's location in a "Priestly matrix" that had itself been "a factor" in creating cultic laws "outside Genesis." Carr, *Reading the Fractures of Genesis: Historical and Literary Approaches* (Louisville, Ky.: Westminster John Knox, 1996), 130.

7. See, e.g., David Noel Freedman, *Unity of the Hebrew Bible,* passim; "The Earliest Bible," 30–31; and "The Formation of the Canon of the Old Testament: The Selection and Identification of the Torah as the Supreme Authority of the Post-exilic Community," in *Religion and Law: Biblical-Judaic and Islamic Perspectives,* ed. Edwin B. Firmage, Bernard G. Weiss, and John W. Welch (Winona Lake, Ind.: Eisenbrauns, 1990), 317.

8. The Minimalists' support for a date during the Second Temple Era differs from that of other biblical scholars, even those whose dating is the same, insofar as Minimalists focus on the theopolitical motivation for the creation of all PH.

9. Richard Elliott Friedman, who believes that P was an Aaronid priest "or at least someone who was representing the Aaronid priests' interests," believes that P was doing his work prior to the Exile. Friedman, *Who Wrote the Bible?* (New York: Harper and Row, 1989), 89.

10. For the formulaic nature and structuring of P, see, e.g., Joseph Blenkinsopp, "The Structure of P," *CBQ* 38 (1976): 275–92. For P as "preoccupied above all else with rankings and classification, chronologies and sequences," see Jean Bottéro, *The Birth of God: The Bible and the Historian,* trans. Kees W. Bolle (University Park: Pennsylvania State University Press, 2000), 163.

11. Although older generations of scholars treated J as early, many today do not. However, Richard M.Wright, whose work is not available to me, still contends J is pre-exilic (*Linguistic Evidence for the Pre-exilic Date of the Yahwistic Source,* Library of Hebrew Bible/Old Testament Studies [London: T&T Clark, 2005], 419). In any case, not only has the *communis opinio* dating of the various redactors been called into question by some

scholars, it is totally rejected by most Minimalists, including myself, who date the entirety of Primary History, be it redacted or not, into some part of the Second Temple Era and view it as a theopolitical creation to shore up the priestly class's claim to power. Significantly, "Contemporary historians, minimalists included, distinguish (1) between a past world where things happened and the narrative representation of that world in ancient writings and (2), between elements in the historiosophical view that contributed to the formation of a particular narrative about the past, the descriptive adequacy of the same narrative in its original literary and historical contexts, and its adequacy for the work of a contemporary historian." Ziony Zevit, "Three Debates about Bible and Archaeology," *Biblica* 83 (2002): 10. Should either the Scandinavian (Uppsala) School's mytholiterary perspective or the Minimalist's theopolitical Second Temple hypotheses be correct, our understanding of the nature of the composition would be decidedly different from what is generally accepted.

12. The distinction between a redactor and an author is a quantitative even more than a qualitative matter. For the use of identical techniques by authors and redactors, see Rolf Knierim, "Criticism of Literary Features, Form, Tradition, and Redaction," in *The Hebrew Bible and Its Modern Interpreters,* ed. Douglas A. Knight and Gene M. Tucker (Philadelphia: Fortress Press, 1985), 151–52. For J and P having different aims, with J's Garden story as etiological, see Mark G. Brett, *Genesis: Procreation and the Politics of Identity* (London: Routledge, 2000), 32.
13. This perception of the resultant unity allows us to conclude that what the Priestly Redactor did was an intentional literary melding rather than a haphazard conjunction between two different literary representations of the creation story, his and that of the Yahwist. He not only wanted his creation story to preface the entire Tetrateuch, but he wanted to alter J's more anthropomorphic account in which Man, not the Deity, was the hero so as to conform to his own theological precepts. But without altering the wording and contents of J's account, the only means he would have to change it would be by that with which he prefaced it. For P's use of J so as to expand on and develop his own narrative constructs, particularly in the Creation-Garden-Expulsion pericope, see, e.g., Bernard F. Batto's "Paradise Reexamined," in *The Biblical Canon in Comparative Perspective: Scripture in Context IV,* ed. K. Lawson Younger Jr., William W. Hallo, and Bernard F. Batto (Lewiston, Maine: Edwin Mellen, 1991), 50–52. For this process in the Tetrateuch, see Frank Moore Cross, *Canaanite Myth and Hebrew Epic: Essays in the History of the Religion of Israel* (Cambridge: Harvard University Press, 1973), 293–25.
14. Moreover, P's literary frame does not require that some type of *inclusio* be present.
15. The implied narrator is nameless. His identification as Moses is a late, theological, nonliterary delineation. We neither know nor have the data to even guess whether there was some Israelite "theogony," showing from whence the deity came, in either the J's or P's time. We have no way of knowing when the Deity came to be perceived as "eternal."
16. It is important that MT does not use "Man" as a proper noun until Gen. 4:25. See, e.g., Ernest Lussier, "Adam in Genesis 1:1–4:24," *CBQ* 18 (1956): 137.
17. For the noun as denoting a "human being" or "humankind," see Howard N. Wallace, *ABD* 1:62. Wallace notes P's use of the term as a collective in Gen. 1: 26–28. He also refers to him as a "human creature" while defining him as "a specific male being" in J's narrative 2:4b–4:25. Nevertheless, Wallace only views him as "restricted" to a specific male being in Gen. 2:18. David Clines, in "'*Adam* The Hebrew for 'Human, Humanity': A Response to James Barr," *VT* 53 (2003): 293–310, points out that the noun is not gendered and has the meaning of both human being and humanity. See Reuven Kimelman, "The Seduction of Eve and the Exegetical Politics of Gender," in *Women in the Hebrew Bible,* ed. Alice Bach (London: Routledge, 1999), 247, for an argument that the translation should be "it" rather than "him," and he uses the generally accepted referent as denoting "mankind."
18. Interestingly enough, the verb as used in Vulgate (*praesum*) implies both caretaking and presiding over, whereas MT (*rdh*) only denotes presiding over or ruling.
19. See, e.g., Hermann Gunkel, *Genesis* (Göttingen: Vandenhoeck and Ruprecht, 1901), 1–2.
20. Although it is logical to attribute the formulation in Gen. 1:1–24b to the influence that Babylonian theology and philosophy exerted on P, it is not necessary to assume that this influence stems from the time of the Babylonian Exile.
21. We must not anachronistically apply the rules of modern scholarship to any type of writing or composition in antiquity.
22. We must distinguish between *lacunae* that are part of the narrative and those that are external to it. The former exist in the narrative as it was presented whereas the latter result from losses in the tradition, be it from erroneous scribal activity or actual mutilation, destruction, or degeneration of the medium on which the work was written.

23. Meir Sternberg notes that, "Whatever the nature and origin of the parts—materials, units, forms—the whole governs and interrelates them by well-defined rules of poetic communication." Sternberg, *The Poetics of Biblical Narrative: Ideological Literature and the Drama of Reading* (Bloomington: Indiana University Press, 1985), 2.
24. Whenever he wrote, J was "a highly creative genius who reshaped prior mythic traditions . . . into a new and original literary myth of origins," as noted by Bernard F. Batto in *Mythmaking in the Biblical Tradition: Slaying the Dragon* (Louisville: Westminster John Knox, 1992), 44, 200 n. 11. Ronald A. Simkins, in "Gender Construction in the Yahwist Creation Myth," *The Feminist Companion to the Bible,* ed. Athalya Brenner, 2nd ser. (Sheffield: Sheffield University Press, 1998), 33–34, deems "the garden narrative" a "creation myth." For Genesis 1 and 2 as etiological, see W. Sibley Towner, *Genesis* (Louisville: Westminster John Knox, 2001), 41.
25. Because there may well have been oral traditions that were handed down concomitant with literary and/or historical, we follow the Scandinavian (Uppsala) school in presuming that P included or at least acknowledged previously oral materials together with written ones in his work just as J did in his.
26. On the other hand, living myth, legend, folktale, and other religio-literary type of stories are treated as historical by those for whom they represent their ideological self-image, that is, for believers. For the reshaping of heroic events "using the structures and patterns of traditional myth," see Frank Moore Cross, "The Epic Traditions of Early Israel: Epic Narrative and the Reconstruction of Early Israelite Institutions," in *The Poet and the Historian: Essays in Literary and Historical Biblical Criticism,* ed. Richard Elliott Friedman (Chico, Calif.: Scholars, 1983), 15. So despite any semblance of narrative historicity, if at all the factuality of epic is only slight. Such things as places, dates, characters, and events themselves are at best presented in a disordered and transformed manner (Cross, "Epic Traditions of Early Israel," 15). For this process, see also A. D. Lord, *The Singer of Tales* (Cambridge: Harvard University Press, 1964), 141–97.
27. We do not know, for example, if he had some now-lost introduction to his narrative. When P placed his narrative of origins in front of this, he did so in such a way that it together with J's narrative of origins from creation to the expulsion of man from the Garden of Eden formed a pericope introducing Primeval History or even the entirety of a longer "historical" work, be it a tetrateuch (four books), a pentateuch (five books), a hexateuch (six books), or something yet longer.

    I do not agree with Jacques Berlinerblau that we need "to temporarily emancipate" ourselves from literary-critical approaches to analyze "texts generated across vast expanses of time." Berlinerblau, "The Bible as Literature?" *Hebrew Studies* 45 (2004): 25.
28. My argument does not demand that a stand be taken in the controversy regarding the translation of this verse. In any case, the formulaic statement in Gen. 2:4a, which is generally deemed to conclude P's creation narrative, in fact both introduces J's narrative and concludes P's at the same time as it does neither. By placing his creation narrative before that of the Yahwist, P combined the two narratives in such a way that his forms a preface or "pre-text" to the entire composite pericope (Gen. 1:1–3:24 or Gen. 1:1–4:26—if we include the coda formed by chapter 4, also attributed to J). This was done in such a way that the pretext of difference is perhaps more clear to the reader than the redactoral unity whereby Gen. 1:1–3:24 or Gen. 1:1–4:26 has become a composite whole. So Gen. 1:1–2:4a is a "pretext" at the same time as it is a "pre-text." Therefore when P states, "this is the origin of the heavens and the earth," which Wiseman then qualifies as meaning "the story of their origin" (see P. J. Wiseman, in *Clues to Creation in Genesis,* ed. Donald J. Wiseman [London: Marshall, Morgan and Scott, 1977], 36), P is at one and the same time referring to his own and to J's creation narrative. And so he makes the pretext that the fact that the latter is more concerned with the creation of Man than of the heavenly entities is not very important, but rather it is to be subsumed into the narrative of the origin of the heavens and the earth.

    Cross, *Canaanite Myth and Hebrew Epic,* 302. See also R. Rendtorff, *The Old Testament: An Introduction* (Philadelphia: Fortress Press, 1986), 132; Thomas W. Mann, *The Book of the Torah: The Narrative Integrity of the Pentateuch* (Atlanta: John Knox, 1988), 12.
29. Wiseman, *Clues to Creation in Genesis,* 36.
30. Hermann Gunkel suggests that both Genesis 1 and 2 are reflective of Canaanite thought regarding rain/water. But he believes the mythology that subtends Genesis 1 would be "totally understandable in Babylonia," having other aspects that *are* Babylonian, whereas that subtending Genesis 2 is purely Canaanite. So Gunkel suggests that creation in Genesis 1 rests on "ancient traditions," whose *Sitz im Leben* is most likely Babylonian, not Canaanite. Gunkel, "The Influence of Babylonian Mythology Upon the Creation Story," in *Creation in the Old Testament,* ed. Bernhard W. Anderson (Philadelphia: Fortress Press, 1984), 32, 33, 44–50. This has been debated by many, with some suggesting that Genesis 1 is a reaction to, and polemic against, Babylonian mythology. For some of the different perspectives see H. W. F. Saggs, *The Encounter with the Divine in Mesopotamia*

and Israel (London: Althone, 1978), 52–53; A. S. Kapelrud, "The Mythological Features in Genesis Chapter 1 and the Author's Intentions," *VT* 24 (1974): 181, 185; W. G. Lambert, "Old Testament Mythology in Its Ancient Near Eastern Context," *VT Supp 40 Congress Volume: Jerusalem 1986,* ed. J. A. Emerton (Leiden: Brill, 1988), 124–43. But William P. Brown's conclusions regarding the treatment of motivation is very important, rendering the nature of some analysis suspect. Brown, *Structure, Role, and Ideology in the Hebrew and Greek Texts of Genesis 1:1–2:3* (Atlanta: Scholars Press, 1993), 222. John D. Currid's belief does raise some interesting questions. Currid, "An Examination of the Egyptian Background of the Genesis Cosmogony," *BZ* 35 (1991): 18–40. For parallels between J's account and the Gilgamesh narrative, for which there is an extensive body of literature, see Batto, *Slaying the Dragon,* 48–62.

31. There is an enormous body of literature about the "World" or "Cosmic Tree." For a discussion of the "Cosmic Tree" in world mythology see, e.g., Mircea Eliade, *The Sacred and the Profane: The Nature of Religion* (New York: Harcourt Brace Jovanovich, 1959), 147–51 et passim.

    For provenience, see, e.g., Jutta Krispenz, "Wie viele Bäume braucht das Paradies? Erwäungen zu Gen II 4B–3 24," *VT* 54 (2004): 301–18; see esp. 303, 308, and 309. For a relationship between Genesis 3 and the story of Adapa, see B. Otzen, "The Use of Myth in Genesis," in *Myths in the Old Testament,* ed. Benedikt Otzen, Hans Gottlieb, and Knud Jeppesen (London: SCM, 1980), 46. See also Batto, *Slaying the Dragon,* 41–47, 200 n. 12. Interestingly enough, Gabriel Germain notes that of the Mesopotamian "descent" themes, only the Gilgamesh's and *Odyssey*'s are parallel. Germain, *Essai sur les Origines de Certains Thèmes Odysséens et sur la Genèse de l'Odyssée* (Paris, 1954), 342. For a relationship between Genesis 3 and Gilgamesh, see Otzen, "The Use of Myth in Genesis," 46. A practice tablet, dating to the fourteenth century BCE, i.e., four centuries prior to the Yahwist's writings, representing the death of Enkidu (Tablet VII GE), was found at Megiddo. See, e.g., Batto, *Slaying the Dragon,* 46; for parallels, see 58–62.

32. For Israelite knowledge of Akkadian literature, which had Sumerian literature behind it, see Samuel Noah Kramer, "Sumerian Literature and the Bible," in *The Bible in Its Literary Milieu,* ed. John Maier and Vincent Tollers (Grand Rapids, Mich.: Eerdmans, 1979), 276. For P's having knowledge of Sumero-Babylonian traditions, see, e.g., Claus Westermann *Genesis 1–11* (Neukirchen-Vluyn: Neukirchener Verlag, 1976, 2nd ed.), 22.

33. Gerhard von Rad's contention that this being is not androgynous can only be valid if in fact the being was mankind or humanity. Its being a single entity does not allow for its status as nonhuman. As much as we want to read the text symbolically, von Rad himself has pointed the way when he indicated that Genesis 1 must be treated literally. Von Rad, *Genesis* (Philadelphia: Westminster Press, 1972), 47, 60.

    For the combination, see Danna Nolan Fewell and David M. Gunn, *Gender, Power, and Promise: The Subject of the Bible's First Story* (Nashville: Abingdon, 1993), 23.

34. See, e.g., Sir James George Frazer, *Folk-Lore in the Old Testament: Studies in Comparative Religion, Legend and Law,* abridged ed. (New York: Macmillan, 1923), 2.

35. While not distinguishing between redactors here, James Barr, in *The Garden of Eden and the Hope of Immortality* (Minneapolis: Fortress Press, 1993), 21, properly argues "that the central theme of the story of the Garden of Eden, along with the theme of knowledge of good and evil, is the theme of immortality." On the other hand, this is not the general interpretation. So Westermann (*Genesis 1–11,* 341) notes the relationship of Gen. 2:25 to what is described in Gen. 3:1–7. But not one of the three schools of thought he discusses really treats the text as forming an explanation for mortality, which cannot be treated as identical to historicity or as serving as part of the ritual for the moralization of man that underlies the entire pericope. On the other hand, Westermann (342) acknowledges that by virtue of eating the fruit, "the man has become altered" insofar as he has expanded his status: "he now knows what he previously did not know"; that is, he now has Wisdom, something he previously lacked. For a discussion of "theme" as applied to Genesis 1–11 as a whole, see David Clines, "Theme in Genesis 1–11," *I Studied Inscriptions from Before the Flood: Ancient Near Eastern, Literary, and Linguistic Approaches to Genesis 1–11,* ed. Richard S. Hess and David Toshio Tsumura (Winona Lake, Ind.: Eisenbrauns, 1994), passim.

36. Northrop Frye, *The Secular Scripture: A Study in the Structure of Romance* (Cambridge: Harvard University Press, 1976), 14.

37. See David Noel Freedman ("The Deuteronomic History," *Interpreters Dictionary of the Bible Supp*., ed. Keith Crim [Nashville: Abingdon, 1976], 226) for some non-P overriding redactor of Primary History who is subsequent to Dtr[2]. See also Cross, *Canaanite Myth and Hebrew Epic,* for P as after Dtr. But see S. Mandell and D. N. Freedman, *Herodotus' History and Primary History,* for P as prior to Dtr. Moreover, if we accept Ivan Engnell's hypothesis that there was a P work and a D work (not to be confused with the redactors we call P and D respectively), and that the Tetrateuch is part of the P work, the entire problem of whether or not P modified J's account may become moot. Somehow or other the two different accounts, representing two different

tradition units, became fused into a tradition complex in the transition process. Engnell, "The Pentateuch," in *A Rigid Scrutiny: Critical Essays on the Old Testament* (Nashville: Vanderbilt University Press, 1969), 50–67.

38. Hence Gunkel (*Genesis 4*) notes that the only use of Yahweh-Elohim in Genesis is in chapters 2–3, which shows it to be later than J. But this does not mean that the pericope itself beginning with Gen. 2:4b should not be treated as J's work, and Gunkel makes no attempt to abrogate J's redactorship.
39. So as noted above, Cross (*Canaanite Myth and Hebrew Epic,* 302) is correct as seeing P's transitional statement in Gen. 2:4a as an introduction to J's account rather than as a conclusion to his own. For stress on the "monotonous reiteration of the fact of death, which increasingly encroaches upon life," in the Primeval History, see Clines, "Theme in Genesis 1–11," 295–96 et passim.
40. Claus Westermann, *Elements of Old Testament Theology* (Atlanta: John Knox, 1982), 90. But for the replacement of this type of creation by creation via the "word," see 91.
41. For the mutual openness of P's and J's creation stories, see G. von Rad, *Genesis,* 42. D. M. Carr (*Reading the Fractures of Genesis,* 115) points out that when there is "interweaving outside the Bible, the author of the combined text has composed some material that links the source documents into a new whole. In this respect, Genesis appears to be no exception."
42. The Priestly Redactor's theological bent, rather than a desire not to change a word of scripture, a stance that cannot be attributed to any redactor of Primary History, may possibly be the best explanation for his willingness to let J's account of the creation of the Man and the Woman stand as an alternative to or even a continuation of his own account. Likewise, P may have seen no need to add some depiction of the hero's likeness to the Deity to the portion of the text that he included in his narrative, but which emanated from (and is now assigned to) J's account since he had already stressed that very matter in his own creation narrative.
43. So Edwin Firmage thinks, as do many others, this is the creation of humanity, and it is the "focal point of the story." Firmage, "Genesis 1 and the Priestly Agenda," *JSOT* 82 (1999): 100–101. For the idea that this is a personified humanity, see, e.g., Thomas L. Thompson, *The Mythic Past: Biblical Archaeology and the Myth of Israel* (New York: Basic Books, 1999), 83.
44. The lack of the article in Gen. 5:2 may well be meaningful. At this point of the narrative, P clearly wants to suggest that it was "mankind" that was created, whereas in Gen. 1:27 that need not be his intent. The use of the article must not be considered arbitrary. Whenever there is determination, a literary or theological basis for it must be considered.
45. There is yet another facet to P's creation account: male power. It is the generic, nonspecific likeness of the deity, that is Man, who is not depicted as having a female part, who was fashioned so as to rule over everything as is indicated by the purpose clause in Gen. 1:26b: "so as to rule over. . . ." This, however, is not relevant to our argument and it has been well pursued by others.
46. Since the alterations of state that a nonparadigmatic initiand experiences are made manifest as a culmination to the events leading up to the peripeteia within the creation narrative itself, it is logical to presuppose that Man or the Man is the model initiand in a creation/birth ritual that every man must experience. But since every ritual holds implicit a rebirth, we must not limit the initiation to physical creation/birth.
47. Although, in the combined Gen. 1:1–3:24, the fact of the androgynous nature of the Man makes it unclear whether we are dealing with a male birth paradigm, we must not forget that, in Gen. 1:1–3:24—as opposed to the Mesopotamian traditions—the Deity himself creates without the midwifery of a woman.
48. In the Yahwist's account (Gen. 2:7), he is not created in the Deity's image. However, Andreas Schüle's suggestion that despite its lack of mention by name, "the different stages of the creation of Adam and Eve display some striking resemblances to the stages of the making of a divine image—however, with a critical overtone" is very important. Moreover, Schüle's linking of this to creation of an icon and the *mīs pī* ritual enlivening it is basic to our realization that Elohim did in fact create an icon of the sort found elsewhere in the Ancient Near East. The difference inherent in the creation of the Female is not relevant to my argument. Schüle, "Made in the 'Image of God': The Concepts of Divine *Images* in Gen 1–3," *ZAW* 117 (2005): 3, 12–13, 14.
49. This is reiterated in Gen. 5:2: "He created them Male and Female; and, on the day in which he created them, he called their name Man."
50. Ruth Adler suggests on philological grounds that the text does not mean that she is created as an inferior helper, but rather as a counterpart. Adler, "The Bible in a Women's Studies Course," *Approaches to Teaching the Hebrew Bible as Literature in Translation,* ed. Barry N. Olshen and Yael S. Feldman (New York: MLA, 1989), 95. See also G. von Rad, *Genesis,* 82. But I believe, also on a philological basis, that she had been created "in confrontation to him," and this too means that she is not an inferior helper. Rather she is to act as do male siblings in the patriarchal narratives that will follow. For creation from the side rather than the rib, and for the implications of this, see Batto, *Slaying the Dragon,* 54.

51. So here it is legitimate to treat the narrative as subject to hypertext.
52. Given the inheritance patterns in Genesis, the implications of this are interesting.
53. For the relationship to "mother earth," see Westermann, *Genesis 1–11*, 365.
54. The "Earth or Sea Diver" creation tradition, delineating male birthing, is common in many societies.
55. J. G. Frazer, *Folk-Lore in the Old Testament*, 17; Northrop Frye, "Theory of Archetypal Meaning: Apocalyptic and Demonic Imagery," in *The Bible in Its Literary Milieu*, ed. Maier and Tollers, 65; Kenneth Burke, "The First Three Chapters of Genesis," in *The Bible in Its Literary Milieu*, ed. Maier and Tollers, 390. For mortalization as a neater term than death, see Burke, "First Three Chapters of Genesis," 384.
56. See, e.g., Sir James George Frazer, *The New Golden Bough* (Garden City, N.Y.: Anchor, 1961), 150–51. But, for the incorrect and ideologically based belief that the Ancient Near Eastern preoccupation with the matter of death is not in operation here since "the Bible dissociates itself completely from" such mythologies, see Sarna, *Understanding Genesis*, 26–27.
57. Frazer, *Folk-Lore in the Old Testament*, 17.
58. See, e.g., Edmond Leach, "Lévi-Strauss in the Garden of Eden: An Examination of Some Recent Developments in the Analysis of Myth," in *Reader in Comparative Religion: An Anthropological Approach*, 2nd ed., ed. William A. Lessa and Evon Z. Vogt (New York: Harper and Row, 1965), 578; Frazer, *Folk-Lore in the Old Testament*, 16–18.
59. But see David Carr, who argues that Genesis 2–3 is actually an against wisdom story that relies on an "artful subversion" of an earlier account now part of Genesis 2, and which is presented so as to set up Wisdom as a pretense against which to argue. Carr, "The Politics of Textual Subversion: A Diachronic Perspective on the Garden of Eden Story," *JBL* 112 (1993): 577–95.
60. Fewell and Gunn, *Gender, Power, and Promise*, 25–26. See also Laurence A. Turner, *Genesis* (Sheffield: Sheffield Academic Press, 2000), 28.
61. I do not accept Bruce K. Waltke's limitation that the terms Good and Evil are "a merism for all *moral* knowledge" (italics mine). Waltke, with Cathi J. Fredricks, *Genesis: A Commentary* (Grand Rapids: Zondervan, 2001), 86.
62. See, e.g., Cyrus H. Gordon, *Before the Bible: The Common Background of Greek and Hebrew Civilizations* (New York: Harper and Row, 1962), 103. See also, e.g., Hans Goedicke, "Adam's Rib," in *Biblical and Related Studies Presented to Samuel Iwry* (Winona Lake, Ind.: Eisenbrauns, 1985), 73–76. The relationship to Sumerian literature has been noted as well. However, it focuses on the relationship of rib, and consequently, Eve to life. See, e.g., Walter Brueggemann, "Of the Same Flesh and Bone, Gn 2:23a," *CBQ* 32 (1970): 538–39. For Egyptian as well as other ANE ties, see Jutta Krispenz, "Wie viele Bäume braucht," 303, 308, 309 et passim. For the combined relationship of the Tree, Existence, and Life as well as Death, see 313.
63. H. N. Wallace, *The Eden Narrative* (Atlanta: Scholars Press, 1985), 111–14, 158. This is not explicitly stated. But both the tone and the sense of the narrative lead the implied reader to attribute more blame to the Woman than to the Man even when the text itself does not do so. This does not reflect the implied reader's patriarchal attitude, but that of the implied narrator.
64. For fruit and tree imagery as sexual metaphors in Ancient Near Eastern love poetry, see Joan G. Westenholz, "Metaphorical Language in the Poetry of Love in the Ancient Near East," *La Circulation des Biens, des Personnes et des Idées dans le Proche-Orient Ancien*, ed. D. Charpin and F. Joannès (Paris: Éditions Recherche sur les Civilisations, 1992), 381–87. But see Sarna, *Understanding Genesis*, 25, for the belief that neither the Man nor the Woman was granted "any special supernatural powers" by virtue of having eaten of this tree.
65. Although I am intrigued by and find correct Cyrus Gordon's belief that good and evil represent totality, I cannot accept it as being the equivalent of omniscience since neither the Man nor the Woman shows him- or herself to be omniscient once they eat. Rather, it must be treated as Wisdom, which comprehends divine creativity amongst other things. Gordon, *The Ancient Near East*, rev. 3rd ed. (New York: W. W. Norton, 1965), 35 n. 3, 36–37, 109.
66. See Fewell and Gunn, *Gender, Power, and Promise*, 24.
67. Carol Meyers, *Discovering Eve: Ancient Israelite Women in Context* (New York: Oxford University Press, 1988), 91 et passim.
68. The blessing of humanity in Gen. 1:28 is correlated with Wisdom: "When Adam and Eve are commanded during creation to cultivate and maintain the garden, wisdom as a coming to terms with life is implied in this commission." Claus Westermann, *Blessing in the Bible and the Life of the Church*. trans. K. Crim (Philadelphia: Fortress Press, 1978), 99, cited by Roland E. Murphy in *ABD* 6:924. I agree with Judith E. McKinlay ("To Eat or Not to Eat: Where Is Wisdom in This Choice?" *Semeia* 86, ed. Athalya Brenner and Jan Willem

van Heuter [Atlanta: Society of Biblical Literature, 1999 (2001)], 1:9) regarding the blurring of, and consequent distinction of, boundaries.

69. I agree with Judith E. McKinlay regarding the blurring of, and consequent distinction of, boundaries. McKinlay, "To Eat or Not to Eat: Where Is Wisdom in This Choice?" *Semeia* 86 ed. Athalya Brenner and Jan Willem van Heuter (Atlanta: Society of Biblical Literature, 1999 [2001], 1:9).
70. Waltke's (*Genesis,* 87) treatment of this as a "spiritual death" belies the nature of myth.
71. See Barr, *The Garden of Eden and the Hope of Immortality,* 9.
72. See Lloyd R. Bailey, *The Oxford Study Bible: Revised English Bible with the Apocrypha* (New York: Oxford University Press, 1992), 13, *ad* Gen. 2:17. But see Barr, *The Garden of Eden and the Hope of Immortality,* 10; von Rad, *Genesis,* 81, 95–96.
73. Although E. Leach ("Lévi-Strauss in the Garden," 580) says that they did "become aware of sexual difference," I myself do not equate this with sexuality itself, only of the potential for and knowledge of the existence of sexuality. And I see no basis in the narrative for Hugh C. White's belief that the awareness of their sexual difference had preceded what he terms the "violation." White, *Narration and Discourse in the Book of Genesis* (Cambridge: Cambridge University Press, 1991), 128. See also Gerda Lerner (*The Creation of Patriarchy* [New York: Oxford University Press, 1986], 196), who presumes that this knowledge is sexual rather than of their potential for sexuality. And without warrant she then treats this pericope as denying women the "free and open sexuality of the fertility-goddess." For a more balanced presentation, but acceptance of the sexual implications in J's story, see Otzen, "The Use of Myth in Genesis," 45, 48–49 et passim. Hence H. Gunkel (*Genesis,* 11) attributes their actions prior to their awareness as childlike and suggests that prior to the opening of their eyes, they had gone naked in the same way that children do.
74. So this pericope does in fact hark back to a Garden of God tale despite the fact that J never uses this particular name for it. (Likewise, First Isaiah's "Song of the Vineyard" may be a literal reference to the Garden of Eden as well as being an allegorical one to the Children of Israel.) For this as the Deity's garden, see Batto, *Slaying the Dragon,* 50–51. But for the more common opinion, see Sarna, *Understanding Genesis,* 25, who believes that we merely have a refinement of this perception so as to stress the planting of the Garden for man, not for the deity; *et alii.*
75. But see Matthieu Casalis, who thinks that Gen. 2:21–25, and particularly 2:23–24, are verses indicating sexuality. Casalis, "The Dry and the Wet: A Semiological Analysis of Creation and Flood Myths," *Semiotica* 17 (1976): 46–47.
76. See Alan Jon Hauser, "Intimacy and Alienation in Genesis 2-2," in *Art and Meaning: Rhetoric in Biblical Literature,* ed. David J. A. Clines, David M. Gunn, and Alan J. Hauser (Sheffield: JSOT, 1982), 25. But I cannot agree with H. Gunkel (*Genesis,* 11 *ad* 2:25) that they resemble children insofar as they go naked and do not know good and evil. Modern psychology suggests that children are far more aware of their world than we would like to believe; they simply may not have the ability to express their awareness.
77. I stress the omniscience of the implied narrator here so as to indicate that lack of reporting does not imply lack of knowledge. If, as by definition he is, the implied narrator be omniscient, then he knows what had happened. Any omission or ambiguity, therefore, represents his conscious choice, not his lack of knowledge. It is inherent in the character of an implied narrator that he picks and chooses what he reports. That the real author makes that choice for him is beside the question. But at the same time this self same omission opens up a plethora of possibilities.
78. Nevertheless the idea of it being an apple is intriguing in light of Heinrich Zimmer's observations about the role of the apple in heroic literate. Zimmer, *The King and the Corpse: Tales of the Soul's Conquest of Evil,* ed. Joseph Campbell (Princeton, N.J.: Princeton University Press, 1971), 46–47). Moreover, I have been informed that the apple had its origin in the far East, most likely in China, and by J's time, it may have been known anywhere along the trade routes leading to the Mediterranean. If so, the presupposition that the fruit of the tree was an apple need not reflect some cultural interaction with eastern Greeks and their myths as is often presumed. Eliade (*The Sacred and the Profane,* 150) meaningfully notes that "the sacred tree or sacred plants display a structure that is not to be seen in the various concrete vegetable species."
79. Batto (*Slaying the Dragon,* 75) notes that "it is difficult to believe other than that the Priestly Writer intended his creation account as a corrective to the Yahwist's version."
80. I use these terms as technical terms in accord with what has been established by the New Critics. Batto (*Slaying the Dragon,* 75) notes the "entirely new look P's 'frame' of the Yahwistic stories creates." See also 91–94 et passim.
81. W. G. Lambert ("The Relationship of Sumerian and Babylonian Myth as Seen in Accounts of Creation," *La Circulation des Biens, des Personnes et des Idées dans le Proche-Orient Ancien* [Paris: Éditions Recherche sur

les Civilisations, 1992, D. Charpin and F. Joannès, ed.], 134) states: "life as the ancients saw it only came from pre-existing life: the plant from the seed." Lambert, "The Relationship of Sumerian and Babylonian Myth as Seen in Accounts of Creation," in *La Circulation des Biens,* ed. Charpin and Joannès, 134.

82. Frazer, *Folk-Lore in the Old Testament,* 16–17.
83. Von Rad, *Genesis,* 47.
84. Westermann, *Elements of Old Testament Theology.*
85. This after all is characteristically the manner in which P treats any anomalous thing or creature, particularly in the "laws" that he included in the Sinai Pericope.
86. So von Rad (*Genesis,* 91) is right in seeing the fruit as coming from a "unique, miraculous tree of Paradise."
87. For an emergence of the species in relationship to their creation, see Westermann, *Elements of Old Testament Theology,* 92. Italics are Westermann's.
88. But see Charles Rowan Beye, "The Epic of Gilgamesh, the Bible, and Homer: Some Narrative Parallels," in *Mnemai: Classical Studies in Memory of Karl K. Hulley,* ed. Harold D. Evjen (Chico, Calif.: Scholars, 1984), 11, who believes that they became sexually aware.
89. So the Serpent and Eve need not have been one and the same in earlier traditions as some believe if in fact the Man ate without question. On the other hand, if there had been traditions in which the Man had been the one tempted, then the equation of the serpent and Eve may be valid.
90. Rather than presume, as most do, that there was only the Tree of Life, and that J added a separate tree, I think it likely that that archetypal tree was of something more than Life, it was a more comprehensive tree by far, and was analogous to the World Tree, which combines Life, Death, and Wisdom, and is a common tradition in world religions. The Yahwist simply separated it into two of its components.
91. But Frazer (*Folk-Lore in the Old Testament,* 16–17) raises another possibility. He suggests that the earlier story did incorporate both trees, and the Deity was actually affording Man the opportunity to choose life.
92. The Man and the Woman, who become Adam and Eve respectively although not simultaneously, undergo similar transitions from sacred time, space, and status to historical time, real space, and human status. While they are in the Garden, they are neither completely mortal nor are they immortal. Only when the Deity curses and expels them do they leave their liminoid time, place, and status. They go to historical time—no matter how different it be from our perception of historical time—and nonliminal, nonsacred space, which we may or may not identify with known places. Inherent in each of these transitions is the distinction between life and death whether freely embraced or imposed against the will. But here too there is ambiguity in the text.
93. Some back and forth interchange in this matter has been noted by others.
94. Dmitri Slivniak believes that the transgression, not the nakedness, is the problem. Therefore, shame is rendered into guilt. Slivniak, "The Garden of Double Messages: Deconstructing Hierarchical Oppositions in the Garden Story," *JSOT* 27 (2003): 443.
95. Again the covering of the genitalia is meaningful. The fact that they do not only cover their genitalia until after they have eaten of the fruit of the interdicted tree, although they had been in the presence of their nonhuman companions prior to this, shows that they did not experience shame regarding nakedness before the nonhuman animals who were not deities. This has been attributed to their being in a childlike state, with which I disagree precisely because they are liminal and therefore are "beyond" that particular classification, and for the lack of shame because the Man lacks "knowledge" (*Erkenntnis, not Wissen*), with which I agree. See Gunkel, *Genesis,* 11 *ad* 2:25.
96. Although some verses may be etiological, I firmly believe that this cannot be said of the entirety of J's pericope.
97. For the sense of shame when they perceive that the Deity is walking in the Garden, see Fewell and Gunn, *Gender, Power, and Promise,* 32.
98. E. van Wolde points out that it was the very "seeing their nakedness" that gave "them knowledge about the difference between man and woman." E. van Wolde, "A Reader-oriented Exegesis Illustrated by a Study of the Serpent in Genesis 2–3," *Pentateuchal and Deuteronomistic Studies,* ed. C. Brekelmans and J. Lust (Leuven: Leuven University Press, 1990), 18.
99. Which may be why the Deity clothes them with skins after defining what their function is henceforth to be (Gen. 3:14–21).
100. For the necessity of observation for shame to be manifest, see T. M. Lemos, "Shame and Mutilation of Enemies in the Hebrew Bible," *JBL* 125 (2006): 228, who cites David D. Gilmore, "Honor, Honesty, Shame: Male Status in Contemporary Andalusia," from *Honour and Shame: The Values of Mediterranean Society,* ed. J. G. Peristiany (London: Weidenfeld and Nicolson, 1965), 101.
101. Gunkel, *Genesis,* 11 *ad* 2:25.

102. We can only speculate as to whether this is pertinent to and reflective of the divine creativity in Genesis 1 that is not accomplished by Elohim's creative word. I cannot agree with Lerner (*The Creation of Patriarchy,* 188), who sees the "immortality that comes through generation, through procreativity" as symbolically softening the "curse of mortality."

103. Michael A Knibb, in "Life and Death in the Old Testament" (*The World of Ancient Israel,* ed. R. E. Clements [Cambridge: Cambridge University Press, 1989], 402), does not attribute man's loss of immortality to disobedience. Rather, he lost the potential for immortality as Barr (*The Garden of Eden and the Hope of Immortality,* 19) indicates when he refers to immortality "as a chance that was lost."

104. See Barr, *The Garden of Eden and the Hope of Immortality,* 58–60 et passim. For the tree in earlier stages of the biblical story, see 58.

105. See Bailey, *The Oxford Study Bible,* 13, *ad* Gen. 2:17. But see R. W. L. Moberly, "Did the Serpent Get It Right?" in his *From Eden to Golgotha: Essays in Biblical Theology* (Atlanta: Scholars Press, 1992), 1–27.

106. For the Tree of Knowledge of Good and Evil as forbidden, and therefore, totem, see Stanley A. Cook, "Israel and Totemism," *JQR* 14 (1902): 423.

107. It is not necessary to treat this as being some type of punishment; rather, it is part of their humanization, which is not necessarily the same as their mortalization.

108. So Fredrick E. Greenspahn is correct in viewing the expulsion from the Garden as "a way of precluding access to" the Tree of Life rather than a type of punishment for the act of disobedience. Greenspahn, "A Mesopotamian Proverb and its Biblical Reverberations," *JAOS* 114 (1994): 37.

109. But see Slivniak ("The Garden of Double Messages," 443–44), who suggests that this may simply be resultant on disobedience.

110. We may presume that like Sophocles' *Oedipus Tyrannus,* they had eyes but did not see once their eyes were opened, and like Teiresius, they had no use of their eyes, and they saw right well.

111. For the blindness see Gunkel, *Genesis,* 13 *ad* 3:4.

112. The way in which this material was later treated reflects a demythologization of the narrative. This is in accord with von Rad's belief (*Genesis,* 19) that when cultic and/or "ethnological tribal sagas" were taken out of their *Sitz im Leben,* they became subject to "every kind of spiritualized literary application."

113. See, e.g., von Rad, *Genesis,* 77. But see 78.

114. And it certainly reflects the Babylonian creation story insofar as man had been construed to do the gods' work for them. But it also reflects native Canaanite traditions as well as other Ancient Near Eastern ones, as has been noted frequently. But the non-Israelite influence is clearly muted by both J's and P's respective theological precepts and aims.

Jeremiah, the Shoah, and the Restoration of Israel

Marvin Sweeney

I

The Book of Jeremiah is unique among the prophetic books insofar as it presents the oracles and activities of the only one of the prophets to live through the Babylonian siege and destruction of Jerusalem. Other prophets may have lived through such catastrophe, for example, Ezekiel received the news of Jerusalem's fall while living in Babylonian exile, and Isaiah lived at the time of Samaria's fall to the Assyrian empire, but Jeremiah is the only prophetic book to give its readers a glimpse of life in the doomed city and the struggles in which its inhabitants engaged as they faced the onslaught of the Babylonian army. Indeed, Jeremiah tells his readers more about himself, his own thoughts, and his struggles with his divine commission than any other prophet in the Hebrew Bible. Jeremiah begins his prophetic career in 627 BCE at the outset of the reign of King Josiah, which promises a restoration of Judean independence and a reunification of Judah and Israel under Davidic rule, but he lives to see the tragic death of Josiah in 609 BCE and the twenty-two-year period that, ultimately, sees the destruction of Jerusalem and Judah in 587 BCE. He is a Levitical priest who knows, teaches, and reflects upon past tradition in relation to the circumstances of his own time. He is a political partisan who employs his reflection on past traditions to stake out a political position opposed to that of the pro-Egyptian King Jehoiakim ben Josiah, one that calls for submission to the Babylonian empire rather than opposition to it. He is a man who suffers when his own brothers or fellow priests seek his life, when he denies himself the joys of marriage and family life because he understands that the catastrophe is coming, when he sees his own nation and people devastated after they failed to heed his advice and fought their former Babylonian allies, when he is arrested for treason for speaking his mind, and when he is forced into Egyptian exile against his will to die in a foreign land.

Modern critical scholarship recognizes Jeremiah's engagement with the destruction of Jerusalem and the Babylonian Exile, although it has not fully recognized the relevance of Jeremiah for issues posed by the Shoah.[1] Overall, Jeremiah is portrayed as a prophet of judgment, who proclaims the destruction of Jerusalem, Judah, and the Temple as a result of the people's failure to observe YHWH's Torah.[2] In general, Jeremiah's message of judgment is viewed uncritically as the just punishment of a sinful people who are led astray by false prophets who proclaim peace in a time of threat. Scholars who attempt to reconstruct the compositional history of the book generally argue that the earliest material appears in Jeremiah 1–20 or 1–25, which contain the bulk of the poetic oracles of judgment against Jerusalem and Judah.[3] Many likewise argue that the narrative material in Jeremiah 26–45, which also includes oracles of restoration in Jeremiah 30–31 and 32–33, is later material that does not necessarily represent the work of the prophet.[4] Because of the prevailing view that prophets and priests are fundamentally opposed to each other, Jeremiah's laments, which are formulated according to the patterns of cultic poetry that would have been sung by the Temple priests, are often viewed as secondary additions to the text that likewise do not represent the work of Jeremiah himself.[5] Indeed, Jeremiah's priestly identity is often suppressed or overlooked in modern study of the book. Because Jeremiah is clearly a true prophet, his polemics against false prophets are directed against cynical manipulators of public opinion who speak oracles of support for the monarchy, Jerusalem, and the Temple for their own personal gain.[6]

Although attempts to reconstruct the history of Jeremiah's composition are both legitimate and necessary, they tend to obscure important aspects of the interpretation of Jeremiah. First is the literary form of the book, which is hardly structured on the basis of an early collection of oracles in Jeremiah 1–25 that has been supplemented by later additions in Jeremiah 26–52. Rather, the literary pattern of presentation of the words of YHWH that came to Jeremiah throughout his lifetime point to a literary structure that portrays the prophet's reflection on the fate of Jerusalem and Judah leading up to and beyond the Babylonian Exile. The literary structure of the book points to such progressive reflection on divine judgment against the city and the prospects for its restoration after the judgment is complete (see Table 1).[7]

Indeed, such an integrative reading of the literary structure of Jeremiah places Jeremiah's oracles of judgment in conversation with his oracles of restoration; it places Jeremiah's prophetic identity in conversation with his identity as a Levitical priest; and it places Jeremiah's laments in conversation with his oracles of judgment. Altogether, a synchronic reading of Jeremiah reveals the prophet's struggles to reconcile his understanding of past tradition, such as the Torah or Isaiah's message of deliverance for

Table 1. The words of Jeremiah Ben Hilkiah concerning the restoration of Jerusalem and the downfall of Babylon

I.	Oracles concerning Israel and Judah	1–6
	A. Superscription	1:1–3
	B. Commissioning of the prophet	1:4–10
	C. Signs concerning YHWH's purpose	1:11–19
	D. Oracles calling for Israel and Judah to return to YHWH	2–6
II.	Account concerning Jeremiah's Temple sermon	7–10
III.	Oracles concerning rejection of YHWH's covenant	11–13
IV.	Oracles concerning drought and marriage	14–17
	A. Drought	14–15
	B. Marriage	16–17
V.	Oracles concerning shattered pot/judgment against Judah	18–20
VI.	Oracles concerning Davidic kingship	21–24
VII.	Narratives concerning Jeremiah's warnings to submit to Babylon	25–29
VIII.	Oracles concerning restoration of Israel and Judah	30–31
IX.	Narrative concerning field at Anathoth	32–33
X.	Narrative concerning YHWH's decision to give Jerusalem to Nebuchadnezzar	34:1–7
XI.	Narrative concerning reneging on year of release	34:8–22
XII.	Narrative concerning fall of Jerusalem	35–39
XIII.	Narrative concerning Jeremiah's removal to Egypt	40–43
XIV.	Narrative concerning Jeremiah's oracles in Egypt	44
XV.	Narrative concerning word to Baruch	45
XVI.	Oracle concerning Egypt	46:1–12
XVII.	Oracle concerning Babylonian conquest of Egypt	46:13–28
XVIII.	Oracle concerning small nations	47–49
XIX.	Oracle concerning Babylon	50:1–51:58
XX.	Narrative concerning Jeremiah's instructions about Babylon	51:59–64
XXI.	Appendix concerning fall of Jerusalem	52

Jerusalem, with the reality of Jerusalem's impending Shoah or destruction for its failure to submit to Babylonian rule. It points to a man who wants no part of YHWH's divine commission, but who is nevertheless compelled to accept his—and Jerusalem's—fate. Examination of a series of texts, including his commission as a prophet in Jeremiah 1; his early oracles concerning Israel and Judah in Jeremiah 2–6; his famous Temple sermon in Jeremiah 7–10; his laments in Jer. 11:18–23; 12:1–6; 15:10–21; 17:14–18; 18:18–23; 20:7–13; and 20:14–18; his diatribes against false prophets in Jeremiah 23, 27–29; and his visions of restoration in Jeremiah 30–31 and 32–33 point to the various dimensions of his struggle with his divine commission to witness and interpret the Shoah of Jerusalem and Judah.

II

Jeremiah 1 presents three important subunits of the larger literary block in Jeremiah 1–6 that are important for defining Jeremiah's perspectives concerning the fall of Jerusalem and the Babylonian Exile. They include the superscription of the book in Jer. 1:1–3, the account of Jeremiah's commission as a prophet by YHWH in Jer. 1:4–10, and the account of the prophet's visionary experiences that convey YHWH's purposes. Altogether, these subunits demonstrate that Jeremiah is a priest in Jerusalem during the last years of the kingdom of Judah, and that he struggles with his prophetic commission to interpret the impending calamity that will overtake his nation.

The superscription for the book in Jer. 1:1–3 immediately signals Jeremiah's priestly identity with its opening statement, "The words of Jeremiah ben Hilkiah from the priests who were in Anathoth in the land of Benjamin." Although the superscription identifies Jeremiah as a "priest" (*kōhēn*), it qualifies that identification by specifying that he is from the priest at Anathoth. This indicates that he is not a member of the Zadokite priestly line that served in the Temple of YHWH at Jerusalem, but that he is a member of the priestly line of Eli, whose only surviving member, Abiathar, was expelled from Jerusalem to Anathoth by King Solomon early in the history of the kingdom of Israel (1 Kings 2:26–27). This means that Jeremiah comes from a priestly line that has no particular sympathy for either the house of David or for the Jerusalem Temple. Abiathar was expelled from Jerusalem by Solomon after having served David loyally throughout his life. Furthermore, he was expelled prior to the construction of the Jerusalem Temple. Subsequent literary blocks in the Book of Jeremiah demonstrate the prophet's capacity to critique king and Temple. Jeremiah 21:11–22:30 presents the prophet's condemnation of kings Jehoiakim and Jehoiachin of Judah, although his statements make his admiration for the righteous King Josiah very clear. Likewise, Jeremiah 7–10 presents the prophet's famous Temple sermon in which he states that the people cannot expect protection from YHWH based on the existence of the Temple alone. In keeping with his perspective as a Levitical priest, he maintains that adherence to YHWH's Torah is the necessary precondition for YHWH's favor and protection. As a priest of the Elide priestly line, Jeremiah would well remember that his own ancestral sanctuary at Shiloh had been destroyed in the premonarchic period (Jer. 7:12–15), and that Jerusalem could just as easily suffer the same fate.

The superscription goes on to specify in verses 2–3 that the word of YHWH came to Jeremiah from the thirteenth year of King Josiah ben Amon of Judah (627 BCE), through the reign of King Jehoiakim ben Josiah, and until the eleventh year of the reign of King Zedekiah ben Josiah in 587–586 BCE when Jerusalem was exiled. The superscription thereby highlights the importance of the destruction of Jerusalem and the Babylonian Exile for the book and for the prophet's career. The attentive reader will recognize, however, that the chronological claims of the book are not quite accurate. Jeremiah does not conclude chronologically with the destruction of Jerusalem. Although Jerusalem's fall is portrayed in Jeremiah 35–39, 52, the narratives in Jeremiah 40–45 portray the subsequent assassination of Gedaliah ben Ahikam ben Shaphan, the Babylonian-appointed governor of Judah in 582 BCE, and Jeremiah's subsequent removal to Egypt against his will, where he spends the rest of his life condemning the people of Judah for their rebellion against the will of YHWH. In considering why the superscription would make such a claim, it should be noted that the span of years from the thirteenth year of Josiah to the eleventh year of Zedekiah totals forty years. Although Jeremiah begins his career in the land of Judah in a time of great optimism over King Josiah's program of religious reform and national restoration at the time of the Assyrian empire's decline, he ends his life and career as an exile in Egypt. In this manner, Jeremiah's life represents a reversal of that of Moses, likewise a prophet and Levitical priest, who had led his people on a forty-year journey from Egypt to the land of Israel.[8]

The account of the prophet's commission in Jer. 1:4–10 indicates Jeremiah's struggle with his prophetic role and YHWH's insistence that he carry it out despite his objections. The passage presents YHWH's statement to Jeremiah in verse 5 to commission him as a prophet:

> Before I created you in the womb, I selected you;
> before you were born, I consecrated you;
> I appointed you a prophet concerning the nations.

Jeremiah resists YHWH's commission to serve as a prophet in verse 6 by stating:

> Ah YHWH, G-d! I don't know how to speak, for I am a boy.

Jeremiah's objection to his prophetic commission is common; for example, Moses responds to YHWH's commission to free Israel from Egyptian bondage by stating that he is inadequate to the task. But YHWH's insistence that he go as instructed in verse 7 indicates an order on YHWH's part that the prophet will not be able to refuse:

> Do not say, "I am still a boy,"
> but go wherever I send you, and speak whatever I command you.
> Have no fear of them, for I am with you to deliver you.

Indeed, Jeremiah's objection here presages his lifelong struggle with his prophetic commission in which he must witness and announce YHWH's judgment against the people of Jerusalem and Judah culminating in their destruction and exile. Although the prophet's message includes the prospect of restoration following the punishment, the content of YHWH's commission to him in verse 10 emphasizes punishment:

> See, I appoint you this day over nations and kingdoms
> to uproot and to pull down, to destroy and to overthrow,
> to build and to plant.

The four verbs of destruction and two verbs of restoration employed in this passage recur as leitmotifs for the prophet's message throughout the book in Jer. 12:14–17; 18:5–10; 24:6; 31:28, 40; 42:10; and 45:4.

Finally, the two vision reports in Jer. 1:11–19 emphasize both Jeremiah's priestly identity and the motif of impending judgment and destruction. The first vision account in verse 12 presents Jeremiah's observation of a branch of an almond tree, which YHWH interprets as a demonstration that YHWH is "watchful" to bring the divine word to pass. The vision is based on a pun involving the Hebrew noun *maqqēl šāqēd*, "branch of an almond tree," and the verb *šōqēd*, "watchful, watching." The pun is intended to evoke the image of the sprouting rods of Aaron representing the tribe of Levi in Num. 17:16–28 to symbolize the selection of Aaron and the tribe of Levi to serve as priests in Israel. The second vision account in verses 13–19 employs the image of a steaming pot tipped away from the north to depict the enemies from the north, that is, the Babylonians, who will assault Judah to carry out YHWH's judgment against the nation. Once again, the image evokes Jeremiah's status as a priest whose responsibilities include tending to the pots employed for cooking food for the priests and people during the sacrificial worship services conducted at the Temple. Not only does the image convey Jeremiah's priestly identity, it serves as the basis for YHWH to insist that Jeremiah carry out his prophetic role of announcing judgment despite his objections when YHWH commends him in verses 17–19:

> So you, gird up your loins, arise and speak to them all that I command you.
> Do not break down before them, lest I break you before them.
> I make you this day a fortified city, and an iron pillar,
> and bronze walls against the whole land—
> against Judah's kings and officers and against its priests and citizens.

They will attack you, but they shall not overcome you;
For I am with you, declares YHWH, to save you.

YHWH's command includes a threat. Jeremiah has no choice but to comply—or suffer the consequences.

III

Jeremiah's identity as a Levitical priest plays a crucial role in his prophetic announcements concerning the events of his day and his understanding of YHWH's role in those events. Leviticus 10:10–11 makes it clear that a central facet of Jeremiah's task as a Levitical priest is to teach the people of Israel and Judah the entire Torah of YHWH concerning the differences between what is sacred and what is impure. The oracles in Jeremiah 2–6, which constitute the largest block of material in Jeremiah 1–6, demonstrate Jeremiah's attempts to carry out his priestly and prophetic role during the early years of Josiah's reforms and in the aftermath of Josiah's death.[9] Indeed, these oracles demonstrate the prophet's capacity to rethink his teachings in relation to the events of his day and to reflect upon earlier tradition in articulating his understanding of divine purpose.

The present form of Jeremiah 2–6 constitutes Jeremiah's lengthy prophetic summons to repentance directed to Judah. Jeremiah points to YHWH's charges of idolatry against Judah and argues that YHWH will bring an unnamed enemy from the north to carry out the divine judgment unless Judah repents and returns to observing YHWH's expectations. Although the present form of this text is directed to Judah, literary tensions and internal references within this block of material indicate that it is a composite text in which an early summons to repent directed to the northern kingdom of Israel was later expanded and shifted so that it would address the southern kingdom of Judah instead. The poetic material in Jer. 2:1–3:5; 3:14–4:2 appears to be directed exclusively to Israel/Jacob or the northern kingdom of Israel. These passages accuse Israel of forsaking YHWH, transferring their allegiance to the foreign gods or Baalim of Egypt, Assyria, and elsewhere. They assert that northern Israel has suffered YHWH's punishment for such actions, and call upon Israel to return to YHWH at Zion:

Turn back, rebellious children declares YHWH.
Since I have espoused you, I will take you,
one from a town and two from a clan and bring you to Zion.
And I will give you shepherds after my own heart,
who will pasture you with knowledge and skill. (Jer. 3:14–15)

If you return O Israel—declares YHWH
If you return to Me, if you remove your abominations from My presence
And do not waver and swear 'As YHWH lives'
In sincerity, justice, and righteousness —
Nations shall bless themselves by you and praise themselves by you. (Jer. 4:1–2)

Jeremiah's call for the repentance of northern Israel and its return to YHWH at Zion articulates the basic goals of King Josiah's program of religious reform and national restoration in the late seventh century BCE. At the time of the decline of the Assyrian empire, which had dominated Judah from the late eighth century BCE., Josiah apparently sensed that the opportunity was ripe to assert Judean independence, reclaim the territory and population of the former northern kingdom of Israel, and thereby restore the ideal Solomonic empire based on the house of David and the Jerusalem Temple. As a prophet whose career began in the thirteenth year of Josiah, that is, 627 BCE, at the outset of Josiah's reform program, Jeremiah appears to serve as a mouthpiece for the king's reform and restoration program insofar as he calls for Israel's return to YHWH, Jerusalem, and Josiah.

The sudden and unexpected death of Josiah at the hands of Pharaoh Necho of Egypt at Megiddo in 609 BCE puts an abrupt end to Josiah's program. With his death, Judah became a vassal of Egypt and later of Babylonia, which led ultimately to Jerusalem's and Judah's destruction in revolt against Babylon in 588–586 BCE. Jeremiah's recognition of the significance of Josiah's death explains the expansion and reformulation of the original summons to repentance directed to Israel into a summons to Jerusalem and Judah in Jeremiah 2–6. Josiah's death indicated that YHWH's plans for punishment were not yet complete, and that Jerusalem and Judah would suffer destruction just like Israel had suffered a century before if they did not observe YHWH's will. The additional material in Jer. 3:6–13 demonstrates the prophet's reflection on his message from the days of Josiah and his recognition that Judah must be even more guilty than Israel before her. As a result, the additional material in Jer. 4:3–6:30 targets Judah as the object of YHWH's wrath and the prophet's summons to repentance:

> Open your hearts to YHWH, remove the thickening of your hearts—
> O men of Judah and inhabitants of Jerusalem—
> Lest My wrath break forth like fire, and burn with none to quench it,
> Because of your wicked acts. (Jer. 4:4)
> Set up a signpost: To Zion.
> Take refuge, do not delay!
> For I bring evil from the north, and great disaster. (Jer. 4:6)

Jeremiah's reformulation of his message from a summons directed to Israel to one directed to Judah indicates his recognition of the danger now facing Jerusalem and Judah in the aftermath of Josiah's death. But it also represents his reflection as a Levitical priest on past tradition and his attempts to teach that tradition to his people. Jeremiah 2–6 is peppered with language and phraseology reminiscent of the prophet Isaiah ben Amoz of Jerusalem. A century prior to Jeremiah's time, Isaiah had offered a message of judgment against the northern kingdom of Israel and deliverance for the southern kingdom of Judah based on his understanding of the Davidic/Zion tradition, which asserted YHWH's promise to defend the house of David and the city of Jerusalem forever.[10] Indeed, Isaiah's oracles envisioned a reunification of Israel and Judah and a restoration of Davidic rule over the north in the aftermath of Israel's downfall:

> In that day, the stock of Jesse that has remained standing
> shall become a standard to the peoples—nations shall seek his counsel
> and his abode shall be honored. . . .
> He will hold up a signal to the nations and assemble the banished of Israel,
> And gather the dispersed of Judah from the four corners of the earth.
> Then Ephraim's envy shall cease and Judah's harassment shall end;
> Ephraim shall not envy Judah, and Judah shall not harass Ephraim.
> They shall pounce on the back of Philistia to the west,
> And together plunder the peoples of the east;
> Edom and Moab shall be subject to them
> And the children of Ammon shall obey them. (Isa. 11:10, 12–14)

Although such an Isaian perspective may well underlie Jeremiah's calls for Israel's return to Jerusalem in Jer. 2:1–3:5, 3:14–4:2, the calls for Judah's repentance together with its potential punishment in Jer. 3:6–13, 4:3–6:30 often quote Isaian oracles as well. For example, Jer. 5:15–17 includes Jeremiah's statements that YHWH will bring "a nation from afar" against the house of Israel:

> Lo, I am bringing against you, O House of Israel, a nation from afar—declares YHWH.
> It is an enduring nation, it is an ancient nation;
> A nation whose language you do not know—you will not understand what they say.
> Their quivers are like a yawning grave—they are all mighty men.
> They will devour your harvest and food, they will devour your sons and daughters,
> They will devour your flocks and herds, they will devour your vines and fig trees.
> They will batter down with the sword the fortified towns on which you rely.

Jeremiah's statement concerning the approach of a foreign enemy to punish Israel or Judah is strikingly similar to Isaiah's statements concerning the approach of the Assyrian army to punish Israel in Isa. 5:26–29:

He will raise an ensign to a nation afar, whistle to one at the end of the earth.
There it comes with lightening speed! In its ranks, none is weary or stumbles,
They never sleep or slumber;
The belts on their waists do not come loose, nor do the thongs of their sandals break.
Their arrows are sharpened, and all their bows are drawn.
Their horses hoofs are like flint, the chariot wheels like the whirlwind.
Their roaring is like a lion's, they roar like the great beasts;
When they growl and seize a prey, they carry it off and none can recover it.

Given the interrelationship between the Jeremian and Isaian oracles, it would appear that Jeremiah draws on the Isaiah tradition to articulate his summons to Judah. Coming in the aftermath of Josiah's death and Judah's subjugation to first Egypt and then Babylon, Jeremiah's vision of a restored and reunited Davidic monarchy had to be altered to one that saw the possibility of continued judgment against Judah and Jerusalem like that suffered by Israel and Samaria. For Jeremiah, the older Isaian message of YHWH's protection for the house of David and Jerusalem could no longer hold sway. Jerusalem and Judah could fall victim to a Mesopotamian conqueror from the north just as Israel had fallen victim to the Assyrians a century before.

IV

Jeremiah's recognition of the potential danger to Jerusalem and Judah appears quite clearly in his famed Temple sermon in Jeremiah 7–10.[11] The sermon appears in the form of YHWH's instructions to the prophet to stand in the gate of the Temple and deliver a sermon to the people that challenges the notion that the presence of the Temple represents YHWH's promise of protection and security for Jerusalem. The narrative in Jeremiah 26 concerning Jeremiah's trial for sedition as a result of his declaration that Jerusalem would be destroyed indicates his compliance with YHWH's instructions. Only the intervention of Ahikam ben Shaphan, a highly placed supporter of Jeremiah, saved the prophet from execution.[12] The narrative in Jeremiah 36 concerning King Jehoiakim's disdainful treatment of the scroll of Jeremiah's sermon indicates that Jeremiah was subsequently banned from speaking publicly at the Temple and sought to work around the ban by having the scribe, Baruch ben Neriah, write a scroll of Jeremiah's words and read it in the Temple in place of the prophet. Jehoiakim's order that Jeremiah be arrested upon hearing the scroll indicates the king's response to the prophet's message.

The sermon is controversial because of Jeremiah's contention that the presence of the Jerusalem Temple will not save the city from potential destruction. It is, therefore, a challenge to the dominant Davidic/Zion covenant theology of the time that posited YHWH's promise of eternal rule for the house of David (2 Samuel 7; 23:1–7; Psalm 110) and security for the city of Jerusalem (Psalms 2, 46, 47, 48). In keeping with classic Deuteronomic theology and literary form, Jeremiah employs the classic form of the Levitical sermon like that employed by Moses throughout the Book of Deuteronomy to argue that the people must observe YHWH's expectations in order to ensure their security in the land (see Deuteronomy 28–30).[13] He cites elements of the Ten Commandments (see Deuteronomy 5) to illustrate what such observance entails. To support his argument, he points to the history of his ancestral sanctuary at Shiloh, which was apparently destroyed by the Philistines (see 1 Samuel 4), to contend that Jerusalem could be destroyed as well. Although one might be surprised that a Levitical priest would present such a critique of the Temple, Jeremiah's role as a priest called for instruction in the proper observance of YHWH's will, including the purification of the Temple (see Lev. 10:10–11). As a member of the Elide priestly line whose ancestor Abiathar had been dismissed from service in the Jerusalem Temple and banished to Anathoth in the days of Solomon, Jeremiah would have little sympathy for the Jerusalem Temple or reason to accept its conceptualization as the center or source for creation in ancient Judean thought.

By announcing the potential destruction of the Temple and Jerusalem like that of Shiloh, Jeremiah challenged the very foundations of Judean self-identity and stood trial for sedition against the king and state for his claims (see Jeremiah 26). The narrative concerning the trial illustrates the desperate nature of Jeremiah's situation. Jeremiah's defense is based on his contention that he speaks on behalf of YHWH, and his supporters point to the example of Micah, whose contention that Jerusalem would be plowed like a field (Jer. 26:17–19; cf. Micah 3:12) prompted King Hezekiah's repentance and the deliverance of the city. The execution by King Jehoiakim of a prophet named Uriah ben Shemaiah from Kiriath Jearim appears to have sealed Jeremiah's fate until the intervention of Ahikam ben Shaphan, who, like his father, had once been an officer in King Josiah's court (see 2 Kings 22:3, 12). Jeremiah's life is saved, although he is banished from Temple service (see Jer. 36:1–8).

Although Jeremiah apparently delivered the sermon as instructed, he clearly struggles with his commission from G-d. Many interpreters contend that the Temple sermon narrative appears only in Jer. 7:1–8:3, but the introductory word transmission formula in Jer. 7:1 and the following formulas concerning YHWH's continuing instructions to Jeremiah in Jer. 7:16, 27; 8:4; and 10:11 indicate that the unit extends much farther, apparently through the end of chapter 10.[14] Within the passage, Jeremiah also speaks to YHWH. Following his admonition that Jerusalem and Judah not follow the way of the nations in Jer. 10:2–5, the text in Jer. 10:6–10, 12–16 presents the prophet's praise of YHWH in typical Levitical fashion. Following YHWH's statement that YHWH will fling away the inhabitants of the land in Jer. 10:18, Jeremiah again addresses YHWH in verses 19–25 to speak about the sickness and wounds that he must bear as a result of the message that he delivers to the people. The culmination of the prophet's address to YHWH in verses 23–25 calls for YHWH to show mercy to the people, chastise Jeremiah, and judge the nations that devour Jacob:

> I know, O YHWH, that man's road is not his to choose,
> That man, as he walks, cannot direct his own steps.
> Chastise me, O YHWH, but in measure;
> Not in Your wrath, lest You reduce me to naught.
> Pour out your wrath on the nations who have not heeded You,
> Upon the clans that have not invoked Your name.
> For they have devoured Jacob, have devoured and consumed him,
> And have laid desolate his homesteads.

In calling upon YHWH in this manner, Jeremiah displays the sense of pathos at the suffering of the nation that Abraham Joshua Heschel deems to be characteristic of both YHWH and the prophet in the Book of Jeremiah.[15]

V

Jeremiah's struggle with his divine commission continues throughout the so-called laments of Jeremiah in Jer. 11:18–23; 12:1–6; 15:10–21; 17:14–18; 18:18–23; 20:7–13; and 20:14–18.[16] Many modern scholars challenge the authenticity of these laments, arguing that their formulation as liturgical poetry presupposes a setting in Temple worship and priestly identity precludes authorship by a prophet such as Jeremiah. But Jeremiah's priestly identity buttresses arguments that the laments are indeed authentic. Because he was a Levitical priest, one of Jeremiah's duties would have been to sing liturgical psalms as part of the Temple liturgy.[17] In this respect, it is noteworthy that Chronicles identifies the Levitical Temple singers as prophets.

The first lament in Jer. 11:18–23 easily builds upon the portrayal of Jeremiah's Temple sermon in Jeremiah 7–10, 26, by portraying the opposition that was raised against the prophet. Following a prophetic discourse in Jer. 11:2–17 concerning Judah's broken covenant with YHWH, verse 14 presents YHWH's instructions to Jeremiah not to intercede on the people's behalf:

> As for you, do not pray for this people, do not raise a cry of prayer on their behalf;
> For I will not listen when they call to Me on account of their disaster.

Jeremiah having heard and presumably announced YHWH's decree against the people, his first lament in verses 18–23 emphasizes the prophet's isolation as the people begin to accuse him and plot his demise. Jeremiah portrays himself as a lamb about to be sacrificed in verse 19 when he states:

For I was like a docile lamb led to the slaughter;
I did not realize that it was against me they fashioned their plots:
"Let us destroy the tree with its fruit," let us cut him off from the land of the living.
That his name will be remembered no more!

Although YHWH reiterates the intention to punish the men of Anathoth who threaten him in verses 21–23, such an announcement of the demise of his own hometown associates can hardly come as much comfort to the prophet. His second lament in Jer. 12:1–6 follows immediately with the prophet's charges that YHWH does nothing to stop the actions of the wicked or to protect the righteous in verses 1–2:

You will win, O YHWH, if I make claim against You.
Yet I shall present charges against You:
Why does the way of the wicked prosper? Why are the workers of treachery at ease?
You have planted them, and they have taken root,
They spread, they even bear fruit.
You are present in their mouths, but far from their thoughts.

Jeremiah continues by stating that YHWH knows that he is righteous, and demands to know when YHWH will act against those who are evil and thereby bring the land to ruin.

The struggle is not Jeremiah's alone, as YHWH also laments over the coming destruction. After stating in Jer. 15:1 that even the intercession of Moses and Samuel would not stop the coming destruction, YHWH laments over the coming punishment in verses 5–6:

But who will pity you, O Jerusalem, who will console you?
Who will turn aside to inquire about your welfare?
You cast Me off—declares YHWH—you go ever backward.
So I have stretched out My hand to destroy you;
I cannot relent.

Jeremiah responds by beginning his third lament in Jer. 15:10–21 with a woe statement that mourns the day of his birth:

Woe is me, my mother, that you ever bore me—
A man of conflict and strife with all the land!
I have not lent and I have not borrowed; yet everyone curses me.

He continues in verses 17–18 by charging that YHWH is untrustworthy:

I have not sat in the company of revelers and made merry!
I have sat lonely because of Your hand upon me for You have filled me with gloom.
Why must my pain be endless, my wound incurable, resistant to healing?
You have been to me like a spring that fails, like waters that cannot be relied upon.

Jeremiah is commanded by YHWH in Jer. 16:1–17:13 not to marry or have children because they will only suffer due to the guilt and coming punishment of Judah. Such a command denies the very first command of Jews in halakhah, "be fruitful and multiply" (Gen. 1:28) and thereby denies the very life that YHWH grants. Jeremiah nevertheless remains committed to YHWH in his fourth lament in Jer. 17:14–18, pleading with YHWH:

Heal me, O YHWH, and let me be healed; save me, and let me be saved;
For You are my glory.

Jeremiah then demands the condemnation of the people after he is denounced for comparing the people to a pot that is spoiled on the potter's wheel. In his fifth lament in Jer. 18:18–23, he once again demands righteousness from YHWH:

Listen to me, O YHWH, and take note of what my enemies say!
Should good be repaid with evil? Yet they have dug a pit for me.

> Remember how I stood before You to plead on their behalf,
> To turn Your anger away from them!

When he is placed in stocks for smashing a pot to symbolize the coming destruction of the people, Jeremiah launches his bitterest tirades in his sixth and seventh laments in Jer. 20:7–13, 14–18, when he compares YHWH to a rapist who overpowers him and impregnates him with the divine word that he can no longer hold inside himself:

> You enticed me, O YHWH, and I was enticed; You overpowered me and You prevailed.
> I have become a constant laughingstock, everyone jeers at me.
> For every time I speak I must cry out, must shout, "Lawlessness and rapine!"
> For the word of YHWH causes me constant disgrace and contempt.
> I thought, "I will not mention Him, no more will I speak His name"—
> But His word was like a raging fire in my heart, shut up in my bones,
> I could not hold it in, I was helpless.

In an ultimate statement of bitterness and self-denial at his divine commission and betrayal by YHWH, Jeremiah takes on the role of the newborn baby to curse the day of his birth in verses 14–18:

> Accursed be the day that I was born!
> Let not the day be blessed when my mother bore me! . . .
> Why did I ever issue from the womb, to see misery and woe,
> To spend my days in shame?

VI

Jeremiah's laments over his sense of abandonment by YHWH run parallel to his charges of false prophecy in Jeremiah 23, 27–29.[18] His questions concerning the trustworthiness of YHWH prompt him to question the trustworthiness of prophecy as well, although his struggles with the earlier prophetic work of Isaiah cause him to weigh the applicability of earlier prophetic tradition in relation to his own time. Whereas earlier prophetic texts in Isaiah spoke of the downfall of northern Israel and its Assyrian oppressors, the statements concerning Jerusalem deliverance would have wrung hollow to Jeremiah in the face of the threat posed by Babylonia. For Jeremiah, Isaiah's statements concerning the downfall of Israel can also be applied to Judah and Jerusalem, namely, Isaiah's prophecies would only attain their fulfillment with the punishment of Jerusalem and Judah as well.

Jeremiah's lengthy discourse in Jer. 23:9–40 condemns those who would prophesy falsely in the name of YHWH. Ironically, this discourse follows Jeremiah's first royal oracle that condemns the "shepherds" or leaders of the people who have "scattered the sheep" and anticipates the rise of a righteous Davidic monarch in terms that recall Isaiah's oracle concerning the rise of a righteous "branch" of David in Isa. 11:1–16. The placement of Jeremiah's discourse concerning false prophets and the fact that Jeremiah's second royal oracle in Jer. 33:14–26 actually applies to the city of Jerusalem rather than to the house of David suggest that the prophet may have had in mind Isaian-inspired prophecies concerning the rise of a new Davidic monarch when he condemned false prophecy.

Jeremiah 23:9–40 begins with a brief superscription that directs his comments "to the prophets" without specifying whether he means true or false prophets. His intentions become clearer, however, when he laments over godless prophets and priests who lead the people into darkness, adultery, and evil by prophesying in the name of Baal. Prophets in the Bible frequently condemn their targets by charging them with idolatry or apostasy; Hosea, for example, charges that Israel has become apostate because it is allied with Assyria rather than with Aram, and Ezekiel charges a group of worshippers at the Temple (that includes a supporter of Jeremiah) with worship of the sun when in fact they are engaged in the morning worship service for YHWH. It is, therefore, imperative that the interpreter determine the specific issue on the prophet's mind. Jeremiah states in verse 17 that false prophets state that "all shall be well with you," which many take as an indication that he condemns in principle those prophets who speak of restoration rather than judgment. But Jeremiah himself speaks of restoration in Jeremiah 30–31, 32–33, so the interpreter must probe the matter more closely. In verse 30 Jeremiah states that YHWH will condemn those prophets who steal YHWH's words from one another to proclaim "the oracle of YHWH."

Although Jer. 23:9–40 does not give readers a full understanding of Jeremiah's concept of false prophecy, the narrative in Jeremiah 27–28 concerning Jeremiah's confrontation with the prophet Hananiah ben Azzur provides some criteria for making a determination. The narrative setting is during the reign of Jehoiakim ben Josiah when the king was consulting with allies to determine how to respond to the Babylonian victory of Egypt at Carchemesh in 605 BCE, although it is also related to the reign of King Zedekiah. Jehoiakim had been placed on the throne by Pharaoh Necho of Egypt in place of his younger half-brother, Jehoahaz, who apparently supported his father Josiah's policy of alliance with Babylon. As an Egyptian client, Jehoiakim was now faced with the prospect of abandoning support for his Egyptian patron to submit to the nation that had just defeated Egypt. In an effort to influence the royal decision, Jeremiah, a consistent supporter of the pro-Babylonian faction in Jerusalem, walked about Jerusalem in a yoke to symbolize the need to submit to the Babylonians. Hananiah confronted Jeremiah, broke the yoke from upon his shoulders, and declared that in two years time YHWH would break the yoke of Babylon and that Jerusalem would once again be free. Hananiah's declaration that Jerusalem would be freed from foreign control reiterates Isaiah's Davidic-Zion theology in which he declared to King Ahaz of Judah that YHWH would protect Jerusalem and the House of David from foreign threats (see Isa. 7:1–9:6). It also takes up Isaiah's admonitions against alliance with the Babylonians (see Isaiah 39). By Josiah's time, Jerusalemites would have understood Isaiah's prophecy to be an announcement of security for Jerusalem, especially since the narratives in Isaiah 36–39 depict YHWH's defense of Jerusalem and Hezekiah once Hezekiah turned to YHWH.

Jeremiah, however, lives in a time and situation far removed from that of Isaiah. As a supporter of alliance with Babylonia from the days of King Josiah, Jeremiah calls for submission to Babylon. But his call for a Babylonian alliance also recognizes Judah's changed status in Babylonia's estimation. Josiah had been an ally of Babylon and died at the hands of Pharaoh Necho of Egypt supporting his Babylonian allies. Jeremiah apparently took Josiah's death as a sign that things had changed. Furthermore, under Jehoiakim, Judah had broken its alliance with Babylonia to ally with Egypt. For Jeremiah, Babylonia posed a threat to Judah now that it had sided with Babylon's chief enemy in the aftermath of the fall of the Assyrian empire. Jeremiah returned to walk the streets of the city with a yoke of iron so that he might announce that YHWH's decision was firm, that is, Babylon would rule with a yoke of iron and Judah would be compelled to submit. To underscore Jeremiah's point, the narrative concludes with an announcement of Hananiah's death. By challenging a prophet who spoke a message of deliverance for Jerusalem in keeping with the earlier prophecies of Isaiah, Jeremiah demonstrates an interest in reflecting on earlier prophetic tradition and its applicability to the present situation, that is, whereas Isaiah prophesied judgment against Israel and deliverance for Jerusalem, Jeremiah recognized that Jerusalem would potentially suffer as well if it did not recognize the lesson to be derived from the experience of northern Israel. Ironically, the Book of Isaiah would expand in the exilic and post-exilic periods to account for the Babylonian exile as well.

Indeed, Jeremiah's position concerning Babylonian exile is stated in his letter to the exiles in Jeremiah 29 in which he tells those Judeans exiled to Babylon in 597 BCE to build houses, plant gardens, raise children, and so on, because they will be in exile for seventy years as an expression of the will of YHWH. Jeremiah's letter was prompted by announcements that prophets among the exiles had apparently spoken a message of deliverance that would soon be realized much like that of Hananiah. Jeremiah instead names those prophets and charges them with deluding the people. He advises the exiles to turn to YHWH and wait; YHWH will first ravage Jerusalem with the Babylonians, and only after the punishment has reached its full course will the exile return. Again, Jeremiah refutes the Isaian-inspired message of deliverance. Jerusalem would suffer before any restoration would begin.

VII

Although Jeremiah's message focuses on judgment and exile for Jerusalem and Judah, he also announces restoration as part of his efforts to discern divine intention in relation to the course of events in the ancient world and his struggle to understand earlier Judean tradition in relation to those events.[19] His commission as a prophet in Jer. 1:10 includes the two verbs of restoration, "to build" and "to plant," in addition to the four verbs of destruction. In this respect, Jeremiah continues the perspective of Isaiah, but he differs by anticipating a long period of judgment that overtakes Judah as well as Israel before the restoration can be realized. Two passages in particular lay out Jeremiah's understanding of restoration, namely, Jeremiah 30–31 and 32–33.

Jeremiah 30–31 anticipates Israel's return to Jerusalem in terms that reflect Josiah's program of religious reform and national restoration.[20] Although the current form of the passage clearly envisions a restoration of both Israel and Judah following the period of punishment, redaction-critical analysis of this passage demonstrates that it is an expanded form of an underlying set of oracles that depicts northern Israel's return to Jerusalem. Whereas the present form of the text presupposes the final editions of the Book of Jeremiah from the exilic period or later, the underlying oracles concerning Israel's return to Jerusalem presuppose King Josiah's program of religious reform and national restoration. Both editions of this text employ a teleological perspective in which the projected outcome of a period of punishment is restoration and YHWH's renewed commitment to secure Israel and Judah.

The final form of Jeremiah 30–31 portrays a restoration for Israel and Judah. This intention is made clear in Jer. 30:1–4 in which YHWH instructs Jeremiah to write down the divine words spoken to him concerning the restoration of both Israel and Judah. The following sequence of oracles in Jer. 30:5–31:40, each of which begins with the formula, "thus says YHWH," or a variant, then lays out a scenario in which the restoration will be realized. Jeremiah 30:5–11 projects the deliverance of Jacob, that is, Israel, so that Jacob might serve the Davidic king. Jeremiah 30:12–17 promises Zion that those who wanted to devour Zion shall themselves be devoured. Jeremiah 30:18–31:1 promises to restore the relationship between Jacob or Israel and YHWH so that YHWH will be G-d to all the clans of Israel and they shall be YHWH's people. Jeremiah 31:2–6 portrays Israel as a maiden who takes up her timbrels to dance as she returns to YHWH at Zion. Jeremiah 31:7–14 depicts the return from the north of the remnant of Israel to the heights of Zion. Jeremiah 31:15 briefly portrays Rachel, the matriarch of the northern tribes of Ephraim and Manasseh, as she weeps for her children who are gone. Jeremiah 31:16–22 calls for the cessation of weeping as Ephraim or Israel repents and returns to YHWH. Jeremiah 31:23–34 portrays the restoration of Israel and Judah in the land of Judah, particularly in relation to YHWH's new covenant with both. Jeremiah 31:35–36 declares Israel's relationship with YHWH to be eternal. Jeremiah 31:37–40 will be eternal, before it describes the rebuilt city of Jerusalem.

Although the final form of Jeremiah 30–31 portrays the restoration of both Israel and Judah, the core of the oracles that begin with the formula, "thus says YHWH," depict northern Israel's return and restoration to Zion or Jerusalem. Those elements of the oracular sequence that begin with the formula, "behold the days are coming," in Jer. 30:3–4, 31:27–30, 31:31–34, and 31:38–40 take up the restoration of both Israel and Judah/Jerusalem. The reference to Zion in Jer. 30:17 is a secondary adjustment of a reference to "prey" (Heb., *ṣēdenû*) to "Zion" (Heb., *ṣîyôn*) in keeping with the larger concerns of the expanded text. It would appear that a text that originally outlined the return of Israel to Zion/Judah has been expanded to take up the restoration of both Israel and Judah. Such an expansion indicates the prophet's attempt to rethink an earlier oracle that supported King Josiah's reform, particularly his efforts to reunite the former northern kingdom of Israel with southern Judah under Davidic rule and thereby to restore the former united kingdom of Solomon. With the realization that judgment would overtake Judah as well, insofar as Babylonia would ultimately invade Judah and destroy Jerusalem, Jeremiah's expanded oracle envisions the ultimate restoration of both Israel and Judah once the punishment is complete.

Jeremiah 32–33 presents a scenario of restoration for Jerusalem and Judah once the period of judgment is complete. Although chapters 32 and 33 are frequently treated as separate texts due to their seemingly different concerns, the introductory word transmission formula in Jer. 32:1 and successive word transmission formulas linked by waw-consecutive construction in Jer. 32:26, 33:1, 33:19, and 33:23 point to Jeremiah 32–33 as a coherent unit. The unit begins with a portrayal in Jer. 32:1–25 of Jeremiah's efforts to redeem family property in Anathoth during a lull in the Babylonian siege of Jerusalem. The prophet has the legal documents written, including "the sealed text and the open one" (v. 14), which is a common means in ancient Judah to provide a public document with the general provisions of the deed and a sealed document that includes the details of the transaction.[21] Jeremiah 32:26–44 then lays out the prophet's understanding of his purchase of land as an act that symbolizes YHWH's intention to restore Judah following the period of punishment, namely, Jeremiah's redemption of land symbolizes YHWH's coming redemption of the land once the war and exile are over. Jeremiah 33:1–18 follows with an oracle sequence that announces YHWH's willingness to explain "wondrous things" and "secrets you have not known" (v. 3). Those secrets project the restoration of Israel and Judah under the rule of a righteous Davidic branch, which includes the restored city of Jerusalem and the line of Levitical priests. Jeremiah 33:19–22 promises that YHWH's covenant with David will never be broken, and Jeremiah 33:23–26 promises that YHWH will never reject the offspring of Jacob and YHWH's servant David.

Redaction-critical analysis once again points to a text that has been expanded in relation to later times and circumstances. Most notably, the reference to "the sealed text and the open one" in Jer. 32:14 apparently prompted writers to attempt to discern divine purposes in relation to Judah's restoration following the period of punishment. Jeremiah 33:1–26 attempts to project restoration as the secret that is hidden in the symbolic action of Jeremiah's redemption of land at Anathoth. Although the portrayal of Judah's and Benjamin's restoration in Jer. 33:1–13 may well be the work of Jeremiah, the material concerning the righteous Davidic branch in Jer. 33:14–26 appears to be much later, particularly since this material is entirely absent in the Septuagint form of Jeremiah. Overall, the scenario laid out in Jer. 33:14–26, which is introduced once again by the formula "behold, the days are coming," presupposes the circumstances of the early Persian period. As Yohanan Goldman's analysis of this material demonstrates, the oracles concerning the restoration of a Davidic branch are formulated to refer to the city of Jerusalem, not to a new Davidic monarch.[22] Likewise, the text envisions the restoration of the Levitical priesthood together with the Davidic "branch." According to Jer. 33:14–26, the Davidic monarchy is not reestablished, but the city of Jerusalem is restored and the Levitical priesthood emerges as the leadership of Judah under Persian rule. Altogether, this restoration fulfills the eternal promise to Israel's ancestors, Abraham, Isaac, and Jacob in Jer. 33:26. As Goldman demonstrates, this scenario is derived from an exegetical reformulation of the monarchic oracle in Jer. 23:1–8; statements concerning YHWH's promise concerning the house of David in 1 Kings 2:4; 8:24–26; 9:4–6, and Jeremiah's portrayal of YHWH's covenant with Israel and Judah in Jer. 31:35–36, 37–40. Unlike the reformulation of Jeremiah 30–31 noted above, the reformulation of Jeremiah 32–33 appears to be the product of a hand much later than that of the prophet himself. The most likely setting for such a reformulation of Jeremiah's material in Jer. 32:1–33:13 is the early Persian period when the house of David faltered at the time of the building of the Second Temple and the Temple priesthood rose to fill the void left by the absence of the monarchy.

VIII

The remaining portions of the Book of Jeremiah in chapters 34–52 focus on the fall of the city of Jerusalem to Babylonian forces; the destruction of the city and the exile of much of its surviving population; the assassination of Gedaliah, the Babylonian-appointed governor of Jerusalem; the removal of Jeremiah to Egypt and his activities there; and the oracles against the nations. Nevertheless, the material from Jeremiah analyzed here points to the prophet's struggle with his divine commission from the time of Josiah's reform through the last years of Judah when it becomes increasingly apparent to him that Judah will fall to the Babylonian empire. Overall, Jeremiah struggles repeatedly with YHWH for forcing him into his role as the prophet who will oversee and interpret YHWH's actions to the people, and he struggles with past tradition, particularly the work of the prophet Isaiah whose oracles concerning the downfall of Assyria and YHWH's support for the Davidic monarch and the city of Jerusalem were read in relation to Josiah's program of national restoration and reunification in the aftermath of the Assyrian empire's collapse. In struggling with his divine commission and past tradition, however, Jeremiah ultimately grapples with the challenges posed to Judah by the power of the Babylonian empire and the reality of Jerusalem's and Judah's impending demise. For a Levitical priest like Jeremiah, such an act could only come at the direction of YHWH, who sought to punish Judah and Jerusalem for failing to observe YHWH's Torah. In order to defend the sanctity, righteousness, and power of YHWH, Jeremiah's only recourse was to argue that the people—and not YHWH—were responsible for their own fate and that YHWH would ultimately act to restore Jerusalem, Judah, and Israel once the period of exile and punishment was over.

Notes

1. For discussion of Jeremiah, see Jack Lundbom, "Jeremiah, Book of," *Anchor Bible Dictionary,* ed. D. N. Freedman et al (Garden City, N.Y.: Doubleday, 1992), 3:707–21; Joseph Blenkinsopp, *A History of Prophecy in Israel* (Louisville: Westminster John Knox, 1996), 129–47; David L. Petersen, *The Prophetic Literature: An Introduction* (Louisville: Westminster John Knox, 2002), 97–135; Marvin A. Sweeney, *The Prophetic Literature, Interpreting Biblical Texts* (Nashville: Abingdon, 2005), 85–125.
2. E.g., Ronald E. Clements, "Jeremiah 1–25 and the Deuteronomistic History," in his *Old Testament Prophecy: From Oracles to Canon* (Louisville: Westminster John Knox, 1996), 107–22.
3. Winfried Thiel, *Die deuteronomistische Redaktion von Jeremia 1–25,* WMANT 41 (Neukirchen-Vluyn: Neukirchener, 1973); William L. Holladay, *The Architecture of Jeremiah 1–20* (Lewisburg, Pa.: Bucknell University Press, 1976).
4. Claus Rietzschel, *Das Problem der Urrolle. Ein Beitrag zur Redaktionsgeschichte des Jeremiabuches* (Gütersloh: Gerd Mohn, 1966); W. W. Nicholson, *Preaching to the Exiles: A Study of the Prose Traditions in the Book of Jeremiah* (New York: Schocken, 1970); Winfried Thiel, *Die deuteronomistische Redaktion von Jeremia 26–45,* WMANT 52 (Neukirchen-Vluyn: Neukirchener, 1981); Christopher R. Seitz, *Theology in Conflict,* BZAW 176 (Berlin: Walter de Gruyter, 1989); Carolyn J. Sharp, *Prophecy and Ideology in Jeremiah: Struggles for Authority in the Deutero-Jeremianic Prose* (London: T&T Clark, 2003).
5. Christl Maier, *Jeremia als Lehrer der Tora. Soziale Gebote des Deuteronomiums in Fortschreibungen des Jeremiabuches,* FRLANT196 (Göttingen: Vandenhoeck and Ruprecht, 2002).
6. Cf. Thomas W. Overholt, *The Threat of Falsehood: A Study in the Theology of the Book of Jeremiah,* SBT 2/16 (Naperville, Ill.: Allenson, 1970).
7. For the following structure, see Sweeney, *Prophetic Literature,* 85–95; cf. Louis Stuhlman, *Order Amid Chaos: Jeremiah as Symbolic Tapestry,* Biblical Seminar 57 (Sheffield: Sheffield Academic Press, 1998).
8. Christopher R. Seitz, "The Prophet Moses and the Canonical Shape of Jeremiah," *Zeitschrift für die Alttestamentliche Wissenschaft* 101 (1989): 487–516.
9. For discussion of Jeremiah 2–6, see esp. Marvin A. Sweeney, "Structure and Redaction in Jeremiah 2–6," in his *Form and Intertextuality in Prophetic and Apocalyptic Literature,* Forschungen zum Alten Testament 45 (Tübingen: Mohr Siebeck, 2005), 94–108.
10. Cf. Ute Wendel, *Jesaja und Jeremia. Worte, Motive und Einsichten Jesajas in der Verkündigung Jeremias,* BibThS 25 (Neukirchen-Vluyn: Neukirchner, 1995); Sweeney, "The Truth in True and False Prophecy," in *Form and Intertextuality,* 78–93.
11. See now Louis Stuhlman, *Jeremiah,* Abingdon Old Testament Commentaries (Nashville: Abingdon, 2005), 86–113; Douglas Rawlinson Jones, *Jeremiah,* New Century Bible (Grand Rapids, Mich.: Eerdmans, 1992), 141–81; cf. Jack R. Lundbom, *Jeremiah 1–20,* Anchor Bible 21A (New York: Doubleday, 1999), 446–613; cf. Helga Weippert, *Die Prosareden des Jeremiabuches,* BZAW 132 (Berlin: Walter de Gruyter, 1973), 26–48; Maier, *Jeremia als Lehrer der Tora.*
12. For discussion of the ben Shaphan family and its support of the prophet Jeremiah, see Jay Wilcoxen, "The Political Background of Jeremiah's Temple Sermon," in *Scripture in History and Theology,* ed. A. Merrill and T. Overholt, Fest. J. C. Rylaarsdams (Pittsburgh: Pickwick, 1977), 155–66.
13. For discussion of the Levitical sermon, see Gerhard von Rad, "The Levitical Sermon in the Books of Chronicles," in his *The Problem of the Hexateuch and Other Essays* (London: SCM, 1966), 267–80; Rex Mason, *Preaching the Tradition* (Cambridge: Cambridge University Press, 1990).
14. Sweeney, *Isaiah 1–39, with an Introduction to Prophetic Literature,* Forms of the Old Testament Literature 16 (Grand Rapids, Mich.: Eerdmans, 1996), 546–47.
15. Abraham Joshua Heschel, *The Prophets* (New York: Harper and Row, 1969), 1:103–39, 2:1–11.
16. For discussion of Jeremiah's laments, see Kathleen O'Connor, *The Confessions of Jeremiah: Their Importance and Role in Chapters 1–25,* SBLDS 94 (Atlanta: Scholars Press, 1988); Mark S. Smith, *The Laments of Jeremiah and Their Contexts,* SBLMS 42 (Atlanta: Scholars Press, 1990).
17. See David L. Petersen, *Late Israelite Prophecy: Studies in Deutero-Prophetic Literature and in Chronicles,* SBLMS 23 (Missoula, Mont.: Scholars Press, 1977), 55–96.

18. For discussion of Jeremiah and the question of true and false prophecy, see Overholt, *The Threat of Falsehood*; Sweeney, "The Truth in True and False Prophecy"; cf. Armin Lange, *Vom prophetischen Wort zur prophetischen Tradition,* FAT 34 (Tübingen: Mohr Siebeck, 2002).
19. Ronald E. Clements, "Jeremiah: Prophet of Hope," in *Old Testament Prophecy,* 123–41.
20. See Marvin A. Sweeney, "Jeremiah 30–31 and King Josiah's Program of National Restoration and Religious Reform," in *Form and Intertextuality*, 109–22.
21. Andrew G. Shead, *The Open and the Sealed Book: Jeremiah 32 in Its Hebrew and Greek Recensions,* JSOTSup 347 (London: Continuum, 2002), 114–24.
22. Yohanan Goldman, *Prophétie et royauté au retour de l'exil. Les origins littéraires de la forme massorétique du livre de Jérémie,* OBO 118 (Göttingen: Vandenhoeck and Ruprecht, 1992), esp. 12–21.

Part 2

Jewish-Christian-Muslim and Other Dialogues

Jewish-Christian Relations

A Dialogue with Zev Garber

Eugene Fisher

I have been in active dialogue, both personally and in print, with Professor Zev Garber for over fifteen very satisfying and enriching (certainly for me) years. In the process I have been constructively challenged by and learned much from him. I hope that he has, at least on some occasions, picked up a useful insight or two from me. I consider Garber to be one of the most thoughtful scholars on either "side" of the contemporary and historic Jewish-Christian dialogue. So if the following summary of some of our exchanges, along with some related follow-up points, reveals that he has not always won me over to his point of view, or him to mine, I trust that my continuing respect for him, and my respect for his views precisely where they differ from mine, equally comes through to readers of this essay written in his honor.

Edith Stein: Daughter of Israel, Catholic Martyr

In the volume of essays on Edith Stein (1891–1942) collected by Harry James Cargas, of blessed memory, are two articles. First is a reprint of an exchange between myself and Rabbi Daniel Polish (first published in the journal *Ecumenical Trends* in 1987 and 1988) on the occasion of the beatification by Pope John Paul II of the philosopher Edith Stein, a Jewish woman who converted to Catholicism, became a cloistered Carmelite nun, and was murdered in Auschwitz. The second is an essay by Garber in which he disputes my own argument that Stein should be understood as having been killed by the Nazis because she was a Jew while simultaneously dying the death of a Catholic martyr, as the beatification process proclaimed.[1] Polish, also a good friend, saw in the beatification two serious concerns from a Jewish perspective: first, he feared that the gesture of honoring a Jewish convert to Catholicism could precipitate organized Catholic attempts to convert Jews; second, he felt that it represented an attempt by the "protean" Catholic Church to appropriate for itself the Jewish *sanctum* of the Holocaust as Christianity had centuries earlier "appropriated" for itself a "gamut" of Jewish symbols, theological constructs, and forms of worship, especially when the beatification was viewed in the light of the then only recently resolved controversy over the establishment by the same religious order, the Carmelites, of a convent in an abandoned theater adjacent to Auschwitz itself.[2]

While noting and praising the sensitivity with which Polish raised his concerns, I responded to the first by citing a statement of the U.S. Catholic Bishops' Committee for Ecumenical and Interreligious Relations issued on April 23, 1987:

> Catholic respect for the integrity of Judaism and the ongoing validity of God's irrevocable covenant with the Jewish people is solidly founded on our faith in the unshakable faithfulness of God's own word. Therefore, in no way can the beatification of Edith Stein be understood by Catholics as giving impetus to unwarranted proselytizing among the Jewish community. On the contrary, it urges us to ponder the continuing religious significance of Jewish traditions, with which we have so much in common, and to approach Jews not as potential "objects" of conversion but rather as bearers of a unique witness to the Name of the One God of Israel.

I rejected Polish's perception of the two cases as "part of a pattern of Catholic actions," which I deemed a rather "conspiratorial" view.[3] Likewise, I argued that "appropriation" is a misleading term to use when in point of fact the founders of Christianity were Jews not appropriating but reinterpreting their own traditions in response to the traumatic events of the first century of the Common Era. In short, Christianity was born out of the experience of a group of Jews who had a unique experience of the Jew, Jesus of Nazareth, who died but rose again.

In his response to my reply, Polish acknowledged that, in its official statements on the subject, "the Catholic Church has, thankfully, moved beyond supersessionism and the desire to displace the Jewish People," but notes as well that the "transformation" of so vast an entity as the Catholic Church simply "cannot be accomplished in a brief quarter of a century."[4] So Jews are right to react to actions on the part of the Church that might reasonably be understood as slipping back into the old, triumphalist "reflexes" of Catholics toward Jews. He was right. If I was Jewish, I would not entirely trust me either!

Polish, then, briefly engages my argument that, *halachically* (according to the principles of Jewish law as interpreted over the centuries in rabbinic tradition), a Jew who converts to Christianity is to be understood as still a Jew, albeit an apostate one. So, I reasoned, Stein can be seen by Jews as still Jewish after her conversion, along with being a Catholic martyr. "Despite the distorted and perverse assumption of Nazi policy which would define her as Jewish on the basis of spurious racial doctrine, Edith Stein," he concludes on this point, "died as a Catholic and not as a Jew."[5]

Garber picks up on the discussion at this point in his own essay which he includes also in his own collection of his essays on the Shoah published in the same year, an essay written from the perspective of her canonization, which precipitated a second round of the Edith Stein controversy. He sets as his goal answering the question, "Was she a Jewish martyr or Christian martyr or both?" He presents, in admirably succinct detail, the understandings of the Jewish people as a religion, as a nation, and as a lineage, arguing (correctly, in my view) that it is in a real sense a nexus of the three. One can be Jewish and not practice Judaism, he argues. *But* when one chooses to practice a religious tradition other than that of the Jewish people, like Edith Stein, "it is clear that [she] does not fulfill the categorical definitions nor obligations of one who is a Jew," Church claims to the contrary notwithstanding.[6]

Garber then engages the Catholic Church and its teachings directly. He acknowledges and accurately summarizes the advances made in official Church documents, pointing out some elements that he considers "disappointments" in them (to which I will return later in this essay), seeing the canonization of Edith Stein, Sister Teresa Benedicta of the Cross, as a direct challenge to the trust built up between our two communities in the then almost thirty years of dialogue. While acknowledging the evidence that Stein considered herself still to be a Jew after her conversion to Christianity, Garber takes on my own argument that *halachah* would consider Stein to be an apostate Jew, but still a Jew, and interprets it differently than I did. I must acknowledge that I am not sufficiently grounded in *halachah* to do anything more than note that my understanding of the text was not based on my own limited expertise, but that of rabbis who can claim such expertise. So for my part I will abide by Garber's well-articulated principle that it is up to Jews to decide who is a Jew, just as it is up to Catholics to decide who is a Catholic martyr, and leave the discussion to the rabbis to resolve.

The opinion of Rabbi Avda bar Zavda (Sanhedrin 44a), which I had adduced to argue my case, Garber notes, had to do with the specific situation of forced conversions, such as those of the First

Crusade in 1096 who, afterward, wished to return to the practice of their ancestral faith. They were not required to go through the traditional ceremony for converting to Judaism, as they would have had they been considered not to be Jews. Garber notes, saliently, that Stein's was not a forced "abandonment" of her people's faith, but voluntary, so she would not fall under the category covered in the ruling I cited.

To identify with the Jewish people (*guf* = body) but not practice the Jewish religion (*neshama* = soul) is not in itself grounds for group or self-excommunication. However, to proclaim Jewish ethnicity and to practice voluntarily another religious *sancta* (e.g., Christianity) is grounds for self and group removal from Jewish identity.[7] Garber than raises the case of Brother Daniel Rufieson, a Carmelite who converted to Catholicism, also voluntarily, but who was responsible for saving Jewish lives during the Holocaust and for actively resisting Nazism. When he appealed to become a citizen of Israel under the Law of Return, he was denied by the Israeli Supreme Court on grounds that were specifically secular and not religious, that is, the ordinary usage of the term "Jew" as understood in the national-historical understanding of Jews. In my view, it must be noted, Garber's appeal to the secular ruling of Judge Silberg, which specifically excluded the rabbinic, *halachic* understanding of the Jewishness of converts to Christianity, weakens rather than strengthens Garber's interpretation of Sanhedrin 44a, since, if the Israeli Supreme Court felt that rabbinic tradition cohered with its secular one, it would not have had to go out of its way to state that it was ruling on secular grounds.

Garber then adds another strong point to his own case. While many Talmudic and modern authorities, he notes, have ruled that a Jew murdered precisely for being Jewish "is forgiven of all sins, whether public or private," there are three cardinal sins that one cannot commit even under circumstances of extreme pain or threat of death: idolatry (apostasy), unchastity (incest, adultery), and murder (Sanhedrin 74a).[8] Garber's equation of idolatry and apostasy raises, of course, the very interesting and sensitive question of whether Judaism considers Christianity to be a form of idolatry. But that is perhaps another question I should leave to the rabbis to debate, though I believe that, as the dialogue between us proceeds, Judaism might move beyond the medieval opinions that have placed us in that category.

With regard to Edith Stein, Sister Teresa Benedicta of the Cross, Garber has a nuanced attitude. He states without equivocation that "Jewish fears that the veneration of Sister Teresa would promote conversion among Jews or appropriate the Shoah event as a Church tragedy are properly laid to rest in a statement of the Bishops' Committee for Ecumenical and Interreligious Affairs of the National Conference of Catholic Bishops," quoting then from the statement I cited above in this essay. He welcomes the statement's reaffirmation of the Church's condemnation of antisemitism. But then, referring to Pope John Paul II's homiletic reflection on the occasion of her beatification, he observes that "major problems still exist."[9] "[K]nowingly or unknowingly," he writes, "Pope John Paul II inserted the controversial dynamics of *Verus Israel* in his homily . . . when he made reference to the words of Jesus to the Samaritan woman at a place tradition calls Jacob's well."[10] The reference, of course, is to John 4:22–24, in which Jesus proclaims that "salvation is from the Jews" and continues: "The hour is coming and now here when true worshippers will worship the Father in spirit and truth." While acknowledging the pope's appreciation for Edith Stein "as a great daughter of the Jewish people," and his use of the term "Shoah," which "confirms the inextricable connection between Israel and the Great Catastrophe," the pope's reference to worship "in spirit and in truth" implies that Judaism's "spiritual *Lebensphilosophie,*" which is a more "worldly realism and spirituality," is to be understood as superseded, replaced by Christianity's more otherworldly "truth" and spirituality.

Garber is right to stress that there exists a fundamental difference between Christian and Jewish theologies of redemption. But when he states, "For the Church, it is the Easter faith, spirit over matter, that enables victory to be proclaimed over Golgotha and Auschwitz. For the Synagogue, it is the covenantal oath at Sinai, uniting spirit and matter and resulting in everyday acts of holiness, that permits Zion to triumph over Auschwitz," he misses the element that is what is most distinctively "Catholic" in Catholicism's understanding of the relation between spirit and matter. This is the sacramental view, a reflex of our understanding of the incarnation and its effects on all Creation, in which we see the world, in the phrase of Gerard Manley Hopkins (1844–89), "charged with the glory of God." One has to look to Jewish mysticism to begin to understand this essential Catholic worldview. Say to the emanations of the divine into the world, or the wonderful notion that God, in order to create "space" for Creation, "withdrew" into Himself, leaving divine sparks in all created matter as He did so. We Catholics, too, see those divine sparks in all Creation when we contemplate God's wonders. In the Catholic view, matter and spirit, precisely because God became human and took on a physical body, commingle. Everything that is, in a sense, participates in the divine. So while Garber is right to juxtapose "the Christ event" and "the Sinai event" as fundamentally dividing our two faith traditions (though they remain linked, from the Church's point of view, with a "sacred bond" as the Second Vatican Council and subsequent Church teaching have emphasized, because of the "shared patrimony" of the Hebrew Scriptures and a shared faith in the One God of Abraham and Sarah).

This point about the sacramentality of my Catholic worldview came home to me vividly in several sessions of the ongoing dialogue with Reformed Christians, which I staffed at the time for the Bishops' Committee for Ecumenical and Interreligious Affairs. We were discussing our respective understandings of the sacraments of Baptism and Eucharist. The discussion turned toward the nature of sacraments and our understandings of sacramentality itself. For those in the Calvinist tradition, there is a sharp divide between the physical and the spiritual realms, between the finite and the infinite, the temporal and the eternal. For Catholics, the divide was breached by the incarnation, allowing for the mutual penetration of each by the other. What happens in the Eucharist is just such a moment of interpenetration, rendering Christ, physically as well as spiritually, truly present. Trying to explain this from our side, some of the Catholics brought up the poetry of Gerard Manly Hopkins. I brought up the Jewish mystical traditions alluded to above. Our Reformed counterparts were, to put it mildly, quite taken aback, since in their view the realms are and must remain mutually exclusive, lest Christians slide into idolatry, worshipping the merely temporal, the fleshly, as divine. Hence, one can (I hope) understand why I resist Garber's presumption of a spirit-versus-matter construct of total dichotomy upon Catholicism, since it does not allow for that which is central to my faith: its sacramental basis. Indeed, it may be one of the major differences, I believe, between Catholicism and the heirs of Ulrich Zwingli (1484–1531) and John Calvin (1509–64), a major dividing point in the history of Western Christianity.[11]

At this point, let me back up a bit. The very first article I published in what is now (but was not yet then) the field of Christian-Jewish relations was entitled "Typical Jewish Misunderstandings of Christianity."[12] The essay was the result of my reflections on how my Jewish professors at New York University portrayed Christianity. Over the years, I noticed a pattern of misunderstandings that for a while baffled me. Christianity is said to place mediators between man and God (Christ, Mary, priests), whereas Judaism enables Jews to pray and encounter God directly. Salvation/justification is by faith alone, creed versus deed, while Judaism emphasizes right (righteous) behavior. Christianity espouses blind faith while Judaism is reasonable. Christianity goes to extremes in asceticism, while Judaism holds to the golden mean. For Christianity, the concept of original sin means that the world and flesh are wholly corrupt, fallen humanity is determined not free, and good works are to no avail, while Judaism stresses the opposite in all these cases. Christian sacraments, such as infant baptism, are magical in nature, leading to superstition, whereas Judaism is enlightened and nonsuperstitious. Christians believe that only Christians can be saved, while Judaism allows salvation for Christians through the Noahide covenant.

One of the things that intrigued me about these misreadings of my faith was that they differed from the classic Jewish apologetics and polemics against Christianity, such as the classic *Nizzahon Vetus* (Old Book of Polemics), which focused on debunking Christian claims about what the Hebrew Scriptures "truly" meant. The more I thought about them, the more I realized the nature of the pattern. In each case I could see that the particular misconception could be understood as having taken at face value one or the other side of the internal polemics Protestant and Catholics have thrown at each other since the Reformation. Sometimes the Protestant version of Catholicism was posited on all of Christianity, sometimes the Catholic polemical understanding of Protestantism was taken as true of Christianity as such. One can see these caricatures of Christianity in works such as Martin Buber's *Two Types of Faith,* Trude Weis-Rosmarin's *Judaism and Christianity: The Differences,* and in the essays of Ahad Haam, among many other examples.[13] With this figured out, it was not difficult to trace the misunderstanding back to the works of the *Wissenschafte des Judentuums* movement founded in 1819 in Berlin by Leopold Zunz (1794–1886), Eduard Gans (1797–1839), and Moses Moser (1796–1838), which quite understandably needed a response to the Christian polemics against Judaism of the period. Such polemics, while understandable in the context of their time, I would argue, are less than helpful today. Yet, as the example of the very fair-minded Zev Garber's misunderstanding of the words of Pope John Paul II illustrate, such views as we each have imposed upon the other over the course of our intertwined, too often troubled history, are difficult to unravel and confront within ourselves.

Toward the end of his essay, Garber very aptly notes that "recognition of Jewish self-definition challenges the Church to be a professing Church," a principle mandated for Catholics by the 1974 Vatican Guidelines for Catholic-Jewish relations.[14] I wholeheartedly agree with Garber on this point and have worked to make it a reality for over three decades now. I believe he would agree that the principle is two-sided. Jews, equally, need to allow Christians in general, and, in this case, Catholics in particular, to define themselves. Understanding that the reference to John's Gospel was at one point, but is not necessarily now, understood as supersessionist, and that the spirit/matter dichotomy is not for Catholics a simplistic "either/or" is as good a place as any to start. The figure of Edith Stein, daughter of Israel, Catholic martyr, might yet be one of healing and reconciliation for our two ancient communities, or so I fervently pray.

Demystifying Christology

In a paper presented to the 2003 Scholars Conference on the Holocaust, Garber ably sketches "the perpetual dilemma" of the "antisemitism" in Christian history and contemporary Western consciousness, including its new guise of anti-Zionism.[15] This latter phenomenon, it should be stated, has been unmasked and challenged by the Catholic Church. Successive presidents of the U.S. Conference of Catholic Bishops have gone on record condemning the notorious 1975 Zionism as racism resolution of the United Nations, calling for its repeal until finally, almost three decades after it was passed, it was indeed repealed. In 1985 the Holy See's Council for Justice and Peace issued a statement on "The Church and Racism." It concluded that antisemitism was clearly the worst form of racism to plague the twentieth century, which witnessed the Shoah. And it noted that anti-Zionism, which it distinguished from antisemitism since it could represent opposition to a particular Israeli government and its policies, can often "serve as a screen for anti-Semitism, hiding it and leading to it" (no. 15). More recently, the International Catholic-Jewish Liaison Committee's "Joint Declaration" from its 2004 meeting in Buenos Aires, Argentina, reaffirmed and repeated the Holy See's 1985 admonition and condemnation.

Looking at the long, too-often-tragic history of Christian-Jewish relations before the Shoah, Garber points to the ancient Christian anti-Jewish polemical tradition, aptly called "the teaching of contempt" by Jules Isaac (1887–1963), as a major if not sole contributing factor to the relative ease with which so many European Christians fell into step with Nazi antisemitism. Based on the way he frames his question, Garber would agree with the classical formulation of Yosef Yerushalmi. Writing in opposition to Rosemary Radford Reuther's assertion that, in his words, "genocide against the Jews was an inexorable consequence of Christian theological teaching," Yerushalmi notes that, if that were the case, genocide would have occurred during the Middle Ages when the Church had very real political power, not centuries after it had lost the power to translate theology into public policy. "Even if we grant that Christian teaching was a necessary cause leading to the Holocaust," Yerushalmi writes, "it was surely not a sufficient cause."[16] One must include in any assessment the impact of racial theory, which did not flow from Christian theology but from secular thought, and which was opposed by the Church as a violation of the vision of Genesis that all humans are equally created in the image and likeness of God. Likewise, one must explain the very different reactions of various countries in Europe to Nazism's racial antisemitism. The people of Catholic Austria and the people of equally Catholic Italy, for example, received essentially the same set of understandings and misunderstandings of Jews and Judaism in their catechism classes. Yet the former embraced the Nazi "solution" to the "Jewish problem," while the latter, under German occupation, saved some 70 percent of its Jewish population. Similarly, in those parts of Europe controlled by the Italian army, Jews were not put on trains for the death camps, but protected from the Germans. Likewise among neighboring countries, for example, in predominantly Catholic Belgium, a majority of Jews survived, while in predominantly Protestant

Netherlands a far smaller percentage survived. One could go on. But the point is that, obviously, various economic, social, cultural, and historical factors along with religious teaching must be taken into account to begin to understand the complex reality of the Shoah.

On the other hand, one can only agree with Garber when he states, "Whether or not one holds that there is a direct link between 2000 years of Christian supersessionist teaching and the Shoah, certain core New Testament beliefs and Church teachings in contributing to Nazi ideology and tolerating state-sponsored, technologically administered mass death cannot be denied." Indeed, Pope John Paul II made the same point when he stated that the negative teaching toward Jews and Judaism, which "began as early as the Second Century . . . so lulled the consciences" of so many European Christians that they were not able to organize an effective resistance to Nazi genocide. This is especially true, as Garber notes, of the charges of deicide and misanthropy.[17]

Some of Garber's general statements, while essentially true, require considerable nuancing. For example, shortly after the above, in the same paragraph, he comments:

> In Christian preaching and teaching on the Jews, Catholic Saints (e.g., Augustine [354–430], John Chrysostom [349–407], Thomas Aquinas [1225–74]) and Protestant Reformers (e.g., John Calvin [1509–64] and Martin Luther [1483–1546]) appear united in their teaching of contempt of the Jewish way before God's grace and love.

It is a small point to note that while Chrysostom is acknowledged a saint by the Catholic Church, he was and remains a central figure in Eastern Orthodox Christianity. More significant is to examine carefully the writings of the two. Chrysostom's series of anti-Jewish homilies have a personal venom missing from Augustine's more theologically oriented analyses. This is because Chrysostom's homilies were inspired by the need he felt to dissuade his Christians from continuing in their practice of attending synagogue services. He thus accuses synagogues of being dens of prostitution and debauchery. And while it is true that Augustine does not challenge the by-then-prevailing notion of Jewish collective guilt for the death of Jesus, he makes two important arguments that changed the course of Western Christian history and provided the doctrinal basis for tolerance of Jews and Jewish faith within Christendom. Augustine's mentor, Ambrose of Milan (~337/340–397), had argued that Jews should be forced to convert. Augustine opposed this. First, he argued, Jews give witness to the validity of their Sacred Scriptures as God's Word. This, he felt, was a necessary witness since the validity of the New Testament relies upon its interpretation of the Old Testament. Thus, he argued, Jews should be allowed to worship "as did their ancestors," for theirs is a true worship of God based on God's revelation to them. Second, in a passage that many have pounced on as being anti-Jewish, Augustine (I believe brilliantly) turns the deicide canard on its head. The Jews may be guilty of the death of Jesus, he writes, but they have by that very reason the Mark of Cain on their foreheads. They are protected by God from human punishment. It is not we Christians but God Himself who will judge them. These were the theological bases upon which the medieval Church would, beginning with Pope St. Gregory the Great (~540–604), make it a part of the canonical legal tradition of the Church that Judaism, and only Judaism, among all the known religions of the ancient world, be considered *religio licita*. Synagogues, and only synagogues, albeit regulated, would be allowed to stand, so that the Jews could continue to worship as had their ancestors, and to witness thereby to the world the truth of God's revelation to them.

Likewise, there is a rather large distinction to be made between the writings of Luther and Calvin on Jews and Judaism, though neither confronts the "teaching of contempt." Again, a personal factor seems to be in play. Luther's early writings, perhaps reflecting on Augustine (he was, after all, an Augustinian monk), promote tolerance of the Jews. He seems to have initially believed that his purified Catholicism would, if presented to Jews through love and mercy, inspire them to convert. Toward the end of his life, realizing that his form of Christianity was no more tempting to Jews than that of the Catholicism he had by this time left, Luther wrote two blistering pamphlets calling on Christians to burn down synagogues and convert or exile the Jews ("On the Jews and Their Lies" and "On the Unknowable Name and the Generations of the Christ," both in 1544).

Calvin, on the other hand, had a vision of a society imbued with biblical principles. He therefore took the Old Testament seriously as providing a blueprint for his perfect Christian society, since it grapples with such issues throughout its pages. Calvinist-inspired countries, such as the Netherlands and Switzerland, tended for some centuries to be more tolerant of Jews and Judaism than Lutheran or Catholic ones (with the exception of Italy, which, because of the political authority the pope as head of the Papal States, continued to observe the canon laws protecting the Jews). Many of the Jews fleeing Spain's 1492 decree of conversion or expulsion, for example, ended up in Rome. So, again, my point is that one must take equally into account the differences as well as the similarities within the various Christianities in order fully to understand so complex a matter as two millennia of European Jewish-Christian history. It was not always or everywhere lachrymose. Otherwise, explain why so many Jews still lived and prospered within Christian societies at the beginning of the twentieth century?

In the final section of his 2003 paper, Garber opens a topic he probes more deeply in an article published originally in the journal *Shofar* and then included in a book he edited for the Shofar Supplements in Jewish Studies series.[18] In both, however, I am left with questions to raise in my ongoing dialogue with him. And in both, as usual, he himself raises a number of the right questions with which we Jews and Christians will continue to need to grapple together for perhaps centuries to come, until the coming or return of the Messiah resolves them for all of us: "Was (Jesus) the Son of God, necessary for belief in the atonement theory of redemption, or a member of God's firstborn son, Israel (Exod. 4:22)? Was there one Christ? Was his mission false, failed, or fulfilled? Is belief in the death and resurrection of Christ reflective of Mosaic monotheism or expressive of Church Tritheism?" As he notes, part of the problem stems from the varying ways we Jews and Christians use the same terms (e.g., redemption, Messiah), part is history, part theology. It is a very rich dialogue for which Garber is calling, one that has the potential, respectfully done and with mutual esteem, to challenge and enrich our understanding not only of each other, but of our own traditions as well.

Garber, in 2003, notes that he assesses the Easter faith from the vantage point of

> critical scholarship in search of the historic Jesus, not hand-me-down faith affirmation; Jesus did not teach what was to become the Church's understanding of him and his mission; traditional negative teachings about the Jews have been used to justify great acts of evil against them; and that Jesus our Lord points the way to God, meaning that the God-man of the hypostatic union is metaphorical and not the ultimate force called God.

He concludes that in order to move away from its antisemitic heritage, Christians must "demythologize the Jewish guilt in the death of Jesus," but equally "demystify dogmatic Christology." I join Garber without equivocation in working to eliminate all vestiges of the ancient teaching of contempt and collective guilt charge from Christian teaching on all levels. It is not necessary to Christian self-understanding. Indeed, the negative attacks on Jews and Judaism greatly obfuscate what is essential to the teaching of Jesus and the Church, not only for Jews but for Christians as well. We are not, after all, a religion of hate and vengeance, but a witness to divine love and mercy. "Father, forgive them. They know not what they do" is the very core of true Christian teaching about the crucifixion.

But I must say that I recoiled when I read an Orthodox Jew such as Garber so cavalierly dismiss the central role of tradition in my faith. Such phrasing might appeal to some Protestants, whose search for the historical Jesus stems from just such dismissiveness. But it is not a path that can be advocated for Catholics who, like Orthodox and Conservative Jews, see tradition not as a dead thing of the past but a living reality, which may need rethinking in the light of new questions and issues, but which frames and limns our theological horizons. Likewise, to abandon the reality of the Incarnation, to turn it into a merely "metaphorical force," as Garber would have us do, would be to abandon Christianity. Is the price Garber demands for Jewish-Christian reconciliation apostasy from Christianity? Must we become, in essence, Jews (i.e., Christians without Christ) in order to prove to Garber that we have repented our sins against Jews? John Paul II's famous prayer inserted into the Kotel (Western Wall) in Jerusalem straightforwardly repented those millennial sins and affirmed God's enduring covenant with the Jewish people. There was no hint, however, of moving away from the "high Christology" that is the very center of Catholic faith. I applaud him on both counts.

In his 2005 article in *Shofar*, Garber reveals a bit more of his understanding of Jesus, the Jew. He follows the theory of S. G. F. Brandon that Jesus was a revolutionary whose political views were tamped down and replaced by a "portrait of a pacifistic Christ" by the gospel authors in order to make Christianity appear less threatening to the Romans. While I believe he is correct to question the blasphemy charge ("Where in the biblical-talmudic tradition is blasphemy defined as claiming that one is the 'Messiah the Son of the Blessed'?"), I must say that I was not convinced by Brandon 's overall thesis at the time, and remain unconvinced.[19] The nonviolent response of love to force is so radically central to the gospel narratives, and so unique in the history of the religious traditions of Israel (or Greece or Rome), for that matter, that I cannot imagine the historicity of the gospels or the validity of my faith without it, even though the caveat to that teaching—the Justifiable War theory—historically, has made of pacifism a treasured minority position among Christians. If this is clinging to tradition on my part, so be it. I plead guilty. But as a famous Christian once said, "Here I stand. I can do no other."

Garber understands what he calls the Christian Scriptures (I would reject this renaming of the New Testament because "the Christian Scriptures" perforce include the Hebrew Scripture, so Torah is as much Christian scripture, from our viewpoint, as are the Synoptics) to be helpfully understood "in the idiom of Midrash." I believe this to be a very helpful insight and one to be pursued in the Christian-Jewish dialogue. He sees Jesus to have been "not a false but a failed Redeemer of the Jews."[20] This, too, is a positive advance, a move away from the polemical toward the dialogical in our discussions. It allows for the response that Catholic tradition sees Jesus as having "fulfilled" but not "perfectly fulfilled" the biblical promises in His First Coming. The Eucharistic proclamation of the Church is "Christ has Come. Christ is Risen. Christ will Come Again!" This is the eschatological caveat, the "not yet" which must always be added to the "already" of our faith. We proclaim a successful Messiah, but one whose work is not yet done, a Reign of God to come, which we, like the Jews, await and to which we, like the Jews, witness and are called by God to work toward. In this perspective, much is possible between the Church and the Jewish people, and, in our joint witness to humanity of its End, and which, in turn, defines its meaning throughout history.

Finally, at the end of the article (which revolves around Mel Gibson's movie, *The Passion of the Christ,* to which I will turn below), Garber seems to accept the interpretation of the affirmation of Rom. 9:4 that "Christ is the end of the Law" to mean that in Christ the Law is ended, abolished. But the sentence in context can be better read as "Christ is the goal of the Law," in which case it is eschatological, a goal to be fulfilled with His Second Coming. In this case, again, there is an openness to a both/and approach, to replace the either/ors of our disputational past. As the rabbinic saying has it, "These and these are the words of the living God." I would conclude this section with a paraphrase of that saying with which I think Garber might concur: "These Jewish and these Christian words are both, each in their own way, the words of the living God."

Responding to Gibson's *The Passion of the Christ*

Zev Garber responded to the movie, in a sense, by throwing a book at it. I did, too. His was a scholarly book that shed a great deal of light on the complex historical and theological issues raised by the movie. The book I worked on as staff for the U.S. Catholic Bishops' Committee for Ecumenical and Interreligious Affairs was a compilation of the official teachings of the Church on the subject. When asked by the editor of *America* magazine for an article to come out before the movie to help Catholics view it without picking up negative attitudes toward Jews and Judaism, I summarized those teachings. When asked for my reflections after the movie I wrote a piece I called "After the Melstrom," although my play on words did not quite get by the magazine's spellcheck. I reprint them here in honor of the excellent work Garber did with regard to the movie.

The Bible, the Jews and the Death of Jesus

A week or so before Ash Wednesday of 2004, the Bishops' Committee for Ecumenical and Interreligious Affairs (BCEIA) of the U.S. Conference of Catholic Bishops will release a 150-page resource book for use by Catholic preachers, teachers, interested laity, and Catholic-Jewish dialogue groups.[21] Its title will be *The Bible, the Jews and the Death of Jesus: A Collection of Catholic Documents.* The publication will bring together in one place excerpts and, in some cases, entire documents from various levels of

Catholic teaching pertinent to how the Church reads its Scriptures, understands its relationship with Jews and Judaism, and understands and presents its ever deepening reflections on the saving mysteries of the Passion and Death of Christ, the One Savior of all humanity.

In introducing this collection of official Catholic documents, Bishop Stephen E. Blaire, Bishop of Stockton and chairman of the BCEIA, quotes from an address given by Pope John Paul II in 1997 to a group of Catholic, Protestant, and Orthodox scholars assembled by the Holy See to study together "The Roots of Anti-Judaism in the Christian Milieu." Since this papal quote reveals much of the motivation for the reissuance by the BCEIA of the documents, it is worth reproducing in full here:

> Erroneous and unjust interpretations of the New Testament regarding the Jewish people and their alleged culpability have circulated (in the Christian world) for too long, engendering feelings of hostility toward this people. They contributed to the lulling of consciences, so that when the wave of persecutions swept across Europe . . . the spiritual resistance of many was not what humanity rightfully expected from the disciples of Christ. Your examination of the past, in view of a purification of memory, is particularly appropriate for clearly showing that anti-Semitism has no justification and is absolutely reprehensible.

Note the carefulness and clarity of the pope's words: "erroneous and unjust interpretations of the New Testament." These ancient errors in the interpretation of the Passion narratives of the gospels centered around the unjust and unjustifiable idea that "the Jews" (as opposed to some individual Jewish leaders) were and remained in subsequent generations collectively guilty for His death. As embroidered over the centuries in theological tomes, popular preaching and Passion Plays contributed, the Holy Father asserts, to the passive acquiescence and active participation of far too many Christians in the Holocaust in the twentieth century. The Vatican anti-Judaism symposium was one of the major symposia the pope mandated take place to prepare for his breathtakingly honest and historic Liturgy of Repentance in St. Peter's to inaugurate the millennial Lenten season. The explanation for the expression of repentance on behalf of the universal Church for the sins of, again, far too many Catholics in anti-Jewish and even antisemitic teachings and actions over the centuries was likewise succinctly stated by the Pontifical Theological commission just days before the liturgy took place in St. Peter's Basilica in Rome. The prayer from the liturgy was, it is to be noted, that which the Holy Father placed in the Western Wall of the ancient Jewish Temple in Jerusalem only days later. I quote from the theological explanation:

> The *Shoah* was certainly the result of the pagan ideology that was Nazism, animated by a merciless anti-Semitism that not only despised the faith of the Jewish people, but also denied their very human dignity. Nevertheless, "it may be asked whether the Nazi persecution of the Jews was not made easier by the anti-Jewish prejudices imbedded in some Christian minds and hearts. . . . Did Christians give every possible assistance to those being persecuted, and in particular to the persecuted Jews?" This fact constitutes a call to the consciences of all Christians today, so as to require "an act of repentance (*teshuva*)," and to be a stimulus to increase efforts to be "transformed by renewal of your mind" (Rom 12:2), as well as to keep a "moral and religious memory" of the injury inflicted on the Jews. In this area, much has already been done, but this should be confirmed and deepened.[22]

Most recently, in September of 2003 in *L'Osservatore Romano*, Cardinal Walter Kasper of the Holy See's Commission for Religious Relations with the Jews expanded on the above reflections, and Cardinal Roger Etchegaray on December 23 warned of an increase of antisemitism worldwide and particularly in Europe, calling the Church to increased vigilance. Since the charge of collective guilt of the Jews lies historically at the heart of Christian anti-Judaism, the BCEIA's reaffirmation of the teachings of the Church on these matters remains, sadly, quite timely. What Church documents did the bishops select, then, and why?

The idea for the resource volume came out of discussions precipitated by a recent run on the BCEIA's 1988 statement, *Criteria for the Evaluation of Dramatizations of the Passion*, raising the need for republication. *Criteria* has now been posted on the Conference website (www.usccb.org). It was felt appropriate, however, to set the 1988 statement into the larger context of Church teachings that forms its matrix. As Bishop Blaire comments in his introduction, "two developments within the Church awakened and fostered a new understanding of the relationship between the Church and its roots in Judaism. The first was the biblical movement led the Church to a re-reading of the Gospels, and indeed all Scripture, through analysis of literary and historical forms in order to identify a fuller theological understanding. The second development was that the Church in the Second Vatican Council formulated its commitment to re-examining its relationship with the Jewish people."

The readings in *The Bible, the Jews and the Death of Jesus* begin with the Council's reconsideration of Church teaching on Jews and Judaism, *Nostra Aetate, no. 4* ("In Our Time"). The volume then establishes an understanding of how the Church reads its Scriptures, with selections from documents of the Pontifical Biblical Commission: *The Historical Truth of the Gospels* (1964) and *The Interpretation of the Bible in the Church* (1993), which communicate the methodology of biblical and theological interpretation applied to the Passion narratives by the bishops in *Criteria*. The section concludes with the discussion of each of the four gospel Passion narratives in the Commission's *The Jewish People and Their Sacred Scriptures in the Christian Bible* (2002).

Next, the text brings together the relevant sections of the official statements of the Holy See's Commission for Religious Relations with the Jews (1974, 1985, 1998), drawing out the implications of *Nostra Aetate* for the Church's preaching and teaching. These documents of the universal Church were in turn implemented in statements by bishops' conferences around the world. In the U.S., and republished here, are those of the U.S. Conference of Catholic Bishops: *Statement on Catholic-Jewish Relations* (1975), the Bishops' Committee on the Liturgy, *God's Mercy Endures Forever: Guidelines on the Presentation Jews and Judaism in Catholic Teaching* (1988), and, finally, the Bishops' Committee for Ecumenical and Interreligious Affairs, *Criteria for the Evaluation of Dramatizations of the Passion* (1988).

Concluding the documents sections are citations from *The Roman Catechism of the Council of Trent* (I, 5, 11) and the current *Catechism of the Catholic Church* (nos. 595–598), the latter under the titles: "Divisions among the Jewish Authorities concerning Jesus," "Jews Are Not Collectively Guilty for Jesus' Death," and "All Sinners Were the Authors of Christ's Passion." Interestingly, the recent Catechism reaffirms and cites the theological insight of the Council of Trent:

> We must regard as guilty all those who continue to relapse into their sins. Our sins . . . crucify the Son of God anew. . . . And it can be seen that our crime in this case is greater in us than in the Jews. As for them, according to the witness of the Apostle, "none of the rulers of this age understood this, for if they had they would not have crucified the Lord of glory." We, however, profess to know him. And when we deny him by our deeds, we in some way seem to lay violent hands on him.

Rounding out the collection are selections from a papal Good Friday liturgy guiding the Church's understanding of the Passion of St. John and the Stations of the Cross and the text of the gospel passion narratives themselves. As Bishop Blair notes, concluding his introduction, "behind all these statements and gestures was the determination to end prejudices against Jews and Judaism, and in a fuller way to understand salvation in Christ by seeing the unique place of Jews and of the Jewish religion in the unfolding of salvation."

Catholic-Jewish Relations in the Aftermath of the Maelstrom

I write this just after giving a talk on the passion at one of the "brown bag" lunches various departments here at the Conference host to let colleagues know what they are doing (we presume we know what we are doing in our own fields, of course).[23] It drew at least twice the usual crowd, and sold a number of copies of the bishops' collection of Catholic documents, *The Bible, the Jews and the Death of Jesus*. Similarly, bishops across the country have spoken out about the movie, all with the warning that, whatever one thinks of the movie, Catholics should not go away from it thinking that all Jews, then or now, are guilty of the death of Jesus, and that there are four gospels, not one or five, written toward the end of the first century and reflecting the times in which they were written and the needs of the communities for which they were written as much as the events in Jesus' life which they relate. Bishops are sending materials to all their parishes and schools with this message spelled out in some detail, as I did in my article not long ago in these pages. More Catholics are going to learn more about the teaching of their Church on Jews and Judaism this Lent than in any comparable period since the Pope's 1986 visit to the Great Synagogue of Rome, or perhaps even since the Second Vatican Council. Hundreds perhaps thousands of joint groups of Jews and Christians will be viewing the movie together, as was suggested by Cardinal William Keeler, around the country and engaging in quiet dialogue. Underneath the hype, *The Passion of the Christ* has given Catholic-Jewish relations in this country a great boost. So I want to join the rabbi who, after seeing the movie in one such group, commented, "I want to thank Mel Gibson for bringing us all together." God does, indeed, write straight with crooked paths.

How might such a dialogue go, should you be fortunate enough to be in one?

Well, the first thing that should happen is that the Catholics should listen, as also suggested by Cardinal Keeler, with their hearts as well as their minds to the concerns of their Jewish neighbors. They are quite legitimate. They are also based on history. The Jewish people, like the Catholic Church, have a long memory. However, the same is not necessarily true of American Catholics who are, after all, Americans and who dropped European history into the waters at the feet of the Statue of Liberty when we immigrated here. The ahistorical nature of American Catholics has a good side, of course. Even before the Second Vatican Council, most American Catholics had dropped many of the old ethnic and religious animosities, rabid antisemitism being among them. But Jews, understandably after all that has happened to them at the hands of Christians over the centuries, and what happened to them in "Christian" Europe in living, horrified memory, are really not quite yet sure they can trust us not to come storming out of the movie looking for a Jew to take it out on, as, indeed, some of our European grandparents might well have!

So we need to listen. Then we need to do more. We need to act together. The group might go to a Catholic school, for example, and ask together to see what the textbooks actually say about Jews and Judaism. It is not what our grandparents' generation got in catechism class on this subject at all. I know this because my 1976 doctoral dissertation was on the portrait of Jews and Judaism in Catholic religious education materials. It updated one done by Sister Rose Thering, OP (1920–2006), before the Council and was in turn updated by one done in 1992 by Dr. Philip Cunningham of Boston College. Cunningham manages an excellent website devoted to Christian-Jewish relations which makes available many useful resources for Catholic preachers and teachers as well as dialogue groups, http://www.bc.edu/research/cjl.

Jews, then, need to know that the Catholic Church has indeed made great strides in fulfilling the mandate of *Nostra Aetate* to renew its stance toward and teaching about Jews and Judaism. They need, understandably, to see for themselves that the old slot of anti-Judaism, the idea of collective guilt, is really not there anymore for something into which a Passion Play might fit. They need, as Rabbi Balfour Brickner once famously said at a dialogue meeting, to learn how to take "yes" for an answer. While you are at the Catholic school, if it is a high school (the violence will preclude most Catholic grade schools from letting their children see the film), you might want to suggest some educational programming to inform the kids about Catholic teaching with regard to the theological and historical issues raised by any depiction of the Passion.

While Catholics need to know and take to heart that a people one-third of whose entire population was systematically murdered by baptized Europeans not all that long ago, are still struggling with the pain of that loss, a pain that Passion Plays played a role in bringing about, Jews need to know how Christians will essentially view the film, which, in many cases, will be as a religious experience that, for Christians, has nothing to do with Jews as a group, but with Jesus and our own coming to grips with our own sinfulness. This, too, is a legitimate response, just as are Jewish concerns. Most collectively guilty for the death of Jesus, the Catechism of the Council of Trent rightly taught, are Christians, who sin knowing that since Jesus died for the sins of all humanity, while what the relatively few Jews who were involved did was done in ignorance, for which they have already been forgiven by Jesus himself.

Finally, the group might talk about how we talk about and to each other. Though we share common scriptures and have interrelated throughout Christian history, our religious language often uses the same terms in different ways, and our social language is influenced by the different ways our communities are organized and the histories we have undergone. Even our institutional styles of making public pronouncements differ. Not to make light of it, but Jewish agencies tend to talk like New

Yorkers, while the Catholic bishops speak more like Midwesterners, milder in tone and with verbal pyrotechnics. A lot of what went on in the media hype over the movie was (once again) a culture clash as much as a culture war. Many Jews have asked me why the bishops did not outright condemn the movie for its Passion Play elements. They wanted a shout from on high. What they got was a book (see above), a series of clear statements on the teaching of the Catholic Church, and an active educational and pastoral system doing its job communicating that teaching, day in and day out. The Catholic bishops, I keep reminding my Jewish friends, do not need to shout in the newspapers to be heard. The Church teaches and preaches, and will do so long after this movie has had its last showing. What is important is that we get the teaching right. On that, we must be grateful as always for the sensitivity of Jews to the corrosive and at times subtle nature of the profound evil that is antisemitism. As Pope John Paul II has said to us time and again, this Jewish voice is, for the Church, "a saving warning."

Finally, the group might want to visit a Jewish school and take a look at what Jewish textbooks say about Christianity. There are a few inaccuracies there, as well, though none so dangerous as pre-Vatican II Christian teaching.

Notes

1. Harry James Cargas, *The Unnecessary Problem of Edith Stein,* Studies in the Shoah 4 (Lanham, Md.: University Press of America, 1994). Polish received an award from the Catholic Press Association for his explanation of Jewish fears regarding possible implications of the beatification.
2. In ibid., 15.
3. Ibid., 19.
4. Ibid., 24.
5. Ibid.
6. Zev Garber, *Shoah: The Paradigmatic Genocide: Essays in Exegesis and Eisegesis,* Studies in the Shoah 7 (Lanham, Md.: University Press of America, 1994), 79–96; Cargas, *The Unnecessary Problem of Edith Stein,* 61, 65.
7. Cargas, *The Unnecessary Problem of Edith Stein,* 69. At this point, there are several paragraphs in the Cargas volume which are not in the Garber text, presumably added to the former rather than deleted for the latter, from here on my references will be only to that volume.
8. Ibid., 70.
9. The full text can be found in Eugene Fisher and Leon Klenicki, eds., *Spiritual Pilgrimage: Pope John Paul II, Texts on Jews and Judaism, 1970–1995* (New York: Crossroad, 1995), 91–98. Cargas, *The Unnecessary Problem of Edith Stein,* 72.
10. *Verus Israel.* The reference here is to Gal. 6:16, which can be understood to mean "the true Israel," and a reference to the Church as the only true Israel, as some Fathers of the Church understood it. On the other hand, it can also be read to mean "truly Israel," capping Paul's argument throughout Galatians that Gentiles, through Christ, can be considered "adopted heirs" of biblical Israel alongside the natural heirs, the physical descendants of Abraham and Sarah. In this case, Paul's argument is not supersession or replacement but instead an argument against the "Judaizers" who were insisting that Gentiles had to convert to Judaism and be circumcised in order to enter the Church. This fits the context of the passage much better that the supersessionist understanding. It is bolstered by Paul's image in Romans 9–11 of Gentiles being "engrafted" unto the root (Israel) rather than being in any sense a "new" growth in themselves. Many New Testament scholars today read the passage in the latter rather than the former sense.
11. Interestingly, there was a Lutheran scholar present at the meetings who "sided" with us Catholics in the matter of, shall we say, the carnality of sacramental spirituality.
12. *Judaism: A Quarterly Journal* 22, no. 1 (Winter 1973): 21–32.
13. Martin Buber, *Two Types of Faith* (New York: Harper Torchbooks, 1961); Trude Weis-Rosmarin, *Judaism and Christianity: The Differences* (New York: Jonathan David, 1968); Ahad Haam, *Selected Essays of Ahad Haam* (New York: Meridian, 1962), 152.
14. Cargas, *The Unnecessary Problem of Edith Stein,* 74. Pontifical Commission for Religious Relations with the Jews, *Guidelines and Suggestions for Implementing the Conciliar Declaration, Nostra Aetate, no. 4* (December 1, 1974), "Preamble." "Christians must therefore strive to learn by what essential traits Jews define themselves in the light of their own religious experience."
15. "Shoah's Apocalypse: Three Talking Points," unpublished, sent to me by the author.

16. Eva Fleischner, ed., *Auschwitz: Beginning of a New Era? Reflections on the Holocaust* (New York: KTAV, Cathedral Church of St. John the Divine, ADL, 1974), 103.
17. "Shoah's Apocalyse," II, B. John Paul II, Speech to Symposium on the Roots of Anti-Judaism (October 31, 1997), *L'Osservatore Romano* 6, no. 1 (November 6, 1997).
18. "The Jewish Jesus: A Partisan's Imagination," *Shofar* 23, no. 3 (Spring 2005): 137–43; Zev Garber, ed., *Mel Gibson's Passion: The Film, the Controversy and Its Implications* (West Lafayette, Ind.: Purdue University Press, 2006), 63–69.
19. "The Jewish Jesus," 138.
20. Ibid., 141.
21. This section reprinted from *America,* February 16, 2005, with permission of America Press, Inc. © 2004. All rights reserved. Visit http://www.americamagazine.org.
22. International Theological Commission, *Memory and Reconciliation: The Church and the Faults of the Past,* March 2000, 5.4.
23. This section reprinted from *America,* April 5, 2005, with permission of America Press, Inc. © 2004. All rights reserved. Visit http://www.americamagazine.org.

Who Owns the Truth? The Question of the "Other" in Postdenominational Judaism and Christianity (and Islam) in the Next Fifty Years

Steven Leonard Jacobs

Introduction: The Future *Is* Unpredictable Despite . . .

For almost three decades (1974–2000), I labored full-time "in the vineyards of the Lord," serving primarily rabbinically in Jewish congregations in Birmingham, Mobile, and Huntsville, Alabama, and Dallas, Texas, including academic postings in those communities as well. Since 2001, I have been a full-time member of the University of Alabama faculty and part-time rabbi of a small congregation in Tuscaloosa. In all of these viable centers of modern American liberal Jewish life, I repeatedly reminded those whom I had been privileged to serve that, in my studies in those congregations, I kept not one but *three* crystal balls—to remind me that none of them worked! That is to say, for Jews, especially for American Jews (and for Christians and Muslims as well), the future will not be what we wish it to be, but, rather, will be determined largely by our actions today as well as our responses to tomorrow's events, which are themselves equally unpredictable. Questions of diminishing or increasing Jewish numbers not only in this country but worldwide, diminishing or increasing Jewish religiosity here and abroad, the shape and context of Jewish-Christian relations in this country and Jewish-Muslim/Arab relations in the Middle East and elsewhere and their impact upon Jews locally and globally, the phenomenon of Islam's world growth increasingly surpassing Christianity most especially on the African continent, the heretofore little-perceived and only recently addressed rise of the fundamentalisms in all three faith communities as all three conflictually struggle with modernity and postmodernity, the increasingly lessening impact of white Western Christianity and its sad and tragic history of colonialism and triumphalist supercessionism politically and religiously are all arenas worthy of exploration and exposition.[1]

Looming largest, however, is a question so significant in its implications for both the present and the future that it undergirds the rest, and to which our responses may very well determine the next fifty years, most particularly in this country. And this is the question of "Who Owns the Truth: The Question of the 'Other,'" of which I am more and more convinced will be viewed as *postdenominational* Judaism and Christianity in the years to come. If one manner of characterizing post–World War II America is, increasingly with hindsight, an age of interreligious and intrareligious dialogue, then these next fifty years will take us to the very heart of the matter, to a question that has been lurking at the periphery of all of the dialogues and dialogical encounters that have been taking place betwixt and among these faith communities: that of the subjective or objective truth of the claims made by each of them, claims oft-times directly contrary and opposite to those made by the very persons with whom we have been willing to engage in the dialogue, as well as the claim to *ownership* of such truth. How, increasingly, we will relate to the person of the "other"—to use a term comfortable to both the late French Jewish philosopher Emanuel Levinas (1906–95) and German Roman Catholic theologian Johannes Baptist Metz—will ultimately prove the hallmark of these next five decades. Before turning to the question itself directly, what exactly *can* we say with regard to contemporary thinking about the future of Judaism, Christianity, and Islam? Like so much of contemporary intellectual life and discourse, do the vast resources available to us on the Internet embodied on the World Wide Web, itself most assuredly changing the very face of our conversations, have anything of significance and import to say to us regarding what we may comfortably call "the future of religion"? In addition, are there other texts and resources pointing us toward our headlong rush into that future?

The World Future Society, the World Network of Religious Futurists, Signs, Wonders, and Others

Begun in 1966, the World Future Society is, according to its Web site (http://www.wfs.org), "an association of people interested in how the social and technological developments are shaping the future." Comprised of more than 30,000 people in more than eighty countries, it "strives to serve as a neutral clearing house for ideas about the future." Its bimonthly publication *The Futurist*

> publishes articles and reports dealing with (1) significant social and technological trends and informed forecasts about where they may lead, (2) methods for using information about future possibilities in decision making, (3) other topics of interest to people seeking greater success in the future for their organization and themselves.[2]

Its annual conference in 2001 in Minneapolis was entitled "FutureScope 2001: Exploring the 21st Century." While not focusing directly on religion as such, the organization's Web site also included its "top 10 forecasts . . . chosen on the basis of their interest, significance, and plausibility . . . from leading scientists, researchers, and scholars whose views of the future have been published in *The Futurist* during the last year [i.e., 2000]." These included the following:

1. The number of centenarians worldwide will increase from 135,000 today to 2.2 million people by 2050.
2. By 2010, biomonitoring devices that resemble wristwatches will provide wearers with up-to-the-minute data about their health status.
3. Exercise will promote mental well-being as well as a healthier body, helping people fight chronic pain, depression, chemical dependence, and even schizophrenia.
4. Tiny electronic microchips implanted in a person's forearm could transmit messages to a computer that controls the heating and light systems of intelligent buildings.
5. The twenty-first century could see widespread infertility and falling birthrates.
6. Farmers will become genetic engineers, growing vaccines as well as food.
7. The worldwide consumption of meat will double by 2050.
8. Ninety percent of the world's 6,000 languages could go extinct by 2100.
9. Water scarcity could threaten 1 billion people by 2025.
10. Human population will level off by 2035, while pet population will increase dramatically.[3]

Each of these forecasts, if reasonably solid projections based on currently available data and evidence, possesses enormous implications for all communities of faith. Ironically, such faith groups, in the main, tend not to discuss such future realities outside their own religio-theological interests and concerns.[4]

One of two "linked sites," however, more specifically focused on our topic is that of the World Network of Religious Futurists (WNRF), itself an organization twenty-five years old, and meeting conjointly with the World Future Society. According to its own FAQ ("Frequently Asked Questions") as posted on its Web site:

> You "study the future" of religion by extrapolating trends, and by caring about the future, especially the future of religion. And by praying and studying sacred texts and histories of one's own faith tradition—to be inspired by it. . . . Religious future scholarship focuses on predictable occurrences in the future of religion, based on presently observable trends, and past trends in religion, compounded by wild cards or quantum leaps, in the context of society's future as a whole, raging from science to technology. . . . Added to that, futures study of religion thinks in terms of what we want to see as well as what we expect to see. . . . By reflecting on the past, present and like emerging events in religion and religions, we clarify our values, and ask ourselves if these are the events we would like to see. . . . *The study of the future of religion is therefore the pursuit of the ideal, the search for the highest and best truth,* and, by God's grace, the power to improve all things, including religion itself [emphasis added].[5]

In 1997 Jay Gary, resident of Colorado Springs, president of the consulting group Millennium 2000, and cochair of the Christian Futures Network of the World Network of Religious Futurists, received the Earl Award, named for the "founding father" of religious futures research, the late Dr. Earl D. C. Brewer, director of the Center for Religious Research and professor of religion and society at the (Methodist) Candler School of Theology, Emory University, Atlanta. Gary's address was entitled "Ten Global Trends in Religion," and included these observations:

1. The persistence of Religious Persecution.
2. The attraction of Militant Fundamentalism.
3. A rising growth rate of Islam.
4. A shift to non-white Christianity.
5. The growth of Pentecostal and non-denominational Christianity.
6. A decline of Tribal Religion.
7. A level of growth of Non-religious Persons.[6]
8. An increase of Pluralism in society.
9. An increase of Women in pastoral roles.
10. The anticipation of a New Millennium.

While Gary's last trend is now ten plus years old, and the alarmist dangers prior to the year 2000—most specifically that of computer meltdown affecting all manner of global society—proved nonexistent, his observations are by and large correct and bear directly on the central focus of this essay, the ownership of "the Truth" and the question of "the Other." But they tell only half the future story.

Todd M. Johnson, Ph.D., is senior research coordinator of GEM Research, Richmond, Virginia, and coeditor of the (2000) *World Christian Encyclopedia,* and its subsequent updates. In it are two tables relevant to this discussion, abstracted here (see Tables 1 and 2).

Taking both Johnson and his colleagues' numbers and actual percentages into consideration, as well as Gary's trends, we may conclude the following:

1. The "world of religion" is, truly, moving beyond any sense of denominationalism within its own religious traditions into a postdenominational world.
2. The divisions which will yet exist will now be between "traditionalists," now defined as those for whom the structures and systems of the past will remain primary—"fundamentalists" becoming the largest and most vocal among them—and "nontraditionalists," now defined, at the very least, borrowing a phrase from the late rabbinic scholar Dr. Solomon Freehof of Pittsburgh, as those for whom the past shall exercise "a vote, but not a veto."
3. Historically white, male, and Christian dominance of our world and its patterns of thought and action will *not* continue, but will be surpassed certainly by the end of the next century by the equal participation of males and females, nonwhites and non-Christians.
4. Both Christianity and Islam will continue to show *significant* increases in overall populations (as will Judaism to a far lesser degree), and will continue, although percentage-wise, Islam's increase will be far more dramatic (12.4% in 1900 to 20.2% in 2025) than Christianity (34.5%

Table 1. Growth of World Religions, 1900–2025

	1900	1970	2000	2025
Christians	558,056,300	1,222,585,000	2,015,743,000	2,710,800,000
Muslims	200,102,200	558,272,000	1,215,693,000	1,894,436,000
Jews	12,269,800	14,767,000	14,307,000	15,864,000

Table 2. World Religions

	1900	1970	2000	2025
Christians	34.5%	33.2%	33.4%	35.5%
Muslims	12.4%	17.7%	18.5%	20.2%
Jews	0.8%	0.3%	0.3%	0.3%
Hindus	12.5%	13.3%	13.4%	13.1%
Chinese folk religions	23.5%	3.4%	3.4%	2.7%[a]

[a]These last two are included in this percentage abstract listing because they are the only two among the additional world faiths with any statistical significance whatsoever.

in 1900 to 35.5% in 2025), with Judaism actually experiencing a decrease on the world scene (0.8% in 1900 to 0.03% in 2025).

Before turning specifically to the Jewish religious future, I would present one additional set of projections taken from yet a third Web site, that of "Signs and Wonders: Scanning the Future of Faith," which, according to its own introduction, sifts "through the World Wide Web looking for evidence of emerging religious futures." Its "mission is to provide the readers—religious futurists, ministers, and just plain spiritual people—with a guided tour of the web, stopping wherever we see the future of faith before our eyes." (The site is regularly updated.)

In addition to those already included and enumerated by Gary, they have also included six other trends "increasing in prominence," which they believe will, most assuredly, impact communities of faith:

1. The rise of the global teenager, approaching 2 billion before 2010.
2. The rise of postmodernity (defined as more pluralistic and relativistic and becoming mainstream) in Western society.
3. The aging of Western populations.
4. Economic and political globalization (with the increase of power and influence of multinational corporations).
5. The continued growth of the Internet (with its attendant technologies).
6. The advent of revolutionary technologies (e.g., genetic engineering, nanotechnology, materials science) and their challenge for people of faith.

Again, each of these trends, evidences of which are already in existence, will help shape and redefine the way in which Judaism, Christianity, and Islam do their work and attract and lose adherents in the future.

Specifically Judaism and the Jewish People

Jewish modernity begins in 1791 when the nation of France, despite opposition, becomes the first country in Western Europe to grant its Jews citizenship. As the walls of the European ghettos came tumbling down, and Jews began a serious interaction with the larger society, so, too, does the lessening impact and influence of Christianity exert their pulls, while the drive toward secularization and economic expansionism becomes dominant, both which will prove a mixed blessing to and for Jews.[7] As Dan Cohn-Sherbok, professor of Jewish theology at the University of Kent, England, correctly noted in his 1994 book *The Future of Judaism,* "The fragmentation of the Jewish people in the post-Enlightenment age has thus led to the disintegration of a shared religious vocabulary."[8] With the rise of Reform or Liberal Judaism in Germany in the early 1800s, and the rise of Conservative or Positive-Historical Judaism, also in Germany, in the 1850s, this religious disintegration continues. Add to these already existing factors the increasing waves of Jewish emigration to these United States in the mid-1800s and early 1900s of both Western European German modernist Jews and Eastern European Polish and Russian traditionalist Jews, and the devastating impact and far-reaching implications of the Holocaust or Shoah of World War II, and one has the present state of world Jewry, no longer a unified community in any sense but a mythic one, divided on every issue of concern, including the present and future direction of the reborn (1948) Third Jewish Commonwealth, the State of Israel.

Little, if any, evidence exists to suggest that this divisiveness will be counteracted by future trends or present concerns. To be sure, external attacks upon the Jewish people, not only against the State of Israel and its inhabitants, but throughout the world, will result in a temporary renewal of Jewish communal solidarity, but, as in the modern past, it will be short-lived and momentary. The issues of a declining Jewish birthrate coupled with an aging Jewish population, increasing exogamous Jewish marriage versus decreasing endogamous Jewish marriage and how best to address/combat/reverse this phenomenon, and Orthodox versus non-Orthodox ownership of "Jewish truth" will continue to pull at the Jewish people, organizations, institutions, fragile communal structures, and thinkers well into this century and beyond.[9] Among many Jews, however, in all denominational groupings, is the fervent hope (and prayer) that this increasing divisiveness will not degenerate into two "armed" camps: Orthodox versus non-Orthodox, including secularists; fundamentalists versus everybody else; Zionists versus non-Zionists, and not only in this country and Israel but wherever Jews exist in quasi-community.

Who Owns the "Truth" and the Question of the "Other"

In an increasingly pluralistic world, growing increasingly smaller and more aware because of the impact of globalist economic agendas and telecommunications and other technological breakthroughs, where historically, white and male and Western Christianity will no longer dominate modes of thinking and acting, issues of truth and questions of otherness come readily to the foreground. Though written from a decidedly Jewish perspective and with an admittedly Jewish concern and agenda, Cohn-Sherbok's *The Future of Judaism* devotes considerable attention to what he calls "Open Judaism"; the future implications for "Open Christianity" and "Open Islam" are particularly relevant.

Addressing both Jews and non-Jews, Cohn-Sherbok writes that, ultimately, truth, however defined, is not only by the one who perceives it as such but also by those who accept it as well.

> [T]he adherents of the world's faiths must recognize the inevitable human subjectivity of religious conceptualization. A theology of religious pluralism thus calls for a complete reorientation of religious apprehension. What is now required is for Jews [and others] to acknowledge that their conceptual systems, forms of worship, lifestyles, and scriptures are in the end nothing more than lenses through which Reality is perceived, but the Divine as-it-is-in-itself is beyond human understanding . . . universalistic truth claims about Divine reality must be a way to a recognition of the inevitable subjectivity of beliefs about the Real.[10]

Thus, on the concern of the ownership of religious truth, it is not owned as such by any one religious tradition, despite protestations to the contrary, but, rather, properly understood, each and every religious tradition, including Judaism, Christianity, and Islam, is a prismatic lens through which each religious community comes to share in a portion of that truth as it haltingly attempts to forge a relationship with Divine Reality. By implication and extension, on the question of the "Other," in this same future world quickly becoming present, what is required for global survival is the recognition, acceptance, and acknowledgment that this other, too, shares equally in that truth, *without* diminishing the particularity of one's ongoing religious and communal commitments. While admittedly such a foundational lesson may well nigh be unacceptable for those for whom fundamentalist orthodoxies will demand exclusivist adherence coupled with denigration (or worse) of outsiders and even those within a specific religious tradition with a different perspective, we appear to also be experiencing the beginnings of a new, postdenominational interfaith community that draws upon the particularistic traditions of its members but seeks to address shared concerns out of a moral-ethical mandate. The preliminary work of Lutheran professor of theology James F. Moore of Valparaiso University is significantly important.[11]

Addressing Jews specifically, Cohn-Sherbok grounds his own plea for Jewish openness in individual freedom and independence of thought and action, something to which the historically organized and institutionally developed Jewish denominational communities have not been committed.

> A theology of religious pluralism, in which Judaism is perceived as simply one religion among many, calls for an attitude of openness. Aware of the inevitable subjectivity of religious belief, all Jews should feel free to draw from the past elements of the tradition which they may find spiritually meaningful. Unlike all the main branches of Judaism, this new interpretation of Judaism is grounded in an ideology of individual freedom granting each person independence of thought and action.[12]

Focusing on God rather than on Jewish denominational particularity will redirect Jewish energies, according to Cohn-Sherbok, outside of its own into a religiously pluralistic world:

> [I]n the contemporary world the Jewish community needs to adopt a more open stance in which the Divine—rather than the Jewish faith—is placed at the centre of the universe of faiths. Such pluralism would enable Jews to affirm the uniqueness of their own heritage while acknowledging the validity of other religions. The theology underpinning this shift of perspective is based on the distinction between Real *an sich* and Real as perceived. From this vantage point, the truth-claims of all religions should be regarded as human constructions rather than universally valid doctrines.[13]

Thus, for Jews, too, the primacy of the Divine, by definition, takes precedence over any claims for sole possession of religious truth, which has not historically been a Jewish focus except within the Jewish religious community itself. The oft-quoted Talmudic dictum, "The righteous of all nations have a share in the world to come," affirms this understanding, though it certainly must be recognized and accepted that those nations, too, are those that affirm a Yahwist reality as the *only* Divine reality. It does, however, grant a certain lack of inclusiveness to Jewish claims while affirming the validity of other claims to religious truth and the integrity of those possessing such claims.

Conclusion: The Future Is Now

Despite all research, reading, and reflection evidenced in this essay, the aforementioned three crystal balls remain stubbornly unyielding in their ability or lack thereof to predict the future and make their predictions clear or cloudy. This much, however, appears to be certain:

We are, perhaps, moving too quickly into a postdenominational religious world of Jews, Christians, and Muslims, a world where divisions between and among will be between those who claim sole ownership of the truth and a belittling or denigration of the other—or worse—and those who affirm the shared ownership of the truth and evince a respect for the other and a willingness to work together out of a shared concern for the present and the future. Which groups will emerge victorious in what may very well become a battleground on a multiplicity of levels remains open. But, equally, our rejections as well as our affirmations today will, more assuredly, influence the direction of those groups and their decision-making preparations for tomorrow, as will the impact of societal and technological changes far beyond our control. As with so much of human existence, however, the choices are ours and ours alone to make, either individually or in concert and harmony with those who share not only our concerns but our visions and our dreams as well.

Notes

Note: This nucleus of this essay, now expanded, originated as a paper presented at the inaugural conference for the Center for American and Jewish Studies, Baylor University, Waco, Texas, November 1–3, 2000, entitled "The Next Fifty Years: Beginning a Millennium of Hope and Possibility."

1. For example, on the question of the rise of these fundamentalisms, the following works come immediately to mind: Richard T. Antoun, *Understanding Fundamentalism: Christian, Islamic, and Jewish Movements* (Walnut Creek, Calif.: Altamira Press, 2001); Karen Armstrong, *The Battle for God* (New York: Knopf, 2000); Giles Kepel, *The Revenge of God: The Resurgence of Islam, Christianity and Judaism in the Modern World* (University Park: Pennsylvania State University Press, 1994); Michael Karpin and Ina Friedman, *Murder in the Name of God: The Plot to Kill Yitzhak Rabin* (New York: Henry Holt, 1998); Bruce B. Lawrence, *Defenders of God: The Fundamentalist Revolt Against the Modern Age* (New York: I. B. Taurus and Co., 1989); Ian S. Lustick, *For the Land and the Lord: Jewish Fundamentalism in Israel* (New York: Council on Foreign Relations, 1988); Malise Ruthven, *Fundamentalism: The Search for Meaning* (Oxford: Oxford University Press, 2004); Laurence J. Silberstein, ed., *Jewish Fundamentalism in Comparative Perspective: Religion, Ideology, and the Crisis of Modernity* (New York: New York University Press, 1993); Ehud Sprinzak, *The Ascendance of Israel's Radical Right* (New York: Oxford University Press, 1991); Roger W. Stump, *Boundaries of Faith: Geographical Perspectives on Religious Fundamentalism* (Lanham, Md.: Rowman and Littlefield, 2000).
2. *The Futurist* 34, no. 5 (Sept.–Oct. 2000): 3.
3. The World Future Society Web site, http://www.wfs.org/forecasts.htm.
4. Limitations of space, however, preclude a thorough discussion of each of these ten forecasts and their religio-theological implications.
5. World Network of Religious Futurists (WNRF), http://www.wnrf.org.
6. On this particular trend, see Irving Greenberg, *For the Sake of Heaven: The New Encounter between Judaism and Christianity* (Philadelphia: Jewish Publication Society, 2004), where he distinguishes between *pluralism* ("in which faiths retain serious authority claims") from *relativism* ("in which all worldviews are true because none is true, other than in some communally agreed conventional way"), and thus applauds this new encounter.
7. "Modernity itself is, to a large degree, an extension of Christianity, and the secularization of Western culture over the last centuries is both in conflict with and a fulfillment of the Christian West." Marc Ellis, *Ending Auschwitz: The Future of Jewish and Christian Life* (Louisville: Westminster/John Knox Press, 1994), 76.
8. Dan Cohn-Sherbok, *The Future of Judaism* (Edinburgh: T&T Clark, 1994), 179.
9. Exogamous marriage = marriage outside the ethnic community. Endogamous marriage = marriage within the ethnic community.
10. Cohn-Sherbok, *The Future of Judaism,* 185.
11. All by James F. Moore: *Christian Theology After the Shoah: A Re-Interpretation of the Passion Narratives* (Lanham, Md.: University Press of America, 1993); *Toward a Dialogical Community: A Post-Shoah Christian Theology* (Lanham, Md.: University Press of America, 2004); and as editor, *Post-Shoah Dialogues: Re-Thinking Our Texts Together* (Lanham, Md.: University Press of America, 2004). Unpublished works include: "The Akedah in Dialogue: Reading Scripture Together After the *Shoah*" (1995); "Beyond Conversation toward Dialogue: A Proposal for the Next Necessary Step in Jewish-Christian Dialogue" (1998); "Re-Envisioning Christianity: A New Era in Christian Theological Interpretation of Christian Texts" (1998); and "Re-Tthinking the Traditions: Reading John 8 and Exodus 2 Together After the *Shoah*" (2000).
12. Cohn-Sherbok, *The Future of Judaism,* 181.
13. Ibid., 182.

The Backwards Man and the Jewish Giant

Mirrors of Traumatic Memory in the Late Photographs of Diane Arbus

Daniel Morris

> This is how one pictures the angel of history. His face is turned toward the past. Where we perceive a chain of events, he sees one single catastrophe which keeps piling wreckage and hurls it in front of his feet. The angel would like to stay, awaken the dead, and make whole what has been smashed. But a storm is blowing in from Paradise; it has got caught in his wings with such a violence that the angel can no longer close them. The storm irresistibly propels him into the future to which his back is turned, while the pile of debris before him grows skyward.
> —Walter Benjamin, "Theses on the Philosophy of History, IX"

One of Diane Arbus's lesser-known but most-revealing photographs is called "The Backwards Man in his hotel room, N.Y.C. 1961." Part of a series Arbus did on "Eccentrics" for a photo essay published in *Harper's Bazaar,* it depicts a contortionist from Hubert's Museum named Joe Allen.[1] Appearing to be about sixty years old, Allen stands in profile, facing a bright naked lightbulb that hangs from the ceiling of a cramped room. The apartment features a bed and chairs that, as in Van Gogh's painting of his room at Arles, block the only doorway to the room. A ubiquitous clothes hanger—presumably for the man's one suit—is hooked to the door, the blinds are drawn over the one window, and there is a mirror with chest of drawers behind him.

Seemingly out of place and incorrectly dressed for what should be an informal private occasion in a dry indoor space, Allen wears a semitransparent raincoat over a formal dark suit. He is not exactly staring at the ceiling's naked bulb, but in the direction toward the bright light, at nothing visible to viewers. As is typical of Arbus prints, vertical edges frame the image with a thick black stripe, in this case giving the appearance that Allen is staring toward emptiness itself. The picture of Joe Allen in his forlorn and yet cramped Van Gogh–style room, in a raincoat and with that dangling lightbulb and hanger, would be macabre, surreal, and poignant enough to qualify as one of Arbus's Prufrockian examples of what Paul McCartney in "Eleanor Rigby" called "all the lonely people." What is singularly bizarre—"freakish" or "flawed," to use two of the favored Arbus terms for those "aristocrats" who "born with their traumas have already passed the test" of life—and hence characteristically of interest to Arbus in the 1960s is the fact that his long black shoes point in the opposite direction from the facial profile.

In one sense, "The Backwards Man" is part of the eccentric cast of carnival and sideshow "freaks"—sword swallowers, midgets, completely tattooed figures—that represent Arbus's belated fascination with a world of strangeness and strangers to which she felt attracted as a child. It was also a world that her parents protected her from until she cast out as a teenaged photographer fresh out of Fieldston School with her husband, Allan Arbus, in the 1940s. "When you grow up your mother says, 'Wear rubbers or else you'll catch cold.' When you become an adult you discover that you have the right not to wear rubbers and to see if you catch cold or not. It's something like that."[2] For Arbus, however, "The Backwards Man" also embodies her uncanny and proleptic relationship to history as a form of traumatic memory. "Joe Allen is a metaphor for human destiny—walking blind into the future with an eye on the past," she writes in one appointment book. "The Backwards Man: the man who can see where he was . . . nostalgia . . . ," she writes in a notebook entry.[3]

For Arbus, Joe Allen is the Benjaminian Angel of History, but in reverse. The face of Benjamin's Angel is "turned toward the past," to witness a catastrophic history that he is unable to repel as a storm propels him forward, toward a future to which he is blind, or from which he has turned away. Allen, the Backwards Man, is facing forward, in the direction of a naked lightbulb. In *A Streetcar Named Desire,* for example, such a lightbulb represents perception of the world in terms of what Blanche, the illusionist, doesn't want Mitch to see—realism, not magic. Allen does not flinch from this observation of an unadorned "what is," but his feet are planted (not quite retreating) in the opposite direction, which Arbus reads as "an eye on the past" and as "where he was." For Arbus, seeing things with the extreme illumination of the unadorned lightbulb—comparable to the blast flash that characterizes her photographic procedure—is contingent upon bodily contortion that propels the seer, impossibly, in two directions at once. The light blinds and illuminates, fractures an instant of time, and exposes the viewer to the ravages of time.

My understanding of Arbus in general is that her portraits of eccentric characters such as Joe Allen are expressionistic, rather than realistic or documentarian in nature. They are displaced self-portraits exposing traumatic memories. Contemporary psychoanalytic theorists have challenged traditional conceptions of what we mean by accurate testimony. They question the idea of a "reliable" testimony when we refer to statements made by a witness who documents extreme physical suffering, psychological disorientation, and metaphysical despair. In *Unclaimed Experience,* Cathy Caruth writes, "For history to be a history of trauma means that it is referential precisely to the extent that it is not fully perceived as it occurs; or to put it somewhat differently, that a history can be grasped only in the very inaccessibility of its occurrence."[4]

For the victim of a catastrophe, distinctions among remembering, forgetting, and misremembering may become moot. What happened to the living witnesses to terror in the death camps, for example, is unspeakable, if speaking implies the expression of a legible discourse, and if the definition of survival refers to the personal liberation from memory in the form of a recovered sense of identity as whole.

Representing the disaster in the muddled or stammering tone of one's testimony, rather than testifying objectively *about* a disaster as documentary reportage, involves the problem of temporal undecidability. How can we even say when something has happened if, as Caruth argues, "it is not fully perceived as it occurs"? How do we verify the facts when the witness may never have consciously registered the event in the first place? The unreliability of testimony, therefore, can be interpreted as a psychic tremor that exemplifies how the witness may regard the present moment as a painful repetition of the long ago. Metaphorically speaking, testimony may be "written" onto the body of the witness. The pain of the past, which has literally intruded upon the present-tense existence of the speaker, may be expressed through a facial tic, as tears, or even in the silence that follows an interviewee's refusal to answer a question. As is the case with many survivors interviewed about the death camps in Claude Lanzmann's documentary film *Shoah,* trauma can be announced as a stutter, a discursive interruption, and a sudden unwillingness to tell the story. We can interpret inarticulateness, or narrative "failure," as indicating that the past has intruded upon the present self.

It would be a major overstatement and highly inappropriate to make a case for the significance of a historical catastrophe such as the Shoah on Arbus's photography. At the same time, her photographs *do* represent in the displaced form of "freak" photography her experience of a profound psychological wound that at times mirrors survivor testimony. Whether its root cause is physical, psychological, or metaphysical, Arbus represents subjects that suggest her inability to differentiate between "now" and "then." Her picture of Joe Allen, the Backwards Man, or of Eddie Carmel, the Jewish Giant, whose images I will discuss later in this essay, manifest what French theorist Julia Kristeva, following Freud's idea of the uncanny, would refer to as the strangeness within the self. I read Arbus's signature pictures as what Oliver Wendell Holmes, among other things a nineteenth-century commentator on photography, called mirrors with memories, but ones that don't evoke the sitters' memories, for these, as Arbus said, remain unavailable to the photographer, regardless of her efforts to enter the lives of others through representation. Images of Allen and Eddie Carmel, I contend, are mirrors that reflect the photographer's memories of experiences she belatedly recovers through photographs. Arbus's relation to history is mirrored in the situation of the Backwards Man. We note the emphasis on bodily distortion, on how outside and inside commingled (rain gear and formal suit worn inside the private room) and, with the hanger as a metaphor for suicide, Joe Allen is a figure who represents the dangers of gazing into the naked lightbulb that simultaneously and impossibly yokes past and present times and contradictory spaces together into a single frame.

What was that Benjaminian history of catastrophe, for Arbus, which proved to be so informative of her sense of an illumination in the present and yet became unsurvivable? Some pictures that Diane Arbus *didn't* take in the 1920s and 1930s, which represent her childhood in Manhattan and in Europe, will contextualize the pictures she *did* take in the 1960s. The pictures that she didn't take, charming images of Arbus with her mother Gertrude and her brother Howard (who would later become known as the distinguished poet Howard Nemerov), depict a past that became in retrospect for Arbus evidence of her dissociation from a history of material hardship as experienced by others—poverty, geographic displacement, and ultimately erasure via the European catastrophe to which Benjamin alludes. These older images remain as specters in Arbus's mature visual imagination as she makes pictures that emphasize ironic juxtapositions, surreal and absurdist elements, as well as the—in Arbus's term—"freakish" dimensions of human being.

A cutline for a 1936 newspaper of parents David and Gertrude Nemerov aboard the *Conte Di Savoie,* arriving in New York Harbor from Paris, states that the couple had gone on a "tour of Paris shops" and that David, the vice president of Russeks furrier and department store, said, "French women were fur-conscious with mink and Persian lamb predominating in their style designs." The cutline also mentions—and here is the grotesque juxtaposition that would fascinate the mature Arbus—that "Spanish refugees returned on the same boat with them." These words, of course, refer to political dissidents fleeing Franco in Fascist Spain, forerunner to the Nazi regime that would spell the end for millions of Europe's Jews. The parents' blindness to the catastrophe—they turn away from the ship to wave at reporters on shore in New York harbor—visualizes what Arbus called the "unreality" of a childhood in which, for example, Diane was photographed in 1927, strolling with her mother and brother at "an elegant seaside holiday resort on the coast of France," with the onset of the Great Depression less than two years away.[5]

A 1932 photograph by Nat Norman of "Hooverville, A Shanty town in Central Park" illustrates how the Nemerovs' wealth did and did not provide isolation from events in the world surrounding the imposing towers of the San Remo apartment on Central Park West where Diane lived with her parents and maternal grandparents. In the background of this image of ramshackle makeshift huts on the lawn of the great park are the spires of the San Remo Building, where the Nemerovs lived at 146 Central Park West. In a radio interview from 1960 with Studs Terkel, Arbus described the shanty town as "the most palpable potent memory of the other side of the railroad tracks . . . you holding the hand of one's governess and feeling . . . I don't mean to say I envied those people, but that you couldn't just wander down. That there was such a gulf."[6]

The shantytown represents a metonym for lack, displacement, and economic collapse on the level of national politics and macroeconomics, but it is also for the young Diane a site connecting her to the real world. Thus, for Arbus, "the family fortune felt humiliating." Arbus often spoke of the "unreality" of her cloistered upbringing. The Hooverville is an alluringly untouchable and yet visibly palpable realm that symbolizes community, a connection to other lives. Arbus interprets the position of being a "Jewish aristocrat" (rather than what she elsewhere referred to as the aristocracy of the freaks who have already passed their test by surviving traumatic experience) as a source of estrangement from the real America. It is "like being a princess in some loathsome movie of some kind of Transylvanian obscure middle European country and the kingdom was so humiliating." Ironically it is the young Diane, however "normal" her outward appearance, and not the residents of the Hooverville in this reading who becomes the "freak," alien, misfit. At least the Hooverville is named after a contemporary American president, however incompetent! Arbus, whose grandparents emigrated from Poland (maternal) and Russia (paternal), interprets the San Remo as a fictive space (part of "some loathsome movie"—Arbus in adult life would take pictures of Disneyland, the castle especially). The San Remo is also misplaced in terms of political systems (it is associated with aristocracy and monarchy, not democracy) and of location (it is connected to "some kind of Transylvanian obscure middle European country").[7]

Arbus's perception of her childhood as absurd because divorced from history is evident in her comments about a Jewish upbringing in which she was shielded from awareness that Jewishness itself is a sign of difference:

> "I never knew I was Jewish when I was growing up," [Arbus] said. "I didn't know it was an unfortunate thing to be! Because I grew up in a Jewish city in a Jewish family and my father was a rich Jew and I went to a Jewish school, I was confirmed in a sense of unreality. All I could feel was my sense of unreality."[8]

Arbus is recalling the 1932 Shantytown image with Terkel. That same year, 1960, she develops her characteristic style in which ironic juxtapositions imply the estrangement of the familiar, as well as images of naked or veiled characters. The coincidence of her late style as a photographer and her recollection of images from her childhood suggest her mature work bears the trace of her lingering fascination with the subcultures of New York. In characteristic pictures she belatedly recovers images that she was exposed to decades earlier, but denied access to as a child. Thus I read the mature work as representations of her traumatic misplacement, as well as recurring traces of memories that Arbus was exposed to and yet failed, in Caruth's formulation, to "own" at the time of her exposure to them. The iconic image of the child with a toy hand-grenade in Central Park is dated 1962 (Norman Mailer quipped that giving Diane Arbus a camera is like giving a child a hand-grenade). Arbus's depiction of what she called "Pseudo Places" (an *Esquire* project) is also from 1962. One example of a "Pseudo Place" is "A Rock in Disneyland, Cal 1962." Arbus's fascination with Hollywood culture and surrealism include her 1963 portrait of Fellini film star Marcello Mastroianni in his hotel room. From this period Arbus also photographed persons who cross genders and play unusual roles: "Female Impersonators in Mirrors, NYC 1958" and the pictures of the "Jewish Giant" Eddie Carmel, 1960 and 1970, including his appearance at Hubert's Museum dressed up as the World's Biggest Cowboy. These images resemble Mirrors with Arbus Memories when read in conjunction with information about her childhood history. Many of these pictures, as was the case with the Backwards Man, do in fact include mirrors. Challenging the border between sitter and photographer, these images mirror Arbus's self back to her, but reveal the self to be illusory, veiled, transformed, or situated in pseudo spaces.

Arbus said:

> One of the things I felt I suffered from as a kid was I never felt adversity. I was confirmed in a sense of unreality which I could only feel as unreality. And the sense of being immune was, ludicrous as it seems, a painful one. It was as if I didn't inherit my own kingdom for a long time. I could learn things but they never seemed to be my own experience.[9]

Arbus's unauthorized biographer Patricia Bosworth's discussion of the photographer's childhood may explain her sense of "unreality," as well as indicate why she represented the world as she did with her camera in the 1960s. Arbus was born into an extraordinarily wealthy family of Manhattan Jews who lived, as mentioned, in a luxurious apartment, complete with servants, on Central Park West called the San Remo. Her father, David Nemerov, whose parents were born in Kiev and who lived during Diane's childhood years in the 1930s an impoverished life in Brooklyn as Orthodox Jews, had married the beautiful daughter of the founders of Russeks, a fashionable furrier. Her mother's parents, the Russeks from Poland, unlike her father's, were relaxed in their Jewish practices. Bosworth reports that Diane's father, who became an owner of Russeks, felt shame over his parents' Orthodoxy, which he viewed as a form of superstition.

> The Russeks would never entertain David Nemerov's parents, who lived in Brooklyn—David Nemerov rarely if ever invited his father and mother to the San Remo. In that mammoth apartment any suggestion of superstition or poverty had been blotted out (her father's parents were Orthodox Jews; her mother's parents were much more relaxed in their Jewish practices).[10]

As was typical of second-generation Jewish Americans who believed that becoming 100 percent American required dissociation from the customs, religious practices, language, food ways, and fashions of their forebears, David Nemerov wished to "blot out" the existence of his unkempt and impoverished Orthodox parents. Through the marriage to Gertrude, David suppressed the distance between his (from a normative American point of view) "strange" origins as the child of impoverished Russian Jews and the nonobservant Upper West Side Jews who wished to "pass" as mainstream whites. By contrast, Diane associated the rare visits to her paternal grandparents' apartment in Brooklyn with uncanny feelings of being at home while away from what she perceived as the "unreal" (rather than normative) world of Manhattan's wealthy Jewish culture. Bosworth writes of this "strange comfort":

> While "Jewishness" was never central to her life or [to her brother] Howard's (they attended Temple Emanu-El only on holy days and they went to Sunday school grudgingly), their "Jewishness" was still a fact. And always dramatized when, every other year, they celebrated Passover at Meyer and Fanny Nemerov's apartment in Brooklyn. It was practically the only time they ever saw their paternal grandparents, and they found the experience strangely consoling. Surrounded by immigrants and the sons of immigrants who all shared a common past, the awareness that they were Jewish had residual significance.[11]

David Nemerov tried to detach his parents' Jewishness (associated with foreignness and poverty) from his identity, but Arbus, belatedly, understands "Jewishness" as a repressed part of her personal history as well as part of what Bosworth describes as a "common past" that she would explore in her portraits from the late 1960s and early 1970s.

Ironically, the assimilated, decidedly non-Jewish or even anti-Jewish aspects of her upbringing, made possible by her parents' wealth and by their conception of what a rich child's life should look like and how a rich Jew should look (not too Jewish!), had the opposite effect on young Diane. A quality of absurdity, falsification, and concealment—through nose jobs, orthodontia, language training—hangs over how Arbus and her childhood friends recall their upbringing:

> Diane and most of her friends were brought up to have all the accomplishments of the well-bred eighteenth-century English lady—painting, piano, languages, manners, a thorough familiarity with art. [A classmate says] "The kind of money our families had magnified their feelings of inadequacy, of personal failure. We grew up in an emotional desert of shame—never affirmation—and those of us who were taught to be assimilated were filled with self-loathing." . . . Another friend remembers that in spite of the Depression she and Diane and Renee and others like them were raised as "Jewish princesses." They had the "kvelling mamas" who almost daily told them they were special—they had the lessons at Viola Wolff's dancing class, the orthodontia, and, for several of them, later the nose job. "We were isolated, we were pampered, we were spoiled, we knew nothing else but that world on Central Park West, and so we took it for granted."[12]

Arbus's feelings of "unreality" in childhood, as well as the arbitrary nature of her situation as a freakish thing—a rich Jew in the Depression era costumed as a well-bred eighteenth-century English lady—reappears as a symptom of her failure to come to terms with her past.

In a perceptive essay, Leslie Brill argues that freakish subjects in Arbus are not necessarily those who are, by normative standards of beauty, the midgets, transvestites, and giants that she famously pictures. Instead, the "freaks" are those who, through costuming, masking, or exaggerating the marks of sexuality, have attempted to "radically alter" their appearance in a way that "diminishes [their] humanity." For Brill, Arbus's pictures are not, contrary to common opinion, all about unhappy misfits. Instead, her work portrays two types of individuals, those who, however strange in appearance, have accepted their difference, and those who wish to "cover-up" their true selves through self-mutilation or through a hyper-conformism to appearance and manner. Brill is thinking of subjects like the "Blond girl with shiny lipstick" who, she writes, have "been taken over by the social idea of what a sexy young woman should look like and be."[13]

Brill does not focus on the point, but the main examples of subjects who fit into the category of "self-acceptance" rather than "cover-up" are Jewish. Her examples suggest that Arbus, consciously or not, treated sympathetically Jews at home, Jews who are portrayed as comfortable with "themselves, unashamed and cohesive to a degree that Arbus's true freaks never attain." There is an "Elderly couple on a park bench," "A Jewish giant at home with his parents in the Bronx, N.Y." and "A Jewish couple dancing." Brill admits these characters seem "tired," "worried," not "happy," aged, not beautiful by typical standards, or even physically freakish, as in the case of the giant, Eddie Carmel, but they are "at home with each other. They are touching each other. They seem comfortable in their surroundings" and "they make no attempts at disguise."[14]

Brill is onto something important about how Arbus photographs relate to mid-century Jewish American identity. Have not American Jews, and especially those who grew up, as did Arbus, as a daughter of second-generation Americans in the post–World War II era, grappled with the issue of assimilation, of becoming "100 percent American" by dissociating themselves from the language, customs, mannerisms, dress, and physical locations associated with first-generation immigrants to America? The rise of suburbia, the movement toward Reform Judaism (where the yarmulke and kippah are not required), the refusal to speak Yiddish or to learn Hebrew, or to observe the Sabbath, intermarriage, all of these decisions signified how American Jews of Arbus's generation wished to "pass" as white, middle-class, Americans. They wished to underplay their difference from mainstream culture through various forms of disguise, cover-up, or performance. The Jews, more than any other minority group, held a particularly ambiguous relationship to mainstream categories such as whiteness, Americanicity, or middle-class values. For Jews, the ability to "pass" as white, American, and middle class was more available than to other ethnic and minority groups. But such "passing," such ease of "assimilation," would not come for free. Jews would enter an uncanny relationship to the self, both at home and homeless, both the same and always just slightly different from the "real" American. As in the movie *Zelig,* the Jew would be perceived as a ventriloquist, a chameleon, always one who was able to "pass" as a version of the "real" American, but who was always also aware (or made aware) that he or she was not the same. There was always the fear that the Jew would be "too Jewish," as a recent book title of representations of Jews put it. In that book, Norman Kleeblatt discusses the cost of "passing":

> Radical assimilation and clear separation of public persona from private self became standard strategy for Jews who sought entry to humanist and commercial professions. A publisher recently reflected that when he began his career in 1958, the industry "still thought of itself as a respectable profession. The business was being run, for the most part, by men in suits or donnish tweeds, with pipes, who were either Ivy League WASPs or Jews whose highest ambition was to be mistaken for WASPs." The Jewish community thus achieved visible success while its individual members were becoming invisible.[15]

Arbus's obsession with issues of sameness and difference, at home and homeless, self-acceptance and cover-up, freakish and normal, inside and outside the mainstream, the "gap," as she wrote, "between intention and effect" in which even the subject who attempts to conceal the "true self" experiences a slippage in which an excess of meaning intrudes upon the disguise so that the pictures expose the disguise and the face underneath it, the "performance and backstage mixed, posture and striving together," portray the quintessentially Jewish dilemma of being Jewish American, as Arbus understood this concern in ways that are at times poignant, disturbing, sympathetic, and other times caustic and condemnatory.[16] She is concerned with the mark of difference in the context of the apparent sameness of twins, for example. One observer reports that "people found her pictures, like the cover of New Documents, Triplets in Their Bedroom, N.J. (1963) distressing because the subjects did not fit into the American dream, even if they were outwardly trying to do so."[17]

No series of images better illustrates Arbus's ambivalent expression of her uncanny version of Jewishness than her portraits (taken in 1960 and then again in 1970) of Eddie Carmel, the Jewish Giant.[18] Arbus represents Carmel and his parents in a way that affirms the dignity and difference of her subjects, as well as confronts the artist's concern with what I'd call the difference in sameness, or the otherness of the self.[19] Arbus's images of Carmel are themselves enigmatic representations and elliptical documents that defy straightforward interpretation. Brill emphasizes the cohesiveness and unashamed display of affection among "freakish" Jews such as Carmel and his "normal"-sized parents. (In the picture, in fact, it could be argued that Carmel is "normal" sized and the parents are dwarfs.) By contrast, Carol Armstrong sees generational conflict and tension between child and parents. Armstrong suggests that the posture of Carmel's father, with hands in pockets, is asking, "What does this have to do with me?" and that the mother is wondering how "this body bore that?" thus denying responsibility for bearing this monstrous offspring.[20]

Brill is correct to note that, unlike many of Arbus's best-known portraits in which the subjects gaze, often in a trancelike manner, at the camera's bright flash, Carmel family members look at each other. Perhaps speaking to each other, they are certainly engaged with each other in a domestic space. However inhibiting this space is for Eddie, who must hunch over so his head will not hit the ceiling, the apartment feels somewhat homey, familial, and strangely normal. Leslie Fiedler notes the ironic reversal of the David and Goliath myth, with the goyish enemy of the Jews now portrayed as himself a freakish Jew, ambiguously posed in a manner implying he could crush his parents or embrace them. Carmel may also be viewed as a grotesque literalization of the second-generation Jewish parental wish for their children to grow to exceed their financial expectations and social horizons. From this point of view, Carmel represents Arbus's parodic critique of the immigrant mythos of upward mobility. Social climbing becomes a form of abnormality, difference, and an expression of the crisis in the relationship between parents and a child who is quite literally unfit to live at home. Do we read Eddie's cane as a pun on the name of the first Jewish murderer? What did Diane say about Carmel?

> I know a Jewish giant who lives in Washington Heights or the Bronx with his little parents. He is tragic with a curious bitter somewhat stupid wit. The parents are orthodox and repressive and classic and disapprove of his carnival career. . . . They are truly a metaphorical family. When he stands with his arms around each he looks like he would gladly crush them. They fight terribly in an utterly typical fashion which seems only exaggerated by their tragedy. . . . Arrogant, anguished, even silly.[21]

One thing is certain: Arbus followed Carmel throughout the period when she produced her most notable work. She photographed him in 1960 in cowboy suit attire that he wore at Hubert's Museum (the carnival career that Arbus mentions that Carmel's parents disapproved of) as well as in the Bronx apartment with his "little parents" that she would return to photograph ten years later for the famous image that appeared in the Aperture monograph.

In between 1960 and 1970, Eddie Carmel's appearance has changed. The glandular disease that caused his miraculous growth spurt in his teenaged years and that propelled him to a bizarre kind of minor celebrity in the 1960s (he appeared in two B-grade films, Barnum and Bailey's Circus in Madison Square Garden, and worked for the New York talk show host Joe Franklin) has begun to hunch his back, disable him from walking without two canes, stress his heart, and bring him closer to the premature death that occurred at age thirty-six in 1974. In the 1960 picture, in spite of his unusual size and willingness to represent himself as that unlikely thing, a Jewish cowboy, much less a giant Jewish cowboy, in a freak show, Eddie at home appears as a rather well-kempt, clean-cut kid, and loving child. His appearance suggests a desire to conform to parental expectations in spite of the strange fate that has befallen him. Appearing to be in good shape, he doesn't need the two canes he will require to stand up in the 1970 pictures. His white shirt is clean and tucked in, his face is cleanly shaved, and his frizzy hair is neatly cut. Ten years later, Carmel's overall appearance is of someone who is disheveled, down on his luck, uninterested or unable to resemble a young professional. "The Sixties" has happened to Eddie Carmel. And yet Eddie seems more at ease in the 1970 picture, more at home in his rumpled attire, than he was in the clean-cut picture from 1960. Now he is busting out of his untucked shirt. His hair is longer, frizzy, and uncombed, and he has unshaved sideburns. His pants are worn, perhaps stained. He is severely hunched. His parents, ironically, have become even more formal in this picture than in the one from 1960. The father is now in a suit and tie with a handkerchief in the pocket—he wore a dress shirt in the 1960 picture.

There is a framed picture of Jerusalem (Eddie was born in Tel Aviv) on the wall and a TV set behind where the parents stand. Two balled-up Kleenex tissues rest on the couch behind Eddie's cane, a rare bit of mess in an otherwise immaculate apartment. Eddie's expression is enigmatic, but it seems warm and inviting, especially in comparison to the affect-less, zombie-like stare that is characteristic of so many of Arbus's other subjects. Eddie's thick lips are open, as if he might be breaking into a smile. Perhaps he is speaking to the mother whom he gazes upon. Her eyes are exaggerated, as if riveted to Eddie's face. The father's expression suggests, if not outright scorn and contempt for Eddie, then a reserved detachment. As with her famous portrait of the twins on the cover of the Aperture monograph, the two curtains behind the parents are similar but tellingly different. The one closest to the father is completely shut, the one in between Eddie and his mother is partially opened, suggesting a degree of openness between mother and son that is unavailable between father and son. Two lamps are covered in a protective plastic cover, but the lightbulb on the wall behind Eddie's back is, surprisingly, exposed, naked, like the lightbulb in the picture of Joe Allen, the Backwards Man. Eddie's fuzzy hair seems to touch the ceiling, which is lined with old, repaired cracks.

Like "The Backwards Man," a displaced self-portrait with implications to Arbus's relationship to her parents, the Carmel parents embody—twin—elements of the Nemerov parents and grandparents. Like Diane's paternal grandparents, they are Orthodox, of modest means, and reside in an unfashionable New York borough. Like her parents, they are protective (the closed curtains and plastic on the sofa chairs and lampshades signify this), interested in "passing" as mainstream Americans (the father's decision to wear a suit), and, most important, they are critical of expressions of difference (the father's posture signifies this). The decade from 1960 to 1970 has taken its toll on the mind and body of the Jewish giant who will not live long. Eddie is at home again, facing his forebears, facing in the direction of Jerusalem. At the same time, the parents do not fully accept him, and he no longer fits into so limiting a domestic space. All of this suggests Arbus is exploring tensions that she views as absurd and yet archetypal among Jewish families.

Carmel is Arbus's deeply ambivalent attempt to represent a personal homecoming, a return to a repressed past through the palimpsistic image of her own parents and grandparents. Arbus famously pictured those with obvious flaws but also those who unsuccessfully masked their flaws with attempts at normality. "The Jewish Giant" suggests that it is very much a matter of family relativity, if you will, as to whether it is Eddie, the shaggy, open-faced, oversized Jewish hippie, who is "mainstream" in a society in which Jimi Hendrix sang about "flying his freak flag high" and Jim Morrison of how "people are strange," or if it is the parents, perhaps represented as dwarfs in this picture, who are the misfits. Eddie, who was in fact a stand-up comedian, quipped that it was just his luck to have midget parents. Arbus's famous picture of him is so compelling because she has captured the arbitrary nature of normality and the competing claims being made on that term in this picture. Like the Jewish beauty with the thick black hair, fur almost, on her arms and the Star of David on her chest to remind the boys that she is Jewish, Eddie is the one whose Jewishness, read as a term of strangeness, is an open secret, something to come out into the open about, something that contains, as Theolonious Monk would say, an ugly beauty.

Arbus brings to post–World War II photography the Jewish ethical concern with documenting the significance of the least among us. Such a thesis would fit nicely into a discussion of her work as in the tradition of Jewish documentary and "street" photography, the tradition of Paul Strand, in his portrait of a blind street beggar, of Arnold Rothstein, in his iconic image of a father and sons struggling to reach a sand-blown shack in the midst of the Oklahoma Dust Bowl, of Ben Shahn's pictures of striking West Virginia coal miners, of the life and death struggles for political freedoms against tyranny in the work of the war photographer Robert Capa and Joe Rosenthal, of the half-Jewish Margaret Bourke-

White's documentation of the lives of black South African miners and of Gandhi at his spinning wheel, of the dignified portrayals of African American cultures in the work of Weegee, Helen Levitt, and Aaron Siskind, and in the poignant testimonies of hardscrabble life in America's cities in the work of Arbus's teacher, Lisette Model, and immediate predecessor, Robert Frank. Like these forerunners, Arbus tended to document, and to identify with, strangers and outcasts in American fringe society in the 1960s and early 1970s. (Her last series of pictures focused on children with Down syndrome.)

Arbus's work fits into the distinguished tradition of Jewish documentary art, but I have interpreted her representations of "freaks" as a self-reflection, one that dovetails with Arbus's conflicted sense of her Jewishness, understood here as a queer situation that exists in between fixed identity formations. Arbus was born into a state of "unreality," and as one who "did not know she was Jewish," or that being "Jewish was a dangerous thing to be." She was a privileged child of rich parents living in the protected environment of what she calls "a Jewish town." Understood as a belated self-portrait, Arbus's "freaks" represent a return to a repressed sense of otherness. Protected from the ravages of history and from a confrontation with the crisis of her Jewish identity in a way that she described as the product of "chance" (why was she born a rich Jewish child in New York and not a similarly situated child in Austria or Germany, for example), Arbus confronts the otherness within the self in her "freak" portraits. She uncovers aspects of identity that could be likened to the repressed Eastern European ethnic Jewish grandparents that, Arbus recalled, she both longed to connect with and yet was shielded from identifying with in her youth.

Notes

1. *Diane Arbus Revelations* (New York: Random House, 2003), 154.
2. Time-Life editors, *Photography Year 1973* (New York: Time-Life Books, 1973), 35.
3. *Diane Arbus Revelations,* 154.
4. Cathy Caruth, *Unclaimed Experience: Trauma, Narrative, and History* (Baltimore: Johns Hopkins University Press, 1996), 187.
5. *Diane Arbus Revelations,* 123.
6. Ibid., 124.
7. Ibid.
8. In 1967, after her first major exhibit at the Museum of Modern Art, Diane commented to *Newsweek:* "It's irrational to be born in a certain place and time and of a certain sex. It's irrational how much you can change circumstances and how much you can't. The whole idea of me being born rich and Jewish is part of that irrationality. But if you're born one thing, you can dare—venture—to be ten thousand other things." Patricia Bosworth, *Diane Arbus: A Biography* (New York: W. W. Norton, 2005), 22–23.
9. C. Zoe Smith, "Audience Reception of Diane Arbus' Photographs: A Q-Study," *Journal of American Culture: Studies of a Civilization* 8, no. 1 (Spring 1985): 13.
10. Bosworth, *Diane Arbus,* 22.
11. Ibid., 23.
12. Ibid., 22–23.
13. Leslie Brill, "The Photography of Diane Arbus," *Journal of American Culture* 5, no. 1 (1982): 70–71. I would question what Brill means to say by claiming that such persons are attempting to "deny, simplify or conceal their true identities" (74). I wonder what a "true" or "essential" identity might be. Isn't all identity, at least to a degree, performative? As the Jewish American photographer Cindy Sherman suggests in her Untitled Film Stills series, and as gender theorist Judith Butler argues, isn't the self to some degree a "construct," something fashioned, not given? As social critic Erving Goffman argued in *The Presentation of Self in Everyday Life* (Garden City, N.Y.: Doubleday, 1959), don't we all consistently make ourselves up, as we, for example, narrate our lives to ourselves and to others and as we act out our subject positions differently in different contexts, say, at work, and at home, and with friends?
14. Brill, "The Photography of Diane Arbus," 74.
15. Norman Kleeblatt, ed., *Too Jewish? Challenging Traditional Identities* (New Brunswick, N.J.: Rutgers University Press, 1996).
16. Arbus, quoted in Bosworth, *Diane Arbus,* 75.
17. Robert Hirsch, *Seizing the Light: A History of Photography* (Boston: McGraw-Hill, 2000), 382.

18. I use the word *uncanny* in the sense that Arbus at once could claim not to know she was Jewish and yet also find her biannual visits to her Orthodox grandparents in the Bronx to be "strangely comforting" and a sign of a common past that at once she desired and that also eluded her except in the company of the "flawed" and "freakish" in the last decade of her life.
19. As Rachel Adams writes in her chapter on "Freak Photography" in *Sideshow USA*: "[The "Freak" subject's] differences cannot be definitely segregated from an otherwise normal world, nor isolated within one part of the body; they are neither sanitized to appear 'just like us' nor cordoned off as unique and irreplaceable anomalies" (126).
20. Brill, "The Photography of Diane Arbus"; Carol Armstrong, "Biology, Destiny, Photography: Difference According to Diane Arbus," *October* 66 (Fall 1993): 29–54.
21. *Revelations* (1968 ed.), 67.

Developments in Catholic-Jewish Relations

1990 and Beyond

John T. Pawlikowski

The last fifteen years or so have witnessed significant new developments but also the emergence of new challenges in the Catholic-Jewish relationship. In this essay, I will highlight some of the main new developments and discuss the emerging challenges, focusing in particular on four areas: (1) the Holocaust, (2) the theology of the Church's relationship with Judaism in the light of new biblical research, (3) Jewish understandings of the land of Israel, and (4) joint social responsibility. In considering all these issues I shall attempt to be as candid as possible about positive developments as well as continuing tensions. An honest dialogue is, in the end, the only truly respectful dialogue. Such honesty has always been an admirable hallmark of Zev Garber's contribution to the Christian-Jewish dialogue.

March 1998 saw the release of the Vatican statement on the Holocaust *We Remember* by the Holy See's Commission for Religious Relations with the Jews, then headed by Cardinal Edward Idris Cassidy. This long-anticipated statement, first promised by Pope John Paul II in an address to the Jewish community in Miami a decade or so earlier, garnered a mixed reaction. On the positive side, it lays to rest any possibility of Holocaust denial within Catholicism and renders it an important subject for further reflection and for education within the Catholic Church on a global basis. It likewise affirms the religious roots of hostile attitudes toward Jews and Judaism in erroneous interpretations of the New Testament that led to discrimination, attempts at forced conversion, and, at certain moments, outright violence and death. Overall, the document lends the Church's moral authority to the need to understand, and, most of all, to *remember* the Shoah. *We Remember*'s use of "Shoah," now the more acceptable term for Jewish extermination under the Nazis, was also seen as a positive move by many within the Jewish community. Veteran dialogue participant Judith Banki summed up the positive reaction to the statement in the following way:

> The Vatican's *We Remember* opens a rich field for further common study, and its expression of human solidarity should guide the footsteps of those who seek to develop its teaching and preaching implications—to end, in the Pope's moving words (in his introductory letter), of "shaping a future in which the unspeakable inquity of the Shoah will never again be possible."[1]

On the negative side, there was some disappointment that the document was not issued as a formal papal encyclical. The introductory letter from Pope John Paul II did, however, serve to moderate some of this disappointment. In terms of issues, a number of Catholic and Jewish scholars, myself included, raised concerns about certain aspects of the document as did an editorial in the leading American Catholic publication *Commonweal*.[2]

From my perspective, there are three major problematical dimensions to *We Remember* despite its very real accomplishments. The first has to do with the distinction between the sinful actions of the "sons and daughters" of the Church and the fundamental holiness of the Church itself. I am aware, as Cardinal Cassidy has stressed, that this distinction is rooted in classical Catholic ecclesiology, which views the Church as a sacramental reality unaffected by the sinful realities of history. But there are also other ecclesiological understandings, including some emerging from Vatican II, that relate the sacramental church more directly to the historical dimensions of the Church as an institution. Surely, Catholics must take this classical outlook seriously, even if one feels that it can lead to major misinterpretations or that it is overly ahistorical. It clearly appears to be the dominant ecclesiology both for John Paul II and Benedict XVI.

If one were to accept the interpretation of the Austrian Catholic philosopher Friedrich Heer, there is a very dangerous "withdrawal from history" in such an ecclesiological understanding which, in his mind, was responsible for a muted response by Catholicism to the Shoah. According to Heer, the disregard on the part of Christians for the well-being of the Jewish people throughout history, especially between 1918 and 1945, can only be understood as part of a general disregard for humanity and the world. He attributes this attitude to the dominance in Christian theological thinking to what he terms the "Augustinian principle." This attitude views the world under the aspect of sin, and, ultimately, leads to a sense of fatalism and despair about the world. Heer remains convinced that this fatalistic tendency not only influenced Catholic behavior during the Nazi era but remains as much a danger today as it did in the period of the incubation of Nazism. Hence, in not confronting such an ecclesiology, *We Remember* was in effect bypassing one of the root causes of Catholic failure during the Shoah.[3]

Surely the authors of *We Remember* were not in a position to resolve ecclesiological tensions within contemporary Catholicism.[4] Nonetheless, the statement could have, and should have, made it clearer that the "sons and daughters" of the Church who fell into the sin of antisemitism did so because of what they had learned from teachers, theologians (including the Church Fathers), and preachers sanctioned by the institutional Church as well as from depictions of Jews and Judaism in Christian art.[5] Reading the document in its present form leaves the impression that the sinful "sons and daughters" of the Church who espoused antisemitism were led to this pernicious outlook by teachings and teachers outside the context of official Catholicism. This was one of the major criticisms of the document in the *Commonweal* editorial, which rightly argued that *We Remember* failed to urge the need for institutional self-examination and not only personal self-examination within Catholicism. The statement of Pope John Paul II on the first Sunday of Lent 2000, as part of the Vatican's observance of the new millennium, which included an apology for the Church's actions against the Jewish people in the course of history, a statement that the Pope eventually placed in the Western Wall during his historic visit to Jerusalem, did serve to rectify—to some extent—the lack of institutional self-examination of *We Remember* itself.

Having moved into a new papal era, we may legitimately ask where Pope Benedict XVI will stand on the question of the Shoah and antisemitism. From all indications, there is little question that he regards the Shoah as one of the most horrible periods in human history and will be quite firm in condemning present-day manifestations of antisemitism. In his remarks at the synagogue in Cologne in August 2006, the pope spoke quite forcefully:

> Today, sadly we are witnessing the rise of new signs of antisemitism and various forms of a general hostility towards foreigners. How can we fail to see in this a reason for concern and vigilance? The Catholic Church is committed—and I reaffirm this again today—to tolerance, respect, friendship and peace between all people, cultures and religion.[6]

And, in a November 30, 2005, general audience, he referred to the Holocaust of the Jews as "an infamous project of death."[7]

It is with regard to the parentage of the Shoah that Pope Benedict's remarks have raised some eyebrows. He appears to regard it primarily, even exclusively, as a neopagan phenomenon that did not have roots in the Christian tradition but instead constituted a fundamental challenge to all religious belief, including Christianity. No reputable scholar on the Holocaust would deny its neopagan roots or its fundamental hostility to any religious perspective. But equally reputable scholars would also insist on surfacing the Holocaust's links with classical antisemitism, especially on the popular level where it provided a seedbed for its growth in European society during the first part of the twentieth century.

The Holocaust succeeded in a culture that supposedly was deeply impacted by Christian values for centuries. Much of the Nazi anti-Jewish legislation replicated laws against the Jews existing in Christian-dominated societies over a long period of time. We cannot obfuscate the fact that traditional Christianity provided an indispensable context for the widespread support, or at least acquiescence, given by many baptized Christians during the time of the Nazi attack on the Jews and other marginalized groups. Pope Benedict seems to be supporting in his Cologne address a fringe interpretation of the Holocaust that presents it solely as an attack on religion in all its forms rather than a phenomenon that drew in large measure on a previous antisemitic base in the heart of Christianity. His remarks can leave the impression, intended or not, that the Holocaust was primarily the result of secularizing forces not dissimilar from the secularizing forces now affecting Europe in particular, and which, both as cardinal and now as pope, he has strongly attacked.

This same strain of thought can be seen in Pope Benedict's speech at Birkenau death camp in May 2006, at which I was present. Once again, he failed to acknowledge any major institutional responsibility on the part of the Catholic Church for what occurred at that site and many others throughout Europe. His speech was critiqued by the editors of *Commonweal* magazine, a critique I subsequently supported in a published letter to the magazine.[8] The controversial address by the pope at the University of Regensburg in October 2006, in which he accused Islam of having a violent dimension to its religious expression while ignoring a similar pattern in Christian history, including violence against Muslims during the Crusades, represents a further continuation of this papal mentality. David Gibson, writing a Commentary/Analysis released by Religious News Service in connection with the Regensburg speech, rightly describes an ongoing tendency in Cardinal Ratzinger/Pope Benedict to regard any criticism of the Church as a potential threat to its ability to speak the truth to contemporary society. That there were some bad apples, as it were, in Catholicism over the centuries, Cardinal Ratzinger/Pope Benedict seems willing to grant. But the Church, as such, has always been, in the words of Gibson, "an immutable exemplar of the religious ideal." Gibson unfavorably contrasts the current papal perspective with that of Benedict's predecessor, John Paul II, who issued more than 100 formal apologies during his tenure. Gibson notes that Cardinal Ratzinger was known as a behind-the-scenes critic of such apologies, and once publicly described such efforts as "masochistic" and "perverse." An argument could be made that behind Pope Benedict's serious inability to critique Catholicism's historic sinfulness lay an Augustinian outlook along the lines outlined above by Friedrich Heer in Christian theology over the years.

Throughout recent years, the issue of the Catholic Church's response to the Holocaust, particularly the actions of Pope Pius XII, has been the subject of considerable scrutiny. A number of works severely indicted Pope Pius XII for his supposed failures to speak out against the extermination of the Jews and the victimization of other groups such as the Poles. Some authors, such as John Cornwell, painted him as an ally of Hitler. In response, there have been strong defenses of Pius XII published by Robert Graham, S.J., the Protestant scholar Ronald Rychlak, the Jewish scholar David Dalin, and Catholic historian Sister Margherita Marchione. More balanced interpretations can be found in the writings of Michael Marrus, Michael Phayer, and John Morley.[9] Regrettably, the Vatican has sometimes promoted the most defensive volumes, which many critics have faulted for inadequate and even downright poor scholarship. This is certainly the case with respect to the writings of Sister Margherita Marchione, whom a very moderate voice on the question of Pius' supposed moral failure during the Shoah has described as adopting "a pietistic tone, exacerbated by a sickly adulation and combined with outrage that their pope should be so attacked."[10] The Vatican discredits itself by promoting only questionable scholarship on this issue. Ultimately, only by supporting a thorough and open scholarly investigation of Pius XII's record, which is far from complete with much archival work remaining, can it achieve any credibility in this controversy.

There was some hope that the Catholic-Jewish historians group created by Cardinal Edward Idris Cassidy in his capacity as head of the Holy See's Commission for Religious Relations with the Jews and the leadership of the World Jewish Congress might find a constructive path through this controversy by a thorough examination of the Vatican archival materials released by Pope Paul VI. This effort collapsed due to a number of factors, including some mistakes by the organizers and participants, coupled with considerable opposition from the defenders of Pius XII within the Vatican. It did, however, produce a report that does serve to highlight the remaining scholarly questions. Cardinal Cassidy attempted to have Cardinal Kasper restart this project but to no avail, perhaps because of continuing internal opposition within certain Vatican circles. In his Cologne synagogue address, Benedict XVI did make mention of the importance of Catholics and Jews examining the historical record together without any specific reference to the prior historians' project. Whether this reference will generate any interest on the part of Catholic and Jewish leadership to try again in this regard remains an open question. It certainly would be a worthwhile endeavor.

While not related to the Holocaust explicitly, the controversy over the film by Mel Gibson, *The Passion of the Christ,* raised some serious concerns about the depth of Catholic commitment to, and understanding of, its relationship with Judaism. Some 150 scholars, many of them leading figures in contemporary biblical research, raised serious objections to Gibson's use of the biblical passion narratives. Many have pointed to Gibson's use of classical antisemitic images of Jews and Judaism such as the supposed Jewish association with the devil. In the end, one has to say that this controversy had as much to do with internal divisions within contemporary Catholicism as it had to do with Catholic-Jewish relations. But Catholic leadership failed to provide any adequate response in terms of confronting the film's obvious antisemitic imagery. The papal response was ambiguous in the end, and hardly did credit to Pope John Paul II's long-demonstrated commitment to positive Catholic-Jewish relations. After considerable struggle, a statement did emerge from the U.S. Bishops' Secretariat on Ecumenical and Interreligious Affairs warning that the Gibson film could not take the place of official Catholic documents in catechesis. And the French Bishops' Conference also raised serious objections to the film. But *The Passion of the Christ* was also aggressively promoted in certain Catholic circles, and the U.S. Bishops' film office failed badly in its analysis of the film.[11] Professor Garber has been rightly concerned about the overall impact of this film, though Gibson's personal problems may serve to mute any continuing impact on Catholic education.

On a more theological front, the last fifteen years have not seen any major new statement on Catholic-Jewish relations. Cardinal Walter Kasper had initially expressed some hope in 2005 as the fortieth-anniversary *Nostra Aetate* approached that a new declaration might be possible. There has not been a statement other than *We Remember* since the *Notes* of 1985. But this hope never became a reality, for whatever reason. Upon assuming the presidency of the Holy See's Commission for Religious Relations with the Jews, Cardinal Kasper himself began to explore the theological dimensions of the Church's relationship with the Jewish people in some exciting ways, even though what he offered in several addresses would be described as new theological kernels rather than a comprehensive exposition of the issues.[12]

In his various addresses and articles, Kasper has underlined the continuing validity of the Jewish path to salvation. He has insisted that the Jewish-Christian relationship is *sui generis* because Jews are alone in having authentic revelation from a Christian theological perspective. As a result, Kasper has also argued that there is no need for Christians to proselytize Jews because they are already in a covenantal relationship with God. He has likewise underlined his continued belief in the universality of Christ and stresses that there are not two totally disconnected paths to salvation for Jews and Christians. He appears to be saying that while the Jewish and Christian paths may be distinctive, they are not distinct but somehow integrated. Kasper's present position leaves aside a discussion of how his affirmation of the continuing validity of the Jewish path to salvation pursued in a distinctive fashion relates to the universal salvific plan found in the Christ Event. Do Jews now, or at least at the end time, have to acknowledge explicitly the universal reign of Christ? This question requires a more comprehensive answer than Kasper has offered thus far. It also has to be said that, recently, he does not seem to be pursuing the issue of the theological relationship between Jews and Christians with quite the same vigor as in the early days of his presidency of the Vatican Commission. Put another way, are the distinctive paths of Jews and Christians toward ultimate salvation on an equal footing or does the Jewish path, while distinctive, ultimately fall under the sway of the Christian path and require an explicit recognition of Christ at some point? Or is there a way of theologically stating the ultimate integration of the distinctive paths without employing expressly Christological language? Does Christ in the end bring about the salvation of all people, including Jews, but it is not necessary for Jews to expressly acknowledge this reality from a Christian perspective?

The same questions might be posed regarding initial theological reflections on the Christian-Jewish relationship by then-Cardinal Joseph Ratzinger as well as the theological implications of the comprehensive statement from the Pontifical Biblical Commission (PBC) on the Jews and their scriptures as seen in the New Testament which Cardinal Ratzinger approved and for which he wrote a positive introduction.[13] When the document *Dominus Iesus* was issued by Cardinal Ratzinger's Congregation for the Doctrine of the Faith, considerable discussion arose as to whether it was meant to apply to Jews. Cardinals Cassidy and Keeler joined forces with others to argue that it did not, although in all candor that could have been made explicit in the document. In the end, this effort appears to have prevailed, and some even see Cardinal Ratzinger's subsequent writings on the Christian-Jewish relationship and his embrace of the PBC's statement as confirmation of its inapplicability.

Building, it would appear, on the PBC's argument that Jewish messianic hopes are not in vain, something that Ratzinger explicitly mentions in his introduction to the PBC document, he argues, in a manner similar to Kasper, that Jews follow their own distinctive path to salvation. But, in the end, he holds out more explicitly than Kasper for Christological confirmation of the Jewish path. What is not fully clear in his writings, which too must be described as the beginnings of a theology of the Christian-Jewish relationship rather than a fully developed treatise, is whether Jews must affirm this Christological confirmation at some point. This same ambiguity also exists in the PBC's document itself, which adds another interesting statement with some potential for the theological understanding of the Christian-Jewish relationship. The PBC document speaks of the eschatological Messiah as the One who is to come. This eschatological Messiah will exhibit the traits Christians have already seen and acknowledged in the Jesus who has already come and remains with the Church. While there is a small window for new thinking here, an opening seems to be provided for acknowledgment of the future "One" by Jews without necessarily speaking of the "One" in specific Christological terms. This may be reading into the text, but I would at least suggest this as a possible interpretation. The PBC had no mandate to pursue the possible theological implications of its assertion but theologians certainly do. Without doubt, this issue of integrated but distinctive paths will stir considerable debate in the coming years.

While Pope Benedict XVI has not yet offered the Church any focused theological reflection on Jewish-Christian relations, there are implications for such a perspective in an address he gave at St. Peter's Square in Rome on March 15, 2006, as part of the Wednesday general audience. This address began a new cycle of catechesis on the theme "the relationship between Christ and the Church." In this address, Pope Benedict presented some views that are problematical from the standpoint of where Christian-Jewish relations have come since *Nostra Aerate,* as well as from current understandings in biblical scholarship. Several conservative Catholic media outlets interpreted the pope's address as explicitly calling for the conversion of Jews, something that appears to go well beyond the actual papal statement.[14]

In the actual address, Pope Benedict speaks of the arrival of the definitive eschatological time in Jesus, "the time for rebuilding God's people, the people of the 12 tribes, which is now converted into a universal people, the Church." The twelve tribes, the pope adds, are "reunited in a new covenant, the full and perfect accomplishment of the old." In all candor, I have to say that this sounds very close to a classical replacement theology of Judaism, in no way reflecting the theological rethinking that has begun in theologians such as Franz Mussner and Gregory Baum who termed chapter 4 of *Nostra Aetate* the most radical reformulation of the Church's ordinary magisterium to emerge from Vatican II. Nor does it connect in any way to the inchoate, but important, reflections that Cardinal Ratzinger offered for several years, discussed above.

What we seem to have here is another example of a disconnect between theological reflection within the context of the Christian-Jewish dialogue and internal Church theological reflection. But such a disconnect cannot continue if Catholic-Jewish relations are truly to take root in Catholicism. We cannot continue to say one thing when Jews are present in our midst and another when we are doing internal theological reflections. The theological reflections that are emerging from the dialogue must begin to be incorporated into the heart of Christian reflection on the Church's basic identity. We need to mainstream the theological developments that have emerged from the dialogue with Jews and Judaism for the past forty years. As Johannes Baptist Metz, another important theological voice in terms of the Christian-Jewish relationship, has reminded us: the new understanding of the Christian-Jewish relationship has central relevance for all of Christian theology and not merely for the dialogue with Jews and Judaism.

Another questionable assertion by Pope Benedict in this same March 2006 address is his claim that at the Last Supper Christ founded a new community, the Church. This definitive statement appears to go against a growing consensus among biblical scholars that there is little evidence of a distinctive Christian identity prior to the end of the Jewish war with Rome in 70 CE. And, even after that, it took considerable time, in some places several centuries, for the separation between Christians and Jews to be finalized. This is an area where new understandings emerging from biblical scholarship connected with the dialogue are significantly challenging classical ecclesiology. This papal address in no ways reflects this new awareness, an awareness, I might add, that was present in some of the important writings of the late Cardinal Joseph Bernardin of Chicago, an important pioneer in rethinking the Christian-Jewish relations, as well as in the writings of Cardinal Carlo Martini, S.J.[15]

An important theological statement that came from the Catholic-Jewish dialogue in the United States is the document *Reflections on Covenant and Mission,* along with a parallel statement from the ecumenical Christian Scholars Group on Christian-Jewish Relations titled *A Sacred Obligation.*[16] The first document emerged from an ongoing dialogue between the U.S. Bishops' Secretariat for Ecumenical and Interreligious Affairs and the National Council of Synagogues. (It had a companion statement from the Jewish perspective, which generally has been put aside as of inferior quality.) While only a study document (it was misrepresented in the official press release from the U.S. Catholic Bishops' Conference as a more authoritative piece), it was intended in part as a response to Cardinal Walter Kasper's call for national episcopal conferences to pursue the issue of the Christian-Jewish theological relationship in lieu of any imminent statement from Rome on the matter.

Both *Reflections on Covenant and Mission* and *A Sacred Obligation* (which was intended, in part, as a response to the groundbreaking Jewish document on Christianity, *Dabru Emet)* affirm the continuing validity of the Jewish covenant and argue that issues related to Christology and to the evangelization of Jews need considerable rethinking in light of the scholarship that has come forth as a result of the forty years of dialogue. Some very negative reactions ensued to *Reflections on Covenant and Mission,* in particular from the likes of Cardinal Avery Dulles and the Congregation for the Doctrine of the Faith.[17] But the document has also received considerable praise from Cardinal Edward Idris Cassidy in his recent volume reflecting on his work as president of the Pontifical Council on Christian Unity and its subcommission on Catholic-Jewish Relations. While not embracing *Reflections on Covenant and Mission* in every aspect, Cardinal Cassidy terms the statement "an encouraging response that marks a significant step forward in the dialogue, especially in the United States."[18]

Overall, the last decade in Catholic-Jewish dialogue has seen only a modest effort to take up central theological issues from the Catholic side, though there have been some promising developments from the Jewish side. Some of the promising efforts begun in the seventies and eighties by such pioneers as Franz Mussner, Johannes Metz, Clemens Thoma, and others have receded somewhat. The strong attack on *Reflections on Covenant and Mission* no doubt contributed to this. And a more recent article by Cardinal Avery Dulles, in which he questions whether Vatican II really affirmed the continuity of the Jewish covenant and raises anew the texts in the Letter to the Hebrews which appear to abrogate the original covenant, has caused some consternation among both Catholic and Jewish scholars.[19] While both Cardinal Keeler of Baltimore, who heads the U.S. Bishops' Commission on Catholic-Jewish Relations, and Cardinal Kasper have reassured participants in the dialogue that Cardinal Dulles' views do not represent the *official* teaching of the Church but only his personal perspective, there remains some uncertainty within the dialogue how far the Church is willing to go in addressing central theological issues raised by *Nostra Aetate* and the scholarship it has engendered.

On the Jewish side, we have seen some new encouraging beginnings in terms of a Jewish theology of Christianity. *Dabru Emet,* which garnered the support of well over one hundred Jewish scholars and rabbis, and the work by individual Jewish scholars such as Irving Greenberg, who has been working on a theory of seeing Jesus as a "failed" but not a "false" Messiah from the Jewish perspective, certainly have laid the groundwork for further developments.[20]

Moving on briefly to the two other issues raised at the outset of this essay, I turn to the land question. Increasingly, Jewish scholars such as Ruth Langer, Eugene Korn, Edward Kessler, and Michael Kotzin have argued that this is a missing piece in the Catholic-Jewish dialogue that must be put on the table. Langer and Kotzin were especially strong in arguing this position at the September 2005 commemoration of *Nostra Aetate* at the Pontifical Gregorian University in Rome cosponsored by the Gregorian, Boston College, Catholic Theological Union, Georgetown University, and Sacred Heart University in Connecticut. None of the Jewish scholars are calling for a simplistic endorsement of Israeli political policies. But they are insisting, in part based on the well-known assertion in the 1974 *Vatican Guidelines for Catholic-Jewish Relations,* which underlined the importance of Catholics coming to understand Jews as they define themselves, that there needs to be a far better appreciation of how the land of Israel figures in contemporary Jewish identity.

This increasingly vocal assertion from the Jewish side will likely cause some tensions in the dialogue. In some Catholic circles, it will be understood as a call for the Catholic Church to lean toward the Israeli side in the current Palestinian-Israeli controversy. But Catholics need to respond to this new challenge from the Jewish side in some manner while maintaining a necessary commitment to justice for Palestinians and to the survival of a living Christianity in the Holy Land. Partly this issue will involve recognition among Catholics that there are certain forms of anti-Zionist rhetoric, including some that have a classical religious aspect grounded in the discredited claim that Jews killed Jesus, which constitute antisemitism. It will not prove easy to separate legitimate criticisms of Israeli policies from those that verge on an anti-Zionist form of antisemitism. This question emerged in discussions on the final communiqué from the 2004 Vatican-Jewish international dialogue in Buenos Aires, Argentina. While the final communiqué approved by both delegations to the Buenos Aires meeting did include a reference to anti-Zionist forms of antisemitism (perhaps insufficiently clarified), the negative reaction to this part of the communiqué in some circles in Rome serves as an indication of the difficulty it will be for Catholics to respond to the challenge put forward by Ruth Langer, Michael Kotzin, and other Jewish scholars and communal leaders.[21]

The late summer 2006 Israeli-Lebanon war has given new urgency to a discussion of the land question. It has brought to the fore somewhat differing perspectives on ethical dimensions of war/peace. In future Catholic-Jewish discussions, the growth of an antiwar perspective within Catholicism, which emerged initially in discussions at the Second Vatican Council regarding the text of the conciliar statement on "The Church in the Modern World," and was given further impetus by John Paul II, particularly during the 1991 Gulf War and then in the days prior to the outbreak of war in Iraq, will have to receive some serious consideration. In part, the Catholic dimension of the 1974 Vatican Guidelines on Catholic-Jewish Relations will be that in the dialogue Catholics must come to understand Jews as they define themselves. Applying this same central principle, Jews will come to appreciate better the significant transformation of Catholic identity on issues of military conflict. But at the same time Catholics will need to understand that Jews increasingly approach issues of peace and war within the context of the basic survival of Israel as a secure haven for the Jewish people. The dialogue on war/peace issues will not be easy, but it cannot be avoided.

The final issue that I would raise is that of Catholic-Jewish collaboration in the social arena. As I stressed in a major presentation on "Justice and Charity in a Globalized World" in July 2004 to the eighteenth meeting of the International Catholic-Jewish Liaison Committee in Buenos Aires, Catholic-Jewish efforts at improving the condition of workers in the United States during the 1930s and 1940s developed by Msgr. John A. Ryan of the then–National Catholic Welfare Conference (the predecessor to the current U.S. Conference of Catholic Bishops) were instrumental in creating a positive rapprochement between Catholics and Jews that carried over into Vatican II. When we ask why the American bishops so strongly supported chapter 4 of *Nostra Aetate* at key moments when the document was in serious trouble, part of the answer is to be found, in my judgment, in the continuing memory of this constructive cooperation. The question before us at the moment is whether such collaboration can be maintained and even enhanced as the Catholic-Jewish dialogue grows more complicated. The fact that social justice issues were prominent in the 2001 meeting of the ILC and were made the focus of the 2004 meeting provide grounds for some encouragement in this regard.

Clearly, then, we see some changes occurring in the composition of the dialogue in recent years. In its beginning years, the dialogue was largely shaped by Catholics who supported the broad social vision of Vatican II's statement on "The Church and the Modern World" and related documents. On the Jewish side, the major partners tended to come predominantly from the liberal side of the community where a central emphasis on social justice issues prevailed. In the last decade or so, we have seen more conservative parts of both communities enter the framework of the dialogue. This has produced some growing tensions on social issues between the two sectors of the dialogue. How these will play out over the next years will certainly determine the future contours of the dialogue.

One area that will likely continue to produce some intense interaction is the question of justice in the Israeli-Palestinian conflict. This, in turn, may well result in some growing differences on fundamental issues of war and peace as noted above. In terms of Israeli/Palestine, while Pope Benedict XVI seems bent on confronting terrorism in a decisive way, the Catholic Church is obviously very concerned about maintaining a living community in that region and not just a presence rooted in monuments. The impact of the occupation will inevitably be a part of this concern. Jews, understandably, made the issues of safety and security a primary concern. These respective concerns, while not irreconcilable, can and have generated tensions. On the more general level of theory regarding war/peace issues, we may find some fruitful grounds for discussion. A noted Jewish scholar dealing with war/peace issues, Michael Walzer, has made this point relative to the U.S. Bishops Pastoral Letter on War and Peace.[22]

In closing, let me mention two other areas that increasingly will confront the Jewish-Catholic dialogue. The first is the expansion of the dialogue beyond the parameters of Europe and the Americas to the African and Asian contexts. This represents a formidable challenge, given the very tiny presence of Jews in these parts of the world. Some initial efforts have been made and need to continue. As Peter Phan has shown, some of the classical negative images of Judaism have reappeared in sectors of Asian theology.[23] A central issue here will be how theologies in Asia and Africa can legitimately present Jesus and Christianity in a truly inculturated way that at the same time respects the growing scholarly emphasis on the Jewish context of Jesus' message, which has emerged within post–Vatican II biblical scholarship. This issue will require concerted effort in the coming years. On the Jewish side, while the issue is not as pronounced, there is also need to draw into the dialogue representatives of the Jewish tradition with roots in Asia and Africa. The 2004 Parliament of the World's Religions in Barcelona, Spain, made an effort to bring forth the multicultural face of the international Jewish community that must be enhanced within the Catholic-Jewish dialogue itself.

The second question that will increasingly challenge the Catholic-Jewish dialogue is the extent to which it should move to the inclusion of Islam. There has been an increasing pressure in many circles to expand the dialogue into a trilateral reality. Pope Benedict XVI, in a recent address to the leadership of the American Jewish Committee, repeated remarks along this line which he had articulated in a meeting convened in association with the World Jewish Congress. As president of the International Council of Christians and Jews (ICCJ), I have experienced such pressure on a regular basis. There is no question in my mind that there is an urgent need for trilateral discussions. Within ICCJ, we created an Abrahamic Forum some years ago. But I do not believe that moving exclusively to a trilateral model will serve us well. There are differences in the Catholic-Jewish relationship and in the Catholic-Muslim relationship theologically and historically which must be honored. Cardinal Walter Kasper and Archbishop Michael Fitzgerald have both underscored these differences over the years. But, on the other hand, the time has also come for the development of the trilateral dimension, including the theological aspects, while not sacrificing the specific continuing questions in the Catholic-Jewish discussion.[24] There is also a need for a Jewish-Muslim discussion, which Catholics can encourage but not shape. The recent international meetings of rabbis and imans, while not entirely harmonious, do represent a step in the right direction and should be encouraged.

All in all, we can say that the Catholic-Jewish dialogue has matured and developed since 1990 in very important ways. That not all problems have been resolved, and that new ones have emerged, should not surprise us, given the history of the relationship. The large number of conferences throughout the world celebrating the fortieth anniversary of *Nostra Aetate* certainly provides a basis for future hope.

Notes

1. Judith Banki, "Vatican II Revisited," in *Ethics in the Shadow of the Holocaust: Christian and Jewish Perspectives,* ed. Judith H. Banki and John T. Pawlikowski, OSM (Chicago: Sheed and Ward, 2001), 213.
2. Various Jewish and Catholic critiques can be found in *Ethics in the Shadow of the Holocaust.* The editorial titled "Misremembered" appeared in *Commonweal* 125 (April 10, 1998): 7.
3. Freidrich Heer, *God's First Love* (New York: Weybright and Talley, 1970), 406.
4. For a discussion of various ecclesiological options in contemporary Catholicism and their relevance for discussions of the Shoah, cf. Robert J. Schreiter, "The Church as Sacrament and as Institution: Responsibility and Apology in Ecclesial Documents," in *Ethics in the Shadow of the Holocaust,* ed. Banki and Pawlikowski, 51–60.
5. For a comprehensive overview of such depictions, including many pictorial examples, cf. Heinz Schreckenberg, *The Jews of Christian Art: An Illustrated History* (New York: Continuum, 1996).
6. Pope Benedict XVI, "Visit to Cologne Synagogue," *Origins* 35, no. 12 (Sept. 1, 2005): 205–7.
7. This text can be found on the Web site of the Center for Christian-Jewish Learning at Boston College: www.cjlrning@bc.edu.
8. Cf. *Commonweal* 133, no. 12 (June 16, 2006): 5, and 133, no. 13 (July 16, 2006): 2.
9. The best overall discussion of the controversy regarding Pius XII can be found in Jose M. Sanchez, *Pius XII and the Holocaust: Understanding the Controversy* (Washington, D.C.: Catholic University of America Press, 2002).
10. Ibid., 178.
11. For a discussion of the Gibson film controversy, cf. Philip A. Cunningham, ed., *Pondering the Passion: What's at Stake for Christians and Jews* (Lanham, Md.: Rowman and Littlefield, 2004); Zev Garber, ed., *Mel Gibson's Passion: The Film, the Controversy, and Its Implications* (West Lafayette, Ind.: Purdue University Press, 2006); and J. Shawn Landres and Michael Berenbaum, eds., *After the Passion Is Gone: American Religious Consequences* (Walnut Creek, Calif.: Altamira Press, 2004).
12. Cf. Cardinal Walter Kasper, "The Good Olive Tree: The Church and the Jews," *America* 185, no. 7 (Sept. 17, 2001): 12–14; "Spiritual and Ethical Commitment in Jewish-Christian Dialogue," in Ruth Weyl, ed., *From the Martin Buber House* 30 (Summer 2002): 12–20; "Christian, Jews and the Thorny Question of Mission," *Origins* 32, no. 28 (Dec. 19, 2002): 457; and "Issues Concerning Future Dialogue Between Jews and Christians," unpublished paper delivered at the Catholic Theological Union, Chicago, April 17, 2002.
13. Cf. Cardinal Joseph Ratzinger, "The Heritage of Abraham, the Gift of Christmas," *L'Osservatore Romano,* Dec. 29, 2000; *Many Religions—One Covenant* (San Francisco: Ignatius Press, 2000); and *God and the World: Believing and Living in Our Time* (San Francisco: Ignatius Press, 2002). For a Jewish response, cf. David Berger, *"Dominus Jesus* and the Jews," *America* 185, no. 7 (Sept. 17, 2001): 7–12. Cf. the Pontifical Biblical Commission, *The Jewish People and Their Sacred Scripture in the Christian Bible* (Vatican City: Libreria Editrice Vaticana, 2002). Also cf. Donald Senior, "Rome Has Spoken: A New Catholic Approach to Judaism," *Commonweal* 130 (Jan. 31, 2003): 20–23; and the articles by Mary Boys, Leslie Hoppe, Michael O'Connor, John T. Pawlikowski, and Amy Jill-Levine in *The Bible Today* 41, no. 3 (May 2003): 141–72.
14. The text of the papal address with commentary can be found on the www.chiesa.com Web site. Two new theological consultations are in the developmental stage. The first, cosponsored by the Pontifical Gregorian University, Catholic Theological Union, Boston College, and the Catholic University of Leuven, met for the first time in October 2006 with the participation of Cardinal Walter Kasper in a personal capacity. This consultation will involve select Catholic scholars and several Jewish consultants. The second, which had an initial session in December 2004 in London, is more ecumenical on the Christian side and also involves Jewish consultants. It is cosponsored by the International Council of Christians and Jews and the World Council

of Churches. It took place near Zurich in December 2006. Both consultations aim at mainstreaming the new emerging theology of the Jewish-Christian relationship within the Christian churches.

15. For recent developments in rethinking the separation of Christianity and Judaism, cf. Wayne A. Meeks and Robert Wilken, *Jews and Christians in Antioch in the First Four Centuries* (Missoula, Mont.: Scholars Press, 1978); Robert Wilken, *John Chrysostom and the Jews: Rhetoric and Reality in the Late Fourth Century* (Berkeley: University of California Press, 1983); Anthony Saldarini, "Jews and Christians in the First Two Centuries: The Changing Paradigm," *Shofar* 10 (1992): 32–43; Anthony J. Saldarini, "Christian Anti-Judaism: The First Century Speaks to the Twenty-First Century," *The Joseph Cardinal Bernardin Jerusalem Lecture,* April 14, 1999 (Chicago: American Jewish Committee, Archdiocese of Chicago and the Jewish United Fund of Metropolitan Chicago, 1999); Robin Scroggs, "The Judaizing of the New Testament," *Chicago Theological Seminary Register* 75 (Winter 1986); Carlo Maria Martini, S.J., "Christianity and Judaism: A Historical and Theological Overview," in *Jews and Christians: Exploring the Past, Present and Future,* ed. James H. Charlesworth (New York: Crossroad, 1990); Daniel Boyarin, *Dying for God: Martyrdom and the Making of Christianity and Judaism* (Palo Alto, Calif.: Stanford University Press, 1999); and Daniel Boyarin, *Border Line: The Partition of Judaeo-Christianity* (Philadelphia: University of Pennsylvania Press, 2005). Most of these newer views posit a more parallel development of Judaism and Christianity rather than the more classical linear relationship. This has significant implications for both Christology and Ecclesiology.
16. "Reflections on Covenant and Mission, by participants in a dialogue between the United States Conference of Catholic Bishops' Committee on Ecumenical and Interreligious Affairs and the National Council of Synagogues," *Origins* 32, no. 13 (Sept. 5, 2002): 218–24. The text of *A Sacred Obligation* with commentary can be found in Mary C. Boys, ed., *Seeing Judaism Anew: Christianity's Sacred Obligation* (Lanham, Md.: Rowman and Littlefield, 2005).
17. Cf. Avery Dulles, "Evangelization and the Jews," with a response by Mary C. Boys, Philip A. Cunningham, and John T. Pawlikowski, *America* 187, no. 12 (Oct. 21, 2002): 8–16.
18. Cf. Edward Idris Cardinal Cassidy, *Ecumenism and Interreligious Dialogue: Unitais Redintegratio, Nostra Aetate* (Mahweh, N.J.: Paulist, 2005), 252.
19. Cardinal Avery Dulles, "The Covenant with Israel," *First Things* (Nov. 2005): 16–21.
20. Irving Greenberg, Michael Signer, Leon Klenicki, Byron Sherwin, and David Berger have all made important contributions in this regard. Greenberg's is among the most thorough and challenging perspectives. He also regards Moses as a "failed" Messiah. Cf. Irving Greenberg, *For the Sake of Heaven and Earth: The New Encounter between Judaism and Christianity* (Philadelphia: Jewish Publication Society, 2004).
21. International Catholic-Jewish Liaison Committee, "Joint Commitment by Catholics and Jews to Justice," *Origins* 34, no. 13 (Sept. 9, 2004): 208. A recently published volume by Uri Bialer, *Cross on the Star of David: The Christian World in Israel's Foreign Policy, 1948–1967* (Bloomington, Ind.: Indiana University Press, 2005), based on recently released documentation from the Israeli state archives raises some challenging questions regarding the relationship between the Vatican and Israel during and immediately after its establishment. For the text of the Fundamental Agreement between the Holy See and Israel with reflections by John Cardinal O'Connor, Rabbi David Rosen, John T. Pawlikowski, Eugene J. Fisher, and others, cf. Eugene J. Fisher and Leon Klenicki, eds., *A Challenge Long Delayed: The Diplomatic Exchange Between the Holy See and the State of Israel* (New York: Anti-Defamation League, 1996).
22. Michael Walzer, "Reflections on a Man and His Dialogue," in *Harvest of a Dialogue: Hayim Goren Perelmuter,* ed. John Pawlikowski and Dianne Bergant (Hoboken, N.J.: KTAV, 1997), 234–35.
23. One such effort is the essay by Peter Phan, "Jews and Judaism in Asian Theology: Historical and Theological Perspectives," *Gregorianum* 86, no. 4 (2005): 806–36. An essay by Christian M. Rutishauser, S.J., originally given at a conference in Rome in September 2005 celebrating the fortieth anniversary of *Nostra Aetate,* tries to set Christian-Jewish relations in the wider interreligious dialogue: "Jewish-Christian Dialogue and the Theology of Religions," *Studies in Christian-Jewish Relations: An Online Journal* 1 (2005–6): 53–66. On the protestant side Dr. Hans Voko of the World Council of Churches has taken a lead in promoting such dialogue. Cf. Jean Halpern and Hans Voko, eds., *Worlds of Memory and Wisdom: Encounters of Jews and African Christians* (Geneva: World Council of Churches, 2005).
24. For an interesting discussion of the trilateral relationship cf. the dialogue among Reuven Firestone, Mahmoud M. Ayoub, and Archbishop Michael Fitzgerald in *Heirs of Abraham: The Future of Muslim, Jewish, and Christian Relations,* ed. Bradford E. Hinze and Irfan A. Omar (Maryknoll, N.Y.: Orbis, 2005).

Part 3

Judaism as Historiosophy and Thought

Philo and the Dangers of Philosophizing

Louis H. Feldman

Sometimes there is insight to be found in a joke. *In ioco veritas*. There is a story of a yeshiva *bochur*, a student in a yeshiva, who has reached that age when he should be thinking of getting married. And so arrangements are made for him to go out with a young lady. Since he knows nothing about such matters, he inquires as to what he is to talk about with her. Well, he is told, there are three topics—family, food, and philosophy. He meets the young lady and he is tongue-tied. But then he remembers: family. "Do you have a brother?" "No" is the answer. Well, that takes care of family. Then he remembers: food. "Do you like *lokshen* [noodles]?" "No" is the answer. Well, that takes care of food. But philosophy—what does he know about philosophy? Finally, he asks: "Tell me, if you did have a brother, would he like *lokshen*?" I remember that when I received the degree of Doctor of Philosophy, my mother, of blessed memory, who had always wanted me to become a doctor, but a real doctor, not a fake, exclaimed in Yiddish, "Doctor fun Philosophy: *vos far a krankeit iz philosophy*" (What sort of sickness is philosophy?). Somehow, philosophy seems, at least for the most part, to be foreign to the classical sources of Judaism, the Bible, and the rabbinic literature. One thinks of the definition of philosophy ascribed to Mordecai Kaplan: philosophy is the immaculate conception of thought not sired by experience. Judaism seems to be centered on experience: how do you do it? *Halakhah lemaaseh* (the law in practice). And you know the definition of a philosopher: a person who uses many words to describe something that he or she does not quite understand. No wonder there is no treatise on philosophy in the vast Talmudic corpus. Isaac Husik, the historian of medieval Jewish philosophy, is once said to have remarked, "There are Jews, and there are philosophers, but there are no Jewish philosophers." If there had been a Nobel Prize for excellence in philosophy 2,500 years ago, no Jew would have won it.

* * *

To appreciate the uniqueness of Philo as a Jewish philosopher, one should examine how the rabbis of that and succeeding eras viewed philosophers. There are a number of passages in rabbinic literature referring to philosophers, and the rabbis clearly ascribe to them learning and cleverness, particularly in the questions that they ask.[1] Thus they are quoted as asking the elders of Rome, "If your G-d has no desire for idolatry, why does He not abolish it?" (*'Avodah Zarah* 54b). A good question, by the way. But the answer reduces it to absurdity: "If it was something of which the world has no need that was worshipped, He would abolish it; but people worship the sun, moon, stars, and planets; should He destroy the universe on account of fools?" Sometimes (e.g., *Shabbat* 116a) a philosopher is depicted as a heretic, perhaps a Christian. When the Talmud (*Baba Qamma* 82b, *Soṭah* 49b, and *Menaḥot* 64b) imposes a curse on those who instruct their sons in Greek wisdom (*ḥokmah yevanit*), a good guess is that this wisdom is philosophy, *ḥokmah* being a translation of σοφία.

Some light may be shed on this question by an intriguing passage in the Talmud (*Ḥagigah* 14b):

> Four men entered *Pardes* (Paradise, the Garden), namely Ben Azzai and Ben Zoma, Aḥer (Elisha ben Abuya), and Rabbi Akiva. Rabbi Akiva said to them: "When you arrive at the stones of pure marble [i.e., giving the illusion of water], say not 'Water, water!' [i.e., how can we proceed]. For it is said: 'He that speaks falsehood shall not be established before my eyes' (Ps. 101:7). Ben Azzai cast a look and died. Of him Scripture says: 'Precious in the sight of the L-rd is the death of His saints' (Ps. 116:15: that is, a mere glance at the subject is deadly). Ben Zoma looked and became stricken (i.e., afflicted with insanity). Of him Scripture says: 'Have you found honey? Eat so much as is sufficient for you, lest you be filled therewith, and vomit it' (Prov. 25:16, the implication being that one should not attempt to look too deeply into such matters unless one is particularly well qualified). Aḥer (Elisha ben Abuya)[2] mutilated the shoots (the implication being that he entered into a fundamental investigation of the topic and apostasized). Rabbi Akiva departed unhurt" (the implication being that he was so strong in his faith that an investigation of the topic did not weaken his faith).

One is tempted to think that the Pardes that the four entered is the mystical realm of theosophy, that is, religious philosophy or speculation based on mystical insight into the nature of G-d and divine teachings. This would seem to be confirmed by another passage (*Ḥagigah* 15a, Tosefta *Ḥagigah* 2.5) in which we read that the same Ben Zoma, who is here said to have been stricken when he entered into Pardes, told Rabbi Joshua ben Hananiah what he had seen in the *ma'aseh bereshit*, that is, the mysteries of creation, namely that there is only a short distance of two or three fingers between the upper waters (i.e., heaven) and the lower waters (i.e., earth) (Gen. 1:6–7), in other words, that the universe is one; whereupon Rabbi Joshua proclaimed to his students, "Ben Zoma is already without" (presumably out of his mind or a heretic), and a few days later Ben Zoma died.

What does Rabbi Akiva mean when he proclaims, "Say not, 'water, water!'"? One is tempted to guess—admittedly a very wild guess—that he is thinking of how philosophy began, with the question "What is the ἀρχή," "the beginning," the fundamental substance, the single cosmic matter or world-stuff, which lies at the basis of the entire process of nature? Rather strikingly, the earliest of the pre-Socratic philosophers, Thales of Miletus, answered that it was water that is the ultimate substance of which everything is made.[3] Significantly, in the passage quoted above, water is regarded, as we see from the passage in Psalms which is quoted in connection with it, as falsehood, whereas usually (e.g., *Sanh.* 7a; Midrash *Gen. Rab.* 66.1, 69.5, 84.16, 97.3; *Exod. Rab.* 2.5) the Torah is likened to water. It would seem that this kind of water, this kind of theosophical inquiry, is clearly frowned upon. Moreover, Rabbi Akiva is perhaps saying, "Do not seek a simple solution in philosophy to complex phenomena." Or, to paraphrase what H. L. Mencken once said, "There *is* a simple solution to all complex phenomena, and it is always wrong."

The most notorious of the four is, of course, Aḥer, that is, Elisha ben Abuyah. The Talmudic passage (*Ḥagigah* 15a) goes on to explain that the mutilation of the shoots that is ascribed to Aḥer refers to the fact that he saw that permission was granted to the angel Metatron to sit and write down the merits of Israel, whereupon Aḥer expressed wonderment that an angel could be sitting, inasmuch as there is a tradition that in heaven there is no sitting, and he speculated that perhaps there are two divinities. The Talmud then goes to the trouble of proving, in effect, that Metatron is not a divinity by noting that he was punished with sixty fiery lashes. "Permission," the passage continues, "was then given to strike out the merits of Aḥer." Apparently, the mere speculation that there might be two divinities was enough to declare Aḥer a heretic. That Aḥer was obsessed with the question of how a good G-d could have created evil is to be seen in the question which he is said, in the same passage (*Ḥagigah* 15a), to have put to his most famous pupil, Rabbi Meir: "What is the meaning of the verse: 'G-d has made the one as well as the other' (Eccles. 7:14)." Rabbi Meir then explains the passage as follows: "It means that for everything that G-d created He created also its counterpart. He created mountains and he created hills; He created seas and he created rivers." Aḥer is clearly dissatisfied with this answer, whereupon he explains it as follows: "He created righteous and created wicked [i.e., G-d is responsible for both good and evil]. He created the Garden of Eden and created Gehinnom."

Most interestingly, the angel Metatron, who is mentioned in connection with Aḥer in the above passage in the Talmud, is referred to in the following dialogue (*Sanh.* 38b):

> Once a Min [i.e., a heretic] said to Rabbi Idi [a third-century Babylonian rabbi]: "It is written 'And He [i.e., G-d] said to Moses, 'Come up to the L-rd.' But surely it should have stated, 'Come up to me!' "

Whereupon Rabbi Idi explained that it was Metatron, whose name is similar to that of his Master, who spoke those words, for it is written, "For My name is in him [i.e., the angel whom G-d will send before the Israelites]" (Exod. 23:21). Indeed, the great commentator Rashi on this passage remarks that the name Metatron has the numerical value (314) of Shaddai (the Almighty). If so, retorted the Min, we should worship him. Whereupon Rabbi Idi cited the passage that immediately precedes: "Do not rebel (*tamer*) against Him" (Exod. 23:21), that is, playing on the word *tamer,* do not exchange (*tamireni*) Me for him. Indeed, the Karaite Qirqisani claims to have a text of the Talmud that read, "This is Metatron, who is the lesser G-d."[4]

Another indication that Metatron was regarded, in effect, as a second deity may be seen in another passage in the Talmud (*'Avodah Zarah* 3b), where we read that since the destruction of the Temple in the year 70, G-d has been instructing children who died in their infancy, whereupon the Talmud asks who instructed them before the destruction of the Temple. The answer equivocates: "If you like," says the Talmud, "you may say Metatron, or it may be said that G-d did this as well as other things." Clearly, Metatron is viewed, at least by some, as a kind of second G-d.

How did Aḥer—Elisha ben Avuyah—come to such heretical ideas? We may find a clue in the same Talmudic passage (*Ḥagigah* 15b), which speaks of the four who entered Pardes. "Greek song," we are told, "did not cease from his mouth." To the classical Greeks, music was "a second language," of divine origin (Pseudo-Plutarch, *De Musica* 3.1131F–1132A).[5] Indeed, it was a god, Hermes, who was said to have invented the lyre, and a goddess, Athena, who was said to have invented the αὐλός (flute or, rather, oboe). Furthermore, we are told, Heracles, the greatest hero of the Greeks, was instructed by his tutor Chiron in music no less than in the other arts. Even in Sparta, military state that it was, both boys and girls were instructed in music.[6] On the last day of his life Socrates tells of having been urged in a dream to compose music (Plato, *Phaed.* 61A–B). He says that he had imagined that this dream was intended only to encourage him in the study of philosophy, which he claims had been the pursuit of his life, and which is the noblest and best of music. Since, however, he thought that the dream might have meant music in the popular sense of the word, he composed a hymn to Apollo, the god of music par excellence, and versified some fables of Aesop. Indeed, music was an integral part of education, as we learn from Plato's *Republic* (3.398C–402D).

So far as Philo is concerned, music appears at the very beginning of creation (*Plant.* 127–29), for he says that, after all creation had been completed, G-d inquired of one of his subordinates as to whether He had failed to create anything, and He was told that everything was perfect but that He still needed to be praised, whereupon G-d commended this subordinate. It was not long before there appeared a new birth, the family of the Muses; hymnody, in particular, "sprung from the womb of one of His powers, namely virgin Memory, whose name," says Philo, "most people slightly change and call her 'Mnemosyne.' " Classicists will recognize that the passage is closely reminiscent of one in Hesiod (*Theog.* 51–80). In fact, when Philo thinks of the subject matter of the arts and sciences (*Her.* 210), he thinks first of music.[7]

In the past, scholars such as Emil Schürer had attempted to diminish Philo's importance as a theological thinker and to present him merely as a preacher, but Harry Wolfson has demonstrated Philo's originality as a thinker.[8] In particular, Philo was the first to show the difference between the knowability of G-d's existence and the unknowability of his essence.[9] Again, in his view of G-d, Philo is original in insisting on an individual Providence who can suspend the laws of nature in contrast to the prevailing Greek philosophical view of a universal Providence who is himself subject to the unchanging laws of nature.[10]

Philo finds the highest expression of Greek wisdom in Plato, whom he terms nothing less than "most sacred" (*Prob.* 13). It is the synthesis of this wisdom with the Torah that he attempts, and it is Plato's theory of ideas that is the starting point of Philo's philosophy.[11] Indeed, he finds proof of Plato's ideas in the Torah itself, first in the statement (Gen. 1:27) that G-d created man in His image. He understands "image" here to refer to the pattern, according to which G-d created man (*Opif.* 25). Second, he finds the theory of ideas in the biblical passage (Exod. 25:9) in which G-d tells Moses that he is to make the משכן and its vessels according to the form תבנית (form) that He will show him. The Septuagint translates תבנית as παράδειγμα (paradigm), which is one of the terms used by Plato in referring to his theory of forms or models or exemplars of which all earthly things are a mere imitation. Hence, the idea of the tabernacle existed *before* the earthly tabernacle came into existence. Philo thus resolves a major question, namely the process of creation, that is, G-d had ideas or forms on the basis of which the world was created. According to Philo (*Opif.* 29), G-d first created the ideas or patterns, and these had an existence outside of His thoughts. He then created the visible world on the basis of these ideas. Philo thus, long before Julius Wellhausen, explains the so-called two accounts of creation in Genesis, chapters 1 and 2. His explanation (*QG* 1.19) is that the first chapter tells of the creation of the invisible ideas, whereas the second tells of their creation in visible reality.

This, to be sure, corresponds to the tradition found in rabbinic literature that ten items or concepts, including the Torah, existed before the creation of the world (*Exod. Rab.* 40.2). If this is the case, we may well ask what the difference is between Philo and the rabbinic view. In reply, we may answer that the rabbis are not conscious of the parallel between their view and that of Plato. Second, whereas the rabbinic view is presented in midrash, Philo's view is central to his philosophy and is claimed to be a direct interpretation of the Torah. Third, the rabbis do not regard the accounts of Genesis 1 and 2 as referring to two separate degrees of creation. For them the patterns existed from eternity, whereas Philo says that G-d conceived of them only when He decided to create the world (*Opif.* 19). Moreover, when Philo (*Decal.* 134) says that man possesses "in his mind a closer likeness and copy than anything else on earth of the eternal and blessed archetype," the word that he uses for "archetype" is Plato's word ἰδέα (idea). Harry Wolfson says that Philo is here referring to man as a copy of the Logos; hence man is a copy of a copy, but Philo speaks of man as most closely akin to the Father of the world, that is G-d.[12] Judaism, however, insists that G-d is absolutely unique, and we may not assert anything of Him other than that He exists. Furthermore, whereas Plato sometimes speaks of the idea of the good as if it were G-d (*Republic* 2.379 B–C), Philo speaks of G-d as the Good (*Leg.* 1.47).

Philo actually assumes that the Greeks arrived at some truths without revelation. How is that possible? he asks. His answer is twofold. In the first place, he says, some Greek legislators "copied from the most sacred tablets of Moses" (*Spec.* 4.61). The example that he gives (*Conf.* 141) is Exod. 23:1: לא תשא שמע שוא ("Do not accept a false report," where he follows the Septuagint version, ἀκοὴν ματαίαν, "a vain hearing"), which he interprets to indicate that the Torah does not accept hearsay evidence. Moreover, he says, the pre-Socratic philosopher Heraclitus snatched his theory of opposites like a thief from Moses (*QG* 4.152). Second, he asserts, philosophy, operating through reason, is the divine gift to the Greeks parallel to revelation to the Jews (*Spec.* 3.185). Why, then, did G-d decide to give the truth in one way to the Greeks and in another way to the Jews? The answer is that the Torah is intended for the masses. Apparently, G-d realized that not all Jews can get into Harvard. Most are not endowed with superior powers of logic and intellect, whereas the Greek philosophers, notably Plato, are. Through philosophy, says Philo (*Opif.* 77), humans are rendered immortal. "And so," he says,

> carrying its gaze beyond the confines of all substance discernible by sense, it [the human mind] comes to a point at which it searches out after the intelligible world, and on descrying, in that world, sights of surpassing loveliness, even the patterns and originals of the things of sense which it saw here, it is seized by sober intoxication, like those filled with corybantic frenzy, and is inspired, possessed by a longing for other than theirs, and a nobler desire. Wafted by this to the topmost arch of the things perceptible to mind, it seems to be on its way to the Great King Himself. (*Opif.* 70–71)

Moses is described (*Virt.* 178) as one who initiated the Israelites into the mysteries (μυσταγωγῶν). Philo distinguishes, as in the Eleusinian Mysteries, between the Lesser and the Greater Mysteries. It is the latter that enable one to know G-d directly. Indeed, Philo (*Cher.* 49) says of himself, "I myself was initiated under Moses into his higher mysteries." Philo, both Jew and philosopher, searches for the hidden meanings of the Torah and, by means of the allegorical method, interprets the Torah to reconcile it with *mada*. Why, then, did G-d not give all the *mitzvot* to the Greeks? His answer is that G-d used the Jews as missionaries to bring the Torah to the Gentiles (*Mos.* 2.41–44).

Philo asks why G-d did not give the Torah to Abraham, and he, like the rabbis, replies that Abraham was able to figure out the Torah before it was revealed (*Abr.* 275). He was taught not by written law but by unwritten nature, by a kind of natural law. If so, we may ask: why is there a need for revelation? Apparently, he believes that there is a higher law, a kind of Platonic idea, of which the Torah is only a copy.

Philo (*Opif.* 77) asks why human beings were the last to be created by G-d. His answer is that humans should be at a loss for none of the means of living well, and the means of living well come from "contemplation of the heavenly existences, for smitten by their contemplation the mind conceives a love and longing for the knowledge of them. And from this philosophy took its rise, by which man, mortal though he be, is rendered immortal." In contrast to the rabbis' denigration of Greek wisdom, we find the following tribute to philosophy in Philo, in his discussion of G-d's creation of the two great lights, the sun and the moon:

> Banqueting on sights displayed to it one after another, his [i.e., man's] soul was insatiate in beholding. And then, as usually happens, it went on to busy itself with questionings, asking 'What is the essence of these visible objects? Are they in nature unoriginate, or had they a beginning of existence? . . . And what are the principles by which each is governed? It was out of the investigation of these problems that philosophy grew, than which no more perfect good has come into the life of mankind. (*Opif.* 54–55)

Indeed, according to Philo (*Opif.* 8), Moses himself attained the very summit of philosophy.

Of course, we may well ask to what degree philosophizing and the Bible would have constituted a problem for Philo and his contemporaries, as it has for so many Jews in the Middle Ages and in modern times. Surprising as it may seem, we may guess that it did not. Philo was, after all, a very prominent person in the Jewish community both because he belonged to the wealthiest Jewish family in Alexandria and because he had received such an outstanding education in the arts and sciences. That the community was divided in terms of ideology seems clear from Philo's references to excessive literalists (*Somn.* 2.301, *Mut.* 61) and excessive allegorists (*Migr.* 89–91, *Post.* 42).[13] Moreover, the fact that Emperor Claudius, in his letter to the Alexandrians (London Papyrus 1912; *Corpus Papyrorum Judaicarum* 153, ll. 90–91), in his attempt to be even-handed in his treatment of the Jews and the Greeks in Alexandria, warns the Alexandrian Jews in strong terms not in the future to send two embassies to him, "as if they lived in two cities, a thing which has never been done before," indicates that the community must have been sharply divided. And yet, we hear of no criticisms of Philo for his philosophizing, and, in particular, for the manner of his philosophizing—which perhaps is not surprising, since almost all the literature of that era is lost. Nor, more significantly, do we find in the extensive extant works of Philo any answers to such criticisms, whether in Philo's philosophical works or in his historical essays that have come down to us.

Similarly, and significantly, we find no extant criticisms of Philo's younger contemporary, Josephus, for his critical approach to the Bible in the first half of the *Antiquities* and his citation of non-Jewish sources to corroborate biblical references. Nor do we find Josephus' reply to such critics; this is significant, inasmuch as Josephus had many rivals and enemies—both political, such as John of Gischala, and literary, such as Justus of Tiberias—with the possible exception of Josephus' remark that Jews "do not favor those persons who have mastered the speech of many nations" (*Ant.* 20.264).

In terms of methods, the Stoics, beset by the gross immorality found in the description of the gods in the Greek equivalent of the Bible, Homer and Hesiod, developed allegorical and other methods of exegesis, taking liberties in interpreting the "slices from the banquet of Homer," as Aeschylus put it, following the precedent of the famous Greek tragedians. Philo, like Josephus later in the first half of his *Antiquities*, confronted by major problems if one takes the text of the Bible literally, takes similar liberties.

One problem that is very difficult for any believer in monotheism is the sheer remoteness of G-d and the fact that one cannot represent Him or even ascribe any positive attributes to Him, lest one be guilty of anthropomorphism. The pagan has no such problem, since G-d is depicted in human form; but this is clearly a problem for Philo, who so admired pagan Greek literature. Furthermore, the question which the four who entered *Pardes* considered, namely the origin of evil, was deeply pondered by Philo. Philo, as we shall see, resolved both of these problems by positing an intermediary, the Logos—the "Word."

The Nazir (who definitely knew Philo in the Greek), the *talmid* of Rav Kook, in his *Qol ha-Nevuah*, refers to Philo as the giant of ancient Jewish philosophy.[14] He claims that, in his doctrine of the Logos, Philo resisted the approach of Greek philosophy, which is conceptual and contemplative, and instead looks upon Judaism as summoning the Jew not to see G-d, which is impossible, but to understand and listen to Him. In this view of Judaism, he posits that Philo is the forerunner of the Kabbalistic view. But the Nazir's view that hearing is superior to seeing is contradicted by Philo's statement, based upon his interpretation of Exod. 23:1, that the Greek legislators borrowed from the Jews the view that evidence based on what is heard is not admissible. Moreover, Philo, on numerous occasions (*Leg.* 2.34, etc.), explains the meaning of Israel as "seeing G-d."[15] Furthermore, as David Winston has remarked, Philo, in his exhaustive commentary, never expounds on or even mentions the key passage, שמע ישראל (Deut. 6:4: "Hear, O Israel").[16]

As to the remoteness of G-d, Philo solves this problem by explaining that when scripture (Gen. 28:11) says that Jacob came to a certain place, the "place" is the Word (Logos) of G-d, for G-d, not deeming it proper that sense should perceive Him, sends forth His Word to aid the lovers of virtue (*Somn.* 1.68–69). Again, at the burning bush it is not G-d who appears to Moses but rather an angel or herald (*Mos.* 1.66). Philo (*Somn.* 1.232) remarks that if man were merely an incorporeal soul, G-d could reveal Himself to such a soul as He really is, but to souls that are still in a body, He assumes the likeness of an angel, without altering His own nature, "for He is unchangeable, but conveying to those that receive the impression of His presence a semblance in a different form, such that they take the image to be not a copy but that original form itself." Philo was apparently troubled by the vast gulf separating humans from G-d and wondered how they could communicate with one another. His answer (*QE* 2.67) is that even the most lucid and most prophetic mind receives knowledge of G-d not from G-d Himself but from His chief and ministering powers.

The most difficult, and philosophically the most important, chapters in the Bible are the first two chapters in Genesis. In particular, Philo wondered why G-d, who is perfect and incorporeal, should have created a world that is imperfect and corporeal, certainly a good question. He quotes the Septuagint's translation of Gen. 1:2 (it appears that Philo knew only the Greek translation, which he regarded as divinely inspired and, indeed, perfect [*Mos.* 2.37–40]), "And the earth was unseen and unformed" (ἀόρατος καὶ ἀκατασκεύαστος, תהו ובהו), as well as the Septuagint's translation of Gen. 2:5: "And G-d made every green thing of the field *before* it came into being on the earth, and every grass *before* it grew." He concludes from this, following Plato (as the proverb quoted by Jerome [*Vir. ill.* 11] would have it, "either Plato Philonizes or Philo Platonizes"), that at first G-d created the incorporeal and intelligible Ideas before the creation of corporeal copies (*Opif.* 16).[17] Like his younger contemporary, the Stoic Seneca the Younger (*Ep.* 58.18–19, 65.7), he views the Ideas as G-d's thoughts. Through the influence of the Logos, the Ideas become seminal reason-principles (λόγοι σπερματικοί, *Legat.* 55), a concept borrowed from the Stoics, as Dillon has noted.[18]

Philo views the world as being like the Persian empire (*Agr.* 51), ruled by a great king but who has set over it his true Word (Logos) and firstborn Son, who takes upon Himself the government of the world "like some viceroy of a great king." Whereas the Bible (Gen. 1:3) states that "G-d said, 'Let there be light'; and there was light," Philo (*Sacr.* 8) asserts that it was through this Word that the whole universe was formed, and it is through this Word that G-d draws man from things earthly to Himself. He derives this from the biblical statement that "G-d *said* (the verb corresponding to Logos): Let there be light." This Logos, as Henry Chadwick has noted, is termed by Philo "the idea of ideas" (*Migr.* 103; *QE* 2.124), the first-begotten Son of the uncreated Father (*Post.* 63; *Mos.* 2.134; *Conf.* 63), a "second G-d" (frag. *ap.* Eusebius, *Praep. ev.* 7.13.1), the pattern and mediator of creation (*Conf.* 63; *Leg.* 3.96; *Mut.* 57).[19] The Logos, he says, is G-d's shadow. He is the means, the instrument, through which G-d created the world.

It is through the Logos that Philo has an answer to the eternal problem of the origin of evil. God, he insists, in an anticipation of Gnostic doctrine, cannot be responsible for any evil (*Conf.* 161). To be sure, He recognizes that punishment is sometimes beneficial for humans (*Conf.* 182), but G-d decrees that it be exacted by others. In this connection, Philo has a very interesting exegesis of Gen. 1:26: נעשה אדם בצלמנו, "Let us make man in our image." Referring to the plural "us," Philo (*Opif.* 72) asks why G-d would need the help of anyone. Plato in the *Timaeus* (41B–D), similarly confronted with the problem of why G-d would create beings inferior to Himself, has the author of the universe tell the created gods to fashion mortal bodies capable of vice, and says that He Himself will sow in them immortal souls. Philo (*Opif.* 75) says that when men's thoughts and deeds are blameless G-d may be owned as their source, while His subordinates are held responsible for thoughts and deeds of a contrary sort, since G-d cannot be the cause of evil.

If the Logos is the Son of G-d, an interesting question is: who is the mother of Logos? The answer, and it is nothing less than amazing that Philo does have an answer, is that the mother is σοφία, Wisdom (*Fug.* 109), and that it is through Wisdom that the universe came into existence. Wisdom, says Philo (*Det.* 116), "affords to her offspring, as soon as they are born, the nourishment which they require from her own breasts." The next statement is the most important: "Not all her offspring," says Philo, "are deemed suitable for divine food, but such as are found worthy of their parents; for many of them fall victims to the famine of virtue, a famine more cruel than that of eatables and drinkables." What is Philo saying here? Is Sophia a kind of Earth Mother, as Dillon suggests?[20] The Hebrew term for wisdom, *ḥokmah*, is, of course, familiar to us from the Bible, occurring there no fewer than 318 times. It appears personified in Job 28, in Proverbs 1, 8, and 9, and in a number of other places in the Bible, but it is a particularly well-known concept in Greek philosophy and literature. Is Philo, as I should like to suggest, intimating that the marriage of G-d and Philosophy (the love of wisdom) produces the Logos, which, in turn, produces the world as we know it, with its good and evil? Indeed, at one point, as we have noted, Philo identifies the Logos as a second G-d (*QG* 2.62; fragment in Eusebius, *Praep. ev.* 7.13.1). Philo departs from Plato principally in using the term *Logos* for the idea of ideas (*Migr.* 103) and for the ideas as a whole and in his statement that the Logos is the place of the intelligible world. In anticipation of Christian doctrine he terms the Logos the first-begotten Son of G-d (*Agr.* 51), the image of G-d (*Conf.* 147), and second to G-d (*Leg.* 2.86). By virtue of his close relationship with the Logos, Moses, parallel to his position in Samaritan theology, is termed god and king (*Mos.* 1.158) in anticipation of Christology.

That the Logos is a mediator may be seen in Philo's exegesis of the verse (Exod. 25:22): "There [i.e., in the ark] I [G-d] will meet with you, and from above the mercy seat, from between the two cherubim that are upon the ark of the testimony." In this particular passage Philo identifies G-d with the Logos, "inasmuch as it is appropriately in the middle, leaves nothing in nature empty, but fills all things and becomes a mediator and arbitrator for the two sides which seem to be divided from each other, bringing about friendship and concord, for it is always the cause of community and the artisan of peace" (*QE* 2.68). The Logos is compared to manna, "the heavenly incorruptible food of the soul which delights in the vision" (*Her.* 79). The Logos, in turn, is the archetype for further creations (*Leg.* 3.96).

In explaining G-d's creation of man in the image of G-d (Gen. 1:27), Philo says that the Image was made such as representing G-d, and that, in turn, man himself was made after the Image when it had acquired the force of a pattern. It is this Son, the Logos, who, following the ways of His Father, "shaped the different kinds, looking to the archetypal patterns which that Father supplied" (*Conf.* 63). He refers to this incorporeal and imperishable Logos as the archetype of human reason (*Her.* 230ff.; *Leg.* 1.31ff.) and, most strikingly of all, as "the man of G-d" (*Conf.* 41, 62, 146).

When the angel of the L-rd comes to Hagar (Gen. 16:13) he is referred to as G-d's Logos and minister; and it is not strange for her to believe that he is G-d, says Philo (*Fug.* 212, *QG* 3.34). The angels that accompanied Abraham are identified with the words and thoughts that attend G-d; and Philo (*Migr.* 173–74) remarks that as long as a person falls short of perfection he has the Divine Logos as his leader.

Moses is apparently akin to such a Logos, since Philo (*Somn.* 2.189) calls attention to the verse (Exod. 7:1) in which G-d says to Moses, "See, I make you as G-d to Pharaoh," and remarks that Moses was not a man or a G-d but a kind of Logos, contiguous with both extremes. Moses, says Philo, "was named G-d and king of the whole nation, and entered, we are told, into the darkness where G-d was, that is, into the unseen, invisible, incorporeal and archetypal essence of existing things, thus identifying him as a virtual Logos" (*Mos.* 1.158).

Just as those who are unable to see the sun itself regard the gleam of the parhelion as the sun, "so," says Philo, "some regard the image of G-d, His angel the Word, as His very self" (*Somn.* 1.239), though clearly Philo differentiates the two. This Logos holds the eldership among the angels and is their ruler, as it were (*Conf.* 146). This solves the problem of how G-d, Who is pure Form, could condescend to have contact with the lowly world of matter, since G-d, "the Father of all, has given the special prerogative" to his viceroy, the Logos,

> His chief messenger, highest in age and honor . . . to stand on the border and separate the creature from the Creator. This same Logos both pleads with the immortal as suppliant for afflicted mortality and acts as ambassador of the ruler to the subject. He glories in this prerogative and proudly describes it in these words, "and I stood between the L-rd and you" [Deut. 5:5, where the Logos is actually identified with Moses], that is neither uncreated as G-d, nor created as you, but midway between the two extremes, a surety to both sides; to the parent, pledging the creature that it should never altogether rebel against the rein and choose disorder rather than order; to the child, warranting his hopes that the merciful G-d will never forget His own work. (*Her.* 205–6)

Is this a quotation from Origen or Clement of Alexandria or Augustine or some other Church Father? No, it is a quotation from Philo of Alexandria, the Jew. Is it surprising that Henry Chadwick opens his chapter on Philo in *The Cambridge History of Later Greek and Early Medieval Philosophy* with the statement: "The history of Christian philosophy begins not with a Christian but with a Jew, Philo of Alexandria, elder contemporary of Paul"?[21]

Whence did Philo derive this concept of the Logos? He may have obtained it from Jewish sources, since we do find in Psalms (33:6) the statement that the heavens were made by the *word* of the L-rd. Moreover, Prov. 8:22 speaks of Wisdom as being present at the beginning of creation and (8:30) as being beside G-d, like a master workman. Philo, as we have seen, is well acquainted with the concept of angels and, indeed, speaks of the Logos as an archangel (*Conf.* 146, *Her.* 205).

The fact, however, that in mentioning the Logos, Philo assumes that his Greek-speaking audience will understand the references and the fact that Philo was so thoroughly steeped in Greek literature would indicate that his source was more probably a pagan one. In particular, we may note that the Logos serves as divider of the undifferentiated material substance of the world. The Logos, as John Dillon has remarked, is responsible not only for arithmetical equality but also for proportional equality as well.[22]

We may suggest that Philo may have been influenced by the pre-Socratic philosopher Heraclitus in two respects: in the first place, Heraclitus used the term *logos* in the sense of an underlying cosmic principle of order.[23] It is perhaps this role of Logos in the cosmic order that led Philo to adopt this term in connection with the role of the Logos as the agent of creation. That it was Heraclitus to whom Philo was indebted may perhaps be indicated by the fact that Philo, as we have noted, charges that Heraclitus stole his theory of opposites from Moses (*QG* 4.152). In Heraclitus it was the proportional arrangement of things that provided the ultimate order of all phenomena which appear to be disparate in nature, as Thomas Tobin has remarked; and it is proportional equality, as we have noted, for which the Logos is responsible.[24]

In Stoicism, to which Philo is so vastly indebted, reason or *logos* is identified with G-d and nature and controls all of the universe, bringing order into the universe through seminal reason-principles (λόγοι σπερματικοί), the term used by Philo, as noted above.[25] Middle Platonism, like Philo, distinguished between two aspects of divinity and, indeed, speaks of a first and second G-d—the first essentially transcendent, like Philo's G-d, and the second an active, demiurgic power, like Philo's Logos, which was responsible for the ordering of everything else in the universe.[26]

Elsewhere Philo (*QG* 4.8) describes the universe as divided into three parts: the cause of the intelligible world is G-d himself; the cause of the heavenly world is G-d's creative power; and the cause of the sublunary world—the world of growth and decay—is G-d's royal power. The fact that our world is not being ruled by G-d, or at least not by G-d directly, which sounds like something Gnostic or Persian, is like the concept of the Demiurge of the Valentinians and ultimately derives from Plato's *Timaeus*, which, as John Dillon remarks, speaks of the handing over of the formation of the lower soul by the demiurge to the "young gods."[27] Significantly, Plutarch (*De E* 393A) quotes his teacher Ammonius as declaring that all those acts and experiences conventionally attributed to the supreme god are really to be referred "to some other god, or rather daemon, whose office is concerned with Nature in dissolution and generation," that is, the sublunar realm. He thus anticipates the Neoplatonic identification of the sublunary demiurge with Hades.

Furthermore, Plato (*Phaedr.* 246–47), who is described by Philo as "most sacred" (ἱερώτατον, *Prob.* 13), speaks of incorporeal souls that do not descend into bodies. Plutarch (*Is. Os.* 361C) identifies these souls as daemons (δαίμονες). Philo says that "it is Moses' custom to give the name of angels to those whom other philosophers call demons, souls, that is, which fly and hover in the air" (*Gig.* 6).[28] Among these philosophers may have been the fourth-century BCE Xenocrates, who speaks of two types of daemons, good and evil (*ap.* Plutarch, *Is. Os.* 360E). Philo, citing Ps. 78:49, speaks of evil angels. Philo says that "men in general speak of good and evil demons, and in like manner of good and evil souls" (*Gig.* 17). In particular, Philo, like Plato, looks upon the body as a hindrance to the soul. His ideal is the Therapeutae and the Essenes, in effect, monks. Moses, he says (*Mos.* 1.28), had relations only for the sake of having children.

Philo is also novel in his exposition of the mystic love of G-d which G-d has implanted in humans and through which humans become G-d-like. The influence of the mystic notions of Platonism, especially of the *Symposium*, and of the popular mystery cults of Dionysus, Orpheus, Sarapis, and Isis and Osiris on Philo's attempt to present Judaism as the one true mystery is hardly superficial; Philo is a major source of our knowledge of their doctrines, notably that of rebirth.[29] Philo himself says (*Migr.* 34–35) that he has experienced ten thousand times a sudden inability to think or conversely a sudden fullness of thought, so that, under the influence of Divine possession, he was filled with corybantic frenzy. Perhaps, through his mystic presentation of Judaism, Philo hoped to enable Judaism in the Diaspora to compete with the other mystery religions in its proselytizing efforts, as well as in its attempts to hold on to its adherents. But Philo's respect for the literal interpretation of the Bible, his denunciation of the extreme allegorists (*Migr.* 89–99), and his failure to mention any specific rites of initiation for proselytes, as well as the lack of evidence that Philo himself was a devotee of a particular mystery cult indicate that he was essentially in the mainstream of Judaism.

The purpose of Philo's mystic "sober intoxication," to use his phrase (*Prob.* 13), is to lead one out of the material into the eternal world. Philo's admiration for the Essenes (*Prob.* and *Hypoth.* 11.1–18) and the Therapeutae (*Contempl.*), with their extreme views on asceticism, is in line with his view that sexual relations should be engaged in solely to propagate the race (*Det.* 102) and his admiration for Moses for participating in intercourse solely for the lawful begetting of children (*Mos.* 1.28). For him Leah, who is above the passions, is contrasted with Rachel, who is sense-perception (*Post.* 135). Like Plato, Philo regards the body as the prison-house of the soul (*Leg.* 1.108, *QG* 2.69), and indeed in his dualism of body and soul, as in his description of the flight from the self, the contrast between G-d and the world, and the yearning for a direct experience of G-d, he anticipates much of Gnosticism.[30] But, unlike all the Greek philosophers, with the exception of the Epicureans, who believed in limited freedom of will, Philo holds that man is completely free to act against all the laws of his own nature.[31]

In his ethical theory, Philo describes two virtues, under the heading of justice, which are otherwise unknown in Greek philosophic literature—religious faith and humanity. Again, for him repentance is a virtue, whereas for other Greek philosophers it is a weakness.[32] Perfect happiness comes, however, not through man's own efforts to achieve virtue but only (in an anticipation of Paul) through the grace of G-d (*Leg.* 3.136).

In his political theory Philo often says that the best form of government is democracy (*Agr.* 45, *Conf.* 108, *Abr.* 242, *Virt.* 180, *Spec.* 4.237); but for him democracy is far from mob-rule, which he denounces as the worst of polities (*Opif.* 69), perhaps because he saw the Alexandrian mob in action.

For Philo democracy means not a particular form of government but due order under any form of government (*Spec.* 4.237) in which all men are equal before the law, as we find in Stoic doctrine. From this point of view, the Mosaic constitution, which embodies the best elements of all forms of government, is the ideal, he thinks (*Spec.* 3.182). Indeed, the ultimate goal of history is that the whole world should be a single state under a democratic constitution (*Deus* 176). This state, in its divine direction, is anticipatory of Augustine's City of G-d.

What effect did Philo's teachings and writings have? He was not only a philosopher but also the head of what was, in effect, the Anti-Defamation League of the Alexandrian Jewish community, as we see in his leading a delegation to the Roman emperor Caligula. He is closely paraphrased, however, by only one pagan author, the fourth-century novelist Heliodorus (9.9.3). The only Jewish writer until the Italian rabbi Azariah dei Rossi in the sixteenth century who knows his work and who is influenced by his account of creation and his allegorical interpretation of the Temple and its cult is Josephus.[33] Azariah himself, impressed though he was with Philo's philosophical knowledge, criticizes Philo's ignorance of Hebrew, his allegorization of the Bible, and his deviations from the Halakhah as codified by the Talmudic rabbis. Philo is not mentioned at all in the vast rabbinic literature, perhaps because the rabbis felt so strongly about the dangers of his philosophizing, especially his notion of an intermediary divine Logos between G-d and the world or because of his negative attitude toward the body or because they were simply not interested in Philo's ideas.[34] Runia plausibly suggests the possibility that the rabbis rejected Philo's biblical exegesis because his thought had been exploited by prominent Christian thinkers such as Clement, Origen, and Eusebius. Indeed, David Runia has a section of a chapter entitled "How Philo became a Church Father *honoris causa*?"[35] According to Eusebius, Philo met Peter in Rome during the reign of Emperor Claudius (*Hist. eccl.* 2.17.1). According to Jerome, the friendship between Philo and Peter is the reason why Philo was so favorably disposed to the followers of Peter's disciple Mark (*Vir. ill.* 11). Indeed, according to the fifth-century Pseudo-Prochorus (110.6–112.11), Philo discussed the Law and the Gospel with the apostle John and was baptized.

How much influence did Philo's writings have on the Jews of Alexandria? Philo himself (*Migr.* 89–91, *Post.* 42), great allegorist though he was, criticizes the extreme allegorists of Alexandria, who though not constituting a distinct sect, were forerunners of antinomianism, the attack on Jewish legalism associated with Paul. Philo mentions Jews in Alexandria who never act religiously except on Yom Kippur (*Spec.* 1.186). Philo's own nephew, Tiberius Julius Alexander, who attained the governorship of the most important province of the Roman empire, Egypt, did not, we are told (Josephus, *Ant.* 20.100), abide by the ancestral practices. As to possible influence on early Christianity, it would seem significant that Paul, despite his tremendous efforts to seek converts throughout the Mediterranean world, never chose to come to the city that had by far the largest number of Jews in the Diaspora. According to Acts (18:24–28), a Jewish native of Alexandria named Apollos came to Ephesus, where "he powerfully confuted the Jews in public." The fact that he went to Ephesus, we may conjecture, may have been due to an effort on the part of the organized Jewish community of Alexandria to stop his missionary efforts. A letter of Clement of Alexandria discovered by Morton Smith declares that Mark arrived in Alexandria from Rome and composed his Gospel there.[36] We know that the Jewish community of Alexandria, which at its height numbered perhaps 180,000, was greatly diminished by the middle of the second century CE, primarily, it would seem, because of the losses in the revolt of 115–117.[37] We may guess, though, that some were converted to Christianity, perhaps convinced by the identification of Philo's Logos with the Logos of the fourth Gospel and influenced by his praise of the ascetic life. Indeed, according to a tradition preserved by Eusebius, though, to be sure, many have doubted its accuracy, "the number of men and women who were there [at Alexandria] converted at the first attempt was so great, and their asceticism was so extraordinarily philosophic, that Philo thought it right to describe their conduct and assemblies and meals and all the rest of the manner of life [i.e., of the monastic-like Therapeutae described by Philo in his *De Vita Contemplativa*]" (*Hist. eccl.* 2.16.2–17.2). Be that as it may, it does seem plausible to see some kind of connection between the Therapeutae and the later development of Christian monasticism and asceticism in Egypt.[38]

In the works of a tenth-century Karaite named Jacob Qirqisani and in fragments of the Cairo Geniza there are references to an Alexandrian who may be Philo.[39] Qirqisani speaks of a sect, Maghariya, that appeared during the first century BCE. The name is Arabic, meaning "men of the caves," and refers to their practice of keeping their books and sacred writings in caves in the surrounding hills of Palestine. They believed that G-d was too sublime to mingle with matter. They rejected the idea that the world was directly created by G-d, but rather that an intermediary power, an angel, did it. The sect wrote its own peculiar commentaries on the Bible and attributed the Law to this angel. He mentions two writings of theirs of importance—*Alexandrian* and *Sefer Yadua* (can this be Yedidiah, as Azariah dei Rossi translated Philo's name?).

In a ninth-century letter from a Patriarch of Seleucia in Iraq to a Metropolitan of Elam (Iran), he writes:

> We have learned from trustworthy Jews who were then being instructed as catechumens in the Christian religion that some books were found ten years ago in a rock-dwelling near Jericho. The story was that the dog of an Arab out hunting went into a cave in pursuit of game and did not come out again; its owner went in afterwards and found a chamber in the rock in which there were many books.

The Patriarch asked a Jew to whom the books were shown about many passages in the New Testament which are quoted as from the Hebrew Scriptures but which are not found there, and the Jew said that they were among those books and that among others there were 200 psalms of David.[40] May these be identified with the Dead Sea Scrolls, discovered more than a thousand years later? Might the Karaites have had access through these books to the thoughts of Philo? Indeed, Bernard Revel, in his doctoral dissertation, "Karaite Halakah and Its Relation to Sadducean, Samaritan and Philonian Halakah" (Dropsie College, 1913), had argued for Philonic influence on the Karaitic Halakah.

Some have compared Maimonides' debt to and extreme praise of Aristotle with Philo's debt to and extreme praise of Plato. But I should like to point out one major difference, which I think will help to account for the place of Maimonides in Jewish tradition and the lack of such a place for Philo. Maimonides read the Torah in the original and Aristotle in translation; Philo read Plato in the original and the Torah in translation.

Notes

1. Samuel Krauss, *Griechische und Lateinische Lehnwörter im Talmud, Midrasch und Targum*, vol. 2 (Berlin: Calvary, 1899), 446–47, lists thirty-one such passages.
2. On Elisha ben Abuya see now Alon Goshen-Gottstein, *The Sinner and the Amnesiac: The Rabbinic Invention of Elisha ben Abuya and Eleazar ben Arach* (Stanford, Calif.: Stanford University Press, 2000), 21–29, for a critical investigation of the traditions attributed about him.
3. Diogenes Laertius, *Lives of Eminent Philosophers* 1.27.
4. See Gershom Scholem, "Metatron," *Encyclopaedia Judaica* 11 (1971): 1444.
5. See Isobel Henderson, "Ancient Greek Music," in *New Oxford History of Music*, vol. 1, ed. Jack A. Westrup et al. (London: Oxford University Press, 1957), 385.
6. Henri I. Marrou, *A History of Education in Antiquity*, trans. George Lamb (New York: Sheed and Ward, 1956), 17–18.
7. See my "Philo's Views on Music," *Journal of Jewish Music and Liturgy* 9 (1986–87): 36–54.
8. Harry A. Wolfson, *Philo: Foundations of Religious Philosophy in Judaism, Christianity, and Islam*, 2 vols. (Cambridge: Harvard University Press, 1947), 2:439–60.
9. Harry A. Wolfson, "Philo Judaeus," in *The Encyclopedia of Philosophy*, ed. Paul Edwards (New York: Macmillan, 1967), 6:153.
10. Ibid., 152.
11. So Wolfson, *Philo,* 1:200.
12. Ibid., 1:203–4.
13. See my *Jew and Gentile in the Ancient World* (Princeton, N.J.: Princeton University Press, 1993), 74–76.
14. See André Neher, "Les referances à Philon d'Alexandrie dans l'oeuvre du Rav Hanazir, disciple du rav Kook," in André Caquot et al., *Hellenica et Judaica: Hommage à Valentin Nikiprowetzky* (Paris: Leuven, 1986), 385–90; and David Winston, "Judaism and Hellenism: Hidden Tensions in Philo's Thought," *Studia Philonica Annual* 2 (1990): 2–3.

15. See the list of passages with this explanation cited by J. W. Earp, in his index to *Philo*, Loeb Classical Library 10 (London: Heinemann, 1962), 334 n. a, and the extensive and careful analysis by Ellen Birnbaum, *The Place of Judaism in Philo's Thought* (Atlanta: Scholars Press, 1996), 61–127.
16. Winston, "Judaism and Hellenism," 3.
17. On Philo's vast indebtedness to Plato for concepts, imagery, and vocabulary see most recently John R. Levison, *The Spirit in First Century Judaism* (Leiden: Brill, 1997), esp. 151–58.
18. John Dillon, *The Middle Platonists 80 B.C. to A.D. 220* (Ithaca, N.Y.: Cornell University Press, 1977), 159.
19. Henry Chadwick, "Philo and the Beginnings of Christian Thought," in *The Cambridge History of Later Greek and Early Medieval Philosophy*, ed. A. H. Armstrong (Cambridge: Cambridge University Press, 1967), 143.
20. Dillon, *The Middle Platonists,* 164.
21. Chadwick, "Philo and the Beginnings of Christian Thought," 137.
22. Dillon, *The Middle Platonists,* 160.
23. See Hermann Diels and Walther Kranz, *Die Fragmente der Vorsokratiker* (Berlin: Weidmann, 1952), fragments 1, 2, 50.
24. Thomas H. Tobin, "Logos," in *The Anchor Bible Dictionary*, ed. David N. Freedman (New York: Doubleday, 1992), 4:348.
25. Diogenes Laertius 7.135; Plutarch, *Stoic. rep.* 34.1050A.
26. Dillon, *The Middle Platonists,* 46. In particular, note that the Middle Platonist Eudorus of Alexandria, a generation before Philo (126–28), presents as having been held by the Pythagoreans a somewhat similar analysis of two first principles—the first a Supreme Principle which they called The One and which Eudorus called the Supreme G-d, and below that a pair of opposites, a Monad, a second One representing Form, and a Dyad, representing Matter. It is Eudorus' doctrine that the One is the causal principle of Matter, which contradicts both the original Pythagoreanism and strict Platonism and which leads to the kind of Monism favored by Philo.
27. Ibid., 169, 191.
28. See the discussion by Wolfson, *Philo,* 1:382–85.
29. See Erwin R. Goodenough, *By Light, Light: The Mystic Gospel of Hellenistic Judaism* (New Haven: Yale University Press, 1935), 8–10.
30. Hans Jonas, *Gnosis und Spätantiker Geist* 2.1: *Von der Mythologie zur mystischen Philosophie* (Göttingen: Vandenhoeck and Ruprecht, 1954), 70–121.
31. Wolfson, "Philo Judaeus," 152–53.
32. Ibid., 154.
33. See Ralph Marcus, "A Sixteenth Century Hebrew Critique of Philo," *Hebrew Union College Annual* 21 (1948): 29–71; Joanna Weinberg, "The Quest for Philo in Sixteenth-Century Jewish Historiography," in *Jewish History: Essays in Honor of Chimen Abramsky,* ed. Ada Rapoport-Albert and Steven J. Zipperstein (London: Peter Halban, 1988), 163–87; and Charles Touati, "Judaisme talmudique et rabbinique: la découverte par le judaisme de la Renaissance de Flavius Josèphe et de Philon le Juif," *Annuaire École Pratique des Hautes Études,* Ve section: *Sciences Religieuses* 97 (1988–89): 214–17. Others who knew and generally admired the works of Philo were Azariah's Italian contemporaries, the Provenzali (Provencal) brothers (Moses and David) and Rabbi Judah Moscato, and the seventeenth-century Venetian rabbi Simone Luzzatto and the Cretan rabbi, philosopher, and scientist Joseph Delmedigo. See Winston, "Judaism and Hellenism," 1–2. Critical of Philo, we may add, was the eminent sixteenth-century Talmudist Maharal (Judah Loew ben Bezalel of Prague) in his *Be'er* (126 col. b–141a), as noted by Joanna Weinberg, *The Light of the Eyes: Azariah dei Rossi* (New Haven: Yale University Press, 2001), xxii n. 72.
34. A strained attempt has been made by Louis Finkelstein, "Is Philo Mentioned in Rabbinic Literature?" *Journal of Biblical Literature* 53 (1934): 142–49, to find two veiled references to Philo in Talmudic literature, one (*Midrash Tannaim* 6.7, ed. David Zvi Hoffmann, p. 27) warning that one should not, like "Peloni" ("someone"), attempt to mix the wisdom of Israel with that of secular lore, and the other (Tosefta *Yebamot* 3.4.244; Babylonian Talmud, *Yoma* 66b) questioning whether "Peloni" has a share in the world to come. But since "Peloni" is a common word for "someone," it seems hard to believe that it would necessarily refer to a particular person, Philo.
35. David T. Runia, *Philo in Early Christian Literature: A Survey* (Assen: Van Gorcum, 1993), 3–7, 15.
36. Morton Smith, *Clement of Alexandria and a Secret Gospel of Mark* (Cambridge: Harvard University Press, 1973), 446–52.
37. Diana Delia, "The Population of Roman Alexandria," *Transactions of the American Philological Association* 118 (1988): 288.
38. Runia, *Philo in Early Christian Literature,* 220.

39. See ibid., 15, who cites Albert Harkavy, "Abu Yusuf Ya'qub al Qirqisani on the Jewish Sects," in *Ya'qub al Qirquisani on Jewish Sects and Christianity,* ed. Bruno Chiesa and Wilfrid Lockwood, *Judentum und Umwelt* 10 (Frankfurt: Peter Lang, 1984), 49–90, translation of Russian article originally published in 1894; Hartwig Hirschfeld, "The Arabic Portion of the Cairo Genizah at Cambridge VII," *Jewish Quarterly Review* 17 (1905): 65–68; and Samuel Poznanski, "Philon dans l'ancienne littérature judéo-arabe," *Revue des Études juives* 50 (1905): 10–31.
40. See Runia, *Philo in Early Christian Literature,* 16, and the scholarship that he cites.

Exegetical Theology and Divine Suffering in Jewish Thought

Michael Fishbane

It is an honor to participate in this volume in celebration of Zev Garber. His lifework has been devoted to the phenomenon of Jewish suffering and its study, including the pedagogies of its cultural transmission. In this regard, he has also focused on the exegetical uses and transformations of this subject, for good and ill, in both the scholarly and the popular culture. For these reasons, I would like to contribute an essay that shall attempt to set forth some of the Jewish expressions of our subject—in a way that seeks to illuminate some of the inner structures and trajectories of divine suffering in Jewish sources, and the ways they conjoin with the topic of the sufferings of Israel. The topic of divine suffering has many striking resonances in the oldest rabbinic sources, some of which might even unsettle the unsuspecting student on account of their theological boldness and similarity to various non-Jewish images. Indeed, some of the material is replete with images that represent God's body and feelings in highly concrete and dramatic terms. As a result, many readers have recoiled from these strong depictions. In fact, a host of medieval Karaite, Christian, and Islamic authors have repeatedly reviled such images—and even labeled some of them "blasphemies *contra Deum*." There have also been rabbinic commentators on the Talmud and Midrash who have sought to defuse the charged current by contending that these various images of God are either figurative tropes or do not really mean what they say. Rabbeinu Hananel (990–1053), R. Yitzhak ben Yedaiah, and the Maharsha (1555–1631) are all cases in point. *Dor dor ve-dorshav*: each generation has its own exegetical presuppositions and proclivities. For my part, I shall attempt in what follows to take the manifest content of these sources seriously on their own terms—namely, as vibrant exegetical artifacts that formulate their content in and through the process of scriptural interpretation. I wish to call this phenomenon exegetical theology and deem it one of the most basic and constitutive structures of the Jewish religious imagination.

What does exegetical theology entail, and how does it bear on our theme of divine suffering? As I shall understand it here, exegetical theology entails the notion that theological ideas in Jewish sources are variously generated or justified by exegetical acts related to the Hebrew Bible, in the first instance, and that this content is then studied and reinterpreted again and again, with ensuing variations and transformations, in all the subsequent stages of their reception. Accordingly, we cannot separate the theological content from its concrete modes of formulation and presentation—even if (or when) the received literary versions of the material are considerably more condensed or fragmentary than the teachings were at the time of their original production or articulation. This means that we can only know this theology by engaging with the materials as they are now before us. And this brings me to a final introductory point, and that is that the teachings about divine suffering we shall now examine are not abstract theological *dicta*, but concrete and specific exegetical events. Accordingly, their interpretation and appreciation will require a thick description rooted in the inherent nature and complexities of these very exegetical acts and traditions. Only in this way may we hope to enter the circle of evidence and retrieve its meaning on its own terms. I see no other way.

When it comes to exegetical theology, sometimes the smallest textual detail can make the biggest bang. A good case in point is the orthographic variant in Job 13:15, where Job says, *hen yiqteleini lo/lo' 'ayahel*. This can either mean "Though He [God] slay me, yet will I trust in Him" (if one reads the grapheme *lo* pronominally, as does the Massoretic *qere*), or "He may well slay me; I may have no hope" (if one reads *lo'* as the negative particle *lamed-'alef*, as does the Massoretic *ketiv*). The Mishnah (*Sotah* IV.5) preserves an exegetical homily by R. Yehoshua ben Hyrkanos that adopts the first option, and then proposes that Job served God "out of love."

The same orthographic variants also affect the meaning of Isa. 63:9. However, the issue now goes far beyond an individual theological attitude (like Job's) and bears on bold theological predications about God himself—both his feelings and his behavior. Let me briefly remind the reader of the details, since this biblical passage has been of foundational importance for the theme of divine suffering in Jewish thought.

According to the Massoretic text and tradition, Isa. 63:9 is to be read: *be-khol tzaratam lo tzar*, "In all their sufferings [or travails] he [God] suffered [or endured travails]." The terms here all seem straightforward enough, even if it is not really clear just what is entailed by this reference to divine suffering. But our text does not simply pose a semantic difficulty, as important as this is. It also poses a larger problem bearing on the thematic content of the entire passage. For if we read this verse as just recited, then one must also note, first, that it introduces the topic of divine suffering into a unit focused on the mighty acts of divine deliverance and, second, that there is a contradiction between the clause that comes right before it, which speaks of God's independent role as the nation's redeemer, and the one that comes just after, which speaks of an angelic intermediary performing the redemption. Clearly this is a theological mess.

But help is on the way, through the testimony of the Septuagint version at verse 9. For once we observe that the old Greek text has the phrase *ou presbus oude angelos*, "neither a messenger nor an angel," it is immediately evident that it read the Hebrew letters *tzade-resh* as *tzir*, "messenger," and not *tzar*, "trouble," and that it also renders the Hebrew negative particle *lo'* (*lamed-'alef*), and not the pronoun *lo* (*lamed-vav*). This dual evidence resolves the textual difficulties I have just noted and allows one to confidently reconstruct the original phrasing of the passage as follows: "He [God] became their deliverer in all their troubles (*be-khol tzaratam*); neither a messenger nor an angel of his presence delivered them; [but] in his love and pity he himself redeemed them." Significantly just this is also the thrust of a well-known ancient midrash found in *Sifre Deuteronomy* 301, which emphasizes that the deliverance from Egypt was by God alone—not by any intermediary.[1]

Our reconstruction thus fits in with the overall theology of Isa. 63:7–19; but this is not the text that affected Jewish theology so drastically. The one that did—and which recites the phrase "*be-khol tzaratam lo tzar*" (in all their sufferings he suffered)—is clearly a subsequent exegetical transformation of the original scriptural content. Not only does it disrupt the main train of thought, it also clearly cuts across two separate topics. I must underscore this striking point, given the very rich and remarkable afterlife of this topic, all based on the new rendition. I would formulate the matter as follows. The foundational formulation of divine travail or suffering in scripture is itself a radical act of exegetical theology, which inscribed its own voice into the text. Later exegetes would never be so bold. Indeed, for all their theological assertiveness with the language of scripture, and the theologies of suffering they produced, no one ever had the temerity to incorporate his views into the scriptural text itself. For them, scripture was scripture, and Midrash Midrash; but here, for one fateful moment, the two are interfused. *Mirabile dictu!*

Let us now see what this textual transformation produced.

I

Reviewing the range of evidence, found primarily in sources deriving from the Land of Israel and its sages between the second and fourth centuries CE, I would propose that two theological mentalities predominate and provide the poles around which a variety of subtypes constellate. The first of these core mentalities presents a theological structure of divine suffering in which God is *with* the people of Israel in their historical sufferings or tribulations—not as a God of redemptive power, who is with them to protect or rescue them (as one might expect from the biblical formulation and its Ancient Near Eastern cognates), but as a God who endures and partakes of the troubles befalling the people. In these instances, we are dealing with modes of divine suffering oriented toward the conditions of Israel's historical experience or fate. By contrast, the second core mentality presents a theological structure in which God *responds to* the destruction of the Temple and the exile of the nation (which he himself has perpetrated or permitted) in very personal terms—not solely or primarily as an event of sympathetic sorrow, but as a matter of individual loss and lamentation. In these instances we are dealing mainly with a mode of divine suffering oriented toward the conditions of God's own experience, as he is personally affected by the events at hand.

I fully grant that this bifurcation is a bit overgeneralized, insofar as the record is sometimes a bit more mixed. But this said, I would still contend that this twofold categorization does fair justice to the prevailing theological structures and mythic images that have come down to us and provides a preliminary delineation of the evidence.

I begin with the first type which, as just mentioned, involves diverse modes of correlation between the travail or suffering of Israel and God. The texts provide evidence of this correlation in various detail—sometimes focusing on one dominant element, and sometimes presenting several of them together. It is important to be attuned to this, for it provides the basic data for how the subject of divine suffering was formulated and how it developed.

This is evident in one of the earliest strata of materials, preserved in the *Mekhilta de-Rabbi Ishmael, Bo'* 14. Hereby we find the themes of divine servitude, suffering, and exile in one editorial unit, but without any real thematic integration between them. Thus our collection opens with a bold mythic reading of the historical report that "all the hosts of the Lord went out" of Egypt. Without further ado, and beyond any reasonable expectation, we are told that the "hosts" referred to are in fact the "heavenly hosts" themselves. Nothing in scripture has prepared us for this striking reading, or also for its exegetical sequel, which opens with the assertion that "[w]henever the Israelites were in bondage [or enslaved; *meshu'abaddin*], the Shekhinah as it were is in bondage [*meshu'abbedet*] with them." What does this mean? The proof-text adduced hardly seems to help. For the passage cited is the opening clause of Exod. 24:10, which speaks of a vision of God on high, under whose feet there is "*ke-ma'aseh livnat ha-sapir*." Clearly, the plain-sense of these words is that the dome of heaven upon which God is enthroned was of "the likeness of a pavement of sapphire." But this can hardly be its meaning in this exegetical context. We must therefore deduce that what was seen on high was God involved in some manner of brickwork, just like the people Israel on earth. To be sure, this point is not explicated here, but later formulations of this midrash[2] in *Leviticus* and *Songs Rabba* are much more forthcoming and make it clear that the noun *ma'aseh* was understood to refer to some divine labor, and the noun *livnat* (or "pavement") was taken to allude to the *leveinim*, or "bricks," made by the slaves below. But the boldness of this mythic exemplification of divine bondage notwithstanding, we are still left to ponder the nature of the correlation. In what way did Israel's enslavement affect this divine performance? There is certainly no indication that this heavenly bondage was undertaken as a sympathetic participation in the people's plight. That would be a real hermeneutical leap.[3]

The precise nature of the divine travail is also not resolved by the ensuing citation of Isa. 63:9, presented as a supplementary proof-text. Indeed, all that we can presume from its addition here is, I think, that some later tradent understood the divine labor to be a kind of divine suffering, but he tells us nothing about what that means. The statement that "in all their troubles he was troubled" could just as much indicate that Israel's suffering somehow implicates or affects God, as that God sympathetically or willingly identifies with the people's travail. We have no way of knowing. And in any case, however we resolve the meaning of the divine bondage or travail, these two motifs are to be kept completely distinct from the subsequent and independent unit concerning the Shekhinah's accompaniment of Israel in its various exiles. This unit only says that God was *with* the people during her displacements; it says nothing about any divine travail or suffering. It is notable that in other old versions depicting the movements of the Shekhinah, the topic of exile does not even occur. The emphasis is only on God's near or protective presence. Nothing else.

It is only in Amoraic sources that the three themes of divine servitude, exile, and suffering come together in one integrated exegetical unit. This occurs in the remarkable reinterpretation of Lam. 2:3 found in the *Pesikta de-Rav Kahana* 17.5, and elsewhere. This biblical verse is part of a series of passages dealing with God's punishment of Zion and her people, and states that God "withdrew his right arm before the enemy." That is to say, God withdrew his protection of Zion upon the advent of the enemy by putting his arm behind him, so that the enemy could enter Zion and destroy it. The phrase indicating this withdrawn protection is *heishiv 'ahor yemino mipnei 'oyeiv*. In counterpoint, the midrash offers a stunning inversion of this punitive act. God is now said to have responded to the sight of Israelite soldiers being led into exile with their arms tied behind them. And recalling his own scriptural assertion, *'immo anokhi be-tzarah*, which means here, "I shall be with him in trouble" (Ps. 91:15), God says if his people are "in trouble" he will also not be at ease. Thereupon he intentionally puts his own arm behind him—*mipnei 'oyeiv*, a phrase that is now taken to mean "because of what the enemy" had done to his people. Hence God's decision to act in this way is now presented as his deliberate imitation of, and his sympathetic participation in, Israel's suffering. And this act of intentional suffering also extends to the ensuing passage, where the exegete expands upon this mythic correlation and proclaims that for as long as the people of Israel are "in bondage" (*meshu'abbadin*) God's arm would likewise be "in bondage." Quite clearly the old motif of God's servitude has undergone a decisive and fundamental transformation; it is now specifically applied to the sufferings of exile and correlated with the theme of divine travail. Motifs that were only editorially conjoined in the *Mekhilta* are now reused here in a thematically integrated way. Moreover, the mythic realism of this passage, which introduces God as a speaker and actor, boldly infuses these theological assertions with a more poignant and dramatic pathos. The divine suffering is not merely a verbal trope, for the ear, but something to be visually imagined as well. This adds to its imposing tenor.[4]

* * *

I wish now to turn to some deeper emotional valences of divine sorrow or suffering—all in response to Israel's travail. The focus shifts from images of God's arm, to the theme of his cry and tears. They, too, are expressed with a poignant and dramatic mythic realism.

Let us start with a teaching from *b. Hagigah* 5b, which has been transmitted in the name of Rav. It involves an interpretation of Jer. 13:17. Just before this, the prophet called out to the people to "attend" to God's word of warning and not "be haughty" (v. 15). He now goes on to say, "For if you will not give heed, I shall weep in my innermost being [*ba-mistarim tivkeh nafshi*]—because of the pride [*mipnei geivoh*]." This stated, Jeremiah concludes the oracle by reasserting that the onset of tears are because "the flock of the Lord is taken captive." According to the plain-sense of the passage, the entire oracle is spoken by the prophet; but this is not the way it is taken up and transformed in our Talmudic passage. In it, Rav casts God as the speaker of the first part, who is made to say that if Israel will not listen to his warning, he will then go into a "hidden place" (*be-mistarim*) in heaven, and cry there for his people. Subsequent teachers puzzled about the nature of "the pride" because of the odd spelling. One view states that God would cry because of the destroyed Temple, the pride of Israel, whereas the other states that the tears were for the damaged glory of the Kingdom of Heaven.[5]

The reports of this teaching and its annotations are quite brief; but enough is preserved for us to observe several things: first, a prior tradition of divine suffering in heaven clearly conditioned the particular exegesis of Rav—for nothing in the text even remotely suggests this mythic teaching; and second, this topic was studied in the rabbinic academies, and different attempts were made to discern the motivation for the divine tears. In this regard, a close reading shows that yet another stratum follows these two. Its clear purpose is to reconcile the new midrashic predication of divine withdrawal and tears with older biblical and rabbinic traditions stating that there is no such thing as divine sorrow, only joy. A solution is then suggested by drawing a distinction between the inner and outer parts of the heavenly Temple—a distinction imposed on the text by a clever explanation of the word *geivoh*. The conclusion is that while there is only divine joy in the inner sanctum, any sorrow that occurs takes place outside of it. But this is not the end of the unit. With a dogged persistence, yet another contradiction is adduced, now on the basis of Isa. 22:12—since this text clearly asserts that God calls out for mourning and suffering because of the doom wrought upon Zion, and this call was presumed to implicate a divine sorrow from within the heavenly realm. But this additional contradiction is quickly dismissed by the final redactor, who simply states that God's mourning over the Temple must be deemed a special circumstance, in which case God does indeed cry within his heavenly Shrine. Our unit now breaks off, for with this last point we are effectively brought back to the initial interpretation of Rav, who as you will recall had taught that God cries within his Temple if the people would not heed his warnings of disaster.

Though complex, I have presented this brief dissection of the Talmudic passage for good reason. I believe that through it we can draw several conclusions of interest and value for our subject. Indeed, four points can be adduced. First, this unit shows the great power of exegesis to radically transform the theological meaning of a biblical text—in our case, the subject shifts from the prophet to God, and the suffering shifts from something inward to a hidden place within God's own Temple. Second, this unit shows how a piece of exegesis is not necessarily or only conditioned by issues inherent in the text itself, but by living theological notions known to the sages. Third, this unit exemplifies how theological topics derived through exegesis were also taken up in the ancient schools, and their details variously clarified and resolved. Finally, this unit shows how subsequent deliberations of older exegetical matters took them as theological *dicta* that needed to be harmonized with other texts and traditions. Hence, even if we cannot ever directly answer the question as to whether the sages believed their theological myths, we can at least say, from cases like this, that as an exegetical event becomes a part of tradition, and is taken up in the ongoing course or curriculum of study, its status and validity as an act of theological predication changes, and the exegetes themselves are no longer simply proposing or producing a hermeneutical possibility, but are rather participating in a process of its verification and reinforcement. Moreover, as a unit such as this one enters yet other streams of rabbinic culture and theology, different aspects of it are taken up and pondered—all on the strong presumption that the received teaching is now a traditional truth, and only the true status or meaning of its elements are subject to further consideration. I shall return to this point later on, for I deem it to be of much importance.

For now, let us return to the topic at hand and consider other cases of divine suffering that portray an even more emotional portrait. Enter *b. Berakhot* 59a. In this brief unit, a necromancer is asked by a sage to explain the meaning of a certain word used to depict some sort of earth-rumbling, and the diviner forthwith provides a mythic aetiology to the effect that "[w]hen the Holy One, blessed be he, remembers his children sunk in sorrow among the nations of the world, he emits two tears into the Great Sea, and his voice goes forth from one end of the world to the other." Rav Qatina, who was the necromancer's interlocutor, demurred and offered a reasonable rebuttal of the mytheme; by contrast, the anonymous redactor of the unit seems more sympathetic to this proposal and suggests that the real reason Rav Qatina blew off the necromancer was that he did not want other Jews to follow the teachings of such a person. In any event, it is most striking that the diviner simply gives the myth pure and simple, without any added justification or scriptural support. It thus speaks volumes for a certain type of living mythic consciousness in rabbinic antiquity. By contrast, as might be expected, Rav Qatina and his colleagues all offer scriptural proof-texts for the rumbling—a fact that also speaks volumes for their own type of mythmaking. For them, divine suffering is marked in scripture. The variety of their sources also attests to a living mythic reality.[6]

R. Levi takes the process of exegetical theology much further. In one teaching (reported by R. Yehoshua of Sikhnin), the word *tamati* in the Song of Songs (5:2) is applied to Israel. It is not taken literally as "my pure one," but as referring to the symbiosis of God and Israel. Indeed, Israel is actually referred to by God as "My twin [*te'omati*]." The matter is further developed by a parable about twins. "Just as one will feel the head pain of the other, so the Holy One, blessed be he, said, 'I shall be with him in affliction' [*'immo 'anokhi be-tzarah*, Ps. 91:15]." Quite certainly, this mythic exegesis and theology is bold enough, but a variant takes the matter even further. I refer to another teaching of R. Levi, found in *Midrash Eicha*.[7]

He comments there on the lament, "My eye, my eye flows with tears," found in Lam. 1:16. In context, this is the outcry of the human eulogist, and the repeated evocation "my eye" is clearly for stylistic emphasis. But R. Levi does not let matters rest with the plain-sense, and projects a radical theology of divine suffering into the passage. He first evokes the analogy of a doctor who has one eye that ails him, and who says: "Let my [one good] eye weep for the other." With this image, the exegete introduces a formal separation between the two eyes—these being the two eyes of one person. Hence if the biblical verse states, " *'eini 'eini yordah mayim*," where the word "eye" is doubled but the verb is in the singular, this must mean that only one eye was tearing. Thus the physician cries over his one damaged eye (*'eini*), and weeps over it with the other good one (*'eini yordah mayim*). The theological application of this parable is not left to speculation. After giving the parable, R. Levi immediately draws the following conclusion: " 'Israel is called the eye of the Holy One, blessed be he' . . . (thus God) said, as it were, 'Let My eye weep for My eye.' " And if this were not enough, a proof-text is adduced to show that Israel is itself an eye of God, and that he laments over it. The verse used to prove this point is from Zech. 9:1, "*ki la-YHWH 'ein ha-'adam, ve-khol shivtei yisrael*." This statement apparently means something like: "For every human eye is turned to the Lord, and so indeed all the tribes of Israel," and its gist is that all humankind turns to God for aid and salvation. But in this exegetical context the biblical verse must mean no less than "For the Lord has a human eye, and that is the whole nation of Israel."

Here is a mythic theology of divine suffering like no other in ancient rabbinic Midrash, for hereby the tears of God are for a physical wound affecting Israel—who is deemed to be God's own eye. How boldly should we take this image? One may be inclined to take the reference to Israel as the "eye of God" as a mere figure of speech, evoked as a trope for some divine-human symbiosis, and thus not as a bolder mythic configuration. But if so, we still have to reckon with the parable that has been employed, as well as a proof-text that seems to push the tropic envelope. Just what does R. Levi mean when he says something like: "for God has an eye, and that is the [human] people called Israel"? I shall leave the matter open. But however one decides, we must again observe just how the meaning of a rabbinic theology of suffering is inextricable from its concrete exegetical presentation.

* * *

Before we move on to medieval matters, let me briefly mention several cases in the Midrash and Talmud that exemplify the other main type spoken of earlier; namely, cases where the divine suffering focuses on God's personal loss or affliction. Different subtypes can be detected. In one, the emphasis is on God's loss of his Temple. For example, we read in *b. Berakhot* 3a that R. Eleazar answers a query concerning the number of watches in the night. He asserts that there are three, not four, and proves his point by an exegesis of Jer. 25:30. This passage had allowed the prophet to announce God's roar of doom over his land (*naveihu*), soon to be destroyed. It is now midrashically employed to convey God's lament over his ruined Temple (*naveihu*), which he does three times a night, at the onset of each watch. This matter is marked, according to the sage, by the threefold use of the verb "roar" (*sha'ag*) in this passage. Such a divine wailing is therefore periodic and perpetual, a lamentation of loss, enunciated by the perpetrator of the disaster. In other cases, the dual focus of the personal divine lament over the Temple is explicitly conjoined. Note such outcries as "*Oy li 'al beiti*," "Woe is Me for My Shrine," or even "*Oy li meh 'asiti*" "Woe is Me, what have I done?"—for the Temple is destroyed and God fears ridicule among the nations.

In a second subtype of this theme, the emphasis is placed on the extraordinary suffering of God at the dispersion of the nation. A striking instance is found in the *Pesikta de-Rav Kahana* 15.4. Here R. Yohanan depicts the banishment of the northern and southern tribes. After the latter event, God wails aloud, in the words of Jer. 10:19, "*Oy li 'al shivri*," "Woe is Me for My hurt" or even "Woe is Me for I am broken." His brother-in-law, R. Simeon ben Lakish, went even further. He taught that when the northern tribes went into exile God himself "raised a lament" over them, but when Judah and Benjamin were dispersed he was utterly spent and without the power to mourn—hence he called for mourners to lament and cry over the people and over himself, a feature that the sage finds marked in the text itself; he points out that God requests Jeremiah to call the mourners to mourn *'aleinu*, "over us," and to cry tears for both the nation and God as well.

This motif of human tears on God's behalf is developed in a long mythic narrative found in *Midrash Lamentations Rabba* (*petiha* 24). In the boldest of terms, it brings together many motifs found in earlier traditions Thus after God says "Woe is Me" for what he has done, Metatron offers to cry for God but is firmly rejected, and God threatens to withdraw into his innermost chamber. Later, when God goes to the angels to invite them to behold the destruction, he repeats this lament, now wailing "*Oy li 'al beiti*," "Woe is Me for My Shrine," and requests Jeremiah to bring an embassy of the patriarchs to come before him and to mourn his loss. As this event begins to transpire, God again breaks into lament, and now intones this most terrifying conclusion: "*Oy la-melekh*," "Woe to the king who was successful in his youth, but who in his old age was not." One might wonder which is the more awesome point: the mythic presentation of a God who suffers loss and vigor, or the very act of its depiction by the mythmaker, who has not only projected a stunning theology of divine suffering through the sources, but has also suggested that the divine sorrow, so often portrayed in the tradition, may really be the suffering of an aging deity, long past his prime of vigor and might. An old midrashic unit in the *Mekhilta de-Rabbi Ishmael* had once drawn a comparison between God and kings of flesh and blood. Among the distinctions of God is that his power never wanes, that he is ever vigorous and successful, and that he does not age or fall into senescence. Our text has lost this theological confidence altogether, as it depicts an awesome divine sorrow on high.

It calls to mind another astonishing text, this time from 3 Enoch, where R. Ishmael ascends into the heights in order to view God and the mysteries. He is guided on this journey by Metatron, who explains the secret things heaven by heaven—including the letters engraved upon the divine Throne, as well as the deeds of all generations, which are printed upon a curtain spread out before God. It would thus appear that the mysteries included the secrets of history and the nature of divine providence. This is confirmed by the conclusion to Ishmael's vision, which utilizes many of the exegetical motifs we have been tracing. However, these are no longer the constructions of exegesis, but the very content and terms of esoteric myth and truth. As the sage peers behind the curtain, seeing what is beyond mortal sight, he envisions "the right arm of God cast behind him [*nishlahat 'ahor*] because of the destruction of the Temple" (chap. 48a). Ishmael hears the souls of the righteous reciting the old biblical invocation, "Arise, arise put on strength, O arm of the Lord" (Isa. 51:9); whereupon, "at that moment, the right arm of God would cry, and five rivers of tears flowed from its fingers into the Great Sea, making the whole earth quake." Several new citations are then adduced to support this point.[8]

This mythic vision brings us into the supernal realms, where now the sorrow and suffering of God are enacted in the most secret and esoteric sanctuary. Only a trace of this sorrow flows down to the earthly realms, and only for those in the know. The divine arm is portrayed as some hidden and hypostatic reality, in a state of withdrawal, and emitting tears. From it, God's suffering flows into the historical realm in a stream of sorrows. Even the holy souls above know that this suffering has no redemptive effect and thus evoke the hope that the arm will soon arise and put on strength. But the arm only weeps. The time of salvation has not come.

II

Having crossed the bridge into the mystical realms, we may now consider some of the new transformations of our theme in these sources. But let me first briefly advert to a point made earlier; namely that, with the growth and study of teachings in the academies, topics that were formulated as exegetical constructions in one midrashic stratum become truths of tradition that are explored or clarified in subsequent ones. Thus, as midrashic teachings about divine suffering are received and taken up in the stream of medieval mystical speculation and interpretation, these older exegetical formulations become the subject of a profound esoteric mystery and are taken to symbolize or dramatize various features and truths of the supernal structure of the Godhead. This is a remarkable transformation, particularly since some of the dynamics even refer to crises in the very harmony of Divinity. It would be possible to exemplify these matters with reference to many of the themes of divine suffering discussed earlier. But for the sake of focus and concision in this context, let me simply mention one or two that occur in the book of *Zohar* and are taken up later by Rabbi Moshe Cordovero (1522–70). Taking theology to another level, they express a theosophy of suffering in the very depths of the Godhead—even one that extends outward into historical reality, as we shall see.

There are many variations on our theme in the *Zohar*, but the following instance is, I think, both paradigmatic and instructive. It occurs in *parashat Vayera'*, in the context of a discussion of the binding of Isaac (I.220b). We have there a cluster of teachings using Isa. 63:9, taking its content seriously at two esoteric levels—in accordance with the two Massoretic spellings found in the *qere* and *ketiv* traditions. That is, the Zoharic authorship perceives in this verse two levels of esoteric truth: one is derived from the traditional recitation of the verse with the pronoun *lo* (*lamed-vav*); while the other is derived from the traditional writing of the verse with the negative particle *lo'* (*lamed-'alef*). In the first of these instances, the verse is interpreted to mean that when Israel is in distress, the Holy One, blessed be he, is himself "with them," which is to say, in Zoharic parlance, that the masculine gradation called *Tiferet* somehow shares in or partakes of the suffering of the people Israel. This reading is based on the *qere*-reading of *lo* with a *vav*, namely, it understands the reference to the fact that "He" suffers as referring to this masculine dimension of Divinity within the sefirotic hierarchy. And this point is reinforced by the fact that the gradation called *Tiferet* can also be symbolized by the letter *vav*. Thereafter, we are also told that the written or *ketiv* tradition, which has *lo'* with an *'alef*, also marks a profound esoteric truth; and that truth is that the suffering of Israel ascends above the gradation of *Tiferet* to an even more supernal place (*'atar 'ila'ah yetir*)—symbolized here by the primal letter *'alef*. In this exalted realm, we are now told, there is neither anger nor suffering.

Thus in a manner not further explicated, the historical suffering of Israel effects a suffering that extends to the upper reaches of the Godhead, which has been primordially prepared "to suffer with them" (*le-misbal 'imahon*). However, the text adds that this divine suffering also extends downward—to the lowest reaches of the sefirotic gradations; for we are also told that Israel, in the sorrows of exile, constitutes the very dwelling places (*mishkenotav*) of the Holy One, and that his own *Shekhinah* is with them in this suffering. What all this seems to say is that, insofar as the people of Israel are in some sense the historical embodiment or actuality of the divine Presence (that is, they are the feminine gradation of Divinity known as *Shekhinah*), their own historical exile and suffering affect some profound disharmony and loss for *Tiferet* as well, who in some radical sense is separated from a supernal union with his heavenly consort and suffers longingly for her pain and his loss. Clearly, there is some profound interfusing of Israel and a dimension of the divine reality, such that God's suffering for the people is also an inner-divine suffering. Or perhaps we should better say that Israel's own suffering actualizes a vast inner-divine suffering, insofar as historical reality is itself a dimension of, and partakes in, the mystery of the divine Whole.

Three centuries later, Rabbi Moshe Cordovero comments on these matters in his great tract of mystical ethics, *Tomer Devorah*. He does not mince words. For example, when talking about Israel's relationship to God, and the issue of their suffering and his own, he attributes the following lament to the blessed Holy One: "O what can I do to Israel, since they are my relatives, with whom I have a relationship of the flesh" (*ve-hem qerovai, she'eir basar li 'imahem*), and he glosses this point by saying, "For they [the Community of Israel] are the spouse [*bat zug*] of the Holy One"—no more and no less. The great magnitude of this divine suffering is further articulated in Cordovero's explication of the foregoing passage from the *Zohar*. After citing Isa. 63:9 as a proof of God's suffering with Israel, he also speaks of two gradations of this suffering, but he goes on to specify them more fully. In his view, the one first is symbolized by the word *lo*, "He," spelled *lamed-vav*, and pertains to a suffering affecting the chief binary structure of divine providence, called here the *du partzufin* (and referring to the two divine facets known as *Tiferet* and *Malkhut*). Beyond this is a second level of the suffering, symbolized by the word *lo'* spelled with an *'alef*. For Cordovero, this spelling indicates that God's travail ascends to the exalted place he calls *ha-pele' ha-'elyon*, "the Supernal Wonder"—which in his theology must refer to the recondite sefirotic gradation of *Keter*, the supernal "Crown" at the apex of the sefirotic hierarchy—the source of every beneficence that flows down into Being.[9] It may be noted that this supernal place called *pele'*, or "Wonder," is obviously an esoteric anagram of the letters of the word *'alef*—now spelled in reverse, of course. Like the *'alef*, the wondrous mystery of Being is virtually ineffable.

Cordovero also adduces another striking proof-text about divine suffering. This one is taken from Judg. 10:16, which he construes to mean: "And his [God's] soul was grieved for the misery of Israel," and which he glosses as indicating that "He [God] cannot bear their pain [*lefi she-'eino sovel tza'aram*] and disgrace, since they are *she'eirit nahalato*"—that is, the very corporate reality of his being, his very own partner to whom he is related (*she'eir basar . . . 'imahem*).

And if this were not explicit enough, take note of the following. In the spiritual tract just noted, the master informs the reader just what mental intentions he should have in mind while performing certain acts of kindness, so that while doing deeds of beneficence on earth one can also affect certain repairs or benefits (*tiqqunim*) in the supernal realms. Thus while performing the *mitzvah* of visiting the sick (*bikkur holim*), one should concentrate on the two "Supernal Sick Ones" (*ba-holim ha-'elyonim*)—the *Shekhinah* and the Holy One, *Tiferet*, and provide them restoration and sustenance through study of the Torah and performance of the commandments. With respect to the suffering of the *Shekhinah*, who deprives herself of the supernal bounty because of her great travail, Cordovero adduces the verse cited earlier from Judges 10, with appropriate gender changes, namely, "Her soul was grieved for the misery of Israel." With respect to the suffering of the Holy One, who wanders from his place in longing for his beloved, he cites from Isa. 53:5, "For he was wounded because of our transgressions [*ve-hu' meholal mipesha'einu*], crushed because of our iniquities."[10]

Surely this is an astonishing proof-text, for it is taken from the so-called Suffering Servant sections of Isaiah, whose meaning had been contested ever since its application to Jesus of Nazareth in the New Testament. Indeed, no less a person than Nachmanides (1194–1270), in the show-trial in Barcelona, had to rebut the claim that this passage made a precise reference to the suffering and death of the messiah of the Christians.[11]

And here it is applied to no less than the Holy One on high, who, it is now said, "was wounded" by the sins of Israel. For indeed, because of their transgressions, Israel was cast into exile, and this inflicted wounds of suffering upon the *Shekhinah*, to which they are ontologically related, and thus also to the Holy One, who is both the heavenly consort of the *Shekhinah* and also, as we have noted earlier, the marriage partner of Israel—his *bat zug*. And lest anyone think that this wound has been somehow effected upon God, since the verb used is the passive participle *meholal*, Cordovero (or is it a scribe?) dispels all doubt by interpolating the phrase *lirtzono* into the scriptural citation. Thereby all would know that this divine suffering was undertaken "willingly," and not under any compulsion or duress—even if, as the author goes on to say, *u-refu'at sheneihem be-yadeinu*, that "the healing of the two [the *Shekhinah* and *Tiferet*] are in our hands."

Such a formulation leaves one speechless, for now it is humans who must bind and heal the wounds of God. This puts an awesome spiritual burden on human action, which in other contexts of Cordovero's theology must be ground in acts of repentance and the reformation of consciousness into an agent of thinking the good and acting on its behalf at all times. This human dimension is said to take its direction from Divinity itself—and this allows me to mention one other component of Cordovero's theology of divine suffering, which I deem to be truly remarkable. It is given powerful expression through his exegesis of the phrase *mi 'el kamokha*, "Who is a god like You?!," from the beginning of Micah 7:18. The sage takes this clause to be the cardinal expression of divine beneficence. In his view, this phrase "teaches that the Holy One, blessed be he, is a king who is insulted, and bears [or suffers] this insult [*sovel 'elbon*] in a manner that is beyond all human understanding." For, he goes on to say, God is omniscient and providential overall, such that "there is no moment" when humankind and all existence are not nourished by the vast bounty of the divine overflow, which pours down upon each person, "enabling him to live and move his limbs." Hence, even if a person should misuse this vitality, and even pervert it through sinful acts, Cordovero says that "this power is not withheld in any way," but rather, in his awesome forbearance, God "suffers this insult" and continues to pour forth the full vitality and bounty of existence. God is thus a god of enduring suffering, who gives ceaselessly of his great beneficence—despite the fact that it may be misused. For such mercy and goodness the prophet exults, "Who is a god like You?!"

With this teaching, a nobility and dignity is given to divine suffering like no other I know.

III

I wish now, near the end, to turn to a final expression of our theme in Jewish theological sources. It takes us into the depths of the subject of the conjoint suffering of God and Israel, and the power of exegetical theology to transform earlier traditions and present them as religious truth. The teachings I wish to discuss here come from the darkest horrors of Jewish life in Warsaw, between 1939 and 1943. I am referring to the Torah expositions or *derashot* delivered mostly on Sabbaths by the Piezecner Rebbe, Kalonymos Kalmish Shapiro (1889–1943), also known as the "*Esh Kodesh*," after the title of his collection of teachings dealing with the "Holy Fire" of spiritual resistance, amid the conflagration and profanity that consumed Jewish life in Warsaw forever.[12]

Kalonymos Kalman takes us into the depths of an infinite divine sorrow and of an unutterable human desolation that came to find some solace in suffering God's own suffering. In this shared sorrow, something of the abyss of God's vast silence and hiddenness was filled with theological meaning and purpose; and in these awesome and anguished teachings about God's personal suffering the human person finds some meager strength—or strengthening, *mi-meile' yoter yekholim me'at le-hithazzeq*.

In the following, I shall focus on several teachings from the final years, 1940–43.

In one sermon from the winter of 1940, we are struck by the resonance of the "Servant Song" from Isaiah 53. On the one hand, Rabbi Kalonymos echoes Cordovero in a daring predication of this language of suffering on God himself, but he also applies the terms to Israel as well, and in so doing articulates a prayer of protest and anguish. The full human charge is softened somewhat by the assertion that this is a prayer of intercession by the archangel Michael, who sacrifices the souls of Israel on the heavenly altar, and says,

> Master of the universe, if your own sufferings [*yissurekha*] you can bear [*sovel*], and are forbearing regarding your wounded honor [*kevodekha ha-mehollal*], how nevertheless can you bear the sufferings of your children, and be forbearing regarding their wounds—*kol kakh*, to such an extent?![13]

Rabbi Kalonymos speaks further of divine forbearance a couple of weeks before Purim in 1943, when he speaks of God's "infinite" (*beli gevul*) and great suffering for the Jews. Here he offers a dramatic transformation of the old midrash in *Lamentations Rabba*, where God enters the innermost parts of his heavenly Temple to weep for Israel and rejects an angelic offer to weep on his behalf. The Rebbe now interprets this in an unexpected way. In his view, the angel requested that he cry for God precisely because he wanted these divine tears (which he strikingly calls *bekhiyas ha-Kivyokhl*) to descend into the world, for once this would happen the world could not bear it and would explode (*yitpotzetz*), and the enemies would be consumed by the spark of a single tear. But God did not heed this request, in part because the time of redemption was not at hand, and thus ascended even more into the recesses of his own hiddenness and sorrow, where his sorrow and suffering were hidden from all earthly and angelic comprehension. This place of hiddenness is not only the supernal depths of heaven (called *batei gava'i*, in an image recalling an older Talmudic midrash); this place of divine tears is also the Torah, and it is just here that the people of Israel can go to hear God's laments and to experience his sorrow.[14]

Let me conclude with one final teaching from the time of horrors, July 11, 1943. Here Rabbi Kalonymos distinguishes two poles of suffering. On the one hand, there are human sufferings endured "for our own sakes" (*ba'ad 'atzmeinu*)—whether these be for sins or for self-purification—and in these sufferings "he, blessed be he, just suffers with us" (*raq 'immanu sovel*); but there are also other sufferings—these being the sufferings of martyrdom for God's sake (*shel kiddush ha-Shem*)—in which "we, as it were, suffer with him" (*raq 'immo kivayakhol sovelim*). Such a suffering for God's sake may give a person the strength to endure the terrors, says the Rebbe; but he nevertheless calls out to God for salvation: "O save us [*hosha'na*], who learn your teaching, who are smitten on the cheek [*merutat lehi*], who are given to beatings [*netunim le-makkim*], [and] who suffer your suffering [*sovelim sovelakh*]."[15] No doubt you will again discern in this cry the language of Isaiah 53, though now with a surprising turn. In the prophetic passage, the sufferer suffers for another's sins; here Israel suffers with and for the suffering of God. But there is even more that must be noted. We are alerted to it by the cry of *hosha'na,* and the specific sequence of sufferings that are mentioned. From all this I have no doubt that Rabbi Kalonymos is citing and applying one of the *hosha'not* petitions recited during Sukkot and Hoshanah Rabba (this being the prayer called *'Om 'anokhi homah*).[16]

In that litany, the people that cry for salvation are called *golah ve-surah*, "exiled and cast-off," *kevushah ba-golah*, "crushed in the exile," and so on. Indeed all the tribulations refer to the sufferings of the people Israel. What is more, they bear the burden of God's punishment—as for example in the phrase, "*to'enet 'ulakh*," where the people are said to "bear your yoke"—the yoke being the tribulation imposed by God upon them (that is, "your yoke" is an objective genitive). I say all this because the later phrase, *sovelet sovlakh*, must be similarly understood; that is, it falls in line with the rest of the prayer and means that Israel suffers the suffering imposed by God upon them—and not that Israel suffers God's own suffering. But it is just this latter reading which the Rebbe finds in this text, and which he boldly utilizes in his homily. For him, the word *sovlakh*, "your suffering," is a subjective genitive that forcefully denotes that Israel suffers along with the suffering of God.

This is a most remarkable reversal of the primary sense of the prayer, and also a remarkable reversal of the entire theology of suffering that had developed since antiquity. For at the very beginning, on the basis of a reworking of an old prophetic passage (Isa. 63:9), there emerged a bold new theology of God's participatory and anguished suffering for the sorrows of Israel; whereas now, on the basis of a reconception of an old prayer, in which suffering Israel calls upon God for salvation and aid, we have an astonishing instance of the participatory and anguished suffering of Israel for God himself—no less.

Such is the power of exegetical theology. Through it, ancient truths and texts are received and revised, are lived and relived. In the present instance, it even makes possible a modality of self-transcendence; or at least a capacity to overcome evil and suffering with some strength—*u-vazeh mithazzeqet me'at.* "Because (Israel) knows that she suffers your sufferings," says Rabbi Kalonymos Kalman Shapiro, "she is able to be strengthened—somewhat."

And so, much depends upon where the observer is standing with respect to this theology. For those who have stood on the outside, all the teachings of this sort found in the Talmud can lead to the derisive label: *nefanda scriptura*, "abominable writings." But for those within, this imagery breathes pathos and compassion—even when spoken with the utmost irony and in darkest despair. Let the survivors therefore have the last word. The following lines are taken from a collection of poems written by Yankev Glatshtayn (1896–1971), entitled *Fun Mayn Gantsen Mi* (From All My Pain; 1953). They are part of an outcry called *Tefile.*[17]

> *Gist unz toyzenter yor af barg*
> *Un farhoylt dayn punim fun unz.*
>
> ....
>
> *Ch'daven zu dir fun a shtumen siddur,*
> *Mayn troyeriker Gott.*
>
> You pour out thousands of years on credit
> but hide your face from us.
>
> ....
>
> I pray to you from a mute prayer-book,
> O my suffering God!

Notes

1. See my fuller discussion in *Biblical Myth and Rabbinic Mythmaking* (Oxford: Oxford University Press, 2003), 132–35 (hereinafter BMRM). In the ensuing discussions, I have occasionally drawn from fuller analyses in that work, and provide the references to it in the notes.
2 Cited above (*Mekhilta de-Rabbi Ishmael, Bo'* 14).
3. See BMRM, 134–38.
4. Ibid., 147–50.

5. Ibid., 164.
6. Ibid., 162–64.
7. Edition of S. Buber (Vilna: Romm, 1899), 88.
8. See text published in *Synopse zur Hekhalot-Literatur,* ed. P. Schäfer (Tübingen: Mohr-Siebeck, 1981), 34–35 (Mss. Munich 40 and Vatican 228, respectively; paragraphs 68–70).
9. See *Tomer Devorah*, chapter 1 (phrase 4, *le-she'erit nahalato*).
10. Ibid., chapter 5 (practice 3).
11. See in *Kitvei RaMBaN,* ed. H. Chavel (Jerusalem: Mosad Ha-Rav Kook, 1964), 1:307 (and paragraphs 25–28); in his own interpretation of the passage (325) he takes the verb to mean "trembling" (not "pierced").
12. I have used the edition published in Jerusalem, 1960.
13. Ibid., 81.
14. Ibid., 158–61.
15. Ibid., esp. 191.
16. See in *Mahazor Sukkot, Shemini Atzeret, ve-Simhat Torah,* ed. D. Goldschmidt, completed by J. Fraenkel (Jerusalem: Koren, 1981), 175–76.
17. Yiddish text reprinted with English translation in *The Penguin Book of Modern Yiddish Verse,* ed. I. Howe, R. Wisse, and K. Schmeruk (New York: Penguin Books, 1988), 468–69.

Rabbi Abraham Joshua Heschel's Paths to God

Harold Kasimow

In his best-known work, *God in Search of Man,* a book that has been called "the single most sophisticated, profound and comprehensive statement within modern Judaic theology," Abraham Joshua Heschel (1907–72), one of the most significant Jewish thinkers of the twentieth century, expresses his deep concern over the decline of religion today.[1] This concern extends beyond the survival of Judaism to the survival of humanity itself. In a 1967 article he says:

> The cardinal problem is not the survival of religion, but the survival of man. What is required is a continuous effort to overcome hardness of heart, callousness, and above all to inspire the world with the Biblical image of man, not to forget that man without God is a torso, to prevent the dehumanization of man. For the opposite of human is not the animal. The opposite of the human is the demonic.[2]

It is with this prospect (essentially, the destruction of humanity) in mind that Heschel says, "The most serious problem is the absence of the problem."[3] What he means is that the modern world has been so taken over by atheism, agnosticism, and indifference to religion that most people do not even recognize that the absence of God in their lives is actually an issue.

From the first paragraph of *God in Search of Man*, Heschel seeks to examine the causes for the modern-day decline of religion. He starts with a provocative thesis. The central cause for the decline, he says, is not the rise of rationalism or secularism. The central cause lies within religion itself.

> Religion declined not because it was refuted, but because it became irrelevant, dull, oppressive, insipid. When faith is completely replaced by creed, worship by discipline, love by habit, . . . when religion speaks only in the name of authority rather than with the voice of compassion—its message becomes meaningless. (*GSM,* 3)

But Heschel acknowledges that the rationalistic and scientific worldview prevalent today is partly responsible for the disappearance of faith.

> It is characteristic of the inner situation of contemporary man that the plausible way to identify himself is to see himself in the image of a machine. . . . Man is simply "a machine into which we put what we call food and produce what we call thought." The definition itself goes back to the eighteenth century. Never before, however, has it been so widely accepted as plausible.[4]

As the rationalistic-scientific worldview becomes more sophisticated, it becomes more deeply materialistic. In a materialistic society our sense of immediacy begins to dominate more and more, while our sense of transcendence diminishes considerably.

When the exponents of reason went so far as to proclaim reason to be the only guide to truth, they in effect were saying that there was no longer any mystery that the human mind could not penetrate. "Whatever there is to know, that we shall know someday" (*GSM*, 34). When reason became the be-all and end-all, revelation became unnecessary.

Eighteenth-century thinkers attempted to harmonize reason and revelation by making revelation subject to the laws of reason, but they only made religion more irrelevant. As Heschel notes, "If science and religion are intrinsically identical, one of them must be superfluous. In such reconciliation religion is little more than bad science and naïve morality" (*WM*, 13). This opened the way for widespread atheism, agnosticism, and indifference to religion.

The rise in rationalism meant, in effect, that humanity no longer needed God. But starting with his dissertation in 1933, Heschel made a highly original contribution to biblical thought: he asserted that not only do we need God, but God needs us. For Heschel, God is a God of pathos who suffers when we suffer. Alongside God's actions affecting us, our actions affect God. Heschel finds evidence for his highly controversial claim in scripture. "In all their affliction he was afflicted" (Isa. 63:9). Also "For a long time I have kept silent. I have kept still and restrained Myself; Now I will cry out like a woman in travail, I will grasp and pant" (Isa. 42:14).

Heschel brings in passages from other Jewish sources:

> When Israel performs the will of the Omnipresent, they add strength to the heavenly power; as it is said, "To God we render strength!" When, however, Israel does not perform the will of the Omnipresent, they weaken—if it is possible to say so—the great power of Him who is above; as it is written "Thou didst weaken the Rock that begot thee." (Deut. 32:18)
>
> The Holy One, as it were, said: "When Israel is worthy below, My power prevails in the universe; but when Israel is found to be unworthy, she weakens my power above." (The Zohar)[5]

To provide a practical guide for how the modern mind can open itself to God, or more precisely, through which the contemporary mind can respond to a God who is in search of human beings, Heschel illustrated three paths to God in his seminal work *God in Search of Man*:

> There are three starting points of contemplation about God; three trails that lead to him. The first is the way of sensing the presence of God in the world, in things; the second is the way of sensing His presence in the Bible; the third is the way of sensing His presence in sacred deeds. (*GSM*, 31)

Most of Heschel's other major works are primarily devoted to one of these three ways, or paths. *Man Is Not Alone* is concerned with the first path, the way to God via the world, whereas *The Prophets* and *Heavenly Torah: As Refracted through the Generations* are devoted to the second, the way to God through the Bible. Heschel's "Man's Quest for God" is largely given to the third path, the way to God through sacred deeds.

The Path to God through the World

To sense the presence of God in the world, modern humanity must do something quite radical. We must transform the way we view the world around us. We must go beyond the Greek philosophers who have become our guides and immerse ourselves in the viewpoint of biblical men and women. According to Heschel,

> There are three aspects of nature that command our attention: its power, its beauty and its grandeur. Accordingly, there are three ways in which we may relate ourselves to the world—we may exploit, we may enjoy it, we may accept it in awe. (*GSM*, 33–34)

But the modern mind, writes Heschel, understands only the power of nature and responds with a desire to control and exploit nature (*GSM*, 34). The biblical mind, on the other hand, was enchanted by the grandeur of nature, and responded with a sense of awe and wonder.

Fritz Rothschild, a specialist on Heschel's thought, writes,

> To recover the sensitivity to that dimension of reality which engenders wonder and worship Heschel turns to the experience of religious men and the classical document of such experience, the Bible. There he finds six terms that describe grandeur and man's reaction to it in three correlative pairs: the sublime and wonder, mystery and awe, the glory and faith. It must be borne in mind that in each of these three pairs of terms the first one refers to an objective aspect of reality and the second one to man's mode of responding to it. All these terms refer to the realm of the ineffable.[6]

Heschel illustrates the first pair of terms, "sublime" and "wonder":

> The sublime is that which we see and are unable to convey. It is the silent allusion of things to a meaning greater than themselves. . . . It may be sensed in every grain of sand, in every drop of water. Every flower in the summer, every snowflake in the winter, may arouse in us the sense of wonder that is our response to the sublime. (*GSM,* 39)

This is a most crucial idea in Heschel's thought, for Heschel himself states, "Awareness of the divine begins with wonder" (*GSM,* 56). Wonder is the fundamental attitude of the truly pious person.

To explain the word "mystery" Heschel turns to Wisdom literature. According to Heschel, there was nothing that did not hold a great secret for the biblical mind: "What stirred their soul was neither the hidden nor the apparent, but the hidden in the apparent; not the order but the mystery of the order that prevails in the universe" (*GSM,* 56). Just as a pious person cannot exist without the sense for the sublime, a pious person cannot exist without the sense of mystery. Heschel writes, "[T]he root of worship lies in the sense of the 'miracles that are daily with us.' There is neither worship nor ritual without a sense of mystery" (*GSM,* 62).

Heschel explains that biblical men and women did not respond to the mystery with a sense of resignation, with fear or terror, but with awe. "Awe . . . is the sense of wonder and humility inspired by the sublime or felt in the presence of mystery." He argues that just as there is no faith without wonder, there is no faith without awe, explaining, "We must grow in awe in order to reach faith" (*GSM,* 77).

After examining "mystery" and "awe," Heschel turns to the third pair of terms and begins with one of the central concepts in Judaism, the "glory" of God. Here his thought takes up the ancient dynamic between two concepts found in biblical literature: the transcendence of God and the immanence of God. According to some scholars, Judaism has suffered from an undue stress on God's transcendence and has neglected God's immanence. But Heschel turns to the Book of Isaiah to show us the coexistence of the two concepts:

> In his great vision Isaiah perceives the voice of the seraphim even before he hears the voice of the Lord. What is it that the seraphim reveal? "Holy, holy, holy is the Lord of Hosts; the whole earth is full of his Glory." "Holy, holy, holy"—indicates the transcendence and distance of God. "The whole earth is full of his glory"—the immanence or presence of God. (*GSM,* 89)

As Professor Israel Efros explains, "Holiness tries to lift the God-idea ever above the expanding corporeal universe, and Glory tends to bring the Creator ever nearer to man."[7]

Heschel describes what the glory of God means for humanity:

> Standing face to face with the world, we often sense a presence which surpasses our ability to comprehend. The world is too much for us. It is crammed with marvel. There is a glory, an aura, that lies about all beings, a spiritual setting of reality. (*WM,* 90)

According to Heschel, we are citizens in two realms.

> The tangible phenomena we scrutinize with our reason, the sacred and indemonstrable we overhear with the sense of the ineffable. The force that inspires readiness for self-sacrifice, the thoughts that breed humility within and beyond the mind, are not identical with the logician's craftsmanship. The purity of which we never cease to dream, the untold things we insatiably love, the vision of the good

> for which we either die or perish alive—no reason can bound. It is the ineffable from which we draw the taste of the sacred, the joy of the imperishable.[8]

Heschel says the possibility of experiencing the glory is not closed to contemporary humanity. We are certainly capable of responding with wonder and radical amazement to the grandeur and the sublime. We are capable of responding with awe to the mystery, with faith to the glory. Why then do we so often fail? We fail, says Heschel, because of indifference.

> This is the tragedy of every man: "to dim all wonder by indifference." Life is routine, and routine is resistance to wonder . . . said the Baal Shem[,] "Just as a small coin held over the face can block out the sight of the mountain, so the vanities of the living block out the sight of the infinite light." (*GSM,* 85)

But even if we are able to overcome our indifference and react to God's presence with a sense of awe and wonder, we have not yet completed our journey to God, says Heschel.

> It is not a feeling for the mystery of living, or a sense of awe, wonder, or fear, which is the root of religion; but rather the question what to do with the feeling for the mystery of living, what to do with awe, wonder or fear. (*GSM,* 108)

"What to do" with these feelings is taken up in the second and third paths.

The Path to God through Revelation

With regard to the Bible, Heschel writes, "This generation does not know how to study nor what to study. We have lost the way that leads us to the Bible. We do not learn how to sense the presence of God in the words of the Bible."[9] With his second path, Heschel intends to show us a way to encounter God through the words of the Bible. As he says, "The presence of God is found in many ways, but above all God is found in the words of the Bible."[10]

Heschel understands that the modern mind, raised in a tradition of rationalism and skepticism, wants proof of the authenticity of revelation. But proof relies on reason, and Heschel points out that reason and science on the one hand and revelation on the other work on different levels.

> The Bible and science do not deal with the same problem. . . . Science deals with relations among things within the universe, but man is endowed with the concern of the spirit, and spirit deals with the relationship between the universe and God. Science seeks the truth about the universe; the spirit seeks the truth that is greater than the universe. Reason's goal is the exploration and verification of objective relations; religion's goal is the exploration and verification of ultimate personal relations. (*GSM,* 16–19)

Nonetheless, Heschel attempts to use reason to "prove" the truth of revelation. How does he do it? By trying to show that the prophets were authentic. In his examination of the prophets, Heschel says there are only three ways of looking at these biblical figures. Either "they told the truth, deliberately invented a tale, or were victims of an illusion." He dismisses the second possibility based on the improbability of prophets, "men of highest passion for truth," conspiring over many years to deceive the people of Israel. He discounts the third based on the widespread recognition of the prophets' wisdom: "Their message being ages ahead of human thinking, it would be hard to believe in the normalcy of our minds if we questioned theirs" (*GSM,* 223, 227).

Heschel is not attempting to prove the authenticity of the prophets in any traditional sense. He admits that there are no empirical criteria for proving conclusively that the prophets were right or that the Bible is true. Rather, he is trying to show that the authenticity of the prophets cannot be conclusively *disproved.* If it cannot be disproved, it may be true. In effect, Heschel is demonstrating that reason is not an obstacle to accepting revelation as true, but it is also not—and can never be—the key. Reason is one step. To take that final step, from the possibility of revelation to the confidence in revelation, one must have faith.

> The goal of our "examination" of the prophets was not to furnish the prophets with a letter of recommendation, but rather to point to the difficulty of an outright rejection of their claims. Proofs cannot open the gates of mystery for all men to behold. The only thing we can do is to open the gates of our own soul for God to behold us, to open the gates of our minds and to respond to the words of the prophets. (*GSM*, 233–34)

Once we "open the gates of our own soul" to belief in the truth of revelation, we can go on to more specific questions: What does revelation mean? Where did revelation come from? To understand Heschel's views on these questions, we first must understand the three major views of revelation in modern Judaism.

The oldest view of revelation was formulated by the rabbis. They believed that the Torah in the broadest sense, including the Mishnah, Talmud, and Haggadah, was revealed by God to Moses. The great medieval Jewish philosophers, including Moses Maimonides (1135–1204) and Moses Nachmanides (1194–1270), accepted this formulation. Today, modern Orthodox Jewish thinkers continue to concur with this view of the Torah.

The first major break with this traditional idea of revelation came from the Reform movement. In order to understand the revolutionary concept of revelation formulated by the Reform movement, let us consider one of its major platforms.

> God reveals himself not only in the majesty, beauty and orderliness of nature, but also in the vision of moral striving of the human spirit. Revelation is a continuous process, confined to no one group and no one age. Yet the people of Israel, through its prophets and sages, achieved unique insights in the realm of religious truth. The Torah, both written and oral, enshrines Israel's ever-growing consciousness of God and of the moral law.[11]

It is quite apparent that this interpretation of revelation conflicts with the Orthodox position. According to the Reform view, it does not simply flow from God to human beings. Revelation comes about through the insight and discovery of human beings. Human beings, in response to God's inspiration, are the creators of the Bible, yet the statement "God reveals Himself" suggests that the truths discovered by human beings are the truths of God. This would seem to be the implication of the meaning of revelation that is presented by one of the major Reform theologians of the twentieth century, Bernard J. Bamberger.

> The adherents of modern liberal religion profess the theory of "progressive revelation." They believe, that is, that the truth of God is made manifest through the continuing search of all men for enlightenment and goodness. All the scientists, poets, philosophers and religious teachers are the channels of God's revelation to mankind.[12]

A third unique view of revelation, in opposition to both the traditional and the Reform views, prevails in the contemporary world. The major spokesman for this position was Martin Buber (1878–1965), whose works have become important for many thinkers today. In what is now a famous passage, Buber presents his position on revelation:

> My own belief in revelation . . . does not mean that I believe that finished statements about God were handed down from heaven to earth. Rather it means that the human substance is melted by the spiritual fire which visits, and there now breaks from it a word, a statement, which is human in its meaning and form, human conception and human speech, and yet witnesses to Him who stimulated it and to His will.[13]

As Maurice Friedman perceptively says, "Buber rejects the either-or of revelation as objective or subjective in favor of the understanding of revelation as dialogical."[14]

There is certainly an affinity between Heschel's and Buber's approaches to revelation. Both agree that revelation must be viewed as a dialogue between the prophet and God, and contend the prophet "is not a passive recipient" (*GSM*, 259). Heschel says, "prophecy consists of a revelation of God and a co-revelation of man. . . . Thus the Bible is more than the word of God: it is the word of God and man; a record of both revelation and response" (*GSM*, 269–70).

But Buber's position that "the laws of the Bible are only the human response to revelation and, therefore, are not binding on future generations" is very problematic for Heschel, as it is for the entire Jewish tradition.[15] For Buber, "the core of revelation is not the communication of content but the event of God's presence."[16] Heschel's view of revelation as both an event and a content that is binding on all future generations brings him much closer to traditional Judaism than to either the Reform or Buberian view.

To understand the binding content of the Bible, we turn to Heschel's third path, the way to God through sacred deeds.

The Path to God through Sacred Deeds

Heschel stresses that "life is a partnership of God and man" and argues that "this is why human life is holy." It is at this moment that we are able to understand not only why God entered into a "marriage contract" with Israel but also the importance of mitzvot; the mitzvot are the way that the "partnership," the "marriage contract" between Israel and God, is fulfilled.[17]

Heschel's position is that the person who is open to the holy dimension, who is aware of the presence of the ineffable, and for whom revelation becomes a reality will realize that Judaism is not only a religion of love, but is also a religion of yoke: "The first thing a Jew is told is: You can't let yourself go; get into harness, carry the yoke of the Kingdom of Heaven. . . . The predominant feature of Jewish teaching throughout the ages is a sense of constant obligation."[18] We are obligated to God not only in the way we think, but also in the way we live our everyday lives. Heschel repeatedly emphasizes that Judaism is a way of thinking *and* a way of living (*GSM*, 197). Although Heschel is perhaps best known for his study of the inner life of the pious man, he understood that the spiritual life of the Jew is determined by his concrete actions. Heschel is true to the Jewish tradition when he states that "man is above all a commanded being, a being of whom demands may be made" (*WM*, 107).

> The soul is endowed with a sense of indebtedness, and wonder, awe and fear unlock that sense of indebtedness. Wonder is the state of our being asked. . . . We are driven by an awareness that something is asked of us, that we are asked to wonder, to revere, to think, and to live in a way compatible with the grandeur and mystery of living. (*WM*, 109–10)

From this quote it is possible to perceive the interrelationship between the different aspects of Heschel's "path to God." The way begins with our response to the world with wonder and awe; this in turn leads to action, to the performance of sacred deeds. Heschel writes, "Sacred deeds are designed to make living compatible with our sense of the ineffable. The mitzvot are forms of expressing in deeds the appreciation of the ineffable" (*GSM*, 350).

In his movement from the ineffable to mitzvot, Heschel makes what Maurice Friedman refers to as "the transition from his general philosophy of religion to his specific philosophy of Judaism."[19] Any man or woman can respond to God with wonder; any person open to traditional Western religion can accept the authenticity of revelation; but only the Jew is expected to perform the ritual mitzvot of Judaism. Heschel develops this philosophy in *Man's Quest for God* and in the third part of his major work *God in Search of Man*, which is titled "Response."

What is Heschel's understanding of "Response"? By response Heschel means worship of God (*avodat Ha-Bore*), which encompasses all the commandments (*mitzvot*), including prayer. Heschel believes that the modern Jew who begins to sense the ineffable in the world and in the Bible will respond with acts of worship.

For the modern Jew who still cannot open his or her eyes, however, Heschel presents a most challenging and provocative claim. He contends that the mitzvot, the performance of the commandments, are not merely our response to the demands of God, *they may also serve as a path to God's presence.*

> A Jew is asked to take a leap of action rather than a leap of thought. He is asked to surpass his needs, to do more than he understands in order to understand more than he does. In carrying out the words of

> the Torah he is ushered into the presence of spiritual meaning. Through the ecstasy of deeds he learns to be certain of the hereness of God. Right living is a way to right thinking. (*GSM*, 283)

Further along Heschel explains more fully why the Jew is asked to take a "leap of action":

> The mitzvah is a supreme source of religious insight and experience. The way to God is a way of God, and the mitzvah is a way of God, a way where the self-evidence of the Holy is disclosed . . . a mitzvah is where God and man meet.
>
> To meet Him means to come upon an inner certainty of His realness, upon an awareness of His will. Such a meeting, such presence we experience in deeds. (*GSM*, 312)

Heschel's contention that "the mitzvah is a supreme source of religious insight" helps us understand more fully the interrelationship of the three "paths to God." The outline of *God in Search of Man* leads us to believe that the path moves from the ineffable to the reality of revelation and finally to worship. Here, however, the direction of the path is reversed. The mitzvot may lead one to sense the ineffable, then to the study of the Torah. If the roads to the Bible and the ineffable are closed, the "leap of action" is an alternate route to discovering God in our lives.

A number of contemporary Jewish thinkers who are receptive to Heschel's thought and have praised his work, including Maurice Friedman, find this "leap of action" problematic. Friedman writes:

> But if we who are not observant Jews do not now feel ourselves commanded by God to perform the law, how can we perform it with integrity even on the strength of Heschel's assurance that we shall know this to be God's will for us through our observance?[20]

Rabbi Dudley Weinberg holds something of the same position when considering the phenomenon of prayer:

> How utterly appropriate is the inscription so frequently inscribed over the ark in our synagogues: *Da lifne mee attah ohmed*—"Know before Whom you stand." Without this recognition prayer can never occur. Introspection may occur; we may engage in psychological self-examination; we may study liturgical texts and even find them interesting as sources of stimulating ideas; but prayer cannot occur.[21]

Heschel responds in several ways to these criticisms. Heschel was well aware of the view found in rabbinic and medieval sources that without devotion to God (*kavanah*) the performance of the mitzvot is worthless. He even quotes the extreme view found in the Talmud: "the Rabbis call a person who performs a commandment without the proper intention a transgressor" (*GSM*, 408 n. 2). He is also highly critical of those who would perform mitzvot without any concern for proper intention, "as if all that mattered is how men behaved in physical terms; as if religion were not concerned with the inner life."[22]

But Heschel defends against this possibility by explaining that his "leap of action" may be a key to knowledge of God:

> Judaism insists upon the deed and hopes for the intention. . . . While constantly keeping the goal in mind, we are taught that one must continue to observe the law even when one is not ready to fulfill it "for the sake of God." For the good, even if it is not done for its own sake, will teach us eventually how to act for the sake of God. (*GSM*, 403–4; *IF*, 140–41)

Nonetheless, Heschel would agree with Friedman that the Jew who does not feel commanded by God to perform the mitzvah does not perform it with integrity. But in his article "Confusion of Good and Evil," Heschel meets the question of integrity itself in a new way. In this article, profoundly influenced by kabbalistic and Hasidic thought, Heschel argues that even the saint cannot perform the commandments with complete integrity. He cites the Jewish mystical view "that in this world neither good nor evil exists in purity, and that there is no good without the admixture of evil nor evil without the admixture of good."[23]

Heschel then raises the question, "If an act to be good must be done exclusively for the sake of God, are we ever able to do the good?" and responds to his question in the following way: although our deeds may never become perfect, will never become entirely free of self-interest, there is great value in their performance and in our struggle to attain greater integrity.[24]

Further, contemporary Jews are in a uniquely precarious position. The majority of them live among Christians in a Christian world and are exposed to the Christian emphasis on love rather than yoke, on faith rather than action. Heschel writes: "Paul waged a passionate battle against the power of law and proclaimed instead the religion of grace. Law, he claimed, cannot conquer sin, nor can righteousness be attained through works of law. A man is justified 'by faith without the deeds of law'" (*GSM*, 293).

Attempting to recenter assimilated Jews' attitudes, he writes, "The first word in God's approach to man is: 'The Lord God commanded the man . . .' (Genesis 2:16). It is the commandment we must first listen to."[25] The danger today is not Jews performing mitzvot without proper intention, but Jews neglecting the mitzvot altogether. Better they perform the mitzvot without intention, says Heschel, than not perform the mitzvot at all.[26]

Thus far we have dealt with only one aspect of worship, the performance of holy deeds. The two other aspects of worship are study of Torah and prayer. Since the rabbinic tradition considers prayer to be a commandment, Heschel deals with prayer in his discussion of the third path. Throughout his works, Heschel repeats the idea that God needs humanity, and we can interpret this to mean that God needs humanity's worship. Heschel argues that even in Talmudic times the rabbis debated this issue of whether or not God needs humanity's worship. A reading of the Midrash reveals many statements supporting Heschel's contention that there were rabbis in Talmudic times who emphasized God's need for human worship. The following Midrash is a good example. "Why were the matriarchs barren? R. Levi said in R. Shila's name and R. Helbo in R. Johanan's name: Because the Holy One, blessed be he, yearns for their prayers and supplications."[27]

For Heschel the great power of worship lies precisely in the fact that God needs man's prayers. Heschel writes:

> Moreover we must not overlook one of the profound principles of Judaism. There is something which is far greater than my desire to pray, namely God's desire that I pray. . . . How insignificant is the outpouring of my soul in the midst of this great universe! Unless it is the will of God that I pray, unless God desires our prayers, how ludicrous is all my praying! (*MQG*, 58)

The following statement presents Heschel's central contention about prayer.

> Great is the power of prayer. For to worship is to expand the presence of God in the world. God is transcendent, but our worship makes Him immanent. This is implied in the idea that God is in need of man: His being immanent depends on us. (*MQG*, 62)

By explaining to us the idea of a God of pathos and by offering us a threefold path to encounter God, Heschel has given us an innovative way to understand religion that is grounded in Jewish tradition. In his review of *Man Is Not Alone*, a book devoted primarily to the first path, Maurice Friedman claims, "Actually, *Man Is Not Alone* has as much power to speak to the uncommitted as any book that American Jewish thought has produced."[28] Through the first path Heschel shows us how to see the spiritual dimension of the world. The second path shows a way to access the ancient scriptures. In the third path, a specifically Jewish path, he shows us how to live a life of mitzvot that could help us find God.

For Heschel, the contemplation of the role of human beings and their relationship to God was never simply a form of intellectual gamesmanship. It is important; it is vital; there are drastic stakes. As Heschel says,

> Mankind will not die for lack of information. It will perish for lack of appreciation. Unless there is appreciation there is no mankind. The great marvel of being alive is the ability to discover the mystery and wonder of everything. . . . Unless we learn how to revere, we will not know how to exist as human beings. (*MNA*, 37)

Heschel's paths to God bring out the spiritual dimension of Judaism, a Judaism that can no longer be dismissed as a dry religion. For Heschel authentic Judaism is essentially "a way of developing sensitivity to God and attachment to His presence" (*GSM*, 26).

Soon after Heschel's major books began to appear in the 1950s, Christian thinkers did not fail to see the profound nature of his work. Reinhold Niebuhr, one of the great Protestant theologians of the twentieth century, in his review of *Man Is Not Alone*, wrote: "This volume is so impressive because it is the work of a poet and mystic who has mastered the philosophical and scientific disciplines and who with consummate skill reveals the dimension of reality apprehended by religious faith." By the time of his death, Heschel had emerged as an important authentic Jewish voice among Jews and members of other religious traditions. The prominent Hindu scholar K. Sivaraman wrote: "Heschel is one of my favorite thinkers of religion of this century." The Christian scholar W. D. Davies stated: "I speak for Christians and other non-Jews. To encounter him [Heschel] was to 'feel' the force and spirit of Judaism, the depth and grandeur of it."[29] I believe that today Heschel's works are more widely read than ever before and that his interrelated paths to God still have the power to move the hearts and minds of contemporary human beings.

* * *

This essay is written as a tribute to Zev Garber. I first met Zev when I enrolled at Yeshiva Salanter in the Bronx a few days after I arrived in the United States in August 1949. This *Yeshive bukher* has given me a great deal of *naches*. I am amazed by Professor Garber's contribution to Jewish scholarship. His contribution to Christian-Jewish relations and Holocaust studies has been immense. In this essay I have incorporated material from my book *Divine-Human Encounter: A Study of Abraham Joshua Heschel.*

Notes

1. Jacob Neusner, *American Judaism: Adventure in Modernity* (Englewood Cliffs, N.J.: Prentice-Hall, 1972), 156.
2. Abraham J. Heschel, "What We Might Do Together," *Religious Education* (March–April 1967): 135.
3. Abraham J. Heschel, *God in Search of Man: A Philosophy of Judaism* (New York: Farrar, Straus and Cudahy, 1955), 168 (hereafter *GSM*).
4. Abraham J. Heschel, *Who Is Man*? (Stanford, Calif.: Stanford University Press, 1968), 23–24 (hereafter *WM*).
5. Quoted by Abraham J. Heschel, "The Mystical Element in Judaism," in *The Jews, Their History, Culture and Religion*, ed. Louis Finkelstein (New York: Harper Brothers, 1949), 604–5.
6. Fritz A. Rothschild, *Between God and Man: An Interpretation of Judaism* (New York: Free Press, 1959), 11.
7. Israel I. Efros, *Ancient Jewish Philosophy: A Study in Metaphysics and Ethics* (Detroit: Wayne State University Press, 1964), 7.
8. Abraham J. Heschel, *Man Is Not Alone: A Philosophy of Religion* (New York: Farrar, Strauss, and Young, 1951), 9 (hereafter *MNA*).
9. Abraham J. Heschel, "Israel and Diaspora," in *The Insecurity of Freedom: Essays in Applied Religion* (New York: Farrar, Straus, and Giroux, 1965), 220 (hereafter *IF*). Heschel's major work on the meaning of revelation for rabbinic Judaism, which focuses on the views of Rabbis Akiva and Ishmael, has just been translated from Hebrew into English by Gordon Tucker: *Heavenly Torah: As Refracted Through the Generations.*
10. Patrick Granfield, *Theologians at Work* (New York: Macmillan, 1967), 77.
11. W. Gunther Plant, *The Growth of Reform Judaism* (New York: World Union for Progressive Judaism, 1965), 97.
12. Bernard J. Bamberger, *The Bible: A Modern Jewish Approach* (New York: Schocken Books, 1963), 89–90. Note: It appears to me that this concept of revelation is closer to the Hindu understanding of revelation than to the traditional Jewish concept. "For the orthodox, the Veda is eternal, and not the product of human minds. Yet it is not like the Bible or the Koran; it is the record of the truth as it was 'discovered' by the great rishis, or saints of ancient time rather than a revelation from God." Ainslie T. Embree, ed., *The Hindu Tradition: Readings in Oriental Thought* (New York: Vintage Books, 1972), 6.
13. Martin Buber, *Eclipse of God: Studies in Relation Between Religion and Philosophy* (New York: Harper Torchbooks, 1957), 135.
14. Maurice S. Friedman, *Martin Buber: The Life of Dialogue* (New York: Harper Torchbooks, 1960), 246.
15. Maurice Friedman, *Encyclopedia Judaica*, vol. 4 (New York: Macmillan, 1972), 1433.
16. Emil L. Fackenheim, "Martin Buber's Concept of Revelation," in *The Philosophy of Martin Buber*, ed. Paul Arthur Schilpp and Maurice Friedman (La Salle, Ill.: Open Court, 1967), 290.
17. Heschel, "Sacred Image of Man," in *IF*, 160. For an excellent discussion of the "marriage contract" metaphor to describe the relationship between God and Israel, see Jakob J. Petuchowski, *Ever Since Sinai: A Modern View of Torah* (New York: Scribe Publication, 1968).

18. Heschel, "Religion in a Free Society," in *IF*, 13.
19. Maurice Friedman, "Liberal Judaism and Contemporary Jewish Thought," *Midstream* (Autumn 1959): 24.
20. Ibid.
21. Dudley Weinberg, "The Efficacy of Prayer," in *Understanding Jewish Prayer*, ed. Jakob J. Petuchowski (New York: KTAV Publishing, 1972), 124.
22. Abraham J. Heschel, *Man's Quest for God: Studies in Prayer and Symbolism* (New York: Charles Scribner's Sons, 1954), 53–54 (hereafter *MQG*).
23. Abraham J. Heschel, "Confusion of Good and Evil," in *IF*, 134.
24. Ibid., 140.
25. Abraham J. Heschel, "Protestant Renewal: A Jewish View," in *IF*, 174–75.
26. It is interesting to point out that the Lubavitcher Hasidim are in full agreement with this controversial position of Heschel's. For many years now the Lubavitcher movement has been engaged in a tefillin campaign, whereby Jewish strangers are approached and asked to put on tefillin. The leaders of this movement are certainly aware that these Jews who are encouraged to put on tefillin and pray will do so without kavanah ("devotion to God"). Apparently they believe, like Heschel, that the repeated performance of this action may eventually lead to true intention.
27. *Midrash Rabbah: Genesis*, vol. 1, trans. H. Freedman and M. Simon (London: Soncino Press, 1951), 381.
28. Maurice Friedman, "Abraham Joshua Heschel: Toward a Philosophy of Judaism," *Conservative Judaism* 10, no. 2 (Winter 1956): 2.
29. Reinhold Niebuhr, "Masterly Analysis of Faith," *New York Herald Tribune Book Review*, April 1, 1951; K. Sivaraman, letter to Harold Kasimow, Feb. 3, 1986; W. D. Davies, "Conscience, Scholar, Witness," *America* (March 10, 1973): 214.

The Reception of Early German Haskalah in Nineteenth-Century Haskalah

Moshe Pelli

One of the most intriguing topics in the study of Haskalah literature, which has not been addressed in the critical literature so far, is the "reception" of early German Haskalah in the nineteenth century.

We know that at the end of the nineteenth century, the Berlin Haskalah was severely criticized by various Maskilim and post-Haskalah writers. However, what is less known is the historical and literary process that led to this critical position. That is to say, the transition in attitude toward early Haskalah as the centers of the Haskalah moved to the Austro-Hungarian empire and Galicia as well as to Russia, Lithuania, and Poland. The latter part of the Haskalah was the area of concentration of the late professor David Patterson, whose work in Hebrew Haskalah and his contribution to Jewish studies we are commemorating here.[1]

In this context, the following questions are raised: What was the attitude toward the Berlin Haskalah in the various other phases of Haskalah? How did the later Maskilim regard the literature of early Haskalah, and if indeed there was a change in attitude, when did it take place? What is the essence of this change, and what brought it about? In this essay, I will try to address some of these questions, especially in the area of reception.

As a working hypothesis, I can state, on the basis of first-hand impression from reading eighteenth- and nineteenth-century texts, that the reception of early German Haskalah in the second period of Haskalah, in the Austro-Hungarian empire, especially in Galicia and Italy, and in the beginning of the third period in Russia was generally rather positive.

My assessment of the reception of early Haskalah is based on four general criteria of literary acceptance as guidelines.

Criteria for the Evaluation of Early Haskalah's Reception

The first general criterion of reception looked for reprints and new editions of books, periodicals, and articles from the early period, which were reproduced in the nineteenth century; similarly, reprints of biographies of the early Maskilim, and lists of published books by printers and publishers for these reprints.

Another criterion examined the influence of early Haskalah: namely, in imitation of style, themes, and genres from the early period; also, the acceptance and recycling of early Haskalah's ideas and ideology, or the possible rejection thereof.

A third criterion is based on memoirs of nineteenth-century Maskilim who reported about the impact of early Haskalah on them and the reception of its authors.

The fourth criterion examined in-depth as well as cursory evaluation of early Maskilim and their works by nineteenth-century authors and critics and their assessment of the formers' contribution to the development of Haskalah. Also, inclusion in literary histories and surveys of Haskalah literature.

The theory of reception, such as the one proposed by Hans Robert Jauss, is not included in this essay.[2]

Editions of Early Haskalah Books Republished in the Nineteenth Century: *Hame'asef* and Scriptures

The first criterion that may be used to assess the reception of early Haskalah is based on studying reprints and new editions of early materials. My general impression is that early Haskalah books were published in many editions in the first part of the nineteenth century and afterward, and actually provided seminal materials to Maskilim who wished to read about the foundation of Haskalah and its ideology.

Among the basic books that could be found on the proverbial "Jewish bookshelves" were many of the Haskalah books. Displayed prominently were the editions of Scriptures with translation into German, commentaries, and introductions by the Maskilim, as well as Hebrew textbooks, and works on grammar and linguistics.

A full treatment of this subject will require a detailed, comprehensive bibliographical probe, which is beyond the scope of this essay. Here I propose to present examples of major categories of important Haskalah material that was recycled in the nineteenth century. My intention is to show the prevailing trends in Haskalah reception. It should be emphasized, though, that these examples deal with the quantitative aspect of Haskalah materials, disregarding at this point their qualitative evaluation.

In the future I may expand this study and attempt to address the topic of reception by checking the actual circulation and dissemination of these early books, and the presumed number of readers, authors, and literary activists.[3] But this kind of information is scarce, if available at all.

The starting point of my discussion is the reception of *Hame'asef*, the Hebrew monthly of Haskalah, published from 1783 to 1811 with some interruptions. An early phenomenon that attests to the impact of the work of the early Maskilim may be found in the republication of articles, essays, and poems from *Hame'asef* in *Bikurei Ha'itim*. Published in Vienna from 1820 to 1831, this journal of Haskalah represents the second phase of Haskalah in the Austro-Hungarian empire. *Bikurei Ha'itim* published some 207 different items (of the sum total of 1,916 entries in *Bikurei Ha'itim*) taken from the first four volumes of *Hame'asef*. This is a clear indication of the continuous influence of the first journal and the special role it continued to play beyond its own time and place. The material was recycled without any editing or changes, and thus it became sort of a semicanonical body of literature in early modern Hebrew. In my book on *Bikurei Ha'itim* I discuss the question of the recycled material and the editor's policy regarding materials that were eliminated from republication.[4]

An indication of the viability of *Hame'asef* even beyond the mid-century point was the republication of *Hame'asef* in 1862 as the Galician writer and editor Meir Halevi Letteris published a new edition of volume one of *Hame'asef* for the year 1783/84.[5]

A similar trend may be discerned by several attempts to revive the periodical (*Hame'asef*) and to issue something that resembled it. In 1829 Rephael Fürstenthal issued a publication under the same title, *Hame'asef*, for 1829. And in 1866 Yehuda Leib Reinhartz published a one-time volume which was also called *Hame'asef*.[6]

The continuous influence of *Hame'asef* on rank-and-file Maskilim may be seen also from a few attempts to write such a periodical with the title *Hame'asef*. Walter Röll discovered a manuscript titled *Hame'asef* Kassel of 1799,[7] and I found at the Rosenthaliana library a manuscript of a periodical titled *Keter Torah Hame'asef* from the years 1815–16.[8] Neither of these manuscripts was published. In addition, in 1818, there was an attempt to issue selections from the original *Hame'asef* by the editor of the German Jewish periodical *Jedidja*, Jeremiah Heinemann, and the poet Moshe Büschenthal.[9] It was not published.

Even more impressive was the republication of Haskalah editions of the Hebrew Scriptures, which were very popular in the nineteenth century, having been printed in several editions and were widely circulated.

Mendelssohn's *Be'ur*—the commentary on the Torah with translation into German in Hebrew characters—had a long-lasting impact on Haskalah Judaism, and it was republished in nine different editions by various printers during the century.[10] Following the *Be'ur*, other Maskilim followed in Mendelssohn's footsteps and published commentaries and translations of other books of the Hebrew Bible. Such was the *Sefer Mishlei* (Proverbs) by Yitzhak Euchel, which was published in five different editions in thirty years following its initial edition in 1790.[11]

Among other works were the Five Scrolls by Aaron Wolfssohn and Joel Brill, with Mendelssohn's translation into German of Song of Songs, Brill's edition of Psalms, and Juda Leib Ben Zeev's introductions to the books of the Hebrew Bible. These books and others came out in many editions during the nineteenth century and afterward.[12]

It should be pointed out that traditional editions of Hebrew Scriptures with the classical commentaries were generally in wide circulation, being a permanent feature in Jewish homes. Yet, the dissemination of Haskalah editions is definitely indicative of their reception by nineteenth-century Maskilim. However, at the end of the century we have a report by Berdichevsky that most people bought traditional texts rather than the Maskilim's editions.[13]

Republication of Literary Materials in Chrestomathies, Primers and Catechisms, Ideology Books and *Belles lettres*

Another category of republished books of early Haskalah is found in the practical Hebrew language textbooks, primers, chrestomathies, and catechisms, which were much needed "products" in Jewish schools and among private teachers and Maskilim.

The Hebrew linguistics books and textbooks of Ben Zeev, one of the prolific Haskalah linguists and writers, were widely circulated in many editions throughout the nineteenth century. The literary historian Joseph Klausner reported twelve different editions of Ben Zeev's *Talmud Leshon Ivri*, published from 1796 to 1874, while the bibliographer Chaim Dov Friedberg noted fifteen editions.[14] Similarly, Ben Zeev's lexicon *Otzar Hashorashim* had five editions. Klausner summaried its influence by writing that this book "showed ten of thousands of young people the linguistic treasures of the Bible [. . .] and thus taught them the Hebrew language."[15] Ben Zeev's catechism, *Beit Hasefer*, was printed in nine editions.[16]

Similarly, primers, catechisms, and language textbooks recycled literary texts such as fables, parables, moral tales, and stories, written by the Me'asfim—the circle of writers contributing to *Hame'asef*—and published initially in *Hame'asef*, for the use of students and young Maskilim.[17]

An important source of information about the reception of early Haskalah and the acceptance of its ideology in the following century may be found in the republication of its ideological books. Issuing new editions of such books is indicative of the need to examine and to explore the ideas and ideals of early Haskalah.

One of these books was Naftali Hertz Wessely's educational treatise *Divrei Shalom Ve'emet*. It is one of the basic ideological books of early Haskalah and the most seminal one. In it, Wessely delineated in 1782 the ideological platform advocating the introduction of reforms—especially secular subjects—in Jewish education. His writings had a great impact on the Maskilim of its time and afterward. The demands for educational reform continued to be expressed by nineteenth-century Maskilim, and the republication of Wessely's book in 1826, 1827, and 1886 is indicative of its popularity and its acceptance.[18]

Early Haskalah ideas have been circulating in later writings, signaling the influence of the founding fathers of Haskalah. Thus, echoes of Wessely's proposed educational reforms are resonating in the writings of later Maskilim, such as in *Te'udah Beyisrael* by the influential Russian Maskil Yitzhak Beer Levinson, and others.[19]

Also, the acceptance and reception of original works of prose and poetry may be deduced from their republication at a later date. For example, Wessely's biblical epos, *Shirei Tiferet*, which was originally published in Berlin in 1789, was published in a complete edition in 1809, after Wessely's death, and then appeared in seven subsequent editions.[20] Moreover, as I shall discuss later, Wessely's masterpiece inspired many Haskalah authors to write similar biblical epics and dramas.

Another belletristic work, the travelogue *Masa Ba'rav*, by the Italian Maskil Shmuel Romanelli, was printed in nine editions (including in the twentieth century) since its publication in 1792.[21] The biblical drama *Meluchat Sha'ul*, by Yoseph Ha'efrati, which was also published first in 1792, was reissued in twelve different editions.[22] These new editions and many others are definitely impressive signs of acceptance, which will be elaborated upon below.

Commentary on Classical Texts and Linguistics, Books on Science, and Biographies of Early Maskilim

Commentaries on classical texts, in addition to early Maskilim's commentaries on biblical books, which I discussed before, serve as another source for evaluating reception in our context. One such book is *Yen Levanon* by Wessely, which is a commentary on *Pirkei Avot*. The book was published in three editions.[23]

The study of Hebrew linguistics, grammar, and etymology, to which many of the early Maskilim have devoted their creative energies in their desire to revive the Hebrew language, is another popular channel of influence. Wessely's *Gan Na'ul* deals with synonyms and terms of "wisdom" in the Bible. It was published originally in Amsterdam in 1765 and then, being quite popular at this age of "reason," it was published in six more editions.[24]

One of the stated goals of Haskalah was to foster secular studies among the Jews, particularly in general and natural sciences. Among the first Maskilim in Germany who wrote on natural sciences was Baruch Linda. He published a series of articles on science in *Hame'asef*,[25] which were published in 1789 in his book *Resheet Limudim*. Subsequently, six more editions were published, as an indication of the book's popularity and reception.[26] A further acknowledgment of Linda's acceptance as late as 1873 is found in Shalom Yaakov Abramovich's own book in natural science, *Toldot Hateva* (1862–73), where he paid tribute to Linda's work.[27]

The category of biographies, either republished or new biographies, on the founding fathers of Haskalah in Germany serves as an indicator of their reception by later Haskalah. Some of these biographies were written to glorify the exemplary figures of early Haskalah such as Mendelssohn and Wessely. The first Hebrew biography by the editor and Haskalah activist Yitzhak Euchel on Mendelssohn, titled *Toldot Rabenu Moshe Ben Menahem*, was first serialized in *Hame'asef* and then published in 1789 as a book. This biography was republished in three more editions in the next century.[28]

Not only did reprints of biographies mark their acceptance but also new biographies written on the luminaries of early Haskalah. One such biography on Mendelssohn was published in 1820 in *Bikurei Ha'itim* (German, in Hebrew characters).[29]

The other major figure in German Haskalah, Wessely, was the subject of several biographies in the nineteenth century. It started with the biography by the Amsterdam Maskil David Friedrichsfeld in 1809, and another, serialized in 1857 in *Hamagid*, and then in 1886 two more biographies by Kalman Schulman and Shlomo Mandelkern.[30] Those four different biographies of Wessely testify to the high esteem he has been accorded in later Haskalah.

Among other Maskilim who were deemed to be worthy of a biography in nineteenth-century Haskalah was Yitzhak Euchel. Its author, Meir Halevi Letteris, felt a special empathy, if not an affinity, with Euchel, the editor of *Hame'asef*. Letteris, an editor himself, had a special place in his heart for *Hame'asef* as I mentioned before; he reprinted a new edition of volume one of *Hame'asef* for the year 1783/84.[31]

Publishers' Listings and Personal Libraries; Imitation of Styles and Genres Prevalent in Early Haskalah

Another reliable source of information about the potential dissemination and possible circulation of Haskalah books in the nineteenth century may be found in publishers' lists of books they had published.

From book lists circulated by the Viennese publisher Anton Schmid and the Prague publisher Moshe Landau—to cite two of the important printers and publishers—we can learn about the republication of Haskalah books, and in effect to reconstruct the contents of the maskilic "bookshelf."[32] An earlier list of available books published by the Haskalah publishing house in Berlin, חברת חנוך נערים, is found at the end of Nahman Barash's book *Ein Mishpat*,[33] and it reflects the maskilic book production at the turn of the century.

Searching for information about personal libraries and special collections of Hebrew books may bring interesting results. For example, in 1783/84 *Hame'asef* published several notices about Judaica libraries.[34] It is known that some of the late Maskilim, such as Yoseph Perl, had comprehensive libraries in Hebraica and Judaica.[35] Further investigation of the contents of these libraries can give us information about the availability of early Haskalah books. The Hebrew critic and editor Reuven Brainin reported in his memoirs that he had started some sort of a "library."[36] This aspect should be investigated further.

One of the ways to assess the influence of early Haskalah authors and their writings on later writers is to probe any emulation of style, themes, and literary genres that were prevalent in early Haskalah. Thus, it will be rewarding, for example, to look into the impact of Wessely's *Shirei Tiferet* on other biblical epics.

There are references to its impact on the following writers and their epics: Shalom Hacohen's *Mata'ei Kedem Al Admat Tzafon* (1807) and *Nir David* (1834), Bernhard Schlesiner's *Hashmona'im* (1816), "Toldot Yoseph" by Moshe Mendelssohn-Frankfurt in *Pnai Tevel* (1872), and Ziskind Rashkow's *Hayei Shimshon* (1824).[37] The literary historian Fischel Lahover reported that there were some twenty imitations of Wessely's *Shirei Tiferet*.[38] But this requires another study.

Some authors openly acknowledged their indebtedness to early Haskalah writers. The Breslau Maskil, Ziskind Rashkow, for example, declared in the introduction to his biblical epic *Hayei Shimshon* (1824) Wessely's influence on his work.[39] Also the Amsterdam Maskil Gavriel Polak asserted in the introduction to *Kikayon Leyonah* (1853), an epic on the biblical story of Jonah, that he followed in the footsteps of Wessely.[40] Even if Polack attempted to promote his own book by such an acknowledgment, it nevertheless serves as an indication of some affinity to Wessely's epos and his continuous influence.

Emulating literary genres that were prevalent in early Haskalah by later writers is another indication of reception; for example, "the dialogues of the dead," a popular genre in eighteenth-century Enlightenment literature. This genre continued to be used by late Maskilim throughout the nineteenth century; these writers were Shlomo Levissohn, Juda Leib Mieses, Meir Halevi Alter (in *Bikurei Ha'itim*), and others, as a testimony of a continuous impact of early Haskalah.[41]

A study of literary motifs may be rewarding as well, and it may show some affinity to an early literature. Such is the use of the "spring" motif that continued to be cited in Haskalah poetry throughout the century.[42]

Literary Assessment of Writers and Critics; Authors' Memoirs about Reception

Comprehensive literary analyses and critical discussions of early German Maskilim and their writings may serve as good indicators for reception and acceptance. Thus, Shlomo Levisohn's literary analysis in *Melitzat Yeshurun* in 1816, which deals with theories of poetics and rhetorics, discussed Wessely's literary work. It is indeed indicative of Wessely's reception at that time as a canonical writer.[43]

Also, the Galician poet Dov Ginsburg in his essay on poetics cited Euchel's poetical definitions of Wessely's epos (from the former's review published in *Hame'asef* in 1790), and carried on a serious discussion about them. Obviously, this is another indication of the impact of Haskalah's early writings.[44]

More discussion on direct assessment of the early literature will be discussed in another article.

Another important criterion for assessing early Haskalah's acceptance in the nineteenth century is based on Maskilim's memoirs. These memoirs may shed light on the question of the circulation of Haskalah books, specifically, whether the early Maskilim's books and the volumes of *Hame'asef* were available to second and third generation Maskilim.

For example, the Galician and Russian Maskil Avraham Gottlober reported in his memoirs that thirty-five years after Mendelssohn's death, namely in 1821, when he—Gottlober—was ten years old, there were in his hometown copies of Mendelssohn's *Be'ur*, some of Wessely's books, Ben Zeev's grammar books, and volumes of *Hame'asef*. He also mentioned that he saw Saul Berlin's satiric work *Ktav Yosher* (published in 1795).[45] But Gottlober was unique in that his father allowed him access to these books, whereas many young Maskilim did not have such privilege.

Nineteenth-century autobiographies serve as another source of information. Mordechai Aharon Gunzburg related in his autobiography, *Aviezer*, that in his youth he had read Mendelssohn's *Phaedon*, after which Mendelssohn gained esteem in his eyes.[46] Another autobiographer, Moshe Leib Lilienblum, reported that he had purchased the apocryphal book *Hochmat Shlomo* with Wessely's commentary *Ru'ah Hen*, and that he was very much impressed by it. He also reported of having access to other Haskalah books which were originally printed in Koenigsburg—thus, transposing him metaphorically through this medium of literature closer to the center of Haskalah in Germany; among other books, he also reported seeing Ben Zeev's *Talmud Leshon Ivri*.[47] Reuven Brainin, too, reported of the influence of Ben Zeev's *Talmud Leshon Ivri* on him as well as of Mendelssohn's *Be'ur*.[48]

We can assume that in the centers of Haskalah in the nineteenth century, early Haskalah books have been handed over from one Maskil to another. In more remote and secluded places, there were apparently no Haskalah books unless owned by an established Maskil who lived there. Thus Lilienblum, for example, related how he got acquainted with a young man who owned Haskalah books. Also Brainin wrote in his memoirs about a teacher-Maskil who had had in his possession "a trunk full of Haskalah literature," yet he mentioned the difficulties to get Haskalah books.[49] Another young writer, Mordechai Zeev Feierberg, wrote to Ahad Ha'am that when he grew up he did not have (Haskalah) books.[50]

Such testimonies, which should be further studied, do indicate the availability of early Haskalah books and their influence on the followers of Haskalah in the nineteenth century.

This, however, changes in the 1860s upon the emergence of the critical approach to German Haskalah literature, expressed by such writers as Abraham Uri Kovner, Avraham Yaakov Paperna, and especially Peretz Smolenskin.

But this is a topic for another essay.

Notes

1. This essay was presented in its initial form as a paper at the 38th Annual Conference of the Association for Jewish Studies in December 2006, commemorating the works of the late professor David Patterson.
2. Since most of the source material and references are in Hebrew the endnotes were kept in their original language, namely, Hebrew. על התקבלות טקסטים ראה Hans Robert Jauss, *Toward an Aesthetic of Reception*, Theory and History of Literature 2 (Minneapolis, 1982), 3–45, ובמיוחד עמ' 18 ואילך. אברהם באנד החיל את התיאוריה של האנס רוברט יאוס בדבר התקבלותם של טקסטים סיפרותיים על ספריהם של ויזל, *שירי תפארת*, ושל רמח"ל, *לישרים תהלה*. ראה Arnold Band, "The Beginning of Modern Hebrew Literature: Perspectives on 'Modernity,'" *AJS Review* 13 (Spring–Fall 1988): 1–26. באנד טען שאכן הדפסתם החוזרת של מהדורות שתי היצירות הנזכרות מעידה על התקבלותן. אך הוא סבור שיצירתו זו של ויזל שימשה כ"אופק משתנה" ולא מילאה את "אופק הציפיות" של הקורא משום שהיא הציעה צורה חדשה של שירה (במאמרו, עמ' 17).
3. דן מירון, *בודדים במועדם* (תל-אביב, 1988), עמ' 58–67, דן בהיבט זה של הסיפרות העברית בשנות 1880.
4. על *בכורי העתים* ראה מונוגרפיה ואינדקס מוער: משה פלאי, *בכורי העתים – ביכורי ההשכלה: מפתח מוער לבכורי העתים, כתב-העת העברי של ההשכלה בגליציה* (ירושלים, 2005).
5. מאיר הלוי לטריס, מהדיר, *המאסף לשנת התקמ"ד*, מהדורה ב' (וינה, תרכ"ב).
6. *המאסף* שהוציא יהודה ליב ריינהערץ: *המאסף* יבואו בו שירים ומליצות נשגבי הרעיון גם מכתבים שונים [.] ונצמד לזה הספר היקר **מאמר הברור הפילוסופי** מאת הרב החכם הכולל ר' משה בן מנחם מענדעלסזאהן ז"ל (ורשה, 1866). מובא בו גם קטע *מקהלת מוסר* של מנדלסון שנדפס גם ב*המאסף* הראשון.
7. *המאסף מקיץ תקנ"ט לפ"ק פה קאסל*, כתב-יד (1799) של כתב-עת המצוי בסיפרייה הלאומית והאוניברסיטאית בסטראסבורג, שעליו פירסם וולטר רול מאמר. ראה: Walter Röll, "The Kassel 'Ha-Meassef' of 1799: An Unknown Contribution to the Haskalah," in *The Jewish Response to German Culture*, ed. Jehuda Reinharz (Hanover and London, 1985), 32–50.
8. כתב-יד *המאסף* נמצא בסיפריית הרוזנטליאנה באמשטרדם: *כתר תורה המאסף דברי מליצה הגונים ועריבים ומשלי מוסר וספורי[ם] נחמדים שנאספו יחד* (קוברדן, תקע"ה) מאת מאיר דה וולפט (Meier de Wulft).

9. *Ankündigung für Freunde der hebräischen Litteratur* (Berlin, 1818) חוברת בת 15 עמ', כרוכה בסוף כרך א' של *המאסף החדש* (1809) בעריכת שלום הכהן, המצוי בספריית המדינה בברלין. בתוכניתי לפרסם על כך מאמר נפרד. הכרוז נדפס גם בעברית (בלא הדוגמאות) כמאמר ב*ידידיה*: "Ankündigung für Freunde der hebräischen Litteratur," *Jedidja*, II, 1, 1, S. 117–122.

10. משה מנדלסון, *נתיבות השלום* (ברלין, תקמ"ג); מהדורות שעברו תחת ידי יצויינו להלן בפירוט ביבליוגרפי (וכן להבא): *ספר נתיבות השלום* עם תרגום אשכנזי ובאור מאת החכם המפורסם מוהר"ר משה מדעסויא כפי אשר נדפס בברלין התקמ"גל (וינה, 1817; 1818). ראה גם חיים דב פרידברג, *בית עקד ספרים*, ד' (תל-אביב, 1956), עמ' 1074.

11. יצחק אייכל, *משלי* (ברלין, תק"ן), וכן: אופנבאך, תקס"ה, 1826; דסאו, 1804; וינה, 1817; פיורדא, 1817, וכן *כתבי קודש*, וינה, 1817.

12. יואל ברי"ל, *ספר זמירות ישראל* (ברלין, תקנ"א); *ספר זמירות ישראל הוא ספר תהלים* עם [...] תרגום אשכנזי מאת רבנו משה בן מנחם ומבואר מאת ר' יואל ברי"ל (וינה, 1817); אהרן בן-וואלף [וולפסון] ויואל ברי"ל, *חמש מגלות* (וינה, 1807; 1818). מהדורות חדשות נדפסו בכותרת *כתבי קודש* כגון ספר איוב עם תרגום אשכנזי ובאור מאת אהרן וואלפסזאהן (וינה, 1817; 1826). וכן, יהודא ליב בן זאב, *מבוא אל מקראי קדש* (וינה, 1810).

13. מיכה יוסף ברדיצ'בסקי, *כתבי מיכה יוסף בן-גָריון*, ב', *מאמרים* (תל-אביב, תש"ך), עמ' רמ"ה.

14. יוסף קלוזנר, *הסטוריה של הספרות העברית החדשה*, א' (ירושלים, 1960), עמ' 182–183. ראה גם חיים דב פרידברג, *בית עקד ספרים*, ד' (תל-אביב, 1956), עמ' 1105.

15. קלוזנר, שם, עמ' 183–184. פרידברג, *בית עקד ספרים*, א' (תל-אביב, 1951), עמ' 43.

16. קלוזנר, שם, עמ' 184, מדווח על תשע מהדורות; פרידברג, שם, א', עמ' 145, מדווח על שבע מהדורות.

17. עוד על סיפרות ילדים וסיפרי לימוד, ראה אוריאל אופק, *ספרות הילדים העברית – ההתחלה* (תל-אביב, תשל"ט), וכן, זהר שביט, "'הריהוט של חדר ההשכלה היהודית בברלין' – ניתוח המקראה המודרנית הראשונה לילדים יהודים", *כמנהג אשכנז ופולין ספר יובל לחנא שמרוק* (ירושלים, תשנ"ג), עמ' 193–207.

18. ראה נפתלי הירץ ויזל, *דברי שלום ואמת* (וינה, 1826); *מכתבים שונים* [כולל *דברי שלום ואמת*] (וינה, 1827); נפתלי הערץ ווייזיל, *ספר דברי שלום ואמת* (ורשה, 1886), מהדורת קלמן שולמן. השווה, פרידברג, שם, א', עמ' 225.

19. יצחק בער לעווינזאהן, *תעודה בישראל* (וילנא, תקפ"ח; מהדורת צילום: ירושלים, תשל"ז).

20. פרידברג, *בית עקד ספרים*, ג' (תל-אביב, 1954), עמ' 997. בין המהדורות הנמצאות בידי: נפתלי הירץ וויזל, *שירי תפארת* (ברלין, תקמ"ט); *שירי תפארת* (פראג, תקס"ט); *שירי תפארת* (ורשה, 1840).

21. כולל במאה העשרים. מהדורה א': שמואל רומאנילי, *משא בערב* (ברלין, תקנ"ב). ראה רשימת המהדורות בפרק על סיפרות המסעות בסיפרי *סוגות וסוגיות בסיפרות ההשכלה העברית [:] הז'אנר המשכילי ואביזרייהו* (ישראל, 1999), עמ' 208.

22. יוסף האפרתי מטראפלוויץ, *מלוכת שאול* (וינה, תקנ"ד); (למברג, 1820); (וינה, 1829); (ורשה, תרל"א). פרידברג, *בית עקד ספרים*, ב' (תל-אביב, 1952), עמ' 608, מדווח על 12 מהדורות. בשנת תשכ"ט נדפסה מהדורת 'דורות' של מלוכת שאול בההדרת גרשון שקד.

23. נפתלי הירץ ויזל, *יין לבנון* (אמשטרדם, תרל"ה); (ורשה, תרמ"ד); (ורשה, תרנ"ח).

24. פרידברג, *בית עקד ספרים*, א', עמ' 199.

25. ראה משה פלאי, *שער להשכלה: מפתח מוער להמאסף, כתב-העת העברי הראשון (תקמ"ד–תקע"א)* (ירושלים, תשס"א), עמ' 113, רשימת מאמרי ברוך לינדא ב*המאסף* בפיזיקה ובביולוגיה: על חיות, מודד החום, הברומטר, הפנינים.

26. פרידברג, *בית עקד ספרים*, ג', עמ' 931; ראה גם קלוזנר, *הסטוריה של הספרות העברית החדשה*, א', עמ' 191–192; ואופק, *ספרות הילדים העברית – ההתחלה*, עמ' 18.

27. שלום יעקב אברמָוביץ (אברמוביץ) משבח את *ראשית למודים* ואת מחברו, ברוך לינדא, במבוא, "עת לדבר" לסיפרו *תולדות הטבע*, ג' (וילנה, תרל"ג), עמ' xxviii–xxix.

28. איצק אייכל, "תולדות רבנו משה בן מנחם" (תולדות גדולי ישראל), *המאסף*, ד' (שבט, תקמ"ח), עמ' קי"ג–קמ"ד; (אדר ב', תקמ"ח), עמ' קע"ז–ר"ח; (אב, תקמ"ח), עמ' של"ז–שס"ח; ה' (מרחשון, תקמ"ט), עמ' ל"ג–ס"ד. המהדורה הראשונה, *תולדות רבנו החכם משה בן מנחם* (ברלין, תקמ"ט); בין המהדורות האחרות: *תולדות הרב הכולל החכם החוקר אלהי רבנו משה בן מנחם* (וינה, תקע"ד); *תולדות החכם החוקר אלהי רבנו משה בן מנחם* בתוך *זמירות ישראל* (למברג, 1860).

29. "תולדות רבנו משה בן מנחם" [מאמר בגרמנית באותיות עבריות], *בכורי העתים*, א': 20–26. תקפ"א.

30. על ויזל: *זכר צדיק* שחיבר דוד פרידריכספלד בראשית המאה, וכן הביוגרפיה שכתב יחבי"ק על ויזל: יחבי"ק, "תולדות ר' נפתלי", *המגיד*, א', גל' 26, 30, 33, 36, 37, 51 (תרי"ז). *ספר דברי שלום ואמת* (1886), עמ' 1–31, מהדורת קלמן שולמן; שלמה מאנדעלקערן, "תולדות ר' נפתלי הירץ וויזל זצ"ל", *האסיף*, ג' (תרמ"ז), שיצא בוורשה בתרמ"ו, עמ' 404–417.

31. מאיר הלוי לטריס, "תולדות החכם ר' איצק אייכל ז"ל", *המאסף* לשנת תקמ"ד בהוצאת לטריס (וינה, תרכ"ב), עמ' מ"א–נ'.

32. ראה פלאי, *בכורי העתים – ביכורי ההשכלה: מפתח מוער לבכורי העתים*, עמ' 34, הע' 92, 93, עמ' 48, הע' 156. ב-1807 התפרסמה הודעה בת שני עמודים בשם אנטון שמיד על הוצאת מחזורים בתרגום לגרמנית מאת וואלף היידנהיים, בשם *קול מבשר*, ב-1815 פירסם שמיד "מודעה" ארוכה על תוכניתו להוציא לאור את המהרש"א, המצוייה בסיפרייה הלאומית ומיספרה L1047. סיפרי מישניות, מאמר על דיקדוק לשון המישנה "מאת המשכיל ר' שלמה לעזויזאהן", ובו הוא מציע תוכנית לרכישת הספרים על ידי חתימה מראש. *מודעה זה שנים רבות* (וינה, 1815), המצוייה בבית הספרים הלאומי והאוניברסיטאי בירושלים, 4 עמ' בגודל פוליו, שמיספרה L736. רשימת ספרים שנדפסו בבית הדפוס של לנדא נתפרסמה בשנת תקצ"ו: *רשימת הספרים הנמצאים בבית דפוס משה הלוי לנדא בפראג תקצ"ו* (פראג, תקצ"ו), 8 עמ'; רשימה נוספת נדפסה בכותרת דומה בשנת תקצ"ט. הרשימות מצויות בבית הספרים הלאומי והאוניברסיטאי בירושלים ומיספריהן L2428 ו-L2429. חומר רב על סיפרי השכלה שנדפסו במאה הי"ט נמצא

בספריו של חיים דובעריש פריעדבערג, *תולדות הדפוס העברי בערים האלה שבאירופה* (אנטוורפן, תרצ"ז), לדוגמה, על הספרים שהוציא אנטון שמיד, עמ' 95–99, וכן הכרך *תולדות הדפוס העברי* שנדפס בתרצ"ה.

33. נחמן בן שמחה בר"ש בר"א, *עין משפט* (ברלין, תקנ"ו).

34. ראה *שער להשכלה: מפתח מוער להמאסף, כתב-העת העברי הראשון (תקמ"ד-תקע"א)*, עמ' 145–146.

35. ראה יוסף קלוזנר, *הסטוריה של הספרות העברית החדשה*, ב' (ירושלים, 1960), עמ' 290.

36. ראובן בריינין, "זכרונות", *כתבים נבחרים* (מרחביה, 1965), עמ' 415–418.

37. שלום הכהן, *מטעי קדם על אדמת צפון* (רדלהיים, 1807; זולקווא, 1818); הכהן, *ניר דוד* (וינה, 1834); יששכר בר שלזינגר, *החשמונאים* (פראג, 1816); משה מנדלסון (פרנקפורט), "תולדות יוסף", *פני תבל* (אמשטרדם, תרל"ב), עמ' 111–138; זיסקינד ראשקאוו, *חיי שמשון* (ברסלוי, תקפ"ד).

38. פ. לחובר, *תולדות הספרות העברית החדשה*, א' (תל-אביב, תשכ"ג[12]), עמ' 76, 146. קלוזנר טוען שבוודאי אחדים הושפעו על-ידי המיקרא עצמו ולאו דווקה על-ידי *שירי תפארת*.

39. זיסקינד ראשקאוו הלוי, *חיי שמשון* (ברסלויא, תקפ"ד), עמ' 6.

40. גבריאל פאלק, *קיקיון ליונה* (אמסטרדם, תרי"ג), בהקדמה, עמ' 3: "ונסיתי בהם את מצער כחי לדרך בעקבי החוקר הנשגב, החכם הגדול בתורה ולשון קודש, המשורר אין כמוהו בדורות האחרונים, הרב המפואר כמהור"ר **נפתלי הירץ וויזל זצ"ל**, אשר אין ערוך אליו כנעים זמירותיו בספרו הנחמד **שירי תפארת** העומד לנס ישרון לתפארת עולם". פולק נסמך על ביקורתו של אייכל על *שירי תפארת* ב*המאסף* ומצטט אותו באומרו על יצירתו האפית של ויזל, ש"במתכונתה לא נעשתה כמוה מיום שגלו ישראל מעל אדמתם" (שם)).

41. על פירוט השיחות השונות, ראה בסיפרי *סוגות וסוגיות בסיפרות ההשכלה העברית [:] הז'אנר המשכילי ואביזרייהו*, בפרק על שיחות המתים, עמ' 49, הע' 6, 7.

42. ראה דיוני על התופעה בראשית התקופה בפרק על שירת *המאסף* בסיפרי *דור המאספים בשחר ההשכלה:* תרומתם הסיפרותית של חלוצי *המאסף*, כתב-העת העברי הראשון, להשכלה העברית בראשיתה (תקמ"ד–תקע"א) (ישראל, תשס"א), עמ' 42–45, ועל התפתחותה ב*בכורי העתים* בסיפרי *בכורי העתים – ביכורי ההשכלה:* מפתח מוער ל*בכורי העתים*, כתב-העת העברי של ההשכלה בגליציה (ירושלים, 2005), עמ' 74–75, 108. דוגמה לשירה המוקדשת לאביב: סיפרו של שמואל זינוויל זעליגזאהן, *האביב* (ברלין, תר"ה). ראה מאמרו של יוסף האפרתי, "דרכי התיאור בשירת ההשכלה, לפואטיקה של השירה העברית בתקופת ההשכלה, בייחוד בהשוואה לשירת דור ביאליק", *הספרות*, ב' (1, ספטמבר 1969), עמ' 26-39. נדפס גם בסיפרו *המראות והלשון* (תל-אביב, תשל"ז).

43. שלמה לעוויזאהן, *מליצת ישֻׁרון* (וינה, 1816), דף נ"ב ע"ב, נ"ה ע"א.

44. ב ג מבראד [דב בר גינצבורג] בהקדמתו למהדורת *לשון למודים* לרמח"ל (לבוב, תק"ע; המהדורה שבידי: סדילקוב, תקצ"ו), עמ' 114.

45. אברהם בר גוטלובר, "הגיזרה והביניה: לקורות התפתחות ההשכלה בישראל בארץ רוסיה ופולין", *זכרונות ומסעות*, ב', מהדורת 'דורות' (ירושלים, תשל"ו), עמ' 72; אברהם בער גאטטלאבער, *זכרונות מימי נעורי*, א' (ורשה, 1880), עמ' 26: על *תלמוד לשון עברי* לבן זאב; עמ' 19: באור *מלות ההגיון* עם ביאור הרמבמ"ן [מיספרי העמודים משובשים]; ב' (ורשה, 1881), עמ' 11: על ויזל ובעלי המאספים; ג' (ורשה, 1881), עמ' 31: על *כתב יושר*, הסאטירה של שאול ברלין להגנת ויזל, ו*תולדות הרמבמ"ן*; עמ' 34: על אייכל. וכן במהדורת 'דורות', כרך א', עמ' 78: על *תלמוד לשון עברי* לבן זאב; עמ' 81–82: באור *מלות ההגיון* עם ביאור הרמבמ"ן; עמ' 229: *כתב יושר*.

46. מרדכי אהרן גינצבורג, *אביעזר* (וילנה, 1873), עמ' 115–119, וכן הוא מזכיר סיפרי השכלה נוספים.

47. משה ליב ליליינבלום, *חטאת נעורים*, *כל כתבי משה ליב לילייענבלום*, ב' (קראקא, תרע"ב), עמ' 219, 231. וכן המהדורה הראשונה: צלפחד בר חשים התוהה [משה ליב ליליינבלום], *חטאת נעורים* או וידוי הגדול של אחד הסופרים העברים (וינה תרל"ו); מהדורה מצולמת הוכנה על-ידי פרופ' ג. אלקושי בתל-אביב, תשכ"ז, על-פי מהד' קראקא, תרע"ב. ראה בסיפרי *במאבקי תמורה* (תל-אביב, 1988), בפרק "השכלה והִתמשׂכלות", עמ' 35–45.

48. ראובן בריינין, "זכרונות", *כתבים נבחרים* (מרחביה, 1965), עמ' 407, 477.

49. משה ליב ליליינבלום, *חטאת נעורים*, *כל כתבי משה ליב לילייענבלום*, ב', עמ' 226; ראה מהדורות נוספות בהערה 42. וכן, בריינין, "זכרונות", *כתבים נבחרים*, עמ' 396–399, ואילך.

50. צרור מכתבים אל אחד-העם", *כתבי מרדכי זאב פייארברג* (תל-אביב, ללא שנת ההדפסה; מהד' 5), עמ' 163".

Part 4

Reflections from the Field and the Classroom

Traveling in Ga(r)berdine

G. Jan Colijn

It is early March 1991. The Dutch would shrug "March wags its tail" about the South Jersey weather we are experiencing: snow, high winds—the kind of foul weather that makes you want to curl up with a book, but there will be no curling this night, not even the funny kind with a broom. In a few days, the Richard Stockton College of New Jersey will be hosting the Annual Scholars Conference on the Holocaust and the Churches, and scholars strictly observing the Sabbath are beginning to arrive before the weekend. They will be housed at the Marriott Seaview, a swank resort (and LPGA tournament site) halfway between the College and Atlantic City—where, under its previous ownership, Jews were decidedly unwelcome: local Shoah survivors who ran chicken farms made deliveries under a false name: Green, not Greenman.

We have arranged for dozens of volunteers to meet the conference participants at Atlantic City International (a bit of a joke, that) and other airports. Given the weather, there are substantial delays. The host team is *kvetching* anxiously. Gail Rosenthal, our Holocaust Resource Center's supervisor, is supposed to meet a California participant, but her husband, Bob, does not want her to drive in this mess. He will go with her to our airport while their teenage daughter Toby will stay at home by the phone.

There is just one terminal at Atlantic City International, not a football field in length. There is no way Gail and Bob will miss their pickup. They arrive and the terminal is deserted. Supposedly, the flight is in. Toby is called and she insists their contact has arrived (he has called) but Gail and Bob are not so sure: Allegheny Airlines (May you have as many landings as departures!) knows nothing, but, besides the service counter jockeys, the terminal is empty—except for what appears to be a homeless transient, covered in a sweater, multiple scarves that do not match, no overcoat, woefully underdressed for the winter storm outside. You guessed it: Zev Garber.

In retrospect, assume that those scarves find their provenance in Zev's days around Fleetwood Mac, and stories best left out of this book. At any rate, that night, fully thawed, Zev speaks at Beth El Synagogue in Margate. The rebbe concludes, ". . . as the snow melted, so did our hearts." That was the beginning, and it was good.

A few years later we met again, in Berlin, at a large Holocaust conference. Those involved with the organization had received some death threats from neo-Nazis. Your interlocutor decided better safe than sorry, borrowed a bulletproof vest from our campus police, and wore it everywhere but on the night we went to Kreuzberg and had a feast (liquid and solid) in a Turkish restaurant where we knew we were safe. It goes without saying that Zev was among the merry pranksters: he remembers getting there by subway but not that it was a Turkish place.

Zev-the-wanderer's tales continued. Sometime post-9/11, he was on a Greyhound bus from New York to our house. Unbeknownst to him, his suitcase tumbled out the luggage hold in the tight loop that links the Lincoln Tunnel with New Jersey. The NYPD bomb squad got onto that one in a hurry. It took us days to get it resolved. Eclectic readings in that luggage undoubtedly raised some eyebrows. Take it from good authority: Zev does not look good in my pajamas. Onward . . .

When Steven Jacobs sent out the calls for this *Festschrift*, I looked over the suggested topics. They ranged from Judaism as Historiosophy (paradigmatic hermeneutics) to Hebrew Bible and New Testament: Exegesis and Eisegesis. Hm, I thought, perhaps this will not work. I may contain multitudes, in Whitman's phrase, but a theologian I am not. I am an agnostic. I am also of the view that among the many closed worldviews at the ideological genesis of genocide and at the well-springs of most human carnage, we find religion, especially in its scourging, fundamentalist representations. Herein I am not alone. Sam Harris notes, in *The End of Faith*, that

> A glance at history . . . reveals that ideas which divide one group of human beings from another, only to unite them in slaughter, generally have their roots in religion. . . . Our situation is this: most of the people in the world believe that the Creator of the universe has written a book. We have the misfortune that there are many such books on hand, each making our exclusive claim on its infallibility.[1]

Harris proceeds to list a variety of invocations from various Holy Books about killing the infidels and concludes that much of these texts "contain mountains of life destroying gibberish."[2] Such gibberish, when taken not allegorically, but as literally error-free, certainly seems to bring us a ton of genocidal grief. Harris once more:

> Anti-semitism is as integral to church doctrine as the flying buttress is to a Gothic cathedral. . . . Anti-semitism is intrinsic to both Christianity and Islam; Both traditions consider the Jews to be bunglers of God's initial revelation.[3]

The Iranian filmmaker Mohsen Makhmalbaf, borrowing from the great Persian poet Rumi (1207–73), once suggested that the truth is a mirror that broke when it fell from God's hand. Everyone picked up a piece and thought the truth was his, not realizing it had been fragmented among us all. The results we know.

Having staked out my position, the reader will understand that to make this particular view the *centerpiece* of my contribution to the joyous occasion for which this volume is written would not be quite cricket. There is also the serious forensic possibility I would be engaged by email, over a meal, in a conference corridor somewhere yet in the future, by a torrent of Zev's views on the matter. Frankly we have better things to talk about than luggage and God (although in a discourse about soccer, the most important such alternative, Zev would be a Know Nothing).

However, Steven Jacobs solved my predicament: there were, reflecting Zev's remarkable range, many other suggested topics, from teaching Jewish and Shoah studies to Jewish/Christian/Catholic dialogues, among others.

Thus, it is to the vast intellectual bandwidth of Zev's astonishing scholarly productivity and to his teaching, rather than to his expertise in theology, that I now gladly turn.

His scholarly output is, of course, remarkable. By the time this *Festschrift* will be in print there will be a baker's dozen of authored and edited books, some hundred book chapters and articles, some five hundred book reviews, and innumerable encyclopedia entries. As productive and wide-ranging as this scholarship is, it takes on even greater prestige because Zev is not adverse to roll up his sleeves and to serve his fields [*sic*] in tasks that require time, self-sacrifice, and patience. I note his role as founder and editor-in-chief of Studies in the Shoah for the University Press of America, and his role as co-editor of *Shofar: An Interdisciplinary Journal of Jewish Studies,* published by Purdue University. In these roles, one is dependent on others to make deadlines and production schedules, and scholars march to their own drummers. Most of us with some experience in editing anthologies come to the point where we say: "never again." Not Zev. I think it was Anthony Burgess who once mused that one ought not to write book reviews after reaching fifty—even for money. Not Zev (and, of course, there is hardly ever any pay). There are very few who can match him, especially among those who teach: more about that next.

On teaching I am decidedly not an agnostic. My decanal duties require that I spend a good deal of time on the oversight of instruction as one of the pillars of my institution's growing distinction (Stockton is now ranked as the sixth public liberal arts college in the United States, according to *US News and World Report*). I want to discuss teaching foremost because it is the central, rabbinical core of what Zev does, in the classroom, in his writing. It is the way wherein he expresses love.

Most of us who work in what, in the parlance, are called Research I institutions have absolutely no idea what happens in a place like Los Angeles Valley College, in America's two-year sector, where Zev toils. Our careers are shouldered by the juried *gravitas* and the scope of our research, by our success in grant and contract acquisitions, and by our penchant for "plump little vanities"—in the words of V. S. Pritchett—that lead us to build think tanks, hopefully named after a donor with deep pockets, and dedicated to worthy specialties (or tailored to fit the esoteric hobbyhorse of that donor).

In this environment students are, more or less, the enemy, the bothersome "others" who interfere with the activities just noted. Professors in Research I institutions spend an alarming portion of their hours in proving the theory of mind over matter: faculty do not mind and students do not matter. Despite exhortations by prominent observers of higher education in the United States, for example, the late Ernst Boyer, and despite a constant stream of reports by higher education's national associations, little has changed at the beginning of the new century. Granted, those in the four-year sector may strike the teaching-research balance differently, but only to a degree. Rare is the institution where teaching is axiomatically, automatically, and always the primary consideration for tenure and promotion decisions, and I do not believe it is much different beyond the water's edge, certainly not in my English and Dutch experiences.

When someone running an institute at a Research I university is asked to teach, one may, under great duress by one's departmental chair or dean, agree to one, *but just one*, graduate seminar—for the year, of course, not per term! In our self-image we are not faculty employees of our academy but more or less independent contractors, carefully deigning to choose whatever the least onerous (and minute) contribution we can make to the university's commons, while we pursue the Cartesian windmills of our mind, as much as we can get away with.

Teaching in the two-year sector is of an entirely different nature. The norm may be five courses *per term* (not per academic year), with thirty to thirty-five students or more in each class, often bright and eager, but woefully unprepared by their high school preparation for college work, with students who are at the bottom rung of the economic ladder in the United States, with students who juggle jobs, sometimes multiple jobs, and responsibilities for children or parents. This is the reality in the trenches of American higher education. It is hard work, for overburdened faculty—otherwise often a contradiction in terms—and for students. For the latter to achieve and to thrive under these conditions is truly a marvel. Among the former it is unheard of to publish like Zev.

Anyone who even casually knows Zev cannot come away without the clear impression that he loves these trenches, the open-minded eagerness of his charges who, unlike their counterparts in the most selective universities, are not born with a silver spoon in their mouths, bored with their education, jaded because their future beds are already made, on the upside of the tracks of disparity running across this country. He loves the fabulous diversity in the background of his charges, and situated in the most diverse state in America he knows, like an alchemist, how to wring magic from that diversity and to create acres of diamonds, as the founder of Temple University once said. Successful teaching at this level would be quite enough, and anyone who succeeds in this environment is worthy of a *Festschrift*, too.

Of course, in Zev's case, we have only just begun. It bears repetition to note that, despite his teaching load, his research productivity compares favorably with those in the Research I institutions I gently (or, perhaps, not so gently) lampooned above. Let me now turn to the qualitative aspects of Zev's teaching.

The generation of 1960s students (of which I am a member) had high hopes that the authoritarian model of lecturing dons, orating to deferential students, would not survive our frontal attack on higher education. Our legacy, however, was not permanent. First, the narcissism of my generation was at least focused on change beyond individual advancement. That intent is lost to a good many of the entitlement-driven, grade-conscious, uncurious whiners in college today (and there are plenty of those): we left no enduring legacy there. Second, even when encountering many disciplined students, citizens in the making, concerned with the direction of America, it remains clear that the 1960s iconoclasm against 1950s pedagogy has not worked in one major part. It is true that we have learned a great deal on *how* to teach but there is no reason for cheers because, in terms of *content*, we are sliding backwards in a hurry.

Despite many advances in pedagogy, *qua content,* much contemporary teaching is faith based: many faculty give students a piece of secular or religious fish, marinated in a rich tradition of ideological conviction, buttressed by texts considered sacred or incontrovertibly authoritative. Such faculty do not teach students how to fish.

Zev Garber does not teach like that. One hastens to add he is not bereft of strong opinions, but he does not pour his views upon students as if they are *tabulae rasa.* Let me illustrate my point. When Larry van Meter, head of Moorestown Friends School (Moorestown, N.J.) welcomed my daughter's freshman class five years ago, he said:

> This is a Quaker school but we are not here to make you Quakers. If you are Catholic, we hope to help you become a better Catholic; if you are Jewish, we hope to help you be a better Jew.

Zev will appreciate this. His teaching is essentially postmodern, but not in the way postmodernism typically is defined. His teaching does not succumb to the moral and cultural relativism fashionable today that results from a bewildering array of views peddled to our students (a relativism that may be the biggest internal threat to our society as it faces formidable external challenges), but operates in a context wherein I intend postmodernism to mean teaching students how to fish; how to think; how to empower oneself with an apparatus of critical skills and divergent (inter)disciplinary toolkits that allow students to live rational and moral lives after they leave us. We should "profess" no more by conveying the truth as we hold it, but teach the paths whereby students can discover their own truths—and using the plural here does not endorse the empty-headed notion that all truths are equal. In one of Zev's most tightly argued, succinct, and elegant articles[4] he writes:

> The college classroom should not serve as a podium for intellectual exhibitionism or be a forum for unbridled ranting. Instruction in the classroom ought to be student-oriented so that students are involved in comprehension, application, analysis, synthesis, and evaluation rather than becoming amen-sayers to classroom instruction.[5]

Zev then describes his binary *midrashic* model: *midrash 'atsmi* (self exegesis and eisegesis) and *midrash tsiburi* (explorations of others).[6] And I know he walks the talk.

I have seen Zev in action at my college. Whether by Socratic means, by close textual analysis, or by audiovisual tapestries, he exudes no rank-based authority, but the legitimacy of wisdom. He does not monopolize the hour with the imprint of his views, but he tries to facilitate learning by fostering a hierarchy-free dialogue. Sure, there will be an occasional and collective stumble across the learning community that is his class. Like all of us, he will lose focus, digress in monologue, but he will catch himself. Learning takes place because student learning, not faculty professing, is the primary focus. Writing this should be self-evident but it is also a necessary reminder how much work still lies ahead.

In the meantime, Zev's students will continue to learn not by passively memorizing truths, truths that may remain unexamined (and hence not really mastered, Zev's "amen sayers") but by actively learning to interpret the cognitive, seamless, vast, and invariable complex map that constitutes our world. As a fly on the wall during a Garber hour, you know that authentic, communal, valuable "teachable moments" have been woven into a string of memorable pearls by a master craftsman, and it has been good.

As an agnostic, there is no seat for me at the table when colleagues like Zev, Steve Jacobs, Hank Knight, and Jim Moore apply the *Midrash,* that interpretational minuet of interreligious dialogue, to matters metaphysical, or to the interstices of religion and genocide, an area of great concern to me as noted earlier in this essay. But if religions are ever to emerge from the shackles of zero sum gaming (rubbing against one another like tectonic plates, moving in opposite but very lethal directions), it will be because those daring to engage in genuinely deep dialogue—and here I do not mean diversity or tolerance prattle—have found a way out of the genocidal chasms wherein humanity falls time and again. In his thoughtful writing about interreligious tension points, from an Auschwitz convent to Mel Gibson's *Passion*[7] to his musings on the broad canvass of meta-questions addressed by others in this book, Zev plays a substantial role, a role one can only admire, though not by trying the impossible in striving for compromise, in splitting the difference. As he has written: "equality in dialogue does not mean ready acceptance of the other's religious doctrines and theology."[8] Instead, he tries to engage in a finer and more subtle art, finding common ground.

It will be beyond the time of our existence before it is known whether this interfaith dialogue will have begun to make a difference. You may understand that I do not share the fearless, believing sentiments of Ps. 23:4, but if we are ever to emerge from this genocidal valley, it will be because those with a belief in a metaphysical entity have found a way to stop killing each other. Zev will have been at the genesis of the first stirrings toward finding that path out of the valley. It will also be because scientists, from the natural to the social, will have found ways to have humanity think beyond those nonreligious worldviews that have proven to be equally genocidal: imperialism, nationalism, racism, and totalitarianism in all its manifestations.

We will not succeed in our lifetime. We may not succeed in even the most marginal and modest improvement of the human condition. But that is all right. The late and legendary Catholic chaplain at Cambridge, Monsignor Gilbey, taught that the duty of the Christian is not to leave the world a better place but to leave the world a better man.

What we can say, on the occasion of Zev's sixty-fifth *Jahrzeit* is that he will not give up on the first part, but that he already passes Gilbey's test. Let's give him an A.

Notes

1. Sam Harris, *The End of Faith* (New York: W. W. Norton, 2005), 12–13. See also G. Jan Colijn and Izaak Colijn, *Ruin's Wheel* (Margate, N.J.: ComteQ Publishing, 2006), 110–13.
2. Harris, *The End of Faith,* 23.
3. Ibid., 92–93.
4. Zev's summary of his teaching philosophy is found in a brief, gorgeous recent piece: Zev Garber, "The Flood and the Fig Tree: Teaching, Text and Theology," *CSSR Bulletin* 35, no. 3 (2006): 1–3.
5. Ibid., 1.
6. Ibid., 3.
7. I refer here to, for instance, Zev Garber and Bruce Zuckerman, "The Furor over the Auschwitz Convent: The Inside and Outside of the Language of Bias," in *From Prejudice to Destruction—Western Civilization in the Shadow of Auschwitz*, ed. G. Jan Colijn and Marcia Sachs Littell (Münster: LIT Verlag, 1995), and Zev Garber, ed., *Mel Gibson's Passion: The Film, the Controversy and Its Implications* (West Lafayette, Ind.: Purdue University Press, 2006).
8. Garber, "The Flood and the Fig Tree," 3.

Jewish Studies without Jews

The Growth of an Academic Field in Austria and Germany

Klaus Hödl

In the last few decades, Germany and Austria have experienced a staggering expansion of the field of Jewish studies.[1] They have been set up either as separate institutes within a faculty or as programs that consist of courses related to Jewish history and culture offered by various departments. The development of Jewish studies is closely connected to political and cultural processes in society at large and cannot be described properly without taking them into account. The link between them became especially conspicuous in the former East Germany, where the crumbling of the Berlin Wall in 1989 led, among other institutions and positions, to the founding of the Moses Mendelssohn Zentrum für europäisch-jüdische Studien at the University of Potsdam (MMZ), which is headed by Julius Schoeps; the Simon Dubnow Institut für jüdische Geschichte und Kultur at the University of Leipzig, directed by Dan Diner; and the Lehrstuhl für Judaistik at the University of Erfurt, directed by Andreas Gotzmann.[2]

From an American perspective, this boom of Judaic studies in Germany may come as a surprise. It cannot be explained by the same reasons that account for their establishment in the United States: due to the attractiveness of leading a life without any assertive affiliation to a religious/ethnic group, a growing number of Jews cut their ties to their communities. The institutionalization of Jewish studies is frequently designed to countervail and reverse this development. It often serves the goal of strengthening Jewish identity.[3]

In Germany and Austria, the number of Jews interested in as well as ready to finance Jewish studies, and of Jewish students who would attend their courses, is too small for the issue of identity to play a decisive role and to sufficiently explain the growth of this academic field.[4] In addition, the majority of its teaching staff consists of non-Jews. This fact also stands against a utilization of Judaic studies for advancing Jewish consciousness,[5] as may be confirmed by comparing the situation in Austria and the United States: the first institute of Judaic studies founded in the German language area after World War II was set up at the University of Vienna and from its beginning in 1945/1966[6] until 1993 was headed by Kurt Schubert, a devoted Catholic.[7] His religious denomination was not considered to be a problem; rather, it was regarded as an indication of growing reconciliation between Jews and non-Jews after the Shoah. In the United States, the appointment of a Catholic as head of a Jewish studies program at a well-known college in New York City raised strong criticism by the local Jewish community and finally led to his replacement.[8]

Against this background it seems obvious that Jewish studies in Germany and Austria have primarily been designed to meet the increasing interest of a non-Jewish population in the culture and history of the Jews. The founding of this academic field is hardly propelled by identity policy; rather, as will be delineated below, it is an expression of the reconfiguration of collective memory.

The following pages provide a short overview of the development of Jewish studies in Germany and Austria. The focus will be directed to the question of how their proliferation in countries being largely bereft of Jews can be interpreted. What does the establishment of Jewish studies reveal about the lives of Jews in these societies? Furthermore, it remains to be asked what "Jewish" means in an environment where Jewish studies are mostly taught by non-Jews, and even Jewish cultural productions are largely performed by non-Jews. How can Jewish studies be taught to students who know Jews and Judaism only by hearsay?

Early Efforts to Establish Jewish Studies

The beginning of Judaic studies can be traced to the early nineteenth century, when a few Jews banded together in Berlin in order to deliver papers on and discuss scientific and cultural issues.[9] Among these people were Leopold Zunz (1794–1886), Isaac Markus Jost (1793–1860), and Eduard Ganz (1798–1830), who were to become renowned representatives of the *Wissenschaft des Judentums*. At that time, however, they were hardly interested in Judaism and had not yet embarked on modernizing it; rather, they dedicated their intellectual prowess to general topics. Their interest in the cultural life of society at large is indicated by the papers given in the *Wissenschaftszirkel*, as the group called itself: only one of them dealt with Judaism.[10]

This attitude changed strikingly within a few years. The emergence of romanticism and its concomitant erosion of Enlightenment ideas, the birth of nationalist thinking and the stress on (German) folklore that excluded the Jews from (German) peoplehood, and especially the upsurge of antisemitism in the years following Prussia's victory over Napoleon obscured the vista of full Jewish integration into the society.[11]

Largely alienated from traditional Judaism, but painfully aware of the hindrances to integration into larger society, these Jews now strove for a concept of Judaism with which they could identify and which, at the same time, would be acknowledged by non-Jews and thereby render their social acceptance—as Jews—possible.[12] For this reason they set up the Verein für Kultur und Wissenschaft der Juden (1819–24), which gave them a forum to discuss Jewish history and identity in an informal way and thereby to evolve their new understanding of Judaism.[13]

The innovative element of the Verein was its challenge to the Christian monopoly of studying Judaism in a nonreligious way.[14] Out of these activities there originated the *Wissenschaft des Judentums* (WdJ). It was conceived of as an interdisciplinary study of Judaism. According to the aforementioned Leopold Zunz, it comprised disciplines such as Theologie, Jurisprudenz, Ethik, Geographie, Mathematik, Astronomie, Medizin, Kunst, Sprache, Geschichte et al.[15] The WdJ embarked on a critical interpretation of Jewish writing by taking into account the historical context of its production. This approach enabled them to point out that Judaism was not static but had changed over time, and to criticize many Jewish customs in use as well as to demand their adaptation to contemporary social conditions, that is, to modernize them.[16]

The very link between the *Wissenschaft des Judentums* and Jewish/Judaic studies in contemporary Germany or Austria lies in the fact that the members of the WdJ wanted to establish the "scientific" study of Judaism in a university setting. For this reason Leopold Zunz petitioned the Prussian minister of education in 1843 as well as in 1848 to create a professorship in Jewish literature and history at the University of Berlin, but his request was declined. The explanation of its rejection by the university said that such a position would "strengthen Jewish existence in its particularity, and give spiritual support to its alienating laws and usages."[17]

Even though the *Wissenschaft des Judentums* did not become institutionalized at a university, the attempt to make it part of the already existing academy should be stressed, since it indicates the intention to involve non-Jews in the study of Jewish religion and culture. It attests to an openness toward non-Jews that in the present, as has been mentioned already, sometimes seems to be lacking.

As a consequence of the failure of Zunz's efforts, Jews set up their own institutions. In 1854 the Jüdisch-Theologische Seminar Fränklscher Stiftung was established in Breslau, and in 1872 the Hochschule für die Wissenschaft des Judentums in Berlin.[18] The clear separation of these Jewish institutions from public universities did not change until World War I.

In the subsequent years, the first if very cautious steps toward an integration of the study of Judaism into the existing academic institutions were taken. At the University of Frankfurt/Main, for instance, a position for Religion und jüdische Ethik was established; it never reached the status of full professorship, though. This goal was only achieved at an international level: professorships were introduced at Harvard and Columbia, and in Jerusalem the Hebrew University was opened.[19] Whereas these institutions flourished, the very modest beginnings in Germany came to an end with the rise of National Socialism.

After World War II, the situation improved tremendously. The awareness of the monstrous atrocities perpetrated by the German people during the Nazi regime was the driving force behind an emerging interest in Jewish history and culture.[20] Efforts to disseminate a basic knowledge of Judaism among the population at large, and to divest the Jews of their image as the "exotic other" were taken in various areas, and the academic field was one of them.

All these trends notwithstanding, Jewish and non-Jewish cultures were still regarded as different entities. Yet, they were no longer located at two opposite ends of an axis; rather, their encounter and the consequences of their contacts were seen as worth being examined, and thus their mutual influence. *Symbiose* was the widely used term for these relations.

In this intellectual atmosphere, the first chair for the Science of Judaism, or, more appropriate, for Judaistik, was established at the Free University in Berlin in 1963/64. Other institutions were soon to follow, such as the Martin-Buber-Institut für Judaistik at the University of Cologne in 1966, and the Seminar für Judaistik at the University of Frankfurt/Main in 1969. In Hamburg the Institut für die Geschichte der deutschen Juden was established in 1963, and in Duisburg in 1974 the program Geschichte und Religion des Judentums, which was to become the Solomon Ludwig Steinheim-Institut für deutsch-jüdische Geschichte in 1987. Chairs in Freiburg i. Br., belonging to the department of Orientalistik, in Munich and other universities must also be mentioned. In Heidelberg, the Hochschule für Jüdische Studien was established in 1978.[21]

The Distinction between Judaistik and Jüdische Studien in Germany

The 1990s saw not merely an extension of the field of the study of Judaism but a shift in the research agenda. Most of the new institutions founded in these years called themselves *Jewish*—instead of *Judaic*—Studies and claimed to pursue an innovative approach to the history, culture, and religion of the Jews. In many cases implicitly, in some bluntly, Jewish Studies considered themselves to be more relevant than Judaistik. The latter did not acquiesce to its denigration but lashed out against its new rival as well. For some years, Jewish and Judaic studies were caught in an acrimonious dispute over which was the more appropriate and legitimate representative of the academic study of Jewish history, culture, and religion.[22]

Intimately bound up with the different methodologies to study Judaism was the question of which of the two disciplines provides a more appropriate picture of Jewish life. Jüdische Studien claimed that Judaistik has little to say about Jewish activities outside the framework of religion, that is, about a large part of Jewish existence in Western and Central Europe from the period of Enlightenment onwards.[23] Conversely, Jüdische Studien were criticized for their supposedly low level of teaching as well as their teachers' insufficient knowledge of Judaism and Hebrew.[24] The lack of pertinent language skills allowed them, as was pointed out, to do research only on a restricted scope of topics; in addition, it barred their access to many important sources and thereby favors the creation of images of the past that do not reflect "reality."[25]

Lately, the controversy between Jewish and Judaic Studies has subsided and given way to their rapprochement, which has led to stressing common grounds between the two academic disciplines.

This development finds its expression in the fact that newly established positions are called Jewish Studies, although they teach a Judaistik curriculum.[26]

Jewish Studies in Austria

In Austria, circumstances were different from those of its northern neighbor. Until the turn of the twenty-first century, the former's academic landscape had been dominated by the aforementioned Viennese Institut für Judaistik. Other universities offered only a few courses related to Jewish history and culture/religion. This situation changed in summer 2000, when a Jewish Studies program was introduced at the University of Salzburg.[27] Around the same time, the Center for Jewish Studies (CJS) was established at the University of Graz. It was designed, first and foremost, as a research institute. Its major task consisted of editing a journal (*transversal*) and a book series reflecting its research activities, as well as organizing conferences.[28] In cooperation with the Hochschule für Jüdische Studien in Heidelberg, the CJS started a joint-degree program on Jewish Studies in 2007.

In contrast to Germany, where the establishment of institutes for Jewish Studies was accompanied by vitriolic assessments of their academic performances by the already existing Judaic Studies, the new organizations hardly caused a controversy in Austria. Some consternation on the part of Vienna about the new initiatives in Graz and Salzburg could not be overlooked, however.[29]

The CJS tries to distinguish itself from other institutes and programs of Jewish Studies in Central Europe by adamantly pursuing a cultural studies approach. It draws upon the theoretical framework provided by postcolonial studies, gender studies, and so on, and applies it to the study of (Jewish) culture. Consistently, Jewish culture is understood as dynamic, always changing, and constantly produced by interactive processes that involve non-Jews. Both Jews and non-Jews are seen as working together in the production of cultural meaning. Under this perspective, the contentious issue of non-Jews teaching Jewish studies does not seem to be of much relevance.

What Is Jewish Culture?

The rapidly growing interest of non-Jews in "things Jewish" can also be observed outside the academic world, in the culture of society at large. In fall 2003 Liliane Weissberg gave a lecture sponsored by the Leo Baeck Institute in New York and the German Historical Institute in Washington, D.C., on perspectives of German-Jewish studies. In her presentation she mentioned the craze for Klezmer music sweeping Germany at present. "Berlin may not be unique—the Klezmer scene described may be distinctive, but ultimately not much different, perhaps, from the music played in the outskirts of Polish Krakow today. The description of a thriving musical scene evokes haunting images of the past."[30]

The intriguing point of this phenomenon lies with the fact that non-Jews seem to relish an aspect of Jewish culture that alludes to a past to which they have no personal relations and that is not part of their (collective) memory.[31] The foundation of this culture—a vibrant Jewish life in Eastern Europe—no longer exists. It did not disappear under the onslaught of processes of modernization but was eradicated by the grandparents of those young people who nowadays enjoy Klezmer performances. In this way, the interest in the music must not be seen as a renaissance of a part of Jewish culture that for some decades had receded and thereby escaped attention; rather it may be interpreted as taking a stand against one of the outcomes of the Shoah, namely a cultural landscape that is largely deprived of its "Jewish flavor."

Even more stunning than the growing resonance of Klezmer performances among non-Jewish Germans is the fact that also many musicians are "Goyim." Entire Klezmer concerts are thus performed and attended mostly by non-Jews. This means, according to Weissberg, that

> those young Germans performing in Berlin's Hackesche Höfe or its former Scheunenviertel, a section of town that was populated by poor Eastern European immigrants before the war, are not just playing music. They are playing Jews. This role play has become very successful, and gives apparent satisfaction to actors and listeners alike, many of them tourists visiting the German capital, who encounter this phenomenon for the first time and wonder what it is that they encounter here.[32]

The issue to which Weissberg tries to call attention refers to the fact that Jews, some decades after they were killed, "become alive again." This does not happen through commemoration but through mimicry, through their representation as entertaining figures. Against the background of the Shoah, the conception that Germans "play Jews" for distraction may be perceived as deeply disturbing.

Another strain of perturbation stems from the source that also causes the uneasiness about the issue of non-Jews teaching Jewish Studies. It originates from the notion of a clearly definable Jewish culture and is linked to the apprehension that non-Jews may "remodel" Jewish culture in accordance with their own perspectives, largely divest it of its Jewish "ingredients," and thereby distort it.

Weissberg mentions in her lecture a paradigmatic example of a warped image of Jewish culture produced by non-Jews:

> An event called "Klezmer as in Herder's time" was announced as the entertainment program for a conference celebrating the two-hundredth anniversary of the birth of the German philosopher and Protestant theologian Johann Gottfried Herder (1744–1803) in Weimar in November 2003. It was sponsored by the city's *Kulturamt* and the Protestant Academy of Thuringia in a place that was largely deprived of a Jewish population in Herder's time, the eighteenth century.[33]

In this instance, a historical image is being fabricated that corresponds to the expectations and wishes of non-Jewish Germans, but which definitely is not in congruence with the "actual" past. The non-Jews' preoccupation with Jewish culture and their lack of historical knowledge create a historical narrative that is based on particular interests. This process is reminiscent of warnings enunciated by Peter Schäfer with regard to Jewish Studies: he claimed that a lack of pertinent knowledge of Judaism might lead to the production of "false history."[34]

Trends in the field of Judaic Studies as well as in the culture of society at large are thus part of a development tending to lead to a new understanding of what Jewish culture is and Jewishness means, of a Jewishness that becomes more and more interpreted by non-Jews. This is the background against which some people feel disconcerted about the so-called renaissance of Jewish culture in Germany. Y. Michael Bodemann describes this development succinctly:

> It is important to see then that to a considerable degree Jewish culture is being manufactured . . . by these Judaizing milieux—by German experts on Jewish culture and religion. There can be no doubt, however, that they enact Jewish culture from within German biographies and from within German history; this has an important bearing on the type of Jewish culture that is actually being produced: a culture that is not lived, that draws heavily from the museum, and that is still no less genuine for that.[35]

A cultural studies approach, as pursued by the JCS in Graz, deals with the issue of non-Jews engaged in "things Jewish" in a different way. It questions the purported bipolarity of Jewish versus non-Jewish cultural productions and stresses the complexity of interaction between Jews and non-Jews as the ground on which (Jewish) culture strives. It does not presuppose the existence of a given Jewish culture against which deviations or distortions of cultural articulations may be measured. This approach is illustrated in the following by a concrete example.

Is There Authentic Jewishness?

A few years ago, Ruth Ellen Gruber published a book on the virtuality of Jewish culture. In a certain way, this publication is a telling expression of the concern many Jews harbor about Jewish cultural life performed by non-Jews. Gruber in her publication mentions many examples that nourish such an uneasiness:

> It can be simpler for non-Jews to pursue their interest in Things Jewish on their own. More than a few may even find it more satisfying to fulfil or devise their own idea of what "Jewish" means rather than risk being contradicted by living sources: their own Jewish cultural products become more "real" than "real" Jewish life. "No, I don't know any Jewish people," Michael, a curly haired twenty-year-old working as a volunteer at the Westfalen Jewish Museum in Dorsten, told me in

> 1997. "There is no Jewish life here in Dorsten." Yet the aim of the museum, he told me, was to reach visitors about the everyday life of Jews. . . . The only Jews he had ever met were the occasional visitors, like me, who turned up at the museum.[36]

In her writing, Gruber departs from the notion of an authentic Jewish culture and contrasts it to virtual, reinvented Jewish culture. The latter refers to Jewish culture that is cut off from a Jewish milieu. It is defined by Gruber as a realm "in which Jewish cultural products may take precedence over living Jewish culture: a realm in many senses constructed from desire rather than from memory or inherited tradition." An authentic Jewish culture, on the other hand, is not possible without intimate ties to Jewish community life. Consistently, Jewish culture in present-day Europe, largely deprived of this foundation, becomes increasingly influenced by non-Jews. Or, as Gruber describes the present-day situation in her own words:

> Today in Europe the public idea of Jewish culture—or what is Jewish—is shaped very much from outside as well as from within the Jewish community. Likewise, the wealth of performance, instruction, talk, and exhibition that today consciously advances an idea of collective Jewish identity as often as not end up advancing it in the minds of a non-Jewish rather than a Jewish audience.[37]

Once again, the contentious issue in the realm of Jewish culture is comparable to the argument in the controversy about Jewish studies: how legitimate is the involvement of non-Jews in these two fields, and to which extent do their contributions lead to images of Judaism/Jewish culture deviating from assumed standards of authenticity?

According to critics of Jewish studies in Central Europe taught as well as productions of Jewish culture performed and consumed by non-Jews, current developments differ widely from the past when the existence of large numbers of Jews provided a milieu in which "authentic Jewishness" could flourish and was not at risk of being (mis-)interpreted by non-Jews. It remains to be asked, however, if there has ever been an "authentic Jewish culture," and if contemporary Jewish cultural manifestations are really that different from artifacts produced before the Shoah.

In the following it will be shown that the notion of a dichotomy between an authentic Jewish culture and a virtual Jewish culture must be questioned. This shall be done by analyzing an instance that R. E. Gruber mentions in her book in order to exemplify her distinction between authentic and virtual.

Authenticity at the Viennese Jewish Museum?

In 1895 the world's first Jewish museum opened in Vienna. The primary reason for its establishment was the outburst of antisemitism that Jews wanted to fight by presenting a positive image of Judaism to non-Jews.[38] Among the museum's major attractions there was the Gute Stube, a room for celebrating Sabbath. It was installed by the painter Isidor Kaufmann (1854–1921), who collected the items of its interior in Eastern Europe.[39]

For R. E. Gruber, the Gute Stube is a paradigmatic expression of authentic Jewish culture:

> Kaufmann's Sabbath room installation appealed to nostalgic recollections of the urbanized (or urbanizing) Viennese public, for many of whom the twin image of the *shtetl* and traditional Jewish ways of life had already achieved mythic status. When they stepped into Kaufmann's installation, both Jewish and non-Jewish visitors felt that they were stepping into the past. . . . But it was a past that had a direct link with the present—either via their own childhood memories or via the "authentic" old-fashioned ways that still existed, like an endangered species, in some remaining eastern outposts.[40]

Gruber contrasts the Gute Stube to present-day exhibitions, that, in her opinion, represent instances of virtual Jewish culture: "Today's 'Seder table' installations are sometimes elaborate in every detail— . . . but often they are demonstrative reconstructions, aimed at illustrating concepts rather than evoking real warmth or real memory."[41]

The assumed difference between the kind of Judaism expressed by the Gute Stube and the one reflected by present-day Seder table installations is claimed to be caused by the existence, in the former case, and lack, with respect to the Seder table, of a living Jewish culture. With respect to the Gute Stube, the link to an extant Jewish milieu was forged either by memory or by actual relations to the East European Shtetl world supposedly congruent with traditional Judaism, that in Central Europe had long since gone. In contrast, the Seder table installations were seen as based on a concept of Judaism only.

The Gute Stube

The Gute Stube was the most important part of the Viennese Jewish museum. It was not merely a room that showed the visitors how Jews once used to celebrate Sabbath, but it also evoked the image of the Jews as a family-loving people. The notions of Sabbath and family had increasingly become fused into a metaphor of Jewishness from the second-third of the nineteenth century onward.[42] This was partly the result of the Jews' secularization that divested the Sabbath of its religious content and reinterpreted it as a day that was ideally spent in communion with one's family.[43] The secular reinterpretation of Sabbath was also the outcome of the Jews' attempt to present themselves toward the gentile population as suitable for being acknowledged as equals. Their self-representation as a family-loving people should convince non-Jews that values highly esteemed in society at large at that time were central to Judaism.[44]

This strategy had already been pursued, for instance, by the Jewish painter Moritz Daniel Oppenheim (1800–1882), and finds its paradigmatic expression in his painting entitled *Die Rückkehr des Freiwilligen aus den Befreiungskriegen zu den nach alter Sitte lebenden Seinen* (The Return of the Jewish Volunteer from the Wars of Liberation to his Traditional Family). Oppenheim depicts traditional Sabbath life through a family gathering on Sabbath. Its religious aspects were clearly relegated into the background, as can be concluded from the presentation of the Jewish soldier traveling home on a Sabbath. To be with his family was more important than the observance of religious laws. Sabbath and family were associated with each other.

Oppenheim's paintings mirror not only the secularization of Sabbath that took place in the nineteenth century; they also construct a concept of Judaism that was predicated on its instrumentalization in the fight against antisemitism. In order to make the dedication of Jews to family life on Sabbath not appear as an outcome of their assimilation, Oppenheim projected it back into traditional Judaism, when the two were not unknown but not yet so intimately bound up. In pre-emancipatory, traditional Judaism, large families, and not the modern middle-class family that Oppenheim depicted, were prevalent; and the gathering of the whole family on Sabbath was frequently more a wish than a fact, since in many cases the father, plying his trade, was—often for weeks, months, and even years—not at home. In making the family communion a characteristic of the pre-emancipatory time, Oppenheim creates an image of traditional Judaism that largely consisted of the values and expectations that Jews harbored in the second half of the nineteenth century. It did thus not reflect "reality."

Oppenheim's paintings were well received by Jews and non-Jews. Reviews of his works in non-Jewish newspapers show that the notion of an intimate link between Sabbath and family was widespread in society at large and that Jews were respected for it. Consequently, the Viennese Jewish museum, whose major task was to counteract antisemitism by presenting a positive image of Judaism, had every reason to draw upon Oppenheim's approach. The Gute Stube was thus the three-dimensional realization of Oppenheim's paintings.[45]

Conclusion

The Gute Stube, as well as Oppenheim's paintings, presented an image of Sabbath that was less designed as an accurate reproduction of the past but served the goal of showing to non-Jews that certain norms, highly appreciated by the larger society, such as one's dedication to family life, have always been an integral part of Judaism. It was also a strategy to convince fellow Jews that they could integrate into society and, at the same time, hold fast to their Judaism, since it did not contradict values cherished by non-Jews; just the opposite: Judaism expressed them in an exemplary mode.

This leads to the conclusion that the Gute Stube was not linked to the past, as Gruber assumed. It was based on a concept of (traditional) Judaism that served specific goals. Similar to so-called virtual Jewish cultural manifestations, the Gute Stube was influenced by desires. Furthermore, it was the outcome of an interaction between Jews and non-Jews. The presentation of Sabbath as a day central of which was the family was directed to non-Jews in order to enhance a positive image of Judaism among them. It thus had as much to do with a "living Jewish culture" as with non-Jews. Against this background, there were not many differences between the Gute Stube and present-day Seder table installations. The dichotomy between authentic and virtual is not warranted.

Notes

1. In Germany and Austria, the terms *Jewish Studies* and *Judaic Studies,* mostly translated as *Jüdische Studien* and *Judaistik*, denote different approaches to the study of Judaism. In the 1990s a fierce debate raged between the representatives of the respective fields. Before touching upon this controversy (see below), the two terms will be used alternately, understood very broadly as the study of Jewish religion, culture, and history.
2. Margarete Schlüter, "Judaistik an deutschen Universitäten heute," in *Wissenschaft vom Judentum. Annäherungen nach dem Holocaust*, ed. Michael Brenner and Stefan Rohrbacher (Göttingen: Vandenhoeck and Ruprecht, 2000), 91.
3. Michael Brenner, "Jüdische Studien im internationalen Kontext," in *Wissenschaft vom Judentum,* ed. Brenner and Rohrbacher, 48.
4. There are fewer than 20,000 Jews in Austria. Vienna and its surroundings are home to a scarce 7,000 Jews registered at the Viennese Jewish community. In addition, there are around 8,000 Jews who are not members of the community, and among them there are some 3,000 Orthodox and Ultraorthodox Jews. In Linz, Salzburg, Innsbruck, and Graz, other cities with Jewish communities, there live around 100 Jews respectively. See Sylvia Steinitz, "Shalom Wien," *Profil* 8 (Feb. 20, 2006): 91. In Germany the number of Jews has recently increased, due to immigration from the countries of the former Soviet Union. Between 1994 and 1999 there was "a threefold increase . . . in the membership of Jewish communities throughout Germany." In 2002 there was a total of around 180,000 Jews, and 87 percent of them had come to settle there since 1989. Doris Bensimon, "Jews in Today's Germany," *Jewish Journal of Sociology* 45, no. 2 (2003): 20, 28.
5. The reason given for the purported inability of non-Jews to meet the scholarly requirements for teaching Jewish/Judaic studies refers to their estrangement from Jewish cultural surroundings. See Dean Philipp Bell, "Historical Memory and the State of Jewish Studies in Germany," editor's introduction, in *Shofar* 15, no. 4 (1997): 2–3.
6. The first efforts to establish the institute took place in 1945; there was no full professorship until 1959, and the institute was founded only in 1966.
7. Evelyn Adunka, *Die vierte Gemeinde. Die Wiener Juden in der Zeit von 1945 bis heute* (Wien: Philo Verlag, 2002), 169.
8. Brenner, "Jüdische Studien im internationalen Kontext," 48–49.
9. Siegfried Ucko, "Geistesgeschichtliche Grundlagen der Wissenschaft des Judentums (Motive des Kulturvereins vom Jahre 1819)," *Zeitschrift für die Geschichte der Juden in Deutschland* 5 (1935): 3–4.
10. Michael A. Meyer, *Von Moses Mendelssohn zu Leopold Zunz. Jüdische Identität in Deutschland 1749–1824* (München: C. H. Beck, 1992), 189.
11. See Rainer Erb and Werner Bergmann, *Die Nachtseite der Judenemanzipation. Der Widerstand gegen die Integration der Juden in Deutschland 1780–1860* (Berlin: Metropol Verlag, 1989), 41–46.
12. Ismar Schorsch, *From Text to Context: The Turn to History in Modern Judaism* (Hanover, N.H.: University Press of New England, 1994), 207.
13. Klaus Hödl, "Zwischen den Welten. Jüdische Studien und kulturelle Selbstreflexion," in *Jüdische Studien. Reflexionen zu Theorie und Praxis eines wissenschaftlichen Feldes,* ed. Hödl, Schriften des Kentrums für Jüdische Studien 4 (Innsbruck, 2003), 173.
14. Ismar Schorsch, "Das erste Jahrhundert der Wissenschaft des Judentums (1818–1919)," in *Wissenschaft vom Judentum,* ed. Brenner and Rohrbacher, 11.
15. Peter Schäfer, "Judaistik-jüdische Wissenschaft in Deutschland heute. Historische Identität und Nationalität," *Saeculum* 42 (1991): 202.

16. An excellent case in point is Brit Mila. See Michael A. Meyer, *Antwort auf die Moderne. Geschichte der Reformbewegung im Judentum* (Wien: Böhlau Wien, 2000), 147.
17. Shaye J. D. Cohen, "Gentiles and Jewish Studies," *Jewish Studies Quarterly* 3, no. 2 (1996): 185.
18. Peter Schäfer, "Jewish Studies in Germany Today," *Jewish Studies Quarterly* 3, no. 2 (1996): 149.
19. Brenner, "Jüdische Studien im internationalen Kontext," 8.
20. Siehe Klaus Hödl, *Wiener Juden—jüdische Wiener. Identität, Performanz und Gedächtnis im 19. Jahrhundert* (Innsbruck: Studien Verlag, 2006), 29.
21. Schäfer, "Judaistik-jüdische Wissenschaft in Deutschland heute," 209.
22. The major line of argument brought forth by the representatives of Jewish studies can be found in the attempt by the Moses Mendelssohn Center for European Jewish Studies in Potsdam to distinguish itself from the renowned institute for Judaistik at the Free University in Berlin. See Christoph Schulte, "Judaistik or Jewish Studies? The New Construction of Jewish Studies at the Universities in the Former German Democratic Republic," *Shofar* 15, no. 4 (1997): 32–40. Criticism was directed to the latter's curriculum that stresses the study of Hebrew and thereby de-emphasizes other subjects. The probably most outspoken opponent to Judaistik in Berlin, Christoph Schulte, questioned the relevance of the philological approach by claiming that as little as a Jew is "defined solely by his mastery of Hebrew. . . . Jewish Studies could be equally little defined solely by Hebrew philology." It is not possible, as Schulte stated, to gain a comprehensive view of Jewish culture and history without drawing upon the work of other academic fields. Schulte, "Judaistik or Jewish Studies?" 34.

    This censure was directed to the very core of the Berlin institute's self-definition. Its declared task to present Judaism from its beginnings to the present (Niko Oswald, "Judentum als Gegenstand von Wissenschaft. Eine Kritik des Faches Judaistik in Deutschland," *Babylon* 8 [1991]: 47) is so comprehensive an undertaking that it cannot be accomplished without several professorships. The gap between the outlined intention and actual achievements was even maintained by its representatives and found its expression by the institute's emphasis on ancient and medieval Jewry, the Hebrew Bible, and the rabbinical tradition. Liliane Weissberg, "Reflecting on the Past, Envisioning the Future: Perspectives for German-Jewish Studies," *GHI Bulletin* 35 (2004): 23. Yet, this self-limitation in the curriculum did not lead to a reformulation of its task.

    Whereas Jüdische Studien criticize the Judaistik's emphasis on Hebrew, the former frequently think that they can circumvent the issue of language, and that Jewish religious tradition was not of much importance to the study of the Jewish past. Instead of religion, Jewish culture, also its encounter with non-Jewish cultures, and thereby processes such as assimilation or acculturation, are considered to be of primary relevance to be dealt with. Weissberg, "Reflecting on the Past," 23. And such developments took place above all in the nineteenth and twentieth centuries. Jewish studies thus highlight the more recent past of Jewish history. In this way, both of them, Judaic as well as Jewish studies, focus on specific time periods and exclude large parts of Jewish history and culture.
23. Oswald, "Judentum als Gegenstand von Wissenschaft," 63.
24. Schäfer, "Jewish Studies in Germany Today," 156–57.
25. Schäfer, "Judaistik-jüdische Wissenschaft in Deutschland heute," 212.
26. Schlüter, "Judaistik or Jewish Studies?" 86.
27. Gerhard Bodendorfer, "Ein Forschungsinstitut für Jüdische Kulturgeschichte in Salzburg!?" in *Jüdische Studien,* 58.
28. See Klaus Hödl, editorial, in *Transversal* 1 (2000): 3. See also www.uni-graz.at/cjs-graz.
29. In 2001, at the first conference organized by the Center for Jewish Studies at the University of Graz, a representative of the Viennese Institut für Judaistik maintained that there was no need for any additional institution for Jewish/Judaic studies in Austria, since the Viennese Judaistik covers the whole range of approaches and topics in this academic field.
30. Weissberg, "Reflecting on the Past," 12.
31. See Jan Assmann, *Das kulturelle Gedächtnis. Schrift, Erinnerung und politische Identität in frühen Hochkulturen* (München: Beck, 1999), 35–37.
32. Weissberg, "Reflecting on the Past," 12.
33. Ibid.
34. Schäfer, "Judaistik-jüdische Wissenschaft in Deutschland heute," 210.
35. Y. Michael Bodemann, "A Reemergence of German Jewry?" in *Reemerging Jewish Culture in Germany: Life and Literature since 1989*, ed. Sander L. Gilman and Karen Remmler (New York: NYU Press, 1994), 57–58.
36. Ruth Ellen Gruber, *Virtually Jewish: Reinventing Jewish Culture in Europe* (Berkeley: University of California Press, 2002), 50–51.

37. Ibid., 27.
38. *Führer durch das Jüdische Museum*, ed. Curatorium (Wien, 1906).
39. Klaus Hödl, "The Turning to History of Viennese Jews: Jewish Identity and the Jewish Museum," *Journal of Modern Jewish Studies* 3, no. 1 (2004): 25.
40. Gruber, *Virtually Jewish*, 28.
41. Ibid.
42. David Sorkin, *The Transformation of German Jewry 1780–1840* (Oxford: Oxford University Press, 1987), 89.
43. Hödl, "Turning to History of Viennese Jews," 22.
44. Hödl, *Wiener Juden*, 91–111.
45. Bernhard Purin, "Isidor Kaufmanns kleine Welt. Die 'Gute Stube' im Wiener Jüdischen Museum," in *Isidor Kaufmann, 1853–1921*, ed. G. Tobias Natter (Vienna: Jüdisches Museum der Stadt Wien, 1995), 132.

The Story of *Shofar*

An Editor's Personal Account

Joseph Haberer

Introduction

In this, the twenty-fifth year of its publication, a retrospective account of the founding and growth of *Shofar* is altogether fitting. Also appropriate, as we honor Zev Garber, is to note how closely connected he has been to the journal.

This is a *personal* account, depending to a considerable extent on memory, flawed and partial as it may be.[1] I will describe the challenges, hurdles, frustrations, and satisfactions that have gone into the creation of what is now, perhaps, a premier journal of Jewish studies. I will frame the narrative in the context of the institutions in which this journal has taken its form. *Shofar* has been made possible through the interstices of a university (Purdue), of a college (Liberal Arts), of a program (Jewish Studies), a network of scholarly organizations (the Midwest Jewish Studies Association and the Western Jewish Studies Association), and a series of university presses (Nebraska University Press and Purdue University Press). I will conclude with some comments on the changing environment in which scholarly editors now operate.

Beginnings

Founding acts are important, since they shape the contours and directions of a human enterprise.[2] Small beginnings may have large consequences. In 1981 as the Jewish Studies Program at Purdue was initiated, my involvement began in a very circuitous and peripheral way, not as a founder but an interested supporter.[3]

My professional identification was in the area of science, technology, and public policy, a program that I had headed in the Department of Political Science. That program was unilaterally abolished during my sabbatical in Israel by the then-head of the Political Science Department (without consulting me about it)—the manner of which had left a rather bad feeling on my part. For several years as head of the STPP program I had edited an interdisciplinary newsletter which included mostly useful information, some short book-notes, and available materials. The *STPP Newsletter* had a wide national circulation. When I returned the newsletter was not resumed.

Approximately a year after the Jewish Studies Program at Purdue (JSP) became part of (Humanities, Social Science, and Education), Robert Melson, who chaired the program in its first year, approached me and suggested that I do something like that for the program. I was looking for a new challenge. I proposed a "newsletter," which would include short book-reviews, book-notes, and mini-articles, and set about putting together a prototype. I was willing to edit and put together the thing, but someone had to get the materials to print it on, the postage to distribute it outside of the university—in short, funding!

Robert Melson and I marched off to the dean's office and requested his support. As good deans will, he responded in a positive but guarded way: he would give us $200 to put out the first two issues, but after that we were on our own. I responded by asking whether he would allow us to raise our own money for the program, to which he responded positively. The key to the future of the Jewish Studies Program and *Shofar* lay in that "yes." We were now confronted by the need to raise money. I was in a situation where I felt I had to take the lead, since this new opportunity had come about through a funding request for *Shofar*.

Though I had no experience in fundraising or proposal writing, it was clear enough that there was no point in asking for financial support unless the program expanded its scope beyond the existing course offerings and the occasional public lecture. If there was to be a viable and perhaps vibrant newsletter there had to be news to report. Purdue was viewed as a predominantly technological institution. Building our program would require projects that were not simply duplications of what was done at, for example, our sister institution at Bloomington.

So I set in motion, in conjunction with a Jewish Studies Committee that had been formed, the following a biweekly "Noon Series" of talks, presentations, and discussions based on work or ideas or interests of faculty and community members that had some bearing on Jewish Studies or the Jewish experience. This was cost-free and gave the program some visibility.[4] Since we Jews were considered "the people of the book," making the acquisition of Jewish books a priority was a logical step. This led to my assuming the role of de facto Jewish Studies librarian. I canvassed the Purdue library to assess its holdings of key works and serials—and then appealed to potential donors.

From the outset, then, *Shofar* and JSP were intricately interwoven, and especially so early on when the publication still served as a newsletter. The governing structure of the JSP consisted of a Jewish Studies Committee made up of any faculty member who attended meetings and self-identified as being interested in Jewish studies. This committee met twice a semester and voted on the issues before it. Each year it elected a chairperson, who made the agenda and presided at the meeting.[5]

I decided that our newsletter would be issued quarterly. A cover and format were designed (see Figure 1).[6] In the back of my mind was the notion that it might eventually become more than a source of information and news. Above all, I wanted my investment of time and effort to have some impact (or else why bother) and become a source of adding books to the judaica collection through a book-review section.[7] However inchoate it appears in retrospect, the germ of what became the scholarly journal of later years was there from the start.

The Early Years (1982–1988)

For the title I hit upon *Shofar*. The first few issues were typed by Rose Haberer; the age of the office computer was still some years ahead. An editorial in our first issue—"To Our Readers—A Message and Request"—made our intentions quite explicit:

> *The prayer for knowledge is first among the Benedictions.*
>
> —Amni B. Nathan, Talmud, Berakot, 33a
>
> Jewish Studies Programs are committed, among other things, to the dissemination of knowledge about the Jewish experience in its manifold dimensions.
>
> In starting this quarterly publication, the Jewish Studies Program at Purdue hopes to contribute in a modest way to that purpose. We want to provide scholars, teachers and supporters of Jewish Studies Programs at the college and university level with a publication that will at the very least be *useful*, and at times stimulating. Our primary purpose is to disseminate information and news that will be *useful* to our readers. If we fail in that we will close shop. We also want to encourage

Shofar

FALL 1982

הקשיבו לקול שופר

A FIRST YEAR'S RETROSPECTIVE

Since my tenure as Chairman of this august body is passing and *Rav Gordon Young* is about to take over, I wanted to share some thoughts and musings, some end-notes, and some thank-you notes with you about what has been accomplished and what I would like to see done.

Having the Jewish Studies minor approved by the Curriculum Committee and the Senate this past semester, we became officially part of the Purdue Community, and we made our presence known. None of this could have been done without the help of many competent and sympathetic people. Thanks go to *Rabbi Gedalya Engel* of Hillel who was encouraging and helpful all year. Thank-you's go to the various Heads and the Dean who not only approved the program but helped to shape it. Special thank-you's go to *Joan Marshall* who helped shepherd it through. Once the program was approved, we had the obligation of making it available to students. The job of collating information on courses and advertising these courses on posters was done with efficiency and alacrity, if not panache, by *Gordon Mork*. Though, of course, we cannot take credit for the numbers, it is of interest that this Spring Semester there were 251 students enrolled in various Jewish Studies courses. May they multiply!

To my mind, the most important objective of the Jewish Studies program at Purdue is to help create a content in which faculty and students who are interested in the scholarly and artistic pursuit of the Jewish experience will find support.

[Continued on page 6]

MODERN JEWISH POETS: I

Miklos Radnoti (1909-1944)

Miklos Radnoti was born of Jewish origin in Budapest on 5 May, 1909, and died near Abda, a small town in northeastern Hungary, between 6 and 10 November, 1944. He was an orphan by age twelve (his mother died giving him birth), and he was brought up by a maternal uncle, a well-to-do wholesaler in textiles. During his childhood he knew little emotional security and in his youth never lived long in one place.

After completing business school in Budapest, he matriculated at Szeged University in 1931 in Hungarian and French literature. During the summer of 1931 (and again the summers of 1937 and 1939) Radnoti was in Paris. In June, 1934 he earned his doctorate, summa cum laude, from Szeged University, with a dissertation on the novelist Margit Kaffka.

From 1920 to 1944, Hungary was governed by the pseudo-parliamentary regime of Nicholas Horthy. Horthy was an ultra-conservative, cautious authoritarian who attempted to stifle all forms of progressive political movements or opposition, and ultimately opened the country to Hitler. Radnoti's response to the rise of Hitler was almost immediate. Fearful of the future, Radnoti nonetheless enjoyed domestic happiness. In 1935 he married Fanni Gyarmati whose love was to sustain him through the suffering of the years to come.

Between September, 1940 and the date of his death, he was drafted no less than

[Continued on page 5]

Shofar

Jewish Studies Program
c/o Department of Political Science
Purdue University
West Lafayette, Indiana 47907

TABLE OF CONTENTS

Figure 1. First cover of *Shofar*

the sharing of ideas, teaching materials, humor (don't we all need it?) and poetry (to lift the spirit) among the interdisciplinary community of those in our "field." We would like to believe that SHOFAR could help strengthen the network of Jewish Studies people.

While our program is centered at Purdue, we seek through this publication to reach the larger Jewish Studies community in Indiana, the Mid-west, and the rest of the country. This publication does not intend to become a p.r. vehicle for Jewish Studies at Purdue. Rather we intend to make it an open forum, and, therefore we solicit, welcome, urge that those on our mailing list send us news, information, materials, pertinent newspaper clippings, curriculum materials, and anything else of interest.

Obviously, we are not in a position to print scholarly articles of any length. There are in any case a fair number of journals devoted to that purpose. But we welcome smaller articles, opinion pieces, comments, with the understanding that they should typically be no longer than a 1000 words, and preferably shorter.

The value of this publication will depend in part upon the willingness of our readers to engage. . . .

This clarion call certainly cast a wide enough net and was ambitious in its intentions without going overboard in its objectives. It also informed readers that financial support for the first two issues came from the dean's office, and that some secretarial assistance was provided by the Department of Political Science. Our mailing list, we said, was slightly over 200, half of it from the Purdue community, the rest across the country.[8] We suggested that "individuals who wanted to receive our publication donate $5.00 for each volume and libraries, organizations, and programs send us $10.00." A plea for larger donations was also included!

The first issue (twenty pages in all) consisted of Robert Melson's "A First Year Retrospective," Laslo Kovacs' "Modern Jewish Poets: Miklos Radnoti," Stanford Pinsker's "The Holocaust Must Be Taught,"[9] and Jan Wojcik's "The Uncertain Success of Isaiah's Prophecy: A Poetical Reading." Except for Pinsker's piece, all these were done by Purdue faculty. Also included were "The Poetic Voice," "New Books," "Periodical Literature: Current and Culled," "Periodical Literature: Special Issues,"[10] "News and

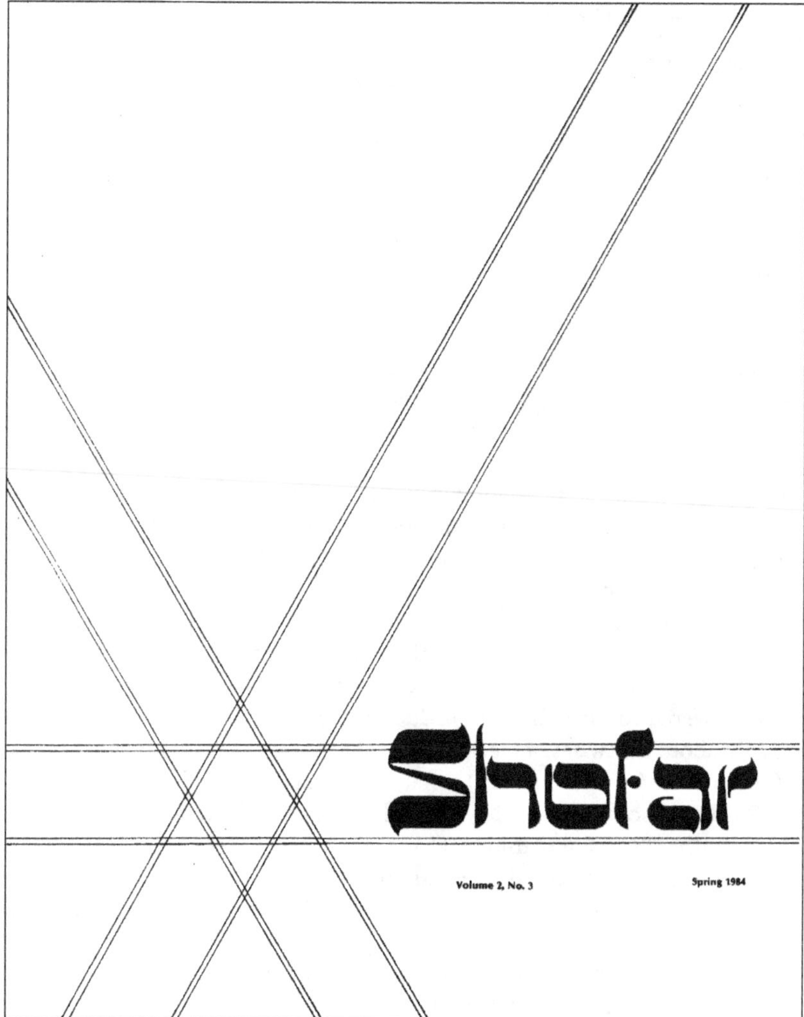

Figure 2. Cover for volumes 2–6

Information," "Film/Media," and "The Lighter Side." I also placed three poems and four cartoons with a Jewish theme on pages that had room for them.

Four issues later *Shofar* had expanded to thirty-eight pages. Volume 1, number 4 also formalized the Book Review section which had expanded to ten pages. In the first volume contributors of articles were all affiliated with Purdue University Three of the issues carried some news about the Purdue program, but this practice ended with volume 1.[11]

With volume 2 some changes took place. The cover was redesigned (see Figure 2). An editorial committee was formed, consisting of professors Walter Hirsch (Sociology), Robert Melson (Political Science), Samuel Shermis (Education), Leon Tiche (Department of Foreign Languages and Literatures), and Gordon Young (History). Subscriptions were raised to $15 per volume. All submissions for publication were to be reviewed by the editorial committee. By the end of volume 2 we had reached seventy-six pages.

The size of *Shofar* increased substantially over the years, as the figures in Table 1 indicate. This was largely due to my own temperament and somewhat compulsive nature. My predisposition was to aim high and to make efforts to improve and expand where possible.[12] Very early on it also became clear that unless some clerical help was forthcoming, we—the active core of the faculty—would undergo rapid

Table 1. Growth in Pages

Volume and Issue	Year	Pages
1, no. 4	1983	38
2, no. 4	1984	76
3, no. 4	1985	80
4, no. 4	1986	100
5, no. 4	1987	102
6, no. 4	1988	122
10, no. 4	1992	240
15, no. 4	1997	182
20, no. 4	2002	210
23, no. 4	2005	230

"burnout." Dr. Ben Klatch, affiliated with the Purdue University Hospital and a key supporter, urged us to approach the philanthropic arm of the Indianapolis Jewish Federation and ask for their financial assistance. We almost immediately received funding from them.[13] With it we hired a half-time secretary, who, among other tasks, took on that of "subscription editor."

Because of expanding program needs, *Shofar* itself was now "outsourced" for typing, an arrangement that worked unevenly. Our dependence on the Political Science Department was also frustrating and not dependable. To send out *Shofar* in a timely fashion we needed some other printing source. Volumes 2 through 7 were produced by the Purdue Printing Services, which did a more professional job, but also brought about a new set of frustrations.

By 1988 (volume 6), *Shofar* was substantial in size and content. Almost all the papers came from outside of Purdue. The "Book-Review," "Book-Notes," and "Articles Noted" sections had expanded considerably. The "News and Information" and "Media" sections were small, and provided material I thought would be of special interest to our academic readers. Cartoons moved to the *JSP Newsletter*. In its stapled, unbound form our journal still had a distinct amateurish and unprofessional appearance.

Subscriptions were modest and to my mind quite inadequate. During this period, we were able to augment the numbers by giving a "complimentary" subscription to donors to our Program regardless of the size of their contribution.[14] This practice was eventually vetoed by the university administration because of IRS tax laws that were applicable to "gift" subscriptions. When this happened, we lost nearly half our subscriptions![15]

In those early years, I was convinced that if they became familiar with *Shofar*, every Jewish Studies scholar and teacher should/would subscribe. On my sabbatical in Israel, I remember hawking some copies to faculty at Hebrew University, who probably looked at me in amazement. Such almost blind faith in one's cause, project, or "product," together with an almost obdurate persistence, is a necessary condition for overcoming initial hurdles. Looking back I am almost embarrassed at my earlier naiveté.

From Newsletter to Interdisciplinary Journal (1989–1997)

Shofar was quickly turning into a big production! It required four issues a year, sent out on a dependable schedule. It was taking up a great deal of my time, as well as that of the JSP staff. Marilyn Fleeter had been hired as a half-time secretary and was fully occupied with the daily tasks of running the program. We used several students from a work-study pool—an inexpensive form of labor, but more often than not hardly worth the time and trouble. Using an outside typist from the community was also not working out very well. Something else was needed. The program successfully applied for additional funds from the Indianapolis Jewish Federation. This enabled us to hire Nancy Lein as a half-time secretary to work on the production of *Shofar*.

Nancy Lein quickly proved to be a very able, reliable, conscientious individual, who I thought did the work of a full-time employee in the half-time position which she now occupied. At my insistence, and with the usual administrative hedging, she was nonetheless quickly promoted from a clerical to the administrative position of managing editor.[16] Beginning with volume 7, preparing *Shofar* was now in her hands.

Around this time Robert Melson suggested that we begin a formal peer-review process to validate the various papers that were submitted. He pointed out it was important, especially for non-tenured academics, to have their publications appear in a peer-reviewed journal. This carried more weight in the promotion process. I fully agreed and was even more enthused by the idea that we could now call upon scholars in various fields to read papers.[17]

So far we had depended on the editorial committee at Purdue and my layperson's judgment.[18] We now began to send out each submission to two qualified readers. The key matter was to find readers. As long as we still had to depend on regular mail to communicate with people, this was a slow, time-consuming, arduous process.

With volume 7 *Shofar* took on a subtitle to reflect more accurately its purview: *An Interdisciplinary Journal of Jewish Studies.* We also finally came out with a redesigned and professional looking journal (see Figure 3).[19]

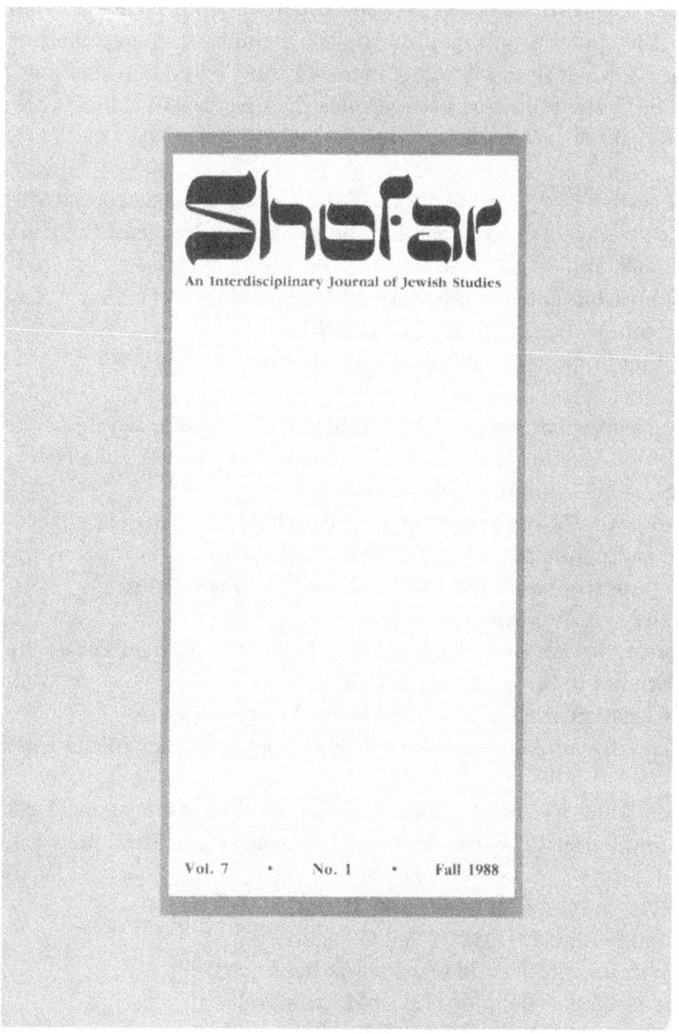

Figure 3. Cover for vol. 7, Fall 1988

Some years earlier, Gordon Young and I had thought of forming a Consortium of Midwest Jewish Studies Programs. Our initial impulse came from what we saw as the disinterest of the national Association of Jewish Studies in assisting smaller programs like ours. I was particularly irked at the palpable condescension emanating from those that were in charge of that organization and the unfriendly atmosphere at their conventions. We believed small programs and isolated Jewish Studies faculty deserved more attention and assistance. So I sent a questionnaire to dozens of Jewish Studies scholars and faculty at Midwestern colleges and universities to find out whether there was an interest in forming a regional consortium.

Responses to the questionnaire were positive and brought about an initial exploratory meeting at Purdue University during the 1989 fall semester. The Consortium idea was quickly dropped as too difficult and cumbersome to put into practice. Instead, the group decided to form the Midwest Jewish Studies Association (MJSA). The first annual convention took place the following year in Chicago at the Spertus College of Judaic Studies. Officers were elected, the organization was incorporated, and policy was set. One of these was to make *Shofar* the official publication of the MJSA with a subscription included in the membership. This increased our subscription rate somewhat, provided greater visibility to our program, and added some cachet to the journal. We also agreed that the annual conferences and *Shofar* should encourage papers and presentations that focused on the teaching of Jewish studies at the college and university level.

We now decided to devote some issues to specific topics. Our plan was to alternate special issues with general issues. The contents and quality would depend on the special issues editor, and not on the peer review process. My task of finding readers was now eased considerably. *Shofar* has followed this pattern since 1988.[20] The following list indicates the diversity of subjects covered over the years, together with the editor(s) of each issue.

6:1 (Su88): Teaching Jewish Christian Relations in the University Classroom (Michael Shermis)
7:3 (Sp89): The Image of the Arab in Israeli Literature and the Image of the Jew in Arabic Literature (Gila's Ramas-Rauch and Aida A. Basia)
8:1 (Fl89): Studies in Jewish Identity and Folklore: Essays in Honor of Henry A. Fischer (Elissa R. Henken, Carolyn Lipton-Walker, and Guy H. Haskell)
8:4 (Su90): Highlighting Books and Bibliography (Joseph Haberer)
9:1 (Fl90): Jewish Ethics (Byron L. Sherwin)
9:3 (Sp91): Teaching Hebrew Language and Literature at the College Level (Zev Garber)
9:4 (Su91): Eastern Jewish Women Immigrants: To America and to Pre-State Israel (Norma Fain Pratt)
10:2 (Wi92): Rabbinics and Talmud (David Kraemer)
10:3 (Sp92): Sephardi Jewry Before and After 1492 (Michael M. Laskier)
10:4 (Su92): Yiddish and Ashkenzic Studies (David Neal Miller)
11:1 (Wi93): Literary Approaches to the Hebrew Bible (Stanley Goldman)
13:1 (Fl94): Perspectives on Zionism (Zev Garber)
14:1 (Fl95): Engendering Jewish Knowledges (Laura Levitt and Miriam Peskowitz)
14:3 (Sp96): Jewish Studies in France (Alan Astro)
15:1 (Fl96): Jewish-Christian Dialog After the Shoah (James F. Moore)
15:3 (Sp97): Teaching African American/Jewish American Relations in the United States (Riv Ellen Prell)
15:4 (Su97): Historical Memory and the State of Jewish Studies in Germany (Dean Phillip Bell)
16:2 (Wi98): Israel and America: Cross-Cultural Encounters and the Literary Imagination (Naomi Sokoloff)
16:4 (Su98): The Spectrum of Jewish Feminism (Rochelle Millen)
17:1 (Fl98): Studies in Jewish Geography (Neil G. Jacobs)
17:2 (Wi99): Women in Jewish Life and Culture (Esther Fuchs)
17:3 (Sp99): Judaism and Asian Religions (Harold Kasimov)
18:1 (Fl99): Crypto-Judaism (Schulamith C. Halevy)
18:4 (Su00): Jewish Music (Ofer Ben-Amots)

19:1 (Fl00): Philip Roth (Jay L. Halio)
19:3 (Sp01): The Jewish Diaspora of Latin America (Nelson H. Vieira)
19:4 (Su01): Sephardic Studies as an Interdisciplinary Field (Bruce Mitchell)
20:1 (Fl01): American Jews (Leonard Dinnerstein)
20:3 (Sp02): New Trends in Yiddish Literary Studies (Jan Schwarz)
21:1 (Fl02): Jewish Poetry (Elizabeth Klein)
21:3 (Sp03): The New York Intellectuals and Beyond (Ethan Goffman)
22:1 (Fl03): Jewish Film (Lawrence Baron)
22:2 (Wi04): The Catholic Church and the Jews (Samuel M. Edelman)
Judaism, Christianity and Modernity: Papers from the Conference on Violence and Religion (2002) (Sandor Goodhart)
22:3 (Sp04): Unfinalized Moments in Jewish American Narrative (Derek Parker Royal)
23:1 (Fl04): *Kindertransporte* 1938/39—Rescue and Integration (Wolfgang Benz, Claudia Curio, and Andrea Hammel)
23:2 (Wi05): Shoah and Israeli Writing (Zev Garber)
23:3 (Sp05): Mel Gibson's *Passion:* The Film, the Controversy, and Its Implication (Zev Garber)
23:4 (Su05): Race and Jews in America (Daniel Itzkovitz)
24:1 (Fl05): Israeli Cinema (Nurith Gertz, Anat Zanger, Nitzan Ben Shaul, and Judd Ne'eman)
24:2 (Wi06): The Cultural and Historical Stabilities and Instabilities of Jewish Orientalism (Ranen Omer-Sherman)
25:1(Fl06): Beyond Klezmer: The Legacy of Eastern European Jewry (Sander L. Gilman and Elizabeth Loentz)
25:4 (Su07): Cool Jewz: Jews and Popular Culture (Mikel J. Koren)
26:1 (Fl07): Abraham Joshua Heschel (Harold Kasimov)

Altogether forty-four out of one hundred are special issues. Three are on the teaching of Jewish studies in the college classroom. I usually suggested special issue editors include a pedagogical piece relating to the theme and a "review essay" of the current literature. This injunction was rarely heeded; since it was difficult to find people to undertake either of these I left it at that and just hoped for the best.

During this period a number of other changes took place. One of these was to set up an editorial board (Fall 1991, vol. 10, no. 1). It consisted of thirty-eight scholars, over half of which came from the Midwest, while national and international members made up the rest.[21]

Several factors went into the selection of the editorial board. Recommendations from colleagues and people I met at the MJSA meeting were helpful. Some volunteered. I was looking for "working" board members, on whom one could depend to review papers, encourage submissions in their area, and set policy. Since we were an interdisciplinary journal, a mix of members covering various fields was also useful. There was no way to guarantee the level of involvement and it would vary considerably. Board members left only at their request or for some reason beyond my control. Changing the board composition was a very touchy matter, and where I might have wished to replace someone, I took the easy way out, that is, I did nothing. Editorial board meetings took place annually at the MJSA meeting. Nancy Lein and I set the agenda. Issues were discussed and voted on by those present. The majority carried the day. The reasons for this were clear enough: if one wanted serious involvement one would need to abide by the votes of the majority.[22]

Photographs were first used in issue 11:2. *Shofar* began to be abstracted and indexed around that time.[23] Beginning with volume 10 Nancy Lein added an annual "Author/Title/Subject Index." With volume 16 (1997) *Shofar* became the official journal of the newly formed Western Jewish Studies Association. At that juncture we added members from the WJSA to the editorial board.[24]

I had also been looking for associate editors and was especially interested in finding people who could focus on specific areas of Jewish studies. Zev Garber was the first appointed in 1996. I had been impressed by the quality of the special issue he edited, the book reviews he provided, as well as the evident editorial skills, conscientiousness, and reliability he demonstrated in his work. He was also professionally active in the areas of the Yiddish and Hebrew languages, and in Holocaust studies. Two other editorial appointments were made: Alan Astro, who was especially knowledgeable about Jewish studies in France, and Dean Bell, an expert in early modern German Jewish studies.[25] Unfortunately because of other commitments they were able to serve only for a short period.

The transformation to a professional journal had taken place by 1990 when *Shofar* became the official organ of the MJSA. Subsequent developments were primarily a form of improving the structure and contents. We had gone through the stages of infancy and adolescence, to maturity. There lurked also the possibility of senescence and decline. Time would tell.

University Presses and Contracts (1996–2006)

In 1996, we arranged for the University of Nebraska Press (UNP) to publish *Shofar*. To the best of my recollection they contacted us, and we, in conjunction with the Purdue Contract Office, drew up the necessary papers. I had been impressed by the quality of their Judaica list; they also had considerable publishing resources and staff available. A three-year contract was drawn up, and it contained a formula for sharing any profits that might accrue.[26] We were to send them camera-ready copy, which they would print and distribute. We no longer had to contend with the subscriptions, a task that we gave up gladly. They also redesigned the cover, adding a four-color scheme for each volume (see Figure 4).

Figure 4. Redesigned cover, vol. 16, Fall 1977

The University of Nebraska Press did an excellent job of producing and sending out *Shofar*. My efforts to work with them to find ways to bring about a larger readership were simply ignored. They seemed indifferent to the problem of a static and very small subscriber list. Given the high quality of their performance, I was willing to leave well enough alone. The contract was extended for an additional three years.

During this second contract period, a new development occurred which was to change our relationship considerably: Project MUSE.[27] Founded in 2001, Project MUSE is a consortium of sixty-eight academic and university presses, under the auspices of the Johns Hopkins University Press, that includes an online database of over 300 humanities and arts journals. Access is available to members of subscribing institutions, which are mostly college and university libraries. Nonsubscribers have access to the base on the Internet but are charged a user fee. Affiliated publishers receive a share of the profits. It became clear to us that these could become substantial.

In the next contract renegotiations we insisted that some of that profit would have to be shared with us. However, UNP was categorically unwilling to make any changes in the contract taking into account the potential Project MUSE income. Their position was "take it or leave it." Since we produced a camera-ready copy of *Shofar,* and bore a lion's share of the costs and overhead in producing it, their stance appeared unreasonable and inflexible. We decided to move the journal to the Purdue University Press (PUP). I had earlier discussed this possibility with Tom Bacher, director of the press, and had found him cooperative and enthusiastic. They took over in 2005 with volume 23.

For us, this move had some distinct advantages. Not least it would bring Project MUSE income to the PUP, which they would share with the Purdue Jewish Studies Program. We found PUP willing, even eager, to undertake additional Judaica projects.[28] One quick result was the creation *Shofar Supplements*, a series edited by Zev Garber, based on special issues of *Shofar* and turned into a classroom or discussion group format.[29] All this pleased me to no end.

Transitions (1994–2006)

The issue of continuity had been on my mind for some years. I recognized the temptation to hold on to an enterprise one had started and invested so much of one's psychic energy. In 1994, at age sixty-five, I retired from Political Science and as director of the Jewish Studies program.[30] In 2001, I finally decided to step down as editor as well. I informed the dean and the JSP program of my decision, pointed out that there were enough papers and book reviews for the next volume or two, and recommended that Zev Garber become my replacement.

Since 1989, Zev Garber had demonstrated his versatility, scholarship, and commitments in an impressive list of *Shofar* contributions, including becoming associate editor in 1996. A perusal of issues published to date shows the following: one editorial viewpoint (20:2), response to 9/11; three articles (10:1, 12:1, 15:1); five special issues (9:3, 13:1, 22:4, 23:2, 23:3); and ten reviews (9:3, 20:1, 20:3, 20:4, 21:1, 21:3, 22:2, 23:1, 23:3, 23:4).

My recommendation was followed and proved to be a fine choice indeed. Purdue University also appointed Dan Morris (English Department) as coeditor. With these appointments *Shofar* was now in good hands and a smooth transition followed.

In a talk at that time I concluded with a set of generalizations based on my twenty years of editorial experience.[31]

- Think carefully and long before you undertake a new venture; you will probably end up doing a lot more than you had originally bargained for.
- There needs to be some sort of vision, a conception of what direction you want to go, but flexibility and creativity are essential for making a go of it. Learn to seize opportunities when they arise. Think big and take one step at a time. As always the right mix of patience and impatience is crucial in moving toward your goal.
- An editor will cast his/her imprint on a publication. This will be reflected in a number of ways, of which the style of editing will be the most important. Two styles predominate: the

one man/woman, "do it my way or else" style or the democratic, more participatory style. Both have their virtues and drawbacks. My preferred style, based on temperament and philosophy, is the democratic one.

- Publishing an academic journal is a precarious enterprise. Journals fold for any number of reasons: lack of money, insufficient subscribers, declining talent, lack of institutional support, and one may get tired or bored.
- To succeed as an editor you have to have an inordinate faith in your "product." Only faith and some sort of obstinacy will carry you through. You will undoubtedly believe your publication is something your peers and others should subscribe to. However, what you think is important may only be of peripheral interest to others.
- Academic journals are usually underwritten by an institutional network within the university or college, sometimes in conjunction with an academic association. Subscriptions do not cover the costs involved. Advertising is atypical and sparse at best for journals that are published by university presses. Universities and colleges typically subsidize and underwrite our efforts.
- There is a fair amount of drudgery in editing and publishing. There are also tricks and shorthands of the trade to be learned: for example, how to find competent book reviewers, solicit papers, handle disgruntled academics, edit and copyedit manuscripts.
- Find and use competent, reliable, talented people. The most important is a good managing editor who will do the bulk of the work putting the journal into a publishable shape.[32] Delegate a great deal, and then let people do their thing. Avoid micro-managing like the plague. Supervise as far as necessary, praise good work always, and reward it whenever possible.
- Avoid procrastination at all costs. A good journal is turned out in a timely fashion. Answer inquiries and correspondence quickly. Learn from experience, which often means learn from your mistakes, omissions, and blind spots. Solicit advice and pay attention to it. Keep at it. Patience and persistence often carry the day.
- Yet a time will come when it may be wise to retire. Be of good cheer when you place the journal into other hands. If you are fortunate and lucky those who take over will infuse the journal with new energy and creativity. If not, remember nothing lasts forever. The problem of continuity has to be faced at some point, because you will not live forever!

My connection to *Shofar* was, however, by no means over. The masthead now listed me as "Founding Editor." I had agreed to continue informally as book editor until someone would take over. It very quickly became clear that this was not about to happen and no one to my knowledge was about to volunteer. Book editing for a major journal is a time-consuming activity, with few rewards in the academic milieu. I could, of course, have forced the issue by retiring *in toto*, but decided against that for several reasons.

The book review section is probably the most widely read section of *Shofar* and it is most useful because of its broad and extensive coverage. What had in earlier years been an arduous and time consuming task was now, given the new Internet technologies, astonishingly effective. With the advent of Google one was able to obtain quickly the location of potential reviewers, their departmental Web pages and e-mail addresses. Publishers' information was also readily accessible. E-mail form letters could be sent in seconds; replies that formerly took weeks, even months, now could be returned within the hour or within a few days. If there was no response one could quickly try someone else. Internet communications did not require postal expenditures and thus eased considerably our financial burden. We now also had reviewers from the four corners of the world, though books mailed to them still involved a substantial financial cost on our part.

Under these new conditions locating books for potential review or book-note inclusion, entering the appropriate information into our data bank, sending out letters to publishers, keeping track of books received, then finding a reviewer—all this had become much easier and faster. It also resulted in a dramatically improved acceptance rate from those contacted.[33] What had in years past been somewhat of a chore now was an activity I began to enjoy. Not least, continuing the book review operation at Purdue meant that books not reviewed or ending up as book-notes would continue to flow into the Purdue Library. With volume 23, no. 4 (Summer 2005) the masthead listed me as "Book-Editor" and thus formalized a return to this ongoing involvement with *Shofar*.

New Directions, New Opportunities, New Challenges

Over the years I made it a practice to attend regularly the annual meetings of the MJSA. Involved in its formation I took a kind of paternal interest in its development. These occasions also provided a source of materials for possible inclusion in *Shofar*. In its early years, I sometimes had doubts about the association's survival. The MJSA nonetheless withstood the test of time and was now firmly established.

In the September 2006 meeting someone in a casual conversation told me that he thought *Shofar* had become the "premier" journal in Jewish studies. Naturally, this was sweet music to my ears. But instead of asking, "What makes you think that?" I thought to myself, "you must be kidding!" and the biblical image of Sara, laughing when told she would give birth in old age, came to mind. After all, there was the long history of almost minuscule subscription rates alluded to earlier.

To be sure, Project MUSE was now a new development, but so far I had no real sense of how this was affecting the use of the journal by those who subscribed to the online database. I was also somewhat chagrined to discover that Purdue was one of the few major universities that was not a subscriber. In October 2006, at one of the Purdue Libraries "Internet Data Base Workshops" I had again complained that *Shofar* was not available online at our august institution. Wrong! I was told: it was in fact now part of an EBSCO data journal database, which faculty and students at Purdue could access.[34]

At this juncture I began to contact people at the Project MUSE and the EBSCO organizations to get some information about usage patterns for *Shofar*. I was interested specifically in the number of institutions that subscribed to each, the total number of "hits" or "visits" per year, and, if possible, which items were being requested. The results were, to say the least, surprising—indeed, for me, staggering. MUSE *Shofar* text access began with issue 19:3 (Spring 2001). The number of *Shofar* subscribers via Project MUSE in 2006 was 1,298.[35] In 2004 *Shofar* items were accessed 10,966 times; in 2005 that number increased to 25,321, and in 2006 it was 36,019. EBSCO *Shofar* text access began with issue 19:1 (Fall 2000).[36] As of volume 24, the number of *Shofar* subscribers via the EBSCO database was 2,750. The total number of times *Shofar* items were accessed in 2006 was 39,529.

The contrast to the pre-Internet period is, to say the least, considerable. Before placement on the Project MUSE and EBSCO databases the subscription base hovered between 135 to slightly over 200. Consider this: In its basic format, length of articles, and the quality of its contents *Shofar* remained much the same for the past fifteen years. Yet until a few years ago with its small subscriber base, it had at best a very limited readership. Nor was it likely that library copies of it were in large use. I sometimes wondered, "Why are we bothering to put out this journal, when only a handful of people are going to read the thing, when the return is so small, the investment of time and resources so considerable?!" Now, however, it dawned on me that a new age of scholarly publishing was upon us, one that was enlarging our readership in a dramatic way.[37]

The new age of information technology had manifested itself with the advent of word processing, the arrival of the Internet, the omnipresence of Web pages, the ever-increasing capabilities of search engines, the expanding access to knowledge through online databases. A process was at work, profoundly transforming the world of scholarly activity and scholarly publishing. Moreover, these developments were occurring with increasing speed. This change was taking place in the creation of knowledge itself, in its transmission and was made available globally, speedily, and in easily handled forms.[38] All this was bound to have long-range effects, the outcome of which at present we may have only a faint glimmer.[39]

Ease of accessibility is an important characteristic of the new search engine and database technology. An example of this is one that I learned about while writing this chapter. To my question, "what has been the impact of internet technology on scholarly journals, their readerships, and libraries at institutions of higher learning?" initial efforts seemed to produce few results that could be used.

A Purdue librarian pointed me to the H. W. Wilson Data Base: Library Literature and Information Index/Full Text, which covers 406 library-related journals and makes available the full text for most of them to subscriber institutions.[40] I now had at hand a vast compendium of library and information technology journals. Then I found Google Scholar, new search engine of considerable power and potential.[41] From both I found a profusion of materials ready at hand.

Search engines now enable one to locate materials in record time. But they also direct searchers to materials in which they are specifically interested. For journals like ours, that now means that key words that appear in the title of special issues (Israeli Cinema) or author names (Gal Raz) or special issues (Mel Gibson) are likely to be discovered through a search engine by an inquiring scholar, which will lead to a database lead. Project MUSE items found on Google are typically listed on the first page of the search. In short, this process, whether on a database or in a search engine, brings the material to the potential user in a radically new and targeted way.[42]

Most scholarly journals will also have benefited by having manuscripts submitted electronically or mailed in on disk. These electronically produced materials can now be forwarded to readers for their evaluation, resulting in a much more rapid return of their comments, with accruing benefits both to author and publisher and also much less retyping by the journal with fewer errors accidentally introduced into the text.

Scholarly journals on databases ought ideally to be included in their entirety. Most are not. *Shofar*, as indicated, is available online only from volume 19. One of the major objectives in the years ahead should be to make journals once they are online as fully accessible as resources permit. Obviously this will call for some kind of prioritization, since this process takes time and is not cost-free. Such a transformation may seem daunting at this point. But so did the earlier changeover in libraries from a card-catalog system—which did yeoman service in its day—to a completely computer-based catalog, now virtually universally applied. This transformation took time and no doubt had its problems, but does anyone nowadays yearn for a return to card catalogs! Or for that matter for the good old days of manual typewriters!

One of the important issues is how to deal with the matter of duplication of resources. Why place a print version of a journal in the library stacks when an online version is available? Print subscriptions are often costly and library budgets are under considerable pressure, often shrinking in actual purchasing power. Library space is limited and materials are expanding what at times may appear an exponential rate. Something has to give. On the other hand, there is the nagging question, "what happens when we no longer subscribe to Database X, and we have stopped the print subscription?" The literature on these themes is already considerable, and the debate will no doubt continue indefinitely.[43]No easy answers are likely. At this point an increasing number of scholarly journals offer a print version, an online version, or a combination to their subscribers.

New technologies make it possible to print on demand precisely as many copies as one might want, and to do this at a reasonable cost. This avoids overprints and the need to warehouse. In some cases bound, printed subscription orders may increase, once readers become familiar with a journal and would like to receive it on a regular basis in hand, rather than in the computer databased form. Furthermore, benefits may accrue in the use of online and database materials for use as tailor-made textbook materials for teaching. Utilizing such materials in institutions that subscribe, for example, to Project MUSE and EBSCO, is cost-free for students, and lessens their financial burdens. Options thus increase rather than narrow.[44]

Editors and copyeditors will have a much easier time evaluating and refining work on the computer, at least in terms of the format in which it is presented. The cogency of the argument, the clarity of the writing, these are not intrinsically shaped by the technology itself and remain, as before, in the hands of the scholar. It is still a truism that the end result of scholarly work is only as good as the person who creates it. New technologies, however sophisticated and enabling, are only a means to an end, not ends in themselves. Impressed or infatuated as we initially may become with these new ways, there is no gainsaying that the hard work of thinking, researching, and writing cannot be taken over by the electronic technology.

And what of the downside of these new approaches? With spell-checks and other built-in computer features, there is the danger of easing up on our editorial or copy editing oversight. The technology will not *ipso facto* overcome sloppy, unclear writing; it may even add to it. E-mail correspondence, as a case in point, is not particularly noted for maintaining high standards. There may well have been virtues in the way journals were produced in the older, precomputer age which will be diluted or lost in the profusion of new technologies. Nor is the speed with which work can now be transmitted necessarily or inherently a good thing. It may well diminish the time for reflection. Quite the contrary, there is the possibility that one may become inundated with material, even overwhelmed by its plenitude. The equation between quantity and quality, between the limits time and energy impose on our efforts, will undoubtedly settle themselves somewhat—as they have done in the past—although we know not at what cost.

On balance, nonetheless, I believe that the age ahead will bring about a democratization of knowledge, will enhance the scope of our publishing efforts, and will enable students and faculty, especially at smaller institutions, to enter into the larger world of scholarship on a more equitable basis. This provides a challenge that we should welcome and for which we should prepare ourselves.

Notes

1. A historian might be appalled by the scarcity of records that remain of the daily operation of *Shofar.* Almost none of the letters, memos, reports, and so on were stored indefinitely. The primary sources of record are the quarterly volumes of the journal. For the rest, I depend on my memory. Though I try to be fair in my judgments, since this is a personal account I make no claim to be objective or impartial.
2. See Joseph Haberer, *Politics and the Community of Science* (New York: Van Nostrand Reinhold, 1969), chaps. 1–3, for a discussion of the importance of founding acts in the history of modern science. The personality and aims of founders, in this case Bacon and Descartes, played a critical role in setting the directions and the styles of the scientific enterprise.
3. The program came into being after a year-long faculty "seminar" on the Holocaust initiated by Robert Melson. We met about once a month and read papers, reviews, and so on. It went well and led some to suggest it was time to consider putting together a Jewish studies program. Enough faculty and courses were in place to undertake the process of getting a proposal through the HSSE Senate (Humanities, Social Science and Education School). In all of this I was on the sidelines as a supporter, not an initiator. According to Robert Melson's "A First Year's Retrospective" (*Shofar* 1, no. 1) Walter Hirsch (sociology), Victor Raskin (English), and Larry Axel (philosophy) were "under Walter's leadership . . . the subcommittee which drew up the first plans for a Jewish Studies minor and discussed the feasibility with Dean Ringel." Robert Melson (political science) served the first year as chair of the program. Gordon Young (history) took on the responsibility the second year, followed, I believe, by Larry Axel.
4. I simply copied this idea from what had been a weekly "noon-series" in the STPP program.
5. The core elements of this governing structure remained in place for the next eighteen years and worked remarkably well. When I became director of JSP we added an "executive committee" consisting of two elected committee members and myself to deal with issues that came up between committee meetings. This provided some oversight, and a guard against the pitfalls of arbitrary behavior. It was also a useful device in dealing with administrators.
6. My daughter Leila drew the covers for the first four issues. I also added a Hebrew inscription, "Hark to the Sound of the Shofar." The cover changed completely with volume 2, when Don Carter from the Purdue Office of Publications designed the logo, and Reed Benhamou the cover; both of these remained in place through volume 6.
7. The STPP newsletter had included a small book-note section, consisting of paragraph-long descriptions extracted from book blurbs, or publishers' press-releases, minus the hyperbole. Making a "book-note" was an easy enough thing to do and the book could subsequently be sent to the Purdue Library. This accomplished two things: it helped the library, and the STPP program could take some satisfaction in adding to a collection that needed all the help it could get. I applied the same approach on becoming the book editor of the quarterly journal *The Bulletin of Science, Technology and Society* (*BSTS*) in the early 1980s. This journal carried only book-notes, thus enabling me to obtain over the years a considerable number of books for the Purdue library. Almost all of this was done through the JSP office, which underwrote the expenses involved (such as postage and printing of form letters). I had the library keep annual records of the books we donated and their dollar value for both *Shofar* and *BSTS* and sent an annual JSP library report to the dean's office.
8. A mailing list over 200 was needed to enable us to use the "bulk rate"—a considerable savings in postage! I don't recall how I put together this initial list.

9. Professor Pinsker was then a member of the Department of English at Franklin and Marshall College. The piece was a reprint from the *Chronicle of Higher Education,* March 17, 1982, 23. I rather doubt that I asked for copyright permission to include it. I blush to recall what liberties I took in the early years about such matters. Poems and cartoons that I found interesting were simply reprinted.
10. We reproduced the tables of contents for *Semeia: An Experimental Journal for Biblical Criticism,* their special issue on "Anthropological Perspectives on Old Testament Prophecy"; *Tradition: A Journal of Orthodox Jewish Thought,* the issue on "Symposium—The State of Orthodoxy"; and *Judaism*'s issue on "The Sabbath Is Forever: A Symposium."
11. In the third year of the program I undertook to edit a quarterly *Purdue Jewish Studies Newsletter.* As activities expanded this newsletter focused exclusively on the involvement of our faculty and program in the areas of teaching/education, research/scholarship, and community/outreach—and (not least) to drum up financial and moral support.
12. Some faculty felt that in expanding so rapidly we were losing the "heimishness" (conviviality) of a small program. Since the majority disagreed, I continued to push ahead.
13. Throughout its existence JSP and *Shofar* have received substantial financial support from the Indianapolis Jewish Federation. Without it we simply would not have been able to expand the program or publish the journal!
14. This is how we were able to reach our 200 bulk-rate number. It also provided goodwill.
15. Increasing the subscription base was a challenge that continued throughout my years as editor. I was never able to increase substantially the low numbers despite several efforts on my part. This was perhaps my most important disappointment. The reasons for that failure—whether personal or structural—are manifold.
16. This change meant increased salary and benefit costs to the program. However, this was a matter of principle. I felt strongly that Nancy Lein's talents ought to be properly recognized and rewarded.
17. Comments from peer-reviewers enable authors to improve their papers, whether they are accepted for publication or not. Over the years I have been impressed by the quality and extent of comments made by many of our reviewers. We owe them a considerable debt of gratitude.
18. I could now also deflect papers that were sent by colleagues and friends, on behalf of themselves or their students.
19. This designation appears first in volume 7, number 1 (Fall 1988). Henceforth through volume 15 (1997) we used a printer in Indianapolis.
20. The first special issue, which appeared in volume 6, number 4, "Teaching Jewish-Christian Relations in the University Classroom" edited by Michael Shermis, started us off on the right pedagogical tone. Looking at it now, I'm impressed by its very high quality.
21. Purdue 5, Indiana University 1, Ball State 1, Midwest 15, South 2, East Coast and New England 7, Western 2, Canada 1, England 1, Israel 2, Poland 1. The current composition is as follows: Purdue 7, Midwest 15, Western 9, South 3, East Coast/New England 2, Poland 1, Canada 1.
22. I proposed that we change our name to something like *Interdisciplinary Journal of Jewish Studies.* The majority decided to keep a name that was already well established. I also liked the idea of including poetry in our pages. The majority thought this would take away from the perception that we were a scholarly, not literary journal. In all cases the will of the majority prevailed.
23. *Index to Jewish Periodicals* 11, no. 2; *Old Testament Abstracts* 12, no. 3. In recent years the following have been added: *Religious and Theological Abstracts, Jewish Abstracts, Historical Abstracts and America: History and Life, Academic Search Premier,* and *Religion and Philosophy Collection.*
24. Lawrence Baron (San Diego State University) founded the WJSA. He had earlier consulted me about our experience in setting up the MJSA. I did make one foray into the deep South, Tulane University, to see whether there might be an interest in organizing a Southern Jewish Studies Association, but nothing ever came of it.
25. Special issue on Jewish studies in France (14, no. 3) and special issue on Jewish studies in Germany (15, no. 4).
26. Despite some nagging on my part, I cannot recall ever receiving a financial report from them.
27. For an overview and history of Project MUSE see http://muse.jhu.edu/about/muse/overview.html.
28. PUP has taken on *Studies in Jewish American Literature* and *Philip Roth Studies.*
29. *Mel Gibson: The Film, the Controversy, and Its Implications,* edited by Zev Garber, was the first of these and came out in 2006. It combined a section that had appeared in *Shofar,* with some additional essays and a list of "Discussion Questions" after each.
30. Gordon Young and Robert Melson became interim directors for the next two years. Sanford Goodhart (English) was director from 1996 to 2001; Gordon Young served again from 2001 to 2004; Daniel Frank (philosophy) is the current director.
31. "Twenty Years of *Shofar:* Reflections of an Editor," talk given at Temple Israel, West Lafayette, March 3, 2001.

32. Nancy Lein would type all the manuscripts, copyedit, correspond with authors on particulars of style and content, and schedule papers and reviews, all in a timely fashion. With the electronic age, the typing has largely been eliminated. My job was to keep the flow of potential publishable papers going, select books for review, find reviewers, and deal with the big issues, questions, and problems, calling on the editorial board when this seemed appropriate.
33. We have reviewed virtually no books written in French, Italian, Hebrew, or Russian. I consider this a serious failure on my part. Obtaining reviews of German books was easy enough, since I was dealing with my native tongue and also had a very personal interest in many aspects of German Jewish history. We still use the U.S. Post for mailing letters to publishers, not having quite worked out how to move that process into smooth Internet format.

    My guess is that since the advent of effective search engines my total time spent has been reduced from approximately ten hours a week to no more than five. The success rate in obtaining reviewers is now also significantly higher. I estimate that at least seven out of ten books will find a reviewer. In some cases, especially with clearly significant books I may have to send out half a dozen requests or sometimes more to land someone. Typically, I try three times on my own. If a potential reviewer turns it down but sends a list of others I might contact, I will use that list. I have also found that such help is on the increase. I attribute some of this success to the reputation of *Shofar* as a premier journal and its higher recognition among Jewish studies scholars.
34. EBSCO HOST: Academic Search Premier. Coverage started in 1984. Full text coverage started in 1990 for selected journals and for *Shofar* in 2000. A "Shofar" database search on February 15, 2007, indicated that 1,131 items were now accessible.
35. Data provided by Project MUSE office. For information and list of subscribers go to htpp:/muse.jhu.edu/about/index.
36. Data provided by EBSCO. Usage figures only available for period October 1, 2005–September 30, 2006. At the time of the contract signing in 2005 EBSCO agreed to provide full text coverage starting with volume 19.
37. For a classic treatment of scholarly publishing at the dawn of the Internet age see Lewis Coser et al., *Books: The Culture and Commerce of Publishing* (Chicago: University of Chicago Press, 1982); also Robin B. Peek and Gregory B. Newby, eds., *Scholarly Publishing: The Electronic Frontier* (Cambridge: MIT Press, 1996).
38. For a comprehensive bibliography see Charles W. Bailey Jr., *Scholarly Electronic Publishing Bibliography: Version 41: 2/22/2002,* University of Houston Libraries, 148 pp. (retrieved Feb. 14, 2007, from http://info.lib.uh.edu/sepb/sepb.html); Leonard J. Stephen McGinty, *Gatekeepers of Knowledge: Journal Editors in the Sciences and Social Sciences* (Westport, Conn.: Bergin and Garvey, 1999).
39. R. King and E. Callahan, "Electronic Journals, the Internet, and Scholarly Communication," *Annual Review of Information Science and Technology* 37 (2003): 127–77, touches on some of these matters. Marshall McLuhan's influential work, e.g., *The Gutenberg Galaxy* (Toronto: University of Toronto Press, 1962), was prophetic. Cf. http://en.wikipedia.org/wiki/marshall_mcluhan. For a more cautious view see Andrew Odlyzko, "The Slow Evolution of Electronic Publishing," *Learned Publishing* 15, no. 1 (January 2002): 7–19 (retrieved Jan. 23, 2007, from http://www.ids-publishing.com/Common/Paper/Paper_51/odlyzko3_the.pdf); Luciano Floridi, "The Internet and the Future of Organized Knowledge," *Canadian Materials* 1, nos. 5–7 (1995) (retrieved Jan. 25, 2007, from http://www.umanitoba.ca/cm).
40. H. W. Wilson Data Base: Library Literature and Information Index/Full Text, http:/www.hwilson.com/Databases/liblit.htm.
41. For details see http://scholar.google.com/intl/en/scholar/about.html. See also Bill Bradley, "Search Engines: Where We Were, Are Now, and Will Ever Be," *Ariadne* 47 (April 2006), examines the development of search engines since 1996 (retrieved Feb. 15, 2007, http://www.ariadne.ac.uk/information). For a sense of the diversity of new search engines, Bill Bradley, "Search Engines: New Search Engines in 2006," *Ariadne* 50 (January 2007).
42. Liwen Vaughn and Mike Thelwall, "Scholarly Use of the Web: What Are the Key Inducers of Links to Journal Web Sites?" *Journal of the American Society for Information Society and Technology* 54, no. 1 (January 2003): 29–38.
43. See "A Bibliography of Books and Journal Articles on Scholarly Publishing," *Journal of Scholarly Publishing* 37, no. 1 (October 2005): 48–54. This item is accessible on both the Project MUSE and EBSCO databases.
44. Tom Bacher, director of Purdue University Press, brought this to my attention. Indeed, print subscriptions to *Shofar* have gone up in the last two years. Major university libraries may still continue to order bound copies.

"But It Isn't on the Test!"

Holocaust Education in the Age of "No Child Left Behind"

Louanne Clayton Jacobs

A Wake-up Call

I currently teach in the School of Education at a state university that is considered one of the Historically Black Colleges and Universities (HBCU). By the time students have enrolled in one of the education courses I teach, they have typically completed most if not all of their required coursework in history, English, mathematics, and science. By the time students enter my classroom they have learned most of *what* they will teach and have begun preprofessional courses designed to help them learn *how* to teach it.

Two semesters ago, I taught a course in the materials and methods of teaching secondary (seventh- to twelfth-grade) social studies. In a general introductory survey of background knowledge relating to literature commonly used to support content teaching, I was surprised to find that only two of my students had read anything beyond Elie Wiesel's *Night* or the frequently anthologized theatrical version of *The Diary of Anne Frank*. Since this was a relatively small (fifteen-student) class, I decided to give the same general survey to my considerably larger (fifty-one-student) Introduction to Education class. Only three students had read either text; all others reported that they had *never* read a Holocaust-related text in any high school or university English class and had had little or no exposure to it in their social studies/history courses. I repeated the survey the following semester with my Introduction to Education students with similar results: four of forty-eight having read one or both literature selections with the remainder having read neither and reporting little or no emphasis on the Holocaust in social studies/history coursework.

Puzzling over the meaning of this information, I decided to conduct some focus-group research to determine what Holocaust content my students would report as having been taught in their middle school/junior high school and high school social studies/history classes. Since all of my students were the products of public education and reportedly intended to spend their teaching career in public education, I believed and still believe that the information gathered would shed some light on the current state of social studies/history instruction in public schools. It must be said that this research was purely empirical in nature. It was, and remains, an exploration rather than an indictment. It is all too common in public education for teachers at one level to blame those in the level preceding them for deficiencies in student knowledge or performance. University professors typically blame high school teachers, high school teachers blame middle school teachers, middle school teachers blame elementary school teachers, and elementary school teachers blame early childhood teachers, leaving kindergarten teachers no one to blame other than pregnant mothers who spend too much time standing in front of the microwave oven. The results of this research are not intended to contribute to any part of that blame game. Rather, they are intended as a basis for dialogue and advocacy on the part of educators, scholars, and others. In the remainder of this essay I will present the results of my findings, contributing factors to the critical situation of Holocaust education in public schools, suggestions for using children's and adolescent literature (fiction and nonfiction) as a viable tool to present Holocaust education in public school content-area classrooms, and provide reasons for advocacy on the part of the Holocaust/genocide scholarly community.

"But It Isn't on the Test!"

After conducting focus-group interviews with my students, the following became clear: while they were *aware* of the Holocaust, they had little knowledge of the event other than the fact that during World War II the Nazis had imprisoned and exterminated large numbers of Jewish people. They could not provide information about how or why this had occurred, had no knowledge of Jewish resistance, could not name any concentration/extermination camps without prompting, and could not identify key terms such as "Shoah," "ghetto," "Warsaw," or "French Resistance." They also could not name a country other than Germany in which the Holocaust had taken place and could name no other group targeted for extermination. The few students who had read *Night* had done so when enrolled in some sort of advanced English class, and no student could provide information about Anne Frank after her capture, the closing scene of the play.

While discussing just what had comprised their study of the Holocaust in particular and social studies/history in general, students frequently referred to concentrating on events and topics that would most likely be covered on standardized tests, particularly those used as high stakes assessments by the schools they attended. Several students saw the importance of studying the Holocaust, particularly in light of current and recent genocides, but were quick to remind me, in the words of one student, "It isn't on the test. And the most important thing in school right now is doing well on the test. So if it isn't on the test, it isn't being taught."

How is standardized, high-stakes testing impacting Holocaust education in public schools? Is it causing teachers to put on the back burner or ignore altogether historical events that are critical for an informed and educated society because they are not emphasized at test time or do not lend themselves conveniently to being answered in a multiple-choice format? And if those critical events, the Holocaust in particular, are left out or marginalized from curricula, are we not inadvertently accomplishing that which Holocaust deniers would wish—a population that not only does not contemplate the events of the Holocaust, but which is open to questioning their veracity?

Holocaust Education and "No Child Left Behind"

In a 1993 Roper poll conducted in the United States, 20 percent of students and 22 percent of adults polled responded that they thought it possible that "the Holocaust had never happened."[1] Another poll conducted in the same year found 12 percent of Americans unsure if the Holocaust happened.[2] In the same year, the National Council of Teachers of English (NCTE) responded to the results of these two polls by issuing a position statement, "On Teaching about Intolerance and Genocide," affirming that "students should read and discuss literature on genocide and intolerance within an historically accurate framework with special emphasis on primary source material." In addition, NCTE created a task force that developed a three-volume compilation of resources to assist teachers in planning and producing instructional materials on the rhetoric and literature of genocide and intolerance, which is unfortunately no long available according to the council's Web site. Rather, the council offers a single volume including the Holocaust in a resource on social responsibility.[3]

At the present time, six states (California, Mississippi, New Jersey, Florida, Illinois, and New York) and Washington, D.C., have adopted legislation supporting Holocaust education. Only three specify grade levels for implementing those studies with the majority encouraging it at the middle and high school levels. California's legislation includes Holocaust education within a broad human rights context and Mississippi includes it within a study of slavery and genocide. An additional fourteen states have adopted language that encourages teaching of the Holocaust, provides resource materials to teachers, or supports a state Holocaust commission.[4] However, especially in states *without* mandated Holocaust education, if the Holocaust is not included in a state's high-stakes accountability measures, it is unlikely to receive much curricular emphasis.

High-Stakes Testing

In using the term "high-stakes testing," I refer to testing that is required under "No Child Left Behind" (NCLB) as a state and school accountability measure. A high-stakes test is one that can result in students being denied graduation, teachers being sanctioned, and schools losing federal funding when test scores do not meet a capricious quantitative benchmark.[5]

High-stakes tests are administered at both elementary and secondary school levels and are exacting a particularly costly toll on social studies and history education at both levels. Numerous educational researchers have documented a reduced emphasis on social studies at the elementary level.[6] And while Holocaust education does not typically begin in the earliest elementary grades, it is certainly, from both a curricular and developmental standpoint, appropriate for upper elementary-age students and is critical for building background necessary to view the Holocaust in the scope of civics, world history, and politics taught in later grades.

Research conducted within the last two years reveals that time devoted to elementary social studies instruction is diminishing across the nation.[7] This research follows an initial survey of teachers by the 2001 National Assessment of Educational Progress (NAEP, also known as "The Nation's Report Card") which found 37 percent of U.S. fourth graders spending only one to two hours per each instructional week on social studies.[8] Since NCLB requires accountability measures in only reading and math (and more recently science), social studies continues to be the subject covered "when we have extra time." In low-performing schools (typically high-poverty and high-minority—more on this later) and for all low-performing students, that "extra time" is taken up by remediation and intensive test-prep sessions.

High-stakes testing in high schools is increasingly synonymous with high school exit exams. To date, twenty-five states currently require students to pass an exit exam in order to earn a high school diploma. The Center on Educational Policy predicts that "71 percent of students attending public school and 82 percent of minority students will take a high school exit exam by the year 2012."[9] Most states requiring exit exams began with exams in reading and math, later phasing in science and social studies. It is left to the discretion of the state to determine which subjects will be included in exit exams, at what grade level, and the content of the exam itself. However, since NCLB does not currently require accountability measures nationwide in social studies or history, those exams are among the last to be developed, introduced, and required. In addition, an examination of the testing criteria for those states including social studies as an exit exam indicates that little to no test questions refer to anything outside of American history and Western involvement in world affairs. By definition, this would virtually exclude the Holocaust from being included in any meaningful way on a high school exit exam.

The social studies community is divided as to whether this is an insult or a blessing in disguise. Initially, educators were disappointed to find that NCLB did not give social studies the attention it focused on math and reading and "feared that the exclusion of social studies would lead to a diminution in the relative importance of social studies in American school systems."[10] Indeed, this has occurred at both the elementary and secondary levels. However, educators remain convinced that the assessment of social studies/history achievement cannot be measured adequately by standardized testing methods and are now at the forefront of a cry to reorganize NCLB or do away with the legislation altogether.

NCLB in Low-Performing Schools and with Low-Performing Students

Finn and Ravitch wrote, "Liberal learning is critical to young people because it prepares them for 'public life'—not just politics and government, but civic life in which we all should partake. . . . For such engagements to succeed, one need not have a college degree, much less a Ph.D. But it's close to essential to have a broad basic education."[11] Students in low-performing schools (almost exclusively those schools in high-poverty/high-minority neighborhoods or school districts) are least likely to receive this broad basic education. This speaks alarming volumes about opportunity, equal access, and the ability to engage in future civic participation. There, the pressure to avoid NCLB sanctions is most keenly felt with teachers attending almost exclusively to material that will be subject to high-stakes testing and engaging in instructional "triage" to avoid those sanctions.

For those readers outside the K-12 public school educational community, allow me to define "triage" in terms of NCLB testing pressures. It consists of identifying those students who will surely pass the tests and crossing them off your class roster, identifying those students who will never pass the tests and crossing them off as well, and finally identifying those students who can, with intensive instruction, be moved from "failing" to "passing." Those students in educational communities are known as "bubble kids." They are the ones that can be taught just enough to "bubble in" the correct answers and keep the school off of the NCLB radar (or out of its gun sights, however you may perceive it). Those students are routinely (according to the research of Jennifer Booher-Jennings, for example) pulled from social studies, physical education, arts, and electives for intensive remediation and test prep.[12] Imagine a Seinfeld-like Soup Nazi excluding these children from a class lesson on prejudice, tolerance, and justice—"No Holocaust education for you!"

What Are We to Do?

Judith Pace, a professor of education at the University of San Francisco, wrote an outstanding commentary that appeared in the December 19, 2007, issue of *Education Week*. In her commentary, she referred to research conducted by John S. Wills of the University of California, Riverside, who studied what happened when social studies instruction was marginalized as a result of NCLB. He found that "elements of thoughtful teaching were eradicated" and asked "whether the drive for accountability is leading not only to lost content knowledge, but also, and paradoxically, to the elimination of thoughtful, student-centered instruction 'disproportionately from the education of poor students and students of color.' "[13]

Pace's article prompted me to begin to think about what to do to save Holocaust education in public schools in the wake of No Child Left Behind. When reading her commentary I could not help but think of the university students I now teach. Most of them are from poor communities. A majority of them will be first-generation college graduates. A majority of them are African American. Most indicate that they will return to their home communities to teach. They are virtually ignorant of any historical connection between the African American community and the Jewish community and are almost totally ignorant of the Holocaust—they know almost nothing of our shared history of suffering and liberation. What could I do to rectify that situation with my own students so that they could be fully prepared to go forth and teach generations of students? How could I help them to incorporate "elements of thoughtful teaching" that would support Holocaust education across their various curricular areas?

Using Trade Literature to Support Thoughtful Teaching

Planning and delivering quality classroom instruction in spite of the demands of NCLB is a daunting task for any teacher. However, there are tools and strategies that can aid educators in their honest attempts to truly leave no child behind. The reality of public education is that many children and young adults arrive at school already significantly behind; they may have little experiential information with which to make connections to text, they may have little background knowledge about the subject being discussed or that of the text being read, they may not have enough expressive language to communicate what they think, feel, believe, or understand about a topic or about information gained from text, or they may not yet have developed reading abilities sophisticated enough to comprehend some classroom texts.

Elements of thoughtful teaching include creating a classroom environment and culture in which all learners are engaged and each student is valued for his or her classroom contributions. This is quite difficult when a classroom of eighth grade students, for example, typically includes 40 percent of students reading independently below grade-level. Compound this with the fact that as historical events, the Holocaust in particular, fade further into the past, students come to the study of the subject with less and less general background information with which to make sense of text. Further compound the problem with the fact that content-area textbooks, particularly those found in social studies and history classrooms, are written on average two reading levels above the grade for which they are intended and a daunting task has become almost impossible.

Fortunately, writers and publishers have been quite busy over the past few years providing teachers with tools designed for just this situation—books! The selection of Holocaust-related tradebooks (books available on the general market—not commercial textbooks) is larger, more varied, and, frankly, much better than it has ever been. Teachers can, through the thoughtful and judicious use of tradebooks, meaningfully engage both novice and experienced students with this sensitive, complex, and critically significant event while also increasing reading comprehension, reading engagement, and historical literacy.

Using Tradebooks Beyond and in Conjunction with *The Diary of Anne Frank* and *Night*

I am certainly not suggesting that either of these texts is inappropriate for young readers or that they should not be included in classroom instruction or classroom libraries. What I am suggesting is that they present what Philip Rosen has referred to as a slice of the comprehensive Holocaust experience that is "one inch long and one inch deep."[14] Anne's story presents one small window into the Holocaust; one that was tragic to be sure, but one that does not convey the experiences of Jews in hiding who had less real and financial resources and who did not have fathers who carefully prepared for the almost unfathomable possibility that the family may need to have a hiding place and gentile co-conspirators who could maintain the family's clandestine existence. In addition, the Goodrich and Hackett theatrical version of *The Diary of Anne Frank* (1956) (which is included in many English anthologies and is, therefore, the one most students encounter) ends not with Anne's death but with her soliloquy about most people being good at heart, leaving the reader with an unfinished story.

Night requires from all but the most sophisticated readers the ability to negotiate the Yiddish included in the text and the ability to understand the degree to which Wiesel's Jewish Orthodoxy influenced the attitudes, decisions, and disillusionment of the narrator. I have used this book a number of times in my over-two-decade experience with students and have yet to have average students who can comprehend God dying on the gallows without extensive classroom discussion and explanation on my part.

Neither text presents the story of women within the camps, of non-Jewish victims, or of Jewish resistance—stories that offer connections for females and non-Jewish readers, for example. While I am not negating the value of either text, I am suggesting that there are other, more readily accessible alternatives that can open a wider window on the magnitude that was the Holocaust. The following is a survey of various formats of children's and young adult literature that can be utilized by teachers to build background knowledge necessary for a serious study of the Holocaust, suggestions for their use, with whom and for what purposes, and example genre selections within each of the formats.

A Note for College and University Instructors and Professors

While the following is written largely with a public schoolteacher audience in mind, there are certainly implications for use in college and university instruction. Students entering higher education classrooms do not always do so bringing with them a comprehensive understanding of the Holocaust. The following texts and suggestions can be modified and expanded for use in college and university instruction as introductions, further explorations, and research resources. I can certainly imagine the suggested selections under the heading, "Biography (Memoirs and Other Personal Accounts)," for example, being used as a springboard for sophisticated lectures on consideration of survivor accounts.

Picture Books: Supporting Content Understanding and Visual Literacy

"A picture book by definition is a book in which the illustrations carry as much of the meaning as the text itself. Most often associated with young children, picture books are increasingly written about sophisticated concepts using sophisticated language—concepts and language ideal for older students."[15]

Picture books are an excellent format for addressing widely varying reading abilities common within classrooms of children and young adult learners. It is difficult for students to learn new and difficult concepts associated with subjects such as the Holocaust while also attending to challenging and often unfamiliar language and text structures. Routinely, due to the fact that many commercial textbooks are far too difficult for many students to read independently with ease, teachers find themselves *telling* students the material through lecture format rather than asking students to actually read content text material.

Though language and concepts in picture books are presented in sophisticated and challenging ways, the readability level of these books is usually below that of older students. Thus, a student does not have to struggle with both concept development and reading comprehension at the same time. Having "controlled" for text difficulty, a student is then freed to concentrate on understanding the new and difficult concepts to be learned.

Picture books also accommodate struggling readers and second-language learners as they acquire new and difficult language and historical concepts. Not only do the illustrations support language and vocabulary development for these students by helping them to "picture" the word meanings, but lower readability levels of picture books allow struggling readers and students of limited English access to subject matter which would otherwise be beyond their reach.

Building Background Knowledge

Reading comprehension depends upon building connections between the known and the unknown.[16] To comprehend is to seamlessly integrate new information into an existing system of knowledge. Reading comprehension is a process of constructing and reconstructing those systems of knowledge through interacting and transacting with text.[17] Implicit is the assumption that there is a foundational element, some existent knowledge on which to build. That assumption, too often, is false—especially in the area of social studies/history—specifically with complex topics such as the Holocaust/Shoah.

Picture books are typically thirty-two pages in length.[18] They are easily read by most students, and most often address only one topic, concept, or event in depth.[19] These attributes make them perfect tools for building background. They can be read quickly and easily, thus allowing students to read many picture books as opposed to little or no textbook material. This facilitates quickly building background knowledge on a wide range of topics or concepts in a limited time period.

> For example, in a couple of class periods students could read *The Harmonica* (Johnston, 2004), *The Butterfly* (Polacco, 2000), *Luba: The Angel of Bergen-Belsen* (McCann, 2003), *The Yellow Star* (Deedy, 2002), and *A Hero and the Holocaust* (Adler, 2002). In approximately two hours students would have read 160 pages. This would have resulted in acquisition of background information regarding treatment of concentration camp inmates at Dyhernfurth, information related to the legend of King Christian X, rescue and survival attempts at Bergen-Belsen, the French Resistance, the Warsaw Ghetto, child victim stories, and the story of Dr. Yanusz Korczak.[20]

This acquisition of background information establishes a platform for entrée into diverse and more complex texts and for building more in-depth and sophisticated knowledge structures.

The "His and Her" of History

"If history is indeed the story of ourselves, then another limitation of history textbooks is that the people are missing!"[21] A cursory examination of any typical classroom textbook will reveal a tome filled with dates, events, and facts with little real insight into the people who lived the events and created the facts that students are often expected to commit to memory.

If students are to truly comprehend and internalize the content to be learned, a personal connection is essential. Picture books, whether historical fiction or expository texts such as biographies or personal narratives, permit students to connect with the people whose first-hand experiences comprised the history. Picture books give "voice" to history; they breathe life into lifeless dates, events, and facts. Additionally, commercially available classroom textbooks most often present historical figures at a chronological age much older than the reader. One rarely reads about a president, a military hero, or a founding father as a young man. However, a majority of picture books present a protagonist who is of a similar age to the child reading the story and, indeed, many of the stories of the Holocaust (including *Night* and *The Diary of Anne Frank*) feature young protagonists. Though the main character of Ruth Vander Zee's *Erika's Story* is an adult when recounting her story, students are able to connect to the baby, the child, and the young mother. I have yet to have a student or teacher read this book and respond with anything other than, "Oh, I just wanted to cry when the mother threw the baby," or "I can't imagine how she managed to do that," or "If it were my baby . . ." These are the intimate personal connections and interactions that result in comprehension.

Lots of "Bang for the Buck"

Not a week goes by but that a social studies/history teacher voices something like this during one of my professional development workshops: "I'd love to teach the Holocaust/Shoah, but my students don't read well enough to comprehend much of that material, and I just don't have time to teach both history and reading." In that same week I usually hear an English/language arts teacher say, "I'd love to use more Holocaust-related materials in my English class, but I really have to focus on teaching vocabulary (or grammar . . .) and just can't spend time teaching history." I am convinced that using picture books in either of these scenarios offers an opportunity to provide teachers with more "bang for the buck."

Picture books introduce students to difficult historical concepts while also focusing on rich language, vocabulary, and the structure and conventions of written language formats such as poetry and the various forms of prose. The short staccato sentences found in *Erika's Story* afford teachers, particularly English teachers, an opportunity to talk about the relationship of sentence length to tension and mood while at the same time introducing historical information.[22] A passage from *The Harmonica* reads, "My lips loved the harmonica, cool as water. At first my breath panted in and out of its niched sides like a bellows."[23] This passage introduces the reader to the young boy who is later to become the musical pet of the concentration camp commandant and also provides teachers and students with examples of rich language and specialized vocabulary used in unique ways (*niche* and *bellows*). Thus, the economical length of picture book texts added to the richness of language and vocabulary multiplied by exposure to new and varied concepts totals a sum too great for any teacher, regardless of discipline, to ignore.

Picture Books for Building and Developing Visual Literacy

A central pillar of reading comprehension is the ability to visualize that which is occurring in a text (a character, a setting, an action). When reading complex historical events with which many readers are unfamiliar, comprehension demands that students have the ability to hold an image, often several different and competing images, in their minds as they read, visualizing those images changing, evolving, and interacting with other held images. This is quite a sophisticated reading task and is often so complex that students lose the events occurring within the narrative due to the fact that they "lose sight" of the images.

Frey and Fisher noted, "As with reading comprehension, visually literate learners are able to make connections, determine importance, synthesize information, evaluate, and critique. Further, these visual literacies are interwoven with textual ones, so that their interaction forms the basis for a more complete understanding."[24] Visual literacy can be developed and supported through the illustrations found in picture books. High-quality illustrations (often awarded Caldecott honors for illustration), particularly the large, often double-page spreads characteristic of picture books, help students to "see" the character, setting, or action and provide the pictures to hold in their heads as they read.

Purposeful attention to picture-book illustrations can help students to develop visual discernment, determining the precedence and relationships between multiple, often competing, visual information. While "looking" is superficial, "seeing" requires this ability to critically "read" images—visually literacy. There is a vast difference between "looking" at an illustration and "reading" an illustration. Certainly, this ability is essential when "reading" the images often associated with the Holocaust, particularly those produced as Nazi propaganda.

One teaching strategy supportive of visual literacy involves guiding students as they divide an illustration into quadrants, examining the illustration bit by bit, discussing what they notice and what they wonder about the new visual information that is being revealed. This strategy aids students in dissecting an illustration focusing on details often missed at first glance. When attempting to look at the *whole* of an illustration from *The Harmonica*, for example, students often do not notice the expression of joy on the commandant's face in one quadrant, the menacing red eyes of the German shepherd in another, or the skeletal death mask in yet another. This method of guided observation leads them toward close examination and attention to detail. Routine close examination of and attention to illustrations can support students as they begin to visualize illustrations and hold on to those visualizations in their "mind's eye" as they read longer, more grade-appropriate non-illustrated texts.

Classroom Environment and Reading Fluency

Picture books by virtue of size and length beg to be held by a teacher and read aloud. Reading aloud to students, regardless of age, is vital.[25] Regularly including read-alouds as part of reflective thoughtful teaching practices can aid in building community and enhancing the learning environment. This is in addition to the wealth of information students attain as we read aloud to them. Mem Fox put it this way: "The more we read aloud to our kids . . . the more experience they'll have of the world through the things they encounter in books. And the more experience they have of the world, the easier it will be to read."[26] Since a majority of public school students do not have much, if any, experience with the Holocaust, experience which is necessary for motivating students to read widely, reading aloud can be the vehicle with which to provide that initial experience.

Reading Aloud to Middle and High School Students?

In a recent workshop for high school English and history teachers, I distributed Holocaust-related picture books and modeled read-aloud behaviors. A few weeks later I had a serendipitous encounter with one of the participants while shopping for groceries. She told me that she hadn't believed that high school students would welcome their teacher reading aloud from "kiddie books," but that she had been willing to take my suggestion and give it a try. She admitted that she had been shocked when students begged her to read other picture books to them day after day after day. She remarked that her classroom just "felt" different now that they were sharing this time together around a content-related picture book. She said that it was the first time she really understood the term "classroom community." She said that the communal sharing of story had caused something she just could not describe; it was as though they were speaking to one another for the first time using a common language. When I suggested a "conspiracy of learners," she laughed and agreed that it was exactly what her classroom had become and that the more they read together the closer they became and the more they wanted to know.

She noticed also that once she put the book down, students would pick it up to read and reread during their "free" time. As students reread text they unconsciously and almost effortlessly increase reading fluency; for each time they read the same material, they read at a greater rate. As they read at a greater rate while internally replaying and reproducing the vocal inflections, intonations, and expression initially provided by the teacher (fluency) during the initial read-aloud, comprehension increases. As comprehension increases, the ability and motivation to independently read longer and more difficult text increases.[27] A number of middle school and high school teachers with whom I have worked have commented that their use of picture books has increased student enthusiasm for reading chapter books, middle-grade novels, young adult novels, and adult-targeted texts, which further increase their understanding of the Holocaust and enhance reading comprehension. This is a formula for exponentially escalating reading success.

Chapter Books, Middle-Grade Novels, and Young Adult Novels

Typically written for ages seven to ten, chapter books are transitional books that help children move from picture books and early readers to full novels. They may include a combination of text and illustration. Middle-grade novels are usually targeted to readers ages eight to twelve and rely entirely or almost entirely on text to tell the story. Young adult (YA) novels, also sometimes called teen novels, are generally read by children anywhere from age twelve upwards. They are longer books, often 50,000 words or more. Young adult novels often include more age-appropriate material such as sex, violence, and peer pressure.

Historical Fiction Picture Books, Chapter Books, Middle-Grade Novels, and Young Adult Novels

Historical fiction does what textbook expository text cannot—it allows the reader to put a face, vicariously his or her own face, on a historical event. Historical fiction picture books often allow the reader to view history through a protagonist his or her own age, one with whom the reader can most easily relate. Historical fiction picture books may include real, imagined, or composites of characters that actually lived during the time period. Settings also may be real or imaginary. The plot events may be documented historical events or they may be fictional. If they are fictional, it means that the author created the events for the telling of the story. To be high-quality historical fiction, the fictional characters, settings, and plot events must be portrayed authentically as if they actually *could* have happened. The following are examples of high-quality historical fiction picture books to build background knowledge for study of the Holocaust, support text and personal connections, develop necessary vocabulary for further reading, and develop visual literacy.

Selected Text Suggestions

Tony Johnson, *The Harmonica* (Charlesbridge, 2004). Inspired by the true story of Henryk Rosmaryn, this picture book recounts the story of a young boy who survived the horrors of a concentration camp by playing his harmonica for the camp commandant in exchange for food, which he could not take back to his starving fellow prisoners, but was required to eat in the presence of the commandant. It is an outstanding selection for supporting visual literacy, for building background knowledge relating to camp conditions, and for making personal connections by responding to the question, "What would I do to survive when all around are perishing?"

Roberto Innocenti, *Rose Blanche* (Creative Editions, 1985). Rose Blanche was a group of young Germans who died for protesting the war. This picture book, named for but not directly about the group, is a powerful story of how one too young to actually understand war and genocide responds to it. Long out of print, this book is now available once again and is a wonderful resource. It provides a perfect introduction for researching the group Rose Blanche and the fairytale Rose Blanche, and then making connections between them.

William Kaplan and Shelley Tanaka, *One More Border* (Groundwood Books, 1998). Jews fleeing Eastern Europe via Japan? Did that really happen? Photographs and artist illustrations recount the story of Jews fleeing the Nazis which is largely unknown, but was far from unique. This picture book is a perfect companion piece to *Faithful Elephants* (1997), which relates the story of the Ueno Zoo and the dilemmas facing zookeepers in the wake of World War II bombings.

Carmen Agra Deedy, *The Yellow Star: The Legend of King Christian X of Denmark* (Peachtree, 2000). This beautifully illustrated picture book by famed storyteller Carmen Deedy recounts the "legend" of King Christian X of Denmark who committed himself to keeping Danish Jews safe during Nazi occupation. How much is true? How much is legend? Sounds like a research topic to me!

Jerry Spinelli, *Milkweed* (Alfred A. Knopf, 2003). In true Jerry Spinelli style, the author has again woven a tale of friendship, individualism, and of the "outsider." Misha is the outsider—a homeless boy either Gypsy or Jew—taken in by Uri and his band of "lost boys." This book spans Polish Holocaust history from occupation until the end of the war. It introduces the reader to Janusz Korczak, the Warsaw Ghetto uprising, and the horrors of daily life in the ghetto. A haunting tale. Pair with picture books by David Adler.

Irene N. Watts, *Good-bye Marianne* (Tundra, 1998). This middle-grades novel introduces Marianne and begins the *Good-bye Marianne* trilogy. As our young female protagonist boards the kindertransport, she is given charge of seven-year-old Sophie. This story ends on the train, but is taken up once again in the sequel, *Remember Me* (2000), and ends with *Finding Sophie* (2002).

John Boyne, *The Boy in the Striped Pajamas* (Dave Ficking Books, 2006). When a young boy and his family are relocated to *Out-With* in Poland due to the father's work transfer, the child finds himself not in his busy city with friends, family, and things to do, but in a remote location where Father is obsessed with work and the child's freedom of exploration and movement is restricted. Bored, irritated with his father, and searching for adventure, he befriends a boy wearing pajamas on the other side of a forbidden fence. The friendship turns in the final pages of this historical-allegory teaching us all a lesson about fences.

Markus Zusak, *The Book Thief* (Alfred A. Knopf, 2006). Narrated by Death, this YA novel tells the story of Liesel Meminger, a young, non-Jewish foster girl living outside of Munich in Nazi Germany. Liesel's fascination with books leads her to steal books from the wife of the local Nazi leadership and from the piles of books subject to town book-burnings. Liesel uses these books to learn to read and shares them with the Jewish man being hidden in her basement.

Biography Picture Books, Chapter Books, Middle-Grade and YA Novels (Memoirs and Other Personal Accounts)

There has been much scholarly debate concerning the role of personal accounts in Holocaust study. Is memory "truth"? Teachers should carefully address this subject themselves before and as they use these books in their classrooms. It is important that students understand that the way an individual (themselves included) remembers an event is influenced by time, distance from the actual event, maturity, and reflection. That is not to say that the events themselves did not happen or that they did not happen in the way recounted by the author. I only caution that young readers can easily fall victim to revisionist propaganda when well-intentioned classroom teachers do not guide students in thinking critically about this genre.

Selected Text Suggestions

Luba Tryszynska-Frederick, *Luba: The Angel of Bergen-Belsen* (Tricycle Press, 2003). This is the story of the women of Belsen who found and cared for fifty-four children who had been abandoned behind the famous camp. Known afterwards as the *diamond children*, all fifty-four survived the war and are pictured along with Luba in a 1995 reunion photograph in the epilogue of the book. This picture book is ideal for opening discussion relating to various types of resistance.

Ruth Vander Zee, *Erika's Story* (Creative Editions, 2003). In 1995 a child survivor told her story to Ruth Vander Zee. Read this book and the picture-story told by master illustrator Roberto Innocenti, and be forever changed. I love this picture book not only for the story and the careful use of color in the illustrations, which conveys an additional level of understanding the text, but also as a model piece of writing. It is an excellent example of how sentence length can convey mood and intensity.

David A. Adler, *Child of the Warsaw Ghetto* (Holiday House, 1995). This picture book is densely packed with information about the Warsaw ghetto (relocation, starvation, smuggling, and uprising) as told through the experiences of survivor Froim Baum, who was later liberated from Dachau. It makes a super companion piece to *A Hero and the Holocaust: The Story of Janusz Korczak* (2002) and is excellent for building background to read longer and more complex and advanced texts such as *Milkweed* (2003).

David Adler, *A Hero and the Holocaust: The Story of Janusz Korczak and His Children* (Holiday House, 2002). This picture book has one of the best leads I've ever read. Both the words and the illustrations on the first two pages set the stage for this excellent biography of Janusz Korczak. This book provides great background for reading *Milkweed* (2003), and offers young students who typically equate "hero" with "action figure" an opportunity for redefining that term.

Susan Goldman Rubin, *Fireflies in the Dark: The Story of Friedl Dicker-Brandeis and the Children of Terezin* (Holiday House, 2000). Part picture book, part chapter book, and part biography—this resource is a treasure for any classroom teacher. Each "chapter" chronicles the experiences of the children of Terezin from relocation to extermination. Actual drawings and short writing done by the children of Terezin are included. It is a perfect resource for guiding readers toward connected texts such as *I Never Saw Another Butterfly* (Scholastic, 1993) and *Brundibar* (Hyperion, 2003). It's also a nice parallel to any works about Janusz Korczak or the liquidation of the Warsaw Ghetto.

Andrea Warren, *Surviving Hitler: A Boy in the Nazi Death Camps* (Harper Collins, 2001). This recent middle-grades-to-YA edition to survivor accounts is excellent. The author relates the experiences of Jack Mendlebaum as he survives Auschwitz. I particularly love the 1990 photograph of Jack on his return to Auschwitz. The book includes an extensive index and accompanying historical information.

Eleanor Ayer, *Parallel Journeys* (Aladdin, 1995). Don't rely on the age designation of ten and up on the back cover. Definitely a book for middle to high school readers, this book presents the side-by-side stories of two young people who grew up within miles of one another during the time of the Holocaust—she a Jew and he an ardent member of the Hitler Youth.

Peter Lane Taylor, *The Secret of Priest's Grotto: A Holocaust Survival Story* (Kar-Ben, 2007). This text, at first glance, appears to be a picture book. However, it is a hybrid mix of nonfiction adventure/discovery, memoir, and biography. The formal readability level of this book is at the high end of eleventh grade, so while it initially appears to be a picture book, it is really quite an advanced text. The book developed as the result of an expedition by cave veteran Cristos Nicola, when he became one of the first Americans to explore Ukraine's caves after the fall of the Soviet Union. He learned that the caves had been the dark hiding place for forty-eight Jews for almost an entire year. One child survivor is quoted as remembering, "By the time that I came out of the cave, I had forgotten what the sun was. And when we came out . . . I told my mother . . . 'Close the candle! Turn out the light!' I couldn't believe it! I had forgotten completely what the sun was" (57–58). Photographs of artifacts, present-day cavers, and historical and current photographs of those who hid within the caves support young readers of this outstanding book.

Fantasy/ Fairy Tale Books ("Historical Fantasy")

Fantasy literature offers readers an awareness of the magical nature of everyday life. It often opens readers to the possibility of a world better, finer, and more "real" than current reality. Fantasy literature often includes literary devices such as talking animals, magic and magical beings, and time travel. Though often a controversial genre through which to portray the Holocaust—that which is, to some degree, a sacrosanct event—I offer the words of multiple award-winning author Jane Yolen on the rationale for using time travel in "historical fantasy": "That is the child at the instant of reading the time travel novel, 'a little bit gone.' One foot in today and the rest stuck back in 1942 or 1857 or 1066. And though I have heard from at least one editor who feels time travel to be 'a gimmick, a device, a framework' only, I believe it is a straight road into memory, an experimental act for an understanding of the past. It is once-upon-a-very-real-time, making history immediate and accessible for the young reader, letting them see backwards through a clear lens."[28]

Suggested Text Selections

Jane Yolen, *The Devil's Arithmetic* (Viking, 1988). This is my all-time favorite novel to use with middle school and high school students. Its fantasy element is so similar to that of *The Wizard of Oz* that students can understand the novel's plot. The author's careful use of accurate historical detail keeps students asking the question, "How much of this is fantasy and how much reality?" What a perfect opportunity to search for the answer to that question!

Jane Yolen, *Briar Rose* (Tom Doherty, 1992). Again, Jane Yolen has done a breathtaking job of blurring the line between fantasy and reality. In this novel she has placed Sleeping Beauty not in the German forests of the Brothers Grimm, but in that of the Third Reich and imagines a female character who escaped from Chelmno—a historical event that unfortunately did not occur. This book is an advanced read.

Steven Schnur, *The Shadow Children* (Scholastic, 1994). I've had many struggling middle and high school readers choose this book because it has large print text and illustrations, which make it seem to be a "children's book" and therefore an easy book. Those same children become engrossed in the twisted dream-like plot in which child-like wraiths may or may not actually exist. This chapter book, accompanied by bizarre black-and-white illustrations is a favorite of young readers who often choose to reread the book a second and third time.

Poetry

Poetry as richly distilled experience and emotion is essential to any Holocaust library. Poems can serve as a model for individual or whole-class writing. Use one or more as springboards for writing and reflection. Poetry is a great way for young people of any age to express the intense experience of Holocaust study.

Nancy Patz, *Who Was the Woman Who Wore the Hat?* (Dutton Books, 2003). I have placed this book under the heading "poetry," but it could just as easily fit in the picture-book category. While visiting the Jewish Historical Museum in Amsterdam, Nancy Patz saw a display of a lady's hat and she began to imagine the woman to whom the hat had once belonged. What resulted was this wonderful book with marvelous illustrations combining photographs and drawings. The author's notes and chronology following the text are exceptional.

Hana Volavkova, ed. *I Never Saw Another Butterfly . . . : Children's Drawings and Poems from Terezin Concentration Camp, 1942–1944* (Scholastic, 1993). This classic is a must for any Holocaust library and a perfect companion to *Fireflies in the Dark* (Holiday House, 2000).

Phyllis Johnson, *Being Frank with Anne* (Community Press, 2007). In this beautiful slim volume, Phyllis Johnson responds as reader and writer to one of the most powerful and influential diaries of our time. Powerful poetry responds to powerful prose; the heart of the reader responds in writing to the heart of the writer. While reading this book I couldn't help but envision classrooms filled with readers using this text as a model for their own writing responses. What a wonderful book! What a wonderful classroom resource!

Graphic Novels and Comics

The terms "comics" and "graphic novel" are often used interchangeably. Technically there are two types of graphic novels: those that are collections of trade paperbacks originally published as serialized comic books, and those that are stand-alone narratives told in comic format. Comic books and graphic novels produced in Japan for a Japanese audience and those produced in the United States for a Western audience, which borrows heavily from Japanese comic traditions, are known as *manga.* When *manga* is turned into movie or television media it is known as *anime.*[29] Each is currently subject to both acclaim and derision within educational communities.[30] As a self-proclaimed long-time comic book fangirl I have embraced them as a classroom resource as have many other educators.

The most widely recognized graphic novels associated with the Holocaust are Art Spiegelman's *Maus: A Survivor's Tale* (Pantheon, 1991) and *Maus II: A Survivor's Tale and Here My Troubles Began* (Pantheon, 1986). A number of graphic novels and comics have followed the trail blazed (often controversially so) by Spiegelman. These texts often present survivors' own stories as well as those of children of survivors—stories only recently being recounted.

Suggested Text Selections

Etsuo Suzuki, *Edu Manga: Anne Frank* (Digital Manga, 2006). This book in the Edu Manga series tells the story of Anne Frank through the comic art form, manga. Astro Boy, one of Japan's most well-known icons, follows the story from sidebars and helps the reader feel like a traveler in Anne's world.

Pascal Croci, *Auschwitz* (Harry N. Abrams, 2004). This is one of the most beautifully written and illustrated texts I have ever read. One look at the cover art draws the reader into the book through the wide-eyed woman pictured there. Once in the text, the reader is drawn into the depths of the horror that was Auschwitz.

Joe Kubert, *Yossel: April 19, 1943* (ibooks, Inc., 2003). Joe Kubert, noted comic genius and creator of Sgt. Rock, also drew characters such as Hawkman, Batman, and the Flash. In this indescribably beautiful carbon-drawing-pencil illustrated text, Kubert reimagines his possible life had his father *not* gotten his young pregnant bride aboard a ship to sail them to safety in the United States. In his reimagining, he becomes involved in the Warsaw Ghetto Uprising.

Martin Lemelman, *Mendel's Daughter: A Memoir* (Free Press, 2006). Martin Lemelman transcribes his mother's memoir, adding his own illustrations in graphic and photo/graphic formats. The story begins with a view into pretransformation and relocation shtetl life through hiding, partisan participation, and into the depths of the nightmare that was the Holocaust. This *beautiful* black-and-white text is readable for young readers and complex enough for young adult and adult readers.

And Finally

Elements of thoughtful teaching practice and advocacy on the part of the scholarly community to support teachers and young people as they engage in interactions between texts, other readers, and reflective teachers become critically important as living memory fades into the past and becomes only the "stuff of history books." As No Child Left Behind turns classroom communities into test-taking factories and as more than a generation of children skilled not as reflective, critical thinkers but, rather, as careful manipulators of the ubiquitous number two pencil arrive on college and university campuses, please hear this clarion call from one still in the trenches fighting the good fight.

Recognize and support quality teaching, advocate for quality instruction for all children, lobby for Holocaust education deep and wide in public schools, rail against high-stakes testing for those teachers unable to resist mandates themselves, and read and recommend quality literature at all grade levels which can support Holocaust education for *all* readers and *all* teachers. Even if it *never* becomes part of "the test" (and in my mind it should not) together we must stand *for* Holocaust education in public schools and, for the sake of past and present generations in which genocide has been and is a reality and for future generations in which it may—G'd willing—be only a part of the "stuff of history books." Let us work together to *truly* leave no child behind.

Notes

1. W. Reich, "Erasing the Holocaust," *New York Times,* July 11, 1993, 1, 31, 33–34.
2. M. Kakutani, "When History and Memory Are Casualties: Holocaust Denial," *New York Times,* June 30, 1993, B1, B6.
3. National Council of Teachers of English, "On Teaching about Intolerance and Genocide" (1993), http://www.ncte.org/about/over/positions/category/right/107439.htm.
4. The United States Holocaust Memorial Museum. State Profiles on Holocaust Education. http://www.ushmm.org/education/foreducators/states/.
5. A. Kohn, "Fighting the Tests: A Practical Guide to Rescuing Our Schools," *Phi Delta Kappan 82* (2001): 349–57.
6. For example, S. Burroughs, E. C. Groce, and M. L. Webeck, "Social Studies Education in the Age of Testing and Accountability," *Educational Measurement: Issues and Practice* 24 (2005): 13–20.
7. Ibid.
8. K. Manzo, "Social Studies Losing Out to Reading, Math," *Education Week* (March 16, 2005): 16–17.
9. Center on Educational Policy, http://www.cep-dc.org.
10. National Council for Social Studies Position Statement on No Child Left Behind, 2008. http//:www.socialstudies.org/positions/nclb.
11. C. Finn and D. Ravitch, eds., *Beyond the Basics: Achieving a Liberal Education for All Children* (Washington, D.C.: Thomas B. Fordham Foundation, 2007).
12. J. Booher-Jennings, "Below the Bubble: 'Educational Triage' and the Texas Accountability System," *American Educational Research Journal* (Summer 2005): 23–68.

13. J. L. Pace, "Why We Need to Save (and Strengthen) Social Studies," *Education Week*, Dec. 19, 2007.
14. P. Rosen, (1999), "Beyond Anne Frank." Presented at the 19th Annual Holocaust Conference at Millersville University, http://www.millersville.edu/holo-con/Rosen-1999.html.
15. L. C. Jacobs, "A Picture Is Worth Six Million Words: Using Picture Books to Support Teaching the Holocaust to Adolescents and Young Adults," *Journal of Content Area Reading* 4 (2005): 53–64.
16. F. Smith, *Understanding Reading*, 4th ed. (Hillsdale, N.J.: Erlbaum, 1988).
17. L. Rosenblatt, *Literature as Exploration* (New York: Philomel Books, 1985).
18. D. Darigan, M. Tunnell, and J. Jacobs, *Children's Literature: Engaging Teachers and Children in Good Books* (Upper Saddle River, N.J.: Pearson Education, 2002).
19. L. W. Billman, "Aren't These Books for Little Kids?" *Educational Leadership* 60 (2002): 48–51.
20. Jacobs, "A Picture Is Worth Six Million Words." Works mentioned include T. Johnson, *The Harmonica* (Watertown, Mass.: Charlesbridge, 2004); P. Polacco, *The Butterfly* (New York: Philomel Books, 2000); M. R. McCann, *Luba: The Angel of Bergen-Belsen* (Berkeley: Tricycle Press, 2003); C. A. Deedy, *The Yellow Star: The Legend of King Christian X of Denmark* (Atlanta: Peachtree, 2002); and D. Adler, *A Hero and the Holocaust: The Story of Janusz Korczak and His Children* (New York: Holiday House, 2002).
21. Darigan, Tunnell, and Jacobs, *Children's Literature.*
22. R. Vander Zee, *Erika's Story* (Mankato, Minn.: Creative Editions, 2003).
23. Johnson, *The Harmonica.*
24. N. Frey and D. Fisher, eds., *Teaching Visual Literacy: Using Comic Books, Graphic Novels, Anime, Cartoons, and More to Develop Comprehension and Thinking Skills* (Thousand Oaks, Calif.: Corwin Press, 2008).
25. F. Serafini and C. Giorgis, *Reading Aloud and Beyond: Fostering the Intellectual Life with Older Readers* (Portsmouth, N.H.: Heinemann, 2003).
26. M. Fox, *Reading Magic: Why Reading Aloud to Our Children Will Change Their Lives Forever* (New York: Harcourt, 2002), 36.
27. T. G. Gunning, *Assessing and Correcting Reading and Writing Difficulties* (Boston: Allyn and Bacon, 2002).
28. J. Yolen, "An Experimental Act," *Language Arts* 66 (1989): 46–48.
29. L. Jacobs, "Let the Girls (and Boys) Read Comics," http://www.myshelf.com/babetoteen/column.htm/January2008/.
30. Frey and Fisher, eds., *Teaching Visual Literacy.*

Spelling and Kabbalah

A Review Essay of Myla Goldberg's Bee Season

Nancy Shiffrin

I wish to express my appreciation to Zev Garber for helping wandering Jews connect to Jewish academic life.

* * *

As the novel *Bee Season* begins, the protagonist, nine-year-old Eliza Naumann, is the Other, the Outsider, in a family of intense unearthly intellectuals. A disappointment to her Cantor father Saul, distanced from her obsessive/compulsive lawyer mother, Miriam, ignored by her Bar Mitzvah–student brother, and not selected as Aaron was for the Talented and Gifted program at her high school, Eliza seems resigned to a secondary position in her family, appropriate to her birth order and gender.

Then Eliza wins her high school spelling bee championship. With her brother's help, she makes her victory visible to her father. Saul is not able to accompany Eliza to the District Bee, nor is Miriam, so Aaron drives her. There, the contestants are described as terrified prey waiting to be slaughtered. Eliza, however, has a mystical experience. "From the first time she steps to the microphone the words are there, radiant as neon," Goldberg writes. "She hears the word and suddenly it is inside her head, translated from sound into physical form. Sometimes the letters need a moment to arrange themselves behind her closed eyes. An E will replace an I, a consonant will double . . . she knows when a word will reach its perfect form."[1]

Author Myla Goldberg describes her trip to the National Spelling Bee to an interviewer:

> It was intense! If nothing else, that was what made me realize that I could write a novel about this. It's an alternate universe; . . . a microcosm of the childhood experience. . . . You grow up, you have parents who have expectations, who want certain things and you try really hard to fulfill them. And then you realize that you can't always. That kind of moment is defining for a lot of people.[2]

Goldberg acknowledges Charlotte Anne Arch, a friend whose family was involved in "the Spelling Bee culture" and "who generously gifted [her] with the seeds of this novel" and Neil Steinberg's essay "The Spelling Bee," as sources. Goldberg also attended a National Spelling Bee contest and interviewed some of the contestants. Steinberg describes the National Spelling Bee as a unique form of torture. "Out of the nine million children, 8,999,999 will lose, and they will lose in a public and humiliating fashion. It would be hard to think of a way of making failure more demeaning," he writes. Steinberg describes the Comfort Room, where contestants retire after misspelling a word. The room has a curtain for crying kids to hide behind and a punching bag. Most of the words given are not in common usage, for example, "feracious" and "jurimetrician," and the children are told that everyone is a winner. "This constant reinterpretation of the meaning of victory, coupled with the utter disregard for the definition of the words being spelled, reinforces my growing view of the bee as a near-Orwellian mockery of the idea that words convey meaning," Steinberg writes. For Steinberg this ritual is pointless, not the "Baroque horror [he] imagined" but "a large-scaled version of what goes on in schools all the time . . . a sad process [which] magnifies the natural disappointments of childhood to no discernible end."[3]

According to Rahel Musleah, Goldberg was raised in an observant Reconstructionist home in Maryland.[4] She is a graduate of Oberlin. She took a course in Jewish mysticism, did further reading, and the connection between Kabbalah and spelling "just clicked." Goldberg did not set out to write a "Jewish novel"; however, she tells Musleah, "it seemed natural to write what she knew. This is not an autobiographical novel, Goldberg maintains, except insofar as she, herself, felt different. As an artist in a family of scientists, Goldberg had to come to terms with parental expectations."

The connection between Kabbalah and what Steinberg calls "a symbol of The American Dream" begins to come together when father Saul finally attends one of the regional bees. He recognizes in his previously mediocre daughter what she herself has begun to experience. In her father's eyes, Eliza has become "a mystical prodigy."[5] About this moment Goldberg writes,

> Round after round—while the other children nod, shake or bounce, their hands scratching and picking—his Eliza stands perfectly centered, in complete concentration, employing the techniques of the ancient rabbis.
>
> Saul wants to jump to his feet and dance where he stands. He wants to sing, raising his hands in gratitude and humility. Even Isaac Luria needed a teacher. Even Shabbatai Zvi and Rabbi Nahman of Bratzlav required instruction to reach mystical greatness. Saul learned long ago that he was not meant to be another Abulafia. Instead, he has been hoping to encounter a student of whom history is made.

A parallel is drawn between the unrealistic hopes of the parents of the bee contestants, and the unnatural hopes of an intellectual father for his very young, not very intellectual daughter who "does little more than go through the motions of the Shabbat service, and who, until the day before the district bee, had never set foot inside his study."[6] He recalls his own pain in not living up to the expectations of his working-class parents and, ironically, believes he is protecting Eliza from the pain of becoming something "a parent does not intend." Saul is thrilled at his daughter's win, though, lifting Eliza over his head as she waves her trophy.

Meanwhile, mother Miriam is concerned. She, too, is obsessed with an alternate universe, one of her imagination, Perfectimundo, symbolized by a kaleidoscope she has owned since childhood. She offers her treasure to Eliza as a reward for her distinction. Eliza is dubious, though polite, and Miriam's disappointment is palpable. Eliza has made the first of several choices; she has chosen her father over her mother. Miriam's hope for her daughter's recognition dies. Saul is aware of his wife's disappointment. But he is not aware that this is a turning point for Miriam and for the family.

Saul assumes responsibility for his daughter's education. They begin with the dictionary, because "the ancients advised thorough knowledge of the texts before undertaking the *Kabbalah*." For Eliza, the dictionary itself is revelation. "The dictionary's words are the exact size of those she has pictured lining the inside of her head, chest and legs. The dictionary is her body's knowledge made manifest." She feels she has done this before, "is merely ghosting with her hand and eye what her brain has been doing all along."

Saul and Eliza study five hours a day, effectively shutting out Aaron and Miriam. Their intense absorption triggers behaviors in mother and son which will eventually blossom into a family crisis. Miriam begins a series of home-invasion burglaries, continuing a pattern of theft that goes back to a "poor little rich girl childhood," and Aaron, disappointed in the results of his Bar Mitzvah (God no longer appears to him), sneaks books about Asian religions from his father's study and worries about masturbation.

"What do you and a Torah scribe have in common?" Saul asks Eliza at one of their sessions. They are working on the word "amanuensis," which Eliza has spelled perfectly, but which she imagines represents a kind of disease. "Both spelling bees and Torah scribes share the idea that a word should be constructed perfectly or not at all. A little mistake and you're beeped off the stage. If a Torah amanuensis makes even one stray ink mark, he's got to start on a brand-new piece of parchment."

"It's called getting dinged out," Eliza replies.

Throughout, Eliza's youthfulness is contrasted with the profundity of the experience she is having. "Elly— . . . when you're trying to think of a spelling word, what happens?" Miriam asks. The two are watching television together. Miriam wants to help her daughter choose an outfit for a particularly important bee.

> I start out hearing the voice in my head in the voice of whoever said it to me. Then the voice changes into something that's not their voice or my voice. And I know when that happens it's the word's voice, that the word is talking to me. Everything else becomes quiet. Even if there's other noise, I don't hear it, because otherwise it's too weird seeing things around me and not hearing them. But the main reason I keep my eyes closed is so that I can see the word in my head. When I start hearing the word's voice, the letters start arranging themselves. Sometimes it takes awhile for them to look right, but when they do, they stop moving and I know that that's the right spelling. So then I just say what I'm seeing and that's it.

In response, Miriam skips "Final Jeopardy," a segment on her favorite television program. In one of the few scenes of mother/daughter intimacy, the two go up to the attic to look through boxes of old clothes. Eliza finds a shirt she likes,

> with big green buttons and her mother's name sewn into the collar. In the privacy of her room, Eliza tries on the shirt, pressing the collar into her neck until she is sure she can feel each individual letter of her mother's name upon her skin.[7]

After a particularly grueling session in Saul's study, in which Eliza succeeds in discovering all of the possible combinations of the letters in "earth" and "mantle," Saul abandons pretense of his interest in spelling bees and explains his true intention, to teach his prepubescent daughter the meditation techniques of Rabbi Abraham Abulafia, who in 1280 wrote a book entitled *Chayyai Olam HaBah*, or *Life of the Future World.* Goldberg credits Gershom Scholem's *Major Trends in Jewish Mysticism* and Aryeh Kaplan's *Meditation and Kaballah* for an understanding of Abulafia's methods and purposes.[8] The intention of the mystics was, of course, not to win spelling bees, but to focus the practitioner's attention on communion with God, in order to prepare for life after death.

Abraham ben Samuel Abulafia was born in Saragossa in 1240. He grew up in Tudela, in the province of Navarre. According to Abulafia's own writings (as reproduced by Kaplan) he "read Scriptures with all their commentaries, and also learned Hebrew grammar . . . [as well as] Mishneh and Talmud." Most of this learning was under his father's tutelage. When Abulafia was eighteen, his father died and he embarked on a period of wandering. He went to the Holy Land, Greece (where he married), and ended up in Capua. He acquired disciples and at the age of thirty-one, began to learn the *Sefer Yetzirah.* He was interested in philosophy, especially in Maimonides, and published a *Guide to the Guide.* There is textual evidence that Abulafia was influenced by the Christian mystics, and possibly Arabic and Indian sources. He studied *Gematria, Notarikon,* and *Temurah*, the three most significant methods of *Kaballah* (receiving). In 1240, or thereabouts, he felt divinely inspired to convert the pope to Judaism. He was detained for a while by the Franciscan Brothers, who had been given orders to burn him; then was released when the pope's death saved him. Though himself respectful of rabbinical Judaism, Abulafia was denounced by the rabbis of his day for his claims of prophecy, which were felt to be the province of the insane.

Finally Abulafia received the revelation that was to distinguish his work. "And it was in those days that God said to Zecharyahu [a numerical permutation of Abraham], 'Write for you this book, which will go against the sages of Israel in this generation, who boast about that which I do not desire. They say, why should we consider God's Name, how will it help us when we utter it, and how will it benefit us if we calculate it?' "[9] He developed a method of meditation dependent on pronouncing the name of God, and also of writing the letters of the Tetragammon, YHVH, in every possible combination. His authority was the Talmudic teaching that "*Betzalel* [the one given the task to build the Tabernacle in the desert] knew how to permute [*tzaraf*] the letters with which the heaven and earth were created," thereby insuring a "channel for the spiritual energies of creation." Abulafia also points out that the phrase "And God said . . ." appears before every act of creation in the Bible, therefore creation is by the word." It is the letters themselves, Abulafia reasons, which are the building blocks of creation and their permutation, a test and a "refining" for the initiate. Abulafia wrote in a clear accessible style, Kaplan notes, in consonance with his idea that prophecy was for all of the people, through the prophet. The rabbis disagreed, and his work was never printed. It is available in manuscript form in specialized libraries and private collections.

Bee Season is a popular literary novel, with extraordinarily good sales. Reviewers and book discussion groups have noted the family's dysfunction and Eliza's quest for identity. Certainly these are central themes. However, what is more striking to me is the way an obscure Kabbalistic text helps to tell a quintessentially American story. In *Art and Ardor* Cynthia Ozick cites exclusion from the texts of classical Judaism as one of the great losses befalling Jewish women. She imagines a new Yavneh in which Pagan or Universalist influences would be minimized and the covenant, the Torah, would be central. The language of the preservation of Jewish culture would be English, or as Ozick calls it, the new *yiddish.* Ozick felt that Jewish literature that draws on the texts of Judaism as well as the contexts of the gentile culture of domicile is the literature which will have lasting value "unto the generations." She is concerned about the male Jewish writers of her generation who write "outside of the Covenant" and only happen to be Jewish.[10]

In the years since *Art and Ardor* was published, Jewish women have been entering the new Yawneh, via renewed commitment to textual learning and through various strategies of authorship. Scholars, both men and women, have been retrieving lost traditions of Jewish women's authorship. Translator/poet David Rosenberg believes the core manuscript of Torah was written by a woman. Marge Piercy's poetry collection, *The Art of Blessing the Day,* is a modern prayer book, and Annie Dillard's *For the Time Being* is a commentary on the rabbinical texts, to name only a few examples.[11] Revitalization of tradition through critique is the essence of Jewish textual study. *Bee Season* can be read as commentary, even though Goldberg claims not to have read many Jewish/American authors and cites Nabokov as her primary stylistic influence.

Our literary Yawneh is not without its dangers. To return to the Naumann family and *Bee Season:* The mother ends up confined to a mental institution. The son joins the Hare Krishna and rejects his family. The father does not grasp his own failure. The problem is in the purpose of Kabbalistic study itself. According to Kaplan, meditation must keep us focused on the Divine. The Good is attained by transcending physical reality. In one of the last scenes of the novel, Saul tells Aaron what has happened to his mother. "The most fundamental things you take for granted are false," Saul shouts, describing Miriam's bizarre behavior. Saul fails to take responsibility for his own withdrawal from the emotional realities in his own home.

To cope with the devastating losses of mother and brother, Eliza takes the Abulafia manuscript from her father's room and retreats to her room to meditate and chant on the permutation of the letters for light, *Ah-va-reh, va-re-ah, reh-ah-vah.* She has an excruciatingly painful mystical experience. The next day she appears at her last bee, having become someone wiser. She looks at her father as if from a great distance, as if she were his grandmother. When her word, "origami," is finally called, she makes a choice. "Origamy" she spells, facing her father. "Are you sure?" she is asked. "Yes," she says. With her deliberate failure, Eliza returns to earth, perhaps finding the grounding, the reality, lacking in the other members of her family.

We do not know. Like all good novels, *Bee Season* does not clobber us with conclusions. I was left with a resonant sense of wonder, a desire to know more about the power of the mystical worldview, a respect for the rabbinical wisdom that requires a proper grounding in life, law, and reality before kabbalah is made accessible, and a desire to follow Eliza's development somewhere into fictional time. I look forward to Goldberg's next book, even though it probably will not be about Eliza.

Notes

Note: A different version of this essay was presented at the Jewish Women's Caucus of the National Women's Studies Association, Spring 2003. This version was presented to the Western Jewish Studies Association, Spring, 2005.

1. Myla Goldberg, *Bee Season* (New York: Anchor, 2000), 39–40.
2. Laura Buchwald, "Interview with Myla Goldberg," www.randomhouse.com (accessed Nov. 24, 2002).
3. Neil Steinberg, "The Spelling Bee," *Granta* 47 (Spring 1994): 53, 65, 72.
4. Rahel Musleah, www.interfaithfamily.com (accessed Jan. 24, 2002).
5. Goldberg, *Bee Season,* 61.
6. Ibid., 63.
7. Ibid., 95–96.
8. Gershon Scholem, *Major Trends in Jewish Mysticism* (New York: Schocken, 1946); Aryeh Kaplan, *Meditation and Kabbalah* (Boston: Weiser Books, 1982).
9. Kaplan, *Meditation and Kabbalah,* quoting *Sefer HaO.* 71.
10. Cynthia Ozick, *Art and Ardor* (New York: Knopf, 1983).
11. David Rosenberg and Harold Bloom, *The Book of J* (New York: Grove Weidenfeld, 1990); Marge Piercy, *The Art of Blessing the Day* (New York: Knopf, 1999); Annie Dillard, *For the Time Being* (New York: Knopf, 1999).

Part 5

Shoah Theology and Other Shoah Matters, Including Antisemitism

What Do Americans Read When They Read about the Holocaust?

Lawrence Baron

In January of 2006, Oprah Winfrey announced that Elie Wiesel's *Night* would be a selection for her book club because she considered it "required reading for all humanity." Soon thereafter, Wiesel appeared on Oprah's syndicated television show and accompanied her on a tour of Auschwitz. Although *Night* has been a perennial bestseller in the past thirty years, it shot up to number one on the *New York Times*' sales rankings for nonfiction paperbacks by February of 2006. Oprah's Boutique currently markets a DVD of the episode on the Auschwitz trip and *Night* tee shirts bearing the transliterated Hebrew passage from Lev. 19:16, "Thou shall not stand idly by."[1]

To be sure, the large readership for *Night* stems more from its powerful portrayal of Wiesel's experiences in Auschwitz than from Oprah's endorsement. The popularity of the book serves as a starting point for considering which Holocaust books have captured the imagination of the American public and what lessons they convey about the event. For six years, I have tracked the sales rankings of Holocaust books on the Barnes and Noble Web site (see Table 1). I use Barnes and Noble instead of Amazon because it controls a greater portion of the book market.[2] There are more recent books that outsell those on my list of the ten most popular Holocaust works, but I include only works that have sustained their sales five or more years after their publication. The list is fairly stable with only two books having dropped off it since I began recording this data. Analyzing the appeal of these books confirms Alan Mintz's insight that even for an event as singular as the Shoah, "meaning is constructed by communities of interpretation—differently by different communities—out of their own motives and needs."[3]

Most Holocaust scholars recognize the first four books on the latest list as classic eyewitness accounts, but perhaps do not realize how early they developed their popularity. *The Diary of a Young Girl* was released in 1952, *Man's Search for Meaning* (originally titled *From Death Camp to Existentialism*) and *Survival in Auschwitz* (originally titled *If This Is a Man*) in 1959, and *Night* in 1960. With the exception of *Night*, the sales of the others warranted second editions within one to three years of their releases.[4] Moreover Leon Uris's *Exodus* and William Shirer's *The Rise and Fall of the Third Reich* topped the sales charts when first released in 1958 and 1960 respectively, and continue to rank among the twenty perennial Holocaust bestsellers according to the Barnes and Noble figures.[5] The initial reception to books like these requires a revision of the consensus view that Americans displayed little interest in the Holocaust until after the Eichmann Trial in 1961 and Israel's Six Day War in 1967.[6]

The sales bump *Night* received from being selected by Oprah could have been predicted, but why she made this decision merits attention. Despite fears that the memory of the Holocaust will die

Table 1. Barnes and Noble sales figures

Rankings as of January 17, 2007	
1. *Night* by Elie Wiesel [Oprah's Book Club]	44
2. *The Diary of a Young Girl* by Anne Frank	423
3. *Survival in Auschwitz* by Primo Levi	898
4. *Man's Search for Meaning* by Viktor Frankl	1,769
5. *Number the Stars* by Lois Lowry	1,783
6. *The Devil's Arithmetic* by Jane Yolen	3,883
7. *Maus* by Art Spiegelman	4,935
8. *Dawn* by Elie Wiesel	5,921
9. *The Hiding Place* by Corrie ten Boom	6,122
10. *I Have Lived a Thousand Years* by Livia Bitton-Jackson	7,054
Rankings as of May 31, 2001	
1. *The Diary of a Young Girl* by Anne Frank	283
2. *Night* by Elie Wiesel	481
3. *Man's Search for Meaning* by Viktor Frankl	742
4. *Number the Stars* by Lois Lowry	1,808
5. *Survival in Auschwitz* by Primo Levi	1,858
6. *The Rise and Fall of the Third Reich* by William Shirer	2,809
7. *The Hiding Place* by Corrie ten Boom	2,950
8. *The Devil's Arithmetic* by Jane Yolen	3,457
9. *The Sunflower* by Simon Wiesenthal	4,181
10. *Maus* by Art Spiegelman	5,036

with the last survivor, the opposite has been true. The vast majority of Americans believe that the genocide of the Jews happened and that it is imperative to preserve its memory. Wiesel has emerged as the most visible spokesperson for the survivors not only through his books and lectures, but also by the status conferred upon him in 1986 when he won the Nobel Peace Prize.[7] The widespread American acknowledgment of the Holocaust as fact and Wiesel's unimpeachable credentials as a witness to it may have motivated Oprah's choice of *Night*. After all, she needed to restore her tarnished credibility after recent revelations that James Frey had fabricated parts of *A Million Little Pieces*, her previous book-club selection. The Web site for her show stresses Wiesel's veracity in its blurb about an earlier appearance on the program: "At a time when we need it most, this Holocaust survivor shares what he knows for sure."[8]

Wiesel fit the role Oprah's guests often play, namely, someone who has persevered and transcended a terrible adversity. In his book on Holocaust memory in the United States, Peter Novick credits the culture of victimization for the popularization of the Holocaust. Contemporary American society celebrates those who overcome misfortune and grow emotionally stronger for having done so. For many Americans, the Holocaust beckons as the ultimate test of endurance and endows those who survived it with special insights into how their experiences can be channeled into beating addictions, coping with handicaps, or dealing with personal tragedies.[9]

The following questions Oprah posed to Wiesel in an earlier interview indicate she was searching for a silver lining in his darkened past: "Despite all the tragedy you've witnessed, do you still have a place inside you for gratefulness?" "Does having seen the worst of humanity make you more grateful for ordinary occurrences?" "Did you come out of the horror of the Holocaust with your ability to love intact?" To his credit, Wiesel resisted her efforts to transform his story into one of redemptive suffering.[10]

In an article in *Commentary*, Presbyterian minister Christopher Leighton worried that many Christian readers of *Night* interpret it within their own religious framework of death and resurrection. He contended that "where Jews find evidence of God's absence, Christians discover, in the midst of anguish and darkness, a confirmation of God's redeeming presence."[11] Surveying the short reviews of *Night* posted by readers on the book's Barnes and Noble Web page indicates that Leighton's concern is unfounded. Over 90 percent of the responses characterize *Night* as a compelling document of the horrors inflicted upon the Jews at Auschwitz. Conversely, very few of the comments impose a Christian meaning on Wiesel's agony, though some disclose that their writers were far too young to understand his book.[12] This latter finding reflects that *Night* has become the second-most-assigned book in high school Holocaust courses.[13]

The increased prominence of *Night* has redounded to the benefit of Wiesel's second novel, *Dawn*, which attained "Top Ten" status for the first time when it was republished in 2006.[14] *Dawn* explores the moral qualms a Jewish survivor has about killing a British hostage as retaliation for the execution of a Zionist activist by the Mandatory authorities in postwar Palestine. Norman Finkelstein has criticized much Holocaust remembrance in the United States as an "exploitation of Jewish suffering" for the purpose of generating American support for Israel.[15] In this regard, *Dawn* is the sole book among the perennial top-ten Holocaust bestsellers which is primarily concerned with the ramifications of the *Shoah* on the struggle for Israeli independence.

Unlike Leon Uris's *Exodus*, *Dawn* hardly can be construed as a heroic Zionist saga. As Ted Estess has observed, "Wiesel suggests that if one is never again to be a victim one must relinquish the ideal and illusion of innocence." Since the Amazon.com Web site contains considerably more reader comments on *Dawn* than its Barnes and Noble counterpart, I coded these to assess how the novel is currently understood by its readers. About 40 percent sympathized with the Zionist cause for which Elisha, the protagonist of *Dawn*, is fighting. Yet nearly 30 percent saw analogies between Elisha's rationale for killing the hostage and contemporary terrorism. For example, one reader remarked, "It is fascinating to see words come from the mouths of these young Jewish partisans that would fit equally well in the mouths of Palestinians today."[16] Of course, Wiesel rejects such moral equivalency and grounds Elisha's dilemma in a reverence for life that does not lend itself to justifying indiscriminate suicide bombings.[17] Despite his denunciation of contemporary terrorism, readers filter texts through their own experiences, knowledge, and political convictions.[18]

The Diary of Anne Frank holds the distinction of being the sole book that surpassed the popularity of *Night* before Oprah stamped the latter with her *heksher*. It remains the book most assigned in conjunction with high school units on the Holocaust.[19] While the threat of Jews being arrested and deported lurks in its background, the diary foregrounds Anne's aspirations to become a writer, her adolescent clashes with her mother and sister, and her pubescent first love. Anne's optimistic belief that "people are really good at heart" softens the impact of the apprehension of the Franks and their friends that abruptly ends Anne's entries. Her underexposed Jewish identity universalizes her story just as her father had intended when he abridged her diary. Teachers still prefer the original version of *The Diary of a Young Girl* to the definitive edition. A content analysis of readers' reviews demonstrates that only a quarter of them mention Jews at all while another quarter refer to the Holocaust in generic terms. Nearly 40 percent gush with an appreciation of Anne's adolescent awakening, courage, hope, or writing ability.[20] The allure of Anne's teenage metamorphosis in such claustrophobic conditions persists even though a fourteen-page postscript highlighting the history of the Shoah and what happened to the Franks and their friends has been added to the diary.[21]

The definitive edition of the diary would rank number six on my list if I had included different versions of the same book on it.[22] Thirty percent longer than the original, it restores Anne's more explicit passages about her budding sexuality, Jewish faith, and resentment of her mother, sister, and other residents of the Secret Annex which her father deliberately had omitted.[23] The new material changes how readers understand the diary. Forty-six percent of them identify Anne as Jewish; another 31 percent recognize her as a victim of the Holocaust, Germany, Hitler, or Nazism. Only 19 percent focus exclusively on her bravery, optimism, talent, or teenage outlook. One of every ten of them is an adult who is either reading the diary for the first time or interested in the unabridged edition because he or she previously had read the original edition. Teachers who continue to assign the old edition should provide more historical contextualization to prevent the diary from being reduced to a well-told coming of age story.[24]

Three other of the top-ten-selling Holocaust books are intended for children and adolescents. Two developments account for this: 1) the incorporation of the Holocaust into the secondary school curriculum; 2) the teaching of the Holocaust to younger pupils, even those in the third grade. The publisher of Lois Lowry's *Number the Stars* recommends it for eight- to twelve-year-olds. To be sure, the book focuses on the uplifting story of how a Danish gentile girl named Annemarie and her parents help the Jewish family of her best friend evade arrest by the Germans and escape to neutral Sweden on a fishing boat. There are moments of danger and even a concluding revelation that Annemarie's sister and her fiancé were killed for involvement in the resistance movement.

Can an eight-year-old fathom why the Germans were hunting Jews or how exceptional the Danish response to this threat was? A proponent of K-4 prejudice reduction and Holocaust education if it is age appropriate, Harriet Lipman Sepinwall reports hearing from a fourth-grade teacher that she had assigned *Number the Stars* "to help her students learn to be rescuers and not bystanders." Conversely, Samuel Totten maintains that "it is simply and profoundly inappropriate to introduce, let alone immerse, such young children to the various horrors of the Holocaust."[25] The comments posted by juvenile readers of *Number the Stars* on the Barnes and Noble Web site divide evenly between those who appear to have some inkling of the calamity that befell the Jews and others who praise the book because it is an exciting story about the unbreakable bonds of friendship.[26]

Compared to *Number the Stars,* Jane Yolen's *The Devil's Arithmetic* is far more graphic in its depiction of the violence of the Holocaust. Nevertheless, the publisher of the novel classifies it as appropriate reading for nine- to twelve-year-olds. Yolen transports a thirteen-year-old Jewish girl from suburban New York to the Polish shtetl where her ancestors resided until they were deported to a concentration camp. The protagonist Hannah has become bored by Jewish history and rituals, but learns to appreciate both and assess the enormity of Hitler's crime against the Jews by experiencing their suffering firsthand. Hannah ultimately chooses to die in place of her cousin in a gas chamber because she is certain that she will be reborn in the future. When Hannah awakens in the present, she realizes that her aunt was the cousin who had been spared and that she herself bears the Hebrew name, Chaya, of the girl who had been gassed. Four out of five comments posted by readers reveal an awareness of the Holocaust. Some are fairly sophisticated in articulating the book's message of the imperative to remember the Six Million while others do not distinguish between the fictional and factual aspects of the book as evidenced in the following remark: "I felt like I was there living the Holocaust with Hannah/Chaya. It was cool."[27]

Livia Bitton-Jackson rewrote her autobiography, *Elli: Coming of Age in the Holocaust,* specifically for teenage audiences.[28] In *I Have Lived a Thousand Years: Growing Up in the Holocaust*, she recollects the major events from her original account of surviving Auschwitz, but eschews incidents and language that potentially might offend the sensibilities of adolescents, boards of education, parents, and teachers. Its publisher, Scholastic Inc., markets the book directly to schools. Bitton-Jackson addresses her readers as "the third generation" who need to know that the Holocaust "was neither a legend nor Hollywood fiction, but a lesson for the future." She warns them that her story delves into the misery and slaughter she endured and witnessed, but assures them that it also reveals "perseverance, loyalty, courage in the face of overwhelming odds, and never giving up."[29] The comments posted by the readers of *I Have Lived a Thousand Years* testify to its author's ability to convey both her tribulations and triumphs to young adults. In the words of one such reviewer, "This book not only teaches how cruel the world can be, but it also demonstrates that determination and love can defeat anything."[30]

Benefiting from the teaching of the Holocaust in American secondary and higher education too, Art Spiegelman's *Maus* has crept higher on the Top Ten list over the past five years. Its pioneering usage of a comic-book format with animal characters to recount the story of a survivor and his troubled relationship with his son has placed it fourth among "primary" sources for high school units on the Holocaust and third in college and university courses on the topic.[31] The growing respect for comic books and graphic novels as adult fare has boosted Spiegelman's sales as well. In college courses, *Maus* often serves as an example of how a serious representation of the Holocaust can be achieved in a visual medium usually associated with light entertainment.[32] As one reader succinctly puts it, "By relating history through mice and the graphic novel format, Spiegelman can provide just enough distance to relate many of the details (of the Holocaust) which cannot be successfully told otherwise."[33] *Maus's* second-generation theme of gleaning a semblance of what happened from the eyewitness account of a survivor, but then inferring just as much from cryptic remarks and post-traumatic traits parallels the predicament of all nonwitnesses who must reconstruct the catastrophe from documents, films, histories, memoirs, museums, novels, and teachers.[34]

Primo Levi's *Survival in Auschwitz* has supplanted Wiesel's *Night* as the memoir most assigned in college and university courses on the Holocaust. In a survey conducted in the 1990s, *Night* was required in 42 percent of such courses and *Survival in Auschwitz* in 29 percent.[35] Based on syllabi currently posted on the Internet, Levi's book has passed Wiesel's as the one most required primary source:

1. *Survival in Auschwitz* by Primo Levi (40%)
2. *Night* by Elie Wiesel (22%)
3. *Maus* by Art Spiegelman (20%)
4. *The Sunflower* by Simon Wiesenthal (10%)
5. *At the Mind's Limit* by Jean Amery (8%)
6. *The Diary of a Young Girl* by Anne Frank (8%)[36]

As my earlier discussion of *Night* suggests, lecturers and professors might correctly assume that the majority of their students already have read it in high school. The preferences of instructors may mirror the Levi renaissance evidenced by a spate of books published about him since 2000.[37] Levi's rationalistic and universalistic perspective may resonate better in a university setting than Wiesel's distinctively Jewish outlook. Jonathan Druker contrasts the two in these terms: "Wiesel tends to focus on the particularity of the victims, European Jewry; Levi, discounting the ultimate significance of ethnic or racial difference, dwells instead on Nazism's affront to humanity."[38] The Internet blogs by readers of *Survival in Auschwitz* rarely mention that Levi was Jewish.[39] Finally, Levi's concept of the "gray zone" of amoral compromises forced upon camp inmates correlates with the prevailing understanding of camp survival as an unrelenting series of "choiceless choices" between equally terrible alternatives.[40]

Though the consensus among Holocaust scholars echoes Lawrence Langer's view that survival in the camps depended on amoral conduct and good fortune, most American adults gravitate toward the more comforting message delivered in Viktor Frankl's *Man's Search for Meaning,* that is, that internees who invested their suffering with some ultimate meaning improved their chances of withstanding demoralization and the death that inevitably ensued from it. Four editions of Frankl's book rank among the top-ten-selling Holocaust books.[41] In contrast, *The Diary of Anne Frank*, *Maus*, and *Night* are the only other titles that would appear twice on my list if I had included different editions of the same book. Frankl empowers human beings with free will to respond positively or negatively to the worst tragedies they confront in their lives. He summarizes this credo in the conclusion of his book:

> In the concentration camps, for example, in this living laboratory and on this testing ground, we watched and witnessed our comrades behave like swine while others behaved like saints. Man has the potentialities within himself; which one is actualized depends on decisions but not on conditions.[42]

Frankl's appeal lies more in its therapeutic value for individuals coping with hardships than in its analytical validity for explaining why concentration camp prisoners either outlived or succumbed to the brutality meted out by their oppressors. Langer has criticized Frankl for believing that everything that happens to individuals is part of their fate. Langer contends that such wishful thinking mitigates both the absurdity and ruthlessness of the German policy to rid the world of Jews. In his opinion, "Frankl writes as a healer, not as a historian, a psychiatrist whose professional task is to reconcile man with his moments of utter desolation and create a way of liberating the future in spite of them."[43] Americans turn to Frankl to deal with their own adversities. In 1991, when the Library of Congress polled readers to name the books that had "made a difference" in their lives, *Man's Search for Meaning* emerged as one of the ten most influential books in the United States. In keeping with its affirmative philosophy, the latest edition of *Man's Search for Meaning* carries a forward by Rabbi Harold S. Kushner, the author of *When Bad Things Happen to Good People.*[44]

The niche carved out by Corrie ten Boom's *The Hiding Place* on the Top Ten list points to a phenomenon that largely has been ignored by scholars of the *Shoah*, namely the appropriation of the Holocaust as a modern Calvary for Christian evangelicals.[45] The ten Boom family belonged to the fundamentalist wing of the Dutch Reformed Church. Although Corrie's grandfather and brother proselytized Jews, they did so out of a reverence for the "Old Testament" and a sense of religious kinship toward Jews whom they regarded as God's Chosen People and Jesus' ancestors. To them, the eventual conversion of the Jews would herald the Second Coming of Christ. Harboring Jews enabled Corrie and her family to witness Christ's boundless love through acts of compassionate courage. When the ten Booms were betrayed and arrested by the Germans, Corrie did not yield to despair and hatred at Ravensbrück. Instead, she considered her imprisonment a test of faith and an opportunity to preach the Gospels to the victims of a satanic regime.[46]

After the war, Corrie embarked on a career as a globetrotting missionary, sharing her compelling wartime story to exemplify the redemptive power of unconditional faith and forgiveness even for the Germans who bore responsibility for the deaths of her father, sister, and brother. Billy Graham recruited professional writers John and Elizabeth Sherill to assist ten Boom in authoring *The Hiding Place,* which was published in 1971. Four years later, he produced a feature film adapted from it which received widespread theatrical distribution. It remains one of the most popular videos marketed by Christian bookstores and Web sites. In 1997 *The Hiding Place*'s brisk sales earned it a spot on the list of the ten most popular Christian books in the United States. In 2006 *Christianity Today* named it one of fifty "landmark" books that have shaped the way evangelicals "think, talk, witness, worship, and live."[47]

Fundamentalist Christian home and parochial schools often require their pupils to read *The Hiding Place* when they are studying the Holocaust. Rebekah Irwin and Simone Schweber have observed the pedagogical approach employed at an evangelical school where this was the case. On the one hand, the teacher admirably hoped reading ten Boom's book would help her students "become more sensitive to others and have more empathy and compassion for other beliefs." On the other hand, by stressing the literalist Christian message imparted by ten Boom, the teacher portrayed God's initial election of the Jews as the reason why Germany selected them as victims and the righteousness of ten Boom as the natural response of a true believer in a savior whose covenant of grace and love for all human beings superseded supposed Jewish legalism and particularism. Students simply received no instruction about the role of Christian churches and rulers in demonizing and persecuting Jews in European history and how the majority of Christians and their clerics failed to respond to the plight of the Jews under German domination in the exemplary manner of the ten Boom family.[48]

Histories of the Holocaust are conspicuously absent from the most recent Top Ten list. Christopher Browning's *Ordinary Men* and William Shirer's *The Rise and Fall of the Third Reich* respectively occupy the eleventh and thirteenth places.[49] One could not imagine two more different works. Browning's dispassionate analysis of what motivated the members of the Reserve Police Battalion 101 to shoot thousands of Jews ranked behind *Night* and *Survival in Auschwitz* as the most assigned book in college and university Holocaust courses in a survey conducted in 1998.[50] It currently leads all other academic works required for college-level history courses, the discipline in which over 50 percent of Holocaust courses are taught:

1. *Ordinary Men* by Christopher Browning (36%)
2. *The Holocaust,* edited by Donald Niewyck (20%)
3. *War and Genocide* by Doris L. Bergen (14%)
4. *A History of the Holocaust* by Yehuda Bauer and Nili Keren (12%)
5. *A History of the Holocaust* by Rita Steinhardt Botwinick (12%)
6. *Neighbors* by Jan T. Gross (12%)[51]

In his highly publicized tome *Hitler's Willing Executioners,* Daniel Goldhagen disputed Browning's findings by asserting that Germans collectively were ensconced in an "eliminationist" strain of antisemitism that facilitated their transition from discriminating against Jews to eradicating them. While the reading public hailed Goldhagen's attribution of guilt to a deep-seated flaw in German national values, Browning's more nuanced interpretation gained a larger following among history professors.[52] *Ordinary Men* now ranks 7,162nd in sales compared to *Hitler's Willing Executioners* position at 40,387th.

Yet the enduring popularity of William Shirer's *The Rise and Fall of the Third Reich* indicates that the average reader still thinks German executioners willingly implemented Hitler's policies against the Jews because they collectively shared his virulent antisemitic attitudes. Written shortly after the war, Shirer's journalistic account of Hitler's conquest of power exudes a "Germanophobic" bias that perpetuates traditional stereotypes about authoritarianism and antisemitism as the mainstream German intellectual tradition that could be traced "all the way back to Luther."[53] The attraction to Shirer's depiction of Nazism as the logical culmination of German obedience and racism stems from the same impulse that catapulted Goldhagen's book temporarily into a blockbuster in the United States when is was first published. As Mitchell Ash has speculated, there is:

> the need on the part of many Jewish as well as non-Jewish Americans for simple binary images of good and evil with which to structure a moral conceptual grid of easy certainties, and to locate the murderous potential of modernity itself somewhere far from the good old USA.[54]

The Barnes and Noble sales statistics serve as a barometer of why the Holocaust continues to fascinate Americans. They reveal that the institutionalization of the Holocaust into the school curriculum has been a spectacular success story that started with higher education, but gradually spread to the secondary and primary grades. The proliferation of Holocaust courses and curricular units encourages the diversity of lessons teachers want their students to draw from the event. Those teaching the youngest pupils hint at the scope of the catastrophe, but cushion the shock of it by emphasizing how Righteous Gentiles shielded Jews from the wrath of the Nazis or how kids like themselves maintained their convictions and loyalty to friends and family in the ghettos and camps. High school students are exposed more directly to the horrors endured by European Jewry by empathizing with protagonists like Livia Bitton-Jackson, Vladek in *Maus*, or Elie Wiesel, who survive despite all odds. The discomforting actuality is reserved for university students and adults who must grapple with the dilemma of "choiceless choices" and ordinary men (and women) capable of extraordinary evil. Jewish and Christian perceptions of the religious meaning of the Holocaust differ radically as the stark contrast between the crisis and certainty of faith in *Night* and *The Hiding Place* dramatically reveals. The popularity of Frankl's and ten Boom's memoirs is a sign that many readers seek to distill something pure from the murky depths of the Holocaust. As James Young once remarked, "In America, the motives for memory of the Holocaust are as mixed as the population at large."[55]

Notes

1. Edward Wyatt, "Oprah's Book Club Turns to Elie Wiesel," *New York Times*, January 16, 2006; *Night* (book), http://en.wikipedia.org/wiki/Night_(book)#Writing_and_publishing_Night (accessed January 9, 2007). "Oprah's Boutique—'Thou Shalt Not Stand Idly by' Crewneck Tee," http://boutique.oprah.com/product/show/5879 (accessed January 9, 2007).
2. Clea Saal, "Sales Rankings," *An Incomplete Guide to Print on Demand Publishers*, http://www.booksandtales.com/pod/articleviewer.php?article_id=10 (accessed January 8, 2007).
3. Alan Mintz, *Popular Culture and the Shaping of Holocaust Memory in America* (Seattle: University of Washington Press, 2001), 40.
4. Anne Frank, *The Diary of a Young Girl*, trans. B. Mooyart (Garden City, N.Y.: Doubleday, 1952; New York: Pocket Books, 1953). Viktor Emil Frankl, *From Death Camp to Existentialism: A Psychiatrist's Path to a New Therapy*, trans. Ilse Lasch (Boston: Beacon Press, 1959), and *Man's Search for Meaning: An Introduction to Logotherapy*, trans. Ilse Lasch (Boston: Beacon Press, 1962). Primo Levi, *If This Is a Man*, trans. Stuart Woolf (New York: Orion, 1959), and *Survival in Auschwitz: The Nazi Assault on Humanity*, trans. Stuart Woolf (New York: Collier, 1961). Elie Wiesel, *Night*, trans. Stella Rodway (New York: Hill and Wang, 1960).
5. William Shirer, *The Rise and Fall of the Third Reich: A History of Nazi Germany* (New York: Simon and Schuster, 1960). On January 17, 2007, it ranked 7,785 on the Barnes and Noble Web site. Leon Uris, *Exodus* (Garden City, N.Y.: Doubleday, 1958), ranks 11,192 on the Barnes and Noble Web site.

6. For example, see Peter Novick, *The Holocaust in American Life* (Boston: Houghton-Mifflin, 1999), 127–69. For an earlier dating of the rise of Holocaust awareness in the United States, see Lawrence Baron, "The Holocaust and American Public Memory, 1945–1960," *Holocaust and Genocide Studies* 17, no. 1 (Spring 2003): 62–88; Hasia R. Diner, *Before "The Holocaust": American Jews Confront Catastrophe* (Ann Arbor: Jean and Samuel Frankel Center for Judaic Studies–University of Michigan, 2004); Kirsten Fermaglich, *American Dreams and Nazi Nightmares: Early Holocaust Consciousness and Liberal America, 1957–1965* (Waltham, Mass.: Brandeis University Press, 2006).
7. Tom W. Smith, *Holocaust Denial: What the Survey Data Reveal* (New York: American Jewish Committee, 1995), 30–61; Novick, *Holocaust in American Life*, 273–74.
8. Wyatt, "Oprah's Book Club Turns to Elie Wiesel"; Dagmar Barmouw, "True Stories: Oprah, Elie Wiesel, and the Holocaust," March 3, 2006, http://hnn.us.articles/22099.html (accessed January 8, 2007). Barnouw's article challenges the "truth" of any memoir, but insinuates that Oprah's selection of *Night* "redeemed her from her wrong potentially diminishing choice of Frey's *A Million Pieces*." "Elie Wiesel," http://www.oprah.com/tows/pastshows/tows_2002/tows_past_20020102_d.jhtml (accessed January 9, 2007).
9. Novick, *Holocaust in American Life*, 190–203.
10. "Oprah's Cut with Elie Wiesel," http://www2.oprah.com/omagazine/200011/omag_200011_elie_b.jhtml (accessed January 8, 2007).
11. Christopher M. Leighton, "Oprah, Elie Wiesel, and My Fellow Christians," *Commentary* 121, no. 5 (May 2006): 59–63.
12. *Night*, http://www.barnesandnoble.com/ (accessed January 11, 2007). I coded the first 200 reader reviews on the site: 92.5% indicated in one way or another that the book was a disturbing encounter with the terrible treatment meted out to a young concentration camp inmate. Only 4.5% attributed any religious significance to Wiesel's ordeal or derived a spiritual message from it. Interestingly, 16% mentioned that they read the book for a school class, whereas only 5% credited Oprah's selection of the book as the reason why they read the book.
13. Jeffrey Ellison and John Pisapia, "The State of Holocaust Education in Illinois," *Idea* 11, no. 1 (September 7, 2006), http:www.ideajournal.com/articles.php?id=41 (accessed January 15, 2007), 7. In 1990 Illinois became the first state to mandate Holocaust education at the secondary level and the authors of this article surveyed high school teachers in the state on how they taught Holocaust units; 39.3% of those queried listed *Night* as the text they assigned.
14. Elie Wiesel, *Dawn*, trans. Frances Frenaye (New York: Hill and Wang, 1961; New York: Farrar, Straus, and Giroux, 2006).
15. Norman Finkelstein, *The Holocaust Industry: Reflections on the Exploitation of Jewish Suffering* (New York: Verso, 2000).
16. Ted Estess, *Elie Wiesel* (New York: Frederick Ungar, 1980), 44; Timothy Haugh, "Not *Night*, But Excellent in Its Own Right," July 19, 2005, *Dawn*. http://www.amazon.com (accessed January 13, 2007).
17. For Wiesel's condemnation of suicide killers, see this transcript from a recent interview with him: "The Tragedy of the Believer," *Speaking of Faith*, July 13, 2006, http://www.speakingoffaith.publicradio.org/programs/wiesel/transcript.shtml (accessed January 14, 2007).
18. Robert C. Holub, *Reception Theory: A Critical Introduction* (London: Methuen, 1984).
19. Ellison and Pisapia, "The State of Holocaust Education in Illinois," 9. Of the Illinois teachers surveyed, 43% assigned *The Diary of Anne Frank* and 39.3% required *Night*. Primo Levi's *Survival in Auschwitz* came in a distant third at 10.3%.
20. Judith Doneson, "The American History of Anne Frank's Diary," in *Anne Frank: Reflections of Her Life and Legacy*, ed. Aaron Enzer and Sandra Solotaroff-Enzer (Urbana: University of Illinois Press, 2000), 123–38. *The Diary of a Young Girl*, http://www. barnesandnoble.com/ (accessed January 21, 2007). Of the respondents, 26% note that Anne was Jewish or that Jews were persecuted or killed; the same percentage mentions the Holocaust or how they are saddened by the events in the book; 38% praise Anne's courage, hope, perceptions of common teenage problems, and writing style. The remaining 10% do not like the book.
21. Anne Frank, *The Diary of a Young Girl*, trans. B. M. Mooyaart (New York: Bantam Books, 1993), 269–83.
22. It ranked 2,961 on January 17, 2007, on the Barnes and Noble Web site.
23. Anne Frank, *The Diary of a Young Girl: Definitive Edition*, ed. Otto H. Frank and Mirjam Pressler, trans. Susan Masotty (New York: Bantam Books, 1997). On the significance of the added passages in this edition, see Mirjam Pressler, *Anne Frank: A Hidden Life* (New York: Dutton Children's Books, 2000).
24. *The Diary of a Young Girl: The Definitive Edition*, http://www.amazon.com/ (accessed January 21, 2007). Pascale Bos, "Reconsidering Anne Frank: Teaching the Diary in Its Historical and Cultural Context," in *Teaching*

the Representation of the Holocaust, ed. Marianne Hirsch and Irene Kacandes (New York: Modern Language Association of America, 2004), 348–59; Simone E. Schweber, *Making Sense of the Holocaust: Lessons from Classroom Practice* (New York: Teachers College Press, 2004), 119–35.

25. Harriet Lipman Sepinwall, "Incorporating Holocaust Education into K-4 Curriculum and Teaching in the United States," *Social Studies and the Young Learner* 11, no. 3 (January/February 1999). Samuel Totten, "Should There Be Holocaust Education for K4 Students? The Answer Is No," *Social Sciences and the Young Learner* 12, no. 1 (September/October 1999). For a thoughtful analysis of how eight- and nine-year-olds are just too emotionally and intellectually immature to deal with the Holocaust, see Simone Schweber, "'What Happened to Their Pets?': Third Graders Encounter the Holocaust," *Teachers College Record* 110, no. 10 (2008): 2073–115.
26. Of the postings 48% reveal some familiarity with the Holocaust while 46% say only that they liked the story. *Number the Stars*, http://www. barnesandnoble.com/ (accessed January 15, 2007).
27. For an example of the former, see Natalie Bernier, "Review," November 28, 2006. For the source of the quotation, see Megan, "Awesome Book," July 22, 2003, *The Devil's Arithmetic*, http://www. barnesandnoble.com/ (accessed January 16, 2007).
28. Livia Bitton-Jackson, *Elli: Coming of Age in the Holocaust* (New York: Times Books, 1980).
29. Livia Bitton-Jackson, *I Have Lived a Thousand Years: Growing Up in the Holocaust* (New York: Scholastic, 1997), 11.
30. Eliza, "Exceptional," June 20, 2000, *I Have Lived a Thousand Years*, http://www.amazon.com (accessed February 9, 2007).
31. Ellison and Pisapia, "The State of Holocaust Education in Illinois," 9; Stephen R. Haynes "Holocaust Education at American Colleges and Universities: A Report on the Current Situation," *Holocaust and Genocide Studies* 12, no. 2 (Fall 1998): 291. Of the high school teachers sampled by Ellison and Pisapia, 8.4% assign *Maus*; 25% of college and university instructors assign either *Maus I* or *Maus II*.
32. Gillian Banner, *Holocaust Literature: Schulz, Levi, Spiegelman, and the Memory of the Offence* (London: Valentine Mitchell, 2000); *Considering Maus: Approaches to Art Spiegelman's "Survivor's Tale" of the Holocaust*, ed. Deborah Geis (Tuscaloosa: University of Alabama Press); Joseph Witek, *Comic Books as History: The Narrative Art of Jack Jackson, Art Spiegelman, and Harvey Peker* (Jackson: University of Mississippi Press, 1989); Roger Sabin, *Comics, Comix, and Graphic Novels* (London: Phaidon Press, 1996); Marianne Hirsch, *Family Frames: Photography, Narrative, and Post-Memory* (Cambridge: Harvard University Press, 1997), 17–40; Amy Hungerford, *The Holocaust of Texts: Genocide, Literature, and Personification* (Chicago: University of Chicago Press, 2003), 85–96; Efraim Sicher, "Postmemory, Backshadowing, Separation: Teaching Second-Generation Holocaust Fiction," in *Teaching the Representation of the Holocaust*, ed. Hirsch and Kacandes, 262–73.
33. Erica J. Dymond, "One of the Most Accessible Works about the *Shoah* and Its Aftermath," January 28, 2007, *Maus: Boxed Set*, http://www: amazon.com (accessed February 9, 2007).
34. Alan L. Berger, *Children of Job: Second-Generation Witnesses to the Holocaust* (Albany: State University of New York Press, 1997); Efraim Sicher, *The Holocaust Novel* (New York: Routledge, 2005), 133–74; Gary Weissman, *Fantasies of Witnessing: Postwar Efforts to Experience the Holocaust* (Ithaca, N.Y.: Cornell University Press, 2004), 18–24.
35. Haynes, "Holocaust Education at American Colleges and Universities," 291–92.
36. To compile this data, I looked up the first fifty syllabi for college and university Holocaust courses that were posted on Google on February 2, 2007, under the search phrase "Holocaust course syllabi."
37. Carole Anger, *The Double Bond: Primo Levi—A Biography* (New York: Farrar, Straus, and Giroux, 2002); Leo Benchouiha, *Primo Levi: Rewriting the Holocaust* (Leicester, UK: Troubador, 2006); Fredric D. Homer, *Primo Levi and the Politics of Survival* (Columbia: University of Missouri Press, 2001); Roberta S. Kremer, ed., *Memory and Mastery: Primo Levi as Writer and Witness* (Albany: State University of New York Press, 2001); Giuliani Massimo, *A Centaur in Auschwitz: Reflections on Primo Levi's Thinking* (Lanham, Md.: Lexington Books, 2003); Stanislao G. Pugliese, ed., *The Legacy of Primo Levi* (New York: Palgrave Macmillan, 2005); Ian Thomson, *Primo Levi: A Life* (New York: Henry Holt, 2002).
38. Jonathan Druker, "A Rational Humanist Confronts the Holocaust: Teaching Primo Levi's *Survival in Auschwitz*," in *Teaching the Representation of the Holocaust*, ed. Hirsch and Kacandes, 337–47.
39. To determine this, I tabulated how many of the reader reviews posted on the Amazon.com Web page for *Survival in Auschwitz* specifically mention that Levi was Jewish or that the primary victims of the Holocaust were Jewish. Of the sixty-three positive reviews of the book, only eight or about 13% do so.
40. Primo Levi, *Survival in Auschwitz: The Nazi Assault on Humanity*, trans. Stuart Woolf (New York: Collier Books, 1961), 79–91; Primo Levi, *The Drowned and the Saved*, trans. Raymond Rosenthal (New York: Summit

Books, 1988), 36–69. Lawrence Langer coined the term "choiceless choice" in his book *Holocaust Testimonies: The Ruins of Memory* (New Haven: Yale University Press, 1991).

41. The mass-market paperback Viktor E. Frankl, *Man's Search for Meaning*, trans. Ilse Lasch (Boston: Beacon Press, 2006), ranks 1,769th; Viktor E. Frankl, *Man's Search for Meaning: An Introduction to Logotherapy* (New York: Pocket Books, 1984), ranks 5,112th, The two Beacon Press editions (2000 and 2006) rank 5,733rd and 5,735th respectively.
42. Frankl, *Man's Search for Meaning*, 212–13.
43. Lawrence Langer, *Versions of Survival: The Holocaust and the Human Spirit* (Albany: State University of New York, 1982), 15–29.
44. See the "Book Description" for the mass-market 2006 edition of *Man's Search for Meaning* on its http://amazon.com/ (accessed February 8, 2007).
45. Yaakov Ariel, "Jewish Suffering and Christian Salvation: The Evangelical-Fundamentalist Holocaust Memoirs," *Holocaust and Genocide Studies* 6, no.1 (1991): 63–78; Lawrence Baron, "Evangelical Converts, Corrie ten Boom, and the Holocaust," *Holocaust and Genocide Studies* 7, no. 1 (1993): 143–48; Lawrence Baron, "Supersessionism Without Contempt: The Holocaust Evangelism of Corrie ten Boom," in *Christian Responses to the Holocaust: Moral and Ethical Issues,* ed. Donald J. Dietrich (Syracuse. N.Y.: Syracuse University Press, 2003), 119–31; David P. Gushee, *The Righteous Gentiles of the Holocaust: A Christian Interpretation* (Minneapolis: Fortress Press, 1994), 119–24, 141–46.
46. Corrie ten Boom with John and Elizabeth Sherrill, *The Hiding Place* (Washington Deport, Conn.: Chosen Books, 1971).
47. Corrie ten Boom with James Buckingham, *Tramp for the Lord* (Minneapolis: Billy Graham Evangelistic Crusade, 1974). *The Hiding Place,* directed by James Collier (Charlotte, N.C.: World Wide Pictures Inc., 1975). Billy Graham, *Just as I Am: The Autobiography of Billy Graham* (New York: HarperCollins, 1997), 513–14. Rhonda Renee Gamble, "Evangelical Representations of Corrie ten Boom," M.A. thesis, San Diego State University, 1997, 51–53. "The Top 50 Books That Have Shaped Evangelicals," *Christianity Today: A Magazine of Evangelical Conviction* (October 2006), http://www.christianitytoday.com.ct/2006/october/23:51.html (accessed February 10, 2007).
48. Simone Schweber and Rebekah Irwin, "'Especially Special': Learning about Jews in a Fundamentalist Christian School," *Teachers College Record* 105, no. 9 (2003): 1693–719.
49. According to the January 17 Barnes and Noble Web site, *Ordinary Men* ranked 7,162nd in sales and *The Rise and Fall of the Third Reich* ranked 7,782nd.
50. Haynes, "Holocaust Education at American Colleges and Universities," 285–87.
51. These statistics are based on the first fifty different Holocaust history course syllabi posted on http:www.Google.com (accessed February 10, 2007). I stopped at fifty when many of the same syllabi appeared again.
52. Daniel J. Goldhagen, *Hitler's Willing Executioners: Ordinary Germans and the Holocaust* (New York: Knopf, 1996); Geoff Eley, ed., *The "Goldhagen Effect": History, Meaning, Nazism: Facing the German Past* (Ann Arbor: University of Michigan Press, 2000); Norman G. Finkelstein and Ruth Bettina Birn, *A Nation of Trial: The Goldhagen Thesis and Historical Truth* (New York: Metropolitan Books, 1998); Robert R. Shandley, ed., *Unwilling Germans?: The Goldhagen Debate* (Minneapolis: University of Minnesota, 1998).
53. Pierre Aycoberry, *The Nazi Question: An Essay on the Interpretations of National Socialism, 1922–1975*, trans. Robert Huley (New York: Pantheon Books, 1981), 216.
54. Mitchell G. Ash, "American and German Perspectives on the Goldhagen Debate: History, Identity, and the Media," *Holocaust and Genocide Studies* 11, no. 3 (1997): 405.
55. James E. Young, *The Texture of Memory: Holocaust Memorials and Meaning* (New Haven: Yale University Press, 1993), 284.

The Evolution and Devolution of a World Apart

The Nazi Concentration Camps and the Holocaust

Paul R. Bartrop

> [T]he behavior of the SS was ruled by the terrible phrase: "Woe to those who forget that everything that resembles a human being is not necessarily a human being."[1]
> —Fania Fénelon, Auschwitz survivor, 1979

Looming over every positive achievement of the twentieth century is the Nazi Holocaust against the Jewish people, a genocidal explosion that saw a sudden and irrevocable break with all of the secular humanistic traditions that had been developing in Europe over the previous thousand years. The relationship between mass death and the industrial state that became manifested in the Holocaust was both intimate and interdependent, and, as a result of it having taken place, we have forever a yardstick by which all other cases of genocide must be measured. Its message is so powerful that no definition of Western civilization can ever again be constructed without reference being made to where its corruption can lead.

The period of National Socialist rule in Europe was a time of immense upheaval, occasioned by deliberate and massive political violence. It was first confined to Germany, but then spread to Austria, Czechoslovakia, and finally to most of Europe. Its brutality was, until 1938, almost solely directed against political opponents, but later in the decade it targeted Jews, for the sole reason of their Jewishness. The aim of the SS, the Nazi organization responsible for planning and executing the antisemitic measures, was the elimination of every trace of actual or potential opposition to Nazi rule, even from those it considered posed a threat through their very existence. This would be a genocidal struggle, forming part of a much broader campaign that would, it was intended, destroy communism, annihilate the Jews, wipe out the free-thinking opposition, and (after the onset of war) reduce the status of the population in the occupied areas (particularly in Eastern Europe) to that of ignorant and impotent vassals.

In this regard, German historian Hans Mommsen has written, with characteristic insight, that the steps leading to Germany's descent into genocide—what he refers to as "the genesis of the Holocaust"—offer a deterrent example of the way in which otherwise normal individuals can be led astray when they live in a permanent state of emergency, when legal and institutional structures collapse, and when criminal deeds are publicly justified as national achievements.[2]

For the Nazis' aims to be realized, of course, their leader, Adolf Hitler, needed not only the expertise of professionals capable of organizing the murder of vast numbers of people, but also a bureaucratic edifice comprised of men and women capable of carrying it through. In this regard he was able to call on the experts responsible for his ambitious prewar eugenics scheme, which had seen the death of scores of thousands of so-called defective humans, those whom the Nazis referred to as "lebens unwertes Leben" (life unworthy of life)—Germans with congenital illnesses, emotional problems, crippling injuries, or physical deformities, among other features distinguishing them from supposedly "normal" people. The euthanasia experts developed both the techniques and the mindset necessary for the killing of large numbers of human beings, and adapting what they had already been doing to the much larger tasks required in Eastern Europe seemed for many to be a natural progression.[3]

When all was said and done, however, what became most obvious from 1941 onward was that the primary ideological objective of German Nazism was the physical elimination of all of Europe's Jews. Given this, we must search for the best way to approach an understanding of the genocidal nature of the Nazi regime; we must try, moreover, to learn how the Third Reich operated, and why it saw the achievement of racial purity through mass annihilation as its principal goal.

In order to engage with the multifaceted issues presented by the Holocaust, an investigation will be made here into the device developed by the Nazis for the purpose of realizing their genocidal aims, namely, the concentration camp system, which operated from the very beginning of the Third Reich until just before its final collapse.

This system brought men and women together within a single confined space surrounded by barbed wire; it subjected them to harrowing physical and psychological trauma and attempted to destroy their ability to think or act for themselves. Inmates dwelt in an atmosphere of brutality, degradation, and continual physical and spiritual abuse, in which the Nazis sought to crush all opposition. As we will see, the uncertainty of the camps and the arbitrary nature of arrests—of *all* perceived enemies—served the purpose of intimidating the populations under Nazi control so that they would accept the authority and the power of the Third Reich without question. Moreover, the administration of the concentration camps was highly structured and, so far as the inmates were concerned, deadly. The intention of the SS was that the camp network would be a hermetically sealed system of terror and death, and for their principal victims of genocide, the Jews, the camps would become the primary site of their annihilation.

How did this supreme manifestation of political evil surface? As the key institutional mechanism of the genocide, what was the origin of the Nazi concentration camp system? In order to answer this we need to go right back to the very beginning of Hitler's rule, for the ethos that underwrote the concentration camps was to be the vehicle upon which his dictatorship would be based, the means whereby Nazism beguiled the German people—and led them eventually to ruinous destruction.

One final introductory comment is required before proceeding. The genocidal nature of the Nazi regime is such an established fact that it does not require elaboration here. It is, as Zev Garber observed in 1994, the paradigmatic genocide.[4] The perpetrators of the Holocaust had but one aim in mind—the physical removal, through killing, of all human beings belonging to their target group. A change of status through religious conversion or naturalization would not help; in the Nazi view, every Jew, by virtue of his or her very birth, "was the static expression of Evil . . . a natural-born, predestined, non-assimilable heretic, doomed to Apocalyptic hell-fire."[5] There was, in short, no way out. Unlike some cases of genocide, where the accent is on destruction "in part," this was intended to be a *total* annihilation—destruction "in whole," from which none would be allowed to escape. The Nazis intended nothing less than the physical destruction, through murder, of every Jew who fell into their net.

In 1996 a book was published in the United States entitled *Is the Holocaust Unique?*[6] Its appearance stirred up an immense controversy. One of the contributors, Steven T. Katz, tried to withdraw his essay once he learned of the content of some of the other contributions; Katz, a scholar committed to the idea of the Holocaust as a singular event without parallel,[7] apparently had had second thoughts about appearing in a volume with others whose views, he had learned, were at some variance to his own. One of the other contributors, David E. Stannard, had a different experience; on a number of occasions after the book's appearance he was accused of being an antisemite and Holocaust denier for arguing that other genocides were in their own way equally as unique as the assertions being made about the Holocaust.[8]

The passions generated by arguments surrounding the question of Holocaust uniqueness, it can be argued, are misplaced energy. Obviously we have to adopt a workable definition of what is or is not genocide, lest every instance of inhumanity become classified as such so that the term loses its meaning; however, considering the Holocaust as the *only* true case of genocide is just as meaningless an exercise. The key to understanding the importance of the Holocaust is to be found by noting just what genocide is, not what we would prefer it to be. When all is said and done it must be recalled that genocide is a crime, recognized in international law through the United Nations Convention on the Prevention and Punishment of the Crime of Genocide 1948, ratified in national legislatures by all of the Convention's signatories, and reconfirmed in the Rome Statute, which set up the International Criminal Court in 2002. Article 2 of the Convention, which outlines what genocide is and which groups can be defined as victims within it, allows not only Jews during the Holocaust, but many other victim populations before and since, to fall within its reach. In short form, article 2 states that genocide is any one of a number of acts committed with intent to destroy, in whole or in part, a national, ethnical, racial, or religious group. These acts are:

a. Killing members of the group;
b. Causing serious bodily or mental harm to members of the group;
c. Deliberately inflicting on the group conditions of life calculated to bring about its physical destruction in whole or in part;
d. Imposing measures intended to prevent births within the group;
e. Forcibly transferring children of the group to another group.

There is no question that there are certain unique aspects to the suffering borne by all victims of all genocides, including the Shoah, but it can be argued that the person who asks "is the Holocaust unique?" is in reality asking the wrong question. We need not be concerned with the issue of how much more "unique" one instance of genocidal inhumanity is from another; this carries with it an unfortunate potential that can serve the purpose of setting one victim population against another, so that comparison is transformed into competition and the question of uniqueness becomes one in which future generations rank the experience of their people alongside those of others in some sort of macabre contest. Comparative analysis is essential if we are to appreciate why genocides occur, but because of the tragedy of *competitive* suffering that stalks our awareness of genocide we find that injured groups can lose sight of the broader human issues that are at stake. No more disastrous situation can occur than if our perceptions of human hurt only serve to set one ill-treated people as rivals against another. Comparison is not, *and must not imply*, destructive and divisive competition.

It is not sufficient, therefore, to ask "is the Holocaust (or, for that matter, any genocide) unique?" as every historical phenomenon is of itself unique in that it will never again occur in exactly the same way or according to the time-and-place circumstances in which the original event happened. Every genocidal act of the past century, from the Hereros to the Armenians to the Ukrainians, from East Timor to Burundi to Cambodia to Bosnia to Rwanda to Darfur, has been characterized by specific developments that cannot be transferred from one setting to another—if only for the reason that human affairs do not act that way. The best that objective historians can hope to identify in these events is the features that are common or different, and from this ascertain whether some sort of general pattern can be discerned.

What, then, *should* be the key question about the Holocaust? If all cases of genocide have elements that are indeed unique unto themselves, it is less appropriate to ask "is the Holocaust unique?" but, turning the issue upside down, to instead ask "what *is* unique about the Holocaust?"—in other words, to assume its uniqueness and thereafter move straightaway to identifying the feature or features that define its unique character.

American psychologists George M. Kren and Leon H. Rappoport, addressing this issue, have argued that the Holocaust's uniqueness lay in the fact that the Nazis converted the very fabric of Western industrial modernity into a vehicle for the attainment of mass death:

> The Nazi use of scientific technology and, at least as important, their systematic utilization of modern bureaucratic techniques transformed the production of death in much the same way as the industrial revolution transformed the production of goods; both involve a transition from a handicraft mode of production to industrial mass production . . . [which] signifies a fundamental transformation of the nature of the act.[9]

As we will see, the means the Nazis employed in order to achieve their murderous aims, especially from early 1942 onward, was of course the death (or extermination) camp (Vernichtungslager), and it is this institution, thoroughly unprecedented in purpose and design, that is the starkest and most unique feature of the Holocaust.

It can even be argued, with some degree of certainty, that nothing, either before or since, approximates the Nazi death camps in design, intention, or operation. The Ottoman Turks, for example, utilized the caves around the Syrian town of Der-es-Zor as a kind of "subterranean Auschwitz,"[10] but this was a case of exploiting a pre-existing landform rather than constructing an architect-designed, professionally engineered institution such as the Nazis did. And Der-es-Zor, it can be argued, is the closest that any genocidal experience comes even to a near-replication of the Nazi death camps.

This is not to say, of course, that installations under other totalitarian regimes were *not* places of relentless torture and murder, even of mass murder. One has only to look at any example from the Soviet or Chinese gulags, at Tuol Sleng prison in Pol Pot's Cambodia, at the Omarska and Trnopolje concentration camps in Serb-dominated Bosnia, at the Drapchi prison in Tibet, or at the so-called reeducation camps of North Korea, to realize that the Nazi concentration camps of what was called the "Dachau model" had much in common with like institutions elsewhere. But nowhere have any of the regimes that produced malevolent concentration camps introduced establishments like the Nazi death camps, in particular the "Operation Reinhard" camps of Treblinka, Belzec, and Sobibor. They were, and remain, thoroughly unprecedented in human history.

The period of National Socialist rule in Europe was a time of immense upheaval and dislocation, occasioned by deliberate and massive political violence. The aim of the SS was the elimination of every trace of actual or potential opposition to Nazi rule, even from those whom it considered a threat through their very existence. Its brief was to wage a genocidal struggle against the Jews, which, under the direction of Heinrich Himmler and Reinhard Heydrich, it undertook with what can best be described as a religious zeal.

The ideological background to Nazi antisemitism has been examined by numerous scholars in the past, and it would be superfluous to revisit their studies here.[11] It would simply be sufficient to recall, in the words of Yehuda Bauer, that Nazi antisemitism was premised upon a combination "of both traditional Christian and pseudoscientific nineteenth-century antisemitism."[12] Put slightly differently by Richard L. Rubenstein, the search for an explanation of the roots of Nazi antisemitism has led scholars in "a search for historical antecedents":

> From the perspective of the Holocaust, all earlier manifestations of anti-Jewish hostility were seen in a new and more sinister light. It was not difficult for scholars to identify a thread of continuity between the religious defamation of Judaism in the Christian tradition, the policies of the Church towards the Jews in premodern times, the racist attacks on Jews in nineteenth- and twentieth-century Europe, and the so-called Final Solution itself.[13]

The Third Reich, in short, was a thoroughly genocidal state, but—as in all cases of genocide—its targeting of a group for destruction did not appear out of the blue. While a prod was needed to initiate the process, the Nazi genocide of the Jews could not have happened unless a number of pre-existing impulses were already present. While it took no less a force than the extreme radicalism of Nazism to bring this out, once in power the government was able to capitalize on a variety of social, intellectual, religious, economic, and emotional currents in order to achieve its ambition of a Jew-free Germany (and later, through different means, of a Jew-free Europe).

The first step on this journey can be said to have taken place on the night of February 27, 1933, when a message was received by the Berlin police that the Reichstag, the home of the German parliament, was on fire. It did not take long for a culprit to be identified: a young Dutchman, Marinus van der Lubbe, was soon apprehended and charged with arson. He was found carrying an identification card of the Dutch Communist Party, a fact that Germany's recently installed National Socialist government proclaimed as proof that communists had launched a revolutionary takeover of the country.

The fear of communism pervading some sectors of the German public now enabled the Nazis to consolidate their political position and build a totalitarian state. It was in order to combat communism, after all, that the Nazis were put in power in the first place, appointed by the old order to bring an end to the threat of a proletarian uprising. The day after the fire, on the pretext that revolution was imminent, Chancellor Adolf Hitler persuaded the president, Paul von Hindenburg, to sign a Decree for the Protection of the People and the State, suspending all civil and individual liberties that had been guaranteed under the constitution. It empowered the government to take such steps as were necessary to ensure that the current threat to German society was removed. Significantly, it made no specific references to definite adversaries. While directing itself in this instance toward communism, it contained the menacing portent of later restrictions, which might be applied to other "enemies."

Marinus van der Lubbe was not the only one charged with responsibility for the fire; other arrests also took place, in a mass crackdown on all communists, and those suspected of being so. Hundreds were detained in the first few days, and tens of thousands in succeeding weeks. On March 3, 1933, Hermann Goering, the Prussian minister of the interior, instructed the police that not only communists, but "those who work with the communists and who support their criminal objectives, even if indirectly," should receive the same treatment.[14]

The form of arrest leading to these people being taken in was soon referred to as *Schutzhaft*, or "protective custody." As a policing concept, it had greater implications than would be found in the mere removal of a wrongdoer from society. Very few ordinary citizens were aware of what happened to a person who had been apprehended. Men who were imprisoned and then released were frequently cowed into such submission that they refused to discuss their experiences, and the Nazi police authorities—the SS, SA, Gestapo, and SD—revealed nothing. Often a man simply disappeared from his home, his place of work, or even from the street, and his whereabouts were not disclosed.

Ignorance of the fate of *Schutzhaft* detainees served to provoke fear among the general population. As it seemed the authorities were indiscriminately arresting all manner of people on the flimsiest of charges (and often for no apparent reason at all), it did not take long for protective custody to become a concept filled with dread. The tactic of *Schutzhaft* embodied many of the same elements that were soon to be found in the haze surrounding the concentration camps, and uncertainties abounded as people agonized over the motives behind the arrests, the treatment of ordinary citizens at the hands of the Nazis, and the means of avoiding such an arbitrary system of seizure and captivity. *Schutzhaft* was a necessary precursor to the concentration camps in its effect on the psychology of the masses; together, the two would combine to suppress all overt opposition to the Nazi regime.

The wave of early arrests understandably put enormous strains on the existing prison system, and it was soon clear that such a situation could not continue indefinitely. Moreover, the concept of protective custody, some Nazis believed, might become less terrifying if it became known that the detainee had "merely" gone to jail. It thus became desirable for some sort of an institution that would concentrate all the *Schutzhaft* prisoners of a given region within a single, nonpenal, nonpublic detention center. Such an institution had decided practical advantages: it would relieve the overcrowding in local prisons; it would assemble all the political prisoners in one compound far removed from the prying eyes of civil rights groups; and it would serve to give concrete form to the terror accompanying *Schutzhaft* arrests.

German historian Martin Broszat has traced the earliest origins of a "concentrated" form of *Schutzhaft* imprisonment to a letter dated March 13, 1933, from Adolf Wagner, the leading Nazi official at the Bavarian Ministry of the Interior, to Hans Frank, his counterpart at the Bavarian Ministry of Justice. Wagner argued that if the existing prison system should prove unable to carry the strain of the great influx of new prisoners,

> I suggest the use of methods formerly employed [by the Weimar regime] in dealing with mass arrests of members of the National Socialist German Workers' [i.e., Nazi] Party. As is well known they were shut up in any empty ruin and nobody worried whether or not they suffered the inclemency of the weather.[15]

He recommended that "special protective custody quarters separate from the police prisons and those of the Ministry of Justice" be established.[16] These new quarters did not take long to appear. On March 20, barely one week later, Reichsführer-SS Heinrich Himmler announced the establishment of the first: it was a compound about fifteen kilometers northwest of Munich, on the outskirts of the town of Dachau. Other camps soon followed, among them Oranienburg, Papenburg, Esterwegen, Kemna, Lichtenburg, Borgermoor, and Columbiahaus, the SS "special" prison at Berlin.

For the most part these camps were rapidly established, highly improvised affairs. Little regard was paid to administration, discipline, or utilization. Some were run by SS officers; some were staffed by SA men, often locals who knew or were known by those they were guarding. Nicknamed "Wilde-KZ" (Wild Concentration Camps), these camps frequently operated without any obvious system or direction. There was little in the way of planning or procedure, and their very location was often impromptu. The camp at Dachau was a former gunpowder factory; that at Oranienburg was originally a brewery (and later, a foundry); and Borgermoor and Esterwegen were initially simply rows of barracks set down on open expanses of marshy heath land. Elsewhere, prisoners had to build their own habitations, and started their camp life living in tents.

It is important to emphasize that these camps were originally places of political imprisonment. They had political aims and selected their captives using political criteria. In their most basic sense they removed political opposition from the midst of the community and intimidated the population into accepting the Nazi regime—a regime that viewed the incarceration of communists and related enemies as a form of punishment which of necessity had to be imposed on these political "criminals." Put simply, the intention in 1933 was that opponents, whether real, presumed, or potential, would be terrified into submission. All the Nazis demanded was political compliance.

Once the singular function of gagging the opposition had been achieved, however, the Nazis saw the desirability of retaining the camps as a bolster to the regime. A regulation issued on April 12, 1934, by Minister of the Interior Wilhelm Frick acknowledged this, saying that the time was "not yet ripe for the complete abolition of protective custody."[17] Frick produced a series of guidelines clarifying the whole issue, including such matters as how and to whom protective custody was to be applied, its intentions, and its duration. One of his most important points stated that the use of protective custody would be permissible only (a) for the protection of the prisoner, and (b) "if the prisoner by his behavior *directly* endangers law and order particularly by subversive activities."[18] This made the likelihood of arbitrary arrests far greater than before, as it was now unnecessary to justify an "enemy" by seeking out an opponent belonging to a distinct group. By its vagueness the regulation left the choice of who was subject to *Schutzhaft* arrest open to the discretion of the senior Nazi officer on the scene.

The new principles did not, however, result in a renewed bout of widespread arrests or resultant overcrowding. Rather, the reverse occurred. Most of the Wilde-KZs had actually closed down by the spring of 1934, and only the larger camps of Dachau, Oranienburg, Borgermoor, Esterwegen, Lichtenburg, and the Columbiahaus prison remained. In addition to standardizing the principles surrounding *Schutzhaft*, Wilhelm Frick's regulation of April 12, 1934, also "expressed the desire of the administration to restore normal conditions," and it followed that for the rest of 1934 and most of 1935 thousands of prisoners were actually released from protective custody.[19]

It was not until October–November 1935, in fact, that a new wave of widespread arrests took place. These were primarily designed to staunch the growth of any anti-Nazi criticism, by hitting hard and fast at the earliest expressions of dissatisfaction. The incidents for which the new prisoners were arrested were petty, such as casually criticizing the regime over a drink, making light of the Nazi leadership, or grumbling over newly instituted government policies. By the end of 1935 it was clear that the concentration camps had become a permanent part of the Nazi state.

In mid-1934 an official body was established to coordinate the diverse camps throughout the Reich. Theodor Eicke, a former police officer, was appointed to the new position of inspector of concentration camps, his brief to oversee the entire system and bring order to the varied styles of hit-or-miss administration that until then had characterized the camp network. With Eicke's appointment, a man and a mission had found each other. Eicke had been the second Kommandant of Dachau, appointed in June 1933. While there he systematized the treatment, supervision, and punishment of the prisoners, and instilled a new *esprit de corps* into the SS guard organization. As Kommandant he made Dachau a model for the other camps, and when appointed as inspector he set about transforming the whole concentration camp edifice according to the Dachau model. The treatment of prisoners became standardized; clear delineations were made within the authority structure concerning the camps' direction and administration. Eicke's routine for Dachau now became the archetype for camps all over Germany. As Wolfgang Sofsky has shown, existing disciplinary and penal codes in the camps were altered "in order to curtail the arbitrary decisions of the commandants" which ran rife prior to this time. These having been instituted, however, "no limits were set on mistreatment and cruel harassment."[20] In matters of prisoner discipline, Kommandants could instruct their guards to be as imaginative as they liked, in accordance with a set of very stringent general guidelines. And the offenses capable of attracting severe punishment were many.

To take one example, we can consider the list of offenses attracting mandatory execution by hanging. At Dachau, Eicke composed a set of regulations that covered most eventualities:

> Any person who at work, in quarries, kitchens, workshops, toilets or rest places carries on politics for subversive ends, makes provocative remarks, associates with anyone else to this end, forms cliques or loiters with intent, collects, receives, passes, recounts to foreign visitors or transmits to others secretly out of the camp or by any other means lies, false or true news for adverse propaganda about atrocities in the concentration camp or its buildings, hands them on in writing or by word of mouth to released or transferred prisoners, hidden in clothes or other articles, throws them by means of stones, etc. over the camp wall or writes coded messages; in addition, any person who for subversive reasons climbs on to the huts, roofs, or trees, makes signals by lamp or otherwise tries to make contact with the outside or incites others to escape or to commit a crime, gives advice on this or supports them by any other means, will be hanged.[21]

As if a list as comprehensive as this was not detailed enough, numerous other activities also incurred the death penalty under the Dachau model. These were extended to any inmates

> who attacked a sentry or an SS member, who refused to obey a command or to work, who incited or induced others to commit such acts, who complained or shouted. Anyone who caused a fire or tampered with any buildings or wires in the camp faced hanging for sabotage.[22]

The Inspectorate of Concentration Camps was established on July 4, 1934; by the spring of that year most of the smaller camps had been closed down and those remaining converted to the Dachau model. Consolidation of the camp administration meant more than the transfer of all prisoners to centralized control; it also meant, as Sofsky has observed, "the institutionalization of the camp as a social system."[23]

The expansion in the number of crimes for which a German citizen could be arrested from the winter of 1935 onward meant the gradual evolution of a carefully planned Dachau-style camp network. Not only this; the first substantial arrests of prisoners other than avowed political opponents of the Nazis also began. Jehovah's Witnesses, persons charged with "anti-social behavior," and male homosexuals now began to be taken into custody. These arrests were each justified differently by the Nazis. Jehovah's Witnesses went against National Socialist thinking by spreading pacifist philosophies, and "anti-socials," who could count among their numbers elements as diverse as vagrants, itinerant merchants, and so-called work-shy elements, together with male homosexuals, were classed as damaging to the smooth and well-ordered structure of a disciplined society. Unlike the communists, however, none of these prisoners had been active political opponents of National Socialism as such, and their arrest can be viewed more as a tightening of the Nazi grip over free thought and behavior than a move to curb political opposition (which had to a large degree already disappeared by 1936, in any case).

For most prisoners in the earliest stages of their incarceration, one thing remained constant—the seemingly incomprehensible system of rules and discipline that confronted them from the moment they arrived in this new world. Prior to their entry to the camp proper, newly arrested prisoners would be interrogated by the SS in the "Political Department" (Politische Abteilung), at which time they would be registered and their personal details taken down on file cards. They would also be classified according to the nature of their "crime," which might or might not reflect accurately the original reason for their arrest. They would then be stripped, their heads would be shorn (and during the war years, their bodies shaved), they would shower, receive their striped prison clothes, and be released into the camp compound. It was left to the discretion of the SS officer in charge whether the new prisoners would receive any food for the first twenty-four hours. Many did not, and the practice of keeping new inmates in quarantine for a set period was increasingly adopted in order to ensure that "old" prisoners did not smuggle them food.

Once in the camp, the SS were able to recognize at a glance which classification a prisoner belonged to by means of a series of identification badges which, when sewn onto the prisoners' uniforms, explained exactly why each detainee had been arrested. These badges took the form of an inverted triangle, and were sewn on both the prisoner's jacket and on the right leg of his trousers (or the dress, if the prisoner was female). The distinguishing feature lay in the various colors of these triangles. A political prisoner wore a red triangle, while a common criminal had a green one. "Anti-social elements" were designated black, followed by pink (homosexuals), pale blue (German political émigrés who had been recaptured by the Reich), and mauve (Jehovah's Witnesses). Jews underwent the same types of classification, but in addition had an erect yellow triangle superimposed on the original one, in order to form a Star of David. A foreign political prisoner would often have the initial letter of his or her country added to the triangle. And above all triangles, also sewn on, was the prisoner's internment number. (A further practice, developed in Auschwitz during the war years, was that of tattooing the number onto the prisoner's forearm.)

In the push to standardize the camps along Eicke's lines, some sacrifices had to be made, and the rationalization program saw large numbers of *Schutzhaft* prisoners released as the smaller camps were closed down. By the winter of 1936–37 inmate populations reached their lowest total since the camps were originally instituted. The Oranienburg camp had been terminated in 1935 in order to make way for a new one a short distance away at Sachsenhausen, which was instituted in September 1936. A large new camp was established at Buchenwald, near Weimar, in August 1937, and for nearly a year thereafter there were but four camps in Germany: Dachau, Sachsenhausen, Buchenwald, and Lichtenburg. The first three formed a geographically convenient blanket for most of Germany. Sachsenhausen covered north Germany and Berlin, Buchenwald guarded the socialist heartland of Thuringia, and Dachau served Bavaria and the south. Flossenburg, in northeastern Bavaria not far from the Czech border, was established in 1938, and Mauthausen, near Linz, was set up immediately after the Nazi invasion of Austria in March of that year. Lichtenburg, in the lower Elbe region, was employed solely as a concentration camp for women from mid-1937 on, until it also was replaced by another Dachau-style camp, Ravensbrück, in May 1939. That camp was located in Mecklenburg, in northern Germany, and was to remain exclusively for women until just before its liberation in 1945. The only camp left of those established in 1933 was the first, Dachau—the model for all those yet to come, and training school for guards and future Kommandants alike.

By the middle of the 1930s, the range of those who could be sent to the concentration camps had been broadened considerably. Prisoners could even then look around them and see "politicals," Jehovah's Witnesses, "anti-socials," homosexuals, and criminals. Some prisoners had the added "distinction" of also being Jewish.

Jews had often previously been arrested for transgressing within the framework of the existing classifications, but from 1935 onward they were frequently being victimized for their Jewishness alone. This was due largely to the effects of the so-called Nuremberg Laws on Citizenship and Race.

According to these laws, the formal status of Jews in the Nazi state was defined and put into practice. Jewish businesses were boycotted, Jewish doctors excluded from public hospitals and only permitted to practice on other Jews, Jewish judicial figures were dismissed and disbarred, and Jewish students were expelled from universities. Jews were increasingly excluded from participation in all forms of German life. The Nuremberg Laws also withdrew from Jews the privilege of German citizenship. It became illegal for a Jew and a non-Jew to marry or engage in sexual relationships.[24] Life was to be made so intolerable for Jews that they would wish to emigrate; those who did not often found themselves arbitrarily arrested and sent to the camps. These arrests did not become widespread until 1938, and in most cases the victims were only held for a short time. The emphasis was to terrorize them into leaving the country.

The first *large-scale* arrests of Jews were made after November 9, 1938, as "reprisals" for the so-called Jewish-inspired assassination of German consular official Ernst vom Rath in Paris. The event precipitating these arrests has gone down in history as *Kristallnacht*, the "Night of Broken Glass." The assassination of vom Rath by the Jewish student Herschel Grynszpan was painted by the Nazis as a major international crime, for which Germany's Jews would have to pay. The resultant pogrom was thus portrayed as a righteous and spontaneous outpouring of anger by ordinary German people against all Jews—even though it was SA members in plainclothes who whipped up most of the action in the streets. As summarized by Abraham and Hershel Edelheit,

> Synagogues were destroyed and burned, Jewish-owned stores were smashed and looted, Jewish homes were assaulted, and individual Jews were physically attacked. Ninety-one Jews were killed during the pogrom, and more than 900 synagogues were demolished. In the aftermath of the pogrom 30,000 Jews were rounded up and were incarcerated in concentration camps.[25]

Herschel Grynszpan's lone action in Paris thus had a grisly outcome back in Germany.[26] Not only did it result in greater concentrated destruction than any previous anti-Jewish measure under the Nazis, it also spelled out to those Jews who had up to now thought the regime was a passing phenomenon that this was not the case. The Nazis were here to stay; their intention was that the Jews would go. The wave of arrests was as much a warning to get out as it was a punishment for the assassination of vom Rath. More Jews than ever could now see the writing on the wall and, provided they had somewhere to go, the Nazis would oblige by helping them to leave.

The *Kristallnacht* arrests thus served as a push for those still reluctant to leave, and the concentration camps served as convenient places for the Nazis to reinforce their point, namely, the notion that the new Germany was a land of terror for those it did not want. The idea found its ultimate expression in camps like Dachau and Buchenwald. Henceforth, Jews were targeted for the sole reason of their Jewishness—a development that has prompted one author to refer to the *Kristallnacht* as "the day the Holocaust began."[27] In this context, the *Kristallnacht* played a very important role. Prior to this, Nazi persecution of Jews was not premised on acts of wanton destruction or murder; the November pogrom, however, had the effect of transforming earlier legislative measures against Jews into physical harassment on a broader and more indiscriminate scale.

Such a development was eminently rational given the Nazi totalitarian mentality that sought to remove and exclude the Jewish population from within. Forcible expulsions had taken place for many centuries, as Jews knew only too well, and at this time expulsion was the only "reasonable" solution to what the Nazis viewed as an ideological challenge of the first magnitude. The Nazis sought to rid Germany of its Jews, and ideally a pogrom such as the *Kristallnacht* served the purpose of convincing them that they should leave.

The events of November 9–10, 1938, seen in this context, played a crucial role on the road to the *Endlösung des Judenfrage* (the Nazis' "Final Solution of the Jewish Question"). From now on, physical acts of an antisemitic nature became state policy, and Jews frantically began seeking havens to which they could emigrate in order to save their lives. The Free World, in turn, began to close its doors to Jewish immigration, and, with Hitler's foreign policy appetite growing and new areas becoming annexed to the Third Reich, the number of Jews coming under Nazi control increased to far less manageable proportions than they had been.

The influx of Jewish prisoners after *Kristallnacht* was one of two events in 1938 causing a rapid regrowth in concentration camp populations. The second came as a result of the physical expansion of the Third Reich: first Austria (March 12, 1938), then the Sudetenland (September–October 1938), and finally Bohemia-Moravia (March 15, 1939). As in Germany in the immediate post–Emergency Decree period of 1933, all real or presumed opposition was immediately removed from the scene, in what must have been a sudden and dreadful whirlwind for those arrested. So far as the camps themselves were concerned, the new wave of arrests saw them swamped beyond anything previously planned. It was as much in order to relieve this pressure, as well as to cover the newly acquired areas, that camps at Mauthausen and Flossenbürg were set up during 1938.

The outbreak of war on September 1, 1939, further served to enlarge the camp system. Throughout the war's first few months all manner of criminals, so-called pacifists (who could, in reality, be anyone), enemy nationals, and political suspects were swept up in a massive operation that spread from one end of the country to the other. Close to two thousand Germans of Polish descent were taken into "protective custody," and the criminal police, not to be denied the chance to clean up their area of administration, ordered the rearrest of Jews who had not so far seriously tried to leave. Also arrested were "so-called psychopaths who because of mental disorder may be suspected of causing unrest among the population."[28] In October Himmler added all "work-shy elements" and Roma (that is, "Gypsies," a term of disparagement to be avoided) to the list of those for concentration camp incarceration.

As the war progressed, and the camps became swollen by enormous numbers of prisoners of all types, the provision of guards to maintain control of them became progressively difficult owing to the increasing demands placed on German manpower. In order to combat this, the SS relied more and more on the system they had devised in the prewar period, appointing certain prisoners to positions of authority and investing them with powers similar to their own. In return, these "prisoner-functionaries" (*Funktionshäftlinge*) received more food, had better living conditions, and performed less work, this being mainly restricted to the supervision of other prisoners.

Those invested with responsibility for such administration were called *Ältesten* (Elders, or Seniors), of which the main figure was the *Lagerältester*—the most senior prisoner in the camp. In each block there was a *Blockältester*, in each room a *Stubenältester*. These latter were in turn assisted by a number of *Stubendienst* workers, who acted as room orderlies. Every block also had a *Blockschreiber*, a prisoner who acted as a kind of registrar for the barracks and reported to an SS officer in the *Politische Abteilung*.

The system of regulation and punishment in the concentration camp could not have operated without the compliance (sometimes willing, sometimes not) of other prisoner-functionaries who acted in a disciplinary role. These were known as Kapos, and were inmates appointed by the SS to serve as labor bosses.[29] They are mainly remembered as fearsome and harsh, renowned for their brutality and frequent sadism. For much of the war the Kapos could be chosen from among any of the prisoner population, though the granting of power—*any* power—to Jews was anomalous to Nazi racial thinking, even in the concentration camp. In February 1944 Heinrich Himmler issued an order prohibiting Jewish Kapos.[30]

Wolfgang Sofsky has shown how the Kapos and the *Blockschreibers* functioned as integral elements in the Nazi system of terror:

> One of the pillars holding up the camp system was an auxiliary force of *Kapos* . . . and "scribes" . . . who helped maintain everyday routines and relieved the burden on the SS personnel. Through their agency, absolute power became omnipresent. It filled almost every cranny, every niche in the camp. Without that delegation of power, the system of discipline and surveillance would quickly have collapsed. The attendant rivalry for positions in supervision, administration, and supply provided the SS with a welcome opportunity to play the various factions among the prisoners' elite off against each other, keeping them dependent. However, the typical prisoner was at the mercy of a dual authority: the members of the SS, who hardly ever appeared in the camp, and the prisoner-functionaries . . . , who were always around, a ubiquitous presence.[31]

Altogether, the Nazis organized things in such a way that the day-to-day running of the camps was done by the inmates themselves: relative to prisoner size, surprisingly few SS guards were actually needed in the camp compound at any one time. The prisoner-functionaries wielded a real and absolute power over the common prisoners. Any order given had to be obeyed; refusal to do so frequently meant death. And although this authority extended through both types of prisoner-functionary, it was the Kapos who exercised the more telling immediate power over the prisoners.

Kapos, like the *Ältesten*, received enormous benefits from their positions, and both types of functionaries fought hard to preserve their privileges. They usually had more to eat than those below them in the social scale, and their food was often of a higher quality. The Kapos supervised the common prisoners at work, while doing little work themselves. They had more time to sleep than the others, and could requisition any item from the prisoners. In the dormitory blocks, which were mostly overcrowded after 1939, the Kapos and *Ältesten* often had their own rooms, sometimes single beds of their own, and at times even lockers for whatever personal property they possessed (which had all too often been looted from those under their charge). They were allowed facilities to wash regularly, to change their linen and—amazingly in a concentration camp—even to change their underwear.[32] Of course, concessions like these were worth too much to lose, and the natural instinct was to try to keep them. No task set by the SS, it appeared, was worth too much if it meant the continuation of the incumbent's position. (There was an added, and more sinister, factor to consider: if an SS order went unheeded, or was not satisfactorily completed, the functionary might lose much more than just his or her position.)

These inmates were to control the everyday existence of the common prisoners: they woke them in the morning, counted them, distributed their food (or withheld it when they considered circumstances necessary), marched them off to work, watched over them during the day's labor, herded them back to the camp and their barracks, and even organized their latrine times. They arranged and administered punishments, and forced inmates to perform in or witness punitive "entertainments" at their discretion.

This authority was in turn reinforced by the overwhelmingly powerful dominance the SS had over the prisoner-functionaries themselves. The Kapos and *Ältesten* were utterly dependent on the SS for everything. They, like any other prisoners, could be punished for the slightest infraction of the rules, and had to do exactly as they were told, nothing more or less. They were sandwiched in the middle of camp society; while enforcing SS structures and discipline on those below them, before the SS they could never forget that they too were prisoners. They could be killed by the common prisoners as traitors (and often were); they could, equally, be killed by the SS on a whim. With all this, it is perhaps not to be wondered at that the *Funktionshäftlinge* carried out the dictates of the SS eagerly. The only choice they faced was whether to extend the hand of comradeship to their fellow inmates, or to repress them with crushing severity. If the prisoner-functionary was to survive, threats from either side had to be countered.

By creating a prisoner elite, the SS established a system that divided the prisoners in order to rule them. In doing so they reaped enormous benefits, as they were thereafter able to control the inmates with a minimum number of guards exercising a relatively high level of control. If the Nazis were to achieve their aims, this was necessary: as Sofsky has written, "mass murder demands organization."[33] Thus, the SS got the work of running the camps done for them, and had many of their dirtier jobs completed as well. Such an arrangement suited not only the SS; for obvious reasons, the prisoners, too, were glad to have the guards out of the way. In a macabre sense, the SS-imposed administrative system worked so effectively because it was in the interests of both parties that it did so. Prisoners sought to convince the SS, through both direct negotiation and deception, that the routine of camp life was at all times under control. Advantages could be gained if the guards were persuaded that responsible functionaries reduced the number of problems needing to be addressed. The more the SS believed this, the safer—so far as anything could be "safe" in a concentration camp—life became. Prisoners could gain some time out from direct SS depredations.[34]

The physical expansion of this highly sophisticated system of divide-and-rule was inevitable with the outbreak of war in 1939, and more camps were an obvious necessity in order to accommodate the new classifications of prisoners. Accordingly, late in 1939, the Inspectorate of Concentration Camps was authorized to examine the possibility of setting up new camps that could begin operation as soon as possible. One of the first of these, located in southwestern Poland near the confluence of the Vistula and Soła rivers, was to be built just outside the town of Oswiecim. In German the name was Auschwitz.

It would be safe to say that no town anywhere in the world summons up the images that now come to mind when the name Auschwitz is mentioned. It is simultaneously the world's greatest murder site and the world's greatest cemetery. A nondescript town in Silesia, not far from Krakow, Auschwitz has acquired a notoriety unsurpassed by any other location in history, as the principal killing site of a regime dedicated to mass murder.

The choice of this town as the location of the new camp had its origins in the desire of the SS

> to create a camp for Polish prisoners and also find a site centrally placed in relation to all the territories which had not yet been conquered but which, in the course of the next few years, the SS believed would come under Nazi control. The chosen site would require convenient railway access and should be somewhat distant from larger centres of population.[35]

As early as February 21, 1940, Eicke's successor at the Inspectorate of Concentration Camps, Richard Glücks, reported to Himmler that a series of "former Polish artillery barracks" had been found which were "suitable for use" for a new camp "after some sanitary and structural defects have been dealt with."[36] The town of Auschwitz, with a prewar population of about 12,000, seemed the ideal location, though the site selected for the camp had its objectionable side. Surrounded by open swampy moorland, it remained muddy for most of the year; it was unhealthy and malaria-infested, and in winter it turned bitterly cold. Severe winds swept down from the north, unimpeded by any natural obstacles on the Polish plain. It was flat, cold, wet, cheerless, colorless. In aesthetic or environmental terms there was nothing to recommend the area surrounding the little Silesian town.

Despite its ideal location on the transport routes, Auschwitz offered few attractions to the Nazis, but, as Deborah Dwork and Robert Jan van Pelt have shown, there was a strong ideological reason for Auschwitz becoming "the site of a violent concentration camp designed to terrorize and incarcerate Poles, and . . . an extermination camp for Jews."[37] This considered the relationship between the Nazi conception of history and the location of Auschwitz on the farthest eastern border of the old Reich, between German "civilization" and what was perceived as the "uncivilized" Slavic domains that had long been the focus of German imperialist attention. Just as the United States had its "wild" West, Dwork and van Pelt argue, Germany's ambitions had been toward the "wild" east—toward Poland, Ukraine, and Russia. Auschwitz, which had been a German duchy before becoming a Polish, Austrian, and then again a Polish town, lay between Teutonia and the east, and was thus ideally situated as the main center of operations when the time came for Germany to launch itself on a mission of obtaining "living space" (*lebensraum*) in what was destined to become a "racially pure" area.[38]

On May 4, 1940, Hauptsturmführer-SS Rudolf Franz Hoess, the newly appointed Kommandant, began his task. This was, he recalled, "to construct a transit camp for ten thousand prisoners, using the existing complex of buildings which, though well-constructed, had been completely neglected, and were swarming with vermin."[39] Employing prisoners from other camps as slave labor, the compound was soon built. It received its initial batch of permanent inmates on July 14, 1940.

Auschwitz was not, however, constructed on the Dachau model. From the first, the intention was that it would serve a different purpose from the older camps in Germany and Austria. Dwork and van Pelt have shown just how different this was to be:

> [T]he initial purpose of the camp was to terrorize the local Polish population which, engaged in industrial occupations, was not deported by the Germans. Auschwitz was a transit camp for the arrested recalcitrant Poles, who were shipped to camps in the west as slave laborers.[40]

Oswald Pohl, the Nazi chief administrative officer of the Reich Central Security Office (and, as such, thus responsible for the overall administration of the concentration camps), had other ideas for Auschwitz. The region was a source of raw materials that could be of use to the Third Reich. There was plenty of sand and gravel, for instance, which could be exploited for the manufacture of concrete needed to construct Europe's new order. It was therefore "the potential resource of building materials which ensured the future of Auschwitz."[41] Not yet a place known and feared the world over, it was nevertheless from an early date a camp with a reputation for hard work and brutal treatment, from which many never returned. It was, moreover, initially a camp for Poles rather than for Jews.

Auschwitz was the first Nazi concentration camp to be created outside the old Reich, even though the region had been incorporated directly into Germany with the occupation of Poland in September 1939. When Heinrich Himmler inspected the camp in March 1941, he ordered its refurbishment and expansion for the purpose of holding substantially greater numbers of inmates. The plans called for

> intensive construction work in the camp area with a view to accommodating 30,000 prisoners and the establishment at Birkenau (Brzezinka), about 3 km away, of a camp for 100,000 prisoners of war. Three months before the Germans attacked the Soviet Union, Himmler was clearly anticipating prisoners from that future campaign. Expansion plans also called for supplying 10,000 prisoner workers to IG Farben for the construction of a large industrial enterprise in the vicinity of Auschwitz and for agricultural development with the help of prisoner manpower, establishment of workshops, and war effort enterprises in the camp.[42]

The camp would become a vast complex covering fifteen square miles. Capitalizing on the use that had previously been made of prisoners employed as labor in SS-run economic enterprises, several subcamps were also established in which the prisoner-workers would be housed.[43]

With these changes it seemed as though the security function originally embodied in the notion of *Schutzhaft* had been subordinated to the economic exploitation of the prisoners. Few of the Auschwitz subcamps served any other purpose than that of industrial or agricultural production. The transfer of concentration camp administration to the SS Economic and Administrative Department in March 1942 only served to confirm what had been a fact of life since well before Himmler's visit to Auschwitz in March 1941. The camp did not take long to realize its economic potential. With its numerous subcamps Auschwitz soon became an industrial, as well as a detention, complex, the two complementing each other through the common medium of slave labor.

The economic transformation of the concentration camp network, and shift away from its original political character, was paralleled by the development of camps outside the old Reich. Many new centers were built in the Nazi-occupied countries, as it was not always practicable to transport the prisoners to Germany or Poland. The camps lost their purely German content and became a continental phenomenon, spreading throughout Europe for the multiple tasks of exploiting slave labor, extending the network of terror over occupied populations, and killing those targeted for this purpose by the SS.

A vast array of new types of camps also evolved, with at least forty-three different categories existing at the height of the Nazis' power. Czeslaw Madajczyk has identified a number of these; while most could not be said to have fit into the Dachau model, they nonetheless fell under the general jurisdiction of the Inspectorate of Concentration Camps, and thereby differed from ghettos or military prisoner of war camps.[44] Overall, it has been estimated that some 9,000 camps and subcamps were established throughout the Old Reich and occupied Europe.[45] Of these, the majority were purpose-built:

> Most . . . operated only for the duration of a single labor project, some with only dozens of inmates and others with thousands. Once the work was completed—unless a new project appeared in the same region—the camp was liquidated and its Jewish inmates were either transferred or murdered. Non-Jewish inmates in camps made up of different nationalities were, in some cases, released but, in most cases, were sent into Germany as "volunteer" laborers.[46]

All were places of unmitigated horror, where life was characterized by "hard work, poor diet, overcrowded and unsanitary living conditions, and SS cruelty."[47] Death by beating, bullets, or other means lurked around every corner. Prisoners baked in the summer and froze to death in the winter. Throughout the war years, disease and starvation were constant companions; deprived of all rights, ordinary inmates were subjected to the caprice of Nazi guards and the other prisoners placed in positions of authority over them. The range of the camps, in purpose, method, size, and duration, was extremely wide; taken together, they blanketed Nazi-occupied Europe in a terror system as comprehensive as it was effective. The concentration camp came to symbolize the true essence of the Nazi regime.

Six of the camps in Poland—Auschwitz-Birkenau, Belzec, Chelmno, Majdanek, Sobibor, and Treblinka—totally transformed the nature and course of concentration camp development. They were a departure from anything previously visualized, in both their design and character. Auschwitz has already been referred to. Belzec, near Lvov, was established at the end of 1941, as was Chelmno. Majdanek, located in the city of Lublin, had already taken prisoners by the end of 1940, while Treblinka, near the village of Malkinia Gorna, was set up during the course of 1941. Sobibor, a camp built near Vlodawa, was established in March 1942. With the exception of Auschwitz (which must always fit into a category of its own in any discussion of the Holocaust), these camps were different from all the others in that they did not perform any of the functions—political, industrial, agricultural, or penal—attributed to those farther west or north. These were the *Vernichtungslager*, the death (or extermination) camps.

Because of their existence, the image of the Nazi concentration camps was irrevocably transformed, such that *all* camps are now mainly viewed as elaborate and gigantic factories created for the purpose of destroying human lives en masse. Until the creation of the *Vernichtungslager*, of course, this was not always the case; as we have seen, the Nazi camp system performed numerous other functions besides killing.

The death camps were institutions designed to methodically and efficiently murder millions of people, specifically Jews. These mass murders took place in specially designed gas chambers. In Auschwitz, the machinery of death employed crystallized hydrogen cyanide which on contact with air oxidized to become hydrocyanic (or prussic) acid gas. This gas was manufactured under the trade name Zyklon B, ironically produced by the same I.G. Farben corporation that was exploiting concentration camp prisoners as slave labor (and paying the government for doing so).[48] Initially, *Zyklon B* had been developed as a delousing or fumigating agent for the eradication of vermin, a further irony not lost on the Nazis carrying out their mass-murder campaign. In the other camps, where the death machinery had not been equipped for the use of *Zyklon B*, carbon monoxide from diesel engines was used, either in fixed installations or from mobile vans.

The nature of the eastern camps is well understood now, but the people of Europe at the time could not even imagine the truth. Prisoners elsewhere, particularly in transit camps in western Europe awaiting transportation to the east, certainly had no idea what awaited them in Poland. Once transported, they still had little notion of the true character of the eastern camps, often finding out only after the doors to the gas chambers had slammed shut behind them. To the outside world, the intention of these camps was at once unknown and inconceivable, yet in the most bizarre way they were the ultimate consequence of all that had occurred since 1933, removing permanently those whom the Nazis deemed to be their enemies.

By 1943 the concentration camps could be seen to function in the following ways: as the means of removing real or potential opposition from the mainstream of German politics; as penal institutions for German criminals; as unofficial prisoner of war camps, generally for Soviet soldiers; as huge reservoirs of slave labor; as centers of agriculture, mining, and industry; as collection and transit points for so-called racial prisoners; and as extermination installations.[49] The singular aims originally envisaged for the camps had become almost completely submerged within ten years.

Administration of the camps underwent a further change from 1942. In Auschwitz the SS sought to exterminate its racial prisoners; on the other hand, the Economic and Administrative Department was charged with the exploitation of foreign labor. Auschwitz was a major battlefield in this struggle of competing philosophies of tyranny. As Martin Broszat has explained,

> [A]ll the other extermination camps in the East (with the single exception of Lublin-Majdanek) had been set up specially and exclusively for factory-like liquidation. In Treblinka, Belzec, Sobibor and Chelmno the Jews who arrived by train or lorry were regularly exterminated almost without exception shortly after arrival.[50]

His argument is that "these were not camps in the true sense as there was no intention of accommodating prisoners for any length of time."[51] By the term "true sense," Broszat is of course referring to the Dachau model, and looked at from this perspective he is quite correct. Extermination was *one* of the functions of Auschwitz; at the other eastern camps it was the *only* function. Of the camps farther west, in Germany and elsewhere, the process was reversed to the extent that planned extermination was subordinated to economic exploitation. Auschwitz was the junction for the two varieties of concentration camp rationale between 1942 and 1944.[52] Typifying this dichotomy was the fact that at Auschwitz, where extermination and exploitation jockeyed for the ascendancy, a selection process occurred to see who would die immediately and who would be kept alive a little longer as slave labor.[53]

Throughout the war, the camps remained detention centers for political prisoners, but their original political character had almost disappeared by 1943. That which replaced it—forced labor and economic exploitation—was reflected not only in the part Auschwitz played in the German war effort, but also in the important roles of many other camps, for example, Dora-Nordhausen (for rocket and missile research), and Ravensbrück (for the manufacture of armaments), among many others. Hundreds, even thousands, of camps and subcamps played their part in producing something of benefit to the German war effort, an activity that intensified with the deteriorating fortunes of the war from 1944 onward.

As the Nazi armies on the Eastern Front began to retreat before the advancing Soviet forces (and later from American and British troops in the west), renewed efforts were made at annihilating Jews while there was still time. Berlin was declared "Jew Free" (*Judenrein*) on May 19, 1943, and on September 11 the first Jewish "family transports" left Theresienstadt for Auschwitz—where the selection process ensured that only a minority stayed alive. A shock of cataclysmic proportions then fell upon the Jews of Hungary, the last great center of Jewish population still untouched by the Holocaust.

In March 1944 the Nazis, suspecting that the Hungarian government of Admiral Nicholas Horthy might be contemplating a separate peace with the Soviet Union, occupied the country. Immediately, Nazi antisemitic measures were imposed over Hungary's Jewish population, and the first deportations of Jews to Auschwitz began on May 2. In the space of four months 400,000 were murdered, with the killing facilities working nonstop, day and night. This was the fastest killing operation of any of the Nazi campaigns against Jewish populations in occupied Europe. It clogged the murder routine to such a degree that the crematoria could not keep up, and a vast number of bodies were simply burned in open pits in the ground. Mass killing had, of course, been an ongoing process in the six eastern camps since 1942, but never did it reach such proportions as in the spring of 1944. The frenzy with which the Nazis undertook their task defied even the demands of winning the war, with both manpower and transportation being diverted from the front line to assist in the deportations. By the time the campaign against the Hungarian Jews was suspended, in the fall of 1944, only the Jewish community of Budapest remained relatively intact.[54]

When viewing this campaign and the means employed to attain it, one reservation must be made: Belzec, Treblinka, Sobibor, and Chelmno had by this time already been closed down. Only Auschwitz remained to carry out the massive undertaking of spring 1944, as April had already seen the start of the evacuation of Majdanek. With the Soviet armies continuing their advance toward Germany throughout the latter half of 1944, the position of Auschwitz itself seemed uncertain, and in September Himmler ordered Rudolf Hess to oversee its liquidation. When delays ensued and the Soviets drew nearer, on November 26 Himmler issued another order concerning the destruction of Auschwitz. After considerable administrative difficulties—and much debate concerning the method of withdrawal—the complete evacuation of the complex was ordered for January 17, 1945. On the eighteenth, some 22,000 men and women left the camp, and the next day a further 3,500 were evacuated. They were about all that was left of a camp complex that at one time could claim a population of possibly 200,000. The earliest date of free contact with Soviet forces was January 22, 1945; when the site was formally occupied two days later, there were only 2,819 survivors left.

Any prisoners still alive in the eastern camps at the end of the war were evacuated by the Nazis so as not to fall into the hands of the advancing Russians. These evacuations have properly been called death marches, as vast numbers of prisoners died or were killed while en route. Evidence that the Nazis tried to keep their prisoners alive is scant; any prisoners who did not make it to their final destination were treated with the same contempt as when in the camp. Evacuated in the winter and early spring of 1944–45, they had to contend with bitter cold, fatigue, hunger, and the SS guards themselves, as well as their own debilitated condition, and for those who had already reached the limit of their endurance the death marches could have only one result.[55] For others, the experience represented yet another challenge that had to be overcome. Often the Russians were so close while the prisoners were marching away that the sounds of battle could be clearly distinguished, further adding to their distress. When they arrived at their new destination their trials were hardly eased, as they faced massive overcrowding in the camps to which they had been evacuated.

American author Jon Bridgman has written that "the liberation of the Nazi concentration camps has not been the subject of much scholarly attention."[56] The essential reason for this, he argues, would appear obvious. Liberation was a dramatic moment, but very little needs to be explored in depth; the Allies arrived, the SS departed, and the inmates were free. Yet there was much more to the story than that. In all camps, the liberating soldiers were shocked and angry at what they found, but at the same time genuinely troubled at the sight of the dead and near-dead which by mid-1945 occupied the camps in their scores of thousands. The discovery of these emaciated and filthy skeletons, some alive, some not, was sickening in all senses of the word.

Bergen-Belsen was perhaps the supreme example of the chaos, overcrowding, and general horror that struck all the camps. It was yet another of the many types of concentration camps, a euphemistically termed *Krankenlager*, or "sick camp." In its way, Belsen has left just as indelible an image of the Nazi system on the Western mind as Auschwitz has in its. Established during the second half of 1943, the camp is best remembered for the images brought to the world at the time of its liberation by British forces in April 1945:

> [T]he camp area was strewn with corpses; thousands of skeletally emaciated and fatally ill people were crowded into miserable barracks, so spent by hunger and disease that even in the days and weeks following liberation large numbers of them died. Pictures of this horror were circulated throughout the world, and Bergen-Belsen became the first evidence of the inhuman barbarity and total state of terror of the National Socialist concentration camp system.[57]

On April 15, 1945, the day of the liberation, the British found some 60,985 survivors; 10,000 unburied dead lay where they had fallen in the compound, and another 15,000 succumbed to disease and starvation after the British arrived.[58]

Ironically, Konnilyn G. Feig has written, "Bergen-Belsen had never been given formal concentration camp status," even though it was created originally as "a model repatriation and transit center." In the final months of the war,

> a fierce typhoid and typhus epidemic and tuberculosis devastated the camp—with an inmate population that had grown fourfold in two months. As a result the area looked like a charnel house from ancient times when the British arrived. The incredulity with which the British grasped the reality of their first liberated camp created of Belsen a metaphor for horror.[59]

Ideological considerations and the dislocation of the north German rail network caused by Allied bombing meant that the Nazis had not transported food to Belsen; medical science, in the form of both doctors and equipment, was completely lacking. No attempt had been made by the Nazis to clean the place. The camp by the end of the war had become nothing but a dumping ground for enfeebled Eastern deportees who had been transported back to Germany. After the liberation, the British set the captured Nazi guards to work helping gather the dead together prior to their burial. Most of those who had died were simply piled up in what became mountains of putrescent flesh, then shoved unceremoniously into giant pits dug by British army bulldozers.

Across Europe, concentration camp prisoners, dropped into places like Belsen to await liberation through death or an Allied victory, had little time to wait in real terms, though each day dragged by unendingly. Painfully slowly, as German units both west and east surrendered, the camps were liberated. On April 12, 1945, Westerbork, in the Netherlands, was set free. The day before, Buchenwald's inmates had risen against their SS guards and taken over the camp, handing it to the Americans on April 13. Belsen was liberated by the British army on April 15, and on April 23 the SS transferred Mauthausen to the International Committee of the Red Cross. The next day Dachau, after twelve years and twenty-eight days of unrelenting misery, was overrun by the U.S. Army.[60] Five days later, on April 29, Ravensbrück was liberated. Theresienstadt was handed over to the Red Cross by the Nazis on May 2, and on May 8 American troops occupied Mauthausen, the last major camp to be liberated. On May 4 Theresienstadt was transferred by the Red Cross to the Russians.

The consequences of liberation were profound, and not only for the fortunate survivors. The impressions conveyed to Allied populations, particularly those in the West, showed them in the clearest possible terms what they had been fighting against, and thereby confirmed the righteousness of their cause.[61]

By this stage, the military side of the war was over. What now remained was to reconstruct new lives and a new Europe from the ashes of the old, a task that would prove as daunting as it was heart-rending. What was to be the fate of the survivors of the liberated camps? Many of the sites were transformed by the Allies almost immediately into holding camps for the survivors, now renamed "Displaced Persons," and these camps would in many cases operate for years before finally being closed down.[62]

The concentration camps established in Germany and throughout Europe underwent massive changes of role and function during their twelve-year existence, changes that can be seen as part of an overall developmental process. From originally being a practical response to the challenges arising from *Schutzhaft* (which had itself been generated by the ascent to power of the Nazis), they moved into other fields of operation and justification, while still containing the political nucleus that gave them birth. That nucleus contained all the elements of one of the most repressive regimes the world had yet seen, one that rejected the essential ideals and freedoms fought for since Europe had emerged from the Dark Ages. From being "wild" institutions, the camps became massive cities housing tens of thousands of people, all of whom the Nazis identified as some sort of political "criminal." Anybody who fell within the orbit of "enemy of the state" did so because they had (according to the Nazis) committed a political offense, even if that was only to have been born into an ethnic or religious group the Nazis had proscribed. The camps' very *raison d'être* changed, from being compounds for political prisoners to huge economic concerns comprised of giant industrial plants whose sole design was to exploit the abundant slave labor they possessed for the greater good of the German Reich. That itself changed with the establishment of a third strain of camps, which served as extermination centers for those the Nazis deemed racially undesirable.

The essence of the camp system was present in Dachau as early as 1933. With the extension of the system to Nazi-occupied Europe in the years following 1939, and the shift in emphasis from exploitation to extermination, the appearance of places such as Treblinka, Majdanek, and Auschwitz gave the camps their ultimate expression. Wartime concentration camps foisted on their inhabitants a life that was inconceivable, in which so-called opponents of the Nazis were collected in order to be debased, overworked, and destroyed. The death camps of Poland further extended these destructive boundaries. Overall, the camps became the most lucid and unequivocal statement National Socialism made about itself, demonstrating beyond doubt that it was an antihuman ideology in which the individual counted for nothing. Anyone who stood against the Nazi system became a victim of it—which only served to further entrench its influence and power.

Nazi antisemitic policy was something that had deep roots and evolved over time. For the Jews of Germany (and later, Austria and Czechoslovakia), persecution became an established part of life under Hitler, and in this sense the Holocaust was coeval with the Nazi state itself. The regime over which Adolf Hitler presided was a regime of genocide, the outworking of which became manifest after the outbreak of total war in 1941. The Nazi concentration camp system, the ultimate expression of a modern and highly centralized police state, was the major tool employed for destruction, but it was not the only means utilized by the Nazis for their murderous ends: wholesale shooting of entire populations by the Einsatzgrüppen, or mobile killing units, was responsible for up to a million Jewish deaths;[63] starvation, disease, random shooting, and other brutality took hundreds of thousands of lives in ghettos and other Jewish districts throughout Europe; Jewish partisans were killed in action against the Nazis, or struck from behind by local populations who practiced their own forms of antisemitic hatred notwithstanding that they were fighting a common enemy; and Jews were also victims of countries allied to Hitler—with policies which, if not genocidal, were nonetheless debilitating enough and barbaric enough to ensure that fatalities occurred at a steady rate. Hitler did not need the concentration camps in order to make the Holocaust, but their existence and ongoing development assured its success, its efficiency, and its magnitude.

An understanding of the Nazi concentration camp system can add to our knowledge of genocide in three important ways. In the first place, it shows us how a regime dedicated to mass murder mobilized all its resources for the purpose of feeding the demands of an industry that had been deliberately assigned the tasks of incarceration, degradation, and, ultimately, annihilation. Second, the concentration camps provided a focus for all Nazi genocidal activities, a cynosure in an otherwise bleak landscape characterized by war, fear, and police-state gloom. Finally, the camps demonstrate that genocidal regimes can be aware of the fact that their activities are of a criminal nature; the Nazis, it should be noted, chose to carry out their murderous project in places far removed from the major population centers, reinforced by an added effort to destroy as much evidence as possible of the Holocaust prior to being overrun by the advancing Allied forces.

Put together, these three aspects of what the concentration camp represented—full mobilization of a state's resources for genocidal killing, the creation of a focus for the killings, and the secretive nature of the killing—all added up to a new appreciation of genocide that had not been present before. Any assessment must consider the Holocaust as genocide's most extreme limit, what Yehuda Bauer has referred to as the final point on a continuum that runs "from mass brutalization through Genocide to Holocaust."[64] The Nazi concentration camps were the purpose-built *locus in quo* wherein the major genocidal events of the Holocaust were played out, and for this reason alone they deserve our careful study: in so many ways, they were the very essence of what defined the Holocaust as the ultimate expression of the crime of crimes.

Notes

1. The opening epigraph is from Fania Fénelon, *The Musicians of Auschwitz* (London: Sphere Books, 1979), 97–98.
2. Hans Mommsen, "The Realization of the Unthinkable: The 'Final Solution of the Jewish Question' in the Third Reich," in *The Policies of Genocide: Jews and Soviet Prisoners of War in Nazi Germany*, ed. Gerhard Hirschfeld (London: Allen and Unwin, 1986), 129.
3. Several excellent studies of the euthanasia program have been undertaken: see, for example, Gotz Aly, Peter Chroust, and Christian Pross, *Cleansing the Fatherland: Nazi Medicine and Racial Hygiene* (Baltimore: Johns Hopkins University Press, 1994); Robert J. Lifton, *The Nazi Doctors: Medical Killing and the Psychology of Genocide* (New York: Basic Books, 1986); Robert Proctor, *Racial Hygiene: Medicine Under the Nazis* (Cambridge: Harvard University Press, 1988); and Michael Burleigh, *Death and Deliverance: "Euthanasia" in Germany, 1900–1945* (Cambridge: Cambridge University Press, 1994). An account of one of the Nazi participants in the euthanasia program who went on to employ his knowledge in the killing of Jews can be found in Gitta Sereny, *Into that Darkness: An Examination of Conscience* (London: Andre Deutsch, 1974), pt. 1. An interesting study showing how the links between the two types of murder campaigns were established is James M. Glass, *"Life Unworthy of Life": Racial Phobia and Mass Murder in Hitler's Germany* (New York: Basic Books, 1997).
4. Zev Garber, *Shoah, The Paradigmatic Genocide: Essays in Exegesis and Eisegesis* (Lanham, Md.: University Press of America, 1994).
5. David Rousset, *A World Apart* (London: Secker and Warburg, 1951), 64–65.
6. Alan S. Rosenbaum ed., *Is the Holocaust Unique? Perspectives on Comparative Genocide* (Boulder, Colo.: Westview Press, 1996).
7. See especially Steven T. Katz, *The Holocaust in Historical Consciousness*, vol. 1, *The Holocaust and Mass Death Before the Modern Age* (New York: Oxford University Press, 1994), 1–10.
8. David E. Stannard, letter to the editor, *Chronicle of Higher Education*, July 19, 1996, B3.
9. George M. Kren and Leon H. Rappoport, comment, in "Was the Holocaust Predictable?" (a symposium), *Midstream* 30, no 4 (April 1984): 9. See also their book *The Holocaust and the Crisis of Human Behavior* (New York: Holmes and Meier, 1994).
10. This term was first introduced in a television documentary about the Armenian Genocide from 1992, *The Hidden Holocaust* (produced and directed by Michael Jones: a Panoptic Production for Channel 4).

11. In an otherwise huge literature, the following range of accounts may be seen as useful starting points: Hermann Graml, *Antisemitism in the Third Reich* (Oxford: Blackwell, 1992); John Weiss, *Ideology of Death: Why the Holocaust Happened in Germany* (Chicago: Ivan R. Dee, 1996); Sarah Gordon, *Hitler, Germans and the "Jewish Question"* (Princeton, N.J.: Princeton University Press, 1984); Omer Bartov, *Murder in Our Midst: The Holocaust, Industrial Killing, and Representation* (New York: Oxford University Press, 1996, esp. chap. 3, "Antisemitism, the Holocaust, and Reinterpretations of National Socialism"; Daniel Jonah Goldhagen, *Hitler's Willing Executioners: Ordinary Germans and the Holocaust* (New York: Random House, 1996); Walter Zvi Bachrach, "Antisemitism and Racism in Nazi Ideology," in *The Holocaust and History: The Known, the Unknown, the Disputed, and the Reexamined,* ed. Michael Berenbaum and Abraham J. Peck (Bloomington: Indiana University Press, 1998), 64–74; and Raul Hilberg, "The Destruction of the European Jews: Precedents," in *The Holocaust: Origins, Implementation, Aftermath,* ed. Omer Bartov (London: Routledge, 2000), 21–42. Several of these works have extensive bibliographies that can serve as guides to further reading for those interested in pursuing the matter further.
12. Yehuda Bauer, *A History of the Holocaust* (New York: Franklin Watts, 1982), 89.
13. Richard L. Rubenstein, *The Age of Triage: Fear and Hope in an Overcrowded World* (Boston: Beacon Press, 1983), 128.
14. Martin Broszat, "The Concentration Camps, 1933–45," in Helmut Krausnick, Hans Buchheim, Martin Broszat, and Hans-Adolf Jacobsen, *Anatomy of the SS State* (London: Collins, 1968), 403. On the Reichstag fire and its aftermath, see Fritz Tobias, *The Reichstag Fire: Legend and Truth* (London: Secker and Warburg, 1963).
15. Ibid., 404–5.
16. Ibid., 405.
17. Ibid., 416.
18. Ibid., 417 (emphasis in text).
19. Ibid.
20. Wolfgang Sofsky, *The Order of Terror: The Concentration Camp* (Princeton, N.J.: Princeton University Press, 1997), 32.
21. Konnilyn G. Feig, *Hitler's Death Camps: The Sanity of Madness* (New York: Holmes and Meier, 1979), 52–53.
22. Ibid., 53.
23. Sofsky, *The Order of Terror*, 32.
24. A collection of the most important documents concerning the Nuremberg Laws can be found in Yitzhak Arad, Yisrael Gutman, and Abraham Margaliot, eds., *Documents on the Holocaust: Selected Sources on the Destruction of the Jews of Germany and Austria, Poland, and the Soviet Union* (Jerusalem: Yad Vashem, 1981), 77–88.
25. Abraham J. Edelheit and Hershel Edelheit, *History of the Holocaust: A Handbook and Dictionary* (Boulder, Colo.: Westview Press, 1994), 296.
26. On Grynszpan himself, see Michael R. Marrus, "The Strange Story of Herschel Grynszpan," *American Scholar* 57, no. 1 (Winter 1987–88): 69–79.
27. Gerald Schwab, *The Day the Holocaust Began: The Odyssey of Herschel Grynszpan* (New York: Praeger, 1990).
28. Broszat, "The Concentration Camps," 469.
29. Henry Friedlander has written that "the unusual title Kapo, meaning head, was probably introduced into Dachau by Italian workers employed in Bavaria for road construction." See Henry Friedlander, "The Nazi Concentration Camps," in *Human Responses to the Holocaust: Perpetrators and Victims, Bystanders and Resisters,* ed. Michael D. Ryan (New York: Edwin Mellen Press, 1981), 36.
30. Eric Joseph Epstein and Philip Rosen, *Dictionary of the Holocaust: Biography, Geography, and Terminology* (Westport, Conn.: Greenwood Press, 1997), 154.
31. Sofsky, *The Order of Terror*, 19.
32. Ibid., 67.
33. Ibid., 26.
34. I discuss a number of these ways of coping in my book *Surviving the Camps: Unity in Adversity during the Holocaust* (Lanham, Md.: University Press of America, 2000). Several other authors have also addressed the relationship between camp survival and the Nazi form of administration; foremost among such works is Terrence Des Pres's now-classic study *The Survivor: An Anatomy of Life in the Death Camps* (New York: Oxford University Press, 1976).

35. Jozef Garlinski, *Fighting Auschwitz: The Resistance Movement in the Concentration Camp* (London: Julian Friedmann, 1975), 13–14.
36. Broszat, "The Concentration Camps," 474.
37. Deborah Dwork and Robert Jan van Pelt, *Auschwitz, 1270 to the Present* (New York: Norton, 1996), 12.
38. Ibid., 11.
39. Rudolf Hoess, *Commandant of Auschwitz: The Autobiography of Rudolf Hoess* (London: Pan Books, 1961), 116.
40. Dwork and van Pelt, *Auschwitz*, 173–74.
41. Ibid., 174.
42. Yisrael Gutman, "Auschwitz—An Overview," in *Anatomy of the Auschwitz Death Camp*, ed. Yisrael Gutman and Michael Berenbaum (Bloomington: Indiana University Press, 1998), 16.
43. Broszat, "The Concentration Camps," 474. Auschwitz was ultimately expanded to the point where it was split into three administrative sections, respectively called Auschwitz I, II, and III, or Auschwitz *Stammlager* (main camp), Birkenau, and Monowitz. Some of the subcamps that fell within the Auschwitz complex, and their functions, were: Janina, Jaworzno, Jawizowitz, Myslowitz, Sosnowitz, Scweintochlowitz, Fuerstengrube, Guentersgrube, Eintrachtshaette, and Heidebreck (mines); Gleiwitz, Bobrek, Althammer, Blechhammer, and Bunawerke (factory centers); Gollischau and Trzebinia (quarries); and Babitz, Budy, Harmenze, and Raisko (agricultural establishments).
44. Czeslaw Madajczyk, "Concentration Camps as a Tool of Oppression in Nazi-Occupied Europe," in *The Nazi Concentration Camps: Structure and Aims, The Image of the Prisoner, The Jews in the Camps,* ed. Yisrael Gutman and Avital Saf, Proceedings of the Fourth Yad Vashem International Historical Conference, Jerusalem, January 1980 (Jerusalem: Yad Vashem, 1984), 47–68.
45. Edelheit and Edelheit, *History of the Holocaust*, 66.
46. Ibid., 66–67. The Edelheits have been meticulous in their research, identifying the names, opening and closing dates, and number of inmates of all the major subcamps of Auschwitz, Buchenwald, Dachau, Dora, Flossenbürg, Gross-Rosen, Kaiserwald, Kovno, Płaszow, Majdanek, Mauthausen, Natweiler-Struthof, Neuengamme, Ravensbrück, Sachsenhausen, Stutthof, and Vaivara. See ibid., 275–88.
47. Ibid., 67.
48. For an insight into the extent of I.G. Farben's complicity in the Holocaust, see Joseph Borkin, *The Crime and Punishment of I.G. Farben* (London: Andre Deutsch, 1979).
49. For a fuller treatment of the concept and administration of SS policy toward the camps as centers of labor, see Broszat, "The Concentration Camps," 483–94.
50. Ibid., 484.
51. Ibid.
52. See also the arguments offered in Christopher R. Browning, *Nazi Policy, Jewish Workers, German Killers* (Cambridge: Cambridge University Press, 2000).
53. An excellent study of Nazi policies of Jewish slave labor can be found in Benjamin B. Ferencz, *Less Than Slaves: Jewish Forced Labor and the Quest for Compensation* (Cambridge: Harvard University Press, 1979).
54. The extermination of the Jews of Hungary has been chronicled extensively, most notably by Randolph L. Braham. See his *The Politics of Genocide: The Holocaust in Hungary* (New York: Columbia University Press, 1981); Randolph L. Braham and Bela Vago, eds., *The Holocaust in Hungary: Forty Years Later* (New York: Columbia University Press, 1985); David Cesarani ed., *Genocide and Rescue: The Holocaust in Hungary 1944* (Oxford: Berg, 1997); and Vera Ranki, *The Politics of Inclusion and Exclusion: Jews and Nationalism in Hungary* (Sydney: Allen and Unwin, 1999).
55. For an attempt at synthesizing the death march experience from the recollections of a number of survivors, see Bartrop, *Surviving the Camps*, 135–40.
56. Jon Bridgman, *The End of the Holocaust: The Liberation of the Camps* (Portland, Ore.: Areopagitica Press, 1990), 9.
57. Eberhard Kolb, "Bergen-Belsen, 1943–1945," in *The Nazi Concentration Camps*, ed. Gutman and Saf, 331.
58. Edelheit and Edelheit, *History of the Holocaust*, 275; Feig, *Hitler's Death Camps*, 373.
59. Feig, *Hitler's Death Camps*, 373–74.
60. The liberation of Dachau, the first of the concentration camps, has been well captured by Michael Selzer, *Deliverance Day: The Last Hours at Dachau* (London: Sphere Books, 1978).
61. Three examples within the literature—other than Bridgman's fine study—stand out. For the British at Belsen, see Leslie H. Hardman with Cecily Goodman, *The Survivors: The Story of the Belsen Remnant* (London: Vallentine, Mitchell, 1958); and Ben Shephard, *After Daybreak: The Liberation of Belsen, 1945* (London:

Jonathan Cape, 2005). For the Americans, see Robert H. Abzug, *Inside the Vicious Heart: Americans and the Liberation of the Nazi Camps* (New York: Oxford University Press, 1985).

62. On the so-called Displaced Persons, and the camps that housed them, see Jacqueline Giere, "We're on Our Way, but We're Not in the Wilderness," in *The Holocaust and History*, ed. Berenbaum and Peck, 699–715.
63. Edelheit and Edelheit, *History of the Holocaust*, 224. For accounts of how the *Einsatzgrüppen* operated at the local level, see Martin Gilbert, *The Holocaust: The Jewish Tragedy* (London: William Collins, 1986), 154–212. The experience of a single German killing unit has been carefully reconstructed in Christopher R. Browning, *Ordinary Men: Reserve Police Battalion 101 and the Final Solution in Poland* (New York: HarperCollins, 1992).
64. Bauer, *A History of the Holocaust*, 332.

Soft-core Holocaust Denial

Trivialization and Sanitization in the Early Twenty-first Century

Michael Berenbaum

I am pleased to join this volume in honor of Zev Garber's work, which has earned him the respect of colleagues, and pleased more to honor Zev Garber the scholar, the teacher, and the man for the rather unique way in which he embodies his scholarship in his being. To have reached a milestone age of life is a tribute not only to longevity, but productivity, and creativity, and, most significantly in Zev's case, decency.

* * *

Few scholars have done more to sensitize us of the meaning of language related to the Shoah than Zev Garber. Thus, in his honor, I would like to examine the language used to describe the Shoah and what one might term "soft-core denial" implicit in the use of such language.

Much attention has been paid in recent years to Holocaust denial, to those who have claimed that the Holocaust never happened. If truth be told, they are an annoyance and not quite a danger. The *Irving v. Lipstadt* trial in London dealt a significant blow to Holocaust denial as the most effective and the most informed of Holocaust deniers was exposed for what he is: a racist, antisemite, and serial fabricator, falsifying evidence and quotes in an attempt to exonerate Adolf Hitler and to restore his "good name." The case against him (according to English libel law, it was incumbent upon the defendant to prove the points that she had made against the plaintiff) was made not by survivors' testimony but by scholars, not by eyewitnesses but by historians who read original documents and traced footnotes to their sources. The unglamorous work of the younger, post-Holocaust generation compellingly demonstrated how the historicity of the Holocaust can be documented.

The recent flurry of attention surrounding the Holocaust denial of Iranian president Mahmoud Ahmadinejad only underscores my point. His denial of the Holocaust, even if popular among extremists within the Islamic world, has diminished his effectiveness as president of the Islamic Republic and has made his reception in the West and his ability to be taken seriously within the West ever more difficult. His denial of the Holocaust set the context for Columbia University students to roll their eyes and nervously laugh when he denied the existence of homosexuals within his country as if they were saying how much more reality does he want to deny.

Robert Kahn, author of *Holocaust Denial and the Law* and a professor at St. Thomas University in Minnesota, has long suggested that we differentiate Holocaust denial within the West from Holocaust denial within Islam; the former seeks to deny the deed, to exonerate Hitler, and restore the reputation of fascism, while the latter seeks to undo the consequence of the Holocaust—the existence of the State of Israel. In the clumsy rhetoric of Islamic denial is an ineffective and counterproductive way of raising the post-Holocaust question of the uses of Holocaust memory. Were that debate actually joined, Ahmadinejad and his ilk would find far more resonance within the West.

Deborah Lipstadt's 1993 work *Denying the Holocaust* was subtitled *The Growing Assault on Truth and Memory*, which is perhaps the only false note in the book as thanks to David Irving's irresistible wish for attention and his misjudgment as to the fierce response of Lipstadt and her team, it may be more accurate to speak of the *Diminished or Defanged Assault on Memory and Truth*.

But if the larger issue of denial is less problematic than previously feared (please notice the phrasing: I am not claiming that it is not problematic, merely that it is *less* problematic than feared), there is a soft-core form of denial that is gaining currency as we struggle to absorb—and in some sense to tame—the Holocaust into our consciousness. Expressed in language, it manifests itself in ways that are large and small.

Permit me to introduce—as appropriate in Zev Garber's honor—a theological concept. In describing God's overwhelming revelation and how it could be absorbed by humanity, the Midrash employs the term "*himtik lahem hadibur,*" the word—the revelation of God, the very word spoken by God, was sweetened, softened so it could be heard. I think that we often sweeten the reality of the Shoah so that it can be approached, but such sweetening imperils its very truth.

Tragedy/Atrocity

The Holocaust is routinely described as a great tragedy that befell the Jewish people, a Jewish tragedy, or for those who want to universalize it, a human tragedy. Yet as Lawrence Langer has shown, tragedy implies the Holocaust is more properly and more accurately described as an atrocity.

> History assures us that man is superior to time when retrospectively he can explain the unexpected, account, in this instance, for the extermination of a people, uncover a system for surviving and thus reduce the event to a partial intellectual order that somehow theoretically balances the price paid in human lives for that order. But from the perspective of the victims, who of course far outnumbered the survivor, the disorder of meaningless death contradicts the ordering impulses of time. Those who died for nothing during the Holocaust left with living with a paralyzing dilemma or facing a perpetually present grief. To the puzzled inquiry why interest in the Holocaust seems to grow as the event recedes into the past, one answer may be that there is no inner space or time to bury it in.[1]

The difference is not a matter of semantics, certainly not a matter of words; it goes to the root of our perception of the event, to our sense of what happened and what can be done with the memory of what happened. Tragedy implies that what we learned roughly balances the price that is paid for such knowledge and that somehow what occurred is appropriate to the victim. Atrocity permits no such balance. It forces one to confront the void, the abyss, the chaos that preceded creation.

German/Nazi

Scholars and filmmakers, writers and students, Germans, Israelis, and Americans often use the word *German* and *Nazi* interchangeably when writing of the period of World War II as if there was no difference between the two. Thus, one can find many references to "the Nazi army" and "Nazi occupation," to "Nazi laws," and "Nazi policies." Such a description of the institutions and the policies that were employed does not differentiate between those institutions that were part of the State, done in the name of the German people, and that which was done by the Nazi Party or undertaken in service to its ideological mission. Such nondifferentiation between *Nazi* and *German* has been used by those within Germany who wanted to shield the State and the German people from responsibility for what happened between 1933 and 1945 or to minimize those activities as the acts of the few driven by ideological passion and racist and/or antisemitic fury—the good German army versus the SS extremists.

Such lack of distinction is evident in many who intend to label everything German as Nazi. They go to the opposite extreme, sometimes carelessly or haphazardly, but also often with malice of forethought.

Over the past several years I have endeavored to establish a simple rule that permits a consistent—or near consistent—and precise use to the terms *Nazi* and *German:* That which was done by the State and the institutions of the State was German; that undertaken by the National Socialist Party or its driving ideology is Nazi.

Applying this rule consistently entails writing of the German army, German occupation, German laws, German courts, German judges, German officials, German government, German invasion, German allies, and German puppet states. It also entails noting that there were Nazi death camps and Nazi racist ideology and the Nazi genocidal program.

Naturally there are border cases where the State and its institutions undertook acts spurred by the party and most especially in fulfillment of its ideology, but as a working principle it helps to minimize the attempts to rid the State and its institutions, as well as the German people, for the policies undertaken by their government and in their name. It is also useful and, above all, most accurate to remember that certain countries—especially Poland, in which the major deaths camps were situated—were German-occupied or annexed. Thus I always refer to the Nazi death camp of Birkenau in German-occupied Poland.

Perished, Killed, Died, Murdered, Exterminated

While it is technically correct to say that Jews perished in Auschwitz or Treblinka, it rids the occurrence of its true horror. *Perished* is too clean a term, too soft a term, too normal a term.

Jews were *murdered* at Auschwitz and most certainly at Treblinka and Belzec. At Belzec there were but two known survivors; so unless one is writing of two very specific men, one must write that inmates were *murdered* at Belzec. With fewer than 100 known survivors among the 700,000–870,000 Jews who were sent to Treblinka, one is also on safe ground writing that Jews were *murdered* at Treblinka. Because there were many more survivors of Auschwitz and many more ways of dying than gassing alone—for example, starvation, disease, malnutrition, despair—one may properly hesitate but not anguish over the word *murdered* because the conditions established in the camp were clearly not conducive to sustaining life. Elsewhere, in nondeath camps, one may properly write that prisoners died there, but within death camps themselves, unless other information is available, one cannot appropriately use the term *died* without in one sense falsifying the conditions under which their lives came to an end.

There is a difference in use between the words *murdered* and *killed*. The Sixth Commandment in Judaism is "Thou shall not *murder*," though translators routinely translate the word *tirzach* as "killing"; but not every killing is a murder and not every killing is inappropriate and certainly not every killing violates the biblical injunction against murder.

I am equally hesitant to use the word *exterminate* not because it sweetens or diminishes its horror but because it is a Nazi term designed to dehumanize the Jews, to treat them as vermin and to regard their murder as of little consequence. When using the word a writer must ask whether indeed he or she is referring to the victims as insignificant or only to the sense that the killers had of their own sense of the deed. If it is the former, then the use of the term is inappropriate; only in the latter case can the word be used without trivializing the act of murder.

Righteous of the Nations of the Earth/Rescuer

Yad Vashem—and through Yad Vashem the Jewish people—give honor to those non-Jews who at risk to their own lives saved Jews during the Shoah without receiving monetary reward. Their criteria are specific, exacting, and the process judicial. Jews who saved Jews are not honored. Those who received compensation, whether direct monetary payments or property and valuables, are not honored. Eric Saul, who has created the Visa for Life exhibition depicting the role of diplomats in saving Jews, who has pushed for the honoring of diplomats, has time and again been informed that because they were operating with diplomatic immunity, they cannot be honored as their lives were not in danger. There were exceptions, such as Raoul Wallenberg, whose deeds of rescue almost cost him his life by "accident"—one dutifully arranged by German officials, reputedly Adolf Eichmann—and who paid with his freedom as he ended up in a Soviet gulag, where by now we can presumably say he died even if he was not murdered.

One need not quarrel with the specificity of the requirement but one wonders about the exaltedness of the title "Righteous Among the Nations of the Earth" as it so elevates the deed of rescue beyond the aspirations of ordinary men and women, who behaved with ordinary decency and kindness even under the most extraordinary of circumstances. Having listened to the testimony of many rescuers, one notices a use of language.

"Naturally, I said come in."[2]

"I am a human being, I could not do otherwise."

"They were people, friends, neighbors, desperate."[3]

In 1979 I was party to a delegation of the President's Commission on the Holocaust, which traveled to the sites of destruction in Poland and the then–Soviet Union and proceeded to Denmark to honor the Danes for their rescue of the Jews. In what I at first perceived as a bit of false modesty, they protested the honor. "We didn't do anything special. We merely treated the Jews the way one treats one's neighbors when a hostile occupying power comes to murder them." In fact, that is what they did. Their moral accomplishment was best expressed in the statement, "We don't have a Jewish problem in Denmark." The Jews were fellow citizens, not outcasts. They were part of the social fabric and the bonds of society, not outcasts, and therefore they were routinely—and seemingly effortlessly—rescued.

Elsewhere I have argued that the good during the Shoah was banal, ordinary, at least from the perspective of those who behaved appropriately.[4] Elsewhere, in genocidal events other than the Shoah, we notice a similar use of language. If we exalt the decent, the moral, the appropriate, and the humane, beyond recognition, we again falsify. We also make deeds of rescue seem out of the reach of ordinary men and women, with human foibles and human inadequacies, men and women just like you and me. Thus, with all due respect, the mystification of the title given to the honor reflects *our* needs and distorts the depiction of the actual act of rescue.

Permit me one word of clarity and also one of self-protection. In the field of Holocaust Studies the word *banality* is routinely associated with Hannah Arendt's use of the term in her 1963 book *Eichmann in Jerusalem: A Report on the Banality of Evil.* Arendt's controversial work would have been far less controversial had she subtitled it more accurately and more precisely *A Report on the Banality of the Evildoer.* The evil perpetrated by the killers was far from banal. It was on an unprecedented scale using all the instrumentalities of a technologically advanced, highly sophisticated, industrial society. Those who perpetrated the event were banal, ordinary, and in many cases undistinguished. But the sum total of banal plus banal plus banal was far from banal, it was monstrous and demonic, evil on a massive scale.

The same may be said of the good. Those who rescued Jews were ordinary men and women—banal in the precise use of the term—but the sum total of their ordinary deeds was noble, given the circumstances under which it was done.

Survivors/Victims/Heroes

No one who has worked in Holocaust education will ever minimize the encounter between survivors and students in the contemporary classroom. We are all aware—painfully aware—that we are the last generation to live in the presence of survivors. After they are gone, the Holocaust will no longer be living memory but historical memory. And we do not yet understand what will be lost. We are consoled that no generation has left a more complete historical record of diaries, memoirs, and, of course, video testimony that will allow students of future generations to continue to encounter those who were there and to learn from their experience. Fortunate are we that such technology was invented and accessible in time to capture the memories of this generation. By contrast, there are only thirty-six oral-history tape interviews with African Americans who grew up as slaves.

Yet the encounter with the survivors in some way falsifies the event, for the most powerful impression made upon the students is of survival, while the reality is that the overwhelming number of those who lived in the ghettos and entered the camps did not survive. Survivors are not merely survivors, they were victims as well and often victims who felt compromised by the very fact of their survival. Thus, while students see in such survival an image of resilience and the ability to overcome even the worst imaginable of circumstances, the very presence of survivors overwhelms and thus obscures the much larger story of those who did not emerge from the camps. Also, the survivors who come into the classroom are often the "winners" of the historical drama. They have transformed their victimization into an act of witness that morally sanctifies their presence. For every survivor the students encounter, there are others, perhaps much more numerous, who have never overcome their experiences, and for whom defeat and destruction did indeed become the final word.

Permit me to clarify this point once again with some precision: I do not want to minimize the achievements of Holocaust survivors. Holocaust survivors, who were a small minority of the victims—many more were murdered than survived—were faced with the question of what to do with the accident of their survival, "Why did I survive?" Over time they found the answer: It was how they lived their lives in the aftermath—it was how they bore witness and transmitted the legacy.

Because they have faced death, many learned what is most important in life: Life itself, love, family, and community, and they found value even in what Holocaust survivor Gerda Klein called in her acceptance speech at the Academy Awards in 1996 and in a book by that very title "a boring evening at home." They teach us that the small things, the simple things we take for granted, cannot be taken for granted and must be treasured and appreciated anew.

The Holocaust survivors responded to survival in the most Jewish way possible: by remembering evil and suffering to deepen conscience, by enlarging memory and broadening responsibility. It is thus that Jews responded to the Exodus. It is also that its survivors responded to the Shoah.

But still, that is the legacy of the survivors who have spoken, of those who have transformed and been transformed in the act of bearing witness and they represent wonderful qualities for our students, qualities that all too often obscure large dimensions of the story.

Holocaust Revisited—Ever Again, Again, and Again

I have a deeply uncomfortable feeling that Jews, committed and serious Jews concerned with the survival of the Jewish people, are increasingly responsible for trivializing the Holocaust by using it as a rhetorical political tool with little regard to its appropriateness or the consequences of its misuse. Tom Tugend quoted me in the Los Angeles *Jewish Journal* as criticizing the title—not the content—of a recent film entitled *Ever Again*, which clearly meant to evoke the post-Holocaust commitment of "Never Again."[5] By its title, far more than its content, it sought to convey that antisemitism today somehow is analogous to what was experienced between 1933 and 1945.

The vulnerability of the 1930s cannot be compared with contemporary Jewish vulnerability.

It was different!

And we are different.

The Holocaust was unique. Not every Jewish vulnerability is the vulnerability of the Holocaust and not every enemy is Adolf Hitler. As Leon Wieseltier wrote, "Hitler is dead."[6] Hitler ruled most of Europe and before his death Arafat could not travel more than 150 yards from his battered headquarters.

Comparing the contemporary situation to the 1930s is to cede to our enemies a power they do not have, an intent they may not share, and to disparage the great achievement of the Zionist revolution that the Jews become actors in history rather than its passive victims. It is to invite upon ourselves not only nightmare of our own times, but the absolute darkness of another time and another place that is not our own and bears no resemblance to our own. Those who do so manifest considerable ignorance of those times and misinterpret our own.

I neither wish to condone or to minimize contemporary antisemitism nor to presume for a moment that Jews are not vulnerable today. To state that something is not the Holocaust, that a second Holocaust is not pending, is merely to restate the obvious, not to prescribe complacency.

The Borders of Auschwitz/Arafat, Nasrallah, Ahmadinejad, the New Hitlers

For three generations, we falsely compared the Holocaust with Israel's wars of survival.

In *After Tragedy and Triumph*, published in 1990 I argued that Abba Eban and Benjamin Netanyahu, two men of rather different political views, had both argued that a "withdrawal to the borders of 1967 was a withdrawal to the borders of Auschwitz." What should have disturbed their Jewish audiences was that these distinguished men—Jewish leaders both charged with governmental responsibilities—had both significantly misrepresented the situation of Jews in Auschwitz and the power of the contemporary Israel state. The charge was repeated as recently at December 7, 2007, in a *Washington Times* op-ed by Louis Rene, the well-meaning director of the Daniel Project, who presumably does not want to deny or trivialize the Holocaust. Still his comparison does both; it is nothing short of odious. It also denies the great achievements of Zionism and the State of Israel. Jews had no troops, no armies, no tanks, and no planes within the vicinity of Auschwitz; they had precious little to defend themselves, except perhaps their willingness to die. Not all dangers facing the Jewish people—and I do not quarrel that the Jewish people face dangers—are the dangers of Auschwitz and not all enemies are capable of—even were they to desire to do so—systematic state-sponsored murder while dominating the fate of nine million Jews.

That leads us to the second generation's trivialization: a few years ago we heard comparisons between Hitler and Arafat; Hitler, who had a dominant army and who controlled more than a score of European countries and Arafat, who whatever his intentions—and I do not deny that he intended the Jews no good and would have destroyed Israel if it were within his grasp—could not move beyond his compounds. Similar rhetorical invocations of the Holocaust were used to compare Hizbollah's leader Sheikh Hassan Nasrallah to Hitler, and, more recently, Iran's Holocaust-denying President Mahmoud Ahmadinejad to Hitler. The Jewish people have known enemies in the past from Pharaoh to Haman and will know enemies in the future. It seems like rhetorical overkill to invoke Hitler's name in every instance. The comparisons have been offered by people who should know better; Israeli generals, American Jewish institutional leaders, congressmen, and senators.

Please note that I wrote these words before the National Intelligence Estimate of December 2007, which cast doubt on Iran's pursuit of nuclear weapons: I think it is clear that Iran is in much greater danger of an attack by Israel on its nuclear facilities before they become operational—if such an attack is potentially effective—then it is of an Iranian nuclear attack on Israel and the United States. Iran does not yet have the bomb, and were it to God forbid build the bomb, it would need a means of delivery and the willingness to face sure and certain retaliation that would devastate its own population. Surely, if the Holocaust is unique—"unprecedented" to use Yehuda Bauer's term—Hitler deserves his own distinct niche among the enemies of the Jewish people and the evil men in history.

We have all received solicitations for organizations fighting antisemitism who invoke this parallel between our age and the 1930s as if our age did not have dangers uniquely its own.

I write this contribution but a week after the Annapolis conference of November/December 2007 brought together the leaders of Israel and the Palestinian Authority with many Arab leaders and members of the international community to discuss peace. I received the following announcement by e-mail from the Children of Holocaust Survivors, who should know better:

> Annapolis: A *Naqba* (catastrophe) of our very own?
>
> *In 1938, the world was silent while 6,000,000 Jews were systematically brutally murdered.* More than 20,000,000 men, women, handicapped, aged, sick, prisoners of war, forced laborers, camp inmates, critics, homosexuals, Slavs, Serbs, Germans, Czechs, Italians, Poles, French, Ukrainians, and many others were murdered along with the Jews. Among them 1,000,000 were children under eighteen years of age.
>
> Hitler told Himmler that it was not enough for the Jews simply to die; they must die in agony.
> —Robert Payne, *The Life and Death of Adolf Hitler*

(Incidentally anyone who knows the Holocaust knows that the systematic killing of Jews did not begin until 1941, but that is merely trivial.) Therefore, they argued that urgent calls should be placed to the White House, the Congress, and local senators and representatives to forestall this doom. Aside from borrowing the history of the Palestinians who call into question the very foundation of the State of Israel and observe May 15 as the anniversary of the Naqba, we see such fierce opposition to the possibility, however remote, of the peace process or the silence of the world to the genocidal endangerment of the Jews. It is both rhetorical overkill and soft-core denial of the Holocaust. The message it sends to our children and to ourselves is just plain horrific. Were this the only instance of such language and such expectations, it would be unworthy of comment, but given what I and many readers have received on the Internet, it is essential to comment. Even the most serious of students of the Holocaust, those who defend its distinctness and its importance in the consciousness of the Jewish people and in the very identity of the individual Jew can inadvertently feed the soft-core denial of the Holocaust.

Thane Rosenbaum has written brilliantly, convincingly, and seriously on the Holocaust. Yet in a recent *New York Times* op-ed, the paper read by more Jews than any other in the United States, on Holocaust survivors and the issue of restitution, he wrote:

> After 60 years, Holocaust survivors are inching toward extinction. According to Ira Sheskin, director of the Jewish Demography Project at the University of Miami, fewer than 900,000 remain, residing primarily in the United States, Israel and the former Soviet Union.[7]

It is generally accepted that there were nine million Jews in Europe in the countries invaded by Germany or allied with Germany; approximately two of three were murdered. Even if we low-ball the figure and rely upon the important work of Raul Hilberg, who writes of 5.1 million killed, then five of nine were murdered. Thus, 3–3.9 million Jews who lived in countries where the Holocaust occurred, were somewhere in the world in 1945 in these countries when the Nazis came to power. Sixty-three years later, if we measure from liberation, or seventy-five years later, if we begin our count in 1933 when Hitler came to power, the survival ratio could not be 25–30 percent. Clearly Rosenbaum, whom I respect, does not deny the Holocaust, would not want to deny the Holocaust, but a misplaced quote in an influential newspaper can be cited to aid those who would.

To avoid soft-core denial, we must relearn the lessons that Zev Garber has taught us well. Our language must be precise, disciplined, and accurate, our rhetoric measured and considered, and our use of historical material critical and exact.

Notes

1. Lawrence Langer, *Versions of Survivor: The Holocaust and the Human Spirit* (Albany: State University of New York Press, 1982), 79.
2. This was the language used by Magda Trochme in Le Chambon. See Philip Hallie, *Lest Innocent Blood Be Shed: The Story of the Village of Le Chambon and How Goodness Happened There* (New York: Harper and Row, 1979). See also Pierre Sauvage's film, *Weapons of the Spirit* (Pierre Sauvage Productions and Friends of Le Chambon, 1989).
3. These two phrases come from an interview within a film *Desperate Hours* on Turkey and the Holocaust—Main Street Productions in association with the Berenbaum Group, LLC and Shenandoah Films, 2001.
4. Michael Berenbaum, "The Mystifying Burden of Goodness," *Dimensions* (Fall 1990).
5. *Ever Again* (Moriah Films, 2007).
6. *The New Republic* (May 16, 2002).
7. "Losing Count," Opinion section, *New York Times*, June 14, 2007.

The Scroll of the Shoah

The Case for the Writings of Yitzhak Katzenelson as the Basis of a Future Jewish Post-Shoah Jewish Theology

Samuel M. Edelman

This essay is written with Zev Garber in the forefront of my mind. He has always been a whirlwind of energy and activity. For the amount of teaching he does, his level of scholarly productivity is mind-boggling. Not only that, but Zev has been the mentor of many younger scholars. He inspires, he encourages, and he finds ways to get their work published. In short, Zev is an inspiration for scholarly achievement and passion. In the area of interfaith dialogue, Zev has been a pioneer with the Scholars Conference on the Holocaust and the Churches Post-Shoah Midrash Reading Group. In this, he and his colleagues Hank Knight, Steve Jacobs, and Jim Moore, all represented in this book, have done critically important work. Zev Garber is following a tradition that is now strong and healthy after more than sixty years after the liberation of the camps and the ending of the Shoah. There has been an extensive effort on the part of Catholics, Protestants, and Jews to come to grips with the impact of the Shoah on theology. Unfortunately, within Judaism itself the discussion of the impact of the Shoah on Jewish theology has, at best, been muted. This contribution will explore the history of this discussion and review some of the major thinkers from the Jewish community including Greenberg, Rubenstein, Garber, and others. The writing of Yitzhak Katzenelson will also be explored to discuss the impact of the voices of the victims themselves in the discussion on what Judaism should be in the light of the Shoah.

Memoria is one of the five canons of rhetoric discussed by classical rhetors from Aristotle to Cicero to modern rhetorical scholars. In many ways, the definition of memoria has been degraded over the centuries in the Western Christian world to simply refer to the act of memorizing a speech or text of some sort. For post-Shoah Judaism, memoria must become a central concern. Do we want the sacred memory of the Shoah to be represented by memoirs of survivors, fictional accounts of the Shoah, statements and writings of the perpetrators? Or do we want the words of the victims themselves, written and uttered at the moment of their torment, to represent how the Shoah will be seen in Jewish memory centuries after the event?

This essay will argue the case for the use of the writings of Yitzhak Katzenelson as the basis for that future sacred text. Included in the analysis will be Katzenelson's "Woe to You," "Introduction to an Evening of Tanach," and other poetic representations of the Shoah.

This essay will also argue that we must begin now to be concerned about post-Shoah Jewish memory and its impact on post-Shoah Jewish theology. It is therefore critical that we begin to analyze the writings of the Shoah from the perspective of what they communicate about our vision of G-d and belief in a post-Shoah world.

Meyer Waxman in his monumental history of Jewish literature began by saying that "the literature of a people is very often described as the mirror of its soul. In it are reflected its strivings and desires, its expression and ideals, its failures and achievements."[1] Jewish literary responses created during the Holocaust are, finally, after fifty years, being analyzed and considered by a small group of scholars. One thing becomes clear after working with much of this literary and creative effort is that it truly offers us a "mirror" into the souls of the victims of the Holocaust. These works are so compelling, so passionate and detailed in their descriptive force, that they need to be considered by future generations of Jewish scholars as more than just something to be studied.

Waxman also noted that "whatever actions and deeds a people performed in the course of its history were prompted by the ideals and emotions expressed in its literature, while the mere records of these acts and deeds known as history."[2] For fifty years now, Holocaust scholarship has focused solely on the recording of the acts and deeds without regard for the "souls" of the people who were the victims. A result of our overwhelming concern with history alone has been the vast creation of museums and memorials to the victims of the Holocaust that represent significant public expressions of history.

It is interesting, however, that, when one looks at the long history of the Jewish people, it is not edifices, museums, and memorials that survive the eons of time, it is literature. It is significant that the Jewish people have been called for centuries "the People of the Book." It is in our literature that we as a people have had our monuments. Those literary monuments have been, as David Roskies points out, responses to catastrophes much like the catastrophe of the Holocaust.[3] In every epoch in the history of the Jewish people that there has been a severe wrenching or catastrophic upheaval, there has resulted a new body of sacred literature as a response, "mirroring" the souls of the people who lived through that period. It follows, then, that the Holocaust as the major catastrophic upheaval of the twentieth century ought to also produce a literary heritage that, over time, will be incorporated into the larger body of Jewish sacred literature. It is time that we begin to move away from the dryness of history into what Waxman calls the "passion of literature" and create a new and longer-lasting memorial to the Jewish victims of the Holocaust: a new addition to the Jewish canon, a book of the Holocaust.

It is the purpose of this essay to explore the history of Jewish literary responses to catastrophe, to describe some of the qualities of that literature that makes it sacred, and to explore a few selected pieces of poetry written during the Holocaust by the victims of the Holocaust to show their potential as candidates for future canonization.

The History of Jewish Response to Catastrophe

The sacred liturgical and canonical corpus of Judaism is almost in total based in some fashion on a response to catastrophe. Even a cursory examination of the history of the Jews can show a clear relationship between the various traumatic wrenchings suffered by the Jewish people and their creation of various bodies of literature. Even the earliest sacred writings—the Tanach (the Five Books of Moses), the Prophets, the Writings—were transformed from an oral literature to a literary form probably beginning during the reign of King Josiah of Judea somewhere between 700 and 600 BCE. This period marked the "discovery" of the Book of Deuteronomy, and it also marked the period of great mourning for the loss of the northern kingdom of Israel and the exiled Ten Tribes. The restoration of the law under King Josiah may have ushered in the period of redaction where the general corpora of literary sources at hand were beginning to be winnowed down into the final canon of biblical text.[4] That canonization process began with the exile from and destruction of Jerusalem by the Babylonians in 587, and continued through to the return under Ezra and Nehemia. It is significant that the return from Babylonian exile was under the leadership of a scribe, and this marks the clear importance of the development of a literary base for Jewish religious and cultural life of the period. We shall discuss later the qualities of a text that made it acceptable for inclusion.

The next major literary response comes in the form of the development of the Midrash, Mishnah, and Gemara or the Talmud. The development of the Talmud was a parallel development to the first exile.[5] While much of the energy of scholars of the period was in the canonization of the Tanach in around 445 BCE and the creation of a Greek translation of the Bible somewhere between 300 and 200 BCE a significant growing discussion of and interpretation of the canon was begun in around 400 BCE. This interpretive ongoing discussion became the basis of what would eventually become the Talmud. Much of the Talmud was written during the period of great Roman persecutions of Jews, the eventual destruction of the Second Temple, the exile of the Jewish population from Jerusalem, and, indeed, later from all of what the Romans would eventually call Palestine. The Jewish response to this catastrophe was the canonization of both the Palestinian and the Babylonian Talmud. The Midrashic collection took place from between 400 and 200 BCE; the Mishnah from between 200 BCE and 200 CE; the Palestinian Talmud was written between 200 CE and 400 CE and the Babylonian Talmud was written between 200 CE and 500 CE (130 years after the destruction of the Second Temple in 70 CE). This process came out of the Temple desecration by the Syrians in the Maccabean period and the destruction of the Temple by the Romans later on.

The next major response to destruction came during the period of the Crusades and their aftermath. The Jewish literary response to this period was significant as a period of interpretation and an expression of the martyrdom of the Jews. The writings of the great Rashi (1040–1105) and the work of Talmudic codification by Alfasi (1013–1103) took place during this period from 1000 to 1400. Central aspects of Ashkenazic liturgy were developed during this period including works by Solomon bar Simson, Isaac bar Shalom, Meir of Rothenberg (1215–1293), and, even somewhat later, in the works of Isaiah Halevi Horowitz (1565–1638). Each of these works added to the corpus of interpretation of Tanach, understanding of the Talmud, or to the catharsis of daily and Shabbat prayer. Following the Crusade period was the advent of the various Spanish exiles, the first of which produced the *Mishnah Torah* of the great Maimonides (1135–1204), and the last of which produced an additional wealth of literary output including some of the most important Cabalistic writings of Isaac Luria (1534–1572) and the crucial and central *Shulkan Aruch* or Codification of the Law by Joseph Karo (1488–1575). The massacres of Jews by various Cossack groups in eastern Poland and the Ukraine produced both legalistic and Hasidic responses to the trauma of the massacres in the 1700s–1800s.

The continued pogroms and outright persecution in czarist Russia may have acted as the catalyst for a burgeoning Hebrew and Yiddish literary explosion at the end of the nineteenth and the beginning of the twentieth century that included writings by modern literary luminaries such as Chaim Nachman Bialik (1873–1934) and Isaac Lamdan (1900–1955). But the most crucial wrenching and trauma were caused by that event called the Holocaust.

The Process of Canonization

Before we proceed on to our examination of Holocaust literature we must spend a brief period of time describing some of the qualities of sacredness that seemed to be the basis of the canon of Jewish sacred texts. Michael Grant, in his *History of Ancient Israel,* points out

> that "Torah" in its ancient meaning meant more than "the Law." Torah with its intersection of law, morality and religion probably was more like "instruction," especially in practical conduct, with particular emphasis on the rules of the cultic worship. But then the use of the word became extended to every conceivable form of teaching that emanated from Yahweh's direction, designed to train the people in holiness and conformity with the covenant. . . . The Torah contains doctrine and creed, regulation and ritual, history and prophecy, memory and aspiration, proverbs, riddles, legends, myths, etiologies, fables, short stories and novellas.[6]

The Christian historian-theologian James Sanders shows that those who did not assimilate into Babylonian or Persian society needed to have a body of literature they could identify as sacred so as to deal with "that experience of death and life was made possible in exile by reviewing and repeating and reciting a selected grouping of old preexilic traditions that provided the vision and conviction necessary to endure." He notes that this grouping of literature eventually became known as the Torah. Sanders suggests that, in this context, Torah meant "prophetic oracle or teaching or priestly instructions. It provided its life-giving power to those who had read and reread its traditions in that way. It was called the *sefer hayyim* (Book of Life) for that reason." Sanders's most important point is that "the move in early Judaism to the concept of a sacred text came not about because of scholarly desires to be accurate but because of the needs of the believing communities."[7]

Neusner also speaks of the qualities of the literary texts that make up the canon of the Talmud. For Neusner, doctrines in the Talmud stress the "conviction" that "Israel makes its own history, therefore shapes its own destiny. This lesson, sages maintained, derives from the very condition of Israel even then, its suffering and its despair." Neusner's point is crucial: it is not the world events that are important in the canon but the Jewish response to those events. "Israel's own deeds defined the events of history. Rome's role, like Assyria's and Babylon's, depended upon Israel's provoking divine wrath as it was executed by the great empire."[8] So the canon of sacred literature in some ways gives evidence of the choice confronting the Jewish people: acceptance of the rule of the more powerful nation confronting Israel or accepting God's rule. Israel's choice is emphasized by the canon. (All of this discussion implies an acceptance of—or at least a recognition of—God's rule.)

The Book of Job, though, offers a different perspective, even though it too is a part of the canon. It is in Job that we see a true questioning of God. We also see the question, why do good people suffer and evil people thrive? Grant points out that we are provided no answers in the Book of Job, rather we are permitted to see open conflict with God.

> Nevertheless, we are given no answers. He (Job) has been made devastatingly aware that Yaweh's way is not man's, and that he himself is not of the smallest significance. "What reply can I give you, I who carry no weight? . . . I know you can do all things and that no purpose is beyond you." . . . Yet these last words of Job's offer food for thought. After all his struggles, he has accepted the power of Yahweh responsibly, neither proud nor abased. But his capitulation is due entirely to inferior strength. He feels shame because he stood out so long against it; but he does not express any guilt or remorse. He is still a virtuous man who has suffered, apparently through no fault of his own.[9]

We are given no answers by God. We are left with only the ambiguity.

So let us recapitulate what these scholars have provided us about the qualities of sacredness that permitted these earlier works to become incorporated into the canon of sacred Jewish texts. First, the concept of instruction is important for the development of a canon. Second, it provides the community with spiritual support with which to endure the pain and hardship to come. Third, it provides the ambiguity and openness to permit conflict to take place between people and God and to permit people to make choices between good and evil even when they see evil succeed all around. Finally, canon seems to permit the development of a corporate memory that transcends time and place.

These are only a few of the possible characteristics that seem to be important in developing a canon of sacred literature. They are a beginning point. Certainly much more effort has to be placed on the criteria for sacredness, but for the moment this will suffice. Before we move on to the poetry, we must spend a brief bit of time exploring the scope of creative activity that took place during the Holocaust so as to be able to better gauge the importance of the writing that we shall examine.

A Brief Examination of the Extent of Jewish Creativity during the Holocaust

The true extent of the literary production that took place in the ghettos and concentration camps may never be known. Too much was destroyed by the Nazis, their supporters, or the ravages of time and the environment. What we do know from historical references and survivor testimony is that cultural activity took place in every major ghetto, in most smaller ghettos, and in the host of labor camps and concentration camps and even in the killing centers. Hundreds and possibly thousands of pieces of music, poetry, drama, and prose writing survive today in archives all over the world, much of it uncatalogued and untranslated. In the collections of Yad Vashem and Lohamei Haghetaot in Israel are representative pieces that cover all aspects of the cultural history of the Jews during the Holocaust. Some of the many authors who wrote during this period include Itzkah Katzenelson (1886–1944), Yeshayahu Spiegel (1906–90), Isaac Rosenfeld (1918–56), Abraham Sutzkever (b. 1913), Leah Rudnitsky (1913–43?), Shmaryahu Kaczerginski (1908–54), Hirsh Glik (1920–44), Wadyslaw Szlengel (1914–43), Simkhe-Bunem Shayevitsh (1907–44), and a host of others. Much of the writing took place in Warsaw, Vilna, Lodz, and Bialistok. The creative acts included poetry, prose literature, diaries and chronicles, theater, opera, a variety of music including folksongs and cantorial renditions, works of history and works of remembrance, as well as journalistic works in different forms.

It is out of these prodigious sources that any future liturgical or canonical additions will be made to the corpus of Jewish sacred literature. These works represent the most authentic, unchanged, unfiltered responses of the Jews suffering under Nazi rule; in this state they represent the most clear voice of the victims themselves. It is this voice, the voice of the Jews who suffered, that has greatest significance for the development of a post-Shoah canon. This is not to demean the many writers of significance who wrote after the war, writers like Wiesel (b. 1928), Nelly Sachs (1891–1970), Andre Schwartzbart (b. 1928), and others. Rather, it is our observation of the canon of Jewish sacred works that points to the seeming first-hand immediacy and knowledge in much of the prophetic canon and liturgy of events that affected the Jewish people such as the destruction of the First and Second Temples and the cruelty of Roman rule and medieval and renaissance exile. Therefore, we shall arbitrarily look at only that literature written during the Holocaust by the victims themselves in ghettos and camps. This essay will only focus, by way of example, on two poems from the works of Yitzak Katzenelson.

Selected Examples of Holocaust Literature that Ought to Be Considered for a Post-Holocaust Sacred Canon

The four criteria we discussed earlier for post-Holocaust sacred literature were memory, instruction, support for the pain and suffering, and the ability to be in conflict with God. The curse and the lament have been central aspects of a significant proportion of Jewish sacred liturgy and canon, primarily because both of these poetic and rhetorical forms have been so successful in creating memories, instructions for future generations, and ameliorating the pain and anguish suffered by the Jewish people. From the biblical curses of Moses in Deuteronomy to the jeremiad of Jeremiah and Lamentations (attributed to Jeremiah), these two forms of Jewish rhetorical tradition have made a mark. The curse gives the weak a word weapon against the strong. The curse acts rhetorically by debasing or demeaning the enemy; power or control are placed in the hands of the one doing the cursing. The lament is also a powerful rhetorical tool because its major focus is on remembrance of past events, often with the intent that one should learn from the recounting of the event. The lament is also a form of instruction. It is logical to assume that these two traditions of the curse and the lament would also reside in the body of literature written during the Holocaust.

One of the preeminent poets of the Holocaust was Yitzak Katzenelson. An already established teacher, poet, and scholar before the war, Katzenelson became, for the underground of the Warsaw Ghetto, a kind of poet laureate. He was considered so important by the underground that he and his one remaining son were smuggled out of the ghetto under his protest prior to the ghetto revolt. He was interned until almost the end of the war in the Vittel internment camp in France until the summer of 1945, when, as the Allies were within kilometers of rescuing the camp, he and his son were sent off to Auschwitz to their deaths. His poetry, plays, and diary entries are primary examples of the depth and breadth of rhetorical poetic activities in the ghettos and camps worthy of inclusion in any future liturgy and canon.

One poem stands out in his corpus of literary activity in the war years. This poem is clearly in the curse format.

"Woe to You"

Yechiel Szeintuch writes:

> this poem (*Weh Dir*), cursing the whole Nazi nation, was written after information about the liquidation of the Jews of Lublin reached Warsaw at the end of April 1942. Yitzhak Katzenelson was one of the first and one of the few in the Warsaw Ghetto to believe the news and comprehend the possible ramifications of the mass murders for all of Eastern European Jewry.
>
> The date noted at the end of the manuscript is 31/V. No year is given. Taking into consideration the content of the poem and the various recorded testimonies about it, there is no doubt that the full date of the poem is 31-5-1942. Before the mass deportations, the poem was prepared for print as part of a planned, special edition of Yitzhak Katzenelson's Zorn Lieder (Poems of Wrath). Together with an original typescript from the Warsaw Ghetto, the original manuscript has been preserved, in a half-torn state, in the Yitzhak Katzenelson Archive in Ghetto Fighters' House, Kibbutz Lohamei Haghetaot. In deciphering the ragged manuscript, we have also consulted the copy. The original is registered under the no. KII/1024, and the copy, KIIa/1024.[10]

Woe to You

Woe to you, who have murdered all my children
and all my old ones, the oldest of my people.

Woe to you, who have entirely exterminated my peaceful people,
burned down my houses of worship,
all my shuls together with the Jews in them,
and my holy Jewish cities.

Woe to you, who have destroyed an unarmed people,
who have destroyed a people unprotected by anyone.
I tell you, those who were unprotected will punish you:
you will be judged by the people without weapons!

Woe to you, nation of child-killers, murderers of the old,
who have annihilated my children and my old ones.
I tell you, murdered old people cannot be hidden,
murdered children heave from the grave as from their mother's womb.
silent, silent, silent as the grass;
mutely we'll stand and mutely we'll ask,
why have you murdered us, why?

Bloody, unclean, you'll run away
and a savage terror will seize you:
we, the dead, will head you off on every road,
we'll block you on every path.

I tell you, nation of murderers, children are never lost,
the aged never die before their time.

I tell you, innocent murdered Jews do not die,
a people is not destroyed without reason.
I tell you, nation of murderers, Jerusalem cannot be laid waste,
Shoot! Shoot into my heart . . . that is your last shot!

Woe to you, your evil hour—listen—has struck,
soon, soon, a plague on you and you're finished:
We'll pursue you on every road,
we'll burst out of our graves.
With wife and child, with grandpa and grandma,
those shot by you for no reason,
the people you buried alive,
we shall stand up and bleakly stare at you.

We shall stand up on every single road,
It lies in ruins, torn apart, and demolished;
hide yourselves in crevices, in caves and secret places,
you, the lowest murderers on God's earth!

Hide yourselves! No . . . only those with shame hide themselves,
you, child-killers, you are without shame!
Crawl, shameless ones, like aliens over your familiar ruins,
and may the crumbling rocks be alien to you.

We, the slain, will stand up and stare at you,
stare at you mutely in our anguish,
and, staring at you, devour you in silence:
we'll cling to your very bones.

In your disgusting body, in your red neck,
as in a filthy swamp, in mud and clay,
you have killed us, the living, and dragged us, dead,
dragged us on your shoulders to your home . . .

To your home! Your home no longer exists!
not knowing where to run! You murderers, may the
trees on the roads and the blades of grass curse you,
and every frog on the bank of every river.

Run, every German with a murdered Jew around your neck!
Dying, we cling silently to your throat—
we'll choke you, choke you, but you'll not choke to death—
turn your heads, your heads, and look around you . . .

It is we . . . we, we! These are our fingernails
that grew sharper after death;
You have slain us along every road
and stained every stone red with us.

Now carry us, carry us in fear and terror—
you can't find the way? March! Forward! Forward!

They raise themselves up, blind, blind and frozen,
they come close to you and shake their heads—
your wives and your children come face to face with you,
and we behind—we won't let you go.

They face to face, and we, we from behind—
why did you destroy us, tell us, why?
You can't stand it, you run with every wind,
you can't drain the bitter cup.

You run, troops of Cain, a wild horde of murderers—
run, guilty ones, run, without pause or rest.
Wherever you set foot, you have committed a murder,
on every morsel of earth you have spilled blood.

Search, murderer, for your home and may you never find it . . .
Wander, as we do, over the earth, and search—
and searching through the ruins, may you lose your mind
and in your madness be cursed!

Run! Run like mice after the war is lost,
We, we! We'll now lead you home,
we'll lead you, each of you, into his own house.
We'll bear witness and observe the scene:
how you greet your wife and child,
how you fall on each other's necks . . . we shall see it,
we'll stand and look with our dim and blinded eyes.

No! No! May you, like us, never live to see this.
May each of you find his way to his ruined house
and not find your wives among the living
and find your children dead on their laps.

Dead. Through open doors and cracked walls
hear the curses . . . Your skin shudders with cold—
your wives are the ones who cursed you
and your own children before they died.

In every city and in each forgotten village
you have plunged your hands in Jewish blood;
each of our homes is a dark page
in your book of blood, cowards that you are!

You have chosen the weakest of all,
plundering the forlorn—the easiest prey!
You have fallen on a helpless people
and trampled them, reducing them to dust.

You have been marvelously brave against children
and against the aged . . . oh, you know, you know the art
of murdering the innocent, the most innocent, you dirty sinner,
you, in your cowardice, have made your selection . . .

You have maimed other nations, but you have exterminated us,
spit you out of her mouth with loathing
and let you lie dead in the streets, like us, like us,
huddled together with your wife and child.

tortured us, eaten us like bread,
you drank our old blood like wine, both old and cheap,
oh, who on earth, like us, has been killed without remorse?

You have sated your lust with us as with corpses,
nation of hyenas, you have drunk our blood—
who helped you—was it God? or was it the devil?
If God—may it smell good to him!
But if it's the devil . . . may all of you, may you all be cursed,
cursed by God and man, you wild beast!
May you sink deep into the fractured earth with Mephistopheles,
and there, deep in the earth, may you never know peace . . .

May the earth in her great fury and her hatred
how cities are rebuilt and bloom in freedom.

With dried-out rotten brains,
with plugged-up putrid ears, listen—
how the sky has brightened after you,
how the earth has smiled when you are gone.

Listen, listen, a marvelous song is ringing out
in love and faith over the whole world—
listen, listen to the mighty voice, free and exalted—

And may your sister the hyena
suck the last drops of venom out of your body
and may sparrows peck out your eyes
and your deep lying wicked murderous heart.

May you feel with your devoured hearts,
may you see with your eyes oozing out,
as lights flicker and twinkle
from what? and from where? and how? and when?

With worm-eaten hearts you'll feel, rapers of mankind,
with plucked-out eyes, look, guilty ones, and see
how nations rise up in all the lands,
he is singing in the choir of nations, the eternal Jew.

Listen, listen and may a wild storm soon grind you to dust,
and blow you into the deserts with your wife and child—
let no memory of you remain!
Nightmare, be erased, be blown away in the wind!

May 31 1942

Weh Dir, "Woe to You," represents the curse in all of its myriad aspects. Similar in many ways to the curses contained in Deut. 28:15–69, where Moses inveighs against the Hebrews for their sins and portrays for them their life without G-d, the curses in *Weh Dir* focus on shifting the power relationship between the victim and the persecutor. In this poem the victims become the ultimate persecutors of the Nazis. In an expression of prophecy, Katzenelson paints a bleak picture for the Nazis, hunted down on every road in every path by the Jews they have killed. Even today, we see the questions of German guilt still being discussed and argued.

The poem acts as an angry denunciation of the Nazis. Yet it does even more, for the Jewish victims find redemption not in their own mortification as seen in Deuteronomy but, rather, in their victimization of their persecutors through all times in the act of memory. Jewish redemption is brought about in the poem by the continued memory and rememory used to afflict the children and children's children of the Nazis. Kenneth Burke, in his own analysis of religious rhetoric, discussed the idea that often when we use rhetoric we are in some fashion attempting to expiate guilt.[11] We expiate this guilt through some kind of purification. Burke suggests that there are two kinds of purification: mortification, or self-blame; and victimization, or the blaming of someone else for the difficulty. In the case of mortification, expiation can only be obtained by changing oneself in some fashion, thus leading to redemption. In victimization, the change must take place within the one blamed for causing the guilt for redemption to take place. The concept of the scapegoat, Azazel at Rosh Hashanah, is a kind of a scapegoat for the guilt and sins of the people. It is in this image that we see the potential solace the victims may have felt in hearing the poem. In essence, the curse in *Weh Dir* provided the victims with an act, however symbolic it might have been, of power reversal. This symbolic act was transformed into reality in the post–World War II Nazi hunting that is still with us.

While the poem never mentions either the Nazis or the Germans, the context is clear. But the poem's universal nature comes through in that the curse can refer to any enemy of the Jewish people. This poem therefore offers to the modern liturgy an alternative to mortification. It suggests that blame need not always be placed upon the Jew for conditions he or she may suffer. It is in this fashion that this poem becomes useful for a post-Shoah liturgy in an age where anti-Jewish sentiment exists even in places where no Jews reside. The poem is an expression of paranoia when paranoia is completely justified. It is, therefore, instructive because it provides the worshipper with powerful and dramatic word magic over his or her persecutors. It provides a force of words that leads to a maintenance of strength against present and future enemies who no longer can be viewed as supermen and unconquerable. Katzenelson has provided us with a curse for all ages.

"Introduction to an Evening of Tanach"

In a more positive approach Katzenelson provides us with a possible addition to the post-Shoah sacred literature with his poetic introduction, *Efenung zu a Tanach-Ovnt*. This work was written somewhere around November 26, 1940, eleven days after the Warsaw Ghetto had been sealed off on November 15. The original manuscript can be found in the Yitzhak Katzenelson Archives in Ghetto Fighters' House, Kibbutz Lohamei Haghetaot (catalogue number KII/1031).

This poem is about the centrality and significance of the Bible in the lives of the Jews of the ghetto. Katzenelson, ever the teacher, translated many passages of the Bible into Yiddish and Polish to make them accessible to more people in the ghetto. Szeintuch writes that there were seventeen such Tanach presentations. Katzenelson's theme in this poem is that the Jews "are not only the people of the Book but that the Bible is a book that shapes their everyday lives."[12]

Katzenelson looked on life in the Ghetto as a series of sufferings (as experienced by Jews throughout history). To him, the Bible was an example of the description of such sufferings and offered comfort and hope through one's relationship to God. Therefore, this poem clearly fits the characteristics of sacred canon of consolation and instruction emphasized in this essay.

Introduction to an Evening of Tanach

Tanach:
it's the first evening of Tanach!
Remember the date:
you came, tired, worn,
with a tearful eye, an aching heart—
you can't avoid it . . .
wherever you go, your sorrow follows!

Today, my neighbors, my brothers, my dear sisters,
today you will offer your sorrow for sale,
today, on the evening of Tanach—
Tanach!

It's our ancient fortress:
the strongest and largest of them all!
Watch, listen, and learn to recognize
the Tanach,
the fortress!
The sky is its roof,
the four corners of the world its walls,
the earth its foundation,

and even though you can't see its lord
and ruler,
in every corner, in each and every crevice,
you feel and sense
God.[13]

If there was any poem that represented the continuation of life even in the midst of death this is it. Throughout this brief poem a new world is created far from the tortures of the ghetto and the hate surrounding it. That world is the embodiment of Judaism and its 5,000-year existence. Contained within this poem is the kernel of hope that Jews having survived 5,000 years of exile, torture, and harrowing existence would even survive this, the Holocaust.

The poem is as eloquent an expression of Jewish theology and continuity as any work of the current liturgy and ought to find a central place in any post-Shoah sacred literature because of its innate hopefulness consolation and because of its promise of Jewish continuity. Ultimately the Tanach poem is a song of praise written in a far different tone and context from the previous poem, *Weh Dir*. Nevertheless, both "The Evening of Tanach" and "Weh Dir" were written with similar rhetorical goals in mind. In both cases, the poem was to create a positive vision of the Jew for the Jew. "The Evening of Tanach" gave to the Jewish audience an image of strength and continuity, or longevity and protection, whereas "Woe to You" acted as an expression of the juxtaposition of the image of the innocent Jew as a victim who in turn will victimize his persecutors. This, too, is an expression of strength and power and both poems may be considered as catalysts for action. For if one no longer believes that his or her enemy in invincible, and one begins to have pride and respect for oneself, then it becomes easier to act in opposition to those who would persecute. While there may never be proof of a causal relationship between the poetry of someone like Katzenelson and the active resistance of the Warsaw Ghetto Jews, there is a close enough proximity of the two events and the understandable and necessary need of the Jewish community to develop a sense of community before it could act collectively against the Nazis. In essence, both poems also act as catalysts for the development of a communal image. Their importance and significance for the development of a future liturgy for the post-Shoah theology cannot be understated.

The inclusion of a poem such as this as a kind of prayer/lament holds within it both accusation and lamentation. The accusation of "where are you, God?" is not couched in an angry tone; on the contrary it is spoken in deep sadness, in a clear lament. This piece echoes many liturgical pieces over the centuries used to remember other destruction or hurbanim. While God is called upon in many of the other Jewish laments to do something, Sutzkever in this poem is asking nothing more than to be comforted and is denied even that.

Conclusion

What is important here are not these special poems as examples of Jewish writing during the Holocaust by the victims of the Holocaust. What is important is that these very same writings may be at some future date far beyond our own lives the basis of what future generations of Jews synthesize out of the vast and horrific period of the Shoah, the Holocaust, the Hurban. We are not arguing that any of these poems are our candidates for sacredness. What we are arguing is that like previous generations of Jews, when confronted with destruction, death, degradation, and defilement, the result was some new body of sacred literature developed to aid those generations that followed in both dealing with the horror and gaining some deeper understanding and comprehension of both the relationships between people and between people and G-d.

These poems by Katzenelson are only a tiny portion of the volume of literary, artistic, and creative materials that currently exist in museums and archives (without even beginning to calculate the materials existing in private archives or held by various survivors). Yet they are quite representative of much of the literary effort of the victims of the Holocaust. It is up to the scholarly community to now begin to examine and reexamine these literary creations; to translate them, analyze them, and understand them as a first step to creating a cultural history of the Holocaust. This cultural history will then offer to future generations the raw material for future liturgical additions. This cultural history will over time become the material read when Holocaust commemoration is observed. Possibly a century or two from now our descendants will read among their sacred Jewish texts the Book of the Shoah, the Hurban, the Holocaust.

Notes

Note: This essay was based on an earlier paper by Drs. Carol and Samuel Edelman delivered at the International Communication Association Conference in Jerusalem, Israel, in July 1998.

1. Meyer Waxman, *The History of Jewish Literature* (Cranbury, N.J.: Associated University Presses, 1980), xv.
2. Ibid.
3. David Roskies, ed., *Literature of Destruction: Jewish Responses to Catastrophe* (Philadelphia: Jewish Publication Society, 1992).
4. Max I. Dimont, *Jews, God and History* (New York: Signet Books, 1964), 55–71; Harold Bloom and David Rosenberg, *The Book of J* (New York: Vintage Books, 1990), 7–50; Paul Johnson, *A History of the Jews* (New York: Harper and Row, 1987), 50–95.
5. Dimont, *Jews, God and History,* 162–81.
6. Michael Grant, *The History of Ancient Israel* (New York: Scribner's Sons, 1984), 147.
7. James Sanders, *From Sacred Story to Sacred Text* (Philadelphia: Fortress Press, 1987), 182, 184.
8. Jacob Neusner, *Scriptures of the Oral Torah* (New York: Harper and Row, 1987), 37.
9. Grant, *The History of Ancient Israel,* 181.
10. Yechiel Szeintuch, "The Work of Yitzhak Katzenelson," *Jerusalem Quarterly*, no 26 (Winter 1983).
11. Kenneth Burke, *The Rhetoric of Religion: Studies in Logology* (Berkeley: University of California Press, 1970).
12. Yechiel Szeintuch, "The Work of Yitzhak Katzenelson," *Jerusalem Quarterly*, no. 26 (Winter 1983).
13. All the poems here published were translated from deciphered manuscripts by Ruth Whitman with Menachem Rotstein. They were printed before in the *Jerusalem Quarterly*, no. 26 (Winter 1982/83), and edited by Yechiel Szeintuch.

"Thou Shalt Teach It to Thy Children"

What American Jewish Children's Literature Teaches about the Holocaust

Peter Haas

I

Although a good deal has been written about Holocaust education at the college and university level, little attention has been paid to what is being taught in Jewish institutions for younger students, that is, in day schools, supplementary schools, synagogues, and the like. Even less is known about what Jewish children who have no formal Jewish education after Bar/Bat Mitzvah age know about the Holocaust. Our interest in this project was sparked by a desire to know what "Millennials"—children coming of age in the last decade or so—know or think they know about the Holocaust. It is our assumption that what they learn when they arrive on our college campuses is not only a result of formal Jewish education. It is also a product of popular culture, be it films like *X-Men* or material read in high school such as *The Diary of Anne Frank*. There is, however, a third medium which may also be highly influential and yet is not widely studied by scholars, namely fiction books about the Holocaust written especially for children below seventh grade. What follows is our first step to survey this literature and to draw some preliminary conclusions about its history, development, and message.

We want to stress at the outset that in no way are we claiming to be comprehensive. The amount of material out there that could arguably be included under the rubric "Children's Holocaust Literature" is immense. What we have done, we believe, is looked at a varied enough sample to be able to draw some reasonably accurate, if tentative, conclusions. The conclusions themselves lead to some interesting broader questions about how the Holocaust might well be seen and understood by children today, and so about the nature of Holocaust awareness in the next generation of American Jewish leadership.

Before turning to our discussion, we wish to bring certain central questions to the front. There is, first and foremost, an inherent tension in the genre of children's Holocaust literature. On the one hand, the Holocaust is such a significant part of the contemporary Jewish narrative that it cannot, nor should not, be ignored. The younger generation needs to be made aware in a responsible way of this formative event in contemporary Jewish culture. On the other hand, the very nature of the Holocaust is such that it is not suitable for all children, especially those below fourth grade or so. Jewish educators and librarians thus find themselves in an awkward situation. In essence, they have to decide whether or not to make Holocaust information available to children below fourth grade and, if so, how to present a proper sense of the Shoah to young children without exposing them to its atrocities. This is an issue for parents as well, which in turn creates some market demand for writing Holocaust books for ever younger audiences.

In most communities, the Holocaust is usually not taught until fifth grade, whether in secular or synagogue schools. As a result, many educators and librarians do not discuss the subject before fifth grade, leaving parents with the task of determining whether to shelter their children from this information or to prepare them for it in some manner, a job for which parents may or may not be prepared. Yet, for a variety of reasons, many parents do feel a need to expose young children to the Holocaust in some way at some time. Some feel this need so as to socialize their children into the Jewish community and give them some background for the classes they will have during the middle school years and for the many books about the Holocaust that were written for pre-teens. Others introduce children to the topic because of family members who were refuges or survivors. So the first question is, what should characterize children's books on the Holocaust for this younger age group?

A second question has to do with what one hopes to accomplish through a children's book on the Holocaust. At all grade levels, there is the issue of how accurate and detailed an author needs to be when dealing with the Holocaust. It is important, of course, for children's textbooks and novels to be accurate, but how graphic should they be especially in relation to atrocities? And if an author makes the story age-appropriate for young readers, then is one really being faithful to the event and its victims? We have found books that fall virtually everywhere on the possible spectrum, indicating that this question is far from a universally accepted solution. An example of precisely this tension occurred in the well-known children's Holocaust book *Daniel's Story* by Carol Matas (Daniel Weiss Associates, 1995). According to Adrienne Kertzer:

> Matas insisted on retaining the following passage even after readers of the manuscript suggested that it was too much for children: After living for a while in the Lodz Ghetto, Daniel was sent to Auschwitz. There, he said that "he almost committed suicide after seeing burning bodies in a pit." This passage goes against the traditional image of children's books as a place for simple heroism, resistance, and spiritual uplift. But Matas felt that the need to inform children about atrocities (the "unbelievable") took precedence over the need to console and inspire children.[1]

Matas made a choice for accuracy over "delicacy" or what is generally regarded as age-appropriateness. Our goal here is not so much to judge the decision Matas made as to point out that this is an issue with which many of the authors discussed below have had to deal.

With these basic questions in mind, we are ready to proceed. Before doing so, we want to point out that we will be limiting ourselves to Holocaust fiction and some biographies for children. That is, we have purposefully decided against looking at textbooks or history books. The reason is, first of all, that we are including a good deal of material for an audience that is too young to understand history. In addition, we are interested in books that relate information about the Holocaust in an informal, personal manner rather than an abstract, detached manner. A novel or picture book puts a "face" on the Holocaust and allows, or maybe forces, a child to identify with someone who had some connection with the Holocaust, and in that way to experience, vicariously, that person's story. These books do not so much provide factual information about the Holocaust as a sense of what the Holocaust was and what it means. And it is this meaning of the Holocaust that we are interested in adducing.

The question we propose to explore here, then, is how authors and illustrators of Jewish children's books have negotiated these various shoals over time. As we shall see, a number of strategies have developed over the last several decades for how to portray and present the Holocaust. Ultimately, we hope to learn from this what moral or religious lessons are being taught in this medium. To that end, we will be keeping an eye on the connection between the solutions authors and illustrators have come to, on the one hand, and what these authors and illustrators are actually conveying to the next generation of Jews, on the other. In short, we intend to explore the connection between the "form" of children's Holocaust books (what is being told, how it is being told, and the role illustrations play) and the content and interpretation of the events. As we proceed, we shall try to maintain a double focus on literary strategy and on the heuristic effects of those strategies.

We begin our study by turning to the very basic question, as alluded to above, concerning whether or not young children should be exposed to the Holocaust, or the more brutal parts of the Holocaust, at all. Many librarians and other educational professionals contend that children should not read books about the Holocaust before fourth grade. They feel that below fourth grade, children have no historical perspective and that they should not be traumatized by reading or hearing about some of the darkest periods of modern history. Young children should be sheltered from this kind of knowledge first because of their age and also because of their poor ability to distinguish real from make-believe. This tension is nicely articulated by Lydia Kokkola, who notes:

> In a sense, one can argue that any writing about the Holocaust for children breaks a strict taboo: that children are not to be frightened. Holocaust literature introduces the child to a world in which parents are not in control, that survival does not depend upon one's wits but upon pure luck, where evil is truly present, and worst of all, a horror story that is true. . . . Holocaust literature for children can therefore be distinguished by its combination of challenging subject matter, ethical responsibility, and its position outside the normal boundaries of children's literature.[2]

The other school of thought argues that in the post-Holocaust world, children should be exposed to, rather than sheltered from, what happened. There are many reasons that one could put forward for early exposure—that children will hear about the Holocaust anyway from Jewish communal events and so should have some foundation for understanding it; that this is an important component of post-Shoah Jewish identity; that being aware of antisemitism in the world today has to do with the very survival of the Jewish people, and so forth. Consequently, there are books that relate to the Holocaust in varying degrees that are being written for children as young as first grade.

Needless to say, such books for young children cannot be as comprehensive or graphic as books for teenagers. Some of these books for very young children are parables about the Holocaust and so can be read differently by children and adults. But, as we will elaborate more fully below, recent illustrated books for very young children are now becoming much more explicit, mentioning Nazi soldiers, concentration camps, hidden children, and other traumatizing events and in ways that would have once been unthinkable. Holocaust picture books for young children have been published in greater number since the beginning of the 1990s.

II

With these thoughts in mind, we turn to our periodization of the literature and the conclusions we have drawn. Holocaust books for children began to appear already in the 1950s. The plots of these first books centered around evasion and escape. The book *Twenty and Ten* by Claire Huchet Bishop (Puffin, 1952) is a short book that closely resembles the mystery/adventure books commonly written for third- to sixth-grade children at that time. The story is about twenty French children and their teacher, Sister Gabriel, who were sent to a refuge in the mountains during the German occupation of France. Shortly afterward, Sister Gabriel agreed to take in ten Jewish children and warned her students about the importance of never telling anyone about the Jewish children. Later when she became fearful that the Jewish children might be discovered, she asked the French children to look for a hiding place for their Jewish guests. The children discovered a hidden cave that proved to be the perfect solution when the German soldiers came, and the Jewish children successfully evaded the enemy.

What is notable here is that in this book the children were the real heroes of the story, finding a way to help each other in the face of mean adults. There is no reference to torture or violence. The action takes place in the mountains of France, not a "typical" Holocaust setting. In fact, on one level, this work can be seen as a typical children's adventure book of the period with the Holocaust background being only incidental. And yet, there is a historical cast to the story that the conventional adventure stories for children do not have—the German invasion of France. We mention this book because it was one of the earliest, and in fact one of the very few children's books of the 1950s altogether that even allude to the Shoah.

This overall character of the very earliest children's literature on the Holocaust persisted into the 1960s. One popular author who wrote from a child's perspective, in this case from the point of view of a German child, was Hans Peter Richter. A good example is his *I Was There* (Puffin, 1962), a roughly autobiographical book written in the first person and originally published in Germany. This book, written for teens, tells about three friends who joined the Hitler Youth movement. The narrator and one of the other boys were enthusiastic about serving the Fuhrer, but the third boy joined only because of pressure put upon him and his family. He was part of a minority of German citizens who felt very uncomfortable with the political events of the time and tried, as long as possible, not to go along with the crowd. In the course of the story, the book not only informs the reader about the activities of the Hitlerjugend but also shows how those who disagreed with the prevailing political sentiment were shamed and humiliated. The book opens with the following powerful statement written as the author looks back many years later on his experiences:

> I am reporting how I lived through that time and what I saw—no more. I was there. I was not merely an eyewitness. I believed—and I will never believe again.

This and other books by Hans Peter Richter were translated into English and became part of the stock of Holocaust books available to American children in the early to mid-1960s.

Overall, however, we found that Holocaust-related children's books were few and far between in the 1950s and 1960s. This is hardly surprising for a number of reasons. For one, the Holocaust was really not talked about much in any case. Jews were uncomfortable talking about the Holocaust in general, all the more so to their children. In addition, the Shoah had not really become part of the Jewish or secular educational agenda. What was transmitted about the Holocaust took place within Jewish families and maybe in unstructured ways in synagogues and religious schools. So a market for children's Holocaust books was largely undeveloped. This began to change by the 1970s. At that time, the Holocaust became a more open topic of discussion in both the Jewish and the non-Jewish worlds. Many have attributed this to the trauma of the 1967 "Six Day War," but there was also a change in generations, with the Holocaust now twenty-five years in the past. Whatever the reason, the number of juvenile Holocaust books increased significantly, and the messages they conveyed about the Holocaust became more varied and textured. The subject was still handled with a certain emotional distancing, however. For example, this decade saw the publication of books such as Sonia Levitin's *Journey to America* (Atheneum, 1970) and Judith Kerr's *When Hitler Stole Pink Rabbit* (Dell, 1971). Both of these books describe the hardships of being a refugee—the poverty, family separation, loneliness, and difficulty in learning a new language, for example. Like earlier books, the focus was on children's and families' ability to evade and/or escape. Now, however, the physical and emotional suffering that occurred came more to the surface. Yet even as these and similar books were more explicit about the physical and psychological difficulties of refugees, they usually ended on a positive note—on survival and the triumph over adversity.

Another popular book of this time, but one that took a very different angle, was *Summer of My German Soldier* by Bette Greene and Robert Hunt (Puffin, 1973). The story is about a teenager in Arkansas who experienced the Holocaust only indirectly. The heroine of the story came into contact with the events in Europe when she met a German soldier who was interred in a POW camp near her town. As she became friendly with the soldier, the girl from Arkansas realized that the German soldier had a lot of the same feelings, thoughts, likes, and dislikes as the Americans that she knew. Like the stories of Hans Peter Richter, the suffering of the Holocaust was personalized and was not limited only to Jews. The Holocaust here bore a more universal message.

The literature from this period, then, seems to show how the Holocaust and the war affected the lives of ordinary people, whether Jewish or not. These books did so by depicting events related to the Holocaust and the war in terms that teens were likely to understand, namely, experiences of kids like themselves. In many cases the characters were not Jewish, or at least not Jewish in any particularly overt way. The novels also put a very human face on the Holocaust. The reader of *Summer of My German Soldier* realizes that, despite the brutality of the Nazis, not all Germans were monsters. At the same time, the book exposed young Jewish readers to a small aspect of the Holocaust, enough to enable a child to understand and relate to some of the stories he heard in synagogue or from relatives. Overall, we see, the market for Holocaust-related books for children was growing, but allusions to the Holocaust were still somewhat indirect. The anti-Jewish threat was certainly there, but it was backgrounded and subdued.

III

Another significant change occurred in the 1980s. During this decade, we witnessed a virtual eruption of children's Holocaust fiction, some of it taking on the character of "coming of age" literature. Many of these stories had to do much more explicitly with the physical and emotional challenges faced by youngsters as they and their families struggled to survive the war. One example is Carol Matas's *Lisa's War* (Scribner, 1987), which depicts the experiences of a young girl who joined the Resistance. More explicit in its depiction of Holocaust reality is Uri Orlev's *Island on Bird Street* (Houghton-Mifflin, 1984). Here we read the story of a young boy who struggled through the harsh winter of 1941–42 in the Warsaw ghetto. We also find, for the first time, children's books that dealt explicitly with life in the concentration camps. A good example is Clara Asscher-Pinkhof's collection, *Star Children* (Wayne State University Press, 1986). Asscher-Pinkhof presents the reader with stories that describe the lives of Dutch children throughout the Holocaust from arrest to life in camps like Westerbork to their transport and experiences in Bergen-Belsen. Another sensitive theme was explored by Ida Vos, who wrote in *Anna Is Still Here* (Penguin, 1986) about the trauma of a young child who was separated from her family for a number of years and then struggled to return to a normal life after the war. Also, significantly, books from this era tended to bring to the front the victimhood of Jews at the hands of Nazis. Clearly by the 1980s, many of the earlier taboos on treating the Holocaust were being broken.

Moreover, just as these books were becoming both more explicit about the Holocaust and also more focused on the Holocaust as a Jewish event, they also dealt more with the complexities of the Holocaust. As one example, we can point to Doris Orgel's novel, *The Devil in Vienna* (Dial Press, 1978). The book describes the friendship between a Jewish girl and a Catholic girl in Vienna and how both were negatively affected by the Holocaust. A second example is Lois Lowry's telling of the Danish rescue of Jews in *Number the Stars* (Houghton-Mifflin, 1989). Overall, books of the 1980s were much more graphic and true to the Holocaust than previously, more focused on Jewish suffering, and open to introducing complexities and ambiguities. It is hardly surprising that these developments evoked some criticism.

An interesting comment on the sensitivity of the times appeared in the publication of *The Number on My Grandfather's Arm* by David Adler (UAHC, 1987). The story is about a child who noticed numbers tattooed on her grandfather's arm one night when her parents were away and her grandfather was washing dinner dishes. She asked him about the tattoo, and her grandfather told her about the persecution and humiliations that the Jews of Poland suffered and some of the horrors of the concentration camps. The story is fairly realistic, but is of course told by a survivor and so has, as it were, a happy ending. The story is accompanied by photographs in black and white, subtly highlighting the somberness of the story. One of the photographs, however, showed a German soldier pointing a rifle at a mother clutching her baby. Should this have been included? In this case, the photo was a bit more than what was deemed appropriate for it was removed in the subsequent edition.

What is interesting about this period is that we see a beginning of a bifurcation in what children can learn about the Holocaust. On the one hand the accounts of hardship and suffering became somewhat more graphic and realistic, and on the other, we saw many stories of rescue and friendship. Children were learning about the horrors of the Holocaust, but also about instances of resistance, friendship, and rescue. A working synthesis had evolved which allowed the Holocaust to be more or less accurately conveyed to young readers without being traumatic.

IV

We can say that in some sense children's Holocaust books really came of age in the 1990s. A number of factors might account for this. One, no doubt, was the fact that the Jewish audience had changed by this time. Fewer and fewer Jewish children were hearing about the Holocaust directly from survivors. Thus books began to fill in the gap that once was covered by family members and neighbors who had survived the Shoah.

A second factor, we would argue, was the maturation of academic studies of the Holocaust. Scholars began to bring out many more of the subtleties, complexities, and intricacies of the Shoah. These studies had an impact on writers and illustrators of juvenile Holocaust books as they themselves became exposed to a much more polychromatic view of the Holocaust. Children's authors now had a greater array of themes with which to work.

Third, the dwindling number of Holocaust witnesses (whether survivors, refugees, or liberators) created—and continues to create—a sense of urgency for recording oral histories, publishing survivor narratives, and making sure through novels and history books that the events of the Holocaust are remembered and passed on to a new generation. Many books from the 1990s were based on or inspired by true personal accounts.

Finally, we have to mention the fact that Holocaust readings (like *The Diary of Anne Frank*) were becoming part of secular school curricula. This was itself a function of the greater willingness to talk about the Holocaust, a tendency fueled to some significant degree by the TV miniseries *Holocaust*, which first aired in 1978. But the introduction of the Holocaust into general public education greatly accelerated the growing awareness of, and interest in, the Holocaust not only for the Jewish, but also for the non-Jewish, community. Consequently, many children's authors began to write for a more general audience. The growth in demand was answered not only by an increasing number of authors and publishers who entered the field, but also by a much broader range of topics and themes. In the 1990s, for example, the award-winning *Star of Fear, Star of Hope* by Jo Hoestlandt was published (a 1993 book written in French and published in the United States by Walker Publishing Company in 1995). The story was narrated by an elderly French woman named Helen, who was looking back on an event that occurred in her childhood. Despite the 1942 German invasion of northern France, she and her Jewish friend Lydia continued to play and go to school together. On her ninth birthday, Helen invited Lydia to sleep over at her house. But late in the evening, the "Midnight Ghost" knocked on the door (a code name for someone who came to warn Lydia to go home because of an impending round-up of Jews). When Lydia handed Helen a gift and told her she had to leave, Helen got angry at Lydia for ruining her birthday celebration and said, "You're not my friend anymore." Helen wrote that she never saw Lydia again, and she has always regretted her words. She lives with the hope that Lydia survived and that perhaps some day she will read this book and call her. Children who read the story learn how an incident, that would have been long forgotten had it happened in ordinary times, can be so painful and haunting when it happens in a time of war and persecution. They also get a sense of what was lost during the Holocaust. The shaded illustrations by Johanna Kang, all in tones of brown, black, and white, add to the somberness of this story.

Also, in the late 1990s we see more books related to the Holocaust for children below fourth or fifth grade. As noted above, this development has been a controversial issue among librarians and Jewish educators. Some of these books have been sensitive to the issues mentioned above. Many of these books, for example, deal with the Holocaust through allusions or parables that can be understood at different levels by children and adults. Thus we might have a story in which a grandmother explains how during World War II, she did not have a menorah for Chanukah, but lit candles by inserting them in a potato (*One Candle* by Eve Bunting, HarperCollins, 2002). This story does not have any explicit and direct mention of the Holocaust, but the setting is hardly going to be a secret for an adult. Another example is the picture book *Elisabeth* by Claire A. Nivola (Farrar Straus Giroux, 1997). An elderly lady explains how a doll, which had been slightly damaged by her dog, was lost "when the soldiers came." Many years later, she found the doll in an antique shop in America. She recognized it because of the teeth marks that her dog had made. The technique of using vague references like "when the soldiers came" is another way of referring to the Holocaust without directly saying so.

A classic example of the "parable" style of children's books is *Terrible Things* by Eve Bunting (Jewish Publication Society, 1989). In this book, small animals lived together in a forest, all coexisting well with each other. The birds and squirrels lived in the trees, the rabbits and porcupines on the ground, and so on. Then one day the "Terrible Things" came. All of the animals were frightened until the "Terrible Things" said that they only wanted to take away animals that fly. The other animals, assuming that they were now out of danger, remained silent as the birds disappeared. After the birds were gone, everyone breathed a sigh of relief. But the "Terrible Things" returned and took away all the animals with bushy tails. Again, no one spoke up for the squirrels and skunks. The "Terrible Things" returned several more times until the only animals left were the rabbits. When the "Terrible Things" came once more, there was nobody left to speak up for the rabbits. This allegory, built on Pastor Niemoeller's famous statement, can be understood by young children as a cute story that teaches the importance of supporting others in need, while older readers will of course realize the other meaning of the story.

However, sometimes efforts to make vague references to the Holocaust backfire and leave children requesting further explanations from parents or teachers. The picture book *Don't Forget* by Patricia Lakin (William Morrow, 1994), written for grades 1–3, falls into this category. The book tries to deal with the Holocaust obliquely. It is set in a post–World War II American city. Sarah, an eight-year-old girl, wanted to surprise her mother by baking a birthday cake for her. With a list of ingredients in hand, she visited several different stores and finally went to the Singers' mom-and-pop grocery store. Sarah made a point of not looking at the numbers tattooed on the Singers' arms but "like a magnet" her eyes were eventually drawn to them. Sarah told Mrs. Singer, "I tried not to stare. I know how you got them. And that they are your secret." Mrs. Singer replied that the numbers should never be a secret. "If no one knows about bad things, they can happen all over again." But the story about the tattooed numbers was never told and in effect, the "secret" that must not be forgotten is for all intents and purposes forgotten in the rest of the book. The remainder of the book is devoted to telling how Mrs. Singer helped Sarah bake her cake. Although Lakin tried to couch the Holocaust within an otherwise upbeat story, she did not adequately deal with the numbers tattooed on Mr. and Mrs. Singer's arms. And so her story leaves children with questions that have to be explained by adults. We might count this as an example of an unsuccessful children's book on the Holocaust.

At the other end of the spectrum, we sometimes encounter a book that goes a little too far in its efforts to bring the Holocaust to the attention of young children. In fact this period sees many books aimed at children as young as first grade and that do not hesitate to make reference to Nazi soldiers, round-ups, and other tragedies. These books bring starkly into question just how graphic one should be. One book that in the view of many went too far is *Let the Celebrations Begin* by Margaret Wild with illustrations by Julie Vivas (Orchard, 1991). The story is about women in a concentration camp who made toys for some of the children there. The rather vivid description of the camp and the lives of the children, and especially the illustrations depicting starving and skeletal women with shaven heads, have been criticized as inappropriate by many educators.

Other books of this period, however, seem to find a better balance. One such is *The Butterfly* by Patricia Polacco (Philomel Books, 2000). In this book Polacco tells about a French family that hid a Jewish family in a room of their basement. At night, when the household was asleep, the young daughter of the Jewish family (Sevrine) secretly climbed upstairs to the bedroom of the French family's daughter (Monique) and played with some of Monique's toys. One night Monique, who was unaware of the hidden family, woke up and thought she had seen a ghost. After this occurred a few more times, Monique learned who Sevrine was and was shocked to realize that people had been living in the basement and she never knew about it. The two girls became friends and had many night-time meetings. But one night, they got too close to the window and a neighbor saw both of them. The girls told Monique's mother, and the Jewish family was forced to leave. Monique's family helped get them to the next refuge. This story is based on an event that happened to Polacco's Aunt Monique, whose mother was part of the French resistance. A note at the end explains that Sevrine was the only family member to survive the escape and that Sevrine and Monique still are friends. Although this book deals quite openly with a round-up of Jews, there is something of a happy ending (in that Sevrine survives). The illustrations are much softer and less frightening than what we find in, say, *Let the Celebrations Begin*.

Another example of a book that finds a good middle ground is *The Lily Cupboard* by Shulamith Levy Oppenheim (HarperCollins, 1992). The story here is set on a farm where a young Jewish girl was sent by her parents so that she could be hidden during the Holocaust. The book describes the child's disorientation at being separated from her home and her parents. While the story itself is psychologically difficult, the illustrations are more muted and so make the story less traumatic than it might otherwise have been.

A different kind of approach that deserves mention is *Brundibar*, authored by Tony Kushner and illustrated by Maurice Sendak (Hyperion, 2003). The book is really a retelling of the opera *Brundibar*, which was written in 1938 and then performed in the Theresienstadt Ghetto in 1943, where the actors and writers (except for the librettist) found themselves reunited. There is no mention in the story itself of the Holocaust, and in Sendak's version, there are only slight hints in the illustrations that what is being told is connected to the Holocaust. The occasional person will be wearing a yellow star, for example, or the organ-grinder wearing what looks like a Nazi Party (i.e., brownshirt) uniform. Like the *Terrible Things*, and other "parable" type approaches, there are only indirect allusions to the Holocaust, both in the text and the accompanying illustrations. In fact the story itself has nothing overt to do with the Holocaust at all (it was written in 1938) and yet its production and history have everything to do with the Shoah.

Another approach was pioneered in *The Grey Striped Shirt* by Jacqueline Jules (Alef Design Group, 1993). One day when Frannie was visiting her grandparents, she discovered an old striped shirt in a basement closet. When she asked her grandparents what it was and why it was there, they seemed reluctant to talk about it. But gradually, over the course of a year, they told Frannie bits and pieces of their story about life in Germany before the war, their expulsion to a ghetto, and finally their experiences in a concentration camp. The Holocaust accounts are interspersed with modern-day activities such as gardening and trips to the synagogue. A good deal of information about the Holocaust is transmitted in the course of the book, but it is doled out gradually and intermittently to break the tension. Furthermore, the book enables Jewish children to understand something of the survivor community.

We turn for a moment to books designed for middle school children. For this age group as well, the 1990s brought about considerably more diversity in what was previously available. This possibly is a response to the introduction of Holocaust themes, like Anne Frank's diary, into public education. As students learned about the Holocaust in secular and religious schools, many developed a fascination with these events and wanted to read books with more detail, and with personal recollections that did not mute some of the hardships that were endured. As a result a flurry of more graphic Holocaust books for this age group appeared. An excellent example of a book designed to meet this market is Isaac Millman's autobiographical story, *Hidden Child* (Farrar Giroux Strauss, 2003). Isaac's father and, later, his mother were arrested. However, his mother managed to bribe a prison guard to take Isaac to their landlady's house and ask her to shelter him. When the landlady refused, the guard left Isaac on the street and went away. Deep in despair, Isaac fortunately was rescued by a Jewish neighbor who kept him until she herself was arrested. Throughout the war, Isaac was shuffled to a number of other homes and institutions and finally ended up in an orphanage. He never saw his parents again. After the war, Isaac was adopted by a family in the United States who cared for him until adulthood. He eventually married the daughter of the woman who saved him when he was left on the street. But he mourns the fact that he was never united with his parents again while many others at the orphanage were.

This book reflects a number of elements that characterize the most recent permutations in children's books on the Holocaust. Most obviously, it relates a wide variety of Holocaust experiences directly, that is, not by allusion. It clearly deals with disturbing facts, informing students about how families were separated, ways in which children were saved, how luck often played an important part in whether or not an individual survived, the hardships that individuals endured, and the bittersweet endings that often occurred. That it is a first-person account of course adds to the impact.

An even more striking example of the kind of diversity that characterized the Holocaust literature of the 1990s is the award-winning *Hana's Suitcase* by Karen Levine (Albert Whitman and Company, 2003). Here we are told the true story of a young girl, Hana Brady, who died at Auschwitz, but whose suitcase ghoulishly survived. The book consists of two stories that are told in alternating segments. One is the fate of Hana and her brother. The other story is about a Japanese teacher who teaches about the Holocaust and her class—how the children wanted to see something tangible from the Holocaust, how the teacher traveled to Poland and obtained the suitcase, and then how the students in her class wanted to know something about the person whose name was on the suitcase. This amazing story reached its climax when the Japanese teacher made contact with Hana's brother who was at that time a plumbing supplies salesman in Toronto. It is hard to imagine a book on the Holocaust written in the 1970s or earlier that centered on Holocaust education in Japan. In some ways this book can be seen as transitional in another way. It is not so much about the Holocaust itself as about the aftermath in the world contemporary to young readers.

Another story that speaks to contemporary middle school children is *The Journey That Saved Curious George* (Houghton Mifflin, 2005), an illustrated book written by the authors of the Curious George picture books. (These popular books, written for preschoolers, are about a mischievous monkey.) In *The Journey*, the authors tell how they escaped from Paris on their bicycles with the manuscript of the first Curious George story hidden in the basket of one of the bikes. Many schoolchildren today are likely to remember hearing the Curious George stories when they were three or four years old. This book thus helps them see how the Holocaust has had an impact even in their own lives. Learning that the authors of these memorable picture books were Holocaust survivors gets their attention and makes World War II come alive.

We can conclude this section by just noting that some books from this period deal with the Holocaust only incidentally. An unusual story that nicely illustrates this category is *Bridge to Freedom* by Isabel Marvin (Jewish Publication Society, 1997). In this engaging story, a young German soldier deserts his unit and hides in a cave in Germany. There he discovers a Jewish girl who has fled Berlin and is also hiding in the cave. The two young people are not sure what to make of each other. As each one considers what their next course of action should be, they notice a third individual—an injured dog, who like them is taking refuge in the cave. After hesitatingly deciding to trust each other, the soldier and the Jewish girl assist the helpless dog. The soldier makes a splint for the dog's leg, and after the German troops have left, they whisk the dog out of the cave and go to the girl's house. By the end of the story, the soldier has joined the Jewish family as all of them escape to safety in Belgium. Although this story has some slow parts in the middle, there is enough adventure and danger to hold the interest of middle school–age children and to teach what happens when Jews and Germans see each other as individuals.

V

For high school students, the taboo against graphic depictions no longer holds, if it ever did. At this age, students begin reading adult books as well as books written specifically for teens. One example, the collection *Salvaged Papers,* edited by Alexandra Zapruder (Yale University Press, 2002), has selections from diaries of teenagers from different countries. These journals describe hunger, living in a forest, betrayal by non-Jews, narrow escapes, and so on, with an unblinking gaze. Since *Salvaged Papers* is comprised of diaries, the reader learns about Holocaust experiences from day-to-day accounts. A diary is not fiction; nor is it a "wide canvas." Rather, the reader encounters what happened day by day with the same uncertainty of the writer. The reader experiences directly on some level the everyday life of individuals who lived through the Holocaust: what they ate (or did not eat), if their food supply was reduced because more people moved into the ghetto, how their mother worked all day and did sewing at night to bring in a little extra income, if the person providing food to a family in hiding met them the day as he agreed to do so, where they slept, how they survived the cold weather, and the many other anxieties, hardships, humiliations, and close calls that people endured each day. Even though the book's editor published only selections from each diary, one still gets a fairly unvarnished sense of what daily life was like in the various situations described.

VI

There are a couple of conclusions we can draw. We started off by noting that the overwhelming majority of children's books about the Holocaust are written for students in grades 4 through 6. This is not surprising. Children above grade 7 or 8 are beginning to be ready to read regular adult literature and so do not comprise a significant market for children's books of any sort. On the other hand, as we have seen, there is some reluctance to write Holocaust books for children in grades 3 and below. In this regard, matters have persisted over the last fifty years.

Yet within this structure there are changes. As a whole, books for middle school readers have become much more varied in theme and approach. They offer a wide range of topics and formats that meet the diverse interests of American pre-teens, Jewish and non-Jewish. Many of these books describe universal themes like love, loss, and friendship as they occur in the context of the Holocaust. On the other hand, other books deal more directly with events of the Holocaust. Some of the books for this age still tend to be somewhat circumspect in their depictions of the horrors of the Holocaust. But a considerable number are much more explicit in both text and illustrations when it comes to depicting violence, cruelty, suffering, life in the concentration camps, and death. We have suggested above that this may be due to a number of factors. One is the much more graphic nature of books designed for older teenagers, a tendency that is filtering down into lower grades. Another factor may be the increased violence to which American children are being exposed in movies, TV, and video games. It is probably a rare twelve-year-old who has not mowed down at least a couple score enemies in a video game or seen someone do so on the screen. What seemed traumatic in the fifties appears almost tame today. This raises the rather interesting question as to whether or not it still makes sense to "water down" the Holocaust for a twenty-first-century middle school child.

Another change is the increasing number of books on this subject for youngsters in second and first grade or younger, an audience that was not even on the horizon until a few years ago. Publishers, teachers, and librarians are still not in agreement about how much exposure to the Holocaust, if any, is appropriate for children this young. One could argue that many picture books and fairytales nowadays feature stories and illustrations that would once have been considered too frightening for that age group. Think, for example, of the very popular *Where the Wild Things Are* by Maurice Sendak. Children also hear fairytales with unhappy endings, such as the works collected by Hans Christian Andersen, stories that were originally told to adults. One solution, as we have seen, is to tell a story that is not explicitly about the Holocaust or that has illustrations that only subtly allude to the Holocaust. The book then gently introduces the Shoah but leaves it to the parent or teacher to decide what else to say. Given the trends noted above, however, it is not out of the question that just as the Holocaust is being written about more and more openly for middle school audiences, so too will the Holocaust be increasingly a subject for lower grades. Today there seems to be a supposition that, rather than be sheltered, young children, especially Jewish children, should receive some exposure to the Holocaust early on.

In the end, then, it appears that "Millennials" are learning both everything about the Holocaust, and yet nothing in particular. They are learning everything insofar as children's Holocaust literature has become widespread and seems to touch on every imaginable scenario and take every imaginable point of view. You can read about Jewish victimhood, partisan resistance, the pressure on German youth, or the memory of survivors. You can even encounter the Holocaust as the backdrop to stories about perennial themes of growing up, loss of friends, and first love.

Millennials learn nothing in the sense that there is no common theme, lesson, or approach. Each book has its own tale to tell and its own lessons to be drawn implicitly or explicitly. Like so much in the lives of Millennials, the world is a marketplace in which every imaginable interest can be addressed. So no part of the Holocaust seems to be inherently privileged in the literature; no single message is being sent; we are bequeathing no particular lesson or story about the Holocaust. In fact, as we have seen, it is possible to read about the Holocaust without any explicit reference to Jews or Judaism at all; it is another tale of human cruelty and human good, of persistence and survival. If this literature is a fair representation of what is out there in Jewish popular culture, then the Holocaust, like every other aspect of Jewish life in the twenty-first century, has no universally agreed-upon essence. This is perfectly consistent with everything else we know about the Millennials. They have lots of information, an overflow of facts, but no master narrative.

Nevertheless, this vast array of literature illustrates the generally accepted view that the Holocaust should not be forgotten. We are approaching the time when there will be no living survivors or refugees of the Nazi terror. The Holocaust should not be simply a footnote in Jewish and world history.

The literature written for children of all ages, like the books and articles written for adults, assures that it will be remembered.

Maybe the best way to conclude our survey is to cite the closing passage of Jacqueline Jules's *The Grey Striped Shirt:*

> I still visit my grandparents whenever I can. We still walk to synagogue on Shabbat and work in the garden on Sundays. Every once in a while I go down to the cedar closet to look at the grey striped shirt. Grandpa Herman says it will belong to me someday. He wants me to show it to MY grandchildren. "You must tell them our story," he said. I promised I would.

Notes

1. Adrienne Kertzer, "The Problem of Childhood, Children's Literature and Holocaust Representation," in *Teaching the Representation of the Holocaust,* ed. Marianne Hirsch and Irene Kacandes (New York: Modern Language Association of America, 2005), 255.
2. Lydia Kokkola, *Representing the Holocaust in Children's Literature* (New York: Routledge, 2003), 11.

Once More to the Jabbok

The Place of Midrashic Dialogue in Post-Shoah Hermeneutics

Henry F. Knight

For Zev

Do midrash.[1] Work dialogically.[2] Attend to the missing faces.[3] These three simple sentences guide my work as a post-Holocaust theologian, educator, and religious professional. Indeed, if by midrash I mean not simply the formal interpretive work of rabbinic tradition but the hermeneutic practice of reading sacred texts and other important documents with an interruptive logic that kindles what the rabbis call the "white fire" of the texts, then these three admonitions describe my understanding of public responsibility in a post-Shoah world.

Of course, these imperatives are not exhaustive. A summons to attend to missing faces articulates a sense of responsibility to the presence of every face, a distinguishing feature of Emmanuel Levinas's important contributions to modern moral life. The fact that his work was self-consciously undertaken in the "after-life" of the Shoah simply underscores this point. Likewise, a summons to work dialogically does not negate solitude. Rather, a dialogical imperative qualifies solitude as a reminder that even our most solitary moments are occasions for us to be mindful of the relationality at the heart of life. Similarly, the call to midrashic discourse signals a respect for the otherness of all forms of texts, not simply the sacred texts that provide primary orientation in my world. To be sure, this summons can be discerned in meaningful social action when it, too, is considered as a text.[4] Moreover, midrashic sensibilities highlight the important role imagination plays in shaping the worlds in which we live and in honoring the plenitude (or richness) of life even and especially in the presence of life-denying scarcity. In our time after the Shoah, these imperatives orient and, I hope, characterize my work and my sense of responsibility in the world.

To be sure, I did not come to this place in my life easily or intentionally. Indeed, I am tempted to say I stumbled here. But that may be too clever a way of putting the matter before recording a bit of midrashic dialogue of my own.

Back to the Jabbok

Since 1993 I have been engaged with three colleagues in pursuing this kind of midrashic dialogue.[5] Working self-consciously as two Christians and two Jews, we have tried to do theology as post-Shoah

Jews and Christians in dialogue and to do it midrashically, wrestling with each other's texts. Each occasion has led to unexpected insights and allegiances. In over a decade of working together, we have learned to anticipate each other's points of view and at the same time be surprised by comments we still do not expect. We have found much common ground. At the same time, we have learned that we cannot assume that we understand the issues that separate us in the same way. Often we have aligned ourselves on topics across confessional boundaries and not infrequently found ourselves summoned by our dialogue to ask questions we hitherto had not considered. On more than one occasion, for example, we have found ourselves reading each other's texts with Moore, a Christian, and Jacobs, a Jew, raising similar questions evoked by the texts before us while Garber and I, through different hermeneutical paths, have aligned ourselves across our religious boundaries to articulate a contrasting set of shared concerns, more often than not reading more traditionally than our colleagues but with midrashic twists that allow us to retain our reading in the face of the questions all four of us have brought to the encounter.

In my case, I have learned that I do my midrashic work limping. That is, my approach to the text is tied up in a problematic relationship with my covenantal other and to my significant other's texts. In fact, I find that relationship mirrored in the first text I faced with my three colleagues, Gen. 32:22–33, Jacob at the Jabbok. Jacob brought a mixed legacy of deceit and struggle to his night of wrestling, including the history of his relationships with his father, his mother, and his brother as well as the accompanying shame and fear. Likewise, he brought his relationships with his uncle and his wives. In short, Jacob brought an entire lifetime to that night. As I joined my colleagues in that first encounter and entered that story and its dynamics, I was facing my own mixed legacy with estranged siblings, and with this text and texts like it. I was bringing a historic lifetime and its accompanying shame and fear. I, too, was facing a history of usurpation that marked my historic relationship to Jewish brothers and sisters over the centuries. Indeed, I was facing up to it; and I was doing so in the aftermath of a distinctively tragic night. Addressing the text, I found that my questions opened its world for me at the same time they opened my own personal history for new exploration:

- Who was the figure that Jacob faced?
- Why was that figure unnamed in the story?
- Could the figure be more than one significant other Jacob faced in his life?
- Why did the unnamed assailant ask Jacob his name but not give one in return?
- Why, after the night of struggle, did Jacob name the place as he did, but not his assailant?
- Why did Jacob limp?
- What does it lead us to ponder when we remember that Jacob emerges from this night with the reconfigured identity of Israel, but that in doing so he limps thereafter?

Raising questions like these, my colleagues and I wrestled with the text as Jacob wrestled with his other—facing manifold others at the riverbank. Like Jacob, we held on, insisting that the text bless us by addressing (not answering) our questions as it, in turn, asked questions of us. And, like Jacob, I was wounded and blessed in the process, moving from the Jabbok to the promised land beyond—walking with a limp. (I cannot speak for my colleagues with regard to *how* they emerged from this night.)

I have returned to this text too often to count. Each time, new questions arise and I discover more about myself, more about this text, and more about the act of midrashic return in the process. Sometimes the return is made with others in dialogue—my midrash partners (Zev Garber, Jim Moore, and Steve Jacobs) as well as with students and other occasional colleagues. Sometimes the return has been made in solitude, but never really alone. Each time, the landscape has changed as a dimension that escaped an earlier observation or an aspect that lay deep in the background has emerged to enlarge this place Jacob called Peniel/Penuel—the face of God. Yet every time, I return as I leave—limping.

Midrashic Dialogue

My approach to Torah and to the New Testament is wounded. Therefore, I make my way wrapped in contrition fully aware of past misreadings and supersessionary distortions. In other words, facing any text in its full, inquiring otherness means I face it limping. But such an approach is more than penitential. Limping translates into a fundamental assumption for me as I work with texts in this manner: our past encounters as well as our present and future ones are and will remain flawed. Therefore, dialogue is fundamental to our work, not just incidental. We do our wrestling with the text ever aware that we must listen closely to what others in the conversation have to show us about the texts and about ourselves, no matter how discomforting that might be. My partners in the exploration have proceeded with similar assumptions. However, our task is not to convince each other that our interpretations are right, since we know they are unfinished and incomplete at best. Rather our task is to venture as we are able into the world of the text, prepared to encounter ourselves as well as the witness of the text in what may be reorienting ways.

For example, since we began our first dialogue, I have become aware of the way the larger canon of the Hebrew Bible records without apology the limping walk of the people Israel. While I had become sensitized in my post-Shoah perspective to beware of taking the confessional tone of the combined texts of Tanach as a reason to conclude that Israel has failed as God's people, it took longer to see the midrashic power of a people called to walk with God in *halakah* who remember not just their walking but especially their limping. The story of Israel's walk with God is imperfect, flawed. Nonetheless, it is a way of walking and it is remembered faithfully, with its human limitations. Reading midrashically and informed by my trips to the Jabbok, I now read Micah 6 in light of Jacob's transfiguring experience. What does God require of Israel but doing justice, loving steadfastly and compassionately, and walking humbly (read *limping*) with God. When Israel forgets and walks without limping, then Israel acts as Jacob. Whether the scribe who compiled the final version of the Genesis text had this in mind or not, a midrashic imagination invites me to read the mixed references to Israel as Jacob and Jacob as Israel after the Jabbok with increased understanding. Dialogue with others has led to dialogue with unexpected faces and facets in the biblical text.

In other words, midrashic dialogue unfolds between and within texts as well as among human partners. In most cases, this multifaceted conversation transpires with a larger interpretive community. Its role is to discern the strengths and weaknesses of the dialogue and its faithfulness to the texts and persons in question. In our case that community includes the participants in the Annual Scholars' Conference on the Holocaust and the Churches (our usual venue) as well as the 1.5 million Jewish children who were murdered in the Shoah. That is, we have added J. B. Metz's admonition to Fackenheim's and make our way in solidarity with the victims of the Shoah now viewed as partners with a haunting stake in the interpretive enterprise we have undertaken. We do so with a sense of scripture's "narrative stubbornness" but always committed to an "unyielding realism" that holds us accountable to the burning children of Auschwitz.[6]

Douglas John Hall, perhaps the preeminent North American Christian theologian of the last fifty years, expresses a similar commitment. Drawing upon what he calls "the Jerusalem tradition shared by Christians and Jews," Hall argues for a truly dialectical faith that lives and thrives in the tension between honest confrontation with human suffering and the promise that death does not have the last word in creation. Adopting language similar to Dietrich Bonhoeffer's, he calls this "costly hope."[7] It shares with Fackenheim the tenacity of holding tight to the humanity that binds us all together while never letting go of the God of creation who intended and still intends an abundant life for all creation. That is, one does not let go of suffering victims in order to affirm what our theology tells us. Rather, suffering humans summon us to demand *even more* from our theological traditions than we have in the past. In short, in midrash we have found a way to proceed that moves forward as we stumble ahead. We limp when we walk.

To be sure, midrashic dialogue does not produce or look for a single voice in a text; nor does it demand agreement on the meaning of the texts we might be facing with others. Neither does it mean that in the context of dialogue that there will not be conflict. Instead, midrashic dialogue reconfigures the conflict so that even in the midst of disagreements we are not seeking to win arguments but searching instead to open the world of the text. Our goal: to face the text together and step more responsibly into its orchard of narrated meaning and grace.

We do this in multiple ways. Indeed the very notion of facing a text implies something of the richness as well as the corrective dynamics employed in our post-Shoah hermeneutics. When we face a text, we do it in dialogue facing each other. To be sure, we work in solitude a great deal of the time, reading commentaries (each other's and our own), but even then we are reading and writing with an awareness of each other's presence. It is a face-to-face experience, even when it is undertaken in moments of solitude. Furthermore, when we read a text midrashically, we recognize that there are several, sometimes many, faces present in the text. The characters, named and unnamed, have real, identifiable faces if we would just take the time to ponder them. For example, the other whom Jacob faced at the Jabbok could just as easily have been Jacob, himself, his brother Esau, his father, his mother, or all of the above. That same richness may be found in the social texts that we "read" on a daily basis.

Midrash proceeds by taking with absolute seriousness the otherness of the text, wrestling with it as other, and not presuming to master it in the process. Very much like Jacob and his *ish*, the text becomes the other that we grasp and insist bless us in our wrestling. In the process we face the text by facing the figures, the others in the text itself. We also face the others missing in the text.[8] Likewise we face the gaps and open spaces, even the shadows in the text as we give faces to the world configured in and by the text. Most important, we face our texts by facing up to the difficulties they all too frequently present to us.

A Way Beyond Supersessionism

Humility and contrition can lead penitent Christians beyond the contempt that stalks the culture of Christendom and its attitude toward Jews and Jewish life. But contrition alone leaves deeper matters untouched. Feeding Christian disdain is an imaginative mindset about God's ways with creation that Regina Schwartz, in her book *The Curse of Cain,* calls "a logic of scarcity" that she claims permeates all three monotheistic traditions, not just Christianity. According to Schwartz, that interpretive lens describes the tendency of monotheistic thinking to treat their truths as requiring singular expression and allegiance.[9] That is, if God is one, then God's truth and God's revelation of that truth are also one. Moreover, if this is the case, then there is only one true version of that knowledge. This attitude is challenged, of course, by midrashic thinking, especially when its logic of plenitude is exercised with regard to fundamental texts and root experiences of the tradition. Fackenheim recognized that this dimension was absolutely critical for post-Shoah hermeneutics to be able to find meaning in the core biblical texts and root experiences that ground Jewish life. Only then could its interpreters interrogate their core experiences and biblical sources with the unprecedented questions occasioned by the suffering of the children in their dark night of the Shoah.[10]

To be sure, midrashic hermeneutics have been an essential feature of our dialogue; however, as Schwartz's work makes clear, midrash's logic of plenitude is equally significant in finding a way beyond supersessionism—the real stumbling block for post-Shoah respect between Christians and Jews. Supersessionism, the thorn in Christianity's hermeneutical side, participates in or embodies a logic of scarcity that views its pursuit of the truth as the search for a single and singular rendering of God's Word that is manifest in or through the text of scripture. When each community reads shared texts as the Word of God viewed through the lens of scarcity, then only one reading is possible, even if it remains inadequately grasped. Each interpretation is judged with regard to that singular reference. If there is a conflict of interpretations, then one or more of those interpretations must be false when compared to the one that is privileged as true. The conflict is irreconcilable.

Supersessionism provides either a hierarchical structure for relating competing interpretations as they move closer and closer toward fulfilling the original intention known by those who exercise authority with regard to that structure of meaning; or more starkly, supersessionism operates with an either-or framework of choices that are guided by an overtly shared logic of replacement.[11] Regardless, since only one path is the true path, then only those interpretations that point to the one true path are of value. In the case of Jewish messianic expectations, any that do not point to Jesus cannot be true from a Christian perspective. They must be replaced with interpretations that confirm specific Christian truth claims. Or they must be seen as incomplete and then later fulfilled by more complete understandings on the part of Christian understandings.

Midrash provides an alternative way, an offering of possible meanings, each of which may be an authentic way of reading a text or situation like a text that has called forth the need to understand it. Its richly textured path becomes an interpretive bridge of dialogue whereby the conflict of interpretations may be viewed as a consequence of the text being approached as a vibrant and fertile garden of meaning, bearing a variety of fruit. Instead of seeking a single interpretation that is right, the text supports numerous readings, each of which points to the bounty of its narrated world and its capacity to speak to multiple generations and even competing circumstances. Recovering the richness of the text, whether its world is expressed in legal discourse or through the rhetoric of narrative, is the goal of midrashic reading. Supersessionary readings, on the other hand, seek a single meaning that in the end take the place of the text and foreclose their capacity to speak anew to later, unanticipated situations and circumstances. Moreover, when supersessionism's meaning is expressed as *the* Word of God, human words are elevated beyond measure and confused with the Mystery they claim to mediate.

In other words, midrashic dialogue offers a way beyond the often-irreconcilable conflict Judaism and Christianity experience when they argue over who has faithfully interpreted the Word of God mediated by their sacred texts. Importantly, midrashic engagement does not do away with the conflict; instead, it reconfigures the conflict as testimony to the importance of what is at stake in our interpretations and the richness of creation to which they point, even in the face of undeniable barrenness and scarcity.[12]

Facing Unfinished Work

As I think about this process with its literal and metaphorical dependence on textual and human faces, I cannot conclude without commenting on the recurring images of my colleagues with whom I read on a regular basis. Their presence across the text—sometimes imagined, other times quite tangible and very real—is a continuing reminder that our midrashic dialogue is always unfinished, even when we decide we have completed one project sufficiently to move on to another. Indeed, my reflections on this particular text bear this out. My first encounter with the midrashic magic of this story began a good eighteen years ago. I have re-entered its spell again and again, each time discovering new insights, new dimensions of the richness of its narrative. This occasion is no different. Of course, I am well aware that the text does not yield its secrets by way of magic. Rather, diligent study and the hard work of close reading and thoughtful reflection are essential for its spell to be experienced—not to mention probing conversation about the text with steadfast friends and reading partners. Still, there remains an enchanting quality to the experience that fits a story of pitching camp on a riverbank of such threshold proportions.

It is no exaggeration to say that each encounter takes me back to the first time I faced Jacob at the Jabbok and limped away from that meeting. I continue to limp as I return and leave the environs of that riverbank empowered by what happens there. Likewise, I am drawn back again and again in hopes that subsequent visits will continue to challenge and transfigure the many faces of my world who meet me there. And not least in this enterprise, each return to this sacred place reminds me of how grateful I am for my colleagues with whom I explore the midrashic garden of this and other texts.

Notes

1. Emil Fackenheim has described the task of post-Shoah Jewish hermeneutics in haunting fashion. As a Jewish reader, he contends that the only faithful way to read and interpret scripture after the Shoah is midrashically. That is, the questions one brings to the text and the world one expects the text to address shatter any strategy that does not provide for reading that resists conventional interpretations and easy solutions to overwhelming problems. See Emil L. Fackenheim, *God's Presence in History: Jewish Affirmations and Philosophical Reflections* (Northvale, N.J.: Jacob Aronson, 1970, 1997), 3–34, esp. 20–25.

   Emmanuel Levinas also highlights this dialectical quality in his midrashic reading of Exodus 20: "We will do then we will understand." He calls it, rather provocatively, "the temptation of temptation." When one faces a problematic text, the temptation is to yield the text to the problem and to seek freedom from the problem by disengaging the text as well—the temptation of temptation. Levinas proposes a stronger strategy consistent with the resistant reading of midrash. He begins with the understanding that Jewish readers are summoned first and foremost by the text and its witness. That is, they should not let go of the text but insist that it deal with the issue that makes it problematic. Indeed, the task is to wrestle with the text until it blesses the reader with a meaning that can speak to the issue at hand. In other words, faithful readers wrest from the text what it may give only if it is claimed as essential to their identity at the same time they insist that there must be another way of relating the text and its conventional meaning. See Emmanuel Levinas, "The Temptation of Temptation," in *Nine Talmudic Readings,* trans. Annette Aronowicz (Bloomington: Indiana University Press, 1990), 30–50, esp. 35, 48.

2. J. B. Metz has characterized the dialogical imperative of post-Shoah Christian theology in classic fashion: "We Christians can never again go back behind Auschwitz: to go beyond Auschwitz, if we see clearly, is impossible for us of ourselves. It is possible only together with the victims of Auschwitz." J. B. Metz, *The Emergent Church: The Future of Christianity in a Postbourgeois World* (New York: Crossroad, 1987), 19, 32. That is, Christian theology must proceed in dialogue with Jewish partners, preferably those engaged in the same questions from the Jewish side of the ledger in accounting for life lived in the aftermath of the Holocaust.
3. The strategy calls to mind the multicorpus work of Emmanuel Levinas. A more accessible Christian application sensitive to the need for midrash in the face of contemporary violence may be found in Danna Nolan Fewell's *The Children of Israel: Reading the Bible for the Sake of the Children* (Nashville: Abingdon Press, 2003).
4. Paul Ricoeur, "The Model of the Text: Meaningful Action Considered as a Text," in *From Text to Action: Essays in Hermeneutics, II,* trans. Kathleen Blamey and John B. Thompson (Evanston, Ill.: Northwestern University Press, 1991), 144–67.
5. I continue to explore this foundational text, building on work I first articulated at the Annual Scholars' Conference on the Holocaust and the Churches in 1993 and have revisited in several publications, especially this section. See Henry F. Knight, *Confessing Christ in a Post-Holocaust World: A Midrashic Experiment* (Westport, Conn.: Greenwood Press, 2000), 1–21, and Henry F. Knight, "Introduction to Part III—Wrestling with Biblical Texts: Torah and New Testament," in Steven Leonard Jacobs, *In Search of Yesterday: The Holocaust and the Quest for Meaning* (Lanham, Md.: University Press of America, 2006), 179–84.
6. Irving Greenberg, "Cloud of Smoke, Pillar of Fire," in *Auschwitz: Beginning of a New Era?,* ed. E. Fleischner (New York: KTAV, 1977), 23.
7. Douglas John Hall, *Confessing the Faith: Christian Theology in a North American Context* (Minneapolis: Fortress Press, 1996), 466.
8. Danna Nolan Fewell has captured quite literally what is at stake in this activity. Reading the biblical story of the flood in Genesis 6–9, she asks about the missing children. Interrupting the flow of the story, she recognizes the missing faces of children who pay with their lives the cost of the way of thinking that the story on the surface of its telling presumes. However, by tending these missing persons and entering into dialogue with the friction present in the narrative, she gives voice to the irony in the text, helping readers perceive the way the text "winks" at its readers as it describes God as the only one who changes in the aftermath of the flood. As Fewell points out, "The text knows that it is being read." See Danna Nolan Fewell, *The Children of Israel* (Nashville: Abingdon Press, 2003), 32.
9. Regina M. Schwartz, *The Curse of Cain: The Violent Legacy of Monotheism* (Chicago: University of Chicago Press, 1997), esp. xi, 4–38.
10. Fackenheim, *God's Presence in History.*
11. David Novak describes these options as two different forms of supersessionism: "hard supersessionism" and "soft supersessionism." Hard supersessionism operates with an overt replacement logic whereby Judaism is viewed as a failed embodiment to live as God's representative people and Christianity is viewed as that community that replaces Judaism in the divine economy of salvation history. Soft supersessionism allows for a positive view of Judaism as a community that has embodied God's expectations and served as a limited representation of God's ways with the world. Christianity, in turn, lives in witness to Christ's fulfillment of divine expectations and the full incarnation of what Israel only partially embodied. See his discussion of this matter in David Novak, "The Covenant in Rabbinic Thought," in *Two Faiths, One Covenant? Jewish and Christian Identity in the Presence of the Other,* ed. Eugene B. Korn and John T. Pawlikowski (Lanham, Md.: Rowman and Littlefield, 2005), 66.
12. I have relied heavily on the distinction Regina Schwartz makes between the logics of scarcity and plenitude as hermeneutical lenses that characterize the issues addressed in this essay. As interpretational lenses, these contrasting "logics" are two ways of construing the choices we face in any environment. Nonetheless, they

should not be confused with the lived realities of scarcity and plenty that confound our life together on this planet. In many situations of plenty, the logic of scarcity is at work leading those with abundant resources to horde their wealth, or use it wastefully with attitudes of entitlement regarding what they have. The opposite attitude is often expressed when those with little resources at all go to great lengths to share what they have with visitors to their communities, or others among them who have greater need. In other words, the logics of scarcity and plenitude are hermeneutical lenses that often operate in great contrast to the manifest realities in which they are employed. I am grateful to Joe Bessler-Northcutt of Phillips Theological Seminary for conversations about Schwartz's work and the need to distinguish these imaginative mindsets from the circumstances in which they are embodied. See Regina M. Schwartz, *The Curse of Cain* (Chicago: University of Chicago Press, 1997), esp. xi, 4–13, for Schwartz's discussion of these hermeneutical options.

Portraits of Two Jewries

Experiencing the Shoah through Fiction

Richard Libowitz

Historians, sociologists, and theologians filter the Holocaust through their very specific scholarly prisms, but our primary task remains a telling of the story, permitting students as well as the general public to understand in the most visceral manner—beyond footnotes, charts, and numbers—that a monstrous event occurred. Important as the academicians' efforts are for maintaining historical accuracy and intellectual acuity, it is not enough to rely solely upon learned compilations of data; thus, we turn to the storytellers. Elie Wiesel and Aharon Appelfeld have long been among the most prolific novelists of the Holocaust. Each crafts fiction based upon fact, reflective of the distinct segment of European Jewry in which he was raised and the commonalty of horror that was the *Shoah.*

Wiesel may have been raised in twentieth-century Sighet, but as a youth he followed an earlier lifestyle, studying Gemara by day and Kabbalah at night until, in 1944, the war against the Jews reached his town, he was transported to Auschwitz and confronted by the Kingdom of Night. For five decades, his prolific pen has turned out books, essays, and plays replete with madmen, mystics, and children, wrapped in a world of God, Torah, and *mitzvot*, invoking a Jewish community living alongside but apart from the Poles, Hungarians, and Rumanians who were neighbors. Less familiar to American readers, Aharon Appelfeld's short stories and novels recreate the world that was snatched away from him as a teen, the world of Mittel Europa, whose Jewish men and women eschewed Yiddish for German, summered in rural towns popular with the petit bourgeoisie, read novels rather than *siddurim,* and attended the theatre or symphony instead of the *beis midrash.*

Wiesel's stories reflect upon life, death, and characters trying to live in a shattered universe, uncertain in which world—if any—they belong. In *Dawn*, the year is 1946 and eighteen-year-old Elisha, a survivor of Auschwitz and Buchenwald, studies philosophy at the Sorbonne prior to his recruitment by an organization which might be called the Irgun. Brought to Mandate Palestine and taught the techniques of guerrilla warfare and terrorism, he also gains a rationale for his new life from Gad, his recruiter:

> For generations we've wanted to be better, more pure in heart than those who persecuted us. You've all seen the result: Hitler and the extermination camps in Germany. We've had enough of trying to be more just than those who claim to speak in the name of justice. When the Nazis killed a third of

> our people just men found nothing to say. If ever it's a question of killing off Jews, everyone is silent; there are twenty centuries of history to prove it.

For Gad, the solution was simple: "We must be like everyone else."[1]

When the British capture, try, and sentence a comrade to death, their response is to kidnap an English officer, vowing that the moment the noose slips over David ben Moshe's head, John Dawson will also die. The responsibility for killing Dawson falls to Elisha. On the eve of David's hanging and Dawson's execution, Elisha agonizes over his impending deed.

> I wanted to understand the pure, unadulterated essence of human nature, the path to the understanding of man. I had sought after the truth, and here I was about to become a killer, a participant in the work of death and God. (35)

As he sits, Elisha becomes aware of others crowding into the room: the spirits of his parents, his rabbi, a beggar he had helped, and the little boy he had once been. All who had known him, all who had affected him, were there because "An act so absolute as that of killing involves not only the killer but, as well, those who have formed him" (79). Elisha struggles with their accusing presence, knowing that "He who has killed one man alone is a killer for life" and that "In their frozen world the dead have nothing to do but judge, and because they have no sense of past or future they judge without pity" (90, 92). Unable to justify his act before the shades, he descends to the room holding his intended victim, wishing to meet Dawson, hoping to develop a hate for the man who is making him a killer, knowing that "Hate—like faith or love or war—justifies everything" (118). Together, they spend an hour in fitful conversation, the condemned man seeming far more calm than his executioner. At last, Dawson asks why he is hated and Elisha can think only

> Because my people have never known how to hate. Their tragedy, throughout the centuries, has stemmed from their inability to hate those who humiliated and from time to time exterminated them. Now our only chance lies in hating you, in learning the necessity and the art of hate. Otherwise . . . our future will only be an extension of the past, and the Messiah will wait indefinitely for his deliverance. (122)

At the appointed moment, despite his inner turmoil, Elisha pulls the trigger and John Dawson dies. Rejoining his comrades, the boy looks fearfully toward the window, only to discover that the ghosts he had seen there are gone and the reflection of his face is fading in the dawn's early light.

The Accident, a portrait of questioning survival, represents Wiesel's effort to write in the manner of his French contemporary, Albert Camus. Set in New York, it is the story of an alienated stranger who remains nameless, a decade removed from the camps and Israel's struggle for independence. One stifling summer evening he steps from the curb and is struck by a taxi. As he lies between death and life, the story alternates between events at the hospital and flashbacks recalling the man's near and more distant past.

Death has been at least temporarily defeated but the patient fails to share his physician's elation; too weak to speak, he gives the impression that he might have preferred to die. The body cast enveloping him is symbolic of the psychological straightjacket in which he has been bound since the war, emotionally crippled and mute. "That I was still alive had left me indifferent, or nearly so. But the knowledge that I could still speak filled me with an emotion that I couldn't hide."[2]

He is visited constantly by his lover, Kathleen, whose own emotional needs demand that he choose life. Wiesel has always shown an inability or unwillingness to develop fully realized female characters but, because she is so significant a part of the protagonist's anguish, Kathleen receives greater attention than is the author's want:

> She had a long, symmetrical face, uncommonly beautiful and touching. Her nose turned up slightly, accentuating her sensuous lips. Her almond-shaped eyes were filled with a dark, secret fire: an inactive volcano. With her, there could be real communication. (29)

This portrait of Kathleen, "with the beautiful black hair that she was so proud of" (16), is juxtaposed against the image of the patient's murdered grandmother, her head covered with a long black shawl, symbol of the world of the dead that retained a firm hold upon him.

The patient's characterization of survivors as "spiritual cripples" who have lost "their will and their taste of life" is an accurate self-description. He is ashamed to have survived, ashamed that he may be unfaithful to a destroyed world, ashamed to feel happiness or know love. Kathleen's presence only exacerbates his distress: "what united us was exactly what kept us apart. She liked life and love." Love for the living was too difficult, it "makes everything complicated . . . hate simplifies everything. Hatred puts accents on things and beings, and on what separates them. Love erases accents" (63, 101). Kathleen knows his words of love are lies, which he justifies along with his attitude about the past:

> a man who tells a woman he thinks he loves, "I love you and shall love you forever; may I die if I stop loving you," believes it. And yet one day he sounds his heart and finds it empty. And he stays alive. With us—those who have known the time of death—it's different. There, we said we would never forget. It still holds true. We cannot forget . . . I think if I were able to forget I would hate myself. (104–5)

The other constant visitor to the hospital room is Gyula, an artist who has known, without asking, that the patient's injuries had resulted from an accident "only in the most limited sense of the word. The cab, I had seen it coming. It had only been a flash, but I had seen it, I could have avoided it" (117). Gyula paints the man's portrait, completing it shortly before his discharge from the hospital and—with the help of crutches—a return to the world. The picture includes all the dead who inhabit and control his existence. Insisting upon life over death, with the dead chased away, if necessary, Gyula—whose name in Hebrew means "redemption"—burns his work and walks out of the room as the story ends.

Yet another facet of this struggle to survive is presented in *The Gates of the Forest.*[3] In this one, longer and more convoluted than his other stories, Wiesel introduces Gregor, a young boy whose efforts to escape the Nazis and grow to manhood are linked with an anonymous stranger, whom Gregor called by his own Hebrew name, Gavriel.

Initially meeting in Gregor's hideout, Gavriel appears to be a madman, laughing when others might scream. Gregor's fears of the stranger are eased, however, through a dream in which his grandfather tells him, "In times like these madmen are our only friends. They don't kill us in the name of beliefs or ideas. They're on our side and they get themselves killed."[4] Gavriel's foray into the nearby town for food alerts the police that a Jew remains in their midst. Knowing his hunters are unaware of the presence of a second Jew, Gavriel surrenders, permitting Gregor to escape.

The boy finds shelter with Maria, his family's former servant, who gives him a new identity as the deaf-mute son of her disgraced sister. Quickly accepted in the village, Gregor becomes the silent innocent to whom the peasants—and even the priest—pour out their secrets. He maintains his deception through thoughts of Gavriel, whose voice "vibrated within him, regulating his breathing and giving depth to his silence" (83).

Gregor's safety is lost when the local teacher coerces Maria into allowing her "nephew" to portray Judas in a school Passion Play. Acting turns to mob violence during the performance and Gregor is beaten savagely until he speaks, an action that paralyzes the mob, believing a miracle has occurred. Upon learning his true identity, however, they are again ready to kill him when the local nobleman whisks Gregor away to a "safe house" from which he can seek haven with the forest partisans.

The partisans are led by Leib the Lion, a friend from Gregor's days in yeshiva. Convinced that Gavriel is imprisoned in a nearby town, Gregor, Leib, and the latter's girlfriend, Clara, attempt a rescue; their plan fails, however, and Leib is captured. This time, it is the partisans who are ready to attack Gregor, accusing him of betraying Leib to the authorities, until Clara—who had made no secret of her animosity toward Gregor—vouches for him.

The story resumes years later: Gregor lives in New York and writes for a Jewish newspaper. He is married to Clara, although she has never given up the dead Leib. Gregor seeks relief from his personal anguish within the local Hasidic community, but clashes with the rebbe.

> When he first met the Rebbe, Gregor had said, "Has nothing changed?"
>
> "Nothing."
>
> "What about me?"
>
> "You haven't changed either."
>
> "And Auschwitz? What do you make of Auschwitz?"
>
> "Auschwitz proves that nothing has changed, that the primeval war goes on. Man is capable of love and hate, murder and sacrifice. He is Abraham and Isaac together. God himself hasn't changed."
>
> Gregor was angry. "After what happened to us, how can you believe in God?"
>
> With an understanding smile on his lips the Rebbe answered, "How can you *not* believe in God after what has happened?" (194)

During the evening on which he has decided to leave Clara, Gregor attends a Hasidic celebration and sees a man who might have been Gavriel. The stranger never admits his identity but draws Gregor's story from him. The novel concludes with Gregor believing "Gavriel" to be the prophet Elijah and, deciding to rid himself of all ghosts, to return to Clara and face the future. Unlike Elisha, who lost his past world when he killed John Dawson, and the nameless patient who needed crutches for a life somewhere beyond his past but not quite in Kathleen's present, Gregor can again embrace his Judaism and look to the future.

Aharon Appelfeld's short novels present men and women traveling from life to death and, on occasion, in a direction suggestive of new life. Without being formulaic, his stories depict a Kafkaesque world in which both time and space lose their hold. Appelfeld's characters have their journeys interrupted—shelter is found, lost, abandoned, or given away—but always resume, despite a lack of control by protagonists surrounded by events they do not understand. They live in silence and confusion; some rage, some wonder, others can do no more than wander, unable to focus upon a reality which has become unreal.

To the Land of the Cattails is the story of Toni Strauss, nee Rosenfeld, who left her home in Ruthenia at the age of seventeen to marry an Austrian Catholic who gave her a new name and a son before abandoning her. The quintessential modern Jew, Toni spends half her life in Austria, flitting from lover to lover until, as heir to the estate of her last elderly "benefactor," she has the means to act upon an urge to return home, to make amends with her parents, and to show her teenage son Rudi something of a heritage about which he knows absolutely nothing. "Something within her, something stronger than she, drew her on. 'Home,' she said to one of the border inspectors. 'Don't you understand?'"[5]

Mother and son begin their journey east on a train in the summer of 1938 but, at the novel's opening, they travel by wagon. The remaining distance is no more than several hundred miles but the journey becomes interminable, with wrong turns, illness, and severe weather stretching a few weeks' travel into years. Although the story tends to unfold through Rudi's eyes, Toni is an equal protagonist, the center of her son's world both when she is with him and when she is gone. Toni's emotional swings from excitement to lassitude are paralleled by Rudi's range in feelings between love and contempt. Toni feels at home, speaking the local language with Jews, peasants, and officials; Rudi, knowing only German, becomes the stranger. He neither looks Jewish nor is prepared to identify with his mother's people in terms of attitude or habit. He is at the age of discovery and his patience is thin. Early in their journey, mother and son have an enigmatic conversation:

> "You are no longer frightened?"
>
> "No, darling, I feel a strong desire to do everything my parents did. I also have a strong wish for you to be Jewish."
>
> "I am a Jew, am I not?"
>
> "Certainly you are a Jew, but you need a few more things, not many, not difficult. . . . And here, in these regions, you will learn the secret easily." (23)

As they travel, Rudi attempts to learn that secret.

In November 1938 Toni falls ill with typhus, forcing them to remain at an inn throughout the winter. When the doctor asks, "Do you observe the tradition?" Rudi's response is "No . . . we are freethinkers," but he remains uncertain and retreats to the stable where, in caring for his horses, he can restore his sense of proportion "or rather . . . the way he liked to look at the world and at his mother: from a distance." Complete detachment is impossible, however; on occasion "as if to disrupt the calm with terror, evil tidings would filter through to them, imposing a moment of disquiet on the warm dining room" (42–50).

As the winter continues, Rudi observes the inn's Jewish clientele;

> They seemed clumsy to him, ill-mannered and corrupt. But in the course of time he found that while they were not particularly pleasant, they were not unbearable. They had a sense of humor, were frivolous and extravagant. Even their complaints were just a form of humor. If that is how Jews are, why do people hate them so much? (60–61)

A clerk answered his question.

> "They have no courage. . . . They don't stick to their guns, you understand?"
>
> "How is that?" Rudi challenged him.
>
> "The simple ability to raise their hands, to get angry without boiling over, that natural ability is denied them. That is the source of all evil: fear, cunning, pain and self-abnegation. In short, they weren't meant for life." (60)

Rudi is different, however. Resuming their journey in the spring of 1939, he insists that "We are Jews, and we will not hide that from anyone" (83). Toni seeks coffee at an inn one evening, but

> [t]he owner retorted that he ran a roadhouse, not a café. The innkeeper's brother was more brutish and made a comment about Toni's Jewishness. Rudi did not understand the words, but he felt their malevolence. "No one insults my mother," he said and punched him in the face. . . . The boy's courage impressed them, as if an unpredicted force had caught them by surprise. They stood where they were and shouted curses that only showed how frightened they were. "Shut up!" Rudi shouted at them, and they fell silent. (85)

Aware of her son's difference, Toni repeatedly questioned him.

> "Aren't you afraid?"
>
> "What is there to fear?"
>
> "I'm glad I sent you to a good gymnasium. There one learns well. There one learns sport. Sport strengthens the body. Fear is a despicable emotion. Jews are always fearful. It is good you are unafraid. I'm happy that you're not afraid."
>
> "There's nothing to fear." (90)

Their journey nears its end as the summer of 1939 draws to its close. Just two hours from her hometown of Dratscincz, Toni leaves Rudi at an inn and continues alone. Rudi follows her the next day, only to discover that the Jews of Dratscincz had been deported that morning.

Rudi begins traveling from village to village, seeking his mother among the Jews awaiting the trains that will take them to the east. "The war was already in full tilt, but there was no trace of it here. Except for the railway stations daily absorbing the deportees, the peaceful autumn reigned with its welter of colors" (124). He is joined on his search by Arna, a young girl who has also become separated from her family. Together, they spend the winter of 1939–40 in the ruins of a Jewish home, Arna trading Toni's clothes and jewelry for food and saving Rudi's life when he falls ill. As Rudi slowly surrenders the last pieces of his Viennese past, the child of Eastern Europe assumes a more significant role in his life. Rudi wonders if Arna embodies Toni's early promise as he realized "her small body bore many secrets within it, hidden secrets. He would have to learn from her as long as he lived. At their stopovers he would sit across from her and ask her questions. Strangely she was not embarrassed" (135).

The novel closes as it had begun, with a train ride, but of a different type. Rudi and Arna join a group of Jews waiting patiently as "an old locomotive, drawing two old cars . . . went from station to station, scrupulously gathering up the remainder" (148). A single enigmatic line suggests that Rudi survives the war, to remember his mother many years later, but Appelfeld is deliberately vague and says nothing of Arna's fate.

Whereas Wiesel's survivors have reached Paris or New York by the opening of their postwar sagas, many of Appelfeld's characters are seen in the immediate weeks following liberation. Turned loose by Allied forces in the spring of 1945, those who did not die of starvation, typhus, or the sheer loss of will to live began to walk the face of central Europe. Theo Braun, protagonist of *For Every Sin*, is one such character. There are many similarities between Theo and Rudi Strauss, but the attitudes and tendencies found in Rudi have been magnified in Theo and his family. Like Rudi, the prewar Theo had been a student with a beautiful and frivolous mother, in love with Austrian culture. Unlike Toni Strauss, however, Theo's mother slipped into lunacy, not the Wieselian madness that recognizes truth, but a dementia with few redeeming social virtues.

Rudi had drawn strength, at last, from Arna, the representative of Judaism, but Theo wanted only to detach himself from other Jews and return to his Austrian hometown of Baden-bei-Wien. Having separated himself from the others in his camp, he travels alone, his antipathy for the survivors who fill the hills and valleys "stronger than any fear."[6]

Too weak to sustain his trek for long, he comes upon a deserted German guardhouse, well supplied with food, cigarettes, bedding, and clothing. There he burns his ragged prisoner's uniform "without feeling anything," replaces it with a German uniform, and marches in place, in military fashion.

> That action, which was intended merely to verify and ratify the sturdiness of the boots, raised up within him, unnoticed, a kind of alien and murky feeling. The feeling waxed within him, and he said, "I'll stay here until I uproot all my weaknesses and fears. No one will have contempt for me anymore." (15–16)

For Theo, the war years were to be blotted out of mind, greater reason to avoid other survivors, despite their supplies of food, coffee, and cigarettes. Yet in spite of himself, he assists one woman, in whose eyes "horror was visible . . . horror which had no more fear in it" (19).

> "What can I offer you?" he said, glad to find the right words. That direct, courteous address surprised the woman. Her pursed mouth opened a little as though she realized the world was back to normal. Once again human beings offered you food and drink. (20)

In Appelfeld's assimilated world, the response to horror does not include calls for love or justice and certainly lacks appeals to God. His characters, the German-speaking Jews of central Europe, did not and perhaps could not understand what had happened to them. They had no rejoinder to their tormentors or a justification for their own suffering. All they were able to do was attempt a return to that which had existed before the war, sometimes to their own astonishment. Thus Mina, the woman to whom Theo offered shelter, says, "A cup of coffee and a cigarette. Who imagined such gifts? We've already been in the world of truth, and we've come back from there. It's interesting to come back from there, isn't it?" (25).[7]

Theo's homeward journey is unsteady; his physical weakness demands repeated stops. He remains in various tents and buildings for weeks at a time, resuming his walk for several hours, only to retreat to his shelter. Uncertain and unhappy, he follows a continually narrowing series of valleys, eventually finding himself among other survivors.

> "What's this here?"
>
> "A transit camp," a woman answered matter-of-factly.
>
> "Transit to where?"
>
> "I don't know," she said, spreading her arms . . .
>
> "How do you get out of here?" he asked.
>
> "You can get out from there." The woman pointed at a small passage, where many people had crowded together with their bundles . . .
>
> "I made a mistake. I shouldn't have come here . . ."
>
> "We didn't intend to get here either . . ."

> "The hillcrest is where you move freely. On a hillcrest you're a free man."
>
> "Are you sure?"
>
> "I have no doubt. This togetherness brings only disaster. Anyone can come and block up this valley. We must scatter, walk on the hillcrests, and the sooner the better for us. Anywhere but here." (144–47)

Theo intends to do more than return to Baden-bei-Wien; his ultimate escape would be conversion to Christianity. When another survivor argues with him about it, they scuffle and Theo knocks him unconsciousness. From then on, he fears he is being pursued by a justice committee, of the sort that punished collaborators. His plans are also disparaged by the woman with whom he had spoken at the transit camp. "'I won't go home,' she insists, 'I'll never go home. Anyplace is my home, just not there.'" Theo warns her that "From now on you'll be homeless, always on the road, always with the refugees," but she replies, "The company of the refugees is more pleasant to me than that of the murderers" (151).

Rather than regaining strength, Theo finds himself losing the very gifts that had sustained him. In the camp, his mother's beauty had overwhelmed him. He recalls her addiction to coffee and her love of Bach's music which filled the churches she had so often visited. "All during the war, the music was within me. Now I'm afraid to lose it . . . I am so frightened of being left without music" (125).

Greater than his fear of losing the music is his dread of being a Jew. The woman in the camp had warned him, "Your desire to return home is . . . a dreadful illusion. We have no home anymore. We no longer have anything" (155). No home, no music, not even language. Theo is proud of his careful and proper German; he fears he will lose that, too. "Now he knew that the language had escaped him. The Yiddish of the camps had done it in. From now on he would speak only the Yiddish of the camps. That fear, that his mother had planted in him from the time he was nursing, filled him again" (162). If he could not be the Theo of before the war, what was left to him?

> "Why do you look down on us?" a man called out in a strident voice. "Believe me, we never harmed anyone. We may not be righteous men, but we're not contemptible. We suffered enough in the camps."
>
> "What do you want from me?" Theo spoke to him, trembling.
>
> "Why do you look down on us? You were in a camp too. . . . You mustn't look down on us. Among us are martyrs for the sake of man. That mute man there, sitting at my side, used to give his meager crust to two sick people. You mustn't look down on him."
>
> "I don't look down on him."
>
> "So why are you running away from us . . ."
>
> "I'm going home." Theo shouted as though talking to a deaf man.
>
> "You know very well that no one is waiting for us at home." (164–65)

Sitting in a hut, drinking coffee with other refugees, Theo finally realizes that he will never return to his hometown, that his lot will be forever with the survivors, and that he has lost the language of his mother for the language of the camps, a set of realizations that make him "dreadfully sad."

> "Where did you intend to go?"
>
> "To my hometown, to Baden-bei-Wien."
>
> "There's no need to go there. Stay here. We have everything we need. . . . There's no sense seeking something that can never be attained. We won't bring the dead back to life. You understand that. Here we're together . . . it isn't always comfortable, but still, we're together." (167–68)

As the novel closes, Theo accepts his new fate and collapses.

Neither Wiesel nor Appelfeld is subtle in the use of allegory: Theo represents the Everyman of assimilated Jewry. He adores his mother, who is German culture, Christian-centered, loving Bach and choirs raining their sweet sounds through city cathedrals, town churches, and wayside chapels. She is beautiful in form, well ordered in dress, precise in language, but her life fluctuates between lucidity and aberration before its final descent into madness. Theo's father is Judaism, personified by the quiet bookstore owner, dominated by his wife to the extent that his presence in their home never seemed real. "His mother filled the house, with no space left over," while his father's existence had "lacked reality. . . . It always seemed as if he had already left" (91). As his mother's illness worsens, the father says less and less, finally retreating into total silence. Only once had Theo seen his father alive, but it was within his own world. "In the final year of high school Theo happened to go into the bookstore . . . his father was standing at the counter in conversation with a student. He spoke in long sentences with elegant relative pronouns and a few fine adjectives. His stance was calm and simple, with no awkwardness" (92). Yet it was too late to bring father and son together.

The mother's madness having driven them into poverty becomes, at last, too much for the father to endure. He divorces her, rejecting her world—the union of Judaism and Germanism—impossible to maintain, and she hated him for it. She never fails to fill her son with poison about his father (Judaism). In the camp, Theo's father "was progressively erased from his memory and forgotten" (95); German culture, his mother's beauty, and the music had sustained him. At the end, however, German clothing might fit Theo but German culture would not. He is compelled to confront his worst nightmare, that he is all his mother had taught him to reject. The assimilated one, the Jewish Austrian who would become a Christian, had no choice but to be a Jew. At the novel's conclusion, readers are left to wonder whether Theo can survive the change.[8]

Bringing his characters closer to contemporary times, *The Immortal Bartfuss* presents a survivor who walked from the camps to Italy following liberation; there, he became involved in smuggling. A liaison with another survivor resulted in a child, but he deserted mother and daughter when he fled to Mandate Palestine. Eventually he was found by the abandoned Rosa and settled into a familial relationship of silence and hatred.

As the novel opens, we are met with a seething family situation, reminiscent of Francois Mauriac's classic *Viper's Tangle*. Rosa and Bartfuss rarely speak; she and elder daughter Paula scheme to find the money they are positive he has concealed within their apartment. Bartfuss does feel an occasional sense of kinship with his youngest daughter, Bridget, who is mildly retarded, but she has been suckled on her mother's hatred and knows only to fear her father.

Bartfuss is fifty years old, a dealer in gold and, perhaps, other commodities. Many among the survivor community know of him and consider him a silent legend, the man purported to have survived multiple gunshot wounds in Europe, one who would not be killed. Bartfuss refuses any talk of those events, however. Occasionally lonely but intensely watchful, he has wrapped himself in silence, severing relationships with most people and finding inner peace only in his walks to the sea. He never allows himself to sleep deeply nor does he reveal himself in conversation, remaining "the dark shadow, the unsolved riddle."[9] Having been a smuggler in Italy, "In Israel he cut himself off from the rings, but he didn't stop trading. In fact, because of his trade he grew more introverted and friendless" (30). Bartfuss had taught himself to avoid both thought and curiosity. "It was better not to ask. You might get entangled, leave yourself open, and show something you hadn't intended to reveal" (35). His attitudes are evocative of Theo Braun's desperate desire to avoid other survivors and his insistence upon silence and solitude as the agencies for healing.

Silence had been necessary for Bartfuss's survival. During the war, he had lived for several months in a forest foxhole.

> When sent to that little camp known for its horrors, he had seen many faces but no people. Starved, crushed into freight cars, the people had learned to ignore each other, to steal and push like beasts with the little strength remaining to them. One after another, feelings were numbed. The suffering was ugly. Except for the few visions of the end of the battle, the agonies would have been even uglier. (48)

Only "the prolonged downfall of the Germans" had restored some faith in life; at the transit camp in Italy, he was rather like everyone else although he spoke little, even then. "No one knew what to do with the lives that had been saved. The lives that had been saved strove for great deeds" (36). Yet Bartfuss's "great dream had been buried somewhere in the sands of Italy, and since then his life had been without a dream" (105). He was left an observer of life, filled with emptiness, his own existence void of feelings except for suspicions of his unloving family, occasional sensations of fatherly concern for Bridget, and a protectiveness about his "treasure," the hoard that filled the days, nights, and schemes of his family, and consisted of "Three gold bars, five thousand dollars, two necklaces, a few gold watches, his father's passport picture, and a small photograph, apparently from school, of his sister" (45).

Now, however, Bartfuss was troubled.

> Without being aware of it, and without wishing to, he started thinking. He had invested a lot of energy into blocking up the openings through which thoughts could push out. In recent years he had managed to seal them off almost completely. Now he felt he didn't have the power to stop them anymore. (36)

The man who had cut himself off from his friends in Jaffa began to seek out people he had known for many years. The distant father who had not attended his daughter's wedding looked for Theresa, a woman whom he had remembered for more than twenty-five years and continued to pursue even when she failed to remember him, told him that she lived in the present while he was existing in the past, and rejected him. A dormant will to struggle began to arise within him, even a sudden desire "to be immersed once again in the general good" (76). Although his health began to fail he was certain he would survive, even while his family feared he would die without revealing the "treasure's" location.

In bringing his characters to midlife and beyond, Appelfeld insisted their misanthropy be softened by the readers' understanding that the disruptions that the survivors suffered had not abated over the years. In his silence, Bartfuss returns to Italy and before; unlike Santiago of *The Old Man and the Sea*, whose dreams of lions on the beach and recollections of youthful feats provided strength and inspiration, Bartfuss turns to the past only as a means of avoiding the present. Yet he lives on, "immortal," embodying the plight of many survivors. Appelfeld has stated;

> The survivors have undergone experiences that no one else has undergone, and others expect some message from them, some key to understanding the human world—a human example. But they, of course, cannot begin to fulfill the great tasks imposed upon them, so theirs are clandestine lives of flight and hiding. The trouble is that no more hiding places are available. One has a feeling of guilt that grows from year to year and becomes . . . an accusation.[10]

In his essay "A Plea for the Survivors," Elie Wiesel sounded a similar note. "Time does *not* heal all wounds; there are those that remain painfully open."[11] He described survivors as men and women who lead "a private existence. They stay among themselves closed and uncommunicative, in a kind of invisible ghetto, relating to the outside world with difficulty . . . in spite of appearances, they are not of this world, not of this era."[12] Wiesel's explanations turn to Job and God and an existential loneliness which nonsurvivors can never grasp. Appelfeld's understandings follow in the same direction, as when he writes, "The Holocaust belongs to the type of enormous experience which reduces one to silence. Any utterance, any statement, any 'answer' is tiny, meaningless and occasionally ridiculous. Even the greatest of answers seems petty."[13] His men and women may have no reserve of faith or moral courage from which to draw, but they too have contributed to Judaism. They too have sought an honorable way within the world. They too had not wished to die.

The curious Rudi, the exhausted Theo, and Bartfuss, who finds that even he cannot eradicate his total will, have lost family, friends, the world. Each has been emptied and each—in one way or another—has acted upon that emptiness. Even the assimilated, Appelfeld insists, make a legitimate Jewish contribution, for in them "the Jewish character and also, perhaps, Jewish fate, was concentrated with greatest force." Appelfeld has provided a voice for a lost segment of European Jewry, no less authentic for its untraditional bent than the Hasidim. He has given us secular *lamed-vavniks* and worldly *tzaddikim* who are confronted with a similar plethora of questions and paucity of answers. They are people who "built themselves a structure of humanistic values and looked out on the world from it. They were certain they were no longer Jews and that what applied to 'the Jews' did not apply to them"[14] even though, as pressure mounted, some made efforts at a rapprochement with the Jewish world from which they had previously fled.

Neither Appelfeld nor Wiesel provides the dates, place names, or numbers insisted upon for historical precision. Instead, they present us with damaged men and women who had been abandoned by the world to the horror that was the Shoah and then, having survived, were expected to go on as if nothing had happened. Some Jews *were* able to live "as if": as if the Shoah had not occurred, as if Auschwitz had not existed, as if the world had not closed the gates of refuge to them. For most, however, personal survival came with a price—loss of family, loss of faith, loss of self-worth, loss of self—far too great to ignore. In their painful odysseys they speak to us of the Shoah in a way no chart, map, or list can ever do.

Notes

1. Elie Wiesel, *Dawn* (New York: Hill and Wang, 1970), 41. Subsequent page numbers appear in the text.
2. Elie Wiesel, *The Accident* (New York: Hill and Wang, 1962), 21. Subsequent page numbers appear in the text.
3. *Day*, in the French original, completing the trilogy of *Night* and *Dawn.*
4. Elie Wiesel, *The Gates of the Forest* (New York: Holt, Rinehart, and Winston, 1966), 13. Subsequent page numbers appear in the text.
5. Aharon Appelfeld, *To the Land of the Cattails* (New York: Grove Press, 1986), 6. Subsequent page numbers appear in the text.
6. Aharon Appelfeld, *For Every Sin* (New York: Grove Press, 1990), 13. Subsequent page numbers appear in the text.
7. For a comment on the impossibility of return to their prewar existence, see Jean Amery, *At the Mind's Limits* (Bloomington: Indiana University Press, 1980).
8. Compare Theo to Amery's essay "On Being a Jew," in *At the Mind's Limits.*
9. Aharon Appelfeld, *The Immortal Bartfuss* (New York: Grove Press, 1988), 24. Subsequent page numbers appear in the text.
10. Philip Roth, "A Conversation with Aharon Appelfeld," *New York Times Book Review*, February 28, 1988, 31.
11. Elie Wiesel, "A Plea for the Survivors," *A Jew Today* (New York: Random House, 1978), 222.
12. Ibid., 222–23.
13. Roth, "A Conversation with Aharon Appelfeld," 31.
14. Ibid., 29.

No Vindication to Venomous Verdict

The Poem "Mr. Auschwitz" by Ronny Someck

Yair Mazor

Along all the length of the streets
Skulls are tossed
From the palm of yesterday to the palm of tomorrow.
—David Fogel, "Untitled"

אדון ארשוויץ
קשה להמס מהזיכרון את גוש הקרח הכחול שקפא בעיניו,
את המספרים שקועקעו בזרועו
ואת החגורה שהצליף באשה שהייתה איתו שם
ועכשיו שותקת במרפסת.
”חבל,“ היה קולו חותך, ”שהיטלר לא עבד שעות נוספות,“
והקקטוסים בעציצים היו מתחדדים כגדרות התיל
של המחנה ממנו ברח.
את הקצף שניגר מבאר פיו המורעל היה מנגב
בדגל שהיה תלוי מיום עצמאות אחד ליום העצמאות הבא.
”אדון אושוויץ“ צעקנו כשבאו לקחת אותו לבית המשוגעים,
והוא עוד הספיק להכניס יד לכיס ולקלף
את הצלופן מהסוכריות שזרק לעברנו.

Mr. Auschwitz
It is difficult to compel the recollection melt the blue ice block that froze in his eyes,
The numbers that were tattooed on his arm
And the belt with which he whipped the woman who was with him there
And now she keeps silent on the balcony.
"Such a pity," his voice did sound like a slash, "that Hitler didn't work extra hours"
And the cactuses in the pots turned as thorny as the wire fence
Of the concentration camp from which he escaped.
The foam that poured out of his poisonous mouth, he wiped
With the national flag that he hung from one Independence Day to the following one.
"Mr. Auschwitz" we shouted when he was taken to the mental institute,

And he still had time enough to put his hand in his pocket and peel
The cellophane of the candies that he threw to us.

The most powerful components that protrude in this poem by Ronny Someck are the following two: stupendously scorching, scalding emotions and admirably aesthetic intricacy. That tempestuous "quarry" of emotions may be plausibly considered as the reservoir of the "raw materials" that feed the aesthetic mechanism and enable it to propel and operate its complex "engine." Thus the poem's erupting emotions act in capacity of a bedrock, on which the aesthetic mechanism is set.

Nevertheless, in order to appreciate to the fullest the stormy might of the poem's emotions, one must go "backwards" and commence the reading process while concentrating on the poem's aesthetic mechanism. Such a "reverse" process of reading, practiced upon encountering the poem, seems to be the only way to reach out to the poem's fervent emotions. Hence, while the poem's flaming emotions are the poem's essence and cornerstone, the poem's aesthetic mechanism is both the structure that holds together the emotions and the apparatus that blazes a trail that leads to the very fervid heart of those turbulent, forceful, fiery emotions.

In light of the above, it appears that one must acquaint himself/herself with the poem's aesthetic mechanism prior to addressing the poem's "quarry" of flaming, inferno-like emotions. The latter makes sense also due to the following consideration. After all, the very core and essence of any work of art is its artistic, aesthetic mechanism. The "meaning" of the work of art, the ideas that are invested in the work of art, are secondary in comparison with the work of art's aesthetic, artistic mechanism. Had a writer, for instance, wished to reverse the order mentioned above, and give priority to his ideas, he would have written an article that introduces the ideas, and not write a poem in which the ideas are cryptically hidden behind the aesthetic, artistic mechanism and cannot be unearthed prior to a fastidiously practiced process of an aesthetic interpretation. Thus, what makes a work of art a work of art is the fact that its first function is of an aesthetic nature, while the work of art's ideas, "meaning," and ideological orientation come second, being subordinate to the leading aesthetic mechanism. Hence, one can "excavate," unveil, decode, and "crack" the work of art's meaning, ideas, and ideological tendencies, only after he analyzes and deciphers the work of art's aesthetic mechanism.

The aesthetic mechanism that is practiced most dexterously in this poem may be entitled the dynamics of the textual continuum (or sequence). The dynamics of the textual continuum is founded on the most prominent characteristic of any text: being time-oriented. Hence, since the text's verbal units (words, sentences, paragraphs, chapters) are "inlaid" in the text and introduced sequentially, the textual sequence conditions and dictates the accumulation of information, one that yields a mutual interaction between bulks of information that are installed early (or relatively early) along the textual continuum and bulks of information that are installed late/later along the textual continuum. Correspondingly, time and timing play the most prominent role in the verbal genre of literature: prose, poetry, and drama. Indeed, other artistic mediums share the same time-oriented leading characteristic. Dance, music, theater can also be experienced only along a sequence, one that is conditioned by time. Time dictates and introduces a progressive procession that consists of a reciprocal "dialogue" between early information (verbal, motion-oriented, sound-oriented) and late/later information. Artistic mediums like painting and sculpture, however, are devoid of time-oriented characteristics since they are created, they operate, and they perform in space only. Correspondingly, the space-oriented artistic mediums are "consumed" by their target audience as objects of physical, tangible volume whose "existential status" materializes in space only while it is observed (although not studied fastidiously) in a couple of seconds, a process that is not harnessed to any time-oriented sequence.

The sequential character of the text, one that forces its target audience (the reader) to consume the text and respond to it through time duration, naturally creates and conditions a phenomenon in which early information that is located along the textual continuum is followed by late information. Indeed, that sequential nature of the verbal medium (that produces the text, that can be any kind of text, such as literary text, a text of a book of history, or even a book of mathematics, a newspaper's text, and so on) is the one that bestows upon the text its most paramount, prominent characteristic: the temporal, time-oriented characteristic. In light of the latter, is one in a position to trace three typical kinds of mutual interaction practiced between early (or relatively early) information and late (or later) information, "inlaid" along the textual sequence/continuum?

The first typical kind is the simplest, in the sense that the late/r information neither affects nor changes the way that the early/earlier information was comprehended and interpreted by the reader, before he/she encountered the late/r information.

> This evening I think again
> About many days . . .
>
> —Yehuda Amichai, "Poem Number 3," from *Time*

First, the distinction between the early information (first line) and the late/r information is hereby stressed due to a syntactical device entitled "run-on line." This syntactical device consists of the fact that the syntactical unit (the sentence) does not terminate at the ending of the line and continues in the following line. Quite often, an entire poem is based on one run-on line: the syntactical unit—the sentence—keeps progressing and "gliding" from the poem's first line to the poem's last line. Metaphorically, one may portray the motion of the run-on line as sliding, gliding down from the poem's one line to the poem's following line. Accordingly, the run-on line stems from a lack of congruence between the syntactical unit (the sentence) and the typographical character of the poetic line. Indeed, the run-on line phenomenon is called in Hebrew *g'lisha*, that derives from the verb *liglosh*, which means "to slide down." That and more. One may cogently argue that the run-on line is not only a syntactical device, but also a compositional device and also a rhetorical device.

Accordingly, the compositional nature (and correspondingly function) of the run-on line stems from the fact that the run-on line is materialized according to a compositional consideration, one that determines the arrangement of the poetic line, the placement of the run-on line along the textual continuum (at the end of one line, and in the beginning of the following line). The rhetorical nature (and correspondingly function) of the run-on line stems from the very nature of rhetorics, one that dictates and conditions the reader's reaction to the text. Since the run-on line shapes and forms the reader's response to the text (by forcing the reader to respond to the early bulk of text in light of the consecutively later bulk of information), it is not only of syntactical and compositional characteristics and function, but of rhetorical as well. In light of the above, does one possess the capacity to realize that the run-on line is conceived by a cluster of three aesthetic devices—syntactical, compositional, rhetorical—that "spin" and "sculpt" one aesthetic intersection, where the three devices encounter, interact, and are woven into one literary entity.

One may further realize, however, that the literary device "run-on line" is tracked in poetry only, and never in prose. The latter stems from the following fact. Only in poetry, the length of the poetic line is determined by the artist (indeed, by the literary text's "implied author") according to aesthetic considerations. Since the run-on line is yielded by the length of the line, one that can discern the syntactical unit (the sentence) before it ended, and make it slide down to the following line; and since the length of the line is determined by the poet upon wishing to meet this way a literary goal. The run-on line is so typical to poetry, to the point that the latter is densely populated by phenomena of absence of congruence between the syntactical unit (the sentence) and the line unit (the typographical character of the line unit). In prose fiction, however, the length of the line is determined not by the poet, not according to poetic considerations, but rather by the publisher, according to technical and economical considerations. Thus, even when the sentence in prose fiction does not end at the end of the line and slides down to the following line, such a run-on line is entirely devoid of aesthetic qualities, since it derives from technical and economical considerations (e.g., the book's format, its potential capacity to sell well). Hence, the very essence of the difference between poetry and prose fiction consists of the run-on line: while prose fiction is entirely "disarmed" of aesthetically oriented run-on lines, poetry is saturated with run-on lines that are sculpted by pure aesthetic considerations.

Most certainly, the run-on line effectively stresses the mutual interaction between an early bulk of information "inlaid" along the textual sequence (the first line of the run-on line, before it slides down to the following line) and a late/r bulk of information that is introduced in that following line, after the run-on line materialized by sliding down to that consecutive line. However, the run-on line is not the only case of a mutual interaction between early/earlier and late/r bulks of information. Nevertheless, the run-on line does intensify the density and tension that are produced by the mutual interaction between early and late bulks of information that populate the textual continuum. As previously argued, while the run-on line is limited to poetry only, the mutual interaction between early and late bulks of information is equally shared by all verbal, artistic mediums: poetry, prose fiction, and drama. Also, as previously further stated, the mutual interaction between bulks of early and late information along the textual continuum introduces three kinds of that interaction that consist of increasing stages of both complexity and intensity.

Since the run-on line in poetry plausibly displays the mutual interaction in focus, the following three demonstrative examples are taken from poetry, in an order that "obeys" the three stages of increasing intensity and complexity mentioned above.

The first example was already introduced, although not yet analyzed:

This evening I think again
About many days . . .

To this example one may add the following:

I saw roads that lead
From one man to another woman.

As previously stated, those examples display the first, most simple kind of run-on line. Indeed, the run-on line materializes in both examples according to the core definition of a run-on line: in both examples the syntactical unit (the sentence) does not end where the typographical unit (the line) ends, and thus, the sentence slides down and continues in the next, consecutive line. Indeed, the materialization of the run-on line (that starts at the end of the first line and ends in the beginning of the following line) draw's the reader's attention to both parts of the run-on line's "equation": the end of the first line and the beginning of the following line.

Once the reader reaches the end of the first line and due to a lack of a period or dots she realizes that she faces a run-on line. Hence, her attention focuses on the second part of the run-on line, in the beginning of the second, following line. The latter stems from the fact that once the reader realizes that she faces and encounters a run-on line, does she cultivate expectations and questions formulated in the following fashion: how the second, yet unearthed part of the run-on line will materialize what is going to be the content of the second part of the run-on line? Is it going to be in agreement with the beginning of the run-on line, or is it going to negate, contradict, and contest the first part of the run-on line?

All those questions may be practiced by the reader as fast as a blink of an eye, while without her awareness to the entire process. However, the latter neither challenges nor erases the very valid existence of that process. The fact that a person is not aware of the incredible complexity of the activity of his nerves and muscles upon raising his hand, for instance, does not negate the physiological complexity that enables him to raise his hand. Hence, this intricate process that consists of both aesthetic and psychological activities, which are performed simultaneously and equally swiftly, is practiced by all readers whether they are aware of the process or entirely oblivious to its occurrence.

Thus, despite the fact that the two parts of the run-on line are formally equal—like two components in one equation—the second part is clearly more prominent since it draws most of the reader's attention. Following all the above, upon observing the first two run-on lines in focus, does one realize that despite the complex aesthetic/psychological mechanism of the run-on line, those two demonstrative run-on lines are relatively devoid of intricacy. Hence, in both cases the second part of the run-on line neither emends nor contests the way that a discriminating reader understood the first part of the run-on line. In other words, in those two examples of run-on lines, the late information (the second part of the run-on line) neither sheds a new light on the early information (the first part of the run-on line) nor calls for even a partial updating, certainly not for a drastic change in the way that the reader previously comprehended the early information. Correspondingly, in those two demonstrative simple examples of run-on line, the later information simply joins the early information (while making it more specific and detailed, most certainly), without shedding a new, "provocative" light on the early information or on the way it was previously comprehended. The second kind of mutual interaction between early information and late information that are located and introduced along the textual sequence/continuum (that mutual interaction—between early and late bulks of information—is effectively magnified in a case of run-on line) consists of a more dramatic, intensive, rigorous, and energetic relations between the two bulks of information.

While in the first kind the late information joins the early one, making it more specific and detailed but without changing a thing in the way the early information was comprehended previously upon the first encounter with it, in the second kind of a mutual interaction between the early and late bulks of information the late information updates considerably and changes the previously introduced early information and the way it was comprehended. That change, however, is relatively moderate. Accordingly, although the late information does change significantly the way the early information was comprehended and interpreted at its location along the textual sequence, such a change calls for updating that early comprehension, but certainly not for deleting and dismissing it altogether. The following example appears to demonstrate effectively the above:

> This is a weeping truth
> But sometimes that truth weeps out of happiness . . .
>
> —Yehuda Amichai, "Poem Number 16," from *Time*

The first line—the early bulk of information—introduces "a weeping truth." Since "a weeping truth" cannot be comprehended on a concrete, realistic level (how does truth weep?) does the reader have to take that statement one step further and interpret it on a metaphorical, symbolic level? Hence, on the metaphorical, symbolic level, "a weeping truth" may be interpreted as truth that encounters tormenting, haunting difficulties upon carrying and demonstrating its truthfulness to deliver its message of moral integrity, to the point that that truth finds itself weeping out of its yoking mission, its demanding, challenging task.

Nevertheless, despite the pain that causes that burdened truth to weep, it continues heralding its message of moral integrity, while continuing weeping as well. The following line, however, the one that introduces the later bulk of information, declares the following:

> But sometimes that truth weeps out of happiness.

Hence, the late information, while interacting with the early information, casts a new light on the early information, to the point that the reader is compelled to practice a process of reverse reading, to read backwards, to reread the early information and update his/her previous comprehension and interpretation of that early comprehension (that truth *always* weeps out of pain that is yielded by its burdening moral message). It is more than certain that a declaration about truth that "eternally" weeps out of pain must be emended and updated in light of later information that declares that weeping truth sometimes weeps out of happiness. One may justly wonder, however: how come that "tormented" truth, that its yoking message of moral integrity is a hounding load to the point that makes it weep constantly, may also weep out of happiness? Indeed, the following lines in the poem (which are naturally considered late information that updates the previous interpretation of the early information) unearths the latent logic that explains how truth that weeps out of pain may also weep out of happiness. Nevertheless, even in the typographical proximity of the run-on line, does one plausibly assume how truth that weeps out of pain can equally weep out of happiness? Accordingly, weeping out of pain may be "metamorphosed" into weeping out of happiness. The latter may happen as a result of a soothing relief, one that is experienced when the weeping truth meets a supportive, reassuring reaction to the moral message delivered by that truth. Under such encouraging, rewarding circumstances, the truth that weeps out of pain (early information) can also weep out of happy relief (late information).

Hence, this is the second kind (more aesthetically complex than the first kind) of mutual interaction between early and late bulks of information (an interaction that is sharpened by the run-on line intersection) located along the textual continuum. Thus the late information is not only added to the early information (while making the latter more specific) but it also updates the previous understanding of the early information. However, that updating does not dismiss altogether the previous interpretation of the early information, but only emends and rectifies it.

The third kind of mutual interaction between the early and late bulks of information that are introduced along the textual sequence is the most drastic, dramatic, and aesthetically intricate of the three kinds. In the third kind, the late information is not only added to the early information while making it more specific and detailed (first kind); does not only update, rectify, and emend the way the early information was previously comprehended (second kind); but it entirely erases and expunges the way the early information was previously comprehended. In light of the latter, is the reader compelled to practice a drastic, reverse reading, to reread the early information in light of the late information, to delete altogether his previous interpretation of the early information and replace it with an entirely new one, one that is "sculpted" according to the dramatically extreme novel light that the late information shed on the early information, and on the way it was previously comprehended?

The following run-on line example displays plausibly that the third kind of mutual interaction between early and late bulks of information placed along the textual continuum, in which the new light that the late information casts on the early information drastically "desolates" the way the early information was previously comprehended and replaces that false comprehension with a new, cogently valid one.

> Othello bent down over Desdemona, to put an end
> to the play.
>
> —Nathan Zach, "Doomed to Death"

As previously stressed, the run-on line creates and molds an intersection where the early information and the late information meet, encounter, interact, clash, and consequently, put under a magnifying, elucidating glass, the very essence of the mutual interaction between the two bulks of information: the early and the late ones. That is exactly what is materialized in the run-on line in focus.

Once the reader encounters the first line, does she easily recognize the literary-allusive bedrock on which that line is founded: the tragedy entitled *Othello* by Shakespeare? Indeed, the reader does not have to read *Othello* in order to recognize that Shakespearean allusion that is "mobilized" by that line and prevails over it. Accordingly, the names Othello and Desdemona have become part of public knowledge, shared even by those who have neither read the play nor will ever read it. Correspondingly, once the reader encounters the first line, she shapes and expects a tragic spirit of somber atmosphere, of murderous bleakness, of morbid murkiness and disastrous dustiness. Such an interpretation of the first line on the part of the reader proves to be plausibly valid, since the Shakespearean tragedy *Othello*, to which the first line alludes, is indeed saturated with atmosphere and feelings, of the most somber, bleak, and murderous characteristics and grim, gloomy, murky connotations. That and more. The reading process does not only consist of information that the reader faces, consumes, and interprets upon encountering, in the present, that information ("the present": the first time of encountering the early information). In light of encountering in the present that information does the reader cultivate expectations that address the future (the following line) in light of the way in which she interpreted that information in the present encounter with it? Accordingly, in the case in focus, is the reader, in full, persuasive liberty, to expect that the following line will continue, reassure, and reinforce the murky connotations and somber, murderous spirit that cogently, undisputedly prevails over the previous, preceding line? However, those naturally cultivated expectations are drastically frustrated, breached, and ruptured.

Like in previous cases of run-on line, the first line that encourages and "goads" the reader to cultivate both murky interpretation that aims at the present (the time of encountering the first line, the early bulk of information) as well as somber expectations that aim at the future, the following line (the later bulk of information):

> Othello bent down over Desdemona to put an end . . .

Thus, according to the present interpretation of this first line (the early bulk of information), and consequently, as well as according to expectations that stem from that interpretation and thus address the following line, it is more than natural that the reader's present interpretation of that line, and her expectations (aiming at the future, the following line, the second part of the execution of the run-on line) will conceive both present bleak comprehension and somber and murderous expectations that aim at the future.

Hence, when we read about Othello who bent down over Desdemona to put an end to . . . [the beginning of the run-on line], the only comprehension, interpretation, and expectation that seem absolutely valid are the following: Othello, saturated with stormy, poisonous feelings of fervently, venomous fury and tempestuous, tormenting, haunting pain, is bending "down over Desdemona to put an end to / her life." What could make better sense than such a reading, comprehension, interpretation, and expectation, which are all inspired by the Shakespearean tragedy in which Othello murders Desdemona out of fury, rage, and acid jealousy? Nevertheless, the following line (the late information that follows the early information, the second, concluding line of the run-on line) commences as follows:

> [Othello bent over Desdemona to put an end to]
> *Her life.*

What does it mean? First, it means that the interpretation, comprehension, and the expectation that were cultivated, with much self-assurance (and justly so) in light of the first line (the early bulk of information, the first part of the run-on line), are breached, denied, frustrated, and even mocked upon encountering the consecutive line (the late bulk of information, the second part of the run-on line).

What is the principal function of such a singularly amazing surprise? First, it teaches the reader a lesson that he must be constantly on the alert upon encountering the dynamics of the literary text: nothing can be taken for granted; what is a cogently solid given at one point of the reading process can be proven to be entirely invalid in the following line; nothing can be considered a "done deal" while the reader is involved in the mutual interaction between early and late bulks of information that are introduced along the textual continuum. Second, in this specific case, the purpose of the above is to "mock" the reader by metamorphosing his grave, tragic comprehension and expectation (yielded by the first line) into comic, humorous reunderstanding (conceived by the commencement of the second line). Accordingly, Othello in the first line, who is a fervently furious and tempestuously dramatic literary character, is metamorphosed in the second line into an amusing, entertaining, realistic actor. He is not anymore a tragic, raging, dramatic, literary character who is about to murder his wife, Desdemona, but rather an impatient, mischievous actor who is about to put an (early) end to the fictional "life" of the actress who plays the role of Desdemona, since he is in a hurry to go home (to the pub? to watch TV with friends?) and thus cannot wait until the entire play reaches its end. Hence, while the first line of the run-on line (the early information) strongly encourages the reader to establish a tragic, bleak, murky interpretation, as well as equally somber expectations aiming at the consecutive, second line (the late information and the second part of the run-on line), does that second line drastically shatter those interpretation and expectations, force the reader to practice reverse reading, return to the early information (that is also the first part of the run-on line), dismiss the previously cultivated shadowy interpretation and expectations, and replace them with mischievous, impish, light-hearted ones? In other words, the mutual interaction between the early and later bulks of information placed along the textual sequence, between the early and late parts of the run-on line, metamorphoses the early tragic meaning into a late comic meaning. Hence, in such a dramatically executed case of a mutual interaction between early and late bulks of information located along the textual continuum, between the early and late parts of the run-on line, the late information casts such a drastic light on the early information, to the point that the interpretation of the early information is found entirely invalid and thus, must be dismissed altogether and replaced with a new one that is dictated by the novel, illuminating late information.

Indeed, the theoretical introduction that preambles Ronny Someck's Holocaust poem under consideration is considerably long and equally detailed. Nevertheless, such a lengthy introduction is undoubtedly a must since it provides the theoretical and methodical tools that are required to analyze and interpret artistically the poem in a valid, persuasive fashion, while understanding to the fullest the poem's aesthetic mechanism that operates as a tool that unearths the poem's ideological message and delivers the latter to the reader.

Unlike many Holocaust poems, in which the Holocaust is concealed and cached deep down, under the surface, epidermal layer of the text, in Someck's poem in focus the Holocaust topic is placed in the uppermost "tissue" of the textual sequence, in a most bold, blatant fashion, to the point that it reads and feels like a thrusting blow of a boxing glove, pounded on the face of a reader.

It was already stated that any work of art should consider the haunting peril, that is lurking in a bushy ambush, threatening to metamorphose worthy, touching emotionality (produced by the work of art; poetry in this case) into a landish, kitschy, vulgar sentimentality. Sentimentality may be metaphorically compared with a venomous liquid that menaces to flood the work of art with an avalanche of an emotional deluge, to the point that the delicate balance between proportional, emotional reaction to the work of art and the "dose" of emotions yielded and conceived by the work of art is devastated and drowned in a swamp of sticky sentimentality. Hence sentimentality must be silenced and muted before it shall bury the work of art under a suffocating burden of coarse, crude, boorish overemotionality. During thousands of years of humankind history, there has not been even one single event that has been as atrocious, as satanic, as diabolic as the Holocaust. Correspondingly, the Holocaust is associated with the most unbelievable, immeasurable, uncontrollable cruelty, inhumanity, savagery, that produced the most stupendously scalding, scorching emotions. Thus, putting the Holocaust in the very front of the poem, in its most visible "showcase," takes the risk of deluging, flooding, and drowning the poem with uncontrollable landslide of uncouth sentimentality.

Toward the conclusion of the poem's aesthetic analysis, however, one will realize what a cleverly utilized technique the poem utilizes, in order to overcome the risk of flooding sentimentality and evict the latter from the poem's artistic/ideological realms. It was already stressed that the dynamic nature of the text (in this case, an artistic, literary text) is indeed the very cornerstone of any text whatsoever. That dynamic nature of the text is founded on a mutual intersection between early and late bulks of information that "populate" the textual sequence. That and more. That mutual intersection may consist of one of the following three types: the late information simply joins the early one while making the latter more specific; the late information casts a new light on the early information to the point that the previous comprehension of the early information must be updated and emended; the late information casts such an extremely drastic light on the early information to the point that the previous comprehension of the early information is proven to be entirely wrong, and consequently, it must be dismissed, omitted, and replaced with a completely new comprehension, one that is in congruence with the blatantly novel light conceived by the late information.

The following aesthetic/ideological analysis of Someck's poem in focus proves persuasively that the poem's most plausible, structural "pillar" is not only based on a constant sequence of such mutual intersections, but the latter also acts effectively as a barrier that blocks a sweeping flood of tawdry, kitschy, coarse sentimentality. Indeed, even prior to the commencement of the body of the poem, to its unfolding textual continuum, does the poem's title both contain and declare in a nutshell the very essence of the satanic, monstrous crime committed by the Nazis against their scorched, tortured, torched victim, the poem's agonized protagonist. Accordingly, naming the Nazis' tormented victim after the name of the most diabolic Nazi death camp yields an unbelievably cruel, inhumane, sadistic irony that cannot be put in words. Such a ruthless, savage irony maps and portrays the very essence of the satanic, monstrous, scalding scar afflicting the Nazis' victim by the Nazis' devilishly twisted mind: naming their victim after the demonic place where he was diabolically victimized is an atrocious symbol for injecting in his veins their fiendish venom. The poem's continuation shall prove that their monstrously ironic plot met an everlastingly venomous success. The poem commences with the following two lines:

> It is difficult to compel the recollection melt the blue ice block that froze in his eyes,
> The numbers that were tattooed on his arm

Indeed, these two lines introduce a run-on line: the length of the first syntactical unit (sentence) is "too long" for the shorter length of the typographical unit (line), and therefore, the sentence slides down from the end of the first line to the beginning of the second line.

In light of the poem's title—one that makes one quiver and shiver—"Mr. Auschwitz," it is very evident that the poem's first two lines in focus portray the tormented portrait of a Holocaust survivor.

His blue eyes look like an ice block that shall never defrost. Hence, it seems like his previous human look, the one that his blue eyes reflected, turned into an icy, inhuman look, one that is frozen forever, one that unveils the dead soul that is snared in his deathly human portrait. Hence, the Nazi beast had robbed him of the very essence of life, the very torch of his life, his living soul. In this respect, one cannot imagine a human being that has been more brutally, beastily victimized. His being an everlasting victim is further emphasized by the numbers that are tattooed on his arm, like the numbers that are tattooed on cattle (the Nazis tattooed blue numbers in the victims' arms, in order to control them as one controls domestic animals). That and more. Those tattooed numbers may act in capacity of an allusion to Cain's sign, one that was tattooed on his forehead to mark his being a murderer (despite the practical function of the sign, to protect him from other people who may kill him just because he is a murderer). The analogy between the victimized survivor to Cain displays piercing, throbbing, even cruel irony. Hence, while Cain's sign, tattooed on his forehead, attested to his being a murderer, the innocent Holocaust survivor was tattooed by murderers. That cruel irony (that stems from a contradictory analogy, which derives from a biblical allusion) further stresses the brutal, inhuman way in which the Holocaust survivor was tortured by the Nazi beast, to the point that the very essence of his soul withered, shriveled, wilted, to the bleak, somber point that it turned into a frozen block of lifeless ice.

Nevertheless, the poem's following two lines drastically contradict the poem's two previous lines by metamorphosing "Mr. Auschwitz" from a victimized into a victimizer:

> And the belt with which he whipped the woman who was with him there
> And now she keeps silent on the balcony.

Structurally, as well as rhetorically, the swinging pendulum that consists of vigorous, even violent waving, from one extreme to the opposite one, demonstrates here its first dramatic, drastic oscillation. Content-wise, however, as if the venomous brutality with which he was victimized "there" (meaning in a Nazi concentration camp or a death camp) infiltrated into his tormented blood circulation, and through the most poisonous irony turned the innocent victimized into a brutal victimizer. Following that vein, one may cogently argue that the touch of devilish wickedness, even when that touch is practiced by the tortured one who was victimized by the satanic wickedness, contaminates the victim of that devilish evil and plants in his anguished soul the toxic seeds of merciless cruelty. Apparently this is exactly what happened to "Mr. Auschwitz." That somber ideological and moral message is effectively introduced and stressed by the aesthetic mechanism that consists of the dynamics of the text, in which early information and late information that populate the textual continuum conduct a mutual interaction through which the late information casts a novel, innovative light on the early information.

Hence, the two lines in focus cast a drastically new light on the earlier information, the one that focuses on the evil that victimized "Mr. Auschwitz." Accordingly, while he was victimized in the past, he turned into a victimizer in the present. "Mr. Auschwitz" was contaminated by the Nazis' murderous brutality and consequently turned into a brute. The fact that he is a victimizer in the present (late information), however, neither eclipses nor does it cloud the solid "historical" fact (early information) that he was victimized in the past. Hence, the latter makes the mutual interaction between the early and late bulks of information that are scattered along the textual continuum more impressively complex. Indeed, the late information (he is a victimizer) sheds a new light on the early information (he was victimized). Nevertheless, the latter does not change the way the early information was previously comprehended, but rather makes it more intricate, more multi-layer: his being a victimizer in the present derives from his being victimized in the past; but it equally had ravaged his both present and future.

The above continues to accumulate momentum in the poem's consecutive lines:

> "Such a pity," his voice did sound like a slash, "that Hitler didn't work extra hours"
> And the cactuses in the pots turned as thorny as the wire fence
> Of the concentration camp. . . .

In these lines the cruel brutality of "Mr. Auschwitz" reaches a venomous vortex, to the point that the reader may cultivate a suspicion that "Mr. Auschwitz" was not only victimized in the Nazi camp but also a victimizer. Accordingly, he served as a Kapo (a Jewish guard in the concentration camp, nominated by the Nazis) and became quite cruel while operating in the concentration camp, since he wished to show the Nazis that he served them obediently, even enthusiastically, and this way spared his own life. Hence, such an assumption that is supported by the latest information introduced to the reader casts a new light upon the comprehension of the earlier information. Accordingly, he did not only turn into a victimizer because he had been victimized, but he was already a victimizer in the concentration camp: he victimized his fellow Jews in order to appease the Nazi beast and save his own skin.

Thus, the swinging pendulum produced and propelled by the mutual interaction between early and late bulks of information, spread along the textual sequence, keeps oscillating while maintaining the reading process dramatic, surprising, energetic, and vital. A certain bulk of information is introduced to the reader, the reader comprehends it according to the characteristics of that information, and, consequently, cultivates expectations aiming at the following consecutive information. The latter, however, sheds a new light on the early information and correspondingly the reader realizes that his/her previous comprehension is wrong, and consequently, his/her previously cultivated expectations are breached and shattered as well. Thus, the reader is compelled to read backwards, reservedly, in order to reshape his/her earlier comprehension of the early information, and equally expel his/her previously cultivated expectations and replace them with new ones.

All that intricate aesthetic mechanism (compositional due to the arrangement of the text and rhetorical due to the impact of the text on the reader, one that hereby materializes via the vehicle of cultivated expectations and frustrated expectations) confers upon the text dense energy, animated vitality. That intricate, dramatically executed aesthetic mechanism serves effectively the poem's ideological message, as shall be further detailed. The consecutive lines continue the fluctuation of that briskly waiving pendulum:

> . . . [as the wire fence
> of the concentration camp] from which he escaped.

Once one reads the ending of the line—"from which [concentration camp] he escaped"—does one realize that the previously molded comprehension of the text, as well as the previously cultivated expectations (aiming at the poem's "future," its forthcoming continuity), prove to be wrong? Accordingly, the previously formed assumption that "Mr. Auschwitz" was a cruel Kapo in a concentration camp who brutally victimized his own fellow Jews was just proven to be absolutely wrong. The fact that he escaped from the concentration camp plausibly attests to the fact that he was not a cruel Kapo but rather a "regular" victimized prisoner, one out of numerous prisoners. The fact that he met success upon attempting to escape from the concentration camp (a mission that was almost impossible; just a fraction, a sliver of a percent of the prisoners who tried to run away were not shot to death, burnt, or hung) demonstrates that even under the most deadly circumstances, he had not lost his hope, his courage, his strength, his creative proclivity, his perseverance, his tenacity, his lust for life. Regretfully, however, the brutal bite of the Nazi viper injected an acid venom in his "veins," and consequently, all the worthy characteristics that he displayed upon successfully escaping from the concentration camp were "translated"—through a cruel, ironic process—into untamed ruthlessness.

Thus, the earlier assumption that he was a Kapo is breached by a later bulk of information that is "planted" along the textual continuum. Hence the poem's "turbulent" pendulum continues oscillating, swinging between molded comprehension and updating comprehension, between cultivated expectations and frustrated expectations. This way the reading process earns energetic vitality and stamina, one that does not only bestow appealing intricacy upon the poem's aesthetic mechanism, but also expresses the poem's ideological message (to be discussed). The continuing two lines add an intriguing complexity to his personality. Until now, the way his personality was introduced, "sculpted," was as a swinging pendulum that fluctuated between two contradictory poles: victimized and victimizer.

In the following lines, however, those that establish the poem's sequential continuity, the two contradictory poles are integrated, merged, welded, and melted into one another:

> The foam that poured out of his poisonous mouth, he wiped
> With the national flag that he hung from one Independence Day to the following one.

On the one hand, the swinging pendulum returns to the extremely negative pole, one that "introduces" the repulsive, loathsome, repellent side in "Mr. Auschwitz's" "being," to the point that it clouds and eclipses the rational knowledge that his mouth turned "poisonous" because the Nazis poisoned it to the point that the tortured victim was "reprogrammed," and the acid venom that was forced upon him penetrated his system, "settled" and "nested" there. On the other hand, however, the fact that "Mr. Auschwitz" publicly, proudly hangs the Israeli national flag "from one Independence Day to the following one," plausibly attests to a positive aspect in his "being." Accordingly, he takes pride in his belonging to an independent Jewish state, he is grateful to the country that embraced him, shielded and sheltered him, when he came out "from the valley of shadows of death." Thus, he knows how to spell worthy words such as "gratitude," "respect," "appreciation." In other words, in this late bulk of information, the one that follows the earliest one, in which "Mr. Auschwitz" is introduced from a positive perspective only (he escaped from the concentration camp while proving that he was not a cruel Kapo, but rather a scorchingly tortured victim and he takes pride in being free in his homeland and express publicly his gratefulness), "Mr. Auschwitz" is introduced simultaneously from two conflicting perspectives: negative and positive. The latter is a novel, innovative aesthetic/ideological aspect in introducing "Mr. Auschwitz."

Until now, the mutual interaction between early and late bulks of information along the textual continuum created a swinging pendulum that fluctuated between two conflicting poles: repulsiveness versus compassion toward "Mr. Auschwitz." In this case, however, for the very first time in the poem's unfolding process, does the swinging pendulum "freeze" in the middle of the fluctuating momentum, between the two contradictory attitudes toward "Mr. Auschwitz," repulsiveness and compassion. Aesthetically, the above introduces an unexpected change, one that breaches the previously cultivated expectations (that he cannot be simultaneously a villain and a victim) and correspondingly bestows upon the poem's aesthetic mechanism further praiseworthy intricacy. Ideologically, however, the above introduces "Mr. Auschwitz"'s behavior as a complex one, one that consists of convoluted duality, one that consists of a merger between two contradictory poles that are doomed to be in an everlasting rivalry, one in which he is doomed to be condemned, snared, and caged for the rest of his tormented life. Indeed, all the above brings to mind E. M. Forster's definition of a "flat character" versus a "round character" (*Aspects of the Novel,* 1961).

Accordingly, while a "flat character" has one prominent characteristic (although it may have many characteristics that "echo" each other), a "round character" has characteristics that drastically conflict each other while "dwelling" under one personality roof (the "round character" may have very few characteristics, but they are devoid of a reciprocal congruence among them). Hence, while the earlier bulks of information introduce "Mr. Auschwitz" as a "flat character" (either "plus" or "minus"), the later bulk of information (that "freezes" the pendulum's oscillation in the middle, right between the two contradictory poles) introduces "Mr. Auschwitz" as a "round character," one that consists of a disposition that weaves and spins contradictory characteristics that coexist simultaneously under one embracing umbrella. Most certainly, the poem's surprising progress from "speaking" in terms of a "flat character" to expressing itself in terms of a "round character" does not only contribute bountifully to the poem's artistic, aesthetic intricacy, but it equally confers upon the poem's ideological message, further insightful complexity, one that stresses the convoluted, turbulent, self-contradictory state of mind, of a person who was beastly scalded, tortured, scorched, and scarred in the Holocaust.

Indeed, one may plausibly consider that unexpected transformation in the oscillating momentum of the swing pendulum a pivotal turning point in the poem's attitude toward "Mr. Auschwitz." Accordingly, the first stage of forming that attitude swings and fluctuates like an oscillating pendulum between the positive and the negative extremes, between the fierceful scolding and pitiful understanding. The second stage is the pivotal one: the one that erases the sharp distinction between "good" and "evil," the one that introduces a third option that stems from a psychological and behaviorist merger between the "good" and the "evil." The third stage starts where the second, "compromising," more complex stage ends, the one that terminates and wraps up at the conclusion of the poem.

At this terminating stage, the attitude toward "Mr. Auschwitz" is clearly, entirely, utterly supportive and compassionate:

> "Mr. Auschwitz", we shouted when he was taken to the mental institute, . . .

The previously oscillating pendulum rests and quits fluctuating stormily and rests on one pole of the two; the one that suspends its recoil and resentment toward the violent venom that gushes out of "Mr.

Auschwitz" since it understands that the latter was viciously forced upon "Mr. Auschwitz"; the one that compassionately focuses on "Mr. Auschwitz" as a chastised victim who is haunted and hounded by the atrocities of his cursed past, his satanic, devilish past, atrocities of the past that had victimized him and trapped him in a nightmarish cage psychological/emotional/behaviorist from which he shall never redeem himself, nor shall he ever liberate himself.

Hence, all the above is painfully exhibited in the scene in which the children verbally abuse him, heartlessly mock him, when he is taken, like a sacrificial lamb, to the misery of the mental institute (although the latter tries to ease his suffering) from which he shall never escape as he escaped in the past from the concentration camp (while keeping in mind the unbridgeable gulf between the two!); that mental hospital which will be his last place of anguish and awe, before he shall say his last farewell to all earthly things, those things that had desolated, soiled, and smitten his life. That new leading trend, which concludes the poem, the one that halts and stops the jittery, jumpy oscillation of the pendulum, the one that introduces "Mr. Auschwitz" from two conflicting, fluctuating angles, is further fortified and emphasized in the poem's two concluding lines:

> And he still had time enough to put his hand in his pocket and peel
> The cellophane of the candies that he threw to us.

For the very first time ever in the poem, is "Mr. Auschwitz" (who is brutally tormented by such a horrible "pseudonym") portrayed as neither a victim nor as a victimizer, but rather as a child-like carrying person, who not only gives candies to the children (who kept verbally tormenting him) but also peels for them the wrapping paper, while he is taken, like a piece of lifeless furniture, to the scary, terrifying bosom of the mental institute. On this note, upon completing the reading process, the reader is in a position to appreciate to the fullest the poem's formidable, complex aesthetic mechanism, as well as its admirable capacity to deliver the poem's ideological message.

That aesthetic mechanism has been introduced and portrayed many times upon practicing the reading process, from the poem's very commencement to its very termination. That aesthetic mechanism has been metaphorically depicted as a swinging pendulum, which keeps oscillating between two dramatically different, opposite poles. That oscillating momentum is based on three consecutive stages. In the first stage, the pendulum fluctuates strenuously, "wildly," between the following contradictory extremes: "Mr. Auschwitz" as a tortured victim versus "Mr. Auschwitz" as a venomous victimizer (while understanding that his being victimized "begot" his being a victimizer, but not approving his violent behavior as a brutal victimizer). The second stage is a turning point in the pendulum's inclination of oscillating. Instead of oscillating "frantically" from one pole to its "rival," opposite pole (Stage 1), the pendulum "freezes" its swinging and is "petrified" between the two poles while portraying "Mr. Auschwitz" not according to one pole or its antithetical pole. It portrays "Mr. Auschwitz" as neither a victim nor a victimizer: it portrays "Mr. Auschwitz" as a "round character," one that simultaneously possesses both characteristics of a victim and a victimizer, while comprehending the causal connection between the two. In the third, last stage, the oscillating pendulum "takes off" again, but this time, instead of fluctuating between the "positive pole" and the "negative pole," it does not further fluctuate, while bestowing on the positive pole (the one that displays empathy to the victimized survivor) both prominence and preference. Hence, the structural character of the submechanism in focus is systematic and fastidiously pedantic indeed. Like in a tennis game, in the first stage the tennis ball moves fast from one corner of the court to the opposite one, back and forth; in the second stage the ball "nests" on the net; and in the third stage, the ball finally lands in one corner of the court. Through these three stages, "Mr. Auschwitz" is viewed as a victim, as well as a victimizer. In the third stage, however, he is portrayed as a victim who deserves compassion despite his brutality, since the latter was forced upon him, was seamed in his "being" by the merciless Nazi beast. Indeed, that three-stage aesthetic mechanism operates in capacity of an avenue that delivers an ideological message. That ideological message consists of the following credo: despite the evil side and good-hearted side that coexist in the suffering soul of "Mr. Auschwitz" (even that name shows how his past tormenting demons continue hounding him in the present [Stage 1]); they are not separable, they are spun and interlaced in one another (Stage 2); but the side that calls for compassion must be considered the prominent side (Stage 3). Since the "sinister" side is not a matter of a free choice upon the part of the Holocaust survivor (although this side should not be tolerated) but rather a scalding scar that was brutally engraved in his tormented soul. Hence, according to that bold, blatant message, "Mr. Auschwitz" is a shocking, staggering metaphor for too many Holocaust survivors whose unbelievable agony and humiliation had been translated into venom that had pierced their very veins, their very existence, to the point that they are doomed to meet no redemption.

As previously stated, the "jumpy," "jittery" reading process, in which cultivated expectations are constantly frustrated; early information and its comprehension are denied, challenged, updated, or entirely dismissed by new information that is introduced in a later location along the textual continuum, bestows upon the reading process dynamic, dramatic vitality and stamina, and a captivating, energetic proclivity. That appealing aesthetic mechanism operates in capacity of a bedrock that holds the poem's ideological message, as well as a springboard from which the ideological message launches its "voyage" to the reader's awareness. That ideological message that has been already partially introduced enlists the poem's "tempestuous" aesthetic mechanism, one that operates like a "stormy" pendulum that "wildly" jerks from side to side, in order to deliver its credo: "Mr. Auschwitz," like other Holocaust survivors, is a tragically "round," complex character; one whose victimized soul is doomed to wildly tug between opposite directions; one whose savage, nightmarish past cruelly conditions and dictates his brutal, turbulent present. As previously stressed, the "arch-foe" of any worthy work of art is overemotionality, and even worse, sentimentality (that is "overdosed" overemotionality).

Hence both overemotionality and sentimentality flood the work of art (in this case, poetry) with sweeping, gusting avalanche of fervent, fervid emotions. The latter violently upsets the aesthetically desirable balance between the subject and the content of the work of art, and the prudently measured dose of emotions that should be produced by those subjects and content. Correspondingly, overemotionality and sentimentality devastate the very core of a valuable work of art by clouding and eclipsing the latter's qualities and "contours," and by showering the work of art's worthy characteristics with a bubbling foam of distasteful adhesive, sticky, greasy "schmaltz." The latter becomes extremely likely and consequently perilous when the subject and the content of the work of art are the Holocaust, the greatest "quarry" from which the most dreadfully emotional "raw materials" are carved. Thus, when it comes to a "Holocaust work of art," the medium (in this case, the verbal medium, the literary text) must enlist the most effective, protective mechanism that will mute overemotionality and silence sentimentality. In the poem in focus, the above is performed and materialized in the following fashion. Indeed, that fashion of operation of "self-defense," when it comes to the peril of flooding overemotionality and uncontrolled avalanche of sweeping sentimentality, is integrated in the poem's aesthetic mechanism. As already stated, the latter consists of an oscillating pendulum, one that keeps fluctuating the reader's "wavy" responses to the text, through a constant curvaceous process through which she must keep alternating and updating her reactions to the text, according to the mutual interaction between early and late bulks of information that are introduced along the textual continuum. Most certainly, the reader's full involvement in such an intensively "turbulent" reading process forces her to invest all her intellectual, rational faculties, in order to follow fastidiously the swift, contradictory oscillations of the fluctuating pendulum. The latter channels all her attention to the intellectual deciphering process of the poem's complex aesthetic mechanism to the point that she suspends her reaction (at least, partially) to the emotions that populate, saturate, and soak the poem.

Hence while overemotionality and sentimentality are the "arch-foe" of a worthy work of art, an intellectual/rational reaction to a work of art is the "arch-foe" of overemotionality and sentimentality. The latter stems from the fact that while an intellectual/rational reaction to the work of art can be practiced only under the circumstance of taking distance from the work of art (and correspondingly, suspending an emotional identification with the analyzed work of art), the very essence of both overemotionality and sentimentality is a total identification with the work of art in a way that leaves no space whatsoever for an intellectual/rational observation of that work of art. Thus overemotionality and sentimentality are entirely devoid of an objective capacity to study intellectually/rationally the work of art. This way, they are "robbed" of their unworthy capacity to unleash the undesirable avalanche of scalding, scorching emotions that floods the poem, to deluge and drown all its worthy qualities and characteristics. This way the rhetorical device (the one that "sculpts" the way that a work of art shapes the reader's response to that work of art) utilizes dexterously the poem's aesthetic mechanism, the one that consists of the oscillating pendulum, and uses it as an "Archimedean" launching point, from which it takes off and embarks on its mission: to mute overemotionality, to silence sentimentality, to let the estimable text speak out.

Neither "Mr. Auschwitz"'s beastly torturing past, nor his haunting, tormenting, brutal present can meet remedy. His future is equally devoid of even a sliver of redemption. However, Ronny Someck's praiseworthy poem in focus does an artistic justice to "Mr. Auschwitz," by mirroring his everlastingly victimized life, in such a compassionate sensitivity and splendidly practiced aesthetic skills.

Ronny Someck

Born in Baghdad in 1951, Ronny Someck came to Israel as a young child. He studied Hebrew literature and philosophy at Tel Aviv University and drawing at the Avni Academy of Art. He has worked with street gangs, and currently teaches literature and leads creative writing workshops. He has published nine volumes of poetry (The last called *The Milk Underground*) and a book for children with his daughter Shirly (*The Laughter Button*). His work has been translated into thirty-nine languages. Selections of his poems have appeared in Arabic translation, French (with the exile Iraqi poet A. K. El-Janabi), Catalan, Albanian, Italian, Macedonian, and English.

He is a recipient of the Prime Minister's Award, Yehuda Amichai Award for Hebrew poetry, and the "Wine Poem Award" in Struga Poetry Evenings, Macedonia, 2005. He recorded three CDs with the musician Elliott Sharp: *Revenge of the Stuttering Child, Poverty Line,* and *Short History of Vodka.* In 1998 he made an exhibition "Nature's Factory, Winter 2046" with Beny Efrat in "Israel Museum." In 2004 he made an exhibition, "Hawadja Bialik," in the Museum of Israeli Art, Ramat-Gan. He is a member in the Public Council of Batsheva Dance Company and at the Hebrew-Arabic Theatre.

Holocaust or Shoah

The Greek Category versus Jewish Thought

David Patterson

During my attendance at the 2001 Scholars' Conference on the Holocaust and the Churches a survivor told me that she had come to a horrifying realization about the relation between Holocaust scholars and Holocaust survivors. Speaking in a whisper, as though afraid of her own words, she said to me, "I know now what they want us to do: they want us to die." My initial reaction was shock. For reasons I did not immediately grasp, her words brought to mind one of the conference sessions on Holocaust education. At one point the discussion in that session revolved around the question of whether one should include something about religious tradition in a course on the Holocaust. The religious tradition referred to, however, was Christianity; there was no mention of Judaism, and for a moment I had the sense that the Christians—as well as a number of Jews—would like for Judaism to basically go away. True, it was suggested that the richness of the prewar Jewish *culture* should be included in such a course, but not a word about the *Judaism* that makes the Jewish people who they are.

And then the connection between my friend's words and the discussion on Holocaust education hit me: we teachers and scholars who pretend to deal with the Holocaust do not want to deal with the Jews because we do not want to deal with the flesh and blood of Jewish life that is rooted in Judaism. We do not want to look into the Jewish faces that put to humanity the question of what is ultimate in life, of that for which we live and die. Whether or not this Jew or that Jew believes in the sacred tradition, the very presence of the Jews signifies the teachings of that tradition, a tradition that runs contrary not only to Christianity but also to the postmodern fashions and fads that rule academia. And so the surviving Jewish remnant remains an irritant. While the Holocaust scholars of academia may successfully ignore Jewish thinkers who take Judaism seriously, ignoring the Holocaust survivors can be a bit problematic—especially if those survivors embrace the tradition that the Nazis sought to erase.

Rising up from the depths of Auschwitz, the 614th Commandment, as Emil Fackenheim calls it, reverberates throughout the world.[1] The Voice cries out to the Jews to declare the truth that the Nazis set out to destroy, namely that *as Jews* we are commanded *absolutely* to embrace an *absolute* truth through the embrace of God and humanity. It insists that Jews do not have the luxury of regarding their tradition of Torah and Talmud as a cultural curiosity or even as a highly developed "civilization." It tells the Christians that their Christianity is, at least in its traditional antisemitic forms, a horrific scandal that prepared the European soil to receive an ocean of Jewish blood. And it tells the philosophers that, despite their intellectual achievements, their "enlightened" civilization spawned a generation of intellectual mass murderers. That is why we scholars want the survivors to go away: in their presence we collide with a Commanding Voice that, like a shofar, shakes us—Jews, Christians, and philosophers—from our complacent sleep and questions all that we had thought to be true.

Thus my friend's remark shook me from my own shameful slumber. She opened my eyes to a pattern that pervades what passes for Holocaust studies in academia and Holocaust remembrance in popular culture. It is a pattern characterized by the elimination of the Jews from any consideration of the Holocaust. Less and less do we speak of Jews at all. Instead, we speak of victims and trauma, dialogue and healing, representation and remembrance, textual analysis and ethical implications—everything except the singular assault on Jews and Judaism. Instead of a reverence for the dead, we have an exploitation of the dead to serve all sorts of postmodernist agendas, from culturalism to historicism, from feminism to deconstructionism, and whatever might be the -ism of the day. One can even sit through a talk show featuring Elie Wiesel and a high school essay contest on *Night* without hearing a single utterance of the word *Jew*. Thus the Jew gets thrown into the general category of "victim," along with victims of all sorts of catastrophes, as we forget that at Auschwitz what was murdered was the Jewish testimony to the very human sanctity that makes other catastrophes catastrophic. If it should happen that we do comment on the Jews, we generally say nothing of what it means to be a Jew. But what can it mean to speak of the murder of *the Jews* without addressing the millennial tradition of Judaism that makes them *Jews*?

My use of the word *Holocaust* until now has been intentional. For it turns out that perhaps one reason for the purging of the Jew from Holocaust studies lies in the word *Holocaust*. One scholar who resists the de-Judaization of the mass murder of the Jews is Zev Garber. And one way in which he undertakes this resistance is this: he has always had the wisdom to refer to the Nazi annihilation of the Jewish people by the Hebrew word for the Holocaust (*Shoah*). The difference lies in far more than a matter of personal preference—it is a matter of restoring what the Nazis set out to destroy: the essential link between word and meaning and the essential Jewishness of the Jewish people. The Nazi assault on this linkage is so radical that it eludes language; indeed, it parallels the Nazi assault on the essence and the soul of the human being, beginning with the Jew.

As Primo Levi has said, there is no word "to express this offense . . . : the demolition of a man."[2] There is no word for this offense because the demolition of a man is the demolition of the word, which was, indeed, a defining feature of the Shoah. Sara Nomberg-Przytyk makes this point when she asserts, "The new set of meanings [of words] provided the best evidence of the devastation that Auschwitz created."[3] In place of the word filled with meaning we have the bleeding wound that remains after the word has been torn from its meaning, like the bleeding word *Jude* branded into the forehead of Shlamek's father in Ka-tzetnik's *House of Dolls*, "as though it were quite natural that the word *Jude* should give blood."[4] As for the difference between *Holocaust* and *Shoah*, it is this: from the word *Shoah* the blood of the Jewish people cries out, while with the word *Holocaust* that outcry is muffled in a sameness assigned to all catastrophes.

In this contribution we shall consider what the Hebrew word *Shoah*, over against the Greek *Holocaust*, reveals about the event. Next, we shall examine a strain of German philosophy that (1) is steeped in the categories of Greek ontological thinking and that (2) ultimately contributed to the annihilation of the Jewish people. And we shall see how the philosophical tradition that, according to Franz Rosenzweig, can recommend only suicide ends by committing mass murder.[5] The point is that the choice between the terms used to refer to the event—the Greek *Holocaust* or the Hebrew *Shoah*—has implications that run far deeper than we might imagine. The matter of calling it *Holocaust* or *Shoah* is a matter of whether we shall think Jewishly or whether we shall continue to think in the ontological mode that led to the slaughter of the Jews.

Thinking Jewishly, of course, entails more than calling the event *Shoah:* it entails an understanding of certain categories of Jewish thought, of a way of thinking that must be retrieved if the Nazis are to be denied a posthumous victory. Thus we shall take the issue of suicide identified by Rosenzweig and consider it in the contexts of Jewish thought. Here it turns out that for Jewish thought, the ultimate question is not suicide but martyrdom—or rather *Kiddush HaShem*, a category fundamental to Jewish thinking. This contribution ends, then, with a consideration of the relation between Shoah and Kiddush HaShem. It concludes by arguing that, while the Holocaust may have made martyrdom (another Greek word) impossible, as Emil Fackenheim maintains, the Shoah allows room for a post-Auschwitz understanding of Kiddush HaShem as a pursuit of Jewish thought and Jewish life, over against the evil of Amalek in the guise of the Greek category.[6]

Retrieving the Jewish Word: The Call of the Abyss

The abyss that since 1945 has threatened to engulf the world and humanity is the abyss of the Shoah. *Shoah* means "abyss." It also means "pit," "destruction," and "ruin." It does not mean "Holocaust," a Greek word that signifies a sacrificial offering by fire. The Nazis did not set out to *sacrifice* the Jews. They set out to annihilate them, as suggested by the term mistranslated as "death camp": *Vernichtungslager*, literally "annihilation camp," a place where the Jews were not to be offered up in sacrifice but reduced to nothingness. The Nazis did not want the Jews to be sacrificed or scapegoated or merely purged of their "wealth" and their "power." Nor did they want them dead. No, the Nazis set out to erase every predicate attached to the Jews, which is to remove them from the realm of being, from the scope of memory, whether alive or dead. Both Elie Wiesel and Primo Levi have described the Shoah as a war against memory. And recall the scene from Steven Spielberg's production of *Schindler's List*, where Amon Göth addresses his troops prior to the liquidation of the Krakow Ghetto, proclaiming, "Jews have lived in Krakow for 600 years. By the end of the afternoon those six hundred years will be a rumor." That is Shoah.[7]

Noting the *Vernichtung* in *Vernichtungslager*, we are reminded that a cognate of *Shoah* is the word *shav*, which translates as "lie" or "nothingness." More than an attempt to exterminate the Jewish people, the Shoah is the imposition of the *tohu-vavohu*, the chaos and void, upon humanity. It is the creation of an antiworld in the midst of the world, an undoing of creation in a rain of ashes that have found their way into every human being. For they abide in the very earth from which we harvest the bread that we put into our mouths. "The world around us," Levi recalls in his emergence from Auschwitz, "seemed to have returned to primeval Chaos, and was swarming with scalene, defective, abnormal human specimens." These "specimens" reflect the image not of the Creator but of the Nazi anti-Creator; these are the inhabitants of the land that the Germans had made of the world. Says Levi, "It was more than a sack: it was the genius of destruction, of anti-creation, here as at Auschwitz; it was the mystique of barrenness."[8] The Italian word translated as "barrenness" is *vuoto*, which means "emptiness" or "void."[9] The anticreation is the creation of nothing—or nothingness, as the word *Shoah* suggests—out of something, a return to the abyss of what strives to overcome the abyss. It is Shoah.

Levi's insight into "the mystique of barrenness" brings us to another cognate of *Shoah*, the verb *shaah*, which means to "become desolate" or to "be devastated"; the *hitpael* or reflexive form, *hishtaah*, is to "wonder," to "be astonished," or to "gaze in wonder or awe." What is the Shoah? It is not a Holocaust. It is not even a genocide. Exceeding the parameters of genocide, it is the calculated imposition of the abyss, of the *Shoah*, upon the world, beginning with the Jewish people, who are the chosen witnesses to holiness in the world. It is the lie made truth, the unreal made real, the return of the world to nothingness, to the *shav*, that creation struggles to overcome. It is the astonishment not over what is unimaginable but over *everything* imaginable. For there was no limiting principle at work in the Nazis' actions, hence no possibility of going too far. On the contrary, they could never go far enough—there lay the dimension of the infinite in the Nazi assault on the Infinite One, the God of the Covenant of Abraham.

In the past, Amalek's hatred of the Jews for their devotion to God and the Covenant has assumed a variety of forms. It can be seen among the Egyptians and the Babylonians, among the Greeks and the Romans—all of whom created great civilizations. And all of whom in one way or another attempted to eliminate God from the world by removing Jewish testimony from the world. But the Nazi effort to remove not only all Jewish testimony but every Jew from the world was unprecedented. It was not the result of economic depression or German resentment over having lost World War I. Nor was it a case of scapegoating, xenophobia, or even racism run amok. Such facile explanations amount to no more than feeble attempts to evade the specters that rise from the ashes of murdered Jews and haunt us. As Fackenheim has correctly said, the Nazis were not antisemites because they were racists; no, they were racists because they were antisemites. In the words of their infamous ideologist Alfred Rosenberg, the Aryan "race has been poisoned by Judaism," and not merely by Jewish blood, for the -ism is *in* the blood.[10] The Jewish teaching concerning the human being is that (1) each one is created in the image and likeness of the Holy One, (2) each one has his or her origin in a single one, in Adam, and (3) each is bound to the other through blood and through a common tie to God. Nothing could be more opposed to Nazi ideology—or to the Western ontological tradition inherited from the Greeks.

The Ontological Tradition: Thinking God out of the Picture

The Shoah that most radically isolated the Jews from the world and most irrevocably plunged them into the abyss was the result of a Greek-based philosophical tradition that set out to free people by making them self-legislating, proceeded to equate them with God, and ended by eliminating God altogether. With an insight bordering on the prophetic, Rosenzweig caught a glimpse of its beginnings when he declared,

> Corresponding to the Copernican turn of Copernicus which made man a speck of dust in the whole is the Copernican turn of Kant, which, by way of compensation, placed him upon the throne of the world, much more precisely than Kant thought. To that monstrous degradation of man, costing him his humanity, this correction without measure was, likewise, at the cost of his humanity.[11]

Refashioning himself after his own image, the human being loses his human image and ultimately dehumanizes the *other* human being. For he loses the holiness that defines the human.

Over against a Jewish tradition that affirms all moral good to come from God, Immanuel Kant insists that that God derives from the rational human reflection on a moral good. Correctly perceiving Judaism to be antithetical to his own position, in *The Conflict of the Faculties* Kant declares, "The euthanasia of Judaism is the pure moral religion." Of course, the euthanasia of Judaism amounts to the elimination of the God of Abraham—a project that would ultimately require the extermination of the Jews. Understanding the human being to be determined by the will and commandments of God and not, as Kant would have it, "only by laws which he gives to himself through reason," Judaism is the opposite of Kantian Idealism. That is why Kant wanted to see it eliminated.[12]

G. W. F. Hegel, the most influential philosopher of the nineteenth century, was no better. Like Kant, Hegel associated freedom with human autonomy; also like Kant, he viewed Judaism as a slave religion. Unlike Kant, however, Hegel drew on the Christian notion of the Incarnation to develop a view of God that denies the otherness of the divinity. In Hegel, Fackenheim explains, "divinity comes to dwell, as it were, in the same inner space as the human self." The self that began by appropriating the world through thought now appropriates the divinity. The philosophical result of this incarnation of God in the self unfolds in the thinking of atheistic neo-Hegelians such as Ludwig Feuerbach and Karl Marx, where, Fackenheim points out, "divinity vanishes in the process of internalization, to be replaced by a humanity potentially infinite in its modern 'freedom.'"[13] This infinite freedom is necessarily opposed to the Infinite One: because it is infinite, the "modern freedom" eliminates the Infinite One, to whom the Jews are the world's original witnesses, so that we now may do whatever we have the will and the imagination to do.

Indeed, we are justified by will alone, as Friedrich Nietzsche and the Nazi Martin Heidegger proclaimed (both of whom are among the idols worshipped by postmodernists). "The expression 'will to power,'" says Heidegger, "designates the basic character of beings; any being which is, insofar as it is, is will to power."[14] What is the most famous of all the Nazi propaganda films? It is Leni Riefenstahl's *Triumph of the Will* (1933)—not *Triumph of the Good* or *Triumph of Righteousness*, both of which would have invoked either "capitalistic" or "communistic" Jewish notions. At the very least, terms such as "the Good" or "righteousness" harbor an appeal to conscience, which, according to Nazi ideology, is a Jewish invention and is therefore yet another weakness that threatens "humanity."

Heidegger's membership in the Nazi Party is well known; and it is no coincidence. For also well known is his proclamation that "the Führer himself and he alone *is* the present and future German reality and its law," a statement made in November 1933, well after the enactment of numerous antisemitic laws, book burnings on university campuses, and widespread Jew bashing.[15] All of this is a matter of common knowledge. What is not so readily admitted among Heidegger's postmodern adherents is the fact that Heidegger was not a philosopher who happened to be a Nazi; no, he was a Nazi who happened to be a philosopher, as Karl Löwith discovered in 1936. When he expressed his concern to Heidegger that there was an essential "partnership" between National Socialism and Heidegger's philosophy, he says, "Heidegger agreed with me [about this] without reservation and elucidated that his concept of 'historicity' was the basis of his political 'engagement.'"[16] Thus the twentieth century's greatest philosophical heir to the Greek ontological tradition pledged his allegiance to Amalek. And the Greek inheritance is conscientious. Says Heidegger, "Along with the German language, Greek (in regard to the possibilities of thinking) is at once the most powerful and the most spiritual of languages."[17] Given Heideggerian, totalitarian thinking, we see the implications of the difference between *Holocaust* and *Shoah*.

We also understand the meaning of the passage from the Talmud: "When Ben Damah, the son of Rabbi Ishmael's sister, asked when he may study the wisdom of the Greeks, the Rabbi answered, 'Go find a time that is neither day nor night and then learn the Greek wisdom'" (*Menachot* 99b). The conflict between Greek and Hebrew thought—a conflict felt in the tension between *Holocaust* and *Shoah*—began with the Maccabees, continued with the Romans, on through the Crusades, then the Enlightenment, and culminated in the Shoah. Jean-François Lyotard summarizes this history of antisemitism by saying, "One converts the Jews in the Middle Ages, they resist by mental restriction. One expels them during the classical age, they return. One integrates them in the modern era, they persist in their difference. One exterminates them in the twentieth century"—which is the final, postmodern solution to the Jewish Question.[18]

On this issue we have a profound testimony that comes from the depths of the abyss itself. Writing secretly from the Warsaw Ghetto, Rabbi Kalonymos Kalmish Shapira makes quite clear the connection between Amalek and the Hellenistic, ontological line of German philosophy. It is found in his commentary on Deut. 25:17: "Remember what Amalek did to you on the way when you were leaving Egypt; that he happened upon you along the way." The Midrash translates the phrase *asher karkhah*, "who happened upon you," as "who chilled you," from the root word *kar*, meaning "cold" (see *Tanchuma Ki Tetse* 9). The suggestion is that Amalek cooled the Jews' passion for God and stirred their passion for other things such as power and pleasure, possessions and prestige—that is the evil of Amalek.

Rabbi Shapira also recalls that the teaching that *baderekh*, or "along the way," is a euphemism for "thought." We must beware of the evil of Amalek, for this evil casts us into the abyss by "chilling our thinking" with regard to anything that smacks of religion. Addressing his fellow Jews, the rabbi explains:

> You were impressed with the superficial culture in which Amalek takes such pride. As a result, your response to Jewish culture and the wisdom of Torah was chilly. You were sure that Amalek was very cultured, that his philosophy was quite as good as anything. To be sure, it also had its ethics, and there is profit to be had from it in this world. What did God do? He brought you face to face with Amalek and with all the culture and philosophy he affects.[19]

But Rabbi Shapira was not the first to perceive the source of this evil that threatens to swallow up the Jews. More than one hundred years earlier, with the same clarity of vision that led him to declare that those who burn books will end burning people, Heinrich Heine wrote:

> The German revolution will not be milder and gentler because it was preceded by Kant's *Critique*, by Fichte's transcendental idealism, and even by the philosophy of nature. These doctrines have developed revolutionary forces that wait only for the day when they can erupt and fill the world with terror and admiration. There will be Kantians forthcoming who will hear nothing of piety in the visible world, and with sword and axe will mercilessly churn the soil of our European life, to exterminate the very last roots of the past. Armed Fichteans will enter the lists, whose fanaticism of will can be curbed neither by fear nor by self-interest. . . . But the most terrible of all would be natural

> philosophers . . . , [who] can call up the demoniac energies of ancient Germanic pantheism. . . . A play will be performed in Germany that will make the French Revolution seem like a harmless idyll in comparison.[20]

Why are the natural philosophers the most terrible of all? Joseph Soloveitchik explains:

> The philosopher, an adherent of *religio naturalis*, envisages God as primarily an infinite ideal to which he aspires. His philosophical religiosity is anthropocentric and anthropocratic. The point of departure is not God but the universal experience (of Him), which is considered creative, redeeming, and inspiring—the maximum bonum of mental life. He is absorbed in his own self rather than in a transcendent God.[21]

The German revolution to which Heine refers, then, is the manifestation of a mode of thinking rooted not only in a distancing of the human from the divine but in a usurpation of the divine by the human. Rooted in the abyss of an illusory self, it would lead to the abyss and the nothingness of Shoah.

Which returns us to the relation between word and meaning that the Nazis brought under assault. Just as the body does not have a soul but rather the soul has a body, so the word does not have meaning but rather meaning has a word. And the meaning of the word abides in the soul of the human being; like the life of the soul, the life of the word shines in the embrace of another human being. Wherever meaning is torn from the word, therefore, human beings are torn from one another in a fundamental assault upon the soul. Thus the capo declared to Eliezer in Wiesel's *Night* that in the concentrationary universe there are no fathers or son, no brothers or friends.[22] There is no human relation, no human connection. In the darkness of this night—the darkness of a radical isolation within the self that characterizes ontological thought—we have the Egyptian darkness, as it is written: "A man did not see his brother" (Exod. 10:23). That is the darkness of Shoah, a darkness that the word *Holocaust* cannot convey. In the Egyptian exile we are so preoccupied with self-fulfillment and the lie of the Egyptian dream, so blinded by our own ego, that we are blind to the face of our fellow human being. Thus first isolated, the Jews are then murdered—"legally," "legitimately," and en masse.

Here we come to a crucial realization: unlike the "burnt offering" suggested by *Holocaust*, the abyss signified by *Shoah* is made of murder. It feeds on murder. It insists on murder. It glorifies murder. It is a fundamental feature of the thinking engendered by Amalek in all his forms. And it is fundamentally antithetical to Jewish thought: the principle most basic to human relation, as articulated in the Ten Utterances from Sinai, is "Do not murder." It is the first of the commandments pertaining to the relation *ben adam l'chavero*, between human and fellow human. If anything is more antithetical to Jewish thought than murder, it is suicide, as it is written: "There is none so wicked as the one who commits suicide" (*Kitsur Shulchan Arukh* 201:1). Most antithetical is the conjunction of the two, where suicide becomes a means to murder. Through the antithetical, however, we come to the fundamental.

Holocaust or Shoah: A Matter of Life and Death

By now we realize that the question of whether we refer to the horror by its Greek name *Holocaust* or by its Hebrew name *Shoah* far exceeds the matter of preference, correctness, or convention: it is a matter of life and death, of nurturing or murder, of sanctification or suicide. Albert Camus opens *The Myth of Sisyphus* with one of the most famous lines in modern philosophy: "There is but one truly serious philosophical problem, and that is suicide."[23] Like Rosenzweig, Camus realized that, having thought God out of the picture, the Greek-influenced philosophical tradition thinks itself into suicide, just as Hitler, Himmler, and other Nazis began with mass murder and ended with self-murder, which was the logical, ontological outcome of their thinking. But Camus' answer to the problem—the individual's revolt, freedom, and passion—is no answer at all, as the end of Hitler demonstrates. For it is a revolt that is mounted only against the void, a freedom that is ultimately the freedom to murder, and a passion that is only for the sake of the elusive self.

For post-Shoah Jewish thought, the one truly serious philosophical issue is martyrdom. Indeed, it is crucial, and the difference lies in the difference between thinking in terms of *Holocaust* and thinking in terms of *Shoah*. While the Kantian categorical imperative may prohibit murder in order to preclude others from murdering oneself, it cannot command martyrdom, as the Talmud does (see *Sanhedrin* 74a; *Ketuvot* 19a). For it would entail treating oneself as a means, and not as an end, which is contrary to the categorical imperative.[24] Whereas the Kantian imperative is rooted in a being-for-oneself, the Talmudic dictum is grounded in a being-for-the-other, both as God and as person. In a radical orientation toward to other, the Talmud commands us to choose to be murdered in an act of martyrdom—not "martyrdom," precisely, but a *Kiddush HaShem* or "Sanctification of the Name"—rather than commit murder, adultery, or idolatry.

In fact, the Mishnah teaches that these three transgressions are the cause of the exile of the Jews from the Holy Land (*Avot* 5:9; see also *Yoma* 82a; *Ketuvot* 19a), an exile that also bespeaks a profound spiritual alienation of humanity that found its extreme manifestation in the abyss of the Shoah. Kiddush HaShem imparts meaning to life. Therefore, explains André Neher, Kiddush HaShem "is the negation of the absurd. Everything receives a meaning through the ultimate testimony of the man who accepts that meaning to the very limit. Everything is oriented in relation to that testimony. Everything becomes *sanctified* through it. Jewish tradition calls the *sanctification of God* the martyrdom, which has found its first historical examples in the *lives* of the prophets"—and not in the ruminations of the philosophers.[25] After the unreality of the antiworld, this negation of the absurd is precisely what is needful. After the Shoah the Sanctification of the Name must manifest itself in the *lives* of the Jewish people, just as Rabbi Yitzhak Nissenbaum of Warsaw declared its meaning in the midst of the murder of the Jews: the Sanctification of the Name meant doing everything possible to *live* as Jews, which means not just staying alive but *living* so as to become a *living* testimony to the Torah that the Nazis set out to destroy.[26] After the Shoah there is no other *opposite* to Nazi thinking, no other *opposition* to the Nazi enterprise. And this *opposite*, this *opposition*, is couched in the word *Shoah*.

Couched in the Hebrew word is the Jewish thinking that is life oriented, as it is oriented toward and derives from the Creator of life. According to the Greek thinking that gave rise to the murderous speculative tradition, the aim of wisdom is to "know thyself." According to Jewish thinking, as stated by the twelfth-century scholar Bachya ibn Paquda, the aim of wisdom is to "become cognizant of the Creator," who shows Himself in the very phenomenon of thinking (*Chovot HaLevavot* 2:5). Jewishly understood, our thinking is awakened by the thinking of Another, of One who sanctifies thought itself, who overshadows and disturbs human thought. As the disciple of the Baal Shem Tov, Rabbi Yaakov Yosef of Polnoe states it, "the thought above awakens the thought below" (*Toledot Yaakov Yosef, Emor* 11). And it awakens us to actions as defined by the *mitzvot*, that is, by the "commandments" of the thinking Creator.

Created from a divine emanation, the soul thinks under the canopy of divine thought. I think, therefore I am? No! God commands, therefore I am. From the viewpoint of Jewish thought, I am not a *res cogitans*, not a "thinking thing," as Descartes declared.[27] I am, rather, a "thought thing" and therefore a "commanded thing." For the canopy of divine thought is made not of autonomous self-legislation but of heteronomous commandment, beginning with the commandment that launches our prayers each morning: before we pray, we declare, "I take upon myself the commandment *v'ahavta l'reakha kamokha*, 'you shall love your neighbor as yourself'" (Lev. 19:18). There is no prayer, no genuine thought, without this orientation toward the other human being. This orientation toward the other human being is implied by the word *Shoah* in ways that it is not implied by the word *Holocaust*. Only the relation to the other human being can oppose the nothingness of Shoah that the Nazis would impose on creation. A better rendering of *kamokha*, translated as "as yourself," would be "You shall love your neighbor, for loving the other *is* your self": that loving is the *who* that you are in the depths of your being.

Where lies the meaning of Torah? Not just in the word or even between the words: it lies in the relation to other human beings. Oriented toward Torah, then, Jewish thought is oriented toward the other human being—not toward an idea or concept, but toward the concrete, flesh-and-blood reality of the other person. That is why we call the Event *Shoah*: it is an effort to think Jewishly, which is to think from an orientation toward the other human being. Thinking in terms of *Shoah*, and not of *Holocaust* draws our thinking into the intricacies of Hebrew language itself, so that we are led to think of "education" or *chinukh,* for example, as "sanctification," of "thought" or *machshavah* as "troubled mind," and of "Jewish" or *Yehudi* as a cognate of *hodah,* which is to "offer thanks." It is to think from a stance of an ultimate "responsibility" or *achariyut* in Hebrew, the root of which is *acher* or "other," in his or her concrete, flesh-and-blood need—a need to which the world had grown deaf in the time of the Shoah. This growing deaf is the outcome of the vision-based mode of Greek thought. Enamored of the *idea,* Greek thinking is enthralled by what is pleasing to the eye; to be sure, the word *idea* comes from the Greek word "to see," *idein.* Hence Philo, the Hellenistic Jew of the first century "corrected" the scriptures by changing every instance of hearing God's voice to a vision of God.

And yet hearing—the *Shema*—is what is central to Jewish thought: hearing not only the Voice of God but also the outcry of our neighbor. After the Shoah, it entails hearing the scream "Mama!" as Sara Nomberg-Przytyk heard it: "Suddenly, the stillness was broken by the screaming of children, . . . a scream repeated a thousand times in a single word, 'Mama,' a scream that increased in intensity every second, enveloping the whole camp. Our lips parted without our being conscious of what we were doing, and a scream of despair tore out of our throats. . . . At the end everything was enveloped in death and silence."[28] If silence is a defining feature of the Shoah—of its nothingness—as so many survivors have declared, it is the silence that echoes after the scream "Mama!" Hearing that word and that silence is the basis of Kiddush HaShem. Even Socrates died for no more than an idea, and his example is the highest philosophy can attain.

Why? Because philosophy cannot come to the teaching we receive from the Talmudic sage Shimon bar Yochai in the *Sifre* on Deuteronomy (33:5): "When you are My witnesses," God cries out, "I am God; when you are not my witnesses, I am not God" (see also *Pesikta de-Rav Kahana* 12:6). And to be God's witness is not to articulate a concept of Him but to live and die according to Torah, for the sake of the other, in a sanctification of His Name, through the Shema. What is at stake in Kiddush HaShem—in *living* for the Holy One, particularly after the Shoah—is not the life of my soul in the beyond but the life of God in the world. Contrary to what the Greek-influenced religious and philosophical traditions of the West might suggest, Kiddush HaShem is not about *me.* Rooted not in the fear of my own death but in the fear of the death of the other—not in a fear of dying but in a fear of committing murder—Kiddush HaShem is the diametrical opposite of Greek philosophy and Western ontology, which, in its Heideggerian culmination and postmodern manifestation, seeks *my* authenticity in a fearless being-toward-*my*-death—which is the vanity of vanities, since nobody gets out alive.

Jewishly speaking, on the other hand, Kiddush HaShem is the one truly serious issue because only through this ultimate being-for-the-other, whereby we choose death rather than inflict death, can we affirm the holiness of the Holy One. In the wake of the Shoah, one soon realizes the bankruptcy of the Pauline salvation by "faith" alone (see, for example, Rom. 3:28), of the Kantian categorical imperative, and of the Heideggerian existential resolve. In the wake of the Shoah, one soon realizes that for a Jew *only* the commandment to undertake a Kiddush HaShem by living *as a Jew*—a commandment *from On High,* and not from my own rationality or sensitivity—can preclude murder.

This choosing of one's own death over committing murder is just the opposite of the suicide that the ontological tradition recommends, beginning with the Socratic assertion that the philosopher lives in a preparation for death and leading to the Heideggerian *Sein-zum-Tod,* or "being-toward-death."[29] Whereas suicide is an execration and desecration of life, Kiddush HaShem is an affirmation and sanctification of life. It is the ultimate testimony to the One who commands us to choose life (Deut. 30:19). In choosing life we do not choose merely to stay alive; rather, we choose not to "die the death," as it is written: opting for life, we opt against the *mot tamut,* the "surely die" or the "dying the death" (Gen. 2:17), about which the first human being and every human being is warned from the beginning. That is what makes Kiddush HaShem "martyrdom" or "bearing witness." That is what makes it the first step in the movement of return from the ashes of Auschwitz to the holiness of Jerusalem. That is why we refer to the Event as Shoah: it is not a burnt offering that sacrifices life—it is a rising from the ashes to affirm life.

Just as the Divine Presence, or *Shekhinah,* that came under the Nazi assault dwells in the time of the Sabbath, so does she dwell in the space of Jerusalem, as the mystics have noted. Using gematria (interpretation based on numerical values of Hebrew letters), they note that when the letters of *Shekhinah* are spelled out, the word *Shekhinah* has a numerical value of 596, which is the same numerical value as the word *Jerusalem*.[30] And in the Talmud it is written, "Rabbi Shmuel bar Nachmani said in the name of Rabbi Yochanan: 'Three are called by the Name of the Holy One, blessed be He, and they are the righteous, the Messiah, and Jerusalem'" (*Bava Batra* 75b). And so it is written: "The Word of HaShem [goes forth] from Jerusalem" (Isa. 2:3). Jerusalem, then, represents precisely what the Nazis attempted to destroy at Auschwitz: the Commanding Voice of the Divine Presence as She dwells in the world. That dwelling is what is sanctified in the Sanctification of the Name.

Whereas the problem of suicide is a logical outcome of speculative thought, it is utterly alien to Jewish thought. Here too we can learn from the Hebrew language, as in Hebrew there is no precise equivalent for "suicide." Although we have the modern Hebrew word *hitratsach*, which, like the Latin-based word *suicide,* means to "murder oneself," this verb does not appear in the Holy Tongue, that is, in the language of Torah. Nevertheless, there are other distinctively Hebrew terms for suicide that are extremely revealing. In the *Kitsur Shulchan Arukh*, for example, the phrase meaning to "commit suicide" is *ibed atsmo*, literally to "lose oneself" or to lose one's "essence," one's "substance," one's "strength" (*otsem*), the very "bone" of one's being. And what is the "essence" or "substance" or "bone" of the human being? It is the Divine Image, the human soul, in all its dimensions, as explored in the last section. There is no self-murder because there is no autonomous, independent "self." Rather, who and what we are lies in the Divine Image in which we are created. Therefore suicide is an assault on the Divine Image: *that* is what the suicide murders. As an assault on the Divine Image, that is what the ontological tradition ultimately comes to. And there are those who have succumbed to it, both Jewish and non-Jewish, with the Shoah extending beyond the limits of space and time. Among the most notable are Tadeusz Borowski, Paul Celan, Piotr Rawicz, Primo Levi, and Jerzy Kosinski.

Here we see the confusion, the overturning of categories, characteristic of the confusion between Greek and Hebrew thought, between *Holocaust* and *Shoah*. It is a confusion that led to a time when children were old and old men were as helpless as children, when the righteous had to hide *from their neighbors* the fact that they saved lives, and now, when murderers are deemed martyrs.[31] This post-Shoah confusion that plagues our world is a manifestation of the confusion between *Holocaust* and *Shoah*. If in the Lager there were no madmen or criminals, as Primo Levi has pointed out, so in the post-Shoah confusion are we slipping into a similar condition.[32] In a realm where insanity passes for normalcy—the insanity that results in suicide being the number two cause of death among people between the ages of fifteen and twenty—we have the confusion that results from the loss of the Divine Image within: when the good is whatever feels good, our children kill themselves. They are not stupid: in fact, they are very intelligent, so intelligent as to learn oh so quickly from our example. And so they "go mad," or *nitrefah dato*, according to the Hebrew expression, which literally means to have one's knowledge "confused" or "torn to pieces." Their knowledge is confused because we have been so long in exile of Shoah that our own knowledge is confused. It is so confused that there are those among us who train children for a suicide that is murder and then call them martyrs. This is the ultimate sign of the shadow of the Shoah, and not of the Holocaust, that extends over our world. This is Amalek in his most insidious form. This is Shoah.

Notes

1. See, for example, Emil L. Fackenheim, *The Jewish Return Into History: Reflections in the Age of Auschwitz and a New Jerusalem* (New York: Schocken Books, 1978), 19–24.
2. Primo Levi, *Survival in Auschwitz: The Nazi Assault on Humanity*, trans. Stuart Woolf (New York: Simon and Schuster, 1996), 26.
3. Sara Nomberg-Przytyk, *Auschwitz: True Tales from a Grotesque Land*, trans. Roslyn Hirsch (Chapel Hill: University of North Carolina Press, 1985), 72.
4. Ka-tzetnik 135633, *House of Dolls*, trans. Moshe M. Kohn (New York: Pyramid, 1958), 125.
5. See Franz Rosenzweig, *The Star of Redemption*, trans. William W. Hallo (Boston: Beacon Press, 1972), 4.
6. See Fackenheim, *The Jewish Return Into History,* 47.
7. See Elie Wiesel, *Evil and Exile*, trans. Jon Rothschild (Notre Dame: University of Notre Dame Press, 1990), 155; Primo Levi, *The Drowned and the Saved*, trans. Raymond Rosenthal (New York: Vintage Books, 1989), 31. It is worth noting that Jews had actually been in Krakow for 800 years.

8. Primo Levi, *The Reawakening*, trans. Stuart Wolf (Boston: Little, Brown, 1965), 33, 128.
9. Primo Levi, *La tregua* (Torino: Einaudi, 1989), 250.
10. See Emil L. Fackenheim, "The Holocaust and the State of Israel," in Michael L. Morgan, ed., *A Holocaust Reader: Responses to the Nazi Extermination* (New York: Oxford University Press, 2001), 132; Alfred Rosenberg, *Race and Race History and Other Essays*, ed. Robert Pais (New York: Harper and Row, 1974), 131–32.
11. Franz Rosenzweig, *Franz Rosenzweig's "The New Thinking,"* trans. and ed. Alan Udoff and Barbara Galli (Syracuse, N.Y.: Syracuse University Press, 1999), 96.
12. Immanuel Kant, *Conflict of the Faculties*, trans. Mary J. Gregor (New York: Abaris, 1979), 95; Kant, *The Critique of Practical Reason*, trans. Lewis White Beck (New York: Macmillan, 1985), 101.
13. Emil L. Fackenheim, *Encounters between Judaism and Modern Philosophy* (New York: Basic Books, 1993), 190–91.
14. Martin Heidegger, "Will to Power as Art," in *Nietzsche*, vol. 1, trans. D. Krell (San Francisco: Harper and Row, 1979), 18.
15. From the *Freiburger Studentenzeitung*, November 3, 1933; see Guenther Neske and Emil Kettering, eds., *Martin Heidegger and National Socialism*, trans. Lisa Harries (New York: Paragon, 1990), 45.
16. Quoted in Neske and Kettering, eds., *Martin Heidegger and National Socialism*, 158.
17. Martin Heidegger, *Introduction to Metaphysics*, trans. Gregory Fried and Richard Polt (New Haven: Yale University Press, 2000), 60.
18. Jean-François Lyotard, *Heidegger and "The Jews,"* trans. Andreas Michel and Mark S. Roberts (Minneapolis: University of Minneapolis Press, 1990), 23.
19. Kalonymos Kalmish Shapira, *Sacred Fire: Torah from the Years of Fury 1939–1942*, trans. J. Hershy Worch, ed. Deborah Miller (Northvale, N.J.: Jason Aronson, 2000), 56.
20. Heinrich Heine, "The German Revolution," in *Words of Prose*, trans. E. B. Ashton (New York: L. B. Fischer, 1943), 51–53.
21. Joseph Soloveitchik, *The Halakhic Mind: An Essay on Jewish Tradition and Modern Thought* (New York: Free Press, 1986), 78.
22. Elie Wiesel, *Night*, trans. Stella Rodway (New York: Bantam, 1982), 105.
23. Albert Camus, *The Myth of Sisyphus*, trans. Justin O'Brien (New York: Random House, 1955), 3.
24. See, for example, Immanuel Kant, *Grounding for the Metaphysics of Morals*, trans. James W. Ellington, 3rd ed. (Indianapolis: Hackett, 1993), 30–32.
25. André Neher, *The Prophetic Existence*, trans. William Wolf (New York: A. S. Barnes, 1969), 338–39.
26. See H. J. Zimmels, *The Echo of the Nazi Holocaust in Rabbinic Literature* (New York: KTAV, 1977), 64.
27. See René Descartes, *Meditations on First Philosophy*, 3rd ed., trans. D. A. Cress (Indianapolis: Hackett, 1993), 19.
28. Nomberg-Przytyk, *Auschwitz*, 81.
29. See Plato, *Phaedo*, trans. Hugh Tredinnick, in *The Collected Dialogues of Plato*, ed. Edith Hamilton and Huntington Cairns (Princeton, N.J.: Princeton University Press, 1969), 66; Martin Heidegger, *Sein und Zeit* (Tübingen: Max Niemeyer, 1963), 118.
30. See Matityahu Glazerson, *Building Blocks of the Soul: Studies in the Letters and Words of the Hebrew Language* (Northvale, N.J.: Jason Aronson, 1997), 175.
31. Jan T. Gross, *Neighbors: The Destruction of the Jewish Community in Jedwabne, Poland* (Princeton, N.J.: Princeton University Press, 2001), 129.
32. Levi, *Survival in Auschwitz*, 98.

What Have We Learned from the Holocaust?

John K. Roth

What have we learned from the Holocaust? Reflecting on some events from 2007, my response to that question goes in two directions: (1) *maybe something* but (2) *not enough*. To explain what I mean by those two points, and to identify their content, it is important to consider the governing question in some further detail.

There could be many questions with the form "What have we learned from . . . ?" The "blank" could be filled in by references to fields of inquiry, such as science or economics, or to events, such as some recent election or the Iraq War. The "blank" could also be filled by references to persons, such as Moses, Jesus, or one might add the names of recently problematic figures such as the racial-slurring talk-radio "shock-jock" Don Imus, the embattled and now former U.S. attorney general Alberto Gonzalez, or Paul Wolfowitz, who left the presidency of the World Bank under a conflict-of-interest cloud. The version of the topic question under consideration here, however, asks what we may have learned from the Holocaust, and at the very least it implies that there is something of particular importance about *that* event. One way to consider this importance is to observe that the time of this writing (in the spring of 2007) was close to three significant Holocaust-related anniversary dates.

First, note that Irena Klepfisz, a child survivor of the Holocaust, became an important writer and poet whose best-known works include a poem called "Bashert." Its title, a Yiddish word, evokes senses of inevitability and fate. As the poem expresses grief and protest, "Bashert" does not mention the Holocaust directly, but that event shadows every line: "These words are dedicated to those who survived," writes Klepfisz. "These words are dedicated to those who died."[1]

Klepfisz's father, Michael, was one of those who died. Yisrael Gutman, survivor and historian of the Warsaw ghetto uprising, says that Michael Klepfisz, "who played an important role in the manufacture of armaments in the ghetto," was killed on the afternoon of April 20, 1943, in hand-to-hand fighting against Gen. Jürgen Stroop's German forces, who had been directed to destroy the ghetto.[2] In the summer of 1942 the Germans had deported 300,000 Jews from the Warsaw ghetto. Most were sent to their deaths in Treblinka's gas chambers. Michael Klepfisz and Yisrael Gutman were members of a group of young Jewish men and women (they numbered about 750) who trained and armed themselves as best they could and were determined to resist Nazi efforts to annihilate the 55,000 Jews who remained in the ghetto in the early spring of 1943.

In January of that year, SS chief Heinrich Himmler had ordered further deportations, but Jewish resistance impeded that effort. Aware that they would meet determined resistance, the Germans regrouped and returned on Monday, April 19, the eve of Passover in 1943, to finish the job. What ensued was, in Gutman's words, "the first urban uprising in German-occupied Europe, and, among the Jewish uprisings, the one that lasted the longest, from April 19 to May 16, 1943." The inadequately armed Jewish fighters, who also lacked military training and battle experience, were outnumbered three-to-one by Nazi forces that enjoyed support by tanks and cannons. The Jews' "arsenal" consisted mainly of pistols, Molotov cocktails, and a few rifles, which had been smuggled into the ghetto or taken from Germans who were ambushed in the previous January's resistance.

Using hit-and-run tactics and taking advantage of bunker hiding places, the Jewish fighters kept Stroop's forces off balance during the uprising's early days, but the Germans retaliated by burning the ghetto, building by building. Even then, doomed though it was, Jewish resistance continued. Not until May 8 did the Germans capture the Jewish Fighting Organization's headquarters, a bunker at 18 Mila Street. Mordecai Anielewicz, the organization's commander, perished in that struggle. On May 16 Stroop declared victory, proclaiming that "the Jewish quarter of Warsaw no longer exists." The losses the Jewish fighters inflicted on the Germans were militarily small. Stroop's report noted sixteen dead and eighty-five wounded. Nevertheless, the Warsaw ghetto uprising remains an immensely important example of heroic Jewish resistance against the Holocaust's overwhelming odds.

About four years later, on April 16, 1947, a man very different from Michael Klepfisz also lost his life. On that date, Rudolf Höss was executed by hanging on a gallows that stood near one of the gas chambers at Auschwitz, a site that has become nearly synonymous with the Holocaust itself. Höss, a Nazi SS officer, had been the commandant of that slave labor and killing center on Polish soil, which has rightly been called the epicenter of the Holocaust, for more than a million Jews were murdered there and tens of thousands of Polish prisoners also died in that place. Höss's execution came too late. However just it may have been, it could not bring back the dead. Nor could Höss's hanging repair the damage unleashed by his actions and the antisemitism and racism that provoked and inflamed them.

A third Holocaust-related anniversary worth remembering at the time of this writing is May 14, 1948. On that date the modern State of Israel came into existence. Survivors of the Holocaust were prominent among its first citizens, as they remain in their dwindling numbers sixty years on. The event we call the Holocaust was Nazi Germany's attempt to destroy Jewish life root and branch. Fortunately, that aim was not successful, at least not entirely, but it came far too close for comfort. However much the Holocaust was a factor in making the State of Israel a reality, no sound judgment is likely to claim that the Holocaust was a price worth paying for Israel's existence. Too much was lost to justify even that outcome.

As the three Holocaust-related anniversaries may help to make clear, the Holocaust was not only *genocide* but also a form of genocide that was *unprecedented*, owing to its systematic, unrelenting, technological, geographical, and ideological scope. For those reasons, it seemed possible that *we* (humankind) might learn something from this distinctive disaster, something that would have ethical, political, and perhaps even ecological importance.

Survivors of the Holocaust, at least some of them, thought that such learning might take place if people would *listen* to what had happened to them. In addition, as education about the Holocaust began to be more pronounced, a similar hope was echoed, namely, if people *studied* the Holocaust, the world might become, as we are fond of saying, "a better place." Unfortunately, those hopes were too optimistic. Ethnic cleansing in the former Yugoslavia, genocide in Rwanda, a humanitarian crisis of immense proportions in Darfur, Sudan, are just a few reminders that the slogan "Never again" is less than credible, a fact that led the Holocaust scholar Hank Knight, a songwriting friend of mine, to compose a piece called "Hardly Ever Again." Its apt lyrics go like this:

In '45, remember when
The world said, "Never, never again!
Never again: six million lost;
Never again: the Holocaust."
"Never," we said, "Never again."
But this is now and that was then.
"Hardly ever again."
Is that what we meant to say?

"Hardly ever again."
Will we turn and walk away?
This is now and that was then;
And we meant "hardly ever again."
But this is now and that was then.
When will we ever mean "never again"?

On a less overtly lethal but still immensely problematic note, *we* (humankind) have not even taken sufficiently to heart the harm that words can do. Absent slurs and slanders and the stereotyping that typically accompanies them, the Holocaust and genocide are scarcely imaginable, but the damage produced by ill-meaning words, spoken intentionally or just thoughtlessly or for some so-called shock effect can be incalculable, a fact that the 2007 scandal surrounding the American talk-radio star Don Imus helped to make clear.

Not enough, then, is a response, a sobering one, that must be made to the question, "What have we learned from the Holocaust?" Fortunately, if we not only recognize but also take to heart the fact that *not enough* has been learned, then it could be that the outcome is not entirely bleak. Knowing that we lack something, that we fall short, even that we might do better, is *maybe something* to consider as we keep asking, "What have we learned from the Holocaust?"

At this point, however, caution is advisable. Specifically, the turn from *not enough* to *maybe something* ought not to be so smooth and seamless that it produces a renewed hope that might turn out to be as naive and inadequate as the one that thought attention to the Holocaust would be sufficient to produce credible versions of the slogan "Never again." At the very least, we ought to think further about the content of the *something* that might be learned from attending to the Holocaust and its reverberations. With that aim in mind, at least two basic matters are among those that bear watching.

First, people need to take even more seriously than has been the case thus far that *what happened, happened*, specifically that the Holocaust really happened. The worst that can happen may seem unthinkable, but it is not impossible. Human beings are not able to prevent every catastrophe, but unless we are mindful about what can happen and how our actions have vital parts to play, we are less than responsible, and we put human life needlessly in jeopardy.

Second, while ours may be a world where contemporary concerns (global warming, for instance, or the ongoing war against terrorists) loom so large that attention to the Holocaust sometimes seems beside the point, it remains the case that memory of the Holocaust is something that we ignore at our peril. If we are faithful to that memory, it enjoins us to bear witness for the living and the dead in ways that protest against and resist the forces that lay waste to human well-being. Conversely, as three contemporary events help to show, if we fail to remember the Holocaust, we lose a resource that can aid and help us significantly.

In 2007 the observance of Earth Day took place on April 22. On that occasion, consciousness about the perils of global warming's perils and our accountability for causing them and, if possible, for overcoming them was upon us more than ever. The forecasts can be so grim and daunting as to make us think that attention to the past, even to the Holocaust, would involve a diversion of attention and energy from the world-saving responsibility that is before us. On the contrary, however, in such a case, it might help us (at least some of us, some of the time) to remember Michael Klepfisz and all the others who resisted the great odds against them in the Warsaw ghetto. *They did not despair; instead they gave all they had to battle against human actions that were destructive of life and that produced a world ecologically as well as politically and spiritually scarred by its killing centers, mass graves, and incinerated bodies whose smoke and ash continue to cloud and shadow our environment.*

Disrespect for human life and disregard for the natural world are intertwined. Usually perpetrated under the cover of war, genocide, including the Holocaust, wreaks havoc on the natural world as well as on human life itself. Conversely, where human life is fully respected, the likelihood that the natural world will be better cared for is usually enhanced. Where the natural world is cared for well, it is also likely that respect for human life will be high. Michael Klepfisz and his sisters and brothers in resistance can help us to see those interconnections, if only we do not forget who they were and what they did.

In the spring of 2007, Americans were shocked by the mass killings that took place on April 16 at Virginia Tech. Schools, colleges, and universities are not the safe places that we have hoped, if not assumed, they will be. One may ask what good could it do, is it even appropriate, to spend time remembering and reflecting on Auschwitz when the disaster at Blacksburg was so close at hand. Seung-Hui Cho, the Virginia Tech student killer, was no Rudolf Höss, but like Höss and all of us, that person was an individual embedded in a society. Just as Höss neither administered Auschwitz single-handedly nor accounted for the Holocaust by himself, the Virginia Tech killer, who, like Höss, does bear responsibility for many deaths, was also embedded in a society.

When we study the Holocaust, we pay attention to individual perpetrators such as Höss, but we also have to explore the social context and its pathologies, which may help to show how there came to be a man like Höss. *The right kind of memory of the Holocaust, the kind that probes history deeply, can help us to see that responsible responses to the loss and grief surrounding events such as those at Virginia Tech in the spring of 2007 need to include attention not only to murderous perpetrators and their victims but also to the social order from which they emerge and to what might be done to make it less likely that such acts will take place again.* As we move into uncertain futures, memory of the Holocaust has perspective and guidance to give us if we remember well and do not lapse into forgetfulness.

One of those murdered at Virginia Tech was Liviu Librescu, a Romanian-born Holocaust survivor who had been a professor of engineering at Tel Aviv University in Israel until a 1985 sabbatical year took him to Virginia Tech, which became his adopted home. Professor Librescu lost his life while blocking the door to his classroom with his body so that his students could escape the onslaught. Only a few hours before the shooting started and Professor Librescu was killed in Blacksburg, Virginia, a two-minute siren wailed across Israel. In 2007 that wailing might have anticipated Professor Librescu's death and that of his fellow victims at Virginia Tech. Be that as it may, since 1951, Israelis have observed Yom Hashoah, the annual Holocaust commemoration that brings the country to a standstill to remember the millions killed by Nazi Germany, its allies and collaborators. Significantly, the day falls midway between the time of the Warsaw ghetto uprising and Israeli Independence Day.

The Israeli siren's scream expresses both grief and warning, especially at a time when voices such as those of the Iranian president Mahmoud Ahmadinejad deny the Holocaust's reality and even threaten to remove Israel from the face of the earth. Just as the Holocaust siren in Israel is a reminder of what was lost during the Nazi years and their reverberations, it warns that Israel's future is not guaranteed either but depends on vigilance and integrity. *It seems to me, moreover, that the particularity of Israel's siren on Yom Hashoah has a significant universality as well, one that warns against taking anything good for granted, including a life such as Professor Librescu's, a point that we all do well to take to heart and that memory of the Holocaust keeps driving home again and again in distinctive ways.*

What happened, happened. Do not despair, even against steep odds. Keep attention focused not only on individuals but also on contexts as we try to create a world less prone to violence. Take nothing good for granted. These four insights are important ones that could be part of the *maybe something* that keeps the *not enough* from being dominant when possible responses to the question, "What have we learned from the Holocaust?" are concerned.

To those four points, I would add one more as a kind of postscript: It is important to recognize that even small deeds and modest actions can be life-saving. Particularly with that theme in mind, it can be appropriate to close these reflections about *not enough* and *maybe something* in response to the question, "What have we learned from the Holocaust?" by referring to the late American Jewish philosopher Philip Hallie, who was a distinguished professor at Wesleyan University in Connecticut.

As an artillery officer in World War II, Hallie helped to destroy Nazi Germany, but he was best known as an ethicist whose belief in the preciousness of human life led him to write about cruelty and also about a French village called Le Chambon, where 5,000 Jews found a wartime haven in the 1940s. A fine storyteller, Hallie often recalled a hurricane that battered New England. The storm's devastating power gave him an apt metaphor for the human predicament. "It's the hurricane we're in," Hallie liked to say, amplifying his conviction with the admonition, "Don't forget it."

Philip Hallie's concern about "the hurricane" was not limited to lethal weather. Human existence, he thought, is always contending with hurricane seasons of one kind or another. Significantly, however, when Hallie tracked the hurricane that reached his Connecticut home, havoc was not all that he saw. As the storm raged, he noticed that there seemed to be space for calm and quiet within the hurricane's eye. Hallie's eye, moreover, was drawn to the pale blue sky overhead. That blue was his favorite color, for, as Hallie put it, his passion, his hope, was to "expand the blue." Some persons, he added, "make a larger space for blue, for peace, for love." Such work, he insisted, "takes power as well as love. It takes force of will. It takes assertion and commitment."[3]

Moving beyond *not enough* and adding what is needed to *maybe something* when we think about what has been learned from the Holocaust depends on expanding the blue and on cultivating the qualities that are necessary for steps in those directions.

Notes

1. For more information on Irena Klepfisz, see Carol Rittner and John K. Roth, eds., *Different Voices: Women and the Holocaust* (St. Paul, Minn.: Paragon House, 1993), 324–27.
2. For more detail on these matters, see Yisrael Gutman, *The Jews of Warsaw 1939–1943* (Bloomington: Indiana University Press, 1989), 370–400, esp. 378ff. See also Gutman's article on the Warsaw ghetto uprising in Israel in Gutman, ed., *Encyclopedia of the Holocaust*, 4 vols. (New York: Macmillan, 1990), 1625–32.
3. See Philip Paul Hallie, "Cruelty: The Empirical Evil," in *Facing Evil: Light at the Core of Darkness*, ed. Paul Woodruff and Harry A. Wilmer (La Salle, Ill.: Open Court, 1994), 128–30. Also relevant is Philip Hallie, *In the Eye of the Hurricane: Tales of Good and Evil, Help and Harm* (Middletown, Conn.: Wesleyan University Press, 2001).

On Oil and Antisemitism

Richard L. Rubenstein

An attitudinal sea change has occurred in Europe. The nations of the European Union (EU), formerly the European Community (EC), have turned aggressively against Israel, and the post-Holocaust taboo on antisemitic speech and incitement, observed by the mainstream media and responsible political, religious, and intellectual leaders for decades, has been broken. When and why did this happen? How are we to understand the plethora of vulgarly antisemitic cartoons and caricatures, as well as statements by European leaders of a kind not uttered publicly since the fall of the Third Reich?

A major reason for the shift was Europe's surrender to Arab demands as the price for lifting the oil embargo of 1973. The reverberations of this surrender continue to be felt to this very day. More dependent on Arab oil than the United States, the nations of the European Community under the leadership of France resolved to appease the oil-producing states in order to assure the uninterrupted flow of oil to their petroleum-dependent economies. This was achieved through the creation of the Euro-Arab Dialogue (EAD) consisting of the nations of the European Union and the Arab League. Through the EAD, the Europeans sought to end a dire economic threat while the Arabs employed oil as a weapon to regain the territories lost in the six-day Arab-Israeli war of June 1967 as a first step toward eliminating the State of Israel altogether. As an initial step, the Arabs lobbied the EC to pressure Israel to withdraw from all territories occupied during the Six Days' War. Acting under French leadership, the Europeans sought both an uninterrupted petroleum supply and an anti-American, Euro-Arab alliance.[1]

Once the Arab leaders saw how easily the Europeans acceded to their demands, they pressured the EU to relax its immigration rules and allow a massive influx of Muslims into Europe. At every EAD meeting, starting with the first in Cairo on June 14, 1975, resolutions were passed in support of Arab immigration.[2] The numbers tell the story. In 1952 the French National Office of Immigration put the number of Muslims in France at 500,000. Today estimates place their number at between 4.5 million and 6 million.[3] Most Muslim workers were initially male and came to Europe as temporary or "guest workers." However, on April 23, 1976, the government of then–prime minister Jacques Chirac issued a decree permitting the "reunion of families," thereby rendering temporary immigration permanent and creating the reproductive basis for the rapid increase in the EU's Muslim population. Although most European countries officially terminated labor immigration during the 1970s because of growing domestic unemployment, approximately 500,000 legal immigrants and 400,000 asylum seekers, largely Muslim in both cases, continued to arrive in Western Europe every year. Moreover, Muslims constitute a significant number of the illegal immigrants, estimated at between 120,000 and 500,000, who enter Western Europe every year.[4]

In the three decades since 1975, Western Europe has undergone an unprecedented demographic transformation. In 1982 15.6 million Muslims resided in Europe, excluding Turkey.[5] According to the U.S. Department of State's *Annual Report on International Religious Freedom 2003,* excluding Turkey, 23.2 million Muslims reside in Europe. Commenting on the State Department report, Timothy M. Savage, Division Chief in the Office of European Analysis at the State Department, has noted, "This number is significantly larger than the estimated 13–18 million typically cited by the media or in academic studies, which are based on dated and often incomplete information."[6] As the immigrant population increased in size, it not only reinforced Europe's anti-Israel policy but became the seed bed for the renewal of a virulent strain of antisemitism throughout Europe.

Even before the Arab oil boycott of 1973, there was a residue of latent antisemitism awaiting arousal. Charles De Gaulle knowingly reignited the flame. He became the first major postwar European leader to break the post–World War II taboo when he asserted during a press conference on November 28, 1967, that the Jews "were still what they had always been, that is an elite people, sure of themselves and domineering." He went on to allege that the Jewish people had been responsible for "provoking ill-will in certain countries and at certain times." De Gaulle deliberately used antisemitism to curry favor with the Arab and Muslim world at a time when Arabs were still in resentful shock over their unexpected defeat. Raymond Aron, the celebrated French-Jewish social theorist, had previously been sympathetic to De Gaulle, but he understood immediately the import of De Gaulle's remarks. Characterizing De Gaulle's comment "as ludicrous as it is hateful," Aron rightly concluded that "General De Gaulle knowingly and deliberately initiated a new phase of Jewish history."[7]

Until the end of France's war with Algeria in 1962, France's ties with Israel were exceptionally close, so close that France agreed in 1956 and 1957 to construct for Israel a twenty-four-megawatt nuclear reactor and a chemical reprocessing plant at Dimona.[8] With Franco-Algerian peace at hand, De Gaulle decided to terminate those ties and seek an alliance with the Arab-Muslim world as a rival power center to the United States and the Soviet Union.[9] De Gaulle's decision to reverse course was fully consistent with his hostility to the United States already manifest during World War II. As historian Edward A. Kolodziej and others have pointed out, De Gaulle regarded it as inconsistent with the grandeur of France that Roosevelt, Churchill, and Stalin denied him a role in the deliberations at which the future of Europe was decided.

Even after terminating its ties with Israel, France continued to supply Israel with the Mirage jets and other armaments that were crucial to its victory, but during the June 1967 war De Gaulle denounced Israel as the aggressor and imposed a strict arms boycott.

As war clouds gathered in the spring of 1967, European public opinion was largely pro-Israel. There was widespread apprehension that the world was about to witness a second Holocaust. Jews and pro-Israel non-Jews tended to identify Israel with the victims of the Holocaust and the Arabs as perpetrators. Attitudes began to change when Israel speedily won a sweeping victory. What did not change was the use of the Holocaust as a metaphor for the Arab-Israeli conflict. Arab, Gaullist, and left-wing media quickly perceived that they could turn the memory of the Holocaust into a powerful propaganda tool *against* Israel. No longer viewed as powerless, the Israelis were depicted in pro-Arab propaganda as perpetrators and the Arabs as their innocent victims, implicitly identifying the Israelis as the new Nazis and the Palestinians victims of a new Holocaust. Later on, in some pro-Arab propaganda the Palestinians would be represented as a crucified Christ figure and the Jews their crucifiers. There is an unpleasant subtext to such accusations: the Israelis deserve no better fate than Nazi Germany, utter destruction. *This would allow antisemites something denied to them in the Shoah, genocide without guilt.*

It took time for the reversal to take hold. Before it did, Egypt and Syria attacked Israel in the Yom Kippur War that lasted from October 6 to 24, 1973. On October 16 the Arab oil-producing states unilaterally raised petroleum prices 70 percent to $5.12 a barrel. The next day they announced a production cut of 5 percent and promised further cuts of 5 percent a month until Israel was induced to withdraw from all occupied territory. On October 18 Saudi Arabia announced a production cut of 10 percent until Arab terms were met. Because it supported Israel, the Arab oil producers imposed a total oil embargo on the United States. The Arab attack on Israel was supported by a massive Soviet arms airlift. As Henry Kissinger, then U.S. secretary of state, has explained, the United States began an equally massive weapons airlift to Israel to maintain a military balance between the warring parties and counter the threat of Soviet dominance in the Middle East. According to Kissinger, the warring Arabs and Israelis had become proxies in a contest between the Soviet Union and the United States.[10] A total embargo was also placed on the Netherlands, the only European Economic Community (EEC) member to permit America to use its airfields to resupply Israel during the war. As a reward for having denied U.S. access to their airfields, America's British and French "allies" were effectively exempt from the embargo while the other six EEC members faced only partial cutbacks.

At France's urging, the European response came speedily. It was to cave in to Arab demands, and, as noted above, to propose the creation of a "Euro-Arab Dialogue" (EAD) as a means of restoring harmonious relations with the Arab states. Meeting in Brussels on November 6, 1973, two weeks after the war's end, the nine EEC foreign ministers issued an unambiguously pro-Arab statement listing what they regarded as essential requirements for Middle East peace. These included the termination of Israel's 1967 occupation of Arab territory and the inclusion of the "legitimate rights of the Palestinians" in the final peace settlement. The foreign ministers also asserted the "inadmissibility of acquiring territory by force," a doctrine they applied exclusively to Israel.

Bat Ye'or, an international authority on the condition of non-Muslims under Muslim domination, has pointed out that in their statement the ministers had taken sides with the Arabs by distorting the intent of UN Resolution 242. Originally formulated in English, the Resolution referred only to unspecified Israeli "withdrawal *from territories*." The French translation improperly altered the original meaning to "from *the* territories" (*des territories)* creating the false impression that Israel had *no legitimate claim to any part of the West Bank.*[11] It was an old trick of diplomacy. Wars have been fought over deliberately misplaced commas and accent marks. The statement's final paragraph took note of "the ties of all kinds which have long linked" the EEC members to the states "of the south and east of the Mediterranean."[12] In spite of American opposition, the Europeans had signaled to the Arabs that they would meet their demands vis-à-vis Israel.

The Europeans also wanted the United States to join them in forcing Israel to withdraw from the occupied territories. They were convinced that America's failure to pressure Israel into a settlement had brought about the war and that America had put vital European interests at risk because of "domestic politics."[13] In his memoir, *Years of Upheaval*, Henry Kissinger recalls, "The always latent view that Mideast tensions would suddenly disappear if only Israel would return to the 1967 borders was put forward with increasing explicitness." Nor has this view, which entails a measure of anti-Jewish resentment, lost any of its potency in circles hostile to Israel. European anti-Americanism has a strong and not always latent antisemitic component.[14] The Nixon administration refused to comply. It insisted that capitulating to the Arabs under pressure would demonstrate weakness and lead to demands for further concessions. Instead, Washington sought a unified response by the oil-consuming nations to counter the Arab oil weapon. Speaking in London on December 12, 1973, Kissinger called on the oil-consuming nations of Europe, North America, and Japan to establish "an Energy Action group of senior and prestigious individuals with a mandate to develop within three months an initial action program for collaboration in all areas of the energy problem."[15] Kissinger reasoned that the embargo had been the result of unified action by the producing nations and that only the unified response of the consumers offered any hope of coming to a mutually satisfactory agreement.

The Europeans would have none of it and caved in almost immediately. Kissinger relates that on December 20, 1973, French president Georges Pompidou told him that France would not run the slightest risk of an oil cutoff, nor would it participate in any group or policy involving any possibility of confrontation.[16] As noted, the European response was to propose, at France's urging, a Euro-Arab Dialogue as a means of restoring harmonious relations between the two sides.[17] The first step was taken at a meeting of the nine EC nations in Brussels on November 6, 1973, at which the foreign ministers demanded that Israel withdraw to the 1949 armistice lines and that "the legitimate rights of the Palestinians" be included in any definition of peace for the Middle East. In addition, they hypocritically asserted the "inadmissibility of acquiring territory by force," a norm they applied only to Israel.

In early December 1973 the Dutch joined the European surrender. On December 4 a spokesman for the Dutch Foreign Office characterized Israel's occupation of Arab territories as "illegal," adding that the Dutch government fully adhered to the Brussels declaration of November 6 which demanded Israel's total withdrawal as a condition for peace. It is hardly coincidental that three days earlier the Saudi and Algerian oil ministers had met with the Dutch minister of commerce and demanded a special anti-Israeli "gesture" as the price of lifting the embargo.[18]

During 1974 and 1975 a series of quasi-official meetings took place between European officials and experts and their Arab counterparts with the first official meeting at the ministerial level taking place in Paris on July 31, 1974. The participants agreed to begin the Euro-Arab Dialogue (EAD) at the expert level sometime in 1975. This was the start of a process, which has continued to the present, whose stated purpose has been to create institutional structures to facilitate the integration and harmonization of European and Arab policies in international affairs, culture, education, and the media. In the course of several years, a common Middle Eastern policy was agreed upon and through the EAD European and Arab leaders sought to create "a global alternative to American power."[19] Commenting on the political motives for the creation of the EAD, Kissinger has observed: "it was France that acted as the spearhead of the so-called Europe-Arab dialogue, the European alternative to our Middle East diplomacy, whose rationale—never made explicit—could only be dissociation from the United States."[20]

Two months after the Paris meeting, at a conference of European and Arab parliamentarians in Damascus, September 14–17, 1974, the Arab delegates demanded from the Western Europeans as a precondition for economic agreements the following:

1. The unconditional withdrawal of Israel to the 1949 armistice lines.
2. Arab sovereignty over the old city of Jerusalem.
3. The participation of the PLO and Arafat in any negotiations.
4. Pressure by the EEC on the US to detach it from Israel and bring it closer to policies of Arab states.[21]

Although no time limit was set, the conditions were not negotiable and the Arabs confidently expected the Europeans to fulfill them. Their confidence was rooted in the credibility of the oil weapon and Europe's surrender to it.[22] The Europeans had unmistakably signaled that they had abandoned all pretense of impartiality and that hostility to Israel would henceforth be a cornerstone of European policy.

At the same time, the Arabs initiated a major effort to gain Christian support, stressing the theme of the Palestinians as victims and Israel as the oppressor. At an Arab Summit meeting in Amman, Jordan, on November 25–27, 1980, the speakers stressed the need for contacts with the Vatican and other Christian organizations such as the World Council of Churches to ensure support for "the recovery of full Arab sovereignty over Jerusalem." Even as the mainstream churches, both Catholic and Protestant, continued interfaith dialogue with Jews in the Diaspora, all too often they favored the Palestinians in the ongoing conflict. Unfortunately, the bias against Israel is consistent with a reading of Christian theology that remains deeply rooted in the hearts and minds of many clergy and laity, namely, that the Jews have been punitively exiled from their land for rejecting Christ. Replacement theology is an increasingly influential, albeit radical, version of that theology with its claim that Jews have been replaced by Christians in God's favor and that all of God's original promises to the Jews, including the land of Israel, have been inherited by Christianity. Some Arab Christian thinkers claim that the Palestinians are the "true Israel" and, whether Christian or Muslim, are alone entitled to possess the Holy Land. From such ideas to a total demonization of Jews and Judaism is an easy step and is often taken. For those Christians, and unfortunately there are many, Israel's unmitigated defeat would be a fulfillment of divine prophecy.

The flaw in the anti-Israel policies was that they were formulated by senior public officials and unelected bureaucrats with little, if any, public input. Even after the 1973 oil embargo, mainstream European sympathies had yet to turn against Israel. However, with official encouragement, the media played an important role in eventually bringing public opinion in line with EAD policy.

One of those who understood the problem even before 1973 was Georges Montaron, the influential director of *Témoignage Chrétien*, a left-wing Catholic group with a very strong pro-Arab bias.

On November 27, 1970, Montaron lectured on "The Arab World and Western Opinion" at the Dar es-Salaam Center in Cairo. Taking note of pro-Zionist sentiment prevalent in Europe, he advised his Arab audience, "If you succeeded in making from authentic Oriental Arabs, authentic Frenchmen and Englishmen—what an influence you would yield in Europe."[23]

Montaron had, in effect, invited the Arabs to consider immigration to Europe as a weapon against Israel. He understood that, starting with Germany's Gastarbeiter (temporary "guest" workers) program, Western Europe was for the first time importing Arabs, Turks, Kurds, and other Muslims in large numbers to solve the labor shortage that developed during the postwar reconstruction period in Western Europe.[24] However, these were not immigration programs. The temporary workers were expected to return home when no longer needed. Permanent residence was assured only when either the workers or their children became eligible for citizenship. As in the United States, citizenship in France and Great Britain is governed by *ius soli* (the law of the soil), by which citizenship results from being born in a country. Children of immigrants born in France and Britain are automatically citizens. Until 2000 the situation was different in Germany. An estimated 3 million Muslims were domiciled in Germany in 2000, but German citizenship was based on blood kinship (*ius sanguinis*) rather than place of birth (*ius soli*). On January 1, 2000, new citizenship laws were enacted that made it possible to acquire citizenship by being born in Germany and in some cases through naturalization.[25] Although the Arabs took no reciprocal measures, the Europeans agreed through the EAD to the establishment and financial support of Muslim religious, educational, and cultural institutions for the newcomers.[26]

Whether or not Montaron knew it, his proposal was consistent with an age-old Muslim strategy of utilizing migration to non-Muslim lands as the first step toward an eventual Muslim takeover. As Europe's Muslim population increased, the immigrants could conceivably also become a weapon against Christianity. Ironically, while De Gaulle sought a Franco-Arab alliance before his death in 1970, he was firmly opposed to large-scale Muslim immigration. One of his motives for separating Algeria from France, in spite of the bitter opposition of the *pieds noirs*, the Europeans in Algeria, and much of the leadership of the French army, was that he believed *Algerie française*, the political union of France and Algeria, would eventually lead to a Muslim majority in metropolitan France. On March 5, 1959, De Gaulle told his confidant Alain Peyrefitte:

> Try to mix oil and water. At the end of a moment they will separate again. The Arabs are the Arabs, the French are the French. Do you believe that the French body politic can absorb ten million Muslims, who tomorrow will be twenty million and the day after tomorrow forty million? . . . If all the Arabs and Berbers of Algeria are to be considered French, how could one prevent them from installing themselves in metropolitan France? . . . My village will no longer be called Colombey-les-Deux-Églises but Colombey-les-Deus-Mosquées![27]

Had he lived, in all likelihood De Gaulle would have regarded the EAD-sponsored immigration as a defeat for France and a victory for the Arabs.

Nevertheless, Montaron was by no means alone. As Bat Ye'or has shown, many of the calls for large-scale Muslim immigration into Europe were first floated in *Eurabia*, a journal initiated in the mid-1970s by the European Committee for the Coordination of Friendship Associations with the Arab World. In a July 1975 issue, Tilj Declerq, a Belgian member of the Parliamentary Association for Euro-Arab Cooperation, advanced the view that "policy must be formulated in order to bring about *economic cooperation through a combination of Arab manpower reserves and raw materials and European technology and 'management.'*"[28] Declerq saw the sharing of technology and manpower as gradually bringing about "as complete as possible an economic integration" between an Arab world with a surplus population and a technologically competent Europe with a declining birthrate.

Although the Arabs took no reciprocal measures, the Europeans agreed through the EAD to the establishment and financial support of Muslim religious, educational, and cultural institutions for the newcomers. As noted above, in the course of three decades Western Europe had undergone an unprecedented demographic transformation. Clearly, the introduction of so massive an immigrant population into Europe was bound to have revolutionary consequences for the political and religious life, as well as the foreign policy, of the nations of Western Europe. In the aftermath of the Madrid and

London bombings, as well as the gruesome murder of Theo van Gogh by a Muslim extremist on the streets of Amsterdam, and the French riots of November 2005, there is today much question whether this population can successfully be integrated. Even if one assumes that the majority of Europe's Muslims desire integration, a segment of unknown size not only disdains integration but dreams of a "New Andalusia," a new era of Muslim dominance on the European continent.[29]

As Montaron had foreseen, the massive immigration has had a profound impact on European sentiment toward both Israel and Jews, as evidenced by overwhelming media hostility toward Israel, increased aggression against Jews and Jewish institutions, and Muslim efforts to eliminate Holocaust education in public schools and turn Holocaust commemorative events into propaganda opportunities for the Palestinian "victims" of alleged Israeli genocide. Whatever Europe's Muslims may feel about integration, most are united in hostility to Israel and an indeterminate number are also hostile to Europe's Jews. In France, for example, the unemployment rate among young Muslim males is four times the national average and there has been a string of vicious attacks by young Muslim gangs against Jews including the ritualistic near-decapitation of Sebastien Salem, a Jew of Algerian background and one of France's most popular DJs, in Paris in November 2003 by a Muslim neighbor who told his mother, "I have killed my Jew. I can go to paradise." He later told police he had no regrets because Allah told him to kill Salem.

Many Muslims also object to the teaching about the Holocaust. In January 2005, for example, Sir Iqbal Sacranie, O.B.E., Secretary General of the Muslim Council of Britain, wrote to Charles Clarke, the British Home Secretary, saying that that body would not participate in Holocaust Memorial Day, January 27, 2005, a national observance under the patronage of the queen, unless it included the "Holocaust" of the Palestinian Intifada.[30] In July 2005 some members of the prime minister's all-Muslim advisory committee on Islamic affairs called for the abolition of Holocaust Memorial Day altogether "because it is offensive to Muslims."[31] Continued observance, they warned, would encourage extremism among young Muslims, a not very veiled threat coming shortly after the London subway bombings. In its place, they advocated creation of a day commemorating all genocide victims, including the Palestinians. As of March 2007, the British Muslim Council officially boycotts Holocaust Memorial Day and demands its replacement by a "Genocide Day" that will also mark "the ongoing genocide and human rights abuses of Palestinians" by Israelis. This can be seen as a malevolent attempt to transform a memorial for Holocaust victims into one in which Jews themselves become the perpetrators and the Arabs their victims!

Moreover, both Muslim numbers and the threat of Muslim violence give them political weight. Some European politicians such as George Galloway, MP, and Ken Livingstone, London's leftist Lord Mayor, curry favor with the Muslim population and have taken demagogic positions overtly hostile to Israel. On July 21, 2005, for example, Galloway made an incendiary speech on Syrian television in which he declared,

> Two of your beautiful daughters are in the hands of foreigners—Jerusalem and Baghdad. The foreigners are doing to your daughters as they will. The daughters are crying for help, and the Arab world is silent. And some of them are collaborating with the rape of these two beautiful Arab daughters. Why? Because they are too weak and too corrupt to do anything about it.[32]

In July 2004 Livingstone officially received Sheikh Yusef al-Qaradawi, a highly influential TV preacher who resides in Qatar, as an honored guest. Qaradawi has advocated the killing of gays and expressed his approval of suicide bombers against Israeli civilians as well as the indiscriminate killing of Americans in Iraq, yet in a September 2005 interview Livngstone likened Qaradawi to Pope John XXIII.[33] Galloway and Livingstone are but the tip of the iceberg. Many other European politicians seek to curry favor in less obvious ways, especially in foreign policy.

Other European politicians have looked the other way when attacks on Jews multiplied during the second Intifada, which began in 2000. This was especially true of the former Socialist prime minister of France Lionel Jospin. According to a 2004 report by S.O.S. Vérité-Sécurité, an antisemitism watchdog organization, 147 Jewish institutions—schools, synagogues, community centers, businesses—have been attacked. The slogan "Mort aux juifs" (Death to the Jews) has been scribbled on school blackboards and uttered at mass rallies. Rabbis have been assaulted. Under pressure from Muslim students, secondary school teachers have canceled classes on the Holocaust.[34] One of the most savage incidents was the ritualistic near-decapitation on November 19, 2003, of Sebastien Salem, an Algerian Jew and one of the country's most popular DJs. Earlier that evening, Chantal Piekolek, fifty-three, who was either Jewish or married to a Jew, was stabbed twenty-seven times in the neck and chest by Mohamed Ghrib, thirty-seven, while working in her Avenue de Clichy shoe store. There was no evidence of sexual molestation. Salem's killer was a neighbor who told his mother, "I have killed my Jew. I can go to paradise." Salem's gruesome murder was reported by only one minor French newspaper, the tabloid *Le Parisien.* It was ignored by mainstream journals, *Le Monde, Figaro,* and *Libération.*[35] Moreover, Salem's ritualistic near-decapitation resembled both that of Theo van Gogh in Amsterdam and that of Ariel Sellouk, a twenty-three-year-old Jew of North African descent murdered by his "friend" Mohammed Ali Alayed, also twenty-three, in Houston, Texas, in August 2003.[36]

Not surprisingly there has been a significant increase in French-Jewish immigration to Israel. According to the Israeli government, 7,024 immigrants came from France from 2000 to the first half of 2004.[37] In June 2005 this writer met a brilliant young French woman at the home of her parents in Paris. She told me that she planned to emigrate to Israel. She said, "Jews have no future in France. Some day I expect to have children and I don't want to worry every time they go outside the way my mother worries about me and my sister." In spite of everything I had read about the revival of antisemitism, I was shocked. Her father had achieved an eminent place in the world of French letters and she had the ability to follow his example, yet she saw no future for herself in the country in which she was born.

Thus, the rise of Europe's Muslim population has coincided with the revival of European antisemitism. The phenomenon was long ignored or denied, but in early 2002 the issue could no longer be swept under the rug. The European Union commissioned a report on the prevalence of physical and verbal violence against Jews and Jewish institutions. The 112-page report was prepared by the Center for Research on Antisemitism (CRA) of the Technical University of Berlin, a highly regarded institution.[38] The CRA has an impeccable reputation for its scientific research and its director, Dr. Wolfgang Benz, is an internationally recognized authority on antisemitism and the Holocaust. When the report was completed, the European Union withheld publication. The EU sponsors deemed "inflammatory" one of the report's key conclusions, namely, that Muslim and pro-Palestinian groups have generated a new and violent wave of hatred in Europe.[39] In spite of the European Union's attempt to suppress the report that it had itself commissioned, the full text was leaked by an unknown source. In July 2003 Congressman Robert Wexler wrote to Javier Solana, the EU's foreign policy chief, demanding release of the official report.[40] Forced to respond, the EU finally released an amended report in March 2003 claiming that the original was of "poor quality and lacking in empirical evidence." This claim was refuted by the CRA, which published a detailed account of its dealings with the EU commission and its research methods. The CRA stated, "There is some evidence that it was . . . political pressure from various EU countries on the management board that had led to its non-publication."[41]

The amended EU report concluded that "[t]he largest group of perpetrators of antisemitic activities appeared to be young, disaffected white Europeans" influenced by extreme right ideas on Jews although it did acknowledge that some perpetrators were young Muslims and "people of North African origin." These findings blatantly contradicted the actual report, which stated, "The percentage attributable to the extreme right was only nine per cent in 2002."[42] The report itself declared that most of the 191 violent attacks on synagogues, Jewish schools, kosher shops, cemeteries, and rabbis in 2002 were the work of "youth from neighborhoods sensitive to the Israeli-Palestinian conflict." According to S.O.S. Vérité-Sécurité, a French antisemitism watchdog organization, 147 Jewish institutions—schools, synagogues, community centers, businesses—have been attacked. Rabbis have been assaulted. Under pressure from Muslim students, secondary school teachers have canceled classes on the Holocaust. At least in 2003 Europe's leaders were in no mood seriously to confront the reality of domestic Islamic antisemitism.

Moreover, Europe's Muslim population contains significant elements that are hostile not only to Jews and Israel but to Christians as well. That was evident in the riots by Muslim youth throughout

France in November 2005. Although the same group had been principally responsible for most of the overt antisemitic violence in France in recent years, neither Jews nor Israel/Palestine were the issue that sparked the November riots. According to Amir Taheri, an Iranian-born authority on Islam and editor of the Paris-based journal *Politique International,* the conflict started when the police answered a call in Clichy-sou-Bois, an overwhelmingly no-go Muslim *banlieue* (suburb) into which no police had ventured for years.[43] The young males, who had long regarded the area as their turf, were infuriated by the police "intrusion." A chase ensued in which two boys, who had not been pursued by the police, entered an area housing a power pylon and were electrocuted.

When the news of the deaths broke, angry young Muslims shouted, "Allah is great," and forced the police to withdraw. The government could not tolerate the expulsion of its police from French territory and sent in the very tough, highly trained Special Forces with armored cars. With the entry of the Special Forces, the electrocuted boys ceased to be the grievance. The rioters began to call the police an army of occupation and demanded their withdrawal from the "occupied territories."

Some Muslims even called for the organization of the predominantly Muslim areas on the basis of the "millet" system of the Ottoman empire, in which each religious community would have the power to organize its own autonomous communal life. In reality, a de facto millet system already exists in many of the banlieues. The law of the banlieues is not the law of France. No matter how French politicians and intellectuals may attempt to come up with programs for successfully integrating the Muslim community, the youthful inhabitants of the Muslim ghettos appear to have rejected integration. As the Muslim population increases, not only will separatist pressure increase, but so too will the territory inhabited by Muslims. If as some authorities predict, France will have a Muslim majority by the middle of the twenty-first century, France is likely to be divided into Christian and Muslim territories.

In reality, Muslim alienation was inherent in the original EAD decision to embark on a program of mass immigration and cultural symbiosis. Whether religious or secular, whether or not they speak perfect French and dress and play like Western youth, most young Muslims feel that they are not like the "Franco-French," and the "Franco-French" perceived them to be other. Nor, as Olivier Roy and others have pointed out, do they identify with the countries from which their parents or grandparents have emigrated. For many, the identity question remains unresolved, but when it is, their identity is likely to be a "deterritorialized identity" rooted in loyalty to the *umma,* the universal Nation of Islam *even if they are not especially observant.*[44] And, by its very nature, such a loyalty is inherently subversive of all national political institutions. Some observers have likened the riots to those that attended the 1960s Black revolt against inferior status in the United States. But such a comparison is flawed. The American white majority did not possess a collective memory of Black conquest; the "Franco-French" have the memory of the Battle of Tours and Poitiers in 732 at which the Muslim invaders were defeated and thrown back across the Pyrenees, where they remained for hundreds of years. Even apart from religion, given their history it is questionable whether each side can really overcome the otherness of the other.

To return to the question with which we began: What accounts for the freedom with which mainstream European sources today resort to antisemitic images and speech? Once De Gaulle broke the taboo, old habits and customs resurfaced. Undoubtedly, the European Union's response to the Arab oil weapon facilitated the reawakening. In 1973 the Europeans were unexpectedly and decisively humbled by their former colonial dependents. And, as the years passed, the sight of ever more Muslims in their midst reminded them of their humiliating capitulation.

Unfortunately, defeat and surrender do little for either personal or national self-esteem. Self and group-contempt are likely responses, but such feelings are hard to bear. The Germans could not bear them in 1918, and they put up a far more strenuous fight before giving in than did Europe in 1973. It is much more comforting to blame others as did the Germans after World War I. That is one of the roots of European hostility, sometimes bordering on hatred, for America. America did not surrender and Europe did.

Moreover, surrender often leads to mythmaking. After Europe's ignominious capitulation to the Arabs, its leaders deluded themselves with the myth that if only America had compelled Israel to make peace on Arab terms, in reality surrender as they had done, the Middle East crisis would have gone away and they would no longer be humiliated by Arab demands. And, who was to blame for America's refusal to do what the Europeans were incapable of doing, namely, pressure Israel? The Jews with their allegedly insidious influence. As so often in the past, the mythical subtext was, *Die Juden sind unser Unglück,* The Jews are our misfortune. Only the residue of Auschwitz's stench prevented matters from really getting out of hand.

Oil lay at the root of European antisemitic revival. As a long-term consequence of a temporary crisis, Europe permitted the introduction into its midst of a population that was largely hostile to Israel and Europe's Jews. Moreover, the new immigrants were a victorious population. They were permanently in Europe on Muslim terms because of Europe's capitulation. Why, most thought, should they integrate with those whom they had defeated? With their rapidly increasing population, it was only a matter of time before their victory in Europe would be apparent to all.

Notes

1. On the difference between the American and European responses to the embargo and the initial American perception of the EAD as an attempt under French leadership to undermine American influence in Europe and the Middle East, see Henry Kissinger, *Years of Upheaval* (Boston: Little, Brown, 1983), 874ff., 928–30.
2. Bat Ye'or, *Eurabia: The Euro-Arab Axis* (Madison, N.J.: Fairleigh Dickinson University Press, 2005), 93.
3. A religious census is prohibited by law in France. Hence, the available figures are informed estimates. On the 1952 figures, see Soheib Bencheikh, *Marrianne et le prophète: l'islam dans la France laïque* (Marianne and the Prophet: Islam in lay France) (Paris: Bernard Grasset, 1998), 86–87. For this citation, I am indebted to Shireen T. Hunter, ed., *Islam, Europe's Second Religion: The New Social, Cultural, and Political Landscape* (Westport, Conn.: Praeger, 2002), 6. In 1978 one source places the figure at 2,000,000. See Dominique Norbrook, *Passport to France* (New York: Franklin Watts, 1986). According to the U.S. Department of State's *Annual Report on International Religious Freedom 2005,* France's Muslim population is estimated to be between 5 and 6 million or between 8 and 10 percent of the population. In July 2005, the CIA estimated the population of France to be 60,658,178 with the Muslim population estimated at between 3 and 6 million (5-10%). See CIA, *The World Factbook,* http://www.cia.gov/cia/publications/factbook/geos/fr.html#People. The semi-official Muslim website, Muslim Population Worldwide, estimates that there are currently 6,000,000 Muslims in France or 10 percent of the population, http://www.islamicpopulation.com/europe_general.html.
4. International Organization for Migration (IOM), *World Migration Report 2000* (Geneva: IOM, 2000), 195. IOM, "Facts and Figures on International Migration," *Migration Policy Issues* (March 2003): 2, http://www.iom.int/DOCUMENTS/PUBLICATION/EN/MPI_series_No_2_eng.PDF . For this reference I am indebted to Timothy J. Savage, "Europe and Islam: Crescent Waxing, Cultures Clashing," *Washington Quarterly* (Summer 2004): 27.
5. M. Ali Kettani, *Muslim Minorities in the World Today* (London: Mansell Publishing, 1986).
6. Savage, "Europe and Islam," 26.
7. John Eric Lewis, "De Gaulle and the New Anti-Semitism," *Israel Insider,* November 28, 2003, http://web.israelinsider.com.
8. The story of Israel's development of nuclear weapons is told in Avner Cohen, *Israel and the Bomb* (New York: Columbia University Press, 1998).
9. See Edward A. Kolodziej, *French International Policy Under De Gaulle and Pompidou* (Ithaca. N.Y.: Cornell University Press, 1973), 447–552.
10. On October 26, 1973, Kissinger sent the following message to the West German government, "The U.S. G[overnment] believes that for the West to display weakness and disunity in the face of a Soviet-supported military action against Israel could have disastrous consequences." A similar note was sent to the British and other "allies." Kissinger, *Years of Upheaval,* 714.
11. Bat Ye'or, *Eurabia,* 78–79.
12. Saleh Al-Mani and Salah Al-Shaikhly, *The Euro-Arab Dialogue: A Study in Associative Diplomacy* (New York: St. Martin's Press, 1983), 111; *Keesing's Contemporary Archives* 19 (November 26–December 2, 1973): 9–10.
13. In *Years of Upheaval,* Kissinger recalls, "The always latent view that Mideast tensions would suddenly disappear if only Israel would return to the 1967 borders was put forward with increasing explicitness."
14. On the difference between the American and European responses to the embargo and the initial American perception of the EAD as an attempt under French leadership to undermine American influence in Europe and the Middle East, see Kissinger, *Years of Upheaval,* 874ff., 928-30.

15. Ibid., 897.
16. Ibid.
17. The most reliable European source on the EAD is Bat Ye'or, *Eurabia.* See esp. 147–89. For a somewhat different Arab assessment of the EAD, see Al-Mani and Al-Shaikhly, *The Euro-Arab Dialogue.* Many of the documents relating to the EAD are publicly available on the EU Web site where the EAD is referred to as "the Euro-Mediterranean Partnership" at http://europa.eu.int/comm/external_relations/euromed/conf/index.htm.
18. "Dutch See Israel in 'Illegal' Stand," *New York Times,* December 4, 1973, 17.
19. Bat Ye'or, *Eurabia*, 63.
20. Kissinger, *Years of Upheaval*, 898.
21. Bat Ye'or, *Eurabia*, 55.
22. The Europeans were initially reluctant to recognize the PLO officially although PLO representatives were included among the Arab representatives at EAD meetings. Nevertheless, the Arabs understood that the Europeans had little choice but to follow their lead. For example, in the midst of the turmoil of the Iranian Revolution of 1979, a conference was held at Rimini on the subject of petroleum and Europe Arab relations with the cooperation of the UN, the European Communities, OPEC, and the League of Arab States. In his conference address, Mana Ben Saceed Al-Otaiba, chairman of OPEC and minister of petroleum and mineral resources of the United Arab Emirates, told the European participants: "If there is no political harmony between us, how can we talk about commercial and economical harmony? Economics and politics are two sides of the same question. . . . All we ask is that Europe and the industrialized countries recognize Palestine as a nation and the Palestine Liberation Organization as its sole representative. . . . You all know that this [petroleum] is a highly volatile and inflammable product and that it is located in an area dominated by military and political disturbances. We must all work together to calm this situation—this smouldering in the oil fields must be damped down otherwise it will burst into flames and then there would be no more oil to supply the industrialized countries with. We must all face this reality if we want to find a peaceful solution to the Palestine problem and to the problem of the Middle East." *Europe Arab World: From Clashing on Petroleum to Cooperating for a New Economic Order* (Forli, Italy: Pio Manzu International Centre, December 1979), 77–79. For this citation I am indebted to Bat Ye'or, *Eurabia*, 81–82.
23. "Le directeur de 'Témoignage Chrétien' dénonce la propaganda sioniste," *Informations Arabes,* no. 15, Geneva, November 30, 1970, 6. For this citation, I am indebted to Bat Ye'or, *Eurabia,* 46 and 328.
24. On Germany's *Gastarbeiter* program, see Charles Hawley, "Integration in Europe: How Germany Failed Its Immigrants," *Der Spiegel Online,* December 21, 2004, http://service.spiegel.de/cache/international; for France see Bencheikh, *Marrianne et le prophète,* 86–87; for England see "Muslims in the West: Dim Drums Throbbing in the Hills Half Heard," *The Economist*, August 8, 2002, http://www.economist.com.
25. Details of the citizenship reform, "Reform of Germany's Citizenship and Nationality Law," are posted on the Web page of the German Embassy to the United Kingdom, http://www.german-embassy.org.uk/reform_of_germany_s_citizenshi.html.
26. See Derek Hopgood, *The Relations between the Two Cultures. Acts of the Hamburg Symposium. April 11th to 15th 1983* (London: Croom Helm, 1983), 305–16; Bat Ye'or, *Eurabia*, 91–98.
27. Alain Peyrefitte, *C'Était De Gaulle* (Paris: Fayard, 1994), 52.
28. Tilj Declerq, "A European Point of View," *Eurabia* (magazine), Paris, July 1975; cited by Bat Ye'or, *Eurabia,* 64. The Parliamentary Association continues to play an important role in the EAD. Its Web site is http://www.medea.be.
29. On the idea of the "new Andalusia" as the model for the Euro-Arab symbiosis in Europe, see Gilles Keppel, *The War for Arab Minds: Islam and the West*, trans. Pascale Ghazaleh (Cambridge: Harvard University Press, 2004), 293–95.
30. *Sunday Times,* London, January 23, 2005.
31. Toby Helm, "Holocaust Memorial Day Must Be Scrapped, Say British Muslim Leaders," *Daily Telegraph Online* (UK), September 12, 2005, http://www.telegraph.co.uk/news.
32. "British MP George Galloway in Syria: Foreigners are Raping Two Beautiful Arab Daughters," MEMRI Special Dispatch Series No. 948, August 3, 2005, http://memri.org.
33. On the killing of gays, see Jenny McCartney, "Livingstone Lauds the Man Who Advocates the Killing of Gays," *Daily Telegraph* (UK), November 7, 2004, http://www.telegraph.co.uk/opinion. On suicide bombers against Israelis, see "Al-Qaradawi Full Transcript," *BBC News,* July 8, 2004, http://news.bbc.co.uk/2/hi/programmes/newsnight/3875119.stm. See also "Sheikh Al-Qaradhawi on Hamas Jerusalem Day Online," MEMRI, Special Dispatch No. 1051, December 18, 2005, http://memri.org. On likening Qaradawi to Pope

John XXIII, see Philip Johnston, "Radical Imam Like Pope, Says Mayor," *Daily Telegraph* (UK), September 14, 2005, http://www.telegraph.co.uk/news.

34. Fernanda Eberstadt, "A Frenchman or a Jew?" *New York Times*, February 29, 2004. See also Marie Brenner, "France's Scarlet Letter," June 2003, http://www.mariebrenner.com/articles/france/sl2.html.
35. See Alyssa A. Lappen, "Ritual Murders of Jews in Paris," *Front Page Magazine*, December 4, 2003, http://www.frontpagemag.com/Articles.
36. *Jewish Herald-Voice Online*, http://www.jhvonline.com/news. The *Jewish-Herald Voice* is a Houston Anglo-Jewish newspaper.
37. "Fearful Jews Leaving France," *CBS News*, July 28, 2004, http://www.cbsnews.com/stories/2004/07/28/world/main632610.shtml.
38. The original report, withheld by the EU, is available on the Web at http://uk-org-bod.supplehost.org/EUMC/EUMC.pdf.
39. Bertrand Benoit, "EU Body Shelves Report on Anti-Semitism," *Financial Times*, November 21, 2003; Clifford D. May, "Hatred, European Style," *Washington Times*, December 3, 2003.
40. Congressman Robert Wexler's Web site, http://www.wexler.house.gov/press_releases/Nov_25_03 .htm.
41. "Anti-Semitism in the Spotlight," *Newletter*, no. 26, Zentrum für Antisemitismusforschung (Center for Research on Anti-Semitism), Berlin, December 2003.
42. Ambrose Evans-Prichard, "EU Covered Up Attacks on Jews by Young Muslims," *Daily Telegraph*, January 4, 2004, http://news.telegraph.co.uk/news.
43. Amir Taheri, "Why Is Paris Burning?" *New York Post Online*, November 4, 2005, http://www.nypost.com/commentary/53917.htm.
44. Francis Fukuyama, "A Year of Living Dangerously: Remember Theo Van Gogh, and Shudder for the Future," *Wall Street Journal Online*, November 2, 2005, http://www.opinionjournal.com.

Disraeli's Boomerang Efforts to Combat Antisemitism

The Interplay of Ideas of Race, Religion, and Conspiracy

Frederick M. Schweitzer

Introduction

Throughout his life Benjamin Disraeli (1804–81) was scorned as a Jew: "the Jew scamp," "that damned bumptious Jew boy," "the wandering Jew, with the brand of Cane [*sic*] upon him," and was subjected to bigoted attacks such as Sidney Herbert's provoking a roar of laughter in the House of Commons by questioning Disraeli in solemn mockery, how anyone could adopt "a faith the profession of which must begin with a surgical operation!"[1] Disraeli often lamented, "Ah, it is not my Government they [the people of England] dislike: I tell you it is me they dislike," that he had been "vilified & decried for upwards of forty years," and so on. According to Lady Dorothy Nevill, it was only after his 1874 electoral triumph that he could "divest himself of the idea that the great mass of the people of England were prejudiced against him." Lady Selina Bradford, one of his beloved confidantes, to whom he wrote 1,100 letters of endearment which were reciprocated in considerable measure, nevertheless reflected the aristocratic distrust and dislike of Disraeli, that "somehow he is a man I cannot respect."[2]

The 14th Earl of Derby, under whom he served three times as Chancellor of the Exchequer—"the Jockey and the Jew"—colleagues working successfully in tandem for twenty years despite undercurrents of antipathy and suspicion, never felt any personal regard or friendship for Disraeli: "I know Disraeli has the feeling I dislike him," he said, "I certainly have no prepossession in his favour"; it was simply that Disraeli was indispensable and irreplaceable as a leader of the Tory party.[3]

The great historian of Tudor England and admiring biographer of Thomas Carlyle, James Anthony Froude, wrote a short biography of Disraeli that is a précis of his own and many Victorians' relentless prejudice against Disraeli: the leader of the Tory party for thirty years and twice prime minister "was a Hebrew to the heart of him," only "nominally a member of the Church of England," and "but half an Englishman," "an outsider"; "in his real nature he remained a Jew," did not have "an English temperament," was "English only by adoption, and . . . never completely identified himself with the country he ruled," but remained "a Hebrew to the end." Nor could Froude forbear quoting approvingly Carlyle's denunciation of Disraeli's decisive role in enacting the democratizing Reform Bill of 1867 as the doings of "a Superlative Hebrew Conjuror, spellbinding all the great Lords, great Parties, great Interests of England to his hand . . . and leading them by the nose, like helpless, mesmerized somnambulant cattle." In refusing the prime minister's offer of honors and a pension, Carlyle was chastened enough to acknowledge that Disraeli "is the only man I almost never spoke of except with contempt," but soon reverted to upbraiding the "cursed old Jew."[4]

The same kind of bigotry was given expression by the popular writer Anthony Trollope, whose novels afford a large gallery of Jewish stereotypes. In several of his political novels Disraeli is portrayed as "Mr Daubeny," nicknamed "Dubby," who is "a political Cagliostro" (an eighteenth-century Italian adventurer and imposter), "a conjuror" who is "dangerous" and "should be found out." In real life Trollope was a rival writer and dismissed Disraeli's novels as all having

> the same flavour of paint and unreality. . . . Through it all [Disraeli's ten novels] there is a feeling of stage properties, a smell of hair-oil, an aspect of buhl, a remembrance of tailors, and that pricking of the conscience which must be the general accompaniment of paste diamonds.[5]

It would seem that only Queen Victoria overcame her inherited prejudice against "the Jew," whose admission to the cabinet in 1852 she stoutly resisted, but came to regard him as her favorite prime minister, chivalric defender of her constitutional prerogatives, ennobled by her as the Earl of Beaconsfield, and beloved almost as a member of the royal family.

Biographical

Disraeli's grandfather and namesake, Benjamin D'Israeli, immigrated to England in 1748 at age eighteen and became a successful businessman and financier. His son Isaac (Disraeli's father) was intended for a business career but balked at that, eventually becoming a literary scholar, freethinker, Deist, and follower of Voltaire. Isaac D'Israeli (the son dropped the apostrophe) seems to have been a three-day Jew but followed his devout father as a member of the Bevis Marks Spanish and Portuguese Sephardic synagogue in London. In 1813 the synagogue appointed him *parnas* (head warden) for a year's term; he politely refused; the matter dragged on for three or four years, the correspondence less cordial, a refusal to pay the fine of £40. When Grandfather Benjamin died, Isaac inherited a fortune, moved his family to fashionable Bloomsbury Square, and wrote a nasty letter to the synagogue canceling his membership. In July of the same year 1817, he had Benjamin, nearly thirteen, not become a bar mitzvah but baptized in the Established Church. Benjamin followed his two younger brothers three weeks earlier, and was followed by his older sister Sarah a month later. Why? Did they put up some resistance? Benjamin had been circumcised, and had had some religious education and Hebrew training, his sister perhaps somewhat more—it is not possible to say more than that.

Meanwhile his father, Isaac, remained an "amphibian," swimming between the Hebrew Bible/Torah and New Testament, and was never baptized. He wrote an admiring essay on Moses Mendelssohn and saw in Reform Judaism a positive development, but as befits a devotee of Voltaire and Pierre Bayle, he was highly disparaging and dismissive of both Judaism and Christianity. Disraeli's mother was indifferent, a non-Jewish Jew who regarded Judaism, like Heine, as not a religion but a misfortune. She was an assimilationist as much or more than his father. Isaac wrote a great many dilettantish works about literature and never embarked upon the magnum opus, "A History of English Literature," for which all these other works were prolegomena. He tried his hand at novel-writing and other imaginative works but with little success.

Benjamin's education was rather sketchy: a Dame's School near home; a private boarding-school run by a nonconformist minister, then to Higham Hall, run by a Unitarian minister, where he studied Latin and Greek. "Nothing was thought of there but the two dead languages," he later carped.[6] Somewhat later at age sixteen in his father's library Disraeli immersed himself in the study of the classical languages and texts. Unlike his younger and much less gifted brothers, Disraeli went to neither Eton nor Harrow, nor Oxford nor Cambridge, where he would have been immersed in the classical curriculum devoted to the training of character. His education—more on the model of German *Bildung,* featuring the development of the self, creative individualism, and struggle against convention and barriers to self-realization—was a product of omnivorous reading and free run in his father's library of 25,000 volumes: "I was born in a library." His father tried to muscle Disraeli into a business career, to become a solicitor (for which he served an apprenticeship of three years and was described by his superior as "assiduous" and "showing great ability"), but he preferred the dinner parties given for his father's literary friends and by the publisher John Murray for his authors, and the avenues these opened to his imagination.[7]

Disraeli tried to get rich quick by dabbling in the stock market (1824–25 in mines and railways in the newly independent countries of Latin America; he wrote three essentially fraudulent pamphlets trying to boost the mining stocks, to no avail in what was an 1820s version of "Pump and Dump") and went deep into debt and remained there for thirty years or more. Although dubbed a Shylock, he was naïve in business matters and had nothing of the stereotypical Jewish genius for moneymaking, having "the habit of never attending to shillings & pence," he explained to one of his creditors, "because they make my head ache," and went into Parliament partly to dodge prosecution by his vociferous creditors and to avoid imprisonment.[8] In his 1844 novel *Coningsby*, someone says, "I have the two greatest stimulants in the world to action, Youth and Debt." In 1841 Disraeli's debts were about £30,000 (about a million pounds today) and he often warned his hosts that he was coming "incognito of course" or that they should come discretely to him. He was successful only in marrying or inheriting money.

Disraeli turned his hand to journalism, trying to launch a newspaper, *The Representative,* which was to rival *The Times* of London. He enlisted the support of Sir Walter Scott, whose son-in-law and future biographer J. G. Lockhart was to be editor, John Murray publisher, and Disraeli star writer. That scheme collapsed on Disraeli's twenty-first birthday after six months of "inglorious mediocrity," whereupon he denied having had any connection with *The Representative.* He then turned to writing novels (again partly to get out of debt), publishing anonymously and with great success in 1826 his satirical novel of fashionable life, *Vivian Grey,* that bore the epigraph from Shakespeare's *Merry Wives of Windsor*, "Why then, the world's mine oyster, Which I with sword will open." Interestingly, his first novel features a conspiracy that reflects his experience in launching *The Representative* and a plot against the Canning government. Once he became known as the author of *Vivian Grey*, editors and reviewers turned on Disraeli as a "nobody" whose novel was "a paltry catchpenny," but he became famous, lionized, and a much sought-after guest at great houses like Lady Blessington's. His extravagant dress (putatively coinciding with the stereotype of an Orientalist streak in Jews but actually that of the Byronic dandy that he emulated) was reported as bright-green pants and splendidly rosetted shoes with a yellow waistcoat or "a black velvet coat lined with satin, purple trousers, with a gold band running down the seams, a scarlet waistcoat, white gloves with several rings worn outside them, with long black curly ringlets rippling down to his shoulders, the whole set off by lividly white skin and black mocking eyes."[9] His physiognomy, also, was perceived as "strictly Jewish."

Disraeli suffered much of his life from depression, what he dubbed "lassitude and despondency," for which the age's prescribed remedy was travel. He toured the Mediterranean in 1830–31 and went to Constantinople where he, a Turkophile all his life, admired the Ottoman sultan who, he believed, was forced to struggle against "unprecedented conspiracies," and for a week to Jerusalem, which inspired his messianic-Zionist novel of 1833, *The Wondrous Tale of Alroy.*[10] Having renewed his energy and contracted venereal disease, Disraeli came home just in time for the fracas over the Reform Bill of 1832 and determined to enter Parliament. Since, he said, "Toryism was worn out, and he could not condescend to be a Whig," he ran as a Radical, and lost handily four times, 1832–37, all the while living the extravagant life of a prodigal dandy—he "out-dandied even the leaders in that age of dandies"—and dodging creditors.[11]

Victoria's succession to the throne in 1837 required the election of a new parliament, and this time Disraeli won a seat as a Tory (having passed through the trajectory from Radical to independent to Tory) for Maidstone, despite being hounded on the hustings by the mob shouting, "Judas," "Shylock," "Old Clothes," and holding pieces of pork up to his face. Within a few years Disraeli became a staid dresser in Victorian black or dark brown. His maiden speech was a fiasco, when he was shouted down by the Irish MPs because he had attacked Daniel O'Connell and challenged the Irish Liberator to a duel. In 1839 Disraeli married Mary Anne Lewis, widow of his fellow MP for Maidstone, Col. Wyndham Lewis. She was a dozen years older than he and wealthy, though not so wealthy as he had calculated. All his adult life he needed an older female confidante and correspondent, among others,

Sara Austen, Clara Bolton, and Henrietta Sykes—"all his women were grandmothers," a diplomat remarked caustically.[12]

There were many such affairs, one at least with a younger woman with whom Disraeli is said by his most recent biographer, Stanley Weintraub, to have fathered a child whose descendants live in Australia: She was shipped off to Australia under the name Donovan; there is some evidence in the form of letters, photographs that show a striking likeness, indications of financial help, and assertions by descendants. One of the grand dames, Mrs. Sarah Brydges Willyams, whose father was Jewish and, like Disraeli, was fascinated by her Jewish heritage, left her entire estate of some £40,000 to him. But Disraeli was also drawn to young men, to some of them inordinately so: the three Young Englanders (the "Diz-Union" of Lords Alexander Baillie-Cochrane, John Manners, and George Smythe), Lord Henry Lennox, Ralph Earle, Montague Corry, and others, often noblemen, well connected, good-looking, charming, almost all of whom remained unmarried; they served as his private secretary or were members of his underground intelligence network. Two of Disraeli's biographers spell out his "latent homosexuality," but conclude it was highly unlikely that any of these relationships were physical.[13]

In 1841 the Whigs went out and Sir Robert Peel and the Tories came in. Disraeli expected a post in the new government, which would bring the impecunious MP a much-desired salary. Peel's "interest and gratitude," he felt, required that he gain office. In actuality, without "birth and connection," no membership in the political cousinhood, Disraeli had little claim on Peel; moreover, he was a kind of "unofficial private secretary" to his benefactor Lord Lyndhurst whom he favored to be Tory leader and prime minister, and his very public affair with Lady Henrietta Sykes militated against any offer from Peel.[14] Nevertheless, there are some grounds for concluding that Peel wanted to oblige Disraeli but was dissuaded, ironically, by Lord Stanley, later 14th Earl of Derby, prime minister, and cabinet colleague of Disraeli, who threatened to withdraw if that "scoundrel" came in. In the time-honored way of aspiring politicians excluded from office Disraeli made a nuisance of himself, joining and then leading the "Young England" trio of parliamentary insurgents and noble dandies who had been friends at Eton and Cambridge: Young England was a typical Disraelian idealization of the aristocratic past and represented the medieval merry maypole interpretation of social harmony and contentment, a compound of feudal paternalism and idealized Christianity. One of them, Lord John Manners, said, we "virtually pledged ourselves to attempt to restore, What? I hardly know."[15]

In dudgeon at his rejection by Peel, the Disraelis sped off to Paris, seeking out the Rothschilds, the conservative politician and later president Adolphe Thiers, and King Louis Philippe in an effort to intrigue against Peel by hooking up (one of many such attempts) with Lord Palmerston. Disraeli offered himself as a source of confidential or secret information to the king and as a lobbyist in France's behalf. In June 1844 Disraeli conspired to unseat Peel, expecting it to occur, according to a table companion John Cam Hobhouse, "the very next day" after a dinner party hosted by the Rothschilds that brought him and the Whig chiefs, Lords Russell and Landsdowne, together; such a Whig government would have enacted Free Trade.[16] Disraeli also soon turned back to writing novels: the trilogy, *Coningsby or the New Generation* (1844, on politics), *Sybil or the Two Nations* (1845, on the social question of poverty), *Tancred or the New Crusade* (1847, on religion).

Peel's gradual conversion to Free Trade (1842–45), which was confirmed by the Irish Famine, led to the repeal of the Corn Laws in 1846. Disraeli took the lead in opposition to Peel and brought him down in a series of sarcastic philippics that had begun in 1842 after his rejection for office and culminated in the polemics of 1846 (Peel stole the Whigs' clothes while they were bathing; "his life has been one great appropriation clause. He is a burglar of other's intellect"), when Peel was defeated in a vote on an Irish coercion bill.[17] Disraeli's relentless sparring with Peel was less the issue of protectionism versus free trade than Peel's presumed haughty and dictatorial leadership of the party versus collective leadership and consensus reached by discussion. The Tories split and Lord John Russell and the Whigs came in. With the Peelites sitting as a separate bloc, Disraeli found himself on the front bench with Lord George Bentinck as leader of the Protectionist opposition in the Commons under the 14th Earl of Derby as Tory chief in the Lords. In 1847 Lionel de Rothschild was elected as a Whig to Parliament, although he was blocked from taking his seat by refusal to swear the required Christian oath. A Whig emancipation bill was defeated with Disraeli and Bentinck the only two Tories supporting the bill. The ensuing uproar against Bentinck induced him to resign party leadership in the Commons, and with his sudden death in 1848 the way was open for Disraeli to emerge as Tory leader in the lower house. Attempts to thwart him by turning the leadership into a troika failed because his rivals and colleagues possessed the requisite prejudices but lacked debating power—Disraeli was said to be sandwiched between "two very stale slices of bread." One of the reasons Disraeli became and remained a Tory, and was able to rise to "the top of the greasy pole," was the lack of talent in the ranks of what some called "the stupid party."[18] As Disraeli wrote to Mary Anne in 1849: "They [the party chiefs] are evidently more afraid of lacking me than I them."[19] Thanks to the financial assistance of the Bentincks, Disraeli was able to acquire the estate of Hughenden Manor, thus turning himself into a country gentleman and, although still deep in debt, much more in the image of a Tory leader.

For six years, 1846–52, Disraeli was the leader of the opposition in the Commons, like a second Moses leading the Protectionist remnant through the wilderness.[20] He and the Tories opposed every Whig measure by every means regardless of its merits: The business of an opposition, he explained, is to oppose. In 1852 the Tories came in with, as prime minister, Lord Stanley, the 14th Earl of Derby (the "Jockey" who presumably preferred to win the Derby than cabinet office), and Disraeli (the "Hoax," or as Dickens calls him in *Bleak House,* "Joodle") as Chancellor of the Exchequer and leader of the House of Commons. It was "the Who? Who? Ministry" since it contained so little recognized talent. Lord Derby did not have an easy time persuading Queen Victoria to accept Disraeli "the Jew" as a cabinet member: "Madame, Mr. D[israeli] has had to make his position, and men who have to make their positions will do and say things which are not necessary to be said or done by those for whom positions are provided"—by right of birth (she especially resented his savaging of Peel).[21]

As Chancellor of the Exchequer Disraeli was terribly miscast and was no match for William Ewart Gladstone. By talent and temperament he should have been foreign secretary, but aristocratic prejudice prevented his accession then or later (he was to be chancellor three times). This first Derby ministry lasted only eleven months, and although Disraeli declared Protectionism "dead and damned" (no doubt causing the shade of Sir Robert to smile bitterly!), his budget was defeated and out the Tories went. Yet it is from that time, 1851–52, that Disraeli, having overcome the chief's distrust and aversion by his indispensability, shared party leadership with Derby in double harness. Their second chance to be led out of the wilderness came in 1858–59, after Palmerston stumbled in foreign affairs and the government was defeated on its conspiracy to murder bill (see *infra*). According to *The Times* ("The Thunderer"), "The nominal head of the new government is Lord Derby but it is abundantly plain that the real premier in 1858 is Mr. Disraeli."[22] The second Derby ministry enacted Jewish emancipation (so Lionel de Rothschild could take his seat at last) but went down owing to its failure to carry a reform bill extending the franchise, despite Disraeli's deft parliamentary footwork proposing "lateral extension of the franchise" and "fancy franchises." The bill divided the Tories and caused them and many other MPs to recall their resentment that the House of Commons was led by "a Jew Adventurer."[23] In the election of 1859, the Tories won about 290 seats, showing that Disraeli's reconstruction of the Conservative Party had progressed significantly since the elections of 1852 (about 280) and 1857 (about 260), but 290 fell short and Palmerston came in for seven years and the Tories remained in the wilderness to 1866.

The third Derby ministry of 1866–68 carried the Second Reform Bill in 1867, although both Lord Derby and Disraeli had solemnly warned him many times over against dangerous democratic tampering with the constitution, and one MP typified the Tory squires in wondering how he would explain to his constituents how, if he "refused a bill last year from a good Christian [Gladstone], he were to accept it this year from a bad Jew."[24] In the course of the debate Disraeli, "dishing the Whigs" and detaching Radical Liberals from the opposition, accepted amendments that radically recast the bill and doubled the electorate; he was willing, according to cloakroom quipsters, to "yield anything except his place [in the cabinet]." In carrying the bill, ironically, Disraeli acted exactly as Peel had done in 1846 and threatened to split the party a second time. Lord Cranborne, the future Marquess of Salisbury who detested Disraeli as a "rogue," resigned with two pivotal colleagues from the cabinet in protest and tried to bring him down the way he had brought Peel down but providentially failed. A Tory backbencher writing to Cranborne bewailed that no matter how much Conservatives opposed various provisions and amendments to the 1867 bill, "I fear when it comes to the point, they will conform to the Jew in all things . . . and yield to [Disraeli's] arguments for the sake of keeping the party together."[25] Although Disraeli insisted throughout that he adhered to "Conservative principles," Derby was more accurate in characterizing the act as "a leap in the dark" into democracy, perhaps translating into law the sentiments of Tory democracy of Disraeli's novel *Sybil.* Derby was incapacitated by gout and resigned; he and the queen insisted that Disraeli become prime minister, and so he did. "He and only he," Derby had informed Victoria, "could command the cordial support *en masse* of our present colleagues."[26] Despite vociferous opposition from Tory diehards like Cranborne and his coterie, the lack of talent made any other choice absurd. Owing to divisions in the party, Disraeli went down to an overwhelming defeat in the parliamentary election of 1868, and Gladstone came in as prime minister, 1868–74, the first of four times he led a Liberal government.

Disraeli got his chance and vindication as Conservative premier, 1874–80, after a landslide victory in the 1874 election. In outline, Disraeli's government was as follows:

1. The 1875 purchase of the Egyptian khedive's shares in the Suez Canal, largely on Disraeli's initiative.
2. The enactment of the Royal Titles Bill declaring the queen to be Empress of India.
3. In 1876 Disraeli became Earl of Beaconsfield, Viscount Hughenden: he was honored by Victoria, and being ill with gout, asthma, and Bright's disease, he was slowing down with age and fatigue; it was an easier task to lead from the House of Lords. In 1868, in ill health, Mary Anne had been made Viscountess Beaconsfield. She died in 1872. In 1878 Disraeli was awarded the Order of the Garter in recognition for his role in the settlement of the Russo-Turkish war.
4. 1877–78 Russo-Turkish war

   Bulgarian massacres that inspired Gladstone's crusading demand that "Bag and Baggage" the Turks be ushered out of Europe (as a military, administrative, governing presence, not the removal of the Turkish or Muslim population).

   The choice was between the unspeakable Muslim Turk and the tyrannical Russian Christian bear: supporting a Christian European power and Balkan Christians versus preserving the balance of power.

   The Russian army's advance to Constantinople was halted by a scratch battle at Plevna in Bulgaria, and though Plevna was eventually taken, Russia lost its opportunity to take the Ottoman capitol, one of the principal objects of the war.

   By Disraeli's order 7,000 Indian troops were mobilized and brought to Malta, and the British fleet was posted to Besika Bay close to the Straits, as expedients to check Russian threats.

   Disraeli's brinkmanship induced his foreign secretary, the appeaser, the 15th Earl of Derby, to resign, and Disraeli's erstwhile mortal enemy, Lord Salisbury, came in and affairs went more smoothly for Disraeli with his cabinet.

   When Plevna fell, Russia dictated the treaty of San Stefano, creating a greater Bulgaria and making extensive territorial gains, especially in Armenia and the Caucasus region.

   Unilateralism gave way (thanks mostly to Andrássy and Derby, seconded by Disraeli and Bismarck) to multilateralism at the Congress of Berlin of 1878. It tore up the treaty of San Stefano, cut Bulgaria in half, rolled back some Russian advances, and preserved a weakened Ottoman Empire. Disraeli returned to Charing Cross and red carpet treatment, holding aloft a piece of paper: "This means I believe Peace with Honour, Peace in our time," and so it did, although some critics said it was "the peace that passeth all understanding and the honour that is common among thieves." Such animadversions might better apply to Neville Chamberlain, who uttered the same phrase exactly sixty years later returning home from Munich, yet it strains credulity to say with Howard Mumford Jones that the diplomatic "path led straight from the Congress of Berlin to Munich."[27]

Race

Disraeli claimed aristocratic descent from the aristocratic Sephardic Jews of Spain and Portugal (emblematic of steadfast loyalty to Judaism) who were forced to leave Spain in 1492 and settled in Italy:

> My grandfather . . . was an Italian descendant from one of those Hebrew families, whom the Inquisition forced to emigrate from the Spanish Peninsula at the end of the fifteenth century, and who found a refuge in the more tolerant territories of the Venetian Republic. His ancestors had dropped their Gothic surname on their settlement on the Terra Firma, and grateful to the God of Jacob who had sustained them through unprecedented trials and guarded them through unheard-of perils, they assumed the name of DISRAELI, a name never borne before or since by any other family, in order that their race might be forever recognised. Undisturbed and unmolested, they flourished as merchants for more than two centuries under the protection of the lion of St. Mark.[28]

Yet almost none of this is true. In actuality only one of his eight great-grandparents was Spanish or *Converso*, and that was on his mother's side; on his father's side they were descendants of Italian Jews in the Papal States (Cento near Ferrara) and might have descended from the Jewish deportees brought as slaves and prisoners of war to Italy by Emperor Titus in the first century, or, much more likely, were later migrants from the Ottoman empire. His mother's family, the Basevis, hailed from Verona; his maternal grandmother Rebecca Rieti was his one forebear of eminent Spanish descent among the exiles of 1492, while his maternal grandfather probably descended from medieval German Jews.

Disraeli stoutly believed he was an aristocrat, of eminent birth and connection, as much so as his Tory colleague dukes and earls and viscounts. In the election of 1847 running against a son of the duke of Devonshire, Disraeli said on the hustings, "I am not disposed for a moment to admit that my pedigree is not as good and even superior to that of the Cavendishes"; on another occasion he declared, "Fancy calling a fellow an adventurer when his ancestors were probably on intimate terms with the queen of Sheba" or his rejoinder when an Irish MP attacked him in Parliament as a Jew, "Yes, I am a Jew and when the ancestors of the right honorable gentleman were brutal savages in an unknown island, mine were priests in the temple of Solomon."[29] These claims—of princely birth among the aristocratic Sephardic Jews and claiming their vast superiority to the Ashkenazi Jews of Germany and Eastern Europe—were a psychological necessity for Disraeli and are key to his self-respect and esteem, indeed, the brash self-confidence that underlay his driving ambition. His espousal of race as decisive and his own aristocratic descent reflect his trip to Jerusalem in 1830–31 but, more important, his self-vindication in response to his rejection for office by Peel in 1841.

A number of scholars have addressed this issue of identity and personality. Disraeli was immensely ambitious from childhood, "a narcissistic personality" born to rule, to lead, to dominate: He had to conduct the orchestra or get sick and suffer malaise. He had to force his way into an alien culture and society, which normally would keep Jews beyond the fringe. Such circumstances variously lead to neurosis, self-hate, turning into a non-Jewish or an antisemitic Jew. In Disraeli's case, it led to a nervous breakdown (1826–31) that came on the heels of a series of failures and setbacks: his legal career, his stock market speculations, his attempt to launch a newspaper, crushing debt, and some acerbic reviews of his first novels, which were followed, however, by an intensification of energy and determination. Thus Disraeli was a "successful narcissist."[30] A characteristic example of self-vindication was Disraeli's boast of his Sephardic heritage, that of an elite, "unmixed," ancient race that had attained a "high civilisation when the inhabitants of England were going half-naked and eating acorns in their woods."[31]

As to Disraeli's Jewishness: Although his was not a Jewish home or upbringing, he certainly possessed some degree of Jewish consciousness by the time he was baptized in his thirteenth year, less from what he imbibed from his indifferent parents than what he read in his father's library. He then got a much more thorough Christian education than he had had in Hebrew and Judaism. Yet friends and enemies alike regarded him as Jewish, then and since. Typical of Disraeli's contemporaries were the aspersions of Froude, Carlyle, and Trollope cited earlier. In 1920 *The Spectator* of London identified Disraeli as "the great English statesman, who while a good patriot and sincere Christian was unquestionably also an ardent Jew."[32] But aside from having dinner many a Sunday evening with the English Rothschilds (Liberals though they were) and attending the weddings of their offspring, Disraeli never belonged to, addressed, or was associated with a Jewish organization of any kind, religious or secular. No Jew served in either of the two cabinets he led. In politics Anglo-Jewish community leaders and the Anglo-Jewish press were almost unanimously Liberal. Jewish leaders never approached Disraeli to intercede in their behalf in the quest for emancipation (1830s–1858) or in behalf of persecuted Jews outside Britain, although they persisted in regarding him as a "great Jew." They were hostile or suspicious of Disraeli's justification of emancipation. Rather than on grounds of religious freedom or equal rights, he argued like a Christian missionary or evangelical that because Judaism is the essential basis of Christianity, Jews are entitled to all the rights and privileges of a Christian state and society. Most galling to Jewish leaders was his expectation, never renounced, that emancipation was prelude to conversion.[33] It is also highly unlikely that Disraeli "regarded as a definite possibility the restoration of the Jews to Palestine through both political action and practical up-building," or that he was the anonymous author of a pamphlet that appeared in German at the time of the Conference of Berlin proposing the creation of a Jewish nation in the Ottoman province of Palestine.[34] It was Bismarck and Salisbury who insisted that the Jewish minority in Bulgaria, Romania, and Serbia that gained their independence from the Ottoman empire under the 1878 Berlin treaty be guaranteed civil rights in the constitutions of those new nations.

One may doubt how much Jewish consciousness in Disraeli is signified by his hero Alroy, a heroic messianic, Zionist military leader who has "a deep conviction of superior race" and launches a revolt to restore his people to the ancient homeland, or because Tancred arrives after many vicissitudes at Mt. Sinai instead of the Holy Sepulchre.[35] On the other hand Lord Stanley recalled a conversation on Disraeli's Zionist "plan": In 1851 all the Turkish province of Palestine needed

> was labour. And protection for the labourer: the ownership of the soil might be bought from Turkey: money would be forthcoming: the Rothschilds and other Hebrew capitalists would all help: the Turkish empire was falling into ruin: the Turkish Govt would do anything for money: all that was necessary was the establishment of colonies, with rights over the soil, and security from ill treatment. . . . A man who should carry [the plan] out would be the next Messiah, the true Saviour of his people.[36]

Stanley thought that while Disraeli spoke with "great apparent earnestness," these ideas were Disraelian "mystification" and recorded that he never heard them again in their conversations. Disraeli's Zionist dreams filled the skies but did not touch the ground.

Disraeli always referred to the Jews as "our ancestors," that is, what made Disraeli "Jewish" in his view was race. He had to explain how, though a Christian in religion, he was Jewish "in spirit," what might be termed his nonreligious Jewishness. His answer—which was the answer of the age—was race. In *Tancred* (1847) Sidonia proclaims: "All is race; there is no other truth."[37] In *Lothair* (1870) the "artist" Phoebus preaches the great virtues and strengths of "Aryan principles," and the world-historical significance of the "Aryans." Once there was "a first-rate [Aryan] race . . . but Semitism . . . ultimately triumphed. Semitism has ruined art." It also caused physical degeneration. "Nothing can be done to correct [ruin and decline] until the Aryan races are extricated from Semitism." All this may be intended as Disraelian mockery since Phoebus is a very silly character and Disraeli consistently reserves his praise and exaltation for the Hebrew or Semitic "race."[38] That "Race is the key to history" is affirmed in *Endymion* (1880), where Disraeli insists that "Language and religion do not make a race," that "There is only one thing that makes a race, and that is blood."[39] (This is not much removed from the Nazi rhetoric of "Blut & Boden.") As recorded by Constance de Rothschild, whose dinner guest he frequently was, Disraeli "believed more in the compelling power of a common ancestry than in that of a common faith. He said to me, as he had said over and over again in his novels, 'All is race, not religion—remember that.'"[40]

Among numerous examples of Disraeli's assertion of Hebrew/Jewish racial purity, superiority, power, and unmatched creativity is the elocution he puts in the mouth of Sidonia:

> The Hebrew is an unmixed race. . . . [T]he Mosaic Arabs [Jews] are the most ancient, if not the only, unmixed blood that dwells in cities.
>
> An unmixed race of a first-rate organization are the aristocracy of nature. Such excellence is a positive fact . . . perceptible in its physical advantages, and in the vigor of its unsullied idiosyncrasy.

> In his comprehensive travels, Sidonia had visited and examined the Hebrew communities of the world. He had found, in general, the lower orders debased; the superior immersed in sordid pursuits; but he perceived that the intellectual development was not impaired. This gave him hope. He was persuaded that organization would outlive persecution. When he reflected on what they had endured, it was only marvelous that the race had not disappeared. They had defied exile, massacre, spoliation, the degrading influence of the constant pursuit of gain; they had defied time. For nearly three thousand years . . . they have been dispersed over the globe. To the unpolluted current of their Caucasian structure, and to the segregating genius of their great Lawgiver [Moses], Sidonia ascribed the fact that they had not been long ago absorbed among those mixed races, who presume to persecute them, but who periodically wear away and disappear, while their victims flourish in all the primeval vigor of the pure Asian breed.[41]
>
> The fact is, you cannot destroy a pure race of the Caucasian organization. It is a physiological fact; a simple law of nature. . . . The mixed persecuting races disappear; the pure persecuted race remains. And at this moment, despite the centuries, dozens of centuries of degradation, the Jewish mind exercises a vast influence on the affairs of Europe.[42]

Why, aside from racial purity and Caucasian organization, are the Jews superior? Disraeli answers, "the Semitic principle," that is "the spiritual principle" of Judaism. "Power is neither the sword nor the shield, for these pass away, but ideas, which are divine," as exemplified by "the greatest of lawgivers [Moses], the greatest of administrators [Solomon], the greatest of reformers [Christ]: what race, living or extinct, can produce three such men as these?"[43]

There follows here and many other places in Disraeli's writings a long list of examples—all exaggerated, half imaginary, many false—of "Jews" as the most powerful and creative element in every sphere. Everybody of distinction is a Jew, a crypto-Jew, or of Jewish descent: early Jesuits, German professors who are fashioning "a second and greater Reformation," Russian and Austrian diplomats, finance ministers all over Europe, several of Napoleon's marshals and Napoleon himself, "great poets, great orators, great writers," Thomas Aquinas, Maimonides, and Spinoza, "the catalogue [that] is too vast to enumerate" includes Rossini, among other Italian composers and prima donnas, Meyerbeer, Mendelssohn, and Mozart. All great music is Jewish—"musical Europe is ours." Disraeli anticipated the pernicious racial ideas a decade later of Count Arthur de Gobineau (who, however, was not antisemitic). The two met in 1841, and it may be, according to Léon Poliakov, that Gobineau's treatment of the "English race" and the "Jewish race" derives significantly from Disraeli's novels.[44] The affinity with Gobineau implies that this was a dangerous line for Disraeli to take, if not at the time, then in the light of later genocidal racial ideologies. His defenders say he fought racism with racism: perhaps, but that is not what his detractors make of it. His notions of a hierarchy of races, superior, inferior, and so on, is too reminiscent of the Nazis. Six years after Disraeli's wild claims about Jewish musical genius, Richard Wagner wrote his genocide-inspiring essay, "The Jews in Music."

Over the years Disraeli became more and more obsessed with the racial idea. Lord Redesdale recalled Disraeli's dedication to ideas of "race and purity of blood" and that the usual subject of his conversation was "the [Jewish] Race."[45] He uttered things like, "You and I belong to a race that can do anything but fail," or hailing a new-born Rothschild infant: "I hope he will prove worthy of his pure and sacred race." Conviction grew also. In writing a preface for a new edition of his novels in 1870, Disraeli felt vindicated by his pioneering racial ideas, "the general influence of race on human action being universally recognized as the key to history."[46]

Reactions to Disraeli's Racial Dogma

Typical of those who took Disraeli's assertions to be provocations was George Eliot, before she transformed herself into a philo-Semite and celebrated Jewish culture and religion in *Daniel Deronda* (1876). In a letter of 1848 she wrote,

> The fellowship of race, to which Disraeli exultingly refers the munificence of Sidonia, is so evidently an inferior impulse which must ultimately be superceded that I wonder that even he, the Jew as he

> is, dares to boast of it. My Gentile nature kicks most resolutely against any assumption of superiority in the Jews. . . . Everything *specifically* Jewish is low grade.[47]

Almost predictably, the encyclopedic French antisemite Édouard Drumont exploited Disraeli's fantasies in *La France juive: essai d'histoire contemporaine* (1886), a vast work that went through hundreds of reprintings and remains in print, in which he quotes Disraeli as "the expert" no less than thirteen times.[48]

In 1878 Cosima and Richard Wagner (the composer) were reading *Tancred* together: "We had to laugh over Disraeli's glorification of the Jews. 'I have an idea what he is getting at,' says R, 'racial purity and great men; that ruling genius I dreamed about—only the Jews could produce him.'" She had noted Disraeli's claim in *Coningsby* that "all the great men in art, science, even religion" were Jews, dismissing it as "[a] very curious phenomenon."[49] The Wagners' son-in-law, Houston Stewart Chamberlain, the transplanted English antisemite who admired and was admired by Hitler, detested Disraeli as a Jew and builder of the British empire, but nevertheless regarded him as his "teacher" in race matters. He was fond of quoting the famous pronouncement and wrote his race-deterministic treatise, *Foundations of the Nineteenth Century* (1899), urging the Germans that "in these days, when so much nonsense is proclaimed on this [racial] Question, let Disraeli teach us that the whole significance of Judaism lies in its purity of race, that this alone gives it power and duration." He quotes Sidonia as proof: "Race is everything; there is no other truth. And every race that carelessly suffers its blood to be ruined will go under."[50] Hitler spoke in the same accents, invoking "racial hygiene"—preserving or restoring purity of blood—as the paramount necessity for national greatness. In at least four speeches, Hitler invoked Disraeli as vouching for the absolute truth of Nazi racial ideology, the first time in May 1920. In January 1921 he invoked Disraeli's authority in proof of the claim that race is the decisive factor in history, and in August 1925 that the "Eternal Jew" had a claw-hold on German politics and economy.[51] In his last speech to the Reichstag, 1941, Hitler proclaimed: "The British Jew Lord Disraeli [Beaconsfield] once [*sic*] said that the racial problem was the key to world history. We National Socialists have grown up with that idea."[52] Julius Streicher, Hitler's "World Jew-baiter No. 1" who was executed for crimes against humanity and incitement of racial hatred by the Nuremberg tribunal, cited Disraeli's dictum, "The racial question is the key to world history," in almost every issue of the prurient antisemitic rag that he founded and edited, *Der Stürmer.* It and Treitschke's notorious motto, "The Jews are our misfortune," were his favorite quotations.[53] Disraeli's racial dogmas lend support, or can readily be made to lend support, to conspiracism (see *infra*).

Religion

Disraeli attended Anglican Church services almost every Sunday, received the sacrament each year at Easter, was married and buried as a Christian, defended the Established Church as a great historic institution, and never publicly said or did anything that would suggest that his profession of Christian faith was a cynical masquerade. In private he was an agnostic and was fond of referring to himself as "the blank page" between the Hebrew Bible/Torah and New Testament; in a letter of 1858 he calls Christianity the "popular mythology."[54] In *Lothair* (1870) Disraeli refers in a humorously condescending way to the Anglican Church as "perplexed," because it was "made by Act of Parliament, not by God."[55] Perhaps his views were akin to Marx's "opiate of the masses." Here too one has to reckon with the influence of his father, the freethinker and devotee of Voltaire and Spinoza, who detested Roman Catholicism and regarded Christianity and Judaism alike as "vulgar superstition."[56] In *The Genius of Judaism* (1833), written and published at the same time as his son's *Alroy* with its Zionist enthusiasm for a revived Jewish state in Palestine, Isaac, writing in the guise of the Christian he never was or became, attacks the Talmud for its "barbarousness" and keeping Jews apart in isolation from society. He seems to hope for emancipation (then pending in Parliament, passed by the Commons, but rejected by the Lords), definitely urges assimilation (but not by conversion, which he scorned), and appears to think the Jews are themselves to blame for antisemitism—on conversion and antisemitism father and son diverged.

In his novels, particularly *Tancred,* Disraeli uttered a lot of theological balderdash about Christianity being Judaism for the masses, the completion of Judaism, and so on. His ideas about the relationship of Judaism and Christianity lend themselves to replacement theory and supercessionist theology: "several millions of Jews . . . persist in believing in only half of their religion"; "the most important portion of the Jewish religion" is Christianity; "Christianity is completed Judaism, or it is nothing. Christianity is incomprehensible without Judaism, as Judaism is incomplete without Christianity"; Christianity is "Judaism for the multitude, but it is still Judaism."[57] "I look upon the [Anglican] Church as the only Jewish institution remaining," Disraeli wrote in his *Reminiscences* in the 1860s.[58] (Here he sounds much like a Jews-for-Jesus propagandist.) At times he spoke like a Christian missionary, as when he says in his life of *Lord George Bentinck*: "It is no doubt to be deplored that several million of the Jewish race should persist in believing in only a part of their religion; but . . . time . . . may remove this anomaly," or his assertion that the Jews "owe everything to the Church and are fools to oppose it."[59] He seemed to think that every Jew was a proto-Christian, whereas the history of antisemitism would indicate that every Christian is a potential antisemite.

A more sober exposition of his views on Christianity's debt to Judaism will be found in Disraeli's 1847 speech in Parliament in support of Jewish emancipation, delivered at the same time that he was writing those extravagant assertions in *Tancred*:

> The Jews are persons who acknowledge the same God as the Christian people of this realm. They acknowledge the same divine revelations as themselves. . . . [The Jews] are, humanly speaking, the authors of your religion. They are unquestionably those to whom you are indebted for no inconsiderable portion of your known religion, and for the whole of your divine knowledge. . . . Every Gentleman here does profess the Jewish religion, and believes in Moses and the Prophets. . . . Where is your Christianity, if you do not believe in their Judaism? On every day, you read to the people the exploits of Jewish heroes, the proofs of Jewish devotion, the brilliant annals of past Jewish magnificence. The Christian Church has covered every kingdom with sacred building, and over every altar . . . we find the tables of the Jewish law. Every Sunday—the Lord's day—if you wish to express feelings of praise and thanksgiving to the Most High, or if you wish to find expressions of solace in grief, you find both in the words of the Jewish people. [He went on to say that] every man in the early ages of the Church, by whose power, or zeal, or genius, the Christian faith was propagated, was a Jew. [This caused an uproar in the House, the recorder noting "Interruption."] If one could suppose that the arguments we have heard [against emancipation] . . . are the only arguments that influence the decision of this question, it would be impossible to conceive what is the reason of the Jews not being admitted to full participation in the rights and duties of a Christian legislature. In exact proportion to your faith ought to be your wish to do this great act of national justice. . . . But you are influenced by the darkest superstitions of the darkest ages that ever existed in this country. It is this feeling that has been kept out of this debate; indeed that has been kept secret within yourselves . . . and that is unknowingly influencing you. . . . I, whatever may be the consequences—must speak what I feel. I cannot sit in this House with any misconception of my opinion on the subject. Whatever may be the consequences on the seat I hold [in the next election] . . . I cannot, for one, give a vote which is not in deference to what I believe to be the true principles of religion. Yes, it is as a Christian that I will not take upon me the awful responsibility of excluding from the Legislature those who are of the religion in the bosom of which my Lord and Saviour was born.[60]

A critical subject was the Crucifixion, one that Disraeli addressed frequently. In his biography of *Lord George Bentinck* he explained that traditional Christian accounts were "not historically true" and "not dogmatically sound." The Crucifixion is providential, foreordained by God, for the central teaching of Christianity is the doctrine of the atonement, that Jesus was born into the world to die in expiation of humankind's sins. Jews, he said, provided the victim and the victimizers (ignoring the Roman executioners). How can Christians persecute the Jews for making redemption possible for them? "You should kneel to us [in gratitude]!" Eva, the Jewish heroine, bursts out in *Tancred*.[61] Among much else that is consistent with modern New Testament scholarship, Disraeli points out that the Diaspora cannot be interpreted as punishment for rejecting Christ or guilt for the Crucifixion, since Jews had been dispersed centuries before by the Assyrians, Babylonians, and others. He became confident that "the house of Israel [is] now [1870] freed of medieval misconception" and proposed to himself writing a life of Jesus Christ but never managed to embark on that project, which, he felt, would resolve the question once and for all and have established the Jewishness of Jesus a generation before Julius Wellhausen.[62] But according to the journalist T. P. O'Connor, probably his most venomous biographer, Disraeli "actually claims credit for the Jews for committing that act which . . . must always be regarded as an inexpiable crime."[63] Thus, then and long after, Disraeli's attempts to rebut the accusation of deicide by the criminal Jews, cursed for all time, condemned to dispersion and to wander, and to degradation and humiliation, were to no avail or even backfired.

Disraeli's Conspiracism

Robert Blake, author of the standard biography of Disraeli among the eighty or so that have appeared, says that Disraeli "was addicted to conspiracy." In his short but perceptive study John Vincent remarks on Disraeli's "beloved talent for conspiracy" and notes that much "detective work" needs to be done on "the less respectable areas of intrigue that have so far been hidden from public gaze." Many biographers find the subject embarrassing and ignore it—here the six-volume biography by Monypenny and Buckle is especially at fault—or touch upon it lightly, others discount it as of no significance, while still others believe Disraeli was not serious, that it was a joke, no more than a literary device essential to Disraeli the novelist but not to Disraeli the statesman. In Cecil Roth's judgment, however, Disraeli expressed his "real ideas. . . . and ideals . . . more freely" in his novels than in his speeches or in other media. More typical is Daniel Pipes' skepticism, believing it was Disraeli's "sense of humor and his irrepressible whimsy." But given the lifelong consistency with which Disraeli invoked conspiracies and secret societies as explanation and basis for action, such assertions are dubious.[64]

Disraeli's firm belief in the mythology of conspiracism and secret societies was widely shared—by his father, among others—normal rather than aberrant in the nineteenth century, a mythology to which Benjamin's generation was particularly susceptible. Indeed, father Isaac fanned the fires of the prevailing phobia. His novels *Vaurien: or Sketches of the Times* (1797) and *Despotism: or the Fall of the Jesuits* (1811) are haunted by fears of the French Revolution's violence and fanaticism coming to England: the Frenchman "Vaurien" conspires to overthrow the English government and drown the country in blood. *Despotism*'s aim, Isaac explained, is to "arouse indignation against political fanaticism" as seen in the sinister Jesuit conspiracies that envelope all of Europe and are embodied in their instrument, the "vile and anti-social" Napoleonic regime.[65] From the 1780s to 1850 many secret societies actually existed but while their power or influence or efficaciousness was minimal, their notoriety was enormous, such as to support credence in a great and universal plot. In the nineteenth century this became a paranoid interpretation of history and politics. It is indicative of the profound shock imparted to the European mind and consciousness by the Revolution of 1789, which inaugurated a period of change on an unprecedented, accelerating, and ever-grander scale; only thus can one understand the credulous readiness of educated people and ruling elites to see conspiracies operating everywhere.

There was another series of shocks in 1815–48. The secret societies reached their peak—in numbers, strength, influence, diffusion—in the decade after1815, when they were made notorious by Metternich and his secret police. According to that "Coachman of Europe" the secret societies are "a real power, all the more dangerous as it works in the dark, undermining all parts of the social body, and depositing everywhere the seeds of moral gangrene which is not slow to develop and increase"; secret societies are "that gangrene of society."[66] To Disraeli Metternich was "my dear master" and "the most enlightened of modern statesmen": they maintained a correspondence and personal contact, particularly during Metternich's exile in England after the Revolution of 1848, when Disraeli contributed articles in French to Metternich's journal, in one of which he professes that the people and princes of Italy are "dupes of the [secret] subversive societies."[67]

Most unsettling was the burst of revolutions (1820–25), the years when Disraeli reached manhood: There were, reportedly, nine conspiracies in 1825 alone. The astounding revelations of spies, secret police, turncoats, and the boasts (largely false though they were) of such agitators as Filippo Buonarroti, "the first professional revolutionary," confirmed belief and inflamed hysteria. The Revolutions of 1830 and 1848 corroborated and reanimated the myth—the 1848 scare profoundly impressed

Disraeli. His parliamentary colleague, the Radical David Urquhart, saw the hand of the tsar in Chartism and thought that Lord Palmerston was an agent of the tsar, as Disraeli thought Lord Palmerston was an agent of the Italian secret societies and that he sent his own secret agents to intrigue against Russia in the Black Sea area. More broadly secret-society conspiracism was part and parcel of the prevailing fear of revolution, a constant of Victorian England. In his *Journals* Lord Stanley (later the 15th Earl of Derby, and Disraeli's protégé and cabinet colleague) makes several references to Tory hysteria, that in 1854, for example, they fretted themselves into "a paroxysm of alarm" and were positively phobic at the prospect of an extension of the parliamentary franchise, believing that a republic was inevitable, that they were the last generation to live under the monarchy and would soon see the end of private property.[68] The question is complicated by the undoubted fact that secret societies did exist, such as the Carbonari that played an important part in Italian unification and similar associations that were the authors of mayhem in Ireland, but Disraeli greatly exaggerated their power and influence. Conspiracism, intrigue, sedition, secret societies, and the secret influence of Jews behind the scenes were central to Disraeli's mind and outlook as to his policies and actions.

Disraeli fashioned (part of his self-fashioning) a High Tory/Burkean/conspiracist/anti-Whig interpretation of English history, matching his conspiratorial notions of history in general. He promulgates this most notably in his *Vindication of the English Constitution* (1835). To Disraeli the Whigs had been bent on an oligarchical conspiracy to subvert the constitution since the Revolution of 1689. Far from "Glorious," the overthrow of the Stuarts brought Britain the "triple blessing [i.e., curse] of Venetian politics, Dutch finance, and French wars," that is, a dominant Whig oligarchy and crippled doge-like executive, deficit spending, and wars rather than the Stuart policy of peace and alliance with France.[69] "The Whigs for two centuries have been great dealers in *coups d'état*."[70] To Disraeli the Hanoverian succession in 1714 was another Whig "coup d'état" as were the 1716 Septennial Act (killing the freeborn "Englishman's birthright of triennial parliaments") and the 1719 Peerage Bill (intended to limit the royal prerogative to create peers) all aimed at solidifying and making permanent the "Whigocracy's" grip on power.[71] Disraeli called for a return to Lord Bolingbroke and the ideal of "the patriot king," which he thought had been realized by George III, Lord Shelburne, and the younger William Pitt. Disraeli dismissed the Reform Bill of 1832 as another Whig coup d'état: "by [creating] a system of nomination not less equivocal than that of the boroughmongers they effected to destroy," the Whig magnates assured themselves a perpetual majority of "Whiglings," so that "the House of Commons is no more the house of the people than is the House of Lords."[72] Worse, it was a scheme to restore the ascendancy of the Venetian-Whig oligarchy and the middle class at the expense of king, lords, and people: The Whigs were "pilfering the royal prerogative," turning William IV into the "projected Doge of Windsor," but also killing "the aristocratic principle of government" and "abolish[ing] the Lords" by the "menace" of compelling William to threaten to create new peers to assure the reform bill's passage.[73] The repeal of the Corn Laws in 1846 was the latest conspiratorial blow against the aristocratic constitution.

Historiographically, Disraeli was certainly the son of the father who had idealized *The Literary and Political Character of James I* (1816) and written a thoroughgoing piece of Tory-Cavalier panegyric and apologia, the five-volume *Commentaries on the Life and Reign of [the Martyr King] Charles I* (1828–31); republished by Disraeli after his father's death. For his vindication of the early Stuarts against the Whig historians, Isaac was awarded an honorary doctorate by Oxford. The son went further back in time, seeing in Henry IV, V, and VI the Lancastrian monarchs under whom "the present Constitution was amply, if not perfectly, developed," itself a restoration of the Anglo-Saxon constitution that secured the proper balance between king and lords. Disraeli also singled out Henry VIII as the great despoiler of the monasteries who deprived the people of their sources of charity and education, and who established the economic base of the usurping Whig aristocracy—the "proto-Whigs"—bribing them by his disposal of the monastic estates.[74] The entire narrative of *Sybil* (1845) hinges on this conspiracist historiography, on Disraeli's claim that English history as written up to then had been "a mere phantasm." Two elements were "blotted out": "the monarch and the multitude; as the power of the crown has diminished, the privileges of the people have disappeared; till at length the scepter has become a pageant, and its subject has degenerated again into a serf." In his letters as prime minister in 1868 and 1874–80 to Victoria, Disraeli often urged upon the queen his exalted view of the royal prerogatives, particularly that she was right in exercising them in foreign policy. Ingratiating himself with Victoria and seemingly subverting the constitution, he wrote to her in April 1868: "On great political occasions, it is wise, that the visible influence, as it were, of the Sovereign should be felt and recognised by the nation, and that Parliament should practically comprehend, that the course of a Ministry depends on the will of the Queen."

There was much public discussion of the queen's pursuit of "personal power" that was exercised through her "personal government." Disraeli was accused of "instigating [her] to join in the conspiracy" and "tell[ing] her she can govern like Queen Elizabeth." As it was put by an article in *The Nineteenth Century*, "If the Queen can summon 7,000 Sepoys to Malta [April–May 1878, an incident in the Russo-Turkish war], she might land 70,000 at Southampton and destroy our liberties." The third volume of Sir Theodore Martin's biography of her late husband, *Life of the Prince Consort*, which appeared in 1878, caused a stir by its vindication of Albert's attempted interventions in the cabinet at the time of the Crimean War. An anonymous review of the book in the Tory *Quarterly* may have been by Disraeli himself (Disraeli had read the first volume "with much interest," as he wrote the queen), certainly by an ardent supporter or colleague.[75] With great precision, the review recapitulates Disraeli's conspiracist interpretation of English history, duly invokes his hero Bolingbroke, and extensively quotes or paraphrases *Coningsby* and *Sybil*. Whether Disraeli was embarked on a conspiracy to undermine the constitution or merely indulge in unctuous adulation of the queen, he was assailed by another reviewer of Martin's book, in the Liberal *Edinburgh Review*, for "penning original theories of the constitution and fantastic histories of party," possibly to justify "the supplanting of parliamentary government by [royal] prerogative." For his rapturous support of her claims, Victoria loved her prime minister and detested his rival Gladstone, who, for his part, greatly distrusted Disraeli as a threat to the constitution and suspected him of encouraging rather than putting right the queen's misapprehensions.[76]

The landless Disraeli (until he acquired Hughenden Manor in 1848) was a fervent supporter of the landed aristocracy, of Crown, Church, House of Lords, and the rule of the squirarchy as JPs and parsons, and he believed himself to be an aristocrat, of aristocratic Sephardic descent—although he was as middle class as middle class could be. Like Marx, whose father also had him baptized as a child, he turned against his own middle class, discovered the proletariat, which for Marx was the bearer of revolution against the bourgeoisie, for Disraeli the object of Tory-democracy noblesse oblige and the aristocracy's ally against the bourgeoisie. His attack on the Whig interpretation of history was simply a justification of the Tory ruling class, entry into which he so ardently strove for. Truly, as Robert Blake concluded, "Disraeli has no real historical sense; he wrote propaganda, not history."[77]

Some Disraelian Examples of Conspiracies

When the Russians defeated the Ottoman army and took Adrianople in 1829, the victors won in a standard operation conducted by a superior military force. But Disraeli invoked "a secret history" and explained that victory was gained "by other means than military prowess. . . . The Sultan had to struggle against an unprecedented conspiracy the whole time, and that [on] the morning that Adrianople was treacherously delivered up [to the Russian forces], the streets of Stamboul were filled with the dead bodies of detected traitors [conspirators]."[78]

In Ireland, one of his great bugbears, the peasants were "enrolled in secret societies" like the Ribbonmen, Whiteboys, Fenians, and many others, and carried out atrocious crimes against people, livestock, and property. In a "Runnymede" letter of February 11, 1837, he accused the Whig lord lieutenant of Ireland of being a party to "the plots of those ["rebels"] who are conspiring against [the royal] dignity."[79] In the spring of 1868, when Disraeli was premier for the first time and Gladstone was proceeding with House of Commons resolutions calling for the disestablishment and disendowment of the Anglican Church in Ireland, Disraeli perceived conspiracies and said in debate that Gladstone was in collusion with the Jesuits, that "High Church Ritualists and the Irish followers of the Pope have long been in secret combinations, and are now in open confederacy."[80]

As leader of the Protectionist opposition in the House of Commons, especially 1847–52, a characteristic gambit of Disraeli was to attack the Whig-Liberal coalition as being in alliance with (the great bogey of the time) Continental Jacobinism. He was convinced, with some reason, that secret societies were the principal instigators of the revolutions of 1848, when they "surprised Europe," when Paris sneezed and the rest of Europe caught a cold, when his idol Metternich became "a victim of the secret societies."

> It was neither parliaments nor populations, nor the course of nature, nor the course of events, that overthrew the throne of Louis Philippe. Amid one of those discontents which are appeased by the sacrifice of a favourite or the change of a ministry, the sovereign and the subjects both in confusion, the king [bereft] of his wonted energy by a prostrating illness and the citizens murmuring without convictions, the throne was surprised by the secret societies, ever prepared to ravage Europe.
>
> The origin of the secret societies that prevail in Europe is very remote. It is probable that they were originally confederations of conquered races organised in a great measure by the abrogated hierarchies. In Italy they have never ceased, although they have at times been obliged to take various forms; Freemasonry was always a convenient guise. The Inquisition in its great day boasted that it had extirpated them in Spain, but their activity in that country after the first French revolution [of 1789] indicates a suspension of vitality than an extinction of life. The Reformation gave them a great impulse in Germany, and towards the middle of the eighteenth century, they had not only spread in every portion of the north of that region but had crossed the Rhine [into France].
>
> The two characteristics of these confederations, which now cover Europe like a network, are war against property and hatred of the Semitic revelation [Christianity]. These are the legacies of their founders; a proprietary despoiled and the servants of altars that have been overthrown. Alone, the secret societies can disturb, but they cannot control, Europe. Acting in unison with a great popular movement they may destroy society, as they did at the end of the last century. The French disturbance of '48 was not a great popular movement. It was a discontent which required nothing more for its solution than a change of ministry: but the sovereign and his subjects were in sudden confusion; the secret associations are always vigilant and always prepared; they took society by surprise, but having nothing really to rely upon except their own resources, the movement however disastrous has been an abortion.
>
> It is the manoeuvres of these men, who are striking at property and Christ, which the good people of [Britain], who are so accumulative and so religious, recognise and applaud as the progress of the Liberal cause.[81]

During the Crimean war, in 1856, Disraeli was in Paris—"doing nobody knows what"—dining with diplomats—"all the diplomatists [are] on their knees; all secrets told from all sides," he crowed—and trying to drive a wedge between Napoleon III and Palmerston in an attempt to oust the prime minister, even placing his own mole in the Paris embassy, Ralph Anstruther Earle. One of Disraeli's bright young men, Earle was a leading member of Disraeli's underground intelligence network for a decade, going behind the ambassador's back to acquire secret dispatches, confidential information, gossip, and any kind of ammunition with which to undermine Palmerston's government. Disraeli always sought friendship, alliance, commercial treaties with France (this was Bolingbroke's policy, he said) and accused Palmerston of antagonizing Napoleon III. He had direct access to the emperor through the duchess of Hamilton, among others, but managed to get only one meeting, disappointing and late in the day.[82] Disraeli's and Earle's conduct was treacherous and unscrupulous, but it was especially so on Disraeli's part in using a very young man as his private spy in the Paris embassy from 1856 to 1859 and beyond, who worked in collusion with another young man, John Bidwell, a clerk in the Foreign Office at home. Earle was an unpaid attaché in the Paris embassy under the ambassador, the Whig Lord Cowley; they strongly disliked each other. Thanks to his two secret agents, the leader of the opposition in the Commons received a steady stream of secret and confidential documents, and knew everything that was going on in the embassy. Earle's letters to Disraeli lack any heading, were unsigned or signed "X," and were mailed to Mrs. Disraeli or to Disraeli at one of his clubs.

One of their several abortive attempts to attack Palmerston and unseat the government was contrived in 1857: Earle was to embroil Palmerston in a quarrel with Napoleon III over the unification of Wallachia and Moldavia in Romania. That same year they also sought to entangle Palmerston over a treaty signed in 1854 by Britain, France, and Austria that had been intended to draw Austria in as an ally in the Crimean war and induce Russia to make concessions or stay out. At the time, 1857, the Italophile Palmerston was supporting Sardinia in its ambition to unite Italy, thus violating the 1854 treaty by abandoning Austria. Disraeli had said of Palmerston in House of Commons debate in 1856, in one of his richer conspiratorial perorations: "a British minister [Palmerston] has boasted—and a very unwise boast it was—that he had only to hold up his hand and he could raise a revolution in Italy tomorrow. It was an indiscreet boast, but I believe it not impossible, with the means at his disposal, that he might succeed. What would happen? You would have a republic formed on extreme principles."[83] In the aftermath, Palmerston was embarrassed and lost his temper when Disraeli, thanks to Earle's access to archives, pointed out that Britain was indeed a signatory to the 1854 treaty, that it was a treaty and not a mere convention, and that Palmerston was amateurish and slipshod in his conduct of foreign policy. But the redoubtable Palmerston brazened it out and his government was unimperiled by what was no more than a trivial episode, but one that reveals the leader of the opposition's proclivity for intrigue and directing his own secret service. At the same time, Lord Lennox, another of Disraeli's favored young men, intrigued against Derby in a plot to jettison him from the party leadership and clear the decks for Disraeli's succession.

The Orsini affair of 1858, an attempt by the Carbonari, an Italian secret society, to assassinate Napoleon III (paradoxically, he had once belonged to the Carbonari) that killed several bystanders, was much more serious. The bombs were made and the conspiracy hatched in England, and some of the conspirators found refuge there, where one was acquitted. Earle's letters to Disraeli offer much advanced information and suggestions how to exploit the event and set the emperor against Palmerston and the French foreign minister against Ambassador Cowley. Thus armed, Disraeli took the lead in accusing and lacerating the prime minister, whose reputation was tarnished somewhat more. Palmerston's response to the crime, in an attempt to mollify the French, was the Conspiracy to Murder Bill; it proposed to punish such conspiracies as felonies (rather than mere misdemeanors) with life sentences of penal servitude. It failed of passage by sixteen votes, brought down Palmerston's government, and brought in Derby and Disraeli, who, ironically, neither then nor ever, enacted an anticonspiracy measure of any kind.

In that second Derby government Disraeli was again Chancellor of the Exchequer; he intensely disliked his cabinet colleague, Lord Malmesbury the foreign secretary, and employed Earle, now his private secretary, to circumvent Malmesbury, sending Earle again to Paris to operate on the backstairs to intercede with Napoleon, once more to turn the emperor against Palmerston but also to checkmate the emperor from intervening in Italy. In all his maneuvers, Disraeli's use of his private, anonymous, and more accurate intelligence system kept Malmesbury in the dark and made him and the cabinet very distrustful of the scheming chancellor. But Disraeli was forestalled. According to his friend and sometime agent, the Tory journalist Thomas E. Kebbel, Disraeli "always" insisted that "a secret understanding had been arrived at between Palmerston and Louis Napoleon at Compiegne" to time the outbreak of war with Austria to coincide with the parliamentary elections, enabling the opposition to attack the Derby government for failing to avert war, for provoking it by its support of Austria, and, presumably, costing the Tories the election.[84] Historians have concluded that the timing of the two events was coincidental, not conspiratorial, and that Disraeli never learned that Napoleon III always preferred the wily Whig Palmerston to the wily Tory Disraeli.

In 1860 Earle and Disraeli were at it again, looking to put Napoleon and Palmerston's government at loggerheads at the time when Napoleon was angling to annex Nice and Savoy (he promptly did so). In what Gavin Henderson called "an astounding degree of treachery," Earle and Disraeli sought to persuade the ruler of France to adopt an anti-British policy, providing him with tactical arguments and a summary of a critical cabinet paper. They failed to weaken or unseat the crafty Palmerston, yet that did not prevent them from further machinations in Italy in 1860–61. Earle was active in Florence and Rome, where, with papal approval and Cardinal Wiseman's encouragement, his maneuvers were intended to rally the English- and Irish-Catholic vote for the Conservatives back home. But Palmerston remained immensely popular and in office until his death in 1865. By then Earle and Disraeli had fallen out and were snubbing each other, apparently because Earle felt himself insufficiently rewarded and resented Disraeli's growing favor of Montague Corry as his private secretary. He left Parliament and politics but not before speaking against Disraeli in the debate on the 1867 Reform Bill. Earle probably was the author of a series of anonymous articles in *The Times* attacking his erstwhile mentor; these were taken up and put to antisemitic use by T. P. O'Connor.[85]

At the time of the Polish revolt against Russia in 1863, Disraeli felt that

> At present the peace of the world has been preserved, not by statesmen, but by capitalists. For the last three months it [events on the Continent] has seen a struggle between the secret societies and the European millionaires. Rothschild hitherto has won; [but under the influence of Napoleon III circumstances are shifting in favor of] the brigands.

Disraeli thought European politics hinged on the struggle between the Rothschilds and the Carbonari. Nationalism (as opposed to patriotism) as exemplified by Ireland, Bosnia, Serbia, or Bulgaria was repugnant to Disraeli; their struggles for national self-determination partook of the nature of conspiracies. Typical of him is this farrago in a speech of 1876, at the height of the Bulgarian massacres by Turkish irregular forces: "Serbia declared war on Turkey, that is to say the secret societies of Europe declared war on Turkey."[86] Perpetually clamoring over how the secret societies thwarted peaceful resolution of the Bulgarian revolt and massacres (1875–77), Disraeli also purported to believe that "[a]ll the Liberal journals [of England] are in the pay of foreign Powers." A more skewed reading of Slavic nationalism, Turkish misrule, and the actualities of power and influence is hard to imagine.

One of the main themes of Disraeli's novel *Lothair* (1870) is the competing conspiracies between the Catholic Church and the secret nationalist societies on the Continent to enlist the noble hero and his money for their cause. A Vatican ecclesiastic informs Lothair that the secret societies "have declared war against the Church, the State, and the domestic principle. All the great truths and laws on which the family reposes are denounced. Their religion is the religion of science." The lines are drawn and "it is a death struggle": "It is the Church against the secret societies. They are the only two strong things in Europe, and will survive Kings, Emperors or parliaments," but if the Church is destroyed, "Europe would be divided between the atheist and the communist." More insidious, in Disraeli's view, are "the schemes of the *illuminati* and the freemasons which apparently torture the Continent [with] all the dark conspiracies of the secret societies." "There are more secret societies in France at this moment than at any period since '85 [when the *illuminati* were outlawed], though you hear nothing of them," although France is honeycombed with local cells that he calls "the Mary-Anne." The "*Madre Natura*," in particular, is "the oldest, the most powerful, and the most occult of the secret societies of Italy"; it "assumed many outward forms, according to the varying spirit of the age: sometimes they were freemasons, sometimes they were soldiers, sometimes artists, sometimes men of letters" but since antiquity it pursued the same aim: to restore the Roman Republic and repel "the Semitic invasion." The First International is represented as the "Standing Committee of the Holy Alliance of Peoples," a talk-shop of revolutionary rhetoricians dedicated to an "extreme republicanism" and with branches in England, Ireland, the United States, Rome, and elsewhere. "The secret societies are hurrying the civil governments of the world, and mostly the governments who disbelieve in their existence, to the brink of a precipice, over which monarchies and law and civil order will ultimately fall and perish together."[87] At various points in the novel, Disraeli attacks the Catholic Church as an evil, conspiratorial institution. He was fascinated by the Catholic Church which, by turns, he admired and detested in a no-popery vein: Impressed by its genius for organization, mystical dogmas, magical arts, and so on, he thought the first Jesuits were Jews (*Conversos*) and that the Jesuits were a colossally effective secret society.

Typical of Disraeli's exuberant suspiciousness and exaggeration is his account of how, facilitated by Rothschilds' quick and secret loan of £4 million, in 1875 he purchased the Suez Canal shares. He wrote excitedly about "a great State secret" to his confidante, Lady Bradford, "We have had all the gamblers, capitalists, financiers of the world organised and platooned in bands of plunderers, arrayed against us, and secret emissaries in every corner, and have baffled them all, and have never been suspected." Absurdly, Disraeli adds that otherwise France would have gotten possession of the canal and "might have shut it up."[88]

In a speech at Aylesbury in 1876, after blaming the Serbs for declaring war and attacking the Ottoman empire in support of Bosnia and Hercegovina a few months earlier (June 30), Disraeli said,

> [I]n the attempt to conduct the government of this world there are now elements to be considered which our predecessors had not to deal with. . . . These are the Secret Societies . . . which at the last moment may baffle all our arrangements—Societies which have regular agents everywhere, which countenance assassination, and which, if necessary, could produce a massacre.[89]

Here Disraeli tumbled together incongruously Russian nihilists and revolutionaries (who confined themselves to Russia), Pan Slavists (who were neither secret nor revolutionary), and Serbian nationalists and various Balkan insurgents (whose secret societies played a minute role); as Lord Hartington said in opposition, the Turkophile Disraeli "denounced everybody and everything except the Turkish government."[90]

To be sure, there was a widespread assumption in Britain, and particularly on the part of Disraeli, that Russia—abetted by Gladstone's oratory against the Turks—headed a deep-seated conspiracy with Serbia and the sultan's Christian subjects in the Balkans to overthrow the Ottoman empire, that an army of Russian agents planned and fomented Serbia's aggression and rebelliousness in Bosnia, Herzegovina, and among the Bulgarians and others, that Russia was bent on extensive annexations and would reduce the Balkan peoples to submissive client states. Henry Austen Layard, his ambassador to Turkey and an extreme Turkophile, confirmed Disraeli's conspiracism: Slavic insurrection and Russia's invasion were "part and parcel of a carefully prepared plot and of a distinct policy." Both were impervious to the assessment of keener and more objective observers like Sir Arthur Evans the future archaeologist of Crete, who argued that it was not secret societies and intrigue but "the flagrant and unendurable tyranny" of Ottoman officials. Layard, the archaeologist of Nineveh, purported to believe that the infamous Bulgarian massacres were launched by Bulgarians at the instigation of Russian secret agents or societies. Disraeli badly misread the situation, led astray by his conspiratorial assumptions. In fact, in 1876 Russia refused to support Serbia's declaration of war and intervention in Bosnia, proposing instead a joint declaration with Austria-Hungary and Germany of nonintervention. No wonder Lord Salisbury grumbled he could not find "a clue to the mysteries of Disraeli's conduct" with regard to the Eastern Question.[91]

At the highpoint of Disraeli's career and fame at the Congress of Berlin in 1878, his foreign secretary Lord Salisbury complained, "What with deafness, ignorance of French, and Bismarck's extraordinary mode of speech, Beaconsfield [he had been ennobled as Earl of Beaconsfield in 1876] has not the dimmest idea of what is going on—understands everything crossways, and imagines a perpetual conspiracy"; he was also handicapped by his "perfect disregard for facts." Disraeli's view of continental politics and diplomacy was shaped decisively by his belief in secret societies, particularly when he was concerned with the Eastern Question, 1875–78. As we have seen, when Serbia and Montenegro declared war on Turkey in June–July 1876, he contended it was really "the Secret Societies of Europe [that] declared war on Turkey."[92] In June of that year he wrote to Queen Victoria, who seemed heartily to agree with him, claiming to have "incontestable evidence that the so-called insurgents [in Bosnia and Herzegovina] are not natives of any Turkish province but are simply an invasion of revolutionary bands, whose strength lay in the support afforded to them by Servia and Montenegro, acting on the instigation of foreign [i.e., Russian] agents and foreign [i.e., Panslavic] committees."[93]At the height of the agitations in England over the Bulgarian massacres, April to August 1876, Disraeli denied that the Turks were the perpetrators: The killers were, he said in his speech at Aylesbury, "the Secret Societies of Europe." Although Cardinal Manning enthusiastically took up Disraeli's refrain, arguing that accusations of conspiratorial doings by secret societies were "no hobgoblin," the political commentator J. Fitzjames Stephen derided the prime minister for "degrading" himself and public discourse with all his "blarney about Secret Societies." Historian James Anthony Froude, who opposed the government's Eastern policy and wanted to see Britain and Russia partition Asia between them, was shocked that Disraeli believed secret societies were responsible for the massacres.[94] A few days later, reacting to the uproar in Britain over the Bulgarian atrocities and the imminence of war, Disraeli felt vindicated and wrote to Lady Bradford,

> I am not quite so surprised as my colleagues and the world in general, for you might judge from what I intimated about secret societies at Aylesbury I had an instinctive inkling of mischief. The remark at the time was, of course, deprecated and ridiculed. . . . I certainly did not suppose the vindication of my prescience was so near at hand. I sincerely wish I had been a false prophet.[95]

Nothing and no one could disabuse Disraeli of his "instinctive inkling," which guided him throughout the crisis and beyond. Even after the emergency was resolved and he had returned in triumph from the Berlin Conference, he was impelled in his Guildhall speech of August 3, 1878, to justify his agreement to Austrian occupation of Bosnia because it "permitted us to check, I should hope for ever, that Panslavist confederacy and conspiracy which has already proved so disadvantageous to the happiness of the world."[96] Indeed, Disraeli persisted in seeing networks of conspiratorial secret societies in Albania, Bosnia, Bulgaria, Greece, Herzegovina, Montenegro, Romania, Russia, and Serbia.

In his last novel, unfinished, *Falconet*, a biting satire on Gladstone, the Rothschilds appear as the "Hartmann Brothers," bankers and party to a Nihilist conspiracy. A character says: "Destruction in every form must be welcomed. If it be only the destruction of a class, it is a step in the right direction," and goes on to say, "There is only one principle . . . the destruction of the species." A revolutionary network and communists loom threateningly on the horizon.[97] There had been a series of assassinations in Russia by Anarchist and Nihilist revolutionaries, and on March 13, 1881, Tsar Alexander II was assassinated. Disraeli rose in the House of Lords two days later, his last speech (he died April 19), to support a vote of condolence and implicitly gave expression to conspiratorial ideas—he was correct, of course, with regard to Russia. In the light of his argument that the Jews were indestructible and not weakened by persecution, it would be interesting to know what Disraeli's reaction might have been had he lived to see the pogroms and abuse of Jews triggered in Russia by the tsar's assassination, and continuing until the overthrow of the stardom in 1917.

Jews as Conspirators

The notion of Jews as conspirators has a very long history, for it stems from the New Testament as interpreted by the Church Fathers and medieval theologians: Christian antisemitism is the progenitor of all conspiracy theory.[98] Disraeli, however, owing to his great fame and prominence, imparted an unprecedented degree of legitimacy and authenticity to conspiracism. He unwittingly played into the hands of antisemites, fortifying myth and prejudice, without vindicating the Jewish cause. No doubt Jews, particularly Anglo-Jewry, took great pride in his personal accomplishments, rising by sheer force of ability and determination against every obstacle that antisemitic prejudice could throw in his path to become leader and rebuilder of the Tory party, twice prime minister, and the favorite prime minister of the queen who ennobled him as the earl of Beaconsfield. There are many statements by contemporaries, Jewish and non-Jewish, in praise of Disraeli that are so extravagant that they invite antisemitic quotation to demonstrate that the Jews are the real power behind the scenes—those scenes invoked by Sidonia. For example, during the parliamentary election of 1880 a prominent member of the Metropolitan Anglo-Israel Association urged its members "to support the Earl of Beaconsfield, who, I believe, is not only director of England, but Governor of Europe, who ruled the Congress [of Berlin] entirely, and who has the management almost of Europe, Asia, and Africa, in his own hands."[99]

The all-powerful, omniscient, international, immensely wealthy, slightly sinister Jew, Sidonia, provides antisemites exploiting Disraeli's work with their premier text: "So you see, my dear Coningsby, the world is governed by very different personages from what is imagined by those who are not behind the scenes."[100] This declaration comes after a list of historical personages—finance ministers and high officials all over Europe—whom the novelist identifies as Jews, crypto Jews, or descendants of Jews, although, in actuality, none of them was. Disraeli's baseless thesis is compounded by his equally unfounded assertions regarding the Revolution of 1848, an event that greatly exercised him. He made the revolution "Jewish." It was led by "men of Jewish race," who headed all "the secret societies who [by revolution] form provisional governments, and men of Jewish race are found at the head of every one of them." In the revolutionary cadres one "will recognise everywhere the Jewish element," although

Daniel Manin, a convert, is the only one he manages to name. The 1848 upheavals would have come to nothing "had it not been for the Jews" whose "fiery energy and teeming resources" sustained the struggle in Germany, Italy, and France. The Jews "wish to destroy that ungrateful Christendom . . . whose tyranny they can no longer endure."[101] The events of 1848 were proof for Disraeli that if the Jews, who were decisively involved in all the significant events and turning points of history, were not emancipated and continued to be treated unjustly, they would subvert society—indeed they were doing so already.

Jews/Judaism, Disraeli asserts over and over, are "inherently conservative"; they are a "natural aristocracy" and "a race essentially monarchical, deeply religious, and essentially Tories." Why, then, do they vote for Mr. Gladstone,—whom Disraeli always believed to be a Radical—join the liberals, socialists, revolutionaries, secret societies, and conspiratorial groups? Because the Tories continue to oppose emancipation (to 1858); more, because "existing society has chosen to persecute this race which should furnish its choice allies." Jews are made radical and subversive, and thus become proponents of "the natural equality of men," which is a "pernicious doctrine." The Jew "will not tamely continue under a system that seeks to degrade him." Sidonia goes on to say that although the Jews are trustees of tradition and religion, yet "in every generation they must become more powerful and more dangerous to the society which is hostile to them."[102]

In his last published novel, *Endymion* (1880), Disraeli's semitic racism verges on depiction of the Jews as sinister conspirators: The character Sergius (an ambassador) refers to the Semites who

> now exercise a vast influence over affairs by their smallest though most peculiar family, the Jews. There is no race gifted with more tenacity, and such skill in organization. These qualities have given them an unprecedented hold over property and illimitable credit. As you advance in life, and get experience in affairs, the Jews will cross you everywhere. They have long been stealing into our secret diplomacy, which they have almost appropriated.

Sidonia also insists that

> in another twenty-five years, they will openly claim their share in the government of this country. Now here we are dealing with races: men and cliques of men, who are guarded in their behaviour by their peculiar [secret] organisation, and a statesman must reckon with this situation.[103]

In general, the secret societies rule and threaten Europe as much as ever; the Rothschilds appear as the spider at the center of the web.

John Vincent concludes that "Disraeli came close to the idea of a Jewish world conspiracy or network, managed by a master race defined by purity of blood." He notes also, that in Disraeli's eyes, "The Jews are behind the right, behind the left, control diplomacy, have enormous resources, hold key positions. Disraeli's advocacy was the stuff of which paranoid anti-Semitism was to be made."[104] Disraeli's avowals of Jewish power and threats to punish "an ungrateful Christendom" reanimate stereotypes and pave the way for accusations by antisemites of Jews as global conspirators and, variously, as the driving force behind the secret societies, Jacobinism, the Paris Commune, the Marxist International, and any and all dangers since his time.

Reactions to Disraeli's Jewish Conspiracism

An early reaction to *Coningsby*'s conspiracism and much else was William Makepeace Thackeray's burlesque, *Codlingsby* (1847), which mockingly notes that "Over the entire world spreads a vast brotherhood, suffering, silent, scattered, sympathizing, *waiting*—an immense Free-Masonry." The Jews have lost Jerusalem, "but have they not taken the whole world in exchange?" "Raphael" is a spoof of Sidonia: he is immensely rich from great international loans to foreign powers but also relishes "huxtering" in "disguise," and is the beneficiary of pawnshop transactions; his house in London is "the centre of Europe" where "all the affairs of the world [are] represented."[105] In the 1850s *Punch*—which more than any other journal shaped the image of Disraeli as "mystery-man," trickster, conjurer, charlatan, and so on—chimed in:

> Well! The Jews, it seems, are conscious of their ill-treatment. *They* join secret societies. *They* . . . topple over thrones with delight. . . . "*All is race.*" What a picture of cool malignity is this! Shadrach luxuriates in locking up the Frank in a sponging-house; he charges him for the 'Semitic Element' and sticks it on the chops and sherry.[106]

More seriously, antisemites took up Disraeli's ideas, quoting him as proof of their assertion of a Jewish conspiratorial menace and manipulation of everyone and everything from behind the scenes. Among the first to do so, the French Chevalier Roger Gougenot des Mousseaux cited Sidonia's dictum about how "the world is governed from behind the scenes" as the epigraph for the title page of his systematic denunciation of the Jews in his work of 1869; it includes several pages quoted from Disraeli and commented upon as immensely illuminating and truthful about the Jewish menace.[107] Half a century later, the English queen of conspiracy theory and drawing room antisemite Nesta Webster used an excerpt from Disraeli's speech in the House of Commons on July 14, 1856, as the epigraph for her book, still in print, *Secret Societies and Subversive Movements,* 1924. According to Disraeli,

> There is in Italy a power which we seldom mention in this House . . . I mean the secret societies. . . . It is useless to deny, because it is impossible to conceal, that a great part of Europe—the whole of Italy and France and a great portion of Germany, to say nothing of other countries—is covered with a network of these secret societies, just as the superficies of the earth is now being covered with railroads. And what are their objects? They do not attempt to conceal them. They do not want constitutional movement; they do not want ameliorated institutions . . . they want to change the tenure of land. To drive out the present [noble] owners of the soil and to put an end to ecclesiastical establishments. Some of them may go further.[108]

As mentioned earlier, the antisemitic volcano Drumont exploited Disraeli's own words in the same way. "European politics," Jane Ridley writes, Disraeli "explained in terms of secret societies or the hidden influence of the Jews." The striking fact is that he combined the two into one, forming a poisonous myth: Jews are the founders, leaders, and driving force of all conspiracies and secret societies.[109]

Disraeli and *The Protocols of the Learned Elders of Zion*

In 1920, at the height in Britain of the initial spurt of public attention to the *Protocols,* then designated *The Jewish Peril,* the London newspaper *The Spectator* ran two articles on "Disraeli on the Secret Societies and the Jews."

> The question whether there exist on the Continent or even here Secret Societies with ultra-revolutionary aims inspired and controlled by Jews, and if so, what type of Jews and for what particular purposes, is still causing a great deal of interest . . . indeed, anxiety. . . . Disraeli's writings deal with the matters in question. . . . Disraeli has to deal and find excuses, or at any rate explanations for the revolutionary side of Judaism.

The article then quotes extensively from Disraeli's life of *Lord George Bentinck* and concludes:

> Those sentences . . . should be specially noted. In 1848 [the revolution Disraeli was particularly exercised over], as now, the Jews were accused . . . of having taken a leading part in the subversive Secret Societies, which were held to have engineered the vast upheaval. Disraeli obviously felt the need for explaining the connection of his fellow Jews with those "unhallowed associations." In doing so, his words seem to find a most curious and significant reverberation in the [*Protocols*].

The article notes a second affinity between Disraeli and the *Protocols*: Jews use their wealth as well as ideas like "Liberty, Equality, Fraternity" to subvert Christian society. In the second article, *The Spectator* ruminates on

> whether conspiracies are in existence for the destruction of the civilised world, and whether a portion of the Jewish race are taking the lead in the great plot for world havoc.

> We are inclined to think . . . that there are a great many Secret Societies now existing in Europe, and that in them Jews are very often to the front. We think also that the power of these Secret Societies has been immensely exaggerated, but at the same time we think that these societies and the Jewish extremists ought to be carefully watched, though not persecuted, by all Governments. . . . But watched they ought to be.[110]

Also in the 1920s, Charles L. Graves, the historian of *Punch*, was much taken by "a strange passage in Disraeli's *Life of George Bentinck* foreshadowing the role of world revolutionaries assigned to the Jews in the recent much discussed Protocol," that is, *The Protocols of the Learned Elders of Zion.*[111] In fact, *Punch* and *The Spectator* were part of a pattern by which numerous antisemites cited Disraeli's life and writings to "prove" the existence of a Jewish world conspiracy and establish the authenticity of the *Protocols.* Jean-François Moisan examined fourteen antisemitic works published in England from 1920 onwards; he demonstrates the lengths they went to exploit Disraeli—the man as much as his writings, using seventy-seven citations and quotations, mostly from *Coningsby* and *Lord George Bentinck*—to justify their chimeras and hatreds, often and characteristically grossly misquoting his words and distorting his meaning and intentions. Among the most notorious was the utterly respectable Nesta Webster, several of whose works remain in print.[112]

The same pattern can be traced on the Continent. In America Henry Ford's *International Jew* (a plagiarizing, paraphrasing, Americanizing, updating of the *Protocols*) named Sidonia as the exemplar of Jewish power, citing his creator for his exact description of "Jewish purpose and Jewish method" and as proof of Jewish scheming and plotting. To Ford, Bernard Baruch was "the proconsul of Judah in America," "a Jew of super-power," "the Disraeli of the United States"![113] George Sylvester Viereck, the German-American Nazi sympathizer who spent most of World War II in an American jail, explained, "It is Disraeli, not Adolf Hitler or Henry Ford, who, in *Coningsby,* sponsored the theory that two hundred members of an inner ring control the destiny of mankind." Hence Viereck understood "the existence of a ring of International Jews or Jewish Internationalists who, now under the mask of Bolshevism, now under the mask of Masonry and High Finance, attempt to make all governments their puppets," and the part of the Jews "in the destruction of the established order in law and morals; the fomenting of unrest and revolution, and the attempt . . . to dominate the world by exploiting alternately the evil forces of Mammon and the evil forces of Anarchy."[114]

Such is the specter of the Right Honorable Benjamin Disraeli, Earl of Beaconsfield, Viscount Hughenden, and Knight of the Most Noble Order of the Garter. Much of his life was devoted to defending the Jews and combating antisemitism. Yet, since he based himself on false racial criteria, dubious theology, and mythical history, generations of antisemites have been able to exploit his life and writings in support and justification of every anti-Jewish prejudice and stereotype, a phenomenon for which he was, says Moisan, "an easy prey."

Notes

Note: This much fuller article is based on my presentation "Disraeli's Ideas on Race, Religion, and Conspiracy: A Preliminary Report" at the conference marking the 200th anniversary of his birth, "Disraeli et L'Europe: L'Homme D'Etat et L'Homme de Lettres," June 18, 2004, at the University of Paris-X Nanterre.

1. Quoted in Sarah Bradford, *Disraeli* (New York: Stein and Day, 1982), 32, 37–38, 52; Herbert, reputed to be a kindly, benevolent soul, quoted in the introduction to *Benjamin Disraeli Letters,* ed. J. A. W. Gunn, M. G. Wiebe et al., 7 vols., 1815–59 (Toronto: Toronto University Press, 1982–2004), 6:xv; hereafter cited as *Disraeli Letters.*
2. Quoted in Bradford, *Disraeli,* 294, 307, 361.
3. Quoted in ibid., 193.
4. James Anthony Froude, *The Life of the Earl of Beaconsfield* (1890; repr., London: J. M. Dent and Sons, 1923), 2, 108, 132, 147, 170, 193, 261–62; Bradford, *Disraeli,* 272, 319.
5. Anthony Trollope, *Phineas Redux* (1873–74; repr., London: Folio Society, 1990), 305; Trollope, *An Autobiography* (Berkeley: University of California Press, 1947), 216–17.

6. Quoted in Bradford, *Disraeli,* 8–9.
7. Quoted in Froude, *Earl of Beaconsfield,* 22.
8. Letter to Benjamin, June 1826 in B. R. Jerman, *The Young Disraeli* (Princeton, N.J.: Princeton University Press, 1960), 74.
9. Quoted in Cecil Roth, *Benjamin Disraeli, Earl of Beaconsfield* (New York: Philosophical Library, 1952), 29.
10. Quoted in Stanley Weintraub, *Disraeli, A Biography* (New York: Truman Taley/Dutton, 1993), 100.
11. Quoted in Froude, *Earl of Beaconsfield,* 55; T. P. O'Connor, M. P., *Lord Beaconsfield: A Biography,* 8th ed. (London: T. Fisher Unwin, 1905), 15.
12. Quoted in Bradford, *Disraeli,* 99.
13. Jane Ridley, *Young Disraeli, 1804–1846* (New York: Crown Publishers, 1995), 131; Bradford, *Disraeli,* 218.
14. Jerman, *The Young Disraeli,* 240, 248 (for the quote), 250; Disraeli wrote to Peel seeking office, but denied it in 1845, lying to the House, which would have been fatal to his career, but he got away with it because Peel either did not wish or could not produce the letter to catch Disraeli out.
15. Quoted in introduction, *Disraeli Letters,* 4:xiv.
16. Lord Broughton, *Recollections of a Long Life,* 6 vols. (London: John Murray, 1909–11), 6:15.
17. Quotations from *Hansard,* 3rd ser., vol. 86, col. 675, May 15, 1846; in chap. 33 of *The Vindication of the English Constitution,* 1835, Disraeli strains to vindicate Peel's emancipation of the Dissenters and Roman Catholics, with no imputation of stealing the Whigs' clothing.
18. John Stuart Mill, *Autobiography* (1873; repr., London: Oxford University Press, 1924), 245.
19. *Disraeli Letters,* 7:488, no. 1919R; Pierre-Henri Simon commenting on Pierre Mendès France's defeat in 1955, observed, "When one enters high politics with the handicap of Jewish blood, it is safer to be Tory than Whig; one must be Disraeli or fall." Anti-Semites attack leftist Jews notably more ferociously than those on the Right. Quoted in Pierre Birnbaum, *Anti-Semitism in France: A Political History from Léon Blum to the Present,* trans. Miriam Kochan (Oxford: Blackwell, 1992), 48.
20. He was playing the role he attributed to his hero Bolingbroke in chap. 31 of *The Vindication of the English Constitution* (1835), of laying "the foundation for the future accession of the Tory party to power."
21. Quoted in Robert Blake, *Disraeli* (New York: St. Martin's Press, 1967), 303.
22. Quoted in *Disraeli Letters,* 7:142 n. 3.
23. Quoted in Blake, *Disraeli,* 406.
24. Quoted in Bradford, *Disraeli,* 266.
25. Quoted in Maurice Cowling, *1867 Disraeli, Gladstone and Revolution* (Cambridge: Cambridge University Press, 1967), 15, 166. Disraeli rejected John Stuart Mill's amendment to enfranchise women.
26. Quoted in Blake, *Disraeli,* 486.
27. Philip A. Appleman, William A. Madden, and Michael Wolff, eds., *1859: Entering an Age of Crisis* (Bloomington: Indiana University Press, 1959), 25.
28. Disraeli's introduction to the 1849 ed. of his father's *Curiosities of Literature,* quoted in Ridley, *Young Disraeli,* 9–10; for his political campaigns Disraeli adopted as his heraldic crest the Castle of Castile with the motto *Forti Nihil Difficile*—to the strong nothing is difficult.
29. Quotations in Isaiah Berlin, "Benjamin Disraeli, Karl Marx and the Search for Identity," *Against the Current: Essays in the History of Ideas,* ed. Henry Hardy, intro. Roger Hausheer (London: Hogarth Press, 1979), 273; and in Tom Reiss, *The Orientalist* (New York: Random House, 2005), 233.
30. According to Charles Richmond and Jerrold M. Post, "Disraeli's Mental Illness," who say he did not recover until his marriage in 1839, in *The Self-Fashioning of Disraeli, 1818–1851,* ed. Charles Richmond and Paul Smith (Cambridge: Cambridge University Press, 1998), 77.
31. Quoted in Bradford, *Disraeli,* 2.
32. *The Spectator,* June 5, 1920, 750.
33. Abraham Gilam, "Anglo-Jewish Attitudes Towards Benjamin Disraeli during the Era of Emancipation," *Jewish Social Studies* 42 (Winter 1980): 315–17.
34. Salo W. Baron, Introduction to Georg Brandes, *Lord Beaconsfield: A Study* (New York: Crowell, 1965), xi.
35. Quoted in Bradford, *Disraeli,* 59.
36. John Vincent, ed., *Disraeli, Derby and the Conservative Party: Journal and Memoirs of Edward Henry, Lord Stanley, 1849–1869* (Hassocks, Sussex: Harvester Press, 1978), 32.
37. Benjamin Disraeli, *Tancred,* in *The Works of Benjamin Disraeli, Earl of Beaconsfield, Embracing Novels, Romances, Plays, Poems, Biography, Short Stories and Great Speeches,* Introduction by Edmund Gosse, Biographical Preface by Robert Arnot, 20 vols. (London: M. Walter Dunne, 1904–5), vol.15, chap. 20, p. 191; hereafter cited as *Works.*

38. Benjamin Disraeli, *Lothair,* in *Works* 17, chap. 29, pp. 168, 171.
39. Quoted in Roth, *Benjamin Disraeli,* 71.
40. Quoted in Bradford, *Disraeli,* 186.
41. *Coningsby* in *Works* 12, chap. 32, pp. 292–93.
42. Ibid., chap. 37, pp. 331–32; the last sentence is one of the most quoted by antisemites.
43. *Lord George Bentinck,* in *Works* 4, chap. 10, p. 127; *Tancred,* in *Works* 16, chap. 36, p. 157.
44. Léon Poliakov, *The History of Anti-Semitism: From Voltaire to Wagner*, trans. Miriam Kochan (New York: Vanguard, 1975), 336.
45. Houston Stewart Chamberlain, *Foundations of the Nineteenth Century,* 2 vols., trans. John Lees, introduction by Lord Redesdale (New York: John Lane, 1910), 1:xxxiv.
46. General Preface, *Works* 17:xxiii; Ernest Renan made the same boast that race was the age's great discovery.
47. Quoted in L. J. Rather, "Disraeli, Freud, and Jewish Conspiracies," *Journal of the History of Ideas* 47 (1986): 120.
48. Édouard Drumont, *La France Juive: Essai D'Histoire Contemporaine,* 2 vols. (1886, *115e édition*; Paris: C. Marpon and E. Flammarion, n.d.), 1:46, 49–51, 53, 110, 141, 143–44 and n. 2, 160, 306, 329–31, 333; 2:3.
49. Quoted in Rather, "Disraeli, Freud, and Jewish Conspiracies," 121.
50. Chamberlain, *Foundations,* 1:271; Chamberlain often paraphrased rather than quoted Disraeli; Lord Redesdale greatly admired Chamberlain as "a literary Hercules," but disagreed with his "strong Anti-Semitism" and thought him "unfair" to German Jews, ibid., 1:xxxv, xxxviii; the Nazis hailed Chamberlain as "seer of the 3rd Reich."
51. Jorg Schneider, *Das Bild Benjamin Disraelis in der deutschen Publizistik zwischen 1900 und 1945* (Bonn: Holos, 1996), 210.
52. Nicolaus Sombart, *Die deutschen Männer und ihre Feinde* (Munich: Carl Hauser, 1991), 284, as quoted in Ian Buruma's review of Roy Jenkins, *Gladstone: A Biography* in *New York Review of Books* 42 (February 1995): 12.
53. Randall L. Bytwek, *Julius Streicher* (New York: Stein and Day, 1983), 13, 133.
54. *Disraeli Letters,* 7:266–67, no. 3221.
55. Benjamin Disraeli, *Lothair,* in *Works* 17, chap. 17, p. 88.
56. Quoted in James Ogden, *Isaac D'Israeli* (Oxford: Clarendon Press, 1969), 194.
57. E.g., Preface to *Coningsby,* 5th ed., in *Works* 12:xvi–xvii; *Sybil* in *Works* 14, chap. 18, p. 161; *Tancred,* in *Works* 16, chap. 26, pp. 22–31 passim, and chap. 53, p. 335.
58. Quoted in Bradford, *Disraeli,* 255.
59. *Bentinck* in *Works* 4, chap. 10, p. 130; quoted from Disraeli's *Reminiscences* in Bernard Glassman, *Benjamin Disraeli: The Fabricated Jew in Myth and Memory* (Lanham, Md.: University Press of America, 2003), 71.
60. *Hansard,* 3rd series, December 16, 1847, vol. 95, cols. 1323–31.
61. *Tancred,* in *Works* 16, chap. 26, p. 37.
62. General Preface, *Works* 17:xxiii.
63. O'Connor, *Lord Beaconsfield,* 382.
64. Robert Blake, *Disraeli* (New York: St. Martin's Press, 1967), 50; John Vincent, *Disraeli* (Oxford: Oxford University Press, 1990), 56, 69; William Flavelle Monypenny and George Earle Buckle, *The Life of Benjamin Disraeli, Earl of Beaconsfield,* 6 vols. (New York: Macmillan, 1913–20); Roth, *Benjamin Disraeli,* 61; Daniel Pipes, *Conspiracy: How the Paranoid Style Flourishes and Where It Comes From* (New York: Free Press, 1999), 25–26.
65. Quoted in Ogden, *Isaac D'Israeli,* 67; Isaac, a devotee of the Enlightenment, initially welcomed the French Revolution but, like so many of his generation, soured on it.
66. Quoted in Blake, *Disraeli,* 301.
67. *Disraeli Letters,* 5:523–25, quote on 525; for Metternich, Disraeli's *Lord George Bentinck: A Political Biography* in *Works* 4, chap. 10, p. 130.
68. Vincent, ed., *Disraeli, Derby and the Conservative Party,* 114.
69. Quoted in Paul Smith, *Disraeli, A Brief Life* (Cambridge: Cambridge University Press, 1996), 61.
70. Disraeli's "Atticus" letter to *The Times,* March 11, 1841, in *Disraeli Letters,* 3:392.
71. T. A. Jenkins, *Disraeli and Victorian Conservatism* (New York: St. Martin's Press, 1996), 12.
72. Monypenny and Buckle, *Life of Benjamin Disraeli,* 1:282, 308.
73. For the "projected Doge of Windsor," see Disraeli's "Runnymede Letters" in *Disraeli Letters,* 2:344; for the "menace" see his "Who Is He?" in *Whigs and Whiggism: Political Writings,* ed. William Hutcheon (New York: Macmillan, 1914), 19; for the abolition of the Lords, article in the *Morning Post,* August 28, 1835, ibid., 69.
74. Quoted in Thomas E. Kebbel, *Lord Beaconsfield and Other Tory Memories* (New York: Mitchell Kennerley, 1907), 52–53; Kebbel refers to an article by Henry Dunckley, "The Progress of Personal Rule," *The Nineteenth*

Century 21 (Nov. 1878): 785–808, to which Kebbel wrote a rejoinder, "Personal Rule A Reply," ibid., (Dec. 1878): 1139–50.

75. Monypenny and Buckle, *Life of Benjamin Disraeli,* 5:354.
76. R. W. Seton-Watson, *Disraeli, Gladstone and the Eastern Question: A Study in Diplomacy and Party Politics* (1935; repr., London: Frank Cass, 1962), 397–402, quotes on 401.
77. Isaiah Berlin, "Benjamin Disraeli, Karl Marx and the Search for Identity," 263, 284–86; Blake, *Disraeli,* 271.
78. *Disraeli Letters,* 1:184, no. 109.
79. Benjamin Disraeli, *Whigs and Whiggism: Political Writings,* ed. William Hutcheon (New York: Macmillan, 1914), 359.
80. *Lord George Bentinck: A Political Biography* in *Works* 4, chap. 3, p. 33; quoted in Edgar Feuchtwanger, *Disraeli* (London: Arnold, 2000), 146.
81. *Lord George Bentinck: A Political Biography* (London: Colburn, 1851), chap. 27; quoted in part in Monypenny and Buckle, *Life of Benjamin Disraeli,* 3:173.
82. Monypenny and Buckle, *Life of Benjamin Disraeli,* 4:68; *Disraeli Letters,* 6:xxiii; 504, no. 2871; 511–12, no. 2882.
83. *Hansard,* House of Commons, July 14, 1856, col. 774.
84. Kebbel, *Lord Beaconsfield,* 20.
85. Gavin B. Henderson's two articles, "Disraeli and Palmerston in 1857" and "Ralph Anstruther Earle," in *Crimean War Diplomacy and Other Historical Essays,* ed. W. O. Henderson (Glasgow: Jackson, 1947), 249–89; the pair's secrecy was such that their correspondence's many hints and allusions to other episodes cannot be deciphered.
86. Quoted in Blake, *Disraeli,* 602.
87. Benjamin Disraeli, *Lothair,* in *Works* 17, chap. 52, p. 351; chap. 50, p. 338; chap. 49, p. 321; chap. 32, p. 207; chap. 54, p. 358; chap. 11, p. 57; and vol. 18, chap. 84, p. 157.
88. *The Letters of Disraeli to Lady Bradford and Lady Chesterfield,* 2 vols., ed. the Marquis of Zetland (New York: Appleton, 1929), 1:400; his foreign secretary said, "There was no deep-laid scheme in the matter," and made it a cabinet, not a Disraeli, coup: Edward Henry Stanley, 15th Earl of Derby, *Speeches and Addresses,* 2 vols., Prefatory Memoir by W. E. H. Lecky (London: Longmans, Green, 1894), 1:278–80.
89. Quoted in J. M. Roberts, *The Mythology of the Secret Societies* (New York: Scribner's, 1972), 7 n. 15.
90. Quoted in Seton-Watson, *Disraeli, Gladstone and the Eastern Question,* 149.
91. Quoted in ibid., 139, 205, 214, 284.
92. Quoted in B. H. Sumner, *Russia and the Balkans, 1870–1880* (1937; repr., London: Archon, 1962), 177, 505–6.
93. Quoted in Monypenny and Buckle, *Life of Benjamin Disraeli,* 6:35.
94. Richard T. Shannon, *Gladstone and the Bulgarian Agitation 1876,* 2nd ed. (Hassocks, Sussex: Harvester Press, 1975), 130, 191–92, 214; Herbert Paul, *The Life of Froude* (London: Pitman, 1905), 279–80. Froude was antisemitic and detested Disraeli personally.
95. Zetland, ed., *The Letters of Disraeli to Lady Bradford and Lady Chesterfield,* 2:95.
96. Quoted in Seton-Watson, *Disraeli, Gladstone and the Eastern Question,* 503.
97. For the *Falconet* fragment, Monypenny and Buckle, *Life of Benjamin Disraeli,* 5:531–58, for the quote, 555.
98. Marvin Perry and Frederick M. Schweitzer, *Antisemitism: Myth and Hate from Antiquity to the Present* (New York: Palgrave Macmillan, 2002), 74–84, 98ff.
99. Quoted in Glassman, *Benjamin Disraeli,* 94.
100. *Coningsby* in *Works* 12, chap. 37, p. 334.
101. *Lord George Bentinck* in *Works* 4, chap. 10, pp. 127–30; Vincent, *Disraeli,* 44.
102. *Lord George Bentinck; Coningsby* in *Works* 12, chap. 37, p. 331.
103. Quotes in Roth, *Benjamin Disraeli,* 71; Glassman, *Benjamin Disraeli,* 164.
104. Vincent, *Disraeli,* 30, 44.
105. B. de Shrewsbury, Esq., "Punch's Prize Novelists," "Codlingsby," *Punch, or the London Charivari* 12 (1847): 166, 193, 199, 213, 214, 223; "Raphael" also claims that the pope "is one of us" as are many other rulers, and that artists like Raphael and composers like Rossini are as well; although Thackeray's parody is light-hearted, it evokes many antisemitic stereotypes; Disraeli greatly resented it and long after Thackeray's death depicted him nastily as "St Barbe" in *Endymion* (1880).
106. Quoted in Rather, "Disraeli, Freud, and Jewish Conspiracies," 121.
107. R. Gougenot des Mousseaux, *Le juif: le judaïsme et la judaïsation des peuples chrétiens* (Paris: H. Plon, 1869); it was translated into German in 1921 by the Nazi ideologue Alfred Rosenberg.

108. *Hansard,* House of Commons, July 14, 1856, cols. 774–75.
109. Ridley, *Young Disraeli,* 340.
110. *The Spectator,* June 7, 1920, 750–51; June 12, 1920, 782–83.
111. Charles L. Graves, *Mr. Punch's History of England,* 4 vols. (London: Cassell, 1921–22), 1:109.
112. Jean-François Moisan, "Le Mythe du Complot Juif: Les Protocoles des Sages de Sion: Le Cas Disraeli," doctoral thesis, University of Paris, 1987, 243–57.
113. *The International Jew: The World's Foremost Problem,* Being a Reprint of a Series of Articles Appearing in *The Dearborn Independent* from May 22 to October 2, 1920, 4 vols. (N.p.: n.p., 1920), 2:56; for the "use and abuse" of Disraeli as proof of the *Protocols,* Glassman, *Benjamin Disraeli,* 163–67; Moisan, "Le Mythe du Complot Juif."
114. George S. Viereck, *The Kaiser on Trial,* 8th ed. (N.p.: Greystone Press, 1937), 408; these are Viereck's views and words though he puts them in the mouth of Wilhelm II's attorney at a suppositious trial under Article 227 of the Versailles treaty.

Writing

(for Zev Garber)

William (Zev) Wallis

Prelude

Obsessed with what no longer seems possible,
Lost in the skein of words that no longer holds
Promise of flight from the history of fire
That no longer cleanses but scalds and scars,
I descend from cirrus dreams to a small room
Where remnants of star-birth scald the mind,
Where golden letters born of first fire
Still shimmer bright an instant at the core,
Revealing forms, molten truth in realms
Hidden deep in glacial Siberian wastes,
Roman ghettoes, Ukranian shtetls,
Endless, long, one-way trains crossing
That great, broad even emptiness
Where time's horizon contracts from life promised
To the pale train of time stopped at the edge
Of stony, shifting criteria where frozen waves
Mock numb passengers in thin coats,
Torn unprepared from some little place
To the south or west, some place where pages
Are not bound with crushing force in mind.
Go ahead, add one more page to the bright flames,
Run blindly through streets of red, brown shirts, boots,
Cobblestones littered with smashed windows,
Broken spines, torn bindings, letters cried out
Burning in the air, books piled like trash, burning –
Burning like thought, like mind, like flesh.
Thus we read those times, the impossible times
Of the disappeared, the unreckoned, the lost.
Listen, I will sing you a story of fire risen from roses,
Not Promethean enlightenment, not inspiration,

But simple fire of the flesh – *Shoah* –
Of old books longing for rebirth – *Shoah* –
Longing for what seems now impossible:
Love of divine form in human kind.
Shoah, shoah, shoah, shoah, shoah.
I want to write about survival on earth
In words too plain for poetry, in words
Simple enough for all the children on earth
To read before they are blinded with hate,
Stumble blind into violence, and are lost forever.
Can the soul still long for what seems unlikely,
Perhaps impossible: order in the universe of men,
Acceptance of the paradox of their oneness.
In this moment inscribed, dear friend,
Let us pause by the hidden tracks and consider
The attributes of man, sapphires of mind
To guide us from terror to peace.
Come, gilded box, yield jewels of worth
From the ashes of a thousand books
In your fragrant cedar depths;
Come, sanguine fire, sing out forms
That divine the hidden heart with searching flame,
Here is the diadem of light,
The inner text of necessary longing,
The Sefirot, the mystical text—
The marks honoring the snowy page
With the shadows of the soul's truth.

1. ***Keter*** *(Crown)*

The invisible crown of knowing love
Sits easy on godhead seen from above.

Israel temple of my mind, you are safe.
Your ancient walls will gather my children inside,
Your storms cloud my eyes on the mountain tops of time.
My hands may lose their need to touch the stones
Buried in the wall of walls, but not the ageless
Golden arms I dreamed would open in Jerusalem
For my children and their children's children.

Israel home of my soul, reside in me
Now, never leave this fragile veil of flesh.
I will find you amidst the stony denial of my love—
Hate's scream, searing blast, flames in the tomb.
I do not think I will soar over your stone walls,
But distant seek the pure smoke of your past
Written down in feathering prayer to last.

2. ***Hokmah*** *(Wisdom)*

Great intellects draw from life force well spent,
But considered through veils, scorched and rent.

My family has taught me to love, to finally
Move from passion to compassion, and return.
Still, I afflict them with my pain, the unresolved
Nightmares of a blind child crying in the night.
I howl at them, as well as at the man in the mirror,
I project my ambition and tastes on them,
Desire more for them than they need.
But even so, their patience with me is sweet
As honeyed pages, their pleasant buzz
At my homecoming draws me safe to them.
They humor me and draw me out of moods,
They fill the evening with story and song,
And my sleepless nights with visions of rebirth.
Seasons of growth fill life with dancing mirth,
Charge dreams with sharing and self-worth.
They help me discover my real work:
They can't know and love what I do not reveal.
Sometimes I invent difficulties; I used to think
Trouble followed me, but know it's me in pursuit.
This tendency to see the darker side
And let it threaten their peace is cruel
To those I love. I grasp, I lose patience,
And, seized by old blindness, strike out with words.
So, in the small hours of morning when I walk restless
Through the dark rooms of our house,
Possessed by numbers and past figures,
And long for that certain something more,
I open the window on a sea of roses
Shimmering with moonlight before our house
And sense our little ones swimming the night
Away in dream, dolphins diving deep to translate
The dance of flowers into the mysterious
    currents of their depths.
I thank God for these moments
When I, most fortunate of men,
Pause within the beauty of my home,
Feel its unchanging qualities of light
Enter me, hollow out my bones,
Prepare me for flight.

3. **Binah** *(Openness)*

Each open book reveals a nascent world,
And to breathe its air – the soul's scroll unfurls.

I neglect the roses before my home,
But they in untamed fullness have forgiven me.
Their dry petals fall from bulb to loam,
As each bloom's design melts into a sea of light.
They do not prove their rooted love for earth,
Or draw back a curtain of words to show
The soul's search. The depth of their surface

Is the cloth of sight, cool flakes of the soil's night.
Fascicles of light drift among the stems
And toward me, before my son's tiny hands
Close over my eyes in a petalling veil,
And I must guess who is there behind me.
    Is it the shield and rose of time, my playful
    Responsibility, and the first form of love?

4. ***Hesed*** *(Covenant)*

The bitter song of history's passion
Does not hint at the race with death we run.

Hard, early rays bend her supple lines
    Till they join the hushed folds of cotton sheets –
All defined by my wife's slow, refining breath.

From the near wall beyond our bed
    Photos of trains at rest hang heavy
In darkness, eyes stare out from naked, bony flesh.

Above her sleeping form, ghastly facsimiles
    Of thin faces gaze out through barbed wire—
I know only numbers remain of those eyes.

Sleeping spirits surge under my skin, I rise quick
    To search my infant's forearm
For dark script in the sudden, fragile light.

Oh, blessed pale blankness! I howl silent joy,
    Sing a new song of grace
As the long nightmare fades and dreaming truth awakes.

5. ***Din / Gevurah*** *(Judgment)*

Strict judgment is the moral realm of men,
Who, dreaming of death, imagine they are angels.

I begin to look more often for those figures
Described in the ancient pages I turn and turn,
Those messengers who linger, seemingly without
Purpose, to gaze indirect at the object of desire.
I once thought they would appear as lovers,
Part of my endless search of earthly ecstasy,
But now I know by the webbed pain about
My heart that they are stern ivory figures
That approximate the form of a severe father,
Or friends lost at war or diving near a coral reef.
Shall I describe their unblinking stare, great
Hands — their cool breath from another domain?

Beneath clouds of mountain ash, gaunt stones lean
And whisper, no longer in outrage at edicts stained

With ink and blood—driven by hate and greed—
Or at lonely seedlings consumed in fire.
Wanderers caught here have sent down fragile roots,
Messages thrust down through fissures of dream,
Forcing up gravestones to mark a chthonic shtetl.
Slabs of lettered time converge on each other.
Feet set in clinging grass, this grave minion
Is finally still, no longer longing for fair place
Among settled peoples – those deaf to pain
And the need of a mountain's marbled page.
What of truth, of love in this field of stone,
As bending limbs descend to whisper *Shalom?*

***6. Tiferet** (Beauty)*

Art elevates us to imagined heights;
The craft of the home reflects heaven's light.

Outside the half dark dome of night closes over us.
Here in our room, light tasks insure rest.
In this little ritual of promise,
We unfold, lift, shake, and tuck,
Smooth out the billowing planes
Of life's sometime grave quilt.
Sheets snap out soft before us,
Then we smoothing fit them
About cloth-and-wood frames
Which lie heavy to the touch.
We will lie secure on them in an hour—
Our forms one in sleep, the bones
Of our dancing dreams intertwined.
Look, the curtains are full of clouds.
Here, in our home, after soft suds swirled
Then slipped down the kitchen drain,
Turn to me, then back, as about the bed's square,
We bend and step in domestic grace,
Partners momentarily apart from
Vast questions — the children's paths
And lesser decisions of age and time.
Beneath us, stirring in the house,
The little ones drift deep in travel,
Calling us on a journey far out the window.
The room fills with soft echoes,
Curtains billow gently, the house sighs.
We sit across, a moment silent, unturning,
Secure with the firm design between us.
The shadow cloud of your hair is loosening.
Your lips are rose petals fragrant as a newborn word.
Inside night's cloak hides the child of truth.
Come let us rest, let our work sleep –
This flooding darkness conceals a sea of light.

7. ***Nezah*** *(Victory)*

Each life is an epic of endurance,
Followed, in faith, by a victorious dance.

O God, how majestic is Your evening sky,
The gold and crimson weave of Your airy mantle
Above the cloud-brushed northern expanse.
The dome of darkening blue is awash
With purple fleece and thunder song.
The wind's great wing sweeps eastward toward morning.
Beneath this star-pierced map of an exploding,
collapsing universe,
Under this great layered growth of time and matter
Only sketched for the earthbound
In the cold words of science,
But veiled in the shroud of cosmic distance –
I seek you everywhere,
Architect of eternity's arch.
Far beneath You I dream,
My eyes strain to fix a mere point in the vast swirl,
The numberless movements above the clouds
As stars emerge — the flickering signature of first fire.
Cool wind sweeps down now
From the mountains to the north
And from your interstellar castle of pure line and point.
Lord of river slide and sea shift
And the earth's ride about the darkening sun,
Accept my restless soul
Into the vast ocean of your burning night,
And lessen the distant eternity
BetweenYour need and my final act.

8. ***Hod*** *(Prophecy)*

Imagine one moment's freedom from doubt —
Endless, enraged curiosity cries out!

Who is honored in Your Presence more,
One who accepts, or questions?
Are my doubts anathema?
Am I wrong to see a new wilderness
In this land of unbearable wealth?
Lord beyond space and time, bring peace
To the forked creatures of Your earth
That we may write Your name with our flights
Into the cold heavens we know and study
As airy fire and artless flow.
Who can blame our longing for a sign?
Would one more proof
For the blind and foolish
Beast struggling below
Separated by so many generations

From Your cleansing fire
Shame Your greatness?
Yet my heart echoes still within,
For I know that just as my soul
Is suffused throughout my flesh,
You are here and within me, everywhere —
In all things, in me, in my questions,
Even in my doubts.

9. *Yesod* (Foundation)

The virtues of knowledgeable surrender
Are cloudy, but what charm they render!

Your silence is familiar now, forgotten
The exact words unspoken as you turned away,
But not the ancient dream in your pain.
These are the facts, but dreams remain the same.
What can beasts strive for in angel arms?
For lithe motion, the clutch and shudder that fight
Against gravity's irresistible pull to the dark?
Golden eyes close; monsters retain the blame.
The world spins, charged by endless dull thrusts:
Whole peoples drift, heads bent, from bed to grave,
Lost in a dark game that once discouraged shame.
        But you, wings arched in silent rapture, shared
        A lunar grace with one who had not cared.

10. *Malkhut* (Kingdom)

Knowledge is lustrous, and teachers know
It increases when shared, to a universal glow.

So let us celebrate the love of this place
We call earth, mind, and form;
The elegant weave of patterned words,
Echoing eternal thought longing for shape;
The light and shade of character and art –
And the vast secret spaces between.
Divine inspiration is the bright bird
Who sings, invisibly darts all through the night,
And wakes the sleeping joy of youth.
She makes the deep promise we long to keep,
Sings the unsettling song that draws us
Ever deeper into the dark wood of bright dream,
Where the truth hides silent — expectant, alone.
Her flight is the first joy we should seek,
The final promise we should keep.

Postlude

Is there redemption, then, in the act of writing
For another, for our selves, for God?

As night gathers and circles gracefully
Through day's deep surface, shaping need,
Carving its heady flight of the heart
Through the cloudy foundation of things,
We ask, can this flight of hands,
This motion of the mind hold flooding emotion
Firm, longer than a short pulse of song?
Can it mold an eternity of final thoughts,
    perhaps forever?
Can it slow the babel of many voices,
Slow them in the name of a moment's truth
And in hope that marks born of need
May record love-becoming-truth
And be more than secondary minutiae
Recorded during long minutes, hours,
Fading days, months, years, decades,
Centuries, millennia?
O Shaper of flow and fire,
Can words then assuage the fear of death?
May They become luminous,
May the people of the book live long
In the vast woven pages of history
And their dear ink be a flood of sharing
To celebrate God's greatest gift—
This world resplendent in first qualities.
And if we find on that page
Our primordial humanity,
Or our double — our Cain, Jonathan,
Or any wrestler by the river —
Or our best, our most brilliant colleague,
The pale mirror of self-realization,
A writing hand in search of justice,
A fabric of nerves pulsing joyous on a screen,
Should we not celebrate that delicate,
Powerful pulse of insistent learning,
The teacher and scholar who researches this world
Resplendent, and records its finest qualities,
The qualities of God and human kind?

The Landscape of Memory

Ann Weiss

In honor of Zev Garber
and
In memory of Stephen Feinstein

This article is dedicated to Professor Zev Garber, a teacher of extraordinary gifts, whose thought-provoking dialectics bring to mind our great Talmudic sages—*Mazel Tov* to you, Zev, for all you have achieved, for all the minds you have opened, and most of all, for the *menschlichkeit* you have added to the world—and to *my* world.

* * *

"We remember *in situ*, when the setting of our memory and the setting of our remembering are one and the same."[1] And in this remembering, aspects of ourselves return to a place where memory began, and to a time when we lived these memories for the first time. We become—if only for an instant—the person who experienced these events for the first time, and saw the world, many lifetimes ago, through eyes that were still innocent.

We are individuals created, not only by DNA and muscle tissue and blood corpuscles, but by the choices we make, by the experiences we have, and by the ways we assimilate our choices, and resultant experiences, into our memory. Or as one of my grad school professors at The Annenberg School for Communications, George Gerbner, often said, "We *are* the stories we tell."[2]

In the case of Shoah memories, as well as pre- and post-Shoah memories, although the DNA may be the same, the people who do the remembering, and the people who originally lived the events remembered, sometimes feel as if they are separate and distinct individuals—the person who lived *before*, whose life had a semblance of innocence, despite elements of antisemitism that may have existed; the one who lived *during* the Shoah, who endured the unimaginable; and then the one who emerged *afterward*, someone who survived the atrocities, and who managed to synthesize a new post-Shoah persona from the old. This "new" person will never be as innocent as the first once was, nor as hopeless as the second may have once felt, but somehow out of the two "lives" that were lived, now a third one emerges—one that knows the worst of what is possible, and chooses to go on living anyway. What brutalities one experienced, how one assimilates past events, and how ones creates a post-Shoah future—these are all matters of one's biography, of individual biology and of personal choice.

Despite moving forward to reconstruct new lives, survivors (and others, of course) describe how the past often penetrates the present, and in extreme cases, how painful memories of the past can sometimes, pervasively and consistently, invade the life of the present. These difficult memories might pollute the life being lived, as in the case studies of Max B. and Hela P., or these difficult memories might function in an opposite, even a positive, direction. The same type of events that immobilize some can, in others, inspire action toward good, as in the impact of memories in the case studies of Maurice S., Mike (Motek) C., and Cvi C.

The Names Not Spoken, the Faces Never Forgotten

Hela P. was a survivor from the Midwest, whom I met at the premiere of my traveling photo exhibition. Because she came from the same region of Poland where many of the photos in my research originated, I hoped we might find photos of her loved ones in my *Eyes from the Ashes* collection, so I asked about her family name growing up—a routine-enough question. I was not prepared for the reaction. A pained expression spread across her face, and between sobs, she explained, "I cannot say their names anymore—even to mention the last name breaks my heart, because it brings bad memories back to me. When I say my family name, I can't help it. I just think of the way they all died."

For Hela, the experience of loss is so profound that more than fifty years post-trauma, even the mention of names of her family of origin still remains too painful to utter. She does not let herself think about the names; she does not let herself think about the loss; she does not let herself, as she explained to me, think about the past. "I live in today. That's what I have. I do not have them anymore."

For her, the matter is simple—but not so simple.

Though she says she does not "live in the past" nevertheless the past, de facto, invades her and, in a very real sense, dominates and even haunts her everyday life. She may not acknowledge the impact of the past, but when a woman bursts into tears at the mention of her family name—no, the *thought* of mentioning her family name—she, in fact, does very much live in the past, but not a past that has been subdued and confronted. Rather she lives in a past—or lives at the effect of the past—that is as present as if she had just crawled out of concentration camp. As Charlotte Delbo, another survivor of Auschwitz, on a similar matter, attests:

> Auschwitz is so deeply etched on my memory that I cannot forget one moment of it. So you are living with Auschwitz? No I live next to it. Auschwitz is there, unalterable, precise, but enveloped in the skin of memory, an impermeable skin that isolates it from my present self. Unlike a snake's skin, the skin of memory does not renew itself.... Thinking about it makes me tremble with apprehension.[3]

Hela's "skin of memory" does not renew itself; it does not need to renew itself because it, in fact, has never receded. Her "skin of memory" wraps her life in a skin of painful recollections that make the mere utterance of her family name too much for her to bear. In Hela's case, it is not only that her bad memories have dominated the good memories of her family, but even more so: the excruciating pain that she still feels at the mention of her family's name is so acutely felt that, in some respects, it has almost obliterated the good memories. I am yet hopeful that sometime before she dies, Hela will be able not only to say her family name, but be able to share the memories of the people they once were—and not only the victims they became.

And then, when I least expected it, Hela made this striking confession: "Even if I cannot say their names, even so, every night before I go to sleep, I try to 'see' their faces, to say goodnight to them. You see, I am the last person in the world who still remembers my parents and sisters and brother. When I am gone, I know there will be no one who remembers their faces!" And so Hela continues, day after day, night after night—both to repress and to reflect, both to remember and to forget. Ultimately, she cannot forget, and despite her inability to say their names out loud, she never can and never will forget.

The inverse experience of Hela is the case of Mickey/Maurice, whose name in Poland was Mendel. He, like Hela, is the lone survivor of his entire family, but unlike Hela, he has made the extraordinary decision to honor the names of his murdered family *every time* someone says his name. "Listen," he explains to me, "I had eleven brothers and sisters. Now I have no one left. I am the only one. So I make the decision that I should take for myself the first letter of every name from my brothers and sisters, and I make for me a new name. [His last name is now the reformulation of his murdered siblings' first initials to form an entirely new name.]"

Contrary to Hela, Maurice wants to "wear" his family's names almost like a crown upon his head. Wherever he is, there, too, are they—almost as if they were standing shoulder to shoulder together. In fact, I was so deeply moved by Maurice's unique way of honoring his murdered family that, a few months ago, when I was giving a speech to a group of survivors, I invited Maurice to join me on stage, in order to say all their names out loud—not only with first initials but in their names' entirety, so that the audience could hear and in the hearing help to honor his family's memory as well. Proudly, after uttering each of their names, he concluded to the audience, "When you say my [last] name, you say *their* names, too!" In defiance, in pride and most of all, in love, Maurice Siidmarc remembers his family, and in his remembering, he enlists others to remember too.[4]

Names remembered. Names suppressed.

If names on their own can haunt or inspire, even more powerful are the memories associated with those names, and the attempt not to remember. Yet it is clear that in the *"un-remembering," there is, in fact, another kind of remembering* deeply the people themselves.

A Bathtub of Tears, with Ham and Cheese on the Side

In the case of Max B., a former yeshiva student whose family owned a chain of well-known department stores in prewar Poland, one is profoundly struck with the radical life changes that took place between Max's prewar and postwar persona.

Before the war, Max lived the life of a deeply observant Jew. The cycle of his years followed the cycle of the Jewish calendar, and every day, as well as all his actions, were bound by the prayers and practices that govern the life of a religious Jew. Max was once an integral part of a large and loving family, of a community, and of a culture that knew exactly what to do, when to do it, and, according to *Halakah* (Jewish law, code of behavior), exactly how to do it. He not only observed all manner of Jewish laws, but in his yeshiva studies, he was devoting his life to the very study of it. As an advanced student, he spent his days and evenings studying Torah, an endeavor to which he was dedicating his present and future life as well. And it was a way of life for which he not only had great aptitude, but it was a way of life that he loved, and to which he not only felt bound but by which he felt nourished and filled: Talmud. Judaism. Parents. Siblings. Torah. Mitzvot. His life was ordered, complete, safe, and satisfying.

Then the war intervened. Not only were his studies interrupted, but his entire concept of life was destroyed as well. During the war, he continued to pray. During the war, he continued to hope. During the war, he continued to believe. But when the war was over, he found himself utterly alone. As he put it, "Now no family, no community, no one!" And now, tragically, his entire belief system had been shattered and together with it his life as well.

Max made the decision, as he told me between his sobs, to "punish G-d the way G-d punished me!" He persevered in his narrative with great difficulty, and although I did not press him, he made it clear he wanted to continue to tell me his story. "I believed so much in G-d and I loved so much mine G-d. I tried to do every mitzvot, every commandment, everything so good how I knew to do. Everything I did was for G-d. And my family—everyone was so good Jews and so good people. Everyone was so religious. Why did G-d do this to me? Why??!!"

And so Max and I sat for an indeterminate time, his questions hanging in the air. There are no adequate answers. And although some may offer philosophical interpretations and some may offer theological explanations, I knew there were no answers adequate for the grieving man sitting before me. Max echoes Rabbi Yitz Greenberg, founder and former director of the National Jewish Center for Learning and Leadership (CLAL), in his oft-repeated words, as Greenberg defiantly challenges "any theology to stand in the face of burning children at Auschwitz."

When Max can speak, halting though it is, he resumes his narrative: Max's wife, a woman I had interviewed for *The Last Album: Eyes from the Ashes of Auschwitz-Birkenau,* strongly urged me to interview her husband because, as she said, "He has an incredible story!"[5] In my view, each life shared is, in its own unique way, "an incredible story," so I not only agreed with her, but even before I met her Max, I affirmed this belief.

In our first interview, in fact, during most of the hours of the afternoon we spent together, Max sobbed. He, like Hela, could not manage to utter the names of his murdered family members without dissolving into tears. He, like Hela, had not been able to make even the semblance of an uneasy peace with his past. His memories, whether expressed out loud or only in his heart, continued to pollute his present.[6] It is not only that he could not escape his past—none of us truly can—but it was the way in which his past interferes so persistently with his present that distinctly marks his painful and defiant response to memory.

Between uncontrollable tears, Max explained to me, with eyes spilling over into a sadness I will never forget, and blurted out to me, "You could fill a bathtub with my tears!"

In the tears shed during our afternoon together, I knew Max could fill a bathtub.

And so could Hela, and so could so many others.

As William Faulkner has rightly said, "The past is never past."

Max and I spent the afternoon together. At the end, I did not learn his family's story—only the sparest of details—but I heard the essence, between his unceasing tears, that after he learned the fate of his family, he never stepped foot into a synagogue again. In fact, Max "bragged" to me: "You know what?!" he said in a tone that was astonishing—not to mention the content, which was equally, if not more, astonishing, especially when considering that these words were being uttered by a former *yeshiva bucher* (yeshiva student). Max continued, "I make it my business to eat a ham and cheese sandwich many times, but *dafka* [he emphasized *dafka,* especially] on Yom Kippur!" He concluded by giving me his justification: "If G-d did this [family murdered] to me, then this is what I will do to G-d!"

It is not over. Not the loss. Not the memories. Not the response. Max continues to "punish" G-d for what G-d did to his family. And in truth, Max continues to punish, not G-d, but Max. Given the frailty of his failing body, it is unlikely that a sense of peace or resolution or even a mild sense of acceptance will ever come to Max before his physical life is over. Not with the bathtub of tears he has already, and continues still to fill.

Being an optimist, however, I continue to hope. In the meantime, Max eats his ham sandwiches, waiting for Yom Kippur, *dafka,* to eat especially then. And, further, he affirmed that if he *were* able to step into a synagogue (something he brags he has never done since the war ended, and learned that his entire family was murdered), it would be so that he could step onto the *bimah,* which is where he would most want to eat his ham and cheese sandwich on Yom Kippur this year.

The memories of loss and love that penetrate Max's ham sandwich also propel him to believe that he must "punish" G-d for the rest of his life. His actions have had the net effect, of course, of singularly punishing Max himself, and continuing to hold him hostage to his past and to his unending pain. Despite his happy current life, despite his lovely wife and home and friends, and the outer trappings of a good life—which he certainly has, and in fairness, it is clear that in many ways Max seems quite buoyant—there is also another level, a very deep core level, at which Max remains a prisoner not only of his memories, but also ultimately of his devastating aloneness at having survived when his beloved family did not.

The sense of loss that adversely marks the lives, and memories, of Max and Hela can be the very catalyst that also positively fuels the lives of other survivors.

Take the example of Motek (Mike) Cukier. His childhood wartime experiences were so devastating that, for the rest of his life, they might easily have immobilized him. It would not be difficult to understand how his trauma might have subsequently destroyed his future sense of happiness, purpose, peace, and equilibrium. But it did not. Instead, the trauma he suffered during the war, and the complete loss of his family, inversely served as an inspiration for the rest of his life. Here's his story, told in his own words, of the central pivotal event in his life, and of the terrible circumstances during which he lost his entire family. Known as Mike in America (I continue to call him Motek, the name from his childhood by which he was known), he remembers:

> We were such a nice family. Everybody loved everybody. We were happy together and we always tried to help each other. When Hitler came, we didn't know what to do. By this time, it was already too late to escape. But my mother had a plan. She said we have to stay together. No matter what, we must stay together. My mother said it so many times; we knew just what we were supposed to do.

> When we were taken away, my little sister was taken away with my mother, and I was taken away with my father—so I was with the men. But then they made the selection. "This way, this way, this way, that way." I was only a small boy, so I was sent to the side with the old men and the little boys. I was just a little boy. But they sent my father to the other side, the side with the workers.
>
> I was put on a big truck with the other ones who were going to be taken away. I could see my father in the other group. I remembered my mother's words. "Stay together, no matter what else." I tried to find the way to come to my father. Now I could not see him anymore, but I knew where he was standing before. I had to get to my father, but I could not find him.
>
> The trains were in-between us and there were so many people, I just couldn't see him. I was scared, but I knew only one thing: I heard in my head my mother's words, "Stay together!" My mother's words were all I knew what to do.
>
> So even if I was scared, I knew what I must to do. I was a good boy and I always listened to my parents. I was little, so nobody noticed when I slipped myself off the back of the big truck and smuggled myself into the big crowd. Everything was so confused that they didn't notice me. I was pushed and almost squashed, but I succeeded to get to my father's side. I still could not find him but I knew he must be somewhere here, near to me.
>
> Then suddenly I found him! I saw him at the same moment when he saw me. I will never forget this moment when I understood that all was lost! My father did the same thing, like I did. My father also listened to my mother!
>
> While I was smuggling myself to my father, my father was smuggling himself to me. I saw his face the last time on the truck. We both did the "right" thing by listening to my mother—it was the reason I lived. It was the reason he died! He left the side of the workers and came to my side so I would not be alone! We both did the "right" thing—but it turned out so wrong!

As Motek tells this devastating story of each one trying to reach the other, there is profound sadness in his voice, in his eyes. It is the only time in our multihour discussion that his voice cracks. And then, as if answering a question I did not even dare to ask, he explains, "It's the reason I have to make my life count. I am here and my family is not. I have to live more, I mean, I have to try to help other people more, like it would be if my family was here."

And help he does. Beyond making a good life with (and for) his wife and children, Motek has devoted the last part of his life to helping to improve the lives of Israeli troops. For many years, he has chosen to provide comfort for soldiers, and to do anything he can conceive to make their lives easier. He hosts special events for the soldiers of IDF/Israeli Defense Forces, big banquets; he gives them beautiful gifts by the thousands (I saw—and was given—one of the monogrammed pens that looked like a Mont Blanc); and in any way, in fact, in *every* way, Motek tries to "repay the debt of my life." Far from being immobilized by memories—devastating though they may be—Motek continues to find ways to let the horror inspire him to do more good, and more good, and more good. The rate of interest on his years of doing mitzvot to honor the memory of his murdered, loving family compounds not yearly, but daily.

In a similar way, Cvi Cukierman took the murder of his family, a tragedy that defines his life, to become the positive motivation for the rest of his life that followed. Cvi, like the other survivors discussed, was also the sole survivor of his family. Cvi, like the others, had every reason to let pain or bitterness dominate his actions, but unlike Hela and Max, and very much like Motek and Maurice, he did not. Instead he found ways to honor his murdered family's memory in ways that were both public and private.

Cvi Cukierman, of blessed memory, was a man I interviewed multiple times over the course of ten years. He was both a valuable informant to my research on *The Last Album* and he, with his family, became treasured friends. Cvi and I spoke about many subjects, but the central thread running through all discussions was the strand of memory: the town of Bendin, his friends, his school, how his family celebrated Shabbat and holidays (always together) and most of all, funny, touching, personal tales of the Cukierman family.

The past was never past with Cvi, so no matter what subject may have started our discussions, we always returned to the subject of his murdered family. Yet, in Cvi's stories, his family was not dead.

In Cvi's narratives, and in fact, in Cvi's mind (not that he was confused or could ever forget that they were dead), nevertheless, Cvi almost always chose to remember his family in their vibrant prewar lives, lives that continued to exert a positive and powerful force on Cvi's life—even from the ashes.

Here's what I mean:

In prewar Bendin, Cvi was part of a large, loving, and well-known family—a family known as much for their good actions as for their good baking.[7] The Cukierman family owned the most famous pastry shop in town, Gayle Rifkele (Blond Rebecca) and it was a place much discussed by many survivors during the course of my multiyear interviews. One of the most treasured memories was Cvi's recounting the family's Sabbath ritual, during which all the siblings (Cvi's father Moshe was the oldest sibling who, though living in the neighboring town of Katowice, always brought his family back to Bendin to be together with the other Cukiermans), their spouses, all the children, parents, aunts, uncles, grandparents came together for every Sabbath, every weekend of their prewar lives to the home of Herschel and Rifkeleh (Cvi's paternal grandparents) in Bendin. Cvi explains:

> I come from a family who knows a lot about love and a lot about helping. We spent every Shabbat together but before we put one morsel in our mouths, my grandmother Rifkeleh had baskets prepared, heaped high with food, and she called us to her. "Here," she said, "is a piece of paper with a name and an address. Go to this house and bring the basket. Knock on the door and then, quick, go away."
>
> You know why she told us to go away quickly? So the people who didn't have enough money to buy the food for Shabbes would not be humiliated. We were to bring the food to them and go away before they came to the door. Then all the grandchildren would return home. Then and only then—after the poor people had their food—only then would our family begin to eat our food. This was our minchag [ritual] every Shabbes. It was beautiful for everyone—not just for them (the people who got the baskets) but for all of us![8]

In his recollections, Cvi highlights the deep love between family members, and also the sense of communal responsibility to make sure that the poorer families in town would also have some delicious food for the Sabbath. It was a value that was inculcated, deeply and well, in each of the Cukiermans.

When the war ended, and Cvi found himself alone, he vowed to make a new life and create a new family. As sole survivor of his nuclear family, Cvi tried to replant the values of his family of origin into the new family he created with his wife, Minna, who was also a Shoah survivor, and also sole survivor of her family. Together, they started a new life and started to create a new family.

In addition to his family, his work as chief hospital administrator of his city, K'far Saba, Cvi also displayed a profoundly affecting commitment to Israel. After the war, Cvi got himself aboard a boat bound for prestate Israel, and when the ship was detained by the British and sent back to Cypress (where the rest of the passengers then remained waiting for over a year), Cvi jumped off the other side of the boat with two friends and, under cover of night, swam to shore near Tel Aviv. Halutzim (pioneers) were waiting on shore to help anyone who had taken the chance. In an instant, the wet swimmers were outfitted in dry clothing, so that when the British searched, which they always did, they could not find the men, among them Cvi, who had jumped off the ship.

Though weak and exhausted, Cvi and his friends immediately began to fight to establish and preserve this fledgling entity. Though it was not yet a state, this Palestine/prestate Israeli entity had already become central to Cvi and the others. He immediately began to fight in the Palmach under the command of Yizhak Rabin, "a very good commander," Cvi affirmed. When I asked Cvi why he had risked his life so many times to save others, especially during the Siege of Jerusalem, Cvi explained, "Without Israel, we have nothing. Look what they did to us in Europe. Look how the world watched and did nothing. Now we have a land, now we have *our own* land."

He almost paraphrased Golda Meir's old quote: "What do we have that the Arabs don't? Nowhere else to go!"

As much as he liked to remember—and as much as Cvi took comfort in the act of remembering—that is how much his wife refused to look back, at least publicly, and she felt only pain when asked about her past prewar life. "What's the point?" Minna would answer whenever I asked about her prewar life and family. "What's the point to speak about it? They are all gone. I am alone. I have a new life. I don't look back." Hers is another way of remembering by not remembering—or at least, not remembering out loud.

In Cvi's determined dedication to remember, contrasted with his wife's determined dedication *not* to remember, they represent opposite poles of the same experience.

Memory does not disappear because one refuses to speak about the past, nor does it infiltrate one's present life any less—even if one chooses not to speak of the people lost or the experiences once cherished. The language of memory is insidious. With words or without words, adequate or inadequate, memory persists. With acknowledgment of its impact or without acknowledgment, its impact continues to be felt. Sometimes, Memory's most powerful language is simply Silence.

The Geography of Memory

Memory is tied to place, not simply to the events that occurred in a particular place. It is my view that geography, itself, is a foundation of memory, and it is the sense of being grounded in a specific place that often situates our memories in a particular location and in a particular sense of time. As Plank aptly explains,

> A sense of place inhabits us. Like the migration of natural life, our memory knows a homing, an impulse to belong not only to a time, but to a place deeply our own. We remember, as pilgrims seeking in regions of lived experience, the site where healing occurs and truth is impaired: the healing of broken communities whose rupture has made us strangers in familiar lands; the truth about ourselves, our origins and destination.
>
> (L)oss marks the beginning of memory, a narrative turned toward that place where we know, if only tacitly, who we are. Memory turns homeward.[9]

At our very first meeting, and for years of our discussions that followed, Cvi spoke of a similar sense of home and identity, which was always linked in his mind to the memory of his family and to his own sense of self. I learned of Cvi's existence in Detroit, ironically, from a survivor who *never* (she was emphatic about the fact that she never) attended Holocaust programs but somehow, inexplicably, she came to my speech and photo exhibition premiere. She told me about Cvi, her good friend in Israel, who was the last living member of the beloved Cukierman family. When I arrived in Israel a week later, I went directly to his house and brought Cvi sixty prewar photos of his long-since murdered family; they were the only Cukierman photos in existence. Surrounded by loving family, eyes filled with tears, Cvi blurted, "Now I can show my family *who I am*. Now I can show them *who I come from! And now I can die a rich man!*"

Even without photos, Lunia Backenroth Gartner Weiss, my mother, of blessed memory, was able to create "emotional" pictures with her stories so vivid, laced with details so vibrant, that we could almost "see" the places and people she described. Because her memories were so deeply rooted in the particularity of place—both geographical places like the strawberry patch, as well as the interior geography of the heart—there was a specificity in her remembering that countered the abstractness into which memory can dissolve.

> At distance, memory may become abstract. . . . In return, the true particularity of place counters the impulse to nostalgia or self- interest by keeping before us a reality that is other and more than simply our mental construction of it.
>
> We are identified, and more fundamentally claimed, by our locations of loss.[10]

Lunia took her "locations of loss" and populated them with the people who belonged there. Never disconnected from reality, she nevertheless allowed her sumptuous memories of love help her "return" in memory to a place of normalcy and family—and with her remarkable gift of narratology, to share these memories with her family, especially her daughters and granddaughters.

Similar to Cvi, Lunia sought to integrate her past with her present. And like Cvi and Hela and Motek and Maurice and Max, Lunia, too, is the sole survivor of her family of origin. She was raised in a large and illustrious family. In addition, they were known for their Torah scholarship and for their generous philanthropy. The family (on her mother's Backenroth side) owned oil wells in Schodnica, in the foothills of the Carpathian Mountains, where Lunia spent four months a year (three months in summer and one month in the winter to ski, with her mother, brother, and mother's extended family, while her father came on weekends, after work, as was the practice of many husbands), and (on her father's Gartner side), the family owned lumber and steel enterprises in Stryj, where she spent the remainder of the year, with her parents, brother, and father's extended family.

Although all her family of origin and most of the rest of her extended family were murdered by the Nazis, with, I might add, much enthusiastic assistance from their Ukrainian neighbors, for Lunia—in the essence of whom they were—they remained very much alive.

She felt her family "protected" her when doctors told her she only had six months left to live;[11] she felt they "knew" somehow, or that the essence of their souls knew about the children and grandchildren she had and about the *naches* she *schepped* (pride she had) in them. True or not, this powerful sense of love she felt for her cherished family, a love that transcended bounds of logic or physics, somehow kept Lunia's family *close* to her for the rest of her life. In a sense, although in one (real) sense, she was alone, in fact, in her belief, she was not—because her love for family kept her murdered family close, and kept Lunia, at least in her own heart, loved and "sheltered" in their protection.

Although the actual people had long since been murdered (her parents, her only sibling, a younger brother, her grandparents, almost all aunts and uncles and cousins), nevertheless, she felt as if her loved ones—especially her parents and brother—somehow kept "watch" over her. And as a result of their sense of "present-ness," in her life, she felt their love throughout the rest of her life, and conversely, she transmitted this sense of love to her family.

The stories she told, except when specifically asked about their deaths, which she always answered in age-appropriate ways, were the stories of her life, filled with love and hope, told with a sense of adventure and her ever-present optimism. She laced her stories with vivid details—like the cream-colored damask wallpaper in her grandparents' dining room, whose pattern of delicate spring flowers was matched by the pattern on the dining-room chairs—and she filled our childhood with stories of hope and goodness and love, populated by the people she loved, and who loved her. It was almost as if we *knew* the people she loved, except for the fact that they had been killed long before we were born, a big "except" to be sure, because of the vividness of her stories and the specificity of the pictures she painted with her words. Her memories of life and people were so positive and so loving that, in her tender, funny, nuanced remembering, they continue to live—even now, after Lunia has also died.

We are a people based on memory. As the great Jewish scholar Martin Buber (1932) affirmed when writing about prewar Jews in Germany, "We are a community, and our community is based upon memory. And it is our common memory that has kept us together and enabled us to survive."[12] These words are true, whether speaking about Jews struggling to remain human under Hitler's barbaric coda or Jews struggling to remain Jewish under vicious Roman rule. When a people are not afforded the dignity of freedom—not only freedom of religion but even the basic human right to live out their lives—one understands, better and deeper, the fuller meaning of Buber's words.

Approaches to Shoah Memory

> We the survivors, ankle-deep in our memories, carry an unwilling legacy imprinted on the cells of our minds, embedded in each of our heartbeats: talk of the unspeakable, spread the word of the unbelievable! The survivors of inhumanity to their fellow humans, of the endless variations of perverted physical tortures and diabolical permutations of psychological torments.[13]

The Holocaust affected each person differently, and from each person's experience, we can learn something of value. From some survivors, like Vera Laska above and Maurice and Motek, we learn of the overwhelming burden and responsibility of memory. From other survivors, like Lunia and Cvi, who consistently chose to emphasize the good (while not forgetting the horror), we see how memories of dead family members can coexist comfortably and lovingly with current life and current (living) family members. And there is another class of survivor, like Max and Hela, who consistently and relentless remembers the horror; as if their modus operandi is to "be the chroniclers of . . . inhumanity . . . and . . . of perverted physical tortures . . . and [of] diabolical . . . psychological torments."[14]

Remembering Death and Remembering Life

This approach to trauma, which places its full emphasis almost exclusively on the horror, is important to note both in itself and because of its implications. This class of survivor puts the emphasis, not simply on memory—as if "memory" could ever be described as "simple"—but on the *horror* of the memory. These survivors, who filter the world principally through the brutality of their past life experiences, find it difficult to escape the trauma of the past, and, in a sense, remain forever prisoner to it. To paraphrase the devastating passage in Jean Amery's *At the Mind's Limit* "Torture" essay, "Once tortured, you are always tortured," because, as he affirms, whenever you remember the torture, it is as if you are still there being tortured again. And furthermore, there is rich data—some of it from the Transcending Trauma Research Project of which I am a member—to suggest that the impact of trauma is never over, and that in certain families, the trauma of the parents is passed to the next generation, and the next.[15] Similarly, the transmission from survivor to successive generations can also be one of optimism and other-directedness, love and hope—that too can transcend trauma.

Approaches to Shoah memory, as we have seen, are as extreme as Lasko's view that you must remember relentlessly, and that you can do nothing without remembering the horror. Other views, represented more closely by Cvi and Lunia who keep memory of the past as a constant companion, but it is a memory born of love and comfort, not only nightmare and fear.

And of course, there are still other survivors who try never to remember, like Max and Mina and Hela, who try to push away thoughts of the past. Or failing to fully block these thoughts, nevertheless, they refuse to mention or share their past in utterances—either to their children or to others. From them, one never hears a memory, a random thought, or even a stray word about the Shoah.[16] There have even been extreme examples of people I have met, like Hela, whereby any mention of the past is too painful—even the memory of loved ones, *especially* the memory of loved ones.

I met a middle-aged child of survivors who, when he heard about my work, confessed that his survivor father could not utter one word about the past—not about the Shoah, not about the times before the Shoah. And then the man standing before me at a social gathering disclosed this shocking fact,

> The only thing I know about my father's life is the names—because I and my siblings are named after his murdered family— and the only other thing, from the whole life of his family, my father shared only one other fact: how the wooden handrail on the steps of his house felt under his hand. Smooth. This is the only thing I know about my father's past, that the wooden handrail was smooth—I know it isn't much, but it's all I have—so I hold onto this detail.

Memory is both cultural and personal, embedded both in the society and in the soul. When one loses a home, the memory of that home still invades us and haunts us. And when one loses the people we love most deeply, and who loved us most deeply, that memory is determinative, I conjecture, of how we will continue to live.

In the case of Hela and Max, the memory of, and grief for, their loved ones has cast a pall over the rest of their lives, despite outward trappings of success and contentment. Scratch the surface only a little and their floodgate of tears opens, and their unfinished grieving is exposed. In the case of Motek and Maurice and Cvi and Lunia, on the other hand, the love for their murdered families has never ended, but the grieving has progressed to a degree that it can be confronted without the excruciating pain experienced by Max and Hela at the very utterance of their murdered family's names. For Lunia, Cvi, Motek, and Maurice, grieving has been transformed to a process of remembering their loved ones with acts of caring and *mitzvot* (good deeds, righteous actions) to honor the memory of the dead.

Memory explores the ways we remember, both collectively as a culture and personally as individuals. The linkage between memory and personal history creates a framework for understanding how we remember, what we remember, what we choose to forget, and what our memories say about our lives. In addition, memory helps to frame the way we see our lives, as well as the way others see us. In considering Shoah memories, that is, the intimate memories of survivors remembering their lives before, during, and after the war years of 1939–45, the range of approaches, above, only begins to explore points on the continuum. There is enough left over yet for a lifetime of exploration.

Memory and Eternity

The great Hasidic master, Reb Nachman of Bratslaw, spoke about Memory in another way. Memory is not only what keeps people together as a group, but Reb Nachman said that it is through Memory that we are linked to the Eternal.

But how can we remember that of which we have no memory at all?

We were not at Sinai, yet our liturgy exhorts us to feel as if we were there. We were not in the desert wandering for forty years, nor actually slaves in Egypt, yet we are encouraged to "feel" the truth of each story, to experience it as if we were enslaved and freed. And in a symbolic yet significant way, when we consider ways we have been shackled and enslaved in our own lives—and the ways we have tried to break free—we indeed have been there.

Some would ask, "Why remember at all?"

In closing, I would like to turn to Elie Wiesel, who offers both a question (in true Jewish tradition), and posits an answer: "Is is not [human nature] to push aside memories that hurt and disturb us? The more cruel the wound, the greater the effort to cover it. . . . All we can do is remember. [But] how does one remember and communicate an event filled with so much fear and darkness and mystery that it negates language and imagination?"[17] I give the last word to Elie in sharing with you the answer he suggests:

> We *must* tell the tale. We tell it not to divide people but, on the contrary, to bring them together, not to inflict more suffering but, on the contrary, to diminish it, not to humiliate anyone but, on the contrary, to teach others to humiliate no one. That is why we bear witness.[18]

Notes

Note: Survivor interview excerpts are from the Ann Weiss archive, conducted between 1986 and 2007, including Helga P., Maurice S., Max B., Motek C., and Cvi C.

1. Plank, "The Survivor's Return," 264.
2. George Gerbner was dean emeritus of The Annenberg School for Communications in Philadelphia and is credited by many with creating the field of Communications as an academic discipline. In his later years, he founded the Cultural Environmental Movement, which examined the influence of media on culture and society, pointing out that it was the vast global industrial complex that determined what media prevailed. Most significantly, Gerbner is known for his worldwide research linking the amount and degree of television viewing with the amount and degree of an individual's feelings of ease and safety (or lack thereof) in society and in the cultural milieu. A personal note: He granted me access to Annenberg's sophisticated editing equipment and studio in order to make my first film, *Eyes from the Ashes of Auschwitz-Birkenau*—an experience that led directly to my graduate degree in communications. An émigré from Czechoslovakia, Gerbner was a well-known poet in prewar Europe and once Hitler came to power, he fled to America when his antifascist activities made it dangerous for him to remain in Europe.
3. These words come from Charlotte Delbo's scathing account of Auschwitz, published as *Auschwitz and After*. Its most devastating section, in my estimation, is entitled, "None of Us Will Return," from which this excerpt is taken (xi).
4. Although full names of many interview subjects have been withheld, the full name of Siidmarc is named here as a way of further honoring Maurice's murdered family. His name is now composed of the initials (underlined) of his murdered siblings' names: Sara, Yacob, Yosef (Note: these *Y*s have been written as *I*s), Mordechai Dov, Menashe, Abram Kalman, Rachel, and Cirle (pronounced Tzirel), hence Siidmarc. Maurice also mentioned that his mother, Henna, died when he was only nine—Maurice, born June 20, 1929, was the fifth son—and his father, Eliyahu Israel, married his mother's sister, Zisl, with whom he had another two little children, a boy named Jonah and a girl named Lealeh. The original name of the family was Skoczylis, and as Maurice said, "Our name had a lot of *yichis* [honor, respect, prestige] not only before the war, but during the war, very much. My older brothers, Abram Kalman and Mordechai Dov, saved the Torah when the synagogue was destroyed, and we kept it in a credenza in our house. When my father took it out every

Shabbes [Sabbath] and holiday, people kept guard at both ends of the street, to warn everybody, in case a policeman should come."

5. Weiss, *The Last Album.*
6. It should be noted, however, that on the surface Max's life looks, and in fact *is*, very good. He met me at the door in his tennis whites, having finished some satisfying time on the courts. He has a breathtakingly beautiful wife whom he adores, and who obviously adores him, and he has a cadre of warm and loving friends. The couple lives in an exquisite condominium on an upper floor of a beautiful and prestigious community complex, overlooking an unobscured view of the ocean. By all common measures, Max lives not only a good life, but he lives an *extremely* good life—and yet, it is clear that his past still invades his present, in a way that compromises the peace of his current life.
7. Bendin is the Yiddish form of the Polish city, Bedzin, located in southcentral Poland.
8. Translated from Yiddish discussions with Cvi, by Ann Weiss. (There has been some minor paraphrasing in the translation in order to make the Yiddish conform better to the English.)
9. Plank, "The Survivor's Return," 263.
10. Ibid., 264.
11. When I was in fourth grade and my younger sister was in kindergarten, my mother was diagnosed with breast cancer that had already spread to her lymph nodes. The doctor told my mother, "Listen, Lucy, you have only six months to live. This is my best advice to you since I know it's important for you to raise your children as Jews: Find a nice Jewish woman to raise your daughters." My mom's response, as she explained to me many years later when I was an adult: "I tried and I tried, but I couldn't find anyone good enough, so I had to stay and do it myself!" She did—and lived to see both her granddaughters celebrate their Bat Mitzvahs, even dancing a vigorous *hora* at both *simchas* (happy events).
12. Buber, *Syllabus for the School for Jewish Youth.*
13. Laska, ed., *Women in the Resistance and in the Holocaust,* 39.
14. Ibid.
15. Research findings of Dan Bar-On, Julia Chaitin, Yael Danieli, and Joel Dimsdale, included among them.
16. "Alexithymia, the inability to find words to describe the traumatic events or anything related to them, as a reaction to overwhelming trauma, is common among some survivors, especially those whose capacity to process cognitively, verbally, and emotionally was overwhelmed by the sheer onslaught of pain and loss," explains Dr. Reinhild Muenke, whose clinical practice includes many survivors of trauma. For further information, please consult van der Kolk, McFarlane, and Weisaeth, eds., *Traumatic Stress.*
17. Elie Wiesel, "Let Us Tell Tales," opening address at International Symposium on the Holocaust, Cathedral of St. John the Divine, New York, June 3, 1974.
18. Ibid.

Bibliography

Survivor interview excerpts from the Ann Weiss archive, conducted between 1986 and 2007, including Helga P., Maurice S., Max B., Motek C., and Cvi C.

Bar-On, Dan. *Fear and Hope: Life-Stories of Five Israeli Families of Holocaust Survivors, Three Generations in a Family.* Cambridge: Harvard University Press, 1995 (in English, German, Hebrew, and Chinese).

———. *The Indescribable and the Undiscussible: Reconstructing Human Discourse after Trauma.* Budapest, Hungary: Central European University Press, 1999.

Buber, Martin. *Syllabus for the School and Jewish Youth.* Berlin, 1932.

Delbo, Charlotte. *Auschwitz and After: None of Us Will Return: Useless Knowledge; Measure of Our Days.* New Haven: Yale University Press, 1995.

Laska, Vera, ed. *Women in the Resistance and in the Holocaust: The Voices of Eyewitnesses.* Westport, Conn.: Greenwood Press, 1983.

Plank, Karl A. "The Survivor's Return: Reflections on Memory and Place." *Judaism* 38, no. 3 (Summer 1989): 263–77.

van der Kolk, Besses, Alexander McFarlane, and Lars Weisaeth, eds. *Traumatic Stress: The Effects of Overwhelming Experience on Mind, Body and Society.* New York: Guilford Press, 1996.

Weiss, Ann. *The Last Album: Eyes from the Ashes of Auschwitz-Birkenau.* New York: W. W. Norton, 2001; rev. expanded ed., Philadelphia: Jewish Publication Society, 2005.

Wiesel, Elie. "Let Us Tell Tales." Opening address at International Symposium on the Holocaust, Cathedral of St. John the Divine, New York, June 3, 1974.

Part 6

Zionism and Hebrew Studies

Hebrew Literature, Academic Politics, and Feminist Criticism

A Confessional Essay

Esther Fuchs

Introduction: The Personal Is Political

To what extent can we draw on our personal and professional narratives as a valid source of knowledge in order to substantiate a critique of our respective academic fields? How can we possibly crosscut from a subjective to a critical discourse, from emotion to fact and back? The following attempt to account for the unusual relationship between "my self" and "my work," and between "my work" and "my field" will be partial both epistemologically and chronologically. The possessive pronoun in "my life" suggests ownership and control; yet, it is precisely the relinquishment of this control that I would like to exercise in this writing, opting instead to free-associate about the early stage of my career in Hebrew literature. This free association will comprise select events, filtered through selective memory work with references to a few select texts that I produced over the years. As Rachel Blau DuPlessis articulated the challenges of confessional critical writing: "No innocence in the autobiographical. What with its questions of saying 'I' and the issue 'what I' and how that 'I' negotiates with various selves: and the question how much (a lot) is unsaid or repressed—with resistance to the cheerful 'my'—the I here is very precise, yet more than half unspeakable."[1]

But if the "I" is unspeakable, if autobiography is one of several fictions of the self, is not the marker "a feminist literary critic" equally ambiguous despite its implication of representation? Does not the tentative construction of the subject empty the "feminist" adjective of political meaning? If feminism suggests a political resistance to a gender-related social and epistemological hegemony, can it accommodate an indeterminate, even contradictory definition of subjectivity? And just what do I refer to by "gender"? Am I using this term as a marker for the power relationship between men and women, or as a complex web of discursive and social performances that constitute all speaking subjects?[2] In what follows I would like to use my autobiographical fragment as a critique of power/knowledge relations in the Hebrew literary academe, though mine may very well turn out to be an ex-centric story. If ex-centric, how can my narrative serve a critical position regarding the entire field of Hebrew literature, or even the American branch of the field as it was practiced in the early 1980s? "Can feminist theory be postmodernist and still retain an interest in emancipation?"

For the purposes of the present essay, I will use Benhabib's concept of "situated criticism," which in my understanding refers to subject, agency, and selfhood, as a locus from which to question social hierarchies and discursive hegemonies.[3] Specifically, I will use the concept of "situated criticism" to help me read "my life" in the context of Hebrew literary academic politics, to read my personal crisis as the price of my engagement with feminist criticism at the "wrong" place and time. I would like to think of my situated criticism as "a fluid interaction in constant motion and open to alteration by self-analyzing practice."[4] With Nancy Miller I would suggest that autobiography is a genre of personal writing, and personal writing, despite its reflexive performance, is best understood as an embodied kind of cultural criticism.[5] The recognition of the authority of experience and the interdependence of the personal and the political are two prevalent themes in feminist theory, as Miller reminds us.

Formalist Beginnings and the Politics of Interpretation

I did not begin my literary critical career with feminist theory. The topic of my dissertation was the Nobel Prize laureate S. Y. Agnon, a daunting subject for a young PhD because of the literary complexity of his work, the scope of his writings, and the enormous scholarship, notably in Hebrew, on his work. When I began to write in the mid-1970s, there were several women critics who undertook to read portions of Agnon's work, but only male critics, like Baruch Kurzweil, Dov Sadan, Shmuel Wereses, Gershon Shaked, Baruch Hochman, Arnold Band, and Dan Miron dared undertake an overview of his work *in toto*. Little if anything has been written about the fact that the 1970s was the first decade to allow women literary critics into the field of Hebrew literature. It would take another two decades before any woman critic would be recognized as a serious player in this male-dominated field.

Unaware of the politics of gender and the production of knowledge, my goal was to demonstrate that Agnon was a modernist whose Talmudic erudition often masked revolutionary sensibilities. I rejected the polarization of Agnon as construed by Arnold Band among others.[6] "Nightmare and nostalgia" was a false dichotomy, I argued, that sought to domesticate Agnon as a naïve romantic traditionalist. I argued that Agnon's pious writing, notably his novel *Bridal Canopy*, was a modernist posture, shot through with ironic references to self-contradictory rationalizations of the humiliations of Jewish exile. I argued that Agnon's apparent nostalgia for the Jewish religious past was nothing less than a subversive parody through which he sought to expose the flaws and fissures in the naïve interpretation of the ancestral past. My formalist approach to Agnon was obviously political in its implications. By rejecting the traditionalist construction of the author I questioned the nationalist construction of his oeuvre. Agnon's ironic presentations of the Diasporic past, as well as of the pioneering present, and above all his self-irony ought to have disrupted any critical metanarrative that sought to domesticate him as a national(ist) writer. Nationalism as such has never been particularly notable for its self-irony.[7]

I published my first book on S. Y. Agnon in 1985. My second book, on Agnon's use of self-irony as a thematic, structural, and poetic principle, was published in 1987.[8] In the final chapter of the first book and throughout the second I focus on Agnon's shift from satiric inversion to a sort of self-reflexive, modernist (perhaps even postmodernist) destabilization of narrative conventions and linguistic rules. Throughout the book I work with the concept of "grotesque" and the principle of "irony of irony" as a sort of stylistic *mise-en-abime* of ironic reversals, where the ironic game of distorting mirrors ends in a return to the inescapable arbitrariness of language as a paradoxical medium of communication. If my first book is a deconstruction of Agnon's interpretation as an author of "nostalgia" on the one hand and "nightmare" on the other, my second book is a postmodern reading of his modernist *Book of Deeds*, "Edo and Enam" and "Ad Olam" as well as his so-called traditionalist magnum opus, *Bridal Canopy*.

Feminist Criticism in the Early 1980s

In the late 1970s, after the acceptance of my doctoral dissertation at Brandeis University, I began reading the classic feminist publications in social and literary theory. Virginia Woolf, Kate Millett, and Simone de Beauvoir asked questions that have not been raised within the limited realm of Hebrew literary criticism. I became aware of feminist challenges to and transformations of formalist approaches to the literary text and to aesthetic construction of literary canons. In the 1980s I was hired as assistant professor of Hebrew literature at the University of Texas in Austin. In the brown-bag seminars sponsored by the small Women's Studies program Jane Marcus spoke about Marxist feminism and the need for materialist analysis, and Gayatri Chakravorty Spivak spoke about postcolonialism and the radical implications of Derridean analysis. The possibility of asking political questions of literary texts was nothing less than exhilarating to me. The gender of the writing agent as interpretive clue, indeed a critical approach, was unheard of in my field. Tentatively I began to ask feminist questions of what I proceeded to define as "mythogynous texts" written from androcentric perspectives. The hostility and aggression I witnessed in response to the early papers I delivered in the early 1980s at the national conferences of the Association of Jewish Studies in Boston left an indelible mark on me. In subsequent years I avoided going to these conferences for fear of being attacked and degraded.

During that period the number of feminist papers in any Jewish Studies discipline was small. It would take at least another decade before a women's caucus was organized at the association. The isolation was crushing, but did not prevent me from publishing my essays in both Women's Studies and Jewish Studies journals. Gradually the main thesis of my book began to materialize for me: women have been depicted as national outsiders, as alien to the body politic, as subversive and dangerous enemies. Male-created female characters—or what I referred to in a more condensed neologism as "gyniconologies"—embodied moral emptiness and ideological atrophy, the lack of consciousness and the absence of conscience. Years later, the very same critics who rejected my work in the early 1980s would go on to become the benevolent and protective mentors and advisors of young feminist PhD candidates. Within a decade, the vitriolic response to my work in the early 1980s would be all but forgotten, and a much more reassuring historiography regarding a general openness on the part of male critics to feminist criticism would win the day. But in the introduction to my book, eschewing any details, I would simply write: "the feminist critic in Hebrew literature is an Other, one who is both alien and dismissible."[9] But the greatest disappointment was yet to come as conferences on feminist Jewish scholarship in general, and feminist Hebrew literary criticism would include male "authorities" on women poets, and anthologies would include the work of male critics who have quietly replaced those of us who have been silenced and erased.[10]

Academic Politics

The scholars whose work I criticized in my book were the heads of the few doctoral programs in Hebrew literature in the United States, while I had little to offer to a younger generation of PhDs, because my university was a state school in Arizona, and because my program did not offer a graduate degree. The leaders of the field continued to determine who were the viable candidates for a doctoral degree, who would receive scholarships, and who would be promoted. Though I was promoted to associate professor in 1985, most of the Hebrew feminist scholars were still working to secure tenure and promotion, and could not compete with the academic prestige the fathers of the field could offer to assistant professors and PhD candidates. What Jane Gallop describes in another context as a theoretical seduction transpired in Hebrew literary criticism as an academic seduction: the fathers of the field seduced and have been seduced by their feminist daughters.[11] The introduction to *Gender and Text in Modern Hebrew and Yiddish Literature* dismisses the feminist critique of Hebraic literary history as an "easy task," indicting it as simplistic and reductive. Yet, the exposure of patriarchal bias in literature, or "sexual politics" has been as productive and creative a force in feminist literary theory as "textual politics."[12]

While in other literatures feminist critique is regarded as a vital approach, or as vital as gynocriticism, or the focus on women's writing, in Hebrew literature the former has become since the early 1990s suspect. Yet, synthesizing both approaches into a coherent feminist theory and methodology was one of my main objectives in *Israeli Mythogynies.* I suggested that Amalia Kahana-Carmon's fiction was a challenge to A. B. Yehoshua's and Amos Oz's dehumanizing mythogynies. I argued that her heroines were in a way "speaking back" at the female gyniconologies created by the leading male authors of the "New Wave" generation. In 1998 a feminist anthology on Jewish American literature and culture was published, using as its methodological paradigm the concept of "speaking back."[13] This anthology used the very method that I used to demonstrate a different but related response by Jewish women authors to hegemonic discourse in American Jewish literature. I felt vindicated as I read the anthology, though I wished this very method were used by Hebrew feminist critics as well.

The Politics of Hebrew Literature

Critics and scholars of Hebrew literature have commented on the vulnerability of the field as a whole. As an academic discipline, this is a field in competition not only with the "major" (Western) literatures, those privileged with departments in most humanities colleges and universities in the West. It vies for recognition in the broader context of Jewish Studies on the one hand and Comparative Literature on the other. Hana Kronfeld describes Hebrew literature as a "minor literature" on the margins of modernism. "All too often the selective modeling of minor literature—as of 'international modernism'—on a Euro American geopolitics and linguistics effectively leaves all that is not English, French or German (or 'deterritorialized' versions thereof) outside our purview."[14] The marginal status of Hebrew literature on the periphery of Comparative Literature requires that its practitioners translate the literary achievements of its best authors for a literary market that does not necessarily understand its cultural discourses. In her appeal for an appreciation of the Hebrew literary endeavor, Kronfeld emphasizes the relevance and importance of Hebrew literature as a "modernist" and a minor literature. In this context, a feminist critique exposing the ideological blind spots of Hebrew literature may not be welcome. A radical critique of Hebrew literature, from a feminist or any other perspective, then, would be interpreted as flawed or misguided. Those who would criticize master-narratives, those who question the politics of Hebrew literature will by definition not be considered among the "best" practitioners of Hebrew literary criticism. A radical critique of Hebrew literary and critical discourse, then, cannot be divorced from questioning Zionism and Israeli political culture. But since Hebrew literature is perceived as a "minor" literature, in need of cultural translation and explication, a questioning of its gender and other exclusionary codes of hierarchical validation cannot be accommodated within the larger political economy of the practice of Hebrew criticism. This kind of critique must be expelled, banned, silenced. While most Hebrew critics would argue that Hebrew literature accommodates the most critical questioning of the Zionist metanarrative, my argument in *Israeli Mythogynies* was quite the opposite; despite appearances to the contrary, there are serious "limits" to the moral discourse of Israeli Hebrew fiction.[15] The moral discourse of Israeli Hebrew fiction is contingent on the recognition of a male consciousness as complex and self-critical. Recent "postfeminist" approaches highlight androgyny as a central trope in both male and female writing, emphasizing the poetics rather than the politics of gender in Hebrew literature. Gender wars seem to have been left behind, traceable in female fictions, in masked autobiographies, and in feminist romances.[16]

The Sexual Politics of Hebrew Poetry or the Odyssey of Male Feminism

How is one to explain the absence of women in the first generation of Hebrew poets without at the same time conceding that Hebrew literature as such was conceived and constructed by and for male writers who have become disenchanted with their own religious tradition? Dan Miron does just that in his book on *The Emergence of the First Hebrew Poetesses*. Miron argues that to the extent that women were rejected or criticized by their male peers in the 1920s, they were suppressed as poets, not as women. To a large extent, he maintains, women poets of the 1920s–1940s voluntarily participated in their own self-censorship and confinement to thematic ghettoes. Miron shifts the blame from the male critical establishment to the women poets themselves, detecting in their work flaws and weaknesses that would explain their marginal status within the literary history of Hebrew poetry. According to Miron, the founding generation of poets of the turn of the century, the generation of Bialik and Tchernichovsky was, in fact, open to women authors and poets. The fault lay not with the male purveyors of the literary establishment, but rather with the women themselves. The problem was the women's lack of the cultural background that legitimized the work of their male contemporaries. Though both Bialik and

Brenner essentially rejected the rabbinic yoke, they nevertheless required traditional literacy as a poetic qualification. "Bialik and Brenner did not publish poetry written by women because texts of women's poetry that met their aesthetic and cultural standards did not reach them." The standards that Miron defines as necessary for publication is a thorough acquaintance with classical Jewish texts, yet, he does not explain why or how a poet like Tchernichovsky, or an author like Berdychevsky, neither of whom adhered to such standards, was indeed published and did attain wide recognition. Instead, he presents the linguistic achievements of Bialik, Uri Zvi Greenberg, and Haim Lensky as the standards that their "step sisters" never achieved. Miron argues that the women themselves were the culprits, because they did not dare send their poems to the likes of Bialik, whose aesthetic standards were known.[17]

As proof that the male-dominated establishment was in fact open to women's creativity, Miron uses the example of Dvorah Baron, who according to him won critical recognition not because of her talent, but simply because she was a woman, and as such an exceptional phenomenon, something the male critics wanted to encourage. Though he goes on to mention the author's personal plight and social isolation, he insists that these have nothing to do with what he refers to as her "corrupting status of privilege" (56). Miron's explanation reveals a classic Catch-22: the women who were not published did not pass the required standards. Those who were published (e.g., Baron) were published not because of their originality or creativity, but rather because they were women. Consequently, even the "founding mothers" whom he apparently extols, and whose work he sets out to exonerate, emerge from his critical assessment as somehow flawed, lacking in poetic inspiration and authenticity, and clearly secondary in achievement and skill to their male contemporaries.

As an example of this secondariness, Miron cites the legendary poet Rachel. Miron argues that her famous stylistic simplicity owed much to the poet David Fogel (100). Indeed Miron's reading of Rachel's poetry does not focus on her work, but rather on the social and discursive processes that turned her into a myth and an icon for subsequent generations. This is the focus of chapter 5 in his book, while chapter 6 focuses on her self-performances and her association with the color white, the color of her thin book of poems. The poetic "poverty" or simplicity of Rachel soon emerges not as a symptom of poetic originality, but as an expression of her literary poverty.

Miron goes on to fault the founding mothers' writing about their feminine experiences, including erotic and birthing experiences. He presents this sort of writing as the women's attempt to appease the male authorities (163). He holds the women poets responsible for selling out as it were, for bending to the prescriptions of the male-dominated coterie of critics and publishers. To gain entry into the Hebrew canon, the pioneering women poets agreed to deflate their writing, to perform stylistic and thematic poetic feminine discourses resulting in thematic narrowness and imaginative flatness. While he excoriates Rachel for flaunting her disingenuous poetic poverty, he criticizes Esther Raab for attempting to link herself to a Zionist collective ethos and to a women's poetic tradition (110–11). Rather than victims he sees in both Raab and Yocheved Bat Miriam a suicidal tendency (108). In a way, Miron questions both the introspective poetics of Rachel and the more explosive and tempermental writing of the early Bat Miriam and Esther Raab. Repeatedly, he assures us that it was not the male establishment, but rather the women poets who undermined their own status, because the poverty of their poetic diction (lacking the traditional linguistic wealth of the Yeshiva graduates) blocked their access to the center of the poetic canon (88). Miron does not question the political investments of the cultural process of canon formation as such, and the extent to which canons enshrine the values of particular cultural hegemonies and social classes.[18] He does not consider the possibility that the aesthetic criteria legislated by Bialik were excuses and rationalizations that justified the exclusion of women from the select coterie of first generation poets. Though he is willing to use the term "masculine rationale" (152) without adequately defining it, he does not consider the concept of the masculine hegemony of cultural values.[19]

Finally, Miron arrogates to himself the privilege of distinguishing between "vulgar" and "sophisticated" feminist criticism (55), remaining all but oblivious to the political implications of his own appropriation of feminist discourse as a means of furthering his own professional status as a literary critic.[20] Though he does not mention any feminist critics who preceded him, he presumes to speak as a feminist, though the gist of his work is to exonerate the founding generation of male critics and poets from any responsibility for the fate of the pioneering Hebrew authors and poets. He dismisses the argument about literary misogyny in Hebraic literary culture as "vulgar" while his own apologetic reading of Bialik's aesthetic criteria is implicitly presented as a more sophisticated feminist approach. Yet, what is sophisticated about taking at face value various "pro women" pronouncements by leading male publishers, critics, and poets? Miron states that "the nationalist ideology" of Bialik's period was highly interested in the feminine presence, relating to it as "a great desideratum and as a national-cultural goal" (55). Why should Bialik's formal pronouncements be taken as a simple reflection of the actual editorial practices of his generation?

Back to My Personal Narrative: Women Poets, Women Critics, and Male Criticism

Though I would not presume to compare myself to the founding mothers of Hebrew poetry, I believe that Miron used similar analytic methods in criticizing my work on S. Y. Agnon, particularly on *The Bridal Canopy.* While he begins with praise for my analysis of Agnon's irony, he indicts me for missing Agnon's multiple, ambiguous self-ironies (116–17).[21] Even as he appropriates several of my insights regarding discursive and structural contradictions, tensions, multiple ambiguities, and false resolutions, he attributes to me an inability to perceive self-irony in Agnon's work. As I read his critique I was both shocked and dismayed. How could he miss the multiple references in my work to Agnon's self-reflexive irony? The contrasting narrative versions, the discontinuities and incongruities of Agnon's tales are precisely the focus of the last chapter of my first book and most of my second book, where I emphasize Agnon's use of self-reflexive irony, a complex and multivalent kind of irony that far exceeds a simple reversal of meaning.[22] Despite his claim to a more sophisticated and complex reading of Agnon's text, Miron ends up repeating the original traditionalist interpretations of Baruch Kurzweil and Hillel Barzel regarding the genre of the story of faith. Miron makes repeated statements regarding the multiple meanings of *Bridal Canopy* (136–37), but his allegedly new approach repeats the earlier readings that dichotomized Agnon as satiric and sentimental, modernist and traditionalist. Basically, Miron reverts to an earlier critical assessment of Agnon that situated him between "Nostalgia" and "Nightmare," an approach that he himself criticized.

His having excoriated me for failing to appreciate the pious tale, it is therefore stunning to find the following conclusion: "All these induced Agnon to create in *Bridal Canopy* not a novel but an anti-novel or in other words a subversive parody, seeking to destroy the novel as a formal-aesthetic entity and as a spiritual-cultural option" (263). This is precisely the conclusion I offer at the end of my book *Cunning Innocence: On S. Y. Agnon's Irony.* As a professional academic I expect and accept criticism, but Miron's misrepresentation of my work smacks of vengeance. Miron's rhetoric of force and aggression constructs me as a woman who misreads a great master. None of the male critics he lists is the object of so much criticism. I am tempted to see in his praise for my work (he lists me among Agnon's leading scholars) a tactic similar to the one he uses when first approaching the poetry of Rachel and Yocheved Bat Miriam.

On Sorority, Solidarity, and Feminist Memory

When I wrote *Israeli Mythogynies* in 1985–86, there was not a single anthology of Hebrew women's stories available in Hebrew or English. Anthologies in translation or in Hebrew began to appear in the mid- and late 1990s.[23] In 1989 Amalia Kahana-Carmon published one of the most eloquent critiques of the exclusion of women from the canonic center.[24] In 1999 Yael Feldman published a book in which she would argue that the feminist scholarship of the 1980s did not catch up with the proliferation of writings by women in Israel in the same decade.[25] Feldman does recognize that it took her at least a decade before she herself began to assess the accomplishments of the generation of the 1980s. Was it not Virginia Woolf who spoke of the need for a critical and philosophical sisterhood, something Jane Marcus refers to as "Lupine Criticism"?[26] And was it not Virginia Woolf whose theory of androgyny Feldman finds in or projects onto each of the Israeli novelists she discusses; was it not Virginia Woolf, then, who wrote of the political and poetic necessity to "think back through our mothers"?[27] These mothers, these sisters, are they not literary critics, Israeli as well as British or French? Though she dismisses my work as one of "the pioneering feminist studies of the 1980s," Feldman nevertheless agrees that the Israeli woman, or what she refers to as the "modern Hebrew woman" disappeared on her way to literary representation.[28] Though my analysis of the tension between gender and nationalism differs from hers, it constitutes nevertheless a major topic of discussion in my book and, as her subtitle indicates, certainly plays a role in her study as well.[29]

My question, then, is where common thematic or analytic threads exist, why not mention them, why not flaunt them, why not develop each other's thinking until we create an alternative tapestry, a critical room of our own, indeed a literature of our own within a relatively hostile environment? Are we not, by downgrading, degrading, and dismissing each other's work continuing the work of the very phallic critics who would deny women a room of their own in their literary and critical nations? If these transformations can be summarized as a move from a male-centered canon to a female-centered one, if we continue to work in our own separate, isolated, and competing enclaves, pretending that the subject has changed, but the method is the same, are we in fact practicing feminist criticism? To use Lillian Robinson's formulation: "Feminist criticism, as its name implies, is criticism with a Cause, engaged criticism. . . . It must be ideological and moral criticism; it must be revolutionary."[30]

Personal Narrative as Critique

As academicians we learn early on to suppress the personal "I" when discoursing about knowledge. As Jane Tompkins puts it: "You have to pretend that epistemology, or whatever you are writing about, has nothing to do with your life, that it's more exalted, more important, because it (supposedly) transcends the merely personal."[31] In some sense, the posture of the impersonal, objective, authoritative "male" voice reinstates the false public/private hierarchy. Speaking privately then is a feminist gesture to the extent that it seeks to disrupt the traditionally male privilege of the public voice. The feminist personal narrative subverts the dominant style laid down by the fathers of Hebrew criticism; the authoritative, professorial, rational communication presenting itself as a means for the transference of knowledge, information, and meaning continues to dominate even in feminist critical circles. To the extent that Hebrew women poets and authors have been devalued for failing to represent a collective ethos, Hebrew feminist critics may in fact claim the private voice as a gesture of protest. By reclaiming the personal narrative, Hebrew critics stand to create a new critical idiom turning the aggregate of their stories into a different collective voice. The foregoing tale of feminism as ideal and reality should be understood as an experiment in personal critique, or in taking criticism personally. Though personal, and admittedly subjective it nevertheless points to larger critical trends in a field of study and as such should be recognized as a legitimate method of literary critical investigation. Confessional writing as has been pointed out focuses on the person behind the writing even as it seeks to detect larger problems in cultural or academic politics.[32] Oftentimes, the declared focus of this kind of writing, the subject herself, remains unknown, slippery, ungraspable, and contradictory which is the paradoxical fate of much autobiographical writing.[33] If I have failed in constructing a coherent autobiographical narrative, I hope I have succeeded in introducing the personal narrative as a legitimate mode of investigation and cultural critique. Even as I emphasize the self-limiting authority of subjective discourse, I claim it as an effective approach especially within the context of literary feminist practice.

Notes

1. Rachel Blau DuPlessis, "Reader I Married Me: A Polygynous Memoir," in *Changing Subjects: The Makings of Feminist Literary Criticism,* ed. Gayle Greene and Coppelia Kahn (London: Routledge, 1993), 97.
2. Judith Butler, *Gender Trouble: Feminism and the Subversion of Identity* (London: Routledge, 1990).
3. Seyla Benhabib, "Feminism and Postmodernism: An Uneasy Alliance," in *Feminist Contentions: A Philosophical Exchange,* ed. Linda Nicholson (London: Routledge, 1995).
4. Linda Alcoff, "Cultural Feminism Versus Post-Structuralism: The Identity Crisis in Feminist Theory," in *Second Wave: A Reader in Feminist Theory,* ed. Linda Nicholson (New York: Routledge, 1997), 343.

5. Nancy K. Miller, *Getting Personal: Feminist Questions and Other Autobiographical Acts* (New York: Routledge, 1991), 1–30.
6. Arnold Band, *Nostalgia and Nightmare* (Berkeley: University of California Press, 1968).
7. Terry Eagleton, "Nationalism, Irony and Commitment," in *Nationalism, Colonialism and Literature,* ed. Terry Eagleton, Fredric Jameson, and Edward Said (Minneapolis: University of Minnesota Press, 1990), 23–42.
8. Esther Fuchs, *Omanut ha-hitamemut: On S. Y. Agnon's Irony* (Tel Aviv: Machon Katz, Tel Aviv University, 1985); Fuchs, *Sehok samuy: Comic Aspects in S. Y. Agnon's Fiction* (Tel Aviv: Reshafim, 1987).
9. Esther Fuchs, *Israeli Mythogynies: Women in Contemporary Hebrew Fiction* (Albany: State University of New York Press, 1987), 8.
10. Naomi Sokoloff, Anne Lapidus Lerner, and Anita Norich, eds., *Gender and Text in Modern Hebrew and Yiddish Literature* (New York: Jewish Theological Seminary, 1993).
11. Jane Gallop, *The Daughter's Seduction: Feminism and Psychoanalysis* (Ithaca, N.Y.: Cornell University Press, 1982).
12. Sokoloff, Lerner, and Norich, eds., *Gender and Text in Modern Hebrew and Yiddish Literature,* 13; Toril Moi, *Sexual/Textual Politics: Feminist Literary Theory* (New York: Methuen, 1985).
13. Joyce Antler, "Introduction," in *Talking Back: Images of Jewish Women in American Popular Culture,* ed. Antler, Brandeis Series in American Jewish History, Culture, and Life (London: Brandeis University Press, 1998), 1–11.
14. Chana Kronfeld, *On the Margins of Modernism: Decentering Literary Dynamics* (Berkeley: University of California Press, 1996), 5.
15. Yerach Gover, *Zionism: The Limits of Moral Discourse in Israeli Hebrew Fiction* (Minneapolis: University of Minnesota Press, 1994).
16. Anne Golomb Hoffman, "Bodies and Borders: The Politics of Gender in Contemporary Israeli Fiction," in *The Boom in Israeli Fiction,* ed. Alan Mintz (Hanover, N.H.: University Press of New England, 1997), 35–70; Yael Feldman, "Feminism Under Siege: The Vicarious Selves of Israeli Women Writers," *Prooftexts* 10 no. 3 (September 1990): 493–514.
17. Dan Miron, *Imahot meyasdot, ahayot horgot* (Founding Mothers, Stepsisters: The Emergence of the First Hebrew Poetesses) (Tel Aviv: Hakibbutz Hameuchad, 1991), 56, 100. Subsequent page numbers appear in the text.
18. Paul Lauter, "Race and Gender in the Shaping of the American Literary Canon: A Case Study from the Twenties," in *Feminist Criticism and Social Change: Sex, Class, and Race in Literature and Culture,* ed. Judith Newton and Deborah Rosenfelt (New York: Methuen, 1985), 19–44.
19. Catharine R. Stimpson, "On Feminist Criticism," in *What Is Criticism?,* ed. Paul Hernadi (Bloomington: Indiana University Press, 1981), 230–41.
20. Stephen Heath, "Male Feminism," in *Men in Feminism,* ed. Alice Jardine and Paul Smith (New York: Methuen, 1987), 1–32.
21. Dan Miron, *Histaklut berav nekher* (Study of Agnon's Narrative Art in *Bridal Canopy*; in Hebrew) (Tel Aviv: Hakibbutz Hameuchad, 1996), 38, 46, 58–59, 90, 115–19.
22. Fuchs, *Omanut ha-hitamemut;* Fuchs, *Sehok samuy.*
23. Lilly Rattok, *Hakol ha'aher* (The Other Voice: Women's Fiction in Hebrew) (Tel Aviv: Hakibbutz Hameuchad, 1994, in Hebrew); Risa Domb, *New Women's Writing from Israel* (London: Vallentine Mitchell, 1996); Miriyam Glazer, ed., *Dreaming the Actual: Contemporary Fiction and Poetry by Israeli Women Writers* (Albany: State University of New York Press, 2000); Shirley Kaufman, Galit Hasan-Rokem, and Tamar S. Hess, *The Defiant Muse: Hebrew Feminist Poems from Antiquity to the Present* (New York: The Feminist Press, 1999).
24. Amalia Kahana-Carmon, "Lehitbazbez 'al hatsedadi [To be wasted on the peripheral]," *Yediot Aharonot* (September 15, 1989): 25–27.
25. Yael S. Feldman, *No Room of Their Own: Gender and Nation in Israeli Women's Fiction* (New York: Columbia University Press, 1999), 4.
26. Jane Marcus, "Storming the Toolshed," in *Feminist Theory: A Critique of Ideology,* ed. Nannerl O. Keohane, Michelle Z. Rosaldo, and Barbara C. Gelpi (Chicago: University of Chicago Press, 1981), 217–36.
27. Jane Marcus, *Art and Anger* (Columbus: Ohio State University Press, 1988), 73–100.
28. Feldman, *No Room of Their Own,* 4.
29. Fuchs, *Israeli Mythogynies,* 13–34.
30. Lillian S. Robinson, *Sex, Class and Culture* (New York: Methuen, 1978), 3.
31. Jane Tompkins, "Me and My Shadow," in *Gender and Theory: Dialogues on Feminist Criticism,* ed. Linda Kauffman (New York: Basil Blackwell, 1989), 122.

32. Rachel Brownstein, "Interrupted Reading: Personal Criticism in the Present Time," in *Confessions of the Critics,* ed. H. Aram Veeser (London: Routledge, 1996), 29–39.
33. Shari Benstock, "Authorizing the Autobiographical," in *Feminisms: An Anthology of Literary Theory and Criticism,* ed. Robyn R. Warhol and Diane Price Herndl (New Brunswick, N.J.: Rutgers University Press, 1997), 1138–54.

The Folktales of Rabbi Yosef Hayyim

Lev Hakak

Rabbi Yosef Hayyim (1834–1909) was born in Baghdad, Iraq, into a family of notable rabbis. He was also known as Ben Ish Hai, which is the title of his major work on Jewish law published in Jerusalem in 1898. Yosef Hayyim was considered the most prominent rabbi of the Babylonian Jews in the latest generations. At the age of thirteen he was admitted to the famous Midrash Bet Zilkha, where the great Rabbi Abdallah Somekh taught him. A few years later, he retreated to his attic to study alone. At age twenty-one he was already well known for his vast knowledge and brilliance. At age twenty-five, his father died, whereupon he took his father's place as a Jewish preacher (*darshan*) in Baghdad for fifty years. He preached every Saturday in a synagogue known as Slat Alzariri ("The Small Synagogue"), except for four Saturdays a year in which he preached at Slat Alkabbiri ("The Big Synagogue"). On these four Saturdays, he was the only Jewish preacher preaching in the synagogues of Baghdad.

Yosef Hayyim was renowned in the Jewish world, particularly in all Middle Eastern countries, as a mystic ("Cabbalist") and as a decisor (a rabbinical authority who presides over Jewish law). He responded to questions from many countries about Jewish law. He was also known as a highly gifted preacher, who instituted rabbinical and communal enactments. He authored about 200 liturgies—seventy of which came into our hands—that were used and sung in various countries, including Iraq, Israel, and India. He published sixty books concerning a variety of topics, including Jewish law, liturgies, sermons, biblical interpretations, and mysticism.

Rabbi Yosef Hayyim (who read secular Hebrew literature of his time) was considered a supreme decisor. His book *Ben Ish Hai* (Jerusalem, 1898) was the authoritative code of Jewish law for Babylonian Jews. Even today, many Sephardi Jews consider it to be their concise book of Jewish law.

Rabbi Yosef Hayyim loved Israel and was active in supporting the Jews who settled in it. In 1869 he went to visit Israel. On the way to Israel one Saturday, pirates attacked his convoy in the desert. Seeing Rabbi Yosef Hayyim continuing his studies with serenity, the pirates, confused and astonished, decided to move on.

The rabbis of Jerusalem welcomed him with love and admiration. He went to visit the rabbi of Hebron, Eliahu Mani (see in this book the chapters about Mani's two sons), who was an old friend of Rabbi Yosef Hayyim. When he tried to visit the graves of the forefathers he was attacked and burst into tears. He explained that it was not the danger that caused him to cry, but the status of the graves of the forefathers.

Rabbi Yosef Hayyim was a scholar who kept away from the business world. But, his four brothers were interested in both business and religious studies. They named their business after their famous brother. At one time, they had business difficulties and their embittered creditors sued them. The brothers were acquitted of any wrongdoing, and they later paid all their debts. But Rabbi Yosef Hayyim was so embarrassed by this incident that for several years he would not leave his home.

While Rabbi Yosef Hayyim was a decisor, the Alliance strove to implement changes in Jewish education in Baghdad.[1] Rabbi Yosef Hayyim was in favor of various kinds of changes, but when he felt that they were going too far, he stopped supporting them. Jacob Obermayer, who came from Vienna in 1876 to teach in Baghdad, supported the easing of some religious requirements. He published a harsh criticism in a Hebrew periodical in Europe against Rabbi Yosef Hayyim. When the rabbis in Baghdad read it, they excommunicated Obermayer and protested the publication of the article. They forgave Obermayer only after he publicly asked forgiveness from Rabbi Yosef Hayyim.

Ben-Yaacob published the first twenty of Rabbi Yosef Hayyim's poems in 1970, a chapter in a book in 1979, a monograph, and then a collection of Rabbi Yosef Hayyim's liturgies and poems. Zvi Yehuda edited an important collection of articles about Rabbi Yosef Hayyim.[2]

The Babylonian rabbis wrote poetry as part of their intellectual creativity, and most of their motifs were religious and national. The poems and liturgies of Rabbi Yosef Hayyim have a strong religious-moralistic slant. Rabbi Yosef Hayyim did not achieve the same recognition and status with his poetry that he enjoyed with his rabbinical writing.[3]

Rabbi Yosef Hayyim, a gifted speaker, used folktales in his sermons that deeply touched the hearts of his listeners. Every tale had a clear lesson. These tales were collected by his disciple, Rabbi Ben-Zion Hazan, and published in a book called *Nifla'im Ma'asekha* (Splendid are Your Deeds). The book was published in 1912 in Jerusalem, and another book of folk literature was gathered from Rabbi Yosef Hayyim's works in 1913.[4] These books appeared in numerous editions. Hazan's collection is incomplete. In 1988 a five-volume edition appeared that included additional folktales of Rabbi Yosef Hayyim (Hayyim, 1988).[5]

Rabbi Yosef Hayyim did not author all the folktales that he told. Some of them he heard and some he read and adapted. By these didactic stories, Rabbi Yosef Hayyim captured the attention of his listeners. The stories demonstrate how deeply he understood his people's hearts.

In her introduction to the book *Chacham Yosef Chayim*: *Parables from Baghdad* Nehama Conuelo Nahmoud wrote that Rabbi Yosef Hayyim's place "in the lives and the hearts of Sephardim throughout the world is analogous to that of the Vilna Gaon or the Ba'al Shem Tov in the hearts of Ashkenazi Jews—and the number of his followers is continually increasing" (9). She published English adaptations of these stories.[6]

The folktales of Rabbi Yosef Hayyim are aimed at benefiting the listeners, to teach them something that would improve their lives and characters. These are educational, didactic stories dominated by their moralistic message. The characters and plot are illustrations to a message. The tale is only a sweet wrapper for a plot with a bitter pill.

These folktales illustrate great aesthetic achievement. They contain many literary devices such as intriguing plots, illustrative episodes, dialogues and monologues, direct and indirect speech, imagery, heroes and antiheroes, allegories, humor, passive and active voicing, flashbacks, flash-forwards, symbols, and parallelism.

The folk literature of Babylonian Jews was written in Hebrew, Aramaic, and Judeo-Arabic, depending on the period in which they were written. There is substantial literature about the folktales of Babylonian Jews.[7] We find folk literature of Babylonian Jews in the Babylonian Talmud and in the homiletic interpretations of the scriptures ("midrashim"). We also find folk literature in the work of the Gaonites (highly learned geniuses), who headed the Babylonian Yeshivot.

From the twelfth to the seventeenth century (a difficult period), we have almost no folk literature from the Babylonian Jews. However, from the eighteenth century forward we have substantial folk literature.

Hebrew folktales of Babylonian Jews from the first millennium are rich. In later times, Hebrew folktales were given a special place in the works of Rabbi Yosef Hayyim, Rabbi Shelomo Bekhor Hutsin, and Rabbi Shelomo Twena. Rabbi Shelomo Bekhor Hutsin published three volumes of folk literature.[8] Today, folktales of Babylonian Jews are found in print, or are recorded in manuscripts. Yitzhak Avishur did important work in the field of Babylonian Jewish folk literature.[9] In 1988 Jason published a book in which she presented an index that draws a profile of folktales of Arabic-speaking Jews who immigrated from Babylon to Israel.[10] The first part of the book lists the folktales by the tale-type scheme of Aarne and Thompson. The folktales were told in Judeo-Arabic.

Included in this article are several folktales of Rabbi Yosef Hayyim that I translated and some brief introductory remarks to each one of them.

These folktales were told by one man, and therefore his choices, his values, his style, and his use of various literary devices, such as suspense, humor, and frequent dialogues, are common to them. Some of these stories are about the relationship between two people rather than G-d and man.

In the following folktale a rich man throws a party. A smart and courageous guest encounters him and illustrates and dramatizes to him how he, the rich man, exalted the ignorant guests and demeaned the knowledgeable ones. The guest demonstrated his opinion by using a balance, in which the empty scale was up and the full scale was down. At the end of the tale, Rabbi Yosef Hayyim expresses a pessimistic view of the quality of leaders and rich people. The tale promotes faith, because in such a world we can depend on G-d. At the climax of the story, a face-to-face encounter between the rich host and his smart guest is dramatized by a direct speech. Like other folktales of Rabbi Yosef Hayyim, it is an emotional story, with a short plot and a climactic ending.

> There once was (m'aseh) a smart man who came to a party of his friend, and there were some people who were invited to the feast, and when he entered the party hall, he saw that the seating was upside down, topsy-turvy: he placed the rich people who were unknowledgeable and ignoramuses at the top, and the sages that were full of wisdom and knowledge at the bottom, under the rich men, and he became furious because of it, and he backed up, and left that house, and brought one balance and a heavy stone, and he hung the balance free of weight by a rope that came out of the middle of the ceiling of the party hall, and when the two scales of the balance were empty they stood equally side by side, and then he put the big heavy stone on one of the scales, and the empty scale jumped immediately and came up and the full, heavy one went down. The host asked what did you accomplish by this, and he answered I did the same as you did, that you placed the empty people on the top and the ones full of wisdom down below.
>
> The moral is that in this world the broken part is larger than the sound portion, "the wisdom of the learned will degenerate and the sin-fearing will be despised" [Sotah 49b], "go away impure" they will be shouted at, and all the wicked and the robbers and the swindlers take part as the heads of the speakers and all the affairs of the countries and the communities are decided by them and there is no one wise [among them who walks in] an honest way and "it is for us to rely upon our father who is in heaven" [Sotah 49b].

In this tale Rabbi Yosef Hayyim illustrates how people are prejudiced concerning the poor and the rich. People tend to believe that anything worn by a poor man has to be cheap, no matter how expensive. The same is true about their perception of the rich, that anything they are wearing must be expensive. People's gullibility is illustrated by the following dialogue showing how flamboyant embellishments win their admiration. During Rabbi Yosef Hayyim's time, conversational Hebrew was uncommon. Hebrew was mainly a written language. Nevertheless, he creates a style of dialogue that can be differentiated from the style of a narrator. For example, in one sentence the predicate is missing: "This [is worth]—at least about eighty gold Dinars." In another sentence the style is slang: "What are you talking about?!" ("What are you saying!?"). Of course, the contemporary Hebrew reader feels the absence of the rich colloquial Hebrew at that period. For example, for the term "most" Rabbi Yosef Hayyim uses the rabbinical language of "limrubbeh," while the spoken Hebrew today would be "hakhi harbeh."

The rabbis of Babylon were moderate. Even though they highly valued learning, they were very practical and encouraged success in business. Many of them preferred relying on their work and businesses for a living. They neither encouraged poverty nor supported ignoring the economic needs of people.

> There once were two bridegrooms, one was rich and one was poor, that entered a synagogue. First entered the rich, and he was wearing a belt [sash] made of simple cotton, which he bought for seven

silver Dinars, and he wore on his fingers a ring with a simple stone that he bought for two silver Dinars that looked like a precious stone.

People started looking at him, in their usual way, and one of them said to his friend:

"Look how expensive this belt is, certainly its value is fifty gold Dinars."

His friend responded:

"This [is worth]—at least about eighty gold Dinars."

And he asked about the ring, if one can find one like it for two hundred Dinars, and his friend said to him:

"What are you talking about?! A ring such as this would not be sold even for four hundred gold Dinars!"

And afterward entered the poor bridegroom to the synagogue, and he was wearing an expensive belt that was worth one hundred gold Dinars, that he borrowed from a rich man for one day only, and on his finger there was a ring with a precious stone, that he also borrowed, and it was worth five hundred Dinars.

And one of the people in the congregation said to his friend:

"What do you think, how much did this poor man pay for his belt?"

"Ten Dinars at most, because it is made of cotton."

And he asked him about the ring, and he responded:

"It is worth two silver Dinars at most."

We find that when the poor man wears the clothing and the jewelry, they are ugly in the eyes of the world, and he will be [considered] also ugly as to his deeds and his virtues, and the opposite is true about the rich man, as it was said, "money will even legitimize bastards."

Look how poverty inflicts ugliness on a person in all aspects, and therefore the poverty is called "ugly afflictions," that troubles a man.

In the following tale Rabbi Yosef Hayyim illustrates the importance of "honor thy father and thy mother." The younger generation, represented by the grandson, is the one who reprimands his father. He has compassion for his grandfather and he stirs proper thoughts and feelings in his father's heart. It is important to note that Baghdad's rabbis at that time acknowledged people should be honored and recognized on the basis of their wisdom, and not their age.[11]

Direct speech is used in this tale in important stages of the story. The grandfather's touching request is expressed in a direct speech, which is juxtaposed with the father's unfeeling reaction. Rabbi Yosef Hayyim attempted (like other Hebrew authors of his time) to create a Hebrew dialogue with a style distinguished and lower than the one of the narrator. However, in the short father-son dialogue the son uses the wisdom and style of the sages ("the parents are a good omen for their children").

The story has suspense—the listeners knew before the fathers what the son did in the attic, but they do not know why he did what he did, and the question of the father represents their curiosity too. As to the father, he cannot see what happens in the attic and his son does not respond to his questions, which prolongs the suspense. The story advances within time; the suspense increases when the son ignores the father. The son explains his own enigmatic actions. The listener identifies with the compassion, wisdom, and courage of the son, and then is relieved when he knows that the father changed his ways. As he did in other folktales, Rabbi Yosef Hayyim spelled out the moral of the story, by a mosaic style of allusions, that together close the story with a positive tenor.

There once was a man who had an elderly father, and did not have compassion for his father to bring him to his home to feed him and to clothe him, and this elderly man lived with the poor man of that town.

And it came to pass during one of the cold days that the old man was sitting with the poor man of his town and the grandson of the elderly man passed by, and the old man begged his grandson and said:

"See how the cold is great and mighty, and I am naked [thin clothed] at the peak of the cold, therefore tell your father to send me a raiment to cover myself with and put on during this cold time."

And the grandson went and told his father what his grandfather told him, and his father said to him:

"Go to the attic and find a raiment hanging on a hook, take it and bring it to your grandfather."

And the grandson went up to the attic, and found well-worn raiment that was torn in several places, and he became infuriated. And he took scissors and cut the raiment through its length to two equal halves, and thus he was delayed in the attic.

And his father shouted:

"What's holding you up? And what are you doing there?"

And after he called him several times, the son came down from the attic, and he had half a raiment in his hand.

And his father said to him: "Why did you cut the raiment through its length to two equal halves, and what will you do with the other half?"

And the son said to him: "The second half I placed for you, because when you become old I will take you out of this house, and you will sit among the poor against your will, and during the cold days—when you will ask me for a raiment to dress with—I will send you the half that is left here, because like fathers like sons, the deed of the parents are a good omen for their children, and I will treat you in the same way you are treating your father!"

And the father was ashamed and confounded, and knew that he had sinned terribly by dishonoring his father. Concerned that one day he would experience this same humiliation, he went to his father and asked his forgiveness and brought him home.

Let him that glorieth glory [Jeremiah 9, 23] that he is wise and knows that there is a judging God up above in heaven for every matter of transgression and sin; and that will by no means clear the guilty, heaven forbid, and all the measures came to an end—but measure for measure [tit for tat, punishment fitting the crime] did not come to an end.

Therefore, man, only be strong and of good courage to do good deeds, "and thou shalt do that which is right and good in the sight of the Lord" (Deuteronomy 6, 18) and man, and if you do so—then "thy children like olive plants, round about thy table" [Psalms 128, 3] that is laden, "thy wife shall be as a fruitful vine, in the innermost parts of the house" [ibid], and richness and honor shall not depart out of your home "besides the still waters" [Psalms 23, 2] "in thy presence is fullness of joy" [Psalms 16, 11].

In this tale Rabbi Yosef Hayyim prompts his listeners to accept a small transgression in order for G-d to save them from a larger transgression. The emotions of the man in the story shift from "he began wailing and screaming" to "he began to sing and be joyful"; first he cried "about his bad luck," but once he understood that his insignificant injury and monetary loss saved his life, "he began to sing and be joyful about his good fortune." The opposing feelings in this concise and rhythmic story stir excitement in the hearts of the listeners. It is a story that encourages acceptance of troubles in human life. It provides comfort and encouragement, and inspires faith.

There once was a man who saw a big sailboat sailing overseas. He ran to his home in order to retrieve his merchandise and sail overseas. But before he reached the boat—a nail penetrated his foot, and he could not move. Meanwhile the boat left the dock and embarked.

He began wailing and screaming about his bad luck, because there would not be another boat going overseas for a year, and his merchandise would remain with him.

Three days later he learned that the boat sank. He began to sing and be joyful about his good fortune. And he began kissing the nail that had pinned his foot, because it had spared his life and his property.

It is deducible from the context that no matter what trouble a man encounters he has to be generous-spirited and open-minded and to accept it with love and appreciation, for heavens mandate is never ill willed. And if a man encounters a loss of money or illnesses etc—he should absolutely recognize that the Creator (blessed be Him) was merciful with him, because the merciful One does not take life (G-d forbid), but with the rod of his wrath he would strike him with torture or monetary loss, in order to bring him and his family back to good conduct.

The following tale contrasts the lifestyle between two male characters. Both men are neighbors, living in close proximity to one another (geographically). One "had sheep and oxen", the other one "did not have the means to buy meat everyday—rather, only once a week, enough for Saturdays"; one had "fields and vineyards," while the other one "did not have furniture and utensils"; one—"his house was fine-looking and spacious," the other one—"his house was undersized, small and narrow." In short—one was "very rich," "his table—was a king's table," while the other one "was a craftsman." The difference between the two men is puzzling and surprising (and pleasing to the hard-working, low-income audience): The "very rich" man "was very thin and grew weak" while the craftsman was "very healthy physically and powerful [big, fat] and his face always looked rosy." The main part of the tale is a monologue about the craftsman, who first dwells on the rich man's character, followed by an explanation of his own character.

The explanation also juxtaposes the characters: the craftsman tells the rich man that he (the wealthy man) is by nature "angry and full of rage" while the craftsman is by his "nature and temper, . . . very congenial, and . . . not angry and not furious even when the issue justifies anger." The rich man is "desirous and covetous, and very envious" while the craftsman describes himself as a man with the "virtue of frugality and contentment," who is "not envious of other people."

The craftsman's character is illustrated by his positive self-image, and by the way he addresses the rich man. He is confident and direct. He recognizes his self-worth and does not feel inferior to the confused rich man.

The story provides a comforting message to its readers. The proud craftsman instills confidence in his audience by his manner of speaking to the confused and needy-of-advice rich man. The story cautions its listeners not to equate having wealth to having a fulfilling life.

> There once were two men who were neighbors, and one of them was very rich and had sheep and oxen, fields and vineyards, and his table—was a king's table, and his house was fine-looking and spacious, but he was very thin and grew weak.
>
> And his neighbor was a craftsman—a silversmith, who did not have the means to buy meat everyday—rather, only once a week, enough for Saturdays, and his house did not have furniture and utensils, and did not have a fine mattress, and his house was undersized, small and narrow, but he was as fit as a fiddle, very healthy physically and powerful [big, fat] and his face always looked rosy.
>
> And the rich neighbor asked:
>
> "Why do I look the way I do, and you look the way you do?"
>
> "The reason is, that by your nature you are angry and full of rage, and therefore at least ten times a day you will encounter anger and rage with your servants and your family, and the anger causes a person to be skinny and weakens him and strongly harms him. Moreover, you—your nature is that you are desirous and covetous, and very envious, and thus all your life is painful, because you became confused and troubled, a money chaser, and it is impossible for you to fulfill all your cravings, and therefore sighs and sorrow always consume your flesh and strength, and how can you become healthy by the food that you eat, while all these vices of yours consume your strength and flesh!
>
> Whereas me—as to my nature and temper, I am very congenial, and I am not angry and not furious even when the issue justifies anger, and I also have the virtue of frugality and contentment, and I rejoice in my portion, and I see the little that I have—as plentiful, and I am not envious of other people about everything, therefore I am always very healthy physically, thanks to the comfort that I have!"
>
> It is deducible from the tale that jealousy, lust and ambition were obstacles and stumbling blocks for the children of Israel in all their good pathways, and if the world was cautious about these three essentials—then people would be healthy and well in their body and soul, and they would be happy in this world—and they would have it good in the world to come, may the Lord reward us with it.

In the following tale Rabbi Yosef Hayyim illustrates the importance of setting an example for the younger generation. A parent's proper conduct is not only important for himself, it sets an example for his children. The tale is didactic, and justice is on the side of the son, not the father. One's transgressions do not end there; they continue for generations. Physical punishment illustrates this point.

There once was a man who came to hit his son because the son ate without washing his hands, and the father held the two legs of his son with one hand, and a steak with the other hand, and when the father raised the steak to hit his son's feet, the steak landed on the father's hand instead, on the hand that was holding the son's legs, and the father's hand was hit forcefully and gravely, and the son said to his father:

"Your hand was justly and rightfully hit, because you are hitting my legs for not washing my hands, while you yourself always eat without washing your hands, and by having your own hands hit, they spoke to you from heaven, saying: 'Why are you hitting his legs for not washing his hands, hit your own hands for not washing them,' don't you know that like father like son, that if I saw that you would not eat without washing your hands, then I too would not eat without washing my hands?"

Baghdad rabbis were far from being fanatics; they were moderate. In the following tale Rabbi Yosef Hayyim acknowledges the value of telling a "white lie." Goel ("redeemer") and a creature called Lie hold opposite positions as to the use, need, impact, and nature of lying. The story is structured as a trip that begins in the morning while Goel is still in bed. It also ends in his bed after various encounters with the people who are important in his life, while he is determined not to lie. At the opening of the first scene, Goel is still in his bed and he is vigorous and sure of himself during his encounter with his maid. However, after various encounters, he understands that because he rejected Lie and everything Lie represents, he loses everything. The order in which the tragedies occur go from bad to worse. First, his finances collapse. Then he loses his cook and his inheritance. Then his creditor sues him, and finally he loses his fiancée's love.

The tragic events are obvious; however the tale contains humor, too. Goel says to his uncle: "and if your death day would come earlier—you will truly perform an act of kindness." "He wanted to hit his head against the wall," but instead he hit it "against the head of a passer by," who happened to be his creditor. His fiancée and her aunt were upset because Goel, upon the aunt's request, correctly estimated her age. "She fumes if one tells her that she is of an old age," explains the fiancée.

Nevertheless, since the folktales of Rabbi Yosef Hayyim are aimed at providing comfort and encouragement, the closure of the tale is happy. This closure is in the form of a direct speech from Goel, who changed his view of lying based on the lesson that Lie taught him.

There once was a young man whose name was Goel. On the evening of the New Year, while he was sitting on his bed, he took his clothes off in order to go to bed and fall asleep, and he thought:

"Woe, the world is full of scoundrels and wicked, that speak insincerely. Lies have slain many people and the number of victims is high! This world would have been a paradise, had lying not been so deeply rooted in our hearts; may the curse of God come upon those who follow the path of lying."

And with a heart full of fury because of the ways of the world and its deceitfulness—he went to bed and pulled up the blanket to cover his face.

After closing his eyes, he saw in his sleep a little Creature [little being] standing across from him and looking at him with a mocking smile in its shiny eyes.

And Goel stared at him and called: "Who are you?"

And the small Creature answered:

"I am Lie."

And Goel sat on his bed, and called out with rage and fury and wrath:

"Come here closer and I will speak firmly to you, I will shatter your head and cut you into pieces, and this act will be considered an act of piety, for it saves tens of thousands of people from your evil!"

And when he said that, he wanted to extend his arms to catch the Creature, but the Creature backed up. And Goel stretched his hands out twice, but to his sorrow, his efforts were in vain and he utterly failed, because the Creature slipped away and hid time and again and escaped, until Goel became tired and stopped running after it.

And the Creature said to Goel mockingly:

"Lie will not be caught easily! And now, what use do you have for my blood, so that you maliciously want to kill me? And be it known, that you will harm the world, you will gravely damage it if you harm its benefactor and charitable person."

And Goel called out laughingly and angrily:

"You, the despicable, are the 'benefactor and charitable person' of the world?"

And the Creature responded:

"Indeed I am. You and all the people of the world together could not exist without me. I am telling you the truth now, even though I am the Lie, and I firmly promise you that you could not get through one day peacefully—if I will not walk beside you."

And Goel responded:

"Were you called Lie, so that you will tell the truth? I will live all my life peacefully and happily without ever seeing your face."

And the Creature said:

"All right, let's try that. I surely have justification to leave you for a long time, because you are a man with a quick temper, and you maliciously raised your hand to hit me, but I will not take revenge and will not bear a grudge, and I do not want to disgrace my name and be called Cruel, because I will be considered Cruel if I leave you for a long time. But in order to try you and to educate you, I will leave you tomorrow, and we will see what happens and how will you spend that day. And you—do not call me and do not ask for my help during moments of troubles because I will not listen to you even if it is a matter of risking of [costing the price of] your life, I will not rescue you, so that the trial will be comprehensive. And tomorrow will be a holy day for your brethren and you will remember it. In the evening I will return and ask you whether or not you have use for me."

And the eyes of the Creature seemed odd to Goel, because his look changed time and again, one time they were greenish and one time reddish, and one time azure. And there was a miracle, and the Creature all of a sudden became an old woman, and its face was full of wrinkles; and within a moment he changed and became a tender boy whose face emitted beauty and grace.

And Goel thought:

"Since this Creature is the Lie itself, it is not odd that he changes himself, because it is the way of Lie to be changeable and alter his colors as the wind blows."

And again Goel quickly stretched out his hand to strike the Creature—but this time too he missed the target, because the Creature moved aside, and Goel could not hurt him, and the following words came to Goel's ears:

"Be well, and tomorrow at this time I will come back to see you in person—and we will see how this matter ends."

And Goel said:

"We will see."

And then his eyes closed and he fell asleep.

And Goel did not have a wife and children, and at his home there was only one old woman who cooked for him everyday. And that day—New Year's day—while he was still lying in his bed—the cook served him a glass of water, and when he opened his eyes, she said to him:

"I wish you, dear Sir, for the coming good New Year, that you will have life and tranquility, riches and honor, and I will pray to God with all my heart that you will be successful in everything you do, and that whithersoever direction you turn you will be wise and successful, and we will live a long life together forever."

And Goel said when he opened his eyes:

"If only the day will quickly come that I will be freed from you, relieved of you so that I don't have to see your wrinkled appalling face anymore."

And the old woman said:

"Woe to the ears that hear this! I will not let this man violate my honor, to speak evil to me, because I am a well respected woman."

And Goel said:

"It is the truth indeed, you deceived me!"

And she said to him:

"If I deceived you, take another woman in my place that would know how to appreciate a man like you that instead of giving his maid presents for the New Year—which is the proper thing to do—he speaks haughtily to her and humiliates her!"

And Goel did not answer her at all, only brandished one of his shoes to throw at her. And the cook understood his intent, and she forestalled the evil and left the room. And Goel heard her voice behind the door, as she was talking to herself, saying:

"May he do as he pleases, who could ever have thought that one would hear such words coming out of his mouth on this holy day? It must be that he has gone mad!"

And Goel felt remorse in his heart, and thought:

"Why did I have to quarrel today with this old woman? True, deep in my heart I am dissatisfied with her, and I don't want her if I find someone better than her, nevertheless—I should not have made her bitterly outraged on this holiday, and I did not have to reveal the truth that was in my heart."

And with shattered strength [weakly] and a frightened heart he got dressed, and he remembered the holiness of the day and he closed his heart to grief, and went to the synagogue, and when he came back home—he ate a little bit, and went to look for his friends and the people who loved him.

"I will go first to my uncle's home, because he is sick and going to die, and I will inherit his property, because he does not have a son."

And he did that, he went to his uncle's home, and when he approached the bed of his sick uncle who sat at that time on an ivory bed, instead of saying to him: "I am happy to see that you are doing well", he said:

"I am happy to see you sick, lying on your sick-bed, and that you will never get off the bed that you went to lay on; I am waiting impatiently to inherit your wealth."

He told his uncle the truth that was in his heart, lest he would utter any lie.

And then the uncle, hearing a hard curse instead of a blessing, said to him:

"Your words let you down, dear, are you truly waiting impatiently for your uncle's death, the uncle that profoundly loves you?"

And Goel sighed and said:

"If you would only find a shelter under the aegis of death, dear uncle!"

And he sighed, and said:

"Do you know, uncle, my situation? I need money, and only your property would redeem me from my poverty. Truly, uncle, I love you, but is a man immortal? And even if you would live one or two more years—it is the same for you, and if your death day would come earlier—you will truly perform an act of kindness."

This is how Goel spoke to his uncle, wanting to atone for his first words, but in fact he just continued to heap coals of fire upon his uncle's head, and his uncle shouted loudly:

"Get out of my home, vile! Do not come to see me again! You have neither part nor lot in my house, and you will not inherit one cent! You, hurry up and get out, before I order my servants to chase you and throw you out like an abhorred offshoot!"

And Goel went out, stood up astonished and confused, and he bit his lips with his teeth, his face was pale, his knees shaking, and his heart was likely broken,

And he thought:

"Woe, what got into me and why on earth did I say these words to my uncle? Because of my fickle-mindedness I destroyed all the buildings that I have built with my thoughts! Many years I worked hard to attract his heart to love me, and in one moment—I mercilessly destroyed the entire building that for years I worked to build! I acted foolishly!"

This is how Goel thought in his heart bitterly, and he wanted to hit his head against the wall, because of his immense remorse, but to his regret or to his tragedy—he did not hit his head against the wall but against the head of a passer by, that he did not see because he was immersed in his thoughts and stuck in their sad abyss.

And the passer by felt the impact of Goel's strike, and he said:

"Pay attention to the road!"

And Goel responded:

"To hell with you!"

And when Goel raised his eyes and looked at the man, he saw that it was one of his lenders, a lender to whom Goel owed a lot of money. And instead of telling him properly—"I am happy to see you today and to wish you a Happy New Year"—Goel said to him, to the contrary:

"I am seized by horror and rage when I see you, you chase me and disturb my rest even on a holiday!"

The lender thought that Goel was kidding, and made efforts to show a joyful face, and he said to Goel:

"I am glad to hear you kidding and teasing on this holy day. It must be that you feel fine because you heard good news, and thus your spirit is very joyful, and apparently you are coming out of the house of your honorable uncle, so what did you hear about your inheritance—how much does he intend to bequeath to you?"

And Goel said:

"He will not bequeath to me even one cent!"

Goel said that, because he was angry and out of control, he told the passer by his secret, against his own will.

And the lender said:

"If so, listen to what I am telling you, even though it is improper to discuss business and money issues today, my guts compel me to tell you, that if you don't pay me back my money within a week from now, I will submit your promissory notes to the court and file a lawsuit against you! How long will I wait for you? It is hard to bear anymore!"

And Goel said:

"This too God stored up for me."

And he turned around, and went away sullen and displeased.

From there, he went to his Boss, to fulfill his obligation to wish him a Happy New Year, but he did not find him at his home, and he was very happy about it, because undoubtedly he would have quarreled with him too, because the truth was his guiding light, and the Lie—was the darkness on his road. Therefore he left his Boss's home joyfully, and from there he went to the home of his fiancée to wish her a Happy New Year.

And his fiancée was an orphan, deprived by death of both parents, and she grew up in the home of her aunt. And Goel decided to weigh his words with a scale, and to put a rein on his mouth and to bridle it, but his bad luck once again did not leave him alone because there were issues between him and the fiancée's aunt, and he pained her with his words too, when she asked him:

"Guess how old I am?"

And he said:

"Over fifty."

And she became furious over his response, and the fiancée was on her side, and she said to him:

"What prompted you to shame and disgrace my dear aunt on this holy day?"

And he said:

"What did I do? Did I lie? Isn't she fifty-years-old?"

And his fiancée said:

"Indeed it is the truth, but she—she fumes if one tells her that she is of an old age."

And he said:

"My beloved, may I find grace in your eyes and you will not consider me as guilty of a sin."

And from one issue to another that he discussed with his matched fiancée, he told her that she was his fourth woman that he had married three women before—but he despised them and divorced them. And the fiancée became enraged and she said:

"Get out of here, vile, and don't ever come again to see me! After you have divorced three women—how can I trust you and be your wife?"

By now Goel was frightened by his bad luck, how in one moment he destroyed his future and the towers that he built with his imagination, and he went out of his fiancée's home sullen and displeased.

He went back to his home at the end of the day, and thought about the incidents he had that day, and he fell face down and cried bitterly about the incident he had with the old cook, and the incident he had with his uncle, and the incident he had with the lender, and the incident he had with his fiancée, and he saw that he wanted to tell his heart's truth, but there was no cure for any of these incidents but by telling lies and not expressing the truth which is shut up in his bosom.

And he began praising Lie, and he confirmed and justified the words that the creature told him, and he blessed the creature.

And at the end of this Goel woke up from his sleep and opened his eyes, and saw that he was sleeping on his bed and the sun was shining, and he saw that the old cook was standing near his bed above his head, and in her hand she held a glass of water, and she said to him:

"I wish you, dear Sir, for the coming good New Year, that you will have life and tranquility, riches and honor, and I will pray to God with all my heart that you will be successful in everything you do, and that whithersoever direction you turn yourself you will be wise and successful, and we will live a long life together forever."

And Goel answered her:

"What are you talking about? Is today the New Year holiday, and it is now the first morning of the New Year?"

And she said to him:

"You still don't know, Sir, that today is the first day of the New Year? It appears that you slept well, and therefore I could not wake you up from your sleep, and I stayed standing above the head board of your bed for some time until you woke up by yourself, and they have already begun praying at the synagogue!"

And Goel woke up, and looked at his watch and saw that it was morning already, and at that time he clearly knew that everything he experienced— seeing the Creature, conversing and quarreling with him, his quarrel with the cook, and his visit with his uncle and the conversation he had with him and with the lender and with his fiancée and her aunt—everything took place in his dream, in his vision of the night, and that he was horrified by a terrible dream, and his reins rejoiced and he was happy that he did not lose the riches of his uncle, and did not lose his fiancée, and he said:

"You, angel of dreams, are a faithful messenger. True, you have pained my heart, and you filled me with anger and pain. But you did not inflict any evil upon me, because you taught me how to behave. And you showed me that a man does not have the strength to walk down the road of truth in this life, but that he would encounter times when he would have to decline the truth and bond with a lie. And if he does not do so—he is committing suicide. I thank you, angel of dreams, for this teaching!"

The dichotomy between a righteous man and a wicked man is central to the following story. The righteous man is different from the wicked in life and in death: In life, the righteous man is strong and can endure the predicaments (storms) of life because of his deep roots (like those of a palm tree), while the wicked man is weak and cannot endure any problem (wind) because his roots are shallow (like those of a weed). After life in this world the righteous man is not considered dead, because of his deeds and the people he left behind. Determining the stability of the righteous versus the wicked man's character is delayed until their character traits (and depth of their roots) emerge. This folktale exposes the depth of these roots and the implications of their differences. The differences between the righteous and the wicked are dramatized by a bet that has a winner and a loser, a contrast that is further expounded upon and detailed in describing a palm tree and the weeds that grow around it.

There once were two men that stood near a mulberry tree or a palm tree, and one of them said: "I estimate with my mind that this tree is about 20 cubits [ancient measure from elbow to fingertip] tall." And the second man answered him, and he said: "It is incorrect; the tree is more than 25 cubits tall." And the first man rushed to climb to the top of the tree and took a rope with him and measured the tree and found out that the height of the tree from its top to the ground was 20 cubits exactly. And he said to his friend: "My estimate was correct, I have just measured the tree and it was as I said." And the second one answered: "You are wrong, and I am right, let's bet and I will show you how this tree is more than 25 cubits tall." And his friend said: "Fine", and his heart was glad because he was sure that he would win, because he just measured the tree to be just 20 cubits long. And after they deposited the bet with a referee, the second man took a spade and dug five feet deep around the tree. And the tree was still standing in the soil because it is the nature of a tree to go deep into the thick ground. And he said: "Here are five cubits in addition to the 20 that you measured from the top of the tree to the ground. Altogether, including the five cubits that were hidden in the soil the tree exceeded 25 cubits, as I have estimated." And he took the Dinars that were deposited by the first man with the referee.

And it came to pass a few days later that the first man, the man who lost the bet, went to walk in the fields with another man. And they found long weeds in the field. And the first man who lost asked his friend: "How tall are the weeds?" And his friend said: "I estimate with my mind that the weeds are only five cubits tall." And the first man said: "It is not so, I say that it is over seven cubits tall." And his friend measured the weeds from top to bottom and found that he well estimated that they were five cubits tall. And he said: "Behold I have measured and I found that the weeds are, as I estimated, only five cubits tall." And the first man was glad in his heart, and he thought, now I will recover my loss that I lost that day regarding the tree measurement, because what happened to me that day when it did not occur to me to calculate the estimated part which was hidden beneath the ground, is now happening to this man. Therefore I will now bet with this man who is innocently calculating how tall the weeds are and I will recapture the loss I incurred in measuring the tree. And he said to his friend: "You are wrong in measuring the weeds and saying that they are five cubits tall, I am right, the weeds are taller than seven cubits. Let's bet, we will bet in writing 10 Dinars each, and if I show you that it is as I say, that the weeds are indeed taller than seven cubits, I will win the bet, and if not—you will win it." And his friend said: "Fine." And each one of them deposited 10 Dinars with a referee. And the man who lost the first bet started digging around the weeds, and the weeds fell when he dug one finger deep, because there were no roots inside the soil, and the roots do not penetrate the soil more than half a finger deep.

And the same is true about righteous and wicked people, because the wicked person has no foundation and no deep roots that enable him to exist mightily and courageously, and he resembles a weed. The success of the wicked extends only as far as the eye can see, and this is why it was said about the wicked "and when all the workers of inequity do flourish; it is that they may be destroyed for ever" [Psalms 92, 8], because a soft wind uproots them, but "the righteous shall flourish like the palm-tree" [Psalms, 92, 13] because in addition to what one can see, he has deep roots and all the wind of the world cannot uproot him.

And I am saying that the resemblance of the tree to a righteous man and the weed to a wicked man is as follows: For the wicked man, his days on earth are the only days to be considered as his life, and when he dies he does not have any more life in this world at all, and this resembles a weed because it does not have any other dimension except the one that is readily seen above the ground, and after he falls and is uprooted one can see the dimensions of the weed on the ground, and he will not have any hidden existence beneath the soil. But the righteous man, in addition to his visible life span on earth, has another existence in this world even after he dies, because by having children that he guided to walk in the path of uprightness, and disciples whom he taught to maintain good customs and to perform virtuous and good deeds, that these substitute for him and reflect his good ways and good virtues that are named after him—death does not apply to him. He is still alive and not dead, as our sages of blessed memory wrote: "Why does scripture use 'sleep' with regard to David and 'death' with regard to Joab? 'Sleep' is used for David because he left a son; 'death' is used for Joab because he left no son" [Babylonian Talmud, Bava Batra, 116a].

And the righteous man resembles a tree, that in addition to its overt part, which is above ground and visible to everyone, it has a part that is hidden beneath the ground, that exists but is not visible, but is known and recognized through observing and by estimating through the mind's eye, and therefore he resembles a palm-tree whose major roots lie hidden beneath the soil.

Notes

1. Hakak, *Iggerot.* Collected, and wrote an introduction and lists of abbreviations and publications.
2. Abraham Ben-Yaacob, *Shira U-Fiyyut shel Yehudeh Bavel Ba-Dorot Ha-Ahronim,* 317–19; *Yehudeh Bavel Mi-Sof Tekufat Ha-Geonim ad Yamenu,* 190–200; *Ha-Rav Yosef Hayyim Mi-Bagdhdad; Otsar Ha-Shirim,*

Ha-Hibburim Ve-Ha-Derashot Ve-Sippureh Ha-Ma'asiyyot shel Ha-Rav Yosef Hayyim. Zvi Yehuda edited an important collection of articles about Rabbi Yosef Hayyim; see Yehuda, ed., *Ha-Rav Yosef Hayyim*.

3. Hakak, *Nitsaneh Ha-Yetsira Ha-Ivrit Ha-Hadasha Be-Bavel*, 74–76.
4. Hayyim, *Niflaim Ma'asekha; Mashal Ve-Nimshal.*
5. Hayyim, *Niflaim Ma'asekha.*
6. Conuelo Nahmoud, *Chacham Yosef Chayim.*
7. Noy, *Ha-Narah Ha-Yefifiyyah U-Sheloshet Beneh Ha-Melekh;* Avishur, "Ha-Sifrut Ha-Amamit shel Yehudeh Bavel Be-Aravit Yehudit" and *Ha-Sippur Ha-Amami shel Yehudeh Iraq;* H. Jason (Yazon), "Hassipur al Har Ha-Shemesh" and *Sippureh Am Mi-Pi Yehudeh Iraq;* Hasan-Rokem, "Iyyun Bi-Mkorot Sippureh Ha'am shel Yehudeh Babvel"; Shenhar, "Ha-Sifrut Ha-Amamit shel Yehudeh Bavel Ve-Zikkatah Le-Sifrut Ha-Agadah"; Agasi, *Husham Mi-Baghdahd—Maasiyyot Bavliyyot, Ha-Mikhtav Shenislakh Im Ha-Ruuah, and Ha-Yafa Bat Ha-Ruuah;* Ben-Yaacob, *Ha-Otsar—Hamishim Sippureh Am Veagadot.*
8. Hakak, *Iggerot.*
9. Avishir, *Hassippur*, 1:7–25.
10. Jason, *Sippureh.*
11. See, for example, Hutsin, "Massa Bavel"; Hakak, introduction to *Iggerot.*

Bibliography

Agasi, A. *Husham Mi-Baghdahd—Maasiyyot Bavliyyot*, 1960.

———. *Ha-Mikhtav Shenislakh Im Ha-Ruuah—Sippureh Am shel Yehudeh Bavel*, 1979.

———. *Ha-Yafa Bat Ha-Ruuah, Sippureh Am Bavliyyim*, 1980.

Avishur, Yitzhak. "Ha-Sifrut Ha-Amamit shel Yehudeh Bavel Be-Aravit Yehudit"; *Pe'amim*, no. 3 (1979): 83–90.

———. *Ha-Sippur Ha-Amami shel Yehudeh Iraq*. 2 vols. University of Haifa, 1992.

———. "Shiddud Maarakhot Sifrutiyyot U-Temurut Leshoniyyot Be-Kerev Yehudeh Iraq Ba-Et Ha-Hadasha (1750-1950)." *Mi-Kedem U-Miyyam* 6 (1995): 235–54.

Ben-Yaacob, Abraham. *Ha-Otsar—Hamishim Sippureh Am Veagadot*, 1969.

———. *Ha-Rav Yosef Hayyim Mi-Bagdhdad*. The Baylonian Jewry Heritage Center, 1984.

———. *Otsar Ha-Shirim, Ha-Hibburim Ve-Ha-Derashot Ve-Sippureh Ha-Ma'asiyyot shel Ha-Rav Yosef Hayyim*. Makhon Ha-Ketav, 1994.

———. *Perakim Be-Toldot Yehudeh Bavel*. Vols. 1 and 2. Olam Ha-Sefer Ha-Torani, 1989.

———. *Shira U-Fiyyut shel Yehudeh Bavel Ba-Dorot Ha-Ahronim*. Makhon Ben-Tsvi, 1970.

———. *Yehudeh Bavel Beerets Yisrael Me-Haaliyyot Ha-Rishonot ad Ha-yom*. Reuven Mas, Jerusalem, 1980.

———. *Yehudeh Bavel Mi-Sof Tekufat Ha-Geonim ad Yamenu*. Kiriat Sefer, 1979.

Conuelo Nahmoud, Nehama. *Chacham Yosef Chayim: Parables from Baghdad*. Sephardic Heritage Series 1. New York: Lightbooks, 1981.

Hakak, Lev. "The Holocaust in the Hebrew Poetry of Sephardim and Near Eastern Jews." *Shofar* (Spring 2005).

———. *Iggerot Ha-Rav Shelmo Bekhor Hutsin*. Hakibuz Hameuchad, 2005.

———. *Nitsaneh Ha-Yetsira Ha-Ivrit Ha-Hadasha Be-Bavel*. Merkaz Moreshet Yahadut Bavel, 2003.

———. "Shlomo Bechor Hutsin: L'intineraire d'un Juif 'mskil' de Baghdad." *Reeh: Revue Europeenne Des Etudes Hebraiques* 7, no. 5 (2001): 193–213.

Hayyim, Yosef. *Mashal Ve-Nimshal*. Jerusalem, 1913.

———. *Niflaaim Ma'asekha*. 5 vols. Siyah Yisrael, Jerusalem, 1988.

———. *Sefer Rav Pealim*. Vol. 2. *Hoshen Mishpat*, Jerusalem, 1903.

Hutsin, Shelomo Bekhor. "Massa Bavel." *Hamaggid*, no. 41 (Oct. 21, 1868): 325.

Noy, Dov. *Ha-Narah Ha-Yefifiyyah U-Sheloshet Beneh Ha-Melekh, 120 Sippureh Am Mippi Yehudeh Iraq*. 1965.

Shenhar, Aliza. "Ha-Sifrut Ha-Amamit shel Yehudeh Bavel Ve-Zikkatah Le-Sifrut Ha-Agadah". *Mehkarim Be-Toldot Yehudeh Iraq U-Vetarbutam* 1 (1981): 133–46.

Shohet, Nir. *Sippurah Shel Golah. Ha-Agudda Le-Kiddum Ha-Mehkar Ve-Hayetsira*. Jerusalem, 1981.

———. *The Story of an Exile*. Translated and edited by Abraham Zilkha. Association for the Promotion of Research, Literature, and Art, 1982.

Yehuda, Zvi, ed. *Ha-Rav Yosef Hayyim: Pirkeh Mehkar Ve-Iyyun Bi-Melot Tishim Shana Li-Ftirato*. The Babylonian Jewry Heritage Center, 1999.

The Sha'ar Ha-Shamayim Synagogue (Keniset Ismāʿīlīyah) in Cairo, Egypt

Rivka Kern-Ulmer

May Zev Garber continue to flourish like a palm tree.

A building is a cultural signifier that carries meaning to all that enter or view the building. A synagogue is a building that carries meaning for those who congregate in it as a community. In those cases in which the Jewish community dissipates, the synagogue mainly serves as a building block in the construction of a collective memory and as a teaching tool.[1] The collective and individual memories are not only inscribed on the conscience of a group but also on the stones and walls of edifices which memorialize them. This essay discusses the Sha'ar Ha-Shamayim Synagogue in Cairo, Egypt, and its significance for Egyptian Jews. This synagogue was built early in the twentieth century, a time when the Jewish community of Egypt prospered. One of several architectural vestiges of Jewish life in modern Egypt, it is still owned by the small Sephardic congregation in Cairo, the major remnant of the Jewish community in Egypt. This building is part of the culture of memory of the Egyptian Jewish community since it symbolizes the long history of Jews "dwelling" in Egypt. The building serves as a visual and a textual monument that is inscribed with Egyptian Jewish icons. In order to serve as a focus of the culture of memory and as a teaching tool the synagogue contains Egyptian, biblical, and various Jewish motifs as well as textual references. This essay consists of the following subparts: a description of the synagogue, including motifs that relate to the Judeo-Egyptian tradition; the relationship of the artwork and the inscriptions of the synagogue to Egyptian, biblical, and rabbinic textual traditions; the synagogue as a teaching tool.

A Description of the Synagogue, Including Motifs that Relate to the Judeo-Egyptian Tradition

In contemporary Egypt, one can still find a variety of archeological and architectural remnants of Jewish life.[2] Generally, the recorded history of the Jews in Egypt spans from the sixth century BCE to our times. If one is to include Egypt's first recorded contacts with Semites and some Proto-Israelites/Canaanites, this time frame can be extended to the second millennium BCE.[3] Since this essay focuses upon the Sha'ar Ha-Shamayim Synagogue it is important to note that the Jewish community of Egypt flourished toward the end of the nineteenth century (CE), when European and Turkish Jews were invited by the Egyptian government to participate in the commercial and cultural development of the country. This was especially evident in the major economic centers of Egypt, Alexandria, and Cairo, in which Jews held many significant positions in the commercial and financial sectors.[4]

The capital of Egypt, Cairo, has many attractive Jewish sights.[5] Among them is the famous Ben Ezra Synagogue in Fustat (Old Cairo), which is the location of the Genizah that contained many documents relating to medieval Judaism.[6] Additionally, there are some adjacent buildings with fading Hebrew inscriptions that indicate that they formerly housed Jewish organizations or shops owned by Jews.[7] Furthermore, there is a large Jewish cemetery in the area of Cairo known as Bassatin, where many preeminent figures of the Jewish community of Cairo are buried.[8] There are buildings and homes in the former Jewish quarter (*Ḥāret El-Yahūd*) that give us an impression of Jewish life in the early twentieth century. There are a handful of edifices that used to be synagogues in other parts of the city, but which serve different purposes now.[9] The most magnificent Jewish building in contemporary Cairo is the Great Synagogue, the Sha'ar Ha-Shamayim Synagogue, which still functions as a synagogue for the small Cairene Jewish community, as well as for Jewish tourists.

As in many other countries of the Diaspora with diminished Jewish populations, the formerly Jewish buildings in Cairo have quickly decayed and occasionally they are vandalized.[10] However, one should note that Egypt is a country struggling to feed and house its constantly growing population and which has thousands of antiquities from different historical periods (Pharaonic, Greco-Roman, Coptic, Fatimid, and Mameluk, just to name a few) that are worthy of preservation. Thus, the task of maintenance and renovation seems to be overwhelming for the Egyptians. The Sha'ar Ha-Shamayim Synagogue in Cairo was renovated in the 1980s by the Fédération Sépharde Mondiale (the Sephardic World Federation). In addition, the synagogue is usually protected by Egyptian police.

The Sha'ar Ha-Shamayim Synagogue, which is commonly called "Le Temple Ismailiah" (Arabic: *Keniset Ismā'īlīyah),* is located in the center of Cairo. Presently it is surrounded by modern Egyptian apartment and commercial buildings. It was built in 1903, partially designed by the Italian architect Branchi, and constructed by the family of Mosseri Bey. Joseph Mosseri (1869–1934) received the honorary title Bey from the government of Egypt for his successful financial endeavors on behalf of the country (see Figure 1).[11]

The Relationship of the Artwork and the Inscriptions of the Synagogue to Egyptian, Biblical, and Rabbinic Textual Traditions

The Sha'ar Ha-Shamayim Synagogue contains motifs that are found in the biblical descriptions of Solomon's Temple in Jerusalem; these motifs are merged with features of *art nouveau* and Egyptian stylistic elements.[12] The key motif in the decorative program of the synagogue is the palm tree. As one perceives this motif, it appears that the palm trees are undulating with an assured rhythm throughout the whole building. The motif of the palm tree is often found in synagogue architecture, for example, the ancient synagogues of Capernaum, Eshtemoa, Beth Alpha in the Land of Israel, and in the mosaic from the synagogue in Hammam Lif, Tunisia.[13] Furthermore, date palms were found on ancient ossuaries and coins. A critical aspect of the festival of Sukkot is the shaking of the *lulav* which in part contains leaves from a palm tree. A biblical commandment directly mentions the palm tree in respect to the celebration of the festival of Sukkot: "And you shall take on the first day the boughs of goodly trees, branches of palm trees, and the boughs of thick trees, and willows of the brook; and you shall rejoice before the Lord your God seven days" (Lev. 23:40).

Throughout history the depiction of a palm tree (תמר) has been viewed as a national symbol of the Land of Israel; for example, Jericho was referred to as "the city of palms."[14] The prophetess Deborah dispensed judgment from under a palm tree: "And Deborah, a prophetess, the wife of Lapidoth, judged Israel at that time. And she lived under the palm tree of Deborah between Ramah and Beth-El in Mount Ephraim; and the people of Israel came up to her for judgment" (Judg. 4:4–5).[15] Palm trees in the Jerusalem Temple are mentioned in the Hebrew Bible ("He carved the walls of the house all around about with carved engravings of Cherubim, palm trees, and open flowers in the inner and outer rooms"; 1 Kings 6:29); this description of the palm tree motif comes very close to the palm tree

Figure 1. The Sha'ar Ha-Shamayim Synagogue in the early twentieth century. *Source: The Jewish Encyclopedia* (New York: Funk and Wagnalls, 1905), 5:71.

motif in Sha'ar Ha-Shamayim. Further biblical references to palm trees decorating sanctuaries are found in Ezekiel's vision of the future Temple:

> And there were narrow windows to the little chambers, and to their posts around the gate inside, and likewise to the vestibules; and windows were around inside; and upon each post were palm trees. (Ezek. 40:16)
>
> And its windows, and its vestibule, and its palm trees, were according to the measure of the gate that looks toward the east; and it was ascended by seven steps; and its vestibule lay before them. (Ezek. 40:22)
>
> And there were seven steps to ascend it, and its vestibule was before them; and it had palm trees, one on this side, and another on that side, upon its posts. (Ezek. 40:26)
>
> And its vestibule was toward the outer court; and palm trees were upon its posts; and its ascent had eight steps. (Ezek. 40:31)[16]

Furthermore, a combination of sword-bearing angels and palm trees is mentioned in the following: "And it was made with cherubim and palm trees" (Ezek. 41:18). The placement of the palm trees in the Sha'ar Ha-Shamayim Synagogue resembles the descriptions of Ezekiel. As can be seen, the depiction of palm trees in this synagogue in Cairo is a definite reference to the ancient Temple in Jerusalem.

In order to fully decode the "embodiment" of the palm tree, one has to return to the textual medium to grasp the teaching potential of this symbol. For example, the palm tree, according to the Alexandrian Jewish philosopher Philo, was a symbol of virtue and victorious strength.[17] A similar conception is found in a midrashic text which explains the biblical metaphor of the palm tree. This biblical metaphor characterizes the righteous:

Bereshit Rabbah 41:1

> *And the Lord plagued Pharaoh and his house with great plagues* (Gen. 12:17). It is written: *The righteous shall flourish like the palm tree; he shall grow like a cedar in Lebanon* (Ps. 92:13). As the palm and the cedar have neither crookedness nor excrescences, so the righteous have neither crookedness nor excrescences; as the shadow of the palm and the cedar is cast afar, so is the reward of the righteous far away; as the heart of the palm and the cedar is directed upward, so are the hearts of the

> righteous directed toward the Holy One, blessed be He, as it is written, *Mine eyes are ever toward the Lord, for He will bring forth my feet out of the net.* (Ps. 25:15)

The above midrashic text is based upon a lemma in Ps. 92:13, which is utilized in a simile. The resulting reading is a combination of several lemmata from the biblical verse, and it establishes that righteous people, according to this midrashic passage, are comparable to palm trees.

In the Zohar, the mystical text regularly studied by Sephardic Jews, several passages emphasize the symbolism of the palm tree. A precious quality of a palm tree within the Zoharic framework, namely the unification of male and female forces, is set forth in the following passage which emphasizes the similarity of the righteous character of Abram and Sarai to a flourishing palm tree.

Zohar, vol. 1, 82b

> R. Isaac explained the text: *The righteous shall flourish like the palm tree; he shall grow like the cedar in Lebanon* (Ps. 92:13). Why is the righteous man compared to a palm tree? Because just as, if a palm tree is cut down, it takes a long time for one to grow again, so if the world loses a righteous man, it is a long time before another arises in his place. Further, just as a palm tree does not grow unless the male [palm tree] is accompanied by the female, so the righteous cannot flourish unless they are male and female together, like Abram and Sarai.

The most significant feature on the street façade of the Sha'ar Ha-Shamayim Synagogue is the design of the palm trees, which dominates all other artistic aspects of the façade. The façade of the building is symmetrical; there are two rows of windows. Each window of the first row is divided by a small pillar. At the street level the windows are flanked by two rectangular kiosks, both of which are decorated with a Star of David motif. Above the pillars, on top of the windows, one finds the Tablets of the Law. The façade above the windows has representations of date palm trees that stretch up to the second row of windows, which are reduced to a smaller scale than the first row. Each palm tree is a protruding relief; the tree trunk is crowned by a circle of palm branches from which hang two clusters of dates. The impression of these palm trees is realistic as well as decorative (see Figure 2).

The façade has geometrical cornices with small rounded decorations. The cornices are decorated with wavy lines that are reminiscent of Ancient Egyptian depictions of water, including the river Nile; this decorative element may refer to the location of the synagogue in the city of Cairo, on the banks of the Nile. The top of the façade is marked by a curving contour rather than by an elaborate cornice. The roof is crenellate and the sides of the pediment are shaped like steps. Another striking feature is that the four corners of the building all rise above the roof in four semi-arches that resemble the horns of a ram; these "horns" are comparable to the ancient horned altars found in Meggido and Beer-Sheva.[18] The rounded tops of the semi-arches recall the horns of the altar in the Temple in Jerusalem; for example "and from the altar projecting upward, shall be four horns" (Ezek. 43:15). This serves to remind the worshipers that their prayers are directed toward the site of the Temple in Jerusalem. Additionally, these "horns" on the corners of the roof could be a specific reference to the *Shekhinah*, God's presence, which was represented by the horns of the altar of the Jerusalem Temple.[19] The façade evokes not only the Jerusalem Temple but also an Egyptian temple, particularly the Ptolemaic Temples such as found in Edfu, in its monumental design.

The entrance to the synagogue courtyard does not face the street. One enters the synagogue's courtyard from the right side of the building. The wall facing the courtyard contains a Hebrew inscription on the left side of the entrance door to the synagogue (see Table 1).

This inscription, which is dedicated to the memory of Vita Mosseri,[20] contains many allusions to the Hebrew Bible and to the liturgy of the synagogue that are used to characterize a righteous man. For example, the Torah service is alluded to in the above quote from Psalm 24; other quotes are "laudation" verses. Furthermore, the quote "from the foundation to the coping" is from 1 Kings 7:9; this verse describes in part the construction of the Solomonic Temple in Jerusalem. The name of the synagogue, "Sha'ar Ha-Shamayim" (The Gate of Heaven), is referred to in this inscription. The name of the synagogue is derived from Gen. 28:17: "And he was afraid and said: How awesome is this place! This is none other than the house of God, and this is the gate of heaven." This passage is from the bibli-

Figure 2. Façade (Photo: Ulmer).

cal story of Jacob dreaming of a ladder to heaven. Additionally, the name of the synagogue suggests a reference to Ps. 118: 19–20 ("Open to me the gates of righteousness that I may enter through them and give thanks to the Lord. This is the gate of the Lord; the righteous shall enter through it"). These verses are part of the Hallel Psalms recited in the synagogue during the celebration of the pilgrim festivals.

These inscriptions in the courtyard serve to teach and inspire all those who enter the sanctuary. From the courtyard one enters the synagogue through an elevated kiosk, which again is an element found in the architecture of ancient Egyptian temples; for example, the Philae Temple has several kiosks. The wooden entrance doors of the synagogue are beautifully carved and have the same palm tree motif as the outer walls of the building. The stained-glass windows of the two sections of the entrance door each have a wooden, carved date palm tree in the middle. Also, the brass metal fittings around the door handle are in the shape of palm trees. The door reveals the very strong influence of art nouveau. The same palm tree ornament is repeated again and again throughout the art work of the synagogue.

The floor plan of the synagogue sanctuary includes a vestibule that leads to the synagogue as well as to the stairs that provide access to the galleries. A synagogue vestibule functions as a place where worshipers congregate and greet each other before entering the main sanctuary. The left side of the vestibule bears the French inscription: "A la mémoire de Feu Moïse de Cattaui Pasha 1850–1924" (To

Table 1

[Translation]
[Line 1] For Your loving kindness[a] is better than life; [2] O continue Your loving kindness, God, unto them that know Thee[b] [3] You take pity,[c] Your compassion is great[d] [4] [Dedicated] to the man that has a pure heart and clean hands.[e] [5] Behold the prosperous man, he shall be like a tree planted by the rivers of water,[f] [6] His name shall be praised, in everlasting memory,[g] [7] His good sense is comely; he is reasonable, [8] This is the praiseworthy Gabbai [9] Who endeavored in the construction of this house of our God, and this is the Gate of Heaven (*sha'ar shamayim*)[h] [10] And with his strength and wealth he stood like a hero for its improvement, from the foundation to [11] the coping,[i] a noble and great man, fond of the Torah and its students, [12] R. Vita Bey Mosseri, May he rest in Paradise, [13] Remember him for good, God,[j] Amen.

כי טוב חסדך מחיים
משוך חסדך האל ליודעיך
ורחמיך יכמר המון מעיך
לאיש בר לבב ונקי כפים
הן גביר עץ שתול על פלגי מים
לזכר עולם מהלל שמו
נאה לו טעמו ונימוקו עמו
ה"ה הגבאי המפואר
אשר השתדל בבנין בית אלדינו זה
וזה שער השמים
ובכחו ואונו עמד כגבור לשכללו מהמסד עד
הטפחות איש שר וגדול אוהב התורה ולומדיה
כה"ר ויטא ביך מוצרי נ"ע
זכרה לו אלדים לטובה אמן

[a]Ps. 69:17.
[b]Ps. 36:11.
[c]Gen. 43:30.
[d]Isa. 63:15.
[e]Ps. 24:4.
[f]Ps. 1:3.
[g]Ps. 112:6.
[h]Gen. 28:17.
[i]1 Kings 7:9.
[j]Neh. 5:19.

the memory of Moses Cattaui Pasha). Cattaui Pasha had been president of the Jewish community of Cairo for forty years.[21] One also sees a large marble plaque in the design of the Tablets of the Law with gilded frames containing the names of former synagogue officials. Another plaque in the vestibule commemorates a more recent Gabbai, Zaki Mori (he died in 1965), with a bilingual (Hebrew/French) inscription (see Table 2).

The Hebrew inscription cited in Table 2 is again based upon selective verses from the Hebrew Bible, many of which are part of the synagogue liturgy.[22] This inscription is befitting for the Gabbai.

The Sanctuary

In the synagogue sanctuary the *teva* and the *aron ha-qodesh* (ark) are given equal emphasis by being placed at opposite sides in the center of the large three-naved room.[23] On each of the two sides of the *teva* there is a marble column. The capitals of these columns are scroll-shaped. The *teva* is semicircular and is surrounded by a decorated metal railing with a floral design; seven marble dividers form the divisions of this railing. Next to the *teva* are two large candelabras in the shape of palm trees. The *aron ha-qodesh* is elevated and has a dais in front of it with a decorated metal railing of floral design. The blue velvet *parokhet* (curtain) protecting the *aron ha-qodesh* has an inscription (see Table 3).

The above inscription honors the memory of David Joseph who died in 1977. The wooden doors of the *aron ha-qodesh* are carved in the same date palm tree motif of the entire synagogue building. The *aron ha-qodesh* contains several Torah scrolls, some of them in beautiful wooden cases, others with embroidered cloth mantles. The standing wooden Torah cases are based upon the Sephardic

Table 2

[Translation of the Hebrew:] [Line 1] Blessed be the memory of the righteous,[a] [2] his righteousness endures forever.[b] [3] He worked with all his might and strength for the community [4] and for the *Sha'ar Shamayim* Synagogue [5] all the days of his vigor and strength. [6] He died on Friday the 10th of Cheshvan [7] in the year 5726.[c] May his soul be bound in the bond of eternal life![d]	En Hommage à netre [*sic*] regrette Zaki Mory Gabbay de çe temple 1957–1965 pour son dévouement au service de la kehila les fidèles reconnaissants.	זכר צדיק לברכה צדקתו עומדת לעד עבד בכל כחו ומרצו לטובת הקל ולטובת בית הכנסת שער שמים כל ימי מישך נבאותו נ'ל'ב'ע ביום שישי י חשון התשכו תנצבה

[a]Prov. 10:7.
[b]Ps. 111:3, 112:3, 112:9.
[c]November 5, 1965.
[d]1 Sam. 25:29.

Table 3

[Translation:] [Line 1] This curtain has been sanctified [2] in order to uplift the soul of [3] the learned[a] R. David Josef of blessed memory, [4] who died on the 27th of Tamuz[b] [5] 5737. [6] May his soul be bound in the bond of eternal life!	פרוכת זו מוקדשת לעלוי נשמת ר' דוד יוסף גאון ז"ל שנפטר ביום כ"ז תמוז תשל"ז תנצבה

[a]Hebrew: *gaon.*
[b]July 13, 1977.

custom of reading the Torah scroll while it is in an upright position. Some of the woodwork of these Torah cases has ivory inlays in an Islamic ornamental pattern, which derives from the rich craftsmanship of Cairo. At the top of the scroll handles are silver finials. The hanging brass lamps resemble lamps that are found in mosques; such lamps are, however, a regular feature of synagogues in Middle Eastern countries. The *aron ha-qodesh* has a large wooden carving of date palm trees on its right and left side; this is in contrast to many other synagogues that have columns referred to as Jachin and Boaz.[24] A metal candelabrum with nine branches in the design of a palm tree stands in front of the dais on a small pedestal; the pedestal itself is in scroll form.

The women's gallery is above the *teva*; the parapet is decorated with lotus flowers and ornaments. The seats of the sanctuary are made of the same type of wood that is found throughout the synagogue. The wood is mahogany colored, possibly stained cedar wood. On the back of some of the seats is a "cartouche" consisting of a circular metal plate that bears the name of a former occupant; the practice of placing a "cartouche" on these seats was probably derived from ancient Egyptian inscriptions, which signified the names of Egyptian kings (Pharaohs). Above the center of the sanctuary rises the *copula* to a height of twenty-two meters. The beams that support the light green ceiling depict beige-colored Stars of David and floral ornaments. The beams themselves are supported by columns with proto-Ionic scroll capitals; these columns emanate from the floor of the sanctuary. The walls of the sanctuary are blue in color.

The stained-glass windows in the sanctuary have pointed arches; these windows contain very beautiful geometric designs, including two yellow semicircles and one complete yellow circle within a blue and green patterned ornamental background. The borders of the windows show lotus flowers. The windows are displayed in sets of two; between these pairs of windows are additional date palm tree designs in wood. Metal electric lamps with glass fixtures shaped like lotus flowers are found throughout the sanctuary.[25] The lotus-flower design is a direct borrowing from Pharaonic art. The lotus flower was the emblem of Upper Egypt, one of the "Two Lands" that comprised Ancient Egypt. Temple pillars in Ancient Egypt often had capitals carved in the shape of lotus flowers. The lotus was symbolic of rebirth; for example, one of the Egyptian creation myths describes how the newborn sun-god rose from a floating lotus.[26] In addition to representing ancient Egyptian cultural concepts, the lotus design in the synagogue is reminiscent of art nouveau.[27] This strong influence of art nouveau is found in the polychromed window panes, the lotus-flower lamps, the craftsmanship of the woodwork and the metalwork which reveal a great consistency of form, with elastic proportions, flowing and undulating surfaces. This consistency makes the Sha'ar Ha-Shamayim Synagogue an exquisite place of worship. However, the synagogue rarely has enough participants to constitute a *minyan* (quorum of ten worshipers); the usual number of participants is about five people. The absence of a full Torah service, of a permanent rabbi, and of young people is the sign of a dying community. Nevertheless, the building of the Sha'ar Ha-Shamayim Synagogue in central Cairo serves as a permanent reminder of the longstanding Jewish presence in Egypt.

The Synagogue as a Teaching Tool

The building of the Sha'ar Ha-Shamayim Synagogue shaped and expressed the values of the Jews of Cairo in the early years of the twentieth century. The synagogue integrated the Jewish community of Cairo into the Egyptian environment and reflected the rich history of the community while simultaneously expressing contemporary European art forms, such as art nouveau and French Empire. For Judaism to flourish there is a great need for a vibrant community in respect to maintaining prayer services and the observances of religious festivals; additionally, community is important for Jewish continuity. The Jews who built and supported the Sha'ar Ha-Shamayim Synagogue respected the history of their institutions and the long history of Jews in Egypt from the Israelite presence in Pharaonic Egypt to the more immediate presence of Egyptian Jews. The nineteenth- and twentieth-century Egyptian Jews were emancipated and assimilated into Egyptian society and contributed substantially to the economy and the prosperity of Egypt. In the synagogue building the collective memory and shared experiences of the Jewish people were nurtured. The objective for many decades was that the next generation would learn to appreciate the successes and failures of the prior generation. This was particularly important to the descendants of Egyptian Jews, who after the foundation of the modern State of Israel and the ensuing Egyptian-Israeli wars experienced a "second Exodus from Egypt." The Sha'ar Ha-Shamayim Synagogue serves as a teaching tool for Egyptian society to accept its past and to fully acknowledge the Peace Treaty with Israel in 1979.

This building has several architectural elements that reflect Egyptian art forms—the kiosks, the monumental design of the building, the lotus flowers. The synagogue's inscriptions bear the names of the founding families who lived in Egypt. The community builders acknowledged and affirmed the contribution of the members. Community is by definition made up of many individuals, from the charisma of the designated leaders—the chief rabbis of Cairo—to all members who made gifts and served as a community resource. People still today take their children and visitors to the inscription on the walls and point out their names. Thus, this synagogue articulates values such as education and charity. In a fluid, chaotic, or confused place and time, the building has been a center. The Sha'ar Ha-Shamayim Synagogue in Cairo, Egypt, communicates the values of the past in its magnificent artwork and serves as a teaching tool to any visitor.

Notes

1. With respect to the Egyptian culture of memory that was purposefully preserved in ancient Egyptian stone buildings, see Jan Assmann, "Stein und Zeit: Das monumentale Gedächtnis der altägyptischen Kultur," in Jan Assmann and T. Hölscher, *Kultur und Gedächtnis* (Frankfurt am Main, 1988), 87–114. Jan Assmann, *Das Kulturelle Gedächtnis: Schrift, Erinnerung und politische Identität in früheren Hochkulturen* (Munich: C. H. Beck, 1992; 4th paperback ed., 2002), partial, English translation by Rodney Livingstone, *Religion and Cultural Memory: Ten Studies* (Stanford, Calif.: Stanford University Press, 2006), 51, 76, analyzes the function of "memorialization" concerning buildings and he relates his discussion to Holocaust monuments. The Holocaust museum Yad Va-Shem in Jerusalem derives its name from a passage in Isa. 56:5 ("And to them will I give in my house and within my walls a memorial and a name [yad va-shem] better than sons and of daughters; I will give them an everlasting name, that shall not be cut off"), which combines the notion of a building and a memorial. This notion of a memorial and a name may also be detected in the Sha'ar Ha-Shamayim Synagogue.
2. My description of the synagogue is based upon field work performed during more than a dozen visits to Egypt in the 1980s and 1990s. The synagogue is located at 17 Adly Street, formerly Maghrabi Street. A newspaper article about the synagogue, Samir Rafaat, "Gates of Heaven," *Cairo Times* (September 2, 1999), is available on the Internet (http://www.egy.com/landmarks/99-09-02.shtml); this article contains pictures of the synagogue and its interior. Other literature concerning the synagogue is found in Maurice Fargeon, *Les Juifs en Egypte depuis les origins jusqu'à ce jour* (Cairo: Paul Barbey, 1938), 198–203; Manfred R. Lehmann, "Synagogues du Caire," in Gilbert Cabasso, Ehtel Carasso, André Cohen, et al., *Juifs d'Egypte: Images et textes* (Paris: Edition du Scribe, 1984), 115–37; Jack Mosseri, "The Synagogues of Egypt: Past and Present," *The Jewish Review* 5 (1913/14): 31–44. Concerning the Jews in Egypt in the twentieth century see Gudrun Krämer, *The Jews in Modern Egypt, 1914–1952* (Seattle: University of Washington Press, 1989). A picture of the synagogue is also found in Victor D. Sanua, "Growing Up Jewish in Cairo," *Image Magazine*, April 20, 1997 (repr. in Sanua, *Articles on the Jews from Egypt Which Appeared in the Image Magazine 1997–1998* [Brooklyn: International Association of Jews from Egypt, 1998]; Sanua, "A Jewish Childhood in Cairo," in Victor D. Sanua, *Fields of Offering: Studies in Honor of Raphael Patai* (Cranbury, N.J.: Associated University Presses, 1983), 283–95.
3. See R. Ulmer, "Discovering Mosaistics: Israel's Egyptian Roots," *Bulletin of the Israeli Academic Centre in Cairo* 18 (1994): 24–27, and the sources cited therein; J. K. Hoffmeier, *Israel in Egypt: The Evidence for the Authenticity of the Exodus Tradition* (New York: Oxford University Press, 1997).
4. See, e.g., Raymond Stambouli, "L'activité économique des Juifs d'Egypte (XIXe et XXe siècles)," in *Juifs d'Egypte*, 193–213.
5. Mosseri, "The Synagogues of Egypt," writes: "As a result of the increase of the Jewish population in Cairo in the last twenty-five years, new synagogues have been built in 1890 (Névé Shalom), in 1900 (Ets Haim), and 1903 (Shaar Hashamayim), the two former in the Abbassieh quarter, and the latter, the prettiest and biggest of all, in the Ismailia quarter" (43). Fargeon, *Les Juifs en Egypte*, 199, specifies that the synagogue was established in 1905 (5665).
6. See, e.g., the collection of papers, Jacob Lassner, ed., *Cairo's Ben Ezra Synagogue: A Gateway to Medieval Mediterranean Life* (Chicago: Spertus Institute of Jewish Studies, 2001). A major repository of Geniza fragments is at Cambridge University; see http://www.lib.cam.ac.uk/Taylor-Schechter/GOLD.
7. One inscription reads: "Refuge Ben Ezra; Ralph S. Green, רל[ף] ז. גרין.
8. My Web site contains links to photographs of this cemetery: www.facstaff.bucknell.edu/rulmer/. Pictures of Bassatin are also found in *Juifs d'Egypte*, 144, 184–85, the tomb of the Mosseri family is shown on 187. After the cemetery was subjected to vandalism and "squatting," a process of documenting the inscriptions is under way. See also the Web site of *Bassatine News* vols. 1–20 (October 1, 1995–2005), www.geocities.com/bassatin/bassai.htm.
9. M. R. Lehmann, "Synagogues du Caire," in *Juifs d'Egypte*, 115–37; Fargeon, *Les Juifs en Egypte*, 199ff. Ashkenazi Synagogue, Al-Noubi Street; Kubbeh Synagogue, Misr-Sudān Street, Kubbeh Gardens; Hanan Synagogue, Daher; Heliopolis Synagogue, Heliopolis; Meir Y. Biton Synagogue, Orabi, Ma'adi; Beit Mosseri, *Ḥāret El-Yahūd*.
10. See Victor D. Sanua, "Emigration of Sephardic Jews from Egypt after the Arab-Israeli Wars," *Proceedings of the Eleventh World Congress of Jewish Studies* (Jerusalem, 1994), sec. B, 3, pp. 215–22.
11. See Krämer, *The Jews in Modern Egypt*, 42.
12. Concerning *art nouveau* in a synagogue cf. C. H. Krinsky, "Hector Guimard's Art nouveau Synagogue in Rue Pavée Paris," *Journal of Jewish Art* 6 (1979): 105–11.

13. See E. R. Goodenough, *Jewish Symbols in the Greco-Roman Period* (New York: Pantheon Books), 1:184ff., and also Steven Fine, *Art and Judaism in the Greco-Roman World: Toward a New Jewish Archaeology* (Cambridge: Cambridge University Press, 2005), 140–44; the date palm was a Jewish symbol in the Greco-Roman world. The mosaic from Hammam Lif, Tunisia (Brooklyn Museum) dates from circa sixth century CE; see the publication by the Brooklyn Museum, *The Tree of Paradise* (Brooklyn, N.Y., 2005).
14. Deut. 34:4; Judg. 1:16; Judg. 3:13; 2 Chron. 28:15.
15. The palm tree of Deborah is also found in the title of a major mystical text: Cordovero's *The Palm Tree of Deborah.*
16. See also Ezek. 40:34, 37, and chap. 41; 2 Chron. 3:5.
17. For example, Tamar's name is explained as relating to a palm tree (Philo, *Alleg. Int.*, xxiii.73).
18. See, for example, Y. Aharoni, "The Horned Altar of Beer Sheba," *BA* 37 (1974): 2–6.
19. Compare Ps. 18:3 "the horns of my salvation."
20. See Krämer, *The Jews in Modern Egypt*, 43.
21. Ibid., 45, 86ff., 101–2.
22. A Sephardic prayer book that may have been used in the synagogue is entitled סדור מנחה חדשה (Cairo: J. Hezkiel, 1943); Hebrew, French, Ladino; an earlier Cairene prayer book is depicted in *Juifs d'Egypte*, 233: *Siddur Farhi* فرحي شدور (Cairo: Hillel Yaacoub Farhi, 1917), in Arabic and Hebrew.
23. It should be noted that in Sephardic synagogues the platform for the reading of the Torah is referred to as *teva*. With regard to a short description of the sanctuary, see Lehmann, "Synagogues," 124–26.
24. The Jerusalem Temple had columns designated as Jachin and Boaz, see, e.g., Carol Meyers, *s.v.* "Jachin and Boaz," in *ABD* 3, 597–98; S. Yeivin, "Jachin and Boaz," *PEQ* 91 (1959): 1–15.
25. See B. Kern-Ulmer, *Rabbinische Responsen zum Synagogenbau* (Hildesheim: Olms, 1990), 135.
26. See, e.g., *Knaur's Lexikon der ägyptischen Kultur* (Munich: Knaur, 1960), *s.v.* "Lotos," p. 186. To celebrate this event a hymn was recited in the Egyptian temples on festival days, e.g., the Lotus Offering, especially at the cult center of Edfu. The blue lotus was also the emblem of the god Nefertem, "the Lord of Perfume." Fragrance in Ancient Egypt functioned as a sign of divine presence. The lotus also appears to have been strongly connected with sensual pleasure.
27. For example, the stylized flower designs on Tiffany lamps (see Corning Museum of Glass, Corning, N.Y.).

On Three Early Incidences of Hebrew Script in Western Art

Harris Lenowitz

Though some have theorized that the Hebrew script in the trilingual titulus of the fourteenth-century *Crucifixion* by Giotto is the first appearance of Hebrew in Western art, the script in fact began to appear in that circumstance at least two centuries earlier, at the beginning of the twelfth century. Major changes in the Church's relationship with the Jews occurred between these earliest appearances. For purposes of understanding the significance of the earlier date, the most important change was the renewal (following Jerome [347–420]) of Hebrew study among Christians. At about the same time, with Peter of Cluny (1092–1156) and the Gregorian Reform (1050–1080), the conventional art-image of the Jew begins to shift toward the subhuman and the monstrous. In this history, the use of Hebrew script in works of Western art serves to proclaim, ambiguously, the connections and disconnections between Christianity and Judaism: the particular variety of supercessionism that is in the mind of the artist, the patron and, ultimately, the viewer.

The manuscript illuminations I present here relate to a brief but not altogether unhappy period in Norman England and Aquitaine, of mutual, relatively benign relations between Jewish and Christian scholars. The period is typified historically by Harding's *monitum* to the Vulgate he caused to be made in 1109 and artistically by the Hebrew scripts in the opening page of the St. Alban's Bible Lamentations (ca. 1115) and the illumination preceding a commentary on the Book of Jeremiah (ca. 1120) that shows the prophet addressing King Zedekiah.[1] Though the Hebrew script in both cases is unquestionably Jewish-handed (a third illumination—from the Montalcino Bible [ca. 1150], will illustrate the variances among such scripts) and evidences a cooperative, presumably nonforced, relationship between a Jewish worker and a Christian executive, themes in the presentations of Jeremiah/Lamentations must yet be read typologically within the Church. Decoding such readings, tensed between the making of art and the use of art to define social relationships, helps to clarify the picture that has developed over the last few years concerning the warmth of such relationships, which ostensibly resulted from a Christian interest in the "Hebrew truth" particularly as they developed through the north French Jewish schools such as that of Rashi (1040–1105) and his sons-in-law at Troyes, France.

Christian Hebraism, Hebrew Script in Art and Antisemitism

A Jew recognizing Hebrew script in a work of art that has no function in Jewish culture, as opposed to illuminations in a Passover Haggadah, for example, sees something familiar and yet odd. The Jew who sees Hebrew letters in a painting from the Italian *cinquecento*, for example, reacts with puzzlement, perhaps suspicion and, on occasion, pleasure at being able to respond with amusement (at misspellings and misunderstandings). The experience is rather like that of being in a museum in which the Schatzkammer of a seventeenth-century noble is exhibited and then finding oneself inside it on a shelf. This disorientation stands in contrast to the perceptions of Christian artists, patrons, and viewers of art, who see the Jew and Jewish theology and history through the one lens. Though the Christian viewers will not, for the most part, understand the calligraphic designs constituting artists' representations of Hebrew script as making words and sentences, they can identify its significance. The Jew on the other hand is at best bemused; peering through the Christian lens, he may know that he has been estranged, perhaps even dehumanized. Jews are not the intended or expected readers of Hebrew script in non-Jewish art.

Of course, Hebrew script does appear before the twelfth century in Jewish works (mosaics, frescoes, inscriptions including those of the catacombs). However, these manifestations for the most part do not engage Christianity. Thereafter Christianity makes increasing attempts to appropriate the Hebrew Bible and these efforts come eventually to include the Hebrew script, including the Hebrew letters and vowel points themselves. Indeed, the single most important drive contributing to the appearance of Hebrew script in Christian works of art is the very resolute and tenacious search by Christians to find that the Hebrew Bible, from people and plots to poetry and prophecy, testifies and defines not Judaism but Christian belief and practice. Under what circumstances and in what manner this phenomenon is manifested in a work of art are the important questions to be asked. The investigation should shed light on the varieties of Christian perceptions of the Jew, as it does to the exploration of other symbols, such as the physiognomies and postures, clothing (especially legally required costumes and accessories), appurtenances (moneybags, for example) that encode the Jew, the "Hebrew."

Christian scholars of Hebrew and their works (and, to a lesser degree, their Jewish and converted advisers) served as consultants and inspirations both before Western artists began to picture the script and thereafter. It was they who provided the connection between the two different references a Hebrew word has—the one the Jew knows as his own chief cultural marker, and the one the Christian knows as the mark of the Jew in the identity constructed by his Christian culture. It is the conflict between the two references that produces the ambivalent feelings in the museum patron I have described above. At the intersection of the artistic and scholarly enterprises, the varieties of Christian Hebraism—the pointed study of the Hebrew language by Christians—and the motives of those engaged in it provide important information about the works of art in which Hebrew inscriptions appear while the composite sheds light on contemporary Christian-Jewish relations. The ample quantity of works and artists that have participated in this tradition, from multiple, different origins, schools, and periods, offers the opportunity to investigate a wide variety of social and cultural contexts as well as works themselves from this distinctive prospect.

The term "Christian Hebraist" applies to Christian writers on the Hebrew language and on texts written by Christians in that language.[2] The writers may have many different interests and attitudes but these mostly associate themselves with a single polemic stance toward Jewish texts and culture, one that brings together the early ideology of *verus Israel* and the notion of the *veritas Hebraica*.[3] The composite accepts as true that the Hebrew Bible was in Hebrew and that Jewish/Hebrew commentary relates to that primevality and may or even should therefore be attended to by Christians ("the truth of Hebrew scripture"). Nevertheless, this recognition imposes no restriction on the determination of the proper reading of the original work; that must be the responsibility of the Christian "church" ("the True Israel"). Thus, the Hebrew language, works written in it, and the Hebrew scripts themselves are set within a larger constellation of ideas about Jews held by Christians (and influencing Jewish self-conceptions as well) from the beginnings of Christianity in the mid-first century to the present.

Hebrew script appears in Christian, European drawings, illustrations, illuminations, engravings, carvings, and stone sculpture and paintings. It also may be seen in or on works in metal—such as reliquaries, processional crosses, and cast-works, in stained glass and in sculpture—including seals and medals, in tapestries, and in both still and motion-picture photography (to include video and digital formats). For purposes of discussion, it seems most practical to use the term "Hebrew script" broadly and to include printed and cursive forms of Hebrew that create legible and communicative texts; calligraphic forms that intend to represent Hebrew script but are not readable as such (near-Hebrew and quasi-, or better, pseudo-Hebrew); and stylizations of other alphabets (see Figure 1) made to resemble the forms of Hebrew script (as well as Hebrew script that represents other languages such as Aramaic and Yiddish, Ladino, Judeo-Arabic, et al.). An understanding of the iconography of these forms of Hebrew script in works of Western art ought additionally to comprehend in its program the *absence* of the script both before and after the time it actually began to appear in order to describe the relevant social codes motivating the appearance or nonappearance of Hebrew.[4]

Figure 1. R. Griffin "Hosanna," from Gordon McClelland, *Rick Griffin* (Limpsfield, 1980), 91. (Courtesy of Ida Griffin.)

Elisabeth Revel-Neher hypothesized that the absence of negative images of Jews in Byzantine art, those that display Jews in their assigned roles in the Passion, together with the presence of images of Jews in daily life, argues for the lack of religiously driven antisemitic tendencies in the East, an absence of the constructed Jew of the *adversus Judaeos* conversations and literature emerging in the West.[5] Significantly, Hebrew script does not appear in Byzantine art. Antisemitism expressed in art, it seems, is a Western phenomenon and Hebrew script only appears in Western works. The period of the rebeginning—following the times of the early Church Fathers—of Christian Hebraism coincides with the Crusades and the wars against Arian heresy, and the next major outbreak coincides with the Reformation. In addition to these two main efflorescences, many isolated occurrences of Hebrew script in Western art, which are associated with internecine calumny, made most famous in the lemma of "judaization."[6] The appearance of the script stands for different attitudes—most of them jealous of Christian primacy and inimical toward Jews. Hebrew letters in Christian art in a given work before the modern period may signify the absence of real, that is, ambivalent, human, Jews in the minds and society of the artist and his or her patrons as well. In accord with this hypothesis, I have found that the period of the Crusades (~1095–1272) and that of the Plague (~1340sff.) in Europe are two of the richest for the appearance of the script.

There are obviously traditions that link such appearances together but no one use is exactly like any other. The Christian imagining of the Jew is so complex and its history so lengthy, and the critical importance of one or another image of *a* Jew or *The* Jew so central to it—however various in the *mises en scenes* in which the image appears—that describing the function of Hebrew script in a particular work of art is not exactly applied taxonomy. Sarah Lipton, following Schreckenberg, has demonstrated this complexity in regard to images of the Jew in her exploration of the range of meanings associated with the very familiar—and very familiarly termed "sign of infamy"—the Jew's Hat.[7] Its appearance is not always or simply a negative critique; worn by a Jew stabbing a Host or in a manuscript illuminating the crucifixion, such a hat signifies something different from a hat of similar dimension, color, and placement worn by such a universally admirable figure as Abraham or, indeed, Joseph.

We expect to see our fellows look their parts in our own dramas. Jews grow ugly in art for the first time as they come to figure in the struggles of the Gregorian Reform (ca. 1050–1080). The Jews were a pawn in this contention, their management an important objective, for both concrete and symbolic reasons, to be captured in the Church's triumph over secular rulers. The depiction of Jews in art multiplied thereafter and ultimately the control over the image came to rest in the hands of the Church. Living Jews became subjects of the Church, for the Jews were first Christ-killers and foremost devil worshippers and invincibly ignorant, requiring protection in order to play out their part in the Second Coming, and also to serve certain economic functions, such as money-lending. Their secular rulers had to submit to the Church's authority, supreme in this realm, as in all matters of religious consequence, like investiture. Jews are portrayed as they *Are*—god-killing monsters—and as they *are*, noncitizens of the City of God.

After the time of Peter of Cluny (1092–1156) and Bernard of Clairvaux (1090–1153) Jews are regularly depicted this way and some of that can be seen in representations at the monastery of Vezelay itself, site of Bernard's call for the Second Crusade (1146) (see Figure 2). For a very long, hard time, Jews and Devils had each other for company. Schreckenberg writes "literary apologetic against the Jews combined with an extended pictorial depiction of the [Christian] controversy [with Judaism in the period around 900. From then on, however, it continued into modern times]."[8] The appearance of Hebrew script in connection with Christian art images of Jews becomes common as part of the little reformations, mostly Italian, of the Renaissance, beginning with the discovery of the most important little book and its publication in the early 1400s, Horapollo's *Hieroglyphica*. Hebrew, along with other ancient languages and their scripts, becomes part of the rediscovery of antiquity, and its plantation in Christian society continues beyond the Reformation until very recently.

It is with the Venerable Peter of Cluny that the study of Hebrew for purposes of secular as well as ecclesiastical power—taking control over the Jews away from all but the Church—achieves a certain centrality among other resources for the Christian alienation of the Jew. Here it is only fair to acknowl-

Figure 2. Law and Devil (fr. J. Roubler, P. Claudel, *Vézelay*, Paris, 1948).

edge Petrus Alfonsi's (1062–1110) influence on Peter of Cluny's sermon, "Against the Jews" (published in two parts, one from 1143, chapter 1 through the first half of chapter 4, focusing on Christology; and the rest of the work devoted to demonizing the Jews and leaving them, their history, and rabbinic literature in ruins). This work also serves as the basis for Peter's later composition, "Against the Sect of the Saracens" (ca. 1150). Both are contributions to Peter's two-stage program for his Church: first, ridding the Church of internal dissidence (the treatise *Contra Petrobrusianos)*; second, expanding the realty and social territory controlled by the Church. Both treatises depend on sources and materials with which Peter became acquainted, though never well acquainted, through the sort of materials referenced by Alfonsi (formerly Mosé Sefardi) in his imaginary debate-treatise "Dialogues Rejecting Jewish Opinions." Even though Peter of Cluny's own essays are not dialogues but raving, merciless diatribes, we might look to Alfonsi as the common source for both, perhaps even in person. But if it was not that apostate, informed, and intelligent Jew telling tales out of school to Peter, it was surely another informed and intelligent Jew. (Oddly, Peter does not mention his sources.)[9] The point is that both treatises acknowledge the importance of penetrating the religious literature of Jews and Muslims in order to uncover their errors and their hate of the Lord. This is to be done as a step in the two-part conquest of the world for Christ. To accomplish this step required knowledge of the "sacred" texts of Judaism and Islam and acquiring that knowledge demanded expertise in Hebrew, Aramaic, and Arabic. Christian interest in the religious literature written in Hebrew, as well as in Arabic (the effort produces the first translation of the Quran in the west), attains elevated status. The appearances of Hebrew script in art for some time to come attest to the new cachet. Thus, Giotto's *Crucifixion* which, as initially mentioned is taken by some (see n. 3 above) to be the first non-Jewish work in Christian Europe to display Hebrew script, appears during this period (see Figures 3–4).

To this point I have sought to show when and where a corner was turned in the history of the Christian manipulation of the Jewish image. I have proposed that particular displays of letters of the Hebrew alphabet arise in Christian art from that moment. I have also suggested that Jewish informer(s) sought and found common cause with those they educated at the courts of King Alfonso I of Aragon, from which Alfonsi had come to Cluny, and Peter of Cluny. Now I will propose that a variation of the same ideology-in-action produced what were the earliest appearances of Hebrew script in Christian art, a more or less open, somewhat more benign exchange of information between Jews and Christians concerning Jewish texts and traditions and the Hebrew language. This earlier stage can be associated with a geographical-historical locus, or perhaps more than one, and intellectual leanings common to certain Jewish scholars and certain Christian ones. Evidence can be found in studies of Christian and Jewish literature of the time and place of the meetings and documented as well by images of the Hebrew script in contemporary works of art (see Figures 5–7).

I think that the urban campuses of higher education that were developing at this time, as opposed to the monasteries, appear to be responsible for *this* broadening of intellectual interests. Universities in England and Europe grew out of the need for a more advanced education for church functionaries alongside a turn toward a new hermeneutic practice that rejected the authority of scholasticism and reformulated fields of study altogether. In particular, we can isolate a tradition of scholarly collegiality between Christian and Jewish intellectuals associated with studies of the text of the Hebrew Bible. The studies, beginning with Harding's Vulgate research, were initially undertaken in order to reach conclusions concerning what words the Bible actually contained. (For some time both the Cistercians and the Cluniacs were deeply involved in such investigations.) This impulse is rerouted and continues into the work of the Victorines (participants in the move away from cathedral schools and the monastic life toward the life of the school), especially that of Hugh of St. Victor (1078–1141). The meeting ground has Christians asking Jews, "What is in your text?" In addition to attempting to reread Hebrew texts as expressing Christian theology, these Christians were concerned with the text's simple meaning, the *pshat*—the simple, nonallegorical meaning—of the text and is associated with the north-French Jewish school of Rashi, his daughters and their husbands, the Tosafists, in particular. The exchanges seemed to be friendly ones, at least as this single realm of contact was concerned. Relations in the neighborhood of Cluny had started out well, in fact. We do not know the origins of the Jewish settlement of Burgundy or much of the activities of the early settlers. They lived, on land that belonged to

Figure 3. Giotto, Crucifixion from Sta. Maria Novelle.

Figure 4. Detail of figure 3, the titulus.

Figure 5. Book of Jeremiah, from Cahn, *Romanesque Bible Illumination.*

them, in harmony with their Christian neighbors. Jews in fact borrowed money (!) from Cluny. (Soon, Peter launched a crusade as we know, which included a prohibition on taking *loans* from Jews.) Most interestingly for this essay, in the act of August, 949 lending money to one Joshua and his wife, Tensoretis, on the security of their farm, both the names of Joshua and of his witness, Samuel, are written in Hebrew characters (in CLU 2762, 2.783), recognizing that language as a legal one. Out of this mélange of religion and reasonable investigation and some degree of harmony between Christians as scholars and Jews as scholars arose the two illuminations associated with Jeremiah and, perhaps, the third.

The first two works are contemporaries, from the first decades of the twelfth century, and may be associated with what has been named the "Channel" (north French-British) school. In the one (see Figure 5), illustrating the Book of Jeremiah, Jeremiah, standing over the king, is explaining to Zedekiah that, his regal prerogatives notwithstanding (note the ambiguity in the figure of the king seated upon his *faldstool*), he is not destined to be victorious in a war against Mesopotamia. In the other (see Figure 6) to the Book of Lamentations, thought then to be the work of Jeremiah as well, the commentary that is presented consists of two exegeses of the alphabet. The Hebrew letters in both cases are very likely to have been written by one of those trained in the north French/English book hand of the period, a Jewish scribe, cf. Valmadonna Trust Library 1.

The Hebrew alphabet is in fact what is depicted in both cases, the first, of the king, on account of the second, since the Book of Lamentations is largely a grouping of five laments written in an alphabetic acrostic while the Book of Jeremiah has no associations with the alphabet as an organizing principle. Biblical poems written in acrostics are associated with what is known as the Wisdom school, which proposes that God's rule is demonstrated through rational, human behavior learned through the experience of living. The alef-bet with its principle of organization makes such works easily susceptible to memorization, for one thing. That's what Jeremiah is trying to do for Zedekiah: teach him the *A*s and *B*s of international politics.

The second illumination (see Figure 6) is a bit different. Above each of the transliterated names of the letters of the Hebrew alphabet there appear words that comment on the letters and on the values they teach. This association is carried out through puns on the Hebrew meaning of the Hebrew names of the letters in Hebrew, then interpreted in Latin. (The names of the letters are also to be found alongside the verses they initiate in the text that follows the alphabet table in the margin.) In both these works the Hebrew is that of an experienced Jewish scribe, perhaps a convert to Christianity, working for Christian masters, making one of their holy books in their monastic scriptoriums. By the time of Jerome, the rabbis as well as Eusebius (263–339) have written just that sort of commentary on the alef-bet. They take the meanings of the names of the letters (not of their images, though most of the letters were at first pictographic; the letter alef pictures an ox, *alp* in the semitic dialect of the inventors and is not associated with the verb for "train," as in the super-linears) to be doctrinally meaningful particularly in association with the virtues proclaimed by the Wisdom school. Jerome largely restated Eusebius. In his *Letter to Paula* (XXX), he explains the names of the Hebrew letters to her. The interpretations of the names of the individual letters in section 5 are followed by seven sections in which they are grouped to make sentences.

The words over the letter names in the right column are those of the epistle, so that alef = *doctrina*, bet = *domus*, gimel = *plenitudo*, dalet = *tabularum*, he = *ista*. These are arranged, interpreted, and inflected in section 6 of the letter to make the meaningful sentence "doctrina ecclesiae, quae domus dei est, in librorum repperitur plenitudine divinorum" (The teaching of the Church, which is the house of God, is to be found in the abundance of divine books). The words over the letters in the left column—Alef = *deus*, bet = *filius*, gimel = *vox*—are from later interpretations, some by Jerome himself (he supplied more meanings for letters in his commentary on Psalm 118 [Vulgate references throughout] and again in the *Liber de nominibus hebraicis* and at last in his commentary on Lamentations, though this is often attributed to Bede [672–735]); and some by others: Ambrose (333–397), Isidore of Seville (560–636), and S. Remi (d. 533) on Psalm 118 and Raban Maur (776–856) in the eighth book of his commentary on Jeremiah; and, closest to the time of our manuscript, Paschal Radbert (d. 865) on Lamentations. The first set of meanings, over the right column, is, in general, the least tendentious in reaching for the meaning of the names in Hebrew itself. As mentioned above, Jerome gets alef as *doctrina* from the meaning of the word, or its root, as "train/learn/teach," while the meaning *Deus*, in the left column, may relate to the use of the first letter of the Hebrew and Greek in the alphabetic merismus figure, "I am the Alpha and the Omega." The meaning attached to the second letter in the left column, bet, as *filius* may have come about as a confusion with the Hebrew *ben* and gained its place as the Second Person, following *deus*. Whether in the one case, the bare meanings of the words in both columns, or in the other, Jerome's connected sentences, the alef-bet is being read with Christian meaning, its old meanings—based on the pictographs—superceded.

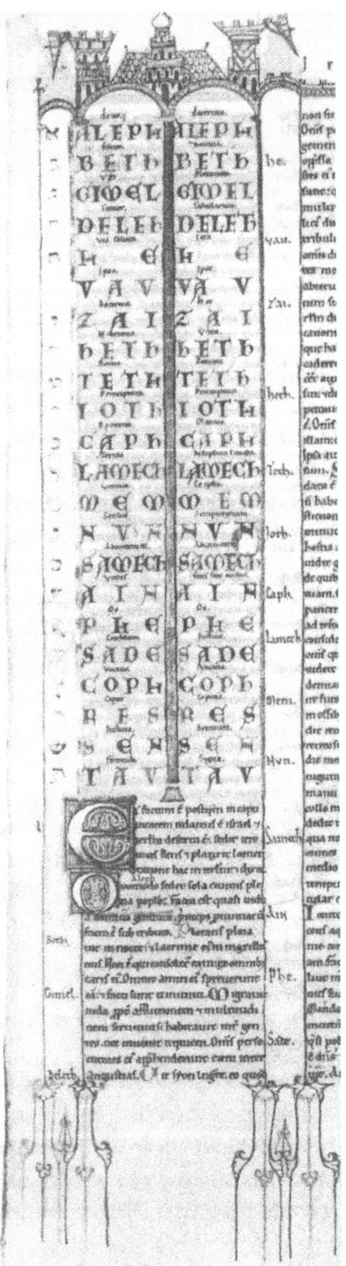

Figure 6. Opening page, Lamentations, from Cahn, *Romanesque Bible Illumination*.

In the Jeremiah-Zedekiah miniature (see Figure 5), Jeremiah holds a scroll on which are found the letters of the Hebrew alphabet—again by a Jewish hand—alone. It is proper for Jeremiah to be represented with this device by reason of his association with the acrostics of Lamentations; moreover, the dependable orderliness of the alphabet as his device associates him with wisdom and judgment as against Zedekiah's belligerence. Briefly, the Jeremiah of much Christian understanding is to be found in his lecture concerning the Good Shepherd of the House of David (22:1–5), or when he proclaims the deliverance from the Babylonian Captivity as the type and pledge of the Messianic deliverance in chapters 30–32. Jeremiah is moreover a type of Christ, a human lamb to be sacrificed (11:19 fulfilling Isa. 53:7), proclaiming the destruction of Jerusalem and its Temple, his concern rewarded with hatred; holy, suffering for no culpable act. The Offices of the Passion use a large amount of language from Jeremiah in fact.

While the order of the alef-bet, derived more or less from the Phoenician, represents more than one way of organizing symbols (of number as well as of sound or character shape) the purpose behind its own order is a mystery.[10] The topos of the order of the alphabet appears first in biblical acrostic poetry, much of it related to themes of the Wisdom school and to didactics. In the apocryphal *Gospel of Pseudo-Matthew*, §31 (Cp. Infancy Gospel of Thomas, Gk A §14, Gk B §6): [Jesus] said to Zaccheus [a teacher],

"Every letter from Aleph to Thau is discerned by the arrangement of it. First say what Thau is and I will tell you what Aleph is." And again he said, "They who do not know Aleph, how can they tell Thau, hypocrites that they are? Say what Aleph is first and then I will believe you when you say Beth."[11] (Other accounts highlight the construction shapes of the letters as meaningful.) If the teacher, Zaccheus, is in fact R. Yochanan ben Zakkai,[12] the tales may stem from another, earlier, rabbinic history-tale, that of R. Akiba,

> He went directly to a schoolhouse, and he and his son began reading from a child's tablet. . . . The teacher wrote down *alef* and *bet* for him, and he learned them; *alef* to *tav* and he learned them. . . . When he was told one Halakhah, he went off to reason with himself. "This *alef*," he wondered, "for what is it written? This *bet*, for what was it written?" (*Avot de-Rabbi Natan*, 6)

The *Sefer Yetzirah* (third to sixth century CE), the most frequently copied manuscript other than the Torah itself, is a treatise on the letters and numbers as the basic elements of creation and quite rare in arraying the alef-bet in groups that do not follow the order alef-bet but instead are grouped as "principial" or "elemental" letter groups in which points of articulation serve to gather the "simples"; the capacity for "doubling," another group (bet/gimel/dalet/kaf, pe, resh, tav); and materialization, the third (alef/mem/shin).

The Giant Bible of Montalcino is not from Britain, the Channel or North France (see Figure 7). It was made in the environs of Siena, perhaps in the scriptorium of the abbey of Sant' Antimo. Its two artists make use of the typical features of central Italian, Florentine, style ("an agitated lineiness, a nervous fussiness and," of particular interest to us, "a disorderly complication of motives."[13] The illumination most clearly evinces this last characteristic. Below the deus artifex and his Greek benediction the initial *I* extends to include six roundels of the days of Creation. To God's left stands Moses holding up in his right hand a cartouche in which Hebrew script appears and in his left a second cartouche containing the Latin translation of the beginning of the Hebrew text. (Cahn mentions the device as "an idiosyncratic . . . depiction of speech," though what is depicted is actually writing.)[14] The statement the illumination seems to make concerning the equality of the Hebrew with the Latin, Moses' own appropriation, even authorship, of both texts equally, together with the primacy granted the Hebrew text, at first brought me to consider the society of Siena as a contemporary circumstance from which the valorization of Hebrew stems. The commune of Siena maintained its independent ways through internal and external strife, preferred strong governmental structures of its own and insisted on legal, proper conduct. Granted, it had its moments of passion, as with San Bernardino or St. Catherine, and was no less devout than its neighbors. But coupling its devotion to the law and the appearance through the centuries of an unusual number of works exhibiting Hebrew script, important frescoes, and paintings in the City Hall, it seemed reasonable to me to think of a judaizing spirit. (Even Bernardino's famous elevation of the Greek-lettered IHS symbol to devotional status can be thought of as a substitution of letter for visual depiction corresponding to the Tetragrammaton.) Eventually and after more reading,[15] I came to pay more attention to two details in particular: the roundels and Moses' beard. The roundels are quite rare in Italy until the thirteenth century; they

Figure 7. Montalcino. Bk of Jeremiah, from Cahn, *Romanesque Bible Illumination.*

are common in earlier north French and British works. Moses' long, pointed, thready beard recalls English manuscripts, like the Lambeth Bible, the St. Albans Bible, and the Bury St. Edmunds Bible, all produced in England in a style displaying the most recently arrived north French fashions. The first two were, it seems, produced at St. Albans under the influence of a lot of north French glossed volumes of individual books of the Bible in the middle of the twelfth century. Most critics write of "gallicizing" stylisms, others of Channel influences on the Montalcino Bible.

Two matters in connection with this depiction and relevant to this essay remain to be discussed: the Hebrew of the upper cartouche and the Person with the scales. The Hebrew has some problems: the marker of the direct object (*'et*) before the word *shamayim* (sky) has been lost; the initial alef of the word *veha-'aretz* (and the earth) was left out, then added back in a superscript; the last word, *va-vohu* (and void) seems to have lost its bet and gained an alef. Both the words *tohu* (formless) and *[v]ohu* have an extra vav following the first consonant. These errors show that the scribe knew quite a bit of Hebrew (especially in the case of the added, vocalic, vavs) and was not working from a copy. Together with the clumsiness of the script itself a scribe who was not a particularly well-educated Hebraist, perhaps a Jew or a convert, perhaps someone trained by a Jew is suggested.

The Person with the scales is not God the Creator. Artistic convention gives the scales into the hand of Justice, a woman, and she shows up, crowned, scales in hand in the initial illumination of the Book of Wisdom (Wisdom of Solomon) in this manuscript. Illuminations in a few early psalters show God holding scales. Psalm 66 is one; it is centered on verse 10 in which God tests, tries, and judges Israel; the theme of Psalm 9 is God as judge and judgment is meted out to the psalmist in Psalm 16. In almost all of the stanzas of Psalm 118 the word *judgment* appears. Psalm 118 is already known to us as one of the sources for patristic and later midrashim based on the alphabetic acrostic form. The scales reach God's hand in Wisd. 11:21 where from the first God orders all things by measure, number, and weight, and acts in accord with his plan of creation and not by whim. This all seems to speak unambiguously for Jewish, not Christian, ideas behind this instantiation, whether indirectly through the

Figure 8. Vezelay, Grinding the Wheat, *Vézelay.*

social order of Siena or not. But to a very large extent the absoluteness of measured law, its logic and universal primordiality as well as its execution, are dissipated by mercy. Wisdom 11:22–27 takes up this second theme and concludes the chapter. Verse 22 is perhaps the source for the arm stretched out, which, though holding the scales, holds them out to the viewer. The arm upraised in blessing promises God's "compassion over all" and goes on to say that "you overlook the sins of men with a view to their repentance for you love all that exists and loathe nothing which you have created." Wisdom did not make it into the Hebrew canon or that of the Protestants, perhaps because of its denial of the "exclusive nationalist tradition of Israel" in favor of a "universalist philosophical tradition which appealed so strongly to the Jewish youth of Roman Alexandria"; perhaps because of its adaptations of the praises of Isis, quite possibly because of its excursus on mercy of which we have heard only the beginning and the extension of mercy to peoples who acted toward Israel and others with great cruelty.

Each of the miniatures I have discussed here testifies to relations between Jews and Christians. The meeting ground is the biblical text in its simplicity and a concern for making sense: literally, what is written there (a question that engaged Jerome deeply as well as Harding) and its significance. But as the Christian abandons his erstwhile companion and regains his school or monastery he grinds the Jews' wheat a second time. As at Vezelay.

Notes

A note to the reader: I have sought to keep the notes to this essay from subverting the main text. The information that they contain documents the main text and expands on it, but, in many cases, the notes offer an alternative reading of the same data; or a descant.

My heartfelt thanks are owed to the staff of the Marriott Library at the University of Utah, the Special Collections Librarians (Greg Thompson and Judy Jarrow), and especially to the staff of Interlibrary Borrowing (Linda Burns and Susan Brusik) without whose kind assistance this work could not have been done. I am also indebted to the Middle East Center of the University for several travel/research grants that contributed and continue to contribute to the endeavor.

1. This grouping follows the presentations and notes on these works in W. Cahn, *Romanesque Bible Illumination* (Ithaca, N.Y., 1982).
2. The most comprehensive studies on this topic include J. Friedman, *The Most Ancient Testimony* (Athens, 1983), H. Oberman, *The Roots of Anti-Semitism* (Philadelphia, 1984), and F. Manuel, *The Broken Staff* (Cambridge, 1992). A rather complete catalog of works and authors preceded by a concise taxonomy and history is Raphael Loewe's article "Hebraists, Christian" in the *Encyclopaedia Judaica* (Jerusalem, 1971), 8.9–71. A complete bibliography of Loewe's work—along with some important contributions to the whole topic—is to be found in N. de Lange, ed., *Hebrew Scholarship and the Medieval World* (Cambridge, 2001), 240–45.

   Although Christian Kabbalists are not all Hebraists, those that are fall within the broader category, *pace* J. Dan, ed., *The Christian Kabbalah* (Cambridge, 1997), 54. C. D. Ginsburg, *The Massoreth Ha-Massoreth of Elias Levita* (repr., New York, 1968, 10), on the other hand, writes that "[the Christian Hebraists] were only doing it for the kabbalah." Comprehensive studies on this subgroup include J. L. Blau, *The Christian Interpretation of the Cabala in the Renaissance* (New York, 1944), F. Secret, *Les Kabbalistes Chretiens de la Renaissance,* 2nd ed. (Milan, 1985), and J. Dan (above); a phenomenon marginal to the matter of Hebrew language and materials draws the attention of C. Swietlicki in *Spanish Christian Cabala* (Columbia, 1986).
3. The most complete survey of Jewish-Christian relations in the literature of the early period in the West (to 425) goes under this name: M. Simon, *Verus Israel,* 2nd ed. (Oxford, 1986). There is a profusion of estimable works on the topic in later periods. An excellent introduction to the topic of antisemitism is M. Shain, *Antisemitism* (London, 1998). E. H. Flannery, *The Anguish of the Jews,* 2nd ed. (New York, 1985), is chronologically arranged and covers twenty-three centuries with concision. Two earlier works remain valuable source collections: S. Kraus, *The Jewish-Christian Controversy from the Earliest Times to 1789,* 2nd ed., ed. W. Horbery (Tübingen, 1995) and A. L. Williams, *Adversus Judaeos* (Cambridge, 1935). The most familiar authorities who shed light on the larger topic of the image of the Jew in Christian art are Blumenkranz, Gutmann, V. Mann, R. Mellinkoff, Revel-Neher, Schreckenberg, Sed-Rajna, C. Roth, and Weitzmann. Mellinkoff devotes a chapter (4) to the phenomenon in her *Outcasts* (Berkeley, 1999) and brings many examples from Northern art. My approach is in general modeled on that of W. Seiferth, *Synagogue and Church in the Middle Ages,* 2nd ed. (New York, 1970), and my findings to the present have been similar to his wherever—particularly regarding patronage and motive—the same periods and localities are under consideration.

This motivational complex does not necessarily inspire the appearance of Hebrew script in every work of Christian art before the nineteenth century. Some appearances seem relatively innocuous, others even benign. One may say that a Christian fascination with Hebrew, rising to religious enthusiasm, typifies many periods and authors without denying that they all have motives for studying it that respond to the absence of a continuous tradition of Hebrew knowledge as against the presence of such knowledge among Jews. They all partake in an artefaction of Jew-and-Christian while studying the language (so much so that Jerome's translation from the Hebrew is also known as "the Hebraica" or the *veritas Hebraica*). They may promote the study of Hebrew but they may do so in order to convince Jews by their own texts in their own language of the truth of Christianity; or, in validating their cultures, they may archaize themselves, claiming that Etruscan is Hebrew as in Rome, or that Hebrew is Egyptian as in Mormon literature, or that Hebrew, Egyptian, Greek, Arabic, and Latin are all in agreement with and substantiate the practices of the Vatican.

Hebrew script, real or pseudo-real, responds to a different set of art-related intentions than do other oriental scripts initially, though there are overlaps (as there are with Egyptian hieroglyphs, see below). Textiles from Arabia and the Silk Route reaching Italy as trade goods are the likely sources for the portrayals of Arabic or Tibetan script, as H. Tanaka first made clear in "Giotto and the Influences of the Mongols and the Chinese on His Art," *Bijutsu shigaku* 6 (1984), esp. 179–181 and in later works such as *Ex Oriente Lux* (Tokyo, 1986) and R. E. Mack, *Bazaar to Piazza* (Berkeley, 2001), have elaborated. Even though oriental scripts may appear in works on religious themes—especially as textile decorations and in ceramics—they are not connected to the same Christian religious polemics as is Hebrew script. (Nevertheless, the frequent appearance of Hebrew letters on textiles including clothing may be a secondary development from this history.) A multimixed statement is made where the letters appear on ritual garments or the like—as in the case of the decorations on headgear on males; the *tallit*, altar covers, etc. In any case, both the religious and secular garments pictured as well as the letters from foreign scripts, but especially from Hebrew script, that decorate them are entirely fictitious at this time. It might be possible to posit a connection to the lettered-garments of God and some angels in traditions from as early as the Enoch literature were it not for the confinement of the scripts in our materials to the borders, etc., of the garments as opposed to their entirety. Cf. the description of the lettered garment in *hekhalot rabbati*, in J. Rothenberg and H. Lenowitz, eds., *Exiled in the Word* (Townsend, 1989), 18. Two overlaps may serve to clarify the distinction. Giotto uses *phags-pa* script on the cloak of Jesus in the Scrovegni Chapel Crucifixion for decor, while in the *titulus* of his Crucifix in S. Maria Novella the Hebrew is a part of the narrative (see below). The second example is that of the Madonna with SS. Lawrence and Julian by Gentile da Fabriano in the Frick Collection. The Moslem prayer known as the *bismillah* appears on the border of her cloak. Here there may be two motives: the one relates to the revival of antiquity in Italian arts and letters of the time of the artist, including foreign scripts (in particular Egyptian and Hebrew in art; Greek and "Etruscan" in letters); the other, to a motive not entirely different from the first perhaps, one concerned with displaying the global truth of the Catholic Church.

In the matter of the scientific study of Hebrew by Christians one may point with pleasure toward the change in purpose that has typified the discipline and the consequent growth of knowledge, with but a few unhappy deviations; see, e.g., M. Pérez-Fernández, *An Introductory Grammar of Rabbinic Hebrew* (Leiden, 1999), and my animadversion, "Honor It and Suspect It: A Resurgence of Christian Hebraism," in *Academic Approaches to Teaching Jewish Studies*, ed. Z. Garber (Lanham, 2000). To select but a single school whose history delineates the different approaches and periods, note the earlier anti-Jewish works of Graf and Welhausen on the Hebrew Bible and then those of Franz Delitzsch, Theodor Noldeke, and Gotthelf Bergsträsser.

4. To the best of my knowledge the few scholarly articles devoted to Hebrew script in Western art deal with isolated periods, artists, places, and approaches and not with the phenomenon in its full breadth. These essays are M. Alexander-Knotter, "An Ingenious Device: Rembrandt's Use of Hebrew Inscriptions," *Studia Rosenthaliana* 33, no. 2 (1999): 131–59; M. Barash, "Hebrew Inscriptions in the Art of the Renaissance" (in Hebrew), in D. Carpi et al., *Scritti in Memoria di Leone Carpi* (Jerusalem, 1967), 141–50, and "Some Oriental Pseudo-inscriptions in Renaissance Art," *Visible Language* 23, nos. 2/3 (Spring/Summer 1989); G. Busi, *Il Succo dei Favi* (Bologna, 1992), 65–115; C. Gandelman, "By Way of Introduction: Inscriptions as Subversion," *Visible Language* 23, nos. 2/3 (Spring/Summer 1989); D. Haitovski, "A New Look at a Lost Painting: The Hebrew Inscription in Lorenzo Costa's Presentation in the Temple," *Artibus et Historiae* 29 (1994): 111–20; B.Harshav, "The Role of Language in Modern Art: On Texts and Subtexts in Chagall's Paintings," *Modernism/modernity* 1, no. 2 (1994): 51–87; A. Parronchi, "*Titulus Crucis*," *Antichitá Viva* 4 (1966): 41ff.; A. Ronen, "Hebrew Script in European Art of the 15th Century" (in Hebrew), in *Proceedings of the Xth World Congress of Jewish Studies*, Vol/Sec.2D (Jerusalem, 1990), 1–7, a summary of "*Iscrizioni Ebraiche nell'arte Italiana del Quattrocento*," in *Studi di storia dell'arte sul medioevo e il renascimento: Atti del Convegno Internazio-*

nale Arezzo-Firenze 1989 (Florence, 1992), 501–624; Sh. Sabar, "Hebrew Script in the Work of Rembrandt" (in Hebrew), in M. Weyl and R. Weiss-Blok, *Rembrandt's Holland* (in Hebrew) (Jerusalem, 1993), 169–87. Rembrandt—the sole focus of the Sabar and Alexander-Knotter essays—would seem not to have been particularly subjected to Christian Hebraism in its anti-Jewish character; on the other hand, what these authors have demonstrated concerning the influence of R. Menasseh ben Israel (1604–57) on him (in regard to the Belshazzar inscription) must be related to that Jewish leader's role as lobbyist for the return of the Jews to England. Likewise, the rabbi's tale of the Lost Tribes and their presence in the Americas is more closely tied to Christian legend (including converso traditions) than to Jewish literature. G. Sarfati, "Hebrew Script in Western Visual Arts," *Italia* 13–15 (2001): 451–547 (which has some errors but does provide a list of 261 works he encountered at random in what he accurately terms, "an 'armchair' research"). The same author's *According to the Language of My People* (Jerusalem, 1997) (in Hebrew) reprints four interesting essays from the journal *leshonenu le'am*. These too contain some misperceptions but pp. 257–68 make significant contributions to the larger field. The dissertation of P. Schöner, published as "Juden bilder im deutschen Einblattdruck der Renaissance: Ein Beitrage zur Imagologie" (Baden-Baden, 2002), has been followed by a recent essay, "Visual Representations of Jews and Judaism in Sixteenth-Century Germany," in *Jews, Judaism, and the Reformation in Sixteenth-Century Germany,* ed. D. P. Bell and S. Burnett (Leiden, 2006), 357–91. Here too there are problems in distinguishing, reading, and representing Hebrew/pseudo-Hebrew inscriptions.

5. *The Image of the Jew in Byzantine Art* (Oxford, 1992). The history of antisemitism in the Byzantine empire is actually not much more pleasant than in the Western empire; no one would want to belittle the unkindnesses of Chrysostom (349–407), the two Justinians (I, 482–565; II, 669–711), Phocas (d. 610), and Heraclius (575–641) in the period before the Islamic conquest. Thus, the representation of Jews in Byzantine art in nonnegative images is, as M. J. Dubois concludes in his introduction to Revel-Neher's book (p. xx), related to the art-image in its association with Byzantine religiosity and its concern with "the representation of eternal mystery." This aggregate results in a slightly different aspect of the construction of the Jew in this Christian/imperial community, one that would preclude the appearance of Hebrew script simply because its appearance would be irrelevant and distracting or noisome to the viewer. (The "eternal mystery" disallows as well the apocalyptic theme of the "conversion of the Jews" so central to western Christian theology throughout its permutations.) N. de Lange, "A Thousand Years of Hebrew in Byzantium," in *Hebrew Study from Ezra to Ben-Yehuda,* ed. W. Horbury (Edinburgh, 1999), writes simply that "Hebrew as a language was virtually confined in Byzantium to Jews. There is apparently no tradition of Hebrew scholarship among Christians, nor have Jewish converts to Christianity left much trace of Hebrew knowledge" (160). It is another form of antisemitism, one motivated largely by social and political concerns rather than by religious ones, that is found in the art of Byzantine culture. Byzantine disinterest in the Hebraic or Judaic history of Jesus shifted around this single pole, for other but similar reasons, arriving at a scholarly deprecation of the Hebrew Bible, its language and texts in the twelfth century that corresponded to an equivalent Western esteem and interest in just those matters: after Origen Hebrew was of interest only in the west. See B. Smalley, *The Study of the Bible in the Middle Ages,* 3rd ed. (Oxford, 1983), n. 6, 361.

6. That is, the Church's attacks against transgressors against many points of received practice and doctrine often label the proponents as "judaizers," accusing them of falling back into Jewish doctrine and practice rejected by the Church. Ronen ("Hebrew Script in European Art of the Fifteenth Century," 601–2) touches lightly on the phenomenon. He finds two points of contact to be typical, the "Hebrew," Aramaic actually, plaint put into the mouth of the suffering Jesus on the cross (Matt. 27:46; Mark 15:34); and the appearances of Hebrew inscriptions on the titulus. He associates the growth of the latter figuration with Abelard (1079–1142). This does go some way toward explaining the role of the anti-Jewish mendicant orders in both Christian Hebraism, and the use of Hebrew script by favored artists as well, though in doing so they may ignore Christian partisan politics including, in this case, the early monastic "reform" movements. See A. Funkenstein, "Basic Types of Christian Anti-Jewish Polemics in the Later Middle Ages," *Viator* 2 (1971): 373–82, "Changes in the Pattern of Christian Anti-Jewish Polemic in the Twelfth Century," *tziyon* n.s. 33 (1968): 125–44 (in Hebrew); cf. chap. 6, "Polemics, Responses, and Self-Reflection," 169–201 of his *Perceptions of Jewish History* (Berkeley, 1993), who favors an early twelfth-century date; and J. Cohen, *The Friars and the Jews : The Evolution of Medieval Anti-Judaism* (Ithaca, 1982), preferring a date about a century later, 24–32; chap. 1 especially 44–50; chaps. 5–7, especially 171–74; and the conclusion, especially 255ff.

   It is a bit difficult to explain the relative lack of consideration either author pays in these works to the social background of the interaction between Christian scholars and Jews from which works like the St Alban's Bible Lamentations embellishment or the Montalacino Genesis initial emerge. On relations between Christian scholars of the Bible, particularly monastics, with Hebrew, Jews, and Jewish texts see, as introductions with notes and bibliographies, Smalley, *The Study of the Bible in the Middle Ages,* esp. xxxii–xxxiii, 78–82, 289–92, 360–66, 340–50; on Hugh, Richard and Andrew of St. Victor and Herbert of Bosham, 83–195; R. Loewe, esp. "Herbert of Bosham's commentary . . . ," *Biblica* 34 (1953): 44ff., "The Medieval Christian Hebraists of England," *Trans. Jew. Hist Soc. of England* 17 (1951–52): 225ff. among others.

7. H. Schreckenberg, *The Jews in Christian Art* (New York, 1996); *Images of Intolerance: The Representation of the Jews in the Bible Moralisée* (Berkeley, 1999), 15–19; and throughout.
8. H. Schreckenberg, *The Jews in Christian Art* (New York, 1996), 13. See his essay, "Die patristische Adversos-Judaeos-Thematik im Spiegel der karolingischen Kunst," in *Bijdragen* 49 (1988): 119–38, for details. Hebrew script is not part of this; and the range of illustrations the author presents show the ambiguity described, as he writes.
9. D. Iogna-Prat, *Order and Exclusion: Cluny and Christendom Face Heresy, Judaism, and Islam (1000–1150)* (Ithaca, N.Y., 2002), 301–2.
10. See, most recently, the essay by J. Brug, "Near Eastern Acrostics and Biblical Acrostics," NEH Seminar papers, The Bible and Near Eastern Literature (New Haven: Yale University Press, 1997). See:http://www.wlsessays.net/authors/B/BrugAcrostics/BrugAcrostics.PDF.
11. J. K. Elliott, *The Apocryphal New Testament* (Oxford, 2004), 90.
12. See D. H. Akenson, *Surpassing Wonder: The Invention of the Bible and the Talmuds* (Chicago, 2001), 476 n. 29, citing J. Neusner, *First-Century Judaisms in Crisis: Jochanan ben Zakkai and the Renaissance of Torah* (Nashville, 1975), 64–66; Akenson extends Neusner's observations to include the Zaccheus of Luke 19.
13. E. B. Garrison, *Studies in the History of Medieval Italian Painting* (London, 1993), 3:47.
14. Cahn, *Romanesque Bible Illumination,* 260.
15. See M-L Thérel, *Remarques sur une illustration du livre de la genèse dans la Bible de Montalcino* (Paris, 1972); D. Winston, *The Wisdom of Solomon* (Garden City, N.Y., 1979).

The Literary Quest for National Revival

From Hazaz's "The Sermon" (1942) to Yehoshua's Mr. Mani *(1990)*

Gilead Morahg

From the earliest settlement period, mainstream Zionist writers have expressed concern that the psychological and ideological deformations that shaped Jewish life in the Diaspora will continue to define Israeli identity and pervert the relationship of the people of Israel to the Land of Israel. This concern, which has its canonical literary expression in Haim Hazaz's story, "The Sermon" (1942), is still very much in evidence in A. B. Yehoshua's masterful novel, *Mr. Mani* (1990). The fact that two works separated by half a century of enormous change in Israeli life share this particular concern is intriguing enough to invite critical consideration. Both "The Sermon" and *Mr. Mani* attempt to determine whether national identity is irrevocable destiny or subject to deliberate choice and intentional alteration. Both are concerned with exploring the question of whether a deeply ingrained communal pathology can be cured and whether the society that has been afflicted by it can be restored to health. Yet, despite these thematic affinities, each of these works presents a different perception of the nature of the national pathology and articulates a different notion of the potential for national regeneration and identity reformation.

In "The Sermon," Hazaz located the pathology that subverted Jewish history in the ethos of abject passivity and perverse exaltation of suffering that evolved in response to the nation's extended experience of "oppression, defamation, persecution, and martyrdom."[1] Fifty years later, Yehoshua believes that an ominously self-destructive pathology still persists in the nation. He also believes that counteracting this malady requires a better understanding of the historical dynamics of modern Jewish identity formation. Much of *Mr. Mani* constitutes an effort to acquire such an understanding. The action of *Mr. Mani* spans the period of the past 150 years with each of its five sections located at a key juncture in this period of the Jewish past. The novel explores the impact and the implications of Jewish attitudes that to a large degree shaped this past on the disposition of the Israeli present and on the future direction Israeli society may take.

One of Yehoshua's long-standing convictions is that, due to the inherent contradictions between religion and nationality, the Jews have historically sought to retain their identity as a religiously defined nation by resisting the responsibilities of independent national existence within distinctly defined territorial boundaries. This, he believes, is the cause of their conscious choice to fashion a culture of Diasporic existence and to seek to sustain it at all costs. At the core of this culture is a deeply ingrained national pathology that repeatedly leads the Jewish people to the brink of annihilation and may, at any moment, drive them beyond this brink and into the abyss. In the tradition of mainstream Labor-Zionism, of which he is clearly a part, Yehoshua regards postexilic Jewish history, from ancient destruction to modern Holocaust, as a colossal and wholly avoidable mistake. Much like Hazaz, Yehoshua argues that the primary perpetrator of this catastrophic error is Judaism itself. Not the Jewish people, he is careful to explain, but Judaism as an ideology, as a system of faith that was willing to take unacceptable risks and make continuous human sacrifices in order to sustain its paradoxical notion of existence as a Diasporic nation that insists on its distinct identity within the social, political, and cultural fabric of other nations that are equally insistent on their own distinct identities.

Yehoshua believes that Judaism bears the ultimate responsibility for the agonies of exile and the horrors of the Holocaust by willfully putting its adherents in the historical position that made catastrophe inevitable. "I do not blame the Jews of Germany or the Jews of eastern Europe," he has said,

> I am talking about Judaism. . . . The failure of Judaism. This is the failure of Moses. This is the failure of the total conception that says that we can stay a people while not in our land, that we can maintain our identity while not in our land. There always were warnings, all through history, that this will end in catastrophe. And it ended in catastrophe.[2]

Mr. Mani suggests that this cultural determinant persists in the post-Holocaust era of Jewish statehood. The novel points to an Israeli society whose actions are still powerfully shaped by religious imperatives and to a Jewish nation still afflicted by a conviction of its ability to sustain its existence within the social tissues of other nations. It reflects a concern that the consequences of this conviction may, once again, be morally and historically catastrophic. It also offers an alternative paradigm; an opposite direction that extends the hope that these consequences may not be inevitable. The novel's five sections conflate the story of five generations of the Mani family with the history of the Jewish nation. Each section occurs prior to the one that preceded it in a narrative regression that seeks to decipher the mystery of the pathology that shaped so much of this nation's catastrophic past, continues to afflict it in the present, and may lead to an even more destructive future.

The first—and latest—section of *Mr. Mani* takes place in 1982. The speaker is Hagar Shiloh, who mistakenly believes she is pregnant and whose lover, Efi Mani, is doing military reserves duty in Israeli-occupied Lebanon. Hagar is trying to tell her mother, Ya'el, the story of her visit with Efi's father, Gavriel Mani, in Jerusalem and of her repeated efforts to prevent him from committing suicide. The key questions that this chapter raises but does not fully answer involve the mysterious cause of Gavriel Mani's compulsive suicidal tendencies. As the novel proceeds, it becomes increasingly evident that Gavriel's predilection is related to the unfathomable heritage of self-destruction that Yehoshua perceives in the Jewish people and that Hagar's efforts on his behalf engage the question of whether anything can be done to counteract this heritage and curtail its effects. The quest for answers to the novel's key questions ends in the novel's fifth section, which takes place in Jerusalem of 1848 and is marked by the acute tension between Avraham, the rigidly conservative patriarch of the Mani family, and his iconoclastic son Yosef.

Yehoshua conceives the character of Yosef Mani as "a precursor of the Canaanite ideology . . . [Yosef] wants to create a nation like all nations are created, by uniting people around territory, language and history, and not through the combination of seed and faith." He wishes "to fuse the inhabitants of the land into a single national body that is founded on nativism and on belonging to the land."[3] Yehoshua is not an advocate of Canaanist views and has welcomed their gradual disappearance from Israel's political and cultural landscape.[4] He does, however, recognize the force of these nativist notions and, through the iconoclastic character of Yosef, draws upon them to expose and examine some of the tensions and dangers inherent in this complicated landscape. These tensions and dangers are evident in Avraham Mani's reaction to Yosef's nativist ideology. He is appalled that his son is prepared to disavow the primacy of universal Jewish solidarity in favor of forging a distinctively local national identity.

The profound tension between Avraham and Yosef Mani is an expression of the contradiction between the national and the religious systems that has continually preoccupied Yehoshua and which he regards as the cause of a deep-rooted anomaly in the Jewish people. "On the one hand," he has said, "there is the normal national system functioning in accordance with the basic needs of national existence in a territory, and, on the other hand, there is the religious system, which sets spiritual goals for the people and tries to subordinate the people's existence to religious and spiritual demands."[5] He believes that the religious system has always had a position of disproportionate power in Jewish culture and that its constant conflict with the national system constituted an untenable danger to the unity of the nation. According to Yehoshua, the Jewish solution to this existential threat was preserving and perpetuating the nation's existence in Diaspora.[6] He believes that the perilous tension between the religious and the national systems has not been resolved by the renewal of national life in Israel. It has been transported and incorporated into the social and cultural fabric of this life, threatening to tear it apart from within. In the fifth section of *Mr. Mani*, this internal danger is reflected in the tension between Avraham Mani's dedication to a universal Jewish faith, which is presented as being inherently Diasporic, and Yosef Mani's aspiration to a mode of national existence that is essentially territorial.

Ultimately, and terribly, Avraham kills his son to preserve the continuity of national and religious unity both within his family and in the larger Jewish community. With this act, the source of the suicidal pathology that afflicts the Mani family and becomes identified with a fundamental infirmity in the Jewish psyche is located in Avraham's adherence to a primeval cultural code that insists on the fusion of religion and nationality, compels the Jews to a dispersed Diasporic existence, and places the value of perpetuating this particular mode of communal conformity above the values of individual life and individual love. For Yehoshua, this perilous fusion of nationality and religion is embodied in the originating figure of the biblical Avraham and reflected most clearly in the foundational myth of his apparent willingness to sacrifice his son as an act of loyalty to the god of his nascent religion.

Avraham Mani's readiness to sacrifice his son in order to perpetuate the unity of religion and nationality that is essential to the traditional conception of Jewish identity clearly associates him with the foundational myth of the biblical Avraham's willingness to sacrifice his son as an act of loyalty to the god of his nascent religion. It is this shared willingness to take inhumane action in order to preserve their common conviction that extends the significance of Avraham Mani's extreme transgression beyond the imagined world of a psychologically and morally impaired fictional character to the realities of a similarly impaired historical nation. Avraham Mani's willingness to sacrifice the love and the life of another in order to preserve his ideological vision is part of a larger signifying structure that integrates *Mr. Mani*'s disparate sections and generates the central subtexts of the novel.

Like the novel's fifth section, both the fourth and the second sections are marked by a willingness of adherents of totalizing national ideologies to sacrifice the lives of others, including those who are very close to them, in order to preserve the principles of their beliefs. But these characters are counterpointed by others, especially Ivor Horowitz in the third section and Hagar Shiloh in the first, who reflect aspects of an alternative moral vision that consistently places the value of human life and individual dignity over the proscriptions of any abstract ideology. This strand of thematic articulation stands in distinct contradiction to the injurious heritage of Avraham Mani. It constitutes the core of the novel's countervailing movement in the opposite moral direction that is perhaps best condensed in the words of Hagar Shiloh, the forthright and often caustic narrator of the opening section, who becomes determined "to do everything I can in order to save life, not to kill."[7]

Hagar's capacity for compassion and willingness to act resolutely on it complete the novel's exploration and ultimate affirmation of empathic compassion as the essential capacity that enables the individual to resist the control of unconscious compulsions and make deliberate moral choices in personal as well as political domains. Her character comes to signify that the same principles that validate the preservation of a single life are equally valid for shaping the future of a victorious nation. The fact that the first and most contemporary section of *Mr. Mani* is narrated by a native of a desert kibbutz is a key facet of the novel's signifying structure. Within this structure, as within Zionist culture, the kibbutz marks the restorative triumph of territorially based secular nationalism over the self-destructive Diasporic claim to the viability of a territorially dispersed, religiously determined Jewish nation. But if, as I have been arguing, the impulse toward self-destruction intrinsically imprinted in Gavriel Mani's personality is, by symbolic implication, also an inherent component of his national identity, then a further implication of the novel's first section is that this triumph is not complete. The encounter between the spirited young woman from Israel's south and the despondent Jerusalem judge marks a fateful contest of forces that are still contending in the national psyche. And it is in the context of this contest that the intersection of Yehoshua's *Mr. Mani* with Hazaz's "The Sermon" becomes most usefully distinct.

Both *Mr. Mani* and "The Sermon" reflect an urgent concern with the persistence of the Diasporic Jewish pathology despite the apparent triumph of Zionist ideology. Both work toward an ideological reconstitution that will complete the Zionist psychological revolution by liberating the Jews of Israel from the pathological heritage of their Diasporic past. Yudka, Hazaz's agitated protagonist, concludes that during their years of exile the Jews developed a masochistic "nighttime psychology" that enabled them to embrace the agonies of exilic existence and to subject themselves to a messianic mythology that made this mode of existence permanent. "It's an obvious thing," he says,

> that if not for this myth it would have all been different. Because without it, they finally would have either had to go right back to Palestine or somehow or other pass on out of the world. At any rate they would have had to think of something, or do something, one way or another, to bring it all to an end.[8]

The central irony of "The Sermon" is that it is delivered by Yudka to his fellow Zionist settlers who had already defied their cultural heritage and taken the crucial step of leaving the Diaspora and settling in the Land of Israel. Still, Yudka feels compelled to inflict his concerns upon this clearly reluctant and unreceptive audience because he does not share their confidence that the transformation of Jewish life has been fully accomplished by the mere physical transition from Diaspora to Zion. He recognizes that it is much easier to take the Jew out of the Diaspora than to take the Diaspora out of the Jew. And, like other Zionist thinkers and writers at the time, he is haunted by the concern that Diasporic attitudes will persist and that the ostensibly new Jewish society being created in the Land of Israel will turn out to be a sad and perilous replica of the Diasporic past. The same concern permeates *Mr. Mani* and culminates in the character of Gavriel Mani in whom the internal heritage of self-destructive tendencies that Yehoshua perceives in the Jewish people constantly threatens to tip the precarious balance between normalcy and pathology in which this people continues to exist.

While "The Sermon" and *Mr. Mani* converge in their postulation of the persistence of the Diaspora pathology, they differ on the precise nature of this pathology and diverge significantly in the remedies they propose for it. In "The Sermon," Hazaz locates the pathology that subverted Jewish history in the ethos of abject passivity and perverse exaltation of suffering that evolved in response to the nation's extended experience of oppression, persecution, and martyrdom. According to Yudka, healing this pathology requires abandoning a debilitating history that "has no glory or action, no heroes or conquerors, no rulers and masters of their fate" and the cultivation of new generations of native "heroes, great fighters, and fearless conquerors" (70, 71). He believes that the ultimate objective of the Zionist revolution is the formation of "a people creating its history for itself, with its own strength and by its own will." Because, as he explains, "a people that does not live in its own land and does not rule itself has no history" (85). Yudka acknowledges that this objective constitutes a profound contradiction to what he perceives to be the essence of Judaism. He sees Judaism as being inextricably bound to its Diasporic existence, soothed by the mystique of messianic redemption, and categorically resistant to an actual return to the Land of Israel. And, in an argument that Yehoshua was to revive several generations later, Yudka concludes that continuous Diasporic existence is a deliberate national choice, a calculated act of national will designed to protect a Jewish way of life that is viable only in exile. "For what if [the Jews] really have something to fear?" he asks.

> What if it is true that Judaism can manage to survive somehow in Exile, but here, in the Land of Israel, it's doubtful? . . . What if this country is fated to take the place of religion, if it's a grave danger to the survival of the people, if it replaces an enduring center with a transient center, a solid foundation with a vain and empty foundation? (81)

Yudka answers his question by proclaiming his willingness to take the risk and suffer the possible loss. Because, as he says, "Zionism and Judaism are not at all the same, but two things quite different from each other, and maybe even two things directly opposite to each other" (82). In close accord with

Canaanite views, Yudka sees Zionism as "the nucleus of a different people . . . Not new or restored but *different*." And he believes "that this land of Israel already is no longer Jewish. Even now, let alone in the future" (84; emphasis in original).

Reflecting a similar concern with the persistence of Diasporic pathologies in Israeli life and similarly seeking a way to reverse them, *Mr. Mani* arrives at a different conclusion as to the originating cause of these pathologies and departs considerably from "The Sermon" in the way it proposes to overcome them. These distinctions are as much a product of the passage of time as they are of differences in ideological temperament. In the half a century that passed between the publication of "The Sermon" and the writing of *Mr. Mani,* the Jews in Israel produced an abundance of great warriors, fearless conquerors, and professed masters of the national fate. Yet, according to Yehoshua's novel, a self-destructive pathology continues to jeopardize the Jewish nation. Much like Hazaz, Yehoshua locates the roots of this pathology in an unresolved, perhaps irresolvable, contradiction between the Jewish national and the religious systems. But *Mr. Mani* does not follow "The Sermon" in concluding that the resolution of this contradiction may require the summary separation of Zionism from Judaism, as advocated by followers of the once-influential Canaanite movement. Yehoshua has come to believe that such a separation is impossible. Consequently, he has welcomed the decline in the influence of Canaanite ideals. Because, as he argues, "discarding the Canaanitic option also allowed us to relate to Judaism more maturely, with less anger and with less hypocrisy. And that, in my opinion, greatly facilitated the absorption of Judaism into Israeli identity."[9] Yet, in *Mr. Mani,* his multifaceted examination of the effects of the primal elements of Judaism on the historical course of Jewish life leads Yehoshua to conclude that this absorption should be carefully qualified.

In tracing the origins of the nation's self-destructive proclivity to the foundational depths of Jewish ideology, *Mr. Mani* locates the generative root of this pathology not in the substance of the ideology but in the peremptory value ascribed to sustaining and transmitting it from one generation to another. Like the primal *akedah*, the sacrificial transgression of Avraham, the patriarch of the Mani family, is intended to perpetuate the unity of religion and nationality that is essential to his conception of Jewish identity. Avraham's willingness to take inhumane action to preserve this ideological conviction is a metaphoric distillation of a fundamental flaw in the psyche of a nation that places the perpetual value of a particular set of communal standards above the values of individual life and individual love. The narrative line that runs through the following generations of Manis and leads to the present time portrays this preference as a skewed scale of values that is both morally and existentially untenable. This predisposition emerges as an inherent internal deformation that was not rectified by the Zionist revolution and that, even in their own land, is still impelling the Jewish people toward self-destruction. In *Mr. Mani*, as in "The Sermon," the problem is no longer the persistence of Diasporic existence. It is, rather, the persistence of identity characteristics that are consistent with the Diaspora experience in the one Jewish community that had deliberately separated itself from this experience.

In *Between Right and Right* (1980), as in many of his subsequent polemical essays, Yehoshua has argued that the complex set of beliefs, practices, customs, and institutions that constituted Diasporic Jewish culture were all subordinate to the purpose of preserving the cohesion, integrity, and uniqueness of the Jewish people while dwelling continuously in the lands of other peoples, interweaving their lives with the lives of other nations while maintaining an adamant separation from them. This view coincides with earlier Zionist analyses of the Jewish condition and is clearly evident in "The Sermon." Hazaz's story also reflects the prevailing Zionist conviction that adherence to this mode of Diasporic existence required a powerful, but ultimately debilitating, ethos of submission, suffering, continuous self-sacrifice, and a constant willingness to risk annihilation. "The Sermon" asserts that this virulent form of national pathology can only be healed by the cultivation of new generations of "heroes [and] conquerors, rulers and masters of their fate," who will take control of Jewish history and restore it to glory. It is on this point that *Mr. Mani* departs from "The Sermon" and much other previous Zionist thinking.

The radical perception that emerges from Yehoshua's novel is that Israel's present realization of Yudka's dream of a new ethos of military might and Jewish will-to-power is nothing but a contemporary transmutation of the long-standing Diasporic ideology of a territorially unbounded Jewish existence. As the second section of *Mr. Mani* demonstrates, the unbridled exercise of military prowess to advance a mythopoetic vision of national destiny does not lead to a revitalized future. It merely recapitulates the self-destructive patterns of the past. The blend of myth, force, and exclusionary supremacist pride that define the vision of national revival that dominates that section becomes a metaphor for the most recent manifestation of the Diasporic conviction that the continuing cohesion of the Jewish people is not predicated on its adhering to particular territorial and communal bounds. With its recurrent allusions to the Lebanon War, the domination of another nation, and the occupation of the land in which its people dwell, the novel's second section demonstrates the devastating results of extending the life of a nation beyond the territorial boundaries that define its singularity and imposing its presence on the unwilling population of another nation.

In addition to tracing the origins and examining the consequences of the deformations embedded in the Jewish psyche, Yehoshua continues to be interested in the possibility of a healing transformation of this psyche. He has remained a believer in both the necessity and the possibility of creating the conditions for the emergence of a truly New Jew. In some of his essays, and more so in his novels, he has sought to determine the characteristics that will define this New Jew. Central to Yehoshua's thinking are the notions that maintaining a fully integrated Jewish identity is possible only in an independent Jewish society, that Israel is the only possible place for the existence of such a society, and that, while retaining many traditional aspects of Judaism, the new Jewish identity that will be forged in this society must be purged of its Diasporic deformations and oriented in radically new directions. The desired new directions that figure prominently in *Mr. Mani* include a reorientation of the traditional Jewish concept of territoriality and a new first principle of personal, social, and political morality.

Yehoshua regards the native-born generation that came of age in the early years of Israeli statehood as the first generation to possess a complete Jewish identity, which he calls *Yisraeliuth* (Israeliness) (46). Unlike the Diasporic Jewish identity that constantly invited calamity by its territorial indeterminacy, this emergent Israeli identity is distinguished by a secure sense of belonging to a clearly defined territory. "The cornerstone in the foundation of *Yisraeliuth*," he writes, "nourishing and fortifying it, remains the consciousness of boundaries, which crystallized in particular between 1956 and 1967." This generation "internalized with utter clarity the transition from *Eretz Yisrael* (the Land of Israel) to Israel. This was highly significant since it provided . . . a clear consciousness of boundaries, and it provided the security that comes with knowing borders. If I had to define Zionism in a single word I would say *boundaries*" (48).

Yehoshua regards the clarity and integration of identity that his generation attained as being jeopardized by the blurring of boundaries that occurred in the aftermath of the 1967 war with the increasing Jewish encroachment beyond the borders of the State of Israel and into the non-Israeli territories of Eretz Yisrael. This, he has written, may well be "the reason why many have been seduced into exchanging their primary and organic consciousness of their national identity for partial consciousness based on ethnic, cultural and political affiliations" (48). The characters of Ya'el Shiloh and her daughter Hagar, who is the voice of the novel's most contemporary perspective, are constructed as an antithesis and possible antidote to this dangerous dissolution. These two women not only retain the integrity of their *Yisraeliuth* but also continue to refine and more deeply define it.

It is obviously no coincidence that Ya'el is made to be an exact contemporary of Yehoshua's and a member of the generation that first attained *Yisraeliuth*. Born in the same year as Yehoshua, in a suburb of the city in which he has long lived, Ya'el decides early on to make a new life for herself on a kibbutz in Israel's Negev desert.[10] This is a symbolic move to a place that has profound significance for Yehoshua. He has long regarded the desert as the only space the Jews can have entirely to themselves and, consequently, as the only place in which the Jewish people can purge themselves of the particular pathologies that continue to impair their existence as a nation. "One of the most problematic of all the problems for the Jewish people," Yehoshua has said, is that "we can never understand ourselves except by being with others, by being with the gentiles." He regards this dependence on living intertwined with other nations in order to sustain a sense of national self as a grievous national defect: "The Jews," he concludes, "cannot be by themselves. This incapacity is a permanent problem of our people."[11] Yehoshua believes that the Negev desert is the only place that provides the Jewish people with the opportunity to free itself from this dangerous dependence by living entirely on its own. Therefore, he has said,

> My feeling is that the remedy for the Jewish state is to turn to the desert. From time to time we have to return to the desert. The desert is the place where we have a lot of space of our own; in the desert we don't take anyone else's land. . . . If we do not encounter the desert, if we do not challenge the desert, if we do not find a way to live in the desert, we will always be in conflict about boundaries. . . . If you speak about the Jewish people, if you speak about the future, if you speak about bringing new methods into the world itself, [this] can be accomplished through working in the Negev and trying to make something valuable for everyone from the desert. . . . So for me it is the way of the Negev that provides the best direction. (130, 132)

For Yehoshua, the Negev desert is the true womb of the new Israeli nation and it is little wonder that he has great affection for the people who have made it a permanent home for themselves and for their descendants. He regards the fact that this desert has become a true home for people who have been living there for over half a century as "an achievement in itself. It proves that it can be done" (133). Ya'el Shiloh is one of these people and to her Negev-born daughter, Hagar, the desert is the only home she knows and loves.

In the preamble to the novel's first section, we are told that Ya'el and her husband, Roni, named their daughter Hagar "as an expression of their commitment to making a life in the desert" (p. 15, *7*). Mordechai Shalev is undoubtedly correct in observing that "Hagar represents the *Yisraeliuth* of the native-born 'sabra' that is rooted in an estranged, secularized Zionism."[12] However, her name also carries the imprint of an ancient heritage from which, according to Yehoshua, secular Zionism, despite its determination to do so, has never been able to fully extricate itself. Hagar's name links her directly to the callous inhumanity of the patriarchal Avraham and, by a subsequent series of correspondences, to the congruent conduct of the patriarch of the Mani family who, with unabashed intent, is also named Avraham.

The name of the woman who bore the son of the biblical Avraham and was later cast out to die in the wilderness together with this son reminds us that the man who pleaded for God's mercy on the strangers of Sodom was capable of utter mercilessness toward his own offspring when it came to perpetuating the purity of his familial and ideological line. This heartlessness is subsequently, and most tragically, reiterated by Avraham Mani, who is also willing to sacrifice one son and abandon another in order to preserve his own dynastic and ideological line. Although she never resorts to inhumane extremes, Ya'el Shiloh is still largely driven by the same predominance of rigid ideology over compassionate humanity, which *Mr. Mani* defines as a heritage of Jewish identity that has been transmitted throughout the ages from the patriarchal Avraham on to the members of the first generation of true Israelis. Like many members of her generation, Ya'el is often dogmatic and consistently doctrinaire in fashioning her positions, conducting her affairs and responding to others, including her daughter. She cannot empathize with the experiences Hagar is struggling to relate to and is often unyieldingly callous toward her. Hagar, however, resists her mother's mode of responding to reality. She insists that other considerations must be taken into account and gradually comes to realize what these considerations are. Ultimately, Hagar comes to measure herself not by her ability to adhere to the doctrines of a preconceived ideology but by her capacity to act on the immediate demands of her humanity.

The first time Hagar stumbled upon Gavriel's makeshift gallows and tried to prevent the judge from making use if it, the struggle between them took place in total silence. "Without a word, without a word. . . . That's the thing," Hagar says with retrospective regret. "If something would have been said, perhaps everything would have been different" (p. 35, *27*). By the time of her return from East Jerusalem, Hagar's intervening experiences have instilled in her a deeper empathic understanding that now enables her to intuit the element that had been missing from her previous attempts to make the necessary difference. Until that time, Hagar's determination to thwart the judge's self-destructive drive had led to recurrent variations of a mute struggle between opposing forces that will not relent. But now, when she once again enters Gavriel's darkened apartment and finds him holding a straight-edged razor and bleeding at the neck, Hagar not only takes firm action but is also able to give clear voice to her compassionate concern for another, imploring him to desist, not only at this time but forever: "I grabbed his hand, held it hard, and said very quietly and very firmly, I beg of you, please don't do this anymore" (p. 72, *64*).

More than anything else, it is this unaffected articulation of the value of his life to someone else that moves Gavriel to recognize the fearsome reality of his suicidal compulsion. "I saw that he was completely surprised by me," Hagar tells Ya'el. "Stunned. He ran his other hand over his face and his neck, saw it come back smeared with blood, and was really scared" (p. 72, *64*). This is the climactic moment of the novel's first section and one of the signifying centers of *Mr. Mani* as a whole. It constitutes the psychological turning point at which Gavriel's attempts to destroy himself appear to end and his communion with Hagar, which is later extended to the rest of her family, begins. It also figures as a symbolic convergence of the psychological and ideological dynamics that form the various thematic subtexts of the novel. If Gavriel Mani embodies the self-destructive heritage of a nation that disdains the need for distinguishing borders and continuously courts annihilation by inserting itself into the tissues of other nations, then Hagar's plea that he cease and desist is also the culminating call of *Mr. Mani* as a whole. The fact that Gavriel appears to awaken to his existential peril in response to Hagar's heartfelt plea introduces the more general prospect of a reversal of this precarious national direction. Subsequent intimations of an alternative orientation are retrospectively evident in the Biographical Supplement to the novel's first section.

Read in retrospect, the Biographical Supplement to the novel's first and most contemporary section constitutes both the chronological and metaphorical culmination of the story *Mr. Mani* tells. In it, constituent elements of this story converge on a transformative desert destination, forming the focal point of its ultimate thematic orientation. Hagar, who eventually does get pregnant and gives birth to a son, leaves Tel Aviv and returns to Mash'abei Sadeh to raise her child there. Gavriel Mani travels with increasing frequency from Jerusalem to this desert kibbutz in order to spend time with his grandson and cultivate his incipient relationship with Ya'el. The characters of both Gavriel and Ya'el undergo positive alteration as a consequence of this new congregation. The catalyst for this transformation is Hagar's baby for whom both of them learn to care.

As is often the case in Yehoshua's fiction, the responsibility for the well-being of a child has a humanizing effect that loosens the strictures of psychological and ideological compulsions that prevent his characters from relating to others with unmediated empathy. Hagar's child draws Gavriel out of his habitual orbit and into a new location and a new set of human relations that appear to diminish, and possibly eradicate, his self-destructive inclination. Having been stirred from his emotional torpor by Hagar's act of unmitigated compassion, Gavriel effects a complete reversal of his forefather's moral direction. Unlike the patriarchal Avraham and the ancestral Avraham Mani, both of whom twice betrayed their paternal responsibilities, Gavriel is moved to assume his human duty and become something of a surrogate father to the child who was abandoned by his own son. When Efi Mani goes off to pursue his studies in London, Gavriel

> took it upon himself to replace him to some degree. He would show up every few weeks, on a Saturday or a weekday, always in his dark clothes, always very courteous, and take his grandson for a walk in the arid hills around the settlement. Afterwards he would join the two women on their lawn, tell stories about his ancestors and about his court cases, and the little boy would run back and forth among them. (p. 80, *72*)

The narrative lines that generate the epic sweep and broad historical perspective of *Mr. Mani* converge to this modest focal point: three very different people on the lawn of a desert home tenuously bound together by their responsibility for a small child. But this small point is charged with associations and implications that provide it with the potential of being the nucleus for a new narrative that may emanate from it.

Gavriel's movement from Jerusalem to Masha'abei Sadeh and his growing affinity with the Shiloh family indicate the alternative direction that needs to be taken in order to alleviate the self-destructive drive embodied in the Mani family. This reorientation involves a transition from the confining strictures of the cultural heritage that configured Jerusalem as Judaism's abstract spiritual center to the desert spaces and transfiguring possibilities of Israel's Negev settlements. The attributes of the new cultural orientation toward which *Mr. Mani* tends are both prefigured and distilled in the nascent emotional bonding of Gavriel Mani and Ya'el Shiloh and in the consequent alteration of Gavriel's sense of territorial affinity. The increasing frequency of Gavriel's visits to the kibbutz is due not only to his sense of responsibility toward Roni but also "to the special connection that had formed between the child's grandfather and Hagar's mother" (p. 78, *70*). And, although he is very different from her in dress, manner, and political passions, Ya'el is "forced to admit that she found this man appealing, even though he comes from a very different world with which she was completely unfamiliar" (p. 79, *71*). Gavriel's insistent avoidance of any political discussion suggests that he also differs from Ya'el on ideological grounds. The nature of this difference remains unspecified, but there are intimations that it is a contemporary manifestation of the novel's extended preoccupation with the historic dangers of the Jewish refusal to recognize the existential imperative of conducting national life within firm territorial bounds.

Ya'el and Gavriel appear to differ on the wisdom of disregarding the national claims of the Arab inhabitants of the territories Israel occupied after the 1967 war as well as on the dangers resulting from the conviction that Israeli Jews may use these territories as they will. When she found out that, on his way from Jerusalem to Mash'abei Sadeh, Gavriel regularly drove through Hebron, "Ya'el warned him against driving through the southern villages of Mount Hebron. But Mr. Mani continued to claim that the way seemed safe and the villagers appeared peaceful so there was really no reason for him not to take the short way to the Negev" (p. 80, *72*). Despite Ya'el's admonitions, Gavriel continued to use the convenience of the road Israel had built through the West Bank, convinced that he would come to no harm. "But in early spring of 1987, his car was hit by a big rock near the village of Dir El Manna, some twenty kilometers south of Hebron. That evening, he admitted to Ya'el that it made good sense not to go through there anymore, even though that route continued to attract him, for some reason" (p. 80, 73).

The reason, of course, is no mystery. As the biblical burial site of Avraham and his beloved wife Sarah, Hebron's place of pride in Jewish consciousness dates back to the patriarchal past and proceeds through epochs to modern times. Hebron epitomizes the claims of those who believe that Jews have the historic right and religious obligation to inhabit the territories of the West Bank with its many sacred sites. The long cultural legacy of these sites also explains why many of those Jews who advocate withdrawal from them do so with a heavy heart. The fact that the most contemporary section of *Mr. Mani* concludes with Gavriel's determination to refrain from traversing these territories is as significant as his reason for doing so. Gavriel concludes that continuing to interject himself into the cities and villages of the West Bank was not wise because it was too dangerous. Within the signifying frame of reference established by the novel's narrative structure, this conclusion signals a recognition that the present refusal of Israeli Jews to contain their national existence within clear territorial boundaries is an extension of the Diasporic Jewish insistence on regarding themselves as a-territorial people who can continue to retain their identity as a separate nation while insinuating themselves into the living tissues of other nations. In *Mr. Mani*, this national self-perception emerges as the primal source of existential danger for a nation that is constantly flaunting itself in the face of annihilation.

According to the Biographical Supplement to the novel's last (and earliest) section, Avraham Mani, the originator of the destructive heritage that was to haunt his descendants, turned his back on the Land of Israel and, leading a life of constant wandering, sought to embed himself as a Jewish cleric in the communities of various Arab nations. Gavriel Mani's decision to cease traveling through Arab lands is a clear move in the opposite direction. His new readiness to recognize the wisdom of remaining within the bounds of Israel's old borders while strengthening his affinities with the Shiloh family and the Negev desert is a hopeful narrative gesture toward the possibility of a new cultural orientation that will alleviate the historic national impulse toward self-annihilation.

Notes

1. Haim Hazaz. "The Sermon," in *Israeli Stories*, ed. Joel Blocker (New York: Schocken Books, 1962), 70, 72.
2. Bernard Horn, *Facing the Fires: Conversations with A. B. Yehoshua* (Syracuse, N.Y.: Syracuse University Press, 1997), 126.

3. A. B. Yehoshua, "Closure: Canceling the *Akedah* by Realizing It" [Hebrew], in *In the Opposite Direction: Articles on Mr. Mani by A. B. Yehoshua*, ed. Nitza Ben-Dov (Tel Aviv: Hakibbutz Hameuchad, 1995), 395, 398.
4. A. B. Yehoshua, "Hebrew Literature and *Dor Hamedinah*: Portrait of a Literary Generation," in *Ideology and Jewish Identity in Israeli and American Literature,* ed. Emily Miller Budick (Albany: SUNY Press, 2001), 50, 51.
5. A. B. Yehoshua, "Exile as a Neurotic Solution," *Diaspora: Exile and the Contemporary Jewish Condition,* ed. Etan Levine (New York: Steimatsky/Shapolsky, 1986), 23–24.
6. Ibid., 24. For a more extensive exposition of Yehoshua's views on this issue see A. B. Yehoshua, *Bizekhut hanormaliut* [A plea for normality] (Tel Aviv, 1980), 48. All subsequent page references to this book will be followed by an italicized reference to its English translation: *Between Right and Right* (New York, 1981), 46–52, 65–66; *44–50, 65–66.*
7. *Mar Mani* [Mister Mani] (Tel Aviv: Hakibbutz Hameuchad, 1990), 65. Parenthetical page references in the text will be to this book, followed by a reference (in italics) to its English translation: A. B. Yehoshua. *Mr. Mani,* translated from the Hebrew by Hillel Halkin (New York: Harcourt Brace, 1992), 75. For purposes of greater accuracy I found it necessary to provide my own translations. Consequently, the quotes given in this article will differ from the text of the English translation.
8. Hazaz, "The Sermon," 76. Subsequent page numbers appear in the text.
9. Yehoshua, "Hebrew Literature and *Dor Hamedinah,*" 50, 51. Subsequent page numbers appear in the text.
10. "Ya'el Shiloh, nee Kramer. Born in Kiryat Hayim in 1936," in *Mr. Mani,* 14.
11. Horn, *Facing the Fires,* 130. Subsequent page numbers appear in the text.
12. Mordechai Shalev, "The Imprint of the *Akedah* in 'Three Days and a Child,' 'Summer—1970,' and *Mr. Mani*" [Hebrew], in *In the Opposite Direction,* ed. Ben-Dov, 444.

The Two-Bodied People, Their Cosmos, and the Origin of the Soul

Ziony Zevit

In 2001 I defined Israelite religions as "the varied, symbolic expressions of, and appropriate responses to the deities and powers that groups or communities deliberately affirmed as being of unrestricted value to them within their worldview."[1] In this definition, I expressed my assumption that religion, like culture in general, is formed, formulated, and expressed through organized groups of people. Both are expressed semiotically and mediated through external realities such as spoken and written language, arts, and ritual. Though some elements of both culture and religion are private and subjective, most are public and objective. In the Ancient Near East, as in many parts of the contemporary world, culture was embedded in religion so that there was no intelligible demarcation between the two.

Pre-exilic biblical texts are expressions of Israelite culture and religion with their attendant values. Written by and for Israelites, earlier tales and texts in the J and E sources of the Torah influenced later productions in D, P, and the Deuteronomistic history because authors of the younger works were educated and education involved memorization, internalization, and repetition.[2] By parsing these texts in order to answer certain questions, it is possible to gain some insights into Israelite cosmology and anthropology and to consider how these changed as a result of the destruction of Jerusalem and dismembering of Judah in the fifth century BCE. Among the questions considered and addressed below with varying degrees of thoroughness are the following: In the Israelite perception of the cosmos, were people thought to be weak but charged with achieving perfection? Were people concerned with what might happen to them after death? Did they think whatever ill befell them was due to their not fulfilling divine commands? Did they conceive of the cosmos as filled with malevolent forces from which they had to seek protection?

This study in honor of Zev Garber reflects his many interests in matters historical, historiosophical, and theological. It also skirts the mythological edge of a *leitmotif* informing much of his thinking, to wit: manifestations of evil in the world.[3]

Two-Bodied People

When I compare pictures of myself from years ago with the individual looking out at me quizzically from the mirror, it is quite clear that whereas I have remained much the same, my body has changed. If, while cutting vegetables for a salad, I happen to cut myself, it is clear that my body did something that was not my intention. Should I engage in some act that brings a sense of pleasure and well-being to my body, I might feel guilty. I pamper my body, train it, trying to align its profile with what I decided it should look like. In other words, I perceive the "me" that is my mind as distinct from my body. The perception raises the question of what happens to the me of my mind when my fleshy body dies. Knowledge of the mind-body dichotomy is deeply rooted in Western cultural tradition and has been scrutinized by philosophers, anthropologists, theologians, and psychologists.

In Western religious traditions, it has given rise to dichotomous conceptualizations such as mind and body, master and slave, reason and desire, order and chaos, which in turn evolved into profound metaphors affecting and justifying the organization and structure of society, and the allocation of political power.[4] We are familiar with the saying from Matt. 26:41 and Mark 14:38 used often to explain away some unacceptable behaviors that occur despite ostensibly good intentions: "the spirit is willing but the flesh is weak." Psychologically, this may be restated: desire and impulse are stronger than reason.

Data collected by scholars of Eastern and non-Christian Western religions indicate clearly that comprehensions of the body and of how people explain and interpret body experiences and feelings differ from culture to culture, teaching, in effect, that they are socially constructed.[5] Consequently, it is clear that our Western interpretation is not innate and does not refer to something objective in human biology or biochemistry and, as a consequence, should not be universalized. It is a matter of our culture and language. If so, in the absence of contradictory evidence and the presence of supporting data, I surmise that there was no mind-body dichotomy in the culture of ancient Israel.[6] This surmise clarifies a persistent problem in the exegesis of a Levitical law.

Leviticus 5:1 reads: "If a person sins—he heard an adjuration (against withholding testimony)—and he is a witness—either he saw or knew—if he does not tell, he will bear (responsibility for) his iniquity." The reluctant witness is held liable for nonperformance, most likely in cases that may have involved a deposit in some transaction or in cases of a lost, stolen, or pawned object (see Lev. 5:24). The individual is classified among those who although they touched a ritually impure thing, or the carcass of an unclean creature, or human impurity, were unaware of the fact that they had become ritually unclean. Only later, when they became aware of it, by whatever agency, were they liable to a guilt offering, an *asham* (Lev. 5:2–3). Also included in this category is a person who swore to do something that would have bettered or worsened somebody or some situation but who forgot to follow through (v. 4).

It is somewhat easier to see the oath-taker in this category than the adjuration-hearer. The former most likely swore an oath invoking YHWH which he then forgot, despite its gravity. He actually did something—undertake an obligation made sacred by an oath that was not fulfilled—that in the broader society may have been taken as a deprecation of the divine name. He swore vainly (Exod. 20:7). The adjuration-hearer did nothing. He was passive. He heard the adjuration, knew that he had information, but decided not to testify. His inclusion at the head of a list of those obligated to bring purification offerings requires explanation.

His classification is odd because what he did involved a moral matter of which he was aware. (The law does not assume that he forgot hearing the adjuration. Had that been the case, the law could have employed the same terminology used by the J author of Genesis 40 in describing what happened after the butler promised to remember Joseph to Pharaoh: "and the butler did not remember Joseph; and he forgot him" [Gen. 40:23].) However, in the absence of a mind-body dichotomy, it is likely that what we call *morality*—be it a matter of reason or of an innate sense—was thought to be embodied in the physical body and to emanate from one of two organs: the heart, if a matter of the reasoning mind; the kidneys, if innate.[7] Under such circumstances, Israelites sought *morality* and *immorality,* that is, actions evaluated positively or negatively within their culture, in bodily acts. His body thought and heard and had been summoned to speak. If the adjuration invoking the divine name proclaimed as a matter of law and cultic potency that not performing with his mouth willfully constituted a malfeasant act adjudged guilty requiring cultic purification, his iniquitous act polluted the body, not the mind.[8] The humorous fortune-cookie message, "clean mind, clean body: take your pick," did not apply in ancient Israel. Likewise, Israelite religion and anthropology had no concept of an eternal soul that could become besmirched.

In Israelite conception, the difference between the living and dead was that the former had a *nefesh*—the word most commonly translated and thought to refer to the soul—while the latter did not (living—2 Sam. 1:9; 1 Kings 17:21; Ps. 66:9; dead—Gen. 35:18; Judg. 16:30; Jonah 4:3). The *nefesh* was activated at birth by breath, its presence altering matter from a lifeless to a living state (Gen. 2:7). It was associated with and present in the blood of both humans and animals (Gen. 9:4–5; Lev. 17:11, 14; Deut. 12:23).[9]

In humans, *nefesh* was involved with emotions such as joy (Isa. 61:10; Ps. 35:9; 86:4) and moroseness (Deut. 28:65; 1 Sam. 30:6; 119:28) that were considered transitive, outwardly directed forces (Gen. 23:8; Deut. 4:29) and such essential drives as thirst and hunger (Jer. 31:14; Ps. 107:9).[10] This corresponds roughly to the Freudian notion of Id in that it does not involve cognition and intellectual activities. The dead, lacking *nefesh* activity when breathing and circulation ceased (described as "pouring out of the *nefesh*" [Ps. 53:12]), would therefore be characterized by apathy.

When humans died, not only Israelites, they went to *sheol*, continuing there in some shadowy state appearing much as they had in life. This is clear from the story of the Witch at Endor who recognized the dead Samuel when he appeared to her eyes in a séance (1 Samuel 28) and from Isaiah's oracle against the king of Babylon in which he described the dead king's entry to *sheol* where "the shades of all earth's chiefs" rise from their thrones to greet him disrespectfully (Isa. 14:9–11).[11] This concept of an after-death body is somewhat akin to that of the *ka* in Egyptian mortuary beliefs, except that in Israelite speculation, no mummified first body was required for the postmortem body to maintain its existence.[12]

To the extent that shades had status in *sheol*, it was dependent on whether or not their first bodies had been properly buried and their bones cared for (Isa. 14:18–20).[13] In the case of Israelites, status may have been affected also by sacrifices made either to or on behalf of the dead (Deut. 26:14; Ps. 106:28) as well as by the proper deposit of grave-goods in their tomb that would guarantee their continued well-being.[14] The dead were believed cut off from YHWH—"the dead will not praise Yah, and not all the descendents of Silence" (Ps. 115:17)—they did not address him and he generally did nothing for them (Ps. 88:11–13), but they were not completely cut off from the living.[15] Laws against necromancy indicate that Israelites believed that certain humans could communicate with at least some of the dead in *sheol* in order to gain information otherwise unavailable to the living except through prophecy (Isa. 8:19; 29:4; Lev. 20:27; Deut. 18:11).[16]

These data suggest that Israelite anthropology of the pre-exilic period as reflected in biblical literature held a view of "personhood" that was physical and simple in conception, and one for which death raised no anxiety.

The Integrated Cosmos

Israelite mythopoeia constructed a three-tiered cosmos: the upper one, called *shamayim*, the heavens, was inhabited by divine beings. Within this tier, YHWH occupied the uppermost part (Ps. 113:6; 123:1; 148:1). Above the *shamayim* was water (Ps. 148:4). The middle one, *arets*, earth, was inhabited by humans and all the flora and fauna created from the third through the sixth days of creation as described in Gen. 1:11–29 (Ps. 115:16). The third and lowest tier was sometimes called *tehom*, Depth (Ps. 33:6–8; 104:2–6) or *dumah*, Silence (Ps. 115:17), but most often, it was called *sheol*, rendered conventionally by *underworld* (1 Sam. 2:6–8; Jonah 2:3; Job 26:6–13). Entered through *sha'arey mawet*, the Gates of Mot/death (Ps. 9:14; 107:18) it was the abode of the dead and the realm of the deity Mot/death (Isa. 28:15; 18; Hosea 13:14; Ps. 49:15). Yahweh was absent from the lowest tier and could not be addressed from there (Ps. 115:17), but under certain circumstances he could reach into it if he wished (Isa. 38:10, 18; Amos 9:2; Ps. 135:6).

Genesis 1:1–3 suggests that before there was quantifiable time and before he manufactured the two upper tiers of the cosmos, there had been a series of great battles in which YHWH had been victorious. This may be discernable in verse 2 describing the state of the cosmos when he began to create *shamayim* and *arets*, the upper and middle tiers: the *arets* was unformed and void and there was a darkness over the surface of *tehom*, and the wind of God was hovering over the face of the water. These lines suggest that initially God's wind kept *tehom* in place, under darkness (conceived as a palpable substance, not merely the absence of light). He then formed *arets* over the *tehom*, but *arets* itself was open to *shamayim* that, like a most distant shore, was too far away for people to reach (Gen. 11:1–9; 28:12–13) but not so far that divine messengers could not descend from there to *arets* through the *sha'ar hashamayim*, Gate of *Shamayim* (Gen. 28:17).

More explicit traces of cosmogonic myths exist elsewhere in the Bible. Psalm 74:12–17 describes God as having driven back Yam and smashing the heads of serpent-monsters on the waters, shattering the heads of Leviathan, arranging the waters, and determining the limits of *arets.* Isaiah 51:9–10 describes the mighty arm of YHWH that hacked Rahab and pierced the serpent-monster and dried up Yam and the waters of the great *tehom*. Other traces are found in Ps. 89:10–11; 104:6–9; Job 38:8–11; 40:25–32. These snippets indicate that in the full stories to which they allude, YHWH destroyed some of his opponents, and that he defeated or contained yet others in an unmentioned place.[17]

In addition to YHWH and his messengers, *shamayim* was inhabited by other deities, the focus of rituals described in different biblical texts, whose myths are not recorded in extant sources: Baal, Asherah, and the Queen of Heaven. Other divinities populating the Israelite pantheon are known from casual references and personal names in the Israelite onomasticon: Molech, Asher, Gad, Horus, Shalem, Min, and Bes.[18] Virtually nothing is known about these gods other than that they had their followers among Israelites. Some of the minor deities mentioned above may have been believed to be resident somewhere on *arets* and to wield their effective authority only there, but this is no more than a guess. Mot, of course, was busy in *sheol*. Every deity and every being had its assigned place and *modus vivendi* and *modus operandi*.

Although prophets generally acknowledged the reality of other deities, a stipulation of covenantal Yahwism as expressed in biblical texts is that YHWH demands total loyalty from native Israelites, or else. This loyalty, however, was not defined in terms of what he expected Israelites to do for him, but rather in their abstention from doing anything for any other deity.

The cosmos, as crafted by YHWH, and complicated by the presence of other divine forces, was a self-perpetuating structure. YHWH alone controlled affairs in *shamayim*. Biblical myth preserves little of what went on there. Once there may have been an assault on YHWH's authority by an underling, if the allusion to Hellel ben Shachar in Isa. 14:12 is about a rebellious figure cast first to *arets* and then lowered to the most distant pit in *sheol*.[19] There was also some trouble in *shamayim* before the flood when divine males mated with attractive human females, an affair for which the humans were faulted even though it was the divine males who had acted (Gen. 6:1–4). The few verses in Genesis dedicated to this incident fail to clarify where the divine-human couples lived and what was done to restore the separation of unlike beings.

Insofar as all the fragments and allusions to cosmology occur in genres that display a historical perspective, that view time linearly and assign cosmogonic events to the most distant past, they indicate that *the myths had been historicized*. The events about which they told were singular and interesting, but of no relevance to Israelite religion. There is no evidence that myths were enacted in Israel's cult or that Israelites fretted about maintaining the cosmos through rituals. As a cultic community, Israel's celebrations were connected only with postcosmogonic, historical events (real or imagined) such as the Sabbath and Passover, and timely, immediate natural events such as rain and harvest on Booths, Matzoth, and Weeks.

Travel and Communication between the Cosmic Tiers

There was traffic between the tiers. In general, biblical narrative or prophetic speeches alluding to known traditions describe YHWH as the main interventionist, involving himself or his messengers in the affairs of Israelites on *arets*. But he was not only involved with Israelites, he also affected nations such as the Philistines, Arameans, Assyrians, and others either directly or through assigned divine messengers (Isa. 10:5–6; Amos 9:7; but see also Deut. 32:8 "when he divided the son of Adam, established the borders of nations according to the number of the sons of El [reading with the LXX]"). YHWH or his messengers came down to monitor affairs on *arets* regularly.

Similarly Mot who resided in the lowest tier also moved in the realm of *arets*, entering buildings through windows (perhaps to avoid apotropaic formulae associated with the doors [?]) (Jer. 9:20), perhaps to conduct those newly invested in their shade-bodies to *sheol*. The story about Samuel's postmortem appearance at Endor in 1 Samuel 28 reflects credulity in the notion that necromancers could summon to *arets* at least some of the departed from *sheol*, granting them limited-stay visas, so to speak.[20]

Humans, however, with the rare exceptions of Enoch (Gen. 5:23–24) and Elijah (2 Kings 2:11) did not ascend from *arets* to *shamayim* nor did they, with the exception of Korah and his people (Num. 16:33), descend to *sheol* in living bodies.

Insofar as deities could and did involve themselves in their affairs, Israelites tried to explain what in their life might be symptomatic of divine interventions. Both prophetic and historiographic traditions maintained two parallel, independent modes of explaining events. The idea of divine causality was used to clarify crucial events such as extreme droughts, bountiful harvests, military victories, or defeats. But these were also explicable through natural or human factors.[21] Not every rainstorm or dry spell, not every spontaneous abortion or successful venture required a theologically minted explanation.[22] Consequently, Israelites could seek and curry divine favors for their various endeavors, but did not depend on it. God did not plow fields, plant crops, or build fences; people did. God did not destroy Israel's enemies; Israel's armies did. All Israel had a covenant with YHWH, but some also had a covenant with Mot, who functioned independently of YHWH, that they believed would save them from an untimely death (Isa. 28:15, 18).[23] Many in different historical periods provided their children with names celebrating him.[24] Consequently offerings were directed both to *shamayim* and *sheol*, blood was placed on YHWH altars but sometimes it was poured into the ground. All efforts were directed to maintaining a well-run cosmos with its comprehensible natural order. People did not seek to buy their way into *shamayim* or to avoid *sheol*; they sought a decent, safe life on *arets*. What Israelites thought to gain by worshipping YHWH is discussed below.

The Divine Image in the Cosmos

The three tiers of the cosmos were integrated in one significant way. Although the permanent residents of each tier were occupied by different activities, they shared one common feature: they were physically alike.

Divine messengers conducting YHWH's business on *arets* appeared as fellow humans to various individuals: Abraham's visitors, Lot's guests, the man at Jericho seen by Joshua (Josh. 5:13–15), Gideon's guest (Judg. 6:11–22), the visitor to Manoah and his wife (Judg. 13:1–23). The last-mentioned narrative is particularly interesting because it provides a detail about how the author imagined his characters might be able to guess whether or not a figure was a human or a divine messenger: "a man of God came to me, and his appearance was like a messenger of God, very frightening" (v. 6). Despite this characterization, the messenger was referred to and addressed as *iysh*, man (vv. 8, 10, 11) because "Manoah did not know that he was a messenger of the Lord" (v. 16) until he disappeared in flames on the altar (v. 20). In the absence of any statement or hints to the contrary in biblical narratives composed over a few centuries, these should not be interpreted as disguised figures, assuming human forms that enabled them to pass among people unhindered. When divine beings are odd-looking, they are described: Isa. 6:2; Ezek. 1:5–14.

Just as Adam's son Seth was born *bidmuto ketsalmo*, in his likeness, according to his image (Gen. 5:3), which means simply that the son looked like the father, so too Adam was created by God *bidmuto*, in his likeness according to Gen. 5:1, or *betsalmo, betselem elohim*, "in his image, in the image of God" according to Gen. 1:27. According to Gen. 1:26, this was the divine intention: "We will make humans *betsalmenu kidmutenu*, in our image according to our likeness." The implication of all this is that many inhabitants of the cosmos were theomorphic.[25] The similarity, however, extended beyond appearance.

As a consequence of what happened in YHWH's garden, Israelites thought that all humans were characterized by the faculty to distinguish between what was more or less preferable, correct or incorrect, right or wrong, *tov vara*, just like divine beings (Gen. 3:2–7). Knowing that they were capable of high order, practical, and moral distinctions, they held those not meeting normed or prescribed standards to account. Inasmuch as this knowledge was innately divine and humanity had acquired it by stealth, I infer that Israelites believed that the affairs of the cosmos were conducted fairly in accord with some vague notions of what we might call natural law.[26]

The Yahwistic Cult and the Hidden Face of YHWH

Israelites during the First Temple period acknowledged the existence of many deities and worshipped some of them. However, judging from the evidence of personal names, the most popular of the gods worshipped by Israelites was the supra-tribal deity, YHWH.[27] Insight into their attitude toward his worship is gained by considering the sacrificial system as set forth in the Priestly document.

The Yahwistic cult is premised on the proposition that Israelites want to serve YHWH and to be in his presence in the space demarcated by his shrine. It assumes that all who come to the sanctuary are Yahwists by choice; they are there because they want to be there. Even though there are specific commands regarding obligatory appearances at the shrine three times a year on the pilgrimage festivals (Exod. 34:23 [J]; Lev. 23:1, 15–21; and in expanded form in Num. 28:16–30:1), these are not compulsory in fact. Absent any penalty for nonappearance or a coercive force compelling the demanded appearance and performance of appropriate rituals, noncompliance always remained an option. The legislator in P, as well as in the later Deuteronomic formulation of the commandment in Deut. 16:1–17, assumes that people will come, prescribed offerings and gifts in hand.

The complicated "lay guide to sacrifice," comprising the first seven chapters of Leviticus, clarifies the conditions that had to be met and the sacrificial rules that had to be followed by those deciding to enter the sanctuary. People are allowed to enter the sanctuary only if ritually pure; if not pure, they are instructed how to purify themselves. Following their entrance in a state of ritual purity and presenting a required purification sacrifice, they may present other sacrifices of their choice from a menu of options. Nothing is compelled and offerings are graded in terms of affordability for people of different status and wealth. People wishing to live in a permanent state of ritual impurity could do so without fear of sanctioned penalty. (Fear of social opprobrium, however, and of angry parents and kinsmen may have been another matter influencing behavior.) They would have encountered actual danger only had they tried to enter the sanctuary in such a state and been apprehended by priestly guards. High-handedly entering sacred courts in a state of ritual impurity, they would have been categorized as *zarim*, encroachers, unauthorized to perform a particular cultic act, and subjected to the death penalty (Num. 1:51; 3:10, 38).[28] In fact, since sources of ritual impurity were commonly encountered—contact with the carcasses of unclean animals or of animals permitted for consumption that died, genital discharges such as menstrual blood and semen, various dermatological conditions, certain molds and mildew infestations on cloth or in buildings, and human corpses (Lev. 11–15; Numbers 19)—and because impurity was transferred between people through contact, most people were either ritually impure most of the time or could have assumed reasonably that they were impure.[29] Purification usually involved waiting a designated period of time after contact with the source of impurity and, depending on the nature of the impurity, bathing, and finally presenting a purification offering. People desiring to go to the sanctuary took the equivalent of a shower and put on their "Sunday best," because that was what YHWH desired.

The Yahwistic sacrificial system in P has no official sacrifices of supplication or request and none to ward off impending disaster. When people wished to ask YHWH for something specific, they did so spontaneously, informally, and prosaically, in what Moshe Greenberg terms "prose prayer." Thus, when Miriam was smitten with leprosy Moses prayed, "God, please, heal her, please" (Num. 12:13, and see Gen. 32:10–13; 2 Sam. 19:20–21).[30] Thanking him, however, should one wish to do so, was done formally with a sanctioned sacrifice.

Private offerings mentioned in the "lay guide to sacrifice" covered the following categories: purification, reparation/guilt, and well-being offerings. The last-mentioned category is divided into sacrifices for thanksgiving, oath-fulfillment, and those presented for no particular reason in a spirit of generosity, *zebach shelamiym*, the so-called freewill offerings (Lev. 3:1–17; 7:11–34).

Even *yom hakkippurim*, the solemn day of atonements/expiations, of covering over or wiping clean, was a benign day. Although few were involved in the actual ritual, the ethic informing the ritual was optimistically communitarian, for the good of all. According to priestly conceptions, over time, impurity, perhaps imagined as some invisible miasmic substance attracted and adhering to the outer and inner altars of the tabernacle/temple—accumulated. P determined that this accumulation, originating from unpurged ritual contaminations, crimes, and priestly accidents, had to be eliminated annually before the Autumnal festival.[31] Accordingly, each year, the place in *arets* at which all common human impurities could be treated, and at which YHWH himself could be present, was cleansed of all contaminants. For Israelites, the rituals of this day (Leviticus 16) guaranteed the presence of God throughout the year.

Ithamar Gruenwald's study of Leviticus 16 emphasizes the tensions underlying the rituals of the day and their mythological underpinnings.[32] But, despite its solemnity and though *yom hakkippurim* was fraught with seriousness for the head priest and his assistants, the actors concerned with the absolutely proper execution of the rites in all their minutiae, it was a very happy day for Israelites looking on in silence. They knew that the rituals would be successful and effective. They always were.

These data suggest that if only a single adjective were allowed for describing the ethos of the relationship between Israel and YHWH, it would be *loving*. In this relationship, however, Israel loved YHWH much more passionately than YHWH loved Israel. My characterization of this relationship is supported by the counselors who monitored and intervened in the relationship.

Israel's prophets condemned many aspects of cultic behavior. Isaiah quotes YHWH, "Why do I need the multitude of your sacrifices. . . . I am satiated with burnt offerings of rams and the suet of fatlings. And I have no delight in the blood of bulls, and sheep and goats" (Isa. 1:11). Amos accused his audience of inappropriate sexual activity and imbibing in the shrine (Amos 2:8) and insincerity to the point that he reports YHWH saying, "I hate, I despise your pilgrimage festivals . . . if you bring me offerings . . . I will not accept them . . . remove the sound of your songs from me; I will not listen to the music of your lutes" (Amos 5:21–23). The theme of rejecting Israel's cultic behavior is found also in Jer. 6:20–21; 7:21; Hosea 6:6; Micah 6:6–7; and even in Ps. 50:8–15, part of the Temple liturgy. These texts illustrate that, if anything, Israelites were overly involved in cultic ritual. But to what end? What did they think to gain by their solicitude?

They received divine attention that promised, pursuant to their behaving in accordance with God's dictates, "rain for your land in season, the early rain and the late. And you will gather your grain and wine and oil. And I will give fodder in your fields for your animals, and you will eat and be satisfied" (Deut. 11:14). Life would be normal. It would rain when it was supposed to rain; and be dry when it was supposed to be dry. God would allow the person observing divine precepts to live out his allotted days (Exod. 23:26). Loyalty to YHWH was not rewarded by superabundance but by reaping the fruit of normal labor. Active disloyalty, however, would be met by unnatural disruptions in nature: "The anger of YHWH will flare against you and he will block the heavens and there will be no rain and the land will not produce harvests" (Deut. 11:17). This notion underlies the Elijah story about the drought in the days of Ahab and the contest with Baal prophets on Mount Carmel (1 Kings 18:1–46), and Amos' interpretation of irregular patterns of rainfall, plant blight, and locusts (Amos 4:7–9). YHWH liked loyalty but did not necessarily reward it; he punished disloyalty, and apparently tolerated indifference. Under such circumstances, both the loyal and indifferent were beneficiaries to the same degree because YHWH took pains only to punish the disloyal. (Complicating matters somewhat after the seventh century, loyal Yahwists sometimes perceived their own misfortunes as unfairly due to a collective punishment occasioned by acts of the disloyal.)

This raises an interesting question: Even if loyalty seemed to have been its own reward, what extra, if anything, accrued to the benefit of those providing sacrifices? What they gained was that their sacrifices attracted YHWH's attention to both the offering and offerer and so long as he held them in his gaze and memory, he did not hide his face from them.[33] This notion operated on both the individual and national level.

The Hebrew expression, *histiyr panayw*, "turn aside/hide/conceal his face," indicates that the subject of the phrase wants to avoid seeing (Exod. 3:6) or to ignore something (Ps. 10:11; 51:11; Isa. 8:17). In psalmody, the expression appears in contexts where bad things are believed to happen not necessarily because they were orchestrated by YHWH as a punishment, but because he ignored people, turning his face away from them so that he could not see what was happening and so that he could not hear if they cried out for help (Ps. 30:8; 22:25; 27:9; 44:25). They were subject to random events perceived as misfortunate that regularly occur in the world. This perception is encapsulated in David's message to Joab when learning about the desired death of Uriah the Hittite. As if to mollify Joab, he said, "Don't let this matter trouble you for the sword consumes, sometimes this one, sometimes that" (2 Sam. 11:25). Although cynical and wry in context, it is realistic in perspective.

In Deut. 31:17–18, God warns Moses that after his death Israel will be unfaithful, that he will get angry, leave Israel, and "hide my face from them and it will become prey and many evils and troubles will find it." In Deut. 32:20, God says, "I will indeed hide my face from them; I will see what their end will be." The point of these passages is that when God turns aside from Israel, the world continues to function naturally with stuff happening all the time. Good stuff and bad stuff. According to Deut. 32:20, God did not necessarily know what bad might befall Israel.

The idea has a succinct expression in postexilic Isaiah 54. The prophet comforts Zion for her suffering and tells her not to fear or feel shame for what happened. In verse 8 he explains: "'In a small moment I left you; but in great love I will gather you; in passing anger I hid my face from you a moment; but in eternal grace I will love you,' said your redeemer, YHWH."[34]

The practical advantage of maintaining good relations with YHWH and sacrificing to him was that when something bad happened to Israel, there would be somebody to whom requests for help could be addressed.

Israelite religion recognized that the world could be, not that it was in essence, a violent place and that bad things—marauding raiders killing children, freak storms panicking herds of sheep and camels, mighty winds collapsing a house on a family (Job 1:13–19)—happened to both good people and to bad people. Good things happened also. The point of ritual piety was to have some advantage, to be sure that in time of need, YHWH would be looking. Whether or not he would act was his decision.

The Post–586 BCE Destabilization of the Cosmos

In Israelite thought, the cosmos was essentially stable, but dynamic. Offerings were made from the second tier and directed both upward and downward to maintain amicable relations. Because people died, there was constant movement between the second and third tiers; because God was concerned with human affairs on the second tier there was movement between the first and second tier. However, because people were free-willed and could violate YHWH's commands there was always the possibility that he would punish them in accord with the penalty clauses of the covenant, bringing against them a congeries of malfeasant natural and human forces. Additionally, as Jon Levenson points out, there was always a theoretical possibility that God might lose partial or full control over the primeval monsters restrained when he first organized the cosmos.[35]

With the dawning of quasi-apocalyptic thought in the second half of the eighth century BCE, after the destruction of the northern kingdom, when the Neo-Assyrian threat to Judah and Jerusalem became real, mythopoeic thinkers conceived that YHWH might destroy the chaos monster Leviathan (Isa. 27:1) and consume Mot (Isa. 25:8), putting an end to death, and even that human dead would recover their wet natural bodies (Isa. 26:19). Yahweh could be imagined as reorganizing the cosmos and declaring in language borrowed from Gen. 1:1: "I create a new *shamayim* and new *arets*, and the former ones will not be mentioned and not brought to mind" (Isa. 65:17).

It was only after the destruction of Jerusalem in 586 BCE, during the exilic and postexilic periods, that allusions to these theoretical possibilities emerged as an important factor in Israelite thought. Then, when YHWH was perceived to have punished Israel as he had promised and when Israel saw its national fabric rent, and its social system of tribes, clans, and extended families unraveling, perceptions of the cosmos, its inhabitants, and its operations altered. The old order was thought disturbed, the primal enemies astir, and the primordial battles renewed. Rantings of the quasi-apocalypticists defined a new reality. The primordial violence of cosmogonic myth was dehistoricized and contextualized within an activating theology of contemporaneity. Through its prism, present time was seen as a refraction of primeval chaos and everything was perceived as hurtling toward a looming, uncertain new constellation of force and power before a new evening and morning of a new first day.

William Morrow proposes that the destruction of Jerusalem gave rise to changes that are aptly, not figuratively, characterized as reflecting post-traumatic stress disorder. One symptom of PTSD is reflected in the violation of various cognitive systems that inject confusion into a coherent worldview. Such shifts in meaning systems include loss of faith, a sense of hopelessness and despair, and a desire to escape violence.[36]

In the fractured cosmos of the Persian and Hellenistic eras, *shamayim* and *sheol* became remote from *arets*; communication between them broke down; anxiety about the presence of the divine became normalized; physical conceptions of the cosmos gave way to more abstract notions under the influence of Hellenism; and the second body of Israelites "metamorphosed" into a soul.

Notes

1. Z. Zevit, *The Religions of Ancient Israel: A Synthesis of Parallactic Approaches* (London: Continuum, 2001), 15, 611.
2. D. M. Carr, *Writing on the Tablet of the Heart: Origins of Scripture and Literature* (Oxford: Oxford University Press, 2005), 110–73, 287–97.
3. Material in this study is drawn from a work-in-progress on the evolution of Israelite religions into what I call, for lack of a better term, "Proto-Judaisms" of the Persian and Hellenistic periods.
4. B. S. Turner, "The body in Western Society: Social Theory and Its Perspectives," in *Religion and the Body,* ed. S. Coakley (Cambridge: Cambridge University Press, 1997), 17–25, 38. M. Midgley traces the dichotomy expressed as antagonism back to Paul's statement in Gal. 5:17: "what the flesh desires is opposed to the spirit. And what the spirit desires is opposed to the flesh; for these are opposed to each other to prevent you from doing what you want." See "The Soul's Successors: Philosophy and the 'Body,'" in *Religion and the Body*, ed. S. Coakley (Cambridge: Cambridge University Press, 1997), 54–56, and see Paul's autobiographical example in Rom. 7:14–15.
5. T. Asad, "Remarks on the Anthropology of the Body," in Coakley, *Religion and the Body*, 46–49.
6. This is not an original observation, but one no longer part of contemporary discussions in bibliology as biblical anthropology has changed its focus from the thought world to that of Realia with the help of archaeological discoveries. See the not-so-recent work of Johannes Pedersen, *Israel, Its Life and Culture, I–II* (London: Oxford University Press, 1926), 99–181. Pedersen, his theological-anthropology just under the surface, wrote: "The relationship between body and soul is quite different from what it is to us. Such as he is, man, in his total essence is soul" (99). I would complete Pedersen's sentence with the word "body." See also H. W. Wolff, *Anthropology of the Old Testament* (Philadelphia: Fortress Press, 1974). Wolff tried to describe an Old Testament "doctrine of man" (23), aware that there was no unified "doctrine" in the Bible that could be derived historically because of the nature of the composite texts in the collection (3).
7. For the *heart* as the seat of what we call "mind" see Gen. 27:41; Ps. 10:4; Prov. 15:4; 23:7; and regularly in Deuteronomy; for *kidneys*, see Ps. 15:7; Prov. 23:16. For the combination of the two see Ps. 26:2; 73:21; Jer. 17:10; 20:12.
8. The word usually referring to treaty curses, used in Lev. 5:1 implies that something negative was uttered.
9. According to Lev. 17:14, blood and *nefesh* were coterminous, though distinct in the living. It is unclear if Israelites thought the *nefesh* to be dissolved in the blood or if the two were considered a mixture. For historical periods when the soul was considered distinct from the living body, the mixture metaphor would certainly be apt.
10. See Wolff, *Anthropology of the Old Testament*, 10–25, for additional details.
11. If there was a belief in actual resurrection of the dead, see Isa. 25:8 and 26:19, the metaphoric sermon of Ezekiel 37 suggests a way of imagining it. When the buried, disarticulated body was reassembled and the revived person walked again, the shade-body was simply gone.
12. An atypical ninth-century BCE Iron Age burial cave from Tel Eton, 18 kilometers southwest of Hebron, contains sculpted bird images that I have associated with Israelite mortuary beliefs. See Zevit, *The Religions of Ancient Israel*, 244–46.
13. Jer. 8:1–2 refers to a ritual that involved removing the bones of illustrious Jerusalem ancestors from their tombs and displaying them publicly. Possibly this may have been a rite of last resort intended to force the shades in *sheol* to intercede somehow on behalf of the living. See Zevit, *The Religions of Ancient Israel*, 543.

S. Olyan provides an up-to-date summary of what is known and what is guessable about Israelite burial beliefs. See "Some Neglected Aspects of Israelite Internment Ideology," JBL 124 (2005): 601–16.

14. E. Bloch-Smith, *Judahite Burial Practices and Beliefs about the Dead,* JSOTSS 123 (Sheffield: JSOT Press, 1992), 63–108, 140–41.
15. Ps. 139:8 contradicts this general statement. This psalmist, and presumably many like him, held other views.
16. Wolff, *Anthropology of the Old Testament*, 100–110.
17. J. Levenson, *Creation and the Persistence of Evil: The Jewish Drama of Divine Omnipotence* (San Francisco: Harper and Row, 1988), 7–25. Levenson points to a disquieting passage, Job 40:25–32, representing a tradition in which Leviathan, whose heads were reported smashed in Psalm 74, is touted a living plaything of God. Levenson interprets this as part of a theological tradition that conceived of dissolution into chaos as an ever-present threat and implied that humanity had a role in keeping it at bay.
18. Zevit, *The Religions of Ancient Israel*, 583–84, 605. To this list, we should add the winged serpent-beings described in Isa. 6:2.
19. Ps. 82:7 provides a context for this. God threatens to punish unjust divine figures: "You will die like humans, like one of the officers/ministers you will fall."
20. In other Ancient Near Eastern cultures and in later Judaism, it was believed that the departed could ascend to earth. See S. M. Paul, "'Emigration' from the Netherworld," in *Divrei Shalom: Collected Studies of Shalom M. Paul on the Bible and the Ancient Near East 1967–2005* (Leiden: Brill, 2005), 263–70.
21. See the crucial article of I. L. Seeligmann, "Menschliches Heldentum und Göttluche Hilfe—Die doppelte Kausalität im altesttestamentlichen Gechichtsdenken," *ThZ* 19 (1963): 385–411. My approach differs from that of Seeligmann who maintained that everything was explained in terms of double-causality in that I find evidence that some harmful events were not explained that way. See the discussion below of *hastiyr panayw*.
22. Amos 4:7–8 interprets odd rainfall patterns leading to near droughts in some communities as a divine warning to Israel. His audience, however, did not comprehend the weather pattern as such. Much of Amos involves theologizing all manner of natural and political events.
23. There is both textual and archaeological evidence for chthonic worship and rituals in Israel, see 1 Samuel 14; Lev. 19:26; and Zevit, *The Religions of Ancient Israel*, 280–86, 292–94, 310–11. The rituals mentioned in Jeremiah and Ezekiel, however, are not related to this worship. Although these rituals were believed, by their practitioners, to have been commanded by YHWH (see Jer. 7:31) and were, perhaps, funerary, they had nothing to do with Mot. See Zevit, *The Religions of Ancient Israel*, 542, 549–52.
24. These are collected and analyzed in Zevit, *The Religions of Ancient Israel*, 588–94. On untimely death, see S. M. Paul, "Untimely Death in the Semitic Languages," in *Divrei Shalom*, 223–38.
25. This will be discussed in great detail in Z. Zevit, *What Really Happened in the Garden of Eden?* (forthcoming).
26. I am aware that this conclusion creates problems for contemporary theologians (as it did for medieval ones), even as it clarifies issues in the informal speculations and metaphorical language of Israelite story-tellers, prophets, and poets.
27. Z. Zevit, "A Chapter in the History of Israelite Personal Names," *BASOR* 250 (1983): 1–16.
28. J. Milgrom, *Studies in Levitical Terminology, 1. The Encroacher and the Levite; The Term 'Aboda* (Berkeley, University of California Press, 1970), 5, 36–37, 39–43. The *zar* is the wrong person in the wrong place. The term is aptly applied, but in a less technical way, to the encroaching/poaching women, *ishah zarah* in Prov. 2:16–17; 5:3, who is no stranger to the enticed male. She too is the wrong person in the wrong place, and this is not only a moral estimation but a juridical one as well.
29. H. Eilberg-Schwartz imaginatively suggests some of the ways in which some of these sources for impurity may have been perceived and experienced in Israel, particularly menstrual blood, semen, and genital discharges. Although natural, these were all beyond human control and hence a source of disorder in what should have been an orderly, comprehensible world. See *The Savage in Judaism: An Anthropology of Israelite Religion and Ancient Judaism* (Bloomington: Indiana University Press, 1990), 177–216.
30. M. Greenberg, *Biblical Prose Prayer as a Window to the Popular Religion of Ancient Israel* (Berkeley: University of California Press, 1983), 1–57.
31. J. Milgrom, "Israel's Sanctuary: The Priestly Picture of Dorian Gray," *RB* 83 (1976): 390–99.
32. I. Gruenwald, *Rituals and Ritual Theory in Ancient Israel* (Leiden: Brill, 2003), 202–30. I take issue with Gruenwald's characterization of the slaughtering of the goat as "violent" (216). It is very difficult to conceive that anybody growing up in a society where people regularly slaughtered their own animals for food and for sacrifice, gutted and skinned them, and then butchered them would blink at the killing of a goat.
33. This statement expands a proposal by B. A. Levine that incense, providing a pleasant odor, was intended to attract YHWH's presence when rituals were performed. See, "Lpny YHWH—Phenomenology of the Open-

Air Altar in Biblical Israel," in *Biblical Archaeology Today, 1990: Proceedings of the Second International Congress on Biblical Archaeology* (Jerusalem: Israel Exploration Society, 1993), 202.

34. In Ezek. 39:23 the expression indicates that the only reason disaster befell Israel was that YHWH had turned his face aside to ignore what happened, but a few verses later, in v. 29, it indicates that by turning his face aside, he didn't hear the cries of the people. Presumably, had he heard them, he could not have withheld his help from them.
35. Levenson argues that a variation on this idea interpreting the subdued creatures as evil, coupled to an implicit threat that God could abrogate his rainbow covenant with an unethical humanity, led to a notion that combating evil in the world with God helped him keep chaos (= evil) under control. While I agree with many of Levenson's specific interpretations and conclusions, I see no evidence that supports dating the broad apocalyptic cast characterizing such thought to the pre-exilic period on which the present article focuses. See Levenson, *Creation and the Persistence*, 46–50, 127. Some of his broad, general conclusions—the point of his book—are obtained by reading texts, biblical and rabbinic, somewhat synchronically. This is not a fault in the book, but a fact that must be borne in mind when appropriating its ideas into a pre-Hellenistic context.
36. W. Morrow, "Post-Traumatic Stress Disorder and Vicarious Atonement in the Second Isaiah," in *Psychology and the Bible: A New Way to Read the Scriptures*, ed. J. H. Ellens and W. G. Rollins (Westport, Conn.: Praeger, 2004), 168–71, and "Comfort for Jerusalem: The Second Isaiah and Counselor to Refugees," *Biblical Theology Bulletin* 34, no. 2 (2004): 80–81.

A Garber Bibliography

Editorial Activities

Academic and Professional Advisory Council, National Center for Hebrew Language (NCHL), member, 1995–present.

Hakirah: A Journal of Jewish and Ethnic Studies, editorial board, 2001–present.

Iggeret (newsletter of the National Association of the Professors of Hebrew), editor, 1982–present.

Mentalities/Mentalitiés: An Interdisciplinary Journal (New Zealand), editorial advisor, 2007–present.

Shofar Supplements in Jewish Studies, founder and editor, 2005–present.

Shofar: An Interdisciplinary Journal of Jewish Studies, associate editor, 1994–2001; co-editor, 2001–present.

Studies in the Shoah (scholarly series on the Holocaust, University Press of America), founder and editor-in-chief, 1990–present.

Traversal (Zeitschrift des Centrums für Jüdische Studien, Karl-Franzens-Universität Graz, Austria), editorial board, 2004–present.

Western States Jewish History, editorial advisor, 1999–present.

Books

Double Takes: Thinking and Rethinking Issues of Modern Judaism in Ancient Contexts (with Bruce Zuckerman). Lanham, Md.: University Press of America, 2004.

Post-Shoah Dialogues: Rethinking Our Texts Together (with Henry Knight, Steven Jacobs, and James Moore). Lanham, Md.: University Press of America, 2004.

Shoah, the Paradigmatic Genocide: Essays in Exegesis and Eisegesis. Lanham, Md.: University Press of America, 1994.

Books and Special Issues Edited

Academic Approaches to Teaching Jewish Studies. Lanham, Md.: University Press of America, 2000.

The Impact of the Shoah in America and in Jewish American Life. *Casden Annual Review* 6 (2008).

Jesus in the Context of Judaism and the Challenge to the Church. *Shofar* 19, no. 1 (Fall 2001).

Mel Gibson's Passion: The Film, the Controversy, and Its Implications. West Lafayette, Ind.: Purdue University Press, 2006.

Methodology in the Academic Teaching of Judaism. Lanham, Md.: University Press of America, 1986.

Methodology in the Academic Teaching of the Holocaust (with Alan L. Berger and Richard Libowitz). Lanham, Md.: University Press of America, 1988.

Peace in Deed: Essays in Honor of Harry James Cargas (with Richard Libowitz). Atlanta: South Florida Studies in the History of Judaism/Scholars Press, 1998.

Perspectives on Zionism. *Shofar* 13, no. 1 (Fall 1994).

Shoah in Israeli Writing, with an Emphasis on Hebrew Poetry. *Shofar* 23, no. 2 (Winter 2005).

Teaching Hebrew Language and Literature at the College Level. *Shofar* 9, no. 2 (Spring 1991).

What Kind of God? Essays in Honor of Richard L. Rubenstein (as consulting editor). Lanham, Md.: University Press of America, 1995.

Sections Edited

"Mel Gibson's *Passion*: The Film, the Controversy, and Its Implications." *Shofar* 23, no. 3 (Spring 2005): 71–143.

"Reflections on Emil L. Fackenheim z'l (1916–2003): The Man and His Philosophy." *Shofar* 22, no. 4 (Summer 2004): 107–35.

Encyclopedia Articles

Encyclopaedia Judaica (Jerusalem: Keter Publishing House, 1972)

Abomination
Alfrink, Bernardes J.
Andrews, Lancelot
Astruc, Jean
Auerbach, Elijah
Baethgen, Friedrich
Bate, Julius
Baumgartner, Walter
Baumgartner, Wolf
Beek, Martinus A.
Bentzen, Aage
Bertholet, Alfred
Bleek, Friedrich
Bungenhagen, Johannes
Cook, G. A.
Cook, S. A.
Corneill, Karl H.
De Lyra, Nicholas
Delitzsch, Franz
Dillman, August
Duhm, Bernhard
Dupont-Sommer, Andre
Fredrich, Karl
Ginsberg, Christian David
Gunkel, Hermann
Haupt, Paul
Hengstenberg, Ernest
Hitzig, Ferdinand
Hupfeld, Hermann
Jerimias, Alfred
Jespen, A.
Jirku, Anton
Kautzsch, Emil
Keil, Karl
Kirkpatrick, A. F.
Kittel, Rudolph
Lehmann-Haupt, Carl
Marti, Karl
Meyer, Edward

Novak, Wilhelm
Orlinsky, Harry M.
Reinhold, Johannes
Rosenmuller, E. F. K.
Rowley, R. H.
Ryssal, C. V.
Schaeffer, Claude
Sievers, Eduard
Smedn, Rudolph
Smith, John Merlin Powis
Smith, W. Robertson
Steuernagel, Carl
Theodore of Mopsuestia
Torrey, C. C.
Tzvi Segal, Moses
Vatke, Johan Karl

Encyclopedia Judaica, 2nd ed. (Jerusalem: Jerusalem Publishing House, 2006)

Fishbane, Michael
Katz, Steven T.
Kugel, James
Levinson, Jon

Ready Reference: Ethics (Pasadena: Salem Press, 1994)

Bahya ben Joseph ibn Pakudah
I and Thou
Ibn Gabirol, Solomon ben Yehudah
Talmud
Tillich, Paul
Torah
Wiesel, Elie

Student's Encyclopedia of the Holocaust (Jerusalem: Jerusalem Publishing House, 1997)

Dibelius, Martin
Schindler, Oskar
Shoah
Third Reich
White Paper of 1939
Wiesel, Elie
Wiesenthal Center

Reader's Guide to Judaism (Chicago: Fitzroy Dearborn Publishers, 2000)

Judaism, Introductions to
Responses to the Holocaust
Samaritans

The Encyclopedia of Judaism (Leiden: E. J. Brill, 1999)

Holocaust, Practice of Judaism during 1933–1945

Reference Guide to Holocaust Literature (Farmington Hills, Mich.: St. James Press, 2002)

Glatstein, Jacob
Heyen, William

Niemöller, Martin
Tec, Nechama
Wiesenthal, Simon
Zeitlin, Aaron

Encyclopedia of Jewish American Popular Culture (Westport, Conn.: Greenwood Press, 2008)

Holocaust Remembrance Day
Lazarus, Emma
Schindler's List

Encyclopedia of the Bible and Its Reception (Berlin: Verlag Walter de Gruyter, 2008)

Abubus
Achior
Alcimus
Antipas 02
Antipas 03 Antipater
Antipas 04 Herod
Antipater 01. Son of Jason
Antipater 02. Father of Herod the Great
Belshazzar, Judaism
Beelzebub, Judaism
Birth, Judaism

Articles and Notes

"37th Annual Scholars' Conference on the Holocaust." *Journal of Ecumenical Studies* 42, nos. 1–2 (2007): 121.

"A Citadel Fitly Constructed: Philo-Semitism and the Making of an American Holocaust Conference." *Casden Annual Review* 6 (2008): 191–217.

"A Psychological Interpretation of the Song of Songs" (with S. Kardener). *Reconstructionist* 42, no. 3 (1976): 25–30.

"Amalek and Amalekut: A Homiletic Lesson." In *Jewish Bible Theology: Perspectives and Case Studies,* ed. Isaac Kalimi. Eisenbrauns (forthcoming).

"American Jews: Then and Now." *Jewish Spectator* 49, no. 2 (1984): 45–47.

"An Interfaith Dialogue on Post-Shoah Jewish-Christian Scriptural Hermeneutics, with a Report on the Case Colloquium (April 10, 2005)." *CSSR Bulletin* (The Council of Societies for the Study of Religion) 34, no. 4 (2005): 76–79.

"Berlin International Conference: 'Addressing the Cycle of Pain.'" *Shofar* 10, no. 4 (1992): 75–76.

"Book Symposium: Constantine's Sword: The Church and the Jews by James Carroll." *Religious Education* 97, no. 2 (2002): 184–97.

Contributor to *The Study of Religion at Two-Year Colleges,* ed. C. Freeman Sleeper and Robert A. Spivey. Missoula, Mont.: Scholars Press, 1975. Also ERIC database, www.eric.ed.gov, ED086269.

"Dating the Shoah: In Your Blood Shall You Live." In *Bearing Witness 1939–1969,* ed. A. Berger, 287–99. Lewiston, Maine: Edwin Mellen Press, 1991.

"Deconstructing Theodicy and Amelekut: A Personal Apologia." In *The Netherlands and Nazi Genocide,* ed. G. J. Colijn and M. S. Littell, 407–28. Lewiston, Maine: Edwin Mellen Press, 1992.

"Dialogue at the Mountain: Thoughts on Exodus 24 and Matthew 17:1–13." In *Confronting the Holocaust: A Mandate for the 21st Century—Part Two,* ed. S. C. Feinstein, K. Schierman, and M. S. Littell, 1–12. Lanham, Md.: University Press of America, 1998.

"Disorder in Order: The Interlocution of Shoah in the Passover Haggadah and Seder." In *The Uses and Abuses of Knowledge*, ed. H. F. Knight and M. S. Littell, 273–92. Lanham, Md.: University Press of America, 1996/1997.

"Do Not Hurt Them." In *Holocaust Scholars Write to the Vatican*, ed. Harry James Cargas, 49–55. Westport, Conn.: Greenwood Press, 1998.

"Editor's Introduction." In *Teaching Hebrew Language and Literature at the College Level. Shofar* 9, no. 3 (1991): 1–5.

"Editorial Viewpoint: Old-New Antisemitism: Fatwa Against Israel." *Shofar* 20, no. 2 (2002): 1–4.

"Encounter in Dialogue." *Shofar* 15, no. 1 (1996): 99–107.

"Fackenheim's Post-Shoah Mandate." *Shofar* 22, no. 4 (2004): 112–15.

"Faith from the Ashes: An Interview with Sibylle Sarah Niemoeller von Sell." *Shofar* 22, no. 2 (2004): 44–55.

"The Flood and the Fig Tree: Teaching, Text, and Theology." *CSSR Bulletin* (The Council of Societies for the Study of Religion) 35, no. 3 (2006): 52–55.

Foreword. In Esther R. Taus, *Torah for Today*. Lanham, Md.: University Press of America, 2008.

Foreword. In Henry F. Knight, *Confessing Christ in a Post-Holocaust World*. Westport, Conn.: Greenwood Press, 2000.

Foreword. In Steven L. Jacobs, *Rethinking Jewish Faith*, xiii–xvi. Albany: SUNY Press, 1994.

"The Furor Over the Auschwitz Convent: The Inside and Outside of the Language of Bias." In *What Kind of God? Essays in Honor of Richard L. Rubenstein*, ed. B. R. Rubenstein and M. Berenbaum, 95–109 (with B. Zuckerman). Lanham, Md.: University Press of America, 1995. Reprinted in *From Prejudice to Destruction: Western Civilization in the Shadow of Auschwitz*, ed. C. J. Colijn and M. S. Littell, 167–80. Münster, 1995.

"*Gastgeschenk: Panim B'Fanim*." *Shofar* 10, no. 4 (1992): 76–80.

"Holocaust in Literature." *Religious Education* 76, no. 2 (1981): 224–27.

"Insiders and Outsiders: For Whom Do We Toil?" In *Holocaust and Church Struggles: Religion, Power and the Politics of Resistance*, ed. H. G. Locke and M. S. Littell, 69–86. Lanham, Md.: University Press of America, 1996.

"Interpretation and the Passover Haggadah." *Journal of Reform Judaism* 26, no. 2 (1979): 83–87. A revised version of the paper is found in *Experiencing the Exodus from Egypt*, ed. D. L. Christensen, 51–60. Berkeley, 1988.

"Interpretation and the Passover Haggadah: An Invitation to Post-Biblical Historiosophy." *Bulletin of Hebrew Higher Education* 2, no. 2 (1988): 24–29.

"Introduction to 'A Family Lost Forever.'" In Steven L. Jacobs, *In Search of Yesterday: The Holocaust and the Quest for Meaning*, 3–6. Lanham, Md.: University Press of America, 2006.

"Introduction, Mel Gibson's *Passion:* The Film, the Controversy, and Its Implications." *Shofar* 23, no. 3 (2005): 71–73.

"Israel and the Arabs." *Jewish Spectator* 36, no. 9 (1971) 25–26.

"It Is Not in Heaven: Interpreting Romans 3 and 10 in Light of Deuteronomy 30." *Mentalities/Mentalités* 21, no. 2 (2007): 1–2, 16–21.

"Jethro, Father-in-Law of Moses." *Forum* 50 (1983/1984): 58–64.

"The Jewish Jesus: A Partisan's Imagination." *Shofar* 23, no. 3 (2005): 137–43.

"Jewish Perspectives on Edith Stein's Martyrdom." In *The Unnecessary Problem of Edith Stein*, ed. Harry James Cargas, 61–76. Lanham, Md.: University Press of America, 1994.

"Jewish Studies at Los Angeles Valley College." *Western States Jewish History* 32, no. 1 (1999): 82–93.

"Jewishly Responding to a Death." *National Jewish Post and Opinion*, June 20, 2001, 8–10.

"The Journal Synthesizing Activity." In *The Academic Study of Religion and Public Schools Religion Studies: 1975,* ed. Anne Carr and Nicholas Piediscalzi, 83–90. Missoula, Mont.: Scholars Press, 1975. Also ERIC database, www.eric.ed.gov, ED 114151.

"The Kislev Dilemma: Origins of Channukah." *Jewish Spectator* 58, no. 3 (1993–94): 22–23.

"Know Sodom, Know Shoah." In *Peace in Deed: Essays in Honor of Harry James Cargas*, ed. Z. Garber and R. Libowitz, 83–98. Atlanta: Scholars Press, 1998.

"Language Violence: Auschwitz Convent Controversy." In *Studies in Jewish Civilization 16: The Jews of Eastern Europe*, ed. L. J. Greenspoon, R. A. Simkins, and G. Shapiro, 329–38. Omaha, Neb.: Creighton University Press, 2005.

"Lübeck International Conference." *Journal of Ecumenical Studies* 35. nos. 3–4 (1998): 548–49.

"Mel Gibson's Cinematic Crucified Christ: The Remedy from Jewish-Christian Dialogue." *Transversal: Zeitschrift für Jüdische Studien* 5 (2004): 62–69.

"Mel Gibson's Cinematic Debauchery: A Dialogical Response." *The American Rabbi* (2007): 380–83.

"Multiculturalism and Educating for Shoah: Enlightenment or Endarkenment?" *Shofar* 13, no. 4 (1995): 86–90.

"Night Encounters: Theologizing Dialogue and Encounter in Dialogue." *Shofar* 15, no. 1 (1996): 38–53.

"The Ninety-three Beit Yaakov Martyrs, Towards the Making of Historiosophy." *Shofar* 12, no. 1 (1993): 69–92.

"The Ninety-three Beit Yaakov Martyrs." In *What Have We Learned? Telling the Story and Teaching the Lessons of the Holocaust*, ed. F. H. Littell, A. Berger, and H. Locke, 373–401. Lewiston, Maine: Edwin Mellen Press, 1993.

"On David S. Wyman's *The Abandonment of the Jews*." *Journal of Ecumenical Studies* 40, no. 4 (2003): 396.

"On Tolerance and Philo-Semitism." *Jewish Spectator* 48, no. 3 (1983): 55–57.

"Pilgrim's Progress." *Jewish Spectator* 65, no. 1 (2000): 24. Reprinted in *Service International De Documentation Judéo-Chrétienne (SIDIC)* 34, no. 1 (2001): 10.

Preface. In *The Holocaust Now: Contemporary Christian and Jewish Thought*, ed. Steven L. Jacobs. New York: Cummings and Hathaway, 1997.

"The Problem of Edith Stein: Jewess and Catholic Saint." In *Women in the Holocaust: Narrative and Representation*, ed. E. Fuchs, 1–7. Lanham, Md.: University Press of America, 1999.

"The Problem with Edith Stein: Jewess and Christian Martyr." *Jewish Spectator* 56, no. 2 (1991): 13–14.

"Problems of American Jews." *Jewish Spectator* 48, no. 1 (1983): 36–37.

"Psalm 138:4: A Religious Polemic in the Haggadah." *Central Conference of American Rabbis Journal* 18, no. 1 (1970): 57–60.

"The Rabin Assassination in the Long View and the Short View: Biblical Radicalism in a Modern Context" (with B. Zuckerman). *Hakirah: Journal of Jewish and Ethnic Studies* 1 (2003): 69–88.

"Reflections on Emil L. Fackenheim z'l (1916–2003): The Man and His Holocaust Philosophy: Editorial Introduction." *Shofar* 22, no. 4 (2004): 107–8.

"Reflections on Jesus: Review Essay." *Shofar* 27, no. 2 (2009).

"*Reichspogromnacht*: First Berlin International Conference." *Journal of Ecumenical Studies* 28, no. 4 (1991): 677–78.

"The Religion Olympiad: A Report on the First International Congress of Learned Societies in the Field of Religion." *Davka* (UCLA) 3, no. 1 (1972): 17–24.

"Remembering for the Future II." *Journal of Ecumenical Studies* 31, nos. 1–2 (1994): 202.

"Remembering for the Future III." Journal of Ecumenical Studies 37, nos. 3–4 (2000): 461.

"Responses to the Holocaust." In *The Holocaust in University Teaching*, ed. G. Shimoni, 82–93. New York: Pergamon Press, 1989.

"Rethinking Jewish Peoplehood." *Forum* 39 (1980): 149–54.

Review essay on *The Jewish Study Bible*, ed. A. Berlin and M. Z. Brettler, *Review of Biblical Literature* 7 (2005): 13–19.

"The Samaritan Passover." *Central Conference of American Rabbis Journal* 22, no. 2 (1975): 41–44. Reprinted in *Experiencing the Exodus from Egypt*, ed. D. L. Christensen (Berkeley: Bibal Press, 1988), 45–49.

"Shoah (Holocaust): To Teach, Learn, Understand." *Shofar* 8, no. 4 (1990): 20–36.

"Shoah in Israeli Writing, with an Emphasis on Hebrew Poetry." *Shofar* 23, no. 2 (2005): 1–8.

"Shoah's Apocalypse: Three Talking Points." *Hakirah: Journal of Jewish and Ethnic Studies* 2 (2006): 5–16.

"The Synoptic Jesus: A Jewish Approach." *Davka* (UCLA) 2, no. 2 (1972): 19–33.

"Teaching Lower Division Hebrew Language and Literature at a Two-Year Public College." *Hebrew Studies* 20–21 (1979–80): 161–66. Also ERIC database, www.eric.ed.gov, ED162703.

"Teaching Shoah Matters: A Personal Memoir." In *Teaching about the Holocaust: Essays by College and University Teachers*, ed. S. Totten, S. L. Jacobs, and P. Bartrop, 65–79. Westport, Conn.: Greenwood Press, 2004.

"Teaching the Holocaust: The Introductory Course." In *Methodology in the Academic Teaching of the Holocaust,* ed. Z. Garber with A. Berger and R. Libowitz, 25–55. Lanham, Md.: University Press of America, 1988. Also ERIC database, www.eric.ed.gov, ED 230226.

"Teaching Zionism: Incident on Campus." *Congress Monthly* 69, no. 4 (2002): 17–19.

"Teaching Zionism: The Introductory Course." *Shofar* 13, no. 1 (1994): 8–37. Reprinted in *Academic Approaches to Teaching Jewish Studies*, ed. Z. Garber, 267–96. Lanham, Md.: University Press of America, 2000.

"Terror Out of Zion: Making Sense of Scriptural Teaching." In *Confronting Genocide: Judaism, Christianity, Islam,* ed. Steven L. Jacobs. Lanham, Md.: Lexington Books/Rowman and Littlefield, 2009.

"Thirty-first and Thirty-second Scholars Conference on the Holocaust." *Journal of Ecumenical Studies* 38, nos. 2–3 (2001): 361–63.

"Thoughts on and from the Thought of Richard L. Rubenstein." In *Hearing the Voices: Teaching the Holocaust to Future Generations*, ed. M. Hayse, D. Pollefeyt, G. Jan Colijn, and M. S. Littell, 21–28. Merion Station, Pa.: Merion Westfield Press International, 1999.

"Thoughts on the Text, Teachers and Talmidim." In *Methodology in the Academic Teaching of Judaism,* ed. Z. Garber, 1–11. Lanham, Md.: University Press of America, 1986. Also ERIC database, www.eric.ed.gov, ED 099077.

"Torah and Testament: Teaching and Learning Scripture in Dialogue and in Hermeneutics." In *Puzzling out the Past: Studies in the Northwest Semitic Languages and Literatures in Honor of Bruce Zuckerman,* ed. Steven Fine, Marilyn J. Lundberg, and Wayne T. Pitard (forthcoming).

"Torah and Testimony: Making Sense of Disputation in Dialogue." *Service International De Documentation Judéo-Chrétienne (SIDIC)* 34, no. 3–35, no. 1 (2001–2): 39–43.

"Understanding the Shoah: Review Essay on *The Holocaust in Historical Context*, by Steven T. Katz." *Shofar* 13, no. 4 (1995): 68–73.

"The Vision Language of the Other: Jedwabne versus Auschwitz Convent Controversy." In *Imaginary Neighbors: Polish Jewish Relations after the Shoah,* ed. D. Glowacka and D. Zylinska, 236–52. Lincoln: University of Nebraska Press, 2007.

"Why Do We Call the Holocaust 'the Holocaust'? An Inquiry into the Psychology of Labels." In *Remembering for the Future: Papers Presented at the International Scholars Conference,* vol. 2, *The Impact of the Holocaust on the Contemporary World,* 1879–82. Oxford, 1988. A revised paper and slightly abridged version of the study (with B. Zuckerman) is found in *Modern Judaism* 9, no. 2 (1989): 197–211.

"Words, Words, Words." *Hebrew Studies* 48 (2007): 231–48.

"Written in the Wind: The Evolution of Jewish Studies at a Public Community College in the United States." In *Juedische Studien. Lehren und Forschen in einer jungen Diziplin*, ed. K. Hödl, 123–32. Innsbruck: Studien Verlag, 2003.

"*Yiddishkeit* or Jewish Studies." *Hadoar* 72, no. 2 (1992): 21–22 (in Hebrew).

Book Reviews

ARBA	*American Reference Book Annual*
CCAR Journal	*Central Conference of American Rabbis Journal*
CJ	*Conservative Judaism*
CM	*Congress Monthly*
HA	*Hebrew Abstracts*
HGS	*Holocaust and Genocide Studies*
JB	*Jewish Bookland*
JRJ	*Journal of Reform Judaism*

JS	*Jewish Spectator*
LBR	*Law Books in Review*
LJ	*Library Journal*
MJ	*Modern Judaism*
NJP&O	*National Jewish Post and Opinion*
RBBR	*Reprint Bulletin Book Review*
RBL	*Review of Biblical Literature*
RBR	*Review of Books and Religion*
SCJ	*Studies in Contemporary Jewry*
WSJHR	*Western States Jewish Historical Review*

The A to Z of Catholicism, by William J. Collinge. *ARBA* 33 (2002).

About the Holocaust, by Dorothy Rabinowitz. *Jerusalem Post Magazine* (March 1980), and *HS* 20–21 (1979–80).

Accounting for Genocide, by Helen Fein. *RBBR* 29, no. 2 (1984).

Act and Idea in the Nazi Genocide, by Berel Lang. *CCAR Journal* 41, no. 2 (1994).

After the Evil: Christianity and Judaism in the Shadow of the Holocaust, by R. Harries. *CM* 71, no. 1 (2004).

AJS Reviews, Volume 7–8 (1982–1983), edited by Frank Talmadge. *JES* 22, no. 4 (1985).

American Academy for Jewish Research Jubilee Volume (1928/29–1978/79), 2 vols., edited by S. Baron and I. E. Barzilay. *HS* 24 (1983).

The American Catholic Bible in the Nineteenth Century: A Catalog of English Language Editions, by Sidney K. Ohlhausen. *ARBA* 38 (2007).

The American Jew: A Zionist Appraisal, by Ben Halpern. *RBBR* 28, nos. 3/4 (1983).

American Jews in Transition, by Chaim I. Waxman. *JS* 49, no. 2 (1984).

Amos of Israel, by Stanley M. Rosenbaum. *RelSRev* 18, no. 2 (April 1992).

Amos, by J. L. Mays. *AUSS* 9, no. 2 (1971).

Ancient Canaan and Israel, by Jonathan M. Golden. *ARBA* 37 (2006).

Ancient Israel's Criminal Law, by A. Phillips. *HA* 15 (1974).

Animal Life in Jewish Tradition: Attitudes and Relationships, by Elijah J. Schochet. *RelSRev* 12, no. 1 (1986).

Anti-Semitism in the New Testament? by S. Sandmel. *RelSRev* 5, no. 1 (1979).

Antisemitism, by Milton Shain. *AJS Review* 25, no. 1 (2000/2001).

Antisemitism, Christian Ambivalence, and the Holocaust, edited by Kevin P. Spicer. *Shofar* 27, no. 1 (2009).

Anti-Semitism, Threat to Western Civilization, by Menahem Rosensaft and Yehuda Bauer. *SCJ* 8 (1992).

Approaches to Ancient Judaism, by William S. Green. *RelSRev* 5, no. 3 (1979), and *Choice* 16, nos. 5/6 (1979).

Approaches to Ancient Judaism, vol. 3, by William Scott Green. *Choice* 19, no. 7 (September 1982).

The Arab-Israeli Dispute, by Don Peretz. *ARBA* 97 (1997).

Ashes in the Wind: The Destruction of Dutch Jewry, by J. Presser. *RBBR* 35, no. 1 (1990).

Aspects of Jewish Economic History, by Marcus Arkin. *Choice* 13, no. 11 (1977), and *HS* 19 (1978).

The Assassination of Yitzhak Rabin, edited by Yoram Peri. *JS* 66. nos. 3, 4 (2002).

Auschwitz: Tales from a Grotesque Land, by Sara Nomberg-Przytyk. *RBBR* 31, nos. 3, 4 (1986).*The Babylonian Captivity and Deutero-Isaiah*, by Y. Kaufman. *HA* 15 (1974).

The Banality of Good and Evil: Moral Lessons from the Shoah and Jewish Tradition, by David R. Blumenthal. *Shofar* 19, no. 3 (2001).

Basic Forms of Prophetic Speech, by C. Westermann. *AUSS* 8, no. 2 (1970).

Bearing the Unbearable, by Frieda W. Aaron. *HGS* 6, no. 2 (1991).

Benya Kirk the Gangster and the Other Stories, by Isaac Babel. *RBBR* 34, no. 1 (1989).

Betrayal: German Churches and the Holocaust, edited by Robert P. Erickson and Susannah Heschel. *Choice* 37, no. 6 (2000).

Between Time and Eternity, by Jacob Neusner. *Choice* 13, no. 3 (1975).
Beyond Innocence and Redemption: Confronting the Holocaust and Israeli Power—Creating a Moral Future for the Jewish People, by Marc E. Ellis. *JES* 29, no. 1 (1992).
The Bible and Criticism in Victorian Britain: Profiles of F. D. Maurice and William Robertson Smith, by J. W. Rogerson. *RelSRev* 23, no. 4 (1997).
The Bible in Human Society: Essays in Honor of John Rogerson, edited by M. Daniel Carroll R., David J. A. Clines, and Phillip R. Davies. *RelSRev* 23, no. 4 (1997).
The Biblical and Historical Background of the Jewish Holy Days, by Abraham Bloch. *Choice* 15, no. 9 (1978), and *RelSRev* 5, no. 1 (1979).
Biblical Books Translated from the Aramaic, by Frank Zimmerman. *JAOS* 98, no. 3 (1978).
Biblical Hebrew Syntax, by Bruce K. Waltke and M. O'Conner. *Choice* 27, no. 2 (1990), and *CRBR* (1992).
Biblical Hebrew, by Page H. Kelley. *CRBR* (1993).
Biblical Text in Palestinian Pointings and Their Accents, by E. J. Revell. *JBL* 98, no. 3 (1979).
Bibliographical Dictionary of Modern Egypt, by Arthur Goldschmidt Jr. *ARBA* 32 (2001).
Bibliography of Hebrew Publications on the Dead Sea Scrolls, by M. Yishar. *JAOS* 89, no. 3 (1969).
A Bibliography of Pseudepigrapha Research, by L. DiTommaso. *ARBA* 35 (2004).
Binah: Studies in Jewish Thought, edited by Joseph Dan. *Choice* 27, no. 3 (1990).
Birth Control in Jewish Law, by D. Feldman. *RBBR* 25, no. 3 (1980).
The Black Book, by I. Ehrenburg and V. Grossman. *RBBR* 27, no. 2 (1982).
Black Zion: African American Religious Encounters with Judaism, edited by Yvonne Chireau and Nathanial Deutsch. *Choice* 38, no. 5 (2001).
Black-Woman-Jew: Three Wars for Human Liberation, by A. Roy Eckardt. *NJP&O* (August 1989).
The Blessings in the Targums: A Study on the Targumic Interpretations of Genesis 49 and Deuteronomy 33, by Roger Syren. *CBQ* 51, no. 1 (1989).
The Book Jeremiah: A New Translation with Woodcuts by Nikos Stravrroulakis. LJ 99, no. 15 (1974).
The Book of Amos, by E. Hammershaimb. *AUSS* 12, no. 1 (1974).
The Book of Amos: An Annotated Bibliography, edited by Henry O. Thompson. *ARBA* 98 (1998).
The Book of Exodus in Jewish and Christian Traditions, by Goran Larsson. *HS* 41 (2000).
The Book of Genesis: With a New Interpretation Accompanied by Introduction, Notes, Maps, and Figures (Hebrew), by Moshe Weinfeld. *JBL* 96, no. 2 (1977).
The Book of Hebrew Script: History, Paleography, Script Styles, Calligraphy and Design, by A. Yardeni. *ARBA* 35 (2004).
The Bridal Canopy, by S. Y. Agnon. *RBBR* 25, no. 4 (1980).
A Brief History of Israel, by Bernard Reich. *ARBA* 36 (2005).
Butler's Lives of the Saints: Supplement of New Saints and Blesseds, vol. 1, by Paul Burns. *ARBA* 37 (2006).
By the Waters of Babylon: An Introduction to the History and Theology of the Exile, by James D. Newsome Jr. *JAAR* 48, no. 1 (1980).
By Words Alone: The Holocaust in Literature, by Sidra DeKoven Ezrahi. *RelEd* 76, no. 2 (1981).
The Canonization of the Synagogue Service, by Lawrence Hoffman. *CJ* 35, no. 3 (1982).
The Catholic Experience in America, by Joseph A. Varacalli. *ARBA* 37 (2006).
The Catholic Internet, by Tim DeRyan. *ARBA* 98 (1998).
Celebrating Elie Wiesel, edited by Alan Rosen. *Shofar* 18, no. 4 (2000).
Censorship in the Arab World, edited by Mona A. Nsouli and Lokman I. Meho. *ARBA* 38 (2007).
The Chosen People in America, by Arnold M. Eisen. *JS* 49, no. 2 (1984).
The Chosen People, by J. M. Allegro. *AUSS* 12, no. 1 (1974).
Christian Origins and Judaism, by W. D. Davies. *RBBR* 20, no. 1 (1975).
A Christian Theology of Judaism, by C. Thoma. *RelEd* 76, no. 6 (1981).
Church and the Jewish People: New Considerations, by Johannes Cardinal Willebrands. *JES* 31, nos. 1–2 (1994).
Claud Goldschmid Montefiore on the Ancient Rabbis, by Joshua Stein. *RelSRev* 4, no. 3 (1978).

Comparative Midrash: The Plan and Program of Genesis Rabbah and Leviticus Rabbah, by J. Neusner. *JBL* 107, no. 2 (1988).

Conservative Judaism and Jewish Law, edited by Seymour Siegel. *Choice* 15, no. 3 (1978), and *HS* 19 (1978).

Constantine's Sword: The Church and the Jews, by James Carroll. *Shofar* 20, no. 3 (2002).

Contemporary Halakhic Problems, by J. David Bleich. *Choice* 14, no. 10 (1977), and *HS* 19 (1978).

Contexts and Content: Higher Jewish Education in the United States, by Byron L. Sherwin. *RelEd* 84, no. 3 (1989).

Conversion to Judaism, by J. Rosenbloom. *RelEd* 74, no. 3 (1979).

Conversion: Halakha and Practice, by Menachem Finkelstein. *Shofar* 27, no. 3 (2009).

Corpus of Jewish Inscriptions, vol. 1, *Jewish Inscriptions from the Third Century B.C. to the Seventh Century A.D.*, by P. Jean-Baptiste Frey, Prolegomenon by Baruch Lifshitz, *RBBR* 20, no. 3 (1975).

The Cosmic God, by Isaac Wise. *RBBR*, 21, no. 1 (1976).

The Covenant: A Theology of Human Destiny, by J. Jocz. *AUSS* 9, no. 2 (1971).

Creator, Are You Listening? Israeli Poets on God and Prayer, by David C. Jacobson. *Choice* 45, no. 5 (2008).

Crisis and Covenant, by Alan Berger. *LA Jewish News* (November 1988).

Culture and Customs of Israel, by Rebecca L. Torstrick. *ARBA* 36 (2005).

Damaged Goods, by Thomas Friedman. *RBBR* 32, nos. 2–3 (1988).

David King of Israel Alive and Enduring? (Hebrew), by O. Lipschitz, A. Mazar, A. Rofe, and Y. Zakovitch. *JBL* 119, no. 1 (2000).

The Dead Sea Isaiah Scroll: A Literary Analysis and Comparison of the Qumran Scroll with the Masoretic Text of Isaiah, by J. R. Rosenblood. *AUSS* 12, no. 1 (1974).

The Deaths of Popes: Comprehensive Accounts, Including Funerals, Burial Places, and Epitaphs, by Wendy J. Reardon. *ARBA* 36 (2005).

Defiance, The Bielski Partisans, by Nechama Tec. *AJS Review* 20, no. 2 (1995).

Dialogue: In Search of Jewish Christian Understanding, by J. S. Spong and J. D. Spiro. *CCAR Journal* 24, no. 1 (1977).

Dictionary of Ancient Rabbis: Selections from the Jewish Encyclopedia, edited by Jacob Neusner. *ARBA* 36 (2005).

The Dictionary of Classical Hebrew, vol. 1, edited by J. A. Clines and John Elswolde. *Choice* 32, no. 1 (1994).

A Dictionary of Jewish-Christian Relations, edited by Edward Kessler and Neil Weinborn. *RBL* (2006), http://www.bookreviews.org.

A Dictionary of the English Bible and Its Origins, by Alec Gilmore. *ARBA* 33 (2002).

Dictionary of the Israeli-Palestinian Conflict: Culture, History, and Politics. ARBA 37 (2006).

Dictionary of the Old Testament: Pentateuch, edited by A. T. Desmond and D. W. Baker. *ARBA* 35 (2004).

Die Worbildung der Hebraischen Adjectiva (German), by F. Werner. *JBL* 104, no. 3 (1985).

Dilemmas in Modern Jewish Thought: The Dialectics of Revelation and History, by Michael Morgan. *AJS Review* 20, no. 1 (1995).

Discussing Cultural Influences: Text, Context and Non-Text in Rabbinic Judaism, edited by Rivka Ulmer. *AJS Review* 32, no. 2 (2008).

Discussing Death: A Guide to Death Education, by Gretchen C. Miller et al. *RelEd* 78, no. 2 (1983).

The Dual Image, by H. Fisch. *JAAR* 41, no. 2 (1973).

Dynamic Judaism, by E. S. Goldsmith and M. Scult. *RBBR* 32, no. 2 (1986).

The Dynamics of Judaism, by Robert Gordis. *Choice* 27, no. 7 (1990).

Early Jewish and Christian Exegesis: Studies in Memory of W. H. Brownlee, by Craig A. Evans and William Stinespring. *JES* 26, no. 4 (1989).

Early Jewish Exegesis and Theological Controversy: Studies in Scriptures in the Shadow of Internal and External Controversies, by Isaac Kalimi. *CBQ* 65, no. 1 (2003).

Early Rabbinic Writings, by Hyam Maccoby. *Choice* 26, no. 12 (1989).

Echoes from the Holocaust: Philosophical Reflections on a Dark Time, edited by A. Rosenberg and G. E. Myers. *RBBR* 35, no. 2 (1990).

The Echoes of Many Texts: Reflections on Jewish and Christian Traditions. Essays in Honor of Lou H. Silberman, edited by William G. Dever and J. Edward Wright. *RelSRev* 25, no. 4 (1999).

Economic History of the Jew, by Salo Baron, Arcadius Kahan, and Nachum Gross. *RBBR* 22, no. 2 (1977).

Elder of the Jews: Jacob Edelstein of Theresienstadt, by Ruth Brody. *Shofar* 8, no. 4 (1990).

Elie Wiesel, Messenger of All Humanity, by Robert McAfee Brown. *RBBR* 35, no. 1 (1990).

Emil L. Fackenheim: A Jewish Philosopher's Response to the Holocaust, by David Patterson. *Choice* 46, no. 2 (2008).

Emphatic Words and Structures in Biblical Hebrew, by T. Muraoka. *JBL* 106, no. 3 (1987).

Encyclopedia of California's Catholic Heritage, edited by Francis J. Weber. *ARBA* 33 (2002).

Encyclopedia of Catholic Devotions and Practice, by A. Ball. *ARBA* 35 (2004).

Encyclopedia of Catholic Social Thought, Social Science, and Social Policy, edited by Michael L. Coulter, Stephen M. Krason, Richard S. Meyers, and Joseph A. Varacalli. *ARBA* 39 (2008).

Encyclopedia of Genocide and Crimes Against Humanity, 3 vols., Dinah L. Shelton, editor-in-chief. *Shofar* 24, no. 3 (2006).

The Encyclopedia of Judaism, vol. 5, supp. 2, edited by J. Neusner, A. J. Avery-Peck, and A S. Green. *RBL* 7 (2005).

Encyclopedia of the Arab-Israeli Conflict: A Political, Social, and Military History, 4 vols., edited by Spencer C. Tucker. *ARBA* 39 (2009).

Encyclopedia of the Vatican and the Papacy, edited by Frank J. Coppa. *ARBA* 31 (2000).

End of an Exile, by J. Parkes. *RBBR* 28, nos. 3/4 (1983).

Eschatology in Maimonidean Thought, by J. I. Dienstag. *Choice* 20, no. 4 (1983).

Essays in American Jewish History, by the American Jewish Archives. *RBBR* 20, no. 4 (1975).

Essays in Greco-Roman and Elated Talmudic Literature, by Henry A. Fischel. *RelSRev* 4, no. 4 (1978).

Essays in Jewish and Comparative Legal History, by Bernard S. Jackson. *JBL* 96, no. 1 (1977).

Essays in Jewish Intellectual History, by Alexander Altmann. *Choice* 18, no. 9 (1981).

Essays in Old Testament Ethics, by J. Crenshaw and J. T. Willis. *Choice* 11, no. 9 (1974), and *HA* 16 (1975).

The Essential Talmud, by Adin Steinsaltz. *Choice* 13, no. 10, and *HS* 19 (1978).

Ethics After the Holocaust: Perspectives, Critiques, and Responses, edited by John Roth. *Shofar* 20, no. 1 (2001).

Ethics and Extermination: Reflections on Nazi Genocide, by Michael Burleigh. *Shofar* 18, no. 4 (2000).

Exile and Restoration, by P. Ackroyd. *AUSS* 8, no. 2 (1970).

The Exile of the Word: From the Silence of the Bible to the Silence of Auschwitz, by Andre Neher. *Choice* 18, no. 8 (1981).

Exploring the Talmud, by H. Z. Dimitrovsky. *RBBR* 22, no. 2 (1977).

Ezekiel: A New Heart, by B. Vawter and L. J. Hoppe. *RelSRev* 19, no. 3 (1993).

Faith and Freedom: A Tribute to Franklin H. Littell, edited by Richard Libowitz. *JES* 25, no. 2 (1988).

The Falashas: Forgotten Jews of Ethiopia, by David Kessler. *RBBR* 32, no. 1 (1988).

Family, Women, and Socialization in the Kibbutz, by Menachem Gerson. *Jerusalem Post* (July 1982).

The Female Face of God in Auschwitz, by M. Raphael. *RBL* 6 (2004).

Fire in the Ashes: God, Evil, and the Holocaust, edited by David Patterson and John K. Roth. *Choice* 43, no. 11 (2006).

The Folk Literature of the Kurdistani Jews: An Anthology, by Yonah Sabar. *JAAR* 54, no. 1 (1986).

Foregone Conclusions: Against Apocalyptical History, by Michael Andre Bernstein. *HS 37* (1996).

Forms of Rabbinic Literature and Thought: An Introduction, by Alexander Samely. *Choice* 45, no. 4 (2007).

Forschungsstelle Judentum Theologische Fakeltät, Leipzig (ed.) Leqach 4: Mitteilungen und Beiträge (German). *CBQ* 67 (2005).

Forschungsstelle Judenum Theologische Fakultät, Leipzig (ed.) Leqach 5: Mitteilungen und Beiträge (German). *CBQ* 68 (2006).

Foundations of Religious Tolerance, by J. Newman. *JS* 48, no. 3 (1983).
Four Paths to One God, by G. Rosenthal. *RBBR* 20, no. 1 (Spring 1975).
The Fourth Commandment: Remember the Sabbath Day, by F. Klagsbrun. *Hadoar* 82, no. 4 (2004), in Hebrew.
Frieden ohne Illusionen (German), by H. H. Schmid. *JBL* 91, no. 4 (1972).
From Eve to Esther: Rabbinical Reconstruction of Biblical Women, by Leila Leah Bronner. *Choice* 33, no. 1 (1995).
From Herzl to Rabin: The Changing Image of Zionism, by Amnon Rubenstein. *CM* 68, no. 4 (2001).
From Ideology to Liturgy: Reconstructionist Worship and American Liberal Judaism, by Eric Caplan. *Hadoar* 83, no. 3 (2004), in Hebrew.
From Reform Judaism to Ethical Culture: The Religious Evolution of Felix Adler, by Benny Kraut. *RelEd* 76, no. 6 (1981).
From Shtetl to Suburbia: The Family in Jewish Literary Imagination, by Sol Gittelman. *RBBR* 25, no. 1 (1980).
Genesis, by B. Jacob. *Choice* 11, no. 8 (1974), and *HA* 16 (1975).
Genetic Diseases among Ashkenazi Jews, edited by Richard M. Goodman and Arno G. Motulsky. *Israel Today* (November 1981).
A Genuine Search: God—Torah—Israel, A Reform Perspective, edited by Dow Marmur. *Israel Today* (January 1982), and *Forum* 49 (1983).
Gershom Scholem and the Mystical Dimension of Jewish History, by Joseph Dan. *Choice* 24, no. 10 (1987).
Getting Our Groove Back: How to Energize American Jewry, by Scott A. Shay. *Hador* 2 (2008), in Hebrew.
Gleanings: A Diary in Verse, by Marie Serkin. *Jerusalem Post* (September 1980).
(God) After Auschwitz, by Zachary Braiteman. *Choice* 36, no. 10 (1999).
God, Humanity, and History: The Hebrew First Crusade Narratives, by Robert Chazan. *Shofar* 21, no. 1 (2002).
God, Man, and History, by Elezer Berkovitz. *RBBR* 24, no. 4 (1979).
The Grammar of Modern Hebrew, by Lewis Glinert. *Shofar* 9, no. 3 (1991).
A Guide to the Dead Sea Scrolls and Related Literature, by Joseph A. Fitzmyer, S.J. *ARBA* 40 (2009).
Guidelines for Catholic-Jewish Relations (Secretariat for Catholic-Jewish Relations, National Conference of Catholic Bishops). *JES* 23, no. 4 (1986).
Handbook of Religious Experience, edited by Ralph W. Hood Jr. *RelEd* 92, no. 2 (1997).
Harvest of Hate: The Nazi Propaganda for the Destruction of the Jews, by L. Poliakov. *RBBR* 24, no. 3 (1979).
The Hasidic Parable: An Anthology with Commentary, by Aryeh Wineman. *RBL* 5 (2003).
Hasidic Responses to the Holocaust in the Light of Hasidic Thought, by Pesach Schindler. *AJS Review* 10, no. 3 (1992).
Heaven at Bay—The Jewish Kulterkampf in the Holy Land, by E. Marmorstein. *JS* 37, no. 4 (1972).
The Hebrew Bible in Art, by Jacob Leveen. *RBBR* 20, no. 2 (1975).
An Historic Encyclopedia of the Arab-Israeli Conflict, edited by Bernard Reich. *ARBA* 97 (1997).
Historical Dictionary of Ancient Israel, by Niels Peter Lemche. *ARBA* 36 (2005).
Historical Dictionary of Israel, by Bernard Rich and David H. Goldberg. *ARBA 40* (2009).
Historical Dictionary of Lebanon, by As'ad AbuKhalil. *ARBA* 99 (1999).
Historical Dictionary of the Arab-Israeli Conflict, by P. R. Kumaraswamy. *ARBA* 38 (2007).
The Historical Jesus in Context, edited by Amy-Jill Levine, Dale C. Allison Jr., and John Dominic Crossan. *Shofar* 27, no. 2 (2009).
History and Literature: New Readings of Jewish Texts in Honor of Arnold J. Band, by W. Cutter and D. C. Jacobson. *RBL* 6 (2004).
The History of Israel, by Arnold Blumberg. *ARBA* 30 (1999).
A History of Jews in Babylonia, vol. 1, *The Parthenian Period*, by J. Neusner. *RBBR* 29, no. 4 (1984).
A History of Judaism, by D. J. Silver and B. Martin. *LJ* 99, no. 18 (1974), and *HA* 16 (1975).

A History of Zionism, by W. Laqueur. *HA* 15 (1974).
Hitler and the Final Solution, by Gerald Fleming. *HGS* 1, no. 2 (1986).
Hitler's Apocalypse, Jews and the Nazi Legacy, by Robert Wistrich. *SCJ* 7 (1991).
Hitler's War Against the Jews: Holocaust, by D. A. Altshuler. *RelEd* 76, no. 6 (1981).
The Holocaust, by Jack R. Fischel. *HGS* 14, no. 1 (2000).
The Holocaust: In Answer. . . Is the Story True? Why Did the World Community Not Respond? What Are the Lessons?, edited by F. Littell, I. G. Shur, and C. Foster Jr. *JES* 27, no. 3 (1990).
The Holocaust and the Christian World, edited by Carol Rittner, Stephen D. Smith, and Irena Steinfeldt. *Shofar* 20, no. 4 (2002).
The Holocaust and World War II Almanac, 3 vols., by Peggy Saari and Aaaron Maurice Saari. *Shofar* 22, no. 1 (Fall 2003).
Holocaust Politics, by John K. Roth. *Shofar* 23, no. 1 (Fall 2004).
The Holy City, Jews on Jerusalem, by A. Holtz. *AUSS* 11, no. 2 (1973).
Holy Root, Holy Branches: Christian Preaching from the Old Testament, by Robert J. Allen and John C. Holbert. *JES* 34, no. 4 (1997).
Homeland or Holy Land: The "Canaanite" Critique of Israel, by James S. Diamond. *RelSRev* 14, no. 2 (1988).
The Honeymoon Is Over: Jonah's Argument with God, by T. A. Perry. *CBQ* 69 (2007).
Hosea, by J. L. Mays. *AUSS* 9, no. 2 (1971).
How Should Rabbinic Literature Be Read in the Modern World?, edited by Matthew Kraus. *AJS Review* 32, no. 2 (2008).
How to Be a Jew: Ethical Teachings of Judaism, by Byron L. Sherwin and Seymour J. Cohen, *JS* 59, no. 1 (1994).
The Human Will in Judaism: The Mishnah's Philosophy of Intention, by Howard Eilberg-Schwartz. *Choice* 24, no. 1 (1987).
Humanism in Talmud and Midrash, by Samuel Tobias Lachs. *Choice* 30, no. 3 (1993).
The Image of the Jew in American Literature, by Louis Harap. *JRJ* 25, no. 3 (1978).
Images of Judaism in Luke-Acts, by Joseph B. Tyson. *JES* 30, no. 2 (1993).
The Impossible Dilemma: Who Is a Jew in State of Israel? by Oscar Krainee. *LJ* 101, no. 21 (1976).
In Queen Esther's Garden: An Anthology of Judeo-Persian Literature, by Vera Basch Moreen. *RBL* 3 (2001).
In Search of Sugihara: The Elusive Japanese Diplomat Who Risked His Life to Rescue 10,000 Jews from the Holocaust, by Hillel Levine. *Literature and Belief* 18, no. 1 (1998).
In the Beginning, by S. Asch. *RBBR* 24, no. 2 (1979).
In the Face of Nations: Israel's Struggle for Peace, by Yoseph Tekoa. *LJ* 101 (1976).
In the Heart of the Seas, by S. Y. Agnon. *RBBR* 26, no. 1 (1981).
In the World of Sumer, by Samuel Noah Kramer. *RBBR* 32, nos. 2–3 (1988).
The Incarnation of God, by J. Neusner. *CRBR* (1990).
Index of Biblical Images: Similes. Metaphors, and Symbols in Scriptures, by Warren W. Wiersbe. *ARBA* 32 (2001).
Interpreting the Bible: A Handbook of Terms and Methods, by W. Randolph Tate. *ARBA* 38 (2007).
Introducing the Holy Land, by M. Miller. *BA* 49, no. 1 (1986).
An Introduction to Modern Jewish Philosophy, by Norbert Samuelson. *JS* 56, no. 1(1991).
Israel, by C. H. Bleancy. *ARBA* 96 (1996).
Israel, The Impossible Land, edited by J. C. Attias and E. Benbassa. *Choice* 40, no. 11 (2003).
Israel in Biblical Times: Historical Essays (Hebrew), by A. Malamat. *CBQ* 47, no. 2 (1985).
Israeli Holocaust Drama, by Michael Taub. *HS* 39 (1998).
Israelis and Jews: The Continuity of an Identity, by S. N. Herman. *JS* 37, no. 4 (April 1972).
Israel's Prophets: An Introduction for Christians and Jews, by David J. Zucker. *JES* 34, no. 4 (1997).
The Itinerary of Benjamin of Tudela (Twelfth Century), by Benjamin of Tudela. *RBBR* 30, no. 2 (1985).
The IVP Women's Bible Commentary, edited by Catherine Clark Kroeger and Mary J. Evans. *ARBA* 34 (2003).

Jesus and the Metaphors of God—The Christs of the New Testament, by Bernard J. Lee. *JES* 33, no. 1 (1996).

Jesus in Focus: A Life in Its Setting, by Gerald S. Sloyan. *JES* 22, no. 2 (1985).

Jesus on Trial: A Study of the Gospels, by Gerald S. Sloyan. *JES* 45, no. 1 (2008).

The Jew and His History, by Lionel Kuchan. *RBBR* 30, no. 4 (1985).

The Jew in the California Gold Rush, by Robert E. Levinson. *WSJHR* (January 1980).

The Jew in the Medieval Community, by James Parkes. *RBBR* 22, no. 2 (1977).

The Jew in the Universe, by S. Goldman. *RBBR* 20, no. 1 (1975).

The Jew, the Gypsy, and El Islam, by Richard F. Burton. *RBBR* 25, no. 4 (1980).

Jewish Ceremonial Art and Religious Observance, by A. Kanof. *JES* 11, no. 3 (1974), and *HA* 16 (1975).

Jewish Ceremonial Institutions and Customs, by William Rosenau. *RBBR* 20, no. 2 (1975).

Jewish Education and Society in the High Middle Ages, by Ephraim Kanarfogel. *Choice* 29, no. 9 (1992).

Jewish Ethics for the Twenty-First Century: Living in the Image of God, by Byron L. Sherwin. *Choice* 38, no. 3 (2000).

The Jewish Family Book, by S. Strassfeld and K. Green. *RelEd* 78, no. 1 (1983).

The Jewish Heritage, by Dan Cohen-Sherbok. *Choice* 25, no. 10 (1988).

The Jewish Jesus, by R. Aron. *AUSS* 12, no. 1 (1974).

Jewish Law and Jewish Life, Selected Rabbinical Responsa, by Jacob Bazak. *LBR* 5 (1978).

The Jewish Law Annual, edited by B. S. Jackson. *RelSRev*, 5, no. 2 (1979).

Jewish Life in Twentieth-Century America, by M. Plesur. *AJS Newsletter* (1984).

Jewish Passages: Cycles of Jewish Life, by Harvey E. Goldberg. *Choice* 41, no. 9 (2004).

The Jewish People in Christian Preaching, by Darrel J. Fasching. *JES* 23, no. 4 (1986).

Jewish Perceptions of Anti-Semitism, by Gary Tobin and Sharon Sassler. *SCJ* 8 (1992).

The Jewish Study Bible, edited by Adele Berlin and Marc Zvi Brettler. *CBQ* 66 (2004).

The Jewish Way in Death and Mourning, by Maurice Lamm. *Choice* 38, no. 10 (2001).

The Jewish Woman in Rabbinic Literature, 2 vols., by Menchem M. Brayer. *Choice* 23, no. 10 (1986).

The Jewish-Christian Debate in the High Middle Ages: A Critical Edition of the Nizzahon Vetus, by David Berger. *Jerusalem Post* (July 1980).

Jewish-Christian Dialogue and Biblical Exegesis, by Torn Fornberg. *JES* 27, no. 1 (1990).

Jews and Judaism in the U.S., edited by Marc Lee Raphael. *JS* 49, no. 2 (1984).

The Jews in Roman Legislation, by Amnon Linder. *NJP&O* (January 1990).

The Jews in Sicily, vol. 2, *1302–1391*, by Shlomo Simonsohn. *Shofar* 21, no. 3 (2003).

Jews in the Protestant Establishment, by R. L. Zewigenhaft and G. W. Domhoff. *JS* 48, no. 3 (1983).

Jews in the South, by L. Dinnerstein and M. B. Palsson. *RBR* 2, no. 9 (1973).

The Jews of Arab Lands: A History and Source Book, by N. Stillman. *JAAR* 49, no. 4 (1981).

The Jews of Germany, by H. G. Adler. *JSSR* 9, no. 4 (1970).

John Paul II and the Jewish People: A Jewish-Christian Dialogue, edited by David G. Dalin and Matthew W. Levering. *ARBA* 39 (2009).

Jonah: A Psycho-Religious Approach to the Prophet, by Andre LaCocque and Pierre-Emmanuel LaCocque. *Iggeret* 57 (Fall 1993).

The Joseph Narrative in Genesis, by E. I. Lowenthal. *JBL* 93, no. 4 (1974).

The Journey Back from Hell, by Anton Gill. *NJP&O* (November 1989).

Judaic Ethics for a Lawless World, by Robert Gordis. *Choice* 24, no. 3 (1987).

Judaism in Society. Evidence of the Yerushalmi. Toward a National History of Religion, by J. Neusner. *Choice* 21, no. 8 (1984).

Judaism in the Beginning of Christianity, by J. Neusner. *JES* 22, no. 2 (1985).

Judaism When Christianity Began: A Survey of Beliefs and Practices, by J. Neusner. *RBL* (2004), http://www.bookreviews.org.

Judaism's Theological Voice, by Jacob Neusner. *JS* 60, no. 4 (1996).

Ki Baruch Hu: Ancient Near Eastern, Biblical, and Judaic Studies in Honor of Baruch A. Levine, edited by R. Chazzan, W. W. Hallo, and L. H. Schiffman. *CBQ* 62, no. 3 (2000).

The Kings Depart, by Alyn Brodsky. *LJ* 99, no. 17 (1974), and *HA* 16 (1975).
The Land of Israel: Jewish Perspectives, edited by Lawrence M. Hoffman. *Choice* 24, no. 3 (1987).
Lawrence of Arabia: An Encyclopedia, by Stephen E. Tabachnik. *ARBA* 36 (2005).
Leo Strauss and Judaism: Jerusalem and Athens Critically Revisited, edited by David Novak. *Choice* 34, no. 2 (1996).
The Letters and Papers of Chaim Weismann, vols. 4–6, edited by Meyer W. Weisgal. *LJ* 100.21 (1975).
Liberal Judaism, by Eugene Borowitz. *RelSRev* 11, no. 1 (1985).
Lies: Israel's Secret Service and the Rabin Murder, by David Morrison. *JS* 65, no. 2 (2000).
The Life and Thought of St. Edith Stein, by Freda Mary Oben. *Shofar* 22, no. 2 (2004).
Like All Nations? The Life and Legacy of Judah L. Magnes, edited by William Brinner and Moses Richlin. *Choice* 25, no. 2 (1988).
Literary-Critical Approaches to the Bible: A Bibliographical Supplement, by Mark Minor. *ARBA* 97 (1997).
A Living Covenant: The Innovative Spirit in Traditional Judaism, by David Hartman. *Choice* 36, no. 6 (1999).
The Logic of Incest: A Structuralist Analysis of Hebrew Mythology, by Seith Daniel Kunin. *RelSRev* 23, no. 1 (January 1997).
Long Night's Journey Into Day: A Revised Retrospective Into the Holocaust, by Alice Eckhardt and A. Roy Eckhardt. *JES* 27, no. 3 (1990).
The Long Shorter Way, Discourses on Chasidic Thought, by Adin Steinsaltz. *NJP&O* (June 1990).
The Lord's Prayer and Jewish Liturgy, edited by J. Petuchowski and M. Brocke. *RelSRev* 5, no. 1 (1979).
Maaserot (Zehnte); Maaser Sheni (Zweiter Zehnt) (German), by Rivka Ulmer. *RBL* 2 (2000).
The Maiden of Ludmir: A Jewish Holy Woman and Her World, by Nathaniel Deutsch. *Choice* 42, no. 2 (2004).
Making God's Word Work: A Guide to the Mishnah, by Jacob Neusner. *Choice* 42, no. 2 (2004).
The Making of a Sage: A Study in Rabbinic Ethics, by Jonathan Wyn Schofer. *Choice* 43, no. 3 (2005).
Medium and Message in Judaism, by J. Neusner. *First Series, HS* 34 (1993).
The Men and Women of Yeshiva: Higher Education, Orthodoxy, and American Judaism, by J. Gurrock. *RelEd* 84, no. 3 (1989).
Messengers of God: Biblical Portraits and Legends, by Elie Wiesel. *LJ* 101.10 (1976).
The Messianic Idea in Judaism, by G. Scholem. *JES* 10, no. 2 (1973).
Messianic Judaism, by Dan Cohen-Sherbok. *Choice* 38, no. 7 (2001).
The Metaphor of God Incarnate: Christology in a Pluralistic Age, by John Hick. *JES* 33, no. 1 (1996).
The Michal Affair: From Zimri-Lim to the Rabbis, by Daniel Bodi. *CBQ* 68 (2006).
The Middle East, 11th ed. *ARBA* 39 (2008).
Midrash in Context: Exegesis in Formative Judaism, by J. Neusner. *HS* 26, no. 2 (1985).
A Midrash on American Jewish History, by H. L. Feingold. *JS* 48, no. 1 (1983).
Midrashic Names Derivations in the Bible (Hebrew), by Moshe Carsiel. *CBQ* 53, no. 1 (1991).
The Mishnah in Contemporary Perspective, by A. J. Avery-Peck and J. Neusner. *Choice* 40, no. 10 (2003).
Mishnah's Theology of Tithing: A Study of Tractate Masserot, by M. Jaffe. *HS* 24 (1983).
The Misunderstood Jew: The Church and the Scandal of the Jewish Jesus, by Amy-Jill Levine. *Shofar* 27, no. 2 (2009).
The Mitzvot: The Commandments and Their Rationale, by Abraham Chill. *LJ* 100, no. 4 (1975).
The Modern Catholic Encyclopedia, edited by Michael Glazier and Monika E. Hellwig. *ARBA* 36 (2005).
Modern Jewish Religious Movements, by David Rudavsky. *HS* 22 (1981).
Modern Jews Engage the New Testament: Enhancing Jewish Well-Being in a Christian Environment, by Michael J. Cook. *Shofar* 27, no. 4 (2009).
Moses Maimonides: The Man and His Works, by Herbert Davidson. *Choice* 43, no. 1 (2005).
Moses Mendelssohn Jerusalem, or On Religious Power and Judaism, translated by Allan Arkish, introduction and commentary by Alexander Altmann. *RBBR* 29, no. 1 (1984).

Moses, the Servant of Yahweh, by D. M. Bregle. *HA* 15 (1974).
Moses: Envoy of God, Envoy of His People, by Mosheh Lichtenstein. *CBQ* 71, no. 1 (2009).
My People: The Story of the Jews, by Abba Eban. *RBBR* 30, no. 1 (1985).
The Myth of the Jewish Race, by Raphael Patai and Jennifer P. Wing. *Choice* 12, no. 10 (1975).
Near Eastern Studies in Honor of William Foxwell Albright, edited by H. Goeldicke. *AUSS* 12, no. 1 (1974).
The Neighbors Respond: The Controversy Over the Jedwabne Massacre in Poland, edited by Antony Polonsky and Joanna B. Michlic. *Shofar* 23, no. 3 (Spring 2005).
New Catholic Encyclopedia, Jubilee Volume: The Wojtyta Years, by Berard L. Marthaler et al. *ARBA* 33 (2002).
The New Interpreter's Bible (CD-ROM). *ARBA* 30 (1999).
A New Jewish Theology in the Making, by E. Borowitz. *JAAR* 37, no. 3 (1969).
No Haven for the Oppressed: United States Policy Towards Jewish Refugees 1938–1945, by S. Friedman. *HA* 15 (1974).
Notes on the New Translation of the Torah, by H. M. Orlinsky. *AUSS* 9, no. 2 (1971).
Notes on the Way to Present Jews and Judaism in Preaching and Catechesis of the Preparation of the Document (Vatican City: Commissioned for Religious Relations with the Jews). *JES* 23, no. 4 (1986).
Number Our Day, by B. Meyerhoff. *Forum* 49 (1983).
The Oath, by E. Weisel. *LJ* 99, no. 1 (1974), and *HA* 15 (1974).
The Official Catholic Directory 2007. ARBA 39 (2008).
The Old Testament, Christianity, and Pluralism, by Christina Grenholm. *JES* 35.3–4 (1998).
Old Testament Theology: Basic Issues in the Current Debate, by G. Hasel. *HA* 15 (1974).
On Jewish Folklore, by R. Patai. *Choice* 20, no. 7 (1983).
One Man's Judaism, by E. Rackman. *AUSS* 10, no. 2 (1972), and *JAAR* 40, no. 4 (1972).
Onions and Cucumbers and Plums, by Sarah Zweig Betsky. *RBBR* 26, no. 3 (1981).
OSV's Encyclopedia of Catholic History, edited by Matthew Bunson. *ARBA* 36 (2005).
Our Sages, God, and Israel, by J. Neusner. *Choice* 22, no. 7 (1985).
Our Sunday Visitor's Almanac 2002, edited by Matthew Bunson. *ARBA* 34 (2003).
Our Sunday Visitor's Catholic Almanac, 2000, edited by Matthew Bunson. *ARBA* 31 (2000).
Our Sunday Visitor's Catholic Almanac, 2004, edited by Matthew Bunson. *ARBA* 36 (2005).
Our Sunday's Visitor's Encyclopedia of Saints, rev. ed., edited by M. Bunson, M. Bunson, and S. Bunson. *ARBA* 35 (2004).
The Oxford Essential Guide to People and Places of the Bible, edited by Bruce M. Metzger and Michael D. Coogan. *ARBA* 34 (2003).
The Pagan Rabbi and Other Stories, by Cynthia Ozick. *RBBR* 22, no. 1 (1977).
The Parody of Anti-Semitism, by Dan Cohen-Sherbok. *Choice* 44, no. 5 (2007).
The Passover Afikomen in Exile, by Ruth Gruber Fredman. *Choice* 18, no. 7 (1981).
People of the Book: Canon, Meaning, and Authority, by Moshe Halbertal. *Choice* 35, no. 8 (1998).
Perpetual Dilemma: Jewish Religion in the Jewish State, by S. Zalman Abramov. *LJ* (1977).
Persons and Institutions in Early Rabbinic Judaism, by William S. Green. *RelSRev* 4, no. 3 (1978), and *JAAR* 49, no. 1 (1981).
Pocket Dictionary for the Study of Biblical Hebrew, by Todd J. Murphy. *ARBA* 35 (2004).
Poetry and Prophecy: The Beginnings of a Literary Tradition, by James L. Kugel. *RelSRev* 19, no. 1 (1993).
The Politics of Compromise: State and Religion in Israel, by E. Birnbaum. *JS* 37, no. 4 (1972).
Pope John Paul II: A Biography, by Meg Greene. *ARBA* 35 (2004).
Portraits of Jews, by Hannah R. London. *RBBR*, 20, no. 2 (1975).
Preaching Biblical Text: Expositions by Jewish and Christian Scholars, edited by Frederich G. Holmgren and Herman E. Schaalman. *JES* 34, no. 4 (1997).
Problems Unique to the Holocaust, edited by Harry James Cargas. *Shofar* 19, no. 4 (2001).
Proceedings of the Second International Symposium on Medicine in the Bible and Talmud (special issue of *Koroth* [Israel Institute of Medical History], 1984). *RelSRev*, 14, no. 2 (1988).

Proclamation and Presence: OT Essays in Honor of Gwynne Henton Davies, edited by J. I. Durham and J. R. Porter. *RBBR* 30, no. 3 (1985).

Profiles in American Judaism, by Chaim Raphael. *Choice* 22, no. 4 (1985).

Progromchik: The Assassination of Simon Petlura, by Saul S. Friedland. *LJ* (1978).

A Promise to Keep: A Narrative of the American Encounter with Anti-Semitism, by C. Belth. *Israel Today* (May 1980).

Prophecy in the Mari Documents and the Bible (Hebrew), by A. Malamat. *JAOS* 90, no. 4 (1970).

The Prophetic Existence, by A. Neher. *AUSS* 9, no. 1 (1974).

The Prophets, by E. G. Kraeling. *AUSS* 9, no. 1 (1971).

The Psalms, by L. Sabourin, 2 vols. *AUSS* 9, no. 2 (1971).

Pseudo-Rabad: Commentary to Sifre Numbers, edited by Herbert W. Basser. *RBL* (2000), http://www.bookreviews.org.

Psychoanalysis and the Bible, by D. F. Zeligs. *JB* (February 1975).

The Quotable Saint, by Rosemary Ellen Guiley. *ARBA* 34 (2003).

Rabbi Paul, by Bruce Chilton. *RBL* (2005), http://www.bookreviews.org.

Rabbinic Authority, by Michael S. Berger. *Choice* 37, no. 2 (1999).

Rabbinic Literature and Greco-Roman Philosophy, by Henry Fischel. *RelSRev*, 4, no. 3 (1978).

Race and Nation, by Clive J. Christie. *HGS* 14, no. 1 (2000).

Rashi: The Man and His World, by E. Shereshevsky. *Choice* 20, no. 2 (1983).

Rational Rabbis: Science and Talmudic Culture, by Menachem Fisch. *Choice* 35, no. 10 (1998).

Reading the Rabbis: The Talmud as Literature, by David Kraemer. *Choice* 34, no. 5 (1997).

Readings in Modern Jewish History, by Eliezer L. Ehrmann. *RelEd* 76, no. 6 (1981).

The Real Anti-Semitism in America, by N. Perlmutter and R. A. Perlmutter. *JS* 48, no. 1 (1983).

The Recent Study of Hebrew: A Survey of the Literature with Select Bibliography, by Nahum M. Waldman. *Choice* 27, no. 9 (1990), and *CRBR* (1992).

Reclaiming Goodness: Education and the Spiritual Quest, by Hanan A. Alexander. *RelEd* 97, no. 4 (2002).

Reclaiming the Jesus of History: Christology Today, by A. Roy Eckardt. *JES* 30, no. 2 (1993).

Recovered Roots: Collective Memory and the Making of Israeli National Tradition, by Yael Zerubavel. *MJ* 18, no. 2 (1998).

Reflections of a Post-Auschwitz Christian, by Harry James Cargas. *Shofar* 8, no. 3 (1989).

Reflections Over the Long Haul, by Robert McAfee Brown. *JES* 42, no. 4 (2007).

Religion in Ancient History, by S. G. F. Brandon. *AUSS* 9, no. 1 (1971).

The Religion of Ancient Israel, by T. C. Vriezen. *AUSS* 8, no. 2 (1970).

The Religions of Ancient Israel: A Synthesis of Parallactic Approaches, by Ziony Zevit. *Choice* 39, no. 10 (2002).

The Religious Side of Judaism: Description, Analysis, Interpretations, vol. 1, by J. Neusner. *RelSRev* 14, no. 1 (1988).

"Remember Amalek": Vengeance, Zealotry, and Group Destruction in the Bible According to Philo, Pseudo-Philo, and Josephus, by Louis H. Feldman. *RBL* (2004), http:www.bookreviews.org.

The Rescue of the Danish Jews, edited by Leo Goldberger. *RBBR* 32, no. 1 (1988).

Responses to Suffering in Classical Rabbinic Literature, by David Kraemer. *Choice* 32, no. 7 (1995).

Returning to Tradition: The Contemporary Revival of Orthodox Judaism, by M. Herbert Danzer. *Choice* 27, no. 12 (1990).

Rituals of Childhood: Jewish Acculturation in Medieval Europe, by Ivan G. Marcus. *Choice* 34, no. 1 (1996).

Roads to the Palace: Jewish Text in Teaching, by Michael Rosenik. *Choice* 33, no. 6 (1996).

Romance She Wrote: A Hermeneutical Essay on Song of Songs, by André La Cocque. *Choice* 36, no. 3 (1998).

Russian-Jewish Literature and Identity: Jabotinsky Babel, Grossman, Galich, Rozner, Markich, by Alice Stone Nakhimovsky. *RelSRev* 20, no. 2 (1994).

Saints of Asia, by Vincent J. O'Malley. *ARBA* 39 (2008).

Salo Wittmayer Baron Jubilee Volume (3 vols., Jerusalem, 1974), edited by Saul Lieberman and Arthur Hayman. *LJ* 100, no. 15 (1975).

A Scholar's Odyssey, by Cyrus H. Gordon. *RBL* 3 (2001).

The Secretaries of Death, by Lore Shelley. *HGS* 3, no. 4 (1988).

Sectarianism in the Russian Empire and the USSR, edited by Albert W. Wardin Jr. *ARBA* 97 (1997).

Self-Fulfilling Prophecy, by J. Neusner. *Choice* 24, no. 8 (1987).

Semites and Anti-Semitism: An Inquiry into Conflict and Prejudice, by Bernard Lewis. *HGS* 2, no. 2 (1987).

Separation and Its Discontents: Toward an Evolutionary Theory of Anti-Semitism, by Kevin MacDonald. *AJS Review* 25, no. 1 (2000/2001).

A Shared Inheritance: A Statement on Israel/Palestine (London: Council of Churches for Britain and Ireland). *JES* 29, no. 1 (1992).

The Sibylline Oracles of Egyptian Judaism, by J. C. Collins. *JAOS* 98, no. 2 (1978).

Sigmund Freud and the Jewish Mystical Tradition, by David Bakan. *RBBR* 20, no. 2 (1975).

The Social Life of the Jews of Northern France in the XIII–XVI Centuries, by L. Rabinowitz. *RBBR* 21, no. 1 (1976).

Solomon Goldman, A Rabbi's Rabbi, by J. Weinstein. *HA* 15 (1974).

The Song of (Solomon) Songs, with English Commentary. RBBR 24, no. 1 (1979).

Speaking of God Today: Jews and Lutherans in Conversation, by P. D. Opsahl and Marc C. Tanenbaum. *RBR* (October 1974), and *HA* 16 (1975).

The Star of Redemption, by Franz Rosenzweig. *RelSRev* 11, no. 1 (1985).

State and Education, Philosophical Essays (Hebrew), by Gerson Weiler. *Forum* 39 (1980).

The Story of Judaism: Bibliographical Essays, by Anti-Defamation League, B'nai Brith. *HA* 15 (1974).

Strangers Within the Gate City: The Jews of Atlanta, 1845–1915, by S. Hertzberg. *RelEd* 76, no. 6 (1981).

The Strife of the Spirit, by Adin Steinsaltz. *NJP&O* (May 1990).

Studies in Bible: 1986 (ScrHier 31; Jerusalem:Magnes/Heb.U.), edited by Sara Japhet. *CBQ* 50, no. 4 (1988).

Studies in Early History of Judaism, vol. 4, *History of Early Talmudic Law,* by S. Zeitlin. *RelSRev* 5, no. 1 (1979).

Studies in Jewish Education, vol. 1, ed. B. Chazan. *RelEd* 79, no. 2 (1984).

Studies in Jewish Jurisprudence, vol. 2. *RBBR* 22, no. 4 (1977).

Studies in Judaica, by Leon D. Stitskin. *RBBR* 20, no. 1 (Spring 1975).

Studies in Rabbinic Judaism, by Alexander Guttman. *RelSRev* 4, no. 2 (1978).

Studies in Targum Jonathon to the Prophets and Pinchas Churgin, Targum Jonathon to the Prophets, by Levi Smolar and Moses Aberbach. *CBQ* 48, no. 2 (1986).

Studies in the Targum to the Twelve Prophets, From Nahum to Malachi, by Robert P. Gordon. *RelSRev* 21, no. 4 (1995).

The Sunflower, by Simon Wiesenthal. *RBBR* 22, no. 1 (1977).

The Sustaining Utterance, Discourses on Chassidic Thought, by Adin Steinsaltz. *NJP&O* (June 1990).

The Tahkemoni of Judah Al-Harizi, vol. 2, translated by Victor Reichert. *CCAR Journal* 24, no. 4 (1977).

Talking with Christians: Musings of a Jewish Theologian, by David Novack. *Shofar* 25, no. 2 (2007).

Talmud Yerushalmi: Avodah Zarah, by J. Neusner. *Choice* 19, no. 9 (1982).

Talmud Yerushalmi: The Talmud of the Land of Israel, by J. Neusner. *Choice* 22, no. 7 (1985).

Targum De Job (Spanish), by Luis Diez Merino. *CBQ* 50, no. 1 (1988).

Targum De Proverbios (Spanish), by Luis Diez Merino. *CBQ* 50, no. 1 (1988).

Targum De Qohelet, by Luis Diez Merino. *CBQ* 52, no. 1 (1990).

Targum De Salmos (Spanish), by Luis Diez Merino. *CBQ* 50, no. 1 (1988).

Targum Neofeti 1: Deuteronomy, by Martin McNamara. *CBQ* 60, no. 4 (1998).

Targum Neofeti 1: Genesis, translated with introduction and notes by Martin McNamara. *CBQ* 56, no. 4 (1994).

The Targum of Chronicles, translated with introduction, apparatus, and notes by J. Stanley McIvor. *CBQ* 57, no. 4 (1995).

The Targum of Job, by Celene Mangan. *CBQ* 55, no. 1 (1993).

The Targum of Judges, by William F. Smelik. *CBQ* 60, no. 2 (1998).

The Targum of Proverbs, by John F. Healey. *CBQ* 55, no. 1 (1993).

The Targum of Qoheleth, by Peter S. Knobel. *CBQ* 55, no. 1 (1993).

The Targum of Ruth, translated with introduction, apparatus, and notes by D. R. G. Beattie. *CBQ* 57, no. 4 (1995).

Targum Pseudo-Jonathan: Genesis, translated with introduction and notes by Michael Maher. *CBQ* 56, no. 4 (1994).

Targum Studies, vol. 2, *Targum and Peshitta*, edited by Paul V. M. Flesher. *RBL* 4 (2002).

Targum Studies, vol. 1, *Textual and Contextual Studies in the Pentateuchal Targums*, by Paul V. M. Flesher. *CBQ* 57, no. 1 (1995).

Teen Life in the Middle East, edited by A. Akbar Mahdi. *ARBA* 35 (2004).

The Temple of Jerusalem, by Joan Comay. *LJ* 100, no. 20 (1975).

The Ten Negudoth of the Torah, by R. Butin. *JBL* 89, no. 1 (1970).

Ten Words of Freedom, by J. G. Williams. *HA* 15 (1974).

Testimony, Tensions, and Tikkun: *Teaching the Holocaust in Colleges and Universities*, edited by Myrna Goldenberg and Rochelle L. Millen. *Shofar* 27, no. 3 (2009).

Text as Pretext: Essays in Honor of Robert Davidson, edited by Robert P. Carroll. *RelSRev* 20, no. 1 (1994).

Texts and Tradition; A Source Reader for the Study of Second Temple and Rabbinic Judaism, by Lawrence H. Schiffman. *RBL* 1 (1999).

Theological Dictionary of the Old Testament, edited by G. Johannes Botterwick, Helmer Ringgren, and Heinz-Josef Fabry. *ARBA* 98 (1998).

There We Sat Down, by J. Neusner. *Haddasah Magazine*, April 1973.

The Tiqqune Sopherim and Other Theological Corrections in the Masoretic Text, by Carmel McCarthy. *JBL* 102, no. 2 (1983).

Torah of the Earth: Exploring 4,000 Years of Ecology in Jewish Thought: vol. 1, *Biblical Israel: One Land, One People; Rabbinic Judaism: One People, Many Lands*; vol. 2, *Zionism: One Land, Two Peoples; Eco-Judaism: One Earth, Many Peoples*, edited by Arthur Waskow. *Choice* 38, no. 7 (2001).

The Torah, vol. 1, by W. Gunther Plaut. *Choice* 12, no. 4 (1975).

Torah: From Scroll to Symbol in Formative Judaism, by J. Neusner. *HS* 26, no. 2 (1985).

Toward a Grammar of Biblical Poetics, by Herbert Chanan Brichto. *Choice* 29, no. 7 (1992).

The Traditions of Eleazar Ben Azariah, by Tzvee Zahavy. *RelSRev* 4, no. 1 (1978).

Translating the Classics of Judaism: In Theory and in Practice, by J. Neusner. *HS* 34 (1993).

A Treasury of Yiddish Poetry, edited by Irving Howe and Eliezer Greenberg. *RBBR* 22, no. 3 (1977).

The Treatment of the Holocaust in Textbooks, edited by Randolph L. Braham. *HGS* 5, no. 1 (1990).

The Triangular Connection: America, Israel, and American Jews, by E. B. Glick. *JS* 48, no. 1 (1983).

Turning Point: Zionism and Reform Judaism, by Howard Greenstein. *Choice* 19, no. 7 (September 1982).

Two Powers in Heaven: Early Rabbinic Reports about Christianity and Gnosticism, by Alan F. Segal. *RelSRev* 5, no. 4 (1979).

An Unacknowledged Harmony: Philo-Semitism and the Survival of European Jewry, by A. Edelstein. *JS* 48, no. 3 (1983).

Understanding American Judaism, vol. 1, *The Rabbi and the Synagogue*, by J. Neusner. *JAAR* 44, no. 4 (1976).

Understanding American Judaism, vol. 2, *Sectors of American Judaism: Reform, Orthodox, Conservative and Reconstructionism*, by Jacob Neusner. *JAAR* 44, no. 4 (1976).

Understanding Judaism, by Eugene B. Borowitz. *RelEd* 76, no. 6 (1981).

Understanding Rabbinic Midrash: Text and Commentary, by Gary G. Porton. *RelSRev* 12, no. 1 (1986), and *JRJ* 34, no. 2 (1987).

Unease in Zion, by Ehud Ben Ezer. *CCAR Journal* 24, no. 1 (1977).

The Unfinished Dialogue, by John M. Oesterreicher. *NJP&O* (November 1988).

An Unknown Jewish Sect, by Louis Ginsberg. *Choice* 14, nos. 5, 6 (1977), and *HS* 19 (1978).
The Urim and Thumim: A Means of Revelation in Ancient Israel, by Cornelius Van Dam. *RelSRev* 25, no. 1 (1999).
Vatican Archives: An Inventory and Guide to Historical Documents of the Holy See, edited by Francis Z. Blouin. *ARBA* 99 (1999).
Vichy France and the Jews, by M. R. Marcus and R. O. Paxton. *RBBR* 28, no. 2 (1983).
The Vow and the "Popular Religious Groups" of Ancient Israel, by Jacques Berlinerblau. *JBL* 117, no. 3 (1998).
Vows in the Hebrew Bible and the Ancient Near East, by Tony W. Cartledge. *JBL* 114, no. 1 (1995).
Walter Benjamin: The Story of a Friendship, by Gershom Scholem. *Choice* 19, nos. 5–6 (July–August 1982).
The War Against the Jews: 1933–1945, by Lucy S. Dawidowicz. *CCAR Journal* 25, no. 1 (1978).
The Way Into Encountering God in Judaism, by Neil Gillman. *Choice* 38, no. 10 (2001).
What Is a Jew? by Morris N. Kertzer. *RelEd* 76, no. 6 (1981).
When All Is Said and Done (1913), by D. Bergelson, translated by B. Martin. *RBBR* 24, no. 1 (1979).
Who Was a Jew? by Lawrence H. Schiffman. *Choice* 22, no. 10 (1985).
Who's Who in the Bible, by Richard Coggins. *Choice* 18, nos. 5–6 (1981).
Who's Who in the Bible, Readers Digest. ARBA 96 (1996).
William Robertson Smith: Essays in Reassessment, edited by William Johnstone. *RelSRev* 23, no. 3 (1997).
Wisdom in Israel, by G. Von Rad. *AUSS* 13, no. 2 (1975).
Women and Jewish Law, by Rachel Biale. *RelEd* 81, no. 1 (1986).
A World Fitly Spoken, by Philip L. Culbertson. *JES* 33, no. 3 (1996).
Wrestling with God: Jewish Theological Responses during and after the Holocaust, edited by Steven T. Katz, Shlomo Biderman, and Gershon Greenberg. *Choice* 44, no. 11 (2007).
Writing and Rewriting the Holocaust: Narrative and the Consequences of Interpretation, by James E. Young. *JES* 29, no. 1 (1992).
Yad Vashem Studies, vol. 13, edited by Livia Trothkirchen. *Jerusalem Post Magazine* (March 1980), and *HS* 20–21 (1979–80).
Zachor: Jewish History and Jewish Memory, by J. H. Yerushalmi. *Reconstructionist* 50, no. 6 (1985).
Zion in America: The Jewish Experience from Colonial Times to the Present, by H. L. Finegold. *CCAR Journal* 24, no. 1 (1977).
The Zionist Ideology, by Gideon Shimoni. *AJS Review* 22, no. 2 (1997).

Selected Editorial Columns from *Iggeret* ("Notes from Here and There")

"The Adult Returner" (1983)
"Anatomy of a Boycott" (2005)
"Armies of the Night" (1991)
"Baukh Dayyan Ha-Emet: A Personal Memoir" (2001)
"By Words Alone" (1986)
"Campus Free Speech" (1993)
"Celebrating Zionism" (1997)
"Commune and Society" (1990)
"Cyrus H. Gordon's Last Words" (2001)
"Danger: Academics at Work" (1996)
"December 6, 1987: An Autobiographical Note" (1988)
"Denouncing Zionism as Racism" (1992)
"Descent to 'Polemicsiomania'" (1987)
"Forty Seconds in the Valley" (1994)
"Gershom Scholem Remembered" (1987)
"The Graying of Academia" (1995)

“Herstory” (1991)
“Israel, Then and Now” (2008)
“Keeping the Dream” (1986)
“The Last Hanging at Auschwitz-Birkenau” (1995)
“Papal Symbology” (2006)
“A Philadelphia Ghost Story” (1996)
“Pilgrim's Progress: The Pope and I” (2000)
“The Prague Phoenix” (1993)
“Preliminary Remarks on the Teaching of Hebrew Language and Literature in American Schools of Higher Learning” (1989)
“Religious Zionism” (1998)
“Remembering and Redefining” (1997)
“Remembering Shoah, The Iranian Factor” (2007)
“Satan in Chicago” (1985)
“A Tale of Two Tombs” (2007)
“TaSHaN: Hebrew Language Year” (1989)
“Teaching Without Prejudice” (1984)
“Teaching Zionism and Israel Bashing” (2003)

Academic Presentations

AAR American Academy of Religion Annual Meeting
AJS Association of Jewish Studies
ASC Annual Scholars' Conference on the Holocaust and Churches
NAPH National Association of Professors of Hebrew Annual Meeting
WJSA Western Jewish Studies Association

1970s

“Children of the Book: Sixteen Million Words about the Jews.” AAR–Western Regional, Oakland, April 1973.
“Lower Division Judaica: Problems and Solutions.” AAR, Chicago, November 1973.
“The Importance of a Western Branch of NAPH.” NAPH–Western Regional, Santa Barbara, March 1974.
“Alternative Teaching Methods in Teaching Introduction to Judaism.” AAR, Washington, D.C., October 1974.
“Teaching Religion in Community Colleges: Innovative Courses.” University of California– Riverside, February 9, 1975. Lecture was sponsored by the American Academy of Religion and the Department of Religion, UCR.
“After Auschwitz: Self Images in Jewish Literature” (panel moderator). NAPH–Western Regional, Los Angeles, March 1975.
“The Study of Religion in Two-Year Colleges.” AACJC annual conference, Seattle, April 1975.
“The Journal Synthesizing Activity: An Innovative Teaching Method.” AAR, Chicago, October–November 1975.
“The Samaritan Passover.” AAR–Western Regional, Fresno, November 1975.
“A Psychosocial Interpretation of the Song of Songs” (with Shelton Kardner). AAR–Western Regional, Los Angeles, March 1976.
“Psalm 138:4: A Religious Polemic in the Midrash.” AAR, New Orleans, October 1976.
“Interpretation and the Passover Haggadah.” NAPH, San Francisco, December 1977.
“Judaism as a Historiosophy.” AAR, New Orleans, November 1978.
“The Teaching of Hebrew Language and Literature in Translation at a Two-Year Public College.” NAPH, New Orleans, November 1978.

1980s

"Jethro, Father-in-law of Moses." AAR, Dallas, November 1980.

"Judaism in the State of Israel: Reflections on a Sabbatical Year 5740." AAR–Western Regional, Pasadena, March 1981.

"Amalek. A Rabbinic Paradigm of Evil." AAR, San Francisco, December 1981.

"Hebrew Teaching Methodology" (session respondent). NAPH, New York, December 1982.

"Methodologies in Teaching about Judaism" (seminar respondent). AAR, New York, December 1982.

"Teaching about the Holocaust at a Two-Year Public College." AAR–Western Regional, Fullerton, April 1983.

"Methodologies in Teaching about the Holocaust" (seminar respondent). AAR, Dallas, December 1983.

"Methodologies in Teaching about Judaism," and "Post-Holocaust Reflection" (seminar respondent). AAR, Chicago, December 1984.

Scholar-in-residence, University of Utah, April 1985 (Shoah Lectures), 1985.

Session on *Methodology in the Academic Teaching of Judaism*, ed. Z. Garber (Lanham, Md.: University Press of America, 1986). AAR, Atlanta, November 1986 (book event).

Respondent to A. and H. Cutler, *The Jew as Ally of the Muslim: Roots of Anti-Semitism* (Notre Dame, Ind.: University of Notre Dame Press, 1986). AAR–Western Regional, Long Beach, April 1987.

"Teaching the Passover Haggadah to Seminarians: An Invitation to Post-Biblical Historiosophy." NAPH, Boston, December 1987. Elected president of NAPH at annual meeting.

"Shoah or Holocaust: An Inquiry into the Psychology of Labels," Remembering for the Future (The Impact of the Holocaust and Genocide on Jews and Christians), an International Scholars Conference, Oxford, England, July 10–13, 1988.

"Responses to the Holocaust," workshop on University Teaching of Contemporary Jewish Civilization, Jerusalem, Israel, July 18–27, 1988. *Methodology in the Academic Teaching of the Holocaust*, edited by Z. Garber with A. Berger and R. Libowitz (Lanham, Md.: University Press of America, 1988), was featured.

"Ellie Wiesel on Sacrifice of Isaac and the Holocaust." Southeast Conference on Foreign Languages and Literatures, Winter Park, Fla., February 1989.

"12 April 1951: The Day That Heaven Stood Still (6 Nisan 5711)." ASC, Philadelphia, March 1989.

Session on *Methodology in the Academic Teaching of the Holocaust*, edited by Z. Garber with A. Berger and R. Libowitz (Lanham, Md.: University Press of America, 1988) (book event). AAR–Western Regional, Claremont, Calif., March 1989.

1990s

"Historic Accountability: German Historians Debate the Holocaust" and "The Meaning of the Holocaust in America: Democracy and Morality." University of Central Florida, March 7–8, 1990.

"The Martyrdom of the 93 Bais Yaakov Girls: The Making of Historiosophy." ASC, Nashville, March 1990.

"Why is the Holocaust Called the 'Holocaust'?" (panel). AAR–Western Regional, Oakland, March 1990.

"The Text of the 93 Beit Yaakov Maidens in the Context of Jewish Martyrdom and Life." NAPH, New Orleans, November 1990.

"The Unnecessary Problem of Edith Stein" (panel). ASC, Stockton, N.J., March 1991.

"Churban Theodicy." ASC, Stockton, N.J., March 1991.

"Shoah and Churban: Inexplicable to Explicable, Through the Power of Language." NAPH, Kansas City, November 1991.

"Insiders and Outsiders: For Whom Do We Toil?" ASC, Seattle, March 1992.

"Teaching the Holocaust at the University, College and Jr. College Level" (panel). ASC, Seattle, March 1992.

"A Tribute to Franklin H. Littell in His 75th Year." ASC, Seattle, March 1992.

"Night Encounters: Theologizing Dialogue" and "Encounter in Dialogue." ASC, Tulsa, March 1993.

"Furor Over the Auschwitz Convent: The Inside and Outside of the Language of Bias." Remembering for the Future II Conference, Berlin, March 1994.

"Memory and Healing." University of California–Riverside, September 29, 1994.

"Oral Tradition and the Book of Genesis" (respondent). NAPH, Chicago, November 1994.

"Thinking the Tradition Anew: A New Reading of Genesis 18 and Matthew 10 in the Light of the Shoah and Dialogue." ASC, Provo, March 1995.

Session on Z. Garber, *Shoah: The Paradigmatic Genocide* (book event). AAR–Western Regional, Redlands, March 1995.

"Shoah Education and the Multicultural Classroom." WJSA, San Diego, April 1995.

"Akeda and Educating from Shoah: Making Sense Through Dialogue." NAPH, Philadelphia, 1995.

"Roundtable Discussion—Exodus 24 and Matthew 17:1–13" (presiding and presenting). ASC, St. Paul, March 1996.

"The Status of Holocaust Education in the Colleges and Universities" (panel). ASC, St. Paul, March 1996.

"Different Settings, Different Missions: The Diversity of Jewish Studies Programs" (panel). WJSA, Denver, April 1996.

"Down from Sinai and Calvary: A Shoah *Shiur.*" NAPH, New Orleans, November 1996.

Plenary session on "The Work of Richard L. Rubenstein" (presiding and presenting). ASC, Tampa, March 1997.

"Dialogue on Exodus 3 and Matthew 20." ASC, March 1997.

"Ala, Roza, Regina, and Estera: The Women Who Revolted Against Auschwitz." WJSA, Tucson, April 1997.

"Post-Shoah Exegesis" (respondent). NAPH, San Francisco, November 1997.

"The David Complex: The Making of a Religious National Tradition" (respondent). NAPH, San Francisco, November 1997.

"Literature in Translation at a Two-Year Public College." University of Arizona, January 25, 1998.

"Post-Shoah Encounters with the Text: Ezekiel 37:1–14 and Matthew 28." ASC, Seattle, March 1998.

"The Significance of the Holocaust to the State of Israel." University of Wisconsin–Milwaukee, April 29, 1998.

"Teaching Religious Studies at Community Colleges" (respondent). AAR, Orlando, November 1998.

"Satan Has Not Created the Revenge for a Death of a Child." NAPH, Orlando, November 1998.

"Post-Holocaust Christian/Jewish Dialogue on Biblical Texts: Luke 9:10 and Numbers 11:27–30." ASC, New York, March 1999.

"Methodology for Teaching the Holocaust at the Community College." ASC, New York, March 1999.

"Plenary Panel on the Church Struggle and the Holocaust." ASC, New York, March 1999.

"Edith Stein, the Holocaust, Judaism, and Catholicism." University of Wisconsin–Milwaukee, September 29, 1999.

"Shoah at the University: New Considerations in Holocaust Education." Annual Tobias Lecture, University of Wisconsin–Madison, September 30, 1999.

"The Vatican and the Jews." University of Arizona, October 11, 1999.

"The Samaritan Joseph." NAPH, Boston, November 1999.

2000s

"The Teaching of Jewish and Islamic Studies" (workshop). University of Texas at Austin, February 10, 2000.

"Post-Holocaust Christian-Jewish Dialogue on Biblical Texts: Exodus 3 and John 8." ASC, Philadelphia, March 2000.

"The Samaritan Passover: Torah and Tradition." NAPH–Western Regional, Los Angeles, April 2000.

"Anti-Judaism in the Gospel of John." Remembering for the Future 2000, Oxford, 2000.

"The Rabin Assassination in the Long View and the Short View: Biblical Radicalism in a Modern Context." Remembering for the Future 2000, Oxford 2000 (with Bruce Zuckerman).

"How Believable Is the Allegory of Hagar and Sarah (Gal 4:21–5:1)." NAPH, Nashville, November 2000.

"Rabbinic Hermeneutics: Making Sense of 'I Am' (Exod. 3:14 and John 8:24) in Light of Slavery, Salvation and Shoah." NAPH–Western Regional, March 2001.

Session on *Academic Approaches to Teaching Jewish Studies,* edited by Z. Garber (book event). WJSA, Tempe, March 2001.

"Jewish Responses to Recent Catholic Supersessionism." WJSA, Tempe, March 2001.

"Rabbis Hillel, Jesus, and Akiba on 'Love Your Neighbor as Yourself.'" Aurora University, May 17, 2001.

"Ruth, Matriarch of the Messiah: End of the Line?" NAPH, Denver, November 2001.

"Pius XII—The Historical Record" (moderator). Millersville University, April 2002.

"Teaching Torah: Akedah and Amalek." A Workshop Colloquium on Violence and Religion (COV&R) 2002, Purdue University, June 2, 2002.

"A Grave New World: Making Sense of Esther and Amalek After 9-11-01." NAPH, Toronto, November 2002.

"Rhetorical Diatribe: Making Sense of Matthew 23" (respondent). AJS, Los Angeles, December 2002.

"The Samaritan Passover: Torah and Tradition." UCLA, February 14, 2003.

"Shoah's Apocalypse: Three Talking Points." ASC, Philadelphia, March 2003.

"Visions of the Other." Annual Zborowski Holocaust Lecture, Queens College, N.Y., April 2, 2003.

"The Children of the Warsaw Ghetto" (moderator). Millersville University, April 2003.

"Judaism and Roman Catholicism: The (Un)Necessary Problem of Supersessionism." Purdue University, April 9, 2003.

"Vision of the Other: Auschwitz Convent Controversy." Creighton University, September 2003.

"The Passover Cup of Elijah: What's Curse Got to Do with It?" NAPH, Atlanta, November 2003.

Panelist, "Deicide *Déjà vu*: Mel Gibson's *The Passion of the Christ.*" WJSA, San Diego, March 2004.

"Mel Gibson's *Passion*: The Film, the Controversy, and Its Implications" (panelist). Purdue University, March 30, 2004.

"Devil Is in the Details: Mel Gibson's Suffering Christ." NAPH, San Antonio, November 2004.

"Mel Gibson's Misguided Cinematic Crucified Christ: The Remedy from Jewish-Christian Dialogue." UCLA, December 1, 2004.

Rosenthal Public Lecture, "Rethinking the Problem of Edith Stein." Case Western Reserve University, Cleveland, January 26, 2005.

"Elie Wiesel's *Night*: Godwords." John Carroll University, February 21, 2005.

"A Commanding Voice Remembered: Emil Fackenheim" (presiding and presenting). ASC, Philadelphia, March 2005.

"Is There a Redeeming Voice: Theological Reflections on Job 38–41 and Matthew 27." ASC, Philadelphia, March 2005.

"The Israelite Samaritans." Purdue University, March 30, 2005.

"A Dialogue on Post-Shoah Hermeneutics: Jews and Christians Reading Scriptures After the Shoah" (symposium coordinator and presenter). Case Western Reserve University, April 10, 2005.

"Rethinking the Problem of Edith Stein." Bucknell University, November 17, 2005.

"Imagining the Days of the Messiah and the World-to-Come: Gleanings from Sinai and Cyanide." NAPH, Philadelphia, November 20, 2005.

"Is There a Redeeming Voice: Theological Reflections on Job 38–41 and Matthew 27." Purdue University, February 27, 2006.

"Interpreting 'Jerusalem' in the Passover Haggadah." NAPH, Washington, D.C., November 19, 2006.

"A Citadel Fitly Constructed: Philo-Semitism and the Making of an American Holocaust Conference." AJS, San Diego, December 2006.

"Christ and Torah: Interpreting Romans 3 and 10 in Light of Deuteronomy 30." ASC, Cleveland, March 2007.

"The Term 'Shoah' in the Hebrew Bible: A Teaching Lesson." NAPH, San Diego, November 2007.

“Probing the Legacy of Dietrich Bonhoeffer: Was He Good for the Jews?” (chair). WJSA, Los Angeles, April 6, 2008.

“Understanding Jewish Christian Dialogue.” Samuel Sandmel Lectures, Greenville College, April 15–17, 2008.

“Faith after Auschwitz: Jewish and Christian Responses to the Holocaust.” Nate and Ann Levine Endowed Lecture, Southern Methodist University, November 12, 2008.

“Michael and Samael: Experiencing Angeolology.” NAPH, Boston, November 2008.

“Jesus in the Context of Judaism and the Challenge to the Church” (coordinator and presenter at conference). Case Western Reserve University, May 24–26, 2009.

Biography

Contemporary Authors
Dictionary of International Biography
Directory of American Scholars
International Who’s Who in Education
Men and Women of Distinction
Strathmore’s Who’s Who
Who’s Who in Biblical Studies and Archeology
Who’s Who in Israel
Who’s Who in Religion
Who’s Who in the West

Miscellany

I have contributed hundreds of journalistic pieces and editorial columns on Hebraica and Judaica for *Iggeret* (editor), *LA Jewish News* (contributing editor), and *Chasm Andaaz* (Persian monthly). Also we were invited to give lectures at a variety of schools of higher education, including U.S. Holocaust Memorial Museum, Aurora University, Baldwin-Wallace College, Bates College, Bucknell University, Case Western Reserve University, Claremont School of Theology, Creighton University, Greenville College, John Carroll University, Long Beach State University, Purdue University, Queens College (CUNY), Richard Stockton State College, San Diego State University, Southern Methodist University, University of Arizona, University of California Los Angeles, University of Central Florida, University of Judaism, University of South Florida, University of Wisconsin–Madison, University of Wisconsin–Milwaukee, Valparaiso University, and Youngstown State University.

Rosh Hashana 5769/October 2008

Contributors

Lawrence Baron served as the Abraham Nasatir Professor of Modern Jewish History and director of the Jewish Studies Program and Lipinsky Institute for Community Jewish Studies at San Diego State University from 1988 to 2006. Before that, he taught at St. Lawrence University for thirteen years. He holds his PhD in modern European history from the University of Wisconsin/Madison. He currently is the chair of the master's program in history at San Diego State University. He has authored *Projecting the Holocaust Into the Present: The Changing Focus of Contemporary Holocaust Cinema* (2005) and *The Eclectic Anarchism of Erich Muehsam* (1976) and acted as the historian for Sam and Pearl Oliner's *The Altruistic Personality: Rescuers of Jews in Nazi Europe* (1988). He has co-edited three anthologies including *Martin Buber and the Human Sciences* (1996) and *Embracing the Other: Historical, Philosophical, Psychological, and Historical Perspectives on Altruism* (1992). He is the founder and current president of the Western Jewish Studies Association and a member of the advisory board of the Association for Jewish Studies.

S. Scott Bartchy is the director of the Center for the Study of Religion at UCLA. His fields of interest include history of religions, Christian origins, and early church history. He received his MDiv from Harvard Divinity School (1963) and his PhD from Harvard University (1971). His publications include "Narrative Criticism" and "Slave, Slavery" in *The Dictionary of the Later New Testament and Its Developments* (1997); "Paul's Letter to Philemon" in *The Anchor Bible Dictionary* (1992); "Table Fellowship" in *Dictionary of Jesus and the Gospels* (1992); "Community of Goods in Acts: Idealization or Social Reality?" in *The Future of Early Christianity: Essays in Honor of Helmut Koester* (1992); and *Mallon Chresai: First-Century Slavery and the Interpretation of 1 Corinthians 7:21* (1985).

Paul R. Bartrop is a graduate of La Trobe and Monash universities in Melbourne, Australia. As an honorary research fellow in the Faculty of Arts at Deakin University, Melbourne, and a faculty member at Bialik College, Melbourne, he teaches courses in comparative genocide studies, Jewish religion, modem history, and international studies. He has published six books, among them *Australia and the Holocaust, 1933–1945* (1994); *False Havens: The British Empire and the Holocaust* (editor, 1995); *Surviving the Camps: Unity in Adversity During the Holocaust* (2000); and *Bolt from the Blue: Australia, Britain, and the Chanak Crisis* (2003). A former president of the Australian Association of Jewish Studies, he serves on the executive boards of a number of Holocaust- and genocide-related journals. He lives in Melbourne.

Herbert W. Basser is Professor of Religious Studies focusing on Judaism at Queen's University, Kingston, Ontario, Canada. He received his BA from Yeshiva University and his MA and PhD from the University of Toronto. His publications include "History of Interpretation to Judges 5:4–5 with Special Attention to Rabbi Yosef Kara" (2005), "A Love for All Seasons: Weeping in Jewish Sources" (2005), *Studies in Exegesis: Christian Critiques of Jewish Law and Rabbinic Responses 70–300 CE* (Leiden: E. J. Brill, 2000), "Priest, Priesthood" (*Dictionary of New Testament Background,* 2000), "Ideas of Human Social Concord and Discord in Judaism" (2000), and *Pseudo-Rabad* (University Press of America, 1998). He regularly teaches such courses as "Judaism in the Classical Period," "The Mythology of Heroes, Heroines, and Saints," "The Interpretation of Sacred Texts," "The Interpretation of Religion," "Comparative Religious Ethics," and "Judaism in the Modern Period."

Michael Berenbaum is the director of the Sigi Ziering Institute and (adjunct) professor of theology at the University of Judaism in Los Angeles. He has served as executive editor of the second edition of the *Encyclopedia Judaica* and is the former president and CEO of the Survivors of the Shoah Visual History Foundation and former director of the Research Institute of the U.S. Holocaust Memorial Museum and project director overseeing its creation. Berenbaum has been author or editor of sixteen books, and his writing centers on the Holocaust and modern Jewish thought and the contemporary American experience.

G. Jan Colijn (Kandidaat, Universiteit van Amsterdam., PhD, Temple University) has served as the division's dean since 1988 at the Richard Stockton College of New Jersey. Earlier he chaired the college's Social and Behavioral Sciences division (1982–85). He was a visiting fellow in the departments of politics and international relations at the University of Warwick in 1986–87, the second time he lived in England, where he had run a hotel in 1968. Jan has been at the college since 1974 when he joined the political science faculty for what was envisioned to be a one-year appointment. While on the faculty, he taught international relations, foreign policy, comparative politics, and a variety of general studies courses. His scholarly interest and publications during the past fifteen years have focused on genocide, a central area within the college's liberal arts curriculum. He serves on the boards of a variety of professional organizations. Born in the Netherlands, he counts marathon speedskating and soccer among his avocations. He resides with his wife Sarah, a college alumna, and his daughter Cory in nearby Port Republic, New Jersey (though their dwellings are ruled by beagles Mack and Vince).

Joseph A. Edelheit is associate professor of philosophy and director of Jewish Studies and Jewish Communal Activities and Resources at St. Cloud State University, St. Cloud, Minnesota. He received his BA from the University of California (1968); his MAHL from the Hebrew Union College–Jewish Institute of Religion (1973); and his DMin from the University of Chicago Divinity School (2001). He has written, published, and edited numerous books and articles in the fields of conversion, Jewish ethics, antisemitism, Jewish-Christian relations, and AIDS. He is also the cofounder and director of "Living India," a nonprofit/nongovernmental organization doing HIV/AIDS prevention education and care and support for AIDS orphans in rural India.

Samuel M. Edelman is the dean, College of Arts and Sciences, University of Judaism, Los Angeles, and codirector of the State of California Center of Excellence for the Study of Holocaust, Genocide, Human Rights, and Tolerance at California State University, Chico. He received his BA from the University of Arizona, and his MA and PhD from Pennsylvania State University. Recipient of numerous honors and awards, he is the author of numerous books, articles, and reviews, as well as many presentations and lectures. He is frequently in demand as a consultant and trainer in the areas of Holocaust, genocide, human rights, and tolerance.

Louis H. Feldman is the Abraham Wouk Family Professor of Classics and Literature at Yeshiva University, New York. He received his BA from Trinity College and his PhD from Harvard University. He is a fellow of the Guggenheim Foundation, the American Academy for Jewish Research, and the Institute for Advanced Study at Princeton University, Princeton, N.J. His publications include *Josephus and Modern Scholarship, 1937–1980* (1984), *Josephus, Judaism, and Christianity* (1987), *Jew and Gentile in the Ancient World: Attitudes and Interactions from Alexander to Justinian* (1993), *Studies in Hellenistic Judaism* (1996), *Studies in Josephus' Rewritten Bible* (1998), and *Josephus' Interpretation of the Bible* (1998). He is also the author of more than 138 published articles.

Steven Fine specializes in Jewish history in the Greco-Roman world, focusing on relationships between the literature of ancient Judaism, art, and archaeology. Professor Fine holds a doctorate in Jewish history from the Hebrew University of Jerusalem, an MA in art history from the University of Southern California, and a BA in religious studies from the University of California, Santa Barbara. Dr. Fine is the author of *This Holy Place: On the Sanctity of the Synagogue in the Ancient World* (Notre Dame, 1997) and

Art and Judaism in the Greco-Roman World: Toward a New Jewish Archaeology (Cambridge University Press, 2005). He is the editor of *Jews, Christians and Polytheists in the Ancient Synagogue: Cultural Interaction During the Greco-Roman Period* (Routledge, 1999, runner-up, National Jewish Book Award), *A Crown for a King: Studies in Memory of Professor Stephen S Kayser* (with S. Sabar and W. Kramer, Magnes Museum and Geffen, 2000), and *Liturgy in the Life of the Synagogue: Studies in the History of Jewish Public Prayer* (with R. Langer, Eisenbrauns, 2005). Dr. Fine was curator of Yeshiva University Muse's *Sacred Realm: The Emergence of the Synagogue in the Ancient World* (Oxford and YU Museum, 1996, winner, best catalog of the year, Society of Architectural Historians), and coauthor of *Where God Dwells: A Child's History of the Synagogue* (with L. Fine, *Torah* Aura, 1999). Professor Fine is an editor *of IMAGES: A Journal for the Study of Jewish Art and Visual Culture* (E. J. Brill), and is currently preparing one-volume histories of Jewish art and of Jewish history during the Greco-Roman period. He is also section editor for Ancient Jewish History and Jewish Art and Visual Culture for the Center for Online Judaic Studies, and planning a major exhibition on Talmudic archaeology for the YU Museum. Dr. Fine's current research project is called "Between Tiberias and Gerizim: Studies in Samaritan-Jewish Relations during Late Antiquity." He taught a research seminar dedicated to this subject in the fall of 2006.

Michael Fishbane is Nathan Cummings Professor of Jewish Studies at the University of Chicago, and was for many years chair of the Committee on Jewish Studies. Professor Fishbane is the author or editor of nineteen books and hundreds of articles and reviews in scholarly journals and encyclopedias. Among his many works are *Biblical Interpretation in Ancient Israel* (National Jewish Book Award, 1985), *Garments of Torah: Essays in Biblical Hermeneutics; The Kiss of God: Spiritual Death and Dying in Judaism* (National Jewish Book Award, 1994), and *The Exegetical Imagination: Jewish Thought and Theology.* He is editor-in-chief of the Jewish Publication Society Bible Commentary, and serves on the editorial board of several scholarly journals and book series. His commentary on the *Haftarot (Prophetic Lections)* is the first full-length treatment of the commentaries, and modern analyses. His most recent book *Biblical Myth and Rabbinic Mythmaking* (Oxford University Press, 2003) is a fresh thinking of the subject. Recipient of many scholarly awards, Fishbane has been a Guggenheim Fellow and three times a fellow of the Institute for Advanced Studies at the Hebrew University. He is also an elected member of the American Academy for Jewish Research. He received his PhD from Brandeis University where he taught for twenty years before coming to Chicago. He has also been a visiting professor at Harvard, Stanford, and the Hebrew University of Jerusalem. He is presently writing a commentary on the *Song of Songs,* comprising the entire history of Jewish literature on the subject.

Eugene Fisher was associate director of the Secretariat for Ecumenical and Interreligious Affairs of the U.S. Conference of Catholic Bishops (USCCB), in charge of Catholic-Jewish relations, a position he held since 1977. He succeeded Father Edward H. Flannery, who had held the post since its establishment in 1967 following the Second Vatican Council. Dr. Fisher is the first layperson to hold the USCCB post. Prior to 1977, Dr. Fisher was director of catechist formation for the Archdiocese of Detroit, as well as adjunct professor of sacred scripture at St. John's Seminary in Plymouth, Michigan, and for the Religious Studies Department of the University of Detroit. His doctoral degree is in Hebrew culture and education from New York University (1976). Dr. Fisher is an active member of numerous learned and professional societies and associations, such as the Catholic Biblical Association, the National Association of Professors of Hebrew, and the Society of Biblical Literature (SBL). He has lectured widely throughout the United States, Canada, Europe, Latin America, and Australia. He has published twenty books and monographs, and over 250 articles in major religious journals, many of which have been translated into French, Spanish, Italian, Portuguese, Polish, and German for publication in Latin America and Europe. In April of 1981, Dr. Fisher was appointed by Pope John Paul II to be Consultor to the Vatican Commission for Religious Relations with the Jews. In 1985 he was named a member of the International Vatican-Jewish Liaison Committee, representing the Holy See.

Esther Fuchs is professor in the Near Eastern Studies Department and the Arizona Center for Judaic Studies, the University of Arizona, Tucson, where she specializes in Hebrew language and literature,

Jewish women's studies, feminist approaches to the Bible, Israeli fiction and poetry, and gender issues in Middle Eastern studies. She received her PhD from Brandeis University, Waltham, Massachusetts.

Susan Adriana Garber is a stay-at-home proofreader, editor, writer, and amateur gardener. She is currently working on a series of fantasy stories revolving around her copyrighted character, "Ziva: Warrior of Light." She lives with her husband, Zev, in Sherman Oaks, California, in a house they share with their two adopted dogs (Ruchie and Nafshie), double yellow head Amazon parrot (Fluffy), and AB (Alpha Betta), a Siamese fighting fish (befta *splendens*).

Zev Garber was professor and chair of Jewish studies at Los Angeles Valley College, Van Nuys, California, and taught as visiting professor in religious studies at the University of California at Riverside. He has written extensively in the fields of Judaica and Shoah. Among his publications are *Methodology in the Academic Teaching of Judaism* (1988), *Teaching Hebrew Language and Literature at the College Level* (1991), *Shoah: The Paradigmatic Genocide* (1994), *Perspectives on Zionism* (1994), *What Kind of God? Essays in Honor of Richard L. Rubenstein* (1995, consultant editor), *Peace in Deed: Essays in Honor of Harry James Cargas* (1998), *Academic Approaches to Teaching Jewish Studies* (2000); and *Double Takes: Thinking and Rethinking Issues of Modern Judaism in Ancient Contexts* (with Bruce Zuckerman, 2004). He is editorial advisor to *Western States Jewish History* and has served as president of the National Association of Professors of Hebrew (United States).

Mayer I. Gruber is professor in the Department of Bible Archaeology and Ancient Near East at Ben-Gurion University of the Negev in Beersheva, Israel. His research and teaching interests include biblical lexicography, women in the biblical world and early Judaism, the history of feminist biblical research, Rashi's line drawings, biblical prophecy, and psychohistory. His publications include *Aspects of Nonverbal Communication in the Ancient Near East* (Rome: Biblical Institute Press, 1980), *The Motherhood of God and Other Studies* (Atlanta: Scholars Press, 1992), *Women in the Biblical World* (Lanham, Md.: Scarecrow Press and the American Theological Library Association, 1995), *Rashi's Commentary on Psalms* (Leiden: Brill, 2004), and the entry "Job" in *The Jewish Study Bible* (Oxford University Press, 2003). Gruber received his PhD in ancient Semitic languages and cultures from Columbia University in the City of New York (1977) and his rabbinic ordination from Jewish Theological Seminary in New York (1970).

Peter Haas received his BA in Ancient Near Eastern history from the University of Michigan (1970), and was ordained a rabbi by the Hebrew Union College–Jewish Institute of Religion (1974). He was an active-duty chaplain, U.S. Army (1974–77), and later received his PhD in Jewish studies from Brown University (1980). He then joined the faculty at Vanderbilt University, Nashville, where he taught courses in Judaism, Jewish ethics, the Holocaust, Western religion, and the Middle East Conflict from1980 until 2000, when he joined the faculty at Case Western Reserve University, Cleveland, Ohio. He has published several books and articles dealing with moral discourse and with Jewish and Christian thought after the Holocaust. His most recent book deals with human rights in the Jewish tradition. He has lectured in the United States, Israel, Italy, Germany, and Belgium.

Joseph Haberer was born in Germany in 1929 and immigrated to England in 1938 via the *Kindertransport*. He received his BA from San Francisco State Teachers College (1950), his MA from Columbia University (1955), and his PhD from the University of California, Berkeley (1965). He is professor emeritus of political science at Purdue University and director emeritus of the Jewish studies program. He served as editor of *Shofar* from 1981 to 2001, and is presently its book review editor. His book *Politics and the Community of Science* was published in 1969, and he contributed to the book *Bitter Prerequisites: A Faculty for Survival from Nazi Terror* by William Laird Kleine-Ahlbrandt (Purdue University Press, 2001).

Lev Hakak received his BA from the Hebrew University and his MA and PhD from UCLA. He is the editor of *Hadoar: The Hebrew Quarterly of America*, and is professor of Hebrew language and literature at UCLA. Professor Hakak has published numerous books and articles in both Hebrew language and Hebrew literature. He received the Friedman Award for Contributions to Hebrew Culture in 1996, and awards from the Memorial Foundation for Jewish Culture in 1974 and 1977. He is also an accomplished poet.

Klaus Hödl is the Head of the Center of Jewish Studies at the University of Graz/Austria; editor of the journal *Transversal,* and has written and edited several books and many articles on Eastern European Jews, the Jewish body, and Jewish identity.

Louanne Clayton Jacobs is an associate professor of education, Birmingham–Southern College, Alabama. She is the mother of Shea Clayton Jacobs, the stepmother of Naomi Pryor and Hannah Beth Cobb, and the proud grandmother of Laun and Jacob Pryor, and Greer and Drew Cobb. Her research interests include using children's and young literature to support content area instruction, the effects of classroom libraries on reading attitudes and abilities, girls and comics, and using literature to support positive female body image in K-12 students. She maintains a "teacher-friendly" annotated bibliography of almost 200 Holocaust and genocide resources for children and young adults which includes teaching tips. This resource is available electronically from the author by contacting her at ljacobs@bsc.edu.

Steven Leonard Jacobs, editor, joined the Department of Religious Studies as associate professor and Aaron Aronov Endowed Chair of Judaic Studies at the University of Alabama in 2001. He received his BA (with distinction) from the Pennsylvania State University, his BHL, MAHL, DHL, and DD *(Honoris Causa)* from the Hebrew Union College–Jewish Institute of Religion. He has taught at Spring Hill College, Mobile; University of Alabama at Birmingham; Birmingham-Southern College; Samford University, Birmingham; the University of Alabama in Huntsville; and Calhoun Community College, Huntsville. His primary research foci are in biblical studies, translation and interpretation, including the Dead Sea Scrolls, as well as Holocaust and genocide studies. His books include *Shirot Bialik: A New and Annotated Translation of Chaim Nachman Bialik's Epic Poems* (1987), *Raphael Lemkin's Thoughts on Nazi Genocide: Not Guilty?* (1992), *Contemporary Christian* and *Contemporary Jewish Religious Responses to the Shoah* (1993), *Rethinking Jewish Faith: The Child of a Survivor Responds* (1994), *The Meaning of Persons and Things Jewish: Contemporary Explorations and Interpretations* (1996), *The Holocaust Now: Contemporary Christian and Jewish Thought* (1997), *Encyclopedia of Genocide* (1999; associate editor), *Pioneers of Genocide Studies* (2002; coeditor), *The Biblical Masorah and the Temple Scroll: An Orthographical Inquiry* (2002), *Dismantling the Big Lie: The Protocols of the Elders of Zion* (2003; coauthor), *Post-Shoah Dialogues: Re-Thinking Our Texts Together* (2004; coauthor), and *In Search of Yesterday: The Holocaust and the Quest for Meaning* (2005). His professional and civic involvements have included the Alabama Holocaust Commission; board of advisors, the Center for American and Jewish Studies, Baylor University, Waco, Texas; international advisory board, the Centre for Comparative Genocide Studies, Macquarie University, New South Wales, Australia; editorial board, "Studies in the Shoah," University Press of America, Lanham, Maryland; editorial board, *Bridges: An Interdisciplinary Journal of Theology, Philosophy, History and Science*; educational consultant to the Center on the Holocaust, Genocide, and Human Rights, Philadelphia; board of advisors, the Aegis Trust for the Prevention of Genocide, Great Britain; editor, *The Papers of Raphael Lemkin*; secretary-treasurer (1997–2007) and now first vice president of the International Association of Genocide Scholars. He regularly teaches the following courses: Introduction to Religious Studies, Introduction to the Hebrew Bible, The Holocaust in Historical Perspective, Introduction to the Judaic Experience, Philosophies of Judaism, Contemporary Jewish Thought, Jewish-Christian Relations, and Religion and Genocide.

Harold Kasimow is the George Drake Professor of Religious Studies at Grinnell College, Iowa, where he has taught since 1972, especially in the areas of comparative religion and Judaism. He has written a number of articles on interfaith dialogue and on Abraham Joshua Heschel that have been published in the United States, Poland, England, India, China, and Japan. He is coeditor with Byron L. Sherwin of

No Religion Is an Island: Abraham Joshua Heschel and Interreligious Dialogue (1991) and *John Paul II and Interreligious Dialogue* (1999), both published by Orbis Press. His latest coedited book is *Beside Still Waters: Jews, Christians, and the Way of the Buddha.* He has just completed the book *The Search Will Make You Free: A Jewish Dialogue with World Religions* to be published in English and Polish by Wydawnictwo Warn, the Jesuit publishing house in Krakow. He serves on the editorial boards of several scholarly journals. A few weeks after arriving in the United States in August 1949, he met Zev Garber at the Israel Salanter Yeshiva in the Bronx, New York.

Rivka Kern-Ulmer holds the John D, and Catherine T. MacArthur Chair in Jewish Studies at Bucknell University, Lewisburg, Pennsylvania. She received her PhD from Goethe Universitat, Germany, in 1985 and has published and/or edited ten books, primarily in rabbinics. She presently serves as the cochair of the Midrash Consultation for the Society of Biblical Literature. She has also received grants from the Memorial Foundation for Jewish Culture, the National Endowment for the Humanities, the Society of Biblical Literature, and the American Academy of Religion. Her primary research foci are medieval Hebrew manuscripts and rabbinic literature.

Henry F. Knight earned his BA in English from the University of Alabama and his MDiv and DMin degrees from Emory University where he concentrated in theology and pastoral hermeneutics. He is the director of the Cohen Center for Holocaust Studies, Keene State College, Keene, New Hampshire. Prior to this appointment, he served as applied associate professor of hermeneutic and Holocaust studies at the University of Tulsa in Tulsa, Oklahoma, where he taught courses on Christian theology, the Holocaust, and Jewish-Christian relations. He is cochair of the biennial Pastora Goldner Holocaust Symposium that he and Leonard Grob of Fairleigh Dickinson University, New Jersey, cofounded in 1996. He serves on the Church Relations Committee of the U.S. Holocaust Memorial Museum in Washington, D.C., and the advisory committee for the master of arts program in Holocaust and genocide studies at the Richard Stockton College of New Jersey. Dr. Knight is the author of *Confessing Christ in a Post-Holocaust World* (Greenwood Press, 2000) and *Celebrating Holy Week in a Post-Holocaust World* (Westminster John Knox, 2005). He is also coauthor, with James F. Moore, Zev Garber, and Steven Jacobs of *Post-Shoah Dialogues: Rethinking Our Texts Together* (University Press of America, 2004) and coeditor with Marcia Sachs Littell of *The Uses and Abuses of Knowledge,* vol. 17, Studies in the Shoah (University Press of America, 1997); his articles have been published in the *Journal of Ecumenical Studies, Quarterly Review, Shofar,* and *Encounter.* Hank, as he is known to his friends, is married to Pamela Damron Knight and they have two grown children, Paul (27) and Laura (23).

Harris Lenowitz has been professor of Hebrew in the Middle East Center and the Department of Languages and Literature of the University of Utah since 1993, having come to Utah the year after he completed his dissertation (1971) at the University of Texas in Austin in linguistics. He began teaching Hebrew language and literature when he came to Utah as an assistant professor of Hebrew after an initial interest in Ancient Near Eastern languages, which led to some articles and an anthology of creation texts from the ancient Mediterranean, and to his work in *Alcheringa: Ethnopoetics* as a contributor and editor. While working with Jerome Rothenberg on *A Big Jewish Book,* he became interested in the dicta of Yakov Frank and has worked away at those to the present. Though this work turned him away from Hebrew per se (toward Polish), he has maintained an interest in Hebrew poetry particularly, and has published on biblical poetry, medieval poetry, and modern Israeli fiction as well as articles and reviews on the study of Hebrew. For the last eight or so years, his chief interest has been the appearance of Hebrew script in Christian art. He continues to teach modern and biblical Hebrew and courses on the Jewish messiahs and Jewish mysticism.

Richard Libowitz is a member of the faculties of Temple University and St. John's University, Philadelphia, and a graduate of the University of Notre Dame, Temple University, and the Reconstructionist Rabbinical College. His first article on Holocaust education appeared in 1973, to be followed by volumes, chapters, essays, and papers delivered at conferences throughout the United States, Great Britain, Germany, and Israel. His current study of the effects of commercial films and novels on Holocaust learning has grown out of his increasing inclusion of such materials within his courses. The recipient of many awards and honors, in 2005, he was inducted as an honorary member of Alpha Sigma Nu, the Jesuit Honor Society, certainly the first rabbi to be so recognized.

Sara R. Mandell's interests and training are in diverse disciplines, and her work has always been interdisciplinary. She has received the Founder's Day Award from NYU, two teaching awards as well as a Distinguished Service Award from the University of South Florida. She earned her BA and MA in Latin and her PhD in Classics from NYU. She also served as president of the Southeastern Regions of ASOR and is currently on the steering committee of the Social Scientific Studies of the Second Temple Era of the Society of Biblical Literature, and has taught both classics and religious studies. She recently retired as professor emerita.

Yair Mazor is director of the UWM Center for Jewish Studies and head of the Hebrew studies program and the certificate program in Jewish studies at the University of Wisconsin–Milwaukee. He is the author of fourteen scholarly books and over 200 articles and book reviews, which have appeared in professional and literary periodicals in the United States, Israel, and many European countries. He is an internationally acclaimed scholar in the fields of modern Hebrew and Israeli literature, Scandinavian literature, and children's literature. He is the recipient of numerous scholarly prizes and accolades, among them, two prestigious book awards from Tel Aviv University, the UWM coveted Teaching Award (1999), and the Friedman Prize in 1998. He was born in Israel and served as a sergeant-major in the Israeli paratroopers.

James F. Moore is Professor of Theology at Valparaiso University, Valparaiso, Indiana. He is codirector of the HIV Symposium project at the Zygon Center for Religion and Science in Chicago. He is author of *Sexuality and Marriage* (Augsburg, 1987), *Christian Theology After the Shoah: A Re-interpretation of the Passion Narratives* (University Press of America, 1993, 2004), *Post Shoah Dialogues* (University Press of America 2004), and *Toward a Dialogical Community* (University Press of America, 2004), as well as numerous articles on Jewish studies, on Christian theology and the Holocaust, and on science and religion. He is on the editorial board of the Studies in the Shoah series of the University Press of America and is an educational consultant to the Philadelphia Center for the Holocaust, Genocide, and Human Rights. His essay, "Cosmology and Theology: The Re-Emergence of Patriarchy," in *Zygon* (December 1995) won the 1996 Templeton award for best essay in theology and science.

Gilead Morahg is a professor of Hebrew Literature at the University of Wisconsin–Madison. He has served as president of the National Association of Professors of Hebrew and of the National Council of Less Commonly Taught Languages. He is the author of over fifty studies and essays on Israeli literature. Among his publications are "Outraged Humanism: The Fiction of A.B. Yehoshua"; "New Images of Arabs in Israeli Literature"; "Breaking Silence: Israel's Fantastic Fiction of the Holocaust"; and "Reliable Sources: Intertextual Meaning in David Grossman's *See Under: Love*."

Daniel Morris is professor of English and Jewish studies at Purdue University, West Lafayette, Indiana. He received his PhD in English from Brandeis University (1992). He has published three scholarly books, one on William Carlos Williams (University of Missouri Press, 1995), one on how contemporary American writers have responded to modern painting (University of Massachusetts Press, 2002), and one on the Jewish-American author Louise Gluck (University of Missouri Press, 2006). He has also edited or coedited two collections of essays: one on the Jewish-American poet Allen Grossman (National Poetry Foundation, 2004), and a second on the legacy of New York Jewish public intellectuals. He has published poems in national journals as well as a collection of his own poetry, *Bryce Passage* (Marsh Hawk Press, 2004). He is editor of *Shofar: An Interdisciplinary Journal of Jewish Studies.*

Jacob Neusner is Research Professor of Theology at Bard College and senior fellow of the Institute of Advanced Theology at Bard as well. He also is a member of the Institute for Advanced Study, Princeton, New Jersey, and Life Member of Clare Hall, Cambridge University, in England. He has published more than 900 books and unnumbered articles, both scholarly and academic and popular and journalistic, and is the most published humanities scholar in the world. He has been awarded nine honorary degrees, including seven U.S. and European honorary doctorates, from the University of Chicago, the University of Rochester, Bologna University in Italy (in celebration of the university's nine-hundredth anniversary), Cologne University in Germany, Tulane University, St. Louis University, and Dowling College. In addition he holds fourteen academic medals and prizes, including the University Medal of Excellence, Columbia University, the Medal of College de France, the University of Tubingen Medal commemorating that University's five-hundredth anniversary, the Queen Christina of Sweden Medal of Abo Akademi (Finland), and the Abraham Berliner Prize in Jewish History of the Jewish Theological Seminary of America, as well as numerous other academic awards. He grew up in West Hartford, Connecticut, and is a graduate of William H. Hall High School (1950). He received his AB from Harvard College in 1953, his PhD from Columbia University and Union Theological Seminary in 1961, and rabbinical ordination and MHL from the Jewish Theological Seminary of America in 1960. During his graduate studies he also was Henry Fellow at Lincoln College, Oxford University, 1953–54, and Fulbright Scholar at the Hebrew University of Jerusalem, 1957–58. In his professional career he was founding chairman of the Department of Hebrew Studies at the University of Wisconsin–Milwaukee (1961–62), held a postdoctoral fellowship at Brandeis University (1962–64), and taught at Dartmouth College and at Brown University (1964–89); he spent a research year at the Institute for Advanced Study, Princeton (1989–90), and served as Distinguished Research Professor of Religious Studies at the University of South Florida (1990–2000). He began to teach at Bard College on a part-time basis in 1994 and moved to New York to assume full-time duties in 2000. He has held two fellowships from the American Council of Learned Societies and two fellowships from the Guggenheim Foundation as well as an NEH Fellowship at the Institute for Advanced Study and many other research awards. He also has held visiting professorships at the University of Minnesota and the Jewish Theological Seminary of America. In 1991 he was awarded the Buber Chair at the University of Frankfurt; in 1992 was a member of Clare Hall, Cambridge University; in 1993 visiting research professor at Abo Akademi in Finland; in 1994 Canterbury Fellow at University of Canterbury, in New Zealand; in 1995, Von Humboldt Research Professor at University of Gottingen; and in 1996 he was visiting professor in Theology at Uppsala University. He was president of the American Academy of Religion (1968–69), the only scholar of Judaism to hold that position, and a member of the founding committee of the Association for Jewish Studies (1967–70). He single-handedly founded the European Association of Jewish Studies (1980–81). He also served, by appointment of President Carter, as a member of the National Council on the Humanities and, by appointment of President Reagan, as a member of the National Council on the Arts (1978–84, 1984–90, respectively). He is editor of the *Encyclopedia of Judaism* (Brill, 1999, I-III) and its supplements; chairman of the editorial board of *The Review of Rabbinic Judaism,* and editor-in-chief of *The Brill Reference Library of Judaism,* both published by E. J. Brill, Leiden, The Netherlands. He is editor of *Studies in Judaism,* University Press of America. He was editor for Judaism of the *Dictionary of Religion* (Harper/AAR), and of the *Encyclopedia of Religion* (Britannica/Merriam Webster). He resides with his wife in Rhinebeck, New York. They have a daughter, three sons and three daughters-in-law, seven granddaughters, and two grandsons.

David Patterson holds the Bornblum Chair in Judaic Studies at the University of Memphis, Tennessee. A winner of the Koret Jewish Book Award, he has published more than 125 articles and chapters on philosophy, literature, Judaism, and Holocaust studies. His writings have been anthologized, and his more than two dozen books include *Honey from the Rock: Jewish-Christian Dialogue—The Next Step* (with Alan L. Berger, forthcoming), *Open Wounds: The Crisis of Jewish Thought in the Aftermath of Auschwitz* (forthcoming), *Wrestling with the Angel* (2006), *Hebrew Language and Jewish Thought* (2005), *Along the Edge of Annihilation* (1999), *Sun Turned to Darkness* (1998), *The Greatest Jewish Stories Ever Told* (1997), *When Learned Men Murder* (1996), *Exile* (1995), *Pilgrimage of a Proselyte*

(1993), *The Shriek of Silence* (1992), *In Dialogue and Dilemma with Elie Wiesel* (1991), *Literature and Spirit* (1988), *The Affirming Flame* (1988), and *Faith and Philosophy* (1982). He is the editor and translator of *The Complete Black Book* of *Russian Jewry* (2002) and coeditor (with Alan L. Berger) of the *Encyclopedia of Holocaust Literature* (2002), as well as coeditor (with John K. Roth) of *Fire in the Ashes* (2005) and *After-Words* (2004).

John T. Pawlikowski, a Servite priest, is professor of social ethics at Catholic Theological Union, Chicago, where he also directs the Catholic-Jewish Studies Program in the school's Cardinal Bernardin Center. He is the author or editor of fifteen books on social ethics, Holocaust studies, and Jewish-Christian relations. He has been a member by presidential appointment of the U.S. Holocaust Memorial Council since 1980, and currently serves as president of the International Council of Christians and Jews.

Moshe Pelli is the Abe and Tess Wise Professor in Judaic Studies and Director of the Judaic Studies Program at the University of Central Florida in Orlando. He is a leading authority on the Hebrew Enlightenment (*Haskalah*) in the eighteenth and nineteenth centuries. He has published extensively on modern Hebrew literature. Among his writings are eight scholarly books on the Hebrew Enlightenment, one book on Hebrew culture in the United States, and over 160 research papers. Long active in Hebrew culture, in 1991, he was awarded the Friedman Prize for his contributions to Hebrew Culture in the United States in teaching, research, and editing Hebrew periodicals. In 1996, he received the Researcher of the Year award at UCF; and, in 2006, he was awarded the Distinguished Researcher of the Year, College of Arts and Humanities, UCF, and the UCF Research Incentive Award. In 2005, he was elected vice president of the National Association of Professors of Hebrew (NAPF).

John K. Roth was the Edward J. Sexton Professor of Philosophy, director of the Center for the Study of the Holocaust, Genocide, and Human Rights, and chair of the Department of Philosophy and Religious Studies at Claremont McKenna College, Claremont, California, before his retirement. He has served on the U.S. Holocaust Memorial Council and the editorial board of Holocaust and Genocide Studies. His many publications include *Holocaust Politics* (2001), *Pope Pius XII and the Holocaust* (2004), *Will Genocide Ever End?* (2002), and a revised edition *of After Auschwitz: The Holocaust and Its Legacy* (with Richard Rubenstein, 2007). He has been visiting professor of Holocaust studies at the University of Haifa, Israel, a 2001 Koerner visiting fellow at the Oxford Centre for Hebrew and Jewish Studies in England, 2004–5, appointment as the Ina Levine Senior Scholar in the Center for Advanced Holocaust Studies at the U.S. Holocaust Memorial Museum, Washington, D.C. In 1988, he was named U.S. National Professor of the Year by the Center for Advancement and Support of Education and the Carnegie Endowment for the Advancement of Teaching.

Richard L. Rubenstein is president emeritus of the University of Bridgeport, Connecticut. A Distinguished Professor of Religion at the university and a life member of the board of trustees, he also serves as director of the university's Center for Holocaust and Genocide Studies. An internationally recognized historian of religion whose writings lie at the root of contemporary Holocaust discourse, his works have been the subject of more than a dozen doctoral dissertations. One of his books, entitled *The Cunning of History*, is currently being translated into French. Professor Rubenstein's writings have also been cited as a key inspiration for the Academy Award–winning film *Sophie's Choice*. Prior to assuming his role as president of the University of Bridgeport, Dr. Rubenstein served as Distinguished Professor of Religion at Florida State University. Recently Florida State University created the Richard L. Rubenstein Chair for Religious Studies in his honor.

Frederick M. Schweitzer is professor emeritus of history and director of the Holocaust Resource Center of Manhattan College, New York, which is a Catholic college of the Brothers of the Christian Schools, located in the Riverdale section of the Bronx. His most recent book, coauthored with Marvin Perry, is *Antisemitism: Myth and Hate from Antiquity to the Present* (Palgrave Macmillan, 2002, paperback edition, 2005). He has been engaged in Christian-Jewish dialogue almost since Vatican II, and has written, edited, or contributed to *A History of the Jews since the First Century AD, Toynbee: Reappraisal, Papers on the Dead Sea Scrolls,* and *Jewish-Christian Encounters over the Centuries,* among others; and has penned numerous articles and reviews, particularly on the Holocaust. At present, he is coediting an anthology of documents illustrating the many myths about Jews. His 1998 testimony was instrumental in the Canadian Human Rights Commission's decision to bar the antisemite and Holocaust denier Ernst Zundel from the Internet. He continues to be active in such organizations as the Annual Scholars Conference on the Holocaust and the Churches.

Nancy Shiffrin is the author of *The Holy Letters* (poems) and *My Jewish Name* (essays). She teaches English for The Los Angeles Community College District, and Creative Writing privately. She received her PhD from The Union Institute of Cincinnati, Ohio, in 1994. She received her MA in English from International College, where she was tutored by the late Anais Nin. She does independent research on Jewish American Women authors, and has her own website at http://home.earthlink.net/~nshiffrin/. She also wishes to express her appreciation to Zev Garber for helping the wandering Jews connect to academic life.

Marvin Sweeney is professor of Hebrew Bible, Claremont School of Theology, Claremont, California. He specializes in Hebrew Bible studies with a particular focus on prophetic literature. He is especially interested in biblical theology, literary-critical methodologies, ancient exegesis of biblical texts, and the interrelationship between religion and politics in both the ancient and modern worlds. In addition, he teaches courses in the history of Judaism and Jewish thought. His recent publications include a study of King Josiah (Oxford University Press) and commentaries on Isaiah 1–39 (Forms of the Old Testament Literature), The Twelve Prophets (*Berit. Olam*), and Zephaniah (*Hermeneia*). He is currently working in the area of Jewish biblical theology and writing a commentary on 1-2 Kings (Old Testament Library).

William (Zev) Wallis is Professor of English at Los Angeles Valley College, and has taught Yiddish Literature in Translation in the Department of Jewish Studies, which was until 2008 headed by Zev Garber. His Selected Poems, 1969-99 was nominated for the Pulitzer Prize and his first novel *Hawk* won the Benjamin Franklin Award for Popular Fiction in 2006.

Ann Weiss is founder and executive director of Eyes from the Ashes Educational Foundation, an organization that both teaches and researches on topics related to the Holocaust, using the past to inform, and work to create, a better future. In addition, she is a director/producer, photojournalist, researcher, filmmaker, public speaker, and teacher in settings that range from international conferences to local classrooms. Weiss has written, researched, produced, and directed documentaries on psychiatry and on the *Shoah*, has done educational consulting for UNESCO in the Middle East for the Gulf Arab States (Saudi Arabia, Bahrain, Qatar, Gulf Arab Emirates, Egypt, and Kuwait) as well as Israel and Yad Vashem. In Cyprus Weiss taught a three-day seminar, with Israel's then–head of education Yossi Sarid, to Israeli and Palestinian educators on "Teaching Tolerance in the Classroom," and is currently involved in intense *Shoah* research and continued interviews. Ann Weiss is author of *The Last Album: Eyes from the Ashes of Auschwitz-Birkenau*, published in America, England, France, and Germany by W. W. Norton, with an expanded, revised edition by the Jewish Publication Society, and has created several versions of traveling photographic exhibitions, based on previously unknown photos carried by Jews to Auschwitz-Birkenau, when they thought they were going to be worked . . . not murdered. Her presentations personalize history, and focus on the common humanity we all share.

Ziony Zevit is Distinguished Professor in Bible and Northwest Semitic Languages at the American Jewish University, Los Angeles. He received his BA from the University of California and his MA and PhD from the University of California, Berkeley. He is the author of more than ninety publications in his fields of specialization, and sits on numerous editorial boards. He is also the recipient of numerous honors and awards including fellowships from the Rockefeller Foundation, the National Endowment for the Humanities, Hebrew University, Guggenheim Memorial Foundation, American Council of Learned Societies, the American Schools of Oriental Research, the Ford Foundation, and the Hebrew Union College, Jerusalem.